CW01217013

Mechanics, Vibrations and Waves

Cover design by Craig Dodd (based on a photograph of an oscillating mass on a spring—copyright, Kodansha Limited).

Mechanics, Vibrations and Waves

T. B. Akrill MA
Senior Physics Master
Clifton College
Bristol

C. J. Millar MA
Senior Physics Master
The King's School
Canterbury

John Murray Albemarle Street   London

© T. B. Akrill and C. J. Millar 1974
First published 1974
Reprinted 1977

All rights reserved. No part of this publication may be reproduced, stored in a retrieval system, or transmitted, in any form or by any means, electronic, mechanical, photocopying, recording or otherwise without the prior permission of John Murray (Publishers) Ltd, 50 Albemarle Street, London W1X 4BD

Filmset in Times New Roman on 'Monophoto' 600 by Fyldetype Limited, Kirkham PR4 3BJ and printed offset in Great Britain
by Cox and Wyman Ltd, London, Fakenham and Reading

0 7195 2882 8

Preface

Fundamental concepts in mechanics are often hazily understood during an O-level course, are assumed to be part of the student's vocabulary at A-level, and then have to be covered again in the early stages of higher education. The authors believe that this text offers a coherent account of mechanical principles and their physical applications, in particular to mechanical waves and oscillations, for use in the 16 to 20 age range. No particular course of physics to O-level is assumed, nor is the text limited to any one A-level syllabus. Whenever possible new topics are introduced through experiments in a manner consistent with modern teaching methods and in this context the authors wish to acknowledge the influence of the Nuffield physics courses at both O- and A-level.

Use of this book is not restricted to those who intend to work through it systematically. Where a more pragmatic approach to basic mechanics is used the reader should, however, note the manner in which velocity and acceleration are treated in the early chapters and in particular the precise use of language and drawing of diagrams used in discussing forces. There is a comprehensive index.

In a book of this kind the authors' responsibility is to select and order the subject matter, to update units, facts, and experiments and to identify and clarify difficult ideas in such a way as to offer the reader a better view of the basic physics. We have tried to do all these things and do not claim a greater originality. The following notes indicate some of the ways in which we believe we have achieved our goals.

(*a*) SI units are used throughout. *Quantities, units, and symbols*, a report by the Symbols Committee of the Royal Society (RS 1971) is followed in detail.

(*b*) Physical quantities are treated in accordance with RS 1971. Thus we write, for example, in Newton's second law

$$(6 \text{ kg})a = 30 \text{ N} \Rightarrow a = 5 \text{ N kg}^{-1},$$

and not $\qquad 6a = 30 \Rightarrow a = 5$ plus an added unit.

(*c*) The mathematical level of the book has deliberately been kept low. Thus calculus is used only as a limit of, for example,

$$\Delta v/\Delta t \qquad \text{or} \qquad \sum F \Delta t$$

on the rare occasions where further operations are unavoidable. A simple vector notation is used.

(*d*) Mathematically difficult sections are indicated by ★ at the beginning and end and are printed in smaller type than the main text.

(*e*) Motion in two dimensions is used to develop kinematics, as the vector nature of displacement, velocity, and acceleration is felt to be vital at this level.

(*f*) Throughout the text the frame of reference used in describing a motion is specified. Non-inertial frames are not used to 'simplify' circular motion.

(*g*) In discussing energy conservation the social implications of using up the world's fossil fuel reserves are considered, as is the environmental problem of noise levels in the chapter on sound.

(h) A chapter on special relativity is based on modern experiments with high-energy particles. Mass–energy conservation and time dilation are developed without recourse to the Lorentz transformations.

(i) By using mechanical waves which are easily demonstrated the book covers all the fundamental properties of waves including the principle of superposition and the phenomenon of diffraction.

Spread through each chapter is a number of worked *examples* (indicated by ▶). The style of these examples is discursive and explanatory. They are definitely not simply illustrations of how to substitute physical quantities in formulae.

At the end of each chapter is a set of *exercises*, in total 650. We consider that these exercises, which are original, and not borrowed examination questions, constitute a major feature of the book and will add greatly to its usefulness. Included are thought-provoking questions, routine and not-so-routine problems, suggestions for essay topics (particularly in the chapters on waves), and occasional lengthy exercises which introduce a new idea or experiment. Exercises for which answers are supplied (at the back of the book) are marked with ●.

The text incorporates some 400 *diagrams*, drawn by the authors, and a sprinkling of photographs. We have chosen not to use photographs of standard apparatus, for example a xenon stroboscope, as a clear diagram is more readily understood. Both examples and exercises contain explanatory diagrams.

A short *bibliography* is given at the end of each chapter. References are given to books or to individual chapters of books, to articles and *Scientific American* offprints, and also to films and film loops. We feel the text should be judged not in isolation but together with these short pieces of additional reading.

December 1973

T. B. A. *Clifton*
C. J. M. *Canterbury*

Acknowledgements

It is impossible to identify the many influences which directly or indirectly helped us in the preparation of this book. Many printed sources of information and ideas are contained in the bibliographies at the end of each chapter. Dr J. W. Warren of Brunel University made comments, both at a general level and of a most detailed nature, on the entire manuscript. The responsibility for all that remains is, however, definitely the authors—the diagrams were drawn by one of us (C.J.M.) and the answers to the exercises are our own.

We would like to thank Jane Akrill for her expertise in typing the final manuscript, mathematics and all, and Helen Johnson of John Murray for her great care in editing the manuscript. Thanks are also due to the following who have kindly allowed us to reproduce their copyright illustrations:

Figures 8-1, 16-1, 16-8, 16-10, 16-12, PSSC *Physics* (1960) and PSSC *College Physics* (1968), D. C. Heath and Co. Lexington, Mass.; 9-12, P. M. S. Blackett and D. S. Lees, *Proc. Roy. Soc., London* (A): (*a*) **107**, 349 (1925), (*b*) **136**, 325 (1932), (*c*) **134**, 658 (1931); 10-4, 10-7, Professor P. H. Fowler, Bristol University; 13-10, John Hadland, New House Laboratories, Bovingdon, Herts; 14-2*a*, Philip Harris Ltd, Ludgate Hill, Birmingham; 15-27*b*, 15-33*b*, 17-18, 18-3, 18-9, Professor A. P. French, Massachusetts Institute of Technology (1971) *Vibrations and waves*, Thomas Nelson; 17-9, 17-10, M. Alonso and E. J. Finn (1967) *Fundamental University Physics*, Addison-Wesley, Reading, Mass.; 17-14, R. A. R. Tricker (1964) *Bores, breakers, waves and wakes*, Mills and Boon; 17-17, Leybold-Heraeus Ltd, Blackwall Lane, London; 17-19, British Broadcasting Corporation (Nov. 1937) *The Listener*; 17-24, based upon the Ordnance Survey Map with the sanction of the Controller of H.M. Stationery Office, Crown Copyright Reserved; 18-2, Griffin and George Ltd, Ealing Road, Alperton, Middx; 19-3, Unilab Ltd, Clarendon Road, Blackburn, Lancs; 19-9*a*, The United States Army Coastal Engineering Research Centre; 19-11, E/D/C Distribution Centre, Newton, Mass.; 19-21, The Hale Observatories, Pasadena, California; 19-23, The British Aircraft Corporation and F. R. McKim (1971) *Supersonic Flight*, Longman; 13-10, John Hadland Ltd, from *Science News* **37** (1955) Penguin Books; 15–24, F. W. Sears (1950) *Mechanics, heat and sound*, Addison-Wesley Publishing Co. Reading, Mass.

Contents

1	Introduction	1
2	Describing motion	15
3	Acceleration	32
4	Motion in a circle	52
5	Mass and force	61
6	Using Newton's laws	76
7	Work and kinetic energy	97
8	Linear momentum	115
9	The principle of conservation of energy	136
10	Relativistic mechanics	154
11	Rigid bodies in equilibrium	177
12	The dynamics of rigid bodies	193
13	Angular momentum	207
14	Gravitation	224
15	Mechanical oscillations	246
16	Waves on a string	275
17	Mechanical waves	299
18	Sound waves	322
19	Wave phenomena	341
	Appendix: conversion factors for non-SI units of energy	363
	Answers	364
	Index	367

1 Introduction

1-1	What is Newtonian mechanics?	1	1-8 Symbols for physical quantities 6
1-2	Length and time	2	1-9 Standards 7
1-3	Errors in measurement	2	1-10 Errors 7
1-4	Measuring length	3	1-11 Relationships 8
1-5	Measuring time	4	1-12 Some useful mathematics 10
1-6	Physical quantities and their dimensions	5	Bibliography 12
1-7	Units	6	Exercises 12

1-1 What is Newtonian Mechanics?

Euclid's geometry consists, essentially, of a number of axioms (assertions made without proof: for example, that vertically opposite angles are equal) and a number of theorems (rather more complicated but important statements which derive from the axioms). Using these axioms and theorems, mathematicians can prove a very large number of other results. This geometry has been widely studied, and has given pleasure to many people, but it is of no *practical* importance unless its theorems hold for situations in the real world. For example, it may give us intellectual pleasure to be able to prove that in a right-angled triangle ABC (with the right angle at B), $AB^2 + BC^2 = CA^2$, but it is of no *use* unless we can be sure that if we have, say, a rectangular field, two of whose sides are AB and BC, we can predict that the length of its diagonal CA is given by $CA^2 = AB^2 + BC^2$. We do in fact find that Euclidean geometry can be applied successfully to situations in the real world, except where the distances involved are very large.

Newton's laws (of motion and gravitation) can be placed in the same category as Euclid's axioms. They are assertions about the way in which material bodies behave, and on the basis of these assertions we can make predictions about what will happen when, for example, one billiard ball strikes another. We can even make plans for sending men to the Moon. The fact that men *do* go to the Moon and return safely is evidence that Newton's assertions about the behaviour of bodies *do* relate to the real world: this is not, of course, surprising, since it is unlikely that anyone (let alone Newton) would make assertions without basing them on some experimental work and without testing them by seeing whether things they predict are fulfilled.

But Newton's laws remain a *model* of the real world: a very accurate model, in that they were successfully used by physicists and engineers to plan the behaviour of their apparatus and machinery for two hundred years without any suspicion that the real world did not correspond *exactly* to Newton's model. Increasing knowledge, however, led Einstein to suggest a model which was different (and we believe better) but Newton's model remains a very good approximation to the behaviour of the real world, and it is worth studying first. We shall, in Chapter 10, show how Newton's model of the world is affected by Einstein's ideas, but basically this is a book about Newtonian mechanics.

In this first chapter a number of useful, and often unconnected, ideas are introduced.

1-2 Length and time

We must first learn how to describe where and when an event occurred. Clearly measurements of both length and time are required. For a meaningful statement of length we require an agreed *standard* of length. The standard used is the metre. It was first agreed that the metre should be one ten-thousandth of the distance from the North Pole to the Equator along the meridian through Paris. Later this was replaced by the distance between two scratches on a certain platinum–iridium bar kept, under specified conditions, at the International Bureau of Weights and Measures at Sèvres (near Paris). This latter standard has now been superseded by the definition of one metre as 1 650 763.73 times the wavelength in a vacuum of radiation corresponding to the transition between the levels $2p_{10}$ and $5d_5$ of the krypton-86 atom. To measure the distance between two points we count how many metre rods, or known fractions of a rod, will fit between the two points.

To measure time we need a clock. With this clock we define our standard of time, the *second*. The second was originally defined as 1/86 400 of a mean solar day; quite recently this was replaced by an agreed fraction of the year 1900. This latter standard has again been superseded and at present (1973) the second is defined as the duration of 9 192 631 770 periods of the radiation corresponding to the transition between the two hyperfine levels of the ground state of the caesium-133 atom. To measure time intervals we calibrate more easily observable repetitive devices against the standard and again use a counting process.

1-3 Errors in measurement

When a physical quantity, such as the diameter of a rod, is measured, the result will be written as a number and a unit; for example, 9.0 mm. A scientist will also attempt to measure the possible error in the result.

The errors which might arise may be *systematic* or *random*. *Systematic errors* are those which arise because of some fault in the measuring instrument or in the technique of measurement. To take the example already mentioned, the diameter of a rod: this is a very straightforward measurement, so the chance of systematic error is very slight, but it would occur if the measuring device were wrongly graduated. Systematic errors can be eliminated by taking care over the choice of technique or by checking the instruments used against other similar instruments.

Random errors are those which arise because of the fallibility of human beings. Measurements of the length of a particular rod, made several times by the same person using the same ruler, will probably differ because of parallax errors, though one person may produce a set of readings of a particular quantity which has a wider spread than the set produced by another person using the same apparatus. The effect of random errors can be reduced by making many measurements of the same quantity, and finding the mean value; however, the greater the spread, the greater the number of readings which must be taken to be as certain of the result. The smaller the spread of the measurements, the more *precise* the measurement is said to be. An instrument which is capable of producing a precise measurement is said to be a *sensitive* instrument.

Obviously a measurement can be precise and yet, because of systematic error, very inaccurate. A measurement which is relatively free of systematic error is said to be *accurate*.

A scientist who has made a measurement (and that will be the mean of several measurements) indicates the *precision* of his measurement by giving the limits within which he thinks the correct value lies: the limits must be determined by statistical methods, in which the spread of the readings, and the number of readings taken, will be considered. He cannot indicate the *accuracy* of the measurement, since he cannot tell what unknown systematic errors there might be. A reading of (9.000 ± 0.001) mm clearly indicates greater precision than (0.025 ± 0.005) kg, but no one can say which of these measurements is the more accurate, at least, not without other evidence.

The work of this section is summed up in figure 1-1, where each mark on the lines represents a measurement of a particular quantity. Parts (*a*) and (*b*) indicate equally *precise* measurements of the quantity, but in part (*a*) the measurement is notably more *accurate*. In part (*c*) the

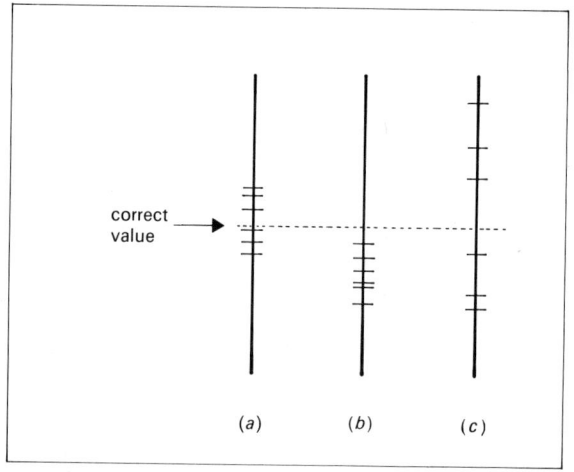

Figure 1-1 Accuracy and precision.

measurement is not *precise*, nor, since only as many readings have been taken as in part (*a*), is it likely to be as *accurate* as in part (*a*). Perhaps in part (*c*) a less *sensitive* instrument was used than in parts (*a*) and (*b*).

1-4 Measuring length

Provided we can use our metre rod, perhaps conveniently divided into 1000 equal parts, or joined end to end with others to form a long tape, we can easily measure lengths. The distance a man can throw a javelin, for example, can be measured as (81.46 ± 0.05) m—a possible percentage error of only $\pm 0.06\%$, and the diameter of a coin as (23.0 ± 0.2) mm—a possible percentage error of $\pm 1\%$.

Large distances

An indirect method known as *triangulation* is used to measure large distances. A distant object will appear in a different place when viewed from two different positions; this effect is called parallax. If the distance between the two positions (the length of the *base line*) is known, and the angles (giving the apparent directions of the distant object) are measured, the distance to the object can be calculated trigonometrically or from a scale drawing.

This technique enables us to survey the Earth's surface, to determine the scale of the solar system, and to measure the distances to nearby stars. When measuring the distance to a star we use as a base line the diameter of the Earth's orbit round the Sun. The apparent position of the star is measured at intervals of six months by photographing the star and recording its position relative to a distant 'fixed' star, that is, a star too far away to exhibit parallax. See figure 1-2.

Another indirect method is the echo method. A pulse of energy which travels at a known speed v is emitted at a point P. The time interval Δt before the pulse arrives back at P, after being reflected from a distant point Q, is measured. The distance PQ is then $\frac{1}{2}v\Delta t$. The measurement involved here is one of time, and the emission and reception of the pulse can be made to start and stop one of the devices described in Section 1-5. The pulse can be of sound energy (sonar) or of electromagnetic energy (radar and lidar). The former is widely used at sea for depth sounding, and the latter in aircraft control and for measuring astronomical distances.

Small distances

When we need smaller graduations than 1 mm, it is possible to perform measurements under a microscope; divisions of

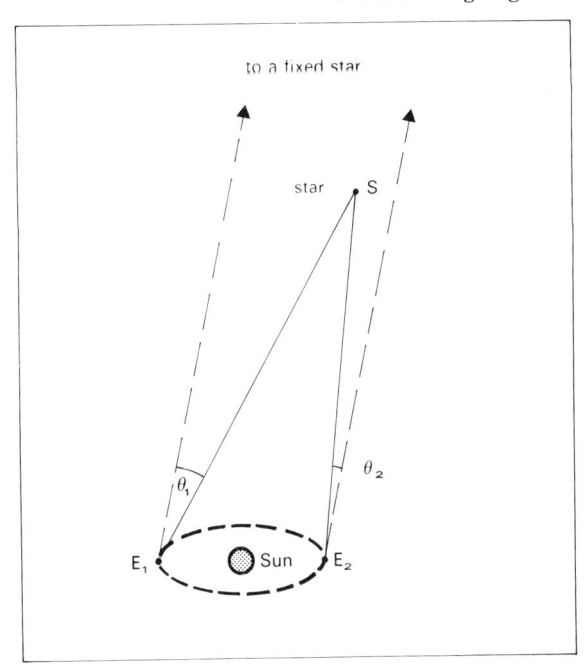

Figure 1-2 The principle of triangulation applied to astronomical distances. The base line $E_1 E_2$ uses the greatest separation we can achieve, the diameter of the Earth's orbit round the Sun. θ_1 and θ_2 are measured from photographs taken through telescopes with objective lenses or mirrors of known focal lengths. The distance of S from the Sun can thus be deduced.

0.01 mm = 10 μm can then be used. Alternatively, we can use a micrometer screw gauge (see figure 1-3) in which a carefully manufactured screw can be designed to advance 0.500 mm per revolution. If a circular scale of 50 divisions is marked on the sleeve of the instrument, and this turns with the screw, a movement of one division of

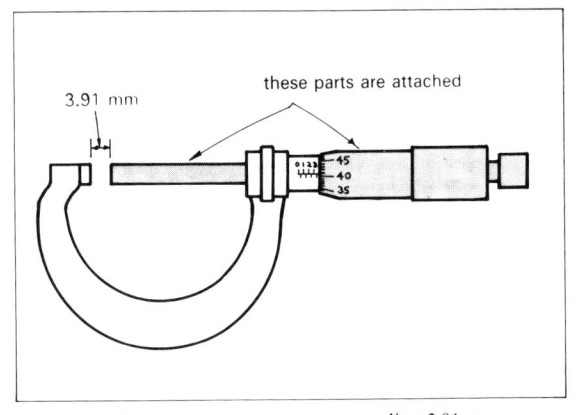

Figure 1-3 A micrometer screw gauge reading 3.91 mm.

the sleeve corresponds to the screw advancing 0.010 mm = 10 μm. If this screw is now used to grip a small object, the width of the object can be deduced by reading the scale before and after the object is introduced. Although this is a sensitive instrument, measurements made with it for objects which are less than 0.5 mm wide will only be precise to $\pm 1\%$. Some special micrometer screw gauges can be read to the nearest 1 μm.

Length/metres	
10^{18}	limit of parallax measurement
10^{17}	distance to the nearest star
10^{16}	distance travelled by light in one year
10^{14}	
10^{12}	distance of Saturn from the Sun
10^{10}	distance of Mercury from the Sun
10^{8}	distance from the Earth to the Moon
10^{6}	distance from Land's End to John O'Groats
10^{4}	height of Mount Everest
10^{2}	height of London GPO tower
10^{0}	height of a child
10^{-2}	width of a finger nail
10^{-4}	diameter of a hair
10^{-5}	diameter of a red blood corpuscle
10^{-6}	limit of mechanical measurement

Table 1-1 Orders of magnitude of distances.

1-5 Measuring time

All clocks have repetitive properties: their behaviour is said to be periodic (see also Section 15-1). The pendulum and balance wheel of conventional clocks and watches oscillate under the action of the pull of the Earth and the push and pull of a spring respectively, with time intervals of between 0.1 s and 2 s for a complete oscillation. This time interval is called the period of the oscillation. In order to turn the to-and-fro motion of these devices into the rotation of the hands of a clock, a ratchet or mechanical valve is used. Clocks of this sort work well enough in measuring the time taken for a man to run 100 metres as (10.6 ± 0.1)s —a possible percentage error of $\pm 1\%$, or for an Earth satellite to circle the Earth as (5414 ± 3)s—a possible percentage error of only $\pm 0.05\%$.

Large time intervals

For larger time intervals we can use days or years (the rotation of the Earth forms a natural clock) and when it is no longer possible to count the years we find that the decay of radioactive elements provides us with a convenient clock. The periodic property of a sample of radioactive material is that the activity of a sample decreases to half its original value in a time called its *half-life* (which varies from element to element). If we can measure the activity of a sample of an element (for which we know the half-life) at two different times, we can deduce the time interval.

Small time intervals

For smaller time intervals we use electrical rather than mechanical oscillations. Some clocks rely on the national supply of alternating current at 50.0 hertz, with one oscillation taking 0.0200 s. This supply is then used to drive a synchronous motor which in turn drives a second hand on a clock at, say, one revolution per second. As the sweep can be broken up into 100 equal parts this sort of clock will be capable of measuring to ± 0.01 s, which will be better than $\pm 1\%$ for time intervals of greater than 1 s, provided that the alternating current has a frequency of exactly 50.0 Hz. By employing electrical circuits which will oscillate at 10^3 Hz or 10^6 Hz, even shorter time intervals can be measured with equal precision. The frequency of the carrier wave of BBC Radio 2 is 200 kHz and is maintained to 5 parts in 10^{10}. It is usual to display the 'ticks' of such clocks not by sweeping a hand round a dial, but by employing a counter called a scaler. For all these clocks used to measure short time intervals there remains the problem of switching them on and off. The human reaction time is quite unreliable (it may be as much as 0.3 s) and so electrical switching is used (see page 25).

A rough value of a short time interval can be achieved using the *calibrated* timebase of a cathode ray oscilloscope, if the start of the interval to be measured can be arranged to trigger the timebase, and if the end of the interval is registered by giving a voltage pulse to the Y-plates. The experiment is repeated many times per second so as to get a steady trace which the eye can see. For example, if the timebase used has a value of 10^5 mm s^{-1} and the trace shows a pulse 30 mm from the start, then the time interval is 3.0×10^{-4} s. This technique is used to measure Δt in the sonar and radar mentioned in Section 1-4.

Time interval /seconds	
10^{17}	age of the Earth
10^{15}	
10^{13}	time since earliest man
10^{11}	half-life of carbon-14
10^{10}	time since the birth of Christ
10^{9}	life of a man
10^{7}	time between successive winters
10^{5}	time of rotation of the Earth on its axis
10^{3}	time needed to eat breakfast
10^{1}	ten seconds
10^{0}	time between heart beats
10^{-1}	time required for a normal blink
10^{-3}	time of contact of two colliding billiard balls
10^{-6}	time for one oscillation of a radio wave
10^{-9}	time for light from this page to reach your eye

Table 1-2 Orders of magnitude of time intervals.

1-6 Physical quantities and their dimensions

The need to have universally agreed standards of length and time has already been noted. Should we continue in this way and agree standards of speed (perhaps the speed of sound in air under certain conditions of temperature, pressure, and humidity), acceleration, and so on? It is *not* necessary to do this. If we have already defined units of length and time (and thus have chosen length and time to be *fundamental quantities*) we can *derive* units for speed and acceleration, using equations which will define the new quantity, and also indicate the unit of this new quantity. Thus, for example,

$$\text{average speed} = \frac{\text{distance travelled}}{\text{time taken}}$$

and the unit of speed will necessarily be the metre/second or $m\,s^{-1}$.

We can similarly define acceleration and thus find a unit for acceleration, but we cannot go much further. Density, for example, cannot be expressed in terms of length and time, so at least one more fundamental quantity is required. What should we choose? We could choose density itself, or we could choose force or mass—the choice is arbitrary. We do in fact choose *mass* as our third fundamental quantity and the internationally agreed standard of mass is the standard kilogram. This was originally the mass of one litre of water when its temperature was 4 °C, but it is now a mass equal to the mass of the international prototype of the kilogram, a cylinder of platinum–iridium kept at the International Bureau of Weights and Measures at Sèvres. Thus the mass of this cylinder is, by definition, one kilogram.

These three fundamental quantities (mass, length, and time) are all we need to derive all the physical quantities we shall meet in this book. Another way of expressing this is to say that if we denote the *dimensions* of mass by M, of length by L, and of time by T, then the dimensions of any derived quantity can be expressed in terms of M, L, and T. For example, density is defined by the equation

$$\text{density of substance} = \frac{\text{mass of body}}{\text{volume of body}}.$$

The dimensions of density are (since volume can always be expressed as the product of three lengths) $M \div L^3$ or ML^{-3}. We shall use the notation

$$[\text{density}] = ML^{-3}, \qquad [1\text{-}1]$$

although some authors prefer to write 'the dimensions of density are $[ML^{-3}]$'. An equation relating physical quantities must (if it is correct) be *dimensionally homogeneous*, that is, each term of the equation must have the same dimensions. This is best illustrated by an example. Suppose we deduced that the mass m of a cylinder of height h, radius r, and made of a material of density ρ, was given by $m = \pi \rho r h$. The dimensions of the left-hand side of the equation are simply M, so those of the right-hand side should be M also. As π is the ratio of two lengths it has no dimensions (see page 52), $[r] = L$, $[h] = L$, and $[\rho] = ML^{-3}$, so that $[\pi \rho r h] = L \times L \times ML^{-3} = ML^{-1}$. We conclude that the statement $m = \pi \rho r h$ is *not* correct. Note, however, that

(a) we do not learn where it is wrong, and
(b) it is a check on the dimensions only, and not a check on any numerical factors. It is even possible for an equation to be dimensionally correct, and physically wrong (see Exercise 3-37).

So if the dimensional check does not tally, the equation is physically wrong; if the check does tally, the equation *may* be physically correct.

1 Introduction

1-7 Units

The units used for the fundamental quantities of mass, length, and time, in the three main systems of units, are given in table 1-3.

The prefixes shown in table 1-4 are commonly used for multiples and submultiples of the gram, metre, and second. Thus a microsecond is 10^{-6} s, and a kilogram is 10^3 g.

	System of units	Mass	Length	Time
Fundamental system (SI)	m.k.s.	kilogram (kg)	metre (m)	second (s)
Related systems (not used in this text)	c.g.s.	gram (g) = 10^{-3} kg	centimetre (cm) = 10^{-2} m	second (s)
	f.p.s.	pound (lb) = 0.453 592 37 kg	foot (ft) = 0.3048 m	second (s)

Table 1-3 *Note.* There are no longer agreed standards for the pound and the foot. They are defined, as in this table, as exact fractions of the kilogram and metre respectively.

Prefix	tera-	giga-	mega-	kilo-	milli-	micro-	nano-	pico-
Multiple	$10^{12} \times$	$10^9 \times$	$10^6 \times$	$10^3 \times$	$10^{-3} \times$	$10^{-6} \times$	$10^{-9} \times$	$10^{-12} \times$
Symbol	T	G	M	k	m	μ	n	p

Table 1-4

1-8 Symbols for physical quantities

In this book we shall use symbols for physical quantities which represent both the number and the unit. Thus m might represent a mass of 14 kg, a an acceleration of 1.60 m s^{-2}, and so forth. When we substitute for a symbol in an equation we shall substitute both the number *and* the unit. In this way the dimensional consistency of our equations will automatically be tested and the consistency of the units is checked. For example, the magnitude of the acceleration a of a particle moving in a circle of radius r with a constant speed v might be found to be given by $a = v^2/r$. If we substitute $v = 60 \text{ m s}^{-1}$ and $r = 400$ m, we find that

$$a = \frac{(60 \text{ m/s})^2}{400 \text{ m}} = \frac{60 \times 60}{400} \frac{\text{m}}{\text{s}^2} = 9 \text{ m s}^{-2}.$$

The dimensions *and* the units are correct. However, on substituting $v = 60 \text{ m s}^{-1}$ and $r = 0.4$ km, we find that

$$a = \frac{(60 \text{ m/s})^2}{0.4 \text{ km}} = \frac{60 \times 60}{0.4} \frac{\text{m}^2}{\text{km s}^2} = 9000 \text{ m}^2 \text{ km}^{-1} \text{ s}^{-2}.$$

The dimension $L^2/LT^2 (= LT^{-2})$ are correct but the unit has been left in an awkward form. We had better start again with

$$a = \frac{(60 \text{ m/s})^2}{(0.4 \text{ km})\left(\dfrac{1000 \text{ m}}{1 \text{ km}}\right)} = \frac{(60 \text{ m/s})^2}{400 \text{ m}} = 9 \text{ m s}^{-2}.$$

We shall employ this technique in the examples in this book. The reader is advised to do likewise when doing the exercises.

1-9 Standards

The two most important criteria of standards of mass, length, and time are *availability* and *constancy*. Advances in technology have thrown doubt on the constancy of some of the earlier standards, and we now sacrifice some availability for the sake of constancy. For example, as stated in Sections 1-2 and 1-6, the original standards of time and mass were, respectively, a fraction of a solar day, and the mass of a certain volume of water. These standards are certainly readily available, but we now believe that the length of a day is increasing (by about 0.001 s in every 100 years) and we know that even the purest water consists of unknown proportions of the different isotopes of hydrogen and oxygen (so that a given volume does not have a fixed mass).

We now try to choose standards based on the subatomic behaviour of the atoms of a particular isotope of an element (see Section 1-2). As far as we know, this sub-atomic behaviour is unaffected by external conditions. We still do not have, however, an atomic standard of mass; our ability to compare the masses of objects is at present much better than our ability to count the number of atoms in a given body. (For further discussion on this topic see the books listed in the bibliography at the end of this chapter.)

1-10 Errors

In Section 1-3 the concept of the possible percentage error in an experimental observation was introduced. It is possible to estimate the random errors when using a familiar piece of apparatus. If the apparatus is wrongly designed or inaccurately made, then further, systematic, errors are introduced which are more difficult to estimate or even (in some cases) to detect. Other systematic errors may be introduced by variations in the physical environment. The effect of the environment on an experiment must be very carefully considered. To take an extreme example, in the experiment to measure g outlined on page 40, the effect of external oscillations set up by Atlantic rollers hitting the west coast of England was considered, though the experiment was performed over two hundred miles away from the west coast!

Random errors

If we have two measurements x and y which have possible errors $\pm \Delta x$ and $\pm \Delta y$, respectively, we shall want to know the possible error in the result if we

(a) find the sum of x and y,

(b) find their difference,
(c) find their product, or
(d) find their quotient.

Any more complicated process (for example, $x^2 y$ or $(x-y)y$) is based on these simple processes.

(a) If we add x and y (and for this to be possible they, and Δx and Δy, must of course be measurements of the same type of physical quantity), the possible sum might be as large as $x+y+\Delta x+\Delta y$ or as small as $x+y-\Delta x-\Delta y$; that is, it is $x+y\pm(\Delta x+\Delta y)$. The possible error in the sum is $\pm(\Delta x+\Delta y)$.

(b) A similar argument holds for the possible error in $x-y$; the possible error in the difference is also $\pm(\Delta x+\Delta y)$.

(c) If x and y might be as large as $x+\Delta x$ and $y+\Delta y$, their product might be as large as $(x+\Delta x)(y+\Delta y) \approx xy+x\Delta y+y\Delta x$ (neglecting the small term $\Delta x\Delta y$). Thus the error would be $x\Delta y+y\Delta x$, or $-(x\Delta y+y\Delta x)$ if x and y had been as small as $x-\Delta x$ and $y-\Delta y$. So

$$\text{the possible error} \approx \pm(x\Delta y+y\Delta x),$$

$$\text{the possible fractional error} \approx \pm\left(\frac{x\Delta y+y\Delta x}{xy}\right)$$

$$= \pm\left(\frac{\Delta y}{y}+\frac{\Delta x}{x}\right)$$

$$= \pm \text{ (the sum of the possible fractional errors in } x \text{ and } y),$$

and the possible percentage error in xy $\approx$ (the sum of the possible percentage errors in x and y). [1-2]

For example, if the possible percentage error in the length of a rectangular field is 2%, and the possible percentage error in its breadth is 1%, the possible percentage error in its area is, approximately, 3%.

(d) The same result holds for x/y: the possible percentage error in $x/y \approx \pm$ the sum of the possible percentage errors in x and y.

▶ **Example 1-1** A quantity E, given by $E = Fl/\pi e a^2$, is being calculated from measurements of F, l, e, and a. These are found to be:

$F = (0.90 \pm 0.01)\,\text{N}$ $e = (1.74 \pm 0.01)\,\text{mm}$
$l = (5.00 \pm 0.01)\,\text{m}$ $a = (0.20 \pm 0.01)\,\text{mm}$.

The percentage errors are: F 1.1
l 0.2
e 0.6
a 5.0 ⎫ (included twice because
a 5.0 ⎭ a is squared)
and π 0.

1 Introduction

These are added to give a percentage error of 11.9% in E. The raw value of E is 2.1×10^{10} N m^{-2}, and the percentage error $\approx 12\%$, that is, $E = (2.1 \pm 0.2) \times 10^{10}$ N m^{-2}. ◀

When a measured quantity x appears raised to a power n and the possible error in x is $\pm\Delta x$, then the possible percentage error in x^n is $\pm n(\Delta x/x)100$; this is an extension of equation 1-2, and is used in Example 1-1. When considering the precision to be expected in an experiment, a rough calculation of the possible errors tells us not only the number of significant figures we may quote in the result and the possible error, but it also pinpoints the *least* reliable measurements. Improving these least reliable measurements will have the greatest effect in improving the experiment. To take a particular case, if we were trying to find the density of a material in the shape of a sphere, using the formula $\rho = 3m/4\pi r^3$ and measuring m and r, a 3% error in r would contribute approximately 9% to the possible error in ρ. If we could make the error in r only 1%, the error in ρ would fall to 3%.

It must be stressed that the errors considered above are *possible* errors; the *probable* errors are less than these. To estimate the probable error involves taking a number of readings of a given measurement and calculating the mean of these readings and their deviation from this mean. Examples of this can be found in books which deal with elementary statistical analysis.

1-11 Relationships

We begin with a reminder of the way in which some algebraic language is used. In this paragraph x, y, and z will represent *variable* quantities and other letters such as a, b, and c will represent *constant* quantities. The statement

$$y = ax$$

means that y is *proportional* to x; from another point of view, of course, $x = (1/a)y$ and x is proportional to y. Proportionality is always reciprocal.

Similarly if

$$y = ax^2,$$

y is proportional to x^2, though not to x. And if

$$y = \frac{a}{x},$$

y is proportional to $1/x$, or *inversely proportional* to x.

The statement

$$y = ax + b$$

(of which $y = ax$ is a special case) implies that there is *a linear relationship* between y and x. That is, if values of y and x were plotted on a graph, a straight *line* would result. However, y and x are not proportional in this case, though $(y-b)$ and x are.

If

$$y = ax^2 + b, \quad \text{or} \quad y = \frac{a}{x} + b, \quad \text{etc.}$$

there is no longer a linear relationship between y and x, and if values of y and x are plotted on a graph, a *curve* is obtained. However, there *is* a linear relationship in $y = ax^2 + b$, namely the relationship between y and x^2, and $(y-b)$ is proportional to x^2; and in $y = a/x + b$, there *is* a linear relationship between y and $1/x$, and $(y-b)$ is proportional to $1/x$.

It should be clear by now that for many relationships, not necessarily linear, between two variables, x and y, it is possible to consider the relationship in such a way that a straight-line graph can be drawn. For example, the relationship between y and x in

$$xy = \frac{a}{x} + \frac{b}{y}$$

is obviously not linear, but the equation can be rewritten as

$$xy^2 = a\frac{y}{x} + b.$$

Now there is here a linear relationship between xy^2 and y/x, and if values of xy^2 and y/x are plotted, a straight line will result.

From now on, therefore, it should be understood that in the general *equation of a straight line*,

$$y = mx + c, \qquad [1\text{-}3]$$

the variables written here as y and x may be more complicated functions of other variables, as in the fourth example in table 1-5: 'y' may be M, and 'x' may be T^2. In every case, however, the *slope* of the line and the value of y when $x = 0$ (the *y-intercept*) are 'm' and 'c' respectively; in the example already chosen, 'm' = $k/4\pi$ and 'c' = $-m_0$.

Suppose we have measured pairs of corresponding values of y and x, and have reason to believe that the relationship between them is of the form, say, $y = a/x + b$. If we plot values of y/y-unit against values of $x^{-1}/(x\text{-unit})^{-1}$, and a straight line results, then we can conclude that our idea was correct and, moreover, we can from the graph find the numerical values of the constants a and b. Figure 1-4 shows how the slope and the y-intercept can be calculated, and table 1-5 gives more examples of this process.

1-11 Relationships 9

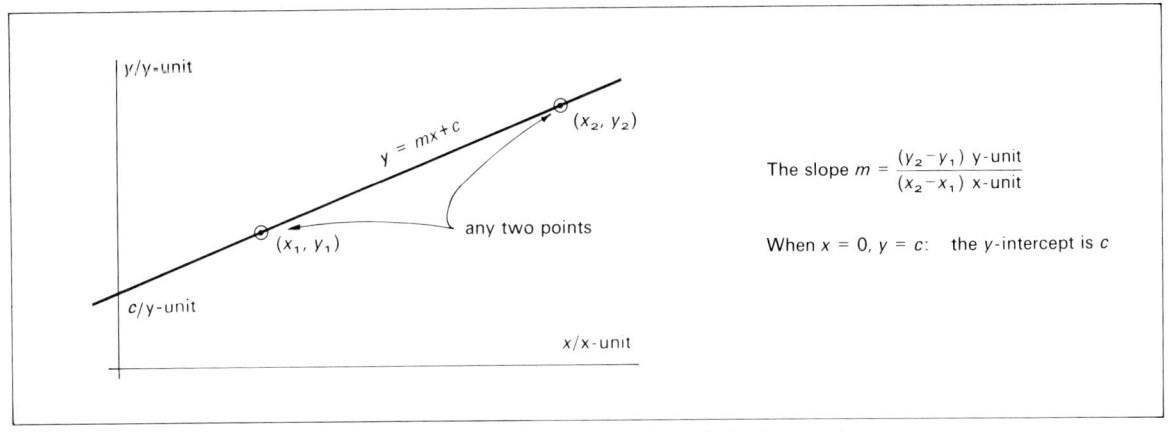

Figure 1-4 When we have a straight-line graph we can find the values of m and c in the equation $y = mx + c$.

▶ **Example 1-2** A scientist measures the following values of the variables ρ and x:

$\rho/\text{kg m}^{-3}$	x/mm
1300	78
1000	61
820	40
700	20
610	1

He thinks there may be some relationship between them of the form $1/\rho = ax + b$, where a and b are constants. Is he right, and if so, what are the values of a and b?

He should plot $\rho^{-1}/\text{kg}^{-1}\text{m}^3$ against x/mm and then he will be able to draw a straight line through the points (see figure 1-5).

Thus the relationship between ρ and x is of the form $1/\rho = ax + b$. The value of b is the y-intercept, that is the value of $1/\rho$ when $x = 0$. $b = 1.65 \times 10^{-3}\,\text{m}^3\,\text{kg}^{-1}$. The value of a is the slope of the graph. Taking points as far apart as possible

$$\text{slope} = \frac{(0.78 - 1.65)\,10^{-3}\,\text{m}^3\,\text{kg}^{-1}}{(80 - 0)\,\text{mm}}$$

$$= -1.1 \times 10^{-5}\,\text{m}^3\,\text{kg}^{-1}\,\text{mm}^{-1}.$$

$$\therefore a = \left(-1.1 \times 10^{-5}\,\frac{\text{m}^3\,\text{kg}^{-1}}{\text{mm}}\right)\left(\frac{10^3\,\text{mm}}{1\,\text{m}}\right)$$

$$= -1.1 \times 10^{-2}\,\text{m}^2\,\text{kg}^{-1}.$$

Note: we calculate the slope using (a) two points as far apart as possible, (b) the actual values of $\rho^{-1}/\text{kg}^{-1}\,\text{m}^3$ (e.g. 0.78) and x/mm (e.g. 80) and not just the distance on the graph paper. ◀

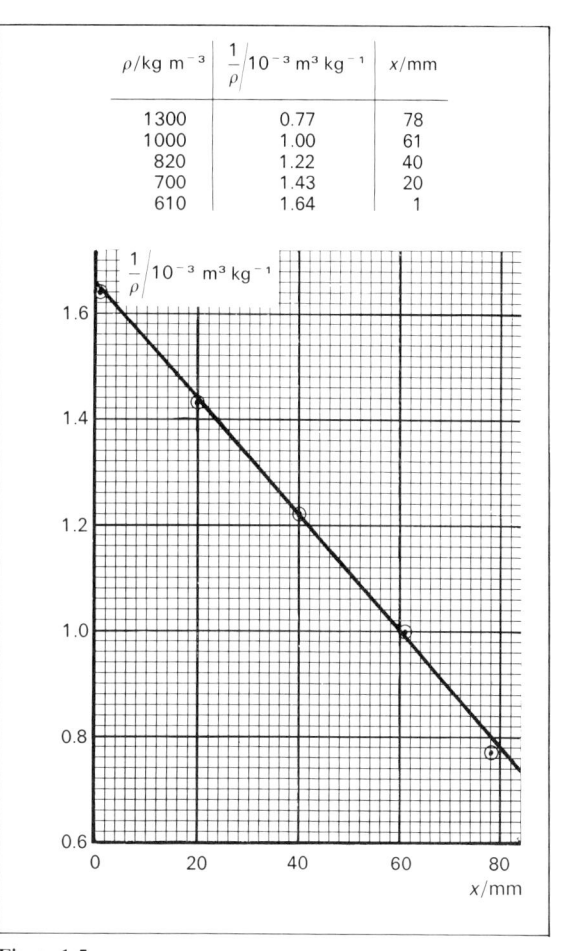

$\rho/\text{kg m}^{-3}$	$\dfrac{1}{\rho}\Big/10^{-3}\,\text{m}^3\,\text{kg}^{-1}$	x/mm
1300	0.77	78
1000	1.00	61
820	1.22	40
700	1.43	20
610	1.64	1

Figure 1-5

Known or deduced relation between quantities on shaded background	Relation reformed into shape $y = mx + c$	Information required	How information can be obtained
$T = 2\pi\sqrt{\dfrac{l}{g}}$	$T^2 = \dfrac{4\pi^2}{g}l$	g	slope is $\dfrac{4\pi^2}{g}$
$M = (V - ax)\rho$	$\dfrac{1}{\rho} = -\dfrac{a}{M}x + \dfrac{V}{M}$	V when M is known	$\dfrac{V}{M}$ is y-intercept
$\dfrac{\Delta F}{A} = E\dfrac{\Delta l}{l}$	$\Delta F = \dfrac{AE}{l}\Delta l$	E when A and l are known	$\dfrac{AE}{l}$ is slope
$T = 2\pi\sqrt{\dfrac{M+m_0}{k}}$	$M = \dfrac{k}{4\pi^2}T^2 - m_0$	m_0	y-intercept is $-m_0$
$p = av^n$	$\lg p = n\lg v + \lg a$	n	slope is n

Table 1-5 Plotting straight-line graphs. If, in any case, the graph when plotted is *not* a straight line, then our guess about the relationship was wrong, or our measurements are faulty.

1-12 Some useful mathematics

This section is not meant to cover anything like all the mathematics used in this text but merely to list a few important results. No attempt is made to deal with the calculus.

The binomial expansion

It can be shown that, when $-1 < x < +1$, then for all values of n

$$(1 \pm x)^n = 1 \pm nx + \frac{n(n-1)}{2}x^2 + \text{terms in } x^3, x^4, \text{ etc.}$$

Thus, if x is very small compared with unity, we can say that

$$(1 \pm x)^n \approx 1 \pm nx. \qquad [1\text{-}4]$$

For example, $\sqrt{(1-r)} = (1-r)^{1/2} \approx 1 - \tfrac{1}{2}r$,

and $\qquad \dfrac{1}{1+3\alpha} = (1+3\alpha)^{-1} \approx 1 - 3\alpha.$

The general angle

The reader will be familiar with the functions $\sin\theta$ and $\cos\theta$ for $0 \leqslant \theta \leqslant 90°$; they can be found from tables. To find their values for other values of θ, we can draw the sine and cosine graphs, as in figure 1-6. We can see from these graphs that, for example,

$$\sin 130° = \sin 50°$$
$$\cos 100° = -\cos 80°$$

and we can find the values of $\sin 50°$ and $\cos 80°$ from tables. In particular we can see that $\sin 180° = 0$ and $\cos 180° = -1$.

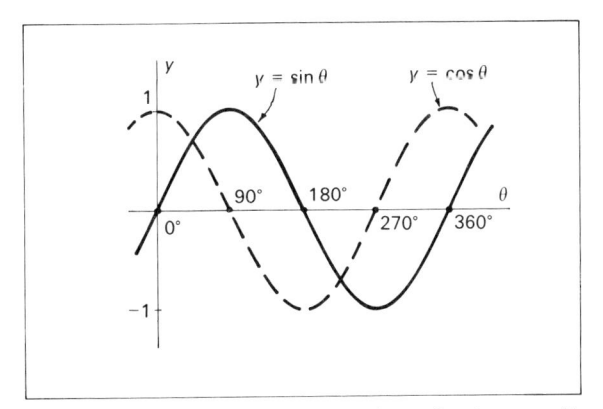

Figure 1-6 The sine and cosine curves drawn for the range 0° to 360°.

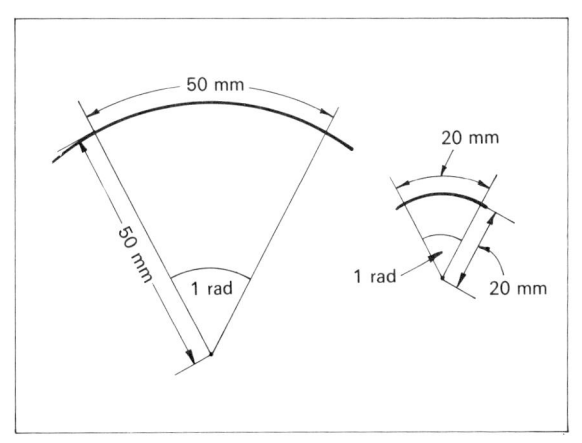

Figure 1-7

The radian measure of angle

The *radian* (rad) is an alternative to the degree as a measure of angle. If, in a circle of radius r, an arc of length s subtends an angle θ (measured in radians) at the centre, then

$$\theta = \frac{s}{r}. \qquad [1\text{-}5]$$

If we now consider a complete circle of radius r (whose 'arc length' is $2\pi r$) this definition implies that the angle θ at the centre is given by

$$\theta = \frac{2\pi r}{r} \text{ radians}$$

$$= 2\pi \text{ radians}.$$

Since the angle at the centre is also 360°, we now see that

$$360° = 2\pi \text{ rad}$$

or $\qquad 180° = \pi \text{ rad}$

or $\qquad 57.3° = 1 \text{ rad}.$

Figure 1-7 illustrates the fact that when the arc length is equal to the radius of a circle, the angle at the centre is 1 radian.

Angles can be converted from degrees to radians, or vice versa, either using the relation $\pi \text{ rad} = 180°$, or using mathematical tables. The next paragraph indicates the sort of situation where it is essential to use the radian measure of angle.

Small angles

When an angle θ is close to zero we find that $\cos\theta$ is close to 1, and that $\sin\theta$ is close to θ, where θ is measured in radians. Table 1-6 examines these approximations more closely, listing $\sin\theta/\theta$ to show how closely $\sin\theta/\theta$ approaches unity as θ approaches zero.

It can be formally proved that

$$\lim_{\theta \to 0} \frac{\sin\theta}{\theta} = 1. \qquad [1\text{-}6]$$

Of course the symbol θ can be replaced by other symbols so that, for example,

$$\lim_{x \to 0} \frac{\sin x}{x} = \lim_{\frac{1}{2}\phi \to 0} \frac{\sin \frac{1}{2}\phi}{\frac{1}{2}\phi} = 1.$$

θ/degrees	θ/radians	$\sin\theta$	$\sin\theta/\theta$	$\cos\theta$
20	0.349	0.342	1.02	0.940
15	0.262	0.259	1.01	0.966
10	0.175	0.174	1.01	0.985
5	0.0873	0.0872	1.00	0.996
1	0.0175	0.0175	1.00	1.00

Table 1-6 Functions of θ as θ tends to zero. All numbers are given to three significant figures.

Bibliography

Austin, A. V. (1968). 'Standards of measurement.' *Scientific American* offprint number 326.

Cook, A. H. (1969). 'A new basis for measurement.' *Physics Education*, **4**, page 353.

Deevey, E. S., Jr. (1952). 'Radiocarbon dating.' *Scientific American* offprint number 811.

Furth, R. (1950). 'Limits of measurement.' *Scientific American* offprint number 255.

Hurley, P. M. (1949). 'Radioactivity and time.' *Scientific American* offprint number 220.

Lyons, H. (1957). 'Atomic clocks.' *Scientific American* offprint number 225.

Phillips, M. D. (1972). 'A simple approach to experimental errors.' *Physics Education*, **7**, page 383.

Symbols Committee of The Royal Society (1971). *Quantities, units and symbols.*

Dorling, G. W. (1972). *Time.* Longman. An elementary text.

PSSC (1960). *Physics.* Heath. The introductory chapters discuss the nature of physics and the measurement of space and time.

SMP (1968). *Advanced Mathematics*, Book 4. Cambridge University Press. Chapter 40 deals with dimensional analysis.

Squires, G. L. (1968). *Practical physics.* McGraw–Hill. A very useful reference for errors and experimental techniques.

Wenham, E. J., Dorling, G. W., Snell, J. A. N., Taylor, B. (1972). *Physics, concepts and models.* Addison–Wesley. Unit One is about models.

Exercises

1-1 In Section 1-2 we said that the standard of length used to be the distance between two scratches on a certain platinum–iridium bar measured under certain conditions. What conditions should have been specified?

1-2 The following measurements of length are made, and the possible error is given:
(a) (6371 ± 1) km (b) (0.90 ± 0.01) mm (c) (798 ± 2) mm.
Which is the most precise measurement? Explain. Which measurement needed the most sensitive instrument?

1-3 Criticize the following information which has appeared on a packet of peanuts. 'Min. net wt. 14 DR 24.808 GRM'.

1-4 Criticize the following arithmetical operations, and suggest correct alternatives:
(a) $3.2 \text{ m} \times 9.6 \text{ m} = 30.72 \text{ m}^2$
(b) $2.0 \times 10^7 \text{ m} + 6371 \text{ km} = 2.6371 \times 10^7 \text{ m}$
(c) 1.54 kg is the mean value of the following four measurements of a particular mass: 1.52 kg, 1.49 kg, 1.51 kg, 1.64 kg.

1-5 Suppose you were given a micrometer screw gauge to measure the thickness of a sheet of paper. You found that its thickness is 0.09 mm, and the possible error is 0.01 mm. Is there any advantage in using the same instrument to find the thickness of one sheet by first finding the thickness of 50 sheets? Can you think of similar examples?

1-6 The 'parallax method' of measuring distances is not easy to apply to the measurement of the distances of stars from the Earth. The diameter of the Earth's orbit round the Sun is about 3×10^{11} m, and the nearest star is about 10^{17} m from the Earth. What maximum angle of parallax does this star produce for an observer on the Earth?

1-7 If electromagnetic radiation (speed in a vacuum = $3.0 \times 10^8 \text{ m s}^{-1}$) were used to measure the distance of a star which was 10^{20} m from the Earth, what would be the time interval between the emission of the pulse and its arrival back on the Earth? Give your answer in (a) seconds and (b) years.

1-8 In talking to astronauts on the Moon's surface there is *always* a pause between question and answer (however simple the question). What can you deduce from this observation?

1-9 Complete some of the gaps in table 1-1 by finding distances which are
(a) 10^{11} m (b) 10^9 m (c) 10^7 m (d) 10^5 m
(e) 10^3 m (f) 10^{-3} m.

1-10 Can an optical microscope be made so sensitive that it can measure to (a) 10^{-6} m (b) 10^{-8} m? What is an electron microscope? Are there any limits to the sensitivity to which it can make measurements?

1-11 Figure 10-2b on page 156 represents the oscilloscope trace produced in an experiment designed to measure the time taken for an electron to travel between two points A and B, 8.4 m apart. One pulse occurs when the electron is at A, the other when it is at B. If the timebase period is 1.0 μs m^{-1}, and the markings on the oscilloscope are at 10 mm intervals, what are
(a) the time interval between the pulses
(b) the speed of the electron?

1-12 Complete some of the gaps in table 1-2 by finding time intervals which are
(a) 10^{14} s (b) 10^8 s (c) 10^6 s (d) 10^4 s (e) 10^{-4} s
(f) 10^{-5} s.

1-13 Are there only three fundamental quantities?

1-14 Mass, length, and time were chosen as the fundamental quantities a long time ago. If you were beginning again today, would you make the same choice?

1-15 If the linear dimensions of *everything* were to double overnight, how would your life be affected?

1-16 Would the loss or destruction of the standard kilogram create any difficulties (*a*) in principle (*b*) in practice?

1-17 Which of the following combinations could have been chosen to serve as the three fundamental quantities:
(*a*) length, time, density
(*b*) length, time, volume
(*c*) length, time, acceleration?

1-18 If we had chosen length and time to be our first two fundamental quantities, and had chosen density to be the third, and had used D as a symbol for the dimensions of density, what would have been the dimensions of (*a*) mass (*b*) acceleration? ●

1-19 If, as in Exercise 1-18, we had chosen density to be the third fundamental quantity, and had chosen as our standard material one with a density to which we had assigned the value one den, what would have been the unit of (*a*) mass (*b*) acceleration? ●

1-20 Does Euclid's geometry hold *exactly* for the calculations a surveyor might make in planning a new road? Explain your answer.

1-21 The diameter of a particular rod was measured on three different occasions (not necessarily by the same person each time, or using the same instrument each time) and the readings were
(*a*) 5.06 mm, 5.08 mm, 5.08 mm, 5.05 mm, 5.07 mm, 5.06 mm
(*b*) 4.98 mm, 4.95 mm, 4.97 mm, 4.96 mm, 4.97 mm, 4.97 mm
(*c*) 5.18 mm, 5.12 mm, 4.98 mm, 5.00 mm, 5.05 mm, 5.07 mm.
Comment on these results. If you were given the results labelled (*c*), what would you try to do before giving an estimate of the diameter of the rod?

1-22 Prove from first principles that if $\pm \Delta x$ and $\pm \Delta y$ are the possible errors in x and y, then the possible error in $3x - 2y$ is $\pm(3\Delta x + 2\Delta y)$.

1-23 Prove from first principles that if the possible percentage errors in x and y are $\pm r$ and $\pm s$ per cent respectively, then the possible percentage error in x/y is $\pm(r+s)$ per cent.

1-24 The density of a gas is to be calculated from the following readings:
mass of container $= 2.3$ kg ± 0.1 kg
mass of container + gas $= 26.3$ kg ± 0.1 kg
volume of gas $= 20$ m^3 ± 1 m^3.
Calculate the density of the gas, giving the possible error in the result. ●

1-25 A simple pendulum is used in an attempt to measure the value of g, assuming the truth of the relationship $T = 2\pi \sqrt{(l/g)}$, where T is the period of the pendulum and l is its length. The time for five oscillations is found to be 10 s $\pm$ 1 s, and the length of the pendulum is found to be 0.990 m $\pm$ 0.005 m. Calculate the value of g, and the possible percentage error in the result. What criticism would you make of the conduct of the experiment? ●

1-26 An optical bench is used to measure the image distance corresponding to a certain object distance for a given lens. The readings taken are:
position of object $= 234$ mm
position of lens $= 434$ mm
position of image $= 734$ mm.
Each position can be assumed to have a possible error of ± 2 mm in it. Find the value of the focal length f, using the formula $1/u + 1/v = 1/f$, where u and v are the object and image distances from the lens, and calculate the possible error in the value of f. ●

1-27 It is proposed to measure the internal diameter of some capillary tubing. Two methods are suggested.
(*a*) A travelling microscope should be arranged to view the cross section of the tubing. The diameter is found to be 0.42 mm. The scale is such that, after making allowance for the thickness of the cross-wire, the possible error is judged to be ± 0.02 mm.
(*b*) Some mercury is introduced into the capillary tube, and the length of this thread is measured with a ruler. It is found to be 82 mm, with a possible error of ± 1 mm. The mass of the mercury is found to be 0.152 g, with a possible error of ± 0.001 g. The value of π (3.14) and the value of the density of mercury (13 600 kg m^{-3}) are assumed known without error. The diameter of the capillary tube is to be calculated using the relationship $m = \frac{1}{4}\pi d^2 l \rho$, where m, d, l, and ρ have the obvious meanings. Calculate the possible percentage error in each case, and comment on the result. ●

1-28 Below are listed some relationships between two stated variables. To produce a straight-line graph in each case, what should be plotted along the y-axis, and what along the x-axis? For your choice, state what will be the slope of the line, and what will be the y-intercept.

	relationship	variables
(*a*)	$T = kl^{1/2}$	T, l
(*b*)	$\dfrac{A}{T^2} = B + Ci$	T, i
(*c*)	$d = kl^p$	d, l
(*d*)	$T^2 l = A + \dfrac{4\pi^2 l^2}{g}$	T, l
(*e*)	$p = p_0 + \rho g h$	p, h

1-29 y and x are thought to be connected by a relationship of the form $y = Ax^n$. The following corresponding values of y and x are available:

x/unit	y/unit
0.50	0.24
0.74	0.84
0.99	2.01

Investigate the relationship between y and x, and if the suggested relationship is true, estimate, by drawing a graph, the values of A and n.

1-30 The length of the side of a cube increases from 10.00 mm to 10.12 mm. To two significant figures, what is the increase in volume of the cube? (Do not find the volume of the cube of side 10.12 mm.) ●

1-31 The radius of a spherical balloon increases by 3 per cent. What is the percentage change in its volume? ●

1-32 The cost of a manufactured article is proportional to the $\frac{3}{2}$th power of its length. If its cost is to be reduced by 6 per cent, by what percentage should its length by reduced? ●

1-33 The period T of a simple pendulum is given by $T = 2\pi \sqrt{(l/g)}$, where l is its length and g is the acceleration due to gravity. If its length is increased by 3 per cent, by what percentage is its period increased? ●

1-34 Find the values, correct to three significant figures, of
(a) sin 140°   (b) sin 173°   (c) cos 110°   (d) cos 158°.

1-35 What angle is subtended at the centre of a circle of radius 20 m by an arc of length 40 m? Give your answer in radians and also to the nearest degree. ●

1-36 What is the length of an arc of a circle if it subtends an angle of 20° at the centre, the radius of the circle being 2.0 m? ●

2 Describing motion

2-1 Vectors and scalars	15	2-6 Velocity and speed	22
2-2 Distance and displacement	15	2-7 Measuring speed	25
2-3 Vector algebra I	16	2-8 Relative velocity	28
2-4 Resolving vectors	19	Bibliography	29
2-5 Vector algebra II	21	Exercises	29

2-1 Vectors and scalars

We are going to be much concerned in mechanics with quantities which do not obey the familiar rules of algebra. Rules, that is, like

$$4 + 3 = 3 + 4 = 7$$

and

$$4 \times 3 = 3 \times 4 = 12$$

which are obeyed when we calculate the cost of our groceries or how long it will take us to do our work. The quantities which do obey these rules are called *scalar quantities* or, simply, scalars. They have only size, and need only a number and a unit for their complete specification. Time is a scalar: thus to say that the ball took 0.40 seconds to fall fully describes how long the falling took.

Not all physical quantities are scalars. Consider the problem

$$4 \text{ paces} + 3 \text{ paces}.$$

The answer is seven paces in the sense that seven steps have been taken but what if we ask how far from the starting point these seven steps have taken us? We now need to know that the problem is really

$$4 \text{ paces forward} + 3 \text{ paces forward},$$

and not   4 paces forward + 3 paces to the right,

if the answer is to be seven paces.

Clearly to solve the problem we need more information about the quantities. We need to know their direction, and then a new rule will be needed if we are to be able to add them. In this text we shall meet only quantities (other than scalars) which require a statement of size and direction relative to some fixed axes for their complete specification. These are called *vector quantities* or, simply, vectors, and to manipulate them we need vector algebra. For example, force is a vector (see Section 6-1) and the answer to the question 'what is the weight of that 10 kg mass?' is '98 N vertically downwards', and not simply '98 N'.

2-2 Distance and displacement

When a particle has two successive positions A and B, we are sometimes interested in the distance travelled in its path from A to B, and sometimes in its displacement, that is, the change of position of the particle. Its displacement is measured by the separation of the two points *and* the direction which must be taken to reach B from A. Since we live in a three-dimensional world, the successive positions of a particle will not generally lie in a plane, but for convenience we shall in this text confine ourselves to movement in a plane. The distinction between distance and displacement is best illustrated by an example; in

2 Describing motion

figure 2-1 we see three successive positions A, B, and C of a particle. The *distances* from A to B and from B to C, measured along the curve, are 71 m and 83 m respectively. The concept of direction does not here arise: in fact the direction of the movement is continually changing. On the other hand, the *displacement* of B from A is 68 m in the direction S 49° E, and the *displacement* of C from B is 55 m in the direction N 17° E. The symbols for distance and displacement are s and $\mathbf{s}$ respectively, the distinction in type-face meaning that the former is a scalar quantity and the latter a vector quantity. However, since both distances and displacements are often to do with *changes* of position, we shall frequently use the symbol Δ prefixed to both s and $\mathbf{s}$; that is, Δs for the distance travelled, and $\Delta \mathbf{s}$ for the change of displacement.

Adding distances and displacements

The sum of two distances (for example, A to B and B to C in figure 2-1) is simply the arithmetical sum, since they are scalar quantities. Thus in figure 2-1 the total *distance* travelled from A to C is $71\,\text{m} + 83\,\text{m} = 154\,\text{m}$. The result of adding the *displacements* B from A and C from B (that is, the total displacement of C from A), however, is clearly not the arithmetical sum of 68 m and 55 m, but is the straight-line distance (68 m, see figure 2-1c) from A to C in the direction of C from A (N 83° E). The addition of displacements is more complicated than the addition of distances; Section 2-3 provides general rules for adding (and subtracting) such vector quantities.

2-3 Vector algebra I

The technique used for adding displacements in Section 2-2 applies generally to the addition of all vector quantities. To add two vector quantities $\mathbf{a}$ and $\mathbf{b}$ (of sizes a and b respectively) we draw lines to represent $\mathbf{a}$ and $\mathbf{b}$ in size and direction, and then place the tail of $\mathbf{b}$ at the head of $\mathbf{a}$ (see figure 2-2). The line which can be drawn directly from the tail of $\mathbf{a}$ to the head of $\mathbf{b}$ represents the sum of $\mathbf{a}$ and $\mathbf{b}$ in size and direction: it is called the *resultant* of $\mathbf{a}$ and $\mathbf{b}$. This process is shown in figure 2-2, in which the symbol $\mathbf{c}$ is used to represent the sum of $\mathbf{a}$ and $\mathbf{b}$.

We can conveniently write

$$\mathbf{a} + \mathbf{b} = \mathbf{c},$$

but when writing these symbols for vector quantities when the distinction of a different type-face is not available either arrows must be placed above the symbols, or else the symbols must be underlined: that is, either $\vec{a}$ or $\underline{a}$. Otherwise there would be confusion, for it is clearly not true (in general) that $a + b = c$, that is, that the size of c is equal to the sum of the sizes of a and b.

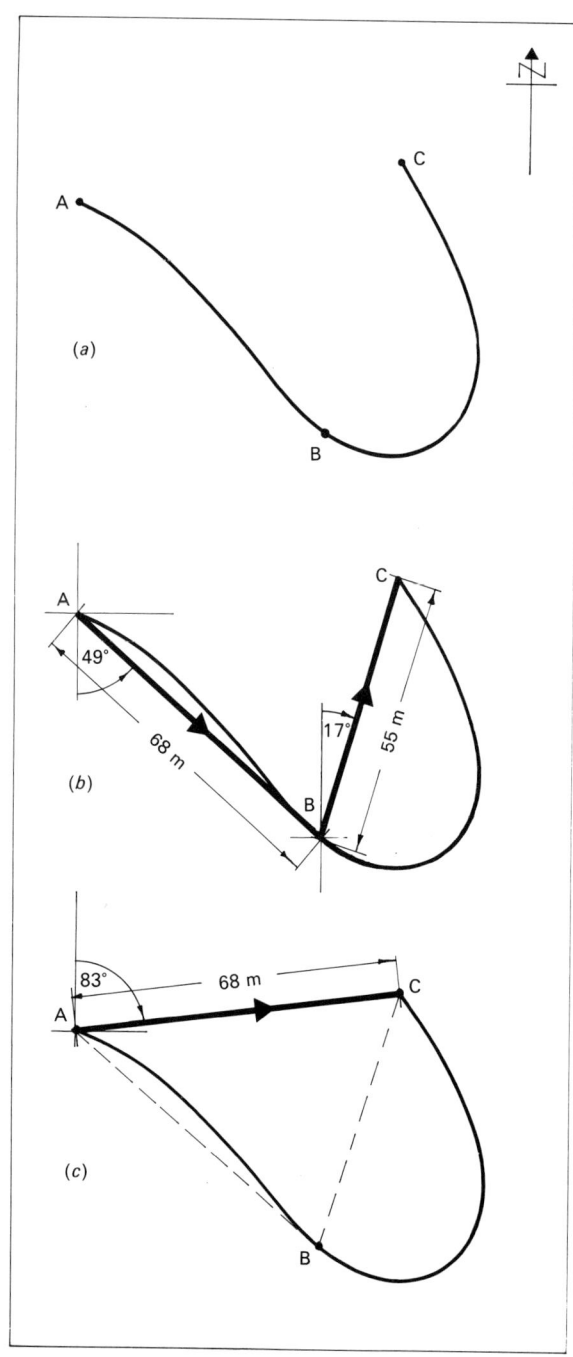

Figure 2-1

successively placed head-to-tail, and measure the direction of this line. If greater accuracy is essential, and a calculation must be performed, it is usually simpler to resolve the vectors first and then find their sum (see Section 2-4).

Vector quantities are in fact *defined* as those quantities which have size and direction and which can be added in this way. We shall meet two distinct classes of vector:

(a) *polar vectors* (or true vectors) such as displacement, or quantities such as velocity, acceleration, force, and momentum which are derived from displacement and implicitly involve the direction of a displacement; and

(b) *axial vectors* (or pseudovectors) such as the moment of a force which involves an axis of rotation. This second class of vector will be noted where it first appears but we shall in general use the single term vector.

The reader will have noticed in figure 2-2 that the vectors have been 'slid' about so as to bring them head-to-tail for adding. This is a legitimate process and is convenient when we do not need to know the line of action of the resultant. Vectors which can be slid about in this way are called *free vectors*. Any two such vectors of the same size and pointing in the same direction are equivalent vectors and we shall generally make no distinction between them. Two other basic properties are that vectors obey simple commutative (equation 2-1) and associative (equation 2-2) laws of addition:

$$s_1 + s_2 = s_2 + s_1 \qquad [2\text{-}1]$$

$$s_1 + (s_2 + s_3) = (s_1 + s_2) + s_3. \qquad [2\text{-}2]$$

The reader should draw sketches like figure 2-2 in order to illustrate these two laws.

Multiplication of a vector by a scalar

The vector $3s$ is defined as the vector sum $s+s+s$ or, for example, $s+2s$. Thus multiplying s by a non-dimensional number n yields the vector ns, which is parallel to s but of different size (figure 2-3). When n is negative the vector ns is in the opposite direction, or the opposite sense, to s. In particular, when n is -1, $-s$, the negative of s, is seen to be the same as s only with the arrow reversed.

When the multiplying scalar is not just a number but a physical quantity x, then the product xs is a different kind of vector, parallel to s, of size xs, but with new units. In Section 5-6 we will see that when the acceleration of a body, a vector a, is multiplied by its mass, a scalar m, the product ma defines a new kind of vector which we call a force F. The problem of multiplying two vectors together is left until Section 2-5.

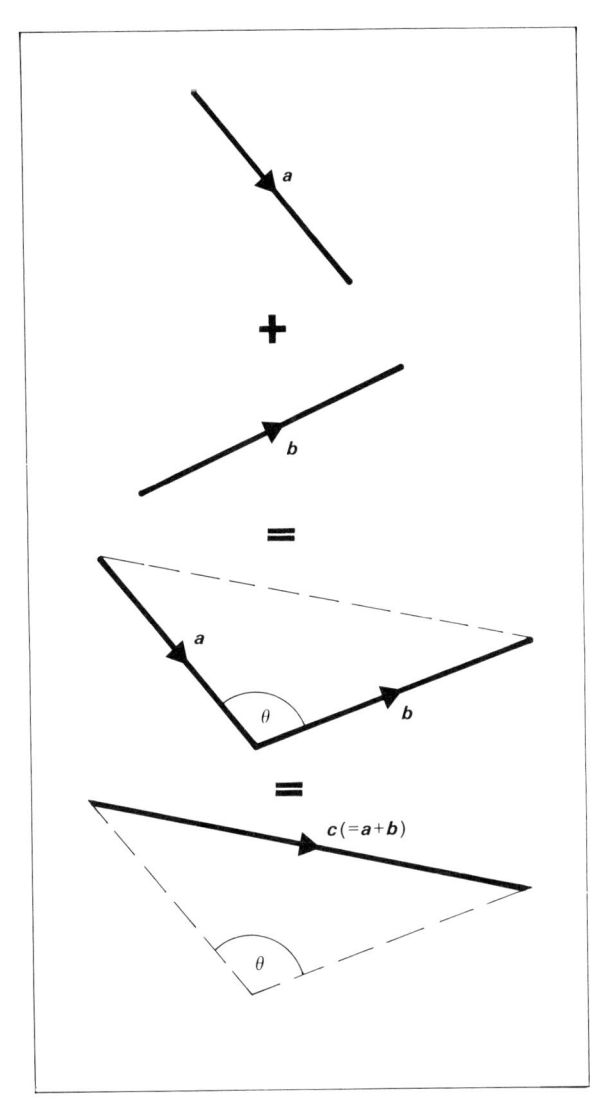

Figure 2-2 The addition of two vector quantities a and b.

Thus, a *scale drawing* can be used to find the resultant of two vector quantities; this method is quick and, with care, gives answers correct to two significant figures. Alternatively, the size and direction of the resultant may be *calculated*. The cosine formula gives

$$c^2 = a^2 + b^2 - 2ab\cos\theta.$$

When more than two vector quantities are to be added, the scale-drawing method is almost certainly quicker. We measure the length of the line drawn directly from the tail of the first vector to the head of the last with the vectors

2 Describing motion

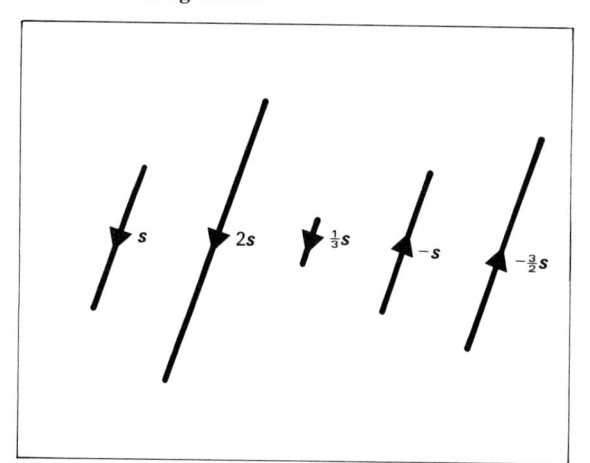

Figure 2-3 The vector s when multiplied by a number n remains parallel to s. The sense of the new vector ns is opposite to the sense of s if n is negative.

Subtracting vectors

The difference between two physical quantities is a recurring problem in mechanics. The change of displacement of a particle Δs, for instance, is defined as $\Delta s = s - s_0$, where s and s_0 are the final and the original displacement respectively.

To subtract two vectors we use the definition of the negative of a vector (see figure 2-4).

Thus $$s_1 - s_2 = s_1 + (-s_2).$$

The algebra of vectors, considered in this section in terms of displacement, applies to all other vector quantities such as velocity and force.

▶ **Example 2-1** An aeroplane is found to be flying in a SW direction at $120\,\mathrm{m\,s^{-1}}$ when there is a steady $35\,\mathrm{m\,s^{-1}}$ NW wind. What would be the velocity of the aeroplane if the wind ceased?

The resultant velocity of $120\,\mathrm{m\,s^{-1}}$ to the SW is the result of adding the aeroplane's own velocity to the wind velocity, that is,

$$\boldsymbol{v}_{\text{aeroplane}} = \boldsymbol{v}_{\text{aeroplane without wind}} + \boldsymbol{v}_{\text{wind}}.$$

Therefore

$$\boldsymbol{v}_{\text{aeroplane without wind}} = \boldsymbol{v}_{\text{aeroplane}} - \boldsymbol{v}_{\text{wind}}$$
$$= \boldsymbol{v}_{\text{aeroplane}} + (-\boldsymbol{v}_{\text{wind}}).$$

This calculation can be performed graphically, as shown in figure 2-5. ◀

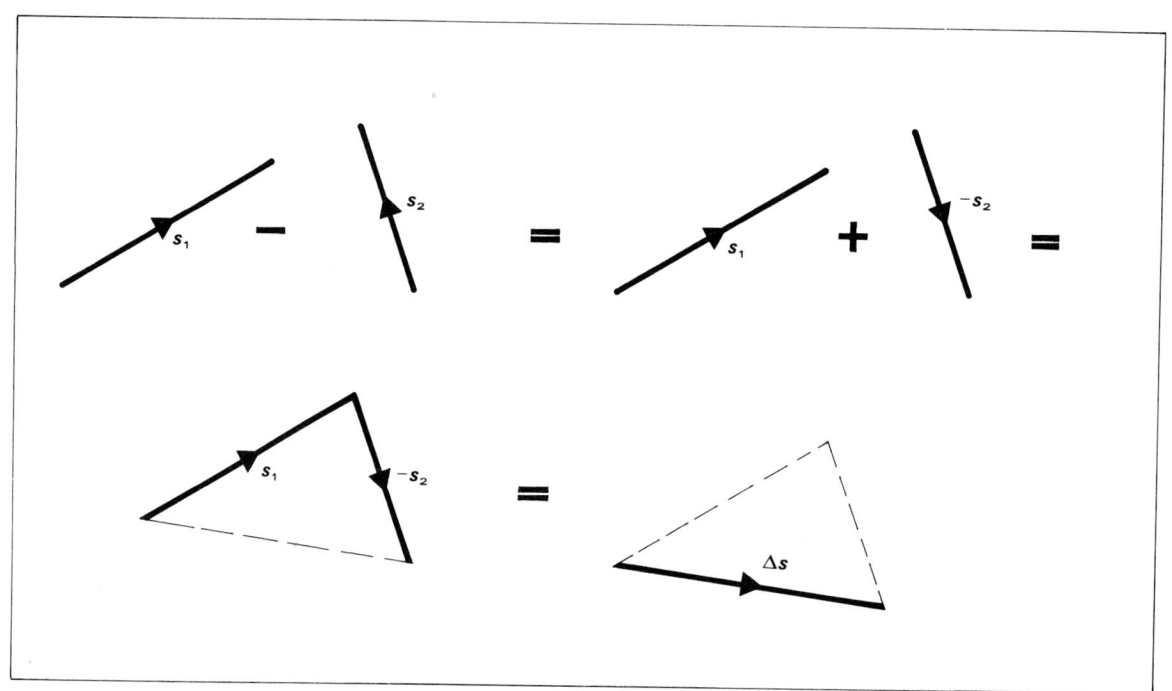

Figure 2-4 The vector difference $s_1 - s_2 = \Delta s$.

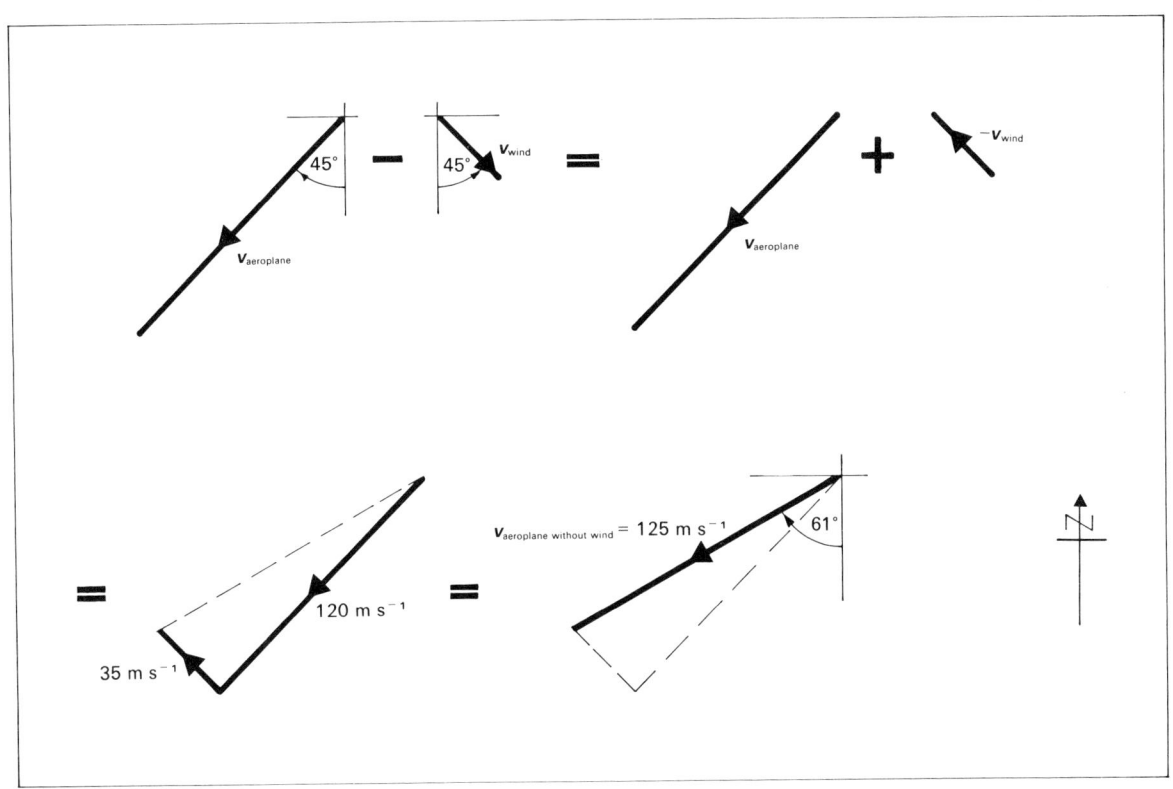

Figure 2-5 The velocity of the aeroplane without the wind would have been $125\,\text{m s}^{-1}$ in a direction $S\,61°\,W$.

2-4 Resolving vectors

When representing vectors in more than one dimension we use coordinate axes. Any displacement can be expressed as the sum of the displacements in the directions of the chosen axes. To consider two dimensions only, the vector OP in figure 2-6a could be described as the sum of a displacement of 49 metres in the x-direction and a displacement of 34 metres in the y-direction for the axes shown in figure 2-6b. These displacements are called the

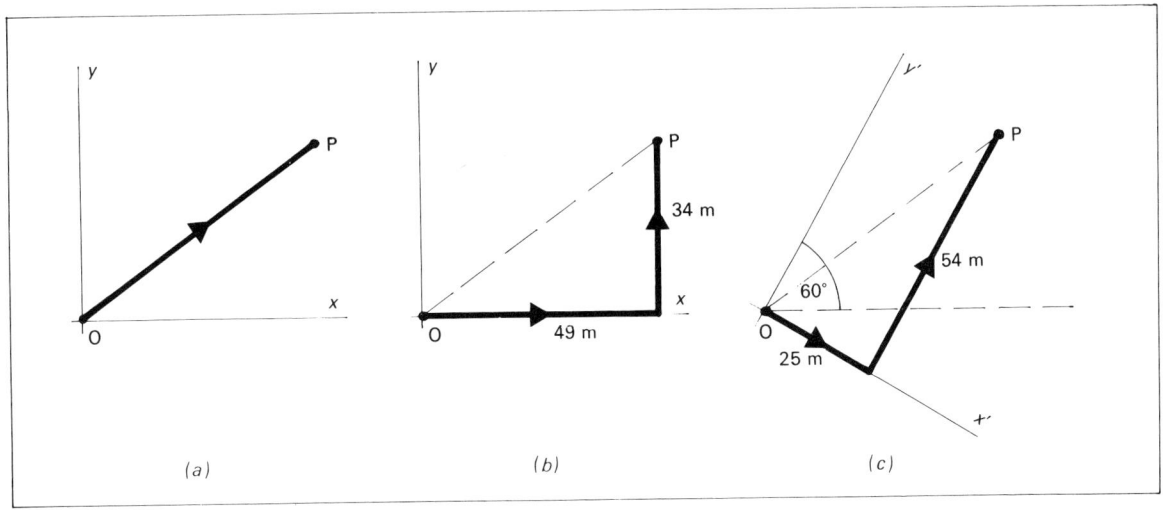

Figure 2-6 The magnitudes of the vectors in the x- and y-directions depend on the orientations chosen for the axes.

2 Describing motion

resolved parts or rectangular components of the original displacement; the process is called *resolving* the vector. Any displacement *s* can thus be written as

$$s = s_x + s_y = s_{x'} + s_{y'},$$

the choice of axes depending on convenience in a particular situation. Thus in figure 2-6c **OP** could be described as the sum of a displacement of 25 m in the x'-direction and a displacement of 54 m in the y'-direction. In three dimensions a similar process is valid,

$$s = s_x + s_y + s_z.$$

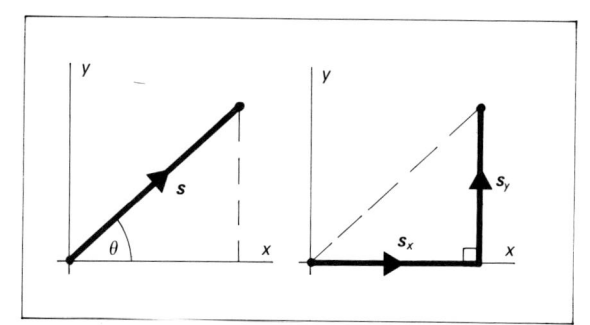

Figure 2-7 Resolving a displacement *s* into two rectangular components or resolved parts.

From figure 2-7 we see that s_x and s_y, the resolved parts of *s*, are related to *s* and θ by the equations:

$$s_x = s\cos\theta \quad [2\text{-}3]$$

and

$$s_y = s\cos(90-\theta) = s\sin\theta; \quad [2\text{-}4]$$

while, if s_x and s_y are known, then *s* and θ can be found from:

$$s^2 = s_x^2 + s_y^2 \quad [2\text{-}5]$$

and

$$\tan\theta = \frac{s_y}{s_x}. \quad [2\text{-}6]$$

Again displacement has been used to introduce the resolving of vectors, but all vectors may be treated in this way. The apparent complication of expressing one vector as the sum of two others has two advantages. Firstly, the two resolved parts are independent of one another. Thus one's progress across a stream can be described by resolving one's displacement or velocity perpendicular to the bank; the pull of a boy dragging a sledge can be resolved so that the effective pull parallel to the ground can be isolated. Secondly, resolving enables several vectors to be added easily. The procedure is as follows.

1. Choose convenient axes so that as many as possible of the vectors to be added are parallel to these axes (we shall call these the *x*- and *y*-axes in what follows).

2. Find the resolved parts of each of the vectors in the *x*- and *y*-directions.

3. Add the resolved parts in the *x*-direction and the *y*-direction, thus finding the resolved parts of the resultant vector.

4. Calculate the resultant by vector addition. As the two vectors are perpendicular this is relatively easy.

It is worth checking your work by roughly sketching a head-to-tail scale vector addition for all the vectors.

▶ **Example 2-2** A particle undergoes four successive displacements:

20 m, N 60° E

10 m, N 30° W

30 m, N 70° W

10 m, N.

Find the resultant displacement.

One method of solution is clearly to join the displacements head-to-tail in a scale diagram; then the resultant displacement is represented by the line joining the tail of the first to the head of the last displacement. Figure 2-8 shows

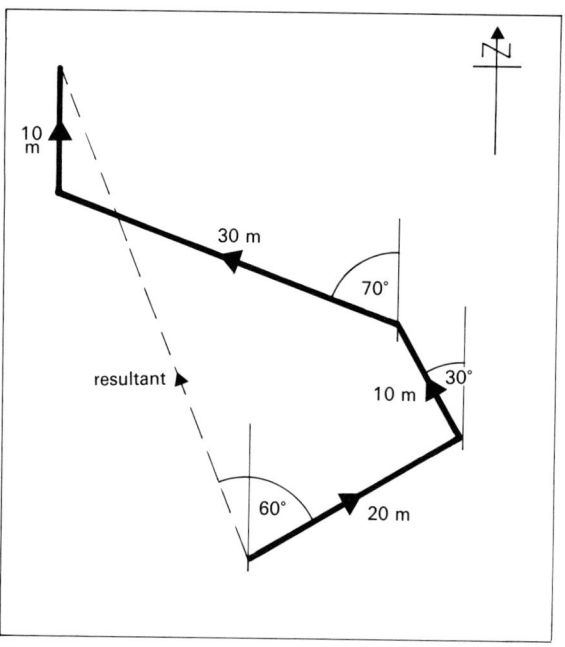

Figure 2-8

the result of doing this: we see that the resultant displacement is 42 m in the direction N 22° W. However, if we wish to calculate the resultant, the easiest method is to resolve the displacements in two convenient directions, although these must of course be perpendicular to each other. We draw (in figure 2-9) the four displacements, from a common origin, and we see that convenient directions are those shown by the p- and q-axes, since two of the displacements lie in those directions. We now resolve

(a) in the p-direction

$20\,\text{m} + (10\,\text{m})(\cos 60°) - (30\,\text{m})(\cos 50°) = +5.7\,\text{m}$

(b) in the q-direction

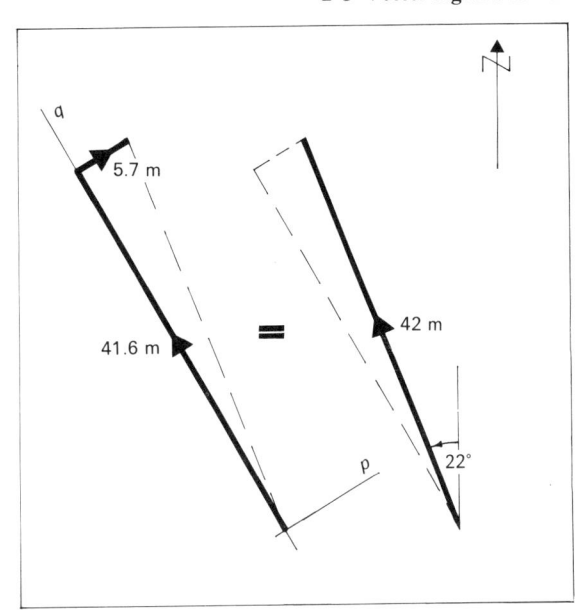

$10\,\text{m} + (10\,\text{m})(\cos 30°) + (30\,\text{m})(\cos 40°) = +41.6\,\text{m}.$

Figure 2-10

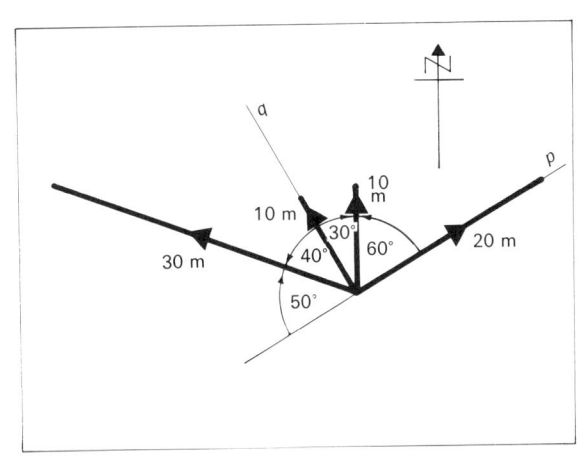

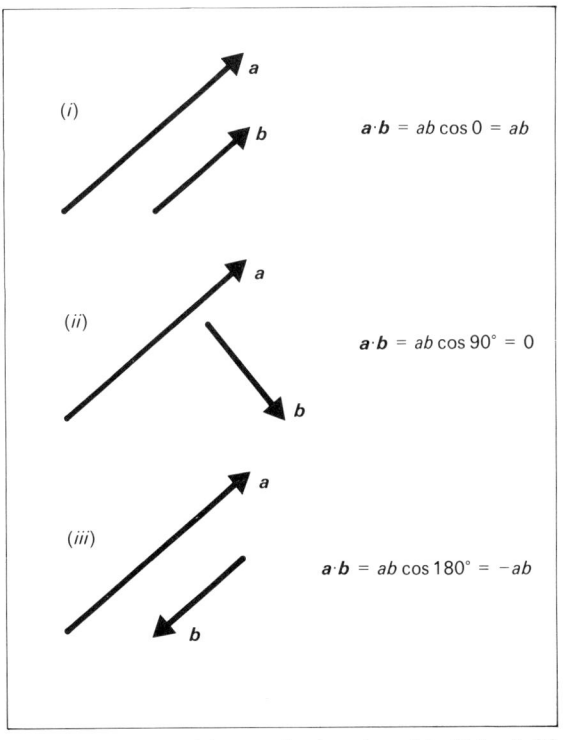

Figure 2-9

The size of the resultant s is given by $s^2 = (5.7\,\text{m})^2 + (41.6\,\text{m})^2$ so that $s = 42.0\,\text{m}$ (= 42 m to two significant figures), and the direction of s is given by $\tan\theta = 5.7\,\text{m}/41.6\,\text{m}$, which gives θ (the angle made by s with the q-direction) as 8°. We do not *need* to draw a diagram to perform this final calculation, but, as so often in problem solving, it probably would help, and figure 2-10 shows the sort of rough sketch we might have made. Therefore the resultant displacement is 42 m in the direction N 22° W, which agrees with the result predicted earlier, and shown in figure 2-8. ◀

2-5 Vector algebra II

Scalar product

The scalar (or dot) product of two vectors a and b is defined by the equation

$$a \cdot b = ab\cos\theta, \qquad [2\text{-}7]$$

where θ is the angle between the vectors. $a \cdot b$ is read as

(i) $\quad a \cdot b = ab\cos 0 = ab$

(ii) $\quad a \cdot b = ab\cos 90° = 0$

(iii) $\quad a \cdot b = ab\cos 180° = -ab$

Figure 2-11 The special cases of $a \cdot b = ab\cos\theta$ for (i) $\theta = 0$, (ii) $\theta = 90°$, and (iii) $\theta = 180°$.

2 Describing motion

'a dot b'. The product is seen to be a scalar quantity (hence the name scalar product) and to be equal numerically to the product of the size of one of the vectors and the size of the other resolved parallel to it. The first occasion when a scalar product is mentioned in this text is in Chapter 3 when two velocities are multiplied. It is again used in Chapter 7, when defining the work done by a force. If a body of weight W is displaced horizontally a distance x, then the work done by the pull of the Earth on the body $= \boldsymbol{W} \cdot \boldsymbol{x} = Wx \cos 90° = 0$.

★ Vector product

The vector (or cross) product of two vectors $\boldsymbol{a}$ and $\boldsymbol{b}$ is defined by the equation

$$\boldsymbol{a} \times \boldsymbol{b} = ab \sin \theta \, \boldsymbol{n}, \qquad [2\text{-}8]$$

where $\boldsymbol{n}$ is a vector whose size is unity and whose direction is perpendicular to the plane containing $\boldsymbol{a}$ and $\boldsymbol{b}$ in the sense in which a right-hand screw would move if rotated from $\boldsymbol{a}$ to $\boldsymbol{b}$ through the angle θ between them. Finding a vector product is a three-dimensional problem. The vector product is sometimes written $\boldsymbol{a} \wedge \boldsymbol{b}$: in either case it is read either as 'a cross b' or as 'a vec b'. Figure 2-12 shows some examples of vector products. Note that the vector product of two polar vectors is a pseudovector.

One occasion where a vector product is mentioned in this text is in Chapter 11, when defining the moment of a force about an axis. If a swing-door of width r is opened by exerting a horizontal pull $\boldsymbol{F}$ on the handle, the moment of this force is $\boldsymbol{r} \times \boldsymbol{F} = rF \sin \theta \, \boldsymbol{n}$, $\boldsymbol{n}$ being a vertical unit vector. Clearly the 'best' direction for $\boldsymbol{F}$ is perpendicular to $\boldsymbol{r}$ giving $\theta = 90°$ and a moment of size Fr. In both $\boldsymbol{a} \cdot \boldsymbol{b}$ and $\boldsymbol{a} \times \boldsymbol{b}$, the product defines a *new* physical quantity with the dimensions of ab. These two types of vector multiplication have developed as a convenient shorthand to help the mathematician or scientist. There is no 'truth' in the methods; they are simply useful. ★

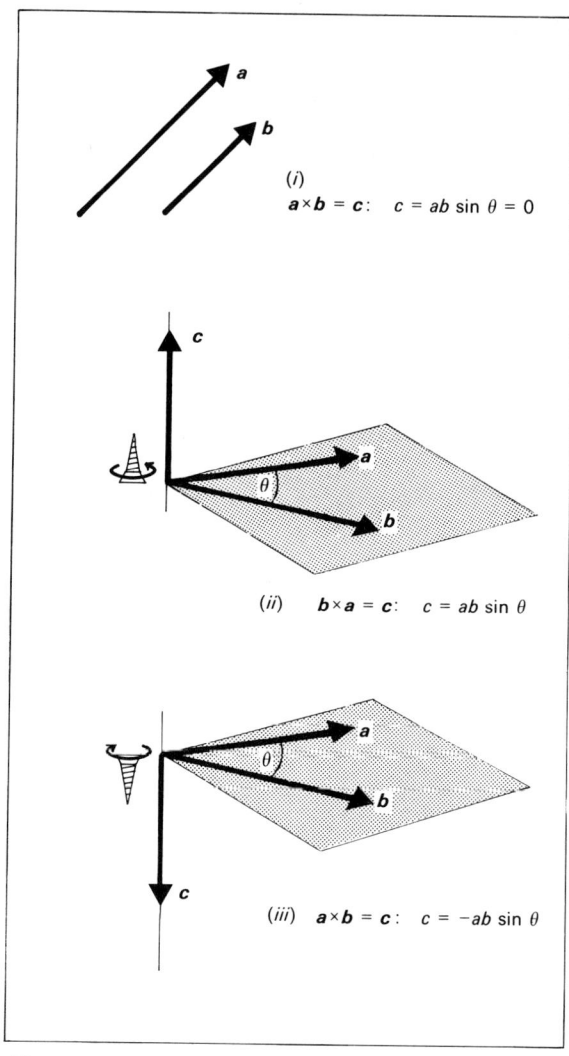

Figure 2-12 Some examples of the vector product $\boldsymbol{a} \times \boldsymbol{b} = \boldsymbol{c}$. Note that $\boldsymbol{a} \times \boldsymbol{b} = -\boldsymbol{b} \times \boldsymbol{a}$.

2-6 Velocity and speed

The average *velocity* $\boldsymbol{v}_{av}$ or $\bar{\boldsymbol{v}}$ of a particle is defined by the equation

$$\boldsymbol{v}_{av} = \frac{\Delta \boldsymbol{s}}{\Delta t}$$

where $\Delta \boldsymbol{s}$ is the *change in displacement* which occurs in a time Δt. $\boldsymbol{v}_{av}$ is a vector, and this is a vector equation, which implies that $\boldsymbol{v}_{av}$ has the same direction as $\Delta \boldsymbol{s}$. The average *speed* v_{av} of a particle is defined by the equation

$$v_{av} = \frac{\Delta s}{\Delta t}$$

where Δs is the *distance travelled* in a time Δt. With speed (as with distance) the question of direction does not arise: both are scalar quantities.

When a particle is moving in such a way that for successive intervals of time Δt its average velocity remains the same, we say that during that time it has a *constant velocity*. Of course this means that the particle moves at a constant speed in a straight line.

The *unit* of both velocity and speed is the m s^{-1}, and the dimensions of velocity and speed are LT^{-1}.

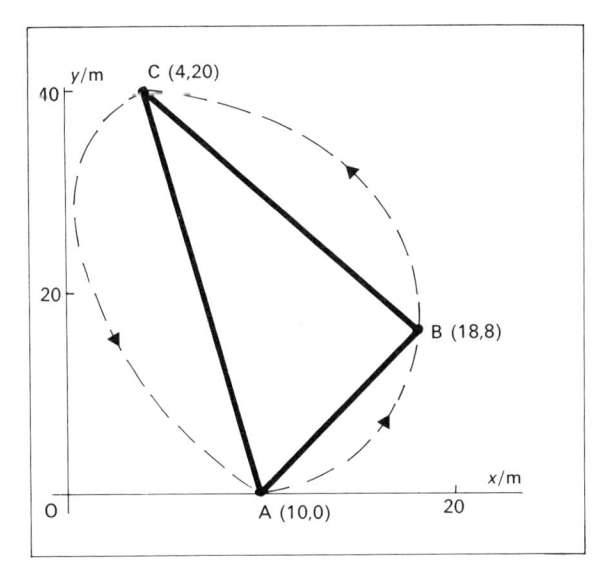

Figure 2-13

(d) $7.0\,\mathrm{m\,s^{-1}}$ in the opposite direction to the answer for part (c)
(e) zero, since the change of displacement is zero.

Note that we know nothing about the actual path taken by the particle (except that it was at those points at those times), although one possible path has been sketched in figure 2-13, or even about its velocities at different points in that path. *The average velocity of a particle is calculated from a knowledge of its changes of displacement.* We cannot calculate the average speed of the particle, for any of these sections, unless we know the distance travelled by it. Suppose, however, we did know that it travelled 60 m from A and back to A again (it must be at least 50 m), then the average *speed* for the whole journey is given by $60\,\mathrm{m}/10\,\mathrm{s} = 6\,\mathrm{m\,s^{-1}}$. Contrast this with the average *velocity* for this journey, which is zero. ◀

Example 2-3 showed how an average velocity could be calculated from a knowledge of the positions of a particle at particular times. Example 2-4 shows the same calculation performed with the data presented in a different form.

▶ **Example 2-3** Figure 2-13 shows a coordinate frame and three points A(10, 0), B(18, 8), and C(4, 20), the units of these lengths being metres. A particle is at A at time $t = 0$, at B at time $t = 5.0\,\mathrm{s}$, at C at time $t = 7.0\,\mathrm{s}$, and back at A at time $t = 10\,\mathrm{s}$. Find the average velocity of the particle
  (a) between A and B
  (b) between B and C
  (c) between A and C
  (d) between C and A
  (e) for the whole 10 s.

We need to find the change of displacement for each section, so that we can find the average velocity for that section. The changes of displacement are:

(a) $\sqrt{(8^2 + 8^2)}\,\mathrm{m} = 11\,\mathrm{m}$ in the direction making $45°$ with Ox
(b) $\sqrt{(12^2 + 14^2)}\,\mathrm{m} = 18\,\mathrm{m}$ in the direction making $130\tfrac{1}{2}°$ with Ox
(c) $\sqrt{(20^2 + 6^2)}\,\mathrm{m} = 21\,\mathrm{m}$ in the direction making $107°$ with Ox
(d) 21 m in the opposite direction to the answer for part (c)
(e) zero,

so the average velocities are:

(a) $2.2\,\mathrm{m\,s^{-1}}\,(=11\,\mathrm{m}/5.0\,\mathrm{s})$ in the direction making $45°$ with Ox
(b) $9.0\,\mathrm{m\,s^{-1}}\,(=18/2.0\,\mathrm{s})$ in the direction making $130\tfrac{1}{2}°$ with Ox
(c) $7.0\,\mathrm{m\,s^{-1}}\,(=21\,\mathrm{m}/3.0\,\mathrm{s})$ in the direction making $107°$ with Ox

▶ **Example 2-4** A particle's initial displacement is 10.0 m in the direction Ox, and after 5.0 s its displacement is 19.7 m in a direction making $24°$ with the x-axis. Find the average velocity $\boldsymbol{v}_{\mathrm{av}}$ of the particle.

Let us first recognize that the data is the same as that presented in Example 2-3. If we refer to figure 2-13 observation and calculation show us that the displacements (from the origin O) of A and B in that figure are indeed 10.0 m in the direction Ox, and 19.7 m in a direction making $24°$ with Ox. So this example is simply an example of a different way in which the same data could have been presented, and (which is more important) an example of the different way in which the problem should then be solved. The simplest technique now is to make a scale drawing, as shown in figure 2-14, where s_1 and s_2 represent the initial and final displacements (from the origin) and $\Delta s = s_2 - s_1$ is the displacement of B from A. (We shall not go on to find the displacement of C from B, as we did in Example 2-3.)

Measurements made from the scale drawing show that $\Delta s = 11\,\mathrm{m}$, and that the angle Δs makes with Ox is $45°$. Therefore the average velocity $\boldsymbol{v}_{\mathrm{av}}$ of the particle is given by

$$\boldsymbol{v}_{\mathrm{av}} = \frac{11\,\mathrm{m}}{5.0\,\mathrm{s}} = 2.2\,\mathrm{m\,s^{-1}}$$

in the direction making $45°$ with Ox. ◀

So far we have calculated only the average velocity of a particle. How can we find its actual velocity at a particular instant, or its *instantaneous velocity*?

24 2 Describing motion

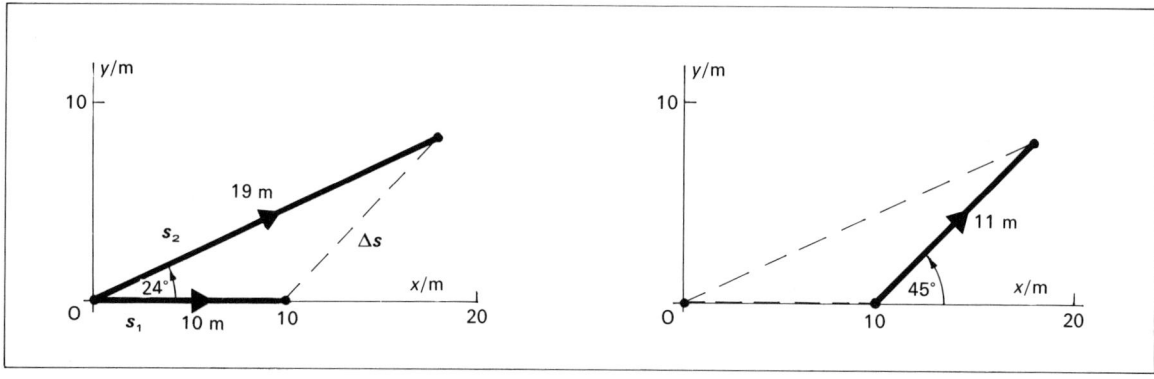

Figure 2-14

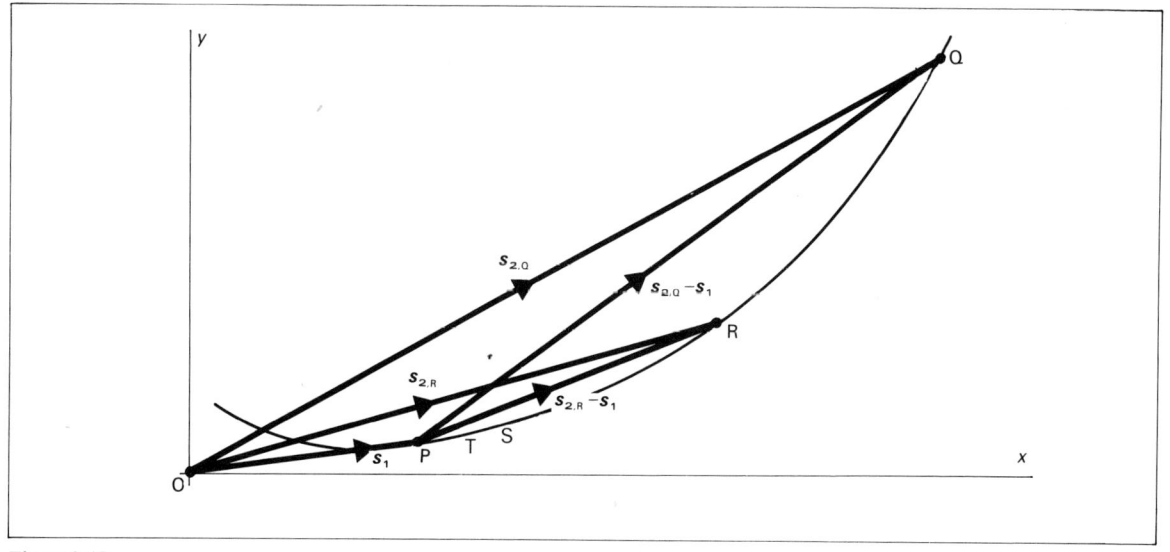

Figure 2-15

Figure 2-15 shows the path of a particle. Initially it is at P, where its displacement from the origin is s_1; later it is at Q, where its displacement is $s_{2,Q}$. During this movement its displacement has been $s_{2,Q} - s_1$, and its average velocity is this displacement divided by the time which it took to travel from P to Q. An approximation to the velocity at P would be obtained by dividing the change of displacement as the particle moves from P to R (a point much nearer P than Q is), $s_{2,R} - s_1$, by the time taken by the particle to move from P to R. We can make better approximations by considering points S, T, etc., which are even closer to P, and we define the instantaneous velocity of the particle at P as the *limiting value* of the ratio $\Delta s / \Delta t$, as Δt (and therefore Δs) tends to zero. The direction of the instantaneous velocity of the particle when it is at P is obviously *tangential* to the curve at P. This might seem difficult to apply in practice, but we shall see in Chapter 4 how we can apply this principle to one particular and most important case. In calculus notation, the instantaneous velocity v, at time t_1, is given by

$$v = \lim_{\Delta t \to 0}\left(\frac{\Delta s}{\Delta t}\right)_{t=t_1} = \left(\frac{ds}{dt}\right)_{t=t_1}, \quad [2\text{-}9]$$

that is, the time rate of change of displacement.

The *instantaneous speed* of a particle is simply the size of its instantaneous velocity. Since we are nearly always concerned with instantaneous (as opposed to average) values of speed and velocity we shall in future refer to them simply as 'speed' and 'velocity'.

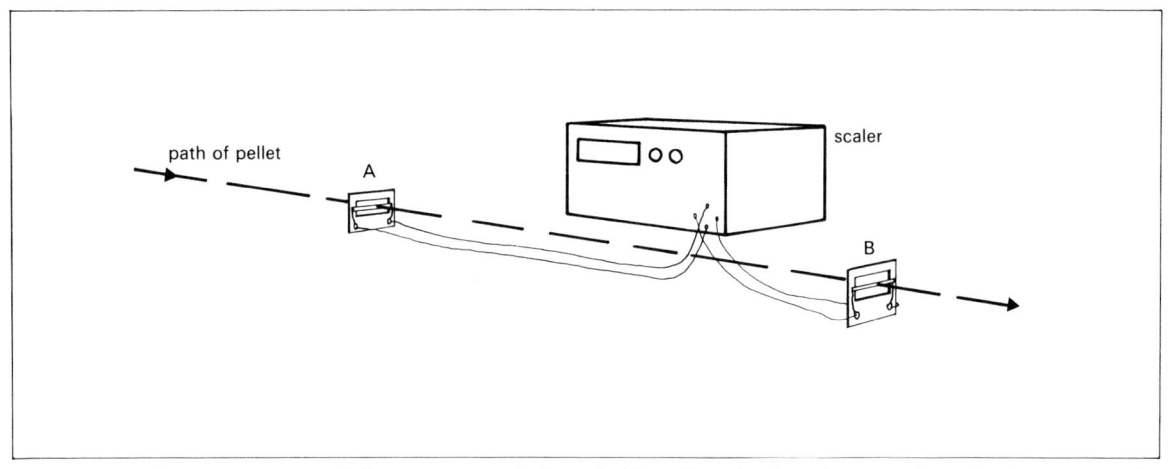

Figure 2-16 A direct measurement of the average speed of an air-rifle pellet. The timer is arranged so that it starts counting millisecond pulses when the strip at A is broken and stops when that at B is broken.

2-7 Measuring speed

If we want to find the average speed of a particle we measure Δs, the distance travelled, and Δt, the time taken, and hence find the average speed $\Delta s/\Delta t$. When doing so it is convenient either to fix the distance Δs and measure the time Δt, or fix the time interval Δt and measure the distance Δs.

Measurement of speed over a fixed distance

(a) In our laboratory investigations the time interval Δt will range from a few milliseconds up to tens of seconds. For example, the speed of a pellet fired by an air rifle can be found by measuring how long it takes the pellet to travel the length of a bench from A to B in figure 2-16. The distance AB between two pieces of aluminium foil (about 2 m) can be precisely measured with a ruler. When the pellet breaks the first foil at A the millisecond scaler-timer starts and when the pellet breaks the foil at B the scaler-timer stops. The scaler-timer contains its own 1 kHz square wave oscillator, the accuracy of which can be checked by comparing it with the mains frequency of 50 Hz which is usually reliable to more than 1%. The limiting feature in this experiment is that the measured time interval is only about 10 ms, and thus there is a possible error of $\pm 10\%$. To improve the precision of this technique it would be desirable to have a 1 MHz pulse generator but the switching devices used in the laboratory do not in general justify such an extension.

(b) On page 118 a small glider which runs on an air track is described. One way of measuring its average speed is to attach to it a piece of opaque material of known length L (figure 2-17). If a narrow beam of light and a photo-diode are arranged on opposite sides of the track so that the material interrupts the beam as it passes then we can measure the time interval Δt for the glider to move a distance $\Delta s(=L)$. If Δs is about 150 mm with a possible error of ± 1 mm, and Δt is about 200 ms, with a possible error of ± 4 ms (depending largely on how sharp the optical cut-off can be made), then the error in the speed $\Delta s/\Delta t$ is $\pm 2\frac{1}{2}\%$, a low figure for speed measurement in the laboratory. The scaler-timer could be replaced by a centi-second electric clock and the speed could still be found to about $\pm 5\%$.

(c) In a device for producing a 'velocity spectrum' for a large number of particles moving with random speeds, for example the molecules of a vaporized metal, a collimated beam of the particles moving in as good a vacuum as possible is allowed to pass through a narrow slit into a hollow cylindrical drum (figure 2-18). If the drum is stationary all the molecules will strike the inside of the drum opposite the slit, but if the drum is rotated about an axis parallel to the slit this will no longer be true. For a given angular speed of rotation of the drum a fast molecule will strike the glass plate at A while a slow molecule will strike the plate at B. The positions of A and B depend on the scale of the apparatus and the speeds of the drum and the molecules. It is left as a problem for the reader. As the drum rotates, a burst of particles enters once per revolution and the glass plate becomes coated with a deposit of the particles, the density of which at a given place (estimated optically) represents

26 2 Describing motion

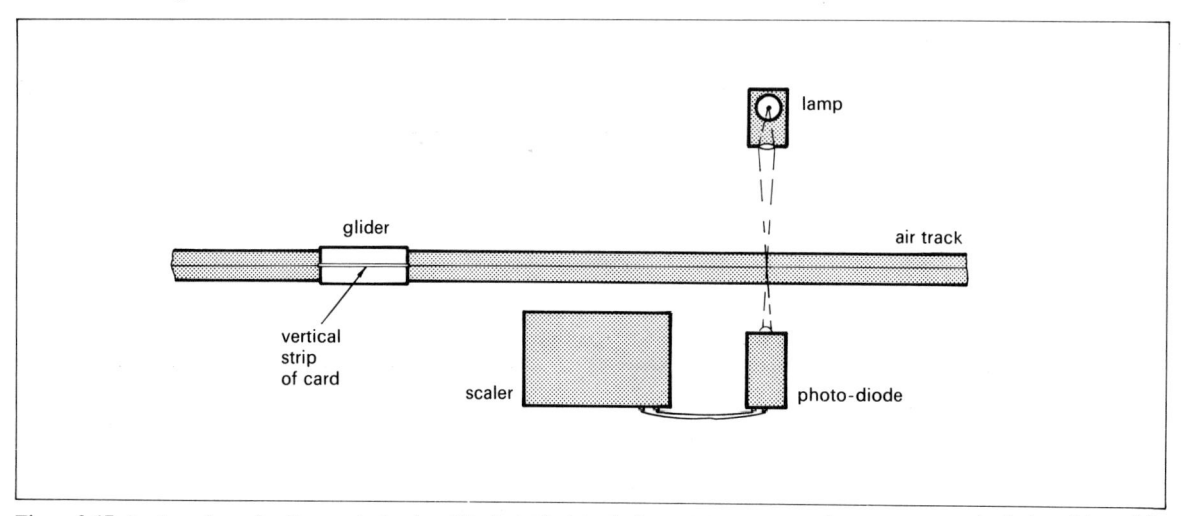

Figure 2-17 A plan view of a linear air track with photoelectric timing set to measure the average speed of the glider while a card mounted on the glider interrupts the light illuminating the photo-diode.

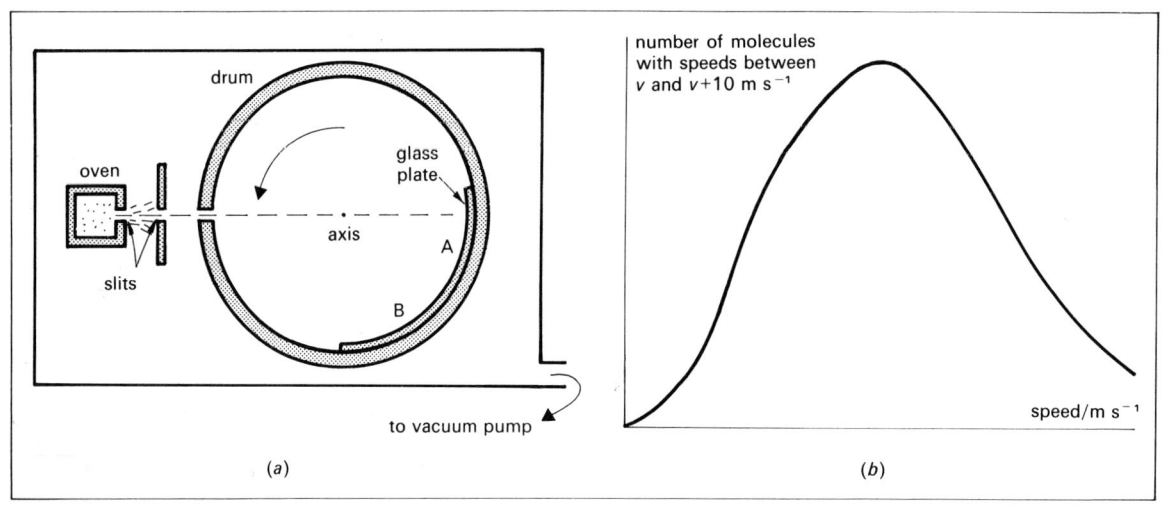

Figure 2-18 Diagram (*a*) shows the apparatus used to establish the speed distribution in (*b*) for the molecules of the substance vaporized in the oven. The drum is a cylindrical shape with its axis perpendicular to the plane of the paper. For a given speed of rotation of the drum the density of the molecules deposited on a part of the glass plate represents the number of molecules moving in a certain range of speeds. Note that the curve, theoretically predicted by J. C. Maxwell, is not symmetrical.

the number of the particles entering the drum with a certain range of speeds. The speed distribution shown in figure 2-18*b* can then be produced. The apparatus can be modified to produce a beam of particles all moving with the same chosen speed by a second slit being made in the drum, for example, at A. The speed of the particles passing out of the drum at A now depends on the speed of rotation of the drum. In this form the drum acts as a *velocity selector*.

Measurement of speed during a fixed time interval
(*a*) In order to record the positions of an object at the beginning and end of the time interval two techniques are commonly used. The simplest is to use a ticker-timer. This is a device which marks a dot on a piece of paper tape which is attached to the moving object as the tape passes under a piece of carbon paper. The dots are marked by a pointed metal object which vibrates up and down at the end of a steel rule fixed at its other end. The rule is

kept vibrating at 50 Hz by making use of a resonance between the natural frequency of the rule and the magnetic field in an alternating current solenoid. The weakness of the method is that the tape, as it is pulled through the timer, exerts a backward pull on the object to which it is attached, and so the ticker-timer can not be used in situations where this pull would be significant. The error in measuring the distance between the carbon dots is unlikely to be less than ± 2.0 mm; if the distance between the dots were 100 mm, the error would be $\pm 2\%$. The error in the time-interval measurement depends much more on the mechanical setting of the vibrating rule than on the constancy of mains frequency at 50 Hz. This error is difficult to estimate, but is certainly a few per cent for adjacent dots, falling as the size of the time interval increases. Thus for two adjacent dots measured to be 124 mm apart the average speed is calculated to be 0.124 m/ 0.020 s = 6.2 m s^{-1} with a possible error of about $\pm 5\%$. Average speeds calculated over longer distances are, of course, found with a smaller possible error.

(b) A second method is to use photographic techniques involving a single photographic plate or film which records the position of the moving object as it is illuminated regularly by a stroboscopic lamp (figure 2-19). The lamp, a small xenon discharge tube, is made so as to switch on for about 10 microseconds per flash at frequencies from 1 to 500 Hz. Provided the moving object is in good contrast with the background and that it moves close to a graduated rule, an analysis of the photograph enables us to measure the distance the object moves in a given time. The stroboscope will need to have its frequency calibrations checked occasionally; the mains supply at 50 Hz provides a useful practical standard but not a reliably accurate one. The photographic method is awkward because of the time needed to process the film, but a Polaroid camera reduces this time to a minimum. The error here lies almost entirely in the distance measurement. If the resulting photograph is enlarged or projected on to a screen it will be possible to keep the error down to 1 or 2 per cent, but measurements taken directly from a Polaroid positive will be much less precise. A lamp used with a motor-driven stroboscope disc can replace the stroboscopic lamp. In this case the time of each flash is larger than 10 µs and the method involves a correspondingly greater possible error in the precision with which distance can be measured.

Other methods

Speeds are also measured by many other methods. For example:

(a) the speeds of distant galaxies, by using the electromagnetic Doppler effect (see page 355);

(b) the speed of an aircraft, by measuring the speed of the air flow past it with a Pitot tube;

(c) the speed of a charged particle such as an electron, by passing it into a region where an electric and a magnetic field can produce precisely opposite forces (and hence no deflection) for a given velocity of the particle;

(d) the speeds of sub-atomic particles in bubble and cloud chambers, by using the principle of conservation of momentum for observed collisions.

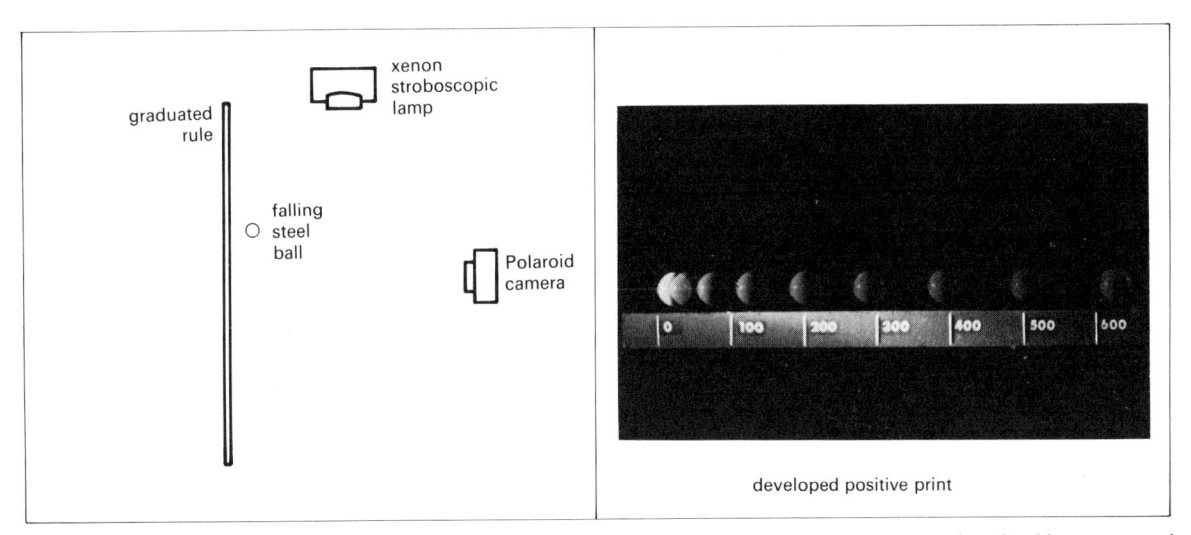

Figure 2-19 The arrangement of illumination and camera to analyse the motion of a freely falling object, in this case a steel ball. The print shows how measurements can be taken if a graduated rule is included in the picture.

2-8 Relative velocity

We shall see in Section 3-9 that all velocities are necessarily relative. For example, an observer on the Earth sees a body A and measures its velocity relative to himself and the Earth; let us call this velocity v_{AE}. A second observer *who is on* A (perhaps on a train) measures the velocity with which he sees the Earth moving relative to himself; he calls this velocity v_{EA}. Clearly

$$v_{EA} = -v_{AE}.$$

The Earth-bound observer now sees another body B, and measures its velocity as v_{BE}. If he now steps on to A, which is still moving with a velocity v_{AE} relative to the Earth, and again measures the velocity of B, the value he gets (v_{BA}) will be less than the v_{BE} by an amount equal to the (vector) velocity which he acquires by stepping on to A.

Thus
$$v_{BA} = v_{BE} - v_{AE} = v_{BE} + v_{EA},$$

which is a special case of a general theorem about relative velocity:

$$v_{XY} + v_{YZ} = v_{XZ}. \qquad [2\text{-}10]$$

This should be thought of in words, as

the velocity of X measured relative to Y	+	the velocity of Y measured relative to Z	=	the velocity of X measured relative to Z.

Figure 2-20 shows an example of how this is applied in practice. M is a missile intercepting a bomber B. Their velocities relative to the Earth are v_{ME} and v_{BE}. If we want to find the velocity of M relative to B (that is, the velocity v_{MB} of M as seen from B) we subtract from M the velocity of B relative to the Earth. In practice the best way of reaching this solution is to add to each moving body the velocity which will 'stop' the body relative to which the other's velocity is required, in much the same way as we believe, in ordinary velocity measurements, that the Earth is stationary. In the above problem to 'stop' the bomber B would clearly involve giving it a speed v_{BE} in the opposite direction to its motion, that is adding a velocity $-v_{BE}$. Adding this velocity, $-v_{BE}$, to the missile M now gives us the velocity of the missile relative to the bomber, as in figure 2-20.

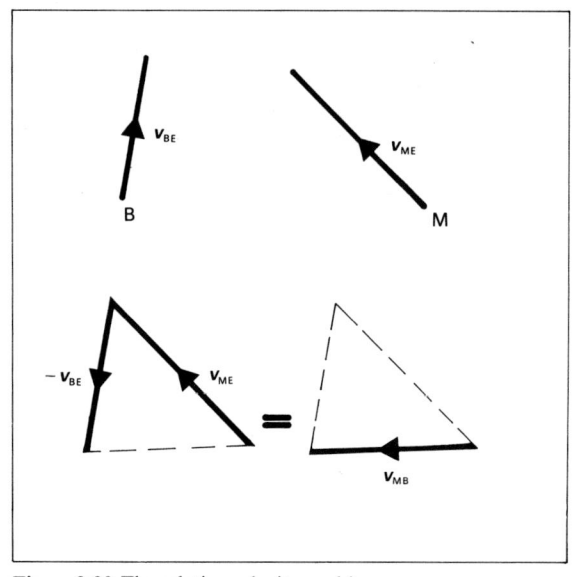

Figure 2-20 The relative velocity problem: $v_{MB} = v_{ME} - v_{BE}$.

▶ **Example 2-5** A cowboy sees a train travelling due north at $7.5\,\text{m}\,\text{s}^{-1}$ when it is 2 km due west of him. If he can ride at $10\,\text{m}\,\text{s}^{-1}$, in which direction must he ride to intercept the train as soon as possible? What is his velocity relative to the train as he rides to intercept it?

(a) We 'stop' the train by adding a velocity of $7.5\,\text{m}\,\text{s}^{-1}$ due south to it, but we must also add this velocity to the cowboy. The resultant of this added velocity and his velocity of $10\,\text{m}\,\text{s}^{-1}$ in the correct direction must be in the direction of the 'stopped' train, that is due west. Thus we have from figure 2-21

$$\sin\theta = \frac{7.5\,\text{m}\,\text{s}^{-1}}{10\,\text{m}\,\text{s}^{-1}}, \quad \text{from which } \theta = 49°.$$

(b) The cowboy's velocity relative to the train, v_{CT}, is the sum of his own velocity and the negative of the train's velocity.

We can see from figure 2-21 that

$$v_{CT} = (10\,\text{m}\,\text{s}^{-1})(\cos 49°) = 6.5\,\text{m}\,\text{s}^{-1}$$

due west. So the passengers in the train 'see' him riding directly towards them at a constant speed of $6.5\,\text{m}\,\text{s}^{-1}$ (to two significant figures). ◀

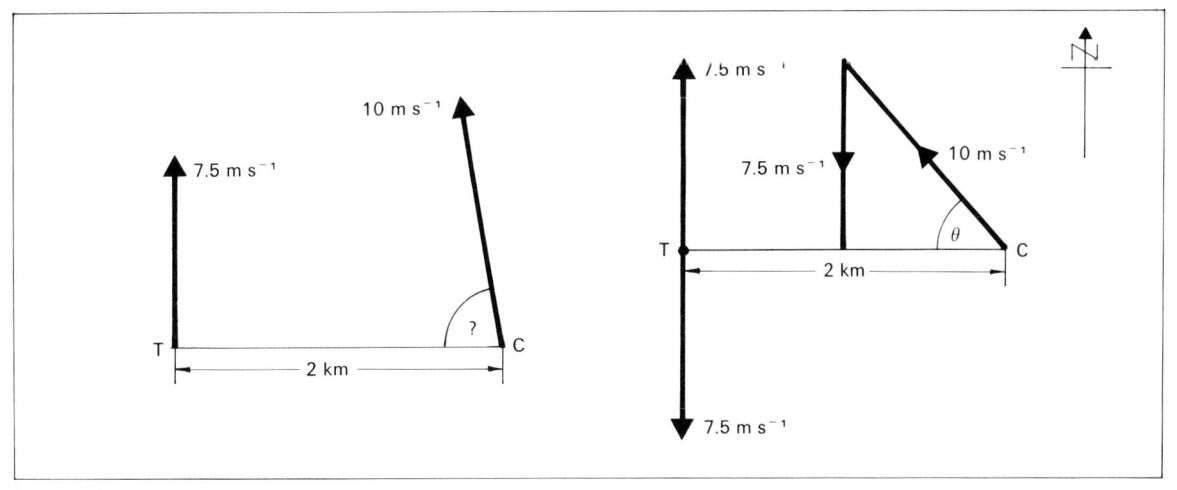

Figure 2-21

Bibliography

Dorling, G. W. (1966). 'Stroboscopic photography.' *Physics Education*, **1**, page 236.

Page, R. L. (1969). 'Velocity analysis of human movement.' *School Science Review*, number 173, page 777.

Nuffield O-level Physics (1967). *Guide to experiments IV*. Longman/Penguin. Appendix I is on multiflash photography.

SMP (1967–68). *Advanced Mathematics*, Books 1 and 2. Cambridge University Press. The chapters on vectors are relevant.

8 mm film loop. 'The Maxwell–Boltzmann distribution.' Longman.

8 mm film loop. 'Vector addition: velocity of a boat.' Ealing Scientific. A loop from Harvard Project Physics series.

16 mm film. 'Measurement.' Guild Sound and Vision. The measurement of the speed of a rifle bullet is taken as the basis of a discussion of the art of measurement.

Exercises

Data (to be used unless otherwise directed):

The angles of a 3–4–5 triangle are 37°, 53°, and 90°.

2-1 A particle is placed in a plane which has a coordinate framework whose y-axis points north and whose x-axis points east. It is observed successively at A(30, 0), B(60, 40), and C(0, −5), the units being metres. Find its change of displacement when it moves
   (a) from A to B   (b) from B to C   (c) from C to A.
Can you calculate the distance moved by the particle? ●

2-2 A particle's initial displacement from an origin is 30 m to the north-east: when next observed its displacement is 50 m, from the origin, to the south-west. What is its change of displacement? Can you calculate how far it has moved? ●

2-3 A particle is initially 200 m east of an origin, and later 150 m north of that origin. What is its change of displacement? ●

2-4 Perform the following calculations:
   (a) 60 m east + 40 m west
   (b) 40 m east + 60 m west
   (c) 40 m east − 60 m east
   (d) 40 m west − 40 m east. ●

2-5 Use a scale diagram to find the sums of the following displacements:
   (a) 10 km in a direction N 20° E, 5.0 km in a direction N 60° W
   (b) 4.0 m in a direction S 30° W, 6.0 m in a direction N 20° W. ●

2-6 Use a scale diagram to subtract the second of the given displacements from the first:
   (a) 2.0 m in a direction N 40° E, 1.5 m in a direction N 30° W
   (b) 4.0 km in a direction S 60° W, 3.0 km in a direction due west. ●

2-7 A particle is initially at an origin, and undergoes the following displacements in the order given: 50 m N 60° E, 60 m N 30° W, 30 m due south. What is its final displacement from the origin? (Use a scale drawing.) Would the result be different if the displacements had occurred in a different order? ●

2 Describing motion

2-8 Use the data of Exercise 2-7 but resolve the displacements into convenient perpendicular directions and *calculate* the resultant displacement. ●

2-9 You travel from the place where you sleep to the classroom or the place where you work; estimate (a) your average speed (b) your average velocity.

2-10 Use the data of Exercise 2-1. If the time intervals for the three stages of the particle's journey are, respectively, 5.0 s, 25 s, and 2.0 s, find the average velocity of the particle during each stage. When the particle has returned to A, what is its average velocity for the complete journey? ●

2-11 A man throws a stone vertically upwards from the ground into the air. It rises to a height of 30 m, and then begins to fall, but is caught by a man leaning out of a window 20 m from the ground. If the time of flight is 5.0 s, what is
(a) the average speed of the stone
(b) the average velocity of the stone? ●

2-12 Can a particle have a constant speed and a changing velocity? Can a particle have a constant velocity and a changing speed?

2-13 A particle moves in a coordinate framework whose y-axis points vertically upwards and whose x-axis points horizontally. The coordinates (in metres) of its position at times $t = 0$, 1.0 s, and 2.0 s are $(0,0)$, $(30, 15)$, and $(60, 20)$ respectively. Find its average velocity
(a) between $t = 0$ and $t = 1.0$ s
(b) between $t = 1.0$ s and $t = 2.0$ s
(c) between $t = 0$ and $t = 2.0$ s. ●

2-14 A particle moving in a vertical plane has at a particular moment a velocity whose vertical resolved part is 25 m s^{-1} upwards, and whose horizontal resolved part is 30 m s^{-1} (north). What is its velocity? ●

2-15 Figure 2-22 shows a particle moving in a circle ABCDA of radius 4.0 m at a constant speed; it completes one revolution in 0.50 s. What is
(a) its average speed from A to B
(b) its average speed for one complete revolution
(c) its average velocity from A to B
(d) its average velocity from A to C
(e) its average velocity for one complete revolution? ●

2-16 A man once wagered that he would drive from Brooklands racing circuit (about 35 km from London) to Piccadilly (in the centre of London) at an average speed of 60 miles per hour (about 27 m s^{-1}). He won his wager. How do you think he did this? What slight, and to the layman, unimportant alteration would you have made in the wording of the wager if you had wanted to defeat him?

2-17 Refer to figure 2-23.
(a) What is the direction of the velocity of (i) the top of the plank (ii) the foot of the plank? Can you think of a point about which the plank may be considered to be rotating (at the instant shown in the figure)?
(b) If the wheel is not slipping, what is the velocity of the point on it which is momentarily in contact with the ground? Can you say anything about the velocities of other points on the wheel (in particular, the centre of the wheel, and the point at the opposite end of the diameter from the point in contact with the ground)?

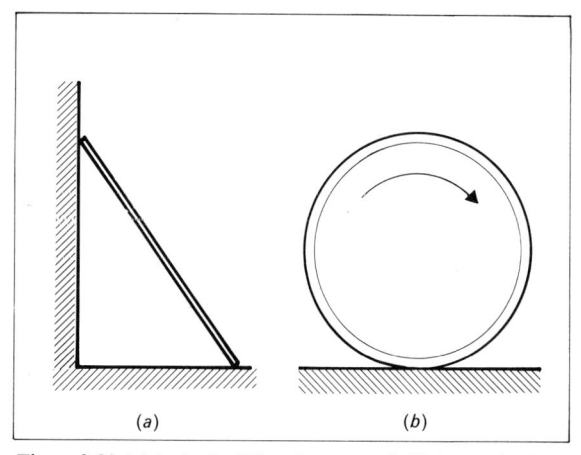

Figure 2-23 (a) A plank sliding down a wall. (b) A wheel rolling (without slipping) along a horizontal surface.

2-18 A particle moving in a straight line has an initial displacement of 50 m, and a constant velocity of 10 m s^{-1}. Find its displacement after (a) 2.0 s (b) 5.0 s. ●

2-19 A particle moving in a straight line has an initial displacement of 20 m, and a constant velocity of -3.0 m s^{-1}. Find its displacement after (a) 6.0 s (b) 10 s. ●

2-20 Refer to figure 2-18a. Suppose the drum has a diameter of 0.4 m, and is rotating at 100 revolutions per second. What is the difference in speed of two particles which arrive on the glass plate at an angular displacement of 36°? ●

2-21 Refer to figure 2-18a. Suppose the drum were used as a velocity selector. Draw a diagram to show where you would cut the slit on the further side of the drum (indicating the direction of rotation of the drum) to allow particles of only a certain speed to pass through. What determines
(a) the average speed of those which get through
(b) the dispersion, about this average, of the speeds of the individual particles which get through?

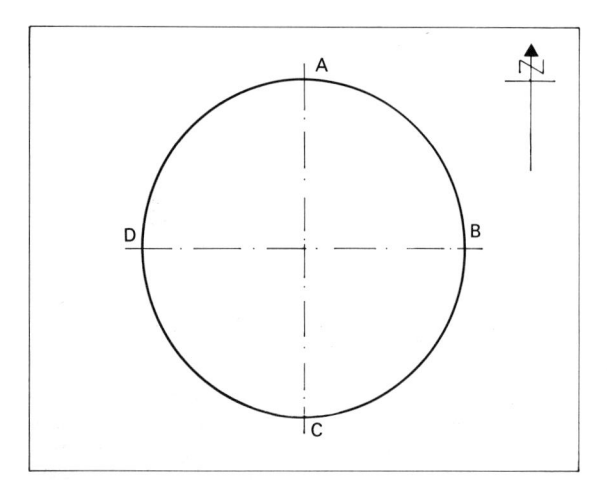

Figure 2-22

2-22 Figure 2-18b is a histogram, that is, the height of the curve at any point shows the number of particles which have speeds within 10 m s^{-1} of that speed. Is the modal speed (the speed most commonly possessed by the particles) the same as the average speed?

2-23 How would you measure the frequency of vibration of the vibrating strip of a ticker-timer?

2-24 The shaft of a motor is rotating at 20 revolutions per second, and a stroboscope lamp flashing at 20 flashes per second is used to 'freeze' it. What would the shaft appear to be doing if the stroboscope flash frequency were
(a) 10 flashes s^{-1}
(b) 19 flashes s^{-1}
(c) 21 flashes s^{-1}
(d) 40 flashes s^{-1}?

2-25 An aircraft capable of a speed of 200 m s^{-1} in still air flies for a distance of $5.0 \times 10^5 \text{ m}$ directly into a wind of speed 25 m s^{-1} (that is, the wind is blowing in the opposite direction to the direction of the aircraft). It then turns round and flies in the opposite direction until it reaches its starting point again, with the same wind still blowing. Find the time for the whole journey. How long would the journey have taken in still air? ●

2-26 A river flows from east to west at 1.0 m s^{-1}; a man who can swim at 0.75 m s^{-1} in still water swims across the river from the south bank, aiming directly across it all the time. What is his velocity relative to the south bank?
   If the river is 900 m wide, how long does it take him to reach the other bank? How far is he downstream of his starting point when he reaches the other bank? ●

2-27 A man who can swim at 0.50 m s^{-1} for 30 minutes wishes to cross the river described in Exercise 2-26. In which direction must he swim? Where will he reach the other bank? ●

2-28 At what speed, v, must a man be capable of swimming if he is to reach the bank of the river in Exercise 2-26 directly opposite his starting point? If he can swim at 1.25 m s^{-1}, in which direction should he swim, and how long will it take him to reach the other bank? ●

2-29 A north–south road and an east–west road meet at a crossroads. A car is travelling at 30 m s^{-1} north on the former, and a truck is travelling at 20 m s^{-1} west on the latter. What is the velocity of the truck relative to the car? What is the velocity of the car relative to the truck? Answer the same questions, but with the truck travelling at 20 m s^{-1} to the east. ●

2-30 A battleship is moving north at 5.0 m s^{-1} and a destroyer is moving at 10 m s^{-1} in the direction N $50°$ E. What is the velocity of the battleship relative to the destroyer? What is the velocity of the destroyer relative to the battleship? If the battleship is initially 6000 m east and 2000 m north of the destroyer, and they maintain their original courses, how close will the destroyer come to the battleship, and after what time? (Use a scale drawing.) ●

2-31 In three-dimensional work we use the three coordinate axes x, y, and z as shown in figure 2-24. It is convenient to define *unit vectors* $\mathbf{i}$, $\mathbf{j}$, and $\mathbf{k}$ which each have a size of one unit and the directions of the x-, y-, and z-axes respectively, and these also are shown in figure 2-24. Find the size of the following vectors, and sketch them in three-dimensional diagrams:
(a) $3\mathbf{i} + 4\mathbf{j}$
(b) $\mathbf{i} + 2\mathbf{j} + 2\mathbf{k}$
(c) $2\mathbf{i} + 6\mathbf{j} + 3\mathbf{k}$.

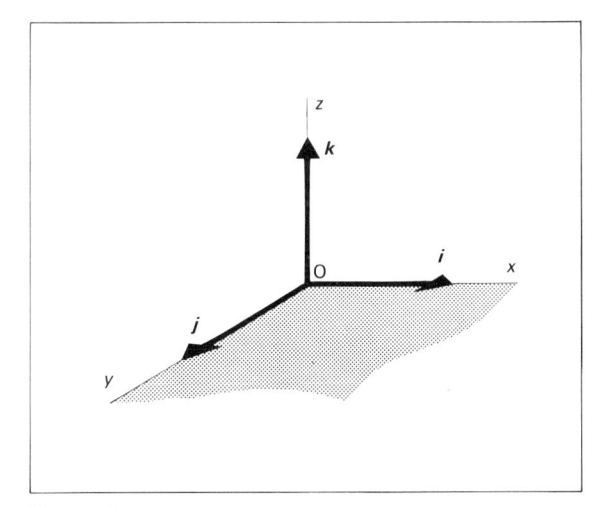

Figure 2-24

2-32 Consider a displacement $\mathbf{r}$ in the positive x-direction and a displacement $\mathbf{s}$ which makes an angle θ with the positive x-direction. Write down the value of $\mathbf{r} \times \mathbf{s}$. Has this product any significance?

3 Acceleration

3-1 Acceleration	32	3-7 The parabola of projectile motion	44
3-2 Planar motion: constant acceleration I	33	3-8 Acceleration as a function of displacement, velocity, and time	46
3-3 Linear motion: constant acceleration	35	3-9 Frames of reference	46
3-4 Linear motion graphs	35	Bibliography	48
3-5 Measuring acceleration	39	Exercises	48
3-6 Planar motion: constant acceleration II	42		

3-1 Acceleration

A body accelerates when there is a change in either the size or the direction of its velocity. The average acceleration $\bar{a}$ or a_{av} of a particle is defined by the equation

$$a_{av} = \frac{\Delta \boldsymbol{v}}{\Delta t} \qquad [3\text{-}1]$$

where $\Delta \boldsymbol{v}$ is the change in velocity which occurs in a time Δt. This is a vector equation, which implies that the direction a_{av} is the same as that of $\Delta \boldsymbol{v}$.

When a particle is moving in such a way that for successive intervals Δt its average acceleration remains the same, we say that during that time it has a *constant acceleration*.

The unit of acceleration is the m s^{-2}.

▶ **Example 3-1** A particle has an initial velocity of 15 m s^{-1} due north; 4.0 s later, it has a velocity of 10 m s^{-1} due east. What is its average acceleration during this time?

Figure 3-1 shows $\boldsymbol{v}_1 (= 15 \text{ m s}^{-1}$ north$)$ and $\boldsymbol{v}_2 (= 10 \text{ m s}^{-1}$ east$)$. We need to find $\Delta \boldsymbol{v} = \boldsymbol{v}_2 - \boldsymbol{v}_1$, which is also shown in figure 3-1. We can find the size of $\Delta \boldsymbol{v}$, and its direction, by measurement from a scale drawing, but when, as here, we have a right-angled triangle, it is simpler to calculate these values:

$$\Delta \boldsymbol{v} = \sqrt{(225 + 100)} \text{ m s}^{-1}$$

$$= 18 \text{ m s}^{-1} \text{(to two significant figures)},$$

and the angle θ is given by

$$\tan \theta = \frac{10 \text{ m s}^{-1}}{15 \text{ m s}^{-1}}$$

so that $\qquad \theta = 34°$ (to two significant figures).

Thus the change of velocity is 18 m s^{-1} in a direction S $34°$ E, and the average acceleration is $18 \text{ m s}^{-1}/4.0 \text{ s} = 4.5 \text{ m s}^{-2}$ in a direction S $34°$ E. ◀

By a process similar to that used to define instantaneous velocity (in Section 2-6) we define the *instantaneous acceleration* of a particle as the limiting value of the ratio $\Delta \boldsymbol{v}/\Delta t$ as Δt (and therefore $\Delta \boldsymbol{v}$) tends to zero. In calculus notation, the instantaneous acceleration a, at time t_1, is given by

$$a = \lim_{\Delta t \to 0} \left(\frac{\Delta \boldsymbol{v}}{\Delta t}\right)_{t=t_1} = \left(\frac{d\boldsymbol{v}}{dt}\right)_{t=t_1} \qquad [3\text{-}2]$$

that is, the time rate of change of velocity. Since $\boldsymbol{v} = d\boldsymbol{s}/dt$, we now have

$$a = \frac{d\boldsymbol{v}}{dt} = \frac{d^2\boldsymbol{s}}{dt^2}. \qquad [3\text{-}3]$$

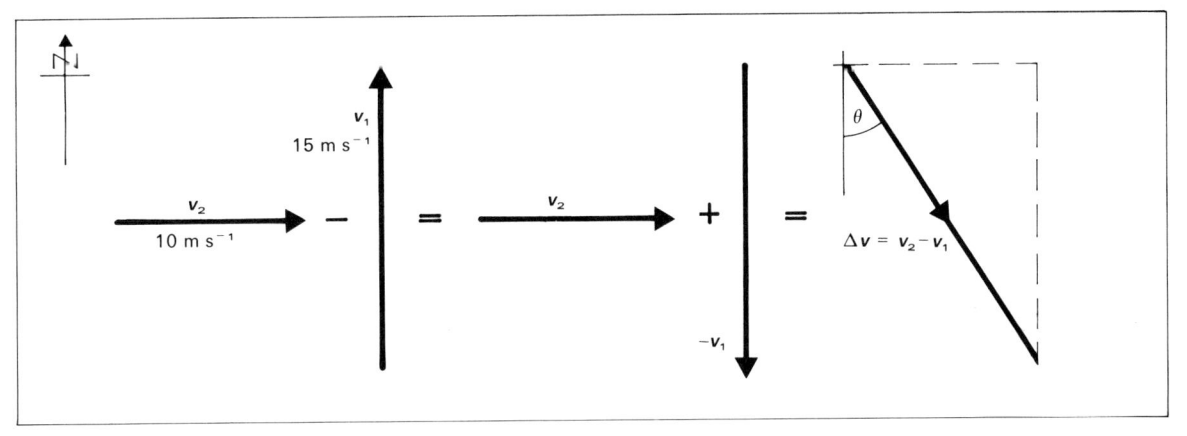

Figure 3-1

Since acceleration is vector quantity, it can be resolved: in Example 3-1, one possible pair of resolved parts is

$4.5 \cos 11°$ m s^{-2} due south-east

and $4.5 \cos 79°$ m s^{-2} due south-west.

Although there are some exercises at the end of this chapter which deal with the general case of acceleration in a plane, we shall normally confine ourselves to the following relatively simple situations.

(a) Straight-line motion, that is, where the direction of the particle's velocity does not change, though its size may do so (Sections 3-3 and 3-4).

(b) Planar motion with a constant acceleration, that is an acceleration which always has the same size and the same direction. This is important because it is the motion of all particles moving in a vacuum in uniform gravitational or electric fields. A stone thrown through the air near the Earth's surface has approximately this behaviour (Sections 3-2, 3-6, and 3-7).

(c) Planar motion where the acceleration has a constant size but its direction, although always towards a fixed point, is changing at a constant rate. This is true of all particles moving in a circular path at a constant speed: an Earth satellite has approximately this behaviour (Section 4-3).

We end this section by producing two results which we shall need at the beginning of the next section. Firstly, if a particle has a constant velocity v_0, the change of displacement s during a time t is given by

$$s = v_0 t. \qquad [3-4]$$

Secondly, what is the change of displacement if a particle starts from rest and has a constant acceleration a for a time t? If its final velocity is v, the definition of acceleration ($a_{av} = \Delta v/\Delta t$) gives

$$v = at.$$

Since the initial velocity is zero, the final velocity v, and the acceleration constant, the average velocity $v_{av} = \tfrac{1}{2}v$. Then the definition of average velocity ($v_{av} = \Delta s/\Delta t$) gives

$$s = \tfrac{1}{2}vt$$

that is $\quad s = \tfrac{1}{2}at^2. \qquad [3-5]$

3-2 Planar motion: constant acceleration I

Suppose a particle has an initial velocity v_0 and a final velocity v, and a constant acceleration a: by definition $a = (v - v_0)/t$, where t is the time which has elapsed, or

$$v = v_0 + at. \qquad [3-6]$$

In general v_0 and a will have different directions, and v will lie in the plane defined by v_0 and a; motion with constant acceleration will necessarily be planar. So far, when adding vectors, we have drawn separate diagrams of the quantities to be added; here for example, if we want to illustrate the fact that $v = v_0 + at$, we would use figure 3-2. However, with increasing familiarity, we can

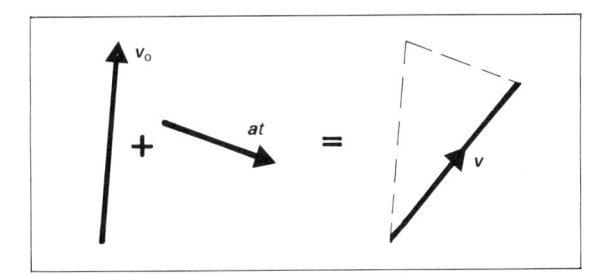

Figure 3-2

34 3 Acceleration

draw all three vectors on the same diagram, as in figure 3-3, and, incidentally, this enables us to see the relationship between the quantities more clearly. Of course the size of at varies with time. Figure 3-4 shows how the size and direction of $\boldsymbol{v}$ changes as t changes from t_1 to t_2.

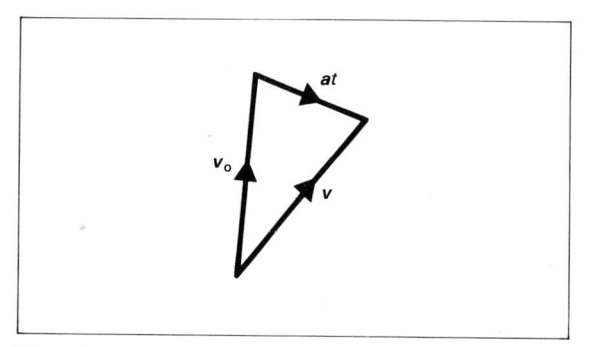

Figure 3-3 $\boldsymbol{v} = \boldsymbol{v}_0 + \boldsymbol{a}t$.

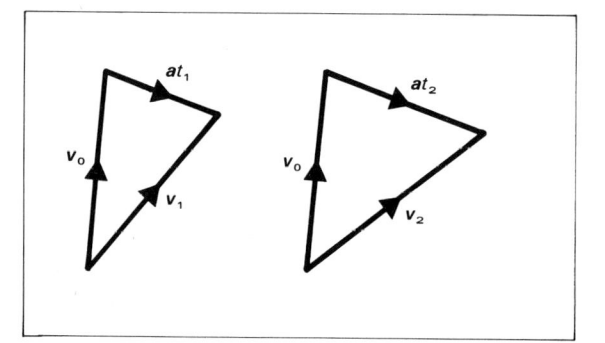

Figure 3-4 The size and direction of the velocity varies with time.

If a particle has a constant velocity $\boldsymbol{v}_0$ its *change* of displacement $\boldsymbol{s}$ after time t will be given by

$$\boldsymbol{s} = \boldsymbol{v}_0 t, \quad [3\text{-}4]$$

the directions of $\boldsymbol{s}$ and $\boldsymbol{v}_0$ clearly being the same. We saw at the end of Section 3-1 that if a particle starts from rest with constant acceleration $\boldsymbol{a}$ its change of displacement $\boldsymbol{s}$ after time t is given by

$$\boldsymbol{s} = \tfrac{1}{2}\boldsymbol{a}t^2, \quad [3\text{-}5]$$

the directions of $\boldsymbol{s}$ and $\boldsymbol{a}$ clearly being the same. The *total* (vector) displacement $\boldsymbol{s}$ for a particle which has an initial velocity $\boldsymbol{v}_0$ and a constant acceleration $\boldsymbol{a}$ will be given by the sum of these two displacements:

$$\boldsymbol{s} = \boldsymbol{v}_0 t + \tfrac{1}{2}\boldsymbol{a}t^2. \quad [3\text{-}7]$$

In general $\boldsymbol{v}_0$ and $\boldsymbol{a}$ will not have the same direction, and $\boldsymbol{s}$ will lie in the plane defined by the directions of $\boldsymbol{v}_0$ and $\boldsymbol{a}$.

Figure 3-5 reproduces the vector diagram shown in figure 3-3 and also shows the result of multiplying each vector by the scalar quantity t; part (c) shows the relationship of $\boldsymbol{s}$ to $\boldsymbol{v}_0 t$ and $\tfrac{1}{2}\boldsymbol{a}t^2$. Figure 3-5c *also* shows that

$$\boldsymbol{s} = \boldsymbol{v}t - \tfrac{1}{2}\boldsymbol{a}t^2. \quad [3\text{-}8]$$

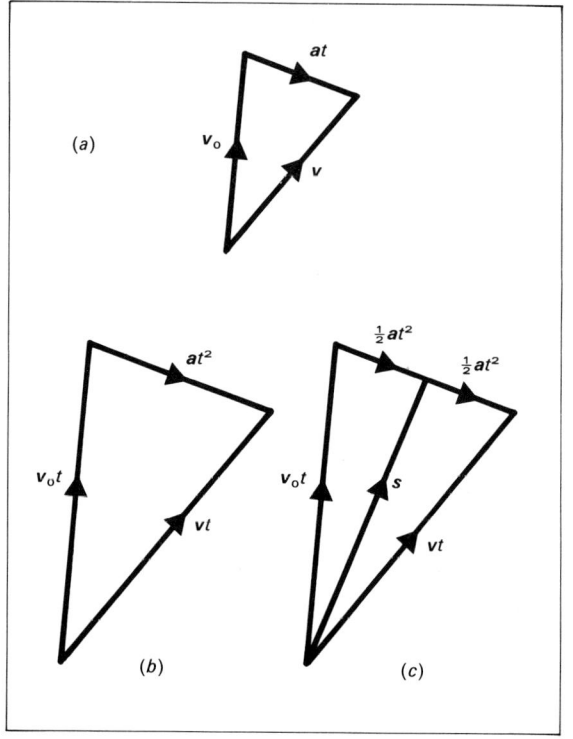

Figure 3-5 (a) $\boldsymbol{v} = \boldsymbol{v}_0 + \boldsymbol{a}t$. (b) $\boldsymbol{v}t = \boldsymbol{v}_0 t + \boldsymbol{a}t^2$. (c) $\boldsymbol{s} = \boldsymbol{v}_0 t + \tfrac{1}{2}\boldsymbol{a}t^2$.

If we extend figure 3-5c by completing the parallelogram of which $\boldsymbol{v}_0 t$ and $\boldsymbol{v}t$ are two sides (as shown in figure 3-6), we can see that $2\boldsymbol{s} = \boldsymbol{v}_0 t + \boldsymbol{v}t$, or

$$\boldsymbol{s} = \tfrac{1}{2}(\boldsymbol{v}_0 + \boldsymbol{v})t. \quad [3\text{-}9]$$

We could of course have obtained this equation by adding together equations 3-7 and 3-8.

We now have four equations relating the quantities s, t, $\boldsymbol{v}_0$, $\boldsymbol{v}$, and $\boldsymbol{a}$; in each of the four, one of the quantities s, $\boldsymbol{v}_0$, $\boldsymbol{v}$, and $\boldsymbol{a}$ does *not* appear. We can obtain a fifth equation, in which t does not appear, from figure 3-6. If we find the scalar product of $(\boldsymbol{v}t - \boldsymbol{v}_0 t)$, which is equal to $\boldsymbol{a}t^2$, and $(\boldsymbol{v}t + \boldsymbol{v}_0 t)$, which is equal to $2\boldsymbol{s}$, we have

$$(\boldsymbol{v}t - \boldsymbol{v}_0 t) \cdot (\boldsymbol{v}t + \boldsymbol{v}_0 t) = \boldsymbol{a}t^2 \cdot 2\boldsymbol{s},$$

that is

$$v^2 t^2 - v_0^2 t^2 = 2t^2 \boldsymbol{a} \cdot \boldsymbol{s},$$

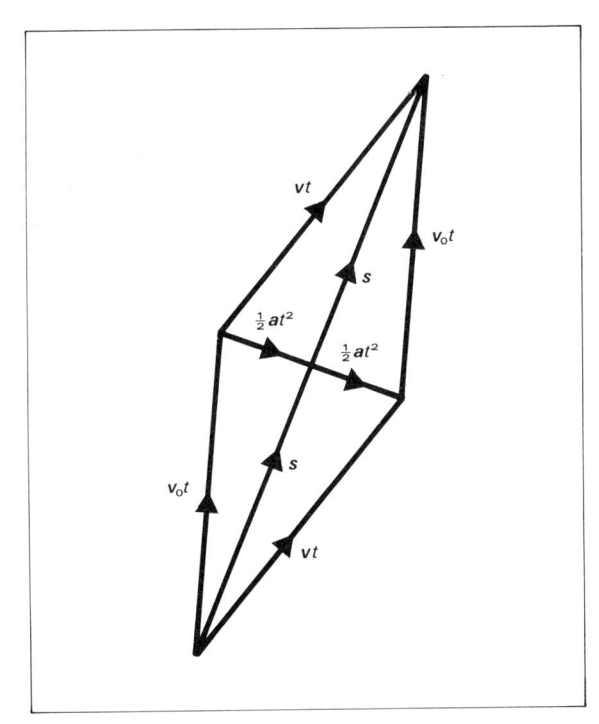

Figure 3-6 The relationship $2s = v_0t + vt$.

or
$$v^2 - v_0^2 = 2as\cos(\text{angle between } \boldsymbol{a} \text{ and } \boldsymbol{s}). \quad [3\text{-}10]$$

This equation is too complicated to be useful unless v_0 and a (and therefore s) have the same direction, when the angle in the equation is zero. Then we have the scalar equation

$$v^2 = v_0^2 + 2as. \quad [3\text{-}11]$$

3-3 Linear motion: constant acceleration

When the acceleration $\boldsymbol{a}$ of the particle has the same direction as the particle's initial velocity $\boldsymbol{v}_0$, the particle's displacement is also in that direction, and the particle moves in that straight line. All the vector equations derived in Section 3-2 will hold (and it will be easier to apply them) and in addition the scalar equation 3-11, since s and a have the same (or opposite) directions.

However, although the equations are easier to apply, we must remember that even in one dimension it is possible for a vector quantity to have one of two directions, and we shall have to decide on a positive sense for the displacement (and that will be the positive sense for velocity and acceleration also). This does not mean that we alter the equations, but the numbers to be substituted in them may have positive or negative signs attached to them. The following example illustrates the method.

▶ **Example 3-2** A glider is placed on a linear air track which is slightly tilted so that one end is higher than the other (figure 3-7): it is given a velocity of $1.5\,\mathrm{m\,s^{-1}}$ up the track. If its acceleration is $2.0\,\mathrm{m\,s^{-2}}$ down the track, find the time when it is $1.0\,\mathrm{m}$ below its starting point.

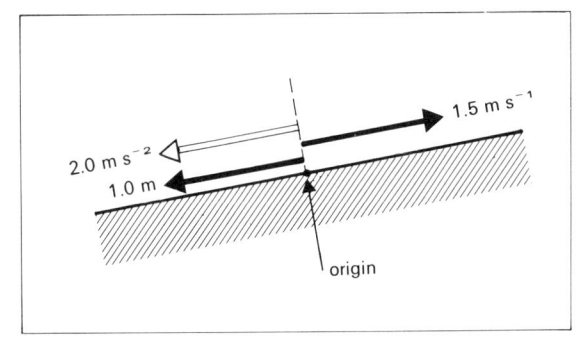

Figure 3-7 The original position of the glider is taken to be the origin for displacements, and the upward direction is taken to be positive.

We take the starting point as the origin for displacement, and the upward direction along the air track to be positive: then $\boldsymbol{v}_0 = +1.5\,\mathrm{m\,s^{-1}}$, $\boldsymbol{a} = -2.0\,\mathrm{m\,s^{-2}}$, and we want to find the value of t when $s = -1.0\,\mathrm{m}$. Using $s = v_0 t + \tfrac{1}{2}at^2$ (since this is equation 3-7 which relates our three known quantities and our fourth unknown quantity), we have

$$-1.0\,\mathrm{m} = (1.5\,\mathrm{m\,s^{-1}})t + \tfrac{1}{2}(-2.0\,\mathrm{m\,s^{-2}})t^2$$

or
$$t^2 - (1.5\,\mathrm{s})t - 1.0\,\mathrm{s}^2 = 0$$

or
$$(t - 2.0\,\mathrm{s})(t + 0.5\,\mathrm{s}) = 0$$

or
$$t = 2.0\,\mathrm{s} \text{ or } -0.5\,\mathrm{s}.$$

The obvious answer is that $t = 2.0\,\mathrm{s}$ when $s = -1.0\,\mathrm{m}$, but the other solution does have a meaning. $t = -0.5\,\mathrm{s}$ gives the time before we 'started the clock' at which the glider, rising at $1.5\,\mathrm{m\,s^{-1}}$ when $t = 0$, would have been $1.0\,\mathrm{m}$ below the starting point.

Note that if we had taken the downward direction to be positive, we should have had $\boldsymbol{v}_0 = -1.5\,\mathrm{m\,s^{-1}}$, $\boldsymbol{a} = +2.0\,\mathrm{m\,s^{-2}}$, and should have wanted to find t when $s = +1.0\,\mathrm{m}$. We should have produced the same equation

$$t^2 - (1.5\,\mathrm{s})t - 1.0\,\mathrm{s}^2 = 0$$

and obtained the same result. ◀

3-4 Linear motion graphs

We can represent a particle's linear motion by drawing three different graphs: a *displacement–time* graph, a *velocity–time* graph, and an *acceleration–time* graph. These have the virtue that they enable us to visualize the motion of a particle far more readily than would a table of numerical data; in addition we find it useful to measure the slopes of the first two of these, and to measure the areas between the graph-line and the time-axis for the second and third.

We can use these graphs to depict only linear motion, since there is no means of indicating on a graph directions other than forward or reverse directions along the line. Before we begin to draw the graph, we need to decide which of these directions shall be chosen to be positive, and which shall be negative. For the displacement–time graph we shall need to choose an origin, that is, to decide at which point on the line the displacement will be said to be zero. There is no need to choose an origin for the velocity–time and acceleration–time graphs: particles at rest relative to the Earth will normally be assumed to have zero velocity and a particle without acceleration relative to the Earth will be assumed to have zero acceleration.

The displacement–time graph

The *slope* of such a graph is the time rate of change of displacement, and therefore by definition the *velocity* of the particle. Figure 3-8 shows the displacement–time graph for a stone thrown vertically upwards from the edge of a cliff; the upward direction has been chosen to be positive, and the edge of the cliff has been chosen to be the origin of displacement. We see at once that the stone slows down, stops, and then increases in speed until (again at zero displacement) it returns to its initial speed (although if its initial velocity was v, its velocity is now $-v$). Its displacement then becomes negative, and its speed continues to increase.

The velocity–time graph

The *slope* of such a graph is the time rate of change of velocity, and therefore by definition the *acceleration* of the particle. Figure 3-9 shows the velocity–time graph for the stone of the previous paragraph. We do not have to choose whether the upward or the downward direction is to be considered positive, since the choice made for the displacement implies that the upward direction must be positive for velocity (and acceleration) also.

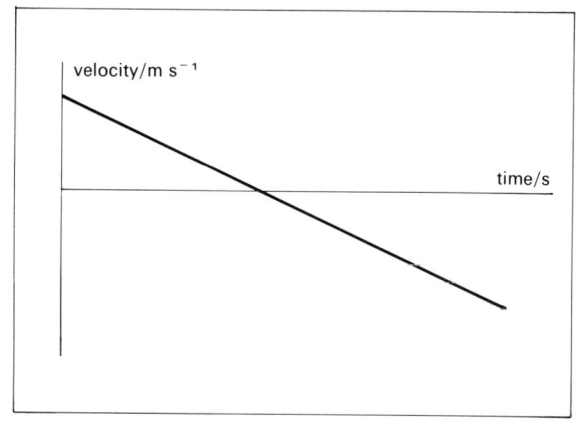

Figure 3-9 Velocity–time graph for a stone thrown vertically upwards from the edge of a cliff.

Further, the *area* between the graph-line and the time-axis is a measure of the particle's *change of displacement*. (If, as is usual, the particle's initial displacement is zero, the area gives the particle's actual displacement.) Consider first a particle moving with a constant velocity of $12 \, \text{m s}^{-1}$, as shown in figure 3-10, from $t = 3.0 \, \text{s}$ to $t = 8.0 \, \text{s}$. We know that the change in displacement is 60 m, and we can see that measuring the area under the graph-line gives the same result.

The velocity–time graph for the stone included some negative values of velocity: the area between the graph-line and the time-axis is then below the time axis. The obvious interpretation of this (which is readily seen to agree with reality) is that this implies a negative change of displacement. Comparison of figure 3-9 with figure 3-8 shows that where the velocity begins to be negative, the displacement begins to decrease.

In general, when the velocity is changing, the area under the graph-line is still a measure of the change of displacement. For, consider the velocity–time graph shown in

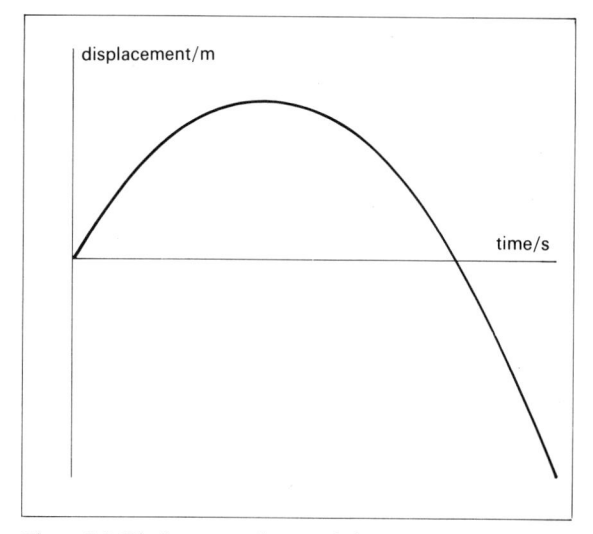

Figure 3-8 Displacement–time graph for a stone thrown vertically upwards from the edge of a cliff.

3-4 Linear motion graphs

curve more closely by using a greater number of narrower rectangles, and in the limiting case, as their width tends to zero, the sum of their areas is *exactly* equal to the area under the graph, from $t = t_1$ to $t = t_2$. In calculus notation, the change of displacement $s_2 - s_1$ is given by

$$s_2 - s_1 = \int_{t_1}^{t_2} v \, dt. \qquad [3\text{-}12]$$

The important point, however, is not the mathematical notation, but the fact that a measure of the change of displacement is provided by the area under the appropriate section of the graph-line, as shown in figure 3-12.

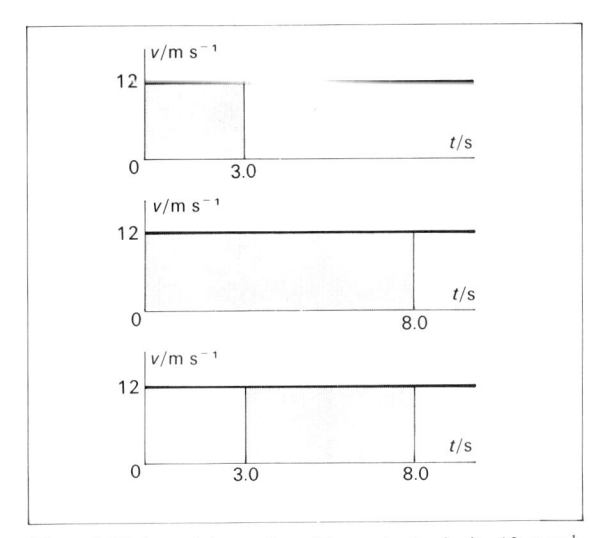

Figure 3-10 A particle moving with constant velocity 12 m s^{-1}. After 3.0 s and 8.0 s, its displacements from the origin are 36 m and 96 m. The change in displacement is 60 m. The area under the graph in the third diagram is $12 \times 5.0 = 60$, which indicates a displacement of 60 m, since one unit of area on the graph represents 1 metre of displacement.

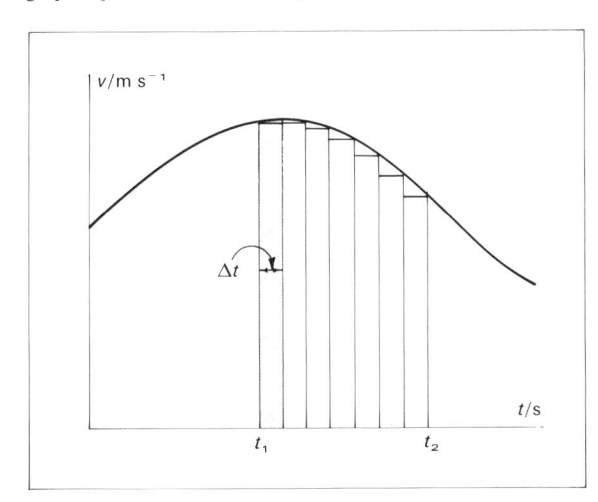

Figure 3-11 The area of the seven rectangles is an approximate measure of the change of displacement between $t = t_1$ and $t = t_2$.

figure 3-11: had the graph-line followed the stepped line, the change of displacement between $t = t_1$ and $t = t_2$ would clearly have been measured by the area of the seven rectangles of width Δt, that is, by

$$\sum_{t=t_1}^{t=t_2} (v \Delta t),$$

where Δt is the width of a rectangle, and v is the height of a rectangle. We can make the stepped line follow the

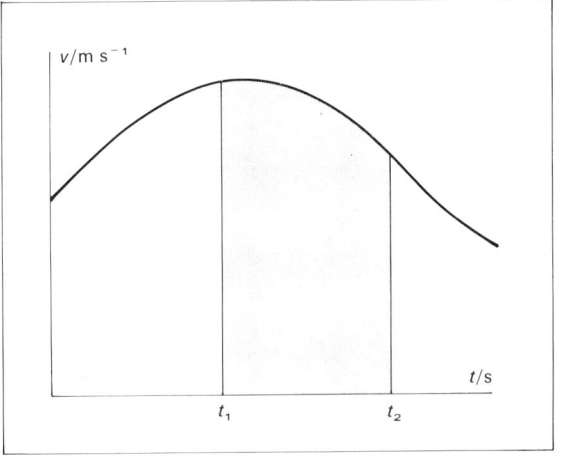

Figure 3-12 The shaded area is a measure of the displacement between $t = t_1$ and $t = t_2$.

Where the particle has constant acceleration, that part of the graph is a straight line, and the area between this and the time-axis can easily be calculated without even drawing the graph to scale. When, as is usual in practice, the graph is curved, as in figure 3-12, and the area under it can only be estimated (unless we happen to know the algebraic relationship between v and t, which is about as unlikely as the acceleration being constant), we can use mathematical techniques such as the trapezium rule or Simpson's rule or, more easily in the laboratory, we can draw the curve on graph paper and estimate the area by counting the squares. This last method is illustrated in Example 3-3.

▶ **Example 3-3** The table gives the speeds, at particular times, of a particle moving in a straight line:

t/s	0	4	8	12	16	20	24	28
v/m s^{-1}	20	35	40	43	50	53	50	40

Find its change of displacement between $t = 0$ and $t = 28$ s.

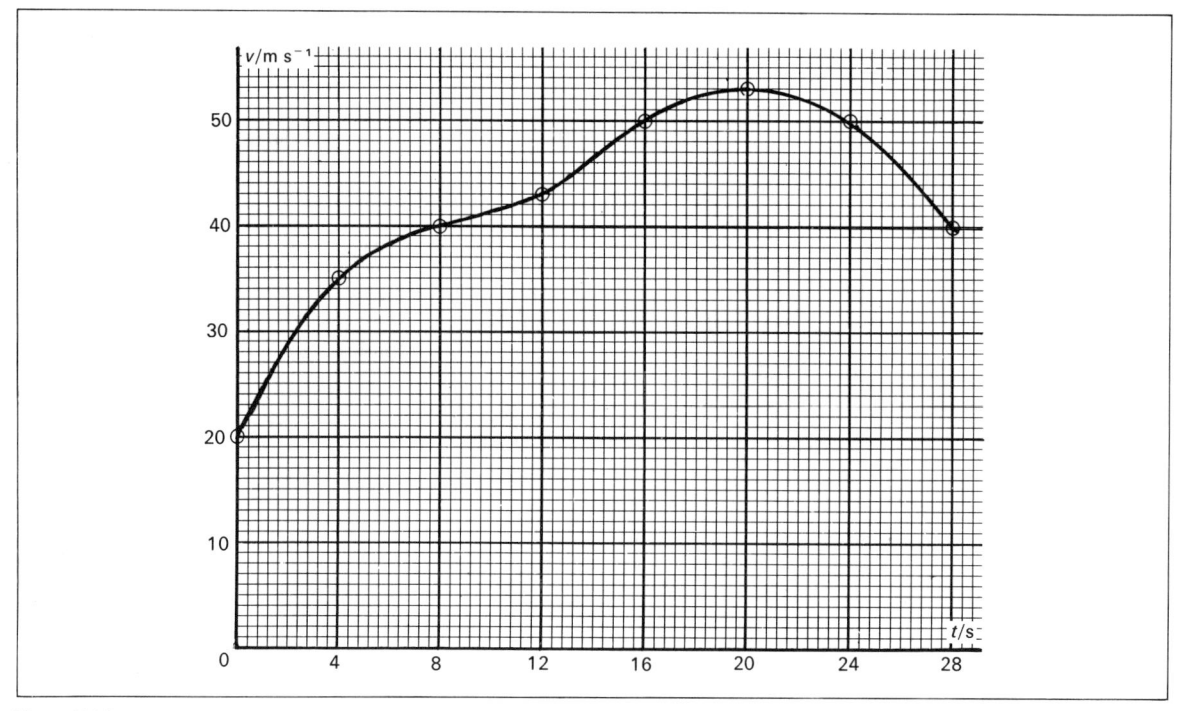

Figure 3-13

We first draw the graph (figure 3-13). We can see (for example, by looking at the bottom left-hand square) that a displacement of 40 m is represented by 100 squares. The number of squares between the graph-line and the time-axis is 3030, so that the change of displacement Δs between $t = 0$ and $t = 28$ s is given by

$$\Delta s = \frac{3030 \text{ squares}}{100 \text{ squares}} \times 40 \text{ m}$$

$$= 1210 \text{ m}. \qquad \blacktriangleleft$$

Distance–time and speed–time graphs

We can also plot *distance–time* and *speed–time* graphs. If we are concerned with distances and speeds, instead of displacements and velocities, we need not concern ourselves with the direction of the movements, and can therefore consider motion which is not linear. The slope of the distance–time graph will give the speed of the particle, and the slope of the speed–time graph will give the rate-of-change of speed (though not, strictly, the acceleration, which is a vector quantity). The area between the speed–time graph-line and the time-axis gives the distance travelled. The essential difference between these graphs and the ones we considered earlier is that distance and speed, being scalar quantities, are necessarily positive quantities, and we do not get as much information as we do from the graphs of the vector quantities. Figure 3-14 shows the distance–time and speed–time graphs which correspond to the displacement–time and velocity–time graphs shown in figures 3-8 and 3-9. We can see that these graphs give us no information about the direction of movement of a particle, nor, since the distance–time graph deals with distances and not displacements, do they enable us to find the position of a particle at a particular time. However, we can use these graphs for the distance travelled, speed, and rate-of-change-of-speed of a particle moving along a curve.

The acceleration–time graph

This is not as commonly used simply because we are more likely to have values of a particle's velocities than of its accelerations. However, for the sake of completeness, figure 3-15 shows the acceleration–time graph for the stone we have been previously considering in this section, and we see that, as the slope of the velocity–time graph implied, it has a constant negative acceleration. However, if we were given a series of values of a particle's instantaneous accelerations at given times, we could use the area under this graph as a measure of the change of velocity of the particle between those times. The change

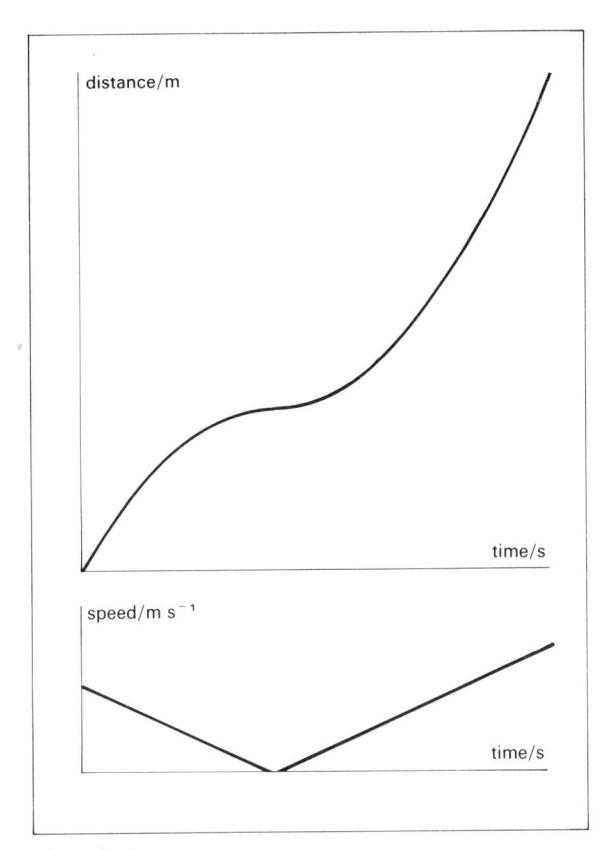

Figure 3-14

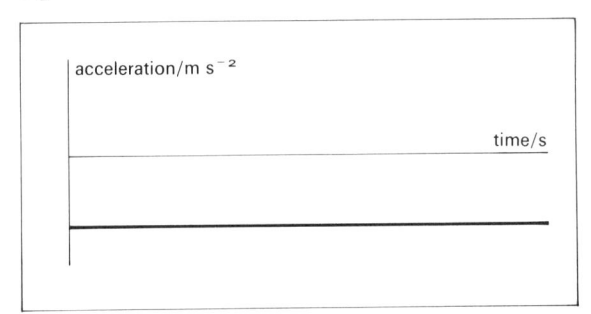

Figure 3-15 The acceleration–time graph for a stone being thrown vertically upwards.

of velocity is given by the limiting value of the sum of the rectangles $a\Delta t$ between $t = t_1$ and $t = t_2$. In calculus notation, just as for change of displacement in equation 3-12, so

$$v_2 - v_1 = \int_{t_1}^{t_2} a\, dt. \qquad [3\text{-}13]$$

The three types of graph are clearly related to each other, and all can be deduced if one is given.

▶ **Example 3-4** A train moves from station A to station B. Its acceleration increases (not necessarily steadily) to a maximum shortly after leaving A, and then falls to zero. When it is approaching B, it begins to accelerate again, its acceleration varying and reaching a maximum shortly before it reaches B. Sketch, beneath each other, acceleration–time, velocity–time, and displacement–time graphs for the train's motion.

The graphs are given in figure 3-16. Note that

(a) on the acceleration–time graph it has been assumed that the maximum value of the acceleration is less than the maximum value of the deceleration, but the total area of the acceleration–time graph must be zero (since the train's change of velocity is zero)

(b) the total area of the velocity–time graph is a measure of the train's change of displacement

(c) the slope of the velocity–time graph is a measure of the acceleration of the train

(d) the slope of the displacement–time graph is a measure of the velocity of the train. ◀

3-5 Measuring acceleration

To find the average acceleration of a particle between two points A and B we need to measure the velocities of the particle at A and B, v_A and v_B respectively, and the time the particle takes to move from A to B, Δt. Then

$$a_{av} = \frac{v_B - v_A}{\Delta t}.$$

In general the only satisfactory way of doing this is to establish the position of the particle at successive known time intervals and to draw a velocity–time graph. The graph can then be used to find either an average or an instantaneous acceleration. Ticker-tape timers and stroboscopic photography both give the necessary information, but they are unlikely to be accurate to more than a few per cent. There are instruments which yield a direct measurement of a: these *accelerometers* depend upon the relationship between force and acceleration. By measuring the force needed to accelerate a particle of known mass which moves with the body, the acceleration of the body can be found. The force-measuring part of the instrument, usually a spring, is calibrated directly in m s^{-2}.

The problem of measuring the size of a constant acceleration, particularly the acceleration due to gravity at a point on the Earth's surface, g, is much more important. The precise and accurate measurement of g was achieved using pendulums until the Second World War, during which the development of techniques for measuring very short time intervals, largely stimulated by the use of radar, allowed a more direct approach to the problem by making it possible to study the motion of a freely falling body.

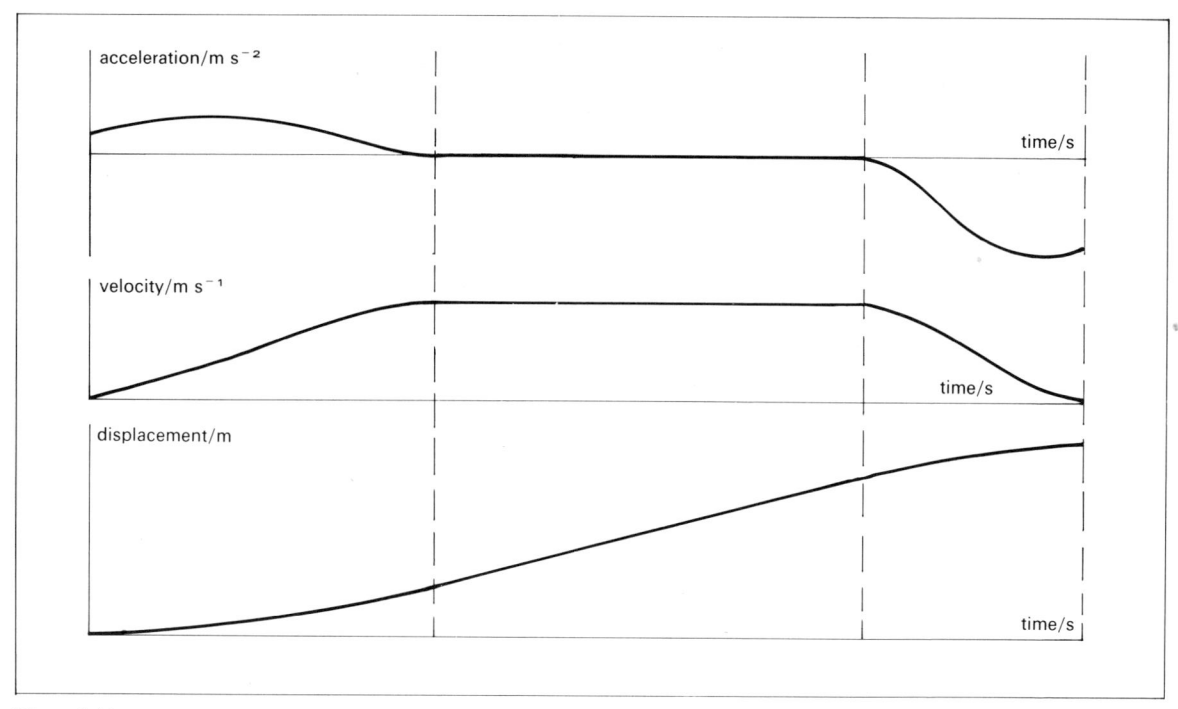

Figure 3-16

(a) The easiest approach is to allow a dense object, such as a steel sphere, to fall a short distance from rest. The switching arrangement is shown in figure 3-17, Δt being measured to ± 1 ms in 500 ms for a fall of 1 m. The error in the experiment is the indeterminacy of h, which can only be measured to about ± 5 mm. Several values of Δt for each of several values of h from 1 to 2 metres should be taken. Assuming that the acceleration is constant, equation 3-5 gives us

$$h = \tfrac{1}{2}g(\Delta t)^2.$$

Thus the slope of the graph shown ($\sqrt{h}/\mathrm{m}^{1/2}$ plotted against $\Delta t/\mathrm{s}$) is $\sqrt{(\tfrac{1}{2}g)}$. Using this apparatus it is possible to measure g to about one per cent. By plotting $\sqrt{h}$ against Δt rather than h against $(\Delta t)^2$, systematic errors in Δt are eliminated when the slope is measured.

(b) *Measuring g by simple pendulum* It is shown on page 256 that for a small body swinging through a small angle ($<10°$) on the end of a thin string suspended from a rigid support, the period of oscillation T is related to the distance l of the centre of the sphere from the axis of rotation by

$$T = 2\pi \sqrt{\frac{l}{g}}.$$

In this experiment the resistance of the air is ignored: T does not depend significantly on the amplitude provided the latter is small. By setting up such a simple pendulum, measuring l with a ruler and nT (the time for n oscillations) with a stopwatch, g can be found. As $T^2 = (4\pi^2/g)l$, a graph of t^2/s^2 against l/m will have a slope of $4\pi^2/g$. The practical details of this experiment and of more complex determinations using pendulums will be found in textbooks of practical physics.

(c) *Accurate determination of g* The latest method of measuring g (performed at the National Physical Laboratory, Teddington), the results of which were published in 1967, involves an analysis of the rise and fall of a freely moving body. In figure 3-18 the times at the marked stages of the flight are given. Using equation 3-5 for

(i) from the lower level to the top:

$$H + h = \tfrac{1}{2}gT^2$$

and

(ii) from the upper level to the top:

$$h = \tfrac{1}{2}gt^2.$$

Subtracting,

$$H = \tfrac{1}{2}g(T^2 - t^2)$$

whence

$$g = \frac{2H}{T^2 - t^2}.$$

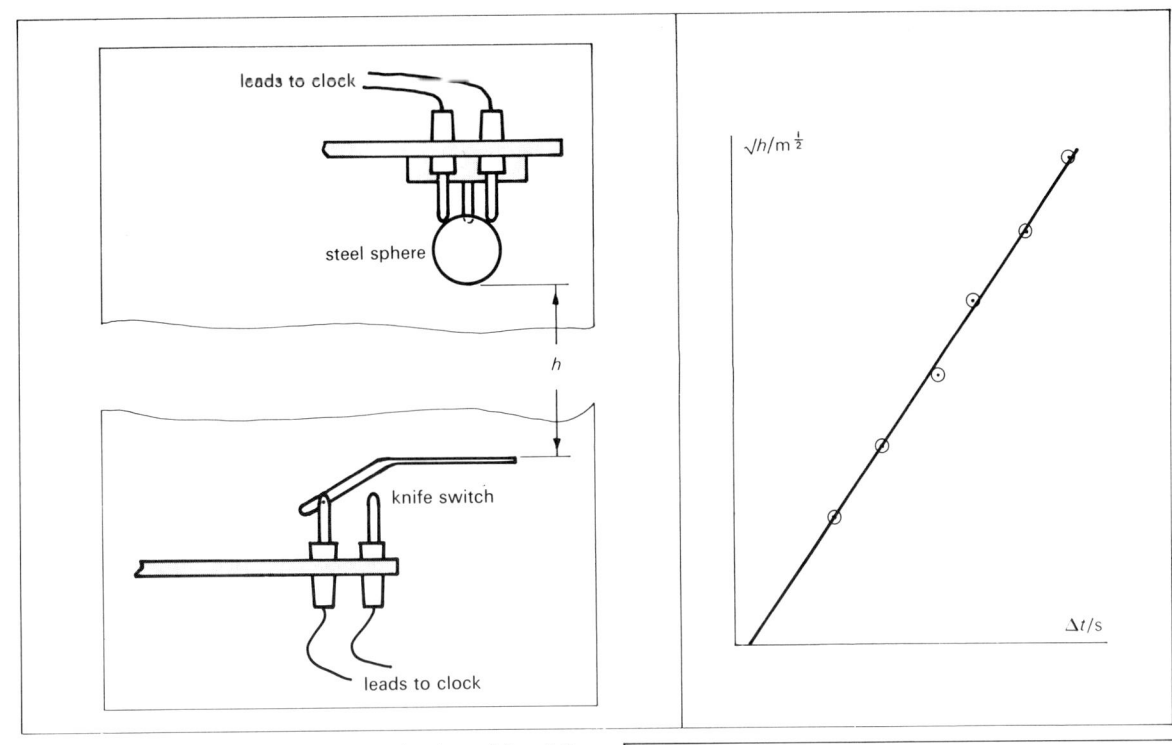

Figure 3-17 An arrangement to measure the time of free fall, Δt, of a steel sphere over a distance h starting from rest. The sphere is held against three pins before release and hits a platform at the end of its descent. The clock could be a millisecond scaler-timer or a one-second-sweep mains-operated clock. Is the measured value of Δt bigger or smaller than it would be in the absence of air resistance?

It was possible to measure T and t very accurately (to better than 1 part in 10^6) using a glass sphere as the moving object. Illuminated horizontal slits were mounted at levels A and B on one side of the evacuated apparatus. Opposite each slit was a narrow strip of photosensitive material. As the ball passed midway between the slit and the strip, its action *as a lens* caused a flash of light to fall on the strip. The pulses so induced were used to trigger a standardized electronic timing device.

There are two reasons why this method is preferable to an equally carefully performed experiment on a body falling downward only—for which the theory is identical. Firstly, the nature of each of the flashes is identical, and secondly the effect of any remaining air is zero, provided that its resistance is small and proportional to the velocity of the ball. In the N.P.L. experiment the pressure was reduced to about $1\,\text{N}\,\text{m}^{-2}$. The experiment was judged to be accurate to better than $2 \times 10^{-6}\,\text{m}\,\text{s}^{-2}$, which is a possible error of less than 2 parts in 10^7.

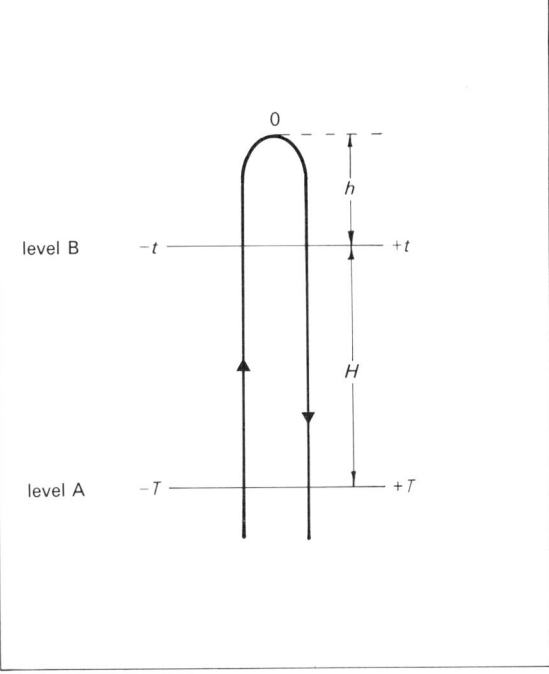

Figure 3-18 The principle of an up-and-down free fall experiment. An object moving in a vacuum has the times for which it is above the lower and upper horizontal lines measured as $2T$ and $2t$ respectively.

3-6 Planar motion: constant acceleration II

We now resume our consideration of the motion of a particle which has a constant acceleration a, the direction of a not necessarily being the same as that of its initial velocity v_0. We look first at a particle for which the direction of v_0 is perpendicular to the direction of a. (The reader will probably visualize this as motion in a gravitational field, but this analysis applies to all planar motions where the direction of v_0 and a are perpendicular.) Figure 3-19a shows the velocity vectors v_0, v_1, v_2, v_3, and so on, which the particle has at times 0, t, $2t$, $3t$, etc. and figure 3-19b shows the corresponding position vectors s_1, s_2, etc.; a coordinate frame, with its origin O at the particle's starting point, has been attached. We can see from figure 3-19b that the particle moves in a curve. We can also see that the curve is a parabola, for at time T the coordinates of the particle are given by $x = v_0 T$ and $y = \frac{1}{2}aT^2$, which, if we eliminate T, gives

$$y = \frac{a}{2v_0^2} x^2.$$

This is the equation of a parabola whose vertex is at the origin, and whose axis is the y-axis.

In figure 3-20 the successive velocity vectors and position vectors are drawn for the more general case where v_0 is not at right angles to a. Choosing an origin of coordinates (arbitrarily) at O, we have, at time T,

$$x = v_0 T \cos \alpha, \qquad y = v_0 T \sin \alpha - \tfrac{1}{2}aT^2,$$

which gives
$$y = x \tan \alpha - \frac{ax^2}{2v_0^2 \cos^2 \alpha}. \qquad [3\text{-}14]$$

This again represents a parabola, the additional complication of the form of the equation being due to our not placing the coordinate origin at its vertex. The axis of this more general parabola is also vertical, and therefore parallel to the direction of a.

This last example does represent the most general case: admittedly we have always chosen to have the direction of a vertical, but if we want to consider the motion of a particle which has constant *non*-vertical acceleration, all

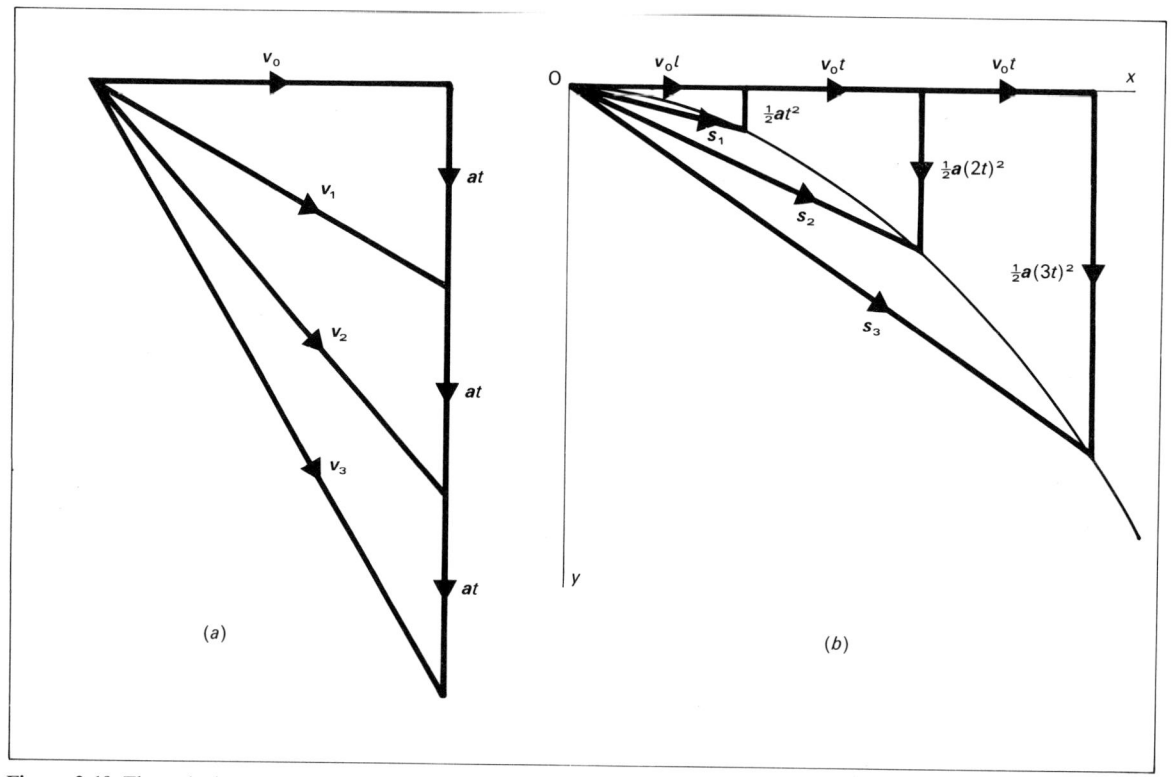

Figure 3-19 The velocity vectors and position vectors, shown at equal time intervals, for a particle which has an initial velocity v_0 which is horizontal, and a constant acceleration a, which is vertical.

3-6 Planar motion: constant acceleration II 43

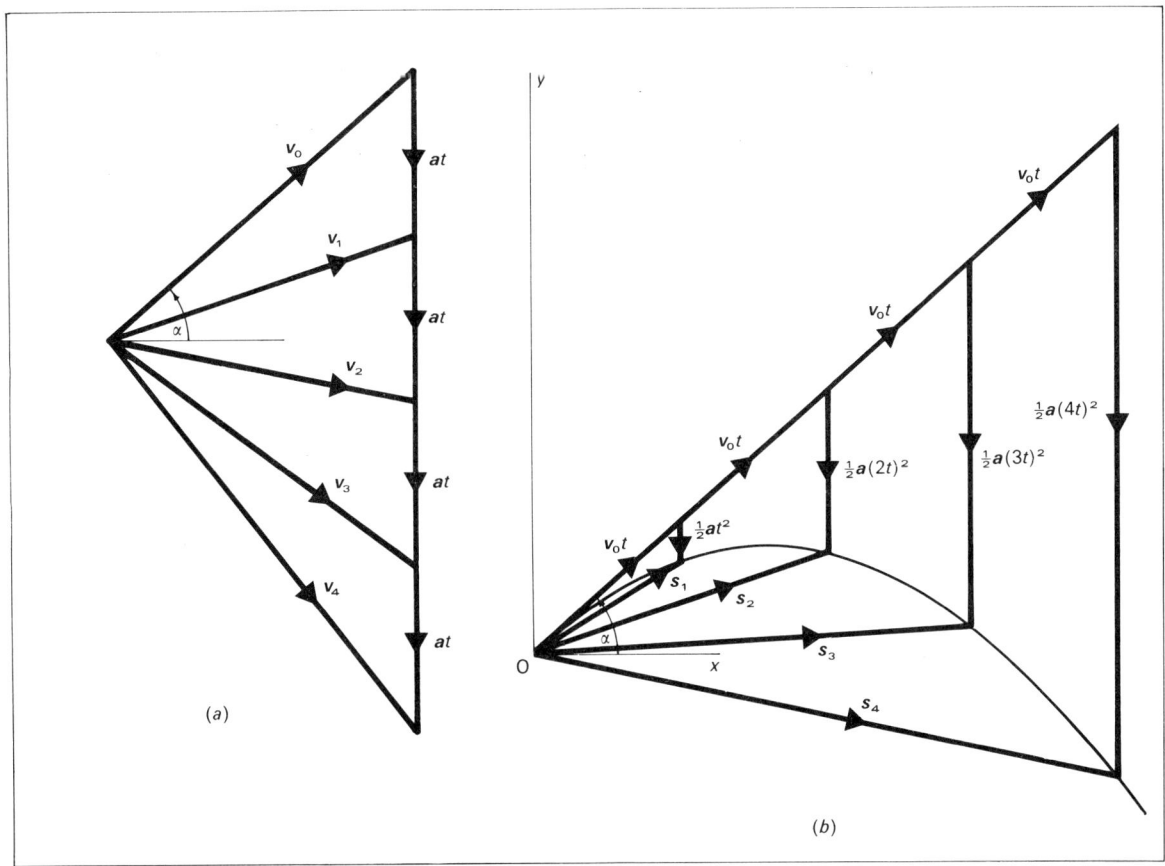

Figure 3-20 This is similar to figure 3-19, but the initial velocity v_0 makes an angle α with the horizontal. The particle again moves in a parabolic curve.

we need do is to rotate figure 3-20, and we have an appropriate diagram. *Any* particle, given an initial velocity v_0 whose direction is not the same as that of its acceleration a, will move in a parabolic path, the axis of the parabola being parallel to a.

One important example of parabolic motion is that of a charged particle moving across a uniform electric field, but here we shall consider only massive particles moving across a uniform gravitational field. In so doing we shall generally assume that the effects of air resistance, the curvature of the Earth, the rotation of the Earth, and the decrease with height of the Earth's gravitational field can be ignored. Figure 3-21 shows two realistic situations in which these assumptions are not made.

Figure 3-21 The path of a body projected under gravity (*a*) in a path which takes it well above the Earth's surface and back again and (*b*) when air resistance noticeably affects the path.

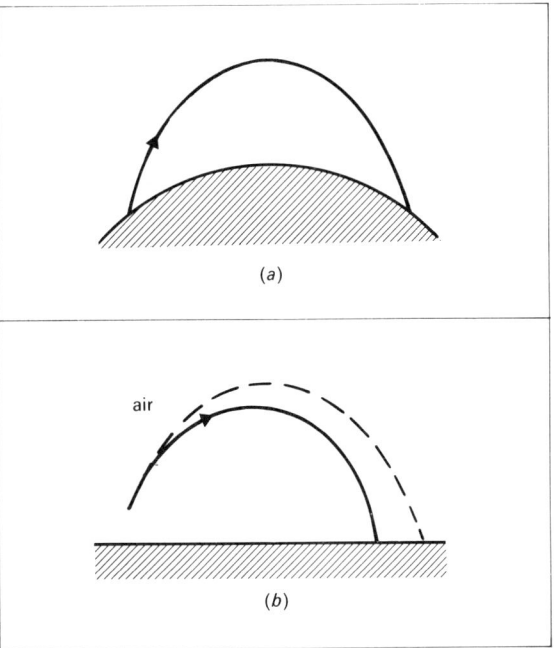

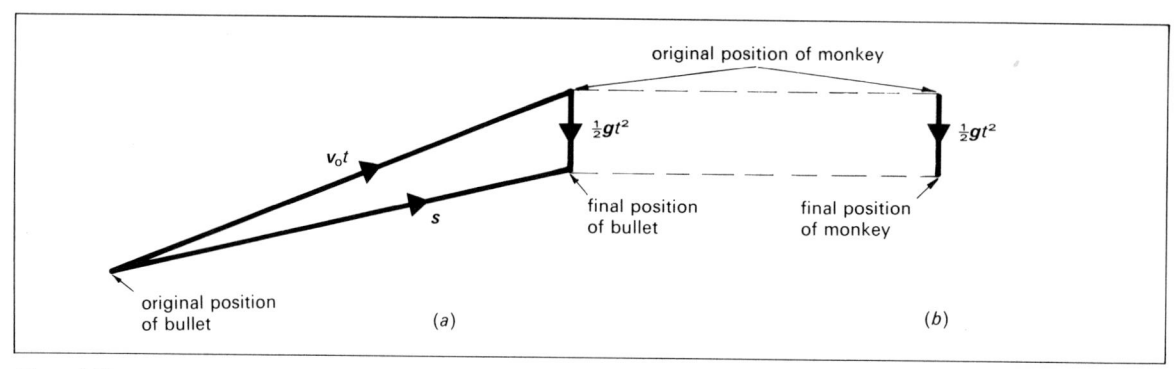

Figure 3-22

The vector analysis of projectile motion is the most successful in a specifically two-dimensional situation, as in the classic monkey and hunter problem, which serves as Example 3-5.

▶ **Example 3-5** A monkey had had several encounters with different hunters armed with rifles. On each occasion a hunter had aimed his rifle at the monkey while it sat in the tree, and had adjusted his sights to allow for distance (that is, to allow for the gravitational effect on the bullet). At the instant the hunter had fired his rifle the monkey had allowed himself to fall vertically, and the bullet had passed through the place where it had been. Another hunter, however, who had heard of this monkey, aimed his rifle at it without correcting for distance, that is, the bullet emerged from the barrel travelling directly towards the monkey. What happened on this occasion?

The monkey was hit. Suppose the bullet takes a time t to reach the vertical line through the monkey: if the bullet has an initial velocity v_0 and the gravitational acceleration is g, the total displacement of the bullet in time t is $v_0 t + \frac{1}{2}gt^2$, as shown in figure 3-22a. In that time, the monkey, with the same acceleration g, falls a distance $\frac{1}{2}gt^2$, so the bullet and the monkey are in the same place at the same time. ◀

3-7 The parabola of projectile motion

We saw in the last section that a directly two-dimensional approach is often very successful. However, when we analyse the motion of projectiles we are often particularly interested in the motion in a particular direction: for example, in the horizontal range of a shell, or the greatest height reached by a ball. So we often choose first to resolve displacements and velocities vertically and horizontally. The situation then becomes relatively simple as in the vertical direction the motion has a constant acceleration g, and horizontally the velocity remains unchanged. We illustrate this technique in Example 3-6.

▶ **Example 3-6** A shell is fired from a mortar on a hillside at a speed of 100 m s^{-1} and at an angle of elevation of $60°$ (figure 3-23). It hits the ground at a horizontal distance of 400 m from the mortar. Neglecting air resistance and taking $g = 10 \text{ m s}^{-2}$, calculate (a) the time interval between the firing of the shell and its hitting the ground, (b) at what distance from the mortar the shell hits the ground, and (c) the angle which the shell's trajectory makes with the horizontal three seconds after firing.

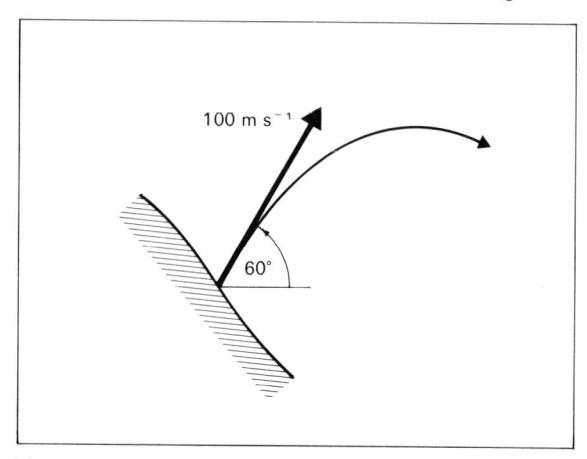

Figure 3-23

The vertical and horizontal resolved parts of the shell's initial velocity are, respectively,

$$(100 \text{ m s}^{-1}) \sin 60° = 87 \text{ m s}^{-1}$$
and
$$(100 \text{ m s}^{-1}) \cos 60° = 50 \text{ m s}^{-1}.$$

(a) Horizontally we have a shell travelling for 400 m at a constant velocity of 50 m s^{-1}. This takes

$$\frac{400 \text{ m}}{50 \text{ m s}^{-1}} = 8.0 \text{ s}.$$

(b) Considering vertical motion, taking upward as being positive, we have

$$v_0 = 87 \text{ m s}^{-1}, \quad a = -10 \text{ m s}^{-2}, \quad t = 8.0 \text{ s}.$$

3-7 The parabola of projectile motion

Therefore
$$s = v_0 t + \tfrac{1}{2}at^2 = (87\,\text{m s}^{-1})(8.0\,\text{s}) + \tfrac{1}{2}(-10\,\text{m s}^{-2})(8.0\,\text{s})^2$$
$$= 696\,\text{m} - 320\,\text{m}$$
$$= 376\,\text{m}.$$

As this is a positive value, the shell hits the ground 376 m *above* the mortar, which is, incidentally, at the top of its trajectory.

(c) After 3 s the horizontal velocity is still $50\,\text{m s}^{-1}$. The vertical velocity has lessened by $30\,\text{m s}^{-1}$, since the shell has an acceleration of $10\,\text{m s}^{-2}$ vertically downwards. Therefore the resolutes of velocity are as shown in figure 3-24, and

$$\theta = \tan^{-1}\left(\frac{57\,\text{m s}^{-1}}{50\,\text{m s}^{-1}}\right) = 49°.$$

(The speed of the shell then
$$= \sqrt{[(50\,\text{m s}^{-1})^2 + (57\,\text{m s}^{-1})^2]} = 76\,\text{m s}^{-1}.)\;\blacktriangleleft$$

We can easily demonstrate that the motion of a projected body is parabolic. A jet of water from a fine nozzle can be broken into a series of drops by vibrating the rubber tube leading from the tap to the nozzle; the drops are thus produced at equal time intervals. When the drops are illuminated stroboscopically at certain frequencies they 'freeze'. These 'frozen' drops are where one drop would be after 1, 2, 3, 4 (etc.) units of time (see figure 3-25). Measur-

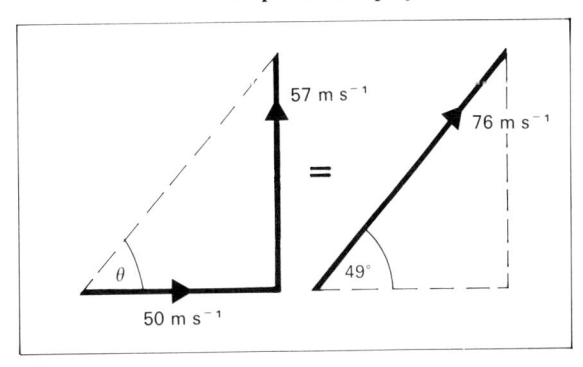

Figure 3-24

ing from a drop at the top of the parabola, the *x*-displacements of successive 'stationary' drops are found to be 1, 2, 3, 4 (etc.) units and the *y*-displacements of these drops are found to be 1, 4, 9, 16 (etc.) units. This is typical of parabolic motion. If the drops are viewed from above, their steady horizontal progress becomes very obvious. Using this apparatus we can also learn that the greatest horizontal range of a drop projected at a given speed occurs when the angle of elevation of projection is 45°.

Another way of analysing projectile motion is to take multiflash photographs of a white painted steel ball which is projected horizontally. Measurements of the displacement of the ball can be made from an enlarged photograph.

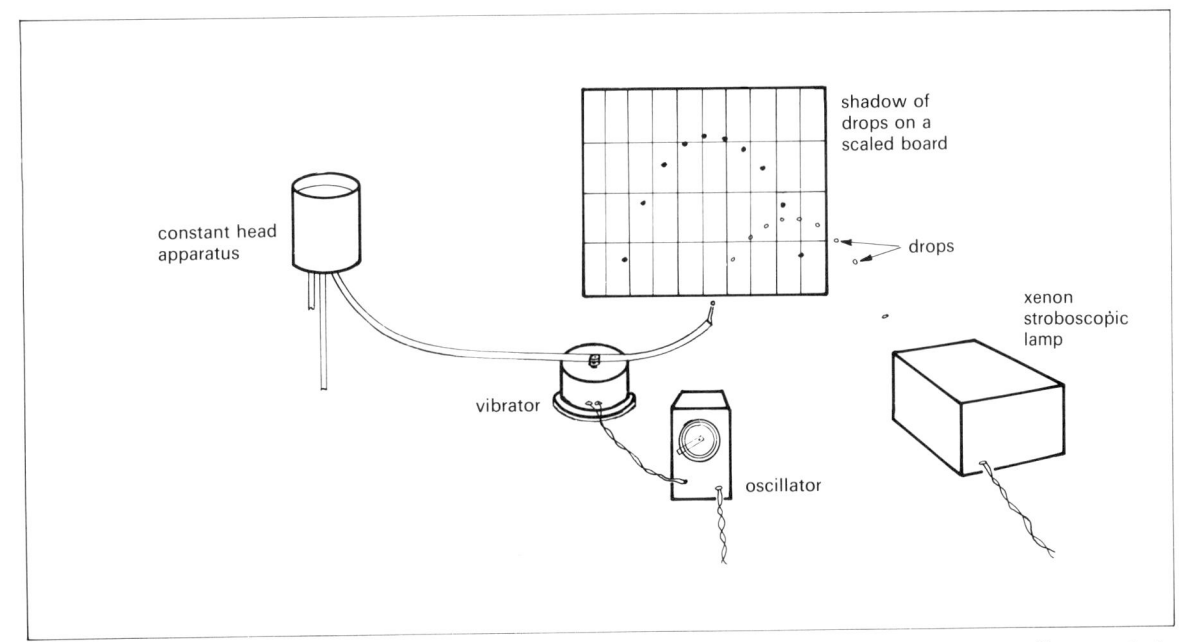

Figure 3-25 'Seeing' the parabola of projectile motion. The drops are 'frozen' by synchronizing the oscillator and the stroboscope. How could they be made to go backwards?

Representations of such photographs, taken from three different positions, are shown in figure 3-26.

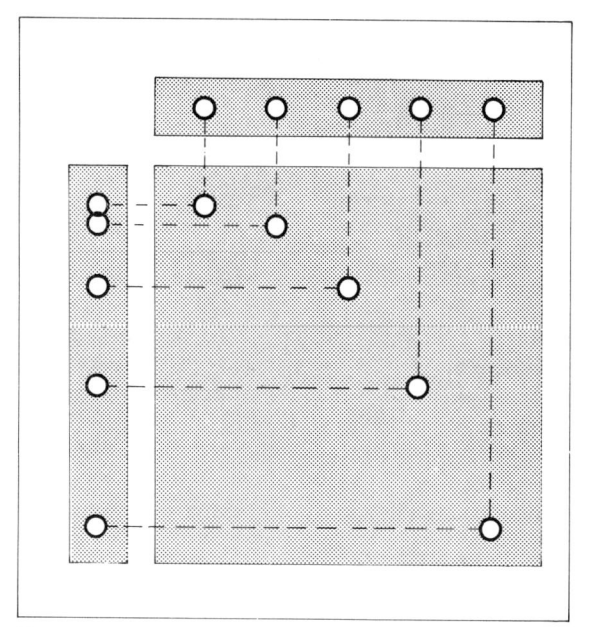

Figure 3-26 Three simulated multiflash photographs of a horizontally projected steel ball.

3-8 Acceleration as a function of displacement, velocity, and time

In earlier sections of this chapter, particularly in Sections 3-2 and 3-3, we have shown how we can relate the displacement, velocity, and acceleration of a particle if we know how one of these varies with time. The appropriate mathematical statements which have already been made for the sizes of these quantities are:

[2-9, 3-2] $$v = \frac{ds}{dt} \quad \text{and} \quad a = \frac{dv}{dt}$$

[3-12, 3-13] $$s = \int v \, dt \quad \text{and} \quad v = \int a \, dt.$$

We have also seen that we can write

[3-2, 3-3] $$a = \frac{dv}{dt} \quad \text{as} \quad \frac{d^2 s}{dt^2}.$$

With these relationships, and the processes of the differential and integral calculus, we can solve some problems involving varying acceleration. First, as an example, however, let us derive the equations of uniform accelerated motion from the definitive statement

$$a = \text{constant}.$$

We integrate to find $\boldsymbol{v}$ at time t; suppose $\boldsymbol{v} = \boldsymbol{v}_0$ when $t = 0$. Then

$$\int_{v_0}^{v} d\boldsymbol{v} = \int_0^t \boldsymbol{a} \, dt,$$

so

$$\boldsymbol{v} - \boldsymbol{v}_0 = \boldsymbol{a}t$$

that is

$$\frac{ds}{dt} = \boldsymbol{v}_0 + \boldsymbol{a}t.$$

We integrate again to find s at time t; suppose $s = 0$ at $t = 0$. Integrating, we have

$$\int_0^s d\boldsymbol{s} = \int_0^t (\boldsymbol{v}_0 + \boldsymbol{a}t) \, dt$$

that is

[3-7] $$s = \boldsymbol{v}_0 t + \tfrac{1}{2}\boldsymbol{a}t^2.$$

From $\boldsymbol{v} = \boldsymbol{v}_0 + \boldsymbol{a}t$ and $s = \boldsymbol{v}_0 t + \tfrac{1}{2}\boldsymbol{a}t^2$ we can eliminate t or $\boldsymbol{a}$ or $\boldsymbol{v}_0$ and get the other three relationships see Section 3-2.

It must be stressed that in real situations such mathematical solutions are seldom possible. We sometimes attempt to make a better model of the actual situation (for example, by assuming certain resistive forces are proportional to the velocity, or the square of the velocity, of a body) but in practice such a simple model is unlikely to be realistic. The need to do this is fast disappearing as numerical techniques (which make use of computers) for solving such problems are developed.

3-9 Frames of reference

In an aeroplane flying at a constant high velocity a passenger is able to toss a coin or walk along the gangway in an entirely normal way. Is this surprising? So far in this chapter we have measured all speeds relative to the surface of the Earth, which we tacitly accept as being fixed. But is it fixed? Answers to questions like these, or even the questions themselves, suggest that any statement about motion is made with reference to a measuring grid attached to some conventional object, such as the Earth or an aeroplane, and that any laws which we deduce about motion do not depend on what the grid is attached to. The scientific name for the measuring grid is a *frame of reference*. For example, two experimenters E_1 and E_2,

3-9 Frames of reference

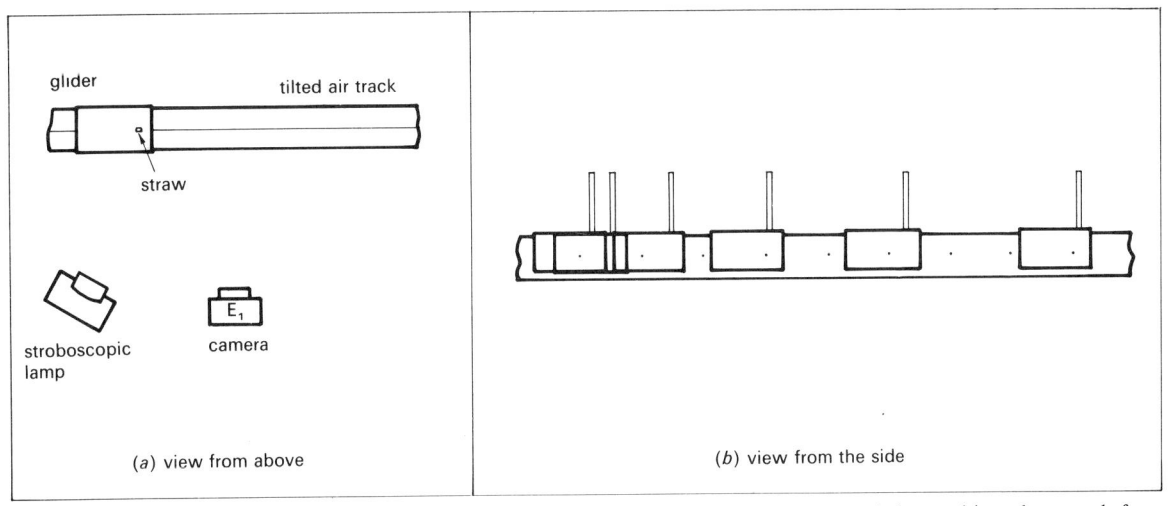

Figure 3-27 In (a) E_1 measures the acceleration of an air-track glider. (b) is a representation of the resulting photograph from which a can be deduced.

using stroboscopic techniques in fast and slow trains, would each establish the equations of Section 3-8 for a uniformly accelerating particle.

Suppose we were to measure the acceleration of an air-track glider such as that shown in figure 3-27a. The track is tilted and the glider is released from rest at the left edge of the field of view of the camera. The resulting photograph using stroboscopic lighting is like that shown in figure 3-27b.

The objection could be raised that the time during which the glider is in the field of view of the camera is too small for a good value of its average acceleration to be calculated by E_1. Would it be better to run the camera on a trolley which moves at a constant speed alongside the air track? (There are many other ways of making better use of the equipment but this suggestion is reasonable.) The result of this second experiment is represented in figure 3-28b and it is certainly true that the glider remains in the field of view of the camera for longer, thus enabling E_2 to perform a better analysis. But will the measured vector acceleration be the same when deduced from figure 3-28b as from 3-27b? *We should find that it is the same.* The reader who really 'believes' this without trying the experiment has an instinctive belief in the *principle of special relativity*.

The result of this experiment then is that if during the time interval Δt, between say the second and fifth flashes, the *changes* in velocity of the glider are

$\Delta \boldsymbol{v}_1$ as measured by E_1 in the first experiment

and $\Delta \boldsymbol{v}_2$ as measured by E_2 in the second,

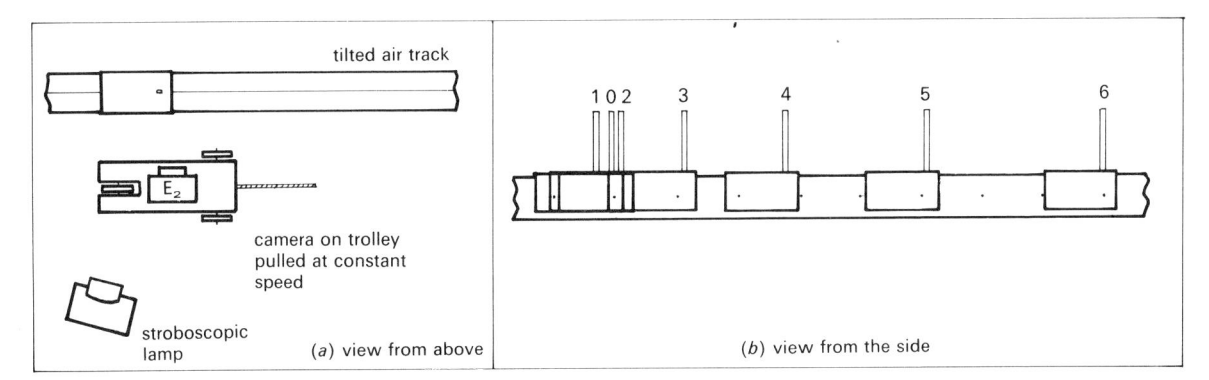

Figure 3-28 In (b) the numbers indicate successive positions of the marker. The glider began by moving to the left relative to the camera, came to rest relative to the camera, and then moved to the right relative to the camera.

then it is found that

$$\frac{\Delta \boldsymbol{v}_1}{\Delta t} = \frac{\Delta \boldsymbol{v}_2}{\Delta t}$$

or $\boldsymbol{a}_1 = \boldsymbol{a}_2$.

As measured accelerations are the same in the two frames of reference then so too will be the experimenters' measured forces (see Chapter 5). They could go on to produce identical mechanics textbooks such as this volume.

*The laws of physics are the same in any two reference frames moving with uniform relative velocity. This is called the **principle of special relativity**.*

Finally, returning to our aeroplane, we notice that we cannot confidently toss and catch the coin or walk along the gangway if the aeroplane is accelerating at take-off, or falling in an air pocket, or turning a corner. Such an accelerating reference frame is said to be non-inertial, whereas the discussion of mechanics which we will develop involves only motion in an *inertial* frame of reference, one, that is, which is *not accelerating*. In practice such a frame is difficult to find (even the Sun rotates in the galaxy); Newton, however, felt justified in imagining the existence of such an inertial frame. His laws apply only in inertial reference frames which are moving slowly relative to each other (by slowly we mean at speeds of less than 10^8 m s^{-1}—see Chapter 10), but they do apply in *all* of these. *Special relativity* is the name given to the mechanics of inertial reference frames moving at high relative speeds; in these the principle of special relativity does still hold, but at the expense of a 'commonsense' view of space and time.

Bibliography

Cook, A. H. (1967). 'A new absolute determination of the acceleration due to gravity.' *Physics Education*, **2**, page 261.

Nuffield O-level Physics (1967). *Guide to experiments III*. Longman/Penguin. The experiments on projectile motion are relevant.

Weidner, R. T. and Sells, R. L. (1965). *Elementary classical physics*, volume 1. Allyn and Bacon. Chapter 4: kinematics in two dimensions; and Chapter 2: straight-line kinematics.

8 mm film loop. 'Galilean relativity—ball dropped from mast of ship.' Ealing Scientific. A loop from the Harvard Project Physics.

16 mm film. 'Free fall and projectile motion.' Guild Sound and Vision. This film includes a breathtaking large-scale version of the 'monkey and hunter' experiment.

16 mm film. 'Frames of reference.' Guild Sound and Vision. An excellent thought-provoking film.

Exercises

Data (to be used otherwise directed):

$g = 10$ m s^{-2}.
Ignore air resistance.

3-1 A particle has an initial velocity of 5.0 m s^{-1} north. What is its average acceleration if, 2.0 s later, it has a velocity of
  (a) 5.0 m s^{-1} east
  (b) 10 m s^{-1} east
  (c) 5.0 m s^{-1} south?

3-2 Figure 3-29 shows a particle which is moving in a circle ABCDA of radius 5.0 m at a constant speed. It completes one revolution in 1.0 s. What is its average acceleration
  (a) between A and B
  (b) between B and C
  (c) between A and C
  (d) for the complete revolution?

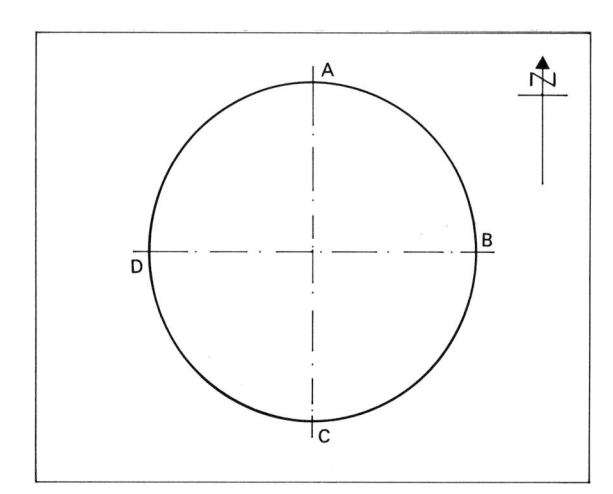

Figure 3-29

3-3 A particle's velocity vectors have the following values of size and direction at equal time intervals of 1.0 s:

Speed (to the nearest half m s^{-1})/m s^{-1}
  43   33½   25   18   15
Angle above the horizontal/degree
       69   63½   48½   33½   0

Draw a scale diagram, similar to that in figure 3-19a or 3-20a, and deduce what you can about the particle's acceleration.

3-4 A particle's velocity vectors have the following values of size and direction at equal time intervals of 0.50 s:

Speed (to the nearest half m s^{-1})/m s^{-1}
  20½   20   22½   32   49
Direction
  N 14° E   N   N 26½° W   N 51½° W   N 66° W

Draw a scale diagram, similar to that in figure 3-19a or 3-20a, and deduce what you can about the particle's acceleration.

3-5 A particle has an initial velocity of 20 m s^{-1}, N 40° E, and an acceleration of 5.0 m s^{-2} E. Draw a scale vector diagram to find, after 5.0 s,
  (a) its velocity   (b) its displacement.
Also find from your diagram the eastward resolved part of its velocity and displacement at this time.

3-6 Repeat Exercise 3-5 for the same particle after 10 s.

3-7 A particle moving along a north–south line has an initial velocity of 16 m s^{-1} north: 5.0 s later, it has a velocity of 4.0 m s^{-1} south. What is its average acceleration? ●

3-8 A particle has an initial upward velocity of 50 m s^{-1}; 6.0 s later, it has a velocity of 10 m s^{-1} vertically downwards. What is its average acceleration? ●

3-9 A particle has an initial velocity of 20 m s^{-1} north, and a constant acceleration of 5.0 m s^{-2} north. What is its velocity after (a) 4.0 s (b) 10 s?

3-10 Estimate the maximum acceleration of (a) a racing car (b) a house fly.

3-11 Figure 3-30 shows a velocity–time graph for a particle. Describe the motion which it represents.

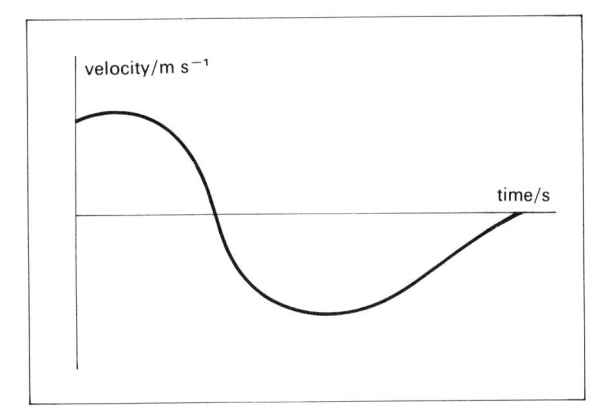

Figure 3-30

3-12 Copy figure 3-30, and beneath it on the same page, using the same scale for the time-axis, draw roughly the corresponding displacement–time graph (assuming that the particle's initial displacement is zero), and the corresponding acceleration–time graph.

3-13 The straight-line motion of a particle is described by the following information: $t = 0$, $v_0 = 0$; $0 < t < 10$ s, $a = 4.0$ m s^{-2}; 10 s $< t < 20$ s, $a = -4.0$ m s^{-2}. Sketch the velocity–time graph, and use it to find the change of displacement of the particle between $t = 0$ and $t = 20$ s. ●

3-14 Repeat Exercise 3-13 for a particle whose motion is given by the following information: $t = 0$, $v = 8.0$ m s^{-1}; $0 < t < 10$ s, $a = 0$; 10 s $< t < 30$ s, $a = -0.50$ m s^{-2}. ●

3-15 A car starts from rest with a constant acceleration of 1.0 m s^{-2} north at the moment that a lorry, with a constant velocity of 20 m s^{-1} north, passes it. Sketch velocity–time graphs for the lorry and the car, using the same axes, and use them to find the time at which the car overtakes the lorry, and the change of displacement of the car at that time. (*Hint*: use the fact that the car and the lorry will then have equal changes of displacement.) ●

3-16 Repeat Exercise 3-15, but this time assume that the car stops accelerating after 30 s, and then has a constant velocity. ●

3-17 The lorry of Exercise 3-15 still has its constant velocity of 20 m s^{-1} north, but now the car starts 5.0 s after the lorry has passed it. Find what constant acceleration the car must have in order to overtake the lorry 50 s after it (the car) has started, and find the speed which it will then have.

3-18 Two cars, each of length 5.0 m, are travelling one behind the other, at a constant velocity of 20 m s^{-1}. There is a gap of nine car-lengths between them, and the second is to overtake the first, that is, to pass it and create a gap of nine car-lengths between it and the first car. Assuming that the second car accelerates at a constant rate of 0.50 m s^{-2}, find
  (a) the speed of the second car when it has overtaken the first
  (b) the time taken for the manoeuvre
  (c) the distance travelled by the second car during the manoeuvre.
(Either draw velocity–time graphs for the two cars, or consider the motion relative to the first car.) ●

3-19 A train whose speed is 40 m s^{-1} is slowing down at a constant rate, and after 600 m has a speed of 20 m s^{-1}. Sketch a speed–time graph, and use it to find the additional distance it travels before coming to rest. ●

3-20 A test report gives the following data for a standing-start acceleration test for a car.

t/s	0	5	10	15	20	25	30	35	40
v/m s^{-1}	0	13	22	27	31	34	36	37	37

Find the car's displacement when it has reached a speed of
  (a) 25 m s^{-1} (b) 35 m s^{-1}
   (i) using the trapezium rule
   (ii) using Simpson's rule
   (iii) drawing a speed–time graph on squared paper and counting the squares between the graph-line and the time-axis.

3 Acceleration

3-21 Draw acceleration–time, velocity–time, and displacement–time graphs (using the same time-axis for all three) for a ball which is bounced down on to the ground and which then rises to about twice its original height.

3-22 Repeat Exercise 3-21 for a ball, attached by an elastic cord to a fixed point in the ground, which is hit horizontally away from the fixed point.

3-23 A car's speed increases steadily from 15 m s^{-1} to 35 m s^{-1} in a distance of 400 m. Find its acceleration, and the time taken.

3-24 If a stone is thrown with a velocity of 30 m s^{-1} vertically upwards, how long does it take to reach its highest point, and how high does it rise?

3-25 If a stone is thrown with a velocity of 20 m s^{-1} vertically upwards how long is it before it has a velocity of 30 m s^{-1} vertically downwards? What is its acceleration when it reaches its highest point?

3-26 How long does it take a particle to fall 8 m in the absence of air resistance if it starts with
(a) a velocity of 30 m s^{-1} vertically downwards
(b) a velocity of 30 m s^{-1} vertically upwards?
In each case explain the significance of any answer you choose to ignore.

3-27 A train slows down at a constant rate from 50 m s^{-1} to 10 m s^{-1} in 80 s. Find its acceleration, and the distance covered in this time.

3-28 Find the time taken for the object to reach the ground in each of the following cases:
(a) a ball is dropped from rest at a height of 1.25 m above the ground
(b) a stone is thrown, from a height of 1.25 m above the ground, with a horizontal velocity of 20 m s^{-1}
(c) a bullet is fired, from a height of 1.25 m above the ground, with a horizontal velocity of 600 m s^{-1}.

3-29 A scientist with a stopwatch says he can measure the speed at which he can throw a stone. What do you think his method is?

3-30 Consider a particle moving from rest with a constant acceleration a: what are its displacements at times t, $2t$, $3t$, and so on? How are its changes of displacement in these equal time intervals related to the change in displacement in the first of these equal intervals? (These facts were known to Galileo; either of them could be used to test whether a body, whose positions at equal time intervals are known, has a constant acceleration.)

3-31 A man stands at a first-floor window in a very tall block of flats, and drops a stone into a pond below him. Other men stand at some of the other windows on other floors and also drop stones into the pond. If they all release their stones at the same time, at which windows should they stand in order that the splashes in the pond may be seen at equal time intervals?

3-32 A stone is thrown with a velocity of 20 m s^{-1} at 35° above the horizontal. Find
(a) the vertical resolved part of its initial velocity
(b) the time it takes to reach its highest point
(c) the time it takes to return to its original horizontal level
(d) the horizontal resolved part of its initial velocity
(e) the horizontal distance it travels, that is its range.

3-33 Repeat Exercise 3-32 for a particle with an initial velocity v_0 at an angle θ above the horizontal, where the gravitational field strength is g. Simplify your answer to part (e), by using the relation $2\sin\theta\cos\theta = \sin 2\theta$, and explain why the maximum range for a projectile occurs when its initial velocity is at 45° above the horizontal.

3-34 Explain (preferably without using the result of Exercise 3-33) why two different angles of projection can give a particle the same range.

3-35 An electron has an initial horizontal velocity of $5.0 \times 10^6 \text{ m s}^{-1}$ north when it enters an east–west uniform electric field which is such that it gives the electron an acceleration of $1.0 \times 10^{14} \text{ m s}^{-2}$ west. The field extends for a distance 1.0×10^{-1} m north. Find the time for which the electron is in the electric field, and its velocity when it emerges from it. How far vertically does the electron fall while it is in the electric field?

3-36 Check the dimensional consistency of the following equations which appear in this chapter:
(a) $s = v_0 t + \frac{1}{2}at^2$, (b) $v^2 = v_0^2 + 2as$, (c) $T = 2\pi\sqrt{(l/g)}$.

3-37 Which of the following equations (where s, v_0, v, a, and t have their usual meanings) are *dimensionally* correct?
(a) $v^3 = a^2 s/t$, (b) $v_0^2 = 3as + s^2 t$, (c) $v_0^4 = 2a^3 t^2 s$.

3-38 A man throws a stone from the edge of a cliff with a velocity of 20 m s^{-1} at an angle of 60° above the horizontal: the point from which he throws the stone is taken as a coordinate origin, with the y-axis vertically upwards, and the x-axis horizontal. Use equation 3-14 to verify that the stone passes through the point (70 m, −124 m).

3-39 The text states (in Section 3-2) that equation 3-10 is 'too complicated to be useful'. Nevertheless, apply it to the stone of Exercise 3-38 to find the speed v of the stone at the point (70 m, −124 m). (You should realize that the value of $s\cos\theta$ can be found without calculation.)

3-40 A particle has an acceleration which is proportional to its velocity, and these vectors have the same direction, that is $a = kv$. Since $a = v(dv/ds)$, we can write

$$v\frac{dv}{ds} = kv$$

where k is a constant. Integrate this equation, given that when the particle's displacement is zero, its speed is v_0. How would you describe the particle's motion?

3-41 A train is travelling in a straight line on a level track at a constant speed of 20 m s^{-1}, and a man drops a stone from an open window. Assuming that air resistance can be neglected, how does the path of the stone appear to (a) the man (b) an observer standing beside the track? What is the effect of air resistance?

3-42 The man of Exercise 3-41 now throws the stone horizontally, and perpendicular to the track. Answer the same questions as before.

3-43 An aeroplane moving horizontally at a speed of $200 \, \mathrm{m\, s^{-1}}$ and at a height of $8.0 \times 10^3 \, \mathrm{m}$ is to drop a bomb on a target. At what horizontal distance from the target should the bomb be released?
Discuss the practical usefulness of your answer.

3-44 A parcel falls from a luggage rack, 2.0 m above the floor of a train which is moving along a horizontal straight track at a constant speed of $10 \, \mathrm{m\, s^{-1}}$. How far does the parcel travel horizontally, relative to the train, in falling to the floor? Answer the same question if the train has an acceleration of $0.50 \, \mathrm{m\, s^{-2}}$.

3-45 A tile slides off a roof inclined at an angle of $37°$ to the horizontal with a speed of $5.0 \, \mathrm{m\, s^{-1}}$. How far horizontally does it travel in reaching the ground 20 m below?

3-46 Answer this as a foretaste of Chapter 4. A car travels in a circular path of radius 100 m at a constant speed of $20 \, \mathrm{m\, s^{-1}}$. Find the size and direction of its average acceleration between two points from which the radii make an angle with each other of
(a) $90°$ (b) $45°$ (c) $30°$ (d) $10°$.

4 Motion in a circle

4-1 Describing circular motion	52	4-5 Circular motion with varying speed	58
4-2 Measuring angular velocity	53	Bibliography	59
4-3 Angular acceleration	55	Exercises	59
4-4 Circular motion with constant speed	56		

4-1 Describing circular motion

The *angular displacement* θ of a line in a plane about an axis through a point O is its position measured relative to a chosen origin line. We also specify the direction (clockwise or anticlockwise) in which the displacement occurs. The anticlockwise direction is usually taken as positive. The average angular velocity of a line, $\bar{\omega}$ or ω_{av}, is defined by

$$\omega_{av} = \frac{\Delta \theta}{\Delta t}, \quad [4\text{-}1]$$

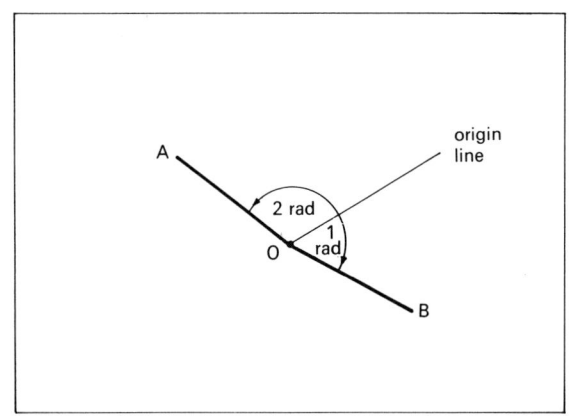

Figure 4-1 The lines OA and OB have angular displacements of $+2$ rad and -1 rad measured from an axis through O perpendicular to the page.

where $\Delta\theta$ is the change in angular displacement and Δt is the time elapsed. Similarly the average angular acceleration $\bar{\alpha}$ or α_{av} is defined by

$$\alpha_{av} = \frac{\Delta \omega}{\Delta t}, \quad [4\text{-}2]$$

where $\Delta\omega$ is the change in angular velocity in time Δt. This is all very similar to the work on linear displacement, velocity, and acceleration. As with linear motion, we can define the instantaneous angular velocity of a line ω and its instantaneous angular acceleration α:

$$\omega = \lim_{\Delta t \to 0} \frac{\Delta \theta}{\Delta t} = \frac{d\theta}{dt}, \quad [4\text{-}3]$$

and

$$\alpha = \lim_{\Delta t \to 0} \frac{\Delta \omega}{\Delta t} = \frac{d\omega}{dt}. \quad [4\text{-}4]$$

The units of ω are rad s^{-1}, and $[\omega] = T^{-1}$. The units of α are rad s^{-2}, and $[\alpha] = T^{-2}$. We could measure these angles in any units which proved convenient, such as degrees or revolutions, and state ω in, for example, rev s^{-1}, or even rev min^{-1}. If we want coherent units we must *calculate* in radians only. The relation between rev min^{-1} and rad s^{-1} is seen to be:

$$1\frac{\text{rev}}{\text{min}} = \left(1\frac{\text{rev}}{\text{min}}\right)\left(\frac{2\pi\,\text{rad}}{1\,\text{rev}}\right)\left(\frac{1\,\text{min}}{60\,\text{s}}\right) = \frac{2\pi}{60}\frac{\text{rad}}{\text{s}}.$$

Constant angular velocity

When a line has a constant angular velocity ω, the angular displacement θ after a time t is given by

$$\theta = \omega t. \qquad [4\text{-}5]$$

The time taken to complete one revolution (2π rad) is called the period T and is related to ω, the angular velocity, by

$$2\pi\,\text{rad} = \omega T,$$

that is
$$T = \frac{2\pi\,\text{rad}}{\omega}. \qquad [4\text{-}6]$$

The number of revolutions completed per second is called the rotational frequency n, and is related to the period T by

$$T = \frac{1}{n};$$

n is measured in rev/s or cycle/s, each of which can be called a hertz (Hz).

▶ **Example 4-1** Calculate the angular velocity of an equatorial radius of the Earth.

The period, T, of the Earth's rotation is 24 hours. Therefore the angular velocity of the Earth

$$\omega = \frac{2\pi}{T} = \frac{2\pi\,\text{rad}}{24 \times 3600\,\text{s}} = 7.3 \times 10^{-5}\,\text{rad s}^{-1}. \qquad ◀$$

Consider now a body (such as a gramophone record) rotating at constant angular velocity. Any point on it is moving in a circular path at a constant speed (though not a constant velocity, since the direction in which it is moving is continually changing). This speed depends on the point's distance from the centre of rotation. For consider the point A in figure 4-2. When the body is turned through an angle θ in time t, A will have moved a distance s given by $s = r\theta$. As the speed of A is given by $v = s/t$, then substituting for s yields:

$$v = \frac{r\theta}{t} = r\omega.$$

The speed is thus proportional to the distance of the point considered from the centre of the body.

$$v = r\omega. \qquad [4\text{-}7]$$

This expression, though derived for the case of a body rotating with constant angular speed, applies equally well

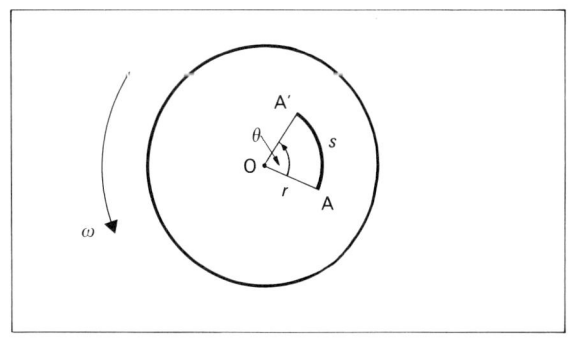

Figure 4-2 A point A on a rigid body rotating about O moves from A to A' in time t.

to instantaneous values of v and ω. If the body is not *rigid*, that is if it bends and stretches as it rotates, this simple relationship between v and ω no longer applies.

▶ **Example 4-2** Calculate the speed of a point on the Equator of the Earth. Take the Earth to be a perfect sphere of radius 6400 km.

Taking the result of Example 4-1, we have

$$[4\text{-}7] \quad v = r\omega = (6.4 \times 10^6\,\text{m})(7.3 \times 10^{-5}\,\text{rad s}^{-1})$$
$$= 4.7 \times 10^2\,\text{m s}^{-1}. \qquad ◀$$

★ Equation 4-7 can be expressed in vector terms. Clearly

$$\mathbf{v} \neq \omega \mathbf{r}$$

as $\mathbf{v}$ and $\mathbf{r}$ are perpendicular. If we express ω in vector terms by a vector *along* the axis of rotation, then we can *define* $\boldsymbol{\omega}$ by the equation (see page 21)

$$\mathbf{v} = \boldsymbol{\omega} \times \mathbf{r}. \qquad [4\text{-}8]$$

This definition is primarily important when we discuss angular momentum in Chapter 13 and we shall not use angular velocity as a vector until then. ★

4-2 Measuring angular velocity

In Section 2-7 various techniques for analysing and measuring the motion of a body in one dimension were described. We can use some of these, particularly multi-flash photography using stroboscopic illumination, to measure the average angular velocity of a rotating line. The average angular acceleration can than be deduced from successive values of ω_{av}, for example from a graph of angular velocity against time.

4 Motion in a circle

Multiflash photography

Figure 4-3 represents a multiflash photograph of a clock with a single hand which rotates once each second, illuminated at regular intervals of a few milliseconds. As the hand covers 18/100ths of a revolution in 18 centiseconds its average angular velocity is clearly 1 rev s^{-1} or 2π rad s^{-1}, as of course we expected! This is not entirely a trivial example, as it provides a method by which a centisecond clock can be used to calibrate a stroboscope, and the calibrated stroboscope can then be used to measure other frequencies. The accuracy of the method depends on the frequency of the mains remaining constant at 50 Hz, a value which is unlikely to vary by more than a few tenths of a per cent. In order to deduce the angular velocity of, say, a flywheel, a line is drawn on the flywheel and the calibrated stroboscope used to take a multiflash photograph. Angular displacements on the photograph can be measured with a protractor and ω_{av} calculated. (Protractors are notoriously imprecise measuring devices and where their use is necessary only rough results can be expected.) If the rotating line has a uniform angular velocity a much more sensitive method is to 'freeze' the line by selecting the correct frequency of the stroboscopic illumination; when this is done we can dispense with the camera.

In relating the frequency of illumination to the frequency of rotation of a line we must take care. Suppose a line is rotating at a frequency n; then the line, drawn as a radius and *not* as a diameter, will be seen to be stationary at a *single* position when the stroboscopic illumination is flashing at n, $n/2$, $n/3$, $n/4$, and so on. It will appear at two diametrically opposite positions when the stroboscopic flash rate is $2n$. The *highest* flash rate for which the line is seen in only one position is thus equal to n, the number of rotations the line makes in one second; its angular velocity is then 2π rad $\times n$. For a rotating body on which more than one radial line is drawn the problem of relating the stroboscopic flash rate to the rate of rotation of the body is more complex. For a body such as a rapidly rotating bicycle wheel it is easier to mark one of the spokes in a distinctive way than to attempt the more complex analysis, while for a slowly rotating wheel the number of rotations it undergoes in a given time interval can be directly counted.

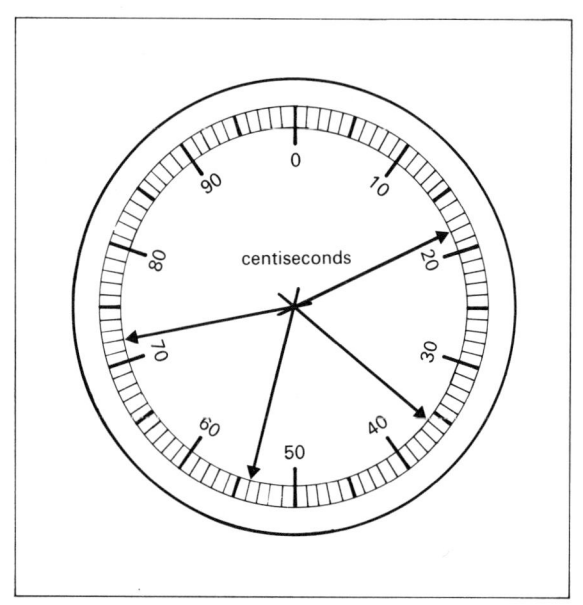

Figure 4-3 Drawing of a multiflash photograph of a centisecond clock. Both angular displacements and time intervals can be read directly from the photograph.

Ticker-tape

When a disc or cylindrical body rotates about its axis of symmetry and this axis is fixed, we can use ticker-tape techniques to measure ω. Figure 4-4 shows two possible arrangements. In (*a*) the tape is shown being wound off the disc; it could equally well be wound on to the cir-

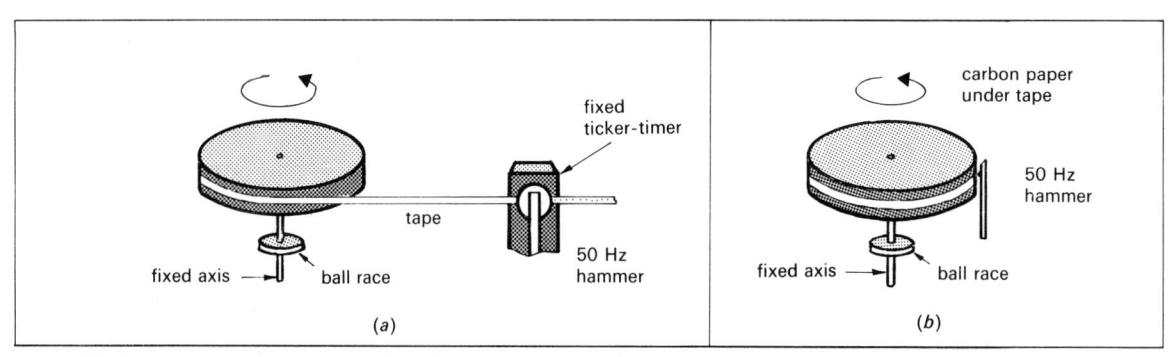

Figure 4-4 Two ways of analysing the motion of the circumference of a rotating disc.

cumference of the disc. The tape travels under a carbon disc which marks dots on it at a known frequency in the usual way. This arrangement enables several rotations of the disc to be analysed although several thicknesses of tape will alter the effective radius of the disc. In (b) the circumference carries a layer of carbon paper with the carbon side out and a single layer of tape wrapped outside this and fixed. The analysis is thus limited to a single rotation and the tape has to be removed before the dots can be analysed. In both cases the tape yields values for the speed v at which the circumference is moving. If the radius r is measured then the angular velocity, $\omega = v/r$, can be found. The precision we can expect from such techniques is of the order of the 5 per cent suggested on page 27 for the linear speeds using ticker-tape timing.

Photoelectric switching

Alternatively, the photoelectric switching technique used, in Section 2-7a, for measuring the linear speed of a moving body can be adapted to measure the angular velocity of a rotating body. The piece of card is attached to the rotating body, so that it forms an arc of a circle which has the axis of rotation at its centre. A beam of light is again arranged to fall on a photo-diode connected to either a scaler-timer or a centisecond clock; when the beam is interrupted by the card, the timer (or the clock) operates. The only measurements needed are the time t recorded by either device, and the angle θ subtended (measured in radians) by the card at the axis of rotation of the body to which it is attached. The average angular velocity ω is then given by $\omega = \theta/t$. In this case it is not necessary for the rotating body to be a disc, and the precision possible in using this method is higher than that for ticker-tape which inevitably produces an unwanted drag on the moving body.

4-3 Angular acceleration

The angular velocity ω of a line drawn from the axis of rotation to a point on, for instance, a flywheel can be measured by the methods described in the previous section. The rate of change of ω, that is the angular acceleration α of the line, can be found from successive values of ω using stroboscopic photography or the ticker-tape methods. The value of being able to measure ω and α will be seen in Chapters 12 and 13 where the dynamics of rotating bodies is considered.

Suppose in figure 4-6 that the angular velocity of the line is ω_0 at OA and ω at OP a time t later. The average angular acceleration from OA to OP is given by $\bar{\alpha}$ or α_{av} where

[4-2] $$\alpha_{av} = \frac{\Delta \omega}{\Delta t} = \frac{\omega - \omega_0}{t},$$

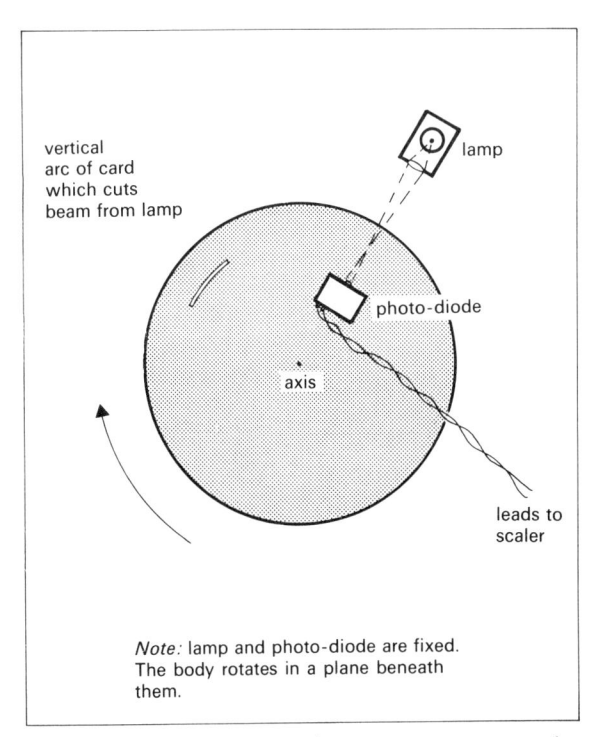

Figure 4-5 Using a photoelectric gate to measure angular velocities.

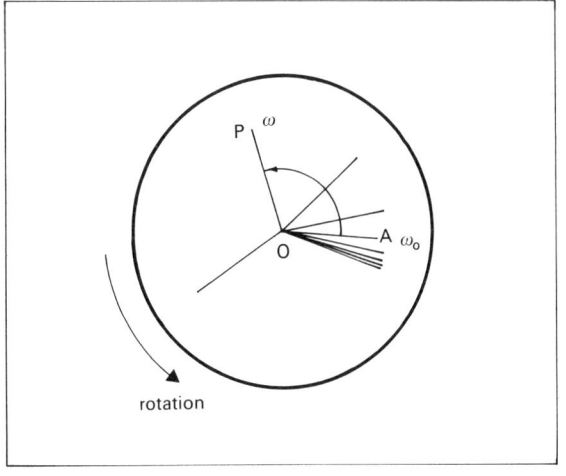

Figure 4-6 Drawing of a multiflash photograph of a line drawn on a flywheel. $\angle \text{AOP} = \theta$.

4 Motion in a circle

and if the motion is one with a constant angular acceleration α

$$\alpha_{av} = \alpha$$

and

$$\alpha = \frac{\omega - \omega_0}{t}$$

or

$$\omega = \omega_0 + \alpha t. \qquad [4\text{-}9]$$

Further, as the average angular velocity from OA to OP is $\tfrac{1}{2}(\omega_0 + \omega)$

then

$$\frac{\theta}{t} = \tfrac{1}{2}(\omega_0 + \omega)$$

or

$$\theta = \tfrac{1}{2}(\omega_0 + \omega)t. \qquad [4\text{-}10]$$

From these two equations we can also deduce that

$$\theta = \omega_0 t + \tfrac{1}{2}\alpha t^2 \qquad [4\text{-}11]$$

and

$$\omega^2 = \omega_0^2 + 2\alpha\theta. \qquad [4\text{-}12]$$

These correspond to equations 3-6, 3-9, 3-7, and 3-11 for planar motion. The angular equations will be particularly useful when we deal with rigid-body dynamics in Chapter 12.

▶ **Example 4-3** A gramophone record takes 4.0 s to reach its (constant) angular velocity of 45 rev min^{-1} from rest. Find its angular acceleration, assuming that it is constant, and the number of revolutions it makes before it reaches this speed.

$$45 \frac{\text{rev}}{\text{min}} = \left(45 \frac{\text{rev}}{\text{min}}\right)\left(\frac{2\pi\,\text{rad}}{1\,\text{rev}}\right)\left(\frac{1\,\text{min}}{60\,\text{s}}\right)$$

$$= \frac{2\pi \times 45}{60} \frac{\text{rad}}{\text{s}} = 4.7 \,\text{rad s}^{-1}.$$

[4-9] $\quad\alpha = \dfrac{\omega - \omega_0}{t} = \dfrac{4.7\,\text{rad s}^{-1} - 0}{4.0\,\text{s}}$

$$= 1.2 \,\text{rad s}^{-2}.$$

[4-10] $\theta = \tfrac{1}{2}(\omega_0 + \omega)t = \tfrac{1}{2}(0 + 4.7\,\text{rad s}^{-1})(4.0\,\text{s})$

$$= 9.4 \,\text{rad},$$

or $\quad\theta = (9.4\,\text{rad})\left(\dfrac{1\,\text{rev}}{2\pi\,\text{rad}}\right) = 1.5\,\text{revolutions.}$ ◀

4-4 Circular motion with constant speed

On page 24 we showed that the instantaneous rate of change of displacement of a particle, the limit of $\Delta s/\Delta t$ as Δt (and thus Δs) tends to zero, was in a direction tangential to the particle's path. In the special case of a particle which moves in a circle the velocity of the particle at any instant, $\boldsymbol{v} = d\boldsymbol{s}/dt$, is thus *at a tangent to the circle* at that instant.

Consider now how the velocity of the particle changes if it moves at a constant speed; its change of velocity is the result only of changes in the direction of its motion. Suppose it moves from P to Q (in figure 4-7a) in a time Δt. The vector triangle of figure 4-7b shows the relationship

$$\Delta \boldsymbol{v} = \boldsymbol{v}_Q - \boldsymbol{v}_P$$

and hence the average acceleration of the particle is this change of velocity divided by the time Δt which elapses:

that is

$$\boldsymbol{a}_{av} = \frac{\Delta \boldsymbol{v}}{\Delta t}. \qquad [4\text{-}13]$$

To find the instantaneous value of the acceleration of the particle *at* P we find the limiting value of the ratio $\Delta \boldsymbol{v}/\Delta t$ as Δt (and therefore $\Delta \boldsymbol{v}$) tends to zero. The direction of this instantaneous acceleration when the particle is at P is obviously perpendicular to $\boldsymbol{v}_P$, that is along $\overrightarrow{PO}$. Similarly, the instantaneous acceleration of the particle at *any* point on its circular path will be *inward along the radius*. This acceleration is said to be *centripetal*.

To establish the *size* of the average acceleration between P and Q, $\Delta v/\Delta t$, we have from figure 4-7c, where $v_P = v_Q = v$,

$$\Delta v = 2v \sin\tfrac{1}{2}\Delta\theta.$$

Also,

[4-7] $$v = r\omega = r\frac{\Delta\theta}{\Delta t}.$$

Thus,

$$\Delta t = \frac{r\Delta\theta}{v},$$

and so

$$\frac{\Delta v}{\Delta t} = \frac{2v \sin\tfrac{1}{2}\Delta\theta}{r\Delta\theta/v}$$

$$= \frac{v^2}{r}\left(\frac{\sin\tfrac{1}{2}\Delta\theta}{\tfrac{1}{2}\Delta\theta}\right).$$

The instantaneous size a_P of the acceleration at P is the value of $\Delta v/\Delta t$ as Δt (and thus $\Delta\theta$) tends to zero.

$$a_P = \lim_{\Delta t \to 0} \frac{\Delta v}{\Delta t} = \lim_{\Delta\theta \to 0} \left(\frac{v^2}{r}\right)\left(\frac{\sin\tfrac{1}{2}\Delta\theta}{\tfrac{1}{2}\Delta\theta}\right)$$

$$= \frac{v^2}{r},$$

for on page 11 the limit of $\sin x/x$ as $x \to 0$ was noted as being unity. This expression, v^2/r, does *not* depend on the

4-4 Circular motion with constant speed

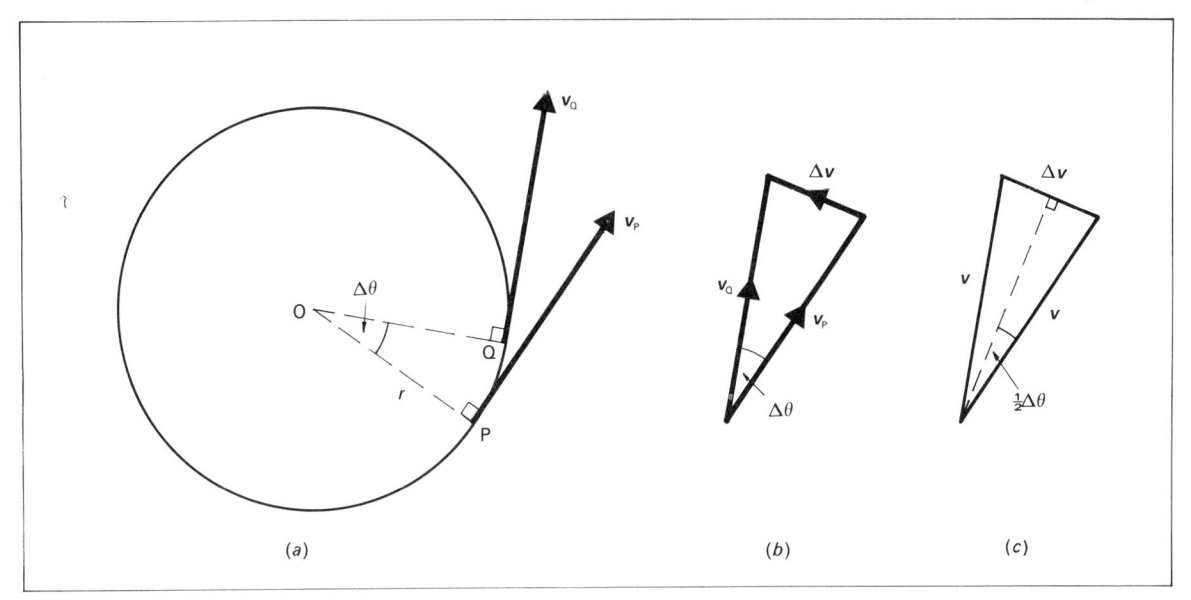

Figure 4-7 A particle moves in a circle with constant speed v.

position of P and so the acceleration, a, of the particle at all points on the circle is the same *size*. Using equation 4-7, $v = r\omega$, we can express a in two ways, either

$$a = \frac{v^2}{r} \quad [4\text{-}14]$$

or

$$a = r\omega^2. \quad [4\text{-}15]$$

So the acceleration of a particle moving in a circle with a constant speed is of constant size v^2/r or $r\omega^2$ and is always directed to the centre of the circle, that is, it is centripetal.

Representing both the size and the direction in one expression we can write

$$\boldsymbol{a} = -\omega^2 \boldsymbol{r}. \quad [4\text{-}16]$$

The minus sign indicates that although $\boldsymbol{r}$ is measured away from the centre O, the acceleration is towards O.

▶ **Example 4-4** A point P on the circumference of a circle of centre O and of radius r moves round the circumference with a constant speed v (figure 4-8). Find its average acceleration while OP moves through $\pi/4$ rad.

Figure 4-8b represents the vector relation $\boldsymbol{v}_2 - \boldsymbol{v}_1 = \Delta\boldsymbol{v}$. As $v_2 = v_1 = v$, then we can see that the size of $\Delta\boldsymbol{v}$ is $2v \sin 22\frac{1}{2}°$. The time taken for P to move from P_1 to P_2 at a speed v is Δt where

$$\Delta t = \frac{\pi/4}{\omega} = \frac{\pi r}{4v},$$

and so the average acceleration is of size

$$2v \sin 22\frac{1}{2}° \div \pi r / 4v$$

$$= \frac{8 \sin 22\frac{1}{2}°}{\pi} \left(\frac{v^2}{r}\right) = 0.98 \frac{v^2}{r}.$$

Notice that this is very close to the size of the instantaneous acceleration of the point at P_1 or at P_2, namely v^2/r. The direction of the average acceleration is such as to bisect $P_1\hat{O}P_2$. ◀

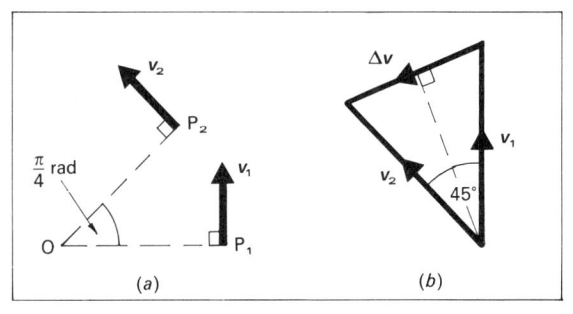

Figure 4-8

4 Motion in a circle

▶ **Example 4-5** A gramophone record has a radius of 150 mm and rotates at a constant angular velocity of $33\frac{1}{3}$ rev min^{-1}. What is the acceleration of (a) a point on the circumference, (b) a point midway between the centre and the circumference?

(a) It is convenient to use equation 4-15, $a = r\omega^2$, since we are given the angular velocity rather than the linear speed. Thus,

$$\omega = 33\frac{1}{3}\frac{\text{rev}}{\text{min}} = \left(33\frac{1}{3}\frac{\text{rev}}{\text{min}}\right)\left(\frac{1 \text{ min}}{60 \text{ s}}\right)\left(\frac{2\pi \text{ rad}}{1 \text{ rev}}\right) = 3.5\frac{\text{rad}}{\text{s}}.$$

Therefore

$$a = (0.15 \text{ m})\left(3.5\frac{\text{rad}}{\text{s}}\right)^2 = 1.84 \text{ m s}^{-2}, \text{ centripetally.}$$

(b) We again use $a = r\omega^2$, but now $r = 0.075$ m and so the centripetal acceleration is just half of what it was before, that is, 0.92 m s^{-2}. ◀

★ Mathematicians may recognize that equation 4-16 can be obtained by two successive differentiations of the position vector s of the particle with respect to time t. For this we define
(i) a unit vector $\hat{n}$, which rotates with the position vector, and
(ii) a unit vector $\hat{t}$, which makes an angle of $+\pi/2$ rad with $\hat{n}$.
We need to know that

$$\frac{d}{dt}(\hat{n}) = \frac{d\theta}{dt}\hat{t},$$

which implies that

$$\frac{d}{dt}(\hat{t}) = -\frac{d\theta}{dt}\hat{n}.$$

Then if the position vector s of the particle (relative to an origin at the centre of the circle in which it moves) is written as

$$s = r\hat{n} \quad \text{(where } r \text{ is constant)}$$

then

$$v = r\frac{d\theta}{dt}\hat{t} \quad \left(\text{where } \frac{d\theta}{dt} = \omega \text{ is constant}\right)$$

and

$$a = r\frac{d\theta}{dt}\left(-\frac{d\theta}{dt}\hat{n}\right)$$
$$= -r\omega^2\hat{n}$$
$$= -\omega^2 r.$$

We mention this not so much for its own sake (since we have already used a method which is closer to the physics of the situation) but because it can readily be extended to the more difficult cases where r and ω are not constant. ★

4-5 Circular motion with varying speed

Let us now consider a particle moving in a circle but not at constant speed. What is its acceleration? Figure 4-9 shows the particle when it has a velocity v, and also when, after time Δt has elapsed, it has a velocity v'. During this time the radius drawn from the centre O to the particle undergoes an angular displacement $\Delta\theta$. The

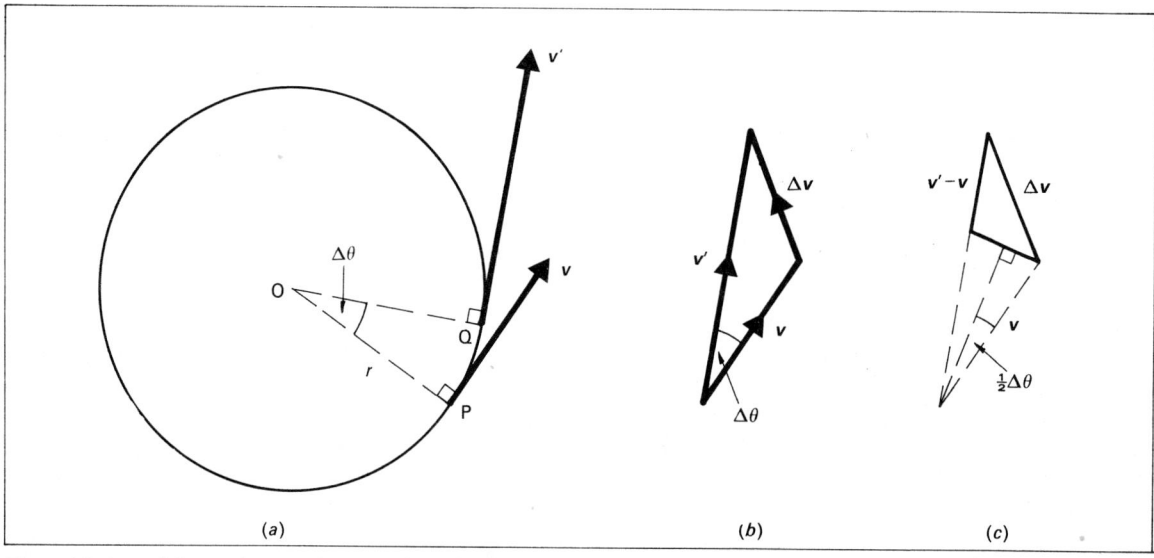

Figure 4-9 A particle speeds up as it moves from P to Q. Its change of velocity Δv as $\Delta\theta$ becomes smaller and smaller is *not* parallel to $\overrightarrow{PO}$ or v.

change in the velocity vector, $\Delta\mathbf{v}$, can be considered to be the result of

(i) the particle's change in direction: in figure 4-9c this contribution to $\Delta\mathbf{v}$ is shown to be $2v\sin\tfrac{1}{2}\Delta\theta$, which in the limit gives a *centripetal* acceleration of v^2/r at P, as before

(ii) the particle's change in speed: in figure 4-9c this contribution to $\Delta\mathbf{v}$ is shown to be $v'-v$. This gives an average acceleration of size $(v'-v)/\Delta t$, the limiting value of which is dv/dt, and the limiting direction of which is *tangential*. Since

[4-7] $$v = r\omega,$$

then
$$\frac{dv}{dt} = \frac{d}{dt}(r\omega)$$
$$= r\frac{d\omega}{dt}, \text{ as } r \text{ is constant,}$$

and the tangential acceleration is equal to $r\alpha$, where α is the angular acceleration of the line joining the particle to the centre of the circle at O.

To summarize, when a particle moves in a circular path (r constant) with a varying speed v and hence a varying angular velocity ω it has

(i) a radial acceleration (which is centripetal) $a_r = r\omega^2 = v^2/r$, and

(ii) a tangential acceleration $a_t = r\alpha$ (if α were constant we could use the equations of Section 4-3).

▶ **Example 4-6** A stationary flywheel of radius 0.20 m is given a constant angular acceleration of 2.0 rad s^{-2}. What is the acceleration of a point on its circumference after 1.0 s?

[4-9] $$\omega = \omega_0 + \alpha t.$$

Therefore, after 1.0 s, $\omega = 0 + (2.0\,\text{rad s}^{-2})(1.0\,\text{s})$
$$= 2.0\,\text{rad s}^{-1}.$$

Therefore after 1.0 s the point has acceleration

(a) $r\omega^2 = (0.20\,\text{m})(2.0\,\text{rad s}^{-1})^2 = 0.80\,\text{m s}^{-2}$ centripetally,

and

(b) $r\alpha = (0.20\,\text{m})(2.0\,\text{rad s}^{-2}) = 0.40\,\text{m s}^{-2}$ tangentially.

Figure 4-10 shows these two accelerations. The size of their vector sum is clearly

$$a = \sqrt{(0.80^2 + 0.40^2)}\,\text{m s}^{-2}$$
$$= 0.89\,\text{m s}^{-2},$$

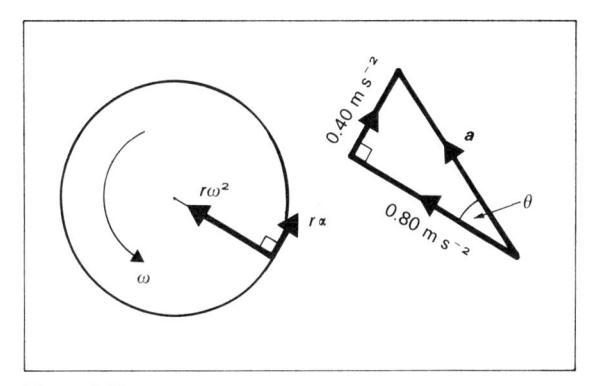

in a direction
$$\theta = \arctan(0.40\,\text{m s}^{-1}/0.80\,\text{m s}^{-1})$$
$$= 26\tfrac{1}{2}°. \quad ◀$$

Figure 4-10

Bibliography

PSSC (1966). *Physics advanced topics supplement*. Heath. The laboratory guide.

Exercises

Data (to be used unless otherwise directed):

$g = 10\,\text{m s}^{-2}$.

4-1 Many electric generators rotate at 3000 rev min^{-1}. Express this in rad s^{-1}. ●

4-2 The period of rotation of a roundabout at a circus is 5.0 s. What is its angular velocity? What is the speed of a point on the roundabout if its distance from the centre of rotation is 10 m? ●

4-3 A disc is painted black except for one *diameter* which is painted white. The disc rotates at 60 rev s^{-1} and is illuminated by a stroboscope. What is seen if the flashing rate is (a) 30 Hz (b) 60 Hz (c) 120 Hz?

4-4 What is the acceleration of:
(a) the communications satellite Earlybird (distance from centre of Earth = 4.2×10^4 km, period of rotation = 24 hours)
(b) a point on the tip of a blade of an electric fan of radius 10 cm when its angular velocity is 20 rad s^{-1}? ●

4-5 Estimate the maximum centripetal acceleration experienced by the driver of a car during a journey

4 Motion in a circle

(a) along a motorway (ignore the possibility of overtaking) and
(b) through a surburban housing estate.
In each case the driver should obey all speed regulations.

4-6 An electric drill rotates at $2000 \text{ rev min}^{-1}$. It is switched off, and takes 4.0 s to come to rest. What is its angular acceleration, assumed constant, and how many revolutions are made before it comes to rest?

4-7 A heavy flywheel is rotating at 80 rad s^{-1} about an axis of symmetry perpendicular to its flat side, and is given an angular acceleration of 0.25 rad s^{-2} for 5000 revolutions. What is its final angular velocity?

4-8 A laboratory centrifuge operates at a working speed of rotation of 200 rad s^{-1}, and, to reach this speed, is given a constant angular acceleration of 50 rad s^{-2}. How long does it take to reach its working speed after it is switched on, and how many revolutions are made in so doing?

4-9 If the end of a rotating test-tube is 0.10 m from the centre of rotation of the centrifuge of Exercise 4-8, what is the acceleration of matter at the end of the test-tube? Express your answer as a multiple of g.

4-10 An electron travelling perpendicular to a magnetic field experiences a force (and hence an acceleration) which is always perpendicular to its velocity. What is the motion of a particle the acceleration of which is of constant size and perpendicular to its velocity? If the acceleration is $1.0 \times 10^{13} \text{ m s}^{-2}$, what quantitative statement can be made about the path of the electron if it is travelling with a speed of $1.0 \times 10^7 \text{ m s}^{-1}$?

4-11 What is the speed of a satellite which is moving in a circle very close to the Earth? (Take the radius of the Earth to be $6.4 \times 10^6 \text{ m}$.) If such a satellite is moving round the Equator, towards the east, how long does one revolution take as seen by an observer on the Moon? How long does it take as seen by an observer on the Earth?

4-12 Find the speed of the Earth (relative to the Sun) in its orbit round the Sun. The mean Earth–Sun distance is $1.5 \times 10^{11} \text{ m}$. Find also the acceleration of the Earth, relative to the Sun.

4-13 Find the speed of the Moon (relative to the Earth) in its orbit round the Earth. The mean Earth–Moon distance is $3.8 \times 10^8 \text{ m}$. Find also the acceleration of the Moon, relative to the Earth.

4-14 Find the speed (relative to the axis of the Earth) of a point on the surface of the Earth (a) at the Equator, (b) at latitude $45°$. Also find the acceleration (relative to the axis of the Earth) of such points. The radius of the Earth is $6.4 \times 10^6 \text{ m}$.

4-15 In the Bohr model of the hydrogen atom the electron moves in a circle of radius $5.1 \times 10^{-11} \text{ m}$ at a frequency of $6.8 \times 10^{15} \text{ rev s}^{-1}$. What is (a) the speed of the electron, (b) its acceleration?

4-16 A space station is made roughly in the shape of the inner tube of a motor car tyre. Figure 4-11 shows a sectional view across a diameter of the station. At what angular velocity must the station be rotated about the axis AA′ in order that a spaceman living in it may experience a centripetal acceleration equal to g? Will the spaceman's head, when he is standing with his feet on what he considers to be the floor, point towards the axis AA′, or away from it? What are the problems likely to be experienced by living and working in such a rotating space station?

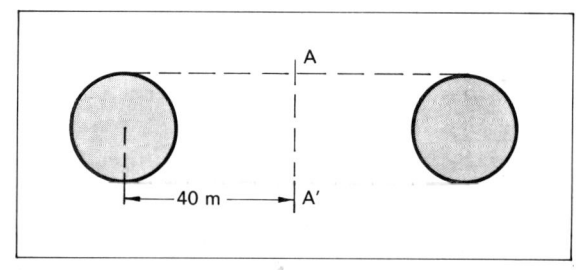

Figure 4-11

4-17 Derive equations 4-11 and 4-12 from the previously deduced relations.

5 Mass and force

5-1 Force	61	5-6 Newton's second law	67
5-2 Newton's first law	61	5-7 Weight	70
5-3 Representing forces	63	5-8 Newton's third law	72
5-4 Inertial mass	65	Bibliography	74
5-5 Measuring mass	66	Exercises	75

5-1 Force

We all have the idea of a force as a push or a pull. The phrase 'the idea of a force' implies that 'force' is a concept rather than something concrete. Another implication is that there must be someone or something to do the pulling or pushing, and there must be someone or something to be pushed or pulled.

A body can be pulled by a rope, pushed by the air, attracted by an electrically charged body, pulled by the Earth, pushed by a hand, and so on. At first sight it would seem that there are very many different types of force. In fact, even if we include the forces exerted by nucleons on each other, and the forces exerted by molecules on each other, as well as such familiar forces as the pull of a hand on a door knob, there are only three different types of force: the nuclear, the electromagnetic, and the gravitational. Of these three, nuclear forces are not considered in a study of Newtonian mechanics.

Gravitational forces are much weaker than electromagnetic forces, that is, in a situation where two bodies have mass and also electric charge, the electric and magnetic forces which they exert on each other are likely to be very much greater than the gravitational force. For example, two bar magnets, placed near each other on a laboratory bench, might well exert sufficiently large forces on each other to cause them to move together; the gravitational forces which they exert on each other would never do that. To take a numerical case, consider two protons A and B: the electric force exerted by A on B is about 10^{36} times greater than the gravitational force simultaneously exerted by A on B. Of course, there *are* large gravitational forces, but usually they are only significant when one of the bodies is of at least planetary size (see figure 5-1a).

5-2 Newton's first law

A force is required to accelerate a particle; that is, a force is required to change the speed of a particle or to change its direction of motion or to change both. This law defines force.

Does our experience justify such a definition? So often it seems that a force is needed just to keep a body moving with constant velocity—let alone to accelerate it. We pull with a constant force, and a garden roller moves in a straight line with a steady speed. In fact in this situation there is a constant resisting force, and this, and the force we exert, annul each other. It *is* a fact of our experience that force causes *acceleration* when the resisting forces are not large. If the garden roller moves off the grass on to a path, so that the friction force is less, and we continue to exert the same pull, the roller begins to move faster. We have to analyse our experience carefully and realize how

5 Mass and force

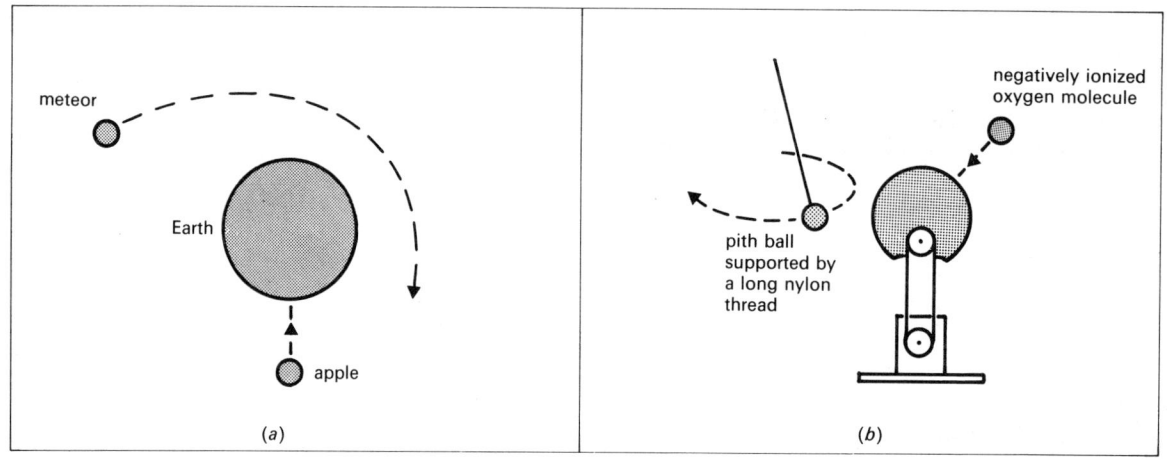

Figure 5-1 The two forces which produce macroscopic effects on the particles and bodies of Newtonian physics. (a) Gravitational forces, (b) electric forces. Each diagram shows the effect of the forces in altering the motions of the bodies on which they act. Note that the gravitational forces are all pulls whereas the electric forces involve both pushes and pulls.

commonly resisting forces occur, so that *in practice* it is always necessary to keep on pulling a body to keep it moving at a steady speed, and in practice it is difficult to demonstrate the truth of Newton's first law with the objects we meet in everyday life. (A historical note: Aristotle stated 'a force is necessary to keep a body moving with constant velocity'. He was considering the final or terminal velocity of a body; that is, when there is a constant resisting force, a constant driving force is needed to maintain motion. In these circumstances he was correct in that he was really saying zero resultant force produces constant velocity.)

We need to examine a particle or body which is moving with constant velocity in the absence of any forces or external influences. The best we can do on Earth is to consider motion in a horizontal plane when frictional forces are reduced as much as possible. In this way we aim to have no horizontal forces acting on the moving body and thus no change in its horizontal velocity. If the 'hovercraft' in figure 5-2 are set in motion, and their motion analysed using multiflash photography (figure 5-3), we find that they continue with their acquired velocity until they are again pushed or pulled in some way. (They do have their speeds very gradually reduced by the horizontal resistance of the air, but the effect is hardly noticeable.) It is tempting to say 'We have verified Newton's first law'. This is not so: Newton's first law is a definition of force. When we see a body moving with uniform velocity our deduction must be, not that Newton's first law is verified, but that what Newton defined as a 'force' is not acting on it. That these experiments are

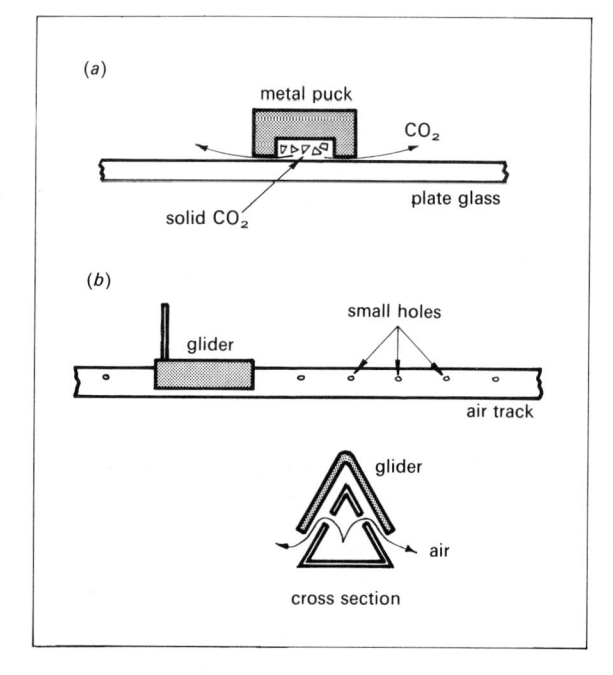

Figure 5-2 Two pieces of apparatus for demonstrating horizontal motion when the frictional force between two bodies is reduced almost to zero. In each case the hover principle is used, the source of the gas layer being an evaporating piece of dry ice in (a) and a reversed vacuum cleaner in (b). The puck in (a) can move in two dimensions while the glider in (b) can move in only one dimension. An air table can be used instead of the glass plate and dry ice in (a), the table being perforated with fine holes through which air is forced, and the puck (or pucks) being made of a light plastic material.

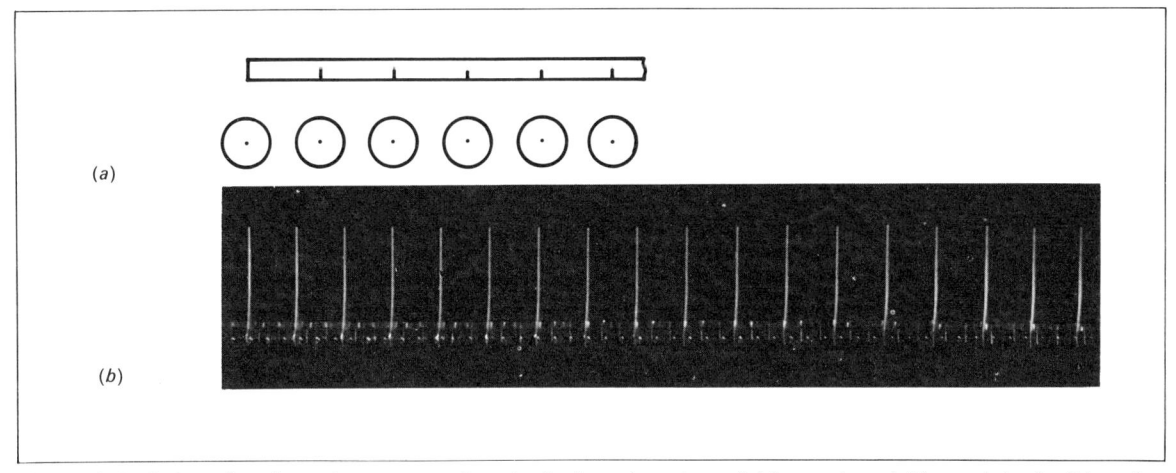

Figure 5-3 Typical results of experiments to analyse the horizontal motions of (*a*) a puck and (*b*) an air-track glider when horizontal forces have been reduced as far as possible. (These experiments do not verify Newton's first law.)

logically predictable was first discussed by Galileo Galilei, who died in the year of Newton's birth. He considered uphill motion as a slowing-down process, downhill motion as a speeding-up process, and thus horizontal motion as... what? (See figure 5-4.) Presumably ideal horizontal motion involved a constant speed.

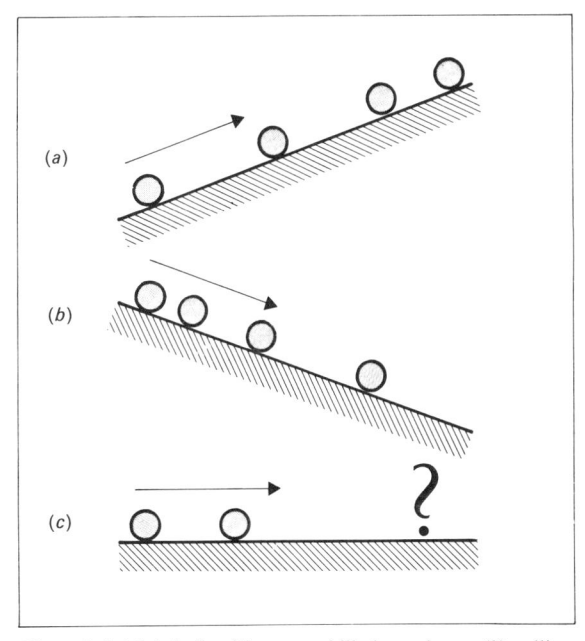

Figure 5-4 (*a*) A ball rolling up a hill slows down; (*b*) rolling down a hill it speeds up; and thus (*c*) in horizontal motion it will logically maintain its initial speed.

5-3 Representing forces

Any force can be described as the push or pull of one body on another. It is *always* possible to describe a force as

the push (or pull) of A on B

where A is the body exerting the force on body B. For example

the push of the chalk on the blackboard
the pull of the dog on the leash.

This technique helps us to avoid confusion about forces and, in particular, about which bodies cause them. We should remember that the forces exerted on a body are always exerted by some *other*, separate, *body*. Beginners sometimes say 'the force is the force of friction' or 'the force is caused by the man's acceleration'; these vague phrases do not help towards understanding the cause of particular forces.

Having formed a phrase to describe a force, our next task is to establish how to represent it on a diagram of the body or particle on which the force is acting. We represent the force by an arrow showing the line of action and direction of the force and where possible make the length of the arrow proportional to the size of the force (figure 5-5).

If only one force acts on a body then according to Newton's first law the body must accelerate. Yet the blackboard in figure 5-5*a* does not accelerate when pushed by the chalk: we conclude that other forces must be

64 5 Mass and force

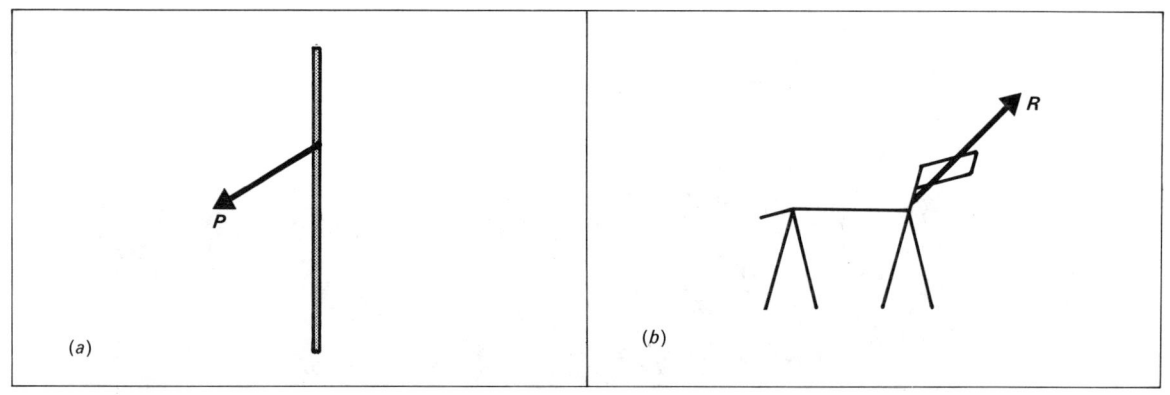

Figure 5-5 Representing forces on diagrams. In (a) *P* is the push of some chalk on a blackboard and in (b) *R* is the pull of a lead on a dog. Note that in each case the diagram shows only the body on which the force is acting and does not include the body causing the force.

acting on the blackboard. To establish the result of several forces acting on one body we need to know how forces are added. In Section 6-1 we show that forces are added according to the laws of vector algebra: thus a force is a vector quantity.

To represent all the forces acting on a body we draw a *free-body diagram* for the body (figure 5-6). All other bodies exerting forces on this body now have their effect shown by the magnitude and direction of the force vector they produce. It is useful but sometimes inconvenient or

P is the push of the ground on the box
W is the pull of the Earth on the box
R is the push of the man on the box

T is the pull of the trapeze on the block
W is the pull of the Earth on the block
F is the push of the air on the block

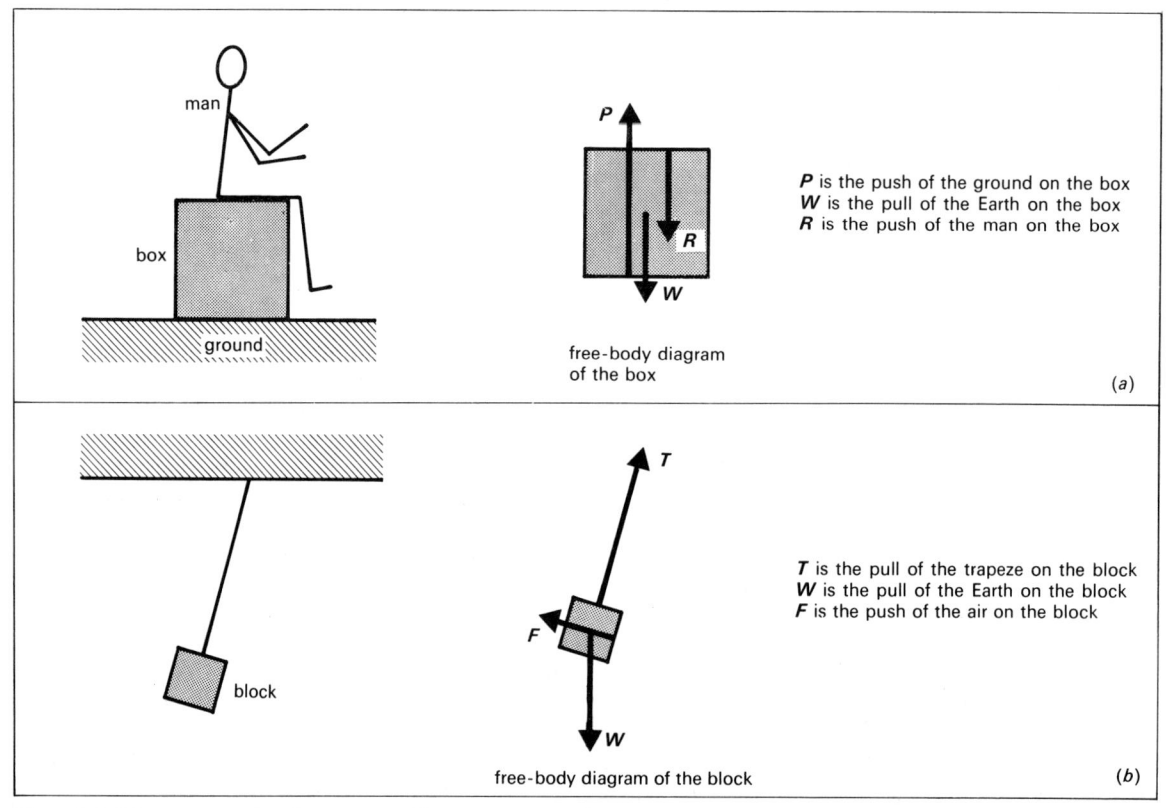

Figure 5-6 When representing forces on a diagram we must first decide which body we are considering and then draw a sketch of this body and mark the force vectors on it. This is a free-body diagram of the body.

even impossible to draw force vectors of lengths proportional to the size of the forces, but we shall do so where possible.

Newton's first law can now be restated in the form in which it is usually used:

a resultant external force is required to accelerate a particle.

Thus if the vector sum of the forces on a free-body diagram is zero, the body will remain at rest or continue to move with constant speed in a straight line.

$$a = 0 \Leftrightarrow \sum F = 0. \qquad [5\text{-}1]$$

▶ **Example 5-1** A child's balloon is seen to fall at a constant vertical velocity, that is its acceleration is zero. Discuss the forces acting on it.

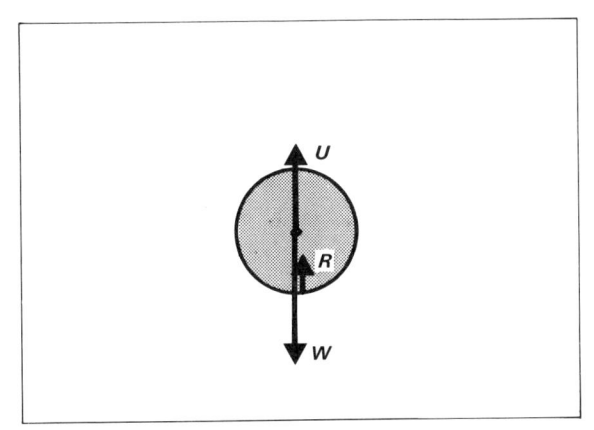

Figure 5-7

The forces on it (figure 5-7) are:

W the pull of the Earth on the balloon (weight)
U the push of the air in which the balloon is immersed (Archimedean upthrust)
R the push of the air (air resistance force) on the balloon.

Since $a = 0, \sum F = 0$,
then $W + R + U = 0$
that is $U + R = W.$ ◀

5-4 Inertial mass

A single force accelerates a body; what effect does the same force have on different bodies? Clearly it produces accelerations of different sizes. The property of the body which determines the size of the acceleration is called its inertia, or its inertial mass. Consider two pucks moving with equal velocities along a line perpendicular to the line joining their centres (figure 5-8a). If they are joined by a rigid rod their motion will be unaffected (figure 5-8b). Suppose we now pull the centre of the rod: the rod will, in general, rotate. This rotation indicates the extent to which the two pucks are willing to change their velocities, that is, it indicates the difference in their inertial masses. The shaded puck in figure 5-8c, which shows the greater unwillingness, is said to have a larger inertial mass than the unshaded puck. If the rod does not rotate, as in figure 5-8d, then we conclude that the two pucks have equal inertial masses. When we join two bodies with a rigid rod and jerk it at its centre in this way we are using an *inertial balance* to compare the inertial masses of the two bodies. Note that our experiment only reveals which of

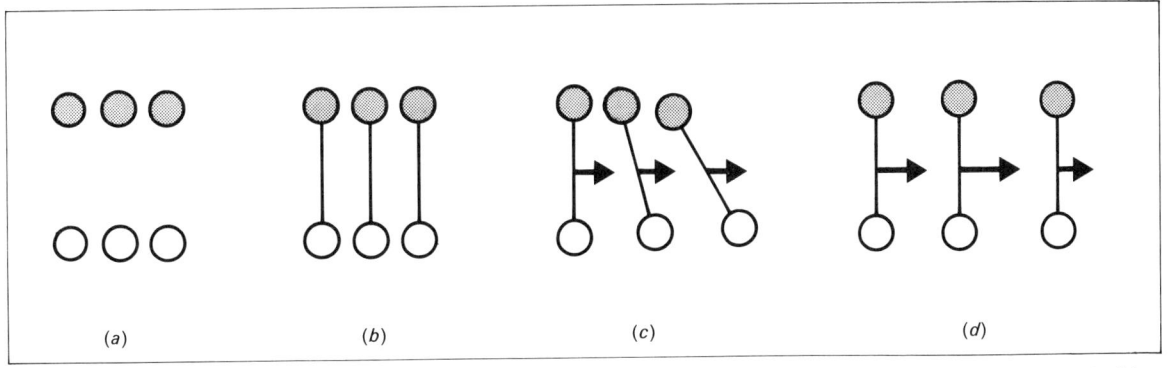

Figure 5-8 Multiflash photographs showing successive positions of two ice pucks moving (*a*) with uniform and equal velocities, (*b*) as in (*a*) but now joined by a rigid rod, (*c*) when the rod is jerked and the pucks have unequal inertial masses, and (*d*) when the rod is jerked and they have equal inertial masses. The pull on the rod need not be a steady one but must be at the centre of the rod. Such an arrangement as shown in (*c*) and (*d*) is sometimes called an inertial balance.

5 Mass and force

the bodies, if either, has the greater inertial mass: it is thus only a comparison—but so also does a beam balance tell us only which is the heavier of two bodies.

The inertial mass, usually called the 'mass' of a body, is found to be a basic property of the body. It is unaltered by the location, temperature, shape, or (for speeds appreciably less than the speed of light) speed of the body. Some scientists consider the inertial mass of a body to depend upon its motion relative to the rest of the Universe—a proposition first stated by Ernst Mach (1838–1916). Newton described mass as being the 'quantity of matter' in a body, a description which would satisfy the list of situations in which it is unaltered.

Experimentally it can be shown that mass is a scalar quantity: that is, the mass of a body is the arithmetical sum of the masses of its parts:

$$m_1 + m_2 + m_3 + \cdots + m_n = \sum_1^n m_r = m.$$

This is true to within any possible experimental accuracy except when we attempt to add the masses of the subatomic constituents of a nucleus, a situation which does not fall within the scope of Newtonian mechanics. Associated with the scalar addition of mass and our idea of the atomic nature of matter is the *principle of conservation of mass*. The principle, first experimentally established by A. L. Lavoisier (1743–1794), can be stated thus:

> *in any system undergoing a physical change the total mass of the system is constant.*

Although one feels intuitively that the principle is correct it rests on experiment: in one such experiment one side of an inertial balance might consist of a puck on which is mounted a closed container in which a chemical reaction is taking place. In view of our modern understanding of the nature of electromagnetic radiation it is now necessary to state the principle of conservation of inertial mass in such a way as to include the equivalent mass of any radiation which might escape from the system.

5-5 Measuring mass

The inertial balance described in figure 5-8 can only tell us when two masses are equal. A very similar device can be designed to measure any unknown mass, provided one known mass is available. The masses are again two pucks: one, A, of known mass, and the other, B, of unknown mass (see figure 5-9). They are attached at different distances from the centre of a rigid rod which is jerked at its centre so as to accelerate the rod. However, positions for A and B can be found such that the moments of the inertial masses about the centre of the rod are equal and when this is so the rod will not rotate. (The moment of a mass m about an axis is defined as being the product mx, where x is the distance of the mass from the axis.)

Let the masses of A and B be m_A and m_B respectively, and let their distances from the centre of the rod be x_A and x_B respectively, when the rod does *not* rotate when jerked at its mid-point. Then

$$m_A x_A = m_B x_B$$

so that

$$m_B = m_A \frac{x_A}{x_B}.$$

If m_A is known, m_B can be calculated.

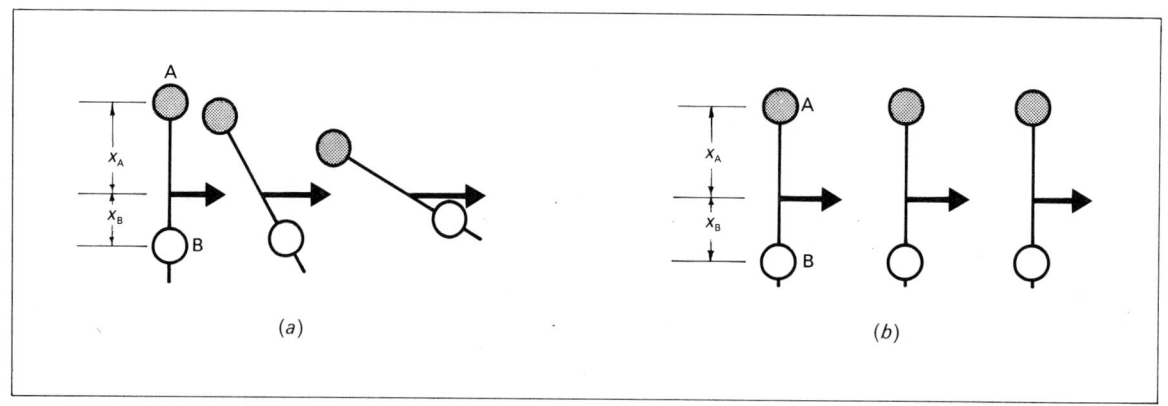

Figure 5-9 Representation of multiflash photographs showing the positions of two pucks A and B of unequal inertial masses m_A and m_B. A and B are attached to a rigid rod which is jerked at its centre. In (a) $m_A x_A \neq m_B x_B$, and in (b) $m_A x_A = m_B x_B$. In (b) the ratio of the masses can be found by measuring the lengths x_A and x_B.

▶ **Example 5-2** Two pucks, one of mass 0.50 kg and the other of unknown mass m, are joined by a rigid rod, as shown in figure 5-9. The pucks are moved along the rod until positions are found such that the rod does not rotate when it is jerked at its centre. These distances are found to be 0.30 m and 0.20 m respectively. What is the unknown mass m?

$$m(0.20\,\text{m}) = (0.50\,\text{kg})(0.30\,\text{m}),$$
so that $\quad m = 0.75\,\text{kg}.$

This type of experiment would work anywhere—even where bodies are not attracted by planets or where they are falling freely. It would in fact be easier to perform it in space than on the Earth because the pucks could be replaced by any two masses. ◀

5-6 Newton's second law

Newton's second law can be expressed as follows for particles of fixed mass.

The mass of a particle multiplied by its acceleration is proportional to the resultant external force acting on the particle. This force acts in the direction of the acceleration.

Represented symbolically, this becomes

$$m\mathbf{a} \propto \sum \mathbf{F}$$

or $\quad m\mathbf{a} = k\sum \mathbf{F}$

where k is a constant. We have still to choose a unit for force: we can make k any value we choose, and so for convenience we put $k = 1$ (a pure number) and define our unit of force to be that which gives unit acceleration to unit mass. Newton's second law becomes

$$m\mathbf{a} = \sum \mathbf{F}. \qquad [5\text{-}2]$$

A more general statement of the law is given on page 126 where we consider bodies whose mass can vary.

	Mass	Acceleration	Force
Dimensions	M	LT^{-2}	MLT^{-2}
Absolute unit (SI)	kg	$m\,s^{-2}$	$kg\,m\,s^{-2} =$ newton (N)

Table 5-1 Absolute units of force derived from Newton's second law.

The dimensions of force are now seen to be MLT^{-2} and the unit will be $kg\,m\,s^{-2}$, which is cumbersome. We measure forces so often that a name is given to this unit: it is called the *newton* (N). The newton is called an absolute unit of force, as its size does not depend on the properties of any particular body, such as the Earth.

▶ **Example 5-3** The resultant force $\sum \mathbf{F}$ on a book of mass 2.0 kg is 10 N. What is the acceleration of the book?

Using $\sum \mathbf{F} = m\mathbf{a}$, we have:

$$10\,\text{N} = 2.0\,\text{kg}(a)$$
so that $\quad a = 5.0\,\text{N}\,\text{kg}^{-1}$
$\quad\quad\quad = 5.0\,\text{m}\,\text{s}^{-2}$

in the direction of $\sum \mathbf{F}$. ◀

We cannot verify the law by experiment but we can use simple apparatus to stress its content. We can

(a) measure the acceleration of a body of fixed mass which is acted on by different forces, and

(b) measure the acceleration produced in bodies of different mass by the same force.

We can use trolleys and exert the forces by means of elastic threads.

(a) *Is $\mathbf{a} \propto \sum \mathbf{F}$ for a particle of fixed mass?* As shown in figure 5-10, a single trolley of fixed mass is accelerated successively by forces F, $2F$, $3F$, and so on, and the accelerations measured with the help of a ticker-timer, the tape being attached to the trolley. If the forces F, $2F$, $3F$, etc., represent the resultant external force acting on the trolley, and we plot these forces against the accelerations, we should expect a straight line passing through the origin (figure 5-11a). In fact the resultant accelerating force on the trolley is less than F, $2F$, $3F$, etc., owing to

 (i) the frictional push of the ground on the trolley
 (ii) the pull of the tape on the trolley
 (iii) the push of the air on the trolley;

and, also, the wheels of this 'particle' rotate relative to the frame of the trolley. However, we can tilt the runway on which the trolley moves so as so produce a 'friction-compensated slope', and we can make the wheels of the trolley of a material of low density; thus the experiment can give results to a precision of about five per cent. With these limitations we can see that $\mathbf{a} \propto \sum \mathbf{F}$ and (perhaps more important) we can in principle measure F if we use a trolley of known mass.

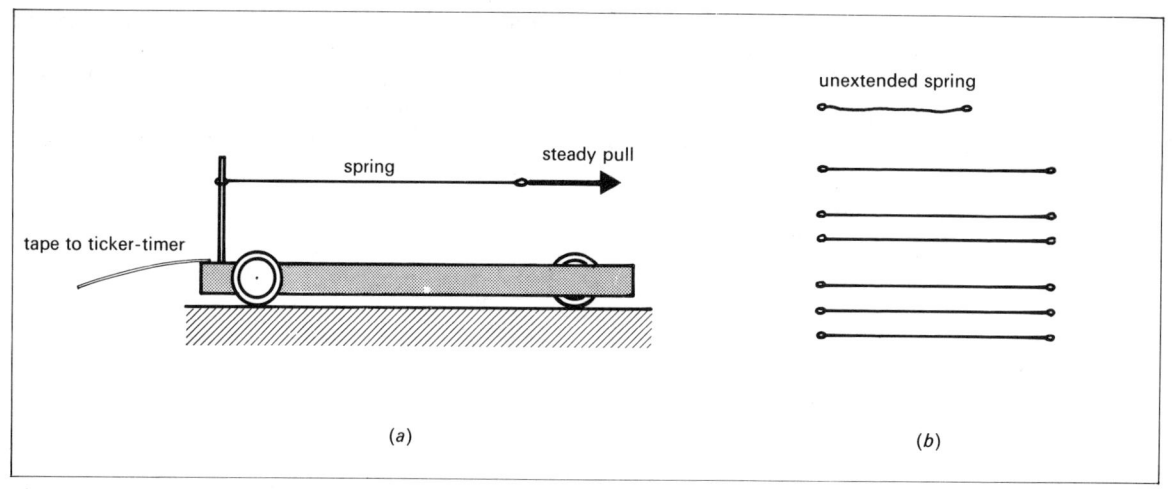

Figure 5-10 (a) The trolley is accelerated along the bench as shown and the dots on the tape are analysed to find the acceleration a. (b) Forces of F, $2F$, $3F$, etc., can be produced by using a number of identical springs and extending each to be level with a fixed mark on the trolley.

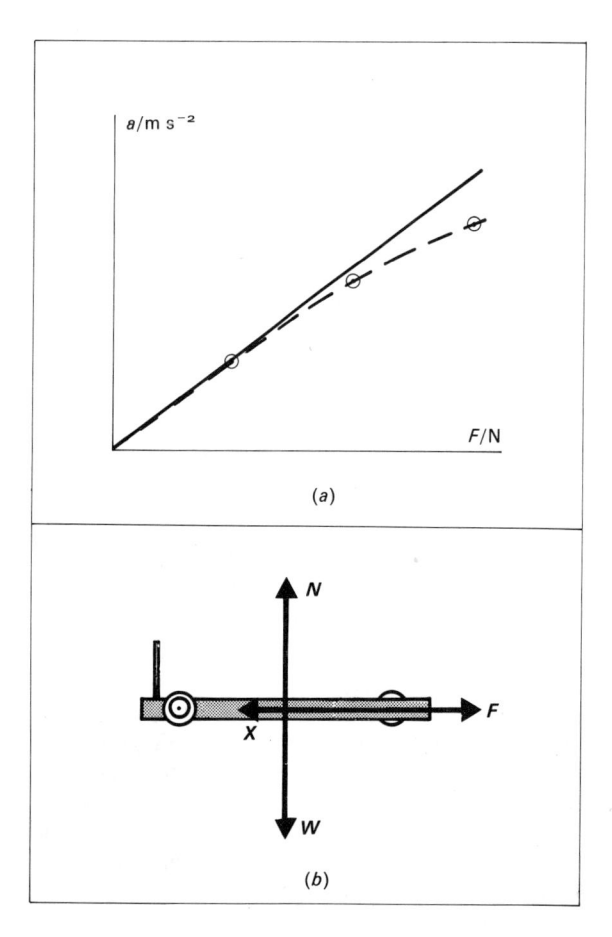

(b) *Is $a \propto 1/m$ when a particle is accelerated by a fixed force?* We can test this relationship by using a number of stackable trolleys and again exerting a steady pull by extending a string by a fixed amount (figure 5-12). The corresponding values of $a/\text{m s}^{-2}$ and m^{-1}/kg^{-1} can be plotted on a graph, and we should again expect a straight line passing through the origin.

There is one facet of Newton's second law which can be more carefully studied. A particle of constant mass which is subject to a constant external resultant force F should undergo a constant acceleration. We can test this with a puck (which we can treat as a particle)—see figure 5-13a. To produce a constant accelerating force we attach a spring to the particle and measure the extension of the spring against an arbitrary scale attached to the puck. If the spring is stretched a fixed amount, we conclude that the pull of the spring on the puck is constant. Provided that the acceleration produced is small, we can assume that the frictional push of the air on the puck is negligible: thus $\sum F$ is a fixed force in the direction of a (for a proper discussion of force as a vector see Section 6-1). But how can we exert a steady pull? The crude

Figure 5-11 (a) A graph showing the expected (full-line) result of an experiment where a trolley of fixed mass is accelerated by a succession of forces. The dotted line shows some experimental results. (b) A free-body diagram of a trolley accelerating along a horizontal table, treating the trolley as a particle. X is the frictional push of the ground on the trolley and F the pull of the spring on the trolley.

5-6 Newton's second law

method of pulling by hand and walking alongside as the mass accelerates is satisfactory for the rough experiments with trolleys, but we might hope for something more reliable. The arrangement shown in figure 5-13a works well, but it must be emphasized that the string–pulley–block system is purely to produce a *steady* extension of the spring pulling the puck. How and why the arrangement does so is unimportant in this context. The system is released from rest and illuminated stroboscopically. The positions of the puck are recorded by each flash on a time exposure of a photographic plate placed above the experiment. If a velocity–time graph is drawn from figure 5-13b we have a straight line, which indicates a constant acceleration. Thus we show that a constant force produces a constant acceleration in a given mass. This apparatus can be extended to repeat experiments (*a*) and (*b*) on pages 67 and 68 more accurately, but as we cannot *prove* a law which defines the way in which we measure mass and force there is little to gain.

The analysis of problems using Newton's second law is left to the next chapter.

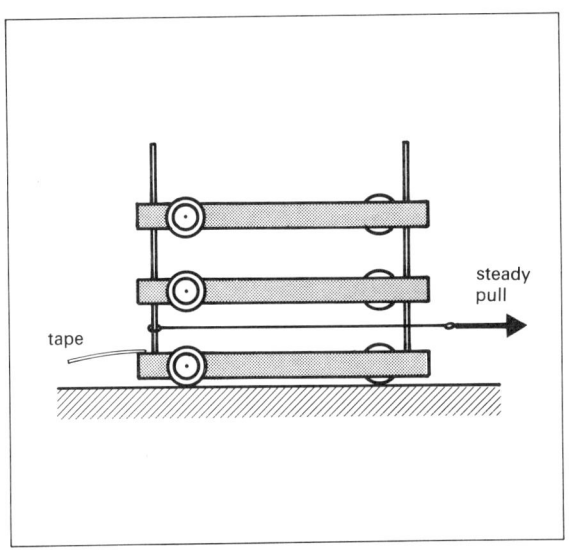

Figure 5-12 A convenient way of producing bodies of mass *m*, 2*m*, 3*m*, etc. is to stack identical trolleys one on top of another. Note that it is only the bottom trolley whose wheels rotate.

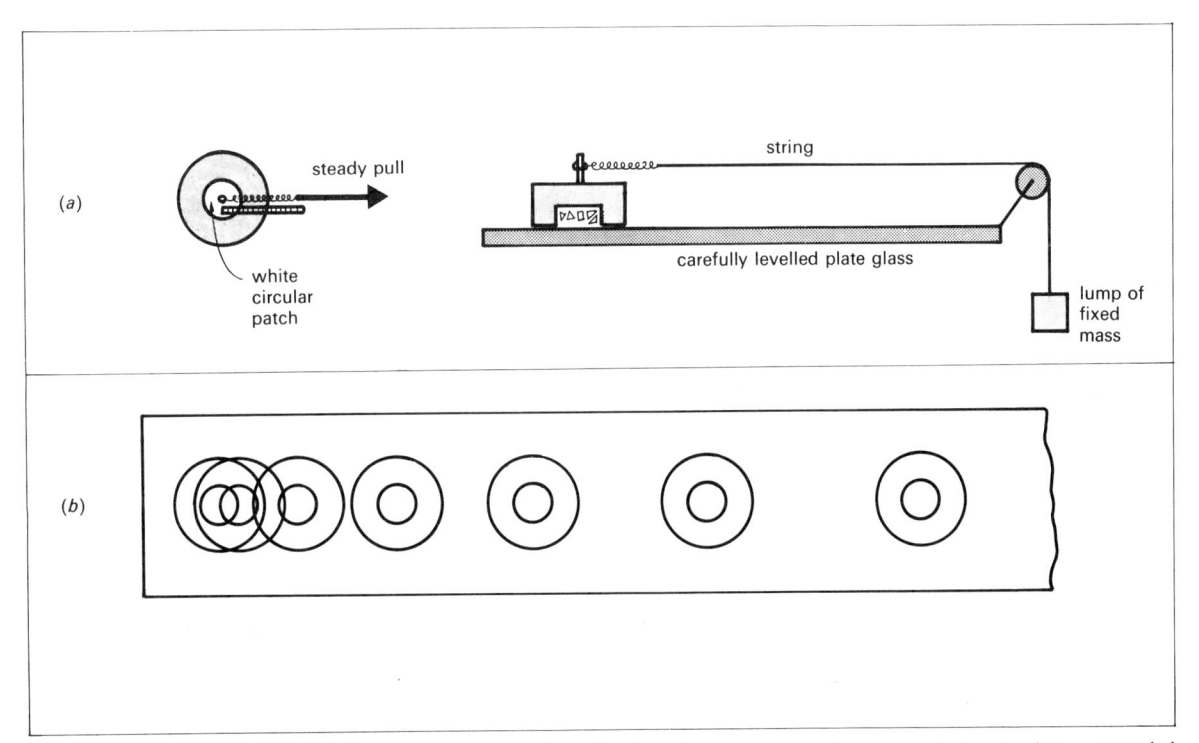

Figure 5-13 (*a*) How to exert a steady pull on a puck. The spring is pulled so as to register a constant extension as recorded by the short ruler attached to the puck. (*b*) Representation of a multiflash photograph of a puck being accelerated by a constant force. The time interval between successive positions is constant.

5-7 Weight

Every particle in the universe attracts every other particle —see Chapter 14. We shall call the pull of the Earth (which can be treated as a particle for objects lying above its surface) on a body, the *weight* of the body.* The body itself acts like a particle placed at its centre of gravity (see page 181). This force, the weight of a body, is always directed towards the centre of the Earth. It is sometimes referred to as 'the force of gravity' meaning 'the pull of the Earth': we shall always use the latter phrase. A body on which the only force acting is the pull of the Earth is said to be in a state of *free fall*. During free fall a body moves with acceleration g_0: in figure 5-14, $\mathbf{a} = \mathbf{g}_0$ in size and direction. Applying Newton's second law to the body, we have

$$m\mathbf{a} = \mathbf{W}_0$$
$$m\mathbf{g}_0 = \mathbf{W}_0. \quad [5\text{-}3]$$

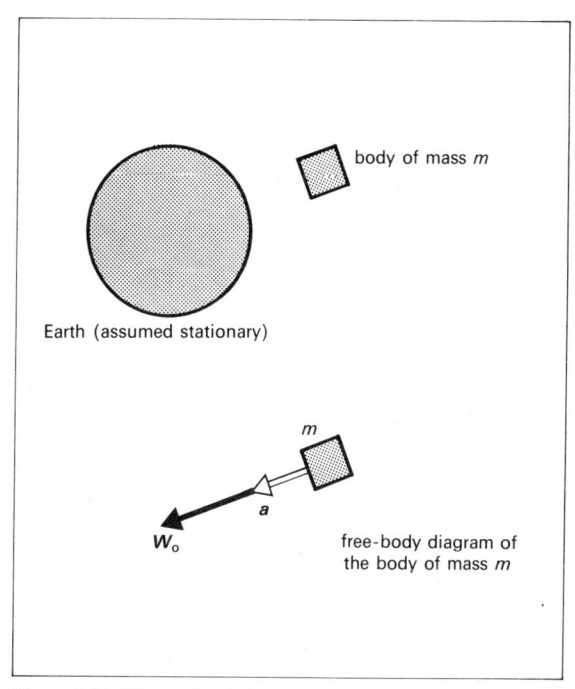

Figure 5-14 The pull of the Earth on a body is called its weight W_0.

---

*Some people define the weight of a body as the force which it exerts on its support. Then it is correct to describe a body in free fall as *weightless*. See Section 6-7.

This equation tells us that the weight of a body is not constant, but depends on the local value of $\mathbf{g}$—see table 14-2.

▶ **Example 5-4** The values of g on the surface of the Earth and on the surface of the planet Mars are $10\,\mathrm{m\,s^{-2}}$ and $3.9\,\mathrm{m\,s^{-2}}$ respectively. Find the weight of a 20 kg mass on the surface of each planet.

$$W = mg$$
and $$1\,\mathrm{m\,s^{-2}} = 1\,\mathrm{N\,kg^{-1}},$$
so that, on the Earth,
$$W = (20\,\mathrm{kg})(10\,\mathrm{N\,kg^{-1}})$$
$$= 200\,\mathrm{N}$$

(towards the centre of the Earth),

and, on Mars, $\quad W = (20\,\mathrm{kg})(3.9\,\mathrm{N\,kg^{-1}})$
$$= 78\,\mathrm{N}$$

(towards the centre of Mars). ◀

(The part of this section which follows in small type is best left to a second reading and until Chapter 6 has been read.)

★ What precisely do we mean by $\mathbf{g}_0$ in equation 5-3? $\mathbf{W}_0$ is the pull of the Earth on the body. The acceleration produced by $\mathbf{W}_0$ is not, however, the acceleration of gravity, $\mathbf{g}$, of Section 3-7, because $\mathbf{g}$ was then measured by an observer in a frame of reference attached to, and therefore rotating with, the Earth. But $\mathbf{g}_0$ is not very different from $\mathbf{g}$ and similarly $\mathbf{W}_0$ is not very different from $\mathbf{W}$, the force which the observer on the Earth thinks produces the acceleration $\mathbf{g}$.

$$[5\text{-}3] \quad\quad \mathbf{W}_0 = m\mathbf{g}_0$$

can thus be replaced by $\quad W = mg \quad\quad [5\text{-}4]$

for most purposes, g now being the measured acceleration due to gravity and W the weight of the body the observer would feel if he were to carry it, or the weight of the body as measured on a spring balance held at rest on the Earth's surface. At the poles, equations 5-3 and 5-4 are identical, as it is the rotation of the Earth which causes the difference.

g and g_0 are of course related. To see how large $g_0 - g$ is, we shall apply Newton's second law parallel to AO in figure 5-15:

$$mr\omega^2 \cos\lambda = W_0 - W\cos\Delta\lambda.$$

As $\Delta\lambda$ is small, $\cos\Delta\lambda \approx 1$. Substituting for W and W_0 from equation 5-3 and 5-4, gives

$$mr\omega^2 \cos\lambda = mg_0 - mg.$$

Therefore $\quad g_0 - g = r\omega^2 \cos\lambda$

or $\quad \Delta g = g_0 - g = r_E \omega^2 \cos^2\lambda$

where $r = r_E \cos\lambda$, r_E being the radius of the Earth.

At the equator, where $\lambda = 0$, and using $r_E = 6.4 \times 10^6\,\mathrm{m}$ and $\omega = [2\pi/(24 \times 60 \times 60)]\,\mathrm{rad\,s^{-1}}$,

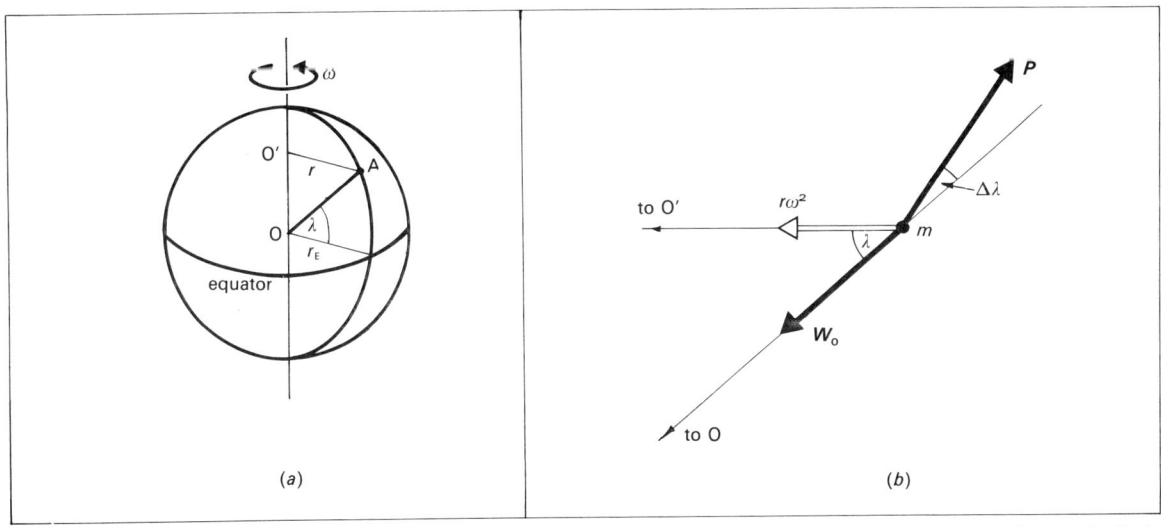

Figure 5-15 An experimenter at A on the Earth's surface at a place of latitude λ holds a body of mass m in what he thinks is equilibrium with a force **P**. He thinks the weight of the body, **W**, is $-\mathbf{P}$. A free-body diagram for the body is also shown in an inertial frame of reference (one in which we can apply Newton's laws of motion) in which, as it is not rotating with the Earth, the body is seen to be accelerating.

we get $\quad \Delta g = 3.5 \times 10^{-2}\,\text{m s}^{-2}$ or $35\,\text{mm s}^{-2}$.

At latitude 60°, $\cos^2 \lambda = 0.25$ and $\Delta g < 10\,\text{mm s}^{-2}$, so our measurements of g in England need to be more accurate than 1 part in 1000 before we need worry about the difference between g and g_0. It is interesting to note that the force which a body needs for support, $\mathbf{P} = -\mathbf{W}$, also varies: that is, the *apparent weight* of a body varies with latitude. This implies that athletic records, for example, should be quoted at a given latitude (as well as at a given height above sea-level), for a javelin thrown 80 m at the North Pole would have travelled 250 mm further at the Equator. See also table 14-2 on page 230 and the Reader to Unit 1 of Project Physics.

To find $\Delta\lambda$, apply Newton's second law perpendicular to AO′ in figure 5-15:

$$W_0 \sin \lambda = W \sin(\lambda + \Delta\lambda)$$

so that $\quad mg_0 \sin \lambda = mg \sin(\lambda + \Delta\lambda).$

Thus when $\lambda = 60°$, $g = 9.819\,\text{m s}^{-2}$, and $g_0 = 9.828\,\text{m s}^{-2}$,

$$\sin(60° + \Delta\lambda) = \left(\frac{9.828\,\text{m s}^{-2}}{9.819\,\text{m s}^{-2}}\right) \sin 60°$$

which gives $\quad \Delta\lambda = 5'.$

A plumb-line therefore defines a line which makes an angle of 5′ with the Earth's radius at a latitude of 60°. We shall use $W = mg$ as if it were $W_0 = mg_0$ unless the difference is especially required. ★

Using equations 5-3 and 5-4 ($W = mg$) it can be seen that the pull W of the Earth on a mass of 16 kg is given by

$$W = 16\,\text{kg} \times 9.8\,\text{m s}^{-2}$$
$$= 157\,\text{kg m s}^{-2}$$
$$= 160\,\text{N (to two significant figures)}.$$

Or, if we write $\quad g = 9.8\,\text{N kg}^{-1}$,

we have $\quad W = 16\,\text{kg} \times 9.8\,\text{N kg}^{-1}$
$$= 157\,\text{N}$$
$$= 160\,\text{N (to two significant figures)}.$$

There is also in use (though *not* part of the SI system of units) a gravitational unit of force called the kilogram force (kgf). 1 kgf is defined as the apparent weight of a mass of 1 kg at a standard station, where the measured value of g is $9.8066\,\text{N kg}^{-1}$. Thus

$$1\,\text{kgf} = 9.8066\,\text{N} = 9.8\,\text{N (to 2 s.f.)}.$$

The usefulness of the gravitational units is that it is *almost* true to say that the pull of the Earth on a mass of 1 kg is 1 kgf *anywhere* on or near the Earth's surface, and it is simple to say that the pull of the Earth on a mass of, say, 45 kg, is 45 kgf. Gravitational units can be used in any situation, and we can talk of a push of 40 kgf or a drag of 120 kgf. If we then want to use Newton's second law ($m\mathbf{a} = \Sigma \mathbf{F}$) we *must*, however, convert these gravitational units to absolute units, and in this text we shall not use this gravitational unit.

5-8 Newton's third law

Newton was the first to appreciate that in an interaction between two bodies two forces are involved and that there is a simple relationship between these forces at every instant during the interaction. His third law states that

if body A exerts a force F on body B, then body B exerts a force −F on body A, that is, a force which is equal in size but opposite in direction.

The forces F and $-F$ are sometimes described as the *action and reaction forces*; this statement leads to considerable confusion, particularly in problems where contact forces are involved. We shall not use these words in this text. The third law implies that a single force is an impossibility: forces *always* occur in pairs.

As the forces involved in Newton's third law act on two different bodies it is necessary, when discussing an example of the application of this law, to draw three diagrams: a situation diagram showing the two bodies A and B and a free-body diagram of *each* of A and B.

▶ **Example 5-6** Consider a block supported by a rope, as in figure 5-16; the pull of the rope on the block is T upwards and the pull of the block on the rope is T' downwards. Newton's third law says that $T = -T'$, that is $T = T'$ and they act in opposite directions. The effect of these two forces on the block-and-rope system is zero: they are internal forces as far as the system is concerned (as, for instance, are the forces which the molecules of the block exert on each other when one considers the block alone). If, in figure 5-16, we wish to consider the third law force accompanying the pull W_a of the Earth on the block we must draw a free-body diagram for the Earth, and mark on it a force W_a', the pull of the block on the Earth, directed from the centre of the Earth towards the block. A very similar force is shown in the discussion which follows. ◀

We must stress that Newton's third law holds at every instant of an interaction. For figure 5-17, where a boy is shown jumping off a wall, we sketch in figure 5-18 two graphs showing how P and P' vary with time before, during, and after the landing.

We shall list some further examples without examining them all in detail. Remember that whenever there is a force which can be described as

$$\text{the } \begin{Bmatrix} \text{push} \\ \text{pull} \end{Bmatrix} \text{ of A on B}$$

there is another force, namely,

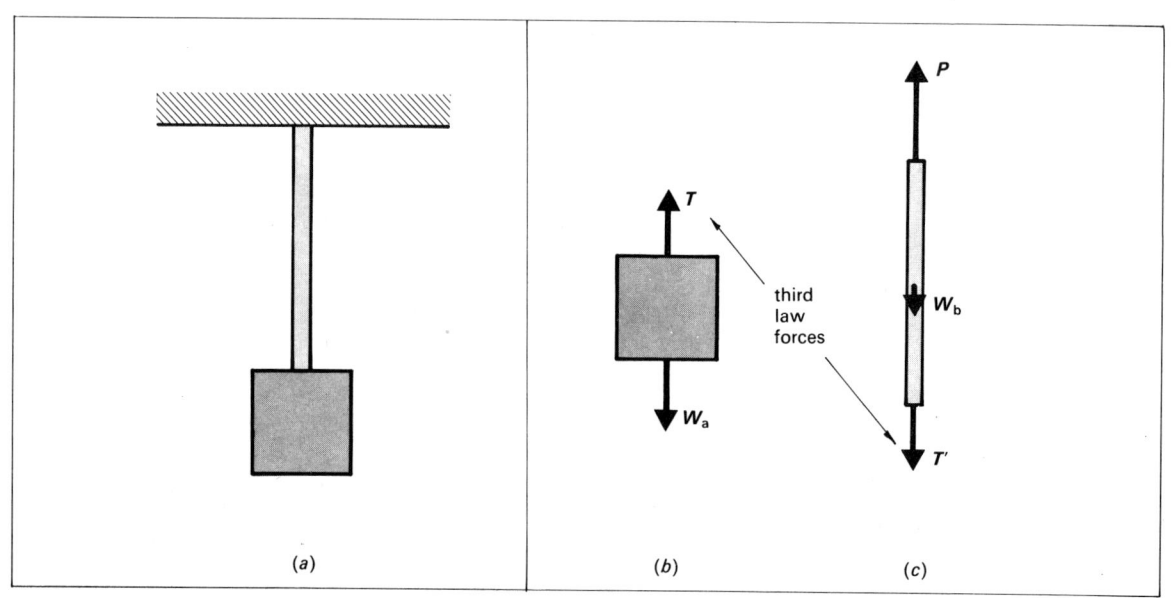

$$\text{the } \begin{Bmatrix} \text{push} \\ \text{pull} \end{Bmatrix} \text{ of B on A.}$$

Figure 5-16 (a) Situation diagram of a block supported by a rope. (b) Free-body diagram for the block. (c) Free-body diagram for the rope. The forces of interaction between the block and the rope are shown as T and T'. Newton's third law states that $T = -T'$.

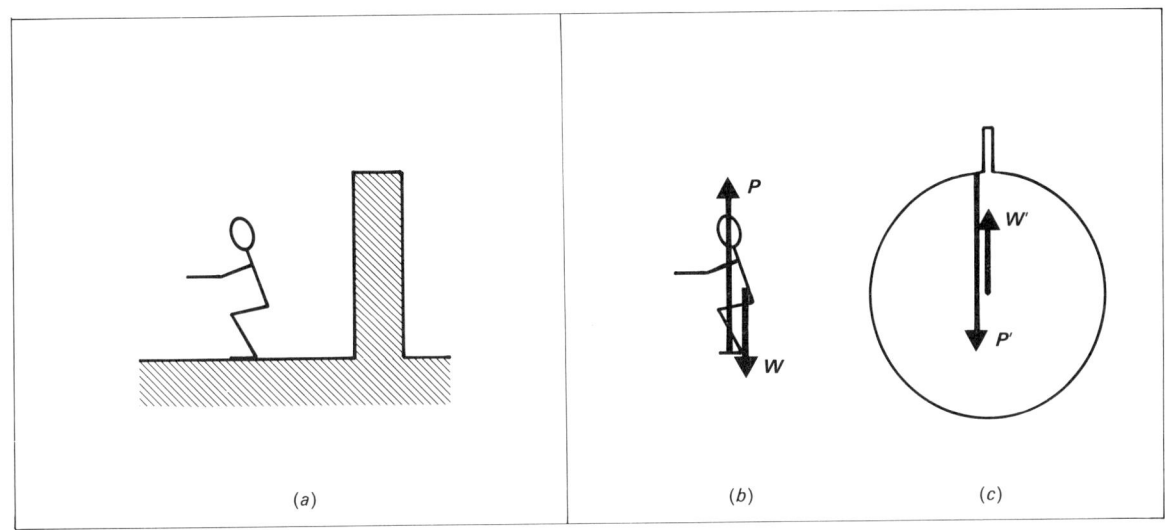

Figure 5-17 (a) Situation diagram. A boy jumps off a wall and lands on the ground, which is part of the Earth. (b) Free-body diagram for the boy. (c) Free-body diagram for the Earth at one instant during the boy's landing. $P = -P'$ and $W = -W'$. Note that there is no resultant force acting on the Earth–boy system.

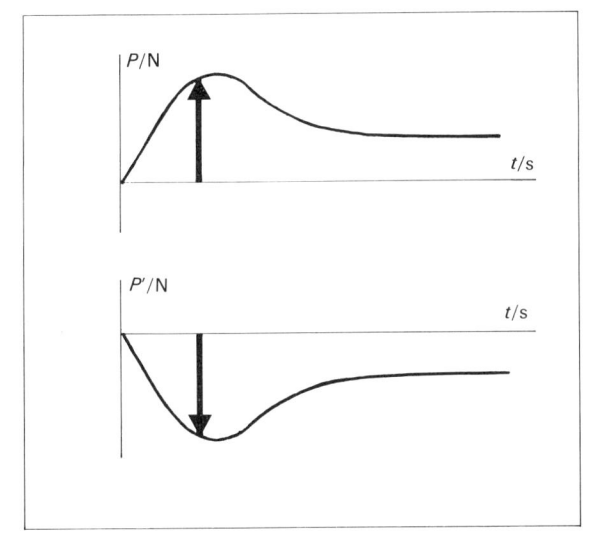

Figure 5-18 Graphs of P and P' against time t for the forces shown at one instant in the above example of the boy jumping off the wall. At $t = 0$ the boy is in mid-air.

(a) One of Newton's own examples reads 'if any person press a stone with his finger, his finger is pressed by the stone'.

(b) If a car wheel exerts a horizontal force of 600 N on the surface of a road, the road surface exerts a horizontal force of 600 N in the opposite direction on the wheel. It is of course this second force which 'drives' the car forward, and the method by which all ordinary cars, trains, and animals arrange for a force to propel themselves is similar. That such an *external* force is required is surely obvious.

(c) If the head of a golfclub exerts a horizontal force on a golfball, the ball exerts an equal horizontal force on the clubhead.

(d) If you step on an egg, the push of your foot on the egg is at every instant equal to the push of the egg on your foot. The force on the egg is more easily able to change the shape of the egg than the force on your foot is able to change the shape of your foot!

(e) If the Earth pulls an apple vertically downwards with a force of 2.0 N, the apple pulls the Earth vertically upwards with a force of 2.0 N.

(f) Finally let us consider (figure 5-19) a man pushing a large box. Whether or not the box is accelerating depends on whether P' is greater than, equal to, or less than G (Newton's first law); it will accelerate unless $P' + G = 0$. The fact that P and P' are numerically equal is irrelevant: when we consider the *box* alone they do not cancel out.

We must remember that in Newtonian mechanics the truth of the third law is not in question and we cannot therefore be asked to describe an experiment to 'verify' it. That Newton's laws give us a technique for analysing and predicting the movements of material bodies with admirable precision means not that the laws are true but that they are accurately relevant to the world we live in.

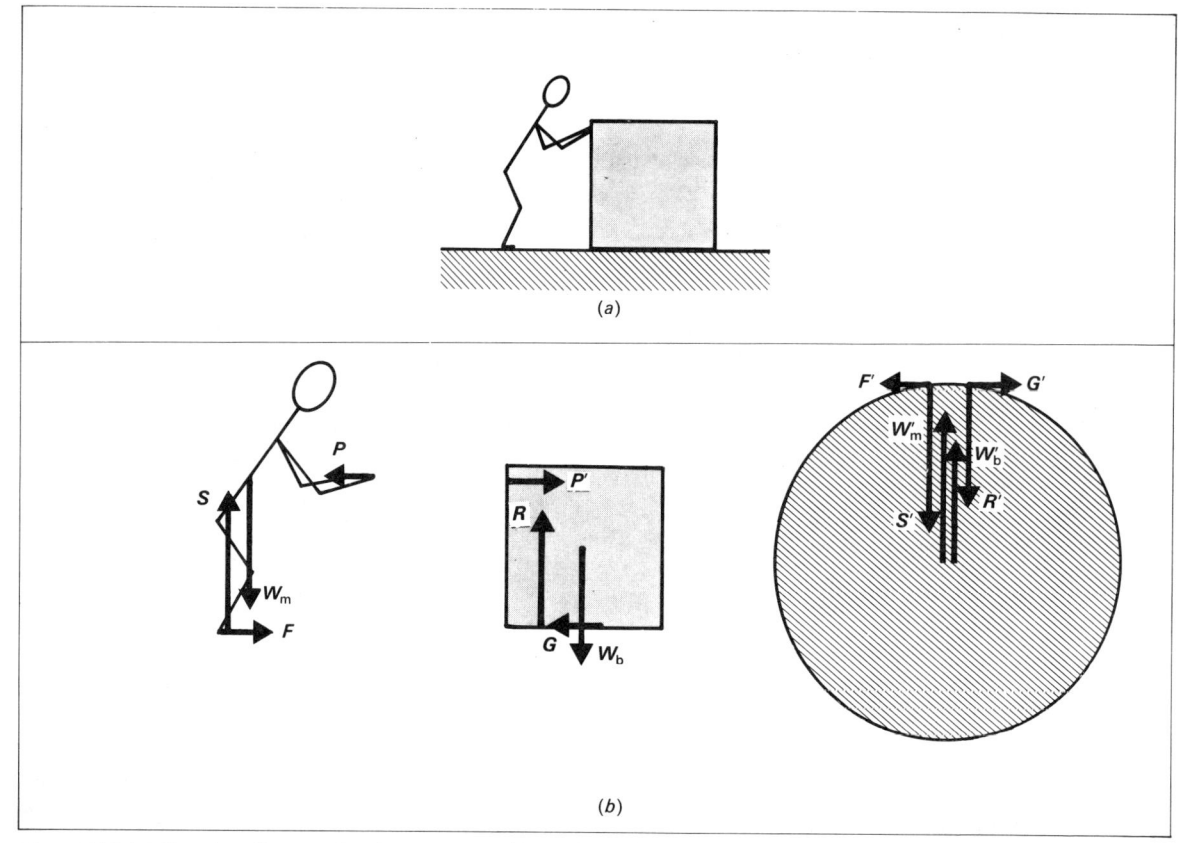

Figure 5-19 (*a*) Situation diagram showing a man pushing a box along the ground to the right. (*b*) Three free-body diagrams for the man, the box, and the Earth. Force pairs connected by Newton's third law are shown as **P** and **P'** etc.

Bibliography

MacLeod, R. R. (1965). 'Towards a sensible definition of weight.' *School Science Review*, number 159, page 372.

Feather, N. (1968). 'The physical basis of Newtonian mechanics, part 1.' *Sources of physics teaching*, part 2. Taylor and Francis. This article, reprinted from *Contemporary Physics*, is an intellectually tough consideration of Newton's laws as formulated in Book One of *Principia*.

Arons, A. B. (1965). *Development of concepts of physics*. Addison–Wesley. A book which stresses the historical development of the concepts of force and mass.

French, A. P. (1971). *Newtonian mechanics*. Nelson. The various forces of nature are discussed in Chapter 5.

Jardine, J. (1966). *Physics is fun*, Book 3. Heinemann. A lively and well-illustrated elementary text.

Nuffield O-level Physics (1966). *Teachers' Guide IV*. Longman/Penguin. The section on the physical basis of Newtonian mechanics is relevant.

PSSC (1971). *Physics*, 3rd edition. Heath. Newton's laws are approached experimentally in Chapter 11.

Rogers, E. M. (1960). *Physics for the inquiring mind*. Oxford University Press. Chapter 7: force and motion.

Toulmin, S. and Goodfield, J. (1963). *The fabric of the heavens*. Penguin. The pre-Newtonian view of motion is presented clearly in Chapter 3.

16 mm film. 'Forces.' Guild Sound and Vision. Both gravitational and electrical forces are discussed.

Exercises

Data (to be used unless otherwise directed):
$g = 10 \,\text{m s}^{-2} = 10 \,\text{N kg}^{-1}$.

5-1 What is a force? Why does a bullet penetrate a block of wood? Why does a pancake leave the pan when it is being tossed?

5-2 You are standing in a bus. When the bus starts, or stops, or turns a corner, you tend to fall over. Why?

5-3 Draw free-body diagrams for the body written in italics in each of the following situations, and describe the forces, as in figures 5-5 and 5-6:
  (a) a *book* resting on a table
  (b) an *electric light bulb* hanging by flex from the ceiling
  (c) a tethered *buoy* floating in water
  (d) a *sledge* being pulled by a rope attached to a dog
  (e) a *horse* pulling a cart.

5-4 List three situations (as dissimilar as possible) where a body is moving with constant velocity. Draw a free-body diagram for each of the three bodies, and describe the forces acting on each.

5-5 Would it be possible to measure mass (as in Section 5-6) by jerking the rod at different places between the two masses without varying the distances of the masses from the rod's centre?

5-6 In the experiment of figure 5-12, trolleys are stacked so as to double, treble, etc. the original mass. Even after compensation for friction, we would not in practice find that $a \propto 1/m$. Can you suggest a reason?

5-7 Find the acceleration when
  (a) a force of 20 N acts on a mass of 20 kg
  (b) a force of 200 N acts on a mass of 20 kg
  (c) a force of 6000 N acts on a mass of 30 kg.
For each situation find also the force-to-mass ratio in N kg^{-1}. ●

5-8 A body at the surface of the Earth is subjected to a horizontal force of (a) twice (b) half its weight. What is its horizontal acceleration in each case? ●

5-9 The value of the gravitational acceleration at a point near a planet varies inversely as the square of the distance of the point from the centre of the planet. Given that the value of g at the surface of the Earth is $9.8 \,\text{m s}^{-2}$, and that the radius of the Earth is 6400 km, find
  (a) the value of g at a height of 200 km above the Earth's surface
  (b) the height above the Earth's surface where the value of g would be half what it is at the Earth's surface. ●

5-10 Do two bodies of different mass, if allowed to fall to the ground from the same height, reach the ground at the same time? Discuss.

5-11 Discuss the idea of 'terminal velocity' of a body. What affects its value, and the time taken for the body to reach it?

5-12 In the following situations draw free-body diagrams for each of the italicized bodies. Describe the forces and say which pairs of forces are equal *because of* Newton's third law:
  (a) a *pen* lying on a *table* which rests on a floor
  (b) a *man* holding a *suitcase* (the man is standing upright on the ground)
  (c) a *suitcase* being dragged off a *table* by a *man* who is standing on the floor
  (d) a *stone* being fired from a *catapult*, while the stone is still in contact with the catapult (the catapult is held by a boy)
  (e) a *man* standing in a bus holding on to a *rail* which is attached to the roof by its two ends.

6 Using Newton's laws

6-1	Is force a vector?	76	6-7 Centripetal forces	89
6-2	The pull of strings	78	6-8 Mass, weight, and weightlessness	91
6-3	Normal contact forces	80	6-9 Accelerating frames of reference	92
6-4	Dry friction	82	Bibliography	93
6-5	Fluid friction	86	Exercises	94
6-6	Applying Newton's second law	87		

6-1 Is force a vector?

It is clear that for full specification of a force more than simply a statement of its size is needed; its direction is very relevant. To a man standing on the edge of a cliff, the difference between being pulled back or pushed forward is of vital importance. This directional property is not enough to make force a vector: to do this we must show that forces obey the rules of vector algebra and in particular that they add vectorially (see page 17). This demands an experimental test.

Suppose a small metal ring rests on a horizontal table and that the ring is attached by a cord to a spring S (figure 6-1). The ring has crosswires so that its centre can easily be located. We now apply two known forces F_1 and F_2 to the ring. Their sizes, F_1 and F_2, could be found by accelerating a known mass with each in turn but in practice they are measured by spring balances calibrated so that they are accurate when lying horizontally. The position of the centre of the ring, O, is noted by marking it on a piece of paper attached to the table, as are the directions of the cords A and B.

The forces F_1 and F_2 are now added as if they were vectors (figure 6-2), the direction and size of $\sum F = F_1 + F_2$ being marked on the paper. The cords A and B are now removed and a single force F_3 applied to the ring.

F_3 is adjusted until the centre of the ring is returned to O. The direction of the cord C is marked on the paper and its size, F_3, read from the spring balance.

If the forces do add as vectors then F_1 plus F_2 should equal F_3: that is $\theta = 0$ and the size of $(F_1 + F_2) = F_3$. The experiment measures θ and compares the size of $(F_1 + F_2)$ with F_3. The result of a single experiment is seldom convincing if ordinary laboratory spring balances are used, as the sensitivity of these instruments is lowered by friction and they are not accurate as they are calibrated for vertical use. The result of numerous experiments, however, convincingly demonstrates that forces are added vectorially.

This experiment can be performed in a more fundamental way by removing the spring S and replacing the ring by a frictionless mass, such as a puck. Accelerations are now measured using first $F_1 + F_2$ and then F_3 adjusted so as to produce the same acceleration. The measured values of $F_1 + F_2$ and F_3 are then compared as above.

Knowing that force is a vector enables $\sum F$ in Newton's second law to be found by vector addition. This technique is not very convenient. However, as the direction of the acceleration is usually known we can resolve each of the forces into parts which are parallel and perpendicular to this direction.

A simple experiment using a trolley (figure 6-3) shows

6-1 Is force a vector?

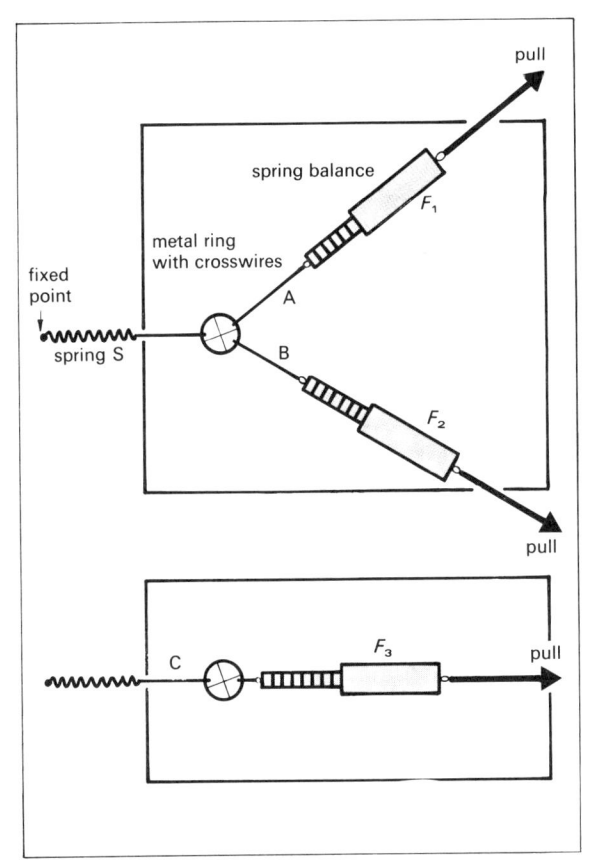

that forces can be resolved in this way and this confirms the vector nature of force. A trolley's motion down a friction-compensated slope is analysed using a ticker-tape timer. To the trolley is attached a large protractor. The radius, r, of this protractor is so arranged that a spring stretched to a length r just accelerates the trolley down the slope when pulled at 85° to the direction of the acceleration. Let this pull of the spring be F; the size of this pull, F, is kept constant during the experiment. Corresponding values of the angle θ, between the direction of motion and a, the acceleration of the trolley, are measured and a graph plotted of $a/\text{m s}^{-2}$ against $\cos\theta$. If the resolved part of F parallel to a is $F\cos\theta$, then the graph should be a straight line through the origin, for by Newton's second law

$$ma = F\cos\theta$$

that is, $$a \propto \cos\theta$$

since, for a friction-compensated slope, the other forces

Figure 6-1 The ring, centre O, is pulled in a horizontal plane first by two known forces F_1 and F_2 and then by a single force F_3 so as to return the ring to the same place. If F_1 and F_2 add geometrically to give a force identical to F_3, then we have shown that force is a vector quantity.

Figure 6-2 (*below*) The values of θ and $F_1 + F_2 - F_3$ will probably not be zero in a single experiment but their average values should be zero if a number of separate experiments is performed.

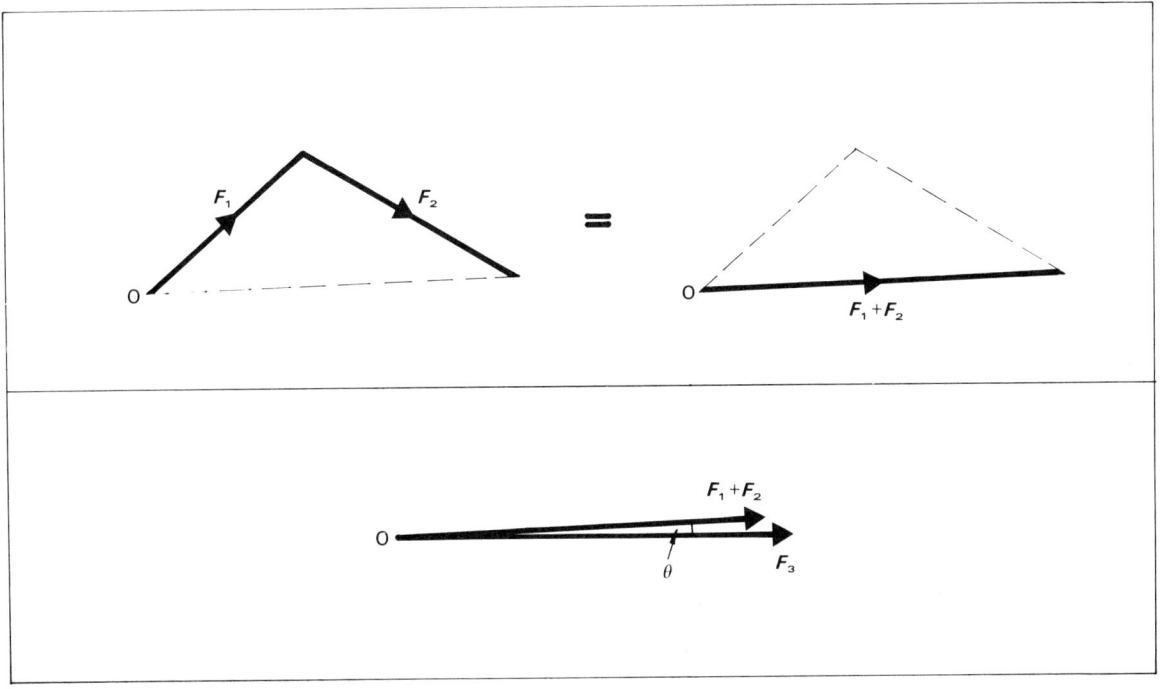

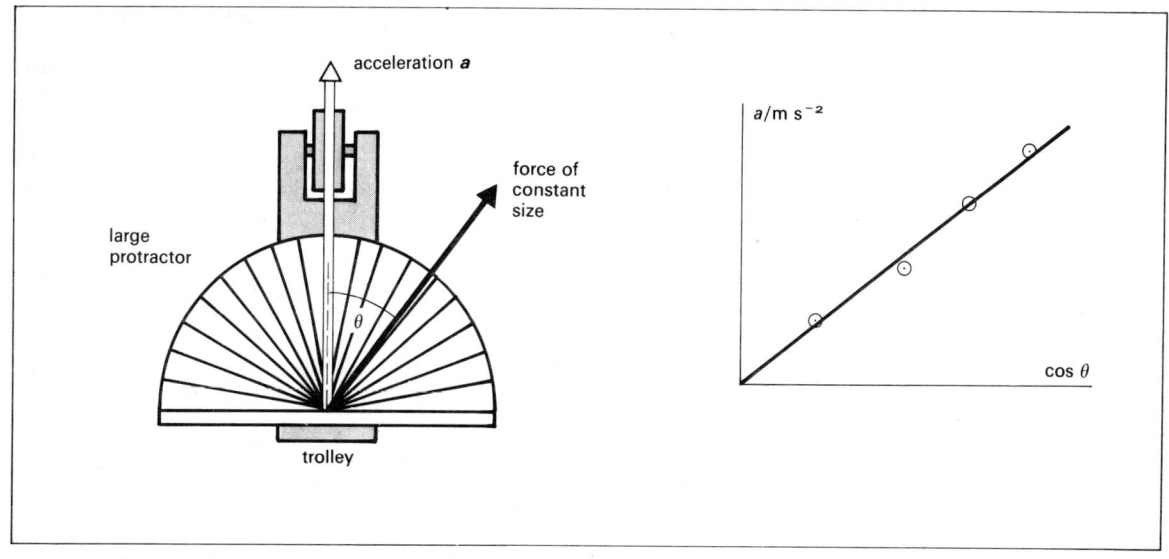

Figure 6-3 The angle θ between the constant pull of the elastic and the direction in which the trolley accelerates is measured from the large protractor which fits over the trolley. a is found to be proportional to $\cos\theta$, thus verifying that we can resolve forces.

on the trolley produce no acceleration. The straight line obtained verifies that we can resolve forces and is itself strong evidence for the vector nature of force.

6-2 The pull of strings

Any fully flexible device, for example a string, being used to pull a body is said to be in a state of tension. To see what this means consider the example shown in figure 6-4a of a kite tethered to a post in the ground. What forces are acting on the *part of* the rope B to C? They are shown in figure 6-4b.

Each of the forces T_1 and T_2 are forces internal to the whole rope and can only be brought into the discussion by cutting the rope, in this case at B and C. They represent the pulls of the molecules of the parts of the rope *that have been removed* on the molecules of the rope at B and C. The kite, in pulling on the post, has pulled all the molecules of the rope slightly further apart than they are in their equilibrium position. It is the presence of these forces that makes us say that the rope is in a state of tension. But what is *the* tension in the rope? Clearly it varies in size from place to place in the rope and although its direction is parallel to the rope its sense depends on which part of the rope is removed after it has been cut. It is best to use the word tension to describe only the size of the force (T_1 or T_2 in this example) and to write *the pull of the rope on the body* when describing the force vector $\boldsymbol{T_1}$ or $\boldsymbol{T_2}$.

> The **tension** at a point in a fully flexible device is thus the size of the force with which one part of the rope cut at the point pulls on the other part.

If a rope ends, for example at A in figure 6-4, then the pull of the rope on the post, $\boldsymbol{T}$, is numerically equal to the tension at A and is directed away from the post in a direction parallel to the rope at A. It is of course related to the pull of the post on the rope, $\boldsymbol{T'}$, by Newton's third law: $\boldsymbol{T} = -\boldsymbol{T'}$.

For real ropes, which have mass, the tension varies from place to place along the rope unless the rope is lying on a frictionless horizontal surface and is not accelerating. Some strings are considered to be so light that their mass, and therefore also their weight, is assumed to be negligible. Such a light string has the same tension at every point and exerts equal, parallel and oppositely directed forces on the two bodies attached to its ends. It is not, however, because of Newton's third law that these forces are equal.

6-2 The pull of strings

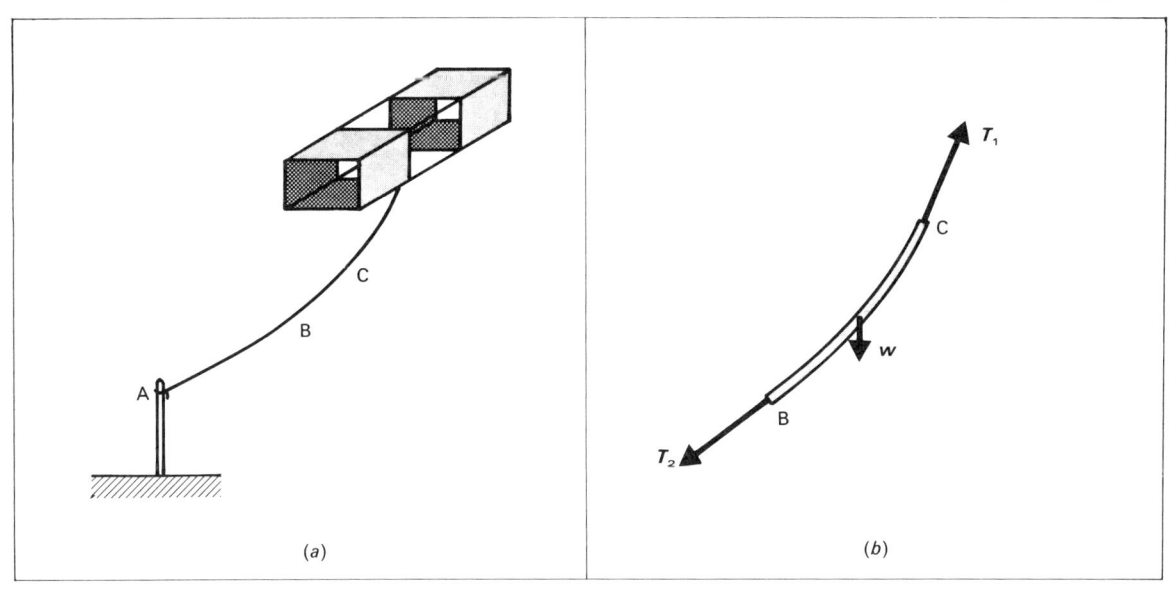

Figure 6-4 (*a*) A kite attached to a fixed post. (*b*) A free-body diagram for a part of the rope BC in which the weight of BC, *w*, affects the relationship between T_1 and T_2. (We assume that the wind does not affect the rope.)

▶ **Example 6-1** A rope is fixed to a ceiling, and a brick is attached to the lower end (figure 6-5). The system is in equilibrium. Draw free-body diagrams for the rope and for the brick and state which forces are equal, giving the reasons for the equalities.

A is the pull of the ceiling on the rope
B is the pull of the Earth on the rope
C is the pull of the brick on the rope
D is the pull of the rope on the brick
E is the pull of the Earth on the brick.

$C = D$ because of Newton's third law (*note:* they act on *different* bodies).
$D = E$ because the brick is in equilibrium (*note:* they act on *the same* body).
$A = B + C$ because the rope is in equilibrium (*note:* they act on *the same* body).

Often we assume that the rope has no mass: then $B = 0$, and $A = C = D = E$, when the rope and brick are in equilibrium. ◀

Ropes and strings often pass round posts or over pulleys. How is the tension in the rope affected? For ropes with mass the problem is difficult but for strings without mass the answer depends on whether or not we can consider the post to be frictionless, and whether or not we can consider that the pulley requires no couple to accelerate it. We are again idealizing the situation: it is legitimate to do so to get an approximation to the solution. If the post or pulley does approximately satisfy the conditions mentioned then we say that the tension in the string is constant and the post or pulley merely (but probably conveniently) alters the direction in which the pull of the rope at its ends can act.

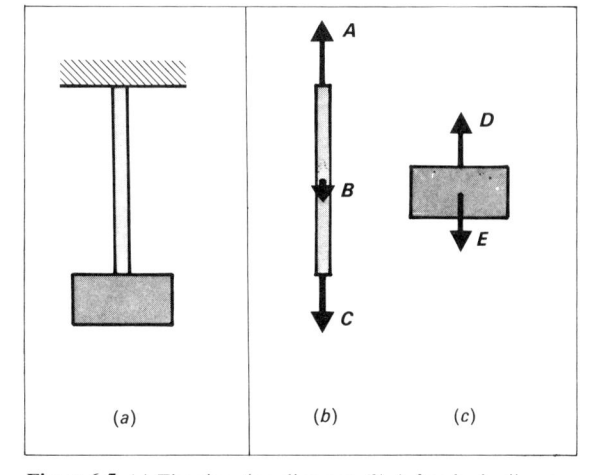

Figure 6-5 (*a*) The situation diagram. (*b*) A free-body diagram for the rope. (*c*) A free-body diagram for the brick.

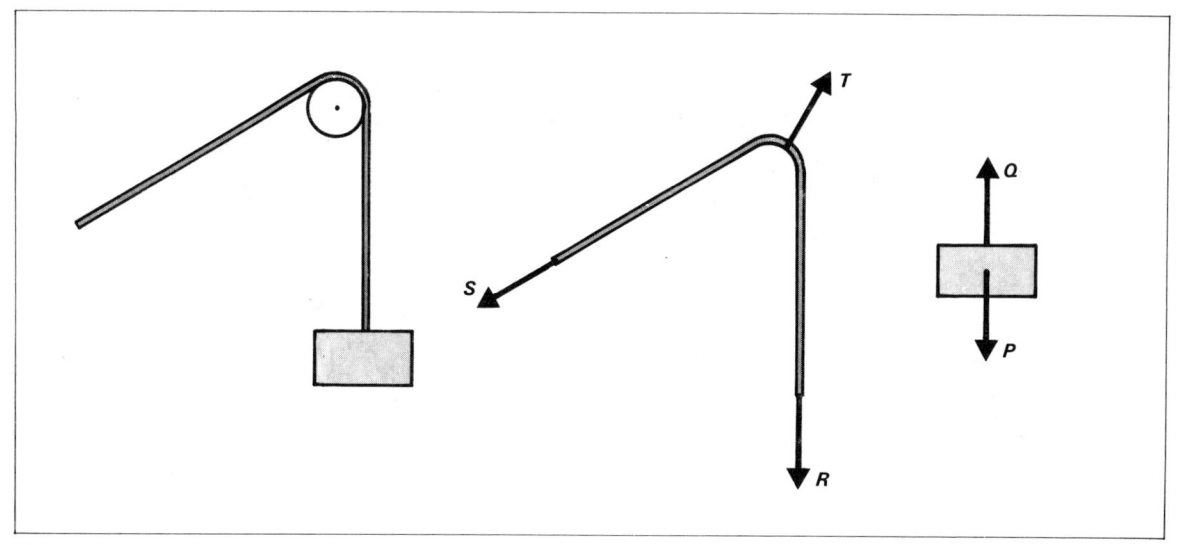

Figure 6-6

▶ **Example 6-2** A man pulls on one end of a rope which passes over a fixed pulley and raises a brick of mass 2.0 kg at a steady speed (figure 6-6). Assuming that the rope has no mass (and therefore no weight) and that the pulley is frictionless (so that it does not exert a frictional push or pull on the rope), find the force exerted by the man on the rope. Take $g = 10\,\text{N}\,\text{kg}^{-1}$.

P is the pull of the Earth on the brick; $P = 20\,\text{N}$ downwards.

Q is the pull of the rope on the brick; $Q = 20\,\text{N}$ upwards, since the brick is in equilibrium. (Of course, $P \neq Q$ if the brick is accelerating.)

R is the pull of the brick on the rope; $R = 20\,\text{N}$ downwards, because Newton's third law gives $R = -Q$, $R = Q$.

S is the pull of the man on the rope; $S = 20\,\text{N}$ parallel to the rope, since the rope has no weight, and there is no frictional force at the pulley, and the rope is in equilibrium: the pulley merely alters the direction of the pull which the rope exerts (and which is exerted on it) at its ends. ◀

6-3 Normal contact forces

Two solid bodies placed close to one another (figure 6-7a) attract each other very, very weakly by a gravitational interaction. If they are placed within a few hundred molecular diameters of one another, about 10^{-7} m, it has recently been shown directly that they attract each other electrically (the forces measured were $\approx 10^{-8}$ N), mostly owing to the proximity of the surface molecules of one body to those of the other. If, however, they are pressed to-

(a)   (b)   (c)

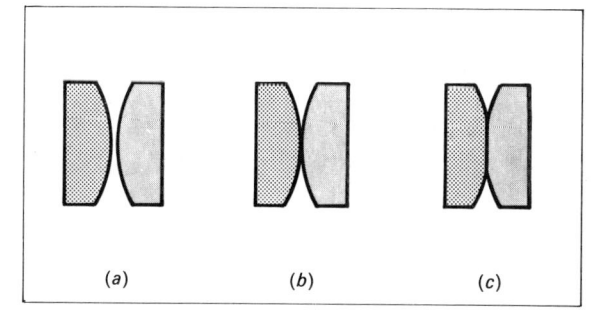

Figure 6-7 Two bodies are held (a) just apart, (b) touching—the surface molecules at the point of contact are at their equilibrium separation from neighbouring molecules in the other body, and (c) pressed together—the molecular structure at the point of contact is strained.

gether by some external agency (figure 6-7c) then they repel each other. This repulsion is the result of some of the surface molecules of the two bodies being pushed so close together that the 'electron clouds' exert strong electrostatic repulsions and keep the bodies apart.

The force exerted by one molecule on another molecule can be described by the graph of figure 6-8a and we shall assume that the forces of interactions between two solid bodies vary in the same general way as this. OP represents the centre-to-centre distance when the two molecules are in equilibrium and thus

$$OP = d_0 = 10^{-9}\,\text{m},$$

6-3 Normal contact forces

d_0 being what we normally take to be the diameter of one molecule. From this we see that for most large-scale contact there is effectively either no force ($r > 10^3 d_0$), or there is a repulsive force which rises very rapidly as r becomes smaller than d_0. Figure 6-8b, in which the scales of r and d are dramatically changed from those in figure 6-8a, illustrates this large-scale situation.

For a body, then, we can take the very large number of intermolecular forces to be represented by a single normal contact force, N. The most common case occurs when a body is in contact with the Earth (figure 6-9).

A normal contact force occurs in many situations and is often the push mentioned when, for example, we push a door or a car. Newton's third law tells us that these normal contact forces always occur in pairs. Thus the normal contact push of a hand on a door is equal in size but opposite in direction to the push of the door on the hand.

If a body is being pushed against a surface in such a way as to tend to make it slide over the surface, the push of the surface on the body will not be normal. It is however convenient in this case to talk of two forces, the normal push of the surface on the body (the normal contact force of this section) and the frictional push of the surface on the body. This second force acts parallel to the common tangent at the point of contact and is discussed in Section 6-4.

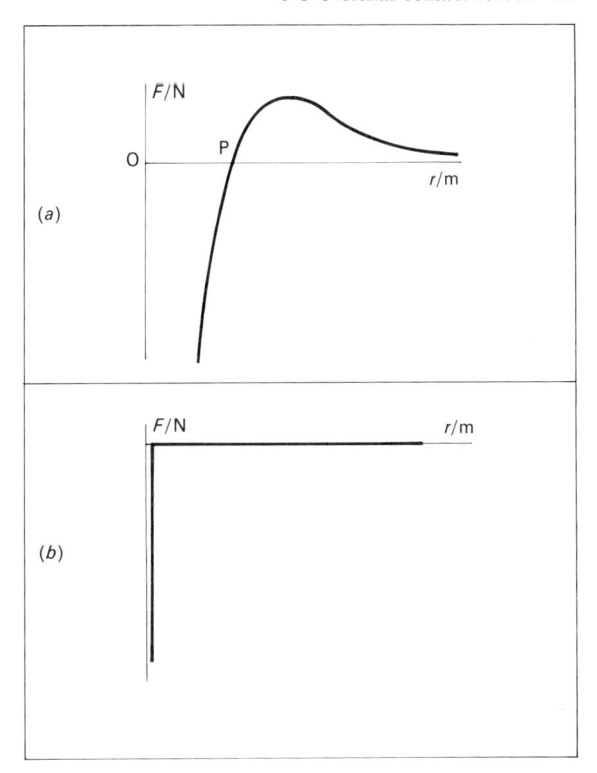

Figure 6-8

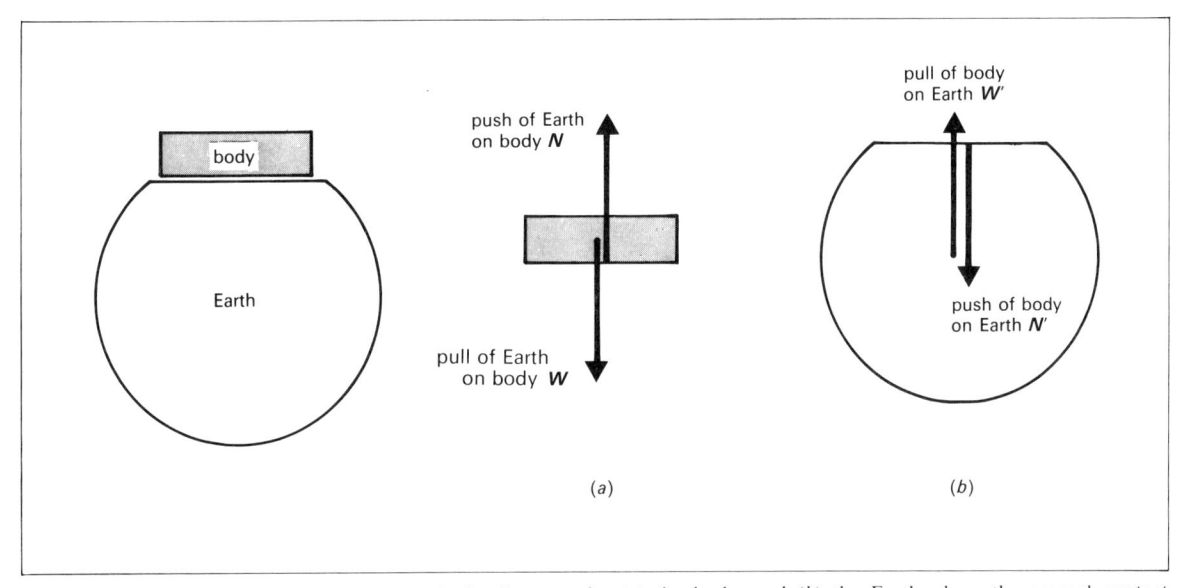

Figure 6-9 A body rests on the Earth. Free-body diagrams for (a) the body, and (b) the Earth, show the normal contact forces and the gravitational interactions. According to Newton's third law $W = -W'$ and $N = -N'$ at all times. Note that the force which acts on the Earth's surface is the push of the body on it—not the body's weight. The body's weight is the pull of the Earth *on the body*.

6 Using Newton's laws

If, for a moment, we consider a body as an extended object, a knowledge of the normal contact force between two surfaces leads to the idea of pressure. The *interfacial pressure* between two solid surfaces in contact is defined by the equation

interfacial pressure between the surfaces

$$= \frac{\text{normal contact push of either body on the other}}{\text{area of contact}}$$

$$p = \frac{N}{A}. \qquad [6\text{-}1]$$

p is a scalar quantity and has dimensions $ML^{-1}T^{-2}$. The unit of pressure is the *pascal* (Pa); $1\,\text{Pa} \equiv 1\,\text{N}\,\text{m}^{-2}$.

The scalar nature of p is not obvious. Area can be represented as a vector—the vector product of two displacements, so that in

$$\mathbf{N} = p\mathbf{A}$$

p is a scalar quantity, the vector $\mathbf{A}$ having a direction perpendicular to the surface in which the area (and so the displacements) lie. $\mathbf{A}$ is thus parallel to $\mathbf{N}$.

What do we mean by the *area in contact*? We could think of A on a macroscopic level as the apparent area in contact; for example, for a book measuring $0.25\,\text{m}$ by $0.30\,\text{m}$ lying on a table, A would be $0.075\,\text{m}^2$. On a microscopic level, A', the real area in contact, is clearly less than A. Typically, $A = 10^5 A'$. A' is effectively proportional to the normal contact force, that is $N/A' = $ constant. What is happening is that the material yields over the actual area of contact until A' has a value which the microscopic structure can support. This local pressure will be *constant* for two given materials and may be of the order of 10^7 Pa. See figure 6-10.

6-4 Dry friction

The idea of solid friction develops naturally from the discussion of the last paragraph. When molecules in contact have settled to a position of constant local pressure N/A', a relative motion between the two materials in a direction perpendicular to N results in a continual breaking of the intermolecular bonds and the continual creation of other intermolecular bonds as different parts of the surface come into contact and form the area A'. On this microscopic level, then, the motion causes a bumpy ride of one surface over the other, the breaking of the intermolecular bonds producing internal energy so that the temperature of the materials rises. This effect can be so great as to melt the surface layers, a procedure which is now used commercially to weld two rotating plates together. For materials P and Q we would expect bits of P to be found stuck to Q after a slide and vice versa. This can be verified directly by experiment even in the case when P and Q are the same materials, such as copper, if one slab of the copper contains some of a radioactive isotope of the metal.

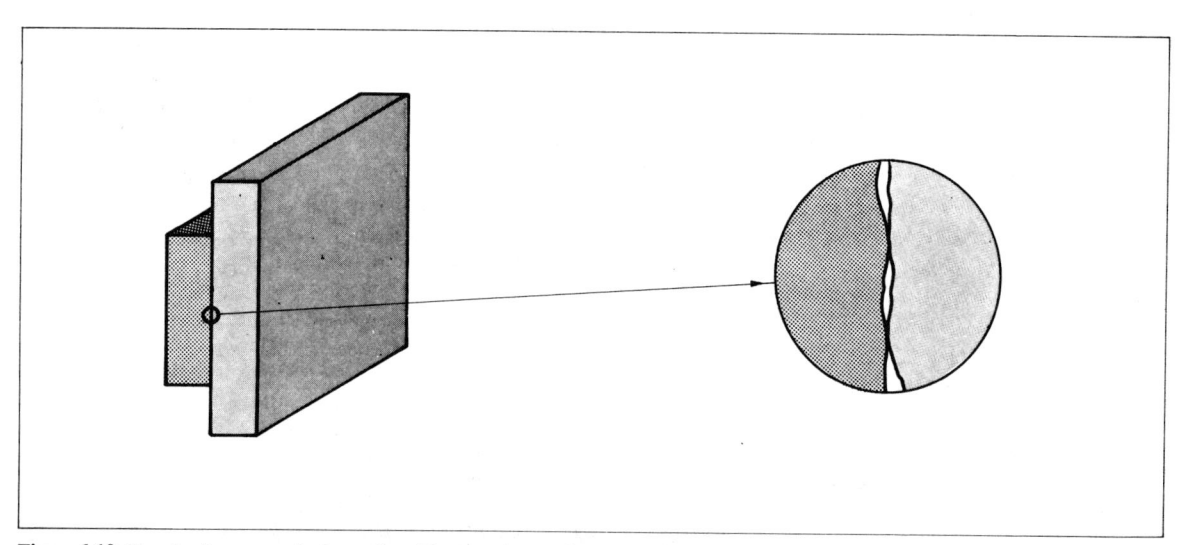

Figure 6-10 Two bodies are pushed together. The actual areas in contact in the magnified diagram are only a small fraction of the apparent contact areas. Over these areas the two materials are 'cold-welded'.

This microscopic view of dry friction predicts that if the force (perpendicular to N) exerted by one surface on the other is F when the surfaces are in relative motion, then

(a) as A' is independent of A, F will be independent of the *apparent* area of contact A for a given normal contact force

(b) as
$$F \propto A' \quad \text{and} \quad A' \propto N,$$
$$F \text{ will be } \propto N,$$

or
$$F = \text{(constant)} N,$$

that is,
$$\frac{F}{N} = \text{constant}$$

(c) F will be independent of the relative speed between the two surfaces but will be equal to the value to which F rises just before the relative movement takes place.

These predictions are all susceptible to experimental tests, but when the macroscopic phenomenon of dry friction is investigated it immediately becomes apparent that no such simple rules hold exactly. The first and second predictions do, however, hold well enough to have been discovered 450 years ago (by Leonardo da Vinci) but it is so difficult to *reproduce surface conditions* that the second can be thought of as only a rough guide. If lubricants and impurities are completely removed, and the surfaces made smooth, then far from producing reliable results for F/N, the surfaces tend to stick together completely!

To test the first and second predictions suppose a block (made so that different faces present different areas of contact) of a given material P is found to slide with constant speed down a slope made of material Q, when the angle of the slope is α (see figure 6-11).

(a) If we find that the block slides with the same constant speed down the slope, whatever the value of A in contact with the slope, we can deduce that the friction force F has not changed. We know that $F = W \sin \alpha$ in each case (because the block is in equilibrium) and we have altered neither W nor α. Hence F is independent of A.

(b) If we find that the block slides with the same constant speed down the slope, even if it now carries a load which makes it n times heavier, we can deduce that the friction force F (still equal to the resolved part down the slope of the weight) is n times larger. Since we know that N is also n times larger, we know that the ratio F/N is constant, and independent of the weight of the block.

Hence we can (and, within the limits of experimental error, will be able to) verify the first two predictions. We use the constancy of the ratio F/N to define

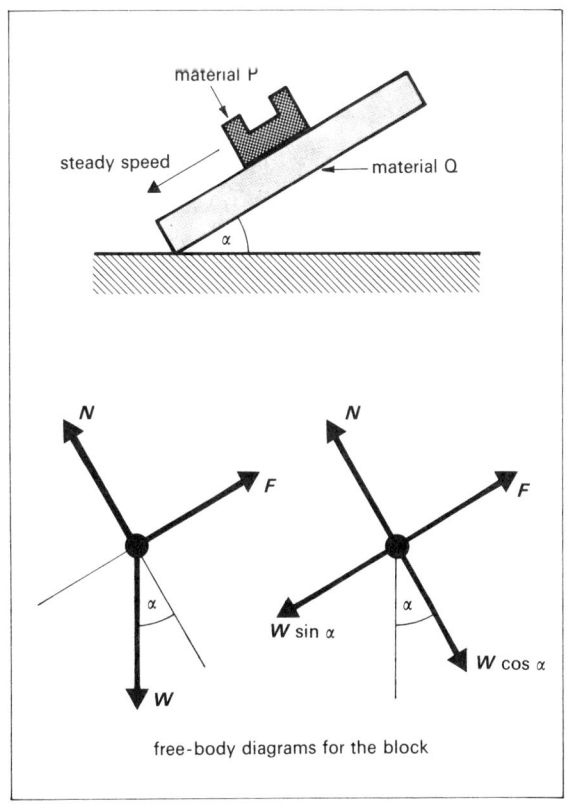

Figure 6-11 A body slides down a slope at a steady speed. The forces acting on the body, treated as a particle, are shown on two free-body diagrams: the second of these shows the resolved parts of W.

the coefficient of kinetic friction μ_k
$$= \frac{\textit{size of tangential friction force}}{\textit{size of normal contact force}} = \frac{F}{N} \quad [6\text{-}2]$$

for one specified material sliding on another specified material.

(c) The first part of the third prediction states in effect that μ_k is independent of the size of the speed of sliding. This is not found to be so, experiment generally showing that μ_k decreases as the relative speed v of the two surfaces increases. One suggested explanation is that the surface molecules in both P and Q vibrate more violently as v increases, but the effects are so complex that it is not safe to generalize. Nor does experimental evidence support the second part of the third prediction: that the size of F during sliding is equal to its value just before the onset of relative motion. If the angle of the slope is gradually increased it is found that the body does not start to slide until the angle is greater than the angle α at which it will move down the slope at a constant speed. The size of F is greater

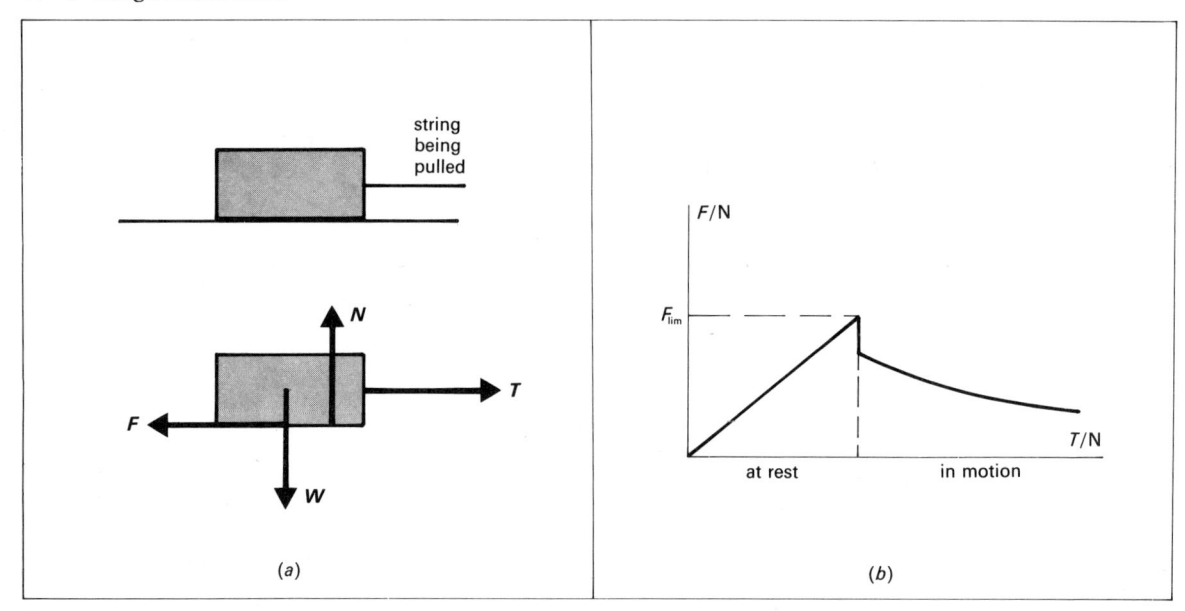

Figure 6-12 In (a) a block is pulled horizontally to the right. Table 6-1 shows the way in which F depends on the coefficients of friction and how the equilibrium of the body is broken if T is increased gradually from zero. In (b) as T becomes large the body will accelerate rapidly to high speeds and the frictional force decreases as shown.

just before the onset of relative motion than during sliding. Let us call this maximum, or *limiting*, value F_{lim}: we define

$$\text{the coefficient of static friction } \mu_s = \frac{F_{\text{lim}}}{N} \quad [6\text{-}3]$$

for one specified material in contact with another specified material.

It is found that μ_s is always greater than μ_k.

As these experiments are notoriously unreliable (and we should not be expecting neat mathematical rules for all the phenomena we meet) the values for the coefficients are vague. Typically, for steel on steel,

$$\mu_s \approx 0.7$$

$$\mu_k \approx \left.\begin{matrix} 0.5 \text{ slow} \\ 0.2 \text{ very fast} \end{matrix}\right\} \text{ relative motion.}$$

Figure 6-12 summarizes the above discussion and table 6-1 relates the graph to the coefficients of static and kinetic friction.

Frictional forces occur in a wide variety of situations but always act so as to oppose or prevent the onset of relative motion between two surfaces which are in contact; they are always perpendicular to N, the normal contact force. Bodies, like human beings or motor cars, move by *using* frictional forces; they try to slide their feet

Value of T	Value of F	What happens to the block	
zero	zero	at rest	equilibrium
$< \mu_s N$	$= T$	at rest	
$= \mu_s N$	$= T$	at rest	
$= \mu_k N$	$= T$	constant speed to right	
$> \mu_k N$	$= \mu_k N$	acceleration to right	

Table 6-1

or wheels backwards over the ground and frictional forces oppose this motion. Such animals and vehicles cannot pull or push *themselves*: an external force is always needed. Can you drag yourself forward by the scruff of your neck or pick yourself up by your shoelaces? Thus a boy standing on a rough floor can walk (accelerate) forward only by trying to push the floor *backwards* with one of his feet; by Newton's third law the floor will exert a push of the same size on his foot, but in the opposite direction, that is, forward. If the floor is smooth the boy must be careful not to push too hard, so as to use the limiting (maximum) frictional force available just before his foot slips. The push his foot exerts on the floor will, of course, accelerate the floor backwards; this acceleration is negligibly small unless the floor forms part of a body having a low mass, such as a rowing boat or a small truck.

The phenomenon of dry friction is often a nuisance and attempts are made to lower its effect with non-stick materials such as Teflon or Fluon or by using rollers; both ideas are in common use, for example in curtain rails.

▶ **Example 6-3** Discuss the frictional forces acting on a bicycle wheel and on the ground when (*a*) the wheel is rolling (that is, free-wheeling) along a horizontal road, (*b*) the wheel is increasing in speed, (*c*) the wheel is being braked.

We must first discuss the origin of the frictional forces. Consider a wheel being pulled horizontally along the ground by its axle. It will rotate because a horizontal force (as well as a normal contact force) will be exerted on it by the ground. This force has two constituents: there is a static friction force (since there is no relative motion between the wheel and the ground) and there is a rolling friction force (due to the deformation of the wheel and the ground). The first of these acts so as to rotate the wheel, and the second acts so as to tend to prevent the forward movement of the wheel. Thus both act so as to oppose its forward movement, and are represented by S and R in figure 6-13. Q is the normal contact force exerted by the ground on the wheel. Q', S', and R' are the forces exerted by the wheel on the ground. By Newton's third law, $Q = -Q'$, $R = -R'$, and $S = -S'$.

Now let us consider a driven wheel, for example a bicycle wheel to which a torque is applied at its axle by means of pedals and cranks. If it is touching the ground, the frictional force exerted on the wheel by the ground will tend to stop it rotating; this frictional force will act as shown in figure 6-14 and will therefore push the wheel in the *forward* direction. The rolling friction force R still acts; for acceleration of the wheel, S must be greater than R. Q', S', and R' are the forces exerted by the wheel on the ground. By Newton's third law, $Q = -Q'$, $S = -S'$, and $R = -R'$.

Finally, let us consider a braked wheel, for example a rotating bicycle wheel to which a torque is applied by means of brake pads at its rim. The ground now exerts a frictional force on the wheel to tend to keep it rotating at the same speed as before; as this must act as shown in figure 6-15, it acts in the *backward* direction. It is the same kind of force as S in figure 6-14. The rolling friction force R still acts. The paired forces are again equal in size by Newton's third law.

Thus for

(*a*) a rolling wheel, S is small and opposes forward motion

(*b*) a driven wheel, S is large and is the external accelerating force on the wheel; it is in the direction of the acceleration

(*c*) a braked wheel, S is large and is the external braking force on the wheel; it is in the backward direction. ◀

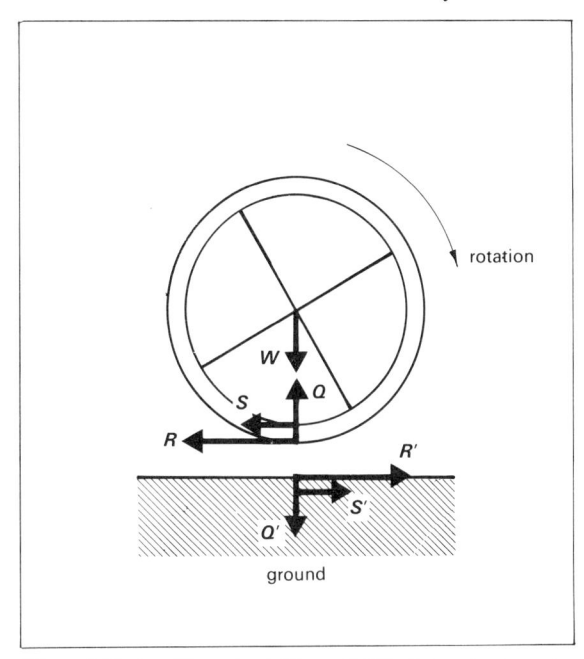

Figure 6-13 A rolling wheel. The pull W' of the wheel on the Earth is omitted.

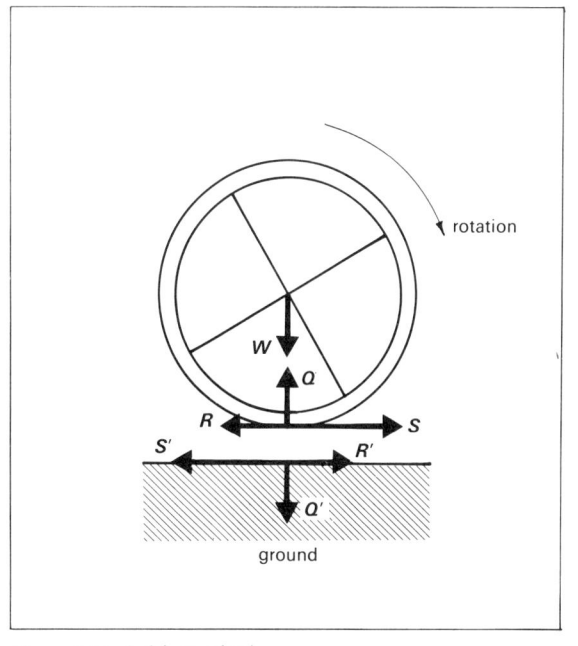

Figure 6-14 A driven wheel.

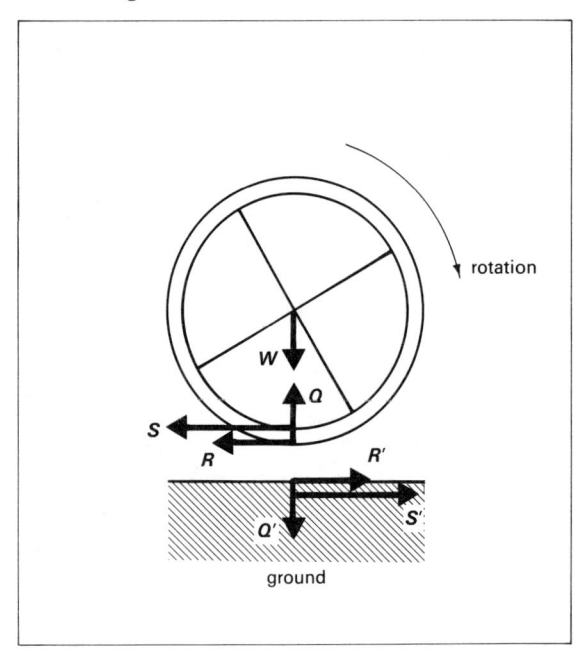

Figure 6-15 A braked wheel.

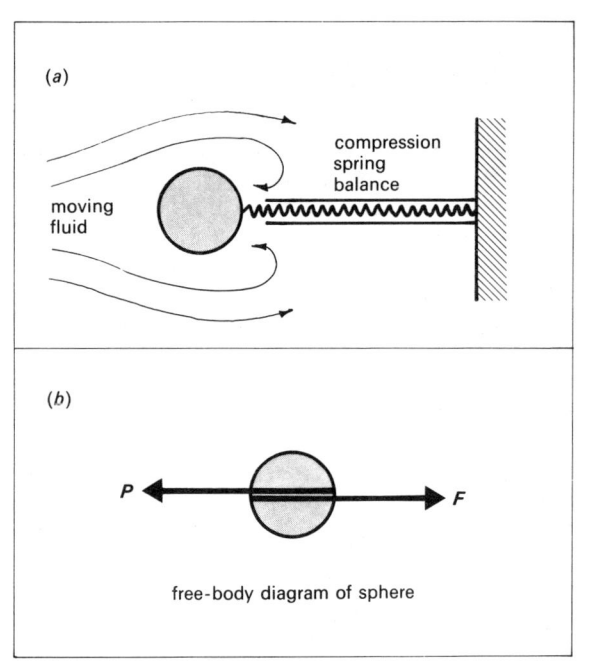

Figure 6-16 (*a*) A body, in this case a sphere, held at rest in a stream of fluid. Only horizontal forces are shown in the free-body diagram (*b*).

6-5 Fluid friction

When a body moves through a fluid with a velocity v there is a frictional force F, the push of the fluid on the body, which acts in the opposite direction to v. More generally v is the relative velocity of the body and the surrounding liquid or gas. From experiments of the sort illustrated in figure 6-16 the size of $F(=P)$ for a range of values of v can be measured for bodies of simple shapes. In general it is found that

$$F = av + bv^2,$$

a relationship which is illustrated in figure 6-17.

This implies that at sufficiently low speeds

$$F(\text{low speed}) \approx av \qquad [6\text{-}4]$$

and that at sufficiently high speeds

$$F(\text{high speed}) \approx bv^2. \qquad [6\text{-}5]$$

The size of a and b depends on the dimensions and the shape of the body and on the nature of the fluid. (See Exercises 6-21 and 6-22.) A more detailed analysis shows that equation 6-4 represents the action of non-conservative internal forces between adjacent layers of the fluid while equation 6-5 is associated with the turbulent motion of the fluid clearly noticeable at high relative speeds. It is

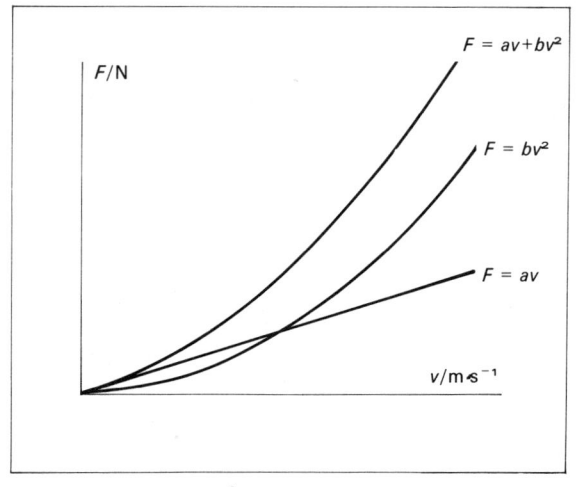

Figure 6-17 $F = av + bv^2$.

usual to refer to the first of these as a *fluid friction* or *viscous* force and to refer to the second as a *fluid resistance* force (air resistance for example).

For cars, bullets, children on bicycles, and so on—the common bodies we meet in mechanics—equation 6-5 is the relevant one, the term av being negligible. We shall sometimes omit these fluid friction and fluid resistance forces, assuming them to be negligible. A case where they are obviously not so is given in Example 6-4 below.

▶ **Example 6-4** A car of mass 1200 kg accelerates from rest to a speed of $8.0 \, \text{m s}^{-1}$ in 2.5 s. Calculate the average horizontal force which the ground exerts on the car, assuming that at these low speeds the fluid and other frictional forces are negligible. If the engine is used so that the ground continues to exert the same forward horizontal force on the car, find the value of b in the equation $F(\text{high speed}) = bv^2$ when the car reaches its maximum speed of $50 \, \text{m s}^{-1}$.

The car's average acceleration $= 8.0 \, \text{m s}^{-1}/2.5 \, \text{s} = 3.2 \, \text{m s}^{-2}$. The average horizontal force, F, on the car is given by Newton's second law:

$$F = (1200 \, \text{kg})(3.2 \, \text{m s}^{-2})$$
$$= 3.8 \times 10^3 \, \text{N}.$$

The car reaches its maximum speed and stops accelerating when the resultant horizontal force on it is zero, that is when the forward force exerted on it by the ground is equal to the total resistance force exerted on it by the air. Then

$$bv^2 = 3.8 \times 10^3 \, \text{N}.$$

Since we know that the speed of the car is then $50 \, \text{m s}^{-1}$, we can write

$$b = \frac{3.8 \times 10^3 \, \text{N}}{(50 \, \text{m s}^{-1})^2}$$
$$= 1.5 \, \text{kg m}^{-1}.$$

The value of b would be different for different cars: it is one of the factors which determines a car's maximum speed. ◀

6-6 Applying Newton's second law

For a particle of fixed mass m,

[5-2] $\qquad m\mathbf{a} = \sum \mathbf{F}.$

The acceleration, $\mathbf{a}$ is best written first as it is the observable quantity, the presence of which defines the existence of a resultant force $\sum \mathbf{F}$ in the direction of $\mathbf{a}$. As this is a vector equation we can either use the direction of $\mathbf{a}$ and write

$$m\mathbf{a} = \sum (\text{forces resolved parallel to } \mathbf{a})$$

or, for motion in a plane, resolve the acceleration into two resolved parts in directions x and y and write

$$ma_x = \sum F_x \qquad ma_y = \sum F_y. \qquad [6\text{-}6]$$

A procedure for using these equations is as follows.

(a) Choose a body (as a first step this act of choosing cannot be stressed too strongly).

(b) Draw a free-body diagram of the chosen body, marking all the external forces on the body. Ensure that each force is a genuine force by trying to express it as 'the push (or pull) of A on B'.

(c) Mark the acceleration $\mathbf{a}$ on the body.

(d) In numerical problems make sure that forces are expressed in newtons.

(e) Apply Newton's second law in the form expressed in equation 5-2.

Some examples of this procedure follow.

▶ **Example 6-5** A lift is rising with an acceleration of $0.50 \, \text{m s}^{-2}$. What is the push of the lift on a man of mass 60 kg who is standing on the floor of the lift? Take $g = 9.8 \, \text{N kg}^{-1}$.

We draw a free-body diagram for the man (figure 6-18), and mark on it his acceleration and the forces exerted on him. These are

W, the pull of the Earth $= (60 \, \text{kg})(9.8 \, \text{N kg}^{-1})$
N, the push of the floor of the lift, which we have to find.

Using $m\mathbf{a} = \sum \mathbf{F}$ we have

$$(60 \, \text{kg})(0.50 \, \text{m s}^{-2}) = N - 60 \times 9.8 \, \text{N}$$

therefore $\qquad N = 60 \times 10.3 \, \text{N}$
$$= 6.2 \times 10^2 \, \text{N}.$$

The push of the man on the floor of the lift is also $6.2 \times 10^2 \, \text{N}$, though in the opposite direction to N: this is a result of Newton's third law. ◀

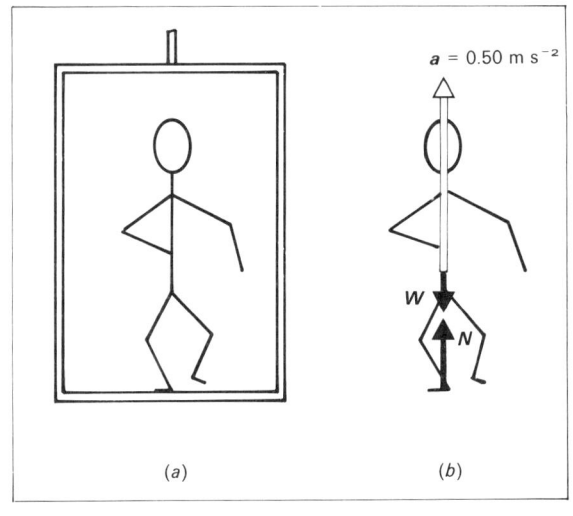

Figure 6-18 (a) Situation diagram. (b) Free-body diagram.

6 Using Newton's laws

▶ **Example 6-6** A plumb-line hangs from the roof of a train which is moving on a horizontal track. If the plumb-line makes an angle of 3° with the vertical, what is the acceleration of the train?

Let the mass of the plumb-bob be m: then its weight, W is mg. The *only* other force acting on it is the pull of the string, T, as shown in the free-body diagram (figure 6-19). The acceleration of the bob is entirely horizontal (since the motion is horizontal and linear); let its value be a. Using $ma = \sum F$ we have

resolving vertically $\quad 0 = T\cos 3° - mg$

resolving horizontally $\quad ma = T\sin 3°$,

so that $\quad \dfrac{a}{g} = \tan 3°$

and $\quad a = 0.052g$

in the direction shown (that is, opposite to the direction in which the bob swings).

If the bob swings parallel to the axis of the train, the train could be moving from left to right and speeding up, or from right to left and slowing down. If the bob swings perpendicular to the axis of the train, it must have a constant speed but be moving in a curve. If the bob swings in some other direction, the train is moving in a curve and either speeding up or slowing down. ◀

▶ **Example 6-7** A block of mass 2.0 kg rests on a rough horizontal table, the coefficient of friction μ between the surfaces being 0.40 (we shall assume that $\mu_s = \mu_k = \mu$). A massless string is tied to the block, passes over a frictionless massless pulley at the edge of the table, and supports a block of mass 4.0 kg. Does the system accelerate, and, if so, what is its acceleration? Take $g = 9.8 \, \text{N kg}^{-1}$.

We draw a free-body diagram (in figure 6-20) for *each* of the blocks. Consider the 2.0 kg block: it has no vertical acceleration, so that, using $ma = \sum F$ we have

$$0 = W_1 - R$$

Therefore

$$R = W_1 = (2.0\,\text{kg})(9.8\,\text{N kg}^{-1}) = 19.6\,\text{N}.$$

The maximum value of $F(= \mu R) = 0.40 \times 19.6\,\text{N} = 7.8\,\text{N}$. If there were equilibrium, T_1 would equal F, and T_2 would equal W_2. As $T_1 = T_2$ for this string, F would equal W_2. But $W_2 = 39.2\,\text{N}$, so that equilibrium is not possible.

Let the 4.0 kg mass have an acceleration a downwards: then the 2.0 kg mass will have an acceleration a hori-

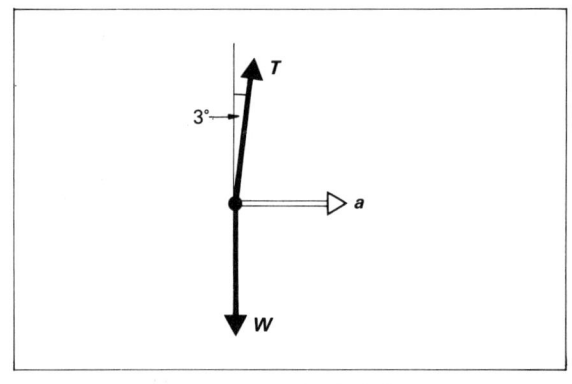

Figure 6-19 Free-body diagram for the bob.

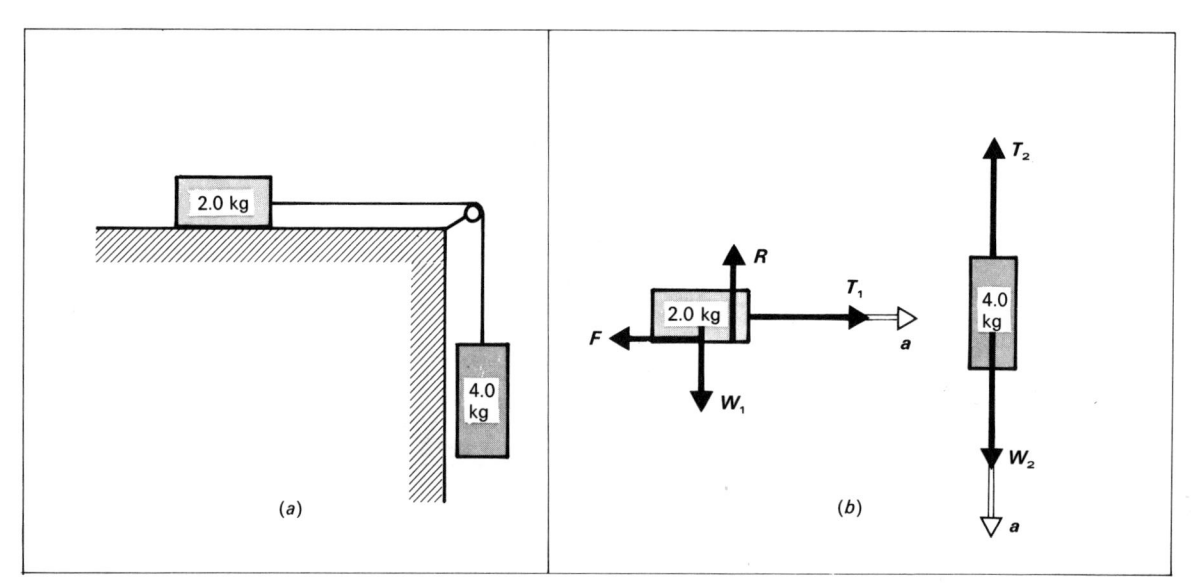

Figure 6-20 (*a*) Situation diagram. (*b*) Free-body diagrams.

zontally. For the 2.0 kg block, resolving horizontally

$$(2.0\,\text{kg})a = T_1 - 7.8\,\text{N}.$$

For the 4.0 kg block, resolving vertically

$$(4.0\,\text{kg})a = 39.2\,\text{N} - T_2.$$

Adding, and remembering that $T_1 = T_2$,

$$(6.0\,\text{kg})a = 31.4\,\text{N}$$

therefore $\quad a = 5.2\,\text{N}\,\text{kg}^{-1} = 5.2\,\text{m}\,\text{s}^{-2}.$

We could now find $T_1 = T_2$ by substituting in one of the earlier equations:

$$T_2 = W_2 - (4.0\,\text{kg})a$$
$$= 39.2\,\text{N} - 20.8\,\text{N}$$

therefore $\quad T_1 = T_2 = 18\,\text{N}.$ ◄

6-7 Centripetal forces

As discussed in Chapter 4, a particle moving in a curved path must be accelerating and thus according to Newton's second law must be acted upon by a resultant force in the direction of the acceleration. For motion in a circle of radius r at a constant speed v, the instantaneous acceleration is of size

[4-14] [4-15] $\qquad a = \dfrac{v^2}{r} = r\omega^2.$

The sum of the forces inward along the radius, which is the direction of $\boldsymbol{a}$, must by Newton's second law be

$$m\dfrac{v^2}{r} \quad \text{or} \quad mr\omega^2.$$

It is this resultant which is called a *centripetal* force acting on the rotating particle of mass m. A centripetal force is therefore not a special kind of force but merely a name given to a force which acts towards a central point.

The size of this force is constant in uniform horizontal motion, and this can be demonstrated with a puck as shown in figure 6-21, provided the centre pivot is itself quite free to rotate. In this example the centripetal force consists only of the pull of the spring on the puck. Some other types of force which can provide the necessary pull or push are

(a) the frictional push of the ground on a bicycle turning a corner

(b) the pull of the Earth on a satellite moving in a circular orbit

(c) the normal contact push of the wall on a wall-of-death rider's motorcycle

(d) the electromagnetic pull on an electron moving in a plane perpendicular to a magnetic field.

According to Newton's third law of motion the body (for example the spring tied to the puck) exerting the centripetal force on the rotating particle will itself experience a force equal in size but opposite in direction to the centripetal force. This is called a *centrifugal* force. So in figure 6-21 we have:

T, the pull of the spring on the puck—this is a centripetal force; and

T', the pull of the puck on the spring—this is a centrifugal force.

By Newton's third law, $\boldsymbol{T} = -\boldsymbol{T'}.$

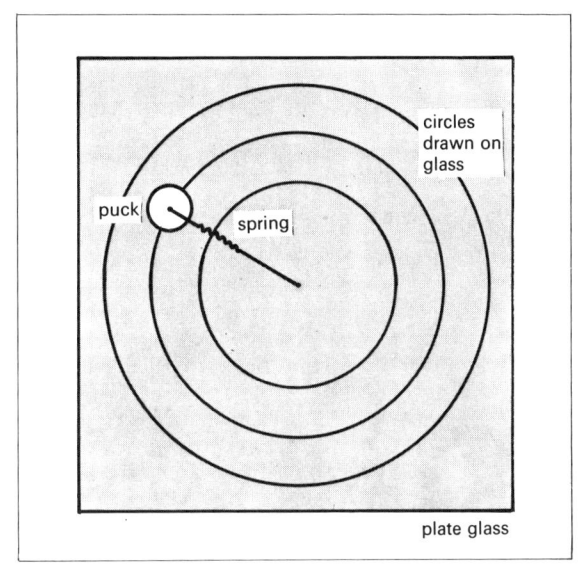

Figure 6-21 If it is possible, by giving the puck a certain speed, to make it follow a circle, that is to move so that the pull of the spring on it is constant, then the constancy of the size of the centripetal force in circular motion is demonstrated. It follows from Newton's second law that we are also verifying that the acceleration is constant in size.

The centrifugal force is seldom of any interest to us. The pull of the string on the support at the centre of the circle is another centrifugal force but this is not directly related to T or T', although it could be roughly the same size as them if the string is light. The reader should consider the other situations listed above and try to locate any centrifugal forces. He should find that these do *not* act on the body which is rotating.

90 6 Using Newton's laws

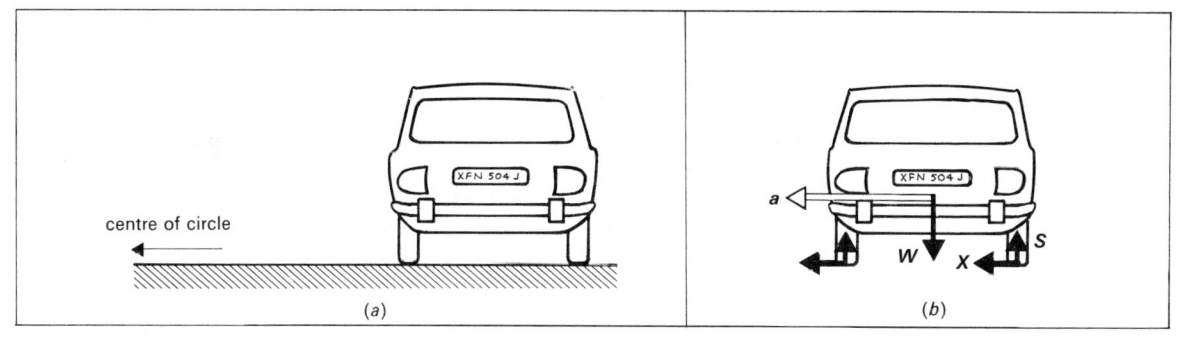

Figure 6-22 A car turns a corner. (a) Situation diagram, and (b) free-body diagram for forces in the radial vertical plane.

▶ **Example 6-8** A car of mass 1000 kg is to be driven along a horizontal circular track of radius 40 m at a speed of $10\,\mathrm{m\,s^{-1}}$. What centripetal frictional force must be exerted by the ground? If the air resistance force is 2000 N, what is the least possible value of the coefficient of friction between the tyres and the road? Take $g = 9.8\,\mathrm{N\,kg^{-1}}$.

In figure 6-22 we have drawn a free-body diagram for the car. The car's acceleration a is given by

$$a = \frac{v^2}{r} = \frac{(10\,\mathrm{m\,s^{-1}})^2}{40\,\mathrm{m}} = 2.5\,\mathrm{m\,s^{-2}}.$$

Resolving horizontally, using $ma = \sum F$, we have

$$(1000\,\mathrm{kg})(2.5\,\mathrm{m\,s^{-2}}) = X$$

therefore $\qquad X = 2500\,\mathrm{N}$.

Since the air resistance is 2000 N, the *forward* frictional force is also 2000 N, so that the total frictional force $F = \sqrt{(2000^2 + 2500^2)}\,\mathrm{N} = 3200\,\mathrm{N}$.

Resolving vertically, using $ma = \sum F$, we have

$$0 = W - S$$

therefore $\qquad S = (1000\,\mathrm{kg})(9.8\,\mathrm{N\,kg^{-1}})$

$$= 9800\,\mathrm{N}.$$

Since the maximum value of the friction force F is μS, the least possible value of $\mu = F/S = 3200\,\mathrm{N}/9800\,\mathrm{N} = 0.33$. ◀

▶ **Example 6-9** A switchback railway at a fairground includes a 'hump' which is part of a vertical circle of radius 8.0 m (figure 6-23). What is the highest speed at which a car may pass over this hump if it is not to leave the rails? Take $g = 9.8\,\mathrm{m\,s^{-2}}$.

Let the speed of the car be v at the top of the hump, and the radius of the hump be r. Then the car's acceleration is given by $a = v^2/r$. Resolving (in figure 6-23) vertically for the car, using $ma = \sum F$, we have

$$ma = mg - S.$$

There will be contact between the car and the rails provided that $S > 0$;

that is if $\qquad mg > ma$
if $\qquad g > v^2/r$
if $\qquad v^2 < gr$
or if $\qquad v < \sqrt{(gr)}$.

When $r = 8.0\,\mathrm{m}$

$$v < \sqrt{(9.8\,\mathrm{m\,s^{-2}})(8.0\,\mathrm{m})}$$

that is $\qquad v < 8.9\,\mathrm{m\,s^{-1}}$.

If $v = 8.9\,\mathrm{m\,s^{-1}}$, $S = 0$, but the weight W is such that it can give the car the inward acceleration needed to move at this speed in a circle of this radius. Thus $v \leqslant 8.9\,\mathrm{m\,s^{-1}}$ for the car not to leave the rails. ◀

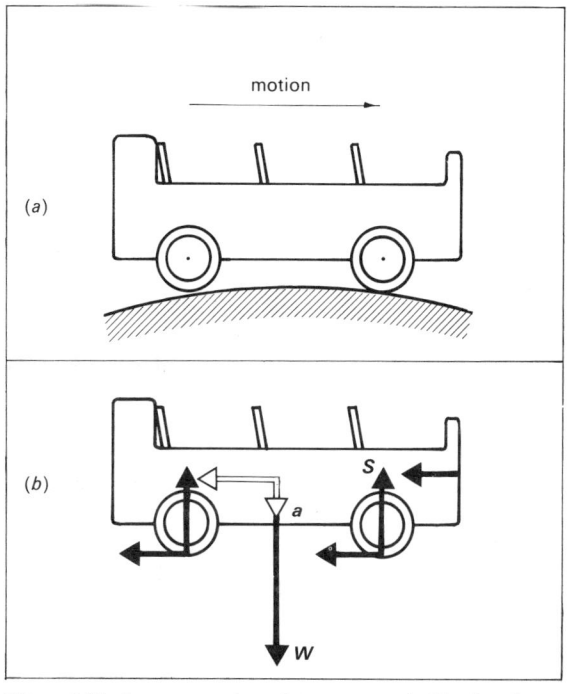

Figure 6-23 A car runs over a hump on a switchback railway. (a) Situation diagram, and (b) free-body diagram.

6-8 Mass, weight, and weightlessness

At an elementary stage students sometimes ask questions like 'But what *is* the difference between mass and weight?' implying that the difference, if any, is subtle and obscure. We hope that having read this and the previous chapter the reader will realize that mass and weight are totally different quantities! Mass is the inertia of a body, and weight is the pull of the Earth on the body. (In some books weight is defined as the push of a body on its support—and this can clearly be zero even in a gravitational field. The word weightlessness derives from this definition. We shall continue to define weight as the pull of the Earth on a body, as we have done so far.)

From this we see that

(*a*) mass is a scalar, but weight is a vector

(*b*) mass and weight have dimensions of M and MLT^{-2} respectively, and units kg and N

(*c*) mass (in Newtonian mechanics) is an intrinsic and invariable property of a body, but weight depends on the distance of the body from the Earth (or some other gravitationally attracting body).

'But', the student may insist, 'can I not measure both mass and weight with a beam balance?'

When we use a beam balance we place a body in each pan. When a balance is achieved the weights of the two bodies must be the same. As the gravitational acceleration is the same at each end of the beam then their masses must also be equal. Thus a beam balance does compare both weights and masses.

The weight of a body is one of its most familiar properties: for example, we lift a body and in doing so exert a force in opposition to the pull of the Earth on it. Mass is an equally familiar property but is less easily recognized. But consider a hammer: whenever we use one we are using the inertia or mass of the hammer, its unwillingness to be stopped. Our hammer would work equally well on the Moon or at a place where there was a negligible gravitational attraction. Again, a spin-drier relies on the inertia of the water held by a piece of fabric. The water will continue to move in a straight line rather than undergo a high centripetal acceleration unless a resultant centripetal force acts on it, and, as such a force does not always arise, the clothes are spun dry. A similar lack of the required centripetal force explains the action of the centrifuge used in chemical analysis. In each case we are using the inertial mass of the body and this rotating technique would again prove equally practicable on the Moon.

Perhaps a lot of the confusion over the quantities mass and weight stemmed from the use of gravitational units for force, in which a body with a mass of *x* kilograms was said to have a weight of *x* kilogram-force or *x* kilogram-weight. The problem was really one of language and is avoided in this text by not using gravitational units. Consider a similar situation: a *year* is a unit of time, a *light-year* is a unit of distance (the distance covered by light waves travelling in a vacuum for a year). Looking at the two units, year and light-year, we might find them at first a little confusing, but our familiarity with the ideas of time and distance prevents us asking 'But what *is* the difference between time and distance?' The question would be absurd: also absurd is the question 'But what *is* the difference between mass and weight?' The equivalence between inertial mass and gravitational mass is discussed in Section 14-9.

Free fall

When the only force acting on a body is the pull of the Earth on it, the body is said to be in *a state of free fall*. Ignoring air resistance, a ball thrown into the air is in free fall at all stages during its motion: on the way up, at the top of its flight, and on the way down.

We can perceive our own weight only indirectly. It would be surprising if we could expect to *feel* the pull of the Earth on each particle of our body any more than we could expect to feel the molecular bombardment of the molecules of the air on our skin. If a force of similar size, however, acts on a small area of our bodies (for example the normal contact push of the floor on the soles of our feet), we do feel it. If temporarily we feel no such supporting force the brain mistakenly thinks that we have no weight either. It is in this way that the idea of *weightlessness* arises. A person might normally *feel* weightless when, for example, he

(*a*) travels in a car over a hump-back bridge, or in an aeroplane entering an air pocket, and he leaves his seat

(*b*) treads on a non-existent floor in the dark (for example when meeting an unexpected step downwards)

(*c*) jumps off a springboard or trampoline.

A peculiar feeling in the stomach is associated with all these states. (Again, we must point out that it *is* legitimate to *define* the weight of a body as the push of the body on its support; in this case the above discussion is not valid.)

▶ **Example 6-10** A man in a space capsule in orbit around the Earth places a block on a spring balance fixed to the floor of the capsule. What does the balance read (that is, what is the push of the block on the balance)?

Let the mass of the capsule and all its contents (except the block) be m_1 and let the mass of the block be m_2. Let their weights at this point in the Earth's gravitational field

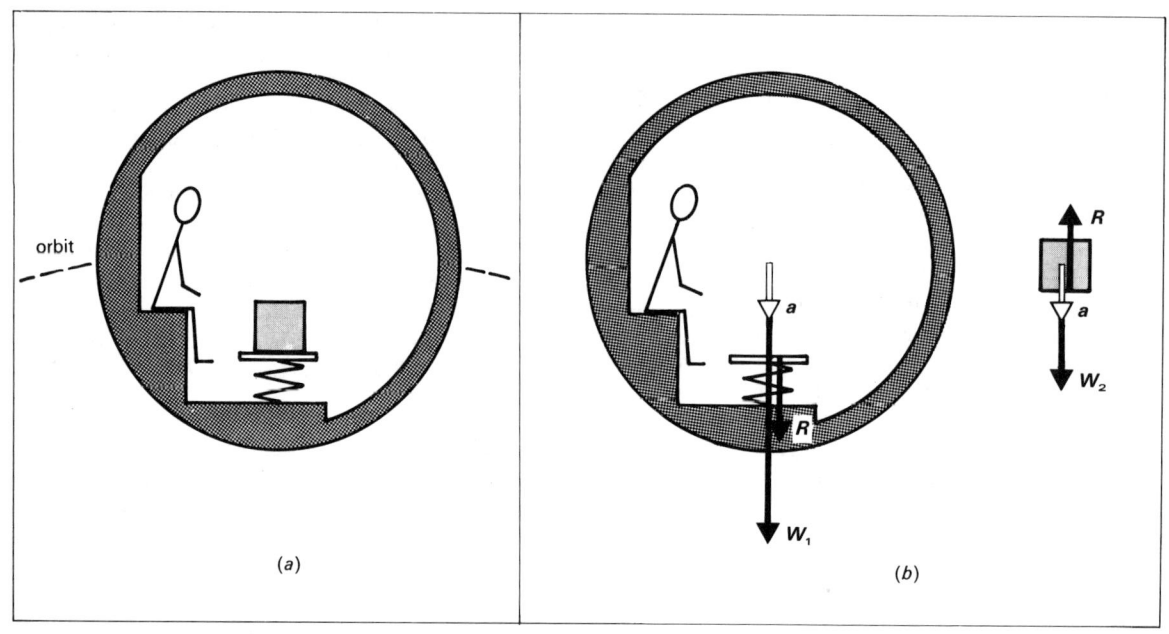

Figure 6-24 A spaceman orbits the Earth in a space capsule and observes the reading on a spring balance. (*a*) Situation diagram, and (*b*) free-body diagrams.

be W_1 and W_2. Then $W_1/W_2 = m_1/m_2$ (see page 188). Both the capsule and the block have the same acceleration towards the centre of the Earth: let this be **a**. If the block and the balance exert a push R on each other, as shown in the free-body diagram in figure 6-24, then, using $m\mathbf{a} = \sum \mathbf{F}$, we have

for the capsule and contents $\quad W_1 + R = m_1 a$
for the block $\quad W_2 - R = m_2 a$
so that $\quad \dfrac{W_1 + R}{W_2 - R} = \dfrac{m_1}{m_2}.$

But we know that $W_1/W_2 = m_1/m_2$ and so $R = 0$.

Thus the spring balance reads zero. Nevertheless the block *does* have a weight (or else it could not be orbiting the Earth). ◀

None of the bodies (including the man) in the space capsule in Example 6-10 would need to have any force acting on it other than its weight, so that all bodies in a space capsule orbiting the Earth are in a state of free fall. These artificial satellites are of great interest as they enable us to study the psychological and physiological effects of free fall on human beings over *long* periods of time.

6-9 Accelerating frames of reference

If you sit in a train with a ball at rest on the table in front of you its property of inertia tells you to expect it to remain at rest unless a resultant force acts on it. A person on a platform of a station through which the train is passing makes the same observation about the ball, substituting the phrase 'moving with uniform velocity' for 'at rest'. Both you in the train and the observer on the platform are (ignoring the rotation of the Earth) making observations in inertial frames of reference (see also Section 3-9). But suppose the train driver applies his brakes, slowing the train? The person on the platform sees the ball roll across the table and says that its inertia demands that it should do so in order to keep its velocity constant: that is, he believes that Newton's first law applies and he expects it to be obeyed by the ball. On the other hand, you, in the train (facing forwards), see the ball roll away from you. What are you to deduce? That Newton's first law is not true? Or that there is a force (whose origin is not obvious) causing the ball to accelerate? The first alternative seems most undesirable, while the second introduces an element of fiction into our understanding of force. Looking out of the window, however, you may realize that for the person on the platform there is no difficulty. Newton's first law seems, to him, to be obeyed, and the reason that it does not seem to you to be obeyed is that the train is accelerating. The frame of reference fixed to the accelerating train is called a non-inertial frame of reference: for measurements made relative to it, Newton's first and second laws do *not* hold. The same reasoning explains why you must exert forces on the ball in order to keep it at rest relative to the train when the train accelerates (remember that an acceleration means any rate of change of velocity, whether the direction is changing or the speed is increasing or decreasing). To summarize: we must not in Newtonian mechanics try to argue from observations made in accelerating (that is non-inertial) frames of reference. We must amend the third of our rules (listed in Section 6-6) for applying Newton's second law to read: mark the acceleration *a measured in an inertial frame of reference*.

As the Earth is rotating, points on its surface are accelerating centripetally. The effect on freely falling bodies of ignoring this rotation is discussed in Section 5-7. We can show by setting up a *Foucault pendulum* that if we refer our measurements to a reference frame fixed to the Earth's surface Newton's first law does not hold. The plane of swing of this long simple pendulum with a massive bob will, if it continues to swing for some hours, rotate relative to the Earth beneath it. Rather than invoke a fictitious force to explain this motion we conclude that the pendulum is obeying Newton's law and swinging *without* rotating in an inertial frame of reference (sometimes called the frame of the fixed stars). Such a pendulum, incidentally, can be seen in the Science Museum in London. The size of the centripetal acceleration of a point on the Earth's surface is so small that for most purposes we

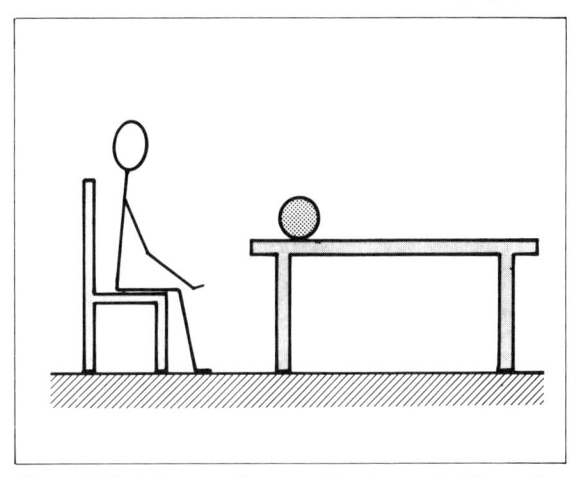

Figure 6-25 A diagram of a man sitting in a train. He watches as a ball, initially at rest on the table in front of him, accelerates away from him. The train must of course be accelerating, that is he is in a non-inertial frame of reference. What does he think if he cannot see the Earth?

can assume that axes fixed relative to the Earth will constitute an inertial frame of reference.

Although non-inertial forces have been dismissed as *fictitious forces*, that is not electromagnetic, gravitational, or nuclear forces, in the above treatment, it is true that they can be useful in certain fields of study to simplify complicated calculations. For example, *Coriolis forces* are invoked in the study of the motion of the Earth's oceans and atmosphere, and in calculations involving long-range missiles. These fictitious forces must not be confused with those which arise from the interaction of two bodies.

Bibliography

Derjaguin, B. V. (1960). 'The force between molecules.' *Scientific American* offprint number 266.

McDonald, J. E. (1952). 'The Coriolis effect.' *Scientific American* offprint number 839.

Tabor, D. (1968). 'Large scale properties of matter.' *Sources of physics teaching*, part 1. Taylor and Francis. This article is reprinted from *Contemporary Physics*.

Warren, J. W. (1971). 'Circular motion.' *Physics Education*, **6**, page 74.

Bowden, F. P. and Tabor, D. (1956). *Friction and lubrication*. Methuen. The microscopic nature of solid contact forces is central to this treatment.

Projects Physics (1971). Reader, Unit 1 *Concepts of motion*. Holt, Rinehart and Winston. Chapters 13 and 14 are of particular interest among a wealth of valuable material.

Resnick, R. and Halliday, D. (1966). *Physics*, part 1. John Wiley. A book of general usefulness which contains some penetrating questions at the end of each chapter.

Rogers, E. M. (1960). *Physics for the inquiring mind*. Oxford University Press. The vector nature of force is discussed in Chapter 3. Chapter 21 is about circular motion.

Sears, F. W. and Zemansky, M. W. (1964). *College physics*. Addison–Wesley. Chapter 2 on equilibrium is very relevant.

Tricker, R. A. R. and Tricker, B. J. K. (1968). *The science of movement.* Mills and Boon. A very readable non-mathematical text. The role of friction in movement is the theme of Chapter 2.

Whelan, P. M. and Hodgson, M. J. (1971). *Essential pre-university physics.* John Murray. Chapter 16 on the structure of matter is a concise summary of the way in which atoms and molecules interact.

8 mm film loop. 'Dynamics of circular motion.' Ealing Scientific. An air table is used to investigate the size of centripetal forces.

16 mm film. 'Experiments in force and motion.' Travelling Films. A film made for science teachers.

Exercises

Data (to be used unless otherwise directed):
$g = 10 \, \text{m s}^{-2} = 10 \, \text{N kg}^{-1}$.

6-1 For the following situations draw free-body diagrams for the bodies italicized (taking the ground to be part of the Earth):
 (a) a *man*, standing on the *Earth*, holds a *box* above his head
 (b) a *lorry* uses a heavy *rope* to tow a *car* along the *ground*
 (c) a *man*, standing on the *ground*, is putting a *shot*
 (d) a *man*, standing on the *ground*, is hitting a cricket *ball* with a *bat*
 (e) a *man* is pushing a *table* over rough *ground*
 (f) a *man* is shooting an *arrow* from a *bow*.

6-2 A brick rests on the Earth. Figure 6-26 shows (a) the situation diagram and (b) the free-body diagrams for the brick and the Earth; *P*, *Q*, *R*, and *S* are the forces which act. If you think any one force is equal to any other force, state which, and give reasons.

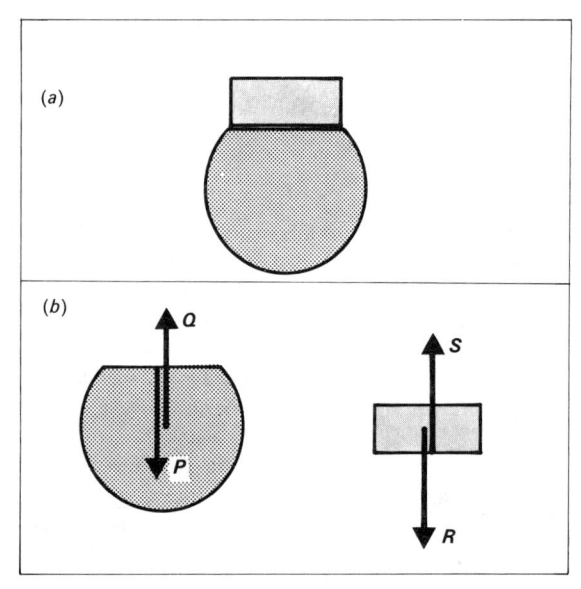

Figure 6-26

6-3 Must a clothes-line sag?

6-4 The coefficient of sliding friction, μ_k, for two surfaces, is generally less than the coefficient of static friction, μ_s. What bearing does this have on the braking of a motor car?

6-5 Can you think of a situation where a body is instantaneously at rest but is accelerating?

6-6 A block of stone has a mass of 20 kg, and rests on a horizontal surface, $\mu(= \mu_k = \mu_s)$ being 0.60. A man attaches a rope to the block and pulls horizontally. What happens if the pull of the rope on the block is
 (a) 100 N (b) 140 N (c) 220 N?

6-7 A massless rope passes over a smooth massless pulley and is attached at its ends to masses of 4.0 kg and 6.0 kg. What is the acceleration of the 4.0 kg mass, and what is the tension in the rope?

6-8 A man stands in a lift which is moving upwards and slowing down at $0.80 \, \text{m s}^{-2}$. If his mass is 70 kg, what is the push of the floor on his feet? What is the push of his feet on the floor? If the lift has a mass of 2000 kg, what is the tension in the supporting cable in the above situation?

6-9 Referring to Exercise 6-6, would there be any difference if the rope exerted a pull of 100 N on the block at an angle of 30° to the horizontal?

6-10 A brick of mass 2.0 kg is placed on a uniform slope which makes an angle of 20° with the horizontal. Find the normal contact force which the slope exerts on the brick. Taking $\mu_k = 0.25$, find the acceleration of the brick.

6-11 A locomotive whose mass is 1.0×10^5 kg pulls two coaches each of mass 5.0×10^4 kg. The ground exerts a forward force on the locomotive of 1.0×10^5 N and the resistance forces total 3.0×10^4 N on the locomotive and 1.0×10^4 N on each of the coaches. Find the acceleration of the train, and the pull which the locomotive exerts on the first coach, and the pull which the first coach exerts on the second coach.

6-12 You try to lift a mass with a thread which you think may break. Why do you try to lift it slowly?

6-13 A brick rests on a plank, the coefficient of friction between the surfaces being 0.20. If a man pushes the plank horizontally, what will happen to the brick if he gives the plank an acceleration of
 (a) $1.0 \, \text{m s}^{-2}$ (b) $1.5 \, \text{m s}^{-2}$ (c) $3.0 \, \text{m s}^{-2}$?

6-14 A tanker of mass 2.0×10^8 kg is being manoeuvred by five tugs as shown in figure 6-27. Each towing rope exerts a force of 2.0×10^6 N on the tanker, and the pulls exerted by the four at the side make an angle of $10°$ with the direction of the tanker's motion. If the water exerts a resistance force of 8.0×10^6 N on the tanker, what is its acceleration?

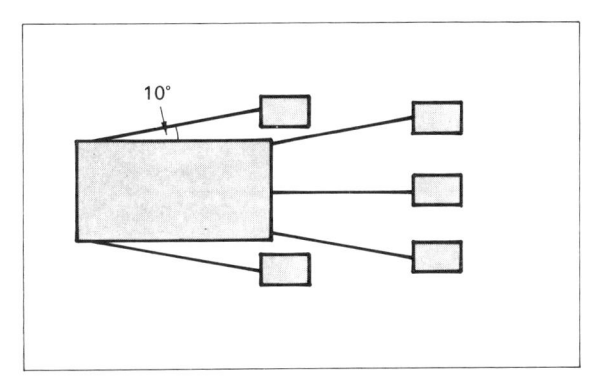

Figure 6-27 Five tugs tow a tanker.

6-15 A man stands on a weighing machine in a lift. The lift moves from rest on the ground floor to rest on the first floor. Making sensible guesses about the sizes of the quantities involved, state, and sketch a rough graph showing what he observes on the weighing machine. If the cable pulling the lift breaks and the lift falls freely, what does he observe on the weighing machine?

6-16 A block of mass 4.0 kg rests on a frictionless horizontal table and a string attached to it is pulled horizontally by a man who exerts a force of 60 N. What is the acceleration of the block? The same block rests on the same table but now the string is led (horizontally) over a smooth massless pulley at the edge of the table, and a 6.0 kg mass is attached to the free end, so this portion of the string hangs vertically. What is the acceleration of the 4.0 kg block?

6-17 A man stands on one pan of a large specially constructed beam balance in a stationary lift. Masses are placed on the other pan to achieve a balance. The lift moves from rest at the first floor to rest at the ground floor. How would the balance behave during the descent? What would be the man's sensations?

6-18 A block of mass 10 kg is placed on a slope which makes an angle of $20°$ with the horizontal and is given a velocity of $5.0\,\mathrm{m\,s^{-1}}$ up the slope. Assuming that the coefficient of sliding friction between the block and the slope is 0.20, find how far the block travels up the slope. How far up the slope would a 20 kg block travel if it were given the same initial velocity? μ_k is again 0.20.

6-19 A man whirls a stone round his head on the end of a string of length 2.0 m. Can the string lie in a horizontal plane? If the stone has a mass of 200 g, and the string will break if the tension in it exceeds 4 N, what is the smallest angle the string may make with the horizontal? What is then the speed of the stone?

6-20 A block of mass m slides down a frictionless slope which is inclined at an angle of α to the horizontal; the acceleration due to gravity is g. What is the block's acceleration? If the slope were rough, what would be the minimum value of the coefficient of static friction which would maintain the block in equilibrium?

6-21 Consider equation 6-4, $F(\text{low speed}) \approx av$. Suppose that the constant a were thought to be related to the linear dimension r of the body, the density ρ of the fluid, and the viscosity η of the fluid (η has dimensions $ML^{-1}T^{-1}$) by an equation of the form $a = kr^x \rho^y \eta^z$, where k is a dimensionless constant. Use the method of dimensions to find the values of x, y, and z.

6-22 A golfball has a mass of 0.045 kg and a radius of 21 mm. Assuming that the value of b in the equation $F(\text{high speed}) \approx bv^2$ is given by $b = 0.25\,\rho A$, where ρ is the density of the medium through which the body is moving, and A is its cross-sectional area, discuss whether a golfball will reach its terminal speed before reaching the ground if it is dropped from a height of 20 m. The density of air is $1.2\,\mathrm{kg\,m^{-3}}$.

6-23 The Moon has a radius of 1.7×10^6 m and the value of the acceleration due to gravity at its surface is $1.6\,\mathrm{m\,s^{-2}}$. At what speed would a rifle have to fire a bullet in order that the bullet might orbit the Moon at ground level?

6-24 A car is to be driven at a speed of $50\,\mathrm{m\,s^{-1}}$ round a circular racing track of radius 250 m. At what angle must the track be banked so that the ground need exert no sideways frictional force on the car?

6-25 A plumb-bob is attached to a massless string, and the other end is held by a man, the plumb-line hanging vertically in equilibrium. Can the man move his end of the plumb-line in a horizontal circle, with the plumb-bob describing a circle of equal radius vertically below his hand? Discuss.

6-26 Describe how the plumb-line in the carriage of Example 6-6 behaves while the train performs the following motions in succession:

(a) starts from rest with acceleration $0.25\,\mathrm{m\,s^{-2}}$ along a straight level track

(b) moves at a steady speed of $20\,\mathrm{m\,s^{-1}}$ along a straight level track

(c) without changing speed, rounds an unbanked curve in the form of a horizontal circular arc of radius 500 m

(d) moves in a straight line again, but down an incline whose angle α with the horizontal is given by $\sin \alpha = 0.050$, and slows down at $0.50\,\mathrm{m\,s^{-2}}$.

6-27 In a machine to investigate the effects on human beings when they are subjected to high accelerations, a cage is attached to a horizontal arm. A man is placed in the cage at a distance of 5.0 m from the vertical axis of rotation. What must be the angular velocity of the arm if the man is to have an acceleration of size $5g$? If the man has a mass of 80 kg, what is the size and direction of (a) the horizontal component of push of the cage on the man (b) the horizontal component of push of the man on the cage?

6-28 When a particle of electric charge q moves with speed v in a plane perpendicular to a magnetic field B, the field exerts a force Bqv on the particle in a direction at right angles to the velocity and in the plane perpendicular to B. An electron of mass 9.1×10^{-31} kg has a speed of $3.0 \times 10^7\,\mathrm{m\,s^{-1}}$ and is in a magnetic field of strength 2.0 T. Taking the size of the electron's charge as 1.6×10^{-19} C, find the radius of the circle in which it moves. (If B, q, and v are expressed in T, C, and m s^{-1} respectively, the force Bqv will be in N.) ●

6-29 When a car rounds an unbanked curve, a passenger tends to slide towards the outside of the curve. Why? Would the passenger tend to slide more or less if the car was increasing its speed as it rounded the curve?

6-30 Explain the action of a spin-drier.

6-31 If the Sun has a mass of 2.0×10^{30} kg, and can be considered to rotate about the centre of our galaxy with a period of 6.3×10^{15} s in a circular orbit of radius 3.0×10^{20} m, what is the force which the galaxy exerts on the Sun? ●

6-32 Figure 6-28 shows a simple pendulum in motion, and a free-body diagram for the bob. Why is it *not* true to say that 'resolving vertically, using $ma = \sum F$, $T \cos \theta - mg = 0$'? Find the value of T.

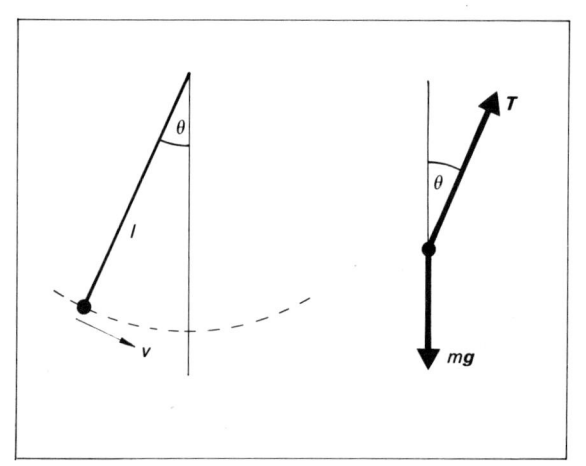

Figure 6-28 A simple pendulum, and a free-body diagram for the bob.

6-33 Figure 6-29 shows a *conical* pendulum in motion, and a free-body diagram for the bob. Find the value of T. (Think what would be the best direction to resolve.)

6-34 A coin is placed on a turntable 100 mm from the axis. The turntable is rotating at 45 rev min^{-1}. What is the least value of the coefficient of static friction at which the coin will not slide? If the coefficient of friction is not great enough, what will be the motion of the coin as seen by (*a*) a fly which is on the turntable and which rotates with it (*b*) a stationary man? ●

6-35 Some eggs are placed in a basket and the basket is (safely) rotated in a vertical plane so that the eggs describe a circle of radius 1.0 m. What is the least speed (at the top of the circle) at which the eggs must move? ●

6-36 Does the Moon fall towards the Earth? In your explanation use an everyday situation to help make your point.

6-37 A pendulum bob has a mass of 0.1 kg, and the string to which it is attached has a length of 1.0 m. When the pendulum is swinging, what is the tension in the string when
(*a*) the bob is at its lowest point, when its speed is 1.0 m s^{-1}
(*b*) the string makes an angle of 16° with the vertical, when the speed of the bob is 0.47 m s^{-1}? ●

6-38 A cube of sugar is placed on a rotating turntable, and the coefficient of static friction is great enough to prevent it sliding. When the speed of the turntable is gradually increased, the cube topples over. Why?

6-39 A man of mass 70.0 kg stands on a spring balance weighing machine at the Equator. What is the reading (in newtons) on the weighing machine? (Radius of Earth = 6.38×10^6 m, $g = 9.81$ m s^{-2}.) ●

6-40 At a fairground people enter a drum of radius 3.0 m which can rotate about a vertical axis with its own axis vertical. They stand with their backs against the inside wall of the drum, and the drum begins to rotate: the floor of the drum is removed when a certain value ω of the angular velocity of the drum is reached. Taking the coefficient of friction between the people's backs and the wall of the drum as 0.40, find the lowest possible value of ω at which the floor may be removed. How would a person in the drum describe his sensations?

6-41 Discover what is meant by saying that 'an aero-engine has a thrust of 45 000 lb'. Express the size of this force in newtons. ●

6-42 Write an essay on 'weightlessness'.

6-43 A Foucault pendulum is set up at the North Pole and set in oscillation above a straight line drawn on the ground. What is observed two hours later?

6-44 Refer to figure 6-25. The windows of the carriage are covered so that the man cannot see out, and he is sensible enough to realize that he may be in a non-inertial reference frame. He sees the ball roll towards him and thinks that this may be because the train is accelerating or because the train has begun to move uphill. Can he decide which of the two possibilities is correct? Do his own sensations help him to decide?

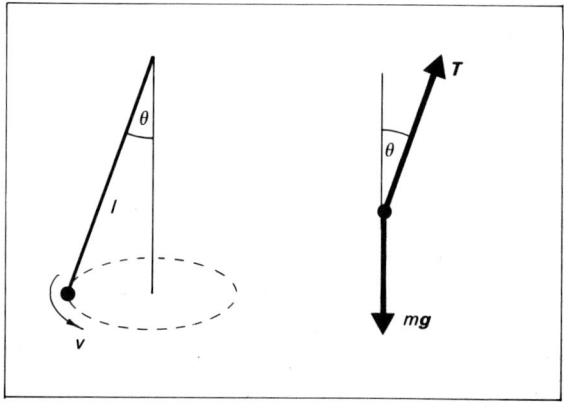

Figure 6-29 A conical pendulum, and a free-body diagram for the bob.

7 Work and kinetic energy

7-1 Work	97	7-6 Kinetic energy	106
7-2 The work done by a constant force	98	7-7 The work–energy theorem	107
7-3 The work done by a variable force	100	7-8 Internal work	110
7-4 Power	103	Bibliography	111
7-5 Principles of machines	103	Exercises	111

When we considered the motion of a particle, and then the forces which can alter its motion, we described force by using the idea that a single force causes a particle to accelerate (Newton's second law). But it will be useful to consider other ways of measuring the effect of a force, particularly as acceleration is difficult to measure. Two possibilities suggest themselves:

(a) Consider the push of a cricket bat on a ball: this is a force which varies from zero to a very large value and down to zero again in a very short time interval. If we do not know the size of the varying force F at each instant, then perhaps we can still evaluate the expression $\sum F \Delta t$. We use this approach in Chapter 8.

(b) Consider the pull of a rope on a cart: here we have a force which pulls the cart along. In this case the value of $\sum F \Delta x$ is a useful measure of F, and it is with $\sum F \Delta x$ that we shall deal in this chapter.

It is interesting to note that for a long time (up to the end of the eighteenth century) a controversy raged between the followers of Descartes and Leibniz as to whether $\sum F \Delta t$ or $\sum F \Delta x$ correctly represented the 'true' measure of the effects of force. In fact, each approach has its merits and its limitations, and we shall use whichever is the more convenient in a particular problem.

7-1 Work

Consider a body which undergoes a displacement Δx as shown in figure 7-1 while a constant force F acts on it. We define

*the **work done** by the force on a particle as the product of the size of the displacement of the particle and the size of the resolved part of the force in the direction of the displacement.*

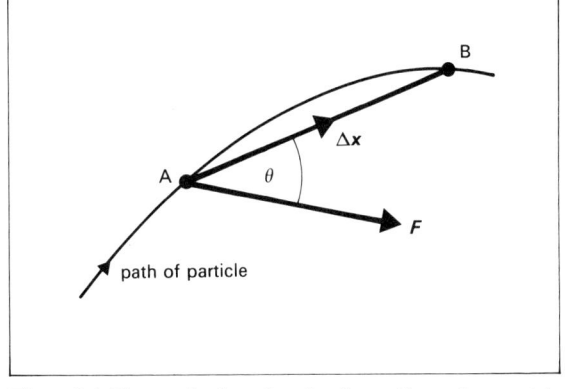

Figure 7-1 The work done by the force F on the particle between A and B is $W_{AB} = F \cos \theta \, \Delta x$.

7 Work and kinetic energy

Using the vector algebra outlined on page 21 this can be expressed as the scalar product of the force and the displacement:

$$W_{AB} = F\Delta x \cos\theta = \mathbf{F} \cdot \Delta\mathbf{x}. \qquad [7\text{-}1]$$

W_{AB} is a scalar quantity, which is one reason why it is a useful measure of the effects of a force. The unit of work will be the same as the unit of $\mathbf{F} \cdot \Delta\mathbf{x}$, and is given in table 7-1. See also the Appendix which shows a conversion table for various units of work and energy now in use.

	Force	Displacement	Work
Dimensions	MLT^{-2}	L	ML^2T^{-2}
Absolute unit (SI)	N	m	N m = joule(J)

Table 7-1 The joule is named after James Prescott Joule (1818–1889).

To answer the question 'what is work?' it is not enough simply to define the quantity as above. In physics it certainly does not mean 'employment' nor does it help very much to say that work is done when a force moves its point of application (at least partly in the direction of the force), although this last remark is certainly true. To explain what work *is*, let us ask instead what work *does*: what is the result of someone or something doing work? When a body is acted upon by a single force, and that force does work, it *accelerates*: we shall see later (Section 7-7) that a knowledge of how much work is done enables us to calculate changes in speed, and vice versa.

7-2 The work done by a constant force

The work done by a force on a body is $F\Delta x \cos\theta$. There are several special cases of the use of this result which occur often enough for us to note them:

(a) The work done by the normal contact force, the push of a surface on a body, is zero, as is the work done by any force which always remains perpendicular to the direction of motion of the body on which it acts. See figure 7-2a and (b).

(b) The work done by a force on a body is negative if θ in the expression $F\Delta x \cos\theta$ lies between 90° and 270°. When the frictional push of a surface on a body does work, θ is often equal to 180°, and so work done by frictional forces is often negative. See figure 7-2c.

(c) The work done by a force on a body is zero if there is no relative motion of the force and the body. In figure 7-2d a man runs forward and the ground exerts a forward push on him. This push depends on the man's foot *gripping* the ground and there is no relative motion between the foot and the ground (or at least only a microscopically small one). There are forces which do work on the man, but these are *internal forces*. (It is still true, however, that the push of the ground on the man is the external accelerating force.)

(d) The work done by a force on a body is zero if there is no motion of the body. In figure 7-2e the pull of the man on the bucket does no work. He does become tired, because his body exerts the necessary upward force by tightening and relaxing a very large number of small skeletal muscle fibres in his arms. Each tightening involves a movement and consequently the performance of some internal work. By our definition of work, however, *no* work is done on

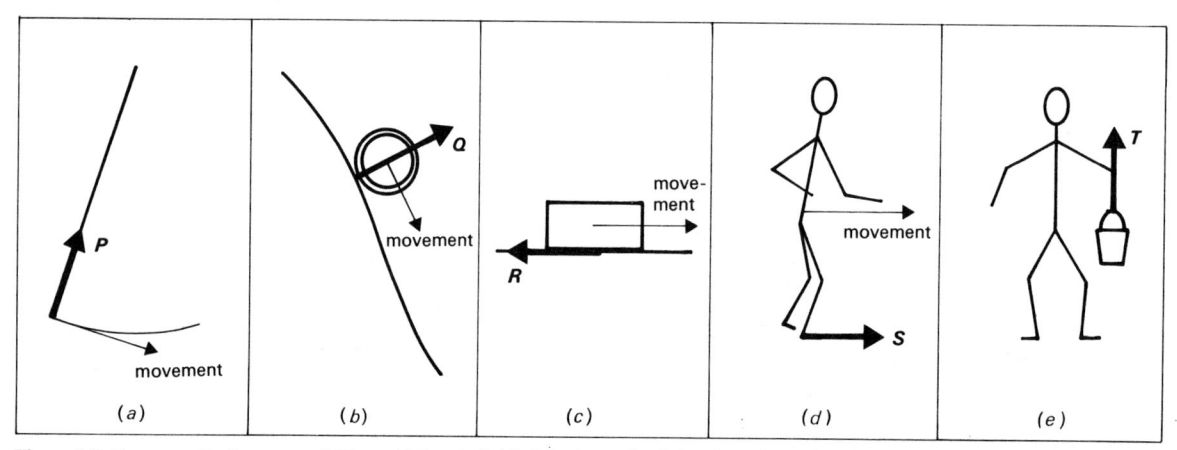

Figure 7-2 Some particular cases of $W_{AB} = F\Delta x \cos\theta$. (a) $\mathbf{P}$ is the pull of the thread on the pendulum bob; (b) $\mathbf{Q}$ is the push of the ground on the hoop; (c) $\mathbf{R}$ is the frictional push of the ground on the block; (d) $\mathbf{S}$ is the push of the ground on the man; (e) $\mathbf{T}$ is the pull of the man on the bucket.

the bucket, just as no work would be done if the bucket were being supported by a hook attached to a fixed beam.

In the particular (but very common) case where the force exerted on a body is constant (that is, in both size and direction) and is independent of the position of the body, the work done by the force can be found easily if the *displacement* is resolved in the direction of the force. It is the displacement and not the distance travelled which is relevant. This implies, for example, that the work done by the pull of the Earth on a body when it is displaced from A to B is independent of the path taken from A to B.

▶ **Example 7-1** A stone of mass 0.20 kg is
(*a*) allowed to fall vertically for a distance of 2.0 m (figure 7-3*a*)
(*b*) tied to a light string of length 2.0 m: the other end of the string is tied to a fixed point, the string is held taut and horizontal, and the stone is then released (figure 7-3*b*)
(*c*) allowed to slide down a frictionless track as shown in figure 7-3*c*, the total vertical displacement being 2.0 m. Find the work done by the forces in each case: ignore the work done by the push of the air on the stone.

Take $g = 10 \text{ m s}^{-2}$: then the weight of the stone = 2.0 N.

(*a*) The only force is the weight of the stone: the work done by this force = (2.0 N)(2.0 m) = 4.0 J.
(*b*) The pull of the string is always perpendicular to the path of the stone, so this force does no work. The weight is a *vertical* force: the *vertical* displacement of the stone is 2.0 m, so that the work done by the weight is (2.0 N)(2.0 m) = 4.0 J. The fact that the *path* of the stone is greater than 2.0 m is irrelevant: all that matters is the *displacement* parallel to the direction of the force.
(*c*) Again, the normal push of the track on the stone is necessarily always perpendicular to the path of the stone, so this force does no work. The *displacement* of the stone parallel to the force of 2.0 N is 2.0 m, so that the work done is (2.0 N)(2.0 m) = 4.0 J.

So in each case the total work done on the stone is 4.0 J. ◀

When several forces act on a body we can sometimes lessen the labour needed to find the total by first calculating the resultant force which acts on the body: Example 7-2 makes this point. In it we first calculate the work done by the separate forces, and sum these amounts of work; then we find the resultant force, and calculate at once the work done by this force.

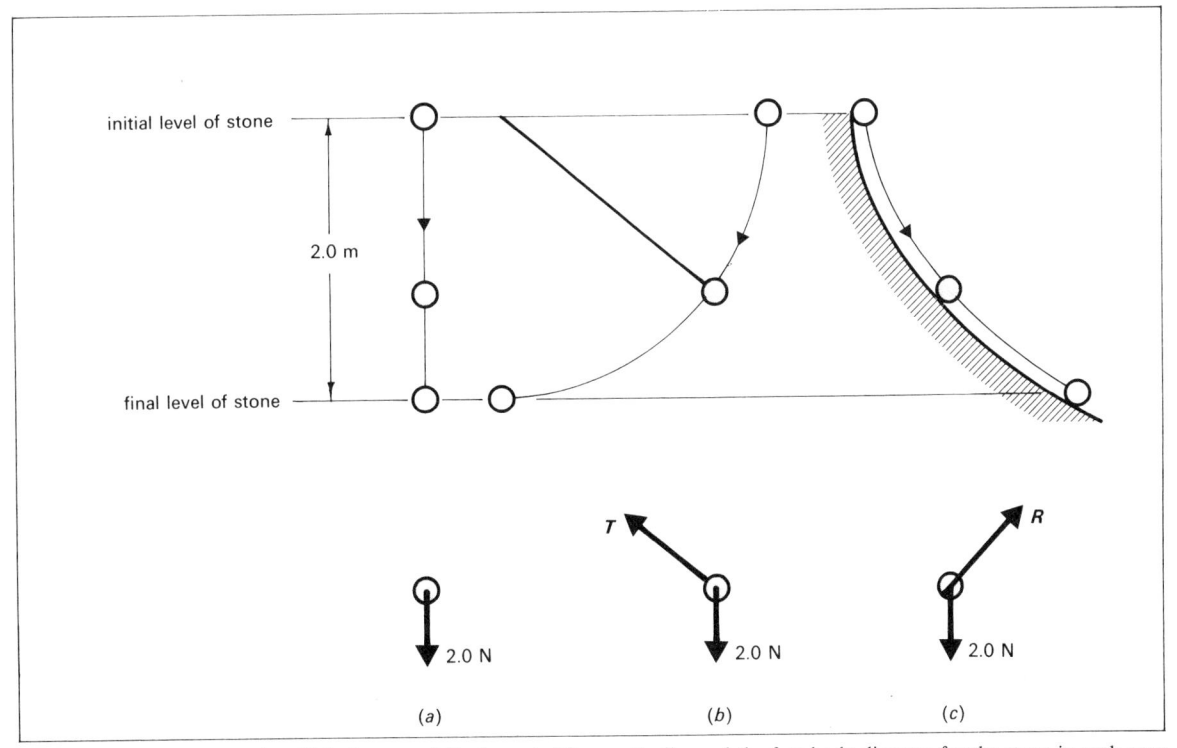

Figure 7-3 The three ways in which the stone falls through 2.0 m vertically, and the free-body diagram for the stone in each case.

7 Work and kinetic energy

▶ **Example 7-2** A block B is being pulled up a rough slope (coefficient of sliding friction = 0.40) by a rope as shown in figure 7-4. The mass of the block is 14 kg, the pull of the rope is 150 N, and the angle of the slope is 30°; the pull of the rope makes an angle of 45° with the slope. Find the total of the work done by all the forces when the block is moved 10 m along the slope.

We can calculate that $S = 15$ N and $F = 6.0$ N, if $g = 10$ N kg^{-1}

First solution The work done on B by

(a) the pull of the rope
$$= (150\,\text{N})(10\,\text{m})\cos 45° = 1060\,\text{J}$$
(b) the pull of the Earth
$$= (140\,\text{N})(10\,\text{m})\cos 120°$$
$$= -(140\,\text{N})(10\,\text{m})\cos 60° = -700\,\text{J}$$
(c) the frictional push F
$$= (6\,\text{N})(10\,\text{m})\cos 180°$$
$$= -(6\,\text{N})(10\,\text{m}) = -60\,\text{J}$$
(d) the normal contact push S
$$= (15\,\text{N})(10\,\text{m})\cos 90° = 0.$$

As work is a scalar quantity, the total work done on B can be found by adding these quantities algebraically, and we find that

$$W = 300\,\text{J}.$$

Second solution The resultant force acting on B is (of course) along the slope, and its value is

$$(150\,\text{N})\cos 45° - (6.0\,\text{N}) - (140\,\text{N})\cos 60° = 30\,\text{N}.$$

When the block moves 10 m, the work done by this resultant force $= (30\,\text{N})(10\,\text{m})$ so that again

$$W = 300\,\text{J},$$

but this method is very much simpler. It is generally true that *the sum of the work done by each of the forces acting on a body is equal to the work done by the resultant force acting on the body.* ◀

7-3 The work done by a variable force

When a varying force does work on a body we have to divide the path into a number of short elements Δx_1, Δx_2, etc. and calculate the work done ΔW_1, ΔW_2, etc. during each:

$$\Delta W_1 = F_1 \Delta x_1 \cos \theta_1,$$
$$\Delta W_2 = F_2 \Delta x_2 \cos \theta_2,$$

and so on.

Adding these up over the whole path from A to B, we have

$$W_{AB} = \Delta W_1 + \Delta W_2 + \cdots$$
$$= F_1 \Delta x_1 \cos \theta_1 + F_2 \Delta x_2 \cos \theta_2 + \cdots$$

so that
$$W_{AB} = \Sigma F \Delta x \cos \theta.$$

To evaluate this expression we could perhaps draw a graph of $F \cos \theta$ against x for the path AB. We see in

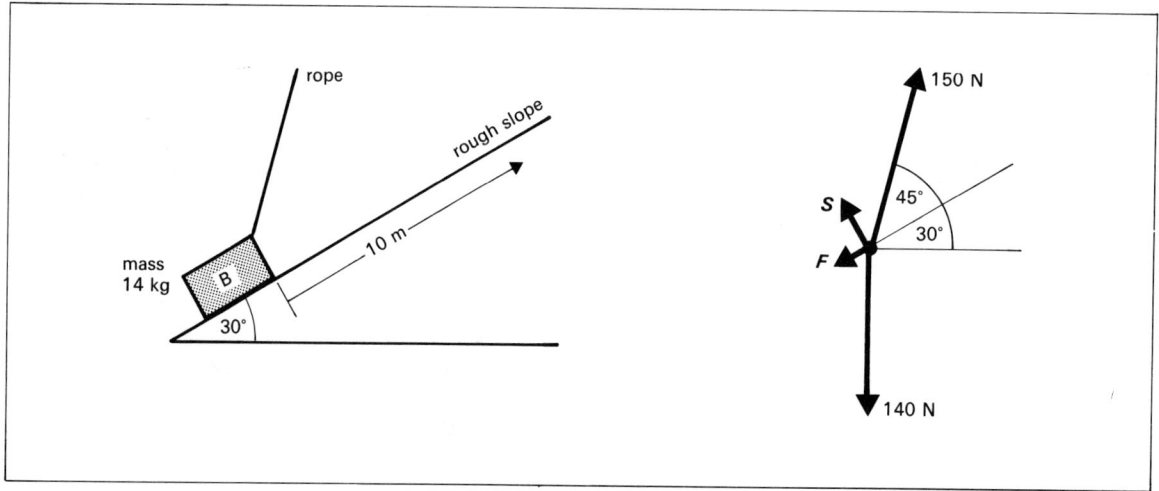

Figure 7-4 The block B of mass 14 kg is accelerated up a rough slope for a distance of 10 m by the forces shown. *g* has been taken to be 10 N kg^{-1}.

7-3 The work done by a variable force

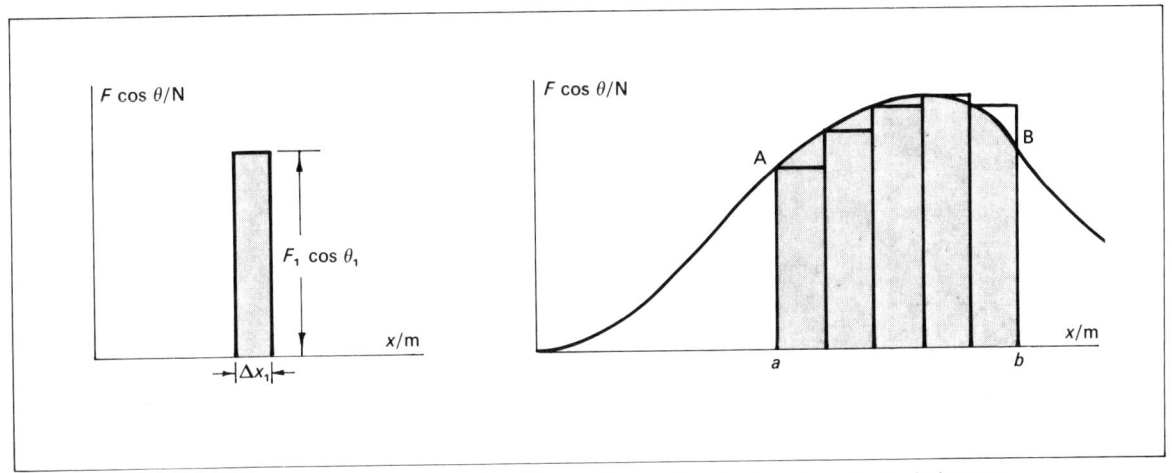

Figure 7-5 The sum of the terms $F_1 \Delta x_1 \cos \theta_1$ from A to B is roughly equal to the shaded area beneath the curve.

figure 7-5 that as for $\sum v \Delta t$ in Section 3-4, $\sum F \Delta x \cos \theta$ is approximately given by the area between the curve and the x-axis. To make the approximation more accurate we can make Δx smaller and smaller, so that in the limit

$$W_{AB} = \lim_{\Delta x \to 0} (\sum F \Delta x \cos \theta) = \text{area beneath the graph of } F \cos \theta/\text{N versus } x/\text{m between A and B}.$$

In the language of calculus,

$$W_{AB} = \int_a^b F \cos \theta \, dx = \int_a^b \mathbf{F} \cdot d\mathbf{x}.$$

We shall usually have to consider only the simple case where $\mathbf{F}$ is parallel to the displacement, that is where $\theta = 0$.

▶ **Example 7-3** Newton's law of gravitation states that the pull F exerted by a particle of mass m_1 on a particle of mass m_2, when they are a distance r apart, is given by

$$F = G \frac{m_1 m_2}{r^2}$$

where G has the value $6.7 \times 10^{-11} \, \text{N m}^2 \, \text{kg}^{-2}$ and is a universal constant (and a 'particle' is a body whose dimensions are infinitesimal compared with r). For *bodies* which have spherical symmetry (they need not have uniform density) the expression for the force F is the same, where m_1 and m_2 are the masses of the bodies, and r is the distance between their centres. Treating both bodies as spheres, find by (a) using calculus (b) drawing a graph to relate F and r, and finding the area beneath it, the work done by the gravitational force when a satellite of mass 5.0×10^3 kg is put into an orbit 10×10^6 m from the centre of the Earth. Take the radius of the Earth to be 6.4×10^6 m, and its mass to be 6.0×10^{24} kg.

(a) *Using calculus* For a small displacement Δr, the work done ΔW by F is given by $\Delta W = F \Delta r$. The total work done W when the force moves from a displacement $r = a$ to a displacement $r = b$ is given by

$$W = \int_a^b F \, dr$$

$$= \int_a^b -G \frac{m_1 m_2}{r^2} dr = Gm_1 m_2 \left[\frac{1}{r}\right]_a^b = Gm_1 m_2 \left(\frac{1}{b} - \frac{1}{a}\right).$$

Therefore

$$W = (6.7 \times 10^{-11} \, \text{N m}^2 \, \text{kg}^{-1})(6.0 \times 10^{24} \, \text{kg})(5.0 \times 10^3 \, \text{kg})$$

$$\times \left(\frac{1}{10 \times 10^6 \, \text{m}} - \frac{1}{6.4 \times 10^6 \, \text{m}}\right)$$

$$= -1.1 \times 10^{11} \, \text{J}.$$

(b) *Using a graphical method* To draw the graph relating F and r we must find corresponding values of F and r. Using $F = (2.0 \times 10^{18} \, \text{N m}^2)/r^2$ in this case, we have:

$r/10^6$ m	$F/10^4$ N
6.4	4.9
7.0	4.1
8.0	3.1
9.0	2.5
10.0	2.0

7 Work and kinetic energy

We now plot the graph (figure 7-6). The area between the curve and the axis consists of 15 large squares and about 187 small squares: that is, about 22.5 large squares, and each large square represents work done of $(0.5 \times 10^4 \text{ N})(10^6 \text{ m}) = 5.0 \times 10^9 \text{ J}$. Therefore the work done (negative because the force and the displacement have opposite directions)

$$= -22.5 \times 5.0 \times 10^9 \text{ J}$$
$$= -1.1 \times 10^{11} \text{ J}.$$

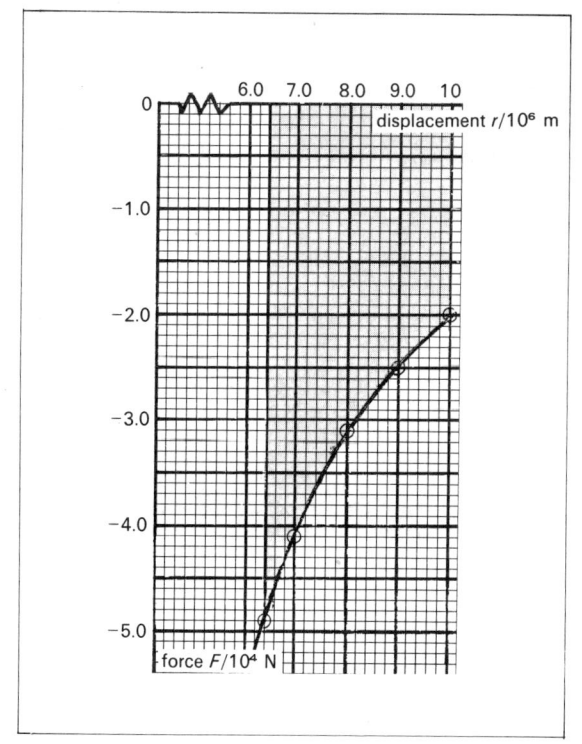

◀

Figure 7-6 A graph relating the gravitational pull F on a satellite of mass 5000 kg at different distances r from the centre of the Earth.

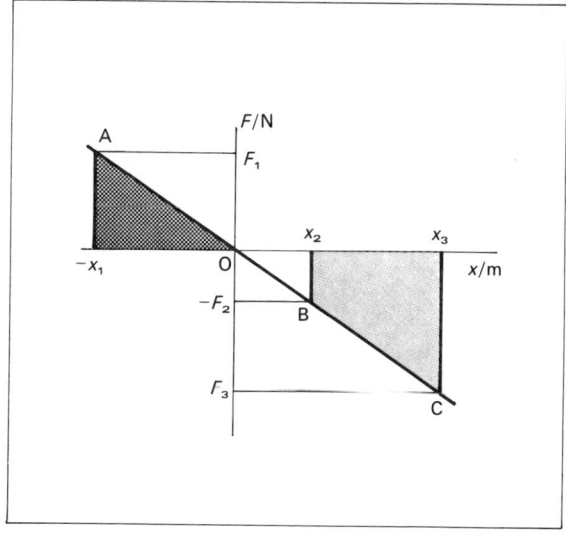

Figure 7-7 The graph $F = -kx$ where F is the force exerted on the body when it has a displacement x. The area between the line and the x-axis represents the work done.

For some situations F is parallel to x and is known to vary with x in a particularly simple manner. We can then calculate $\sum F \cdot \Delta x$ without having to add up a large number of small terms (either by integration using calculus or by drawing an accurate graph). A case of special interest occurs when F is proportional to $-x$, or $F = -kx$, where k is a constant, the negative sign indicating that F and x have opposite directions. Graphically F and x are then related as shown in figure 7-7, where F is the force exerted on the body when it has a displacement x.

From the graph, we see that the work done by F on the body while the body moves from A to O, W_{AO}, is given by

$$W_{AO} = \text{heavily shaded area}$$
$$= \tfrac{1}{2}F_1(-x_1) = -\tfrac{1}{2}F_1 x_1$$
$$= (\text{average force}) \times (\text{displacement } AO)$$
$$= \tfrac{1}{2}kx_1^2.$$

Similarly, $W_{BC} = \text{lightly shaded area}$

$$= \tfrac{1}{2}[(-F_3)+(-F_2)](x_3-x_2)$$
$$= (\text{average force}) \times (\text{displacement } BC)$$
$$= \tfrac{1}{2}k(x_3+x_2)(x_3-x_2)$$
$$= \tfrac{1}{2}k(x_3^2-x_2^2).$$

In general, when such a force F does work on a body,

$$\text{work done} = (\text{average force})(\text{change of displacement}).$$

This special case is important because the force exerted on a body attached to, say, a helical spring (and many other elastic bodies) obeys this law, where x represents the extension or compression of the spring from its unstressed position. The constant k has (for linear deformations) the dimensions $\text{MLT}^{-2} \div \text{L} = \text{MT}^{-2}$ and is called the *stiffness* of the spring (or other elastic body).

▶ **Example 7-4** A spring whose stiffness has a constant value of $40\,\text{N}\,\text{m}^{-1}$ is fixed at one end to a point on a horizontal table, and the other end is pulled slowly with a force equal to the tension in the spring. Find the work done on the spring when its length is increased from (a) 0.50 m to 0.70 m (b) 0.70 m to 0.90 m.

(a) the average force = $(40\,\text{N}\,\text{m}^{-1})(0.60\,\text{m}) = 24\,\text{N}$
so the work done = $(24\,\text{N})(0.20\,\text{m}) = 4.8\,\text{J}$.
(b) the average force = $(40\,\text{N}\,\text{m}^{-1})(0.80\,\text{m}) = 32\,\text{N}$
so the work done = $(32\,\text{N})(0.20\,\text{m}) = 6.4\,\text{J}$. ◀

7-4 Power

When a force does work on a body it can do it quickly or slowly. How quickly the work is done is often as important as what quantity of work is done. We define the rate at which an agent does work (the average power of the agent) P_{av} by the equation

$$P_{av} = \frac{W_{AB}}{\Delta t}, \qquad [7\text{-}2]$$

where W_{AB} is the work done in the time interval Δt considered. P_{av} is a scalar quantity. The dimensions of power are clearly $ML^2T^{-2} \div T = ML^2T^{-3}$, and the unit is the joule/second, which is called the *watt*, after James Watt (1736–1819). Multiples of this unit are in common use (see also the Appendix):

1 kilowatt (kW) = 10^3 watt

1 megawatt (MW) = 10^6 watt.

We should note that the watt, the SI unit of power, is not confined to electrical measurements, but commonly appears in mechanics problems.

▶ **Example 7-5** A lift of mass 1.5×10^3 kg is to be raised 60 m in 10 s. Find the average power needed. (Take $g = 10\,\text{m}\,\text{s}^{-2}$.)

The average force which must be exerted = the weight of the lift = 1.5×10^4 N.
The work done = $(1.5 \times 10^4\,\text{N})(60\,\text{m}) = 9.0 \times 10^5\,\text{J}$.
The average power = $(9.0 \times 10^5\,\text{J})/10\,\text{s} = 9.0 \times 10^4\,\text{W}$ = 90 kW.
(In practice the lift would have a counterweight, so that less power than this would need to be supplied from an external source.) ◀

• We might note some further units of the *work* done by a force on a body:

$$1\,\text{W}\,\text{s} = \left(1\frac{\text{J}}{\text{s}}\right)\text{s} = 1\,\text{J}$$

$$1\,\text{kW}\,\text{s} = \left(10^3\frac{\text{J}}{\text{s}}\right)\text{s} = 10^3\,\text{J} = 1\,\text{kJ}$$

$$1\,\text{kW}\,\text{h} = \left(10^3\frac{\text{J}}{\text{s}}\right)(1\,\text{h})\left(\frac{3600\,\text{s}}{1\,\text{h}}\right) = 3.6 \times 10^6\,\text{J}.$$

The last of these, the kilowatt hour, is widely used as a unit of work, as it is of a convenient size. It is not an SI unit. Other non-SI units of work are given in the Appendix.

Power and velocity

The average power

$$P_{av} = \frac{W_{AB}}{\Delta t} = \frac{\boldsymbol{F}\cdot\Delta\boldsymbol{x}}{\Delta t}$$

$$= \boldsymbol{F}\cdot\frac{\Delta\boldsymbol{x}}{\Delta t} = \boldsymbol{F}\cdot\boldsymbol{v}_{av}$$

where $\boldsymbol{v}_{av}$ is the average velocity of the body on which the work is being done by a force of constant size F. Therefore

$$P_{av} = Fv_{av}\cos\theta = Fv_{av}$$

if the force is parallel to the direction of motion, v_{av} being the average speed. The instantaneous power P is defined by the equation

$$P = \lim_{\Delta t \to 0}\left(\frac{W_{AB}}{\Delta t}\right) = \boldsymbol{F}\cdot\boldsymbol{v},$$

$\boldsymbol{v}$ being the instantaneous velocity.

▶ **Example 7-6** Refer to Example 7-5. We could have solved this problem by realizing that the average speed of the lift was $6.0\,\text{m}\,\text{s}^{-1}$. Now the power needed = $Fv = (1.5 \times 10^4\,\text{N})(6.0\,\text{m}\,\text{s}^{-1}) = 9.0 \times 10^4\,\text{W}$ = 90 kW. ◀

7-5 Principles of machines

A *machine* is a device which does work on a body in a situation where we ourselves either could not have done it at all or could not have done it as conveniently. The principle of all such machines is the same: an *operator* exerts a force which does work on an *object*. (See figure 7-8.) We are not interested here in the equilibrium of the machine, the operator, or the object on which the machine exerts a force, and so we have not marked in figure 7-8

7 Work and kinetic energy

all the forces acting on these bodies. The relevant forces are

(a) the push or pull of the operator on the machine, **P** (there is also the push or pull of the machine on the operator, $-P$, but this is not relevant)

(b) the push or pull of the machine on the object, **Q** (as before the Newton's third law force, $-Q$, is not relevant).

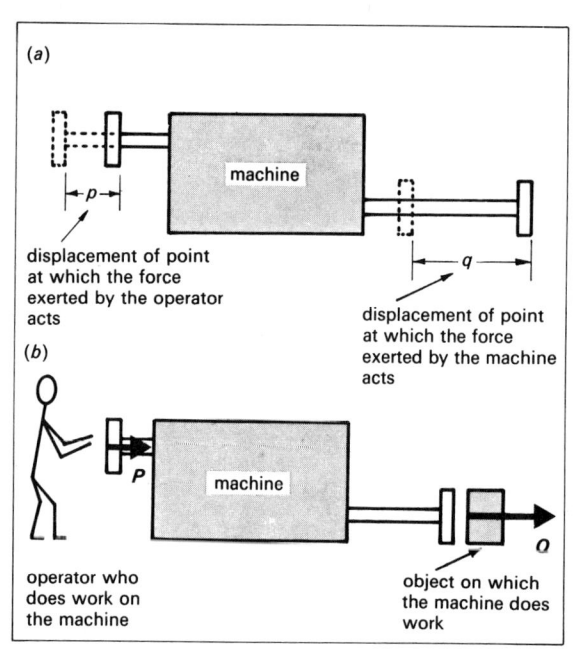

Figure 7-8 The important quantities in the analysis of a simple machine.

From figure 7-8 we have

work done by operator on machine = Pp
work done by machine on object = Qq.

It is found experimentally that $Qq \not > Pp$, and the *efficiency* η of the machine is defined by the equation

$$\eta = \frac{\text{work done by machine on object}}{\text{work done by operator on machine}} = \frac{Qq}{Pp} = \frac{Q}{P} \div \frac{p}{q}.$$

η is a dimensionless quantity and is often expressed as a percentage. Q/P is called the *mechanical advantage* of the machine, and p/q is called its *velocity ratio*. The velocity ratio is determined simply by the geometry of the machine, and is a quantity which can be calculated without experiment: the size of the mechanical advantage can only be measured experimentally.

The efficiency η may be reduced by two causes: firstly, most machines have moving parts on which work must be done to accelerate or lift them, and, secondly, most machines have parts which move relative to each other so that work must be done to move them if the surfaces are not frictionless. The importance of the first reason diminishes as the forces P (and therefore Q) become larger, while friction tends to increase as P increases. A graph of η against Q is typically as shown in figure 7-9.

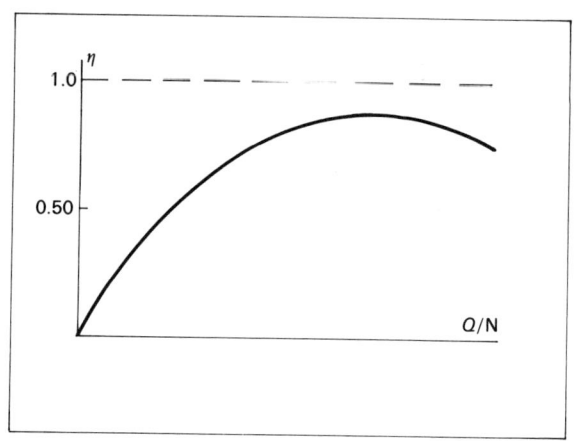

Figure 7-9 This graph of η against Q shows how the efficiency of a pulley system such as that shown in figure 7-10a increases as the pull of the machine on the body increases.

Friction can be reduced by lubrication, or the use of rolling rather than sliding surfaces and by a good design which reduces the number of moving parts. If it were possible to produce frictionless surfaces it would be possible to produce a machine which, when once set in motion, would continue in motion for ever. It is *not*, however, possible to produce 'perpetual motion' machines, when by that term is meant machines which do more work on the object than the operator does on the machine, that is for which $Qq > Pp$. Some interesting (but impracticable) 'perpetual motion' machines are suggested in *Physics for the Inquiring Mind* by E. M. Rogers.

Some machines will not *overhaul*: that is, they will not go into reverse when the operator removes the force P. This can be an advantage in, for example, an inclined plane or a screw when the surfaces are rough. Whether or not a machine will overhaul usually depends on the static limiting friction. This is related to the kinetic friction which controls the efficiency of the machine so it is generally true that a machine of low efficiency ($\approx 30\%$) will not overhaul.

7-5 Principles of machines

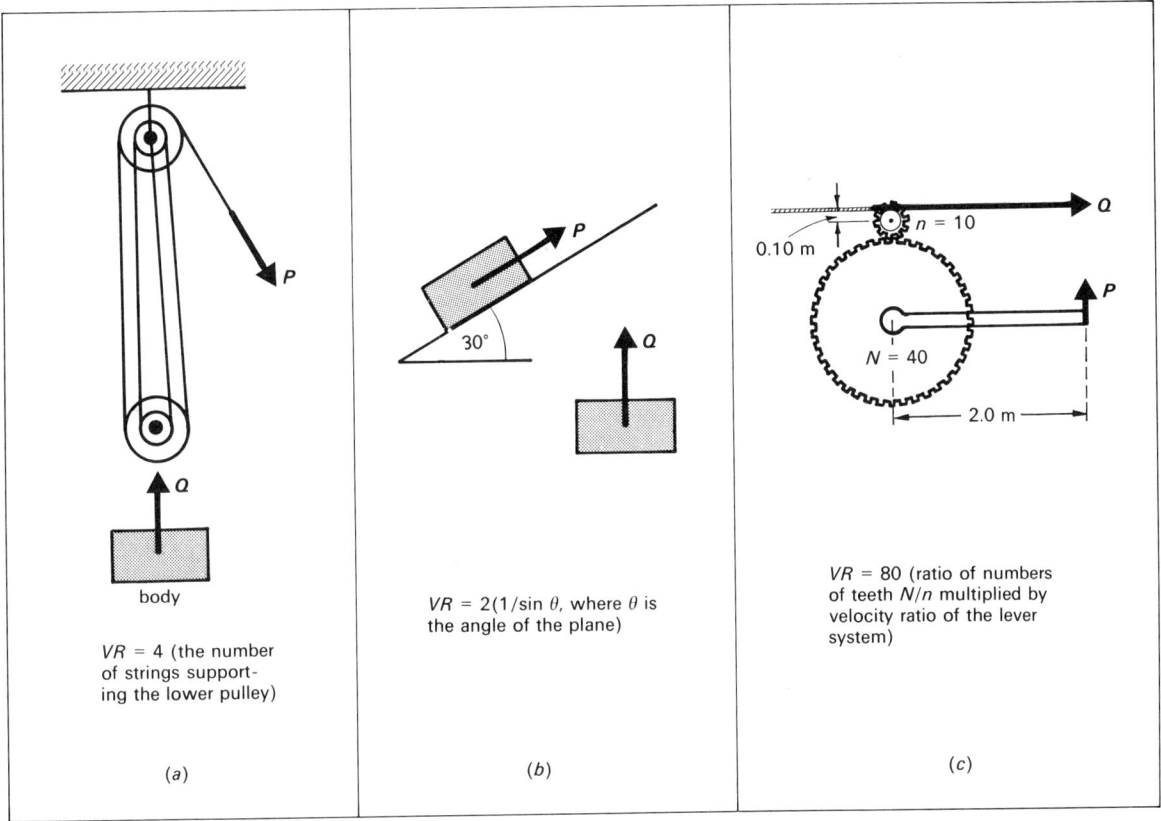

Figure 7-10 Machines of three different types. In these diagrams we show only the forces P and Q although there are of course other forces acting on the bodies. The calculated value of the velocity ratio, VR, is stated on the diagrams.
(a) A simple pulley system, (b) an inclined plane: here we compare the force required to lift the body unaided with that required to drag it up the plane. (c) A simple gear system for winding in a long rope.

(a) $VR = 4$ (the number of strings supporting the lower pulley)

(b) $VR = 2(1/\sin \theta$, where θ is the angle of the plane)

(c) $VR = 80$ (ratio of numbers of teeth N/n multiplied by velocity ratio of the lever system)

▶ **Example 7-7** Figure 7-11 shows a diagram of a screw-jack of the type used to lift a car. The pitch of the screw is 2.5 mm, and the handle moves in a circle of radius 150 mm; find the velocity ratio of the machine. If a man using the jack is willing to exert a force of 60 N, what is the weight of the heaviest car he can lift, if the jack is 20 per cent efficient?

Using the notation of figure 7-8, and considering one revolution of the handle of the jack, we have

$$q = 2.5 \text{ mm}, p = 2\pi (150 \text{ mm}) = 940 \text{ mm}.$$

Therefore the velocity ratio $\left(=\dfrac{p}{q}\right) = \dfrac{940 \text{ mm}}{2.5 \text{ mm}} = 380.$

If the jack is 20 per cent efficient, then using $\eta = Qq/Pp$, we have Q/P (the mechanical advantage) = 76. If $P = 60$ N, then $Q = 76 \times 60$ N = 4600 N. Thus he could, using the jack, lift one side of a car which had a weight of 9200 N (that is a car whose mass was about 1000 kg). ◀

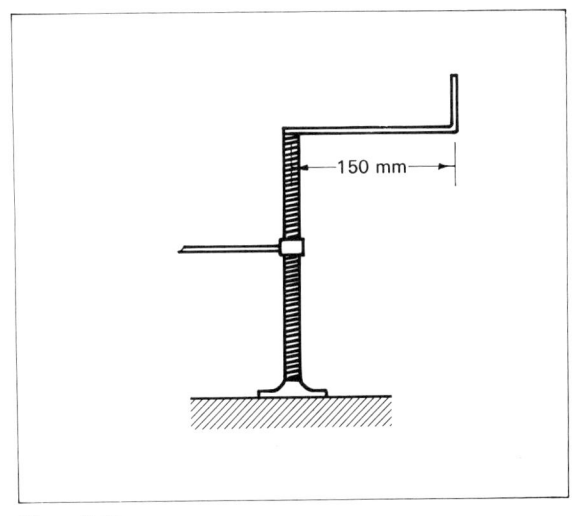

Figure 7-11

7-6 Kinetic energy

The mass m of a particle A is a measure of its inertia. Newton's first law says that A will continue to move with a uniform velocity $\mathbf{u}$ unless a resultant external force $\mathbf{F}$ acts on it. We define

> the **kinetic energy** T of the particle A as the work which A can do on another body B while A is being brought to rest by B.

As the force $\mathbf{F}$ which B exerts on A to bring A to rest is in the opposite direction to $\mathbf{u}$, the velocity of A, then by Newton's third law, A exerts a force $-\mathbf{F}$ on B. This second force is in the same direction as $\mathbf{u}$, so measuring the displacement of A in this direction, the kinetic energy of A is given by

$$T = \sum_{\text{speed } u}^{\text{speed } 0} \mathbf{F} \cdot \Delta \mathbf{x}$$

= area under the graph of F versus x.

To evaluate T from this expression, let us first suppose that $\mathbf{F}$ is constant in size and direction and that the displacement through which A comes to rest is $\mathbf{s}$: then

$$T = \mathbf{F} \cdot \mathbf{s}.$$

In these circumstances the acceleration $\mathbf{a}$ is constant, and thus

$$0 = \mathbf{u} \cdot \mathbf{u} + 2\mathbf{a} \cdot \mathbf{s} \quad \text{and} \quad m\mathbf{a} = -\mathbf{F}.$$

Eliminating $\mathbf{F}$,

$$T = -m\mathbf{a} \cdot \mathbf{s}$$
$$= \tfrac{1}{2} m(\mathbf{u} \cdot \mathbf{u}),$$

that is

$$T = \tfrac{1}{2} m u^2. \qquad [7\text{-}3]$$

Thus the kinetic energy of a particle of constant mass m, moving with speed u, is $\tfrac{1}{2} m u^2$. More generally, when the force $\mathbf{F}$ is not constant, we have

$$T = \int_{v=u}^{v=0} \mathbf{F} \cdot d\mathbf{x}$$
$$= \int_{v=u}^{v=0} (-m\mathbf{a}) \cdot d\mathbf{x}$$
$$= -\int_{v=u}^{v=0} mv \left(\frac{dv}{dx}\right) dx \quad \text{which, if } m \text{ is constant,}$$
$$= -m \int_{u}^{0} v \, dv$$
$$= -m\left[-\tfrac{1}{2} u^2\right]$$
$$= \tfrac{1}{2} m u^2.$$

This is a general proof that the kinetic energy of a particle depends *only* on its mass and speed.

The symbol T will be used for kinetic energy, subscripts being used if needed. It is a scalar quantity ($\tfrac{1}{2} m \mathbf{u} \cdot \mathbf{u}$) and has dimensions of $M(LT^{-1})^2 = ML^2T^{-2}$, the same as those of work, as we should expect. The unit of kinetic energy is therefore the same as that of work, that is the joule. The kinetic energy of a particle is necessarily referred to a given frame of reference, usually the Earth: we shall occasionally find it convenient to use other (inertial) frames.

We cannot design an experiment to 'prove' that the kinetic energy of a particle is $\tfrac{1}{2} m u^2$, as the expression is derived from earlier definitions. However, a simple experiment which would enable us to get the feel of what happens to different bodies when a fixed amount of work W_{AB} is done on them is shown in figure 7-12. A linear air-track glider or an air puck is loaded so as to have a total mass of 1, 2, 3, etc. units of mass. On each occasion there is the same work W_{AB} done by the elastic catapult on the vehicle as it accelerates from rest at A to a speed v at B. The other forces acting on the vehicle do no work as it moves from A to B. If v is measured (using a photocell and scaler-timer or clock situated beyond B), a graph of $v^2/\text{m}^2\,\text{s}^{-2}$ versus m^{-1}/kg^{-1} should give a straight line through the origin. This experi-

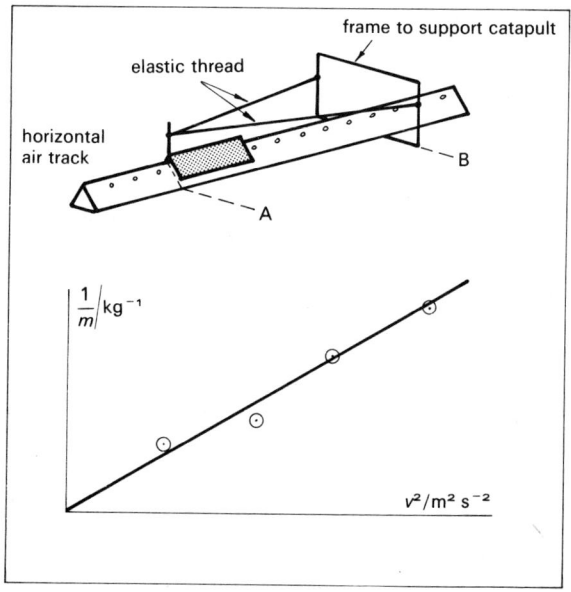

Figure 7-12 A linear air-track vehicle is accelerated from A to B by a thin piece of stretched elastic. The mass of the vehicle is altered and the corresponding speeds measured.

ment *proves* nothing, but the graph obtained could now be used to find the mass of another body if its speed v were measured in the same circumstances. A simple version of the experiment can be performed using trolleys.

7-7 The work–energy theorem

Suppose a particle at A with a kinetic energy $T_A = \frac{1}{2}mu^2$ moves to B where its kinetic energy $T_B = \frac{1}{2}mv^2$. Extending the definition of kinetic energy from the previous section we see that the work done on the particle by the *resultant* force acting on it is equal to the change in its kinetic energy $\Delta T = T_B - T_A$. That is

$$W_{AB} = \Delta T$$

or

$$\sum \mathbf{F} \cdot \Delta \mathbf{x} = \tfrac{1}{2}mv^2 - \tfrac{1}{2}mu^2. \qquad [7\text{-}4]$$

The proof is left as an exercise for the reader: he should consider only the case where the displacement is parallel to the resultant force $\mathbf{F}$, although the result can be shown to be generally true. Note the difference in calculating the work done *on* the particle in this proof as opposed to the work done *by* the particle when deriving $\tfrac{1}{2}mu^2$ as an expression for its kinetic energy. It is often convenient to represent the change in the kinetic energy of the particle diagrammatically, as in figure 7-13a. Figure 7-13b illustrates the equation which defines the kinetic energy of a particle. These two diagrams are examples of *energy flow diagrams*.

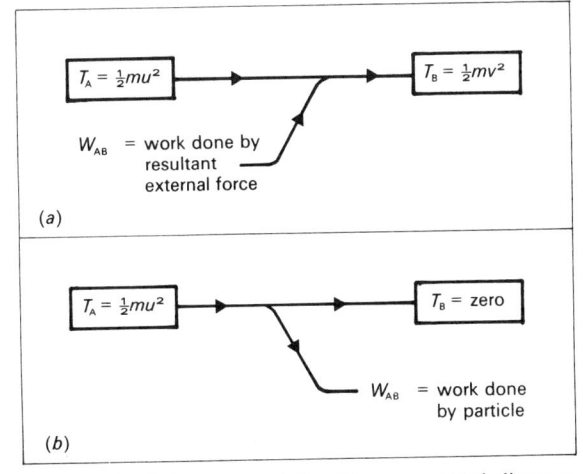

Figure 7-13 Work–energy relationships represented diagrammatically.

The *work–energy theorem*

$$W_{AB} = \tfrac{1}{2}mv^2 - \tfrac{1}{2}mu^2$$

is one of the most powerful in mechanics: it should be remembered in words, not in symbols. As it is a scalar relationship, it is much easier to use than Newton's second law, from which it derives.

▶ **Example 7-8** Refer to Example 7-1. In each case the work done by the forces is 4.0 J: we can now equate this to the gain in kinetic energy of the mass. Thus in each case

$$4.0 \, \text{J} = \tfrac{1}{2}(0.20 \, \text{kg})v^2 - \tfrac{1}{2}(0.20 \, \text{kg})(0 \, \text{m s}^{-1})^2$$

so that $\quad v^2 = 40 \, \text{m}^2 \, \text{s}^{-2} \left(\text{using } 1\dfrac{\text{J}}{\text{kg}} = 1\dfrac{\text{N m}}{\text{kg}} = 1\dfrac{\text{m}^2}{\text{s}^2}\right)$

$$v = 6.3 \, \text{m s}^{-1}.$$

In each case the mass acquires a speed of $6.3 \, \text{m s}^{-1}$. ◀

▶ **Example 7-9** A simple pendulum consists of a massless string and a small massive bob. Prove that in the absence of air resistance it rises to the same vertical height above its lowest point at the end of each swing.

The only forces acting on the bob are the pull of the string and the pull of the Earth. The pull of the string does no work (since it is always perpendicular to the path of the bob): the work done by the pull of the Earth is zero when the bob moves between any two points at the same horizontal level. Thus if the bob starts from rest at one end of its swing, it will neither gain nor lose kinetic energy in moving to another point at the same horizontal level: if it starts from rest at one end of a swing, it will again have zero speed when it is again at that level. Thus it will continue to perform oscillations in which it reaches the same vertical height in each oscillation. ◀

▶ **Example 7-10** A block of mass 1.0 kg has a speed of $1.0 \, \text{m s}^{-1}$ along the horizontal surface of a table. Taking the frictional push of the table on the block as 2.0 N, find the distance the block slides before it comes to rest.

Let the distance the block slides be x: using $F \Delta x = \tfrac{1}{2}mv^2 - \tfrac{1}{2}mu^2$ we have

$$(-2.0 \, \text{N})x = \tfrac{1}{2}(1.0 \, \text{kg})(0 \, \text{m s}^{-1})^2 - \tfrac{1}{2}(1.0 \, \text{kg})(1.0 \, \text{m s}^{-1})^2$$

$$x = \frac{0.5 \, \text{kg m}^2 \, \text{s}^{-2}}{2.0 \, \text{N}} \quad (\text{and } 1 \, \text{N} = 1 \, \text{kg m s}^{-2})$$

$$x = 0.25 \, \text{m}.$$

Note that this problem could have been solved by first

108   7 Work and kinetic energy

finding the acceleration of the block. Using $ma = \Sigma F$ we would have

$$(1.0\,\text{kg})a = -2.0\,\text{N}$$
$$a = -2.0\,\text{m s}^{-2}.$$

Now using $v^2 = u^2 + 2as$, with $v = 0$, $u = 1.0\,\text{m s}^{-2}$, we have

$$0 = (1.0\,\text{m s}^{-1})^2 + 2(-2.0\,\text{m s}^{-2})x$$

which gives $\quad x = 0.25\,\text{m}$

as before, but this method is more cumbersome and we shall always use $W_{AB} = \tfrac{1}{2}mv^2 - \tfrac{1}{2}mu^2$ in preference. In any case we could *only* have used $v^2 = u^2 + 2as$ in situations where the size of the acceleration is constant and we have linear motion. Referring to Example 7-8, we could have used $ma = \Sigma F$ and $v^2 = u^2 + 2as$ for part (*a*) but *not* for parts (*b*) and (*c*): the equation $W_{AB} = \tfrac{1}{2}mv^2 - \tfrac{1}{2}mu^2$ could and should be used for *all three parts*.   ◀

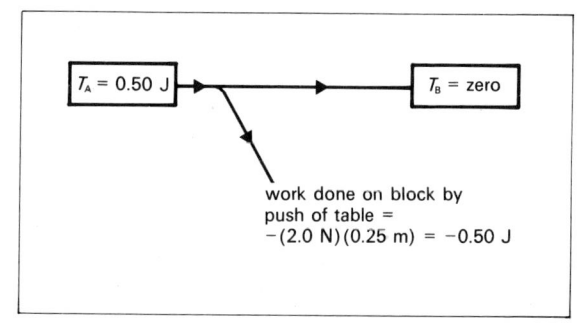

$T_A = 0.50\,\text{J}$ → $T_B = \text{zero}$

work done on block by push of table =
$-(2.0\,\text{N})(0.25\,\text{m}) = -0.50\,\text{J}$

Figure 7-14 Energy flow diagram for Example 7-10.

▶ **Example 7-11** Figure 7-15 shows a rough slope up which a block of mass 2.0 kg is moving with speed 12 m s^{-1}. The frictional push of the slope on the block is 2.0 N. Find the speed of the block when it has travelled 10 m along the slope and has thus risen 4.0 m vertically. Take $g = 9.8\,\text{m s}^{-2}$.

The work done on the block by
(a) the pull of the Earth $\quad = -(19.6\,\text{N})(4.0\,\text{m})$
$\qquad\qquad\qquad\qquad\qquad\;\; = -78.4\,\text{J}$
(b) the normal contact push R of the slope
$\qquad\qquad\qquad\qquad\qquad\;\; = \text{zero}$
(c) the frictional push of the slope $= -(2.0\,\text{N})(10\,\text{m})$
$\qquad\qquad\qquad\qquad\qquad\;\; = -20.0\,\text{J}.$

Using $\qquad W_{AB} = \tfrac{1}{2}mv^2 - \tfrac{1}{2}mu^2$

we have $\quad -98.4\,\text{J} = \tfrac{1}{2}(2.0\,\text{kg})v^2 - \tfrac{1}{2}(2.0\,\text{kg})(12\,\text{m s}^{-1})^2$

$\qquad\qquad 45.6\,\text{J} = \tfrac{1}{2}(2.0\,\text{kg})v^2$

so that $\qquad v = 6.7\,\text{m s}^{-1}.$ ◀

2.0 kg, 10 m, 4.0 m

free-body diagram for the block

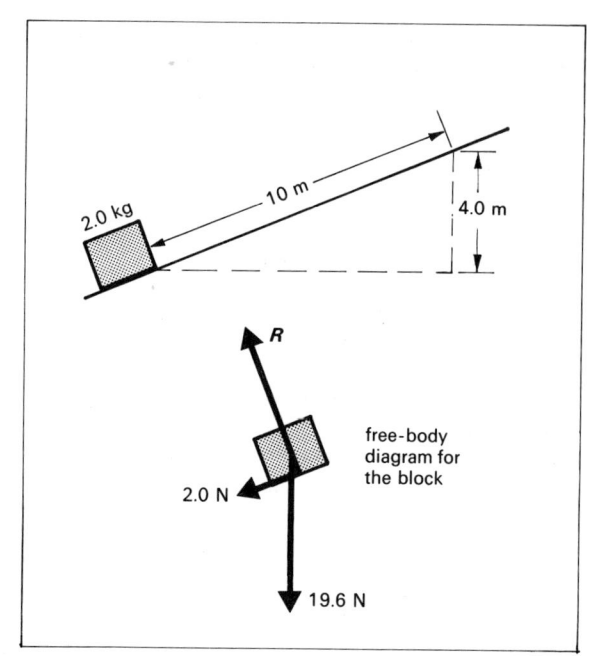

R, 2.0 N, 19.6 N

Figure 7-15

$T_A = 144\,\text{J}$ → $T_B = 45.6\,\text{J}$

work done on block by pull of Earth
$= -(19.6\,\text{N})(4.0\,\text{m})$
$= -78.4\,\text{J}$

work done on block by frictional push of slope
$= -(2.0\,\text{N})(10\,\text{m})$
$= -20\,\text{J}$

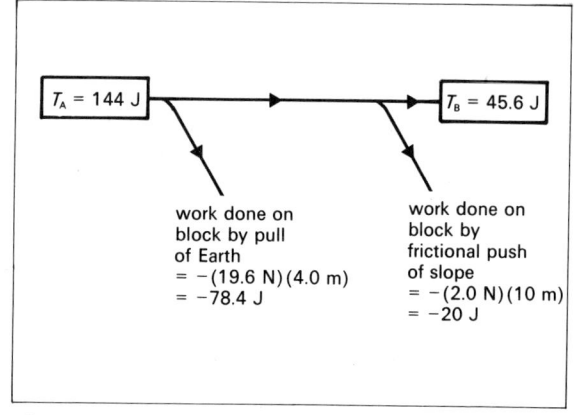

Figure 7-16 Energy flow diagram for Example 7-11.

▶ **Example 7-12** A spring of constant stiffness 12 N m^{-1} and natural length 1.0 m has one end attached to a fixed point on a horizontal table. To the other end is attached a mass of 4.0 kg. The mass is pulled horizontally until the spring has a length of 3.0 m and the mass is then released. If the frictional push of the table on the mass is 10 N, find the speed of the mass when the spring has a length of 2.0 m.

In contracting a distance of 1.0 m, the work done on the block by
(a) the pull of the Earth $\qquad\qquad = \text{zero}$

(b) the normal contact push of the table
   = zero
(c) the frictional push of the table = $-(10\,\text{N})(1.0\,\text{m})$
   = $-10\,\text{J}$
(d) the pull of the spring (= average force × displacement)
   $= \left(\dfrac{24\,\text{N}+12\,\text{N}}{2}\right)(1.0\,\text{m})$
   $= 18\,\text{J}$

so that the total work done on the block = 8.0 J.

Using $\quad W_{AB} = \tfrac{1}{2}mv^2 - \tfrac{1}{2}mu^2$

we have $\quad 8.0\,\text{J} = \tfrac{1}{2}(4.0\,\text{kg})v^2 - \tfrac{1}{2}(4.0\,\text{kg})(0\,\text{m s}^{-1})^2$

so that $\quad v = 2.0\,\text{m s}^{-1}$. ◀

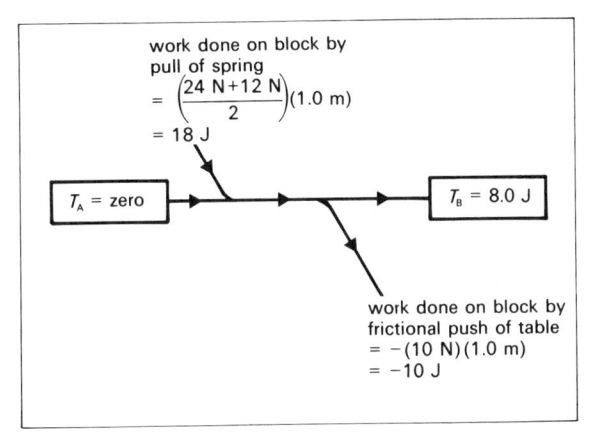

```
work done on block by
pull of spring
= (24 N+12 N)/2 (1.0 m)
= 18 J

T_A = zero  →  T_B = 8.0 J

work done on block by
frictional push of table
= -(10 N)(1.0 m)
= -10 J
```

Figure 7-17 Energy flow diagram for Example 7-12.

▶**Example 7-13** A spring of constant stiffness $4.0\,\text{N m}^{-1}$ is hung vertically by one end and a mass of 0.50 kg is hung at its lower end and held so that the spring is still unstretched but just taut. The mass is then released. What is the speed of the mass when it has fallen 0.50 m? How far will it fall before it next comes instantaneously to rest? Take $g = 9.8\,\text{m s}^{-2}$.

In falling 0.50 m, the work done on the mass by

(a) the pull of the Earth $= (0.5 \times 9.8\,\text{N})(0.50\,\text{m})$
   $= 2.45\,\text{J}$

(b) the pull of the spring (= average force × displacement)
   $= -\left(\dfrac{2.0\,\text{N}+0}{2}\right)(0.50\,\text{m})$
   $= -0.50\,\text{J}$

so that the total work done on the mass = 1.95 J.

7-7 The work–energy theorem

Using $\quad W_{AB} = \tfrac{1}{2}mv^2 - \tfrac{1}{2}mu^2$

we have $1.95\,\text{J} = \tfrac{1}{2}(0.50\,\text{kg})v^2 - \tfrac{1}{2}(0.50\,\text{kg})(0\,\text{m s}^{-1})^2$

so that $\quad v = 2.8\,\text{m s}^{-1}$.

If x is the distance fallen before the mass first comes instantaneously to rest, the work done on the mass by

(a) the pull of the Earth $= (0.50 \times 9.8\,\text{N})x$

(b) the pull of the spring $= -\left(\dfrac{4x\,\text{N m}^{-1}+0}{2}\right)x$.

We again use $W_{AB} = \tfrac{1}{2}mv^2 - \tfrac{1}{2}mu^2$, but in this case $v = u = 0$, so that $W_{AB} = 0$. Hence

$$(0.50 \times 9.8\,\text{N})x - \left(\dfrac{4x\,\text{N m}^{-1}+0}{2}\right)x = 0$$

so that $\quad x = 0$ or $2.5\,\text{m}$.

The answer $x = 0$ refers to the initial situation, when the spring was unstretched and stationary: $x = 2.5\,\text{m}$ gives the fact that the mass will be stationary when it has fallen 2.5 m. ◀

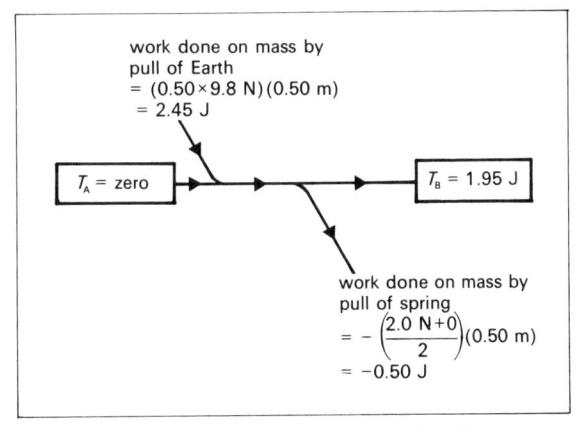

```
work done on mass by
pull of Earth
= (0.50×9.8 N)(0.50 m)
= 2.45 J

T_A = zero  →  T_B = 1.95 J

work done on mass by
pull of spring
= -(2.0 N+0)/2 (0.50 m)
= -0.50 J
```

Figure 7-18 Energy flow diagram for Example 7-13.

Frames of reference

There are some situations for which at first sight the work–energy theorem does not seem to give consistent results. Suppose a horizontal resultant force of 4.0 N is exerted on a mass of 1.0 kg resting on a horizontal table of width 2.0 m. When the mass reaches the far side of the table, after 1.0 s, it will have a velocity of $4.0\,\text{m s}^{-1}$. The work done on the mass is $(4.0\,\text{N})(2.0\,\text{m}) = 8.0\,\text{J}$. This result is consistent with the gain in kinetic energy of the mass: this is $\tfrac{1}{2}(1.0\,\text{kg})(4\,\text{m s}^{-1})^2 = 8.0\,\text{J}$.

But suppose this experiment is performed in a train moving at a uniform velocity of $8.0\,\text{m s}^{-1}$ (this velocity being parallel to that of the mass). An observer in the train will perform the same calculations as we have done above. What will an observer outside the train measure? He estimates that the mass has travelled 10.0 m (2.0 m relative to the train, and a further 8.0 m relative to the ground) and calculates the work done on the mass as $(4.0\,\text{N})(10.0\,\text{m}) = 40\,\text{J}$. From his point of view, however, the final speed of the mass is $12.0\,\text{m s}^{-1}$ ($8\,\text{m s}^{-1} + 4\,\text{m s}^{-1}$); the gain of kinetic energy is thus given by

$$\tfrac{1}{2}(1.0\,\text{kg})(12.0\,\text{m s}^{-1})^2 - \tfrac{1}{2}(1.0\,\text{kg})(8.0\,\text{m s}^{-1})^2 = 40\,\text{J}.$$

Thus in this particular case we see that the truth of the work–energy theorem is *independent* of the inertial reference frame chosen. Exercise 7-46 suggests how this result can be shown to be true in a more general case.

7-8 Internal work

There are many situations where the kinetic energy of a body changes and yet the resultant external force does no work on the body: think, for example, of a boy jumping off the ground, or of a car accelerating along a road. In neither case does the point of application of the accelerating force undergo a (measurable) displacement. For the boy, the upward accelerating force only exists as long as the boy's foot, and therefore the point of application of the force, remains stationary and in contact with the ground. For the car, there is no relative motion between the ground and that part of the wheel which is in contact with the ground, and the accelerating force therefore does no work on the car. (Strictly, there are microscopically small displacements in order to produce the accelerating forces but the work done by these forces is negligibly small—we will assume zero.)

In figure 7-19 we see a trolley which has a spring fixed to it. When the spring is compressed, and the trolley placed against a wall and released, the spring expands and the trolley is pushed away from the wall. The force exerted by the wall on the spring does not, however, do work on the trolley, yet the trolley gains kinetic energy. We might guess that when a boy jumps, or a car accelerates, there is some device inside each of them similar in effect to the spring in the trolley. This device *does work inside them* and the result is an increase in the body's kinetic energy: we call such forces *internal forces* and such work *internal work*. The work–energy theorem is modified in order to meet these situations:

$$W_{AB}(\text{by external forces}) + W(\text{by internal forces}) = \Delta T.$$

We shall, of course, not usually be able to calculate W(by internal forces) unless we know the values of both W_{AB}(by external forces) and ΔT.

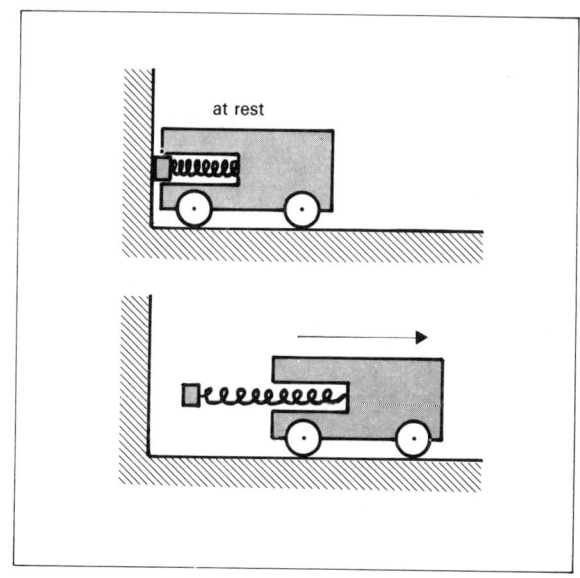

Figure 7-19 The accelerating force, the push of the wall on the buffer, does no work and yet the kinetic energy of the whole trolley certainly changes.

▶ **Example 7-14** Figure 7-20 shows a free-body diagram for a cyclist and his machine which have a total mass of 80 kg, and which are moving at a steady speed of 2.5 m s^{-1} up a hill of constant slope θ (sin $\theta = 0.050$). The wind into which he is cycling exerts a constant force on him of 60 N. What is the rate at which he does internal work?

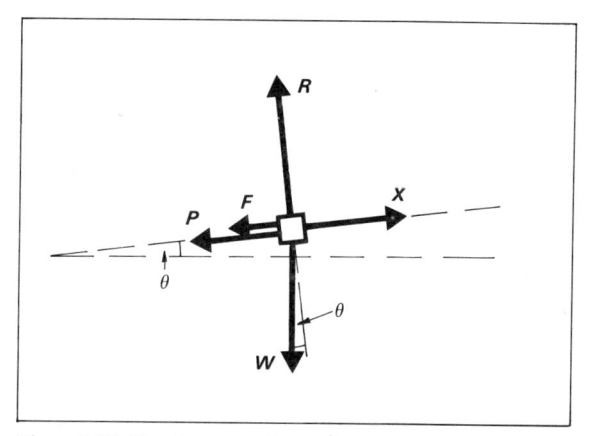

Figure 7-20 The forces on the cyclist and his machine: W is the weight of the cyclist and his machine; R is the normal contact push of the slope; P is the push of the wind; X is the forward push of the ground (the driving force); F is the rolling-friction push of the ground.

Let us take $g = 10\,\text{m s}^{-2}$: we have $W = 800\,\text{N}$, and $P = 60\,\text{N}$. In 1.0 s the cyclist travels 2.5 m, so we can calculate the work done by the external forces on him and his machine while he travels for 1.0 s:

The work done on him and his machine by

(a) the pull of the Earth
 $= -(800\,\text{N})(2.5\,\text{m})(0.050)$
 $= -100\,\text{J}$

(b) the forward push of the ground
 $=$ zero, since there is no relative motion between the wheel and the ground

(c) the rolling friction force
 $=$ zero for the same reason

(d) the normal contact force
 $=$ zero, because its direction is perpendicular to the displacement

(e) the push of the wind
 $= -(60\,\text{N})(2.5\,\text{m})$
 $= -150\,\text{J}$,

so that the total work done by the external forces on the cyclist and his machine $= -250\,\text{J}$. We now use W_{AB} (by external forces) $+ W$(by internal forces) $= \Delta T$: $\Delta T = 0$, since the cyclist is not accelerating, so that

$$-250\,\text{J} + W(\text{by internal forces}) = 0$$

and $\qquad W(\text{by internal forces}) = 250\,\text{J}$.

As this work is done in 1.0 s, the rate of doing internal work is $250\,\text{J}/1.0\,\text{s} = 250\,\text{W}$. At least, this is the rate at which the cyclist contributes energy to the action of cycling uphill: in fact, since he and his bicycle are not 100 per cent efficient, he must work at a rate which is much greater than 250 W. ◀

Bibliography

Magie, W. F. (1935). *A source book of physics.* McGraw-Hill. Excerpts from Descartes and Leibniz.

Nuffield O-level Physics (1966). *Teachers' Guide I.* Longman/Penguin. There is a note to teachers on getting tired while holding an object at arm's length.

Sears, F. W. and Zemansky, M. W. (1964). *College physics.* Addison–Wesley. Chapter 7: work and energy.

Weidner, R. T. and Sells, R. L. (1965). *Elementary classical physics*, volume 1. Allyn and Bacon. Chapter 11: energy.

Wenham, E. J., Dorling, G. W., Snell, J. A. N., and Taylor, B. (1972). *Physics, concepts and models.* Addison–Wesley. The chapter on work and energy contains some nice quantitative examples of energy storage and transfer.

8 mm film loop. 'Direct measurement of potential and kinetic energy during catapult firing.' BBC Publications.

Exercises

Data (to be used unless otherwise directed):
$g = 10\,\text{m s}^{-2} = 10\,\text{N kg}^{-1}$.

7-1 How much work is done on a body when a force of 5.0 N acts on it for a displacement of 3.0 m, the direction of the displacement being the same as that of the force?

7-2 How much work is done on a body when a force of 10 N acts on it for a displacement of 0.60 m, the direction of the displacement being the same as that of the force?

7-3 What is the work done by the pull of the Earth on a mass of 5.0 kg when it
 (a) rises 20 m vertically
 (b) falls 30 m vertically?

7-4 A man holds a mass of 3.0 kg and raises it vertically at a steady speed until it is 6.0 m higher. What work is done on the mass by
 (a) the push of the man
 (b) the pull of the Earth?
In the information given, was it necessary to include the word(s) (i) 'vertically' (ii) 'at a steady speed'?

7-5 A simple pendulum oscillates in such a way that its bob (of mass 0.30 kg) rises at the ends of its oscillations 0.040 m above its lowest point. What work is done on the bob by the pull of the Earth when the bob
 (a) swings from one extreme position to its central position
 (b) swings from its central position to one extreme position?
What work is done on the bob by the pull of the string? Do any other forces do work on the bob? ●

7-6 An Earth satellite has a mass of 1000 kg. How much work is done on it by the pull of the Earth when it makes a circular orbit of length $5.0 \times 10^7\,\text{m}$? The value of g in this orbit is $6.3\,\text{m s}^{-2}$.

7 Work and kinetic energy

7-7 A man pulls a sledge with a horizontal force of 300 N for a distance of 100 m.
(a) How much work does he do on the sledge?
(b) If his pull (of 300 N) was inclined at 20° to the horizontal, how much work would he do on the sledge if it again moved 100 m horizontally?
(c) If the horizontal push of the ground on the sledge is 250 N, how much work does it do on the sledge when the sledge moves 100 m? ●

7-8 A pendulum bob of mass m hangs by a massless string of length l. What work is done in pulling the bob aside until the string makes an angle θ with the vertical? ●

7-9 A block of mass 10 kg slides down a rough slope which is inclined at 40° to the horizontal. The coefficient of sliding friction $\mu_k = 0.30$. When it has slid 5.0 m, how much work has been done on the block by
(a) the pull of the Earth
(b) the normal contact push of the slope
(c) the frictional push of the slope? ●

7-10 A spring has a natural length of 0.20 m and a constant stiffness of 8.0 N m^{-1}. Find the work done by the spring on a man when he stretches it from a length of
(a) 0.20 m to 0.30 m (b) 0.30 m to 0.40 m (c) 0.40 m to 0.50 m. ●

7-11 A spring has a natural length of 1.0 m and a constant stiffness of 8.0 N m^{-1} and is hung up vertically. A mass of 0.50 kg is attached to its lower end, held, and then released. When the mass has fallen 0.50 m, how much work has been done on it by
(a) the pull of the Earth
(b) the pull of the spring?
How far would the mass fall before first coming to rest? Would the mass then be in equilibrium? ●

7-12 A bead is threaded on a frictionless wire which is bent into the form of a circle of centre O and radius 1.5 m, and which lies in a *horizontal* plane, as shown in figure 7-21.

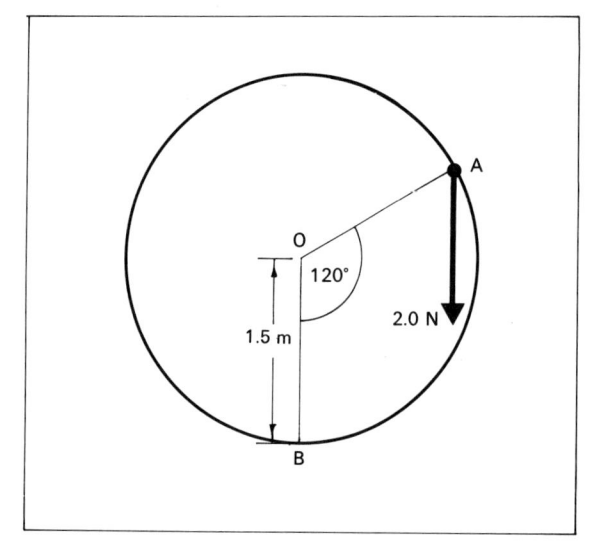

Figure 7-21

The bead is initially at A, and a point B is such that $A\hat{O}B = 120°$. A force of 2.0 N in a direction parallel to OB is exerted on the bead. Calculate the work done on the bead by this force as the bead moves between A and B. ●

7-13 A ski-jump consists of a run (which is not of constant slope) of length 50 m. In this distance there is a vertical fall of 30 m, and there is a fall of 35 m from the end of the run to the ground below. A man of mass 80 kg starts at the top of the run, and the frictional push of the run on him is equal in size to one-tenth of his weight. What work has been done on him by the time he has reached the ground by
(a) the pull of the Earth
(b) the frictional push of the slope
(c) the normal contact push of the slope? ●

7-14 Taking any necessary information from Example 7-3, find the work done by the pull of the Earth on a mass of 1000 kg when it falls to the Earth from a height above the surface of 1.6×10^6 m (a) by drawing a graph relating force and displacement (b) using calculus. ●

7-15 A man raises a bucket of water (of mass 20 kg) from a well. The thin rope pulling the bucket is wound round a shaft of radius 30 mm, and this shaft has at one end a handle cranked so that when the man turns it his hand moves in a circle of radius 150 mm. What is the least force he can hope to exert in order to raise the bucket? If this machine is 80 per cent efficient, what force must he exert? ●

7-16 By making measurements on the structure of a stationary bicycle, calculate its velocity ratio in its lowest gear. How would one measure the velocity ratio experienced when riding the bicycle?

7-17 (a) If using the bicycle of Exercise 7-16 a man exerts a force of 80 N on each pedal alternately, what is the forward force which the ground exerts on the bicycle (assuming it is 70 per cent efficient), when the bicycle is in its lowest gear?
(b) Thinking of a hill as an 'inclined plane' and therefore as a machine for raising loads vertically, find the velocity ratio of a hill which has a slope of 1 in 3 (that is, there is a vertical rise of 1 m for every 3 m travelled up the slope).
(c) Will the man of part (a) be able to cycle up the hill of part (b) if, together with the bicycle, he has a mass of 80 kg? Assume that the inclined plane acts as a perfectly efficient machine.

7-18 An Olympic heavyweight weight-lifter 'snatches' a mass of 160 kg from floor to arm's length, a vertical height of 1.2 m, in 0.55 s. What is his average rate of working? Give your answer in kW. ●

7-19 Find the velocity acquired by
(a) a mass of 2.0 kg, initially at rest, when it is acted upon by a force of 5.0 N due east and it undergoes a displacement of 20 m due east.
(b) a mass of 5.0 kg, initially having a velocity of 8.0 m s^{-1} due east, when it is acted upon by a force of 7.5 N due east, and it undergoes a displacement of 12 m due east.
In (b) would the velocity acquired be the same if the initial velocity had been 8.0 m s^{-1} due *west*? Explain.
Draw energy flow diagrams for these three situations. ●

7-20 Find the speed of the pendulum bob of Exercise 7-5 when it is in its lowest position. Ignore any work done by the push of the air on the bob. Draw an energy flow diagram for the bob as it moves from one extreme position to another. ●

7-21 Estimate the kinetic energy of
(a) a rifle bullet
(b) a man running for a bus
(c) a tennis ball just after it has been served
(d) a family saloon car on a motorway.

7-22 Estimate the kinetic energy of
(a) an oxygen molecule in your lungs
(b) an electron moving along the tube of a television set.

7-23 Estimate the kinetic energy of
(a) the Earth in its orbit round the Sun
(b) the Moon in its orbit round the Earth.

7-24 Refer to Exercise 7-12. If the mass of the bead was 200 g, and its speed at A was $2.0 \, \text{m s}^{-1}$, what was its speed at B? Draw an energy flow diagram for the bead between A and B. ●

7-25 A spring whose stiffness is $30 \, \text{N m}^{-1}$ is supported vertically, and a mass of 1.0 kg is attached to its lower end and then released. Find the work done on the mass by
(a) the pull of the Earth
(b) the pull of the spring
while the mass has fallen 0.50 m. Hence find the velocity of the mass when it has fallen 0.50 m. Draw an energy flow diagram for the fall. ●

7-26 Refer to Exercise 7-25. Draw graphs of the pull of the Earth versus displacement, and of the pull of the spring versus displacement, and hence (by considering the areas beneath the graphs) find
(a) the displacement when the mass first becomes stationary
(b) the displacement when the mass has its maximum velocity.

7-27 Refer to Exercise 7-13. With the ski-jumper starting from rest, find the speed with which he reaches the ground, assuming that no work is done on him by forces other than those in (a), (b), and (c). Is this assumption justified? Draw an energy flow diagram for his jump. ●

7-28 Figure 7-22 shows a bead A of mass 20 g threaded on a frictionless wire which is bent into the form of a circle of radius 0.50 m and which lies in a *vertical* plane. Initially A is at rest, and OA makes an angle of 60° with the vertical. Find the work done by the forces acting on the bead, and hence find its speed when OA has turned through an angle of
(a) 30°   (b) 120°   (c) 210°   (d) 240°. ●

7-29 To find the first answer (a) in Exercise 7-28 would it have been valid to use the equation $v^2 = u^2 + 2as$ with $u = 0$, $a = 10 \, \text{m s}^{-2}$, $s = 0.25 \, \text{m}$? Explain your answer.

7-30 A man throws a stone of mass 0.50 kg up into the air by exerting an upward force of 45 N on it for a distance of 0.40 m and then releasing it. How high does it rise after it has left his hand? ●

7-31 A man throws a stone of mass m up into the air so that it rises for a distance h after it has left his hand. It stops, and falls again. When it has fallen a distance h from its topmost point how much work has been done on it by the pull of the Earth while it has been in free fall? Is the speed of the stone then the same as it was when it left the man's hand? Give *two* answers, (a) ignoring and (b) not ignoring the push of the air on the stone.

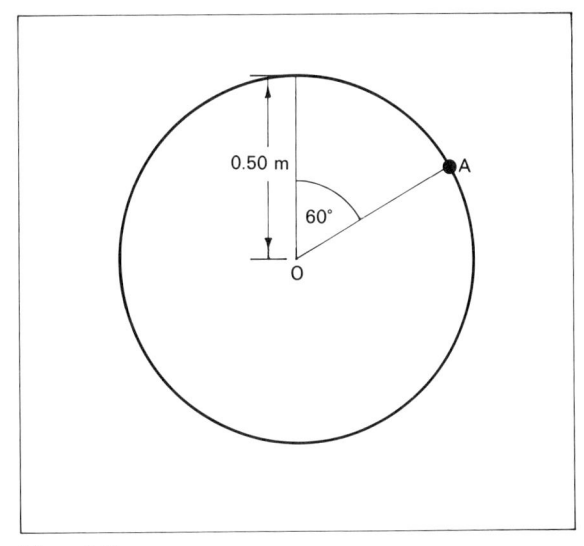

Figure 7-22

7-32 Several people throw stones from the top of a cliff. The stones have different masses, and they are thrown at different angles of elevation, but each person throws his stone at the same speed. Will all the stones have the same speed when they strike the surface of the sea? Will they all reach the surface of the sea at the same time? Ignore air resistance forces.

7-33 A man throws a stone of mass 0.30 kg from the edge of a cliff in such a way that its velocity has an (upward) vertical component of $6.0 \, \text{m s}^{-1}$ and a horizontal component of $8.0 \, \text{m s}^{-1}$. Ignoring air resistance, find the speed of the stone
(a) initially
(b) when it is 1.0 m above its starting point on its way up
(c) when it is 1.0 m above its starting point on its way down
(d) when it is again at the same level as its starting point.
If the man had given the same velocity to a stone of twice the mass, would these answers have been the same? Why? ●

7-34 A block of mass 0.50 kg rests on a horizontal table, the coefficient of sliding friction μ_k between the surfaces being 0.30. A spring of stiffness $5.0 \, \text{N m}^{-1}$ has one end attached to the mass, and the other end attached to a fixed point A on the table. Initially the spring has an extension of 1.2 m: what is the speed of the mass when it has moved
(a) 0.20 m   (b) 0.50 m? ●
Draw energy flow diagrams for the block in the two cases.

7-35 Find the velocity of the block of Exercise 7-34 when it has moved 0.20 m if it starts with a velocity of $1.5 \, \text{m s}^{-1}$ towards A. ●

7-36 Discuss the construction of a 'roller-coaster' for a fairground, with reference to such factors as the need for the coaster to negotiate curves and humps, the desirability of having a high (length of track)/(initial height) ratio, and so forth.

7 Work and kinetic energy

7-37 A frictionless rail is bent as shown in figure 7-23 so that it has a circular loop of radius r. The whole rail lies in a vertical plane. A ball is released from A, at a height h above the lowest point of the circle: what is the least value of h necessary to keep the bead in contact with the rail throughout its motion? (*Hint:* find the speed which the ball must have at the highest point of the loop in order to remain in contact with the rail.) •

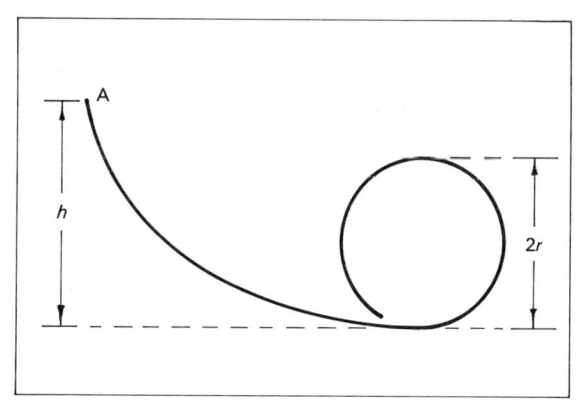

Figure 7-23

7-38 A bullet of mass 0.028 kg and speed $800 \, \text{m s}^{-1}$ is fired into a block of wood and penetrates 0.20 m. What is the average force exerted *on* the wood *by* the bullet? Give a careful explanation. •

7-39 A man who is digging a hole in the ground lifts a pickaxe of mass 10 kg and lets it fall 2.0 m once every 2 s. What is his average rate of working? (Ignore the work done in raising his arms.) If each time the pickaxe strikes the ground, it penetrates a distance of 20 mm, what is the average size of the force exerted by the ground on the pickaxe? •

7-40 A ball of mass 0.50 kg is dropped on to a floor from a height of 2.0 m, and rebounds with a velocity which is -0.8 times the velocity with which it struck the ground. Find
 (*a*) the height to which it rises
 (*b*) the kinetic energy lost on impact. •

7-41 An object of mass 3.0 kg falls from rest through a vertical distance of 20 m and reaches a velocity of $18 \, \text{m s}^{-1}$. How much work is done by the push of the air on the object? •

7-42 A car has a maximum speed of $35 \, \text{m s}^{-1}$ on a level road. If the rate of working of the engine is then 90 kW, what is the total resistance force at this speed? Assuming that the resistance force is proportional to the square of the speed, find the rate of working of the engine when the car has a steady speed of $20 \, \text{m s}^{-1}$. •

7-43 What is the steepest slope up which the car of Exercise 7-42 can travel at a speed of $20 \, \text{m s}^{-1}$, if it has a mass of 1000 kg? •

7-44 A human heart does internal work at an average rate of 6 W. How much work does it do in one day? •

7-45 Why do roads not take the shortest route up steep hillsides?

7-46 Suppose a man on a train moving at a constant velocity V marks out a line on the floor of the train parallel to the direction of movement of the train. He observes that a constant force F (in the direction of V) gives a mass m a velocity v in time t and displacement x, both v and x being measured relative to the train. Write down equations to relate
 (*a*) F, x, m, v (using the work–energy equation)
 (*b*) v, x, t and hence
 (*c*) F, t, m, v.
A stationary observer outside the train observes the above experiment. He sees that the mass m has initial and final velocities of V and $V+v$, and to achieve this the force F is moved a distance $(x+Vt)$ in time t. What equation would he write down to correspond to (*a*) above? Is this equation consistent with equations (*a*), (*b*), (*c*) above?

8 Linear momentum

8-1 The impulse of a force	115	8-7 The rate of change of momentum	126
8-2 The momentum of a particle	116	8-8 Rockets	128
8-3 The conservation of linear momentum	117	8-9 Centre of mass	130
8-4 Simple collisions	118	Bibliography	133
8-5 Recoil	121	Exercises	133
8-6 Interactions in two dimensions	124		

8-1 The impulse of a force

In Section 7-1 it was suggested that one way to measure the effect of a force on a body is to calculate the value of $\sum F\Delta t$, the sum being taken over the time t for which the force acts. $\sum F\Delta t$ or, for a constant force $F\Delta t$, is defined as the *impulse* I of the force on the body.

$$\sum F\Delta t = I. \qquad [8\text{-}1]$$

Its unit is the newton second (N s) or as $1\,\text{N} = 1\,\text{kg}\,\text{m}\,\text{s}^{-2}$, the $\text{kg}\,\text{m}\,\text{s}^{-1}$. The impulse of a force is a vector quantity. The word impulse would seem to imply a violent but brief force such as the push of a tennis racket on a ball or the push of a tennis ball on a racket (see figure 8-1), and the phrase 'an impulsive force' is sometimes thought to be reserved for such situations. But we can think of any force as exerting an impulse on a body; for example, if I push a car with a steady force of 300 N for 12 s, then the impulse of my push on the car is

$$300\,\text{N} \times 12\,\text{s} = 3.6 \times 10^3\,\text{N s}$$

in the direction of the push of my hands on the car. In figure 8-2b it can be seen that the quantity I may have a simple value even though the variation in F and t may be extremely complex.

Figure 8-1 A high-speed photograph of an impact between a tennis racket and a ball.

8 Linear momentum

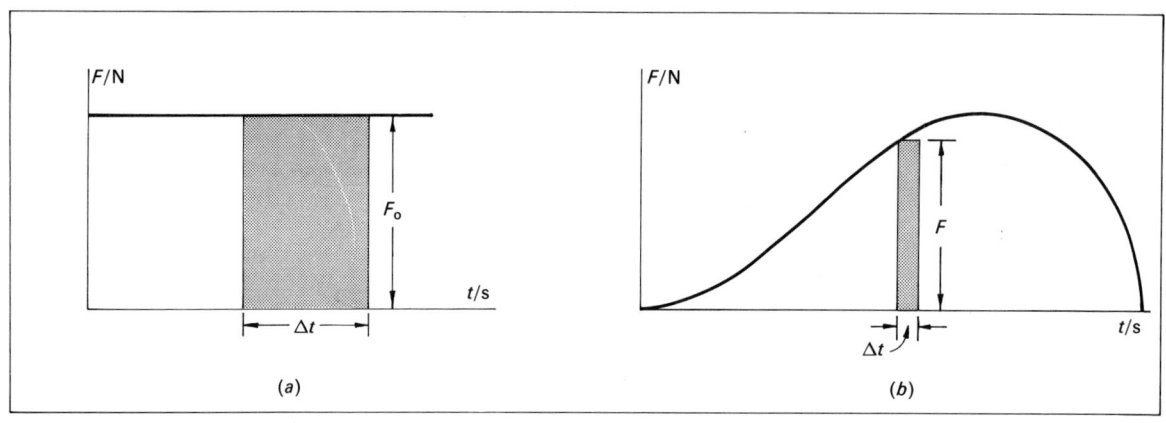

Figure 8-2 (a) The shaded area $F_0 \Delta t$ represents the impulse of F_0 in the time interval Δt. (b) The total impulse of the force is $\Sigma F \Delta t$, and is equal to the area under the graph.

8-2 The momentum of a particle

A particle of mass m moving with a velocity v is defined as having a *linear momentum* p where

$$p = mv. \qquad [8\text{-}2]$$

The unit of momentum is the kg m s^{-1} or as $1\,\text{N} = 1\,\text{kg m s}^{-2}$, the N s. Linear momentum, which we shall often refer to as momentum, is a vector quantity, the direction of p being that of v. Newton's first law is expressed more meaningfully than on page 61, by the statement 'a free particle moves with a constant momentum', as the inertial property of the particle, its mass, is included in this statement.

Consider the particle shown in figure 8-3. In what direction would you push the particle in order to change its momentum by $\Delta p = p_2 - p_1$? The commonsense answer says roughly downwards but we can analyse the motion further using Newton's second law and show that the direction of the momentum change is that of the average force producing the change. Let $p_1 = mv_1$ and $p_2 = mv_2$, and let us assume that m is constant.

$$\Delta p = mv_2 - mv_1$$
$$= m(v_2 - v_1)$$
$$= m\Delta v.$$

It follows that

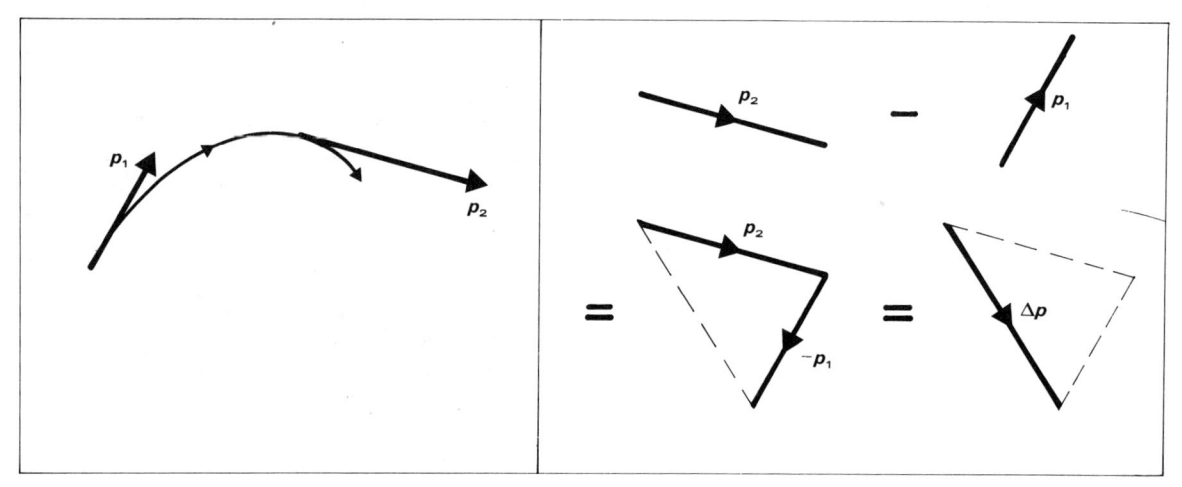

$$\frac{\Delta p}{\Delta t} = m\frac{\Delta v}{\Delta t} = ma = F_{\text{res}},$$

Figure 8-3 The change of momentum of the particle is $\Delta p = p_2 - p_1$.

where a is the average vector acceleration of the particle during the time Δt and F_{res} is the average resultant external force producing the acceleration. This last set of equalities contains two important results. Firstly,

$$\frac{\Delta p}{\Delta t} = F_{\text{res}};$$

we shall consider this further in Section 8-7. Secondly

$$\Delta p = F_{\text{res}} \Delta t,$$

which is the impulse of the force acting on the particle. That is, $\Delta p = I$, and we can express this as:

the change of momentum of a particle = the impulse of the resultant force acting on the particle. [8-3]

Figure 8-4 shows this diagrammatically.

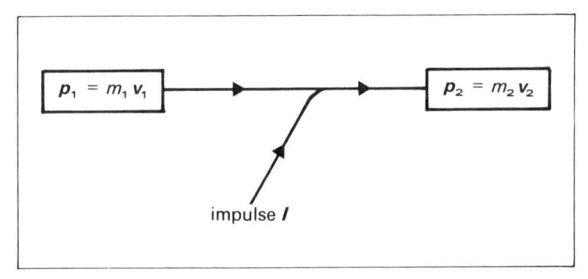

Figure 8-4 A momentum flow diagram.

We shall call this relation *the impulse–momentum equation*. Thus, referring to the car at the end of Section 8-1 which was given a horizontal impulse of 3.6×10^3 N s we deduce that the change of momentum of the car will be 3.6×10^3 N s or 3.6×10^3 kg m s^{-1}. If the car has a mass of 600 kg the change of velocity of the car is Δv where

$$(600 \text{ kg}) \Delta v = 3.6 \times 10^3 \text{ kg m s}^{-1},$$

whence $\Delta v = 6.0 \text{ m s}^{-1}$

in the direction of the push on the car.

▶ **Example 8-1** A hydrogen molecule has a mass of 3.3×10^{-27} kg and a speed of 1.8×10^3 m s^{-1}. If it strikes a surface normally, and rebounds with the same speed, what is the impulse which the surface gives to the molecule?

Taking momenta to the right to be positive, in figure 8-5:

$$p_1 = (3.3 \times 10^{-27} \text{ kg})(1.8 \times 10^3 \text{ m s}^{-1})$$
$$= 5.9 \times 10^{-24} \text{ N s}$$

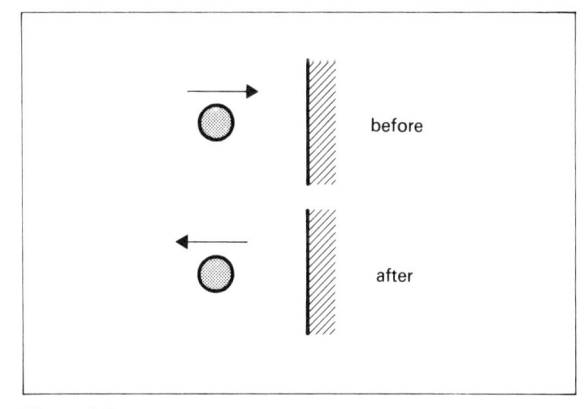

Figure 8-5

$$p_2 = -(3.3 \times 10^{-27} \text{ kg})(1.8 \times 10^3 \text{ m s}^{-1})$$
$$= -5.9 \times 10^{-24} \text{ N s}.$$

Therefore

$$I = \Delta p = p_2 - p_1$$
$$= (-5.9 \times 10^{-24} \text{ N s}) - (5.9 \times 10^{-24} \text{ N s})$$
$$= -11.8 \times 10^{-24} \text{ N s}$$
$$= -1.2 \times 10^{-23} \text{ N s},$$

that is the impulse of the wall is 1.2×10^{-23} N s to the left. If we knew the time during which the wall and the molecule were interacting, we should be able to calculate the average force exerted by the wall. ◀

8-3 The conservation of linear momentum

Before attempting an analysis of what happens when two bodies (which can be treated as particles) interact, the reader should think of some examples from everyday life. Two colliding billiard balls, railway trucks in a shunting yard, and a man stepping out of a small boat are all situations in which two bodies undergo changes in their motions clearly as a result of their interaction. Where we wish to think of the push of A on B and at the same time of the push of B on A we will call the situation an *interaction*.

Looking more closely at a typical shunting yard collision as described by figure 8-6, the push to the right of truck 1 on truck 2 seems at first sight to have a different effect from the push to the left of truck 2 on truck 1. But of course the diagram does not give us the masses of the two trucks. Is it obvious that $mass_1 > mass_2$? If we actually saw the event, it probably would be obvious that this is so.

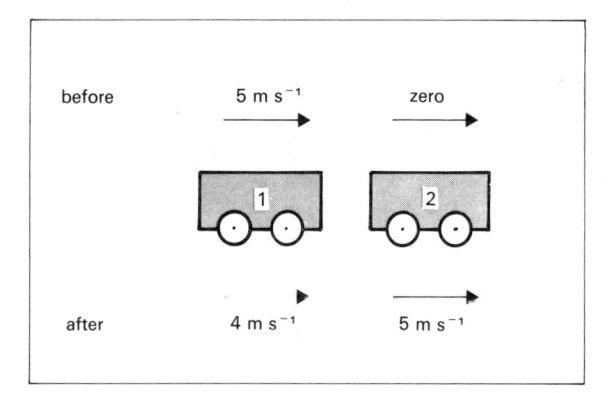

Figure 8-6 A moving truck strikes a stationary one which rebounds from it, the moving truck continuing to move in the same direction as it did initially but with a reduced speed.

The forces of interaction in this example are not the only forces acting on the trucks but let us assume for the moment that we are dealing with situations where the *only* forces are those of interaction.

Consider the impulse–momentum equation, $\Delta p = I$, applied separately to each of two interacting particles denoted by suffixes 1 and 2.

$$\Delta p_1 = I_1 = \sum F_1 \Delta t$$

and

$$\Delta p_2 = I_2 = \sum F_2 \Delta t.$$

But by Newton's third law, $F_1 = -F_2$ at every instant.

Thus also $I_1 = -I_2$

and so $\Delta p_1 = -\Delta p_2$

or $\Delta p_1 + \Delta p_2 = 0.$

This last equation, which states that there is no change in the vector sum of the momenta of the particles as a result of their interaction, is a special case of one of the most important laws of physics—the principle of conservation of linear momentum.

If $\Delta p_1 + \Delta p_2 = 0,$

then $\Delta(p_1 + p_2) = 0,$

and so $p_1 + p_2 = $ constant.

Generalizing $p_1 + p_2 + \cdots + p_n = $ constant,

or $\sum p_n = $ constant. [8-4]

The total linear momentum of a system of interacting particles remains constant.

In the laboratory, or anywhere on Earth, any interacting system will include the Earth itself. Thus a stone thrown into the air, *and the Earth* from which the stone was thrown, form a system for which linear momentum is conserved. We can ignore the Earth and still apply the principle of conservation of linear momentum to familiar Earth-bound systems, if we consider only such situations as collisions or explosions where the forces of interaction between two or more bodies *either* are very large *or* act only in a horizontal plane. These points will be brought out further in this chapter.

As a body, for example a stone, can itself be considered as a system of interacting particles (the molecules of the materials which constitute the stone), we can use this principle for bodies as well as for particles. The most useful statement of the principle of conservation of linear momentum is thus

the total linear momentum of a system of interacting bodies remains constant.

Although the conservation principle is logically deduced from Newton's laws of motion and is thus 'true' if those laws are themselves 'true', the conservation of linear momentum can be quite carefully tested in the laboratory and thus we can show experimentally that the laws apply to the behaviour of real bodies. The three sections which follow deal with practical applications of the principle.

8-4 Simple collisions

In the laboratory a linear air track and its gliders (one of which is shown in figure 8-7) are ideally suited to studying momentum conservation in one dimension. As we are interested in speeds immediately before and after the collisions, the best arrangement is to attach opaque screens of known length to the colliding gliders so that

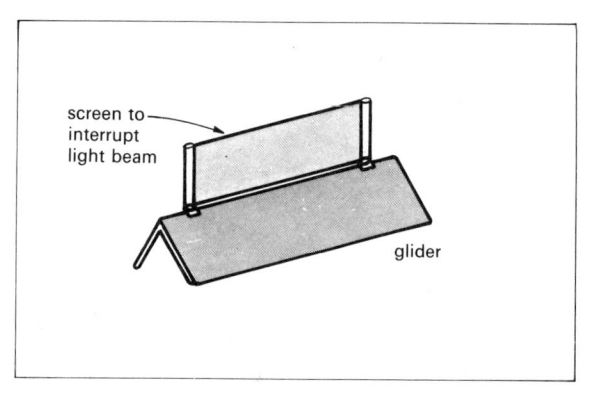

Figure 8-7 A typical linear air-track glider. The mass of the glider can be varied by loading it. Devices such as magnets, spring buffers, and locking buffers can be attached as required.

8-4 Simple collisions

light beams are broken by the screens and the time for which the beam is broken is recorded using phototransistors and either centisecond clocks or millisecond scaler equipment. See also Section 2-7.

When the track is horizontal the main forces acting on a glider during a collision are the push of another glider, the pull of the Earth, and the push of the air from the track. The last two forces are vertical and so their horizontal impulse on the glider is zero. Providing the gliders move fairly slowly, the viscous drag of the air is very small.

Is momentum conserved?

The basic experiment (see figure 8-8) involves two gliders of masses m_1 and m_2 moving towards one another at speeds u_1 and u_2. The gliders then collide and rebound. The switch is thrown connecting clocks 3 and 4 while disconnecting clocks 1 and 2 so that new speeds v_1 and v_2 can be measured as the gliders recede from one another. Typical results might be as shown in table 8-1. The sign convention for velocities in the table is 'velocities to the right are positive'.

The particular arrangement of clocks and light beams shown in figure 8-8 can be used if the gliders rebound or stick together. The springiness of the interaction is discussed further in Section 9-5. The validity of the principle of conservation of linear momentum in this sort of collision can be tested either as shown in table 8-1 or by calculating the total vector momentum before the collision and the total vector momentum after it. For example, for the perspex buffers:

total momentum before

$$= (0.20\,\text{kg})(0.45\,\text{m s}^{-1}) + (0.32\,\text{kg})(-0.24\,\text{m s}^{-1})$$
$$= 0.013\,\text{kg m s}^{-1} \quad \text{or} \quad 0.013\,\text{N s, to the right};$$

total momentum after

$$= (0.20\,\text{kg})(-0.17\,\text{m s}^{-1}) + (0.32\,\text{kg})(0.14\,\text{m s}^{-1})$$
$$= 0.011\,\text{kg m s}^{-1} \quad \text{or} \quad 0.011\,\text{N s, to the right}.$$

The experiment can be performed to better than 5 per cent provided care is taken with the levelling of the air track, and it provides a direct test of the validity of Newton's laws of motion. A simpler set of experiments, with correspondingly less reliable results, using the trolleys and ticker-tapes mentioned in Section 5-6 can also be tried although now the trolleys must not rebound or it is impossible for the tapes to record speed both before *and* after the collision.

There are, however, some questions which should be asked about the glider experiments. How do we measure the masses m_1 and m_2? What happens if we measure the velocities relative to another frame of reference? The

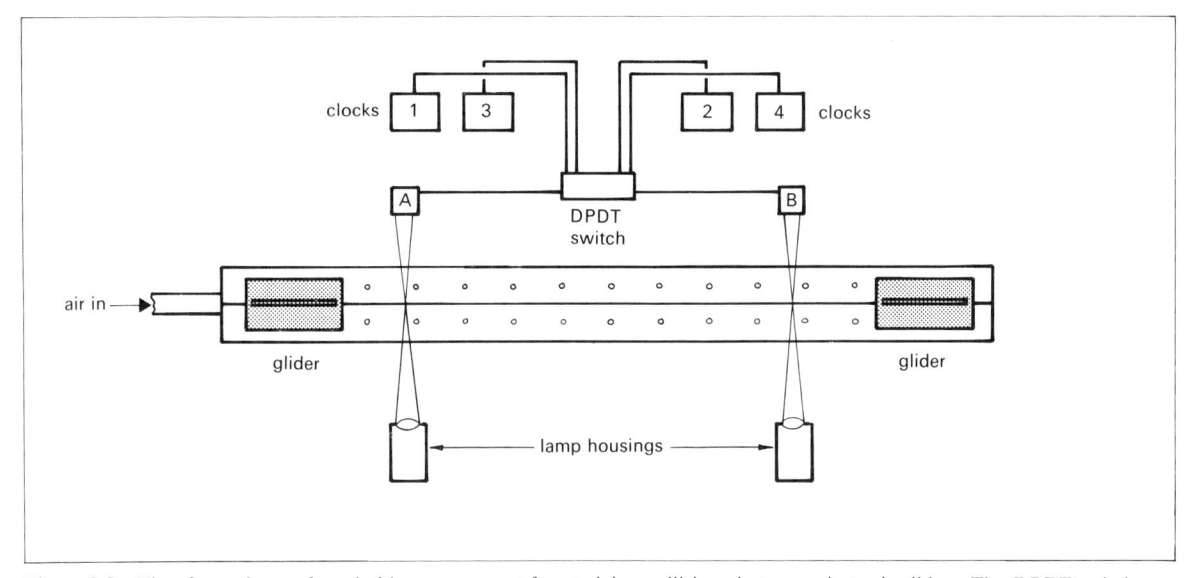

Figure 8-8 View from above of a suitable arrangement for studying collisions between air-track gliders. The DPDT switch can connect either clocks 1 and 2 or clocks 3 and 4 to phototransistor and amplifying units A and B.

8 Linear momentum

Type of buffers	Mass m_1/kg	Initial velocity u_1/m s^{-1}	Final velocity v_1/m s^{-1}	Change of momentum $\Delta p_1 = m_1 \Delta v_1$/N s	Mass m_2/kg	Initial velocity u_2/m s^{-1}	Final velocity v_2/m s^{-1}	Change of momentum $\Delta p_2 = m_2 \Delta v_2$/N s
Perspex buffers	0.20	0.45	−0.17	0.12	0.32	−0.24	0.14	0.12
Magnet buffers	0.20	0.14	−0.26	−0.08	0.25	−0.22	0.10	0.08
Connecting buffers	0.20	0.52	0.11	−0.08	0.20	−0.26	0.11	0.07

Table 8-1 Collisions on an air track: $\Delta \boldsymbol{p}_1 = -\Delta \boldsymbol{p}_2$. The left-to-right direction has been chosen as positive.

first question (which is answered in the next section) stresses that we must be careful as to how much we think we 'prove' by experiments of this sort. The second question can best be answered by referring again to the values obtained from the experiment with perspex buffers. Suppose all the velocities were measured relative to a frame of reference which was moving with uniform velocity of 0.14 m s^{-1} to the right. This would be another inertial frame (assuming the Earth to be one). Then in $\Delta \boldsymbol{p}_1 = m_1 \Delta \boldsymbol{v}_1$, the change of velocity

$$\Delta \boldsymbol{v}_1 = (-0.17 - 0.14) \text{ m s}^{-1} - (0.45 - 0.14) \text{ m s}^{-1}$$
$$= (-0.17 - 0.45) \text{ m s}^{-1} \text{ to the right, as before.}$$

Similarly $\Delta \boldsymbol{p}_2$ is unchanged. Thus the principle of conservation of linear momentum is equally valid for this collision if analysed in two different reference frames. The principle can be shown to hold in any inertial frame of reference.

Measurement of speed

The speed of a fast-moving object, for example a bullet, can be measured by firing it parallel to an air track and at a stationary glider which carries a suitable target, such as a lump of plasticine, in which the bullet becomes embedded (figure 8-9). The mass m_1 of the bullet is measured, and the mass of the bullet plus target plus glider, m_2, after the collision. If the speed of the glider is v_2, as measured by a phototransistor and clock, and the unknown speed of the bullet is v_1, then

total momentum before = $m_1 v_1$ to right

total momentum after = $m_2 v_2$ to right.

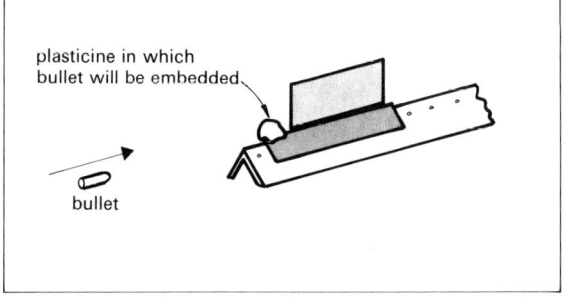

Figure 8-9 A rifle fires a bullet into a stationary target mounted on an air-track glider. It is important to arrange the target so that there are no sudden vertical forces on the glider when the bullet strikes.

Therefore, by the principle of conservation of linear momentum

$$m_1 v_1 = m_2 v_2 \quad \text{or} \quad v_1 = \frac{m_2 v_2}{m_1}.$$

The technique is sensitive enough to show that the muzzle speed of pellets from an *air* rifle is not constant.

Consider finally a collision between the Moon and a falling body such as a stone. Suppose the stone is released from rest a few metres above the Moon's surface and 'sticks' to the surface on impact. The total momentum of the Moon–stone system at the moment of release is zero so that the total momentum *during* the fall and the total momentum *after* the impact must also be zero. Viewed from the Earth the interaction is of no consequence—it is internal to the system comprising the Moon plus the stone: the momentum of the *system* is constant throughout the interaction. But a man standing on the surface of the Moon watching the stone fall sees the downward increase in the momentum of the stone after it is released. He measures its velocity relative to the Moon's surface. Our principle of conservation of linear momentum is *not* refuted, however, because the man's reference frame is not an inertial one, for the Moon must accelerate towards the stone. This discussion stresses that all velocities used in Newtonian mechanics must be measured in inertial frames of reference. From figure 8-10 we have, at the instant shown, by the principle of conservation of linear momentum

$$m\boldsymbol{v} + m_M \boldsymbol{v}_M = 0,$$

numerically
$$v_M = \frac{m}{m_M} v.$$

As the ratio (mass of stone) ÷ (mass of Moon) is of the order of 10^{-23}, v_M is extremely small so that we do not 'feel' the change of momentum of the Moon if we are standing on the Moon, or the similar change in momentum of the Earth when somebody drops a stone on the Earth.

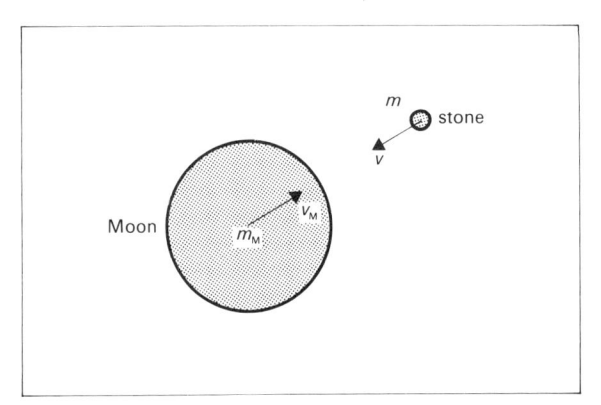

Figure 8-10 A stone falls towards the Moon. All speeds are measured relative to an inertial frame of reference, such as the centre of mass of the Moon–stone system.

▶ **Example 8-2** A stationary body of mass m is struck by a body of mass M ($M \gg m$) moving with speed v. Can one determine the speed of m after the impact?

We cannot use the principle of conservation of momentum alone to determine the speeds of the bodies after impact: we need to know also how elastic the collision is. It is, however, possible to deduce the maximum speed of m after the impact by viewing the collision from a frame of reference attached to the body of mass M. Now, if M is very much greater than m, the impact is similar to that of a ball bouncing on the surface of the Earth. The speed of this rebound is obviously greatest when it is equal to the speed with which the ball struck the Earth. (It is usually less and if it were greater we should wonder where the extra energy had come from.)

We can now see that the greatest speed of the mass m after impact is v relative to the mass M, that is $2v$ relative to the ground. For instance, if a train travelling at 20 m s^{-1} were to hit a football suspended on a length of string from a bridge, the initial speed of the ball would be 40 m s^{-1} relative to the bridge. ◀

8-5 Recoil

If a single stationary body explodes into two parts the principle of conservation of linear momentum predicts that the two parts must move off in opposite directions, that is their paths must form a single straight line. The process is usually described by saying that when one body is fired the other body *recoils*. We cannot prevent the recoil, no matter how firmly we fix one of the exploding parts; for even if it were possible to fix a gun rigidly to the Earth, the Earth itself would recoil. Consider a rifle bullet fired horizontally. Figure 8-11 shows the impulse given to the rifle by the bullet, the (subsequent) impulse given to

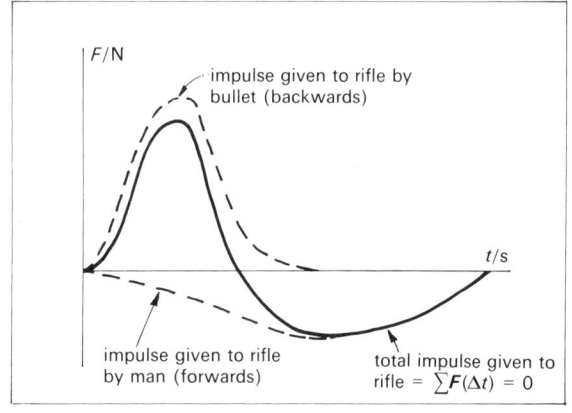

Figure 8-11 A force–time graph for a rifle from which a bullet is being fired horizontally. The gun is at rest before firing and after recoil and so the total impulse given to it must be zero. The propellant gases are assumed to have zero final momentum.

the rifle by the man who is firing the bullet and (with the full line) the total impulse given to the rifle.

In so far as the man can be considered to be a part of the Earth, the Earth will receive a backward impulse but when the bullet hits the Earth its forward impulse on the Earth will exactly cancel the backward impulse given to the Earth by the rifle originally. There was no horizontal momentum in the Earth–gun system before the explosion so there can be none after the explosion.

▶ **Example 8-3** A man of mass 75 kg stands on a horizontal frictionless sheet of ice (figure 8-12). As he cannot exert a horizontal frictional force on the ice, so the ice cannot exert a horizontal frictional force on him—he cannot walk off the ice. However, he finds in one of his pockets a lump of lead of mass 1.0 kg. He throws this horizontally at a speed of $5.0 \, \text{m s}^{-1}$. With what speed does he move, and in what direction?

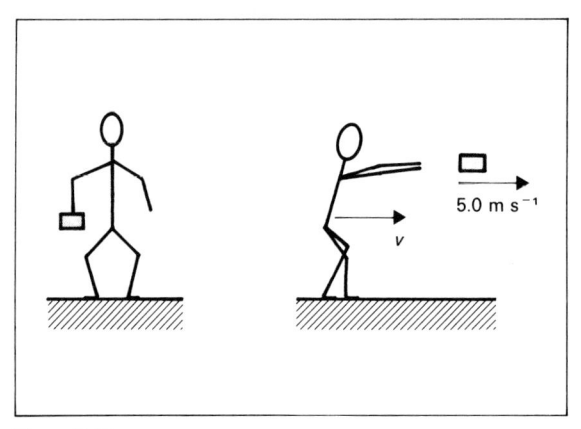

Figure 8-12

Taking momenta to the right (in figure 8-12) as positive:

before the throw:
$$p_1 = 0$$

after the throw:
$$p_2 = (75 \, \text{kg})v + (1.0 \, \text{kg})(5.0 \, \text{m s}^{-1}).$$

Since $p_1 = p_2$
$$0 = (75 \, \text{kg})v + (1.0 \, \text{kg})(5.0 \, \text{m s}^{-1}).$$

Therefore
$$v = -0.067 \, \text{m s}^{-1} \text{ in the direction shown}$$

(that is $0.067 \, \text{m s}^{-1}$ in the opposite direction to that of the lump). (He could also move across the ice if he fired a gun horizontally; astronauts who want to 'walk' in space are 'armed' with gas-guns.) ◀

Measuring mass

Any experiment involving the analysis of the motions of parts of a system of interacting bodies for which

$$\sum p = \sum mv = \text{constant}$$

can be used to find the mass of one of the bodies provided the masses of the other bodies are known. In theory then, to build a set of standard masses we could take the standard kilogram and explode an unknown mass m from it in a region where the only forces acting on the kilogram mass and m are the forces of the interaction. We would measure the speeds and apply the principle of conservation of linear momentum. Then we would take m and explode secondary masses from it until a set of standard masses is achieved. The arithmetic is trivial.

In practice, however, unless the experiment is to be performed in deep space there are practical problems. In the laboratory, measuring an unknown mass m can best be managed if we are provided with two air-track gliders or air-table pucks of known mass which we can conveniently 'explode', for example, by burning a thread which holds them together with a spring compressed between them; a possible arrangement is shown in figure 8-13. The speeds of the gliders after each explosion are measured by clocks 1 and 2 as arranged in figure 8-8.

A series of experiments compressing the spring to different extents is performed and m is deduced from the slope of the graph drawn of the speed v_B of B against the speed v_A of A after the explosion. By the principle of conservation of linear momentum, taking positive to the right:

total momentum before $= 0$

total momentum after $= -(m+m_A)v_A + m_B v_B$

and therefore
$$\frac{v_B}{v_A} = \frac{m+m_A}{m_B}$$

so
$$\text{slope of graph} = \frac{m+m_A}{m_B}.$$

Thus m can be found. The only doubt about the experiment lies in the fact that there are small horizontal external forces acting on the system as the explosion takes place. The horizontal impulse of B on A is however so much bigger than that of the air on A (see figure 8-14) that we can get reasonable results from the experiment even if we ignore the effect of the air.

Figure 8-13 An explosion experiment with air-track gliders. A series of experiments for different initial spring compressions yields a value for the ratio of the speeds of B and A after the explosion—the slope of the graph.

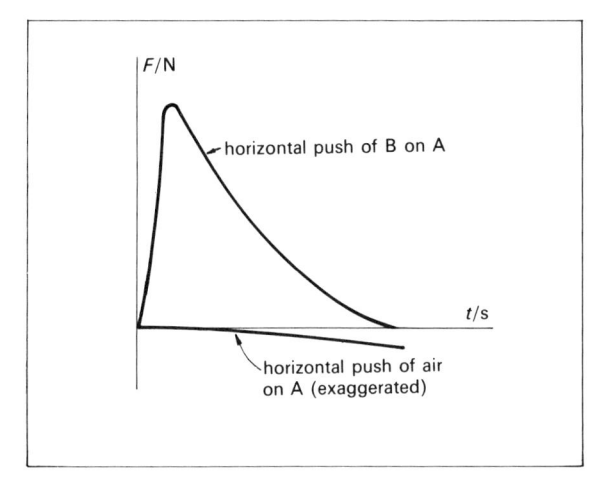

Figure 8-14 The impulses given to an air-track glider during an explosion.

We can summarize the technique used in calculations for analysing interactions in one dimension as follows:

(a) sketch a diagram of the situation (or two diagrams) showing the bodies (i) before and (ii) after the interaction

(b) choose a positive direction and indicate all velocities in that direction on the diagram(s)

(c) calculate the total momentum before and the total momentum after the interaction in the same units (noting the positive direction)

(d) apply the principle of conservation of linear momentum.

▶ **Example 8-4** A stationary railway truck of mass 1.2×10^4 kg is struck by a string of four identical trucks moving with a speed of $10 \, \text{m s}^{-1}$ (figure 8-15). During the impact, all five trucks are coupled together. What is their velocity after the impact?

Taking the right–left direction (in figure 8-15) as positive:

$$\text{momentum before} = (4.8 \times 10^4 \, \text{kg})(10 \, \text{m s}^{-1})$$

$$\text{momentum afterwards} = (6.0 \times 10^4 \, \text{kg}) v.$$

Therefore

$$(4.8 \times 10^4 \, \text{kg})(10 \, \text{m s}^{-1}) = (6.0 \times 10^4 \, \text{kg}) v$$

so that $\quad v = 8.0 \, \text{m s}^{-1}.$

Therefore the velocity of the five trucks is $8.0 \, \text{m s}^{-1}$ from right to left in the diagram. ◀

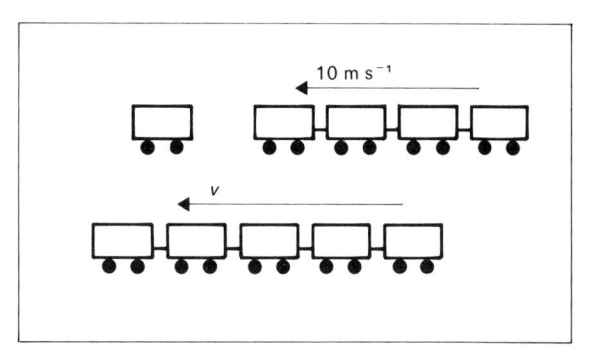

Figure 8-15

8-6 Interactions in two dimensions

Two-dimensional collisions and explosions can be studied experimentally by using frictionless pucks which move over a carefully levelled horizontal surface. The pucks are supported on a thin layer of gas and their motions followed using stroboscopic photography. Pucks which stick together will not be considered in this section as this process usually produces rotation and so the pucks cannot be treated as particles. Groups of pucks can be made to explode by the use of small springs.

Is momentum conserved?

Consider two pucks which collide as shown in figure 8-16 which is a simulated multiflash photograph taken from above. The analysis is most easily done using scale draw-

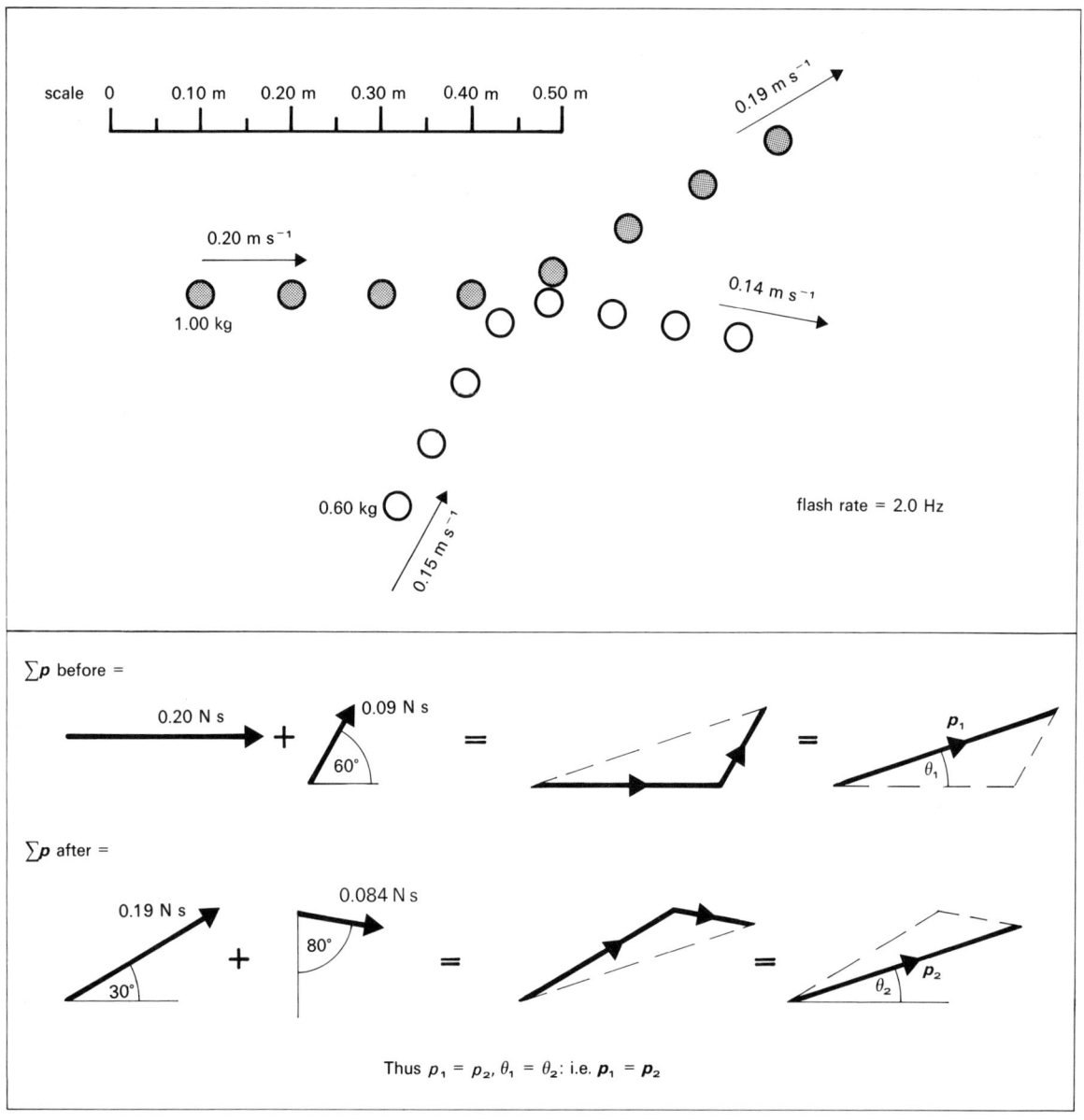

Figure 8-16 Two frictionless pucks collide. The sum of their momenta before and after the collision can be found by vector addition and in this hypothetical example the total momentum is seen to be conserved.

ings to find the respective vector sums of the momenta before and after the collision. Alternatively, we can resolve the momenta in each of two convenient directions and show that the total momentum in any direction is conserved in this interaction. The result of such experiments is to confirm the principle of conservation of linear momentum.

▶ **Example 8-5** Three pucks are placed together on an air table and connected together by threads and compression springs. One puck has a mass of 1.0 kg but the others have unknown masses m_1 and m_2. When the threads are burnt the pucks move with the velocities shown in figure 8-17. Find m_1 and m_2.

First resolve perpendicular to OB, in figure 8-17.
Taking OD as positive:

momentum before $= 0$,

momentum afterwards $= m_1(2.3 \,\mathrm{m\,s^{-1}})\cos 25°$
$\qquad -(1.0\,\mathrm{kg})(2.8\,\mathrm{m\,s^{-1}})\cos 15°$.

Therefore $\quad 0 = m_1(2.3\,\mathrm{m\,s^{-1}})\cos 25°$
$\qquad -(1.0\,\mathrm{kg})(2.8\,\mathrm{m\,s^{-1}})\cos 15°$,

whence $\quad m_1 = 1.3\,\mathrm{kg}$.

Now resolve perpendicular to OA.
Taking OE as positive:

momentum before $= 0$

momentum afterwards $= m_2(1.7\,\mathrm{m\,s^{-1}})\cos 25°$
$\qquad -(1.0\,\mathrm{kg})(2.8\,\mathrm{m\,s^{-1}})\cos 50°$.

Therefore $\quad 0 = m_2(1.7\,\mathrm{m\,s^{-1}})\cos 25°$
$\qquad -(1.0\,\mathrm{kg})(2.8\,\mathrm{m\,s^{-1}})\cos 50°$,

whence $\quad m_2 = 1.2\,\mathrm{kg}$.

The momenta of the pucks was zero before the 'explosion'; since no horizontal force acts on them during the explosion, the vector sum of the momenta after the explosion is also zero, and so the momentum vectors (figure 8-18a) should form a closed triangle as can be seen from figure 8-18b. ◀

Sub-atomic interactions

As in the case of collisions in one dimension, the relative masses of interacting bodies can be deduced if their velocities are known. Thus the analysis of collisions between the particles of nuclear physics enables us to learn a great deal about the nature of the particles, and in particular their mass. The paths of the particles are shown by trails left in bubble or cloud chambers which can be photographed. The speeds of any charged particles can

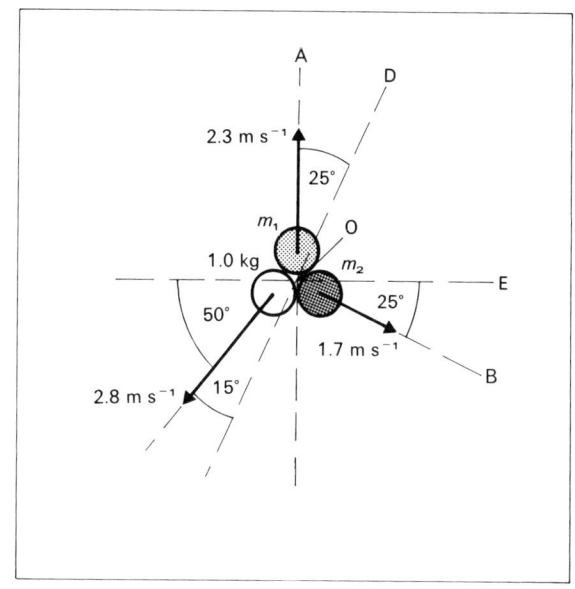

Figure 8-17

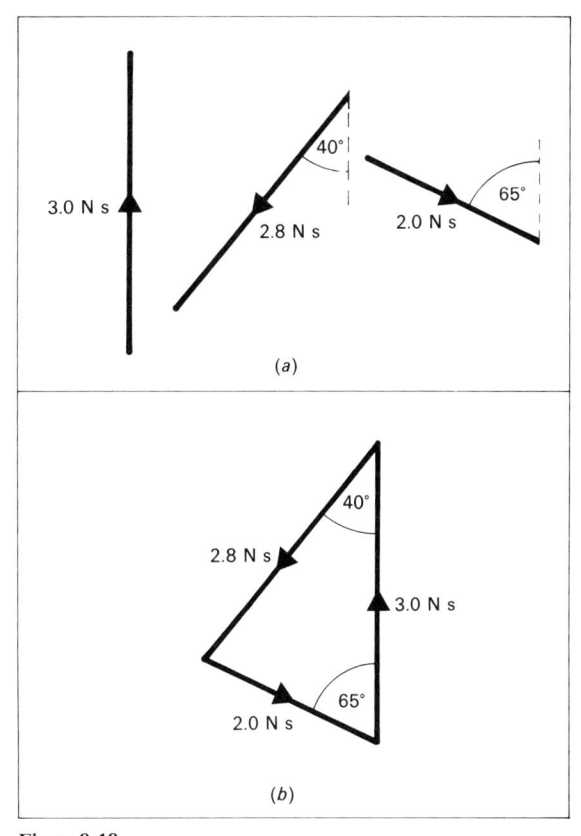

Figure 8-18

8 Linear momentum

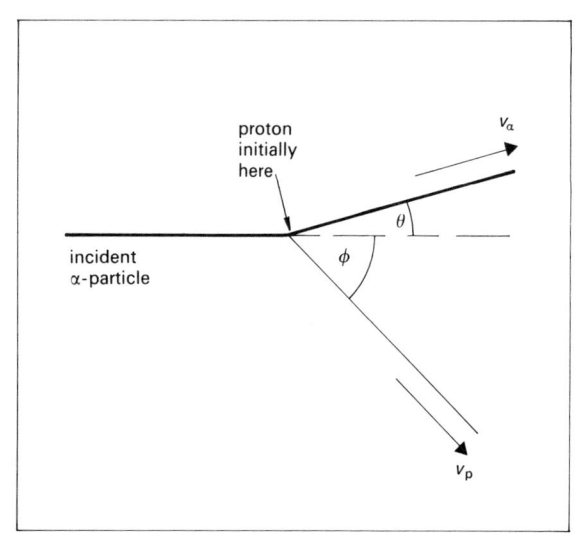

Figure 8-19 A nuclear collision between an α-particle (thick line) and a proton (thin line).

be estimated using magnetic fields to exert known centripetal forces on them and measuring the curvature of their paths. Figure 8-19 shows diagrammatically the result of a collision between a moving α-particle (a helium nucleus) and a stationary proton (a hydrogen nucleus) as recorded in a bubble chamber. From the tracks, the plane of which must be established by taking photographs from two known positions, we can deduce, using the principle of conservation of linear momentum:

(a) parallel to the incident α-particle:
$m_\alpha u = m_\alpha v_\alpha \cos\theta + m_p v_p \cos\phi$
(b) perpendicular to incident α-particle:
$0 = m_\alpha v_\alpha \sin\theta - m_p v_p \sin\phi$.

Generally not enough is known to make these equations alone useful, but by considering the kinetic energies of the particles involved, a complete analysis is possible—see Section 9-5. The speeds of atomic particles are found to be very high, of the order of 10^8 m s^{-1}, and although the principle of conservation of linear momentum can be applied in this region, we shall find that (see Section 10-4) although the linear momentum is still the product of the mass and the velocity of the particle, the mass is not still the *rest mass* of the particle.

It is instructive to investigate further the concept of what we mean by a collision. To say that bodies collide when they hit one another is clearly not helpful. To say that they collide when they exert forces on one another and consequently alter their velocities, that is exchange some momentum, is better, but provides too general a picture. As mentioned in Section 5-1, there are basically only three types of force in nature and collisions are best categorized by the type of force which predominates. Gravitational collisions can best be seen in the motion of bodies like comets; electromagnetic collisions in the everyday bat-and-ball situations (and in a special way in the collisions of charged bodies or magnets), and nuclear forces are observed only when nuclear particles approach each other very closely, for instance when we try to 'split' a nucleus.

8-7 The rate of change of momentum

From page 117 we have the relation between change of momentum and impulse derived from Newton's laws of motion; for an average resultant external force F_{res}

$$\frac{\Delta p}{\Delta t} = F_{\text{res}}. \qquad [8\text{-}5]$$

Instantaneously

$$\lim_{\Delta t \to 0} \frac{\Delta p}{\Delta t} = \frac{dp}{dt} = F_{\text{res}}. \qquad [8\text{-}6]$$

In words

the rate of change of linear momentum of a body is equal to the resultant external force acting on it and takes place in the direction of this force.

This statement is the full *definition of force* in Newtonian mechanics. Up to this point in the text it has been concealed from the reader. Why did we not start with it in Chapter 5? The reason is that it would not have told us very much about force in a way which would have been meaningful. It would not have told us about pushes and pulls. It would not have explicitly told us about accelerations—the observable phenomena. It would have related force to a (then) even more mysterious quantity—the linear momentum of a body.

For bodies of constant mass we have used Newton's second law in the form $ma = \sum F$ and we showed in Section 8-2 that for fixed m this was equivalent to $\Delta p/\Delta t = \sum F$. Adopting this second statement as the fundamental one now enables us to analyse situations in which the mass of a system alters—perhaps a firework rocket attached to a trolley—but leaves our earlier work as correct for the particular case of constant mass.

Consider for example a *stationary* helicopter of mass 1000 kg, in figure 8-20. The forces on the helicopter are the pull W of the Earth on it and the push P of the air on it. By Newton's first law we see that $P + W = 0$, that is $P = W = 9800$ N and P is upwards. By Newton's third law

8-7 The rate of change of momentum

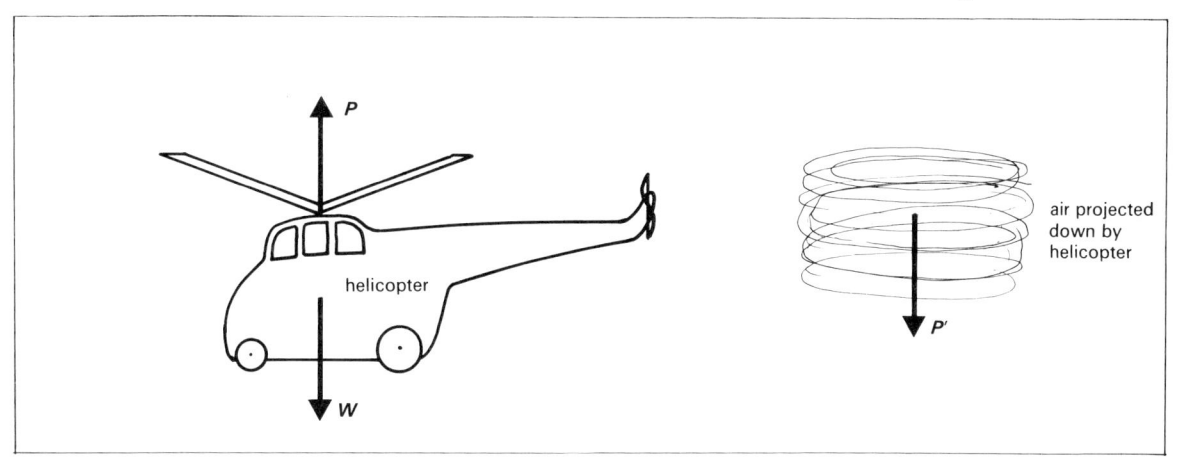

Figure 8-20 A helicopter at rest (or rising or falling at constant speed). $P + W = 0$ (first law); $P' = \Delta p/\Delta t$ of air (second law); $P = -P'$ (third law).

the push of the helicopter on the air is 9800 N downwards. We can use this value in the complete statement of Newton's second law, $\Delta \boldsymbol{p}/\Delta t = \boldsymbol{F}$, to find the rate at which the helicopter pushes the air downwards. Suppose the helicopter pushes the air down at a speed of $20 \,\mathrm{m\,s}^{-1}$; then as

$$\frac{\Delta \boldsymbol{p}}{\Delta t} = \frac{\Delta(m\boldsymbol{v})}{\Delta t} = \boldsymbol{v}\frac{\Delta m}{\Delta t},$$

we have

$$\left(20\,\frac{\mathrm{m}}{\mathrm{s}}\right)\left(\frac{\Delta m}{\Delta t}\right) = 9800\,\mathrm{N}$$

$$= 9800\,\frac{\mathrm{kg\,m}}{\mathrm{s}^2}.$$

Therefore

$$\frac{\Delta m}{\Delta t} = 490\,\frac{\mathrm{kg}}{\mathrm{s}},$$

where $\Delta m/\Delta t$ is the rate of downward projection of mass (air in this case of course). As $1\,\mathrm{m}^3$ of air has a mass of roughly 1 kg, then about $500\,\mathrm{m}^3$ of air are projected downward each second. The reader should work out how this is related to the wing span of the helicopter blades. This example is an interesting example of the use of Newton's laws of motion, as all three laws are used. The argument is quite complicated, but the arithmetic is simple.

In using equation 8-5 or 8-6 to solve problems it is important to be quite sure which body is changing its momentum: in the above example about the helicopter, it is *the air* to which we apply Newton's second law, *not* the helicopter. In a similar way we could analyse the action of ships or aeroplane propellers, or the jet engines on aeroplanes. In each case the medium in which the vehicle moves is gathered and then projected backward at a steady speed, the mass of the ship or plane remaining constant (except for a small reduction in the supply of fuel carried by the vehicle).

▶ **Example 8-6** A wall whose plane is vertical and north–south has a surface area of $100\,\mathrm{m}^2$. A horizontal wind from the east has a speed of $30\,\mathrm{m\,s}^{-1}$, and the air has a density of $1.3\,\mathrm{kg\,m}^{-3}$. What force does the air exert on the wall, assuming that it is all stopped by the wall (that is, none 'rebounds')?

The volume of air which reaches the wall in 1 second

$$= (100\,\mathrm{m}^2)(30\,\mathrm{m})$$

$$= 3000\,\mathrm{m}^3,$$

that is, its volume-rate of arrival $= 3000\,\mathrm{m}^3\,\mathrm{s}^{-1}$. Its mass-rate of arrival,

$$\frac{\Delta m}{\Delta t} = (3000\,\mathrm{m}^3\,\mathrm{s}^{-1})(1.3\,\mathrm{kg\,m}^{-3})$$

$$= 3900\,\mathrm{kg\,s}^{-1}.$$

Then

$$\frac{\Delta p}{\Delta t} = \left(v\frac{\Delta m}{\Delta t}\right) = (30\,\mathrm{m\,s}^{-1})(3900\,\mathrm{kg\,s}^{-1})$$

$$= 1.17 \times 10^5\,\mathrm{kg\,m\,s}^{-2}$$

$$= 1.17 \times 10^5\,\mathrm{N}.$$

But $\Delta p/\Delta t = F$: therefore the force exerted by the wall on the air $= 1.2 \times 10^5\,\mathrm{N}$ and by Newton's third law, the force exerted by the air on the wall $= 1.2 \times 10^5\,\mathrm{N}$. ◀

8 Linear momentum

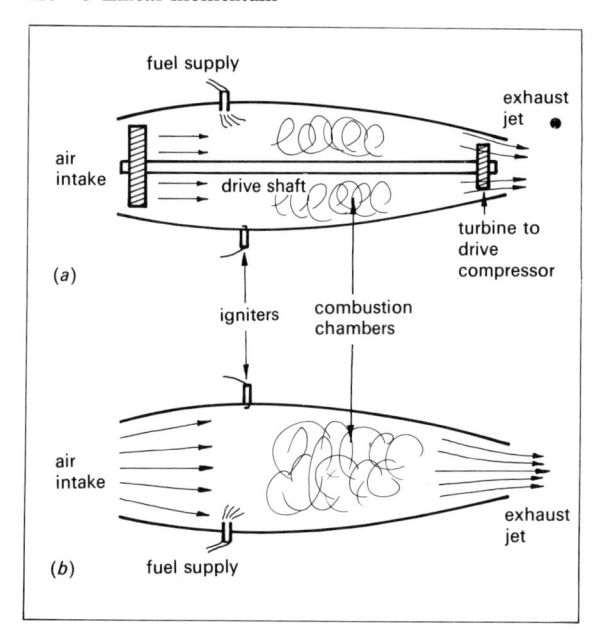

Figure 8-21 The principles of (a) the turbo-jet and (b) the ram-jet.

Jet engines

Figure 8-21 illustrates the principles of two types of aeroplane jet propulsion unit, the turbo-jet and the ram-jet. (The petrol-driven propeller which was used more or less exclusively until 1940 is not shown, nor is the turbo-prop system mentioned below.) The *turbo-jet* is the basic propulsion unit for modern 'jet' aeroplanes. Here the air is compressed after intake and then explosively expanded. The explosion uses the oxygen in the air intake together with a relatively small mass of fuel (paraffin) carried by the plane. The expanded gases rush out of the back of the engine though some of their momentum is used to rotate a turbine which drives the compressor. The design of turbo-jet engines has developed enormously over the past 30 years; in recent types some of the air intake bypasses the combustion chamber and then joins the exhaust gases. The turbo-prop (short for propeller) is much the same as the turbo-jet but almost *all* the momentum of the expanded gases is used to drive a large turbine; this can in turn drive not only the compressor but also propeller blades—that is the jet effect is used to drive conventional rotating blades.

The ram-jet is used in some missile systems (it was the propulsion unit for the 'flying' bombs used against London during the Second World War) and in high-speed aircraft. The compressor is not needed, and hence nor is the turbine, for at very high speeds a sufficient mass of air flows through the engine to provide the required compression. The XK range of high-speed research aircraft use the ram-jet and must be dropped from the underbelly of a carrier aircraft in order to achieve the necessary initial high speed. It must be stressed that the diagrams in figure 8-21 are designed to illustrate fundamentals and are *not* accurate drawings of the two types of engine.

8-8 Rockets

A rifle recoils when a bullet is fired. A machine gun recoils several times every second, each time a bullet is fired. Imagine a machine gun firing thousands of very small bullets every second; the recoil would cease to be jerky. This is illustrated graphically in figure 8-22, where it is assumed that the total mass fired per second is the same for each gun and that their muzzle speeds are the same. Graph (b) of course also represents a *rocket* where the tiny bullets are molecules moving at high speeds as a result

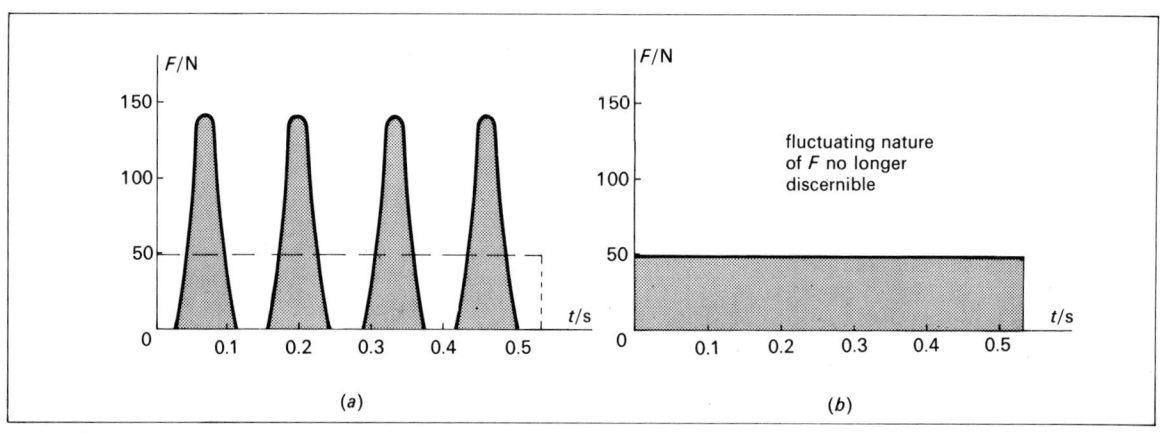

Figure 8-22 Force–time graphs for (a) a machine gun and (b) a gun firing a fine stream of tiny bullets. The impulse over a period of time is the same for both (a) and (b).

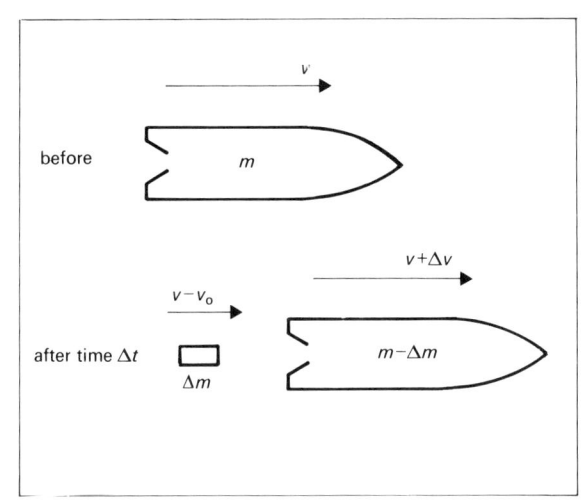

Figure 8-23 A rocket ejects Δm of material in time Δt at an exhaust speed of v_0 relative to the rocket.

of the combustion of the rocket fuel. If we try to analyse a rocket which is fixed (not allowed to accelerate) so that the exhaust gases come out at a constant velocity relative to the Earth, we can apply Newton's laws (and in particular the second law as in equation 8-5) to find the thrust exerted on the rocket housing by the ejected materials. The calculation is similar to that for the helicopter in the previous section. If, however, the rocket accelerates, the problem is more easily solved by applying the principle of conservation of linear momentum to the system consisting of rocket plus fuel. Referring to figure 8-23, a rocket moving in a region where there are no external forces ejects gases at the rate of $\Delta m/\Delta t$, at a constant exhaust speed of v_0 relative to the rocket. When the rocket has mass m, which varies, and has a speed v:

the total momentum before $= mv$

and

the total momentum after $= (m - \Delta m)(v + \Delta v) + \Delta m(v - v_0)$.

The impulse I (from external forces) is zero, so that using equation 8-3 ($I = \Delta p$) we have

$$0 = (m - \Delta m)(v + \Delta v) + \Delta m(v - v_0) - mv$$

whence
$$\Delta v \approx v_0 \frac{\Delta m}{m}. \qquad [8\text{-}7]$$

The acceleration

$$a = \frac{\Delta v}{\Delta t} = \frac{v_0}{m}\frac{\Delta m}{\Delta t}, \qquad [8\text{-}8]$$

and so the thrust at this instant

$$= ma = v_0 \frac{\Delta m}{\Delta t}, \qquad [8\text{-}9]$$

there being no other forces acting on the rocket *in this example*.

To achieve a high thrust we must make v_0 and $\Delta m/\Delta t$ as high as possible. A designer's main task is to increase v_0—a job for a specialist chemical or rocket engineer. There are upper limits to v_0 if the ejection is the result of chemical explosions, 5×10^3 m s^{-1} being about as high as can be hoped for. Thus if $\Delta m/\Delta t$ is 10^3 kg s^{-1} (about 1 ton s^{-1}), the thrust would be 5×10^6 kg m s^{-2} or 5×10^6 N. For use in deep space, ion rockets are being designed where the ejected materials are electrically charged particles which can be accelerated to speeds of the order of 10^8 m s^{-1} using electric or magnetic fields. The expected rate of ejection of matter for such rockets is incredibly low, of the order of 10^{-10} kg s^{-1}, and so they produce a thrust of only about 10^{-2} N! (see equation 8-9).

Now suppose that the rocket is accelerating vertically upwards at the Earth's surface; there is now an external force on the rocket—the pull of the Earth, mg. We cannot apply the principle of conservation of linear momentum but must revert to the impulse–momentum equation, equation 8-4. In time Δt the impulse on the rocket system *upwards* is given by

$$I = -mg\Delta t.$$

The change of momentum in this time is the final momentum minus the initial momentum, so that using equations 8-3 and 8-7,

$$-mg\Delta t = m\Delta v - v_0 \Delta m$$

$$m\frac{\Delta v}{\Delta t} = v_0 \frac{\Delta m}{\Delta t} - mg \qquad [8\text{-}10]$$

$$\frac{\Delta v}{\Delta t} = \frac{v_0}{m}\frac{\Delta m}{\Delta t} - g. \qquad [8\text{-}11]$$

The resultant thrust on the rocket (equation 8-10) is such that if the rocket is to accelerate upward *at all* then

$$v_0 \frac{\Delta m}{\Delta t} > mg.$$

As v_0 is determined by the chemistry of the combustion it is this requirement which demands the initial high value of $\Delta m/\Delta t$, greater than 10^4 kg s^{-1} for a Saturn V rocket, which we see in the launchings from Cape Kennedy. The rate of ejection could be smaller if the total initial mass of the rocket were smaller, but if a high final speed is to be achieved, then the acceleration must continue for some time and so a large mass of fuel must be carried. A rocket, unlike a jet engine, does not collect the material to be ejected as it goes.

Looking at equation 8-11 we see that as the rocket rises, two factors alter so as to *increase* its acceleration $\Delta v/\Delta t$. Firstly, the mass of the rocket decreases as fuel is ejected and, secondly g decreases although the second effect is not very noticeable during the few kilometres of acceleration usually undertaken.

To predict the final speed a given rocket will achieve, suppose that the initial mass is m_0 when it is at rest and that it burns fuel until it has a mass m at which stage its speed is v. Rewriting equation 8-11 in the notation of the calculus (and writing $dm/dt = -\Delta m/\Delta t$ as dm/dt is a measure of the rate of *increase* of mass m of the rocket while $\Delta m/\Delta t$ meant a rate of loss of mass), we have

$$\frac{dv}{dt} = -\frac{v_0}{m}\frac{dm}{dt} - g.$$

Integrating with respect to time t

$$\int_0^v dv = -\int_{m_0}^m v_0 \frac{dm}{m} - \int_0^t g\, dt.$$

Therefore $\quad v = -v_0[\log_e m]_{m_0}^m - gt,$

assuming v_0 and g constant, that is

$$v = v_0 \log_e \frac{m_0}{m} - gt.$$

If the rate of ejection, $-dm/dt$, is constant and equal to R, then $m = m_0 - Rt$.

In particular, if the rocket is in a region where $g = 0$, then

$$v = v_0 \log_e \frac{m_0}{m}$$

whence $\quad m = m_0 e^{-v/v_0}.$

For chemical systems v_0 is limited to about 5×10^3 m s^{-1} and in practice little more than 4×10^3 m s^{-1} is achieved. Therefore to reach the speed of $v = 8 \times 10^3$ m s^{-1} which is the speed neccessary for Earth orbit we have $v = 2v_0$, and thus the final mass m of the rocket $\approx 0.15 m_0$. This is only 15 per cent of the initial mass m_0, that is 85 per cent of the initial mass has been ejected. This calculation is for conditions of zero g, so if the exhaust gases have to support the rocket as well we see that a colossal take-off mass is needed to put a relatively small payload even into Earth orbit, let alone space.

In order to increase the ratio of payload mass to take-off mass, multistage rocket systems are used (see figure

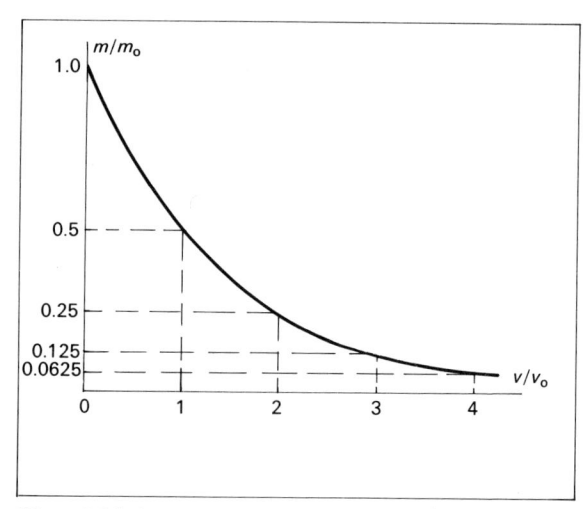

Figure 8-24 An exponential decay $m = m_0 e^{-v/v_0}$. When $v > v_0$ the exhaust gases are moving in the same direction as the rocket as measured by a stationary observer in an inertial reference frame at the starting point.

8-25). Each stage is a complete rocket motor with fuel, oxidant, and combustion chambers. The reader should try to draw a graph similar to figure 8-24 for a three-stage system. The dumping of used fuel containers more than makes up for the need to carry extra motor systems.

8-9 Centre of mass

In Section 5-4 an experiment was suggested for using an inertial balance to compare two masses. If two particles of mass m_1 and m_2 connected by a massless rod rest on a frictionless surface (figure 8-26), then when the rod is struck at C it will rotate unless $m_1 x_1 = m_2 x_2$. C is called the *centre of mass* of the particles m_1 and m_2 and is defined more generally as having a displacement s_{CM} from an origin O where

$$(m_1 + m_2)s_{CM} = m_1 s_1 + m_2 s_2, \qquad [8\text{-}12]$$

and s_1, s_2 are the displacements of m_1 and m_2 from that origin. Therefore

$$s_{CM} = \frac{m_1 s_1 + m_2 s_2}{m_1 + m_2}.$$

The centre of mass of a system of particles can be similarly defined. Adding to equation 8-12 so as to represent a body consisting of a collection of n particles of total mass $m = \sum m_r$

$$(m_1 + m_2 + \cdots + m_n)s_{CM} = m_1 s_1 + m_2 s_2 + \cdots + m_n s_n$$

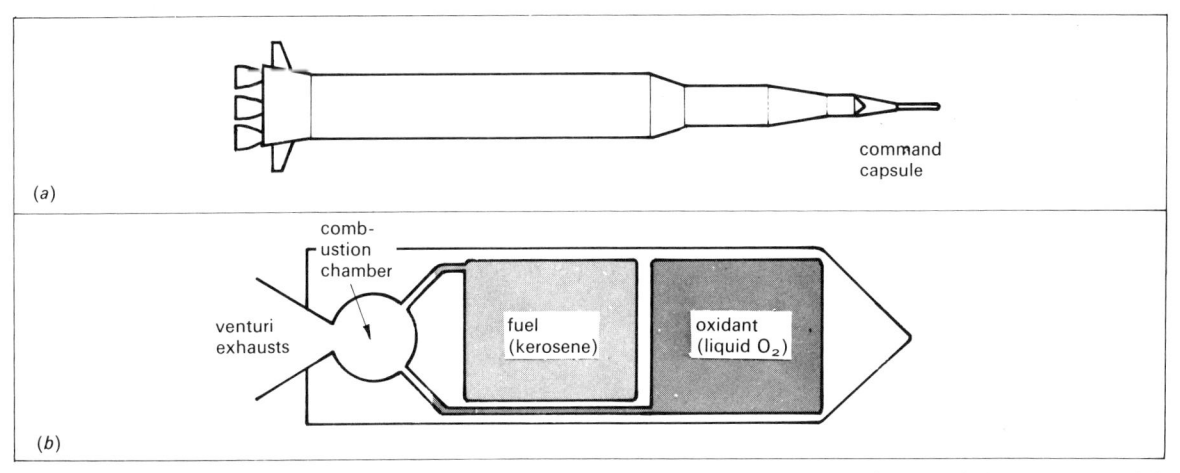

Figure 8-25 (*a*) A scale diagram of Saturn V which launched Apollo 11, the first manned moon landing mission, on 18 July 1969. The payload to fuel ratio is strikingly obvious. (*b*) A schematic diagram of a liquid-fuel rocket motor. Each stage of Saturn V is a rocket of this type.

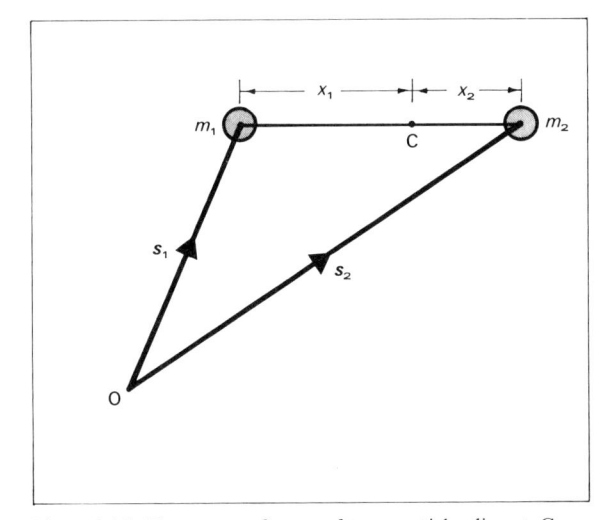

Figure 8-26 The centre of mass of two particles lies at C on the line joining them.

or $$m\,\mathbf{s}_{CM} = \sum m_r \mathbf{s}_r,\qquad [8\text{-}13]$$

which is the defining equation for the position s_{CM} of the centre of mass. As stated, it is a vector equation, but the distance of the centre of mass from a given axis can be established using the relevant resolved part of s_r when an obvious symmetry limits the centre of mass to a line, for example the centre of mass of a uniform cone clearly lies along the axis of the cone. A list of the positions of the centre of mass for a number of simple rigid bodies is given on page 182. In this section, however, we are interested in the motion of the centre of mass of a system of particles rather than in the arithmetic of finding its position.

Consider only two particles which exert forces on one another. Let the total mass be $m = m_1 + m_2$. The interaction will cause the two particles to move together or apart. In time Δt the displacements of the particles from a fixed origin will alter; so will the displacement of their centre of mass. Thus equation 8-12 will give

$$m\frac{\Delta s_{CM}}{\Delta t} = m_1\frac{\Delta s_1}{\Delta t} + m_2\frac{\Delta s_2}{\Delta t},$$

that is $$m\mathbf{v}_{CM} = m_1\mathbf{v}_1 + m_2\mathbf{v}_2, \qquad [8\text{-}14]$$

or $$m\mathbf{v}_{CM} = \mathbf{p}_1 + \mathbf{p}_2. \qquad [8\text{-}15]$$

But $\mathbf{p}_1 + \mathbf{p}_2 =$ constant, for there are no external forces acting on the particles, and so $\mathbf{v}_{CM}$ must be constant if m is constant. This is an extremely useful deduction: in particular it tells us that if we measure $\mathbf{v}_1$ and $\mathbf{v}_2$ relative to the centre of mass then the total momentum of the particles remains zero throughout their interaction. What is more, the centre of mass is an excellent place to fix our reference frame, for when no external forces act on the system $\mathbf{v}_{CM}$ *is constant*, so that a frame of reference fixed to the centre of mass is an inertial frame.

▶ **Example 8-7** A rowing 'eight' has a mass of 300 kg, a length of 21 m, and floats in still water. Its centre of mass is 11 m from the bows. A cox of mass 50 kg stands at the

8 Linear momentum

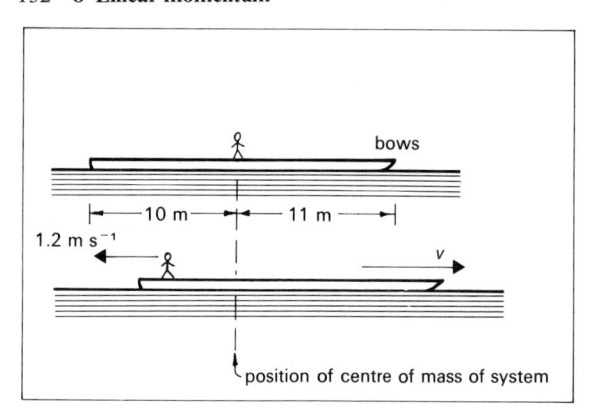

Figure 8-27

centre of mass, and begins to walk at a steady speed of $1.2\,\mathrm{m\,s^{-1}}$ (relative to the water) towards the stern. Assume that the boat does not tilt and that the water exerts a negligible horizontal force on the boat. Refer to figure 8-27; let us discover what has happened to the centre of mass of the system.

Initially, as the positions of the centres of mass of the boat and the cox coincided, it was 11 m from the bows. After, say, 1.0 s, the cox has moved 1.2 m to the left and the boat (by the principle of conservation of linear momentum) has moved 0.2 m to the right, so that their displacements from the original position of the bows are now, respectively, 12.2 m and 10.8 m. Using equation 8-12, we have

$(300\,\mathrm{kg} + 50\,\mathrm{kg})s_{\mathrm{CM}} = (300\,\mathrm{kg})(10.8\,\mathrm{m}) + (50\,\mathrm{kg})(12.2\,\mathrm{m})$.

Therefore

$$s_{\mathrm{CM}} = \frac{3240\,\mathrm{kg\,m} + 610\,\mathrm{kg\,m}}{350\,\mathrm{kg}}$$

$$= 11\,\mathrm{m},$$

that is the mass-centre of the system has not moved. This is a special case of the result that if no external forces act on a system, the mass-centre's velocity is constant. The reader can prove for himself that if the boat-and-cox had initially had a velocity of $5.0\,\mathrm{m\,s^{-1}}$, then whatever the antics of the cox, the mass-centre of the boat-and-cox would still have a velocity of $5.0\,\mathrm{m\,s^{-1}}$.

Alternatively, if we had been told that the cox stepped into the boat without giving it an impulse along its axis and walked, say, 3.0 m (relative to the water) to the right, and had been asked how far the boat had then moved (relative to the water) we should have been able to use the fact that the mass-centre remained at rest to say

$(50\,\mathrm{kg})(3.0\,\mathrm{m}) = (300\,\mathrm{kg})(\text{displacement of boat})$

to find that

the displacement of boat = 0.50 m

whatever the speed of the cox, and irrespective of whether he had walked at a steady speed, or had stopped after walking 3.0 m (relative to the water), etc. Incidentally he walks 3.5 m relative to the boat. ◀

Modifying equation 8-14 so as to deal with the behaviour of a collection of particles forming a body gives

$$m\boldsymbol{v}_{\mathrm{CM}} = m_1\boldsymbol{v}_1 + m_2\boldsymbol{v}_2 + \cdots + m_n\boldsymbol{v}_n,$$

that is $\quad m\boldsymbol{v}_{\mathrm{CM}} = \sum m_r\boldsymbol{v}_r.$ [8-16]

A collection of atoms, such as those forming a molecule of CO_2, or a collection of molecules, such as those forming a man, will move so that their centre of mass has a constant velocity if no external forces act. The significance of the Moon and stone problem discussed on page 121 now becomes clear. The velocities must be measured relative to the centre of mass of the Moon–stone system which is in an inertial frame rather than relative to the centre of mass of the Moon, which is not in an inertial frame. Rifle recoil and rockets can be re-examined using the centre of mass frame of reference.

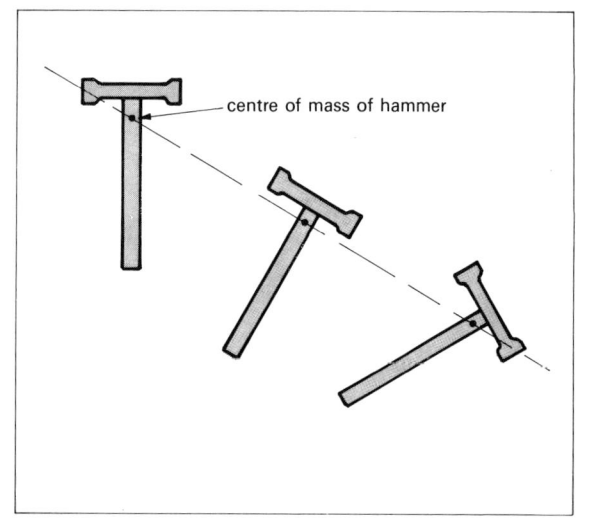

Figure 8-28 A simulated multiflash photograph of a hammer moving over a frictionless horizontal table or thrown by an astronaut working in space well away from the Earth.

Bibliography

Coplin, J. F. (1967). *Aircraft jet engines.* MacDonald. A more detailed look at real propulsion systems.

French, A. P. (1971). *Newtonian mechanics.* Nelson. Chapter 9 on collisions and conservation laws contains a detailed discussion on collisions as viewed from two inertial reference frames.

Gentner, W., Maier-Leibnitz, H., and Bothe, W. (1954). *An atlas of typical cloud chamber photographs,* (out of print), school edition. Pergamon.

Jardine, J. (1966). *Physics is fun,* Book 3. Heinemann. Chapter 7 on momentum contains many excellent photographs.

Project Physics (1971). Reader, Unit 5 *Models of the atom.* Holt, Rinehart and Winston. Chapter 19 is about space travel: problems of physics and engineering.

PSSC (1971). *Physics,* 3rd edition. Heath. Chapter 14 on momentum and momentum conservation stresses in a simple way the vector nature of momentum.

Roberson, E. C. (1969). *Rocket motors* MacDonald. A companion volume to Coplin quoted above.

Rogers, E. M. (1960). *Physics for the inquiring mind.* Oxford University Press. Chapter 8: momentum.

Ryan, P. (1972). *The invasion of the moon 1957–70.* Penguin. A source of information on the Saturn V rockets.

Tricker, R. A. R. and Tricker, B. J. K. (1968). *The science of movement.* Mills and Boon. There are some large scale interactions described in Chapter 6.

8 mm film loop. 'Explosion of a cluster of objects.' Ealing Scientific. This Project Physics loop stresses the vector nature of momentum.

8 mm film loop. 'Dynamics of a billiard ball.' Ealing Scientific.

16 mm film. 'Momentum and collision processes.' Travelling Films. A film made for science teachers.

Exercises

Data (to be used unless otherwise directed):
$g = 10\,\text{m s}^{-2} = 10\,\text{N kg}^{-1}$.

8-1 Estimate the numerical values of the linear momentum of
(a) the Earth
(b) Concorde at its maximum speed
(c) a man running as fast as he can
(d) a hurrying snail
(e) a hydrogen molecule at room temperature.

8-2 What impulse is given by
(a) the ground to a car of mass 1000 kg when it accelerates from rest to a speed of $50\,\text{m s}^{-1}$
(b) a man to a ball of mass 0.15 kg when he throws it at a speed of $20\,\text{m s}^{-1}$?

8-3 What is the change in momentum of
(a) a rifle bullet of mass 5.0 g which slows down from a speed of $600\,\text{m s}^{-1}$ to a speed of $400\,\text{m s}^{-1}$ as it passes through a wall without change of direction
(b) a tennis ball of mass 55 g which bounces vertically on the ground (the speeds before and after impact are $5\,\text{m s}^{-1}$ and $4\,\text{m s}^{-1}$ respectively)?
What are the impulses exerted on the bullet and the ball?

8-4 Referring back to Exercise 8-3, state the impulse exerted on the wall and the ground, respectively. Does their momentum change?

8-5 A golfball of mass 0.045 kg is struck by a golfclub with a force which varies with time as follows:

t/ms	0	1	2	3	4	5	6	7	8
F/N	0	700	1800	2500	2100	1600	900	400	0

Use a graphical method to find the impulse exerted on the ball and hence find the speed of the ball as it leaves the club. ●

8-6 A train of mass 1.0×10^6 kg has a speed of $30\,\text{m s}^{-1}$ and is brought to rest by a resisting force which has an average value of 5.0×10^5 N. How long does it take to slow to $20\,\text{m s}^{-1}$? How long does it take to come to rest? ●

8-7 Two billiard balls collide directly and rebound. What justification is there for saying that the momentum of the balls is conserved? (Is it a conclusion based on innumerable similar experiments? Does it follow from other experiment-based laws? etc.)

8-8 A truck of mass 1.0×10^4 kg travelling at a speed of $4.0\,\text{m s}^{-1}$ is brought to rest by buffers in a time 0.40 s. What is the average force exerted by the buffers on the truck? ●

8-9 A car of mass 1200 kg reaches a speed of $30\,\text{m s}^{-1}$ in 10 s. What is the average force exerted on the car? What exerts this force? ●

8-10 A rifle fires a bullet with a muzzle velocity of $800\,\text{m s}^{-1}$: the total mass of the bullet and propellant gases is 10 g. If the explosion lasts for 1.5×10^{-3} s before the bullet leaves the barrel, what is the average force exerted on the gases and bullet? What is the average force exerted by them on the rifle? ●

8 Linear momentum

8-11 A ball of mass 0.45 kg is thrown up into the air with an initial velocity of $6.0\,\mathrm{m\,s^{-1}}$. Why is its momentum not conserved while it is in the air? What force acts on it? How long is it before it is stationary at the top of its flight? What happens to the Earth while the ball is in flight?

8-12 (a) When a man catches a ball he lets his hands move *with* the ball until it has eventually stopped. Explain this action with reference to the ball's loss of momentum.

(b) Explain similarly why a gymnast who has vaulted over an obstacle may intentionally perform a forward roll (somersault) when he lands on the floor before finally coming to rest.

(c) Explain similarly why delicate instruments may be packed in foam rubber.

8-13 The table shows how the force F exerted on an accelerating car varies with time t.

t/s	0	3	6	9	12
F/N	3000	2880	2720	2520	2140

Find the momentum of the car after (a) 6 s (b) 12 s. Find also its speed at these times if its mass is 1000 kg. ●

8-14 Perform the following momentum additions and subtractions either by scale drawing or by calculation:
(a) 50 N s in a direction N 25° W + 25 N s in a direction N 45° E
(b) 45 N s in a direction S 10° W + 30 N s in a direction N 20° E
(c) 45 N s in a direction S 10° W − 30 N s in a direction N 20° E ●

8-15 A car of mass 1200 kg travelling at $30\,\mathrm{m\,s^{-1}}$ due north rounds a corner so that it is eventually travelling at $30\,\mathrm{m\,s^{-1}}$ due east. What is the car's change in momentum? ●

8-16 A billiard ball of mass 0.40 kg collides obliquely with a cushion. The angles which its path makes with the cushion before and after impact are 52° and 35°, and its speeds are $2.6\,\mathrm{m\,s^{-1}}$ and $1.8\,\mathrm{m\,s^{-1}}$. Find the impulse given by the cushion to the ball and the impulse given by the ball to the cushion. ●

8-17 Consider a number of bodies in an isolated system which exert forces on each other but which do not have forces exerted on them by external bodies. Give a verbal argument, using any or all of Newton's three laws, to justify the statement that the linear momentum of the bodies of the system is conserved. Give two examples of such isolated systems.

8-18 Two billiard balls each of mass 0.40 kg move directly towards each other and collide. The first has a velocity of $4.0\,\mathrm{m\,s^{-1}}$ to the right before the collision and a velocity of $4.5\,\mathrm{m\,s^{-1}}$ to the left after the collision. The second has a velocity of $5.0\,\mathrm{m\,s^{-1}}$ to the left before the collision. Draw a diagram, marking on it all the velocities, and find the velocity of the second ball after the impact. Also find the change in momentum of each ball. ●

8-19 What is the change in the total kinetic energy of the two billiard balls in Exercise 8-18? Account for it. ●

8-20 Repeat Exercise 8-18 from the point of view of an observer travelling *with* the first ball (that is, an observer to whom the first ball appears to be at rest and the second ball to be approaching at a speed of $9.0\,\mathrm{m\,s^{-1}}$). Do your results agree with the answers to Exercise 8-18?

8-21 Repeat Exercise 8-18 for an observer who travels
(a) with the second ball
(b) with the centre of mass of the two balls.

8-22 If the rifle of Exercise 8-10 has a mass of 5.0 kg, find its speed of recoil. ●

8-23 A puck of mass 2.0 kg slides on a frictionless surface at a speed of $0.60\,\mathrm{m\,s^{-1}}$ and collides directly with a second puck of mass 1.0 kg travelling at a speed of $0.20\,\mathrm{m\,s^{-1}}$ in the same direction and sense. If the speed of the second puck is $0.60\,\mathrm{m\,s^{-1}}$ after the collision, what is the velocity of the first puck after the collision? ●

8-24 A truck is travelling horizontally at a speed of $10\,\mathrm{m\,s^{-1}}$ and collides with two similar stationary trucks, with which it couples, and the three trucks move on in the original direction. They collide and couple with a fourth similar stationary truck. What is the speed of the four coupled trucks? What fraction of the original kinetic energy remains? ●

8-25 In an experiment similar to that described in Section 8-4, the following measurements of velocity were made:

	Mass	Before	After
Glider 1	m_1	$0.24\,\mathrm{m\,s^{-1}}$	$0.03\,\mathrm{m\,s^{-1}}$
Glider 2	m_2	$-0.18\,\mathrm{m\,s^{-1}}$	$0.45\,\mathrm{m\,s^{-1}}$

What is the ratio of the masses m_1/m_2? ●

8-26 A small boat of mass 40 kg is tied by a rope to a quay so that the rope is slack and the boat is about 0.50 m from the quay. A boy of mass 60 kg decides to step from the boat on to the quay. Knowing something about the principle of conservation of momentum, would you advise him to step quickly or slowly, or would you suggest any other course of action?

8-27 A shell of mass 500 kg, travelling horizontally at a speed of $100\,\mathrm{m\,s^{-1}}$, explodes into two parts, one four times the mass of the other; the smaller part has a velocity of $700\,\mathrm{m\,s^{-1}}$ in the original direction. What is the velocity of the larger part after the explosion? Does the pull of the Earth affect the momentum of the shell during the explosion? What is the path of the centre of mass of the fragment after the explosion? ●

8-28 What is the change in kinetic energy of the shell of Exercise 8-27 during the explosion? Account for it. ●

8-29 A trolley of mass 18 kg is travelling with a speed of $4.0\,\mathrm{m\,s^{-1}}$ on a horizontal track. A parcel of mass 6.0 kg is dropped vertically into the truck. What is the new speed of the truck? What is the kinetic energy of the system before and after? Account for the change in kinetic energy. ●

8-30 A man picks up a stone from the ground and drops it. Consider the changes in momentum of the stone and the man–Earth system, and discuss whether momentum is conserved for the stone, the man–Earth system, or the stone–man–Earth system.

8-31 Repeat the processes of Exercise 8-30 when a man cues a billiard ball in a direction perpendicular to a cushion. It rebounds normally and he stops it when it reaches him again.

8-32 Refer to Example 8-2. What is the *least* velocity which may be acquired by the mass m when it is struck by a mass M moving with velocity v?

8-33 A *ballistic pendulum* consists of two spherical masses suspended by threads so that when the threads are vertical the spheres just touch each other. One sphere is known to have a mass of 1.0 kg. The second sphere is pulled aside until it is 200 mm above its original level, with the thread taut, and released. When the second sphere strikes the first, the second is brought to rest, and the first rises to a height of 50 mm. Find the mass of the second sphere. •

8-34 A shell of mass 500 kg, travelling horizontally at a speed of $100\,\text{m s}^{-1}$, explodes into three parts. The first, of mass 200 kg, travels vertically upwards at a speed of $150\,\text{m s}^{-1}$, and the second, of mass 150 kg, travels horizontally with a speed of $60\,\text{m s}^{-1}$ but in a direction opposite to that of the original shell. What is the velocity of the third part, assuming that its mass is 150 kg? What is the path of the centre of mass of the fragments after the explosion? •

8-35 A man with a machine gun fires bullets of mass 5 g at a horizontal speed of $900\,\text{m s}^{-1}$ at a rate of 5 per second. He stands on a trolley which runs on frictionless wheels on a horizontal surface. Taking the total mass of the man, the rifle, and the trolley as 180 kg, discuss the trolley's motion. •

8-36 A trolley similar to that of Exercise 8-35 now has a target fixed to it some distance from the gun and the rifleman fires bullets into the target. Explain what happens while the rifleman fires about a hundred bullets. •

8-37 A jet of water travels horizontally and strikes a vertical wall without rebounding. The jet has a cross-sectional area of $1000\,\text{mm}^2$ and a speed of $40\,\text{m s}^{-1}$. If the density of water is $1000\,\text{kg m}^{-3}$, what is the push of the water on the wall? Do you use Newton's third law at any stage in your working? •

8-38 A man and his parachute together have a mass of 120 kg. If air has a density of $1.2\,\text{kg m}^{-3}$, what must be the *effective* area of the parachute if he is to have a terminal velocity of $10\,\text{m s}^{-1}$? •

8-39 Birds and gliders manoeuvre so that upward currents of air (thermals) can strike their undersides and so exert upward forces on them. What must be the speed of an upward current of air which is to support a bird of mass 0.50 kg and effective area (with wings outstretched) $2 \times 10^4\,\text{mm}^2$? Take the density of air to be $1.2\,\text{kg m}^{-3}$. •

8-40 Sand is allowed to fall from a height of 5.0 m onto the pan of a balance at a rate of $10\,\text{g s}^{-1}$. Draw a graph to show the reading of the balance from $t = 0$ (when the sand first arrives) to $t = 20\,\text{s}$. •

8-41 When an astronaut steps outside a space capsule in free fall he uses a gas gun to move himself relative to the capsule. Assuming that together with his space suit he has a mass of 150 kg, and that the gas gun is to give him an acceleration of $0.020\,\text{m s}^{-2}$, find the speed at which the gas must leave the gun if it has a muzzle area of $200\,\text{mm}^2$. Assume that the density of the gas is $0.8\,\text{kg m}^{-3}$. •

8-42 Rain, falling at a speed of $12\,\text{m s}^{-1}$ at an angle of $60°$ to the vertical, falls on a flat roof of area $600\,\text{m}^2$. If 10 mm of rain falls in 1 hour, what is the vertical component of the force on the roof caused by the rain falling? Density of water $= 10^3\,\text{kg m}^{-3}$.

8-43 Water emerges from a constriction at the end of a garden hose. The area of the jet is 0.2 times that of the main hose, and $0.40\,\text{kg s}^{-1}$ of water emerges at a speed of $10\,\text{m s}^{-1}$. Find the force which a man must exert on the hose to keep it still. •

8-44 A rocket has a total mass of 10^4 kg and is at rest on the ground. Taking the exhaust velocity of the gases as $2000\,\text{m s}^{-1}$, find the rate of combustion, that is the number of kg s^{-1} which must be ejected, in order that the rocket may just leave the ground. •

8-45 A rocket has a total mass of 6.0×10^4 kg, of which 5.0×10^4 kg is fuel. Find the ratio of the final velocity v to the exhaust velocity v_0. Assume that the rocket is fired in a region where no external forces, such as the pull of the Earth, act on it. •

8-46 The escape velocity from the Earth is $1.13 \times 10^4\,\text{m s}^{-1}$. Assuming that the exhaust velocity of the gases from a rocket is $3000\,\text{m s}^{-1}$, and the maximum value of the *vehicle mass ratio* [(original total mass) ÷ (mass at burn-out)] is 10, explain why a single-stage rocket cannot be used to send the payload into space. What would be the final velocity of this rocket? •

8-47 In some versions of Saturn V, the original total mass is 2.5×10^6 kg, and the fuel is consumed at a rate of $1.25 \times 10^4\,\text{kg s}^{-1}$. Taking the exhaust velocity as $4000\,\text{m s}^{-1}$, find the initial acceleration. Why will this acceleration increase as the rocket rises, if the rate of consumption of fuel remains the same? •

8-48 The escape velocity from the Earth is $1.13 \times 10^4\,\text{m s}^{-1}$, and a rocket's exhaust velocity is $4.0 \times 10^3\,\text{m s}^{-1}$. Find the vehicle mass ratio which would be needed for a single stage rocket to escape from the Earth. Find also the

$$\text{propellant mass ratio} = \frac{\text{mass of propellant}}{\text{total original mass}}$$

$$= \frac{\text{total original mass} - \text{mass at burn-out}}{\text{total original mass}}$$

$$= 1 - \frac{1}{\text{vehicle mass ratio}}$$

and hence find the percentage of the original total mass which can be used for payload, rocket motor equipment, and so on.

In a multistage rocket the velocity acquired during, say, the second stage is of course added to the velocity acquired during the first stage. Thus in a three-stage rocket, if each stage has the same vehicle mass ratio, each stage must supply one-third of the final velocity. Find the propellant mass ratio for a three-stage rocket with an exhaust velocity of $4000\,\text{m s}^{-1}$ which is to just escape from the Earth.

If the payload (for example in Apollo 13, the LEM, the service module, and the command module) has a mass of 5.0×10^4 kg, what is the mass of the third stage (use the information obtained from the previous parts of the question)? Treating the third stage as the 'payload' for the second stage, and the second stage as the payload for the first stage, find the total original mass of the rocket. What would the thrust need to be in order to give this rocket an initial acceleration of $5\,\text{m s}^{-2}$? •

9 The principle of conservation of energy

9-1 Gravitational potential energy	136	9-6 The first law of thermodynamics	148
9-2 Elastic potential energy	137	9-7 Potential energy graphs	148
9-3 The principle of conservation of energy	138	Bibliography	150
9-4 Collisions	141	Exercises	151
9-5 Internal energy	145		

In the absence of any external forces, a particle moves at a constant velocity. Since its speed is constant, so is its kinetic energy.

Therefore $\quad T = \tfrac{1}{2}mv^2 =$ constant.

The kinetic energy of the particle is *conserved*. What happens when a second particle interacts with the first? The forces involved are linked by Newton's third law and, as $\sum F \Delta t$ is the same in size and opposite in direction for the two particles, linear momentum is conserved for the system as we have seen in Chapter 8. What happens to the kinetic energy of the system? $\sum F \cdot \Delta x$ will usually be *different* for the two bodies, and if one of them is very massive—for example the Earth—the work done on this large body will be negligibly small compared with the work done on the other body. In the early part of this chapter, we shall be taking the second body in the interaction to be the Earth and we shall ignore any change in its kinetic energy as a result of the (small amount of) work done on it. In Section 9-5 this point will be pursued further and the more general case considered. In effect our assumption is exactly that which we make at several places in the text: namely that the Earth is an inertial frame of reference.

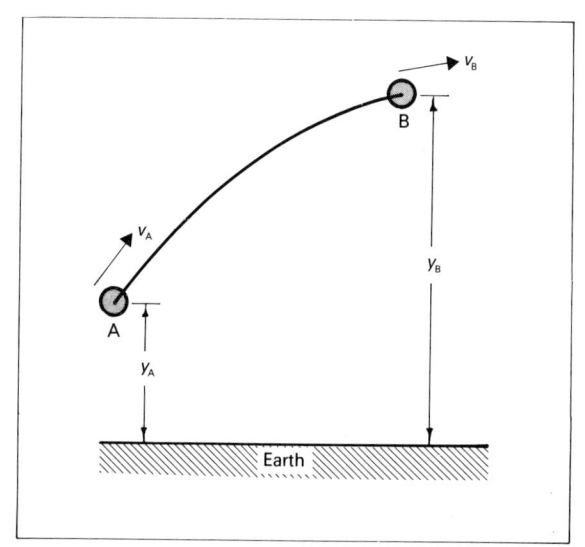

Figure 9-1 A particle of mass m moves from A to B under the action of the pull of the Earth.

9-1 Gravitational potential energy

Suppose a particle of mass m is acted on by only one force, the pull of the Earth, W, or mg, on it. An observer on the Earth measures its speed v and its distance above the Earth's surface y, y remaining small enough to ensure that g can be taken as equal to its value at the Earth's surface. The work–energy equation gives us (see figure 9-1)

$$-mg(y_B - y_A) = \tfrac{1}{2}mv_B^2 - \tfrac{1}{2}mv_A^2$$

(the initial minus sign indicating that $\boldsymbol{g}$ is vertically downwards while y is measured vertically upwards). Rearranging,

$$\tfrac{1}{2}mv_B^2 + mgy_B = \tfrac{1}{2}mv_A^2 + mgy_A.$$

The kinetic energy, T, of the particle is no longer conserved, but the sum of T and the particle's 'mgy' remains constant as a result of the gravitational interaction between the Earth and the particle. If we *define* mgy as the gravitational potential energy of the body, E_g, then, being careful to measure all displacements y from the same arbitrary level,

$$E_g = mgy \qquad [9\text{-}1]$$

$$T_A + E_{g,A} = T_B + E_{g,B}.$$

That is $\qquad T + E_g =$ constant.

The sum $(T + E_g)$ for the particle *is conserved* and we have a case of the principle of conservation of mechanical energy. There is nothing remarkable about this—it is bound to be true as we have defined T and E_g in such a way as to make it so. We should note that in the above discussion

(a) $\boldsymbol{g}$ and y were conveniently parallel. In general, where the displacement $\boldsymbol{s}$ is not parallel to $\boldsymbol{g}$, the work done by $m\boldsymbol{g}$ is $m\boldsymbol{g} \cdot \boldsymbol{s}\, (= mgs\cos\theta$ where θ is the angle between $\boldsymbol{g}$ and $\boldsymbol{s}$).

(b) we have taken g to be constant in size and direction. When this cannot be assumed the evaluation of $E_g = \sum mg\Delta y$ is more complicated but the conservation principle is still valid; see Example 7-3 and also Section 14-8.

▶ **Example 9-1** Refer to Example 7-8: we shall now attempt the same problem using the idea of potential energy.

Let us make all measurements of height (when we calculate potential energies) from the final level of the stone. Initially, when the stone is 2.0 m above this level

$$E_g (= mgy) = (0.20\,\text{kg})\left(10\,\frac{\text{N}}{\text{kg}}\right)(2.0\,\text{m}) = 4.0\,\text{J},$$

$$T = 0.$$

Finally $\qquad E_g = 0,$

$$T = \tfrac{1}{2}(0.20\,\text{kg})v^2 \quad \text{where } v \text{ is the speed of the bob at the lowest point.}$$

Therefore $\quad 4.0\,\text{J} = \tfrac{1}{2}(0.20\,\text{kg})v^2$

$$v^2 = 40\,\text{m}^2\,\text{s}^{-2}$$

so that $\qquad v = 6.3\,\text{m s}^{-1}.$

Note. The result would of course have been the same if
(a) both the potential energies had been measured from a different level
(b) the mass of the bob had been different (so we did not need to know its value) ◀

9-2 Elastic potential energy

Suppose a particle is acted on by only one force, the pull $\boldsymbol{F}$ of a spring on it. Suppose that the spring has a constant stiffness k, so that if it is extended a distance x, $\boldsymbol{F} = -k\boldsymbol{x}$, the minus sign arising because $\boldsymbol{F}$ and $\boldsymbol{x}$ are in opposite directions. The work done by the pull of the spring *on* the particle is given by (average force) × (change of displacement). Thus referring to figure 9-2 where the particle is moving from A to B, the work–energy equation gives

$$(\text{average force})(\Delta x) = \tfrac{1}{2}mv_B^2 - \tfrac{1}{2}mv_A^2,$$

therefore $\quad \tfrac{1}{2}(F_A + F_B)(x_B - x_A) = \tfrac{1}{2}mv_B^2 - \tfrac{1}{2}mv_A^2.$

As $F_A = -kx_A$, etc., we get

$$-\tfrac{1}{2}k(x_A + x_B)(x_B - x_A) = \tfrac{1}{2}mv_B^2 - \tfrac{1}{2}mv_A^2$$

$$-\tfrac{1}{2}kx_B^2 + \tfrac{1}{2}kx_A^2 = \tfrac{1}{2}mv_B^2 - \tfrac{1}{2}mv_A^2$$

or $\qquad \tfrac{1}{2}mv_B^2 + \tfrac{1}{2}kx_B^2 = \tfrac{1}{2}mv_A^2 + \tfrac{1}{2}kx_A^2.$

The kinetic energy, T, of the particle is no longer

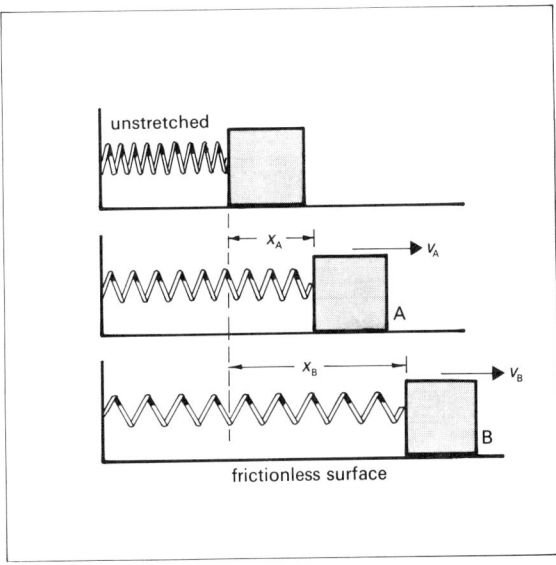

Figure 9-2 A body of mass m moves horizontally from A to B under the action of the pull of a massless elastic spring, the other end of which is attached to the Earth.

conserved, but the sum of T and the '$\frac{1}{2}kx^2$' of the spring remains constant as a result of the elastic interaction between the Earth and the particle. If we *define* $\frac{1}{2}kx^2$ as the elastic potential energy E_e of the body to which the spring is fixed then, being careful to measure all x from the position at which the spring was not distorted,

$$E_e = \tfrac{1}{2}kx^2 \qquad [9\text{-}2]$$

$$T_A + E_{e,A} = T_B + E_{e,B}$$

that is
$$T + E_e = \text{constant}.$$

The sum $(T + E_e)$ *is conserved* and we have another case of the principle of conservation of mechanical energy.

Combining this result with that of the previous section, we have the principle of conservation of *mechanical* energy for a particle, namely

$$T + E = \text{constant}, \qquad [9\text{-}3]$$

E now including both gravitational and elastic interactions between the particle and the Earth. It is often convenient to start problems in Newtonian mechanics by writing down the (scalar) relations of the principle of conservation of mechanical energy rather than the (vector) statements of the second law.

▶ **Example 9-2** A frictionless inclined plane has a slope of 37° and a length of 0.50 m (figure 9-3). To a point which is 0.30 m vertically above the highest point of the slope is attached a mass of 6.0 kg by means of a massless elastic thread of natural length 0.20 m and constant stiffness 100 N m^{-1}, and initially the mass rests on the highest point of the slope. What is its speed when it has arrived at the bottom of the slope?

When the mass is at the bottom B of the slope, the length of the elastic thread is given by

$$\sqrt{[(0.60\,\text{m})^2 + (0.40\,\text{m})^2]} = 0.72\,\text{m},$$

so that the extension is 0.52 m. Let us make all measurements of height from the level of B.

Initially $\quad T = 0$,

$$E_g = (6.0\,\text{kg})(10\,\text{N kg}^{-1})(0.30\,\text{m}) = 18.0\,\text{J},$$

$$E_e(=\tfrac{1}{2}kx^2) = \tfrac{1}{2}(100\,\text{N m}^{-1})(0.10\,\text{m})^2 = 0.5\,\text{J}.$$

Finally $\quad T = \tfrac{1}{2}(6.0\,\text{kg})v^2 \quad$ where v is the speed at B,

$$E_g = 0,$$

$$E_e = \tfrac{1}{2}(100\,\text{N m}^{-1})(0.52\,\text{m})^2 = 13.5\,\text{J}.$$

Therefore
$$18.5\,\text{J} = \tfrac{1}{2}(6.0\,\text{kg})v^2 + 13.5\,\text{J}$$
$$v^2 = 1.67\,\text{m}^2\,\text{s}^{-2}$$

so that the speed of the mass at the bottom is 1.3 m s^{-1}.
Note. In this example we have used the principle of conservation of mechanical energy, but it will nearly always be simpler to use the work–energy theorem. This theorem would have been awkward to use in this particular example because of the difficulty in calculating the work done by the pull of the elastic thread, as the force exerted by it was varying in a complicated manner. ◀

9-3 The principle of conservation of energy

In developing the principle of conservation of mechanical energy we considered only gravitational and elastic forces and only interactions between a particle and the (fixed) Earth. What about frictional or internal forces—is there a potential energy E_f or E_i defined for each of them? *There is not.* To see why, let us think of a gravitational force, the vertical pull W of the Earth on a body, and compare it with a sliding friction force, the tangential push F of a surface on a body. As the body moves, W does work on it: positive work if the body approaches the Earth, negative work if it recedes from it. The net result is that for a journey A → B → C → A, the total work done by W is zero. W is said to be a *conservative force*. Equally (see Example 7-1), the work done by W when the body moves from P to Q is *independent* of the path it takes between P and Q. Contrast these results with what happens when F does work as a body slides about on a rough surface. If it were to travel in a loop, A → B → C → A, the total work done by F is certainly *not* zero: F always acts in such a way as to oppose the relative motion of two surfaces which are in contact. It is called a *dissipative*

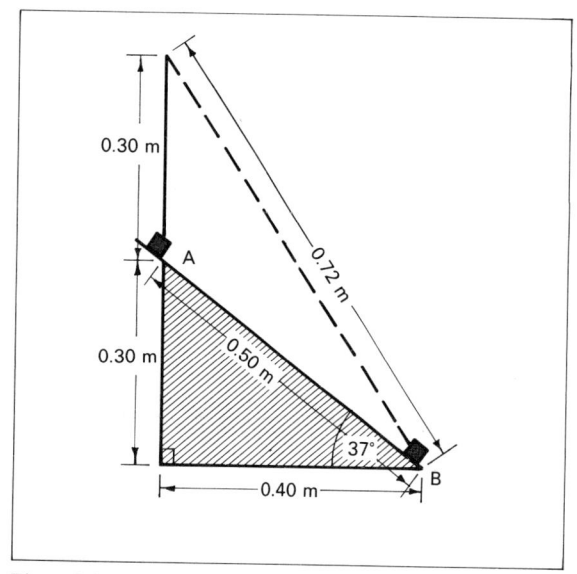

Figure 9-3

9-3 The principle of conservation of energy

force. Further, when the body moves from P to Q, the work done by **F** *does* depend on what distance it travels between P and Q (and also at what speed). Obviously *W* conserves and **F** dissipates the mechanical (kinetic plus potential) energy of the body.

But what happens to the mechanical energy which **F** dissipates? It is convenient to say that it becomes non-mechanical energy, mainly *internal* energy. Physicists (starting with James Joule) have learned how to measure changes in the internal energy of a body, and have found that when a system loses a given amount of mechanical energy, a fixed amount of internal energy is gained by the system. Thus we can extend our conservation principle to include internal energy. Many more 'forms of energy' are now recognized: sound energy, electromagnetic wave (light, for example) energy, chemical energy, nuclear energy (often referred to as 'atomic' energy as it was originally, and wrongly, labelled), and so on, but in this text we will be mainly interested in mechanical energy.

The general principle of conservation of energy states that

in an isolated system the total energy remains constant.

This statement, together with the conservation principles for mass and momentum already considered, lies at the heart of the physical sciences: we will see in the next chapter that the three principles can be further reduced to two.

Where we find mechanical energy being dissipated we look for other forms of energy being produced. For example, consider the energy changes which occur when a bullet, moving horizontally, is brought to rest while penetrating a few millimetres into a block of wood. An energy flow diagram describes the situation (figure 9-4). But where did the kinetic energy of the bullet originate? In the explosion, reactions occur which reduce the chemical energy of the materials; figure 9-5 is an energy flow diagram for the explosion.

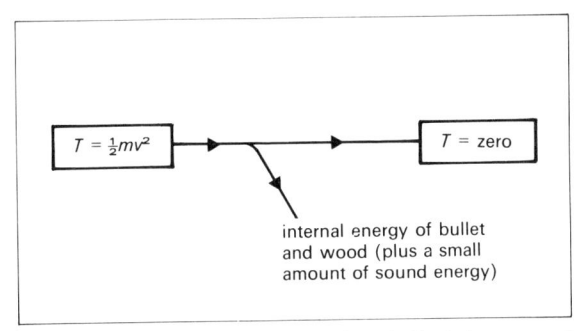

Figure 9-4 An energy flow diagram for a bullet being stopped by a wooden block.

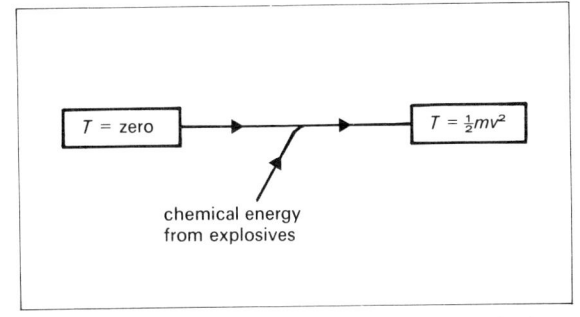

Figure 9-5 An energy flow diagram for a bullet being fired.

According to the general principle of conservation of energy, energy is never created or destroyed: *there is a fixed amount of it in an isolated system.* We simply note it changing its form, for example from mechanical energy to internal energy. Investigating this idea on the grand scale, consider the sources of energy we need for our continued comfort and existence. We use artificial light; we eat. The source of the energy in each of these examples is ultimately the Sun (or, since the early 1940s, nuclear energy liberated artificially on Earth). Energy flows from the Sun to the Earth in the form of electromagnetic waves. Two *useful* energy conversions are the storing of chemical energy in plants (photosynthesis) and the storing of gravitational potential energy in clouds. The first provides a *long*-term energy store in the form of coal, oil, and natural gas deposits and a medium-term store of food for man and animals, while the second process stores energy only in the *short*-term.

It is convenient to use a shorthand to represent very large quantities of energy: let us write

$$10^{21} \text{ J} = Q. \qquad [9\text{-}4]$$

This 'Q' unit is widely used and is exactly defined in terms of an obsolete energy unit, the British Thermal unit; the above equation, though not exactly true, will serve for our purposes. Roughly $5500\,Q$ reach the Earth from the Sun every year. The estimated long-term reserve of fossil fuels is about $250\,Q$ of which one tenth is thought to be readily extractable. The Earth is thus seen to be a very inefficient storage system, the total store representing only 20 days' input, and there will obviously be no noticeable increase in the total available supplies of coal, oil, and natural gas over the next 1000 years—a very small time interval compared with the 5000 million years for which the Earth has had a geological history. Man is currently using about $0.2\,Q$ annually which suggests that his reserves will last not much more than 100 years *if there is no increase in demand*. It is ridiculous to think that there will be no increase in demand and the extrapolation of present trends shows that these reserves, if relied on exclusively, will run out in 50 or 60 years. Much more determined extraction techniques may improve this figure by a factor of five or six. Hydroelectric and other schemes which use the short-term energy storage system seem at first an attractive energy source but man's real hope for the next few hundred years lies in the nuclear fuels which can be extracted from the Earth. Uranium will be the coal of the twenty-first century. Looking further ahead, the prospects again dim unless man can harness fusion reactions so as to supply energy from the fusion of deuterium and tritium (isotopes of hydrogen). The Sun's energy supply comes from the fusion of protons.

All of the above discussion refers to the energy needed for the continuance of a technologically advanced society. There is however a further energy limitation to man's progress—the limitation of food resources in a population explosion. The problem here depends on the following calculation. Of sunlight's supply of $5500\,Q$ each year, suppose 1/1000th or roughly $5\,Q$ *could be* stored in plants as a result of photosynthesis. This estimate is an optimistic one and envisages optimum use of the Earth's land area. An active man's average daily energy requirements are about 10^7 J (that is 100 W over a period of 10^5 s) or roughly 5×10^9 J in a year. As $5\,Q = 5 \times 10^{21}$ J, then the upper limit to the Earth's population would seem to be about 10^{12}. As this calculation takes no account of feeding other animals who in turn supply man with protein and so on, let us put the upper limit at 10^{11}, that is 100 000 000 000, a figure which envisages the world's deserts and jungles to be highly efficient food producers for man. As the population of the Earth is now (1973) approaching 4 000 000 000, we are, from the point of view of feeding mankind alone, already frighteningly near the agriculturally practical limit.

But there does appear to be a loophole in this argument. As energy cannot be destroyed, why should we not recover and reutilize the energy we use? Such an idea involves making use of the internal energy of the Earth, its atmosphere, and its seas, for the end-point of most of the energy conversions which man encourages is an increase in this internal energy. So far in this book we have met no principle to refute such a suggestion: the principle of conservation of energy and the first law of thermodynamics (see page 148) make no mention of the *direction* in which energy conversions can occur. To follow up this point the reader must refer to texts covering *the second law of thermodynamics* which presents just such a limitation on the direction of change. Unhappily the internal energy of the outer layers of the Earth does not offer an easy solution to man's energy problems.

▶ **Example 9-3** Outline the energy changes which are involved in a man sprinting 100 m from rest on level ground.

Throughout he uses his store of chemical energy to enable him to do internal work (as his legs straighten as the ground pushes him forward) but at the same time (since he is an inefficient machine) internal energy is produced in his body. The internal work which is done gives him kinetic energy and also (as he stirs up the air when he runs through it) gives the surroundings internal energy. His feet probably slip as he runs. These frictional forces do negative work and these also give the surroundings internal energy. When he decelerates he does negative internal work (compression forces exist in his legs) and this increases his internal energy. Thus the overall effect is a conversion of chemical energy to internal energy. Figure 9-6 illustrates these energy changes. ◀

Energy/J	Description of system or conversion
10^{29}	kinetic energy of Moon's orbital motion (relative to Earth)
10^{28}	gravitational potential energy of the Earth–Moon system
10^{23}	the Earth's energy reserves in fossil fuels (1970)
10^{22}	solar energy received per day by the Earth
10^{18}	the world's energy requirement each day (1970)
10^{17}	the energy equivalent of one kilogram of matter
10^{10}	the energy dissipated in a lightning discharge
10^{9}	energy content of a day's food for one man
10^{2}	kinetic energy of a running child
10^{1}	kinetic energy of a rifle bullet
10^{-9}	energy of a proton from a large particle accelerator
10^{-10}	the energy equivalent of a proton at rest
10^{-20}	energy of a photon from a red-hot fire
10^{-21}	kinetic energy of an oxygen molecule at room temperature

Table 9-1 Orders of magnitude of some energies. (See page 161 for the principle of conservation of mass–energy.)

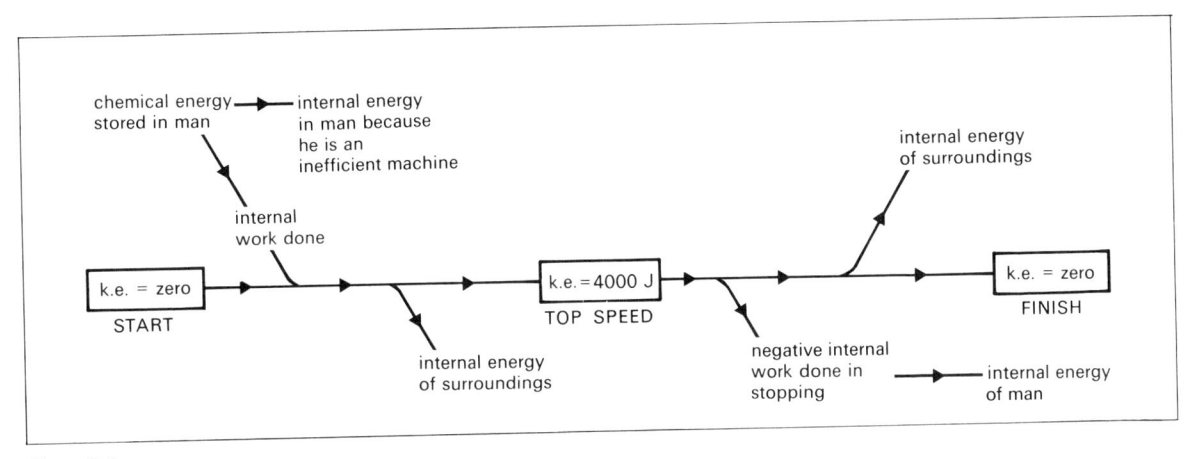

Figure 9-6

9-4 Collisions

When two bodies interact, their total linear momentum is conserved. What of their kinetic energies? We can classify collisions between two bodies, A and B, in a commonsense way by evaluating the ratio of the velocity of B relative to A after the collision to the velocity of A relative to B before the collision. This is more or less equivalent to describing how 'bouncy' the collision is. Referring to figure 9-7 (note the directions of the velocities): if

(a) $$\frac{v_B - v_A}{u_A - u_B} = 1,$$

that is $$v_B - v_A = 1(u_A - u_B),$$

the collision is said to be *perfectly elastic*, and if

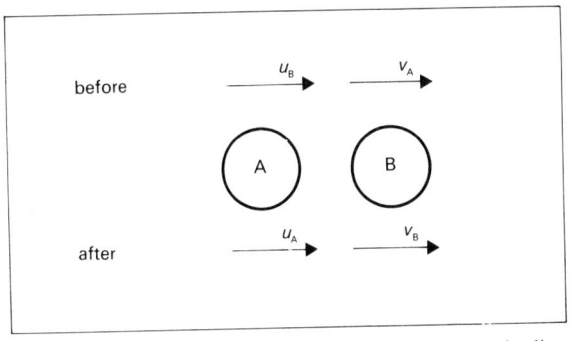

(b) $$\frac{v_B - v_A}{u_A - u_B} = 0,$$

that is $$v_B - v_A = 0(u_A - u_B) = 0,$$

Figure 9-7 A typical head-on collision between two bodies. All velocities are measured relative to the Earth.

the collision is said to be *plastic* or perfectly inelastic (the bodies stick together). In both these cases the equation represents the statement

relative speed of separation
$$= e(\text{relative speed of approach}), \quad [9\text{-}5]$$

the number e being 1 in case (*a*) and 0 in case (*b*). As in collisions between spheres it is always possible to identify which sphere is moving faster after the collision (look at figure 9-7 and ask whether A could be moving to the right *faster* than B after the collision) then, provided we always show unknown velocities in the chosen positive direction, equation 9-5 is unambiguous. It is a form of *Newton's law of impact* and holds only for spherical bodies along their line of centres. It holds for a sphere bouncing on a flat surface as a flat surface may be considered to be part of a very large sphere. e is called the *coefficient of restitution* and depends on the nature of the materials involved. Cases where $1 > e > 0$ are usual; for two glass spheres $e = 0.9$, while for two lead spheres $e = 0.2$. A simple way of measuring e is suggested in Exercise 9-14.

For a perfectly elastic interaction the elastic forces are conservative and the mechanical energy of the system is conserved. Thus the total kinetic energy of the system before the collision is equal to the total kinetic energy of the system after the collision. For such collisions in one dimension the principles of conservation of linear momentum and of mechanical energy are sufficient to predict the velocities of the bodies after the interaction if their masses and velocities before the interaction are given.

When $e < 1$, mechanical energy is lost in the interaction: the lost mechanical energy becomes internal energy. In order to be able to predict the result of such

9 The principle of conservation of energy

collisions we need to know the value of e, for e determines the fraction of the original kinetic energy which becomes internal energy. The common case of $e = 0$ is the easiest to analyse.

If for convenience we measure the speeds, relative to their centres of mass, of two bodies which are colliding head on, then there is an instant during the collision when each body is at rest and their total kinetic energy is zero. Where is the energy? In a perfectly elastic collision it is all elastic potential energy (mechanical energy), while in a perfectly inelastic one, where the bodies remain at rest after the collision, as would two lumps of putty, it is all internal energy. Usually, when $0 < e < 1$, the energy is partly elastic potential energy and partly internal energy at this instant.

If there were to be a release of stored energy at any stage of the interaction, for example from an explosive charge triggered by the two bodies striking one another, the total mechanical energy of the system could increase. The total momentum of the system would, of course, still be conserved.

▶ **Example 9-4** Two billiard balls of equal mass are moving towards each other and collide head-on. The first has a velocity of $0.20\,\mathrm{m\,s^{-1}}$ and the second a velocity of $1.00\,\mathrm{m\,s^{-1}}$, and the balls are perfectly elastic. Find the velocities of the balls after they have collided.

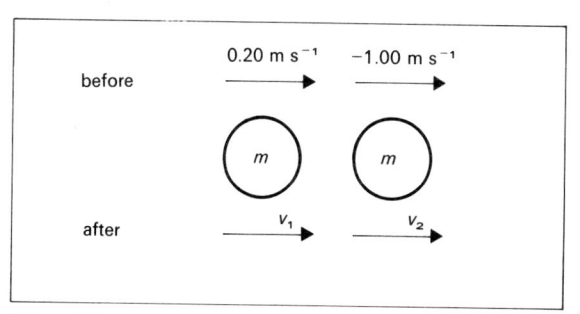

Figure 9-8

Let the velocities after the collision be v_1 and v_2 in the directions shown in figure 9-8. Using the principle of conservation of momentum, and taking the left-to-right direction as positive

$$m(-1.00\,\mathrm{m\,s^{-1}}) + m(0.20\,\mathrm{m\,s^{-1}}) = mv_1 + mv_2.$$

Using Newton's law of impact,

[9-5]   relative speed of separation = e(relative speed of approach)

where $e = 1$, we have

$$v_2 - v_1 = 1.20\,\mathrm{m\,s^{-1}}.$$

The first equation gives

$$v_1 + v_2 = -0.80\,\mathrm{m\,s^{-1}}$$

so that adding, we have

$$2v_2 = 0.40\,\mathrm{m\,s^{-1}},$$

which gives

$$v_2 = 0.20\,\mathrm{m\,s^{-1}}$$

and

$$v_1 = -1.00\,\mathrm{m\,s^{-1}}.$$

Since the value of v_1 is negative the ball (as half expected) moves to the left after the collision. Thus the velocities are

first ball: $1.00\,\mathrm{m\,s^{-1}}$ to the left,
second ball: $0.20\,\mathrm{m\,s^{-1}}$ to the right.

We see that as a result of this *perfectly elastic* collision between two balls *of equal mass* we still have a ball moving to the right at $0.20\,\mathrm{m\,s^{-1}}$, and a ball moving to the left at a speed of $1.00\,\mathrm{m\,s^{-1}}$. They are not the same balls, since they have exchanged their velocities, but the result is the same as if no collision had occurred. ◀

▶ **Example 9-5** A mass of $2.0\,\mathrm{kg}$ which has a velocity of $6.0\,\mathrm{m\,s^{-1}}$ to the right collides head-on with a mass of $4.0\,\mathrm{kg}$ which has a velocity of $3.0\,\mathrm{m\,s^{-1}}$ to the right. If the coefficient of restitution for the impact is 0.50, find the velocities of the masses after the collision.

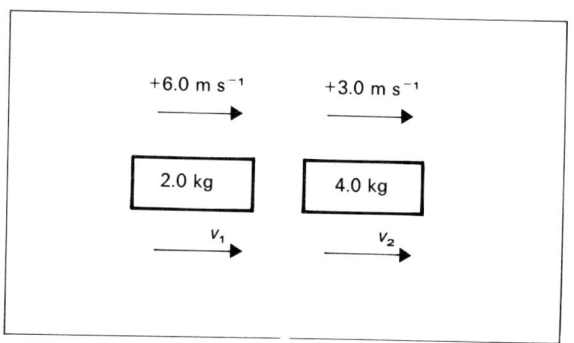

Figure 9-9

Let us first view the collision from a reference frame fixed to the Earth. The situation is drawn in figure 9-9: the left-to-right direction is taken as positive. The principle of conservation of linear momentum gives

$$(2.0\,\mathrm{kg})(6.0\,\mathrm{m\,s^{-1}}) + (4.0\,\mathrm{kg})(3.0\,\mathrm{m\,s^{-1}})$$
$$= (2.0\,\mathrm{kg})v_1 + (4.0\,\mathrm{kg})v_2,$$

and Newton's law of impact gives

$$0.50(3.0\,\mathrm{m\,s^{-1}}) = v_2 - v_1.$$

These two equations yield

$$v_1 = +3.0\,\mathrm{m\,s^{-1}},\ v_2 = +4.5\,\mathrm{m\,s^{-1}}.$$

Let us now view the collision from a reference frame fixed to the centre of mass. The velocity of the centre of mass relative to the Earth is given by

$$(2.0\,\text{kg})(6.0\,\text{m s}^{-1}) + (4.0\,\text{kg})(3.0\,\text{m s}^{-1}) = (6.0\,\text{kg})v_{CM}$$

so that $v_{CM} = +4.0\,\text{m s}^{-1}$.

If u and u' are the initial velocities, measured in the reference frames of the Earth and the centre of mass respectively, we have

$$u'_1 = u_1 - v_{CM}, \quad u'_2 = u_2 - v_{CM}$$

which gives

$$u'_1 = +2.0\,\text{m s}^{-1}, \quad u'_2 = -1.0\,\text{m s}^{-1}.$$

This is illustrated in figure 9-10.

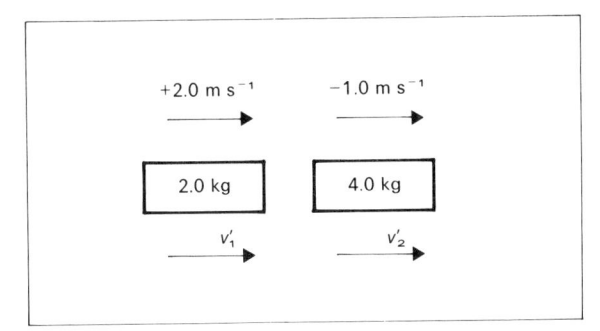

Figure 9-10

The principle of conservation of linear momentum gives

$$(2.0\,\text{kg})(2.0\,\text{m s}^{-1}) + (4.0\,\text{kg})(-1.0\,\text{m s}^{-1})$$
$$= (2.0\,\text{kg})v'_1 + (4.0\,\text{kg})v'_2,$$

and Newton's law of impact gives

$$0.50(3.0\,\text{m s}^{-1}) = v'_2 - v'_1.$$

These two equations yield

$$v'_1 = -1.0\,\text{m s}^{-1}, \quad v'_2 = +0.5\,\text{m s}^{-1},$$

and therefore

$$v_1(= v'_1 + v_{CM}) = +3.0\,\text{m s}^{-1},$$

and

$$v_2(= v'_2 + v_{CM}) = +4.5\,\text{m s}^{-1}$$

as before.

We notice that if we measure the velocities in the reference frame fixed to the centre of mass, the velocity of each of the masses after the collision is minus half its initial velocity. This result suggests that we can find the velocities of masses after a collision by multiplying their initial velocities by $-e$, and indeed this is generally true, provided we work in a reference frame fixed to the centre of mass. So the procedure would be:

(a) find v_{CM}
(b) subtract this from u_1 and u_2 to find u'_1 and u'_2
(c) obtain v'_1 and v'_2 ($v'_1 = -eu'_1$, $v'_2 = -eu'_2$)
(d) obtain v_1 and v_2 by adding v_{CM} to v'_1 and v'_2. ◀

The ionization of gases

In a perfectly elastic collision between a particle of mass m_1 and another of mass m_2, where $m_2 \gg m_1$, for example a low-energy electron striking a helium atom or a ball bouncing on the Earth, the small particle loses *very little* kinetic energy. The more massive particle similarly receives very little kinetic energy. The Earth–ball case is one of common experience (though even a Superball is not perfectly elastic); the electron–atom case is of great significance in interpreting ionization and excitation experiments with gases. An electron could bump elastically into hundreds of gas atoms without losing much of its kinetic energy whereas *one* inelastic interaction could transfer most of the electron's kinetic energy to the atom—perhaps to ionize it.

Nuclear collisions

In the analysis of interactions between nuclear particles using cloud or bubble chambers, we can photograph the tracks of any charged particles involved. If a variety of photographs is examined, the collisions can best be classified according to the angle θ between the two particle tracks *after* the collision. (On a larger scale, for example with billiard balls, collisions are usually classified by the angle between the line of centres of the balls at their closest approach and the direction of the impinging ball. Thus we would talk of head-on or glancing collisions.)

The forces in charged particle collisions are (conservative) electric forces, and so the collisions are perfectly elastic, that is no kinetic energy is lost. Suppose one particle of mass m_1 is moving initially with a velocity $\boldsymbol{u}_1$ and another of mass m_2 is at rest. After the collision let the velocities be $\boldsymbol{v}_1$ and $\boldsymbol{v}_2$; these will not be parallel except in the case of a head-on collision. (*Note*: these are collision situations between nuclear particles, not situations involving nuclear transformations.) Referring to figure 9-11,

$$m_1\boldsymbol{u}_1 = m_1\boldsymbol{v}_1 + m_2\boldsymbol{v}_2 \qquad [9\text{-}6]$$

that is
$$m_1^2 u_1^2 = m_1^2 v_1^2 + m_2^2 v_2^2 \\ - 2m_1 m_2 v_1 v_2 \cos(180 - \theta). \qquad [9\text{-}7]$$

As the collision is perfectly elastic, we also have

$$\tfrac{1}{2}m_1 u_1^2 = \tfrac{1}{2}m_1 v_1^2 + \tfrac{1}{2}m_2 v_2^2. \qquad [9\text{-}8]$$

Multiplying equation 9-8 by $2m_1$ we have

$$m_1^2 u_1^2 = m_1^2 v_1^2 + m_1 m_2 v_2^2. \qquad [9\text{-}9]$$

Subtracting equation 9-9 from equation 9-7 we have

$$0 = m_2^2 v_2^2 - 2m_1 m_2 v_1 v_2 \cos(180 - \theta) - m_1 m_2 v_2^2,$$

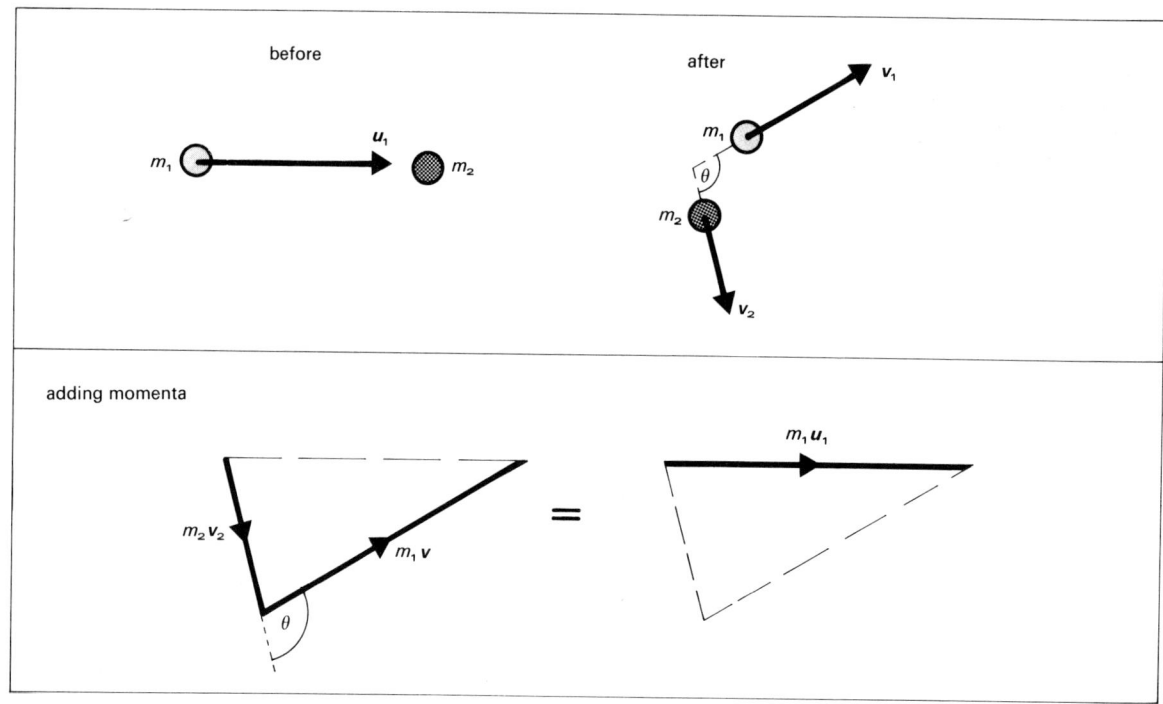

Figure 9-11 The principle of conservation of linear momentum for a two-dimensional collision. The two particles move in directions which make an angle θ with each other after the collision.

whence,

either $m_2 v_2 = 0$ (since we can divide each term by $m_2 v_2$) which gives $v_2 = 0$ and $v_1 = u_1$ (this means that no collision took place),

or, $\quad 0 = m_2 v_2 - 2m_1 v_1 \cos(180 - \theta) - m_1 v_2,$

from which we have

$$-\cos(180 - \theta) = \frac{(m_1 - m_2)v_2}{2m_1 v_1},$$

or $\qquad \cos\theta = \frac{1}{2}\left(1 - \frac{m_2}{m_1}\right)\frac{v_2}{v_1}. \qquad [9\text{-}10]$

So that if we observe chamber tracks, and see that

$\qquad \theta = \frac{1}{2}\pi\,\text{rad},\quad$ we know that $\quad m_1 = m_2,$

if $\qquad \theta < \frac{1}{2}\pi\,\text{rad},\quad$ we know that $\quad m_1 > m_2,$

and if $\qquad \theta > \frac{1}{2}\pi\,\text{rad},\quad$ we know that $\quad m_1 < m_2.$

The relation between $\cos\theta$ and the ratios m_2/m_1 and v_2/v_1 can be demonstrated using a carefully levelled surface and two frictionless pucks with ring magnets as their bases, the magnetic interaction being in this case a perfectly 'elastic' one. If v_2/v_1 is measured using stroboscopic photography, then the dependence of θ on the ratio of the masses can be verified. m_2 can be effectively made very large by holding the second puck still while the 'collision' occurs. If the masses of the pucks are equal, it is particularly striking that $\theta = \frac{1}{2}\pi\,\text{rad}$, *whatever the angle between the line of centres and the direction* u_1. Conversely if we observe $\theta = \frac{1}{2}\pi\,\text{rad}$ in cloud or bubble chamber photographs (see figure 9-12), we can deduce that the masses of the colliding particles are the same. This is an important result for the nuclear physicist. (In nuclear interactions special techniques for determining v_2/v_1 are needed before equation 9-10 and the observed value of θ can yield the ratio of the masses of the particles involved.) It is also a useful result for the billiards player to know. If billiard balls were perfectly elastic it would enable him to predict the results of his play with certainty (we assume that he is skilful enough to cue the ball as he wishes) and even though some energy is lost (*e* for billiard balls is of the order of 0.8) the idea that $\theta \approx \frac{1}{2}\pi\,\text{rad}$ is a good starting point for him when attempting a 'pot' *and* an 'in off'.

9-5 Internal energy

Suppose we can watch the behaviour of two interacting bodies which are so far away from any other objects that it is only the mutual gravitational and elastic forces between them which can alter their positions or their speeds. The situation is deliberately idealized. In figure 9-13 the two bodies are shown with masses m_1 and m_2.

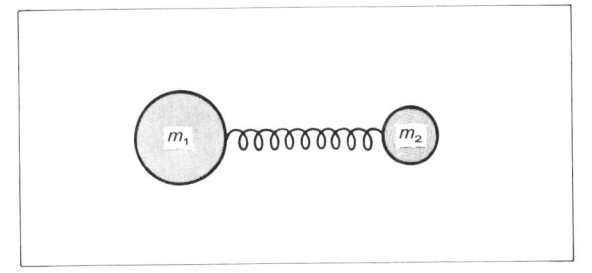

Figure 9-13

If the forces are conservative then the principle of conservation of mechanical energy for the bodies can be written as

[9-3] $\quad\quad\quad T + E = $ constant,

where E is the sum of the gravitational and elastic potential energies of the bodies and T the sum of their kinetic energies. Equation 9-3 can be expanded to

$$T_1 + T_2 + E = \text{constant} \quad\quad [9-11]$$

but E does not become $E_1 + E_2$ as their potential energy is a property of the pair of bodies (the system). To find E we need to know the separation of the bodies, and this can be measured using a reference frame fixed on m_1 or one fixed on m_2. To measure T_1 and T_2 we need to know the speeds at which they are moving, and the choice of reference frame is crucial (which it is not when we measure E). As Newton's laws of motion apply only in inertial frames of reference the only possibility for these two isolated bodies is to use a frame of reference which is fixed at their centre of mass. The absurdity of, for example, measuring the kinetic energy of m_1 from a frame of reference attached to m_2 is easily seen by supposing m_2 to be a tiny body, such as a stone, and m_1 a very massive body, such as a planet (see figure 9-13). The value of T_1 would now vary enormously during an interaction between the stone and the planet while neither T_2 nor E would change very much. So from this viewpoint the mechanical energy of the system would *not* be conserved.

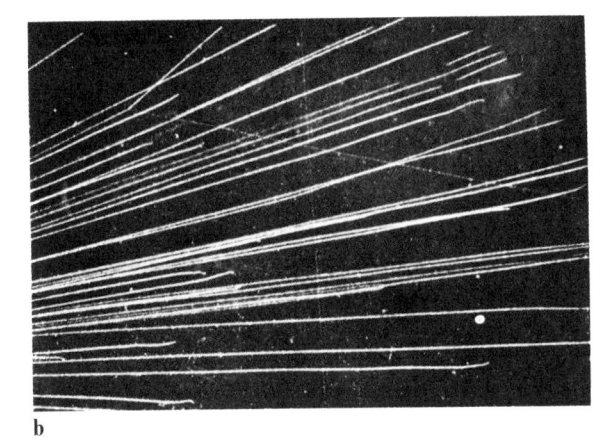

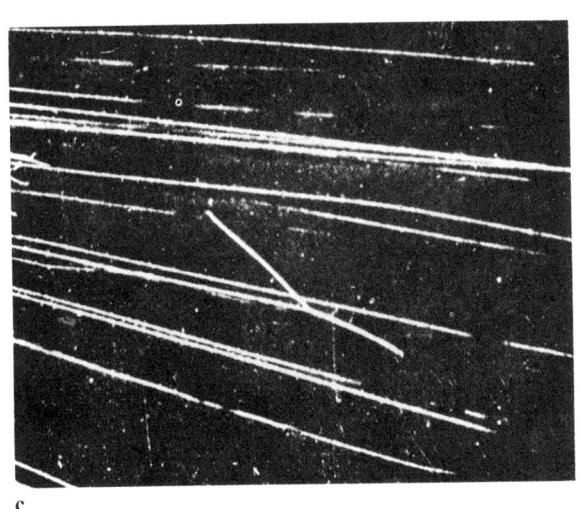

Figure 9-12 Photographs of three cloud-chamber collisions where the angle between the colliding particles after the collision is (*a*) $\pi/2$ rad, (*b*) less than $\pi/2$ rad, and (*c*) more than $\pi/2$ rad.

9 The principle of conservation of energy

One important case where we did not use the centre of mass reference frame but one attached to one of the interacting bodies was on page 136 where we assumed that the Earth, mass m_E, was an inertial frame of reference. Suppose a body of mass m_1 is thrown into the air. We had

[9-1] $$T_1 + E_g = \text{constant},$$

whereas we now see that it should have been

[9-11] $$T_E + T_1 + E_g = \text{constant},$$

T_E being the kinetic energy of the Earth.

But $$\frac{T_E}{T_1} = \frac{\frac{1}{2}m_E v_E^2}{\frac{1}{2}m_1 v_1^2} = \frac{m_1}{m_E}\left(\frac{m_E v_E}{m_1 v_1}\right)^2.$$

Since $m_E v_E = m_1 v_1$ (by the principle of conservation of linear momentum)

$$\frac{T_E}{T_1} = \frac{m_1}{m_E} \approx 10^{-24}.$$

Thus the ignoring of T_E is seen to be quite reasonable and equations 9-1 and 9-11 are effectively equivalent in this case. (The whole discussion fails to take account of the movement of the Earth in its orbit and its spin.)

In establishing equation 9-11 the inertial frame of reference was necessarily the centre of mass frame. If the interaction between m_1 and m_2 were viewed from a second reference frame in which the centre of mass of the system was moving with a speed v_{CM}, then the total kinetic energy of the two bodies (the system) would be

$$T_1 + T_2 = T_1' + T_2' + \tfrac{1}{2}mv_{CM}^2$$

where $m = m_1 + m_2$, and T_1', T_2' denote the kinetic energies measured relative to the centre of mass and $\tfrac{1}{2}mv_{CM}^2$ is the kinetic energy of the system imagined at the centre of mass. The proof of this important result,

the kinetic energy of a system of bodies = the kinetic energy of the parts of the system relative to its centre of mass + the kinetic energy of a mass equal to the total mass of the system which moves with the centre of mass

is left as an exercise for the reader (see Exercise 9-22). It is of particular importance when we have to consider rotational motion and are required to find, for example, the kinetic energy of a rolling wheel.

The principle of conservation of mechanical energy in this new reference frame is thus

$$T_1 + T_2 + E = T_1' + T_2' + \tfrac{1}{2}mv_{CM}^2 + E = \text{constant}.$$

Though T_1', T_2', and E may vary, the observer could remain unaware of these internal changes; he may not even resolve m_1 and m_2 into two separate objects. To him, *the system* of mass $m = m_1 + m_2$ would continue to move with a uniform speed v_{CM}.

Consider now the example of a manned space vehicle drifting at constant velocity through space. The men in it might be moving about and objects would be stored first here and then there. The vehicle would, to an inertial observer, be moving at a constant velocity v_{CM} and with a total mass m would have a kinetic energy $T_{CM} = \tfrac{1}{2}mv_{CM}^2$. Because of the internal interactions (each of which is relatively small and not noticed by the observer) it really has a total mechanical energy of

$$T_{CM} + \sum T_{int}' + \sum E_{int} = T_{CM} + U,$$

where the speeds for T_{int}' are measured relative to the centre of mass of the system. U, which is equal to the sum of the kinetic energies measured relative to the centre of mass plus the mutual potential energies of the parts of the system, $\sum T_{int}' + \sum E_{int}$, is called the *internal energy* of the system.

U = the sum of the kinetic energies of the parts of the system measured relative to the centre of mass + the mutual potential energies of the parts of the system.

When the system contains *very* large numbers of interacting particles, for example a balloon containing a gas, it becomes impossible to treat $\sum T_{int}' + \sum E_{int}$ as the sum of many individual terms. The situation becomes quite literally chaotic. We now consider the energy of the system as $T_{CM} + U$, where T_{CM}, the kinetic energy of the centre of mass, is equal to $\tfrac{1}{2}mv_{CM}^2$, and U, the internal energy, is the sum of all the intermolecular potential energies and molecular kinetic energies measured relative to the centre of mass. Any system which is made up of a very large number of interacting particles, for example molecules, can be treated similarly. Thus a beaker of water or a lump of copper being carried across the laboratory has an obvious kinetic energy of its centre of mass, T_{CM}, and a less obvious (but no less real) internal energy U.

The distinction between T_{CM} (usually written as T as we have for balls and stones in this text) and U can also be thought of as a distinction between ordered and disordered motions. Figure 9-14 illustrates this idea. In (a) the kinetic energy of the centre of mass T can be found. In (b) the centre of mass has a zero velocity but the sum of all the molecular kinetic energies relative to the centre of mass and the intermolecular potential

9-5 Internal energy

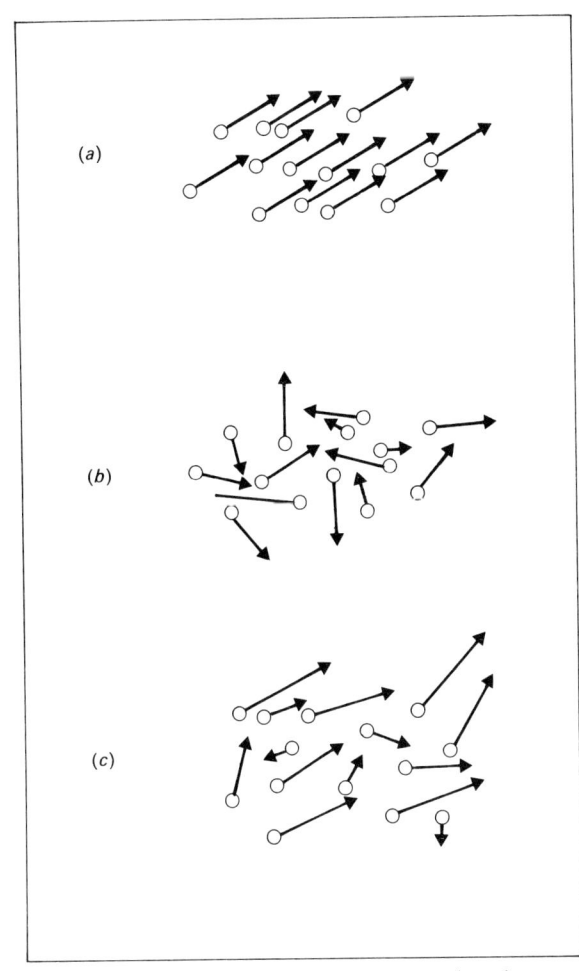

Figure 9-14 A group of molecules (a) all having the same velocity, (b) having random velocities, and (c) having random velocities superimposed on a general drift velocity.

energies represents the internal energy U. (c) shows the usual situation where the total energy is best expressed as $T + U$. In Section 9-4 the kinetic energy of the centres of mass of two colliding bodies was seen to decrease unless the collision was perfectly elastic, so that in any imperfectly elastic intermolecular interaction there will be an increase in internal energy. We can now, with a clearer idea of what is meant by internal energy, follow the transfer of ordered kinetic energy of the bodies ΔT to disordered internal energy ΔU.

For any collision $\quad \Delta T + \Delta U = 0$,

while for perfectly elastic collisions

$$\Delta T = 0.$$

▶ **Example 9-6** A lead bullet of mass 5.0 g travelling horizontally at 1000 m s^{-1} enters a wooden block of mass 495 g which is resting on a horizontal frictionless surface, and becomes embedded in the block. Determine the energy changes. Taking the specific heat capacities of the lead and the wood of the block as 120 J kg^{-1} K^{-1}, and 2000 J kg^{-1} K^{-1} respectively, find the rise in temperature assuming that it is constant throughout the bullet and the block.

Using the principle of conservation of linear momentum, we have

$$(0.005 \text{ kg})(1000 \text{ m s}^{-1}) = (0.500 \text{ kg})v$$

where v is the speed of the block-and-bullet after the impact.

Thus $\quad v = 10 \text{ m s}^{-1}$.

The initial kinetic energy of the block-and-bullet

$$= \tfrac{1}{2}(0.005 \text{ kg})(1000 \text{ m s}^{-1})^2 + 0$$
$$= 2500 \text{ J}.$$

The final kinetic energy of the block-and-bullet

$$= \tfrac{1}{2}(0.500 \text{ kg})(10 \text{ m s}^{-1})^2$$
$$= 25 \text{ J},$$

so that the gain in internal energy of the block-and-bullet is 2475 J (we shall ignore any expansion of the system which will require work to be done on the surroundings).

Using $\quad \Delta Q = mc\Delta\theta$

we have $\quad 2475 \text{ J} = [(0.005 \text{ kg})(120 \text{ J kg}^{-1} \text{ K}^{-1})$
$\quad\quad\quad\quad\quad\quad + (0.495 \text{ kg})(2000 \text{ J kg}^{-1} \text{ K}^{-1})]\Delta\theta$

where $\Delta\theta$ is the rise in temperature.

Therefore $\quad 2475 \text{ J} = (0.6 \text{ J K}^{-1} + 990 \text{ J K}^{-1})\Delta\theta$,

that is $\quad \Delta\theta = 2.5 \text{ K}$.

We could have found the final kinetic energy by viewing the impact from a reference frame fixed to the centre of mass. If v_{CM} is the velocity of the centre of mass, then

$$(0.500 \text{ kg})v_{\text{CM}} = (0.005 \text{ kg})(1000 \text{ m s}^{-1})$$

which gives $\quad v_{\text{CM}} = 10 \text{ m s}^{-1}$,

and the kinetic energy T_{CM} of the centre of mass is given by

$$T_{\text{CM}} = \tfrac{1}{2}(\text{total mass})v_{\text{CM}}^2$$
$$= \tfrac{1}{2}(0.500 \text{ kg})(10 \text{ m s}^{-1})^2$$
$$= 25 \text{ J}.$$

Now this is a perfectly inelastic collision, so the only kinetic energy the system possesses after the impact is equal to T_{CM}. Therefore the block-and-bullet has a kinetic energy of 25 J after the impact. ◀

9-6 The first law of thermodynamics

The most obvious way of increasing the internal energy of a collection of liquid or gaseous molecules (a body) is to stir them in such a way as to churn the molecules about. The equivalent for a solid body is to knock it about. In neither of these operations need we alter the kinetic energy of the centre of mass T of the body. In each case we can describe the process by saying that by doing work ΔW on the body we increase its internal energy by an amount ΔU.

$$\Delta U = \Delta W.$$

The macroscopic effect we notice is that the body becomes hotter—its temperature increases. A quite different way of achieving the same end is to place our body A in contact with another body B which is at a higher temperature. Heat ΔQ is said to flow from B to A, and if it reaches exactly the same state as in the first experiment we can only assume that its internal energy has increased by the same amount ΔU.

$$\Delta U = \Delta Q.$$

These two techniques for increasing the internal energy of a system (doing work on it and giving heat to it) are summed up in the *first law of thermodynamics*:

increase in internal energy of system = heat given to system + work done on system

$$\Delta U = \Delta Q + \Delta W \qquad [9\text{-}12]$$

which is an energy conservation statement. We have not proved anything here and the development of the concepts of temperature, heat, and the experimental equivalence of doing work on and giving heat to a body can be found in textbooks on heat or thermodynamics.

(Conventionally the equation is often written

$$\Delta U = \Delta Q - \Delta W,$$
(work done by system)

which is obviously consistent with our equation: this leads to

$$\Delta Q = \Delta U + \Delta W,$$

which is the form usually quoted.)

As is often the case in a collision, a body gains internal energy because work is done on it (by a sort of hammering process), its temperature rises above that of its surroundings, and it then loses heat until its temperature drops to its initial value. The sequence of events is shown diagrammatically in figure 9-15.

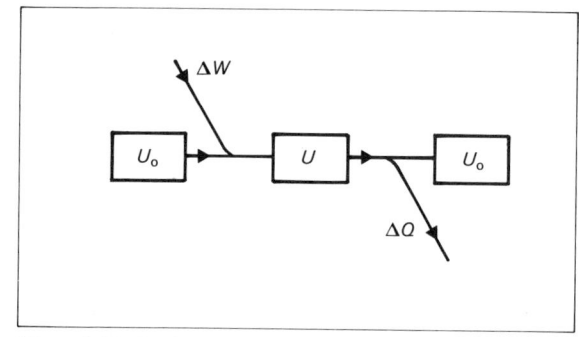

Figure 9-15 Work and energy in an inelastic collision—a typical sequence of events.

The purpose of this section was not to try to deal with thermodynamics but to stress that the study of many particle systems from the mechanical viewpoint leads to such complex situations that a different approach is needed. The concept of internal energy is, however, central to the study of both mechanics and heat.

9-7 Potential energy graphs

The potential energy of a body depends upon its position. Thus $E_g = mgy$ and $E_e = \tfrac{1}{2}kx^2$, where E_g and E_e describe the potential energy of a body pulled by the Earth and a spring respectively. The gravitational pull of the Earth on the body F_g is related to E_g, for

$$\frac{dE_g}{dy} = mg = -F_g$$

(y is measured positive upward and F_g positive downward).

Similarly $$\frac{dE_e}{dx} = kx = -F_e,$$

the elastic pull of the spring on the body. These statements are illustrated graphically in figure 9-16.

In general the force F on a body with a potential energy of E is given by

$$F = -\frac{dE}{dx}$$

where x describes the position of the body relative to some arbitrary origin. F must, of course, be a conservative force.

9-7 Potential energy graphs

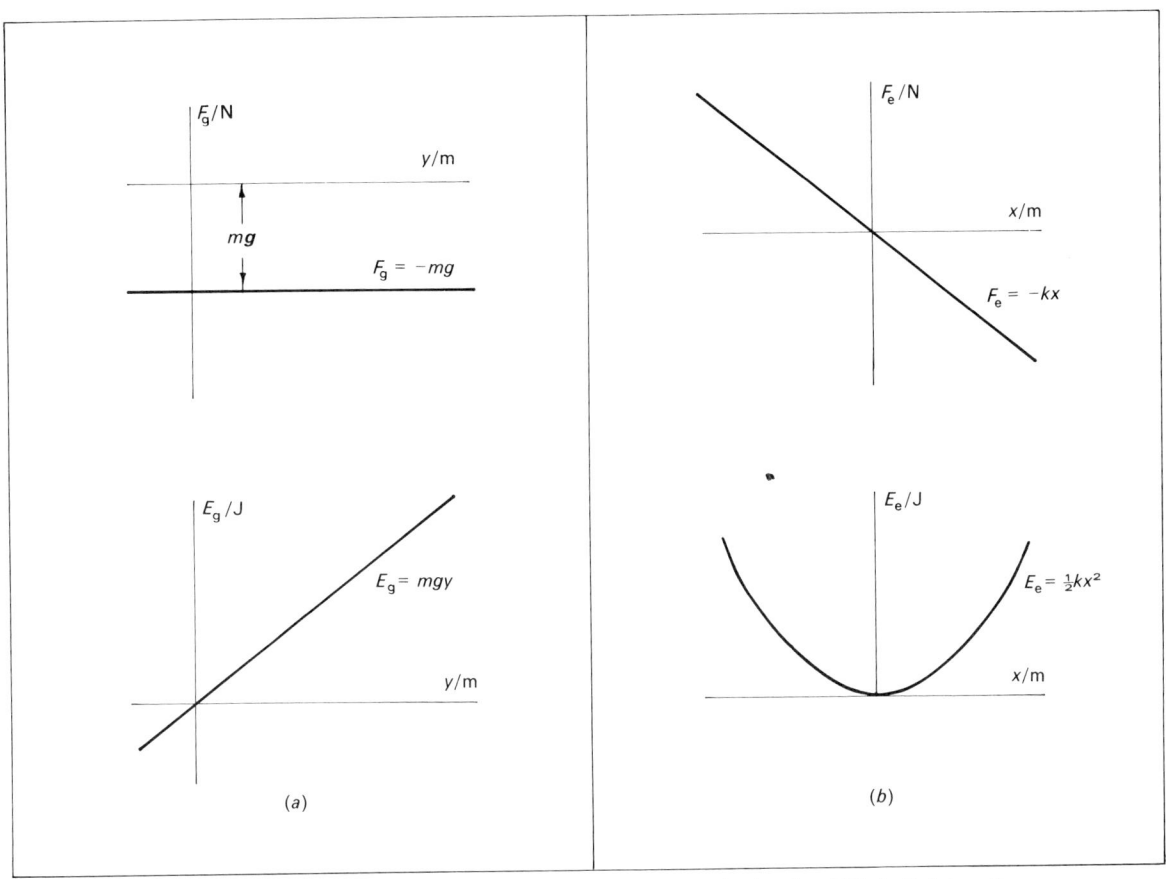

Figure 9-16 Force and potential energy as functions of displacement for (a) gravitational and (b) elastic interactions.

When $\dfrac{dE}{dx} = 0$, $F = 0$.

Thus when the potential energy curve is at a maximum or a minimum the body is subject to no force; that is, it is *in equilibrium* (we assume that there are no other unbalanced forces acting on the body except those involved in the interaction which determines the potential energy). If a minimum, for example point A in figure 9-17, then the equilibrium is said to be *stable*; for small displacements away from A, the body must lose kinetic energy because it is gaining potential energy. If a maximum, for example point B in figure 9-17, then the equilibrium is said to be *unstable*; for small displacements away from B, the body loses potential energy and will therefore gain kinetic energy—thus accelerating from the equilibrium position.

These properties of potential energy graphs are illustrated in the examples which follow.

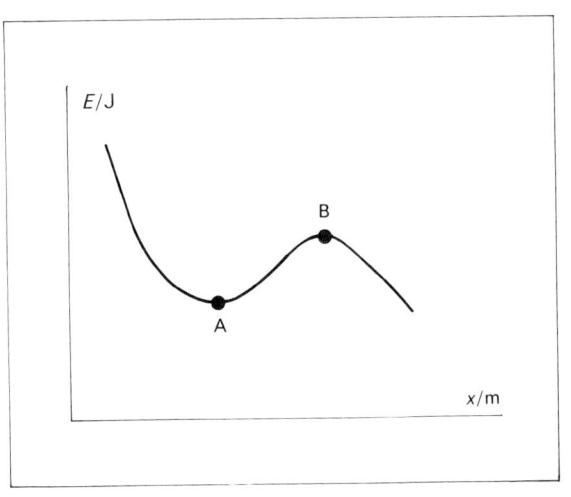

Figure 9-17 A hypothetical potential energy curve.

9 The principle of conservation of energy

▶ **Example 9-7** A space probe of mass 5000 kg has a gravitational potential energy E_g which varies with its distance r from the Earth's centre as shown in figure 9-18. What is the pull of the Earth on the space probe when it is 20 000 km from the centre of the Earth?

As $$F = -\frac{dE}{dr}$$

then F can be found from the slope of the graph. At $r = 2 \times 10^7$ m we have from figure 9-18

$$F = -\frac{20 \times 10^{10} \text{ J}}{4 \times 10^7 \text{ m}} = -5000 \text{ N}$$

away from the Earth, that is 5000 N towards the Earth. Notice that this is about one-tenth of the pull which the Earth would exert on the space probe if it were at the Earth's surface. ◀

▶ **Example 9-8** A spring of natural length 0.30 m has a stiffness of 50 N m^{-1}. It hangs vertically supporting a lump of mass 2.0 kg and oscillates vertically. By writing down the total potential energy of the spring–mass system for various extensions x of the spring establish the value of x_0 for which the lump is in equilibrium.

Let us measure gravitational potential energies from a zero at the support, that is

$$E_g (= mgh) = -(2.0 \text{ kg})(10 \text{ N kg}^{-1}) x.$$

Further $E_e (= \tfrac{1}{2} kx^2) = \tfrac{1}{2}(50 \text{ N m}^{-1}) x^2$,

and so the total potential energy of the system is

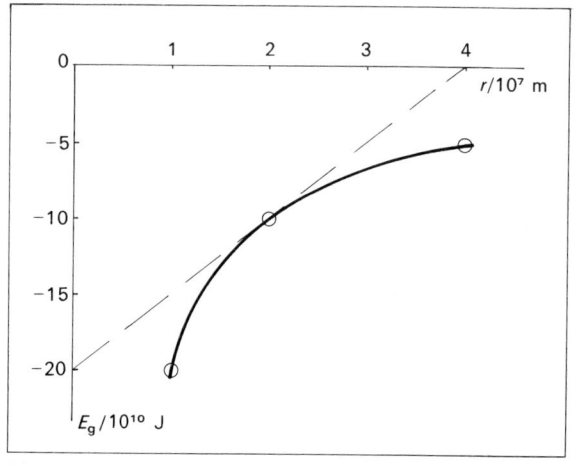

Figure 9-18

given by

$$E = \tfrac{1}{2}(50 \text{ N m}^{-1}) x^2 - (2.0 \text{ kg})(10 \text{ N kg}^{-1}) x.$$

For equilibrium $\dfrac{dE}{dx} = 0$

that is $(50 \text{ N m}^{-1}) x_0 - (2.0 \text{ kg})(10 \text{ N kg}^{-1}) = 0$

or $$x_0 = \frac{20 \text{ N}}{50 \text{ N m}^{-1}} = 0.40 \text{ m}.$$

This is a very circuitous way of solving a simple problem but the technique has wide application in more complex situations. ◀

Bibliography

Angrist, S. W. and Hepler, L. G. (1967). *Order and chaos*. Basic Books. There is a particularly relevant chapter on the world's fuel resources.

Nuffield Advanced Physics (1972). Unit 9 *Change and chance*. Penguin. The first two parts discuss the irreversibility of fuel-burning processes, despite energy conservation.

Nuffield Advanced Physics (1971). Unit 2 *Electricity, electrons, and energy levels*. Penguin. Collisions between electrons and atoms are discussed in the last section.

Project Physics (1971). Text, Unit 3 *The triumph of mechanics*. Holt, Rinehart and Winston. Chapter 10 includes a wide view of the principle of conservation of energy.

Project Physics (1971). Reader, Unit 3 *The triumph of mechanics*. Holt, Rinehart and Winston. Chapter 3 is an excerpt from Feynman's book *The character of physical law*.

Resnick, R. and Halliday, D. (1966). *Physics*, part I. John Wiley. Chapter 10 is about collisions.

Rogers, E. M. (1960). *Physics for the inquiring mind*. Oxford University Press. Chapter 26 deals with energy in a wide-ranging manner. There is a delightful section on perpetual motion machines.

Scientific American (1971). *Energy and power: a Scientific American book*. W. H. Freeman. An up-to-date account of such things as energy resources containing many excellent graphs and diagrams.

Weidner, R. T. and Sells, R. L. (1965). *Elementary classical physics*, volume 1. Allyn and Bacon. The idea of internal energy is carefully developed in Chapter 21.

8 mm film loop. 'Transfer of momentum in collision with ground.' BBC Publications.

8 mm film loop. 'Conservation of energy: pole vault.' Ealing Scientific. This Harvard Project Physics loop enables a quantitative analysis of a pole vault to be made.

Exercises

Data (to be used unless otherwise directed):

$g = 10 \,\mathrm{m\,s^{-2}} = 10 \,\mathrm{N\,kg^{-1}}$.

$\tan 37° = 3/4$.

9-1 How much gravitational potential energy is gained by
(a) a mass of 50 kg which is lifted a vertical distance of 4.0 m
(b) a pendulum bob of mass 0.020 kg as it moves from its lowest point to a point which is a vertical distance of 0.050 m above this? ●

9-2 A spring has a constant stiffness of $20 \,\mathrm{N\,m^{-1}}$ and a natural length of 0.20 m. How much elastic potential energy is stored in it when its length is
(a) 0.40 m (b) 0.60 m? ●

9-3 A massless spring has a constant stiffness of $10 \,\mathrm{N\,m^{-1}}$. It is hung vertically and a mass of 0.50 kg is attached to its lower end and released from rest. Find the extension of the spring when the mass first comes to rest using
(a) the work–energy theorem
(b) the principle of conservation of mechanical energy.
Find also the speed of the mass when it passes its equilibrium position using
(a) the work–energy theorem
(b) the principle of conservation of mechanical energy.
Throughout ignore any conversion of mechanical energy into internal energy. ●

9-4 A mass of 2.0 kg falls from rest for a vertical distance of 2.0 m. Ignoring air resistance, find its final speed, using
(a) the work–energy theorem
(b) the principle of conservation of mechanical energy. ●

9-5 A mass of 10 kg is placed at rest at the top of a slope of length 100 m which is inclined at an angle of 37° to the horizontal. The coefficient of kinetic friction $\mu_k = 0.25$. Find
(a) the normal contact force exerted on the block
(b) the frictional force exerted on the block and hence
(c) the speed of the block at the bottom of the slope, using the principle of conservation of energy, including the internal energy (produced by friction) as a term on one side of the equation.
Find also the final speed of the block using the principle 'work done by forces = change of kinetic energy'. ●

9-6 The situation in Exercise 9-5 is repeated but on this occasion, before being released, the mass is attached to one end of a massless elastic thread of natural length 10 m and constant stiffness $10 \,\mathrm{N\,m^{-1}}$; the other end of the thread is attached to the top of the slope. Using any method you like, find the speed of the mass when it has travelled 15 m from rest. ●

9-7 One end of a massless elastic thread of constant stiffness $50 \,\mathrm{N\,m^{-1}}$ and natural length 0.20 m is attached to a point which is 0.30 m above a point A on a frictionless horizontal surface. The other end is attached to a mass of 4.0 kg which is placed on the surface at a distance of 0.40 m from A. Find the speed of the mass when it passes through A. ●

9-8 A trapeze artist of mass 70 kg holds on to one end of a trapeze rope and launches himself from a platform with a speed of $4.0 \,\mathrm{m\,s^{-1}}$. Ignoring air resistance, find his speed when he has fallen a vertical distance of 10 m. ●

9-9 A car of mass 1500 kg on a switchback at a fairground leaves one hump at a speed of $5.0 \,\mathrm{m\,s^{-1}}$ and just reaches the top of the next hump (that is, the car has no speed at the top). If the vertical difference in heights between the two humps is 8.0 m, find the mechanical energy converted into internal energy by the frictional and air resistance forces. ●

9-10 One end of a massless elastic thread of natural length 1.0 m and constant stiffness $50 \,\mathrm{N\,m^{-1}}$ is attached to a point A on a horizontal surface and the other end is attached to a mass of 50 kg which is placed on the surface 3.0 m from A. The coefficient of kinetic friction $\mu_k = 0.10$. The mass is released from rest.
(a) Where will it first come to rest?
(b) Will it then be in equilibrium?
(c) What will be its maximum speed? ●

9-11 Describe the transformations of energy which occur when
(a) a boy fires a stone from a catapult
(b) a motor car is driven down a hill
(c) a cigarette-lighter flint is used to light some fuel.

9-12 A billiard ball which has a speed of $0.50 \,\mathrm{m\,s^{-1}}$ makes an elastic head-on collision with a stationary ball of equal mass. What are their speeds after the collision? ●

9-13 Five steel balls lie not quite touching each other in a straight line on a level frictionless horizontal surface. A sixth ball is rolled towards them along their line of centres so as to collide with one of the end balls. If all the collisions are elastic, what happens, and why? What happens if (a) two, and (b) three balls are similarly rolled together towards the original line of balls? (*Hint*: see Example 9-4.)

9-14 A steel ball is allowed to fall a distance h_1 from rest on to a firmly fixed horizontal steel plate; after rebounding it rises to a height h_2. How are h_1 and h_2 related to e, the coefficient of restitution for the steel–steel impact? ●

9-15 A ball moving with a velocity of $1.5 \,\mathrm{m\,s^{-1}}$ to the right collides head-on with a stationary ball of twice its mass. If the coefficient of restitution for the impact is 0.60, find the velocities of the balls after the collision. ●

9-16 A ball A of speed u and mass m_A makes an elastic head-on collision with a stationary ball B of mass m_B. Find the ratio v_B/v_A of their velocities after the collision in terms of m_A and m_B only, and use your result to find the value of v_B/v_A when
(a) $m_A = m_B/20$ (b) $m_A = m_B/2$ (c) $m_A = m_B$
(d) $m_A = 2m_B$ (e) $m_A = 20m_B$. ●

9-17 Refer to Exercise 9-16. Now find the ratio of the velocities v_B/u in terms of m_A and m_B only, and use your result to find an expression for the ratio $\frac{1}{2}m_B v_B^2 / \frac{1}{2}m_A u^2$ which is a measure of the fraction of the original kinetic energy transferred to the stationary ball B. Use your expression to find the value of this fraction for cases (a), (c), and (e) of Exercise 9-16 and comment on your result. ●

9-18 Examine some photographs of nuclei colliding. Apply the results on page 144 to some of the photographs.

9 The principle of conservation of energy

9-19 An electron of mass 9.1×10^{-31} kg is moving with a speed of 10^7 m s^{-1}. It strikes a stationary helium atom of mass 6.7×10^{-27} kg head-on. What fraction of its kinetic energy does the electron transfer to the helium atom if the collision is elastic? Approximately how many similar collisions would the electron have to make before losing 3.5×10^{-18} J, an energy equal to the ionization energy of a helium atom?

9-20 Consider the general case of an elastic head-on collision between two bodies of mass m_1 and m_2 moving with velocities u and v before the collision and velocities w and x after the collision, all velocities being in the same sense. Use the principle of conservation of momentum and the principle of conservation of mechanical energy to show that

$$u + w = v + x.$$

Use Newton's law of impact to produce the same result. (This shows that using Newton's law of impact, for elastic collisions, is equivalent to using the two principles mentioned above, so that it does not give a third independent equation.)

9-21 A sphere moving with speed u collides with a stationary sphere of equal mass in such a way that on collision the line of centres makes an angle θ with the direction of u. If the speed of the first sphere after the collision is v, and that of the other sphere is w, and the collision is perfectly elastic and frictionless, find the sizes of v and w in terms of u and θ. In which directions are the spheres moving after the collision? ●

9-22 Consider two masses m_1 and m_2 moving with velocities v_1 and v_2 (measured in a reference frame fixed to the Earth) as shown in figure 9-19. Show that if v_{CM} is the velocity of the centre of mass

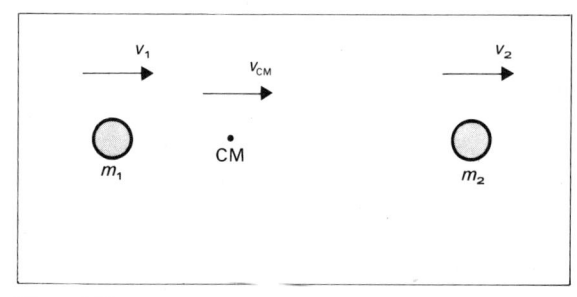

$$(m_1 + m_2)v_{CM} = m_1 v_1 + m_2 v_2.$$

Figure 9-19

Find expressions for
(a) the kinetic energy of the masses, measured in a reference frame fixed to the centre of mass, plus $\tfrac{1}{2}(m_1 + m_2)v_{CM}^2$
(b) the kinetic energy of the masses, measured in a reference frame fixed to the Earth.
Show that these two expressions are equivalent.

9-23 A mass of 2.0 kg with velocity 10 m s^{-1} approaches a mass of 3.0 kg moving with velocity 5.0 m s^{-1} along the same line and in the same direction, both velocities being measured in the same inertial frame. Find the velocity of the centre of mass in that frame.

Find the kinetic energy of the masses as measured by an observer in that frame, and verify that it is equal to the kinetic energy measured relative to the centre of mass plus the kinetic energy of 5.0 kg moving with the velocity of the centre of mass. ●

9-24 Refer to Example 9-5. Calculate the initial kinetic energy of the masses as measured in a reference frame (a) fixed to the Earth, (b) fixed to the centre of mass: let these be T and T' respectively. Also calculate T_{CM}, the kinetic energy of the total mass moving with the speed v_{CM}. Verify that $T = T' + T_{CM}$. ●

9-25 Refer to Example 9-5 and Exercise 9-24. Calculate the values of T, T', and T_{CM} after the collision. Why is the value of T_{CM} unchanged by the collision? For this collision $e = 0.50$, and the value of T' after the collision is 0.25 times the value of T' before the collision. Is it possible to generalize this result to say that the value of T' after any collision is e^2 times the value of T' before the collision? If so, why?

9-26 Refer to Exercise 9-23. If the masses collide, and the value of e for the collision may range from $e = 0$ to $e = 1.0$, within what range of values will the kinetic energy of the masses (as measured by an observer in a reference frame fixed to the Earth) lie after the collision? ●

9-27 A lead bullet travelling at 450 m s^{-1} becomes embedded in a block of wood; assuming that the temperature of the wood does not rise, and that there is no heat loss to the surroundings, find the rise in temperature of the bullet. The specific heat capacity of lead = 130 J kg^{-1} K^{-1}. ●

9-28 A glass tube of mass 0.20 kg contains 0.15 kg of mercury and when placed in a vertical position and inverted the centre of mass of the mercury falls 1.20 m. Find the work done when the tube is inverted 50 times in such a way that the centre of mass of the tube does not move.

If the specific heat capacities of glass and mercury are 500 and 140 J kg^{-1} K^{-1} respectively, find the rise in temperature of the apparatus, assuming that all parts of it rise by the same amount, and that there is no heat loss to the surroundings. Is the rise in temperature of the apparatus the result of heat being transferred to it? ●

9-29 In one of Joule's experiments two masses, each of 3.0 kg, were made to fall 50 times through a vertical distance of 1.0 m. They did not accelerate significantly because while they were falling they rotated a paddlewheel which churned 0.50 kg of water. What was the temperature rise? Assume that the heat capacity of the apparatus was negligible, and that the specific heat capacity of water is 4200 J kg^{-1} K^{-1}. ●

9-30 An elastic thread of natural length l and constant stiffness k is attached at one end to a point A and at its other end to a mass m. The mass is held at A and then released so that it falls vertically. Derive an expression for the total potential energy E of the system when the mass is a vertical distance x below A. Differentiate this expression with respect to x, and hence find the value of x for which the system is in equilibrium. ●

9-31 A uniform rod of length l and mass m is pivoted freely at one end about a point O. To its other end is attached a massless elastic thread of natural length l and constant stiffness k. The other end of the thread is attached to a point A, which is l vertically above O. Derive an expression for the total potential energy E of the system when the rod makes an angle θ with the downward vertical through O. Differentiate this expression once with respect to θ to find the values of θ for which the system is in equilibrium. Differentiate a second time to determine whether the equilibria are stable or unstable ($\sin \theta = 2 \sin \tfrac{1}{2}\theta \cos \tfrac{1}{2}\theta$). ●

9-32 Given that the graph relating the force F exerted by one molecule on another is related to their separation r by the graph shown in figure 6-8a in Section 6-3, deduce the shape of the graph which relates the potential energy E of the interaction to the separation r.

9-33 Consider a long-chain molecule which consists of identical atoms evenly spaced: when the distance between the atoms is x, the potential energy E of interaction between adjacent atoms is given by

$$E = -\frac{A}{x^6} + \frac{B}{x^{12}}.$$

Use the fact that when the resultant force F on an atom is zero, its potential energy is a minimum (or, alternatively, that $F = -dE/dx$) to show that the equilibrium spacing x_0 of the atoms is given by

$$x_0 = \sqrt[6]{\left(\frac{2B}{A}\right)}.$$

If the elastic modulus λ for the chain of atoms is defined by the equation $\lambda = \Delta F \div \Delta x/x_0$ where Δx is the increase in separation (from the equilibrium spacing) caused by an additional force ΔF, prove that $\lambda = -x_0(d^2E/dx^2)$, and show that

$$\lambda = -18 \sqrt[6]{\left(\frac{A^{13}}{2B^7}\right)}.$$

Why is it the value of d^2E/dx^2 at $x = x_0$ which must be used?
Explain why the chain will break when the external force applied to it is the maximum value of $|F|$, and find the spacing x_1 when this occurs. Hence find the breaking strain of the chain. Is its value larger than you would expect? ●

9-34 The remaining fossil fuels in the Earth's crust in 1970 are estimated to represent an energy store of about $250Q$ ($Q = 10^{21}$ J) of which about 90 per cent is coal and 6 per cent petroleum liquids (oil). In 1970 petroleum liquids provided more than 50 per cent of the energy used by man. Discuss the implications of these figures for the future. See also the information on page 140.

9-35 The energy used by one car in one year is about 3×10^{10} J. Estimate the total annual energy consumption of vehicles
(a) in the United Kingdom and
(b) in the world.

9-36 Solar radiation provides an energy input to the Earth of about $5000Q$ each year ($Q = 10^{21}$ J). What input power does this represent? What happens to this energy? Try to give quantitative estimates and perhaps use energy flow diagrams like that of figure 9-6.

9-37 The Earth's store of fossil fuels is being used up, yet the principle of conservation of energy states that no energy ever disappears but is only converted from one form to another. Why then does man worry about his energy requirements in the future?

9-38 Refer to table 9-1. Provide one or more extra examples to fill each of the gaps left in the table of orders of magnitude given; for example what has energy of between 10^{18} J and 10^{22} J?

10 Relativistic mechanics

10-1	The principle of special relativity	154	10-6 The constancy of the limiting speed	166
10-2	The Bertozzi experiment	155	10-7 Moving clocks	170
10-3	The inertia of energy	157	10-8 Summary	173
10-4	The new mechanics	160	Bibliography	173
10-5	Photons	164	Exercises	174

10-1 The principle of special relativity

In Section 3-9 the principle of special relativity is stated. By describing two reference frames moving with a uniform relative velocity as inertial frames we can restate the principle as

the laws of physics are the same in any two inertial frames of reference.

We have illustrated in earlier chapters the way in which problems involving force, linear momentum, and mechanical energy can be solved from more than one inertial frame, that is, we have made use of the fact that the laws of Newtonian mechanics obey the principle of special relativity. Sometimes this assumption can produce great simplification by enabling us to choose an especially convenient reference frame from which to work. If we place the principle of special relativity at the head of our list of laws then it is necessary to test rigorously the rules of Newtonian mechanics to make sure that they do obey the principle; so far we have only assumed this to be so. The experiment in Section 3-9 on page 47 suggests in principle how one might go about this for inertial frames of reference moving slowly relative to one another, while in Section 10-2 another experiment is described for high speeds. The result of the low speed experiment can be arrived at analytically as follows: consider two experimenters E_1 and E_2 who move at a fixed relative velocity v. Figure 10-1, which does not imply that one reference frame is preferred to the other,

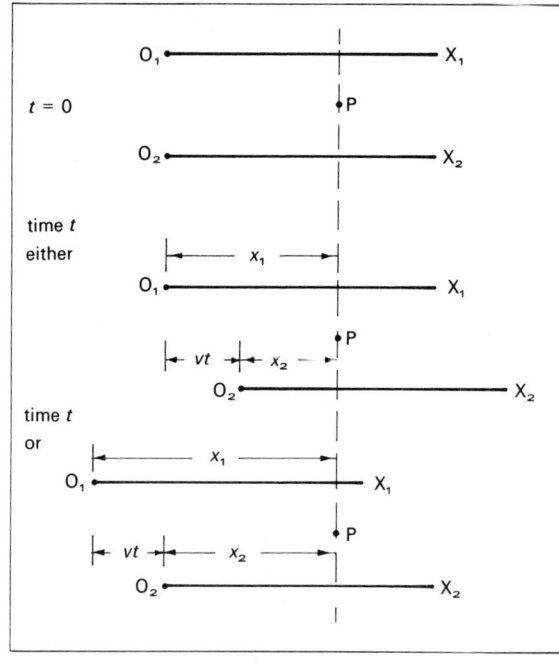

Figure 10-1 The position of P is noted by two observers in inertial frames of reference.

shows how E_1 and E_2 would record the position of P a time t after the observers, at O_1 in O_1X_1 and O_2 in O_2X_2, have passed one another. Clearly

$$x_2 = x_1 - vt. \qquad [10\text{-}1]$$

If P is moving parallel to O_1X_1 then each of the observers could measure P's velocity relative to his own frame of reference. Dividing equation 10-1 by t gives

$$\frac{x_2}{t} = \frac{x_1}{t} - v$$

or
$$v_2 = v_1 - v, \qquad [10\text{-}2]$$

which seems little more than commonsense: the velocities measured by the different observers differ by v.

Differentiating equation 10-2 with respect to time t yields

$$\frac{dv_2}{dt} = \frac{dv_1}{dt} - \frac{dv}{dt}$$

which, as v is constant, gives

$$\frac{dv_2}{dt} = \frac{dv_1}{dt}$$

or
$$a_2 = a_1, \qquad [10\text{-}3]$$

that is the measured acceleration of P is the same in each inertial frame of reference. This was the result established in the experiment on page 47.

If measured *accelerations* follow the principle of special relativity then so also will measured *forces*, and the structure of Newtonian mechanics follows. The only assumptions in the above discussion are our common-sense ideas about displacement and time.

At *high* speeds we find that Newtonian mechanics does not provide the correct predictions to quite ordinary situations and some evidence for this is given in the next section. To preserve the principle of special relativity we have to modify Newton's laws and also alter our preconceived ideas about the nature of space and time. It is this process with which we are concerned in this chapter on special relativity.

▶ **Example 10-1** Two motor cars of length 5.0 m are travelling, with 45 m between their bumpers, at a speed of $35\,\text{m s}^{-1}$. If the second car is capable of an acceleration of $2\,\text{m s}^{-2}$ at this speed (and can maintain this acceleration), find the time taken for the second car to overtake the first and again produce a separation of 45 m between the bumpers. Find also the distance travelled by the second car in the act of overtaking.

Let us view the overtaking from the first car: this will be an inertial frame of reference. For the second car, $u = 0$, $a = 2\,\text{m s}^{-2}$, and $s = 100\,\text{m}$, so that the time taken is 10 s, and the final velocity of the second car is $20\,\text{m s}^{-1}$. We cannot, however, make any statements about the *displacement* or *velocity* of the second car relative to the Earth without considering the velocity of the first car. When we do, we conclude that the final velocity of the second car (relative to the Earth) is $55\,\text{m s}^{-1}$, and that the distance travelled is

$$100\,\text{m} + 350\,\text{m} = 450\,\text{m}.$$

The values of displacements and velocities depend on the frame of reference in which they are measured; times and accelerations (and forces) do not. ◀

10-2 The Bertozzi experiment

All the mechanics studied so far in this text can be investigated experimentally in the school laboratory. The generalizations (Newton's laws of motion, etc.) have followed laboratory experimental results and have been found to be consistent with everyday experience. Does Newtonian mechanics apply to less commonplace situations? What follows in this section is an account of an experiment performed by W. Bertozzi at the Massachusetts Institute of Technology.* The purpose of the experiment is to investigate the dynamics of particles (in this case electrons) at *very* high speeds.

Bertozzi's experiment measures both the speed and the kinetic energy of an electron over a range of high speeds: figure 10-2 gives a diagram of the apparatus. An electron gun produces short bursts of electrons at regular intervals, each burst lasting about 3×10^{-9} s. A Van de Graaff generator accelerates them to a high speed v, and projects them into an evacuated tube over 8 m long in which they move with constant velocity. At the near end of this tube there is a short insulated pipe A (see figure 10-2) which is connected by a cable to a cathode ray oscilloscope. Some of the electrons strike the pipe and a well-defined voltage pulse is displayed on the suitably triggered oscilloscope. At the other end of the evacuated tube the electrons strike an insulated aluminium disc from which a second cable connected to the oscilloscope displays their arrival some tens of nanoseconds later. The oscilloscope has a calibrated timebase and so the time taken, Δt, for the electrons to travel a distance l can be found.

Clearly
$$v = \frac{l}{\Delta t}.$$

The speed is varied by adjusting the accelerating potential

---
* W. Bertozzi (1964). *American Journal of Physics*, **32**, page 551.

10 Relativistic mechanics

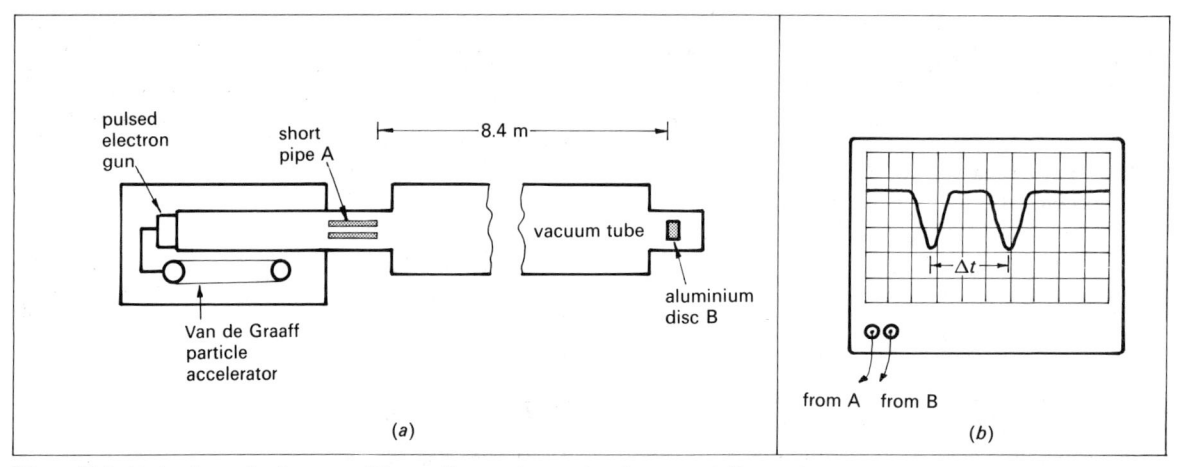

Figure 10-2 (a) A schematic diagram of Bertozzi's experiment showing essentially an electron gun, a long evacuated tube, and a collector. (b) The sort of trace on the oscilloscope for signals produced by a pulse of electrons passing A and B.

of the Van de Graaff generator. As the times taken by the signals from A and B to travel to the oscilloscope will be comparable with Δt, the two cables are carefully matched so that the same delay occurs along each cable.

When the electrons hit the aluminium disc almost all their kinetic energy becomes internal energy in the disc, and its temperature rises. The rise in temperature during several minutes of electron-pulse firing is measured with a thermocouple, the thermal insulation of the aluminium disc being so good that heat losses in this time can be ignored. The thermocouple is connected to a galvanometer which is calibrated to measure increases in internal energy of the disc by separately warming the disc electrically using a small resistor embedded in it. In order that the average kinetic energy T of *each electron* in the beam can be found it is necessary to know how many electrons reach the target in a known time. To do this the electrons striking the aluminium disc are used to charge a capacitor so that the total charge they carry can be found. The capacitor is arranged to discharge when the potential difference across it rises to about one volt and a separate controlled charging and discharging of the disc is used to relate the rate of discharge of the capacitor with the charge reaching it. As we know the charge carried by one electron, this part of the experiment measures the number of electrons hitting the target disc per second and hence the energy of each electron, T, is found. The mass of an electron, m_e, is also known so that the value of T/m_e can be calculated.

The reader should notice that the measurements of v and of T are performed in a very direct way:

      v by a time of flight measurement

and T by a calorimetric measurement.

The results are shown in the table accompanying figure 10-3, and the graph of v^2 against T/m_e. Why do we plot these two variables? Let us think of a particle of mass m_e moving with speed v; its kinetic energy T is, using Newtonian mechanics, given by

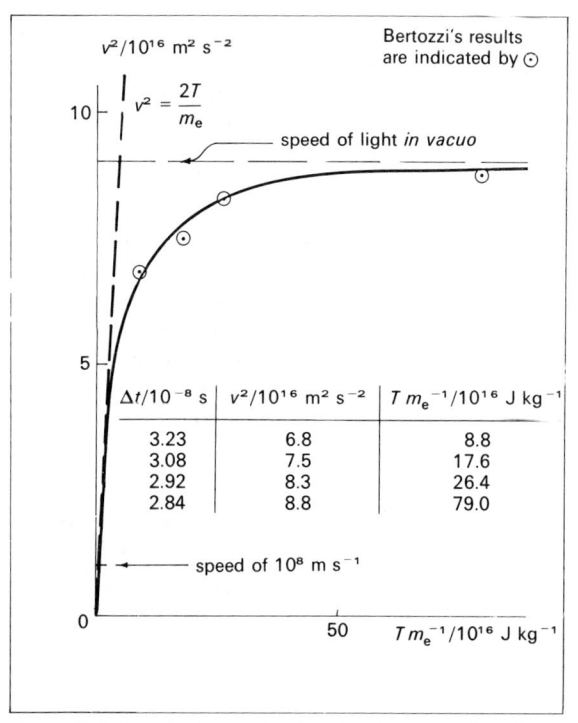

$\Delta t/10^{-8}$ s	$v^2/10^{16}$ m² s⁻²	$Tm_e^{-1}/10^{16}$ J kg⁻¹
3.23	6.8	8.8
3.08	7.5	17.6
2.92	8.3	26.4
2.84	8.8	79.0

Figure 10-3 Graph of v^2 against Tm_e^{-1}. The broken line shows the prediction of Newtonian mechanics. *After Bertozzi.*

[7-3] $$T = \tfrac{1}{2}m_e v^2$$
or $$v^2 = \frac{2T}{m_e}.$$

A graph of $v^2/\mathrm{m^2\,s^{-2}}$ against $Tm_e^{-1}/\mathrm{J\,kg^{-1}}$ should therefore be a straight line of slope 2, passing through the origin. The dotted line on figure 10-3 shows this prediction and we see that the early part of the line agrees with results from, for instance, experiments involving firing bullets into targets, that is, low-speed experiments. Clearly high-speed electrons do *not* obey the prediction of the laws of Newtonian mechanics. We have no reason to doubt the usefulness of the laws of Newtonian mechanics for normal laboratory speeds nor even for the speeds encountered by aeroplanes or even space vehicles, that is, up to about $10^4\,\mathrm{m\,s^{-1}}$, but in this experiment of Bertozzi *very* much higher speeds are involved (to stress this the point on the graphs at which the speed is $10^8\,\mathrm{m\,s^{-1}}$ is noted) and the effect is dramatic. There seems to be a speed, about $3 \times 10^8\,\mathrm{m\,s^{-1}}$, which electrons cannot attain *no matter how much we try to accelerate them.* Bertozzi produced one more result: $v^2 = 9.0 \times 10^{16}\,\mathrm{m^2\,s^{-2}}$, $T/m_e = 260 \times 10^{16}\,\mathrm{J\,kg^{-1}}$ (not plotted on the graph shown, which finishes at $T = 80 \times 10^{16}\,\mathrm{J\,kg^{-1}}$). This very high energy value supports the strange result in italics above. (For this and the highest energy shown on the graph Bertozzi added energy to the electrons during their passage down the evacuated tube so that the two highest values of v are really average speeds. This procedure is justified by the result that the value of v^2 increases only from $8.3 \times 10^{16}\,\mathrm{m^2\,s^{-2}}$ to $9.0 \times 10^{16}\,\mathrm{m^2\,s^{-2}}$ while the kinetic energy increases *tenfold*.)

How do we interpret the result of this experiment? The immediate conclusion is that there is a speed which electrons cannot reach. Let us call this limiting speed c, for it does seem to be about the speed c at which electromagnetic waves (such as light or radio waves) travel in a vacuum. To generalize this result, let us postulate that there is a *common* limiting (or ultimate) speed c which *no* material particle can attain (or exceed), a statement against which no experimental evidence has emerged from the study of high-energy physics in which protons, mesons, and other particles are commonly studied at high speeds.

10-3 The inertia of energy

What explanation can we give of the shape of the graph in figure 10-3? It seems as if work is being done on the electrons (for work and kinetic energy are definitively connected) and yet the electrons are *not* accelerating as we should expect. As the acceleration produced is less than that predicted by Newton's laws we could attribute the effect to an increase in the electron's mass. We think of the mass or inertia of a particle as one of its fundamental properties and the constancy of this property has so far been central to the development of mechanics, but if the laws of Newtonian mechanics do break down then we are justified in questioning such ideas. Let us pursue this line of thought and call the mass of a stationary particle m_0 and the mass of a moving particle m. One interpretation of the Bertozzi experiment on the limiting speed of particles would thus be that

$$m > m_0$$

for very high speeds v, and that m *depends on* v. By very high speeds we mean $v > 10^8\,\mathrm{m\,s^{-1}}$.

What direct support for this suggestion can we find? Firstly let us consider the interaction of atomic nuclei, events which can be studied by cloud and bubble chamber photographs. On page 144 we showed that if a moving particle, such as a proton, collides with an identical particle which is at rest, then they will move along paths which are at right angles after the interaction. However, photographs such as figure 10-4 show that where the

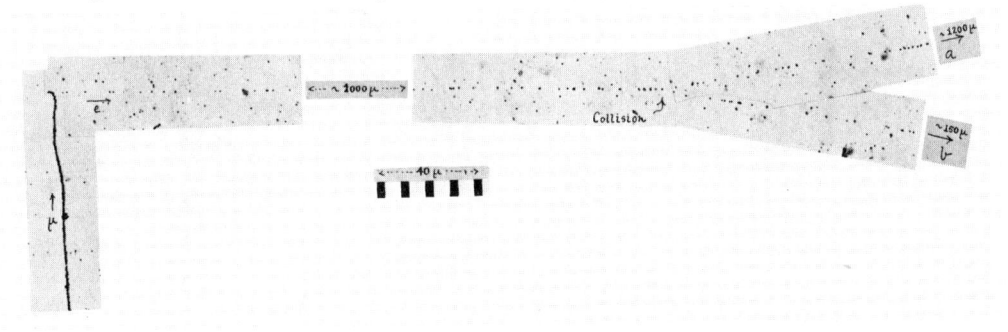

Figure 10-4 A collision between two electrons. The subsequent directions of motion of the two particles are not at right angles, since the speeds are in the relativistic region.

10 Relativistic mechanics

incident particle has a *very* high speed the angle between the paths taken by the particles after the interaction is *less* than $\frac{1}{2}\pi$ rad—a result which indicates that the incident electron has a greater mass than the stationary electron. Secondly, the design of machines such as cyclotrons which accelerate particles to very high speeds has to be modified to allow for an increase in the mass of the accelerated particles as their speed rises beyond about 3×10^7 m s^{-1}—see Example 10-2.

Although this evidence adds to the credibility of our supposition we ought to ask further how any increase in mass can arise. Is it that the extra energy we have given to the electron has itself an inertial property, that energy has mass? To interpret the Bertozzi experiment quantitatively we must put these ideas into algebraic form and try to find an equation which relates the kinetic energy T, the mass m, and the speed v of a particle such as an electron, and which fits the curve of figure 10-3 at all points. We do not expect the mass m in such an equation to be a fixed quantity.

Let us then look again at the classical concept of kinetic energy and consider, for low values of v, a graph of $v/\text{m s}^{-1}$ against $mv/\text{N s}$. Clearly this will be a straight line of slope $1/m$ as shown in figure 10-5a. The area under the graph (the shaded triangle) up to $v = u$ is equal to $\frac{1}{2} \times u \times mu = \frac{1}{2}mu^2$, that is the (Newtonian) kinetic energy T of the particle. For a small increase $\Delta(mv)$ in mv the gain of kinetic energy of the particle is ΔT, the area of the strip shown heavily shaded in figure 10-5a, that is

$$\Delta T = v\Delta(mv)$$

and

$T(v \ll c)$ = area under the graph of v against mv

$$= \tfrac{1}{2} \times v \times mv = \tfrac{1}{2}mv^2.$$

So we have obtained the familiar expression for T: this approach works for low-speed mechanics. Now let us consider high-speed mechanics. We could assume that for $v \approx c$ the statement $\Delta T = v\Delta(mv)$ holds. Thus referring to figure 10-5b we have ΔT, the area of the strip shown heavily shaded, given by

$$\Delta T(v \approx c) \approx c\Delta(mc)$$

$$\approx c^2 \Delta m \text{ (since } c \text{ is constant),}$$

and

$T(v \approx c)$ = area under the graph of v against mv

$$\approx mc \times c$$

$$\approx mc^2,$$

for the shaded area is roughly equal to the area of the rectangle of sides c and mc, provided that v is almost equal to c for most of the area under the graph considered. We see that an increase in kinetic energy $\Delta T(v \approx c)$ implies a proportionate increase in the mass Δm of the particle and that for very high speeds the increase in mass can be expressed approximately as $\Delta T(v \approx c)/c^2$. The reader may wish to pass straight on to the next section where the exact relationships between m and v are given on page 160 and those between T and m are given on page 161. These relationships of course

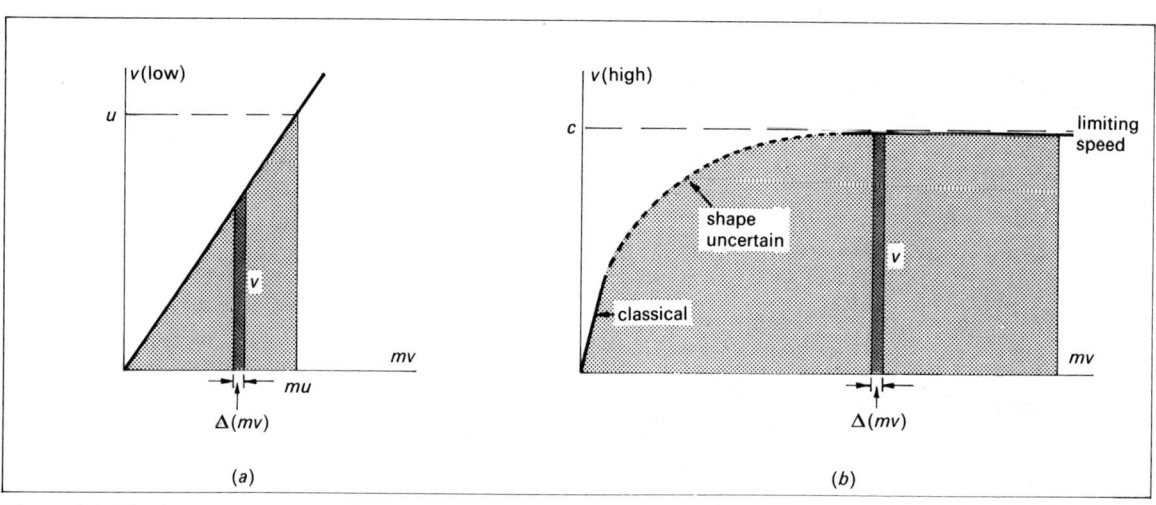

Figure 10-5 Kinetic energy T expressed as the area beneath a graph of v against mv showing (a) the Newtonian situation and (b) the effect of a limiting speed on the graph at high $v \approx c$.

10-3 The inertia of energy

hold for all v, but approximate at high and at low speeds to the expressions above.

★ Suppose we do consider energy to have inertia and that an increase in the kinetic energy of a particle is equivalent to an increase in its mass.* Suppose further that an increase of mass Δm *is equivalent to* a kinetic energy increase of $c^2 \Delta m$, so that we can write

$$c^2 \Delta m = v \Delta(mv)$$

for all values of v. Multiplying each side by m gives

$$c^2 m \Delta m = mv \Delta(mv)$$

and to solve this involves summing each side.

$$\sum c^2 m \Delta m = \sum mv \Delta(mv)$$

or

$$\int c^2 m \, dm = \int mv \, d(mv)$$

$$\Rightarrow c^2 \tfrac{1}{2}(m^2) = \tfrac{1}{2}(mv)^2 + \text{constant}.$$

If we call the value of m when $v = 0$ the *rest mass* m_0, then the value of the constant is $\tfrac{1}{2} m_0 c^2$. Removing the $\tfrac{1}{2}$ and rearranging, we get

$$m^2(c^2 - v^2) = m_0^2 c^2$$

$$\Rightarrow m^2 \left(1 - \frac{v^2}{c^2}\right) = m_0^2$$

or

$$m = \frac{m_0}{\sqrt{(1 - v^2/c^2)}}, \qquad [10\text{-}4]$$

taking the positive value of the square root. The first *direct* experimental evidence for this relation was produced by Bucherer in 1909. Equation 10-4 represents the answer to the question, 'how does the mass depend on the speed?' See figure 10-6 on page 161. On multiplying both sides of the relation by v we have an equation for the middle part of the graph shown in figure 10-5b.

Is this also the key to explaining the shape of the Bertozzi curve on page 156? Is it that the kinetic energy T is given by $T = \tfrac{1}{2} mv^2$ rather than $T = \tfrac{1}{2} m_0 v^2$? Should we simply replace the rest mass m_e of the electrons by our new expression for mass? This would give

$$v^2 = \frac{2T}{m} = \frac{2T\sqrt{(1 - v^2/c^2)}}{m_e}$$

or

$$\frac{T}{m_e} = \frac{v^2}{2\sqrt{(1 - v^2/c^2)}}.$$

This does approximate correctly to the Newtonian expression for low values of v, but for $v = 0.9c = 2.7 \times 10^8 \,\text{m s}^{-1}$ we get

$$\frac{T}{m_e} = \frac{(2.7 \times 10^8 \,\text{m s}^{-1})^2}{2\sqrt{(1 - 0.9^2)}}$$

$$= 8.4 \times 10^{16} \,\text{J kg}^{-1}.$$

---

*The authors are indebted to a treatise by J. M. Ogborn 1967 (unpublished) for this approach.

Thus for $v = 2.7 \times 10^8 \,\text{m s}^{-1}$, that is $v^2 = 7.3 \times 10^{16} \,\text{m}^2 \,\text{s}^{-2}$ the corresponding value of T/m_e should be $8.4 \times 10^{16} \,\text{J kg}^{-1}$, but we can see that the value on the Bertozzi curve is more than $11 \times 10^{16} \,\text{J kg}^{-1}$. The reader can check other points. So we *cannot* simply replace m by $m_0/\sqrt{(1 - v^2/c^2)}$ in the expression $T = \tfrac{1}{2} mv^2$ in order to deal with kinetic energies at high speeds. We saw earlier that the equation $T = \tfrac{1}{2} m_0 v^2$ is not appropriate to high-speed mechanics: now we see that nor is the equation $T = \tfrac{1}{2} mv^2$. To find the correct expression for T we must begin with the definition of T: this we do in the next paragraph.

From the definition of the kinetic energy of a particle given on page 106 we have the change of kinetic energy

$$\Delta T = \text{the work done on the particle by the resultant external force}$$

$$= F \Delta x.$$

We continue to define F by the equation $F = \Delta(mv)/\Delta t$, but now m varies according to the relation $m = m_0/\sqrt{(1 - v^2/c^2)}$, and so our new expression for the kinetic energy of a particle moving with a speed v (see the calculation on page 106) is

$$T = \sum F \Delta x$$

$$= \sum \frac{\Delta(mv)}{\Delta t} \Delta x$$

$$= \int_0^x \frac{d}{dt}\left[\frac{m_0 v}{\sqrt{(1 - v^2/c^2)}}\right] dx.$$

As $v = dx/dt$, and m_0 is constant, we can write this as

$$T = m_0 \int_0^t v \frac{d}{dt}\left[\frac{v}{\sqrt{(1 - v^2/c^2)}}\right] dt.$$

Integrating by parts gives

$$T = m_0 \left[\frac{v^2}{\sqrt{(1 - v^2/c^2)}}\right]_0^v - m_0 \int_0^v \frac{v \, dv}{\sqrt{(1 - v^2/c^2)}}$$

$$= \frac{m_0 v^2}{\sqrt{(1 - v^2/c^2)}} + m_0 \left[c^2 \sqrt{(1 - v^2/c^2)}\right]_0^v$$

$$= \frac{m_0 v^2}{\sqrt{(1 - v^2/c^2)}} + m_0 c^2 \sqrt{(1 - v^2/c^2)} - m_0 c^2$$

$$= \frac{m_0 v^2 + m_0 c^2 - m_0 v^2}{\sqrt{(1 - v^2/c^2)}} - m_0 c^2$$

$$= \frac{m_0 c^2}{\sqrt{(1 - v^2/c^2)}} - m_0 c^2. \qquad [10\text{-}5]$$

Therefore

$$\frac{T}{m_0} = c^2 \left[\frac{1}{\sqrt{(1 - v^2/c^2)}} - 1\right].$$

The reader should show that this expression *does* agree with the results of the Bertozzi experiment as shown in the graph of figure 10-3. Two assumptions inherent in the above calculation are thus made more acceptable. Firstly, the initial equating of the increase in the kinetic energy of the particle with an increase in its mass, and secondly, the continuing use of the definition of force as the rate of change of momentum of a particle.

10 Relativistic mechanics

When we write

$$m = \frac{m_0}{\sqrt{(1-v^2/c^2)}}$$

in equation 10-5 it reduces to

$$T = mc^2 - m_0 c^2$$
$$= (m - m_0)c^2, \qquad [10\text{-}6]$$

or $\qquad \Delta T = c^2 \Delta m. \qquad [10\text{-}7]$

We have now come full circle, for having postulated that an increase in kinetic energy is evidenced by an increase in mass, we have shown that a quantitative expression of this idea is equivalent to the experimental results of Bertozzi. There is no proper deductive proof—the argument involves a guess, a step in the dark—but the whole is justified by the consistency of the conclusions with experiment, and experiment is always the ultimate test of a physical theory.* ★

▶ **Example 10-2** A cyclotron is a device for accelerating charged particles by applying the same potential difference several times in succession. It depends on the particle travelling in a succession of semicircular paths of steadily increasing radius in such a way that the time taken to complete one semicircle is independent of the radius of the semicircle, and this in turn depends on the particle having a constant mass. Given that the device will cease to function satisfactorily when the mass of the particles increases by 1/50th of their rest mass, find the maximum number of times the accelerating potential difference of 2.5×10^5 V can be given to protons (whose charge is 1.6×10^{-19} C and whose mass is 1.7×10^{-27} kg). A particle of charge Q accelerated by a potential difference V in a vacuum gains kinetic energy T given by $T = QV$.

Let the number of times the potential difference can be applied be n: then using $T = QV$ we have

kinetic energy acquired
$$= n(2.5 \times 10^5 \text{ J C}^{-1})(1.6 \times 10^{-19} \text{ C}).$$

We also know that the gain in kinetic energy T can be given by $T = (m - m_0)c^2$ using the above notation. Here we have $m - m_0 = m_0/50$ and so

$$T = \tfrac{1}{50}(1.7 \times 10^{-27} \text{ kg})(3.0 \times 10^8 \text{ m s}^{-1})^2.$$
$$\therefore n(4 \times 10^{-14} \text{ J}) = \tfrac{1}{50}(1.53 \times 10^{-10} \text{ J}),$$
$$\Rightarrow n = 76.$$

The speed v at which $m = \tfrac{51}{50}m_0$ can be calculated from equation 10-4, $m = m_0/\sqrt{(1-v^2/c^2)}$. Transposing we have

$$\left(\frac{m_0}{m}\right)^2 = 1 - \frac{v^2}{c^2}.$$

Here $\qquad \left(\tfrac{50}{51}\right)^2 = 1 - \dfrac{v^2}{c^2}$

or $\qquad (1 - \tfrac{1}{51})^2 = 1 - \dfrac{v^2}{c^2}.$

$$1 - \tfrac{2}{51} + \cdots \approx 1 - \frac{v^2}{c^2}$$

$$\Rightarrow v^2 \approx \tfrac{1}{25}c^2$$

or $\qquad v \approx \tfrac{1}{5}c. \qquad ◀$

10-4 The new mechanics

We now know that Newtonian mechanics breaks down at high speeds. But at speeds of about one-tenth of the speed of light in a vacuum, or 3×10^7 m s^{-1}, the deviations from the results predicted from Newton's laws do not exceed 0.5 per cent, so we must keep a sense of proportion. For *all* normal purposes, including the motions of the atoms or molecules in a hot gas and the motions of planets around the Sun, Newton's laws work magnificently. Who, then, except the philosopher, cares about the new mechanics needed at high speeds? In fact, nuclear physicists and cosmologists are both concerned and both make use of the relations of relativistic mechanics as a matter of course.

We shall use m_0 to represent the classical 'mass' or *rest mass* of a particle and m to represent its relativistic mass (its mass when moving at a speed v):

[10-4] $\qquad m = \dfrac{m_0}{\sqrt{(1-v^2/c^2)}}.$

This particle *will* continue to move with a constant velocity unless acted on by a resultant external force (Newton's first law) but the Bertozzi experiment shows us that we cannot use Newton's second law in the form $m_0 a = \sum F$ to predict its acceleration. In Chapter 8 our statement of the second law for situations in which the mass changed was an equating of the rate of change of momentum to the resultant force in the form

$$\frac{d\mathbf{p}}{dt} = \frac{d}{dt}(m\mathbf{v}) = \sum \mathbf{F}.$$

We continue to define force in this way, although the whole usefulness of the concept of force is diminished when it is no longer simply related to acceleration.

---

*Equation 10-7 was first expressed by Einstein in 1905 in a paper entitled *Zur Electrodynamik bewegter Körpern*.

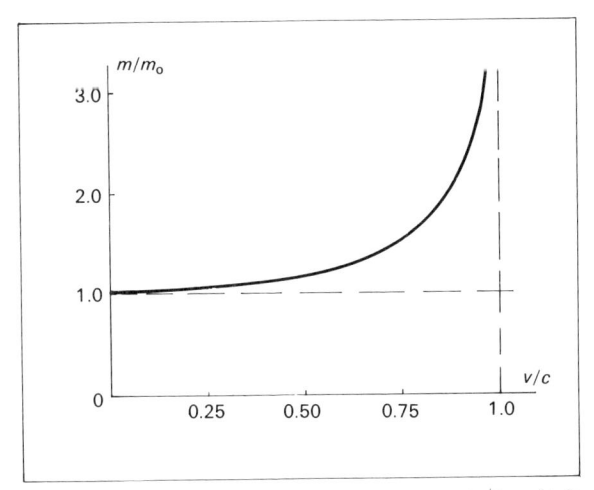

Figure 10-6 The mass increase equation $m = m_0/\sqrt{(1 - v^2/c^2)}$ showing numerical values. For the fastest speed at which man has travelled, $v \approx 10^4 \text{ m s}^{-1}$, we get $v/c \approx 1/3 \times 10^{-4}$ and thus $m = 1.000\,000\,000\,5\,m_0$.

It is correct to write $p = mv$ for high-energy mechanics and the linear momentum of a system of particles $\sum mv$ (though not $\sum m_0 v$) is conserved. This seems to imply that Newton's third law still holds during collision processes, but as our idea of force is now modified we have to abandon the third law and consider linear momentum only in terms of the conservation of momentum before and after the event. Another way of reaching this conclusion is to suppose that during a collision two bodies A and B interact by exchanging a small particle which is 'thrown' backwards and forwards between them. When A has just thrown the particle but B has not yet received it (an inevitable situation as there is a limiting speed at which the particle may travel) then the linear momentum of the system comprising A and B only (but not the particle which we don't 'see') is different from its momentum at the moment before A throws the particle. Once B has caught it, however, momentum for the system is again conserved and so on. Our modern view of the mechanism of interactions *is* of this sort and so we only equate the linear momentum of the system before the mechanism of the collision has begun to the linear momentum of the system after the mechanism of the collision is finished.

Kinetic energy was seen in the last section to be represented by

[10-6] $\qquad T = mc^2 - m_0 c^2,$

where c is the limiting speed of a particle and is the same as the speed of light in a vacuum. For small values of v this reduces to $\frac{1}{2} m_0 v^2 = T$ (see Exercise 10-15). Rearranging the proper relation we get

$$mc^2 = m_0 c^2 + T.$$

This is the basic relativistic equation about mechanical energy and is of very great and general importance. It is a quantitative statement about the inertia of energy or of *the principle of conservation of mass–energy*. The term mc^2 represents the *total energy* of a particle of mass $m = m_0/\sqrt{(1 - v^2/c^2)}$ moving with a speed v; $m_0 c^2$ represents its *rest energy* and T represents its kinetic (mechanical) energy. This kinetic energy T is not a new concept; if a particle has kinetic energy $T = 10^{-10}$ J and it is brought to rest in hitting a target then the target would still gain 10^{-10} J of energy; T is no longer, however, simply $\frac{1}{2} m_0 v^2$ or $\frac{1}{2} m v^2$. The total energy and the rest energy of a particle *are* new concepts, that is they do not appear in Newtonian mechanics.

What do we mean by the statement that the rest energy of a particle is $m_0 c^2$? Does it mean that *if* an electron were to 'disappear' (and the equation tells us nothing about whether or not this *can* happen) then energy

$$m_0 c^2 = (9.1 \times 10^{-31} \text{ kg})(3.0 \times 10^8 \text{ m s}^{-1})^2$$
$$= 8.2 \times 10^{-4} \text{ J}$$

is released as electromagnetic wave energy? It does, but it would be equally true to say that electromagnetic wave energy of mass 9.1×10^{-31} kg is released. We are used to measuring a particle's inertia in kilograms and electromagnetic wave energies in joules, but the new mechanics implies that we may talk of the energy equivalent of a mass in joules or the mass equivalent of some energy in kilograms (if we know the value of c). We should note here that there *are* situations in which an electron, on meeting its anti-particle, the positron, *does* disappear (see Exercise 10-14).

We can still talk of the separate principles of *conservation of mass* and *conservation of energy* although it is now seen that they are two ways of stating the more general principle of *conservation of mass–energy*. Where it is convenient to use one rather than the other the 'rate of exchange' is given by

$$\Delta E = c^2 \Delta m, \qquad [10\text{-}8]$$

where $c = 3.0 \times 10^8 \text{ m s}^{-1}$. The example which follows indicates how careful we must be in our use of words when considering a situation involving mass–energy conservation. Some evidence justifying the general use of mass–energy conservation to all forms of energy, that is not simply mechanical energy, is given after the example.

10 Relativistic mechanics

▶ **Example 10-3** Two balls, each of rest mass 0.18 kg and each moving with the same speed of $0.20\,\mathrm{m\,s^{-1}}$ collide directly. They rebound each with a speed of $0.10\,\mathrm{m\,s^{-1}}$. Find (a) the energy (b) the mass of the system at different stages in the process.

(a) Before the collision the balls have a total kinetic energy given by

$$2(\tfrac{1}{2}m_0 v^2) = (0.18\,\mathrm{kg})(0.20\,\mathrm{m\,s^{-1}})^2 = 7.2 \times 10^{-3}\,\mathrm{J}.$$

At some instant during the collision they are both at rest, and the sum of the elastic potential energy and the internal energy is then $7.2 \times 10^{-3}\,\mathrm{J}$. After the collision their total kinetic energy $= (0.18\,\mathrm{kg})(0.10\,\mathrm{m\,s^{-1}})^2 = 1.8 \times 10^{-3}\,\mathrm{J}$, and so they (or their surroundings) must have an additional internal energy of $5.4 \times 10^{-3}\,\mathrm{J}$. *Throughout the collision energy is conserved.*

(b) Before the collision the balls have an additional mass (because they are moving) equivalent to their kinetic energy. Using equation 10-8 we have

$$\Delta m = \frac{7.2 \times 10^{-3}\,\mathrm{J}}{(3.0 \times 10^8\,\mathrm{m\,s^{-1}})^2} = 8.0 \times 10^{-20}\,\mathrm{kg}.$$

When the balls are instantaneously at rest, they still have an additional mass of $8.0 \times 10^{-20}\,\mathrm{kg}$ (because now they have elastic potential energy and some internal energy). After the collision the balls are not moving so fast, but they (and the surroundings) are hotter. Together the balls and the surroundings have an additional mass of $8.0 \times 10^{-20}\,\mathrm{kg}$. Because we know the balls have a kinetic energy of $1.8 \times 10^{-3}\,\mathrm{J}$ after the collision, we know they have an additional mass of $2.0 \times 10^{-20}\,\mathrm{kg}$ on that account, but we do not know how the remaining $6.0 \times 10^{-20}\,\mathrm{kg}$ (equivalent to the $5.4 \times 10^{-3}\,\mathrm{J}$ of internal energy) is shared between the balls and the surroundings. *Both* are more massive, but we cannot tell how they share the extra mass.
Throughout the collision mass is conserved, for the rest mass of the balls remains unchanged during the collision.

This example should make it clear that we believe it is not only *moving* bodies which are more massive: a body which has energy for *any* reason (for example, it may be hotter, or strained) is more massive for that reason. ◀

We should now want to ask if there is any experimental evidence for the inertial properties of non-mechanical energy. For example, are there any situations in which the rest mass of a particle can be shown to decrease because it has transferred some energy? Or can some form of energy other than mechanical energy (such as light) exert a pressure because of its inertial properties?

To answer the first question: all nuclear reactions involve the equivalence of mass and energy. In order to 'balance' the equations representing such reactions we must either, (a) use the principle of conservation of mass and include the inertia of the kinetic or electromagnetic wave energy involved, or, (b) use the principle of conservation of energy and include the rest energy of the particles involved. Let us take a well-known example from a natural radioactive decay process, that of radon-220 which emits an α-particle from its nucleus. The process has a half-life of just less than one minute and is thus ideal for study in the laboratory. Table 10-1 gives the rest mass of each of the nuclei involved in the reaction

$$^{220}_{86}\mathrm{Rn} \rightarrow {}^{216}_{84}\mathrm{Po} + {}^{4}_{2}\mathrm{He}.$$

The numbers are quoted in the form shown because the relative atomic mass of an isotope is usually given as A_r where

$$\text{mass of nucleus} = A_r \times \frac{\text{mass of nucleus } {}^{12}_{6}\mathrm{C}}{12}.$$

Nucleus	A_r	Rest mass/kg
$^{220}_{86}\mathrm{Rn}$	220.0114	$220.0114 \times 1.66 \times 10^{-27}$
$^{216}_{84}\mathrm{Po}$	216.0019	$216.0019 \times 1.66 \times 10^{-27}$
$^{4}_{2}\mathrm{He}$	4.0026	$4.0026 \times 1.66 \times 10^{-27}$
$^{216}_{84}\mathrm{Po} + {}^{4}_{2}\mathrm{He}$	220.0045	$220.0045 \times 1.66 \times 10^{-27}$

Table 10-1

The table shows that the total *rest mass* of the decay nuclei is less than the *rest mass* of the original radon-220 nucleus by

$$0.0069 \times 1.66 \times 10^{-27}\,\mathrm{kg} = 1.1 \times 10^{-29}\,\mathrm{kg},$$

although it would have been *equal* to the total *mass* of the decay nuclei when they were formed (when they were moving). This difference in rest mass (equivalent to the mass of more than ten stationary electrons), can be measured using a mass spectrometer. The extra kinetic or internal energy which appears as a result of the disappearance of rest mass has an inertia of $1.1 \times 10^{-29}\,\mathrm{kg}$ and this represents

$$(1.1 \times 10^{-29}\,\mathrm{kg}) \times (3.0 \times 10^8\,\mathrm{m\,s^{-1}})^2 = 0.99 \times 10^{-12}\,\mathrm{J}.$$

In fact the α-particle carries almost all of this as kinetic energy (a tiny part of it provides the kinetic energy of the recoiling polonium nucleus), and it is shot away from the decaying radon nucleus. It is subsequently converted to internal energy. The measured kinetic energy of such α-particles is found to be 6.3 MeV (to two significant figures)

$$= (6.3 \times 10^6) \times (1.6 \times 10^{-19}) \text{J} = 1.0 \times 10^{-12} \text{J},$$

which is in close agreement with the value predicted above from the principle of conservation of mass–energy. It is the kinetic energy of the *fission* products of nuclear reactions which is converted to internal energy and used in power stations.

If two nuclei fuse to make one nucleus there is again in some cases a loss of rest mass of the nuclei involved. The most important *fusion* reactions are those which proceed in our Sun and in most stars: hydrogen nuclei are converted to helium nuclei. The production of each helium nucleus involves a loss of rest mass equivalent to that of about fifty stationary electrons and the number of such reactions in our Sun is of the order of 10^{38} per second; the Sun's rest mass is therefore decreasing at the rate of about $4 \times 10^9 \text{ kg s}^{-1}$ and so

$4 \times 10^9 \text{ kg s}^{-1}$ of radiant energy

$$= (4 \times 10^9 \text{ kg s}^{-1})(3.0 \times 10^8 \text{ m s}^{-1})^2 \approx 10^{26} \text{ W}$$

are pouring out into space. It is this energy that provides most of the energy resources of man (see the discussion in Section 9-4). Of course if we learn how to repeat the hydrogen–helium fusion process in a controlled way on Earth (we have already achieved an uncontrolled reaction of this type in hydrogen bombs) then we should have an abundant source of energy in the particular isotope of hydrogen $^2_1 \text{H}$ (necessary for the reaction) found in the seas.

What happens in conventional power stations? Surely we require a knowledge of the principle of conservation of mass–energy to balance the chemical equations of combustion? For if the chemical reactions release energy then the total rest masses of the constituent molecules must decrease. The reason why the nuclear situation seems to demand a mass–energy approach while the chemical situation does not *seem* to do so is that the increase of internal energy per kilogram of material undergoing the nuclear reaction is many thousands of times greater than the increase of internal energy per kilogram of material undergoing a chemical (or atomic) reaction. Nevertheless the production of, say, 10^{12} J of electrical energy by a chemical reaction must be accompanied by a loss in rest mass of

$$(10^{12} \text{ J})/(3.0 \times 10^8 \text{ m s}^{-1})^2 \approx 10^{-5} \text{ kg}$$

(about 10 milligrams) of the coal or oil involved.

A dramatic example of an interchange between kinetic energy and rest mass occurs when cosmic ray particles (nuclei from outer space) strike nuclei in the Earth's upper atmosphere. Figure 10-7 shows a photograph of the tracks left by such an event.

Our second question was whether light can exert a pressure. Experimental laboratory tests show that it can, although the measured pressures, of the order of 10^{-6} Pa, are extremely small and are therefore difficult to detect—see the next section. A further piece of evidence for the pressure which light can exert is the 'tail' of a comet: this always points *away from* the Sun, the particles making up the tail being pushed away by the inertia of the Sun's rays. Bombardment of the comet tail by material particles from the Sun (the solar wind) may, however, be more important.

In conclusion let us stress the *general* relevance of the mass–energy concept to *all* forms of energy. A charged capacitor has a greater *mass* than an uncharged one, a hot potato a greater mass than a cold one, a stretched spring a greater mass than an unstretched one, and so on. The new mechanics, Einstein's creation, really does alter our view of the world but fortunately leaves Newton's mechanics as a valid system for calculations in all everyday situations.

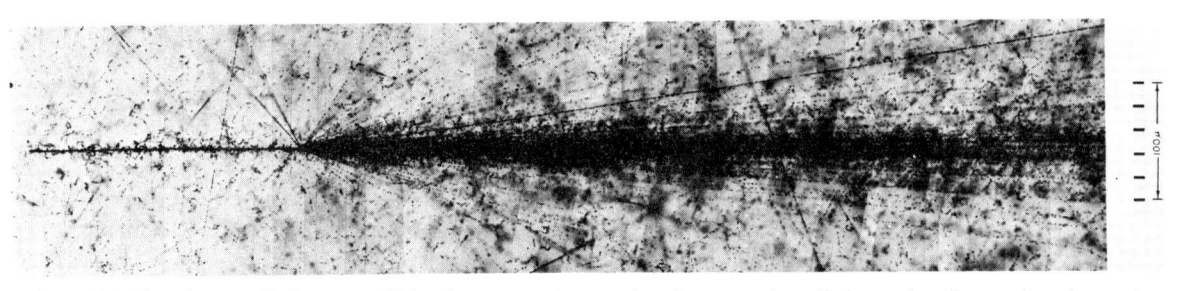

Figure 10-7 The photograph shows a collision between an iron nucleus from cosmic radiation and a silver or bromine nucleus. About 750 mesons were created.

164   10 Relativistic mechanics

▶ **Example 10-4**   A lump of copper of mass 1.0 kg is raised in temperature by 100 K. If the specific heat capacity of copper is 380 J kg^{-1} K^{-1}, find the increase in mass of the lump.

The energy which must be supplied

$$= \left(380 \frac{\text{J}}{\text{kg K}}\right)(1.0 \text{ kg})(100 \text{ K})$$

$$= 3.8 \times 10^4 \text{ J}.$$

Using the mass–energy relationship, $\Delta E = c^2 \Delta m$, we find that the additional mass Δm is given by

$$\Delta m = \frac{\Delta E}{c^2} = \frac{3.8 \times 10^4 \text{ J}}{(3.0 \times 10^8 \text{ m/s})^2} = 4.2 \times 10^{-13} \text{ kg}.$$

We are unlikely to notice this increase in mass. ◀

10-5 Photons

In the last section we gave some evidence that light can exert a pressure. If energy is incident at a known rate on a metal vane in a very good vacuum, the force on the vane can be measured. For an incident power of about 20 mW the force is of the order of 10^{-10} N, for a surface which reflects about half the incident light. Such measurements by Gerlach and Golson in 1923 showed that the relationship between the power P and the force F is of the form

$$\frac{P}{F} = 3 \times 10^8 \text{ m s}^{-1} = c$$

for a variety of surfaces. The relationship has subsequently been extended to other forms of electromagnetic radiation.

During a time interval Δt we can write

$$\frac{P \Delta t}{F \Delta t} = c$$

or

$$\frac{E}{p} = c, \qquad [10\text{-}9]$$

where E is the incident energy and p represents the momentum of the radiation with that energy.

According to the principle of conservation of mass–energy, a change in energy ΔE is equivalent to a change of mass Δm where $\Delta E = c^2 \Delta m$. We have been writing ΔE and Δm as we have been dealing with small changes in the mass of a system of particles. In this section, where we are interested in electromagnetic waves which travel in a vacuum at a speed c and have zero rest mass, we shall write

$$E = mc^2 \qquad [10\text{-}10]$$

where E and m refer to the energy and inertia of a certain amount of radiation. (See Exercise 10-21.)

Combining this energy–inertia equation with the previous energy–momentum equation yields

$$[10\text{-}10] \qquad E = mc^2,$$

but also

$$[10\text{-}9] \qquad E = pc$$

so that

$$p = mc, \qquad [10\text{-}11]$$

a result we might have expected as the answer to the question 'what is the momentum of a mass m travelling at a speed c?'

▶ **Example 10-5**   What force is exerted by the radiation from the Sun on a flat roof which is 10 m square? Assume that the rate of arrival of energy at the Earth's surface is 1.4 kW m^{-2} and that it is all absorbed by the roof.

Assuming that the Sun is directly overhead, the rate of arrival P of energy on the roof

$$= (1.4 \times 10^3 \text{ W m}^{-2})(100 \text{ m}^2)$$

$$= 1.4 \times 10^5 \text{ J s}^{-1}.$$

The force F on the roof is given by the equation

$$F = \frac{P}{c}$$

where c is the speed of electromagnetic radiation *in vacuo*, which we assume has the value $3.0 \times 10^8 \text{ m s}^{-1}$.

Therefore

$$F = \frac{1.4 \times 10^5 \text{ J s}^{-1}}{3.0 \times 10^8 \text{ m s}^{-1}}$$

$$= 4.7 \times 10^{-4} \text{ N}.$$

Let us compare this with the normal contact force S exerted by a layer of water 1 mm deep lying on the same roof: the force S is given by

$$S = (10 \times 10 \times 10^{-3} \text{ m}^3)\left(10^3 \frac{\text{kg}}{\text{m}^3}\right)\left(10 \frac{\text{N}}{\text{kg}}\right) = 10^3 \text{ N}. \quad ◀$$

So far we have been able to imagine the electromagnetic radiation as a continuous progressive wave with a certain mass, momentum, and energy per unit length— rather as we could specify the properties of a mechanical wave on a length of string. When such a wave is shone onto a clean metal surface it is found that electrons can be ejected from the surface; this *photoelectric effect* was first noticed by Hertz in 1887. Suppose a very weak light beam with a power of, say, 10^{-8} W m^{-2} is shone onto a clean piece of potassium metal measuring 1 mm by 1 mm, that is of area 10^{-6} m^2. The rate of arrival of energy on the surface is

$$10^{-8} \text{ W m}^{-2} \times 10^{-6} \text{ m}^2 = 10^{-14} \text{ W}$$

and let us suppose that 10 per cent of this is absorbed: thus energy is absorbed at a rate of 10^{-15} W. It is known that about 2 eV ($\approx 3 \times 10^{-19}$ J) are needed to remove one electron from the surface of potassium and so to eject *one* electron we should expect to have to wait $\approx 3 \times 10^{-4}$ s after switching on the beam. This experiment can be performed but it is found that the first electron is ejected *much* sooner, possibly about 3×10^{-9} s after switching on the beam. It is also found that the ejected electrons are produced not at regular time intervals calculated by dividing the energy required to liberate an electron by the rate of absorption of energy, but *randomly*. Further, for radiation of more than a certain wavelength it is found that no electrons are ejected *at all* no matter for how long or how strongly the metal surface is illuminated.

The reader is referred to texts on modern or quantum physics for a detailed discussion of these results and to the whole study of energy quantization. For our purposes we only require the interpretation first put forward by Einstein in 1905; according to this we should consider light and all other electromagnetic waves to consist of discrete energy packets called *photons*. Each photon has energy E where E is proportional to f the frequency of the wave, or

$$E = hf \qquad [10\text{-}12]$$

where h is called the *Planck constant*, a fundamental constant of nature. h is found experimentally to be 6.626×10^{-34} J s.

As an electromagnetic wave of frequency f has a wavelength λ where $c = f\lambda$ we can also write

$$E = \frac{hc}{\lambda}.$$

Photons behave as particles of inertial mass m, where, as

$$E = mc^2 \qquad [10\text{-}10]$$

and

$$E = \frac{hc}{\lambda},$$

then

$$m = \frac{h}{c\lambda}. \qquad [10\text{-}13]$$

The momentum p of a photon is given by

$$p = mc = \frac{h}{c\lambda} c$$

that is

$$p = \frac{h}{\lambda}. \qquad [10\text{-}14]$$

For example, for visible radiation of wavelength $\lambda \approx 5 \times 10^{-7}$ m, the photon has a mass

$$= \frac{6.6 \times 10^{-34} \text{ J s}}{(3.0 \times 10^8 \text{ m s}^{-1})(5 \times 10^{-7} \text{ m})} \approx 4 \times 10^{-36} \text{ kg},$$

much 'lighter' than an electron of mass about 10^{-30} kg.* Photons have zero rest mass and move at the limiting speed of particles, whatever their energy. If one photon has a greater energy than another, it must have a greater mass m; equation 10-13 shows that it must have a shorter wavelength λ, while its speed c is unchanged. We shall return to this when we consider the electromagnetic Doppler effect on page 356.

The photoelectric effect is only one way in which a photon interacts with an electron (photons do not usually interact with one another but the waves of which one is composed obey the principle of superposition — see page 280). In all such interactions the principles of conservation of mass–energy and of linear momentum can be applied: the photons involved have mass $h/c\lambda$, energy hf, and momentum h/λ. Figure 10-9 illustrates

(a) the photoelectric effect,

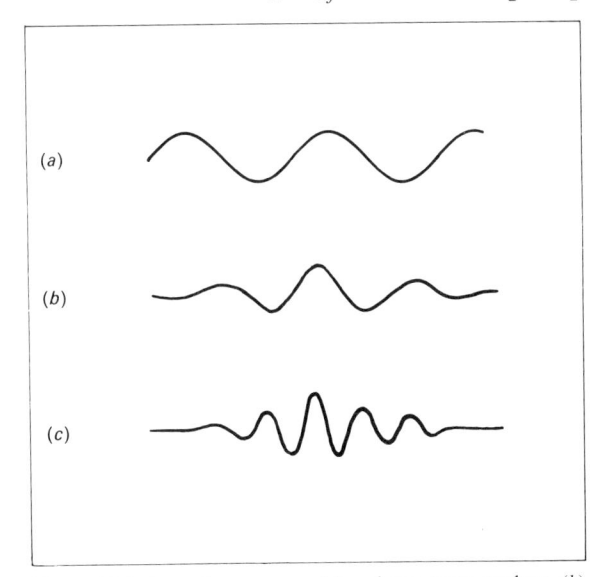

Figure 10-8 A continuous wave (*a*) and two wave packets, (*b*) and (*c*). (*c*) carries more energy than (*b*). If (*b*) were to represent a typical photon then about 10^6 (not half a dozen) waves would be in the wave packet.

---

*These calculations can be reversed to calculate the wavelength of an electron of total energy E. The implications of wave-particle duality lie at the heart of quantum mechanics. See for example, Nuffield Advanced Physics, Unit 10 *Teachers' guide and students' book*.

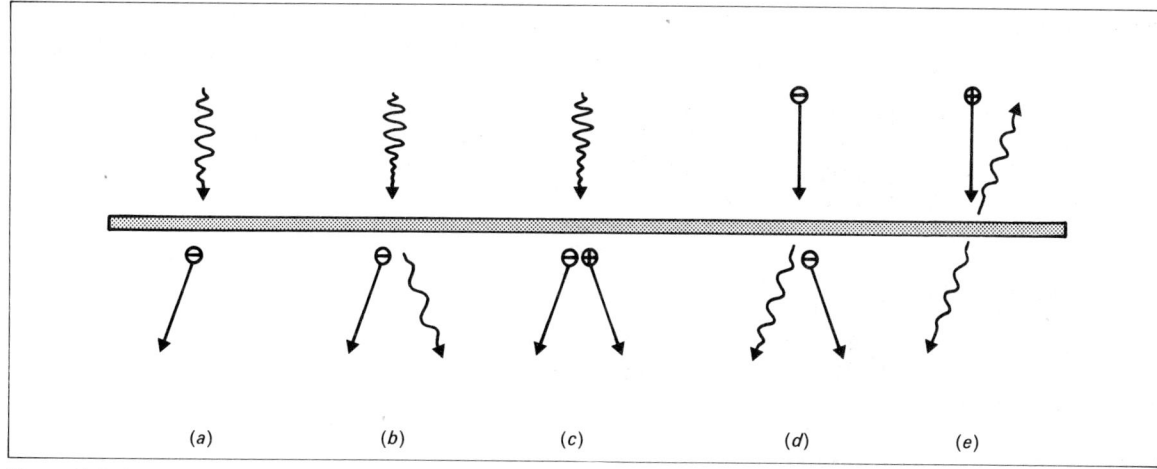

Figure 10-9 A purely diagrammatic summary of photon–electron interactions.

(b) the Compton effect, in which the incident photon collides with a free electron in the material which recoils and scatters a photon with lower energy than the incident one,

(c) pair production (see Exercise 10-17),

(d) X-ray production in which a high-energy electron loses kinetic energy which is conserved as photon-energy in the X-ray region of the electromagnetic spectrum and internal energy, and

(e) pair annihilation in which an incident positron collides with a stationary electron of equal but opposite charge (a positron is the electron's antiparticle) and all the rest mass of the two particles disappears, the mass being conserved by the appearance of a pair of photons in the γ-ray region of the electromagnetic spectrum (see Exercise 10-14).

Finally, if photons have an inertial mass $m = h/c\lambda$, do they experience gravitational attractive forces? They *are* found to be deviated when they pass close to the Sun. The deviation amounts to only 1.7×10^{-5} rad but this is twice what we should expect from a knowledge of Newton's law of gravitation (Chapter 14). We cannot explain this without a knowledge of Einstein's theory of general relativity (1916), which receives a brief mention in Section 14-9.

10-6 The constancy of the limiting speed

The Bertozzi experiment shows us that there is an upper limit to the speed at which electrons can travel: we have called this speed c. Further experiments performed with protons, mesons, and other charged particles in high-energy physics laboratories enable us to assert that the limiting speed to which we can accelerate *any* particle is $c = 3.0 \times 10^8$ m s^{-1} (2.9979×10^8 m s^{-1} to five significant figures).

The speeds of the electrons in the Bertozzi experiment, and the speeds of the other particles, were measured in an inertial reference frame fixed to the Earth. We might wonder what we would have measured their speeds to be in our laboratories had the laboratories been moving at high speed in a frame of reference that was moving relative to the Earth, particularly if the relative velocity of the two reference frames was itself very high, perhaps $0.5c$ or greater. At the moment there is no direct experimental evidence to which we can turn in answer to this question. Rosser* has suggested an experiment using a charged nuclear particle, a π-meson (or pion) which would provide evidence of the sort we require. Pions often decay in flight to a different particle, a μ-meson (or muon). We could arrange for the pions to be moving at a variety of measured speeds close to c and we could study the speeds of the muons produced when they decay in flight. If the speed of the muons was always found to be less than c, no matter how near to c the speed of the pions was, we might postulate that the limiting speed of particles is the same in all inertial frames of reference.

---

*W. G. V. Rosser (1968), *Physics Education*, **3**, page 198.

★ Alternatively, consider another particle, the neutral pion. This decays to two γ-ray photons which travel at the limiting speed $c = 3.0 \times 10^8 \text{ m s}^{-1}$ in the Earth's frame of reference. An experiment has been performed* in which the speed of γ-ray photons emitted by a *moving* source of neutral pions was investigated. The experiment used pions produced at the CERN accelerator referred to in the next section. In the experiment the particles were moving through the laboratory at more than $2.9972 \times 10^8 \text{ m s}^{-1}$, that is more than 99.97 per cent of the limiting speed of particles, and they decayed in flight into two γ-ray photons. The source of the pions is S in figure 10-10, but they have a *very* short half-life and so S is also

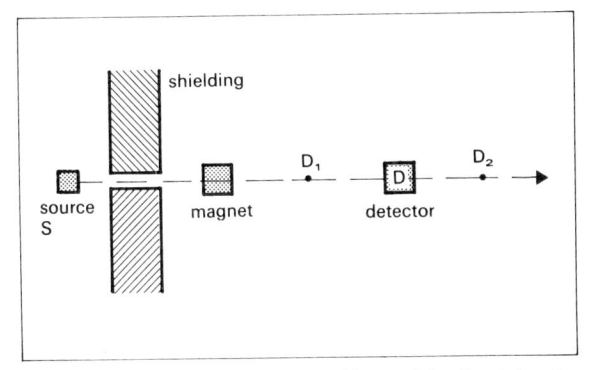

Figure 10-10 The distance $D_1 D_2 \approx 30 \text{ m}$ and the time taken for photons to travel from D_1 to D_2 is measured directly in the Alväger experiment.

effectively the source of the photons. Photons travelling in the direction SD are selected for study and any stray charged particles initially travelling in that direction are deflected from it by a magnet. The pions are produced by a very short burst of protons hitting the source S: thus the pions, and the photons to which they decay, are also produced in short bursts. The arrival of a burst of photons is then recorded by

*T. Alväger et. al. (1964). *Phys. Letters*, **12**, page 260.

the detector D. The time interval Δt_1 between a burst of pions setting out from S and the corresponding arrival of photons at the detector D_1 is measured. With the detector moved to D_2 the time interval is measured to be Δt_2, and so $\Delta t (= \Delta t_2 - \Delta t_1)$ is the time taken for *photons* (emitted close to S by the moving pions) to travel from D_1 to D_2, a distance of about 30 m in this experiment. (As the half-life of pions is less than 10^{-15} s we can be sure that they decay within a very small distance of S, less than 1 mm.)

The speed of the photons was found to be $(2.9977 \pm 0.0004) \times 10^8 \text{ m s}^{-1}$ which is very close to the best values for the speed of photons from sources at rest in the laboratory. The speed of *photons* in inertial frames of reference is thus shown in this experiment to remain constant under quite extreme conditions, and we might postulate that the speed of photons (including light) is independent of the speed of their source. ★

Let us, then, postulate that

the limiting speed of any particle has a constant value ($3.0 \times 10^8 \text{ m s}^{-1}$) when measured in all inertial frames of reference.

This *principle of the constancy of the limiting speed of particles* may, together with the principle of special relativity, be used to establish all the laws and results of relativistic mechanics. As these results are daily being asserted in physics laboratories throughout the world it is unnecessary to await direct confirmation of the above principle; its position among the basic postulates of physics is firmly established. In a similar way we cannot provide experimental proof of Newton's second law of motion, but we continually receive ample evidence of its validity in low-speed mechanics; the above postulate has the same status as one of Newton's laws.

Consider now the situation of figure 10-11. In laboratory A some electrons have been accelerated so that they are moving essentially at their limiting speed: that is, an

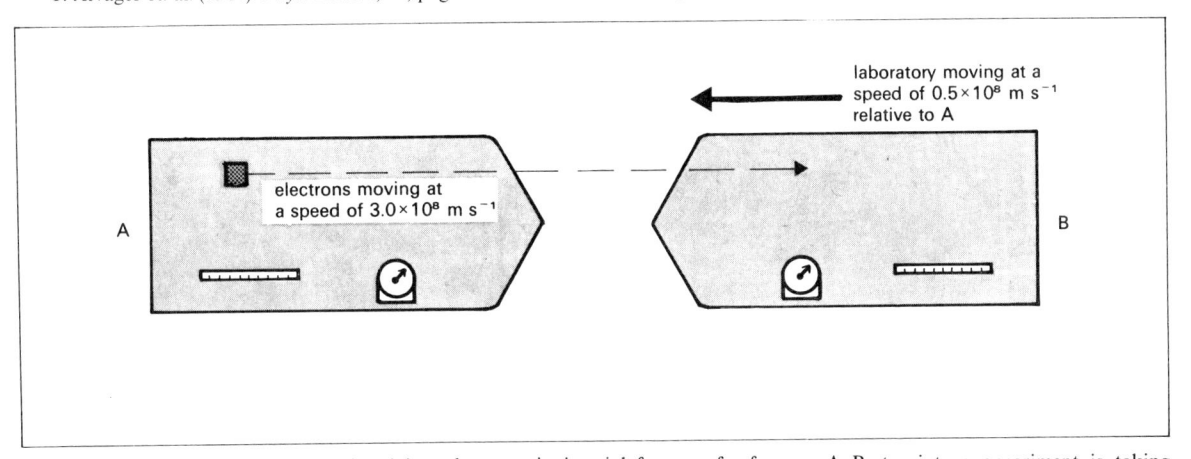

Figure 10-11 A thought-experiment involving observers in inertial frames of reference. A Bertozzi type experiment is taking place in A; electrons from A are investigated in B.

168 10 Relativistic mechanics

observer in A finds that their speed is very nearly $3.0 \times 10^8 \, \text{m s}^{-1}$. Laboratory B is moving (in the opposite direction) at a speed of $0.5 \times 10^8 \, \text{m s}^{-1}$ relative to A. Suppose that an observer in B, using the instruments available in his laboratory, tries to measure the speed of these same electrons which enter B from A as indicated schematically in the diagram. Commonsense predicts that he will find their speed to be

$$3.0 \times 10^8 \, \text{m s}^{-1} + 0.5 \times 10^8 \, \text{m s}^{-1} = 3.5 \times 10^8 \, \text{m s}^{-1},$$

but the principle of the constancy of the limiting speed of particles demands that their speed cannot be greater than $c = 3.0 \times 10^8 \, \text{m s}^{-1}$. Similarly if the electrons in A are accelerated only to $2.8 \times 10^8 \, \text{m s}^{-1}$, the commonsense prediction that B will measure their speed to be $3.3 \times 10^8 \, \text{m s}^{-1}$ cannot be correct as this again exceeds the limiting speed c.

The natural reaction to this is to conclude that the principle of the constancy of the limiting speed is absurd, yet as already stated the principle (sometimes called the second postulate of the theory of special relativity) is firmly believed by physicists the world over. *It is the commonsense which is wrong.* Two questions which immediately arise are:

(a) Is our method for measuring velocities (which we have been taking for granted) wrong?
(b) If it is wrong, can it still be used as an approximation when adding small velocities?

The second question is taken up in more detail in Exercises 19–37 to 19–39. The first question provides special relativity with a peculiar difficulty for it involves a reappraisal of our appreciation of the concepts of space and time. Our *apparent understanding* of these concepts is so deep-rooted as to make us prejudiced in favour of the *status quo*. But the *experimental evidence* is overwhelming and we must, with Einstein, learn to be more precise in how we measure time intervals and distances—because this is all that is required to resolve the difficulties.

Let us look more closely at the *clocks* of two observers A and B moving relative to one another at a fixed velocity v (figure 10-12). Both A and B are in inertial frames of reference and so we can apply the principle of special relativity (our first postulate) to any laws of physics established by A or by B. Suppose the observers A and B synchronize their clocks as B passes A (or A passes B). If they are to check their clocks again then they must communicate with one another. How can they do this? The obvious method is to use light (which in the vacuum between them travels with speed c) but to maintain continuity with the previous arguments in this section let us suppose that they fire bursts of *very* high-

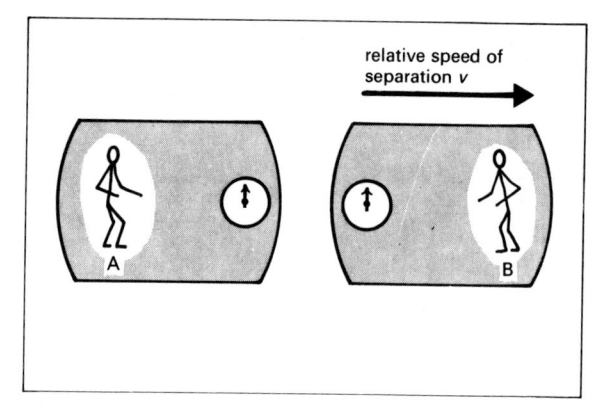

Figure 10-12

energy electrons which travel at speed c as measured by both the sender and the receiver: the principle of the constancy of the limiting speed ensures that this will be so. Suppose the observer A fires bursts of electrons at time intervals Δt_a as measured on his clock.

What A thinks: B will travel away from me between each of my signals. If B receives my signals at time intervals Δt_b then he will travel $v\Delta t_b$ between receiving signals. As the electrons travel at a speed c *as measured by either of us* the extra time for which B travels while the signals catch up with him is $v\Delta t_b/c$, so that B will receive my signals at time intervals greater by $v\Delta t_b/c$ than Δt_a, the intervals at which I send them.

That is
$$\Delta t_b = \Delta t_a + \frac{v\Delta t_b}{c},$$

or
$$\Delta t_a = \Delta t_b\left(1 - \frac{v}{c}\right).$$

Therefore A thinks

$$\frac{\Delta t_b}{\Delta t_a} = \frac{1}{1 - v/c}. \qquad [10\text{-}15]$$

What B thinks: I am receiving A's signals at time intervals $\Delta t_b'$ (we do not write Δt_b, which is only what A expects, and $\Delta t_b'$ may not be equal to Δt_b). As I am moving away from A then he must have sent out signals at shorter time intervals than this; suppose he is signalling at time intervals $\Delta t_a'$. Each signal will travel an extra distance $v\Delta t_a'$ to get to me and this will take a time interval $v\Delta t_a'/c$ (for the electrons travel at c as measured by both of us).

Thus
$$\Delta t'_a + \frac{v\Delta t'_a}{c} = \Delta t'_b,$$

or
$$\Delta t'_b = \Delta t'_a \left(1 + \frac{v}{c}\right).$$

Therefore B thinks

$$\frac{\Delta t'_b}{\Delta t'_a} = 1 + \frac{v}{c}. \qquad [10\text{-}16]$$

Are the ratios of the time intervals predicted by A and B the same?—not according to equations 10-15 and 10-16 which we have deduced (a result which justifies our having distinguished between Δt and $\Delta t'$). Let us investigate a numerical example: suppose that $v = 3 \times 10^4 \text{ m s}^{-1}$, so that as $c = 3 \times 10^8 \text{ m s}^{-1}$ then $v/c = 10^{-4}$, and

$$\frac{\Delta t_b}{\Delta t_a} = \frac{1}{1 - 10^{-4}} = (1 - 10^{-4})^{-1}$$

$$= 1 + (-1)(-10^{-4}) + \frac{(-1)(-2)}{1 \times 2}(-10^{-4})^2 + \cdots$$

$$= 1 + 10^{-4} + 10^{-8} \ldots,$$

while

$$\frac{\Delta t'_b}{\Delta t'_a} = 1 + 10^{-4}.$$

The difference is of the order of 1 part in 10^8, and this is the result for $v = 3 \times 10^4 \text{ m s}^{-1}$—faster than any man has ever travelled relative to the Earth at the time of writing. The differences are thus of no practical relevance even for man travelling in space, *but there is a difference*.

The principle of relativity demands that the ratio of the time intervals as measured by A or B *must be* the same. Yet we have shown that

[10-16]
$$\frac{\Delta t'_b}{\Delta t'_a} = 1 + \frac{v}{c}$$

$$= \frac{1 - v^2/c^2}{1 - v/c}$$

$$= \left(1 - \frac{v^2}{c^2}\right)\left(\frac{\Delta t_a}{\Delta t_b}\right),$$

from equation 10-15. That is, the ratio of the time intervals as measured by the two observers moving relative to one another at a speed v is

$$\frac{\Delta t'_b/\Delta t'_a}{\Delta t_b/\Delta t_a} = 1 - \frac{v^2}{c^2},$$

whereas the two quantities should be identical.

To resolve the problem let us start from the other end and *take the demands of the principle of relativity as axiomatic*; thus we must have

$$\frac{\Delta t'_b}{\Delta t'_a}(\text{correct}) = \frac{\Delta t_b}{\Delta t_a}(\text{correct}) = k,$$

for this statement has the required symmetry. We must now adjust equation 10-15 or equation 10-16 so as to arrive at this result. But if we adjust equation 10-15 by saying, for example, that A sees B's clock running slow by a factor D, giving

$$\frac{\Delta t_b}{\Delta t_a}(\text{correct}) = \frac{\Delta t_b/D}{\Delta t_a} = \frac{1}{D}\left(\frac{1}{1 - v/c}\right),$$

we must *also*, according to the symmetry required by the principle of relativity, adjust equation 10-16 by saying that B sees A's clock running slow by the same factor D, that is

$$\frac{\Delta t'_b}{\Delta t'_a}(\text{correct}) = \frac{\Delta t'_b}{\Delta t'_a/D} = D\left(1 + \frac{v}{c}\right).$$

Thus
$$D\left(1 + \frac{v}{c}\right) = \frac{1}{D}\left(\frac{1}{1 - v/c}\right) = k,$$

or
$$D^2 = \frac{1}{1 - v^2/c^2},$$

that is
$$D = \frac{1}{\sqrt{(1 - v^2/c^2)}} \qquad [10\text{-}17]$$

and
$$k = \frac{\Delta t_b}{\Delta t_a}(\text{correct})$$

$$= \frac{\Delta t'_b}{\Delta t'_a}(\text{correct}) = \sqrt{\left(\frac{1 + v/c}{1 - v/c}\right)}. \qquad [10\text{-}18]$$

D, the factor by which each sees the other's clock running slow, is the *time dilation factor*. As v^2/c^2 is always positive and less than unity, D is always positive and more than unity. *Clocks moving relative to the observer run slow.* If D had emerged as less than unity from the algebra, then we should have concluded that moving clocks run fast. The time dilation factor depends only on the ratio v/c and in no way on the frequency of the signals involved in the experiment. Looking back at the problem which arose from figure 10-11 we see that it is indeed the case that our appreciation of the concept of time has changed, and with it the whole basis of kinematics. In Section 10-7 and Section 19-7 some of the consequences of this change are outlined.

10-7 Moving clocks

The time dilation factor $D\,[=1/\sqrt{(1-v^2/c^2)}]$ from the previous section has a familiar look. Such a function of v/c has appeared before and we know that the factor will only be significant for very high values of v, say $v > c/100$. Can we find any experimental evidence for the existence and size of D? It is not wholly satisfactory that it was deduced from the principle of special relativity and the principle of the constancy of the limiting speed of particles in all inertial frames of reference (in support of which no *direct* experiment has yet been performed). If, however, we can find any direct evidence for D then the whole story will hang properly together. What sort of observable clocks travel at speeds of 10^6 m s^{-1} or more? If the clock is to be of the conventional type, we have only a few microseconds in which to check it as it passes through our laboratory! The reader will probably have guessed that the clocks provided by the decay of unstable sub-atomic particles are the key to our problem.

Consider first the design of large, and very expensive, accelerators such as that at the Centre for Nuclear Research (CERN) at Geneva (figure 10-13). One type of experiment involves producing a beam of charged pions, nuclear particles, by arranging for very high energy protons to hit a metal target at T. (Pions or π-mesons are particles with a rest mass a few hundred times the rest mass of an electron. They are thought to be involved in the mechanism whereby neutrons and protons are bound together in the nucleus of an atom.) This beam is detected by a bubble chamber placed nearly 120 m away at B at the end of the East Hall. As the pions are travelling at speeds of only just less than 3.0×10^8 m s^{-1}, they will take about

$$120 \text{ m}/3.0 \times 10^8 \text{ m s}^{-1} \approx 4 \times 10^{-7} \text{ s}$$

or 400 ns to reach the bubble chamber. It is known that charged pions, at rest in or moving at low speeds through the laboratory, decay randomly with a half-life of 1.7×10^{-8} s or 17 ns, that is that after 17 ns only half of the original number of pions will remain, after 34 ns only a quarter of the original number, and after 400 ns only about 1 in every 2^{23} (≈ 1 in 10^7) pions setting off from the target will not have decayed. (*Note:* these pions are charged, and their half-life is different from that of the neutral pions used in the Alväger experiment described on page 167.) The scientists who designed this system, a routine experimental system at CERN, either made a grave and expensive mistake by thus arranging to detect less than 1 in every 10^7 of the pions produced, or else they accepted time dilation as a fact. In practice the experimenters at CERN do find many charged pions in the beam reaching the bubble chamber—the designers were not stupid.

So pions moving through the laboratory live longer than pions which are at rest in the laboratory! The radioactive clock operates according to our new idea of time dilation and this experiment could be quantified to check our expression for D. Incidentally, the slower decay rate of the moving pions is a useful result for the high-energy physicist for it gives him more room in which to organize his experiments.

The study of cosmic rays provides another situation in which we can test equation 10-17. Very high-energy particles, cosmic rays, bombard the upper atmosphere from space and produce, among other things, a μ-meson or muon which decays randomly with a half-life of the order of microseconds, producing an electron. Muons pour down to the Earth at speeds close to $c = 3.0 \times 10^8$ m s^{-1}, and we on the Earth would expect to observe their decay clocks slowing down if there is time dilation. If we could measure the factor D of this decay process directly and at the same time measure the speed v of the muons, we could verify the expression $D = 1/\sqrt{(1-v^2/c^2)}$.

Figure 10-14 illustrates an experiment carried out by Frisch and Smith at Cambridge, Massachusetts, USA

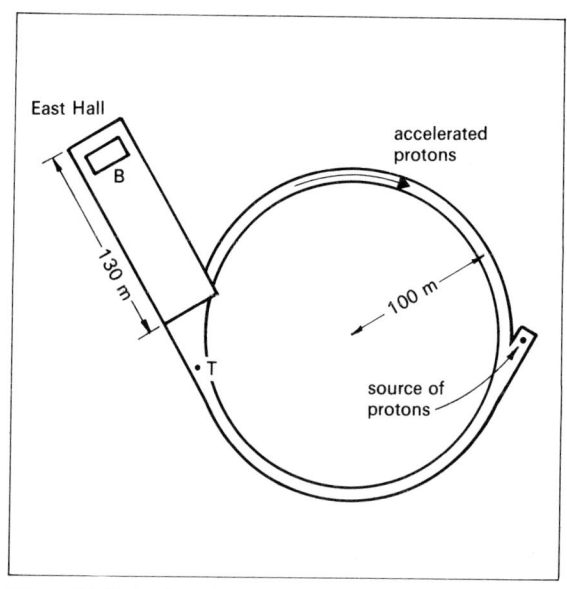

Figure 10-13 A plan of the CERN proton accelerator drawn roughly to scale. The protons hit a target at T. In some experiments the resulting shower of nuclear particles is detected in a bubble chamber at B.

10-7 Moving clocks

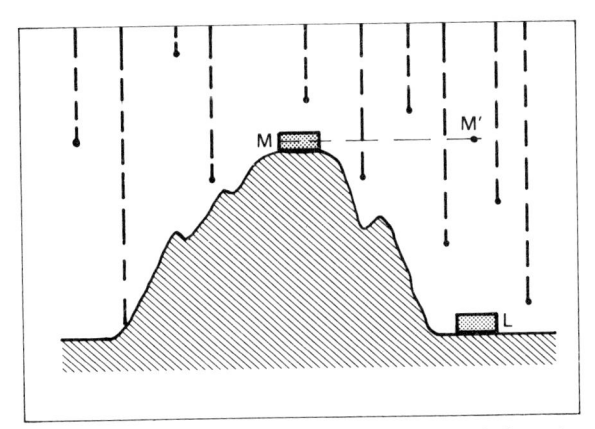

Figure 10-14 Muons travelling vertically downwards from the upper atmosphere. The rate of their arrival at L is less than at M because they decay in flight.

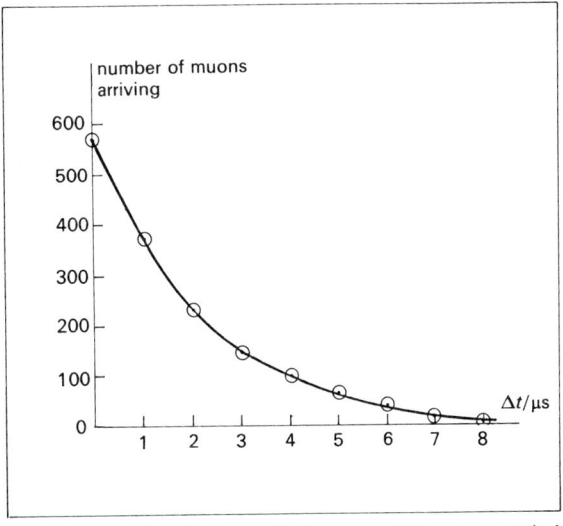

Figure 10-15 Statistical record of muons at M over a period of one hour.

and at the top of nearby Mount Washington.* The two laboratories are called L and M in the diagram and are separated by a vertical distance $LM' = 1900\,\text{m}$. Only muons with a speed of $2.98 \times 10^8\,\text{m s}^{-1}$ ($=0.994c$) were used in the experiment. This was achieved by considering those muons which, after passing through a known thickness of material, were brought to rest in the detector at M or at L; that is the energy of the muons was chosen and used to define their speed. The time interval between the arrival of each muon at M and its subsequent decay at rest there in the detector was measured, and the graph of figure 10-15 was plotted to show the result of one hour's experimenting.

As the time Δt for a muon moving at $2.98 \times 10^8\,\text{m s}^{-1}$ to travel from M' to L (and muons do travel predominantly in a vertical direction) is given by

$$\Delta t = \frac{1900\,\text{m}}{2.98 \times 10^8\,\text{m s}^{-1}}$$

$$= 6.3\,\mu\text{s},$$

then, from the graph, we should expect only about 30 of the more than 500 muons arriving at a level M' to survive to level L. The actual rates of arrival in the experiment were 563 muons per hour at M and 412 muons per hour (far more than 30) at L! The moving muons have decayed *far* more slowly than the stationary muons. The graph shows that according to the muon decay clock the journey from M' to L lasted only about

---
*Frisch, D. H. and Smith, J. H. (1963). *American Journal of Physics*, **31**, page 342.

0.7 μs instead of the expected 6.3 μs. The measured time dilation factor is thus $6.3\,\mu\text{s}/0.7\,\mu\text{s} \approx 9$ (to one significant figure).

Taking the speed of the muons to be $0.994c$ as deduced from their energy, the time dilation factor D should be

[10-17] $$D = \frac{1}{\sqrt{(1 - v^2/c^2)}}$$

$$= \frac{1}{\sqrt{(1 - (0.994)^2)}}$$

$$= \frac{1}{\sqrt{0.01196}}$$

$$\approx 9,$$

so that the experiment *quantitatively* confirms the time dilation factor.

If we were travelling *with* the muons they would be decaying at rest in our frame of reference and we would detect no time dilation effect. Yet the results of the Frisch and Smith experiment still hold: we cannot alter the number of muons reaching the sea-level laboratory L simply by altering *our* frame of reference. The only possible explanation is that, to the moving muons, the distance $M'L$ is not 1900 m but that

$$M'L = \frac{1900}{9}\,\text{m} \approx 210\,\text{m}.$$

An observer travelling with the muons would be able

172   10 Relativistic mechanics

to calculate that in travelling that 210 m, which would take a time of about 0.7 µs, only about 150 muons would decay and so 412 muons would reach sea level *as is the case*. This conclusion is not limited to the example we have given but is a general one: it is usually called *space contraction* (or Lorentz contraction) and is a necessary consequence of the principles of relativity and the constancy of the limiting speed of particles. It is complementary to time dilation.

To sum up: If we observe a clock moving relative to our frame of reference it runs slow: the time dilation factor is

$$D = 1/\sqrt{1 - v^2/c^2}.$$

If we observe a ruler moving relative to our frame of reference it shrinks: the space contraction factor is

$$C = \sqrt{1 - v^2/c^2}. \qquad [10\text{-}19]$$

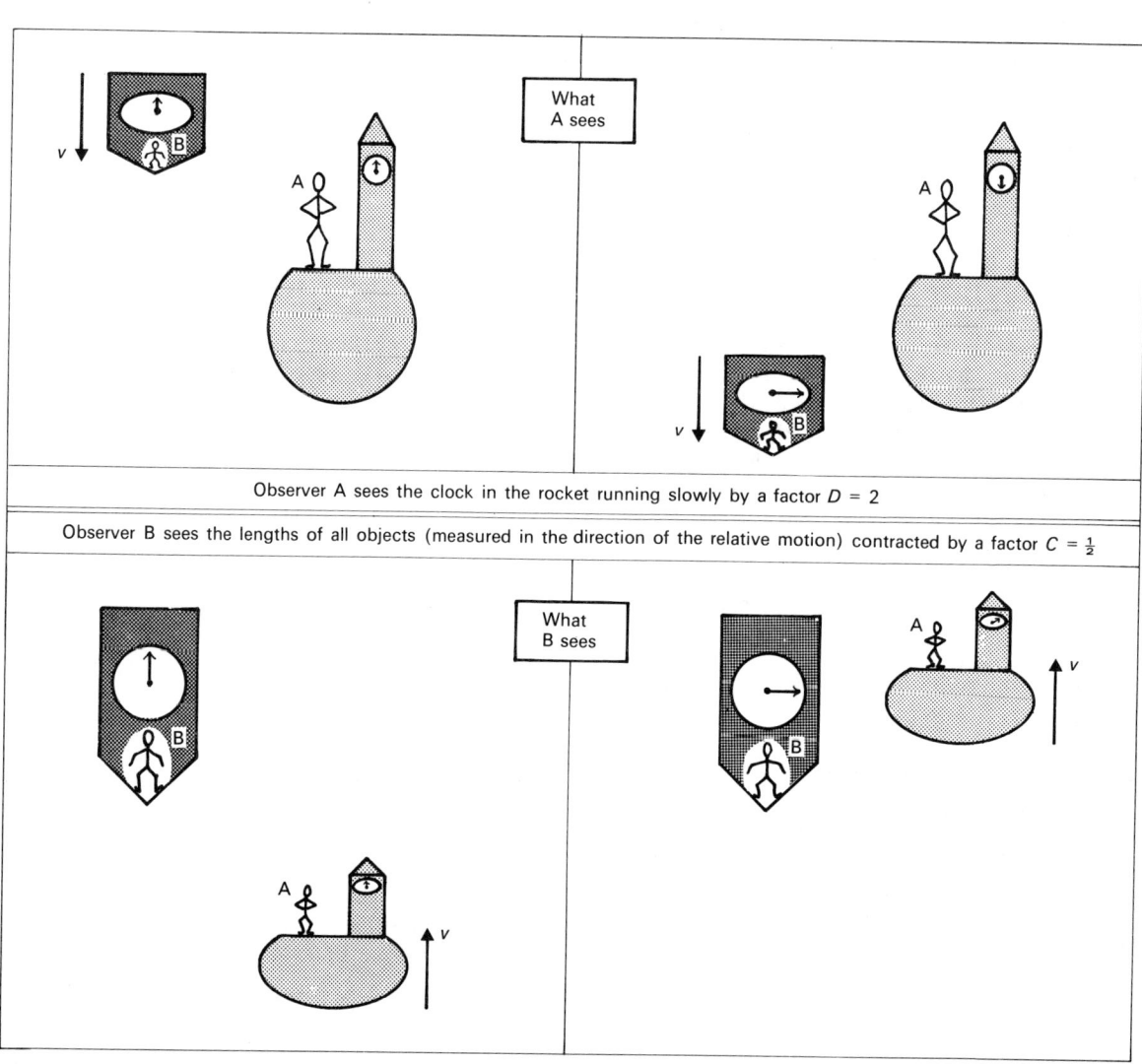

Figure 10-16 A rocket and the Earth approach one another at a relative speed $v = 0.866c = 2.3 \times 10^8 \text{ m s}^{-1}$ so that $\sqrt{(1 - v^2/c^2)} = \frac{1}{2}$.

10-8 Summary

The equations below are lettered [a] to [q] so as to avoid confusion with any numbers given earlier in the text.

A particle of rest mass m_0 has a kinetic energy T given by

[10-6] $$T = (m - m_0)c^2 \qquad [a]$$

which at low values of v, gives

$$T = \tfrac{1}{2}m_0 v^2, \qquad [b]$$

where [10-4] $$m = \frac{m_0}{\sqrt{(1 - v^2/c^2)}}. \qquad [c]$$

[a] can be written [10-7] as

$$\Delta m = \frac{\Delta T}{c^2} \qquad [d]$$

that is

gain of mass = (gain in kinetic energy)/c^2,

or as $$mc^2 = m_0 c^2 + T, \qquad [e]$$

that is

total energy = rest energy + kinetic energy

$$E = E_0 + T.$$

[d] can be generalized [10-8] as

$$\Delta m = \frac{\Delta E}{c^2} \qquad [f]$$

where ΔE represents the change in energy (not necessarily kinetic energy) of the system.

Mass–energy is conserved. [g]

The linear momentum p of a particle is given by

$$p = mv, \qquad [h]$$

which at low values of v, gives

$$p = m_0 v. \qquad [i]$$

The momentum p of electromagnetic radiation of total energy E is given by

[10-9] $$p = \frac{E}{c}. \qquad [j]$$

Linear momentum is conserved. [k]

For particles of zero rest mass, such as photons

[10-12] $$E = hf \qquad [l]$$

where h is the Planck constant = 6.6×10^{-34} J s,

and [10-10] $$E = mc^2, \qquad [m]$$

m representing the inertia of the photon energy.

[j] and [l], together with $c = f\lambda$, yield

[10-14] $$p = \frac{h}{\lambda}. \qquad [n]$$

The limiting speed for particles is $c = 3.0 \times 10^8$ m s^{-1} and is the same in all inertial frames of reference.

Photons *in vacuo* travel at the speed c in all inertial frames of reference.

An observer who measures time intervals on a clock moving relative to him at a speed v notices a time dilation factor

[10-17] $$D = \frac{1}{\sqrt{(1 - v^2/c^2)}}, \qquad [o]$$

while if he measures the length of an object moving relative to him at a speed v he notices a space contraction factor

[10-19] $$C = \sqrt{(1 - v^2/c^2)}. \qquad [p]$$

The ratio of the time intervals transmitted at Δt_a and received at Δt_b between two observers in relative motion at a constant speed v is

[10-18] $$k = \frac{\Delta t_b}{\Delta t_a} = \sqrt{\left(\frac{1 + v/c}{1 - v/c}\right)}. \qquad [q]$$

Bibliography

Bronowski, J. (1963). 'The clock paradox.' *Scientific American* offprint number 291.

Rosser, W. G. V. (1968). 'Special relativity via mechanics.' *Physics Education*, **3**, page 197.

Bondi, H. (1965). *Relativity and common sense*. Heinemann (Science Study Series). This book develops and uses the *k*-calculus.

French, A. P. (1968). *Special relativity*. Nelson. Chapter 1 deals with departures from Newtonian mechanics and includes a discussion of the Bertozzi experiment while experiments on time dilation appear in Chapter 4. A first class book.

Nuffield Advanced Physics (1972). Unit 8 *Electromagnetic waves*. Penguin. Part Four of this unit deals with relativity and in particular with time dilation.

Nuffield Advanced Physics (1972). Unit 10 *Waves, particles, and atoms*. Penguin. Part One gives a simple account of the properties of photons and goes on to consider wave-particle duality.

Project Physics (1971). Reader, Unit 5 *Models of the atom*. Holt, Rinehart and Winston. Chapter 7 is an excerpt from Rogers' *Physics for the inquiring mind*. Several other pieces are relevant.

PSSC (1968). *College Physics*. Raytheon. Chapter 32 is about high-energy mechanics from an experimental viewpoint.

16 mm film. 'The ultimate speed.' Guild Sound and Vision. This is the film of the Bertozzi experiment.

16 mm film. 'Time dilation.' Guild Sound and Vision. The experiment on time dilation with cosmic ray μ-mesons is the theme of this film.

Exercises

Data (to be used unless otherwise directed):

Speed of electromagnetic radiation *in vacuo* $= 3.0 \times 10^8$ m s^{-1}.
Rest mass of electron $= 9.1 \times 10^{-31}$ kg.
Rest mass of proton $= 1.7 \times 10^{-27}$ kg.
Electronic charge $= -1.6 \times 10^{-19}$ C.
The Planck constant $= 6.6 \times 10^{-34}$ J s.

10-1 A train's velocity increases from 20 m s^{-1} to 40 m s^{-1} at a constant rate in 40 s, the velocities being measured by a stationary observer. What acceleration does the stationary observer record? Suppose another train runs on a parallel track at a constant velocity of 25 m s^{-1}, both trains moving in the same direction. What are the initial and final velocities of the first train as measured by an observer in the second train, and what is the first train's acceleration, as measured by him?

10-2 Find the increase in mass of an electron and hence its kinetic energy when it has a speed v where
(a) $v = 0.10c$ (b) $v = 0.90c$ (c) $v = 0.99c$. ●

10-3 An electron is moving in a straight line with speed $0.90c$ in the absence of gravitational, electric, and magnetic fields. It enters a region where there is an electric field perpendicular to its original direction. What is the effect on its velocity in the original direction?

10-4 Find the gain in mass of an electron which has been accelerated by a potential difference of 5000 V in a television tube. ●

10-5 Find the greatest potential difference through which an electron can be accelerated before its mass increases by 1/50 of its rest mass. ●

10-6 What is the rest energy of (a) an electron, (b) a proton? How fast must each be moving for its total energy to be twice as great as its rest energy? ●

10-7 Find the total energy of a proton when it has a speed of
(a) $0.90c$ (b) $0.99c$. ●

10-8 Find the decrease in mass of the following bodies when they undergo the changes stated:
(a) a golf ball (of mass 0.045 kg) moving at a speed of 50 m s^{-1} is brought to rest, and it is allowed to reach its original temperature
(b) a 12 V car battery with a stated capacity of 50 ampere hours is fully discharged, without its temperature rising
(c) a red-hot poker made of iron cools down to room temperature (fall in temperature = 800 K, effective mass of poker = 0.50 kg, specific heat capacity of iron = 500 J kg^{-1} K^{-1}). ●

10-9 If it takes 2.2×10^{-18} J to remove the electron from a hydrogen atom, by how much is the rest mass of a hydrogen atom less than the sum of the rest masses of the proton and the electron? ●

10-10 Energy is received from the Sun at the surface of the Earth at a rate of 1.4 kW m^{-2}. Calculate the pressure exerted by this radiation, if it is all absorbed. ●

10-11 The nucleus $^{210}_{84}$Po decays to form $^{206}_{82}$Pb with the emission of an α-particle, $^4_2$He. Assuming that their rest masses are 209.9829 u, 205.9745 u, and 4.0026 u respectively, and 1 u $= 1.7 \times 10^{-27}$ kg, find the kinetic energy of the emitted α-particle. ●

10-12 If a proton has a kinetic energy of 3.0×10^{-10} J, what is the size of its momentum? ●

10-13 A nucleus of rest mass 2.0×10^{-25} kg emits a γ-ray of energy 3.0×10^{-14} J. Find the speed of recoil of the nucleus. Find the kinetic energy possessed by the nucleus (its velocity is small enough for its kinetic energy to be given by $\frac{1}{2}m_0 v^2$) and find the loss in mass of the nucleus as a result of the γ-emission. ●

10-14 If an electron and a positron meet and annihilate each other, so that no rest mass remains, how much energy is possessed by the photons which result? Why must there be at least two photons? If only two photons are produced, what is the frequency of the wave associated with each? ●

10-15 Take equation 10-4 ([c] in the summary) and use the binomial expansion to obtain an approximate expression for m in terms of m_0 when $v^2 \ll c^2$. Substitute this value for m in the equation $T = (m - m_0)c^2$, and show that this expression reduces to the Newtonian expression for kinetic energy when speeds are low.

10-16 An electron (mass 9.1091×10^{-31} kg, charge 1.6021×10^{-19} C) is accelerated from rest through a potential difference of 5.0000×10^6 V. Find its kinetic energy and its increase in mass. (Take c to be 2.9979×10^8 m s^{-1}.) Hence find the ratio v/c for the electron. (You will need either five-figure logarithm tables or access to a calculating machine.) ●

10-17 What is the minimum energy of a photon if it is to produce an electron and a positron? ●

10-18 The carbon monoxide molecule CO is a fraction 4×10^{-11} less massive than the sum of its constituent atoms C and O. How much energy is transferred when one mole of CO is formed from its atoms, given that the relative molecular masses of carbon and oxygen are 12 and 16 respectively? [This is an important chemical reaction, but we cannot use the result to calculate the energy produced by burning, say, 1 kg of coal in air. From the energy produced by burning 1 kg of carbon in oxygen we should have to subtract (a) the energy required to dissociate the O_2 molecule, (b) the energy required to evaporate the carbon atoms from the solid state, and (c) the energy required to push back the atmosphere (since the volume of CO is twice that of the original O_2). Also the equation $2C + O_2 = 2CO$ almost certainly does not adequately represent all that happens when coal burns in air.] ●

10-19 The nucleus $^{231}_{91}$Pa decays to form $^{227}_{89}$Ac with the emission of an α-particle, $^4_2$He, and a γ-ray photon. If the kinetic energy of the α-particle is known to be 8.0×10^{-13} J, what is the energy of the photon? The rest masses of the nuclei are, respectively 231.0359 u, 227.0278 u, and 4.0026 u. (Take $1\text{ u} = 1.66 \times 10^{-27}$ kg.) ●

10-20 Figure 10-17 shows a view from above a toy radiometer. J, K, L, and M are vanes which have their faces vertical: one face S of each vane is silvered and the other B is dull black. The whole assemblage of vanes can rotate, in a partial vacuum, about a vertical axis through O. Would you expect the vanes to rotate clockwise or anticlockwise (as seen from above) when placed near a source of light as a result of the radiation falling on them?

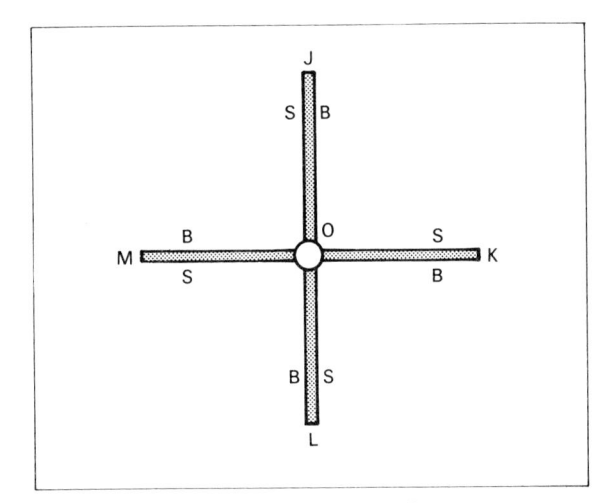

Figure 10-17 A view from above a toy radiometer.

In practice the vanes rotate in the opposite direction to that expected: discover the reason for this.

10-21 Figure 10-18 shows a closed box AB of mass M and length d. There is a lamp at A and an absorbing screen at B. Imagine that a burst of photons of energy E travels from A to B and is absorbed.

(a) What is the momentum of the photons as they travel down the box?
(b) At what speed must the box be recoiling while the photons travel to B?
(c) What time do the photons take to travel from A to B?
(d) How far to the left will the box move during this time?

Suppose the answer to part (d) is Δx. As the centre of mass of the system must not move (there are no external forces acting on it) then *supposing* the photons to have a mass m, show that their mass can be expressed as $m = E/c^2$. [This *gedanken* or thought experiment was first suggested by Einstein in 1906.]

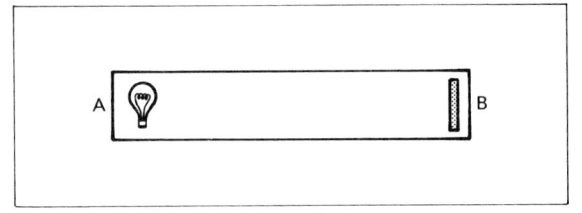

Figure 10-18

10-22 Verify that the values of v and T/m_e given in the table of figure 10-3 satisfy equation 10-5.

10-23 In a collision between two nuclear particles some of the kinetic energy of the colliding particles may be conserved as mass–energy of the particle or particles created during the interaction. In Exercises 9-24 and 9-25 it is suggested that the centre of mass kinetic energy cannot be used to produce internal energy when two masses collide. Similarly the centre of mass kinetic energy must remain after a nuclear collision and only the particles' kinetic energy relative to the centre of mass can be conserved as mass–energy.

Discuss how this conclusion affects the design of nuclear collision experiments. Would it be better to have, for instance,

(a) a moving proton strike a stationary proton
(b) a moving proton strike a stationary lithium nucleus
(c) a moving proton strike another proton moving in the opposite direction
(d) a moving α-particle strike a stationary proton, etc.?

10-24 Consider figure 10-16 on page 172. Why is there a separate diagram for each observer?

10-25 Consider a clock which consists of a tube of length d with a mirror at each end. A burst of photons travels up and down the tube and the clock 'ticks' each time the photons are reflected from one of the ends. When the clock is at rest, the time interval Δt between ticks is given by

$$\Delta t = \frac{2d}{c}.$$

If the clock now moves in a direction perpendicular to its length at a constant speed v, the photons must travel a greater distance between ticks. Draw a sketch of the new situation and calculate the new time interval $\Delta t'$ between ticks using your knowledge of the principle of the constancy of the limiting speed of photons. What is the relationship between Δt and $\Delta t'$? Does it agree with the time dilation phenomenon described in Section 10-7?

10-26 Suppose that a star at a distance of 50 light years from the Earth is thought to have a planetary system on one part of which intelligent life thrives. *Could* they know that we on Earth exploded our first nuclear bombs in 1945? Is this an event which lies, for them, in the future or in the past? Discuss how the limiting speed of particles (and photons), and the way in which this limits the speed at which information can be communicated, affects what we mean by 'now'.

10-27 A writer of science fiction predicts that in 40 years the internal combustion engine will be banned in Great Britain. He hopes to live to see whether his prediction is verified but he is already 60 years old and he realizes that his chances of living to the age of 100 are slender. He knows, however, that if he were to go on a journey at a very high speed v relative to the Earth his own biological clock would, to his friends on the Earth, appear to run more slowly. Could he arrange to return to test his prediction when he himself was only 80?

10-28 A physicist comments to a stout colleague that if he were to move quickly past his friends he would appear slimmer: see figure 10-19. How fast must he move in order to achieve a 25 per cent reduction? What, as a result of this special slimming technique, would happen to his mass?

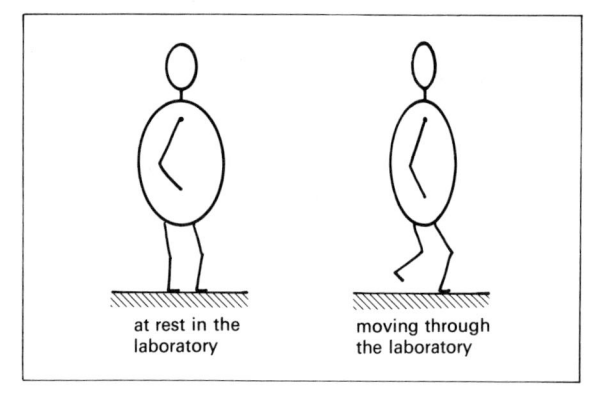

Figure 10-19

11 Rigid bodies in equilibrium

11-1 Bodies and particles	177	11-5 Couples and torques	186
11-2 The moment of a force	178	11-6 The beam balance	188
11-3 Centre of gravity	181	Bibliography	189
11-4 Conditions for equilibrium	182	Exercises	189

11-1 Bodies and particles

This chapter is concerned with rigid bodies—that is collections of particles which always remain in the same positions relative to one another. No such bodies actually exist but if molecules A and B in a boxwood ruler are separated by say 24 mm at one moment then they will remain separated by this distance, despite any sub-microscopic vibrations of A or B, unless the ruler is subjected to large external forces. In considering bodies to be rigid we are using a simple approximation which most solid bodies obey. We shall not attempt to discuss the reason *why* the two molecules in the ruler do remain 24 mm apart.

If the vector sum of the forces acting *on a particle* is zero then, as Newton's first law states, the particle will have zero acceleration, that is the velocity of the particle will be constant. This velocity may or may not be zero. Such a particle is said to be *in equilibrium*.

A body is a collection of particles. Each particle may have internal forces (that is, forces exerted by the other particles of the body) as well as external forces acting on it. Suppose that as shown in figure 11-1 a particle of mass m_1 is acted on by a resultant internal force $\boldsymbol{F}'_1$ and a resultant external force $\boldsymbol{F}_1$. Applying Newton's second law to the particle gives us

$$m_1 \boldsymbol{a}_1 = \boldsymbol{F}'_1 + \boldsymbol{F}_1,$$

while for other particles of the body

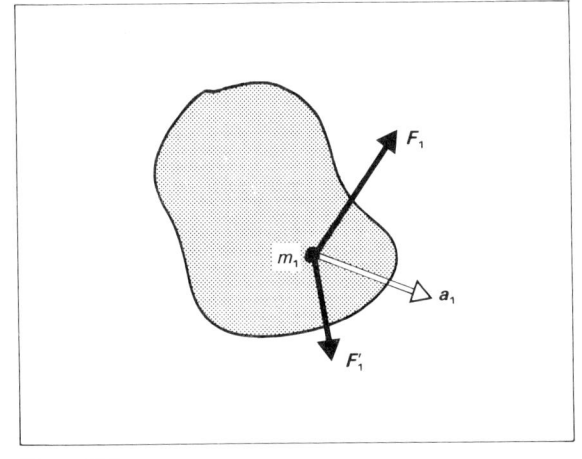

Figure 11-1

$$m_2 \boldsymbol{a}_2 = \boldsymbol{F}'_2 + \boldsymbol{F}_2, \quad \text{etc.}$$

Adding for all the particles of the body

$$\sum m_r \boldsymbol{a}_r = \sum \boldsymbol{F}'_r + \sum \boldsymbol{F}_r.$$

But the vector sum of the internal forces (the interactions between the particles) must, by Newton's third law, be zero, that is

$$\sum \boldsymbol{F}'_r = 0.$$

Therefore

$$\sum m_r \boldsymbol{a}_r = \sum \boldsymbol{F}_r. \qquad [11\text{-}1]$$

11 Rigid bodies in equilibrium

On page 132, in discussing the motion of the centre of mass of a group of particles, we have

[8-16] $$\sum m_r v_r = m v_{CM}$$

where $m = \sum m_r$ and v_{CM} is the velocity of the centre of mass.

Clearly, then $$\sum m_r a_r = m a_{CM} \qquad [11\text{-}2]$$

and so from equation 11-1

$$m a_{CM} = \sum F_r. \qquad [11\text{-}3]$$

This is Newton's second law for a body, a collection of particles. It states that

the mass of a body times the acceleration of the centre of mass is equal to the sum of the external forces acting on the body.

The law, which is central to a study of the dynamics of bodies, has been assumed in earlier chapters. Equation 11-3 is a vector equation but we shall often use it in situations where the resolved parts of the external forces are found in a direction for which a_{CM} is known.

If the vector sum of the external forces acting on a collection of particles is zero then clearly the acceleration of the centre of mass is zero (this is Newton's first law). More particularly, if the particles form a rigid body then the body as a whole will have no translational acceleration. It may have a constant linear velocity and it might be rotating about its centre of mass, in which case individual particles may be accelerated relative to an inertial frame of reference fixed at the centre of mass.

Forces acting on a single particle inevitably act through a point (the particle), while external forces acting on a body need not, and usually do not, act through a point. As forces are free vectors we can still add the external forces acting on a body by the normal vector methods of Sections 2-3 and 2-4: see figure 11-2.

If a particle *is* in equilibrium then it is *necessary* that

$$\sum F = 0,$$

or $$\sum F_{\text{resolved}} = 0,$$

where the resolved parts are taken in *any* convenient direction.

In order to show that a *particle* is in equilibrium it is *sufficient* to show that

$$\sum F_{\text{resolved}} = 0,$$

in *any* three directions (though all three must not lie in the same plane). For a set of forces which all lie in one plane—coplanar forces—we need resolve in only two directions, and for most problems this is all that is required.

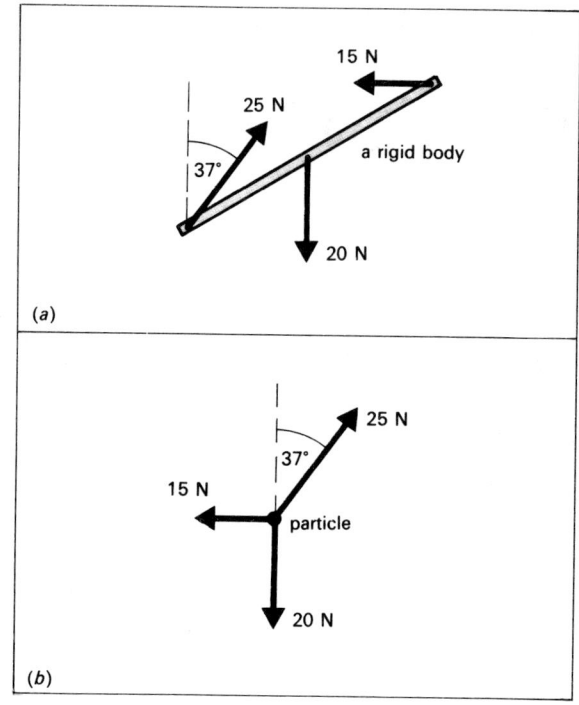

Figure 11-2 The three forces shown acting on a rigid body in (*a*) can be added in the same way as the three forces shown acting on a particle in (*b*).

For a *body* both the above statements apply but they determine only its translational equilibrium. Because bodies rotate, we must also establish rules about their rotational equilibrium.

11-2 The moment of a force

It is a matter of common experience that when a force is being used to produce a turning effect the position of the line of action of the force is important as well as the size and direction of the force. We know that to push open a door it is best to push it at a point as far from the hinges as possible, and perpendicular to the door. In figure 11-3, F_1 has the greatest effect in turning the rod about the axis OO′ in the sense shown, F_5 and F_6 exert no turning effect about OO′, F_2 and F_3 exert smaller turning effects than F_1, and F_4 turns the rod in the wrong sense.

For a force whose line of action lies in a plane perpendicular to the axis about which we want to measure its turning effect, we define the *moment of the force*, to be M where

$$M = r_\perp F, \qquad [11\text{-}4]$$

11-2 The moment of a force

then the resultant moment is found as the sum of all the moments $r_\perp F$, due care being taken of sign. This very important result is proved below. If all the forces act in one plane then they can be dealt with in this way and the resultant moment about any axis perpendicular to the plane of the forces can be found.

Moment as a vector

The force F in figure 11-5 is a vector, as is the displacement $OP = r$. The moment of a force is an axial vector (or pseudovector); by definition the moment of a force (or torque) about a point is M where

$$M = r \times F$$

(vector products—see page 22)

$$= rF \sin \theta \, n, \qquad [11\text{-}5]$$

where θ is the angle between r and F and n is a unit axial vector perpendicular to the plane of r and F with the sense in which a right-hand screw would move if rotated from r to F through θ. Thus M is out of the page towards the reader in figure 11-5. As $r \sin \theta = r_\perp$, then the size of M is $M = r_\perp F$ (or $rF_\perp$, where $F_\perp$ is the resolved part of F perpendicular to r), which was how we previously defined the size of a moment in equation 11-4.

If several forces act on a body then to find the total moment about a point we must calculate the vector sum

$$M_1 + M_2 + M_3 + \cdots + M_n = \sum M_r.$$

In general M_1, M_2, M_3, etc. will be in different directions,

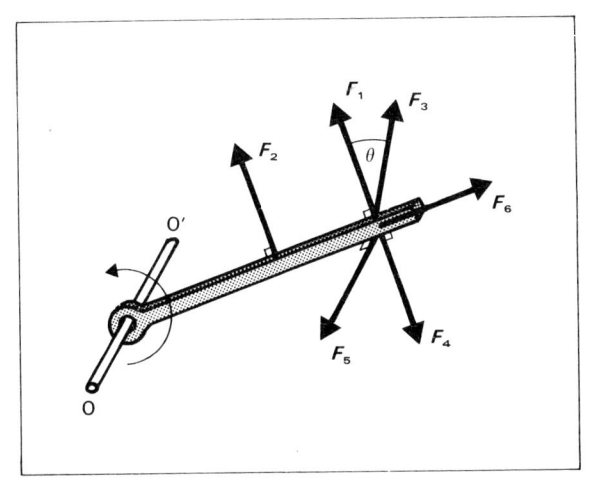

Figure 11-3 All the forces have the same size, F, but they differ in direction, sense, or line of action.

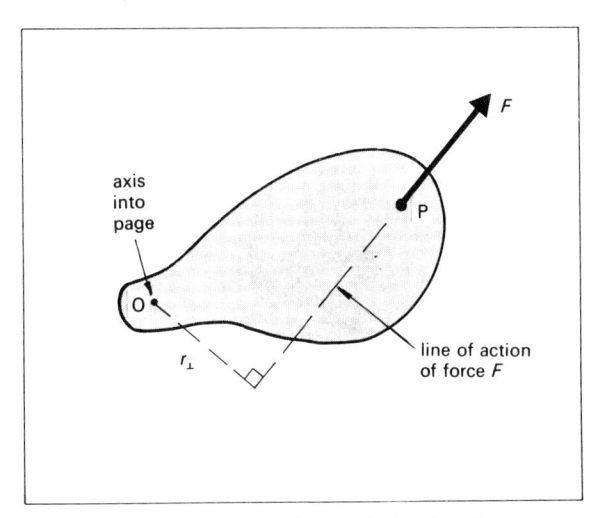

Figure 11-4 A force F acts at P on a rigid body. The moment of the force F about an axis through O is calculated as $r_\perp F$.

where (see figure 11-4) F is the force and $r_\perp$ is the distance from the axis to the line of action of the force. There is a sign convention for M, for some forces tend to rotate a body clockwise and some anticlockwise. We shall adopt the convention that 'anticlockwise is positive'.

M has dimensions of ML^2T^{-2} and units of N m. If the push on a door as above were 30 N and the push was exerted 0.80 m from the hinge the moment of the force about a vertical axis through the hinges would be $(30 \text{ N})(0.80 \text{ m}) = 24$ N m.

If several forces act on a body and the line of action of each lies in the plane perpendicular to the axis through O,

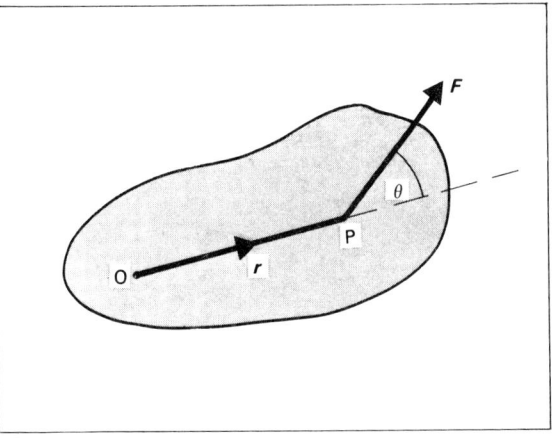

Figure 11-5 The moment M of F about O is defined as $M = r \times F$. The direction of M will be out of the page on this occasion.

11 Rigid bodies in equilibrium

but if the forces are coplanar (or lie in parallel planes) then all the moments will be parallel and

$$\sum M_r = n \sum M_r.$$

That is their sum has a size $\sum M_r$ (though in adding the moments we must be careful about their signs). In this chapter we shall deal only with systems of coplanar forces and we shall not include the vector nature of M in our arguments although the sign convention (anticlockwise is positive) will of course be used.

▶ **Example 11-1** Figure 11-6 shows a rectangular lamina which measures 3.0 m by 1.5 m, and which is subjected to forces as shown. Find the sum of the moments of the forces about the axis through A perpendicular to the lamina.

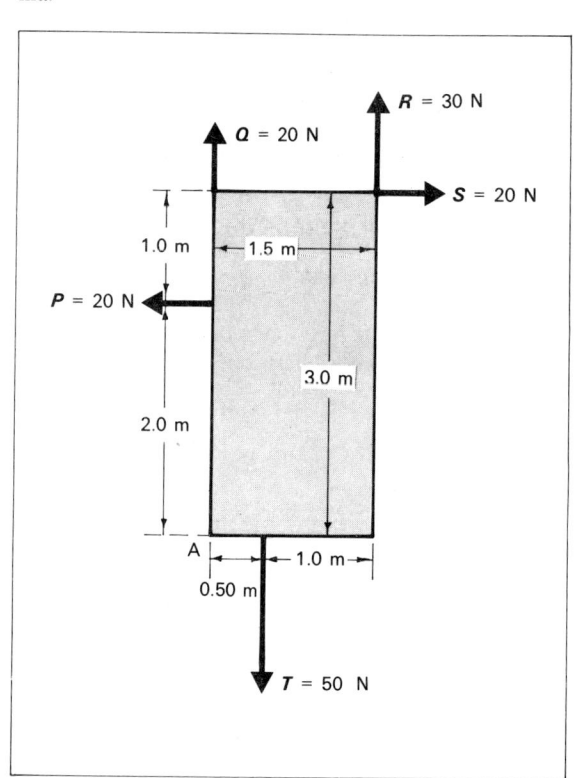

Figure 11-6

Moment of $P = +20\,\text{N} \times 2\,\text{m} = +40\,\text{N m}$
moment of $Q = 0$ (since the moment arm is zero)
moment of $R = +30\,\text{N} \times 1.5\,\text{m} = +45\,\text{N m}$
moment of $S = -20\,\text{N} \times 3\,\text{m} = -60\,\text{N m}$
moment of $T = -50\,\text{N} \times 0.5\,\text{m} = -25\,\text{N m}$.
As all the forces lie in one plane the sum of their moments about $A = 0$, and so the lamina is in (rotational) equilibrium. ◀

The moment of a force F about a point is equal to the sum of the moments of the resolved parts of the force about the point. This general result is easy to prove and is left to the reader in Exercise 11-11. It is seen to be true in the particular case described in Example 11-2 below, and will be useful in analysing the equilibrium of rigid bodies later in this chapter.

▶ **Example 11-2** Figure 11-7a shows a set of forces acting on a rod. In figure 11-7b the force of 100 N is resolved into two components.

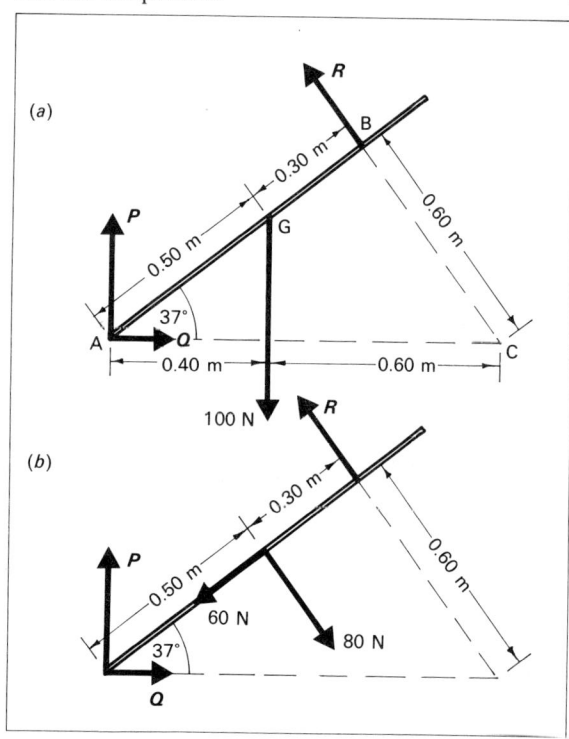

Figure 11-7

Let us take moments for the force of 100 N in (a) about A and about C:
about A: moment $= -100\,\text{N} \times 0.4\,\text{m} = -40\,\text{N m}$
about C: moment $= +100\,\text{N} \times 0.6\,\text{m} = +60\,\text{N m}$.
Let us now take moments in (b) for the resolved parts of the force of 100 N:
about A: moment $= -80\,\text{N} \times 0.5\,\text{m} = -40\,\text{N m}$
about C: moment $= +80\,\text{N} \times 0.3\,\text{m} + 60\,\text{N} \times 0.6\,\text{m}$
$= +24\,\text{N m} + 36\,\text{N m}$
$= +60\,\text{N m}$.
These results are clearly the same as those obtained when we took moments for the single force. Note that when we took moments about A for the resolved parts, one of them had zero moment; this does not *always* happen. ◀

11-3 Centre of gravity

We have assumed up to this point that we can replace the pull of the Earth on a body by a single force, $W = m\mathbf{g}$, acting through a fixed point in the body. This point is called the *centre of gravity* of the body; its position is defined as being that point about which the sum of the moments of the pull of the Earth on the particles comprising the body is zero. In figure 11-8, the total moment of the gravitational forces about the z-axis is numerically

$$x_1 m_1 g + x_2 m_2 g + x_3 m_3 g + \cdots + x_n m_n g$$
$$= \sum x_r m_r g = g \sum x_r m_r$$

if g is constant in size and direction for all the particles.

If the centre of mass of the body is at a distance x_{CM} from the y–z plane, then by definition (see page 131)

$$\sum x_r m_r = m x_{CM},$$

where m is the total mass of the body. Therefore the total moment about the z-axis of the weights of the particles is

$$\sum x_r m_r g = m x_{CM} g. \qquad [11\text{-}6]$$

Thus if x_{CM} is zero this total moment is zero, and following a similar process for the body in other positions we see that the point about which the weights of the particles have zero moment is the centre of mass, that is the centre of mass and the centre of gravity coincide. Equation 11-6 tells us further that a single force $m\mathbf{g}$ acting at the centre of gravity can be used to represent the pull of the Earth on the body when the moment of this force is required. By showing that the centre of gravity and the centre of mass are the same point in a uniform gravitational field we also prove the assumption made previously that for translational motion we can treat a body as a particle with $m\mathbf{g}$ acting at the centre of mass.

To locate the centre of gravity of a body experimentally it is only necessary to exert a single external force P on the body (in addition to the pull W of the Earth on it) and find a position of equilibrium. The only possible situation for equilibrium is that $W + P = 0$ *and* that they have the same line of action. As W is vertically down then P must be vertically up and the line of P must pass through the centre of gravity. Figure 11-10 explains how this enables us to locate the centre of gravity of a lamina. For non-planar bodies the problem is more difficult but a rough

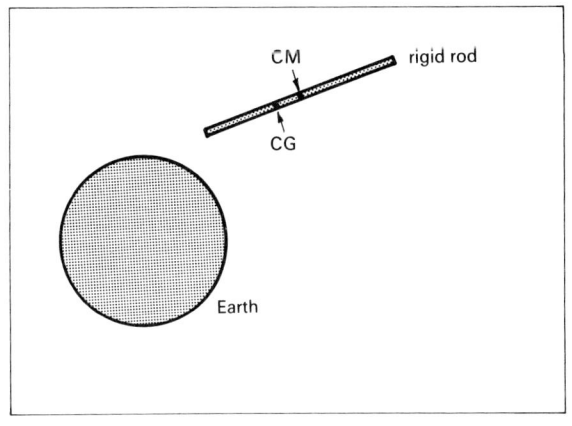

Figure 11-9 A body for which centre of mass and centre of gravity do *not* coincide. $\mathbf{g}$ is obviously not constant at different points on the rod.

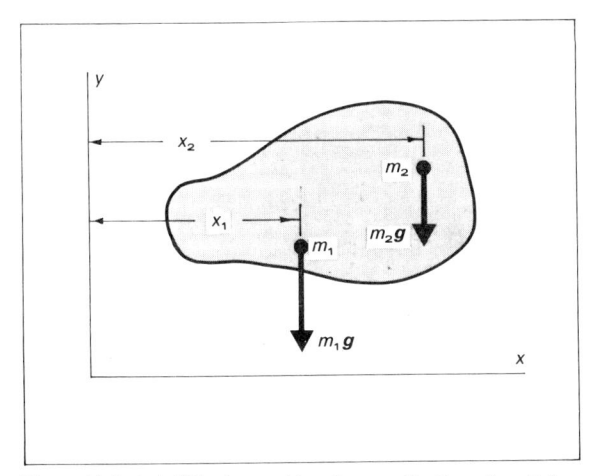

Figure 11-8 A rigid body considered as a collection of particles m_1, m_2, etc., in the Earth's gravitational field.

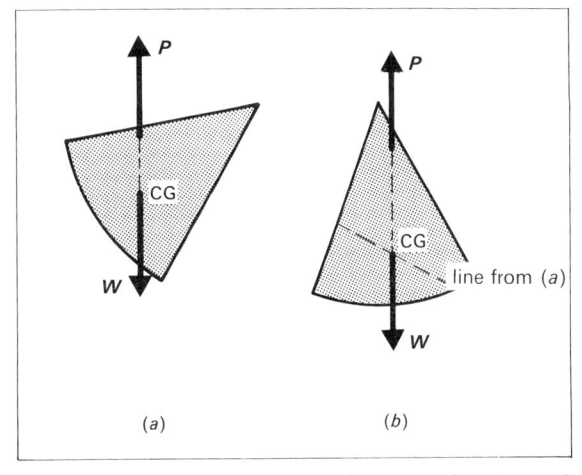

Figure 11-10 Locating the centre of gravity of a sheet of material by supporting it from (at least) two points. The intersection of the lines of action of P in (a) and (b) is CG; the line can be found using a plumb-line if necessary.

11 Rigid bodies in equilibrium

location of the centre of gravity can be found for a human body in a particular position; for example, if the body is firmly strapped to a light board which can be laid across a fulcrum.

For our purposes it is useful to know the positions of the centre of gravity (and the coincident centre of mass) for a few common rigid bodies made of uniformly dense material. The reader should consult texts on calculus for the theoretical arguments leading to these results:

Uniform rod, length d:
  $d/2$ from either end

Uniform rectangular lamina:
  at intersection of diagonals

Uniform sphere (shell *or* solid):
  at centre of sphere

Uniform triangular lamina:
  along any median, $1/3$ distance from base to apex

(In the following the centre of gravity lies on the axis of symmetry)

Uniform semicircular lamina, radius r:
  $4r/3\pi$ from centre of base

Uniform solid hemisphere, radius r:
  $3r/8$ from centre of plane surface

Thin uniform hemispherical shell, radius r (curved surface only):
  $r/2$ from centre of open circular end

Uniform right circular cone, height h:
  $3h/4$ from vertex

11-4 Conditions for equilibrium

In Section 11-1 the conditions for translational equilibrium were listed. If a rigid body is in a state of rotational equilibrium, that is, motion is at constant angular velocity (usually zero) about a given axis, then it is *necessary* that

$$\sum M = 0,$$

about *any* convenient axis. This is sometimes referred to as the *principle of moments*:

> for a body in equilibrium, the sum of the moments, about any axis, of the external forces acting on the body is zero.

If a rigid body is acted upon by a number of known forces then it is possible to test the validity of this statement.

In order to show that a rigid body is in rotational equilibrium it is *sufficient* to show that

$$\sum M = 0$$

for *any* three convenient axes which are not parallel.

To deal with equilibrium, both translational and rotational, we combine these statements with those of Section 11-1. We are, however, usually concerned only with coplanar forces, and so the equations and conditions are reduced to those given in the next paragraph.

Coplanar forces

Consider a rigid body which is acted on by a number of coplanar forces: there are three sets of conditions which, if satisfied, will ensure its equilibrium. The most useful of these sets is

(a) the sum of the resolved parts of the forces in any one convenient direction is zero,

(b) the sum of the resolved parts of the forces in any other one convenient direction is zero, and

(c) the sum of the moments of the forces about any one convenient axis perpendicular to the plane of the forces is zero.

If these results of resolving twice, and taking moments once, are each separately zero, then the body is in equilibrium. Resolving twice, and taking moments once, also gives, for a body in equilibrium, three independent equations relating the forces and distances involved in the problem. Further resolving and moment-taking give no additional equations: see Example 11-3.

▶ **Example 11-3** Consider the rod of Example 11-2. Let us resolve twice and take moments once for this rod.

Resolving horizontally:
$$Q - R\cos 53° = 0$$
$$Q = 0.6 R.$$

Resolving vertically:
$$P + R\cos 37° - 100\,\text{N} = 0$$
$$P = 100\,\text{N} - 0.8 R.$$

Taking moments about A:
$$R \times 0.8\,\text{m} - 100\,\text{N} \times 0.4\,\text{m} = 0.$$

These three equations enable us to find the three unknown quantities P, Q, and R. In some problems the unknown quantities may be angles or lengths, but provided the total number of unknowns does not exceed three, they can be evaluated. We cannot, however, deal with problems where the total number of unknowns exceeds three, since we cannot write down more than three independent equations. In this example we might think that we could get more information by resolving again, for example parallel to the rod:

$$P\cos 53° + Q\cos 37° - (100\,\text{N})\cos 53° = 0$$
$$\Rightarrow 0.6P + 0.8Q = 60\,\text{N}.$$

But if we multiply the first equation by 0.8:
$$0.8Q = 0.48R$$

and the second equation by 0.6:
$$0.6P = 60\,\text{N} - 0.48R$$

and add these:
$$0.8Q + 0.6P = 60\,\text{N},$$

we find we have the fourth equation: that is, the fourth equation is *not* independent of the first three. It will save the reader much time and confusion if he realizes that he can *only* resolve twice and take moments once. (There are two alternative procedures, but this one is the simplest and safest and is the only one which need be quoted in a physics textbook.) ◀

If there are only three non-parallel coplanar forces maintaining a body in equilibrium then their lines of action must all pass through one point. To prove this consider taking moments about an axis perpendicular to the plane of the forces through the point of intersection of any two of them. Unless the line of action of the third force passes through this point it will have a non-zero moment about the axis and the equilibrium will be impossible. This theorem can be useful in solving some problems—see Example 11-4.

▶ **Example 11-4** A beam with weight W is hinged at one end to a wall; its other end is supported by a wire which pulls with a force of 80 N at an angle of 37° with the horizontal (figure 11-11). Find the push R of the wall on the beam. The length of the beam is 2.0 m and its centre of gravity is 0.8 m from the wall.

Where the beam meets the wall, the wall must push upward and to the right on the beam, but the *direction* of the resultant force is not obvious. However, since there are only three forces acting on this beam, and it is in equilibrium, the lines of action of these three forces must be concurrent. We know where the lines of action of the weight and the pull of the wire meet: the push of the wall on the beam must also pass through this point. From the geometry of the figure we can now see that R makes an angle of 48.4° with the horizontal, hence

$$R\cos 48.4° - (80\,\text{N})\cos 37° = 0$$

which gives $R = 96\,\text{N}$ (at 48.4° above the horizontal).
Note. This technique is merely a short cut to the solution. We could have found R and θ by the normal processes of resolving and moment-taking. ◀

To analyse problems on the equilibrium of rigid bodies (the concern of *statics* if the bodies are at rest) we use free-body diagrams and take particular care in isolating the body whose equilibrium we have to consider. This last point cannot be stressed too strongly. In analysing the equilibrium of a man standing on a plank supported by two trestles we could for instance consider

(*a*) the man
(*b*) the plank

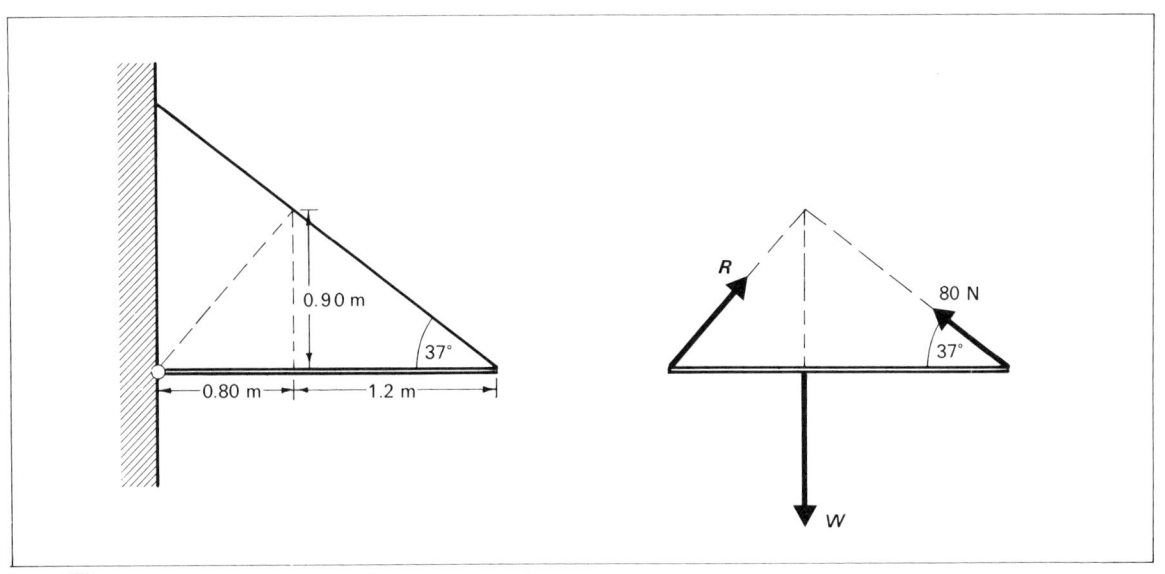

Figure 11-11

11 Rigid bodies in equilibrium

(c) the man plus the plank
(d) one of the trestles
(e) the other trestle
(f) the trestles plus the plank
(g) the trestles plus the man plus the plank.

It is as important to choose the body correctly (or where more than one body must be considered, to choose them in the correct order) as it is to use the resolving and moment-taking techniques effectively. This point and the reason for raising some of the other details met with in this chapter are brought out in the examples which follow.

▶ **Example 11-5** Figure 11-12 shows a gate of width 4.0 m and height 1.7 m. The hinge at the top is in working order, but that at the bottom is missing, so that the gate-post may be assumed to push horizontally against the bottom of the gate. If the gate is of symmetrical design and has a weight of 2000 N, find the forces exerted by the gate-post on the gate.

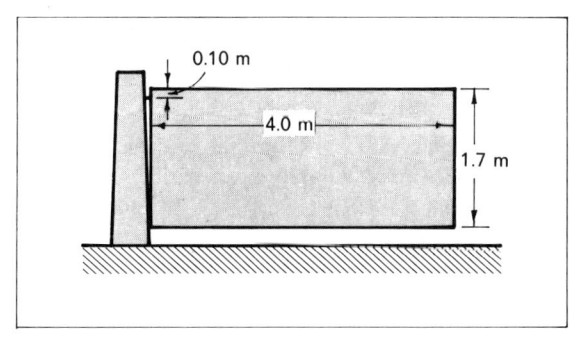

Figure 11-12

We first draw a free-body diagram for the gate, as in figure 11-13a: since the gate is kept in equilibrium by three forces, we can predict the direction of the pull of the upper hinge on the gate-post. As an alternative method, however, we can draw the resolved parts of this pull, as shown in figure 11-13b and we shall adopt this method here.
Resolving vertically:

$$Q - 2000\,\text{N} = 0 \Rightarrow Q = 2000\,\text{N}.$$

Taking moments about the upper hinge:

$$S \times 1.6\,\text{m} - 2000\,\text{N} \times 2.0\,\text{m} = 0 \Rightarrow S = 2500\,\text{N}.$$

Resolving horizontally:

$$P - 2500\,\text{N} = 0 \Rightarrow P = 2500\,\text{N}.$$

The resultant R of P and Q is given by

$$R^2 = P^2 + Q^2 = (2000\,\text{N})^2 + (2500\,\text{N})^2$$

and the angle θ which R makes with the horizontal is

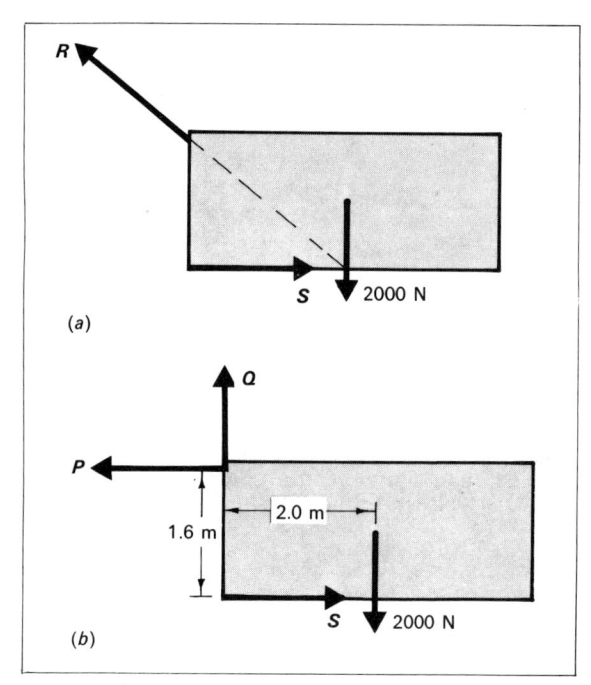

Figure 11-13

given by

$$\tan\theta = \frac{2000\,\text{N}}{2500\,\text{N}}.$$

Hence $R = 3200\,\text{N}$ at an angle $39°$ above the horizontal.
Note. We chose to resolve and take moments in the order which led to a numerical value of each of the unknown forces in turn. We avoided the formation of simultaneous equations. ◀

▶ **Example 11-6** A uniform plank AB of length 2.40 m and weight 150 N supports a man whose weight is 800 N; he stands 0.60 m from A. The plank rests on two trestles, each of which has a weight of 200 N, which are placed 0.20 m and 0.80 m from A and B respectively. What is the total force which the trestle nearer A exerts on the floor?

Refer to figure 11-14. We can find forces only by considering the equilibrium of the bodies: if we want to find the size of a force X, we have to consider the equilibrium of a body on which X is acting, and hope that on this body there will be no other unknown forces acting (or, at least, not more than two others, or else we shall not be able to find X by resolving twice and taking moments once). In our problem the unknown force X is the push of the trestle nearer A on the ground. We cannot consider the equilibrium of the floor, as we do not know anything about the other forces acting on the floor (that is the way in which the floor is supported, the pull of the Earth on the floor, and so forth). But the push of the trestle on the floor is the same size as the push of the floor on the

11-4 Conditions for equilibrium

plank; Q is the push of the man on the plank. At least we can find Q: since the man is in equilibrium, his weight, 800 N downward, is equal to the upward push of the plank on him, and by Newton's third law, the push of the plank on him is equal to the push of him on the plank—therefore $Q = 800$ N. Can we find P? We cannot find P by resolving vertically, because we do not know R, and there is no point in resolving horizontally, since there are no horizontal forces. But if we take moments about the point where R acts, or about any point on the line of action of R, R will not appear in our equation, so let us take moments about the point where the trestle nearer B touches the plank:

$$-P \times 1.4\,\text{m} + 800\,\text{N} \times 1.0\,\text{m} + 150\,\text{N} \times 0.4\,\text{m} = 0$$

which gives $P = \dfrac{860\,\text{N m}}{1.4\,\text{m}} = 614\,\text{N} \approx 610\,\text{N}.$

Returning to our free-body diagram for the trestle, we resolve vertically:

$$610\,\text{N} + 200\,\text{N} - X = 0$$

which gives $\qquad\qquad X = 810\,\text{N}.$ ◀

▶ **Example 11-7** A step-ladder consists of two parts hinged together at the top. Each part may be considered to be uniform, and each part has a length of 3.6 m; the weights of the two parts are 30 N and 6.0 N respectively. The step-ladder is placed with its legs apart on a frictionless horizontal surface, and is prevented from collapsing by a cord tied to each part at a distance of 0.9 m from the lower end. Each part now makes an angle of 53° with the horizontal. Find the pull of the cord on each part.

Refer to figure 11-16. Since the cord is an *internal* part of the step-ladder, we cannot, by consideration of the whole step-ladder, discover anything about the pull of the cord on the legs of the ladder, any more than we could discover the push of the bottom half of one leg on the top half of that leg. We separate the step-ladder into parts, one of which has the cord *external* to itself, as in figure 11-16b, and mark forces on this free-body diagram. X and Y are the resolved parts of the force with which the top of the right-hand leg pushes on the top of the left-hand leg, and S is the upward push of the ground on the leg. T is the pull of the cord. We still cannot solve the problem, however, since this body has four unknown forces acting on it. We have to return to a free-body diagram for the whole ladder in order to find S (X, Y, and T do not of course appear in this diagram, since all are internal forces). We note that the horizontal distance between the feet of the ladder is

$$2 \times 2.0\,\text{m} \times \cos 53° = 2.4\,\text{m}.$$

R is the push of the ground on the right-hand leg, but we do not need to know its value, so we find the value of S by taking moments about the foot of the right-hand leg:

$$6.0\,\text{N} \times 0.6\,\text{m} + 30\,\text{N} \times 1.8\,\text{m} - S \times 2.4\,\text{m} = 0$$

which gives $\qquad\qquad S = 24\,\text{N}.$

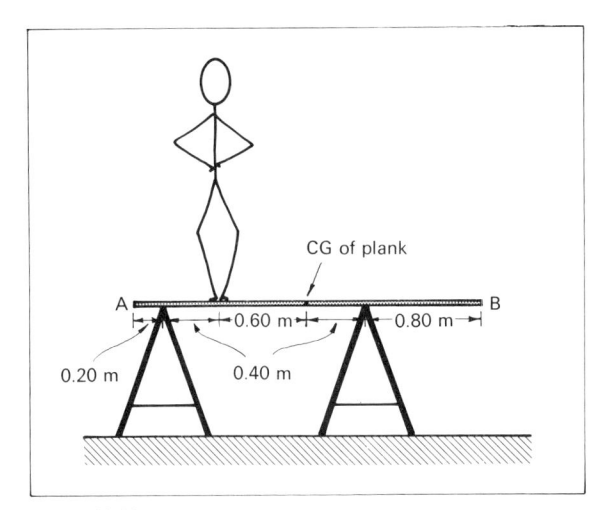

Figure 11-14

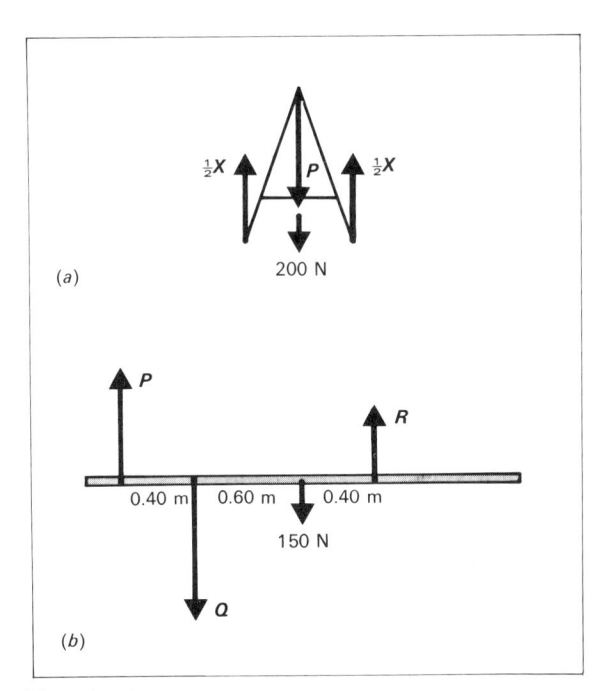

Figure 11-15

trestle, and we do know more about the forces acting on the *trestle*. (We know that the pull of the Earth on it is 200 N; we do not, however, know the size of the push P of the plank on it.) Let us draw a free-body diagram for the left-hand trestle (figure 11-15a). The push P of the plank on the trestle is the same size as the push of the trestle on the plank: do we know enough about the other forces acting on the *plank* to be able to find P? Let us draw a free-body diagram for the plank (figure 11-15b). R is the push of the right-hand trestle on the

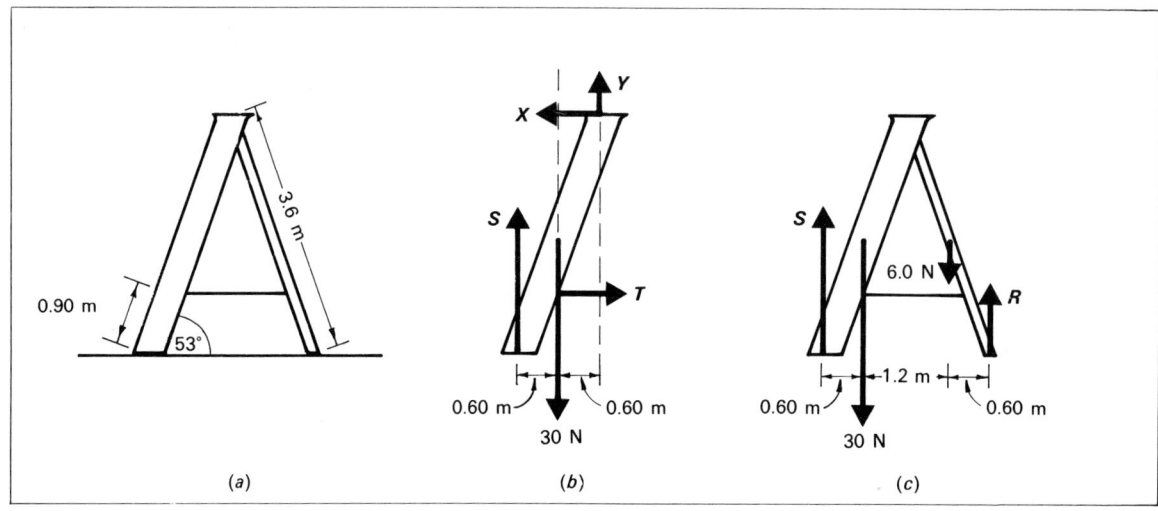

Figure 11-16

Now we return to the free-body diagram for the left-hand leg. We do not want to know the values of X and Y, and we can avoid this by taking moments for the left-hand leg about its top:

$$30\,\text{N} \times 0.6\,\text{m} + T \times 2.7\,\text{m} \times \sin 53° - 24\,\text{N} \times 1.2\,\text{m} = 0$$

which gives $\qquad T = 5.0\,\text{N}.$ ◀

11-5 Couples and torques

If two parallel forces of size P act in opposite directions on a body and have different lines of action, the body will have an angular acceleration, since two such forces do not produce equilibrium even though their vector sum, $\mathbf{P} + (-\mathbf{P})$, is zero. Figure 11-17 shows two such forces. In (a) their moment about an axis perpendicular to the page through A is

$$(x+d)P - xP = dP,$$

which is independent of x, and thus of the position of A. In (b) if $\mathbf{r}$ is a displacement vector between any two points on the lines of action of the two forces, then the total vector moment about A is

$$M = \mathbf{r}_1 \times \mathbf{P} + \mathbf{r}_2 \times (-\mathbf{P})$$
$$= (\mathbf{r}_1 - \mathbf{r}_2) \times \mathbf{P} = \mathbf{r} \times \mathbf{P}$$
$$= r \sin\theta P\mathbf{n} = dP\mathbf{n}.$$

Thus $\mathbf{P}$ and $-\mathbf{P}$ produce zero resultant force and a turning effect dP about *any* axis perpendicular to the plane of the forces. Two such forces are said to form a *couple*.

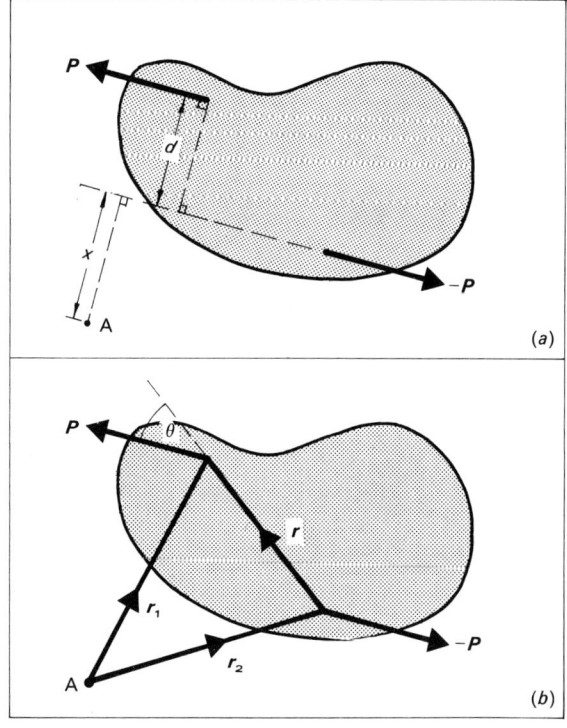

Figure 11-17 The moment about A (or any other axis perpendicular to the page) of the two forces $\mathbf{P}$ acting on the rigid body is anticlockwise and of size dP.

Any system of forces can always be reduced to a single force plus a couple of this type (although in particular cases the force, or the couple, or both, may be zero). For

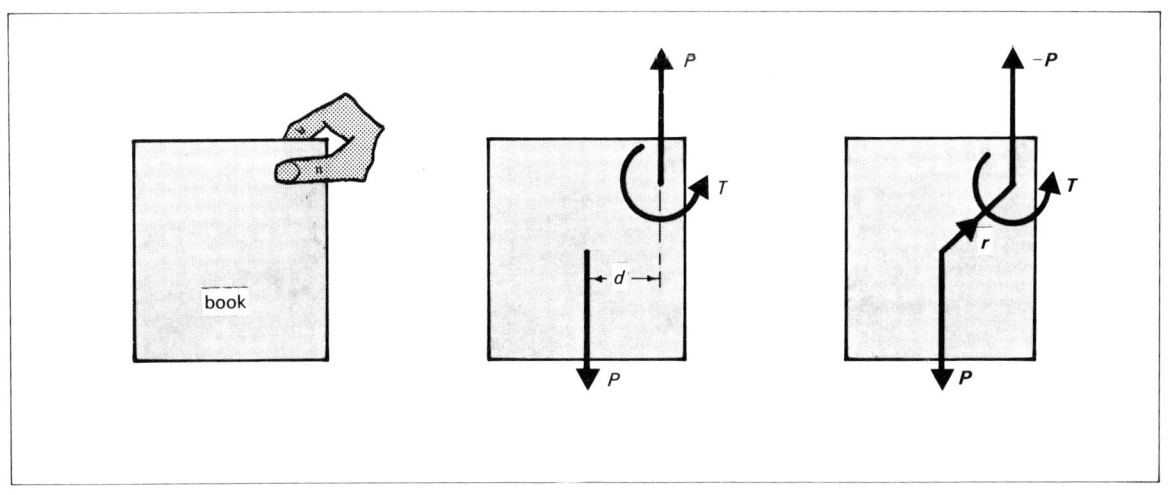

Figure 11-18 A man holds a book. For equilibrium $T = dP$ or, vectorially, $\boldsymbol{T} = \boldsymbol{r} \times \boldsymbol{P}$.

a coplanar system the couple and the force must (as vectors) be perpendicular, and of the statements on page 182, (a) and (b) use the fact that in equilibrium the force must be zero while (c) uses the fact that in equilibrium the couple must be zero.

More generally an action which produces a turning effect only is called a *torque*, T. The translational motion of the centre of mass of a body on which a torque acts will remain unaltered. T is a vector perpendicular to the plane of the turning effect and is in the direction of advance of a right-hand screw which follows the turning effect. T has dimensions $ML^2 T^{-2}$ and the unit N m. For example, vehicle brakes (disc or drum) exert a torque but cannot be represented by a pair of forces. Similarly a man holding a book (as in figure 11-18) exerts a torque as well as an upward force. Other examples of torques include the one which is exerted on the lid of a jar in order to unscrew it and the one which the jar exerts on the lid in trying to prevent the lid being unscrewed. Newton's third law applies to torques: if body A exerts a torque $\boldsymbol{T}$ on body B, then body B exerts a torque $-\boldsymbol{T}$ on body A.

▶ **Example 11-8** An inn-sign, which has a height of 1.6 m and a weight of 300 N, and which may be considered to be uniform, is supported by a rusty hinge at its top edge. It hangs in equilibrium with its plane making an angle of 30° with the vertical. Find the torque exerted by the rusty hinge on the inn-sign.

Figure 11-19 is a free-body diagram for the inn-sign: the hinge must exert a torque T and force P which must act vertically upwards since there are no horizontal forces acting on other parts of the inn-sign. Resolving

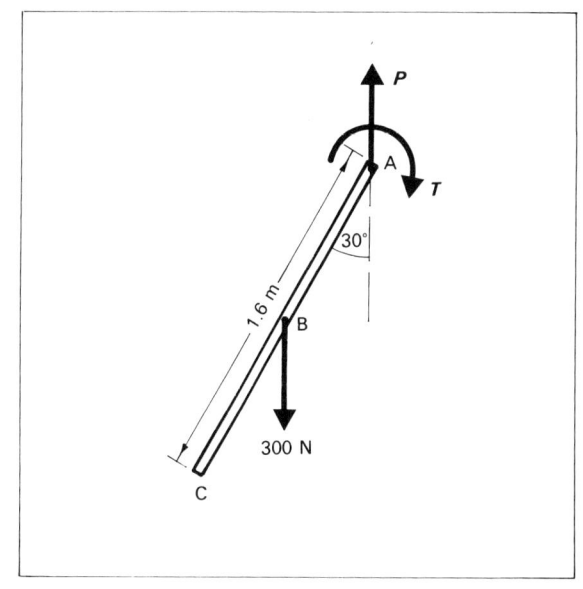

Figure 11-19

vertically,
$$P - 300 \text{ N} = 0,$$
which gives $P = 300$ N.

Taking moments about A:
$$(300 \text{ N})(0.8 \sin 30° \text{ m}) - T = 0,$$
which gives $T = 120$ N m.

(You should take moments about B and C, and see if the results are the same as those obtained above.) ◀

11-6 The beam balance

Although the equal-arm beam or 'chemical' balance is fast losing its importance as the basic laboratory balance its operation illustrates several important principles. In essence (see figure 11-20) it consists of a symmetrical rigid beam and pointer of mass M, the centre of gravity of which is at CG. The beam carries three parallel knife-edges, probably made of synthetic sapphire, symmetrically spaced, and perpendicular to the length of the beam. It can be raised from a held position by lifting the central knife-edge on a horizontal synthetic sapphire block; at the same time the outside knife-edges pick up two scale pans each of mass s. The knife-edges and supports act as accurately located frictionless supports. When the pull of pan A on the beam is equal to the pull of pan B on the beam the beam will be in equilibrium in a horizontal position provided its centre of gravity lies vertically below the central knife-edge. When the beam is in this horizontal position, the pointer is vertical and points to 0 on the scale: then $X_1 = X_2$. The balance is thus a device for comparing forces and is sometimes used directly for this purpose. If the pans contain masses m_1 and m_2, then considering the equilibrium of A we get

$$X_1 = (s+m_1)g,$$

while similarly for B we get

$$X_2 = (s+m_2)g.$$

If the pointer is at 0 on the scale,

$$X_1 = X_2,$$

and so $\quad m_1 g = m_2 g \quad$ or $\quad m_1 = m_2,$

provided g is the same for both masses. The balance can thus be used to compare *masses*, and this is its normal purpose. To achieve a standard set of masses for comparison purposes the standard kilogram can be balanced by two equal masses (as found on the balance), which must thus be 0.5 kg each, and so on. In this discussion the buoyancy forces acting on the masses being compared, that is the Archimedean push of the air on the masses, have been ignored; if the masses are made of the same material then there is no correction to be made.

A balance of the type shown will be *accurate* if (a) the centre of gravity lies vertically below the central knife-edge when the beam is horizontal, (b) the pans are of equal mass, (c) the side knife-edges are equidistant from the centre, and (d) the masses used for the comparisons are true standards. See Exercise 11-29.

Suppose that, when $m_1 = m$ and $m_2 = m + \Delta m$, the beam reaches a new position of equilibrium with the beam at an angle $\Delta\theta$ to the horizontal. The *sensitivity* of the balance is defined as $\Delta\theta/\Delta m$; thus the greater the sensitivity, the larger the angle for which the beam (and therefore the pointer) turns when a mass is added to one scale pan. Taking moments in figure 11-21 about the central knife-edge M we have (assuming that L, M, and N lie in a straight line):

$$Mgh \sin \Delta\theta = (\Delta m) ga \cos \Delta\theta$$

$$\frac{\tan \Delta\theta}{\Delta m} = \frac{a}{Mh},$$

and, approximately, the sensitivity

$$\frac{\Delta\theta}{\Delta m} = \frac{a}{Mh}.$$

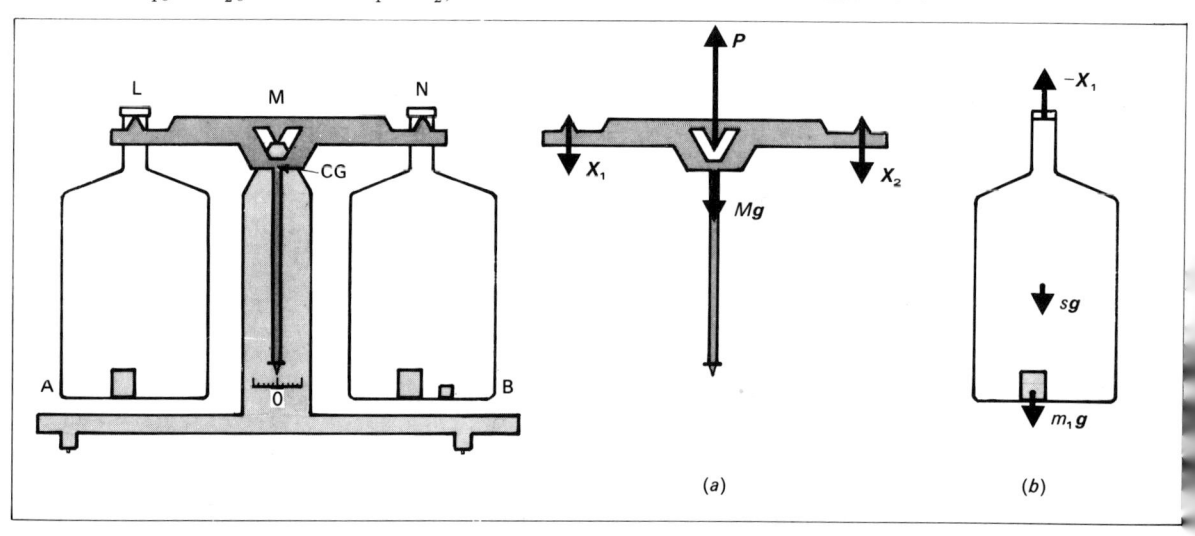

Figure 11-20 An equal-arm balance, and free-body diagrams for (a) the beam plus pointer, and (b) a pan plus mass m_1.

To increase the sensitivity of the balance, M is made as small, and a as large, as is compatible with rigidity and h is made as small as is compatible with the user being able to find a position of horizontal equilibrium quickly—for if h is too small the beam swings very slowly and if it is zero it will balance in any position with $m_1 = m_2$ as it will then be in neutral equilibrium. Another factor which affects the period of swing is the value of g: the period of swing increases as g decreases, and tends to ∞ as g tends to zero.

Figure 11-21 A schematic diagram of the beam of a balance when it makes an angle $\Delta\theta$ with its normal position. All the forces in figure 11-20a still act (as shown).

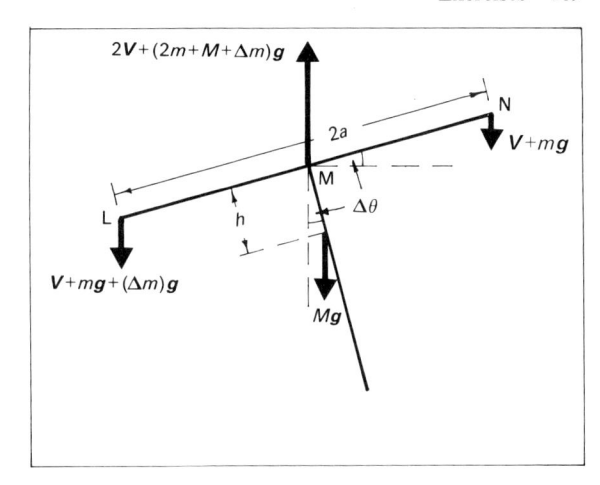

Bibliography

French, A. P. (1971). *Newtonian mechanics.* Nelson. Chapter 4 on forces and equilibrium gives a physicist's view.

Tricker, R. A. R. and Tricker, B. J. K. (1968). *The science of movement.* Mills and Boon. Chapters 3 and 15 discuss the physics of balance.

Quadling, D. A. and Ramsay, A. R. D. (1959). *Elementary mechanics.* Bell. These two volumes contain the traditional approach of the applied mathematician.

16 mm film. 'Gravity.' Gateway. A very elementary film showing the importance of the position of the centre of gravity in vehicle design.

Exercises

Data (to be used unless otherwise directed):

$g = 10 \text{ m s}^{-2} = 10 \text{ N kg}^{-1}$.

Use the convention that anticlockwise moments are positive.

11-1 Figure 11-22 shows forces of 4.0 N, 5.0 N, and 8.0 N on a rectangular coordinate framework of unit one metre. Find the moments of
 (a) the 4.0 N force about the points $(0,0)$, $(0,4)$, $(4,0)$
 (b) the 5.0 N force about the points $(0,0)$, $(2,1)$, $(4,3)$
 (c) the 8.0 N force about the points $(1,2)$, $(3,2)$, $(5,5)$. ●

11-2 A plank AB of length 4.0 m and weight 160 N lies on horizontal ground. Its centre of gravity is 1.5 m from the end A. If a man lifts it slowly at A, what vertical force must he exert? What vertical force must he exert if he lifts it at B? ●

11-3 A wooden bench is horizontal and has a length of 2.0 m and two legs each 0.50 m from an end. The weight of the bench is 100 N, and can be considered to act at the centre of the

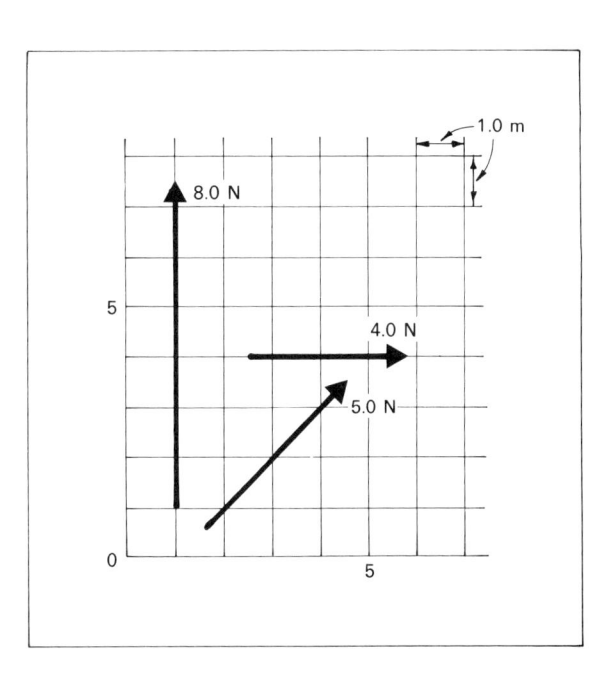

Figure 11-22

11 Rigid bodies in equilibrium

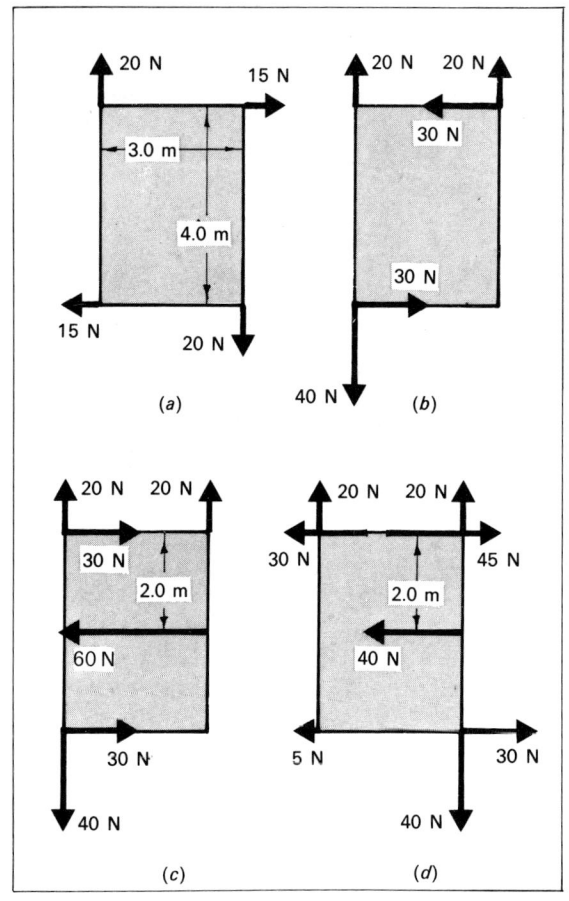

Figure 11-23

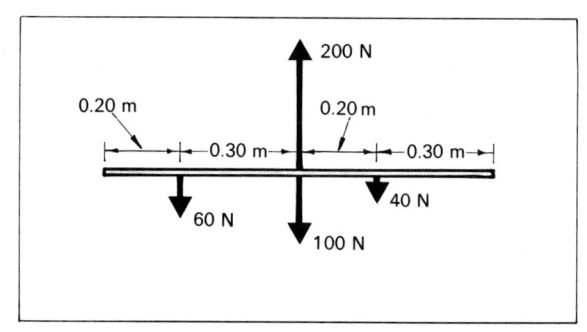

Figure 11-24

bench. What is the weight of the heaviest person who can sit 0.25 m from one end of the bench, without it being upset? •

11-4 Figure 11-23 shows a rectangular lamina under the action of four sets of forces of various sizes. The lamina measures 4.0 m by 3.0 m. Which of the laminae are in equilibrium? •

11-5 A horizontal metre rule AB has a weight of 1.0 N. The only other force acting on it is a force of 1.0 N which acts vertically upwards 0.10 m from B. Find the sum of the moments of the forces about
 (a) A
 (b) a point on the rod 0.10 m from A and
 (c) a point 0.10 m from A on BA produced. •

11-6 A man holds a metre rule of weight 1.0 N horizontal at a point which is 0.30 m from the centre. Find (a) the force (b) the torque exerted by the man on the rule. •

11-7 Figure 11-24 shows a uniform plank under the action of several forces. Is it in equilibrium? If not, what must be added to the system of forces to produce equilibrium? •

11-8 A uniform beam of length 3.0 m and weight 200 N is fixed at one end to a wall so that it projects horizontally without any other support. Find (a) the force (b) the torque exerted by the wall on the beam. •

11-9 A rectangle and an isosceles triangle are cut out of a sheet of wood. The rectangle measures 1.8 m by 1.5 m, and the triangle has a base of 1.5 m and a height of 1.8 m. The base of the triangle is fixed to one of the shorter sides of the rectangle so that the composite figure has an axis of symmetry. Taking the surface density of the wood as 8.0 kg m^{-2}, find the resultant of the weights of the two parts and the points on the axis of symmetry through which it acts. Hence find the centre of gravity of the composite figure. •

11-10 Repeat Exercise 11-9 for a composite figure consisting of a rectangle (3.0 m × 2.0 m) surmounted by a semicircular lamina (radius 1.0 m) fixed to the shorter side of the rectangle. The wood has the same surface density as before •

11-11 Figure 11-25 shows a force F which acts at a point P. Show that the moment of the force about O is $Fd \sin(\theta - \phi)$. The resolved parts of F are F_1 and F_2 in the directions shown: find the sum of the moments of these resolved parts $F \sin \theta$

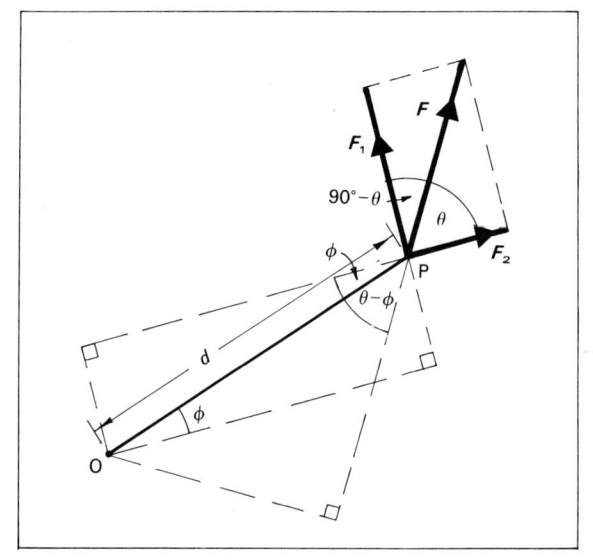

Figure 11-25

and $F\cos\theta$ respectively. Use the trigonometrical identity $\sin(A-B) = \sin A \cos B - \cos A \sin B$ to show that the moment of F is equal to the sum of the moments of its resolved parts. (This is the result which was stated without proof in Section 11-2.)

11-12 Find the values of X and Y in Example 11-7. ●

11-13 The cubical box shown in figure 11-26 has a side of 1.0 m and a weight of 200 N. It rests on a rough horizontal surface and is to be made to pivot about the edge passing through O by a horizontal push applied at A, B, or C. Find the size of the force required at each point.

If the push were not necessarily horizontal, and was to have as small a value as possible, at which point would you apply it, and in what direction? What would be its size? ●

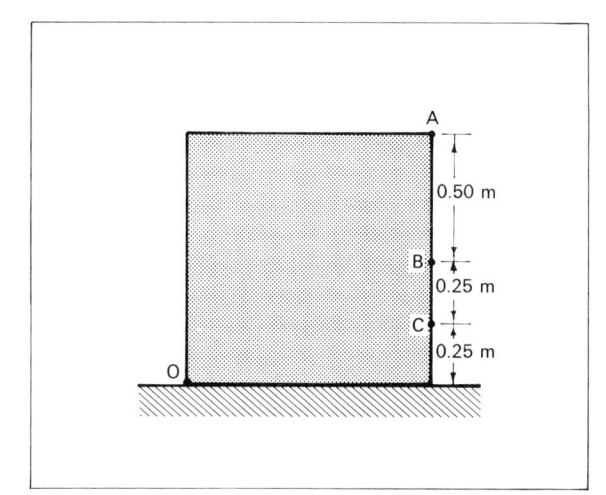

Figure 11-26

11-14 How would you set about designing
(a) a wheelbarrow
(b) nutcrackers of the conventional type (two arms pivoted at one end)?

11-15 A ladder, which may be considered to be uniform, of weight 100 N, rests with its top end against a frictionless wall, and its bottom end on rough horizontal ground. The ladder makes an angle of 53° with the horizontal. Find the forces exerted on the ladder by (a) the wall (b) the ground. ●

11-16 A door-closing mechanism is such that it exerts a constant torque of 60 N m on a door. The door is 1.2 m wide. If a man opens it slowly by pushing horizontally, perpendicular to the door, at its edge, what is the size of the force he must exert? If he continues to push in the same direction (that is, perpendicular to the original position of the door) what is the size of the force when the door has turned through 60°? ●

11-17 A uniform beam AB of length 2.0 m and weight 150 N is freely hinged to a vertical wall at A, and to B is attached a wire which keeps the beam in equilibrium at an angle of 37° to the horizontal, B being higher than A. The other end of the wire is fixed to the wall at a distance of 2.0 m above A. Find the force exerted on the beam by (a) the wire (b) the wall. ●

11-18 The two legs of a step-ladder are the same length (2.0 m) and have weights of 200 N and 80 N respectively. Find the vertical force exerted by the ground on each leg, when the feet are 1.0 m apart. Would the answers be different if the feet were 0.50 m apart? ●

11-19 A uniform plank of weight 300 N and length 4.0 m rests in equilibrium with one end on rough horizontal ground and supported at a distance of 1.0 m from the other end by a vertical post of height 0.8 m with a frictionless top. Find the force exerted on the plank by (a) the post (b) the ground. Could the problem have been solved if the top of the post had been rough? ●

11-20 A step-ladder consists of two equal legs each of length 2.0 m and weight 150 N. There is no cord to help to keep the legs together, and it rests with its legs making an angle of 53° with the horizontal on a rough horizontal floor. What is the size of the horizontal force which the ground must exert on each leg? What is the least possible value of the coefficient of static friction? ●

11-21 Refer to Exercise 11-20. A boy of weight 250 N begins to climb slowly up one side of the step-ladder, while it still makes an angle of 53° with the horizontal. Which leg is likely to slip first? If the coefficient of static friction is 0.50, how far up the ladder can he climb? ●

11-22 A uniform square trapdoor (of side l) has weight W. It is hinged at one side, and raised by a rope attached to the opposite side and passed over a frictionless pulley which is a distance l vertically above the hinge. Find the pull of the rope if the trapdoor is in equilibrium and makes an angle θ with the horizontal. ●

11-23 A ball of radius 30 mm is attached by a thread of length 20 mm to a point on a vertical frictionless wall. The ball rests in equilibrium, touching the wall. If the weight of the ball is 8.0 N, find the push of the wall on the ball, and the pull of the thread on the ball. ●

11-24 Figure 11-27a shows a mass of 4.0 kg suspended by a massless cord from a ceiling; another cord exerts a horizontal force of 30 N on it. Figure 11-27b is the free-body diagram for the mass. Clearly (since $T\cos\theta = 40$ N and $T\sin\theta = 30$ N), $T = 50$ N and $\theta = 37°$, and we can see in figure 11-27c that the vectors representing the forces form the sides of a (necessarily closed) triangle. Will it always be true that, when a body is in equilibrium (under the action of three or more forces), the vectors representing the forces acting on it will form a closed figure? What is the size of the resultant of such forces? Does the closing of the figure illustrate this result? Will *all* the vectors always point in the same sense round such a figure?

(This result is commonly known as the *principle of the triangle of forces*, although it can be applied to bodies on which more than three forces act, when the figure would of course not be a triangle. Its usefulness is similar to the usefulness of the fact that the lines of action of three forces which maintain a body in equilibrium are concurrent; that is, it may provide some information more quickly than the straightforward techniques of resolving and moment-taking. It does not provide *additional* information. The principle could be used in Examples 11-2, 11-3, and 11-5 and in Exercises 11-15, 11-17, 11-22, and 11-23.)

11 Rigid bodies in equilibrium

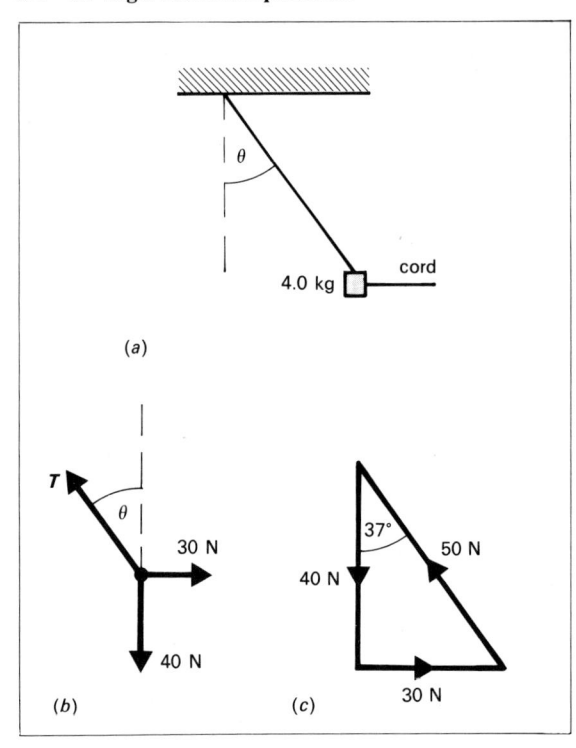

Figure 11-27

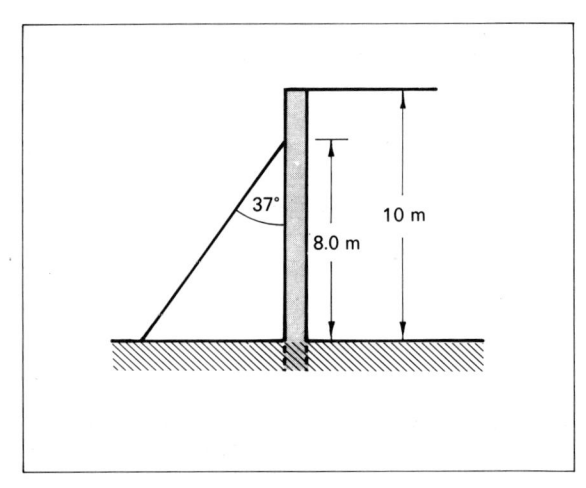

(a) [Diagram showing a 4.0 kg mass suspended from ceiling by a rope at angle θ, with a horizontal cord attached]

(b) [Force diagram with T at angle θ, 30 N horizontal, 40 N downward, 40 N vertical]

(c) [Triangle force diagram with 37° angle, 40 N, 50 N, 30 N]

Figure 11-28
[Diagram of vertical post with wire at 37° attached 8.0 m from ground, and horizontal wire at 10 m]

11-25 Figure 11-28 shows a vertical post of weight 8000 N which is sunk into the ground. A horizontal wire exerts a force of 500 N at its top, which is 10 m above the ground, and another wire, which makes an angle of 53° with the horizontal, and is attached at a point 8.0 m from the ground, exerts a force of 700 N. Find the vertical and horizontal components of the force exerted by the ground on the post, and the torque exerted by the ground on the post. ●

11-26 A rope of mass 12 kg is hung between two posts, the points of attachment being at the same level so that the rope hangs symmetrically. At each point of attachment the tangent to the rope makes an angle of 37° with the horizontal. Find the tension in the rope at its lowest point. ●

11-27 In Section 11-6 it is stated that 'the beam will be in equilibrium in a horizontal position provided that the centre of gravity lies vertically *below* the central knife-edge'. Could the beam be in equilibrium with the centre of gravity vertically *above* the central knife-edge? Comment on your answer.

11-28 Figure 11-29 is a diagram of the beam (of mass M) of a beam balance in which the knife-edges L, M, and N are *not* collinear. The central knife-edge M is a distance p above the line LN. Each arm has a length a, and the centre of gravity of the beam is a distance h below the line LN. Find the sensitivity $\Delta\theta/\Delta m$ of the balance when the scale pans have a mass s and contain a mass m to one of which is added a mass Δm.

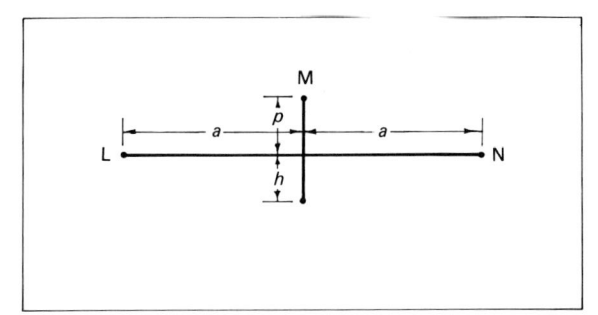

Figure 11-29
[Diagram of beam balance with knife-edges L, M, N; M above line LN by distance p, centre of gravity distance h below, arms of length a on each side]

11-29 Suppose that a certain beam balance has unequal arms (the left-hand arm and right-hand arm having lengths a_1 and a_2 respectively) and it is to be used to find the mass of an object. If the object (mass x) be placed on the left-hand side, a mass m_1 is needed for balance. If the object is placed on the right-hand side, a mass m_2 is needed for balance. Determine x in terms of m_1 and m_2. ●

12 The dynamics of rigid bodies

12-1 Introduction	193	12-6 The work done by a torque	201
12-2 Angular kinetic energy	194	12-7 Summary	202
12-3 Moment of inertia	196	Bibliography	204
12-4 Torque and angular acceleration	198	Exercises	204
12-5 Toppling	200		

12-1 Introduction

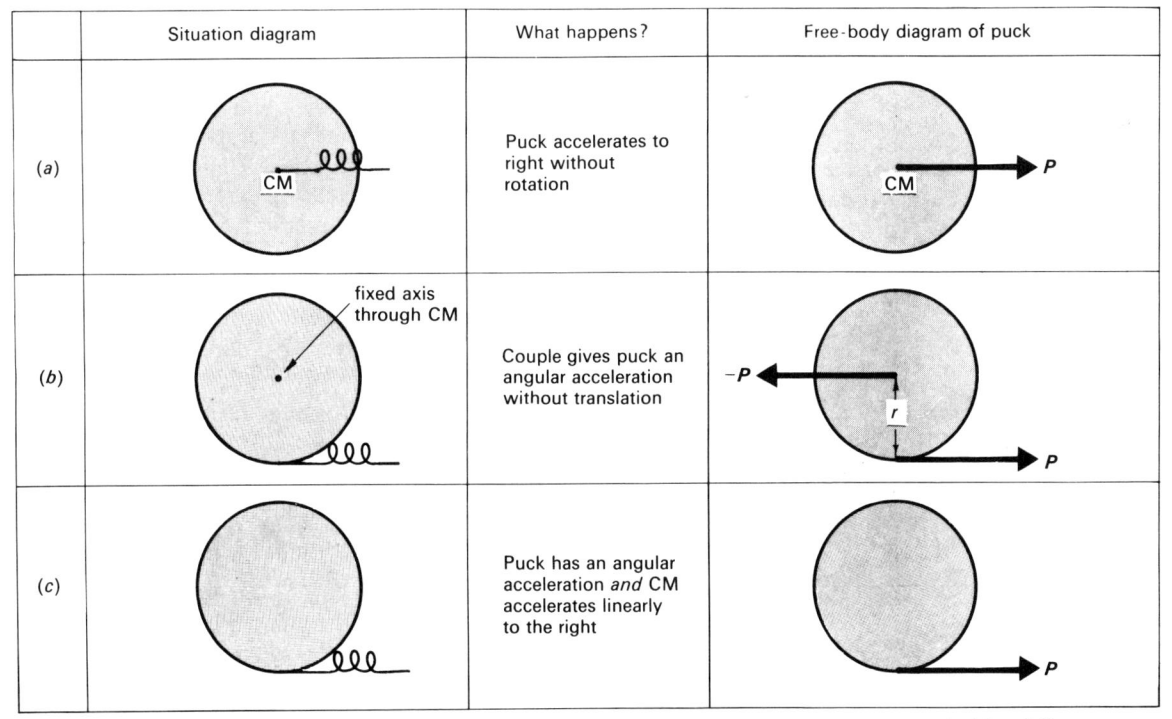

	Situation diagram	What happens?	Free-body diagram of puck
(a)	CM	Puck accelerates to right without rotation	CM → P
(b)	fixed axis through CM	Couple gives puck an angular acceleration without translation	−P ← ↕r → P
(c)		Puck has an angular acceleration *and* CM accelerates linearly to the right	→ P

Figure 12-1 The motion of a puck. Experiment (c) shows that the puck's motion is the sum of that shown in (a) and (b).

194 12 The dynamics of rigid bodies

Consider three disc-shaped pucks which are supported on a frictionless horizontal surface. Suppose each puck is acted on by a constant horizontal force, the pull of a spring P as shown in figure 12-1. If the pucks in (a) and (c) are free to move in a horizontal plane and the puck in (b) is free to rotate about a fixed axis through its centre of mass, CM, what happens to them? Figure 12-1 shows that the pucks in (a) and (b) behave as we would expect, the free-body diagrams which show the external horizontal forces clearly indicating why this happens. The result in (c) may not be so much expected and the free-body diagram does not perhaps help us very much. If however we imagine two opposite forces parallel to P and equal in size to P acting through the centre of mass (figure 12-12), then, while they do not themselves alter the motion in any way, they help considerably in explaining it. The puck is now clearly acted on by a couple of torque rP (equal to the turning effect of P about the centre of mass), which will simply rotate it, and a force P acting at the centre of mass, which will produce a linear acceleration. This is a very important result for it enables us to completely separate the translational and rotational motions of free rigid bodies; now if we meet (c) of figure 12-1, we can replace it by (a) and (b) and treat them separately.

The quantities used in describing angular motion are angular displacement θ, angular velocity ω, and angular acceleration α. For the definitions of these quantities and a summary of techniques of how to measure ω the reader should refer to Sections 4-1, 4-2, and 4-3.

12-2 Angular kinetic energy

Suppose a force does work in increasing the angular velocity of a rigid body about a fixed axis. With the apparatus shown in figure 12-3, a constant horizontal force F can be exerted on the disc by pulling the spring balance (which should be one calibrated for horizontal use). The disc starts from rest. The work done on the disc is found by measuring the distance x moved by F and the final angular velocity can be deduced from the tape if r_2 is known. Several conclusions can be drawn from a series of such experiments, using different values of r, and different values of F and x. Some of them are:

(a) The size of the final angular velocity ω depends on the work done, Fx, and is independent of either F or r taken separately.

(b) The relation between ω and the product Fx is not linear: a graph of $\omega^2/\mathrm{rad}^2\,\mathrm{s}^{-2}$ against Fx/Nm, however, is a straight line (see figure 12-4). (If the disc is rotating at ω_0 at the start of the measured part of the tape, that is where $x=0$, the line crosses the vertical axis at $\omega^2 = \omega_0^2$.) As the

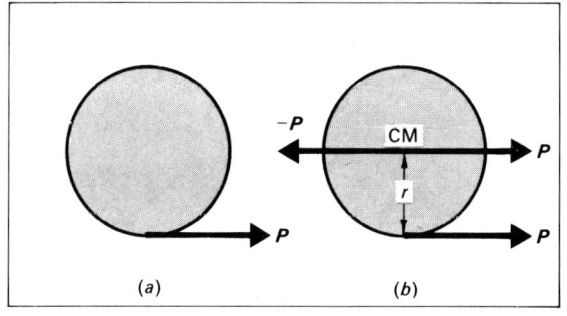

Figure 12-2 The system of forces in (a) is equivalent to that in (b) in all respects.

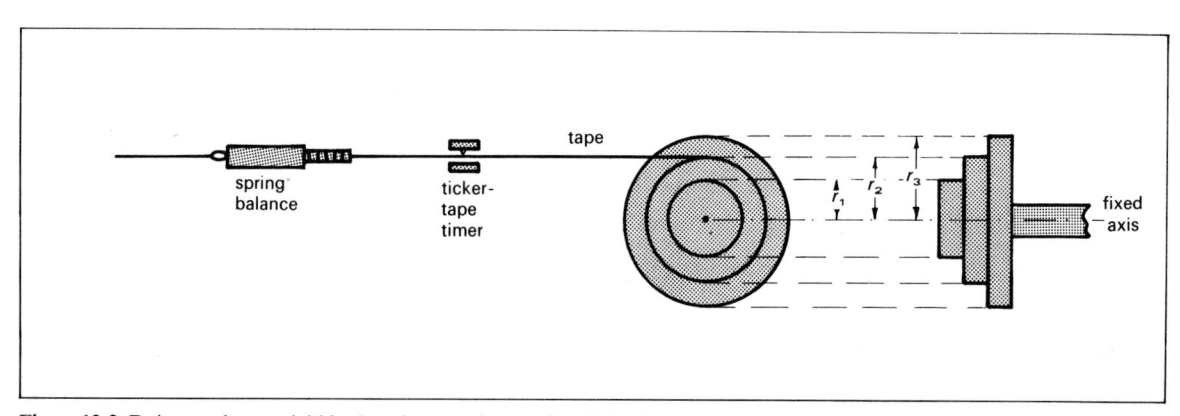

Figure 12-3 Doing work on a rigid body to increase its rotational kinetic energy.

12-2 Angular kinetic energy

The experiment as described is a rough one. To improve it the disc-shaped body could be suspended on a gas layer, or magnetically, thus reducing friction at the axis, and the constant force F could be produced by suspending a small mass on the end of a string passing over a pulley. To eliminate the drag of the ticker-tape, stroboscopic photography could be used to measure ω. The real purpose of the experiment is, however, not to measure I but to show that I is a fixed quantity for a rigid body rotating about a fixed axis; I is called the *moment of inertia* of the body.

Does I have any relation to other known properties of the body, for instance the inertia, or mass, of the body? Consider a rigid body of mass $m(=\sum m_i)$ rotating about a fixed axis perpendicular to the page through O (see figure 12-5). When the angular velocity of the body is ω then a line drawn from the axis to every particle of it has this angular velocity (this is a basic property of a rigid body)—but each particle of the body has a different velocity. For example, the speed v_1 of a particle of mass m_1 is given by $v_1 = r_1 \omega$ and its kinetic energy

$$T_1 = \tfrac{1}{2} m_1 v_1^2$$
$$= \tfrac{1}{2} m_1 r_1^2 \omega^2.$$

Thus the total kinetic energy of the body about the axis through O is

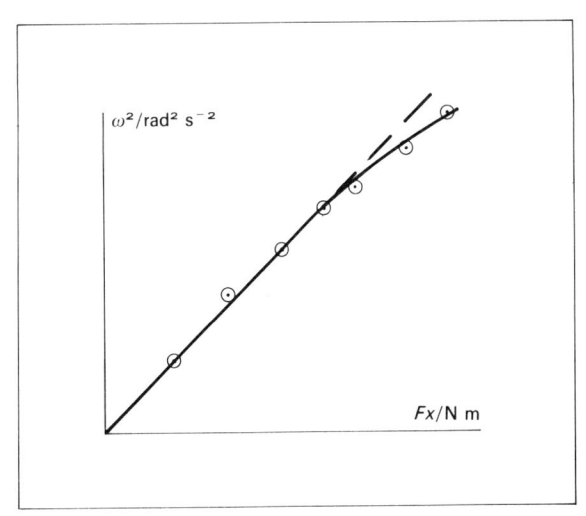

$$T = \sum T_i = \tfrac{1}{2} m_1 r_1^2 \omega^2 + \tfrac{1}{2} m_2 r_2^2 \omega^2 + \cdots + \tfrac{1}{2} m_n r_n^2 \omega^2,$$
$$= \tfrac{1}{2}(m_1 r_1^2 + m_2 r_2^2 + \cdots + m_n r_n^2)\omega^2,$$
$$= \tfrac{1}{2}\left(\sum_1^n m_i r_i^2\right)\omega^2.$$

Figure 12-4 A constant force F increases the angular velocity of a rigid body about a fixed axis doing work Fx. For large values of ω the graph is non-linear owing to friction.

increase in kinetic energy of the disc is equal to the total work done on it by external forces and no force other than F does work in this case (assuming friction forces are negligible):

rotational kinetic energy of the disc

$$\propto \omega^2$$

$$T = \text{constant} \times \omega^2$$

or, by analogy with $\tfrac{1}{2} mv^2$,

$$T = \tfrac{1}{2} I \omega^2. \qquad [12\text{-}1]$$

The constant I can be deduced from the graph,

for $$I = \frac{2T}{\omega^2}$$

and $$T = Fx,$$

so that $$I = 2/(\text{slope of graph}).$$

Suppose, for example, that the graph passes through the origin and through the point $Fx = 0.50\,\text{N m}$ and $\omega^2 = 20\,\text{s}^{-2}$,

then $$I = 2 \div \left(\frac{20\,\text{s}^{-2}}{0.50\,\text{N m}}\right)$$

$$= 0.05\,\text{N m s}^2$$

$$= 0.05\,\text{kg m}^2$$

This constant I is a property of the body.

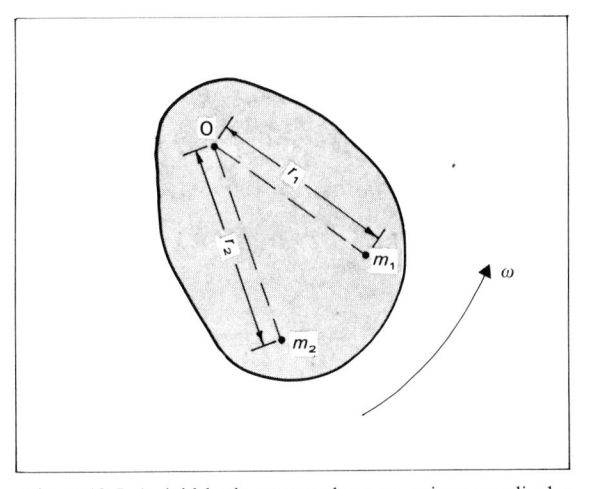

Figure 12-5 A rigid body rotates about an axis perpendicular to the page through O.

12 The dynamics of rigid bodies

But we know that

$$T = \tfrac{1}{2}I\omega^2$$

from equation 12-1, so that our constant I is given by

$$I = \sum m_i r_i^2,$$

and this result verifies the fact that I is a property of the body. The unit of I is the kg m^2 and $[I] = ML^2$.

To summarize the ideas of this section we can say that the work–energy equation for a rigid body of moment of inertia I rotating about a fixed axis is

$$\tfrac{1}{2}I\omega^2 - \tfrac{1}{2}I\omega_0^2 = \sum(\text{work done by external torques on body}).$$

▶ **Example 12-1** A thread, to which is tied a mass of 0.020 kg, is wrapped round the axle of a flywheel. The radius of the axle is 20 mm, and initially it is rotating at 4.0 rad s^{-1} and the mass is rising vertically. After the mass has risen 1.50 m the angular velocity of the flywheel has fallen to 2.0 rad s^{-1}. Find its moment of inertia. Take $g = 10$ N kg^{-1}.

The gain of potential energy of the mass is equal to the loss of kinetic energy of the flywheel and of the mass:

the gain in potential energy of the mass

$$= (0.020\,\text{kg})(10\,\text{N kg}^{-1})(1.50\,\text{m})$$
$$= 0.30\,\text{J}.$$

If the moment of inertia of the flywheel is I, the loss of kinetic energy of the flywheel is

$$\tfrac{1}{2}I[(4\,\text{rad s}^{-1})^2 - (2\,\text{rad s}^{-1})^2]$$

and the loss of kinetic energy of the mass is

$$\tfrac{1}{2}(0.020\,\text{kg})[(0.08\,\text{m s}^{-1})^2 - (0.04\,\text{m s}^{-1})^2],$$

but this second quantity ($=0.00048$ J) is so small in comparison with the other terms that we may safely neglect it. Therefore

$$0.30\,\text{J} = 6I\,\text{s}^{-2}$$
$$I = 0.05\,\text{kg m}^2. \quad \blacktriangleleft$$

When the axis of rotation is not fixed we can consider the motion as translation *of* the centre of mass (CM) together with rotation *about* the centre of mass. Thus the total kinetic energy of a rigid body can be expressed as

$$T = \tfrac{1}{2}mv_{CM}^2 + \tfrac{1}{2}I_{CM}\omega^2, \qquad [12\text{-}2]$$

and this applies to even the most complicated situations. This equation is a special case of the discussion of Section 9-5. An observer, who measures the speed of the centre of mass as v_{CM}, sees the particles of the body moving in complex paths and could sum the individual kinetic energies to be T'. An observer moving with the centre of mass would find the kinetic energy of the particles of the body to be $T'_1 = \sum \tfrac{1}{2}m_i r_i^2 \omega^2 = \tfrac{1}{2}I\omega^2$. The relation on page 146 ($T = T' + \tfrac{1}{2}mv_{CM}^2$) now gives $T = \tfrac{1}{2}mv_{CM}^2 + \tfrac{1}{2}I\omega^2$ as above.

▶ **Example 12-2** A bicycle wheel has a mass of 2.0 kg, a moment of inertia of 0.18 kg m^2, and a radius of 0.30 m. What is the kinetic energy when it is rolling along the ground at a speed of 5.0 m s^{-1}?

Its angular velocity $= \dfrac{5.0\,\text{m s}^{-1}}{0.30\,\text{m}} = 16.7\,\text{rad s}^{-1}.$

Using

$$T = \tfrac{1}{2}I_{CM}\omega^2 + \tfrac{1}{2}mv_{CM}^2 \quad \text{we have}$$

$$T = \tfrac{1}{2}(0.18\,\text{kg m}^2)(16.7\,\text{rad s}^{-1})^2 + \tfrac{1}{2}(2.0\,\text{kg})(5.0\,\text{m s}^{-1})^2$$
$$= 50\,\text{J},$$

so that the kinetic energy of the wheel is 50 J. ◀

12-3 Moment of inertia

In rotational motion the moment of inertia of a body is the equivalent of mass in linear motion. I, however, depends upon the axis of rotation we choose. To take a simple example to illustrate this, consider the situations of figure 12-6. Which arrangement would be the easiest to bring to rest? If all the angular velocities are the same, clearly it would be arrangement (c); thus we can say that this has the lowest moment of inertia.

I can be measured experimentally using the work–energy equation as in the previous section but a more versatile technique is to use collision processes similar in principle to those we have already used to measure mass and these are discussed in Section 13-5. We can *calculate* $\sum_1^n m_i r_i^2 = \int r^2\,dm$, but only if the body has a suitable degree of symmetry unless laborious numerical techniques are used. Consider (figure 12-7) a solid ring of mass m and radius a which is rotating about an axis perpendicular to its plane through its centre of mass. If we imagine the ring to be split up into elements each of mass Δm then

$$I_{CM} = \sum_1^n m_i r_i^2 = \sum(\Delta m)a^2$$
$$= a^2 \sum \Delta m = ma^2, \quad \text{as} \quad \sum \Delta m = m.$$

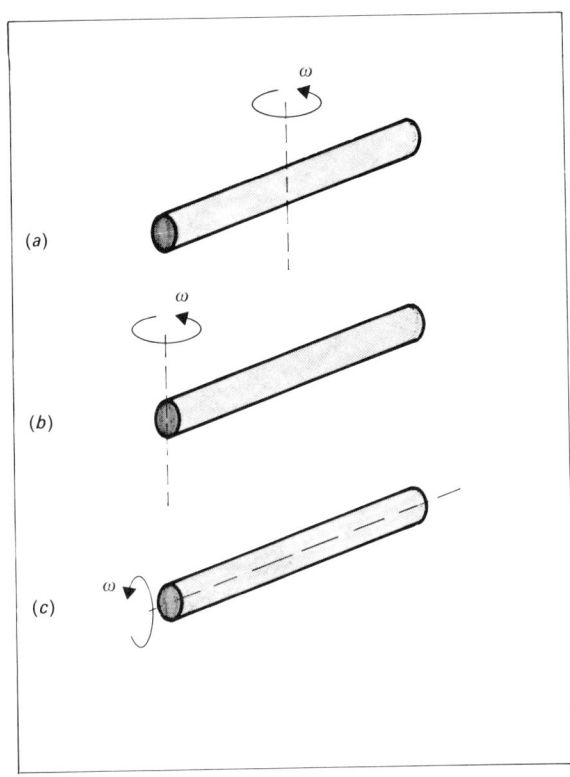

Figure 12-6 Which arrangement has the greatest rotational kinetic energy? As $T = \frac{1}{2}I\omega^2$ it will also be the one in which the bar has the greatest I.

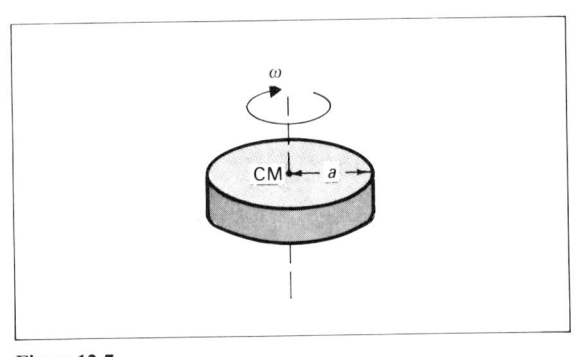

Figure 12-7

In this case then, $I_{CM} = ma^2$, the calculation being simple because the ring possesses a high degree of radial symmetry about the chosen axis.

Figure 12-8 gives the values for the moment of inertia of other common bodies about axes through their centres of mass. The reader should consult mathematical texts for proofs. In each case the mass of the body is m, and the moment of inertia is that about the axis OO'.

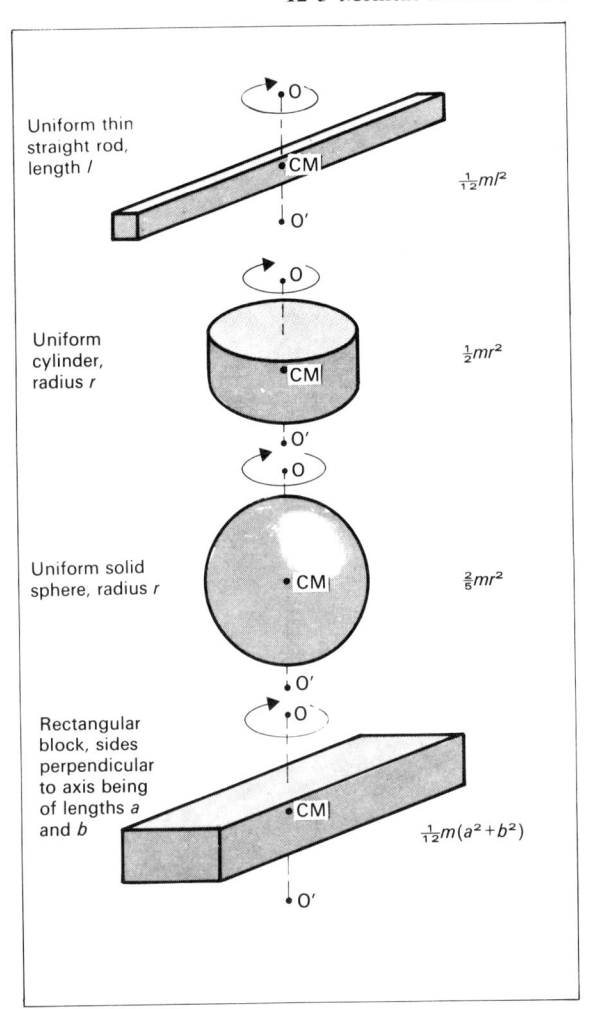

Uniform thin straight rod, length l	$\frac{1}{12}ml^2$
Uniform cylinder, radius r	$\frac{1}{2}mr^2$
Uniform solid sphere, radius r	$\frac{2}{5}mr^2$
Rectangular block, sides perpendicular to axis being of lengths a and b	$\frac{1}{12}m(a^2+b^2)$

Figure 12-8 Some useful expressions for moment of inertia I about axes passing through centres of mass.

For each case in figure 12-8 the moment of inertia could be expressed in the form $I = mk^2$, for example for a sphere $k^2 = 2r^2/5$ and thus $k = (2/5)^{1/2}r$. k is called the *radius of gyration* of the body. Its physical significance is that if all the mass of the body were placed at a distance k from the axis the moment of inertia would be unchanged. It is common to quote values of k rather than values of I.

If we want to know the moment of inertia I of a rigid body about a fixed axis not through its centre of mass (CM), and we know the moment of inertia I_{CM} of the body about a parallel axis through the centre of mass, then

$$I = I_{CM} + mh^2, \qquad [12\text{-}3]$$

where h is the distance between the parallel axes and m

198 12 The dynamics of rigid bodies

is the mass of the body. This is called the *parallel axis theorem*: its proof is left as an exercise for the reader—see Exercise 12-12. As h^2 cannot be negative, this also tells us that, of several parallel axes, that with the minimum moment of inertia will pass through the centre of mass.

There is also the so-called *lamina theorem* (or *perpendicular axis theorem*) for moments of inertia. The use of this is discussed in any textbook on applied mathematics.

▶ **Example 12-3** A dumbbell consists of a rod of negligible diameter and of length 1.20 m, and mass 10 kg, and at its ends two uniform spheres which have a mass of 45 kg each and a radius of 0.10 m. Find the moment of inertia of the dumbbell about an axis (a) coincident with the axis of the rod (b) passing through the centre of the rod but perpendicular to it. Find also its radius of gyration about these axes.

(a) The dumbbell here consists essentially of two uniform spheres, as the rod of negligible diameter has no moment of inertia about its own axis. From figure 12-8 we see that the moment of inertia about a diameter of a uniform sphere of radius r is given by $2mr^2/5$, and so the total moment of inertia is

$$I = 2 \times \tfrac{2}{5}(45\,\text{kg})(0.10\,\text{m})^2 = 0.36\,\text{kg m}^2.$$

The radius of gyration k is given by $I = mk^2$, so that

$$0.36\,\text{kg m}^2 = (100\,\text{kg})k^2,$$

which gives $k = 0.060\,\text{m}.$

(b) The dumbbell now consists of a rod (for which the moment of inertia is $ml^2/12$) and two spheres, but the axis of rotation is not now through the centre of the spheres. The moment of inertia of each sphere about an axis through its centre is (see above) $0.18\,\text{kg m}^2$, so that about a parallel axis through the centre of the rod (0.70 m away) it is (using the parallel axis theorem) given by

$$I = 0.18\,\text{kg m}^2 + (45\,\text{kg})(0.70\,\text{m})^2$$
$$= 22.1\,\text{kg m}^2.$$

So for the two spheres

$$I = 44.2\,\text{kg m}^2.$$

The moment of inertia of the rod is given by

$$I = \tfrac{1}{12}(10\,\text{kg})(1.20\,\text{m})^2$$
$$= 1.2\,\text{kg m}^2,$$

so that the total moment of inertia about this axis is $45\,\text{kg m}^2$ (to two significant figures).
The radius of gyration k is given by $I = mk^2$, so that

$$45.4\,\text{kg m}^2 = (100\,\text{kg})k^2,$$

which gives $k = 0.67\,\text{m}.$ ◀

12-4 Torque and angular acceleration

Consider a body rotating about an axis through O—see figure 12-9. Let us consider only those external forces which lie in planes perpendicular to the axis of rotation. If they do not pass through O they will alter the angular velocity of the body, giving it an angular acceleration α. Internal forces between the particles of the body will, according to Newton's third law, be equal in size and opposite in direction and act along the same line, so that any pair of them will have zero net moment about O. Suppose a force F_1 (the resultant of all internal and any external forces) acts on a particle of the body of mass m_1. F_1 can be resolved into tangential (X_1) and radial (Y_1) parts, and as m_1 has a tangential acceleration $r_1\alpha$ and a centripetal acceleration $r_1\omega^2$ (see page 57), then by Newton's second law

$$m_1 r_1 \alpha = X_1 \quad \text{and} \quad m_1 r_1 \omega^2 = Y_1.$$

Y_1 exerts no torque about O while that exerted by X_1 is $T_1 = r_1 X_1$, so multiplying each side of $m_1 r_1 \alpha = X_1$ by r_1 we get

$$m_1 r_1^2 \alpha = r_1 X_1 = T_1.$$

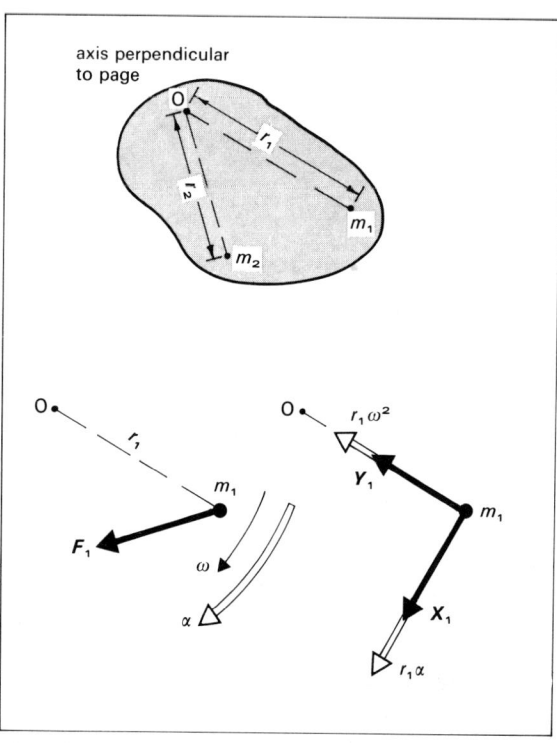

Figure 12-9 A body rotating about O is subject to external forces (not shown). A particle of the body experiences a resultant force F_1 which is the sum of all internal and external forces acting on it.

Similarly we can apply Newton's second law to every other particle of the body and adding we get

$$m_1 r_1^2 \alpha + m_2 r_2^2 \alpha + \cdots + m_n r_n^2 \alpha = T_1 + T_2 + \cdots + T_n$$

$$\sum_1^n (m_i r_i^2) \alpha = \sum_1^n T_i$$

or, for a rigid body, $\qquad I\alpha = \sum T,\qquad$ [12-4]

$\sum T$ being the sum of the torques of all the *external* forces about the axis through O, the internal torques appearing in pairs as discussed above, and therefore having no effect.

Vectorially, $\qquad \mathbf{r}_1 \times \mathbf{F}_1 = r_1 F_1 \mathbf{n}.$

Equation 12-4 is not a new fundamental relationship but stems directly from Newton's laws of motion; it holds only for rigid bodies. It should be remembered in words: the angular acceleration of a rigid body multiplied by the moment of inertia of the body about a certain axis is equal to the sums of the torques (about that axis) of the external forces.

There is here no question of our hoping to prove by experiments that $I\alpha = \sum T$ (since this is derived from Newton's laws) but we can use the apparatus of figure 12-3 to stress its content. For example we can exert a fixed force on the ticker-tape and vary the moment of the force about the axis by altering r so that we can show that α is proportional to r. Similarly, we can load the turntable with other bodies of calculable moment of inertia and measure how α varies for a fixed accelerating torque.

Equation 12-4 can also be used where a rigid body is rotating about an axis which is not fixed in an inertial frame of reference, provided we use its moment of inertia I_{CM} about an axis through its centre of mass and the sum of the torques about the centre of mass. There is no simple reason for this useful result, it is rather a mathematical fluke and the reader is advised to refer to more advanced books on mechanics for a formal proof.

The equation derived above is the scalar counterpart of the vector relation $I\boldsymbol{\alpha} = \sum \mathbf{T}$. The direction of $\boldsymbol{\alpha}$ is parallel to the axis of rotation and obeys a right-hand rule for its sign (see page 22), while $\mathbf{T}_1 = \mathbf{r}_1 \times \mathbf{F}_1$ and is also parallel to the axis if $\mathbf{F}_1$ is perpendicular to it.

▶ **Example 12-4** A turntable in a children's playground has an external radius of 2.0 m, a moment of inertia of 500 kg m^2, and an angular velocity of 2 rad s^{-1}. A man stops it by applying a tangential force of 100 N at its circumference while running round its outside. The bearings of the turntable exert a frictional torque of 50 N m. Find (*a*) the angular acceleration of the turntable, and (*b*) the distance he has to run.

(*a*) Taking the sense of its rotation to be positive and using $I\alpha = \sum T$ we have

$$(500 \text{ kg m}^2) \alpha = -50 \text{ N m} - (100 \text{ N})(2.0 \text{ m})$$

$$\Rightarrow \alpha = -0.5 \text{ rad s}^{-2}.$$

(*b*) The time taken for the turntable to stop

$$= \frac{2.0 \text{ rad s}^{-1}}{0.5 \text{ rad s}^{-2}} = 4.0 \text{ s}.$$

The average angular velocity = 1.0 rad s^{-1}, so that the turntable turns through 4.0 radians, and the man runs a distance of (4.0 rad)(2.0 m) = 8.0 m. ◀

▶ **Example 12-5** A uniform disc of mass 6.0 kg and radius 0.10 m is made to roll without slipping along a horizontal surface by means of a horizontal force of 80 N which is applied to its centre. Find the acceleration of the disc and the frictional force exerted by the surface on the disc. Take $g = 10 \text{ N kg}^{-1}$.

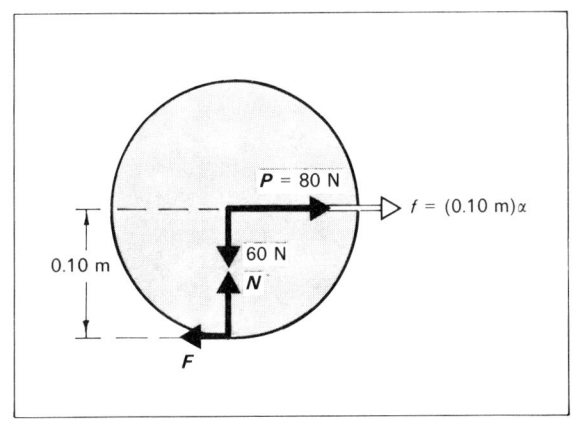

Figure 12-10

Figure 12-10 is a free-body diagram for the disc: if its angular acceleration is α, its linear acceleration (since it does not slip) is (0.10 m) α. Let the frictional force be F. Applying Newton's second law for linear motion:

$$80 \text{ N} - F = (6.0 \text{ kg})(0.10 \text{ m}) \alpha.$$

Applying Newton's second law for rotational motion, about the centre of mass:

$$(0.10 \text{ m}) F = \tfrac{1}{2}(6.0 \text{ kg})(0.10 \text{ m})^2 \alpha.$$

Dividing the second equation by (0.10 m) and adding the result to the first equation we have

$$80 \text{ N} = (0.90 \text{ kg m}) \alpha$$

which gives $\qquad \alpha = 89 \text{ rad s}^{-2},$

and $\qquad F = 27 \text{ N}.\qquad$ ◀

12-5 Toppling

There are many common situations in which rigid bodies topple over, or begin to rotate, as in figure 12-11, where the box will topple if the acceleration of the truck is too great. Considering the free-body diagram of the box, Newton's second law gives

vertically $\quad m(0) = N - mg,$

horizontally $\quad ma = F,$

which gives
$$\frac{F}{N} = \frac{a}{g}. \qquad [12\text{-}5]$$

We can also treat the forces as causing the body to rotate about the centre of mass. If the moment of inertia of the box about an axis through the centre of mass and perpendicular to the page is I_{CM}, then as the angular acceleration of the box about the axis is zero before it topples, we have from Newton's second law for rotation

$$I_{CM}(0) = Nx - Fh$$

$$\frac{F}{N} = \frac{x}{h}. \qquad [12\text{-}6]$$

Combining equations 12-5 and 12-6,

$$\frac{x}{h} = \frac{a}{g},$$

$$\Rightarrow x = \frac{ah}{g},$$

that is, the normal contact push of the truck on the box, N, acts on a line $x = ah/g$ to the left of the centre of mass. As this is only possible if $x \leqslant l$ (for otherwise N will lie outside the box, which is impossible) then the box will *not* topple; that is α will be zero, only if

$$\frac{ah}{g} \leqslant l,$$

that is
$$a \leqslant \frac{gl}{h}.$$

Thus there is a maximum possible acceleration for the truck if the box is not to topple. For boxes of other shapes, a knowledge of the position of the centre of mass enables a similar calculation to be made.

The box could of course slide before it topples. If it is to slide then the required frictional push F of the truck on the box must be $> \mu_s N$, where μ_s is the coefficient of static friction between the box and the truck. As $ma = F$ then this means the box will slide if

$$ma > \mu_s N$$

$$> \mu_s mg$$

that is if $\quad a > \mu_s g.$

Summarizing, the box will slide if $a > \mu_s g$ and will topple if $a > gl/h$. Which of these occurs first thus depends on the relative sizes of μ_s and l/h.

An observer on the truck (a non-inertial observer) finds Newton's laws inadequate if the box slides (see the discussion on page 48). Similarly, if the box topples the non-inertial observer again must either abandon Newton's laws or invent fictitious forces. To avoid these difficulties we must always set the observer in an inertial frame of

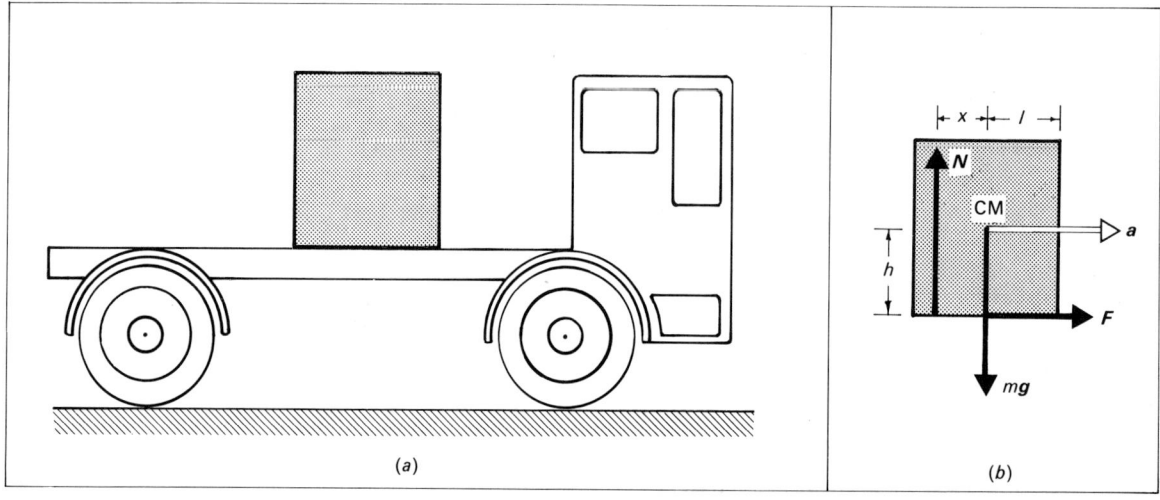

Figure 12-11 A truck carrying a rectangular box accelerates to the right. (b) A free-body diagram of the box.

reference or, for the special case of rotating rigid bodies, at the centre of mass of the body.

A common case of rigid bodies accelerating in such a way as to be in danger of toppling occurs when cars and trains go round corners, thus accelerating centripetally. The method of solution is very similar to that given in the case of the box on the truck.

▶ **Example 12-6** A racing car has a mass of 500 kg and a track of 1.50 m. Its centre of mass is 0.25 m above the ground. Assuming that the frictional forces exerted by the ground on the tyres are great enough to prevent it sliding, find the maximum speed at which it may turn in an arc of radius 100 m on level ground if it is not to topple.

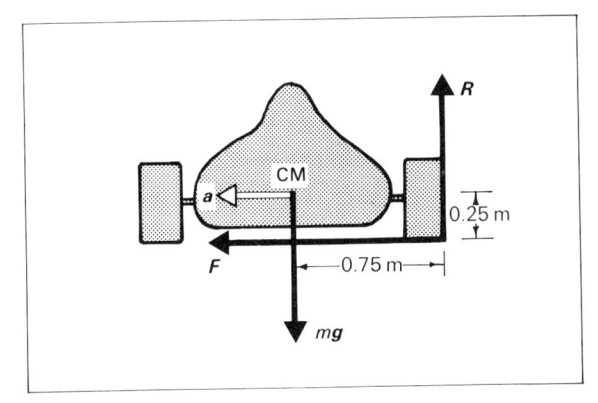

Figure 12-12

Take $g = 10\,\text{m s}^{-2}$. Figure 12-12 is a free-body diagram for the car: if it is just not to topple, the upward push R of the ground must act as shown, that is wholly on the 'outside' wheel. F is the radial resolved part of the frictional force. Applying Newton's second law for translational motion

vertically $\qquad m(0) = R - mg,\qquad$ [12-7]

horizontally $\qquad ma = F.\qquad$ [12-8]

Applying Newton's second law for rotational motion, taking moments about the centre of mass

$$I_{CM}(0) = F(0.25\,\text{m}) - R(0.75\,\text{m}).\qquad [12\text{-}9]$$

From equation 12-7 we have

$$R = 5000\,\text{N},$$

and from equation 12-9 we have

$$F = 15\,000\,\text{N}.$$

so that in equation 12-8 we have

$$(500\,\text{kg})\,a = 15\,000\,\text{N}$$

which gives

$$a = 30\,\text{m s}^{-2}.$$

Since (equation 4-14) $\quad a = \dfrac{v^2}{r}$

then $\qquad v^2 = (30\,\text{m s}^{-2})(100\,\text{m})$

$$v = 55\,\text{m s}^{-1}.$$

This presupposes a very high value for the coefficient of static friction μ_s: the ratio $F/R = 3.0$, so that $\mu_s > 3.0$. In fact, therefore, the car is much more likely to slide than to topple. ◀

12-6 The work done by a torque

A force $\boldsymbol{F}$ acting on a rigid body as in figure 12-13 exerts a torque $T = rF_\perp (= r_\perp F)$ about the axis of rotation through O perpendicular to the page ($\boldsymbol{r} \times \boldsymbol{F} = rF_\perp \boldsymbol{n}$). When the body rotates through an angle $\Delta\theta$, the work done by the force on the body in moving its point of application from P to P′ is ΔW where

$$\Delta W = (\Delta s)F_\perp.$$

As $\qquad \Delta s = r(\Delta\theta),$

then $\qquad \Delta W = rF_\perp \Delta\theta$

that is $\qquad \Delta W = T\Delta\theta.$

The unit of ΔW is the N m rad = N m = J, as expected (the radian being a dimensionless ratio).

If several external torques act on the body then the total work done is the sum of all the various quantities,

$$\sum T\Delta\theta = T_{\text{resultant}}\,\Delta\theta.$$

The sign of ΔW is positive if T and $\Delta\theta$ are in the same sense about the axis, and then the rotational kinetic

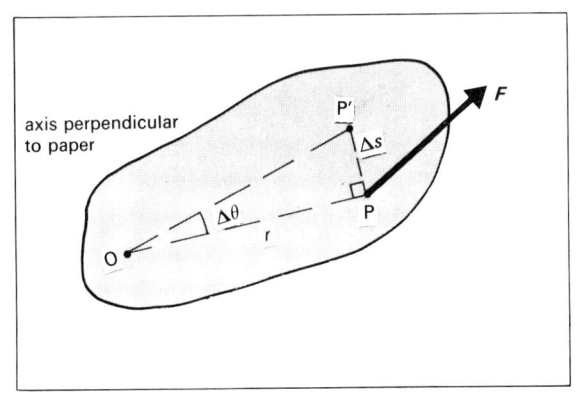

Figure 12-13

12 The dynamics of rigid bodies

energy of the body increases. The work–energy equation still holds and is now written

$$T\Delta\theta = \tfrac{1}{2}I\omega_f^2 - \tfrac{1}{2}I\omega_i^2,\qquad [12\text{-}10]$$

ω_i and ω_f being the initial and final angular velocities respectively and I being the moment of inertia about the axis of rotation.

If the work done in $\Delta W = T\Delta\theta$ is done in time Δt then, dividing each side of the equation by Δt gives

$$\frac{\Delta W}{\Delta t} = T\frac{\Delta\theta}{\Delta t}$$

and we get the power equation for rotational motion,

$$P_{av} = T\omega_{av}$$

or, instantaneously, $\quad P = T\omega.\qquad [12\text{-}11]$

Electric motors and internal combustion engines—in fact almost any device man uses for converting energy into mechanical energy—are usually designed to drive a shaft about a fixed axis. In dynamic terms their output is not a force which does work in moving along a line but a torque which does work in rotating through an angle. If the mechanical torque produced by a machine on a load is T, then the rate at which it does work on the load is $T\omega$, which is equal to $2\pi nT$, where n is the number of revolutions the drive shaft makes per second, it being assumed that T is constant. The expression $2\pi nT$ will give the power in watts $(J\,s^{-1})$. To measure the power at which the machine does work when it is rotating the shaft at a rate of revolution n it is necessary to measure T while the shaft rotates at this speed. A simple torquemeter could be designed as shown in figure 12-14. If the spring balances read F_1 and F_2, then for a pulley of radius a the applied torque about the axis of rotation is $(F_1 - F_2)a$. Thus a human being turning the driving shaft by suitably arranged foot pedals and gears might record, at two revolutions per second, $F_1 = 200$ N and $F_2 = 50$ N, on a pulley for which $a = 0.20$ m. The power delivered to the shaft is thus

[12-11] $\quad P = T\omega = 2\pi na(F_2 - F_1)$

$$= \left(2\pi\frac{\text{rad}}{\text{rev}}\right)\left(2\frac{\text{rev}}{\text{s}}\right)(0.20\,\text{m})(150\,\text{N})$$

$$\approx 380\frac{\text{N m rad}}{\text{s}},$$

that is $\quad P \approx 380$ W.

Many other forms of torquemeter can be designed but the one shown in figure 12-14 illustrates the principle well enough.

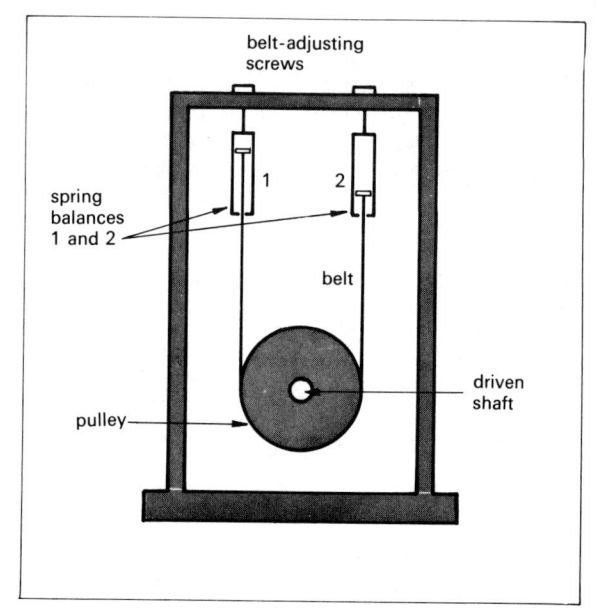

Figure 12-14 A torquemeter. The pulley is attached to the driven shaft in which the torque is to be measured.

▶ **Example 12-7** A motor is to be started by pulling a cord attached to a pulley of radius 0.050 m. A spring exerts a constant resisting torque of 0.50 N m, and the cord is pulled with a constant force of 50 N for a distance of 1.0 m. Taking the moment of inertia of the pulley and the rotating parts of the motor as $0.20\,\text{kg m}^2$, find the angular velocity acquired.

The pull of the cord exerts a torque of $(50\,\text{N})(0.050\,\text{m}) = 2.50\,\text{N m}$ so that the resultant torque is $2.50\,\text{N m} - 0.50\,\text{N m} = 2.0\,\text{N m}$. The angle through which the pulley turns is $(1.0\,\text{m})/(0.050\,\text{m}) = 20\,\text{rad}$, so that using the work–energy equation we have

$$(2.0\,\text{N m})(20\,\text{rad}) = \tfrac{1}{2}(0.20\,\text{kg m}^2)\omega_f^2 - \tfrac{1}{2}(0.20\,\text{kg m}^2)(0)$$

so that $\quad \omega_f^2 = 400\,\text{rad}^2\,\text{s}^{-2}$

$\quad\quad\quad\omega_f = 20\,\text{rad s}^{-1}.\qquad$ ◀

12-7 Summary

The general case of the motion of a rigid body will involve both translation and rotation. To analyse such situations we can, firstly, imagine all the mass of the body to be concentrated at its centre of mass (CM) and for all external forces to act through the centre of mass. The translation of the body now follows Newton's laws of motion for the dynamics of a particle. Secondly, we can

Translation		Rotation	
Force	F	Moment of force, torque	$T = r_\perp F = rF_\perp$
Mass	m	Moment of inertia	$I = \sum_1^n m_i r_i^2$
Newton's second law	$ma = \sum F$	Newton's second law	$I\alpha = \sum T$
Work	$F\Delta x \cos\theta$	Work	$rF_\perp \Delta\theta$
Translational kinetic energy	$\frac{1}{2}mv^2$	Rotational kinetic energy	$\frac{1}{2}I\omega^2$
Power	Fv	Power	$T\omega$

Table 12-1

imagine an axis through the centre of mass and consider the torques exerted by external forces about this axis. The rotation of the body now follows Newton's laws of motion for the dynamics of a rigid body about this axis. Table 12-1 summarizes the basic relationships used in the translational dynamics of a particle and in the rotational dynamics of a rigid body about an axis which is either fixed in an inertial frame or passes through the centre of mass of the body. They are written in scalar form for simplicity. The analogy between the two sets is obvious. Momentum is noticeably absent, but the next chapter deals with angular momentum; the reader should be able to guess the expression in angular motion for a rigid body which will be analogous to mv for linear momentum of a particle.

Some problems on the acceleration of rigid bodies can best be solved by writing down an energy equation, that is applying the principle of conservation of mechanical energy to the body and differentiating it with respect to time.

★ Consider a uniform solid sphere of mass m and radius r rolling from rest at O down a rough slope without slipping (figure 12-15). The rolling friction is negligible. Suppose the slope makes an angle α with the horizontal. When the sphere has rolled a distance x it will have a translational kinetic energy of

$$\tfrac{1}{2}mv^2 = \tfrac{1}{2}m\left(\frac{dx}{dt}\right)^2$$

and a kinetic energy about its centre of mass of

$$\tfrac{1}{2}I\omega^2 = \tfrac{1}{2}I\left(\frac{1}{r}\frac{dx}{dt}\right)^2.$$

Calling its gravitational potential energy zero at O it has a

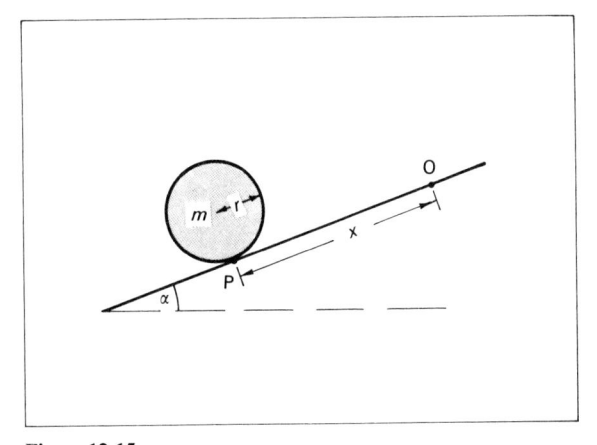

Figure 12-15

gravitational potential energy of $-mgx\sin\alpha$. Thus as its mechanical energy must remain constant, we have

$$\tfrac{1}{2}m\left(\frac{dx}{dt}\right)^2 + \tfrac{1}{2}\frac{I}{r^2}\left(\frac{dx}{dt}\right)^2 - mgx\sin\alpha = \text{constant.}$$

Differentiating with respect to time we get

$$m\left(\frac{dx}{dt}\right)\frac{d^2x}{dt^2} + \frac{I}{r^2}\left(\frac{dx}{dt}\right)\frac{d^2x}{dt^2} - mg\sin\alpha\left(\frac{dx}{dt}\right) = 0.$$

Either

$$\frac{dx}{dt} = 0 \quad \text{or} \quad \left(m + \frac{I}{r^2}\right)\frac{d^2x}{dt^2} = mg\sin\alpha.$$

As $I = \tfrac{2}{5}mr^2$ for a sphere, this gives

$$\tfrac{7}{5}m\frac{d^2x}{dt^2} = mg\sin\alpha$$

that is, the linear acceleration is

$$a = \tfrac{5}{7}g\sin\alpha.$$

★

Bibliography

Page, R. L. (1971). 'Measuring the moment of inertia of the human body.' *School Science Review*, number 182, page 103.

Nuffield Advanced Physical Science (1973). *Teachers' guide III*. Penguin. Option G3 deals with rotational motion.

Quadling, D. A. and Ramsay, A. R. D. (1959). *Elementary mechanics*. Bell. The second volume gives examples of how to calculate moments of inertia.

Weidner, R. T. and Sells, R. L. (1965). *Elementary classical physics*, volume 1. Allyn and Bacon. Chapter 14 is about rotational dynamics.

Exercises

Data (to be used unless otherwise directed):
$g = 10 \text{ m s}^{-2} = 10 \text{ N kg}^{-1}$.

12-1 Estimate the moments of inertia, about the axes stated, of the following bodies:
 (a) a long-playing gramophone record, about an axis through its centre, perpendicular to its plane
 (b) a door (of the usual type) about an axis through its hinges
 (c) a golfclub, about an axis through one end, perpendicular to its shaft
 (d) a motor car wheel and tyre, about an axis through its centre and perpendicular to its plane
 (e) a garden roller, about the axis of the roller.

12-2 What are the radii of gyration of the following bodies about the axes stated:
 (a) a uniform disc of radius 0.30 m, about an axis through its centre, perpendicular to its plane.
 (b) a uniform rod of length 0.80 m, about an axis through one end, perpendicular to its axis.
 (c) a hoop of radius 0.20 m, about an axis through its centre, perpendicular to its plane? ●

12-3 What is the moment of inertia about its axis of a uniform cylinder of mass 0.30 kg and radius 0.10 m if its height is
 (a) 0.10 m (b) 0.010 m? ●

12-4 What is the moment of inertia of a point mass of 2.0 kg about an axis 0.50 m from the mass? What is the moment of inertia of a hoop of mass 2.0 kg and radius 0.50 m about an axis through its centre and perpendicular to its plane? ●

12-5 A uniform disc has a mass of 0.20 kg and a radius of 0.10 m. What is its moment of inertia about an axis through its centre and perpendicular to its plane?
 The disc is now cut along a diameter and one half is folded on to the other so as to make a semicircular disc of twice the original thickness. What is the moment of inertia of this body about the original axis? ●

12-6 What is the kinetic energy of a trapdoor which measures 1.0 m by 1.0 m and has a mass of 10 kg if it is turning about an axis along one side with an angular velocity of 2.0 rad s^{-1}? ●

12-7 What is the kinetic energy of a level-crossing gate of moment of inertia 1500 kg m^2 about an axis through its hinges when it has an angular velocity of 0.50 rad s^{-1}? ●

12-8 What is the kinetic energy of a baseball bat of mass 2.0 kg and length 0.80 m when it has an angular velocity of 10 rad s^{-1} and is moving about an axis 0.20 m from one end and perpendicular to its length? (You may assume that the baseball bat is uniform but of negligible thickness.) ●

12-9 A bicycle wheel of radius 0.30 m and moment of inertia 0.20 kg m^2 is rotated by a boy who places his hand on its circumference and exerts a tangential force of 10 N while the wheel turns through one-tenth of a revolution. If he does this 15 times, and frictional forces at the bearings are negligible, what angular velocity does the wheel acquire? ●

12-10 A thread is wrapped round the circumference of a flywheel of moment of inertia 0.50 kg m^2. Find the angular velocity acquired when the thread is pulled for a distance of 1.5 m with a force of 10 N. ●

12-11 A mass of 2.0 kg is attached to a thread which is wrapped round an axle to which is fixed a flywheel of moment of inertia 0.20 kg m^2. What is the angular velocity of the flywheel when the mass has fallen 2.0 m? Assume that the gain of kinetic energy of the falling mass is negligible. ●

12-12 Consider a body of mass m rotating about a fixed axis O with angular velocity ω; its centre of mass is a distance h from O (figure 12-16). Find

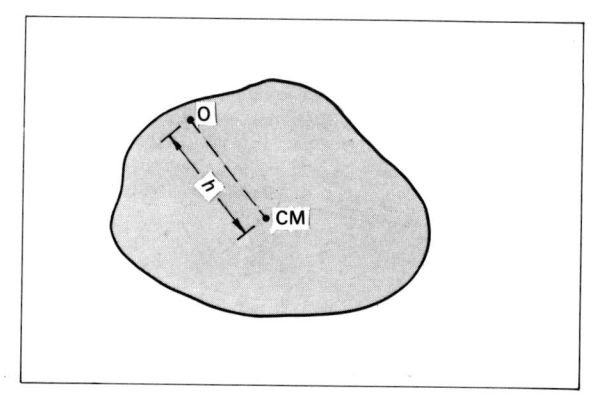

Figure 12-16

(a) the kinetic energy of the body as measured by an observer moving with the centre of mass
(b) the kinetic energy of a mass m moving with the velocity of the centre of mass
(c) the kinetic energy of the body as measured by an observer who is stationary.
Use the fact that 'the k.e. of the body = the k.e. of the body measured relative to the centre of mass + the k.e. of the centre of mass, to prove that

$$I_O = I_{CM} + mh^2.$$

12-13 A bicycle wheel of radius 0.30 m is rolling along the ground with a linear velocity of $3.0 \, \text{m s}^{-1}$. What is the angular velocity of the wheel?
If its mass is 2.0 kg and its moment of inertia about its axis is $0.20 \, \text{kg m}^2$, what is its kinetic energy as measured by an observer who moves with the axle of the wheel? What is the kinetic energy of the mass of the wheel moving with the velocity of the centre of mass? What is the kinetic energy as measured by an observer who is at rest relative to the ground? ●

12-14 If the total mass of a bicycle is 10 kg, and each of its wheels has a radius of 0.30 m and a moment of inertia about its axis of $0.20 \, \text{kg m}^2$, how much work must be done to stop it when it has a speed of $9.0 \, \text{m s}^{-1}$? ●

12-15 The total mass of a car is 800 kg, and this includes four wheels each of mass 25 kg, a radius 0.50 m, and a radius of gyration of 0.30 m. Find the kinetic energy of the car when its speed is $10 \, \text{m s}^{-1}$. What fraction of this kinetic energy is absorbed in the rotation of the wheels?
Suggest a reason why the wheels of sports cars and sports bicycles are made as light as possible. ●

12-16 A sphere slides without rolling down a uniform frictionless slope which makes an angle α with the horizontal. What is its acceleration?
A sphere rolls without sliding down a uniform rough slope which is inclined at an angle α to the horizontal. Find the gain in kinetic energy when it moves from rest a distance $h/\sin \alpha$ down the slope (and therefore falls a vertical distance h) and hence find its final speed and its acceleration.

12-17 A uniform disc of radius 0.20 m and mass 5.0 kg rolls, without rolling friction and without slipping, down a slope, falling a vertical distance of 2.0 m. What is the final linear velocity of the disc?
If the same disc slides on a frictionless slope without rolling, falling the same vertical distance, what would be its final linear velocity? ●

12-18 If you were given two apparently identical spheres (that is, with the same mass, the same radius, and the same surface) and were told that one was hollow and one was solid, how would you try to discover which was which? If you were given *one* sphere, how would you try to discover whether it was hollow or solid?

12-19 A rail is bent as shown in figure 12-17 and a ball is placed at A.
(a) If the rail is frictionless, to what level does the ball rise after it has left the rail at B?
(b) If the rail is rough enough to enable the ball to roll without slipping (no internal energy is produced) will it rise to the same height after it leaves B?

12-20 A coin, which may be assumed to be a uniform disc of radius 10 mm and mass 0.010 kg, is tossed and rises 1.8 m. In so doing it completes 30 revolutions, rotating about a diameter. How much work is done on the coin (ignore air resistance)? (The radius of gyration of a disc of radius r about a diameter is $r/2$; take $\pi = 3$.) ●

12-21 A ladder has a mass of 20 kg and a length of 4.0 m and can be assumed to behave like a uniform rod. If it stands upright with its lower end on the ground, and then falls to the ground without its lower end slipping, what is the angular velocity as it strikes the ground? If its lower end had slipped, would its angular velocity have been the same? Describe the motion of the ladder if the ground had been frictionless. ●

12-22 A uniform circular disc has a mass of 5.0 kg and a radius of 0.10 m and is free to rotate about a frictionless horizontal axle passing through its centre perpendicular to its plane. What is its angular acceleration when a thread passing round its circumference
(a) is pulled with a steady force of 10 N
(b) has a mass of 1.0 kg hung on it? ●

12-23 A pulley is supported in frictionless bearings and has a mass of 4.0 kg and a radius of gyration of 0.040 m; the radius of the groove in it is 0.060 m. A massless thread passes over the pulley (and the contact is rough enough to prevent the thread slipping) and to its ends are attached masses of 5.0 kg and 3.0 kg respectively. Find the acceleration of the masses and the tension in the two parts of the thread. ●

12-24 A merry-go-round has a moment of inertia of $2000 \, \text{kg m}^2$. What torque is needed to give it an angular acceleration of $0.5 \, \text{rad s}^{-2}$? ●

12-25 The rotating part of a telephone dial has a moment of inertia of $2.5 \times 10^{-4} \, \text{kg m}^2$, and a force of 0.50 N is applied tangentially at a distance of 40 mm from the centre. If a spring exerts a constant resisting torque of $1.8 \times 10^{-2} \, \text{N m}$, what is the angular acceleration of the dial? What is the angular acceleration of the dial when it is released, if the spring continues to exert the same constant torque? ●

12-26 A metre rule has a mass of 0.150 kg and is pivoted freely about an axis through one end. The other end is raised until the rule is horizontal and is then released. Find the angular velocity and the angular acceleration of the rod when it makes an angle of 60° with the vertical. ●

12-27 The engine of a motor car works at a rate of 75 kW when it is turning at 5000 revolutions per minute. What torque does the engine exert? ●

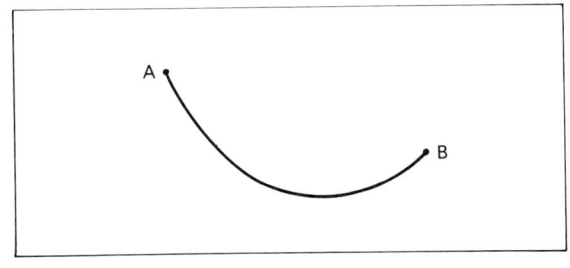

Figure 12-17

12 The dynamics of rigid bodies

12-28 A bicycle wheel rotates freely about its axis and has a kinetic energy of 200 J. How many revolutions will it make before it comes to rest if brakes applied at a point 0.30 m from its axis exert a frictional force of 30 N? If the moment of inertia of the wheel is $0.20\,\text{kg}\,\text{m}^2$, what is the angular acceleration of the wheel?

12-29 A 'brake-tester' consists of a rectangular uniform block of wood which measures 0.20 m by 0.16 m by 0.12 m. In use, it is placed on a horizontal part of the floor of a moving vehicle and then the brakes are applied. If the acceleration is great enough, the block topples over: what are the six accelerations which will cause the block to be on the point of toppling when it rests on its different faces? Assume the floor is rough enough to prevent slipping.

Discuss the use of the brake-tester if the coefficient of static friction between the block and the floor is 0.78.

12-30 In elementary problems about strings passing over pulleys, certain simplifying assumptions are usually made:
(a) the contact between the string and the pulley is such that the string does not slip but there is no rolling friction (causing dissipation of energy)
(b) there is no friction at the pulley bearings
(c) the pulley is massless.
In figure 12-18 two masses m_1 and m_2 ($m_1 > m_2$) are attached to the two ends of a massless string passing over a pulley. With all the assumptions above the tensions T_1 and T_2 in the two parts of the string are equal. What is the effect on the values of T_1 and T_2 if each of the assumptions (a), (b), and (c) is removed in turn?

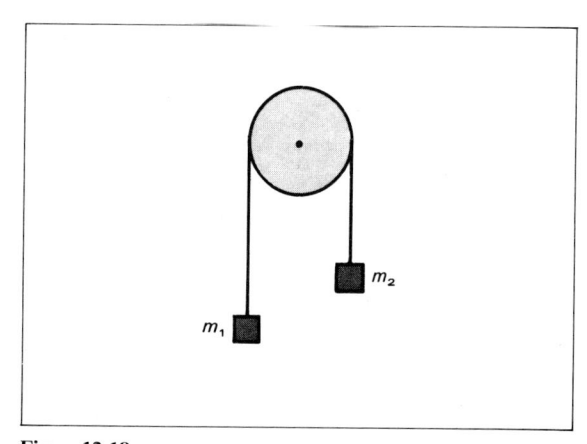

Figure 12-18

12-31 A car has a mass of 1000 kg and a wheelbase of 3.0 m: its centre of mass is 0.6 m above the ground and a horizontal distance of 1.2 m from the front axle. Find the normal contact pushes P and Q exerted by the ground on the front and rear wheels respectively when the car is at rest on level ground. If it accelerates from rest at $5.0\,\text{m}\,\text{s}^{-2}$, find the new values of P and Q.

12-32 A cyclist and his machine together have a mass of 80 kg and their centre of mass is 1.0 m above the ground. He wishes to cycle in a circular arc of radius 50 m at a speed of $10\,\text{m}\,\text{s}^{-1}$. What is the least value of the coefficient of static friction, and at what angle must he lean to avoid toppling outwards?

12-33 Explain how a wall-of-death rider is able to cycle in a horizontal circle on the inner surface of a vertical cylindrical wall.

12-34 A uniform sphere rolls without slipping and without dissipating energy down a uniform inclined plane which makes an angle α with the horizontal. Use Newton's second law for the translational and the rotational motion of the sphere to find its linear acceleration. Compare your answer with the answer you obtained in Exercise 12-16. What is the size and direction of the frictional force which the slope exerts on the sphere?

12-35 A cotton reel is a uniform wooden cylinder of radius r and mass m. The free end of the cotton is unwound and held and the reel allowed to fall vertically, more cotton unwinding as it falls. Find the linear acceleration of the reel, its angular acceleration, and the tension in the cotton.

12-36 A stationary billiard ball of mass 250 g and radius 32 mm is given a horizontal impulse passing through the centre of the ball. It slips at the point of contact, the frictional force F giving the ball a linear acceleration a and an angular acceleration α. If the coefficient of kinetic friction μ_k is 0.80, find the values of F, a, and α.

This motion continues until the decrease in its linear velocity and the increase in its angular velocity are such that it begins to roll without slipping with a linear velocity v. Use the kinematic equation $v = u + at$ and $\omega_2 = \omega_1 + \alpha t$ for the ball while it is slipping (given that the initial linear velocity is $2.0\,\text{m}\,\text{s}^{-1}$) to eliminate t and find v. How far does the ball slide before it begins to roll without sliding? (Ignore the rolling resistance force throughout.)

12-37 A bus developed for use in Switzerland has fitted to it a flywheel of moment of inertia $500\,\text{kg}\,\text{m}^2$. This is given an angular velocity ω at each terminus, and the kinetic energy of this flywheel is to be used to drive the bus for a distance of 10 km against an average resistance force of 2500 N. Assuming that hill-climbing, acceleration, and so on, will require an additional 60 per cent of the energy needed for motion on level ground at a constant speed, calculate the minimum value of ω.

13 Angular momentum

13-1	Angular momentum	207	13-5 Measuring moments of inertia	214
13-2	The rate of change of angular momentum	208	13-6 Non-rigid bodies	215
13-3	Central forces	209	13-7 The vector nature of angular momentum	218
13-4	The principle of conservation of angular momentum	211	Bibliography	221
			Exercises	222

13-1 Angular momentum

By analogy with the linear momentum p of a particle ($p = mv$) we define the angular momentum L of a body about an axis of rotation by the equation

$$L = I\omega, \qquad [13\text{-}1]$$

where I is the moment of inertia of the body about that axis and ω is its angular velocity. The unit for L will be kg m² s⁻¹ which, as 1 J = 1 kg m² s⁻², is equivalent to J s. The dimensions of L are ML^2T^{-1}.

As, in figure 13-1a,

$$\begin{aligned} L = I\omega &= \left(\sum m_i r_i^2\right)\omega \\ &= \sum mr_i(r_i\omega) = \sum mr_i v_i \\ &= \sum p_i r_i, \end{aligned}$$

we see that the angular momentum of a rigid body is the sum of the moments of the linear momenta of its particles. In figure 13-1b a single particle is shown; its linear momentum is mv and its angular momentum about an axis

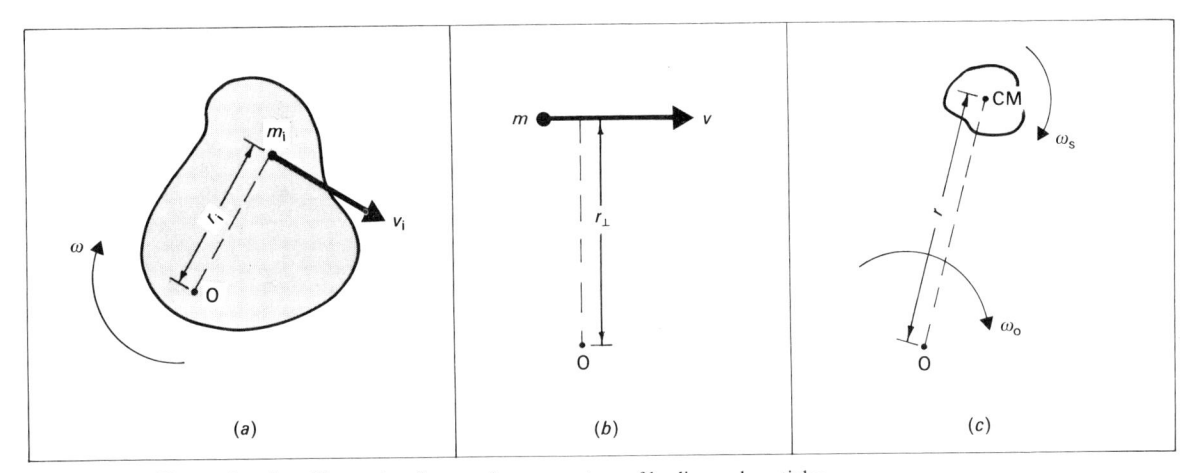

Figure 13-1 Different situations illustrating the angular momentum of bodies and particles.

through O perpendicular to the paper is $mvr_\perp$, that is the angular momentum about that axis of the particle is $pr_\perp$. In figure 13-1c a rigid body is rotating about an axis through O and at the same time spinning about an axis through its centre of mass CM. If ω_o and ω_s are the respective angular velocities and the body has a mass m and a moment of inertia I_{CM} about the spin axis through its centre of mass, then we can refer to

(a) the orbital angular momentum $mr^2\omega_o$
(b) the spin angular momentum $I_{CM}\omega_s$.

(Note that I_{CM} in the spin angular momentum *must* be the moment of inertia about the centre of mass.)

The total angular momentum of the body can be shown to be

$$mr^2\omega_o + I_{CM}\omega_s$$

if the two axes are parallel and the rotations have the same sense. This result, which is stated without proof, does not hold when the axes are not parallel, for L is a vector quantity. Many bodies possess both orbital and spin angular momentum. At the extremes of the scale an electron in an atom and a planet in the solar system each possess both forms of angular momentum, a fact which has had much to do with the development of theories of the atom and of the origin of the solar system.

★ In the equation $L = I\omega$, L must be a vector quantity for $I\omega$ is a vector quantity of size $I\omega$ and with the direction of ω. In vector terms we have $\boldsymbol{L} = I\boldsymbol{\omega}$. As

[4-8]
$$\boldsymbol{v} = \boldsymbol{\omega} \times \boldsymbol{r},$$

then rewriting $L = pr_\perp$ in vector terms,

$$\boldsymbol{L} = \boldsymbol{r} \times \boldsymbol{p}.$$

This will interest the reader who is familiar with the cross product and he should be able to check the consistency of these three vector equations. (See Exercise 13-25.) Note that $\boldsymbol{L}$ is an axial vector or pseudovector.

The adding of two angular momenta can now be seen to involve a vector sum. Thus a body whose spin angular momentum $\boldsymbol{L}_s$ and orbital angular momentum $\boldsymbol{L}_o$ are about non-parallel axes—for example the Earth (see page 234)—will have a total angular momentum $\boldsymbol{L}$, where

$$L^2 = L_o^2 + L_s^2 - 2L_oL_s\cos\theta,$$

θ being the angle between the axes. ★

A torque which lasts for a short time only is called an impulsive torque. For instance, when two rotating discs engage we cannot measure either the torque exerted by each on the other (which would be varying) or the time of interaction, but the effect of such an impulse can be described by the product $T\Delta t$, or, as T varies, as $\sum T\Delta t$.

$$\text{Impulse of a torque} = \sum T\Delta t. \qquad [13\text{-}2]$$

By analogy with the discussion leading to the impulse–linear momentum equation of Section 8-2, we see that the impulse of a torque is equal to ΔL, the change of angular momentum of the body on which the torque acts, so that

$$\Delta L = \sum T\Delta t. \qquad [13\text{-}3]$$

▶ **Example 13-1** If the same face of the Moon is always seen by an observer on the Earth, what is the rate of rotation of the Moon about its own axis? Find the total angular momentum of the Moon about an axis passing through the centre of the Earth. Take the Moon to be a uniform sphere of radius 1.7×10^6 m and mass 7.3×10^{22} kg moving in an orbit of mean radius 3.8×10^8 m with a period of 2.4×10^6 s.

The period of its rotation about its own axis must be the same as the period of its rotation about the Earth. Its orbital angular momentum ($= mr^2\omega$)

$$= (7.3 \times 10^{22}\,\text{kg})(3.8 \times 10^8\,\text{m})^2 \left(\frac{2\pi\,\text{rad}}{2.4 \times 10^6\,\text{s}}\right)$$

$$= 2.8 \times 10^{34}\,\text{kg m}^2\,\text{s}^{-1}.$$

Its spin angular momentum ($= I_{CM}\omega_s$)

$$= \tfrac{2}{5}(7.3 \times 10^{22}\,\text{kg})(1.7 \times 10^6\,\text{m})^2 \left(\frac{2\pi\,\text{rad}}{2.4 \times 10^6\,\text{s}}\right)$$

$$= 2.2 \times 10^{29}\,\text{kg m}^2\,\text{s}^{-1},$$

so that the spin angular momentum is insignificant in relation to its orbital angular momentum. ◀

13-2 The rate of change of angular momentum

Equation 13-3, which we can rewrite as

$$\frac{\Delta L}{\Delta t} = \sum T \qquad [13\text{-}4]$$

can be expressed in words as

the rate of change of angular momentum of a body is equal to the sum of the external torques acting on it.

(Note that it is analogous to the definition of force given in Section 8-7.) This statement is the full *definition of torque* in Newtonian mechanics. We did not start with this definition in Chapter 11 as it would not have told us very much about torques in a way which would then have been helpful. It would not have told us about twists or about angular accelerations—the observable phenomena. It would have related torque to a (then) even more mysterious quantity—the angular momentum of a body. In applying equation 13-4 we must restrict ourselves to bodies which rotate about an axis which is fixed in an inertial frame of reference; when dealing with bodies without such an axis of rotation, we may only measure the values of L and T about an axis passing through their centre of mass.

For bodies of constant moment of inertia I we have

[13-4] $$\frac{\Delta L}{\Delta t} = \sum T, \quad \text{and}$$

[13-1] $$L = I\omega.$$

Therefore $$\frac{\Delta(I\omega)}{\Delta t} = \sum T$$

or $$\frac{I\Delta\omega}{\Delta t} = \sum T.$$

But $\Delta\omega/\Delta t = \alpha$, the angular acceleration of the body, and thus we get

$$I\alpha = \sum T,$$

which is equation 12-4. Using equation 13-4 as the fundamental one now enables us to analyse situations where the moment of inertia of a system about a given axis changes—perhaps a Catherine wheel (firework) or someone making a springboard dive—but leaves our earlier work correct for the particular case of constant moment of inertia.

The full definition of torque in vector terms and using a calculus notation is given by the equation

$$\frac{d\mathbf{L}}{dt} = \sum \mathbf{T}. \quad [13\text{-}5]$$

▶ **Example 13-2** A marine engine's moving parts have a mass of 30 kg and a radius of gyration, about the axis of the crankshaft, of 0.20 m. If they are to reach a speed of 2400 revolutions per minute in 10 s, what is the average rate of gain of angular momentum? What is the average accelerating torque exerted on the moving parts?

The moment of inertia of the moving parts ($= mk^2$)

$= (30 \text{ kg})(0.20 \text{ m})^2$

$= 1.2 \text{ kg m}^2.$

The angular velocity to be reached

$$= \left(2400 \frac{\text{rev}}{\text{min}}\right)\left(\frac{1 \text{ min}}{60 \text{ s}}\right)\left(\frac{2\pi \text{ rad}}{1 \text{ rev}}\right) = 80\pi \text{ rad s}^{-1}.$$

The gain of angular momentum ($= I\omega$)

$$= (1.2 \text{ kg m}^2)\left(80\pi \frac{\text{rad}}{\text{s}}\right)$$

and the average rate of gain of angular momentum

$$= \frac{96\pi \text{ kg m}^2 \text{ s}^{-1}}{10 \text{ s}}$$

$= 30 \text{ kg m}^2 \text{ s}^{-2}$

$= 30 \text{ N m}.$

Therefore the average torque $= 30$ N m. ◀

13-3 Central forces

Consider a body P of mass m which is projected as shown in figure 13-2a. If P is a magnetic puck free to move on a frictionless horizontal surface and O is a fixed magnetic puck with the same circumferential polarity then a stroboscopic photograph of the ensuing motion will be like that represented in figure 13-2b. In the absence of frictional forces the resultant external force acting on P will be $\mathbf{F}$, the push of the puck O, which will lie in the horizontal plane and be directed along the line OP. Here we have a fixed axis (through O) and a body (P) on which the force is always directed along the line joining the body and the axis: such a force is called a *central force*. The velocity of P varies in both its size and its direction. This is not simple to analyse as there is no simple relation between $\mathbf{F}$ and $\mathbf{OP}$. However if the area swept by the line OP in successive time intervals Δt is measured by counting squares on some transparent graph paper laid over the photograph, we find that

area $P_1 OP_2 =$ area $P_2 OP_3 = \cdots =$ constant.

If this area is put equal to ΔA,

$$\frac{\Delta A}{\Delta t} = \text{constant}. \quad [13\text{-}6]$$

This surprisingly simple result (equal areas are swept in equal time) can also be established experimentally if the circumferential polarity of the pucks is opposite or if the central force is provided in some other way, for example

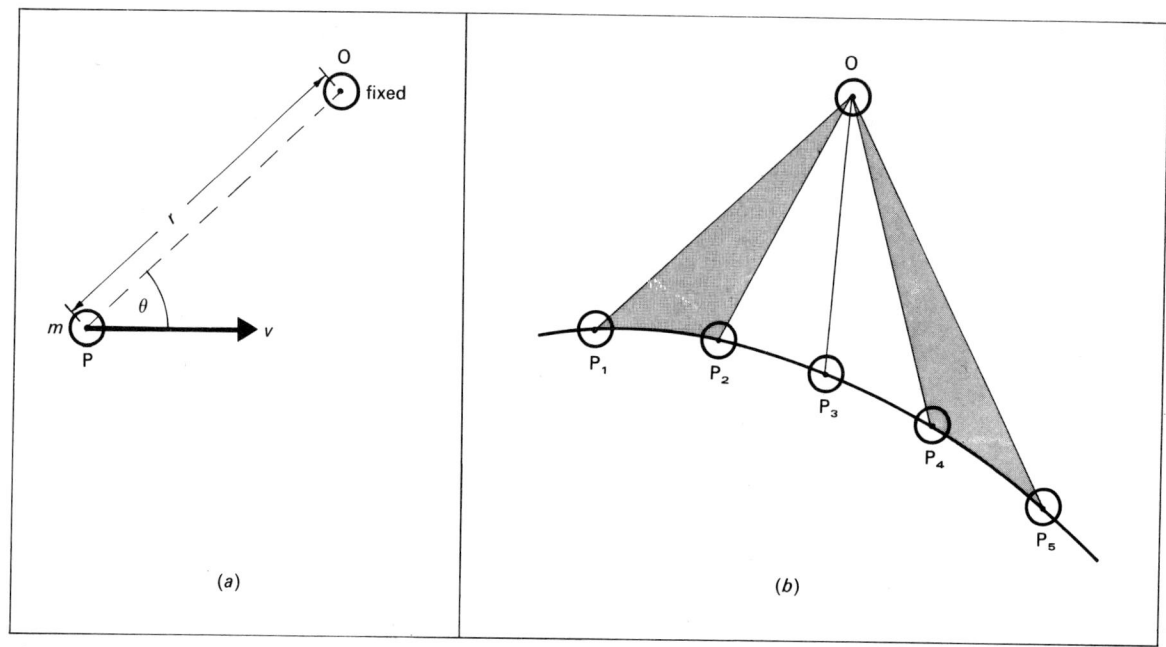

Figure 13-2 A magnetic puck P is projected with speed v and initial angular momentum $L = mvr \sin\theta$ ($\boldsymbol{L} = \boldsymbol{r} \times m\boldsymbol{v}$) about an axis through O perpendicular to the figure.

by a thin elastic band, or by the electric attraction or repulsion between charged particles. The result has been found to be of fundamental importance: the gravitational attraction of two bodies provides central forces, as with the motions of the planets around the Sun. The law of equal areas swept in equal times was discovered from astronomical observations by Kepler, and Newton based his Law of Gravitation partly on this (see Section 14-2). Also, detailed study of the scattering of α-particles by gold nuclei analysed by Geiger and Marsden led Rutherford to establish the nuclear model of the atom.

To return to figure 13-2a: as the resultant external force on P acts through O, that is it is a central force, then the torque it exerts about an axis through O is zero.

$$\sum T = 0.$$

From Newton's second law

$$\frac{\Delta L}{\Delta t} = 0,$$

or
$$L = \text{constant, for motion under a central force.} \quad [13\text{-}7]$$

The angular momentum of P about O remains constant under the action of a central force. Note that *no* assumption as to the nature of the central force (it does not, for example, have to obey an inverse-square law) is made in this statement. The fact that L is constant, and our experimental deduction $\Delta A/\Delta t = $ constant, must be equivalent, as we shall now prove.

Consider a particle of mass m moving along the trajectory AB under the action of a central force through O. Let the velocity of the particle be $\boldsymbol{v}$ at P. (See figure 13-3.) In time Δt the particle moves to P' where $PP' = v\Delta t$.

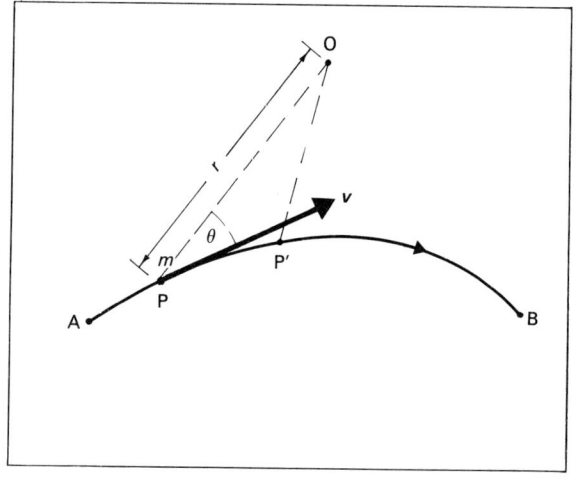

Figure 13-3 The law of equal areas and the conservation of angular momentum.

Therefore

$$\text{area POP}' = \tfrac{1}{2}rv(\Delta t)\sin\theta$$
$$= \tfrac{1}{2}(\Delta t)rv\sin\theta.$$

But $\qquad L = mvr\sin\theta,$

therefore $\qquad \text{area POP}' = \tfrac{1}{2}\Delta t\left(\dfrac{L}{m}\right)$

and $\qquad \dfrac{\Delta A}{\Delta t} = \dfrac{L}{2m}.$

This is only approximately true for the line PP' is not straight and POP' is not really a triangle. Using calculus techniques, however, we could show that dA/dt is exactly equal to $L/2m$. The above result holds approximately if Δt is small. The vector proof is left as an exercise for the reader.

Note also that the orbit of the particle moving under the action of a central force must lie *in a plane*. This follows immediately from the vector nature of L, for if $L = $ constant, it must be constant in direction as well as in size.

▶ **Example 13-3** A mass of 0.50 kg rests on a frictionless horizontal plane and is tied to one end of a massless string: the other end is wrapped round a vertical post of circumference 20 mm and arranged so that, when taut, 1.0 m of the string is free from the post. The string is then given an angular velocity of 10 rad s^{-1} in a direction such that more of the string becomes wrapped round the post. Assuming that the radius of the post is sufficiently small (compared with the length of the string) for the pull of the string on the mass to be considered a central force, find the angular velocity of the mass when it has made five revolutions.

Let the initial and final values of the free length of the string be r_1 and r_2 respectively, and let the initial and final values of the angular velocity be ω_1 and ω_2 respectively, and let the mass of the body be m. Then the initial and final angular momenta (about the post) of the body are $mr_1^2\omega_1$ and $mr_2^2\omega_2$ respectively. Since, under the action of a central force, the angular momentum is conserved,

$$mr_1^2\omega_1 = mr_2^2\omega_2$$

or $\qquad r_1^2\omega_1 = r_2^2\omega_2$

and $\qquad \omega_2 = \left(\dfrac{r_1}{r_2}\right)^2 \omega_1.$

$r_1 = 1.0$ m: after five revolutions, the string has a length of 0.90 m, so that $r_2 = 0.90$ m. Hence

$$\omega_2 = \left(\dfrac{1.0\text{ m}}{0.90\text{ m}}\right)^2 (10\text{ rad s}^{-1})$$
$$\omega_2 = 12\text{ rad s}^{-1}. \qquad ◀$$

13-4 The principle of conservation of angular momentum

In Section 13-3 we discussed the conditions under which the angular momentum of a single particle was conserved: here we are concerned with the angular momentum of a system of particles, including, particularly, those concerning rigid bodies. The essential conditions common to all the systems we consider are that:

(*a*) the resultant external torque acting on the system, measured about the axis of rotation, is zero, and

(*b*) the forces of interaction between the parts of the system are equal in size and act in opposite directions along the same line.

Where these conditions are met, the statement of Newton's second law in the form

$$\dfrac{\Delta L}{\Delta t} = \Sigma T$$

means that

$$\dfrac{\Delta L}{\Delta t} = 0$$

or $\qquad L = $ constant.

The total angular momentum of the system about the chosen axis is constant. This is the *principle of conservation of angular momentum*—one of the most important conservation laws of physics. It is the angular statement of Newton's first law of motion.

Although we cannot do an experiment to 'prove' the truth of the law, there are a number of experiments and demonstrations which can be done to illustrate its meaning and usefulness.

(*a*) Consider a turntable (see page 54) on which is fixed a block of wood. One end of the wood carries a piece of card about 0.1 m long which, when the table rotates, operates a photocell gate to enable a scaler to record Δt, the time interval for which the card breaks the light beam. On the other side of the block is a set of rubber cups which can each hold identical steel balls. The cups are set so that if one of the balls arrives travelling horizontally and perpendicular to the block, it is 'caught' by the cup and the turntable is set into rotation. The principle of conservation of angular momentum should apply to this collision if the angular momentum is calculated about a vertical axis through P, the axis of rotation of the table. Referring to figure 13-4,

$$mvr = I\omega$$
$$= I\dfrac{\Delta\theta}{\Delta t},$$

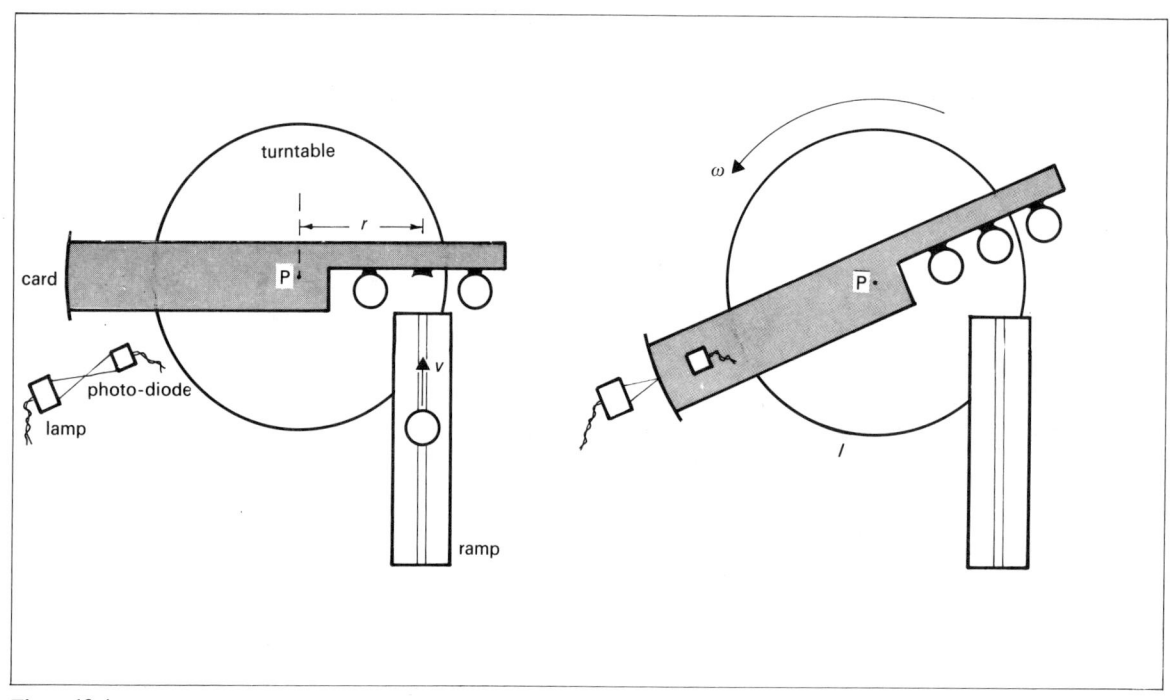

Figure 13-4 The apparatus is seen from above. A ball of mass m is rolled down a ramp so as to stick to the rubber cup with a horizontal speed v.

where mv is the horizontal linear momentum of the ball as it strikes the rubber cup at a distance r from P, I is the moment of inertia of the turntable and *all* the balls about P, and $\Delta\theta$ is the angle subtended at P by the card. If we now project a ball into each cup in turn by rolling it down a ramp the last part of which is horizontal (the other two balls being on each occasion already in their cups), we are performing the above experiment while varying r and Δt, v being the same each time. If the principle of conservation of angular momentum applies, then a graph of r/m against $(\Delta t)^{-1}/\text{s}^{-1}$ should yield a straight line through the origin. The experiment, though not accurate, does help us to understand at the same time both the concept of the angular momentum of a particle about an axis as well as the more obvious concept of the angular momentum of a rotating rigid body.

(b) We again use the turntable, but this time it carries a rim of paper tape fixed over carbon paper (see page 54). We mount the vibrator of a ticker-timer alongside the table and hang a body (for example, a disc) symmetrically over the table by a cotton thread (figure 13-5). We set the table in motion and, about half a revolution after starting the ticker-timer, burn the thread so as to drop the disc. We stop the table before it completes a revolution. The tape will be marked on the reverse side and will record the

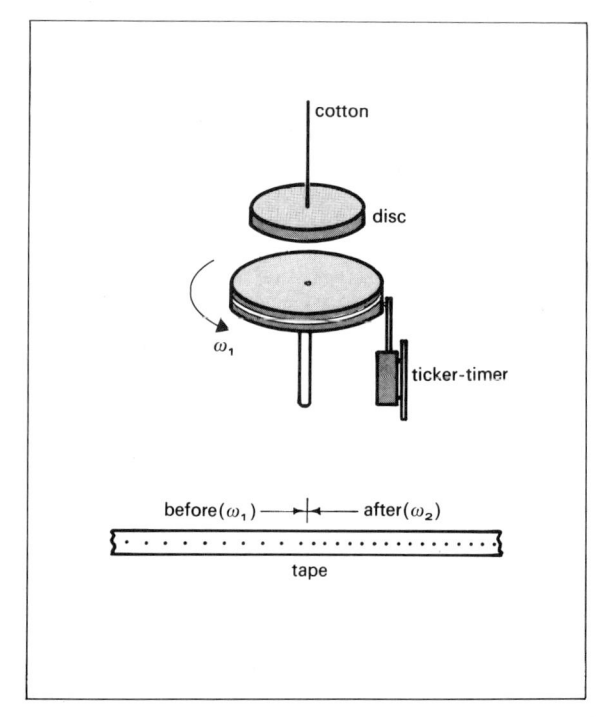

Figure 13-5 An angular collision between two rigid bodies.

13-4 The principle of conservation of angular momentum

peripheral speed of the table. Several experiments can be recorded on the same piece of tape by adjusting the height of the ticker-timer slightly. The ratio of the angular velocities of the table before and after the collision, ω_1/ω_2, can be read off the tape. If the principle of conservation of angular momentum holds, then this ratio should be constant, that is independent of ω_1. A full analysis involves the moments of inertia of the table and the disc: a method for measuring these and other moments of inertia is discussed in the next section.

(c) Consider two spheres which are hung by long light threads from the same point of a high ceiling. If they are projected so as to collide and bounce off one another while their motions are recorded by stroboscopic photography from above, then the total angular momentum of the spheres about a vertical axis through O should be found to be constant. We saw in Section 13-3 that

$$\frac{\Delta A}{\Delta t} = \frac{L}{2m}$$

for a particle of mass m subject to a central force. Thus the test of whether angular momentum is conserved (that is $\sum L$ = constant) is that $\sum m\Delta A$ should be constant (since the time intervals Δt are chosen to be the same and are therefore constant). An analysis of the photograph to measure the areas ΔA for the spheres before and after the collision should therefore give

$$m_1 \Delta A_1 + m_2 \Delta A_2 = m_1 \Delta A'_1 + m_2 \Delta A'_2.$$

(d) The case of non-rigid bodies is dealt with in more detail in Section 13-6. The correlation between the predicted and the practical results of the experiments with non-rigid bodies shows the wide applicability of the principle of conservation of angular momentum. In the collisions described in this section there is always some loss of kinetic energy, the internal energy of the interacting bodies increasing, but loss of mechanical energy is quite consistent with momentum conservation.

▶ **Example 13-4** A shaft with a number of gear wheels has a moment of inertia about its axis of 30 kg m^2 and an angular velocity of 600 rad s^{-1}. A similar shaft (which lies along the same axis as the first shaft) has a moment of inertia of 20 kg m^2 and is stationary. A clutch connects the two shafts end-on so that after the connection they both have the same angular velocity. Find this angular velocity.

The initial angular momentum = $(30 \text{ kg m}^2)(600 \text{ rad s}^{-1})$
$$= 18\,000 \text{ kg m}^2 \text{ s}^{-1}.$$

If the final angular velocity is ω, the final angular momentum
$$= (50 \text{ kg m}^2)\omega.$$

Since no external torques act on the shafts during the connection, the angular momentum is conserved: thus

$$18\,000 \text{ kg m}^2 \text{ s}^{-1} = (50 \text{ kg m}^2)\omega$$
$$\omega = 360 \text{ rad s}^{-1}.$$

We should note that although angular momentum is conserved, the total kinetic energy of the shafts is not. ◀

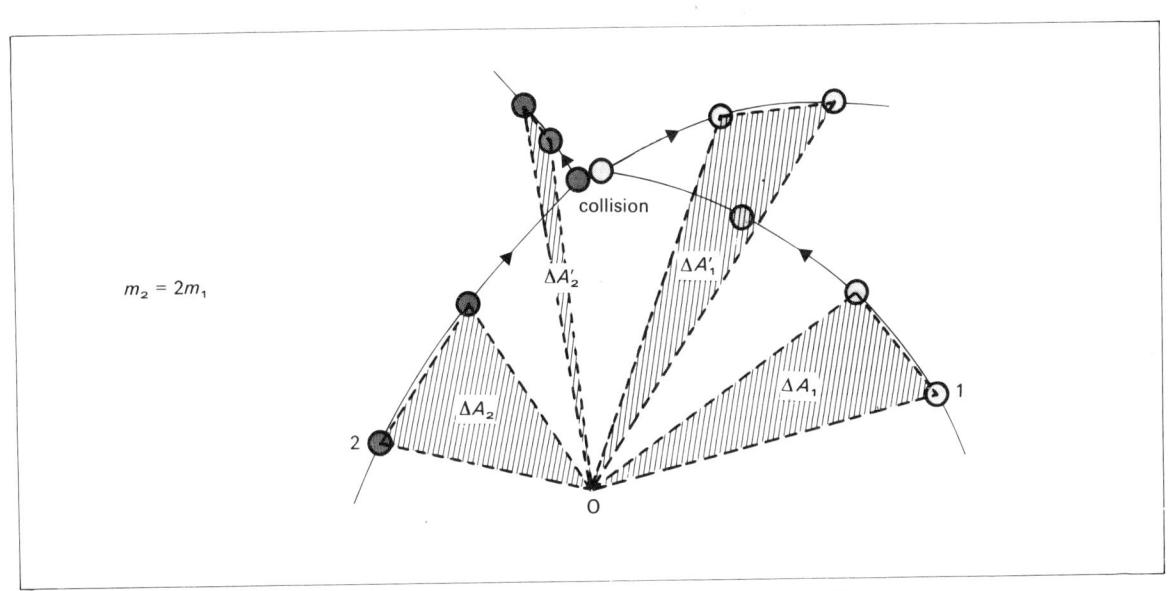

Figure 13-6 Two particles, of mass m_1 and m_2, each subject to a resultant central force from O.

13 Angular momentum

▶ **Example 13-5** The movement of water over the surface of the Earth because of tidal motion is known to result in a gain of internal energy and therefore a loss in the kinetic energy of rotation of the Earth. Thus its spin angular momentum decreases. Does this contravene the principle of conservation of angular momentum?

The cause of the tidal action must be another body, namely the Moon (we can here ignore the relatively small effect of the Sun). Therefore there is an external torque acting on the Earth and this is the cause of the Earth's change in angular momentum. If we consider the Earth–Moon system we should expect *its* angular momentum to be conserved, and if the spin angular momentum of the Earth is decreasing, the orbital angular momentum of the Moon must be increasing. This could occur because

(a) its speed v increases while its radius r remains constant *or*
(b) v remains constant while r increases *or*
(c) v and r both increase *or*
(d) v increases and r decreases but v increases more than r decreases *or*
(e) r increases and v decreases but r increases more than v decreases.

Other considerations show that (e) is the only possible mechanism, so the Moon is gradually receding from the Earth. ◀

13-5 Measuring moments of inertia

The experiment suggested by Example 12-1 in Section 12-2 can be used to measure the moment of inertia of a flywheel. We equate the work done on the flywheel to $\frac{1}{2}I\omega^2$, and find the value of ω by measuring the linear velocity of the thread, for example by replacing it by ticker-tape. Hence we deduce the value of I. Further, in Section 12-3 we saw that we could calculate, using $I = \sum m_i r_i^2$, the moment of inertia of bodies possessing a high degree of symmetry. The most general technique for measuring I depends, however, on using the principle of conservation of angular momentum, just as the mass measurements described in Section 8-5 used the principle of conservation of linear momentum.

If we are to use turntable experiments (such as the one outlined in figure 13-4) to measure a moment of inertia, then we need to know the moment of inertia I_t of the turntable about its vertical axis of rotation. This is too difficult to find from its mass and dimensions and so we perform a preliminary experiment, with a 'standard' uniform disc. We measure the mass m and radius a of a uniform disc to find its moment of inertia I_s; $I_s = \frac{1}{2}ma^2$. If we now perform an angular collision experiment (figure 13-5) between the standard disc and the turntable then, denoting the initial angular velocity of the table as ω_t and the angular velocity of the table plus disc as ω, we have, from the principle of conservation of angular momentum

$$I_t \omega_t = (I_t + I_s)\omega$$

whence
$$I_t = \frac{I_s}{\left(\frac{\omega_t}{\omega} - 1\right)}.$$

Now that I_t is known we can 'drop' any other body on to the turntable and find its moment of inertia I about an axis which is coincident with the axis of rotation of the turntable.

In this case
$$I_t \omega_t = (I_t + I)\omega$$

whence
$$I = I_t\left(\frac{\omega_t}{\omega} - 1\right).$$

The practical difficulties of such experiments are few: we need to reduce friction in the turntable bearings to a minimum, to measure the ratio of the angular velocities before and after the collision ω_t/ω as precisely as possible, and to drop the body of unknown moment of inertia without any rotation and so as to fall on the turntable in the correct position. As the whole experiment takes less than one revolution of the turntable the friction at its bearings and the drag of the air will have so small an effect that the error in the value of ω_t/ω will be less than one per cent but the drag produced by the ticker-timer will be more significant. A scaler-timer recording millisecond pulses can replace the ticker-timer (see figure 4-5 on page 55). The scaler is set at zero and the turntable is spun at about 3 rad s^{-1}; on its first revolution the beam is broken for, say, 232 ms. As soon as the scaler stops recording the cotton is burnt and the collision takes place. On its second revolution the scaler reading goes up to, say, 567 ms from 232 ms and the experiment is over, for

$$\frac{\omega_t}{\omega} = \left(\frac{\Delta\theta}{232}\right) \div \left(\frac{\Delta\theta}{567-232}\right) = \frac{335}{232}$$

whence
$$I = I_t\left(\frac{335}{232} - 1\right) = \frac{103}{232}I_t.$$

The error in ω_t/ω in a single experiment may be two or three per cent but the probable error can be reduced by performing several experiments. The last practical difficulty is that of dropping the body accurately. The body can be suspended vertically above the turntable by a thread, and this thread can be burnt through; if in addition we provide the upper surface of our turntable with tiny rubber suckers then it will grip any flat object dropped on to it. In this way we can measure I for bodies which are asymmetrical or for symmetrical bodies about axes other than their axis of symmetry, and thus test the parallel axes theorem.

The experiment as described is limited to bodies which are flat but by starting with a different form of turntable a similar experiment could in principle be performed to measure the moment of inertia of, for example, a sphere. Another more general method is to time the period of torsional oscillations of the body about the axis for which its moment of inertia is required. This technique is mentioned in Section 15-5.

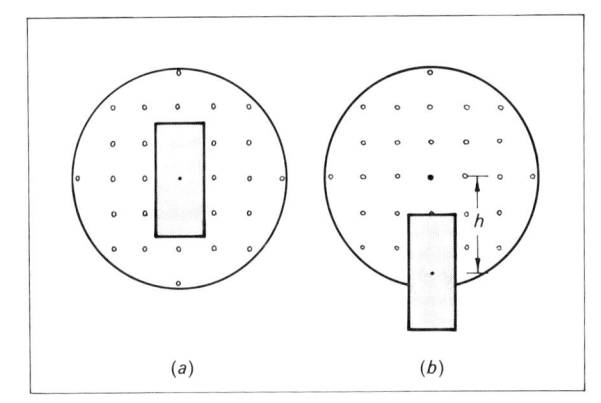

Figure 13-7 Testing the theorem of parallel axes. In (a) I_{CM} is measured and in (b) I. If $I = I_{CM} + mh^2$, where m is the mass of the rectangular plate, then the theorem is verified experimentally. See equation 12-3 in Section 12-3.

13-6 Non-rigid bodies

If you hold a china cat with its paws pointing upward and release it without rotation, it lands on its back, but if you drop a live cat in exactly the same manner it lands on its paws. There is no need for the live cat to 'cheat' in any way by struggling as it is held—you really can release it without rotation, so that its initial angular momentum, about any axis through its centre of mass, is zero. This is perhaps the most intriguing example of the way in which non-rigid bodies (in this case the live cat) seem, at first sight, to flout the rules we learn for rigid bodies and particles, for if a body has zero angular momentum about its centre of mass at the start of its fall it should have zero angular momentum about its centre of mass throughout its fall, as the only external force acting on it is the pull of the Earth, which exerts zero torque about the centre of mass. Perhaps the cat uses air resistance to produce an extra external force? In falling a few metres the air resistance forces are negligible. We shall explain the falling cat problem at the end of this section but first let us look at some simpler examples of the motion of non-rigid bodies.

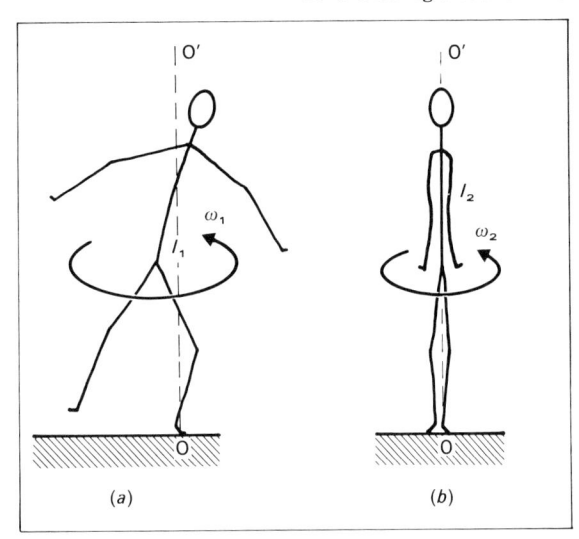

Figure 13-8 An ice-skater goes into a tight spin about a vertical axis OO'. ω_2 is much greater than ω_1.

An ice-skater goes into a spin about a vertical axis with his arms and one leg outstretched as shown diagramatically in figure 13-8a. He has an angular momentum about OO' of $I_1 \omega_1$. If he now contracts as in (b) then by the principle of conservation of angular momentum about OO'

$$I_2 \omega_2 = I_1 \omega_1$$

provided no external torque acts about OO'.

As $\quad I_1 > I_2 \quad$ then $\quad \omega_2 > \omega_1$.

It is possible to make I_1 more than four times as great as I_2 so that a skater can achieve an impressive increase in angular velocity in a tight spin.

As $I_2 \omega_2 = I_1 \omega_1$ and $\omega_2 > \omega_1$, then clearly

$$\tfrac{1}{2} I_2 \omega_2^2 > \tfrac{1}{2} I_1 \omega_1^2,$$

that is the angular kinetic energy of the skater has increased. This kinetic energy comes from the chemical energy of the skater who has to use his muscles to do work in pulling in his arms and leg. A controlled and semi-quantitative experiment of this kind can be done by standing a person on a robust turntable which has a small moment of inertia. By measuring the angular velocities, the different moments of inertia of the person can be found. For a typical human being, for whom I_0 is the moment of inertia about a vertical axis when standing to attention, the moment of inertia rises to $2I_0$ when the arms are raised to the horizontal.

When a non-rigid body is in a state of free fall its angular momentum about an axis through its centre of mass remains constant. Thus a diver who leaves the board with an angular momentum $I\omega$ about a horizontal axis may, just after leaving the board, decide to perform one and a half forward rotations before reaching the water instead of the normal half rotation needed to hit the water head first. He knows that he must increase his forward angular velocity to about 3ω in order to complete the rotations in the time taken to fall to the water and to do this he tucks in his knees and arms so reducing his moment of inertia to about $\frac{1}{3}I$ while preserving his initial angular momentum. You should be able to think of a number of similar examples where a human being uses his agility to perform specialized movements.

▶ **Example 13-6** A diver stands on a springboard and jumps so that his mass-centre (which is initially 1.0 m above the springboard) rises 1.0 m and he has an angular velocity of the value needed in order to enter the water 6.0 m below the springboard vertically after a plain dive—see figure 13-9. At the topmost point of his motion he decides that instead of a plain dive he will perform one complete somersault before entering the water. Assuming that when his fingers touch the water his centre of mass is still 1.5 m above the water surface, and that it takes 0.20 s for him to change the shape of his body from being straight to a shape with a smaller moment of inertia, and a further 0.20 s to straighten out again, calculate the factor by which his moment of inertia would have to be reduced.

If u is the initial upward velocity, and h the height to which the diver rises for the upward motion

$$u^2 = 2gh$$
$$u^2 = 2(10\,\text{m s}^{-2})(1.0\,\text{m})$$
$$u = \sqrt{20}\,\text{m s}^{-1}.$$

For the whole motion $s = ut + \frac{1}{2}at^2$, and taking the upward direction to be positive, $s = -5.5\,\text{m}$, $a = -10\,\text{m s}^{-2}$, $u = \sqrt{20}\,\text{m s}^{-1}$. Therefore

$$-5.5\,\text{m} = (\sqrt{20}\,\text{m s}^{-1})t + \tfrac{1}{2}(-10\,\text{m s}^{-2})t^2$$

$$t = \frac{\sqrt{20} \pm \sqrt{(20+110)}}{10}\,\text{s}$$

$$= 1.59\,\text{s} \quad \text{or} \quad -0.69\,\text{s}.$$

The second of these solutions is the time it would have taken to reach B from A: from considerations of symmetry we see that the time from the springboard to the topmost point is $(1.59\,\text{s} - 0.69\,\text{s})/2 = 0.45\,\text{s}$. To perform a plain dive he has to perform half a revolution in the time of 1.59 s, so that his initial angular velocity ω_1 is given by

$$\omega_1 = \frac{\pi\,\text{rad}}{1.59\,\text{s}} = 1.97\,\text{rad s}^{-1}.$$

Suppose that, to perform the somersault, he gains an *extra* angular velocity ω: in the 1.14 s from the topmost point to the water surface he has 0.20 s in which he has (let us assume) a uniform angular acceleration, 0.74 s in which he has the constant extra angular velocity ω, and 0.20 s in which he slows down again. For the two periods of 0.20 s, his average *extra* angular velocity is $\omega/2$, so that for the whole *extra* revolution we can write

$$2\pi\,\text{rad} = \tfrac{1}{2}\omega(2 \times 0.20\,\text{s}) + \omega(0.74\,\text{s})$$

$$\Rightarrow \omega = \frac{2\pi\,\text{rad}}{0.94\,\text{s}}$$

$$= 6.68\,\text{rad s}^{-1}.$$

The new angular velocity ω_2 is given by

$$\omega_2 = \omega_1 + \omega$$
$$= 8.65\,\text{rad s}^{-1}.$$

The ratio $\omega_2/\omega_1 = (8.65\,\text{rad s}^{-1})/(1.97\,\text{rad s}^{-1}) = 4.4$, so that if his angular momentum is to be conserved during his dive, his moment of inertia will have to be reduced by a factor of 4.4. In fact this is so high a value (the greatest factor by which a human being can reduce his moment of inertia is about 3.5) that he will be unsuccessful. He must jump higher, or change his shape more quickly, or use a higher diving board, or some combination of these remedies. ◀

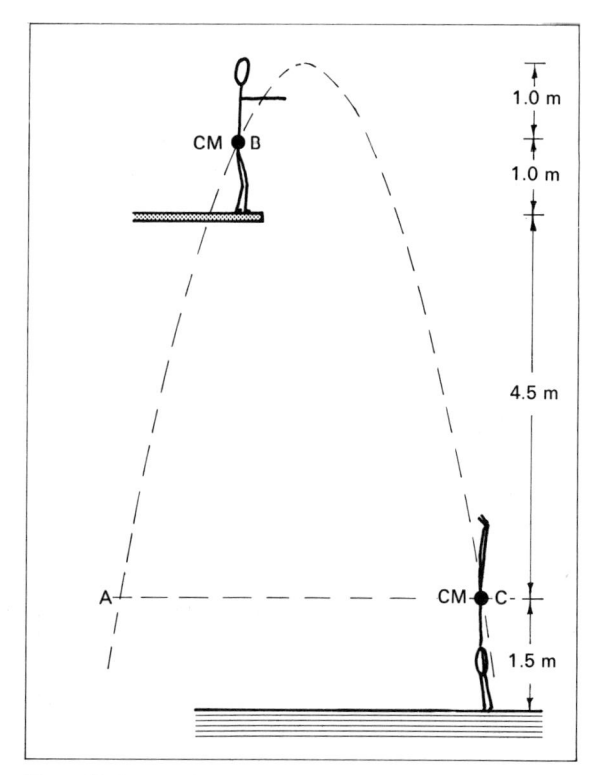

Figure 13-9

13-6 Non-rigid bodies 217

a

b

c

d

e

f

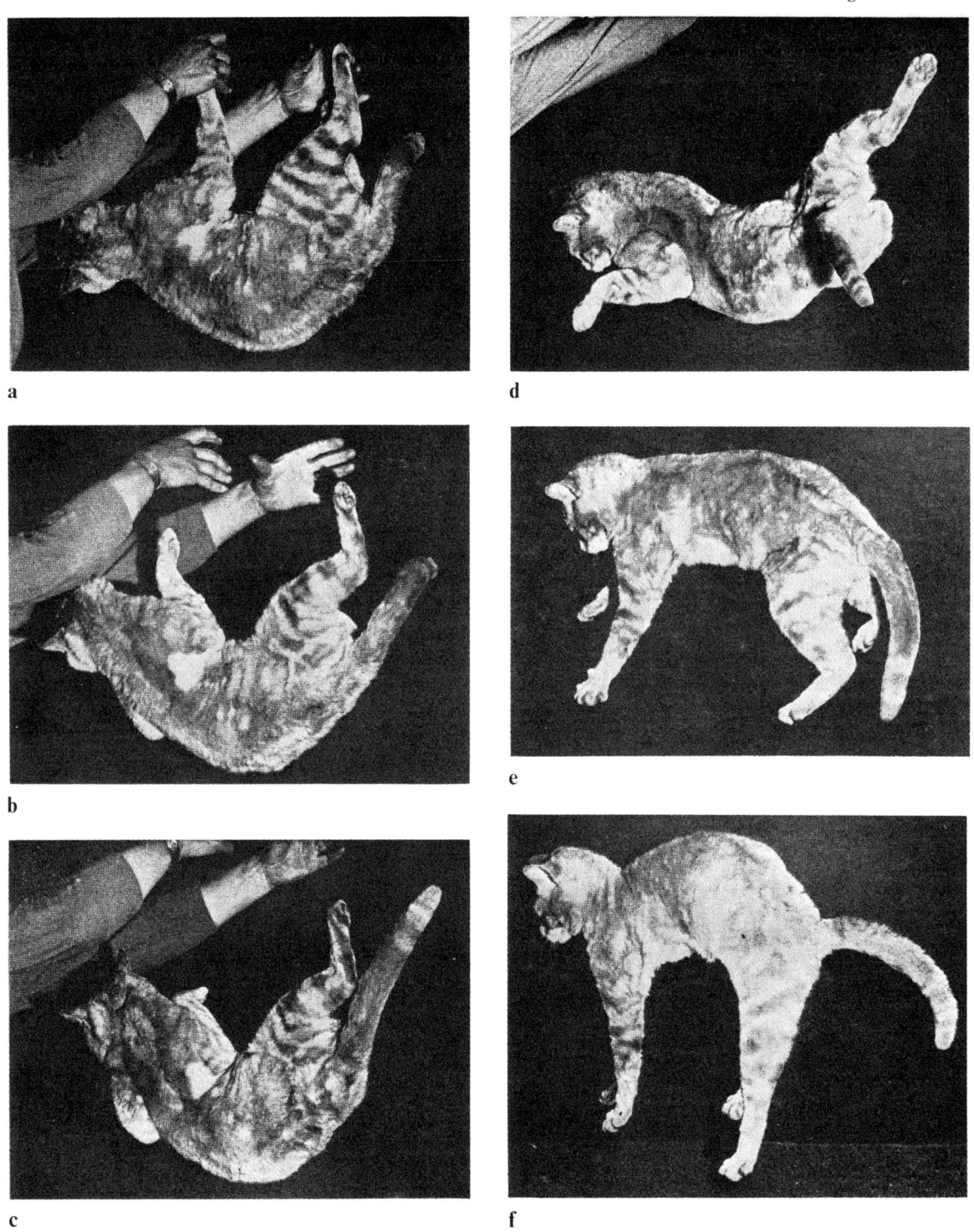

Figure 13-10 A falling cat.

Let us now return to the cat discussed at the beginning of this section. The cat behaves as if it were more than one body: it rotates its hind legs in one sense about a horizontal axis through its centre of mass and rotates its front legs and head in the opposite sense. If it were now to reverse this move it would finish up where it started, but not if it were first to alter the moments of inertia of the upper and lower parts of its body respectively (for example by pulling in its front paws). The process is difficult to imagine but if a sturdy turntable is available you could try to perform the following routine, which allows a human being to perform a rotation about a vertical axis even though no external torque acts on him: he should

(a) place his legs horizontally and arms vertically while sitting on the table

(b) rotate his legs to the right

(c) draw in his legs as far as possible and stretch his arms out horizontally

(d) rotate his arms to the right until his arms and legs are above one another

(e) return to position (a).

With a properly levelled turntable on good bearings a net rotation of at least 30° can be achieved and yet at no time during the process did the whole system possess any net angular momentum about a vertical axis. The cat achieves its rotation in a similar way though its body is so supple and its actions so quick that even with slow motion film it is not easy to reduce them to a sequence such as that given for the human being on the turntable. Moreover the cat has to achieve a rotation of 180° in a matter of less than half a second.

13-7 The vector nature of angular momentum

★ So far in this chapter we have met the following vector relationships involving angular momentum:

for a particle $\quad L = r \times p$

for a body $\quad L = I\omega$

Newton's second law

$$\frac{dL}{dt} = \sum T$$

and $\quad L$ = constant when $\sum T = 0$.

A dramatic illustration of the vector nature of angular momentum is given by a person who sits on a robust frictionless turntable and holds a spinning weighted bicycle wheel by handles attached to its axis, as is shown diagrammatically in

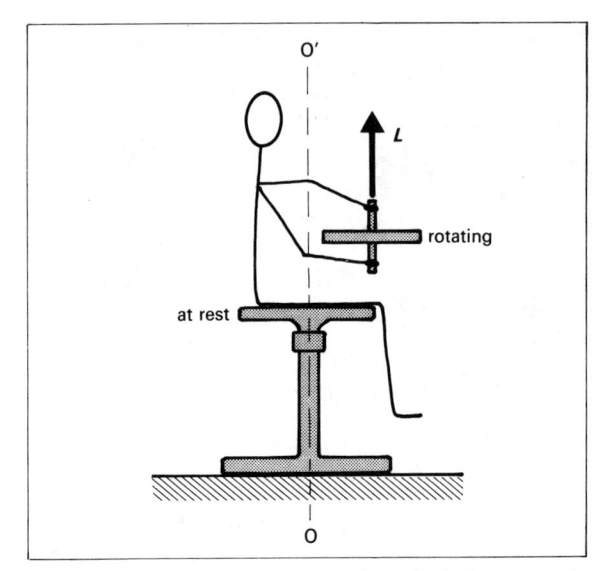

Figure 13-11 A man, holding a rotating wheel, sits on a table which is free to rotate about the vertical axis OO'.

figure 13-11. (The experiment could also be performed while sitting in a floating circular rubber dinghy.) Let the wheel's angular momentum be L (parallel to ω, that is vertically upwards). The angular momentum of the system (made up of man, wheel, and turntable) is initially, therefore, L, the man and the turntable being initially at rest. No matter what the man now does with the wheel the vector angular momentum of the system about OO' will be L, provided no external torques act on the system about OO' Suppose, for example, the man 'stopped' the wheel by letting its rim rub against his chest—the whole system would acquire an angular velocity in the same sense as ω. Suppose the man inverted the wheel: the angular momentum of the wheel would now be $-L$ (that is L vertically downwards) and yet the angular momentum of the system must remain L. Thus the man and table rotate in the same sense as the initial rotation of the wheel with an angular momentum $2L$. The greater the moment of inertia of the wheel, the greater the angular velocity acquired by the man, and to achieve this the rim of the wheel can be loaded with lead. Performing the experiment is an odd experience; the *internal* torque which alters the plane of rotation of the wheel and sets the table rotating can be clearly felt.

The vector property of the equation $dL/dt = T$ can be checked but the analysis is complicated and we shall instead consider the effect of external torques on the motion of a top or a *gyroscope*.

Figure 13-12 shows a form of gyroscope. It is designed so that the centre of mass of the sphere and arm coincides with the geometrical centre of the sphere. The gyroscope can be spun about an axis through the arm to which a small disc, of mass m, can be attached. The gyroscope is like a top which is spun about an axis of symmetry but for a top the fixed point is where it touches the ground; for this gyroscope the fixed point is the centre of the sphere. The behaviour of a gyroscope can be roughly demonstrated using a top or a little gimbal-mounted toy gyroscope.

13-7 The vector nature of angular momentum

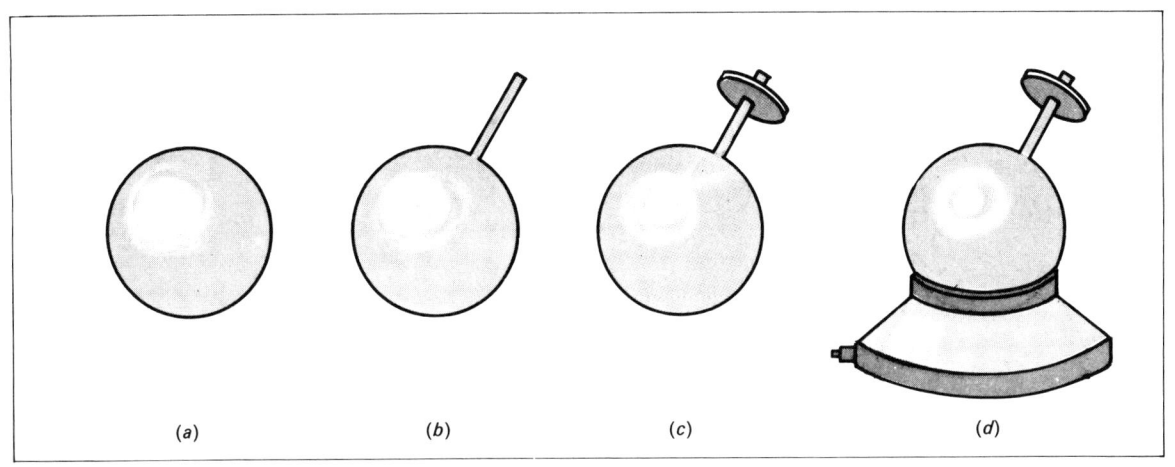

Figure 13-12 An air-supported gyroscope (*d*) is made by placing a carefully machined metal sphere in a hemispherical bowl and blowing air at low pressure through a number of tiny holes so that the sphere 'floats' on a thin cushion of air. The sphere carries an arm (*b*) which is made so that the centre of mass of the whole lies at the centre of the sphere. Asymmetry can be introduced (*c*) by attaching a disc of mass *m* to the arm.

If a *stationary* gyroscope is held with OO' (see figure 13-13) at an angle θ to the vertical and released, it falls sideways in the plane YOO', twisted by the torque $\mathbf{r} \times m\mathbf{g}$. The vertical *forces* balance: $W + mg = P$. If the gyroscope is now spun about the axis OO' and again released when OO' makes an angle θ to the vertical, a very complex motion results. The arm *starts* to fall as before but it now *precesses*, that is the arm OO' rotates about OY, in a clockwise sense as seen from O. This happens because when the arm has fallen a little the vertical component of the angular momentum of the system is lowered; $L \cos \theta$ decreases. As, however, there is no resultant torque about a vertical axis through O, the whole gyroscope must begin to rotate about OY in order to conserve the total vertical angular momentum of the system. As the arm OO' precesses it 'wobbles' up and down—this latter motion being called *nutation*. The motion of O' is something like that shown in

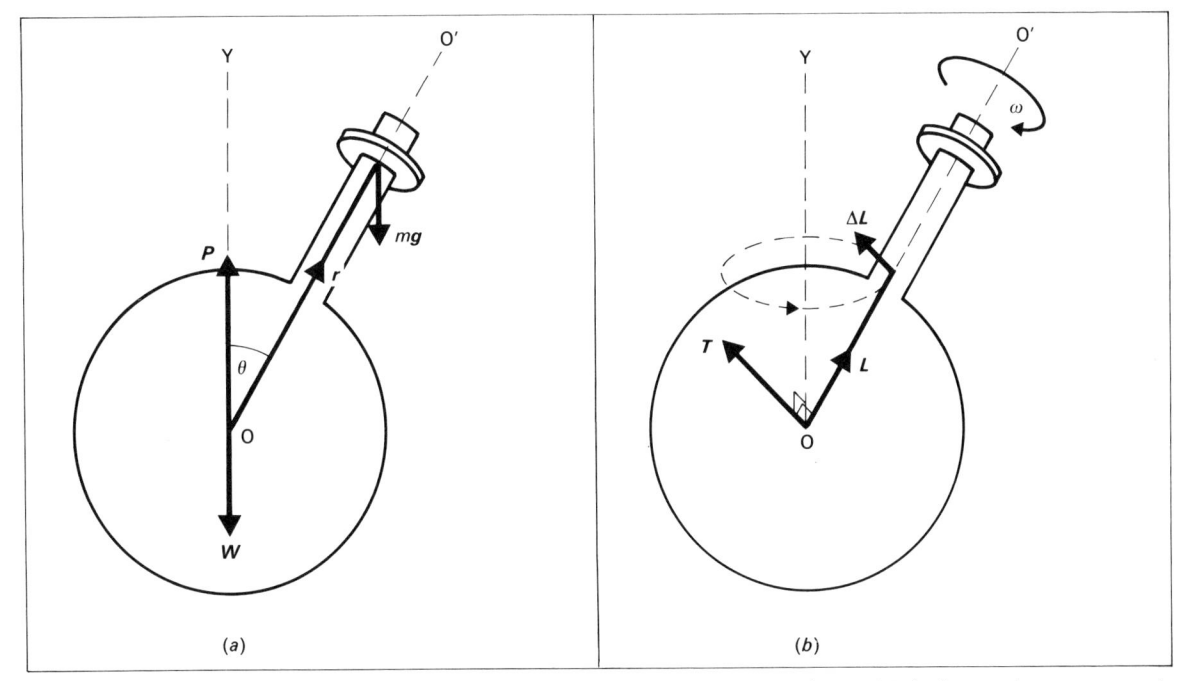

Figure 13-13 The mechanics of the gyroscope. The torque $\mathbf{T} = \mathbf{r} \times m\mathbf{g}$ produces a change $\Delta \mathbf{L}$ in its angular momentum in time Δt.

figure 13-14. In simple toy gyroscopes and tops the nutation is very rapidly damped by frictional forces and the gyroscope's motion becomes one of precession only.

If the gyroscope is spun about OO' and, instead of being released, is projected sideways at a certain angular velocity ω_p, that is it is given angular momentum about OY, then it can undergo a pure precession without nutation. To understand why this happens, and to deduce the value of ω_p, consider the effect of the torque $T = r \times mg$ on the gyroscope in a time interval Δt. It will change the vector angular momentum of the gyroscope, which is $L = I\omega$, by an amount

$$\Delta L = T\Delta t = r \times mg\Delta t,$$

that is by
$$\Delta L = mgr \sin \theta \Delta t$$

in a direction parallel to T (see figure 13-13). Thus ΔL is perpendicular to L and the change in L can be seen to be not a change in size but a change in direction *only* (think of a series of *very* small changes ΔL). There is a close analogy between this precessional motion of a gyroscope and the uniform circular motion of a particle. The particle is acted on by a constant force which is perpendicular to its direction of motion while the gyroscope is acted on by a constant torque which is perpendicular to the direction of its angular velocity, that is to its axis of rotation. The gyroscope needs to be pushed sideways because the torque $r \times mg$ will do no work on it while it precesses and its precessional kinetic energy has to come from somewhere. If, as at first, it were simply released, it would gain the necessary kinetic energy by first falling and this leads to the oscillatory motion of nutation.

To calculate ω_p consider the vector equation $L' = L + \Delta L$ depicted in figure 13-15. The change ΔL results in a rotation about OY of $\Delta \phi$ in time Δt where

$$\Delta \phi = \frac{\Delta L}{L \sin \theta}.$$

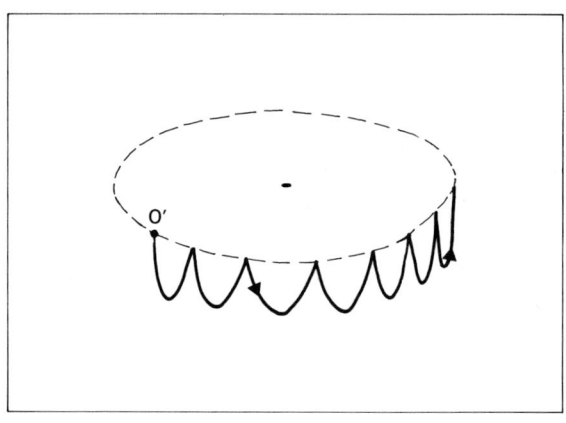

Figure 13-14 The motion of the tip of a gyroscope, showing nutation. The path is a cycloid.

Therefore

$$\omega_p \left(= \frac{\Delta \phi}{\Delta t} \right) = \frac{\Delta L}{L \sin \theta \Delta t} = \frac{mgr \sin \theta \Delta t}{I\omega \sin \theta \Delta t},$$

$$\omega_p = \frac{mgr}{I\omega}. \qquad [13\text{-}8]$$

In general it can be shown that the precessional angular velocity ω_p is related to the angular momentum of the system L and the torque producing the precession T by the equation

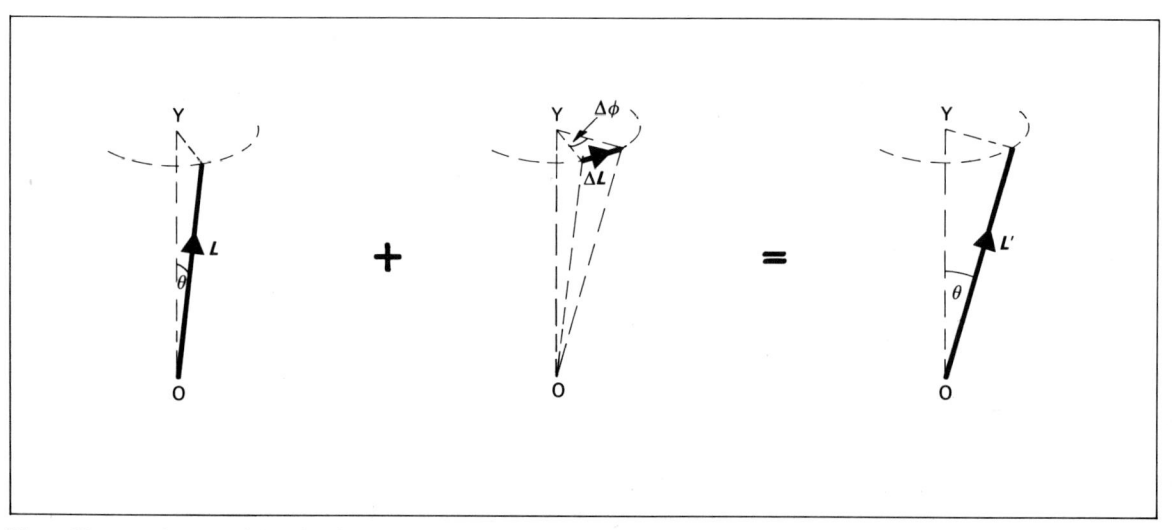

$$T = \omega_p \times L. \qquad [13\text{-}9]$$

Figure 13-15 ΔL is tangential to the circle, but as $\Delta \phi$ becomes smaller and smaller, then L' will tend to L in size.

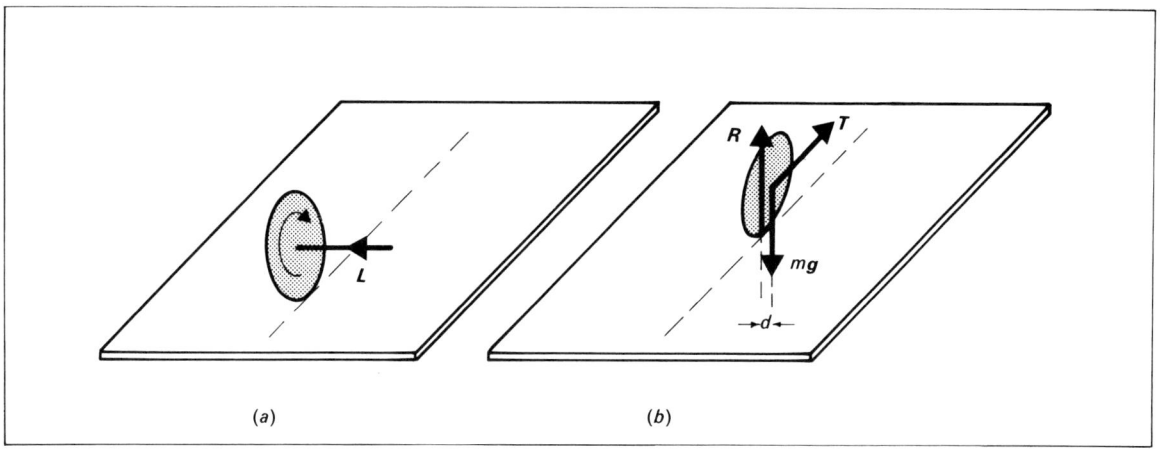

Figure 13-16

▶ **Example 13-7** A coin rolls, upright, along a horizontal table. If a momentary disturbance acts on it, so that it leans over, why cannot it continue to roll in its original straight line while it (presumably) falls over?

Initially it has an angular momentum L as shown in figure 13-16a; after it has been disturbed, a torque acts on it, as shown in figure 13-16b. Suppose the horizontal separation of mg and R is d: the size of this torque T is mgd, and its direction is as shown. In a small time Δt, T produces a change $\Delta L (= T\Delta t)$ in L; as shown in figure 13-17. Since ΔL is perpendicular to L, its effect is to at least change the direction of L. The new spin angular momentum of the coin therefore has a different direction and the coin cannot move along a straight line. If ΔL has a certain size (which depends on T, which depends on the angle of lean) the *size* of L will not be changed, and then the process will continue, the direction of L changing at a constant rate, with the coin rolling in a circular path at a constant speed. (Compare the circular motion of a particle: if the centripetal force has the correct size, it will produce a change in the direction of the velocity of the particle without changing in size.) ◀

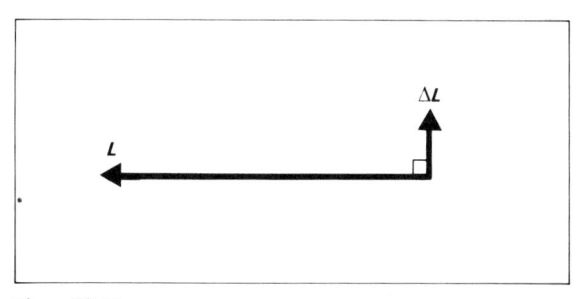

Figure 13-17

The Earth is subject to a very slow precession of its axis of rotation with $\omega_p = 6.7 \times 10^{-12}$ rad s^{-1}, that is a period of rotation of about 26 000 years. This is caused by a torque which the Sun and Moon exert on the slightly asymmetrical Earth (see pages 230 and 234). The Earth also undergoes a very small nutation with a period of 19 years.

Gyroscopes can be used as stabilizers both on a small scale (for example, for a gunsite on a tank) and on a large scale (to prevent a ship from rolling, for example). The principle in each case is that when a bump or a roll tries to alter the vector angular momentum of the gyroscope a couple is produced which tries to preserve its initial orientation. ★

Bibliography

Page, R. L. (1969). 'Moments of inertia of the human body about a vertical axis.' *Physics Education*, **4**, page 221.

Dyson, G. H. G. (1970). *The mechanics of athletics*, 5th edition. University of London Press. The chapter on angular motion is a most comprehensive account of the importance of mechanics to almost all human athletic activities.

Pohl, R. W. (1932). *The physical principles of mechanics and acoustics*. Blackie (out of print). This contains a particularly fine set of 'silhouetted' diagrams—Chapter 7 is relevant.

PSSC (1968). *College physics*. Raytheon. Chapter 19 is on angular momentum and includes a large collection of stroboscopic photographs.

Tricker, R. A. R. and Tricker, B. J. K. (1968). *The science of movement*. Mills and Boon. Several chapters contain relevant material.

13 Angular momentum

Exercises

Data (to be used unless otherwise directed):
$g = 10 \text{ m s}^{-2} = 10 \text{ N kg}^{-1}$.

13-1 Estimate the angular momentum of the following.
(a) A wheel of a bicycle moving at a speed of 10 m s^{-1} (i) about a horizontal axis through the hub and perpendicular to the plane of the wheel (ii) about a horizontal axis through the point of contact with the ground and perpendicular to the plane of the wheel.
(b) A ballet dancer spinning on her points, about her axis of rotation.
(c) A long-playing record, rotating about a vertical axis through its centre and perpendicular to its plane.
(d) An empty wooden beer barrel (to hold $4\frac{1}{2}$ gallons), being rolled along the ground, about the axis of the barrel.

13-2 A bicycle, each of whose wheels has a moment of inertia of 0.20 kg m^2, and a radius of 0.30 m, is travelling due north at a speed of 6.0 m s^{-1}. What is the size and direction of the angular momentum of either wheel? •

13-3 Consider the Earth to be a uniform sphere of mass 6.0×10^{24} kg and radius 6.4×10^6 m which rotates about its own axis which makes an angle of $23.5°$ with the normal to the plane containing the Earth and the Sun. Take the mean distance of the Earth from the Sun as 1.5×10^{11} m and calculate the total angular momentum of the Earth about an axis passing through the Sun and perpendicular to the plane containing the Earth and the Sun. (Consider whether you should add or subtract the two terms which comprise the total angular momentum.) •

13-4 An aircraft of mass 2.0×10^5 kg is travelling at a constant speed of 100 m s^{-1} in a horizontal circle of radius 2000 m whose centre is 300 m vertically above a control tower. Eventually the aircraft leaves the circular path, flying along a horizontal straight path which is a tangent to the circle. Find the angular momentum of the aircraft about a vertical axis through the control tower (a) while the aircraft is in the circle (b) when it is flying straight. •

13-5 In one model of a hydrogen atom, an electron moves in a circular path around a proton; its radius is 5.3×10^{-11} m. What is the orbital angular momentum of the electron? (The force F which electric charges Q_1, Q_2 exert on each other in a vacuum is given by $F = kQ_1Q_2/r^2$ where r is the separation and $k = 9.0 \times 10^9 \text{ N m}^2 \text{ C}^{-2}$. The numerical value of the electric charge on both a proton and an electron is 1.6×10^{-19} C; the mass of the electron is 9.1×10^{-31} kg.) •

13-6 The mass of Jupiter is 1.9×10^{27} kg and the radius of its orbit round the Sun is 7.8×10^{11} m. The period of its revolution is 3.7×10^8 s. The mass of the Sun is 2.0×10^{30} kg and its radius is 7.0×10^8 m. Its average angular velocity about its own axis is $1.5 \times 10^{-6} \text{ rad s}^{-1}$. Assuming that the Sun is a uniform sphere (which in reality is *not* true), find the ratio of the angular momentum, about the Sun's axis, of Jupiter and the Sun (Jupiter's spin angular momentum may be neglected). The result of this calculation is important to cosmologists. •

13-7 A gramophone record of mass 0.10 kg and radius 0.15 m can be idealized as a uniform disc. It is dropped onto a turntable whose moment of inertia is $1.5 \times 10^{-2} \text{ kg m}^2$ and which has an angular velocity of 3.5 rad s^{-1}. What is the angular velocity of the turntable-and-record as soon as they have reached a common angular velocity? Is there any loss of kinetic energy in the process? Assume no external torque acts during the collision. •

13-8 A figure-skater, with her arms pulled in to her sides, and standing upright, has a moment of inertia of 1.2 kg m^2. When she has her arms outstretched, and stands on one leg with the other leg stretched horizontally her moment of inertia increases to 8.0 kg m^2. If her angular velocity in the first position was 25 rad s^{-1}, what is her angular velocity when she changes to the second position? How do you account for the change in her kinetic energy? •

13-9 A turntable in a children's playground has a moment of inertia of 200 kg m^2. Five children of average mass 20 kg stand 2.0 m from its centre, and then start to run round the edge of it, reaching a speed of 3.0 m s^{-1} relative to the turntable. What is then the angular velocity of the turntable? •

13-10 A man sits on a frictionless turntable (as described in Section 13-7) but holds, instead of a bicycle wheel, a mallet. He intends to swing the mallet in a horizontal plane so that he and the turntable will rotate in the opposite sense. He can swing the mallet only through $180°$, and its moment of inertia about the central vertical axis is considerably less than that of himself and the turntable about that axis. Describe and explain how he can perform one complete revolution.

13-11 A flywheel is supported by a horizontal axle which rotates in frictionless bearings. The system consisting of flywheel and axle has a mass of 200 kg and a moment of inertia of 250 kg m^2; and the radius of the flywheel is 1.2 m. A force of 1500 N is applied vertically downwards at the rim. Where is the other force with which this constitutes a couple? What is the angular acceleration of the flywheel? What is the rate of change of angular momentum of the system? •

13-12 Estimate the rate of gain of angular momentum of the rotational moving parts of a motor car engine when a man tries to start it using a starting handle.

13-13 An electric fan can rotate about an axis which makes an angle θ with the vertical, as shown in figure 13-18. Its mounting is free to rotate about a vertical axis. The fan rotates clockwise when viewed from the front. What happens when
(a) $\theta < 90°$ (b) $\theta = 90°$ (c) $\theta > 90°$?

13-14 Explain the presence of a small auxiliary rotor at the tail of a helicopter. State how the direction of rotation of the main and the auxiliary rotors are related.

13-15 A top has a moment of inertia I about its spin axis and an angular velocity ω about that axis; as a result of being subjected to a torque T it is precessing without nutation with an angular velocity ω_p. We have seen that $\omega_p = T/I\omega$: in what sense is this result analogous to the result $\omega = F/mv$ for the motion of a particle of mass m moving at a constant speed v and constant angular velocity ω when the centripetal force is F? (*Hint*: in circular motion the change in velocity caused by the force produces no change in speed; in the motion of a top the change in the precessional angular velocity ω_p caused by the torque produces no change in the spin angular velocity ω.)

13-16 Explain how a bicycle can be steered if the rider is not touching the handlebars. Would this be easier if the bicycle were of the modern small-wheeled type?

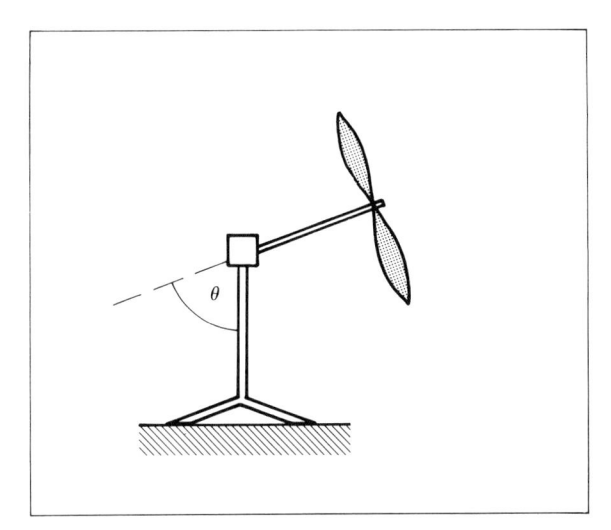

Figure 13-18

13-17 What is meant by the *rifling* of a gun barrel? What is its purpose?

13-18 What effect does the rotation of the moving parts of an aero-engine have when a pilot wants
 (a) to turn the aeroplane in a horizontal plane
 (b) to make the aeroplane climb?
(In jet engines different parts of the engine are made to rotate in opposite senses to reduce gyroscopic effects, if this can be done without introducing additional complications.)

13-19 The rotating parts of a motor-car engine rotate clockwise when viewed from the front of the car and have a moment of inertia of $20\,\text{kg}\,\text{m}^2$ and an angular velocity of $80\,\text{rad}\,\text{s}^{-1}$. The wheelbase of the car is 2.5 m. If it is driven along a horizontal circular arc of radius 100 m at a speed of $20\,\text{m}\,\text{s}^{-1}$, what gyroscopic effect is there? ●

13-20 Some motor-car engines are mounted transversely: can the gyroscopic effect when such a car turns a corner be put to any advantage? See also Exercise 12-37; what should be the direction of the axis of the flywheel of the bus? Is the direction of rotation of the flywheel about the chosen axis relevant?

13-21 Discuss whether the rotation of the wheels of a car has any significant effect on its ability to turn corners without overturning.

13-22 What is the principle of a gyrocompass? Does it have any advantage over a magnetic compass?

13-23 A bicycle wheel is suspended from one end A of an axle AO by a cord attached to a fixed point (figure 13-19). The mass of the wheel is 4.0 kg and its moment of inertia is $0.50\,\text{kg}\,\text{m}^2$ about the axle. The distance of A from O, the centre of the wheel, is 0.20 m. The wheel is rotating, in the direction shown in figure 13-19, with an angular velocity of $16\,\text{rad}\,\text{s}^{-1}$. How could the wheel be enabled to precess without nutation?

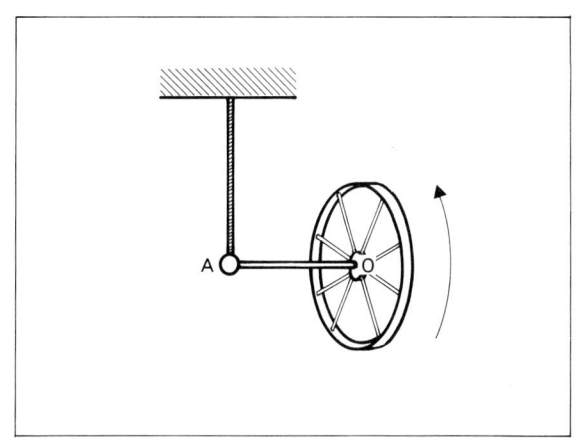

Figure 13-19

Would there by any difference if a more massive bicycle wheel were used, if it had the same radius of gyration, and AO remained the same length? ●

13-24 Figure 13-20 shows a particle of mass m moving in a circle of radius r with constant speed v: the angular velocity ω is given by $v = r\omega$. What is the direction of $\boldsymbol{r} \times m\boldsymbol{v}$ (and hence of $\boldsymbol{L}$)? What is the direction of $\boldsymbol{\omega}$? Are your answers consistent with the fact that $\boldsymbol{L} = I\boldsymbol{\omega}$?

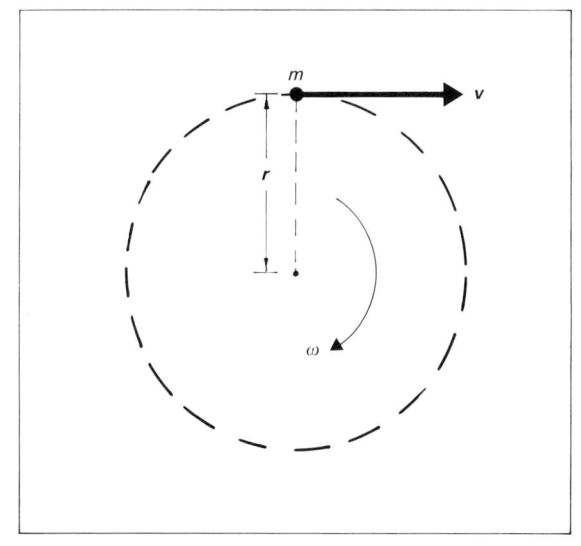

Figure 13-20

13-25 For mathematicians only: find the value of the triple vector product $\boldsymbol{r} \times m(\boldsymbol{\omega} \times \boldsymbol{r})$. Is it equal to $I\boldsymbol{\omega}$?

13-26 Refer to figure 13-3: express the area POP' as a vector $\Delta \boldsymbol{A}$ in terms of $\boldsymbol{r}$ and $\boldsymbol{v}$, and show that $\Delta \boldsymbol{A}/\Delta t = \boldsymbol{L}/2m$.

14 Gravitation

14-1	Historical introduction	224	14-7	Gauss's theorem	235
14-2	Newton's law of gravitation	225	14-8	Gravitational potential	237
14-3	Measuring G	227	14-9	Inertial and gravitational mass	241
14-4	The Earth's gravitational field	228		Bibliography	242
14-5	Satellites	230		Exercises	243
14-6	Sun, Earth, and Moon	232			

14-1 Historical introduction

Man's attempts to explain the motions of the heavenly bodies form a story rich in science and humanity. In this chapter we are not going to attempt a historical development other than a brief outline in this introduction; we would encourage the reader to refer to Eric M. Rogers's *Physics for the inquiring mind*, the second part of which is subtitled 'Astronomy: a history of theory'.

Until near the end of the seventeenth century when Newton produced his great treatise on mechanics, the study of the Sun, the Moon, the planets, and the stars had followed two separate lines of development. Firstly, men had attempted to *describe* the motions of these bodies well enough to predict their relative positions at future times and, secondly, they had tried to suggest a *mechanism* for the motions. The former (kinematical) approach met with considerable success: ingenious compound motions, for example the epicycles of Ptolemy (about A.D. 120), could predict planetary motions more or less to within the accuracy of measurements then available in all but a very few situations. There was little advance on Greek measurements until Tycho Brahe (1546–1601) in a lifetime of careful observation produced very detailed tables of planetary positions. Tycho Brahe did not himself advance the science of planetary prediction but his tables were the experimental results on which the work of Kepler and Newton was based. Johannes Kepler (1571–1630) showed that Brahe's results were consistent with a system of planets moving round the Sun and obeying the following laws:

1. *The planets describe elliptical orbits, with the Sun at one focus.*
2. *The line drawn from the Sun to a planet sweeps out equal areas in equal times.*
3. *The squares of the periods of revolution are proportional to the cubes of the semi-major axes of the planets' paths round the Sun.*

The first law indicates a heliocentric scheme; this had been shown by Nicolaus Copernicus (1473–1543) to fit the then available observations better than a geocentric one, but Kepler's achievement in establishing the elliptical property is amazing. Although he chose to study the orbit of the planet Mars, the most eccentric of those then accurately measured, the path differs from a circular orbit by only, at most, 5 parts in 1000. All three laws are the result of a very great deal of arithmetical work; he did not discover the third law until very late in his life.

So much for kinematics–but *why* do the planets obey Kepler's laws? What are the dynamics of the problem? The story here is a shorter one, for there are only two real contributors: Galileo Galilei (1564–1642) and Isaac Newton himself. Galileo developed the concepts of inertia and of acceleration while Newton codified the dynamics of a particle in his three laws of motion. Gathering these from earlier sections we have:

1. *A force is required to accelerate a particle, that is to alter its motion in size or direction or both.*
2. *The vector rate of change of momentum of a body is proportional to the resultant external force acting on it. For a particle of fixed mass this becomes* $m\mathbf{a} = \sum \mathbf{F}$.
3. *If a body A exerts a force $\mathbf{F}$ on body B, then body B exerts a force $-\mathbf{F}$ on body A.*

Newton now suggested a law of gravitational force which was consistent with both his own laws and Kepler's laws. This final result is undoubtedly one of man's great achievements. The bibliography at the end of this chapter contains several references in which a detailed consideration is given to the story briefly summarized here.

14-2 Newton's law of gravitation

The gravitational pull of one particle on another depends on the mass of each particle and the distance between them. If we postulate that for every particle in the Universe

$$F \propto \frac{m_1 m_2}{r^2},$$

then all the predictions made using this inverse square law relation are found to be verified experimentally. The predictions are astronomical or astronautical and do not involve laboratory experiments.

Laboratory tests of $F \propto 1/r^2$ cannot be made with any precision for as r decreases so must the dimensions of the attracting bodies and their masses depend on their radii cubed. In the sections which follow some of the evidence to support the law is considered. This includes explaining the motion of satellites, both natural and artificial (and therefore Kepler's laws), our tides, the behaviour of comets, and the precession of the equinoxes; the variation of g over the Earth's surface, both on a large and on a small scale; and calculating the masses of those planets which have satellites. Perhaps the most convincing evidence imaginable for a scientific theory is that it predicts the existence of some hitherto unknown object—Newton's law of gravitation predicted the existence of the planets Neptune and Pluto. The law has also helped physicists and astronomers in formulating theories of galactic, stellar,

	Mass/10^{23} kg	Radius/10^6 m	Semi-major axis length/10^{10} m	Period of revolution/10^6 s	Mean density /kg m^{-3}	Acceleration due to gravity at surface/m s^{-2}
Sun	19 800 000	695	—	—	1 420	274.40
Mercury	3.28	2.57	5.79	7.60	5 610	3.92
Venus	48.3	6.31	10.8	19.4	5 160	8.82
Earth	59.8	6.38	14.9	31.6	5 520	9.80
Mars	6.37	3.43	22.8	59.4	3 950	3.92
Jupiter	19 000	71.8	77.8	374	1 340	26.46
Saturn	5 670	60.3	143	930	690	11.76
Uranus	880	26.7	287	2 660	1 360	9.80
Neptune	1 030	24.8	450	5 200	1 300	9.80
Pluto	—	—	591	7 820	—	—
Moon	0.734	1.74	0.038	2.36	3 360	1.67

Table 14-1 The Solar System.

and planetary evolution, and played a part in landing men on the Moon's surface.

If $F \propto m_1 m_2/r^2$, then we can insert a constant, which is called G, the *universal constant of gravitation*, and write

$$F = G\frac{m_1 m_2}{r^2}. \qquad [14\text{-}1]$$

G is universal in the sense that it has the same value for all gravitational interactions, that is it is the same when we use the law to analyse the motions of the satellites of Jupiter as when we use it for Earth satellites. All gravitational interactions are found to be attractions: no gravitational repulsion has ever been observed.

From experiment, $G = 6.670 \times 10^{-11}\,\text{N}\,\text{m}^2\,\text{kg}^{-2}$. Even now it is known to only four significant figures and is the most difficult of all the fundamental constants to measure precisely. The dimensions of G are $M^{-1}L^3T^{-2}$.

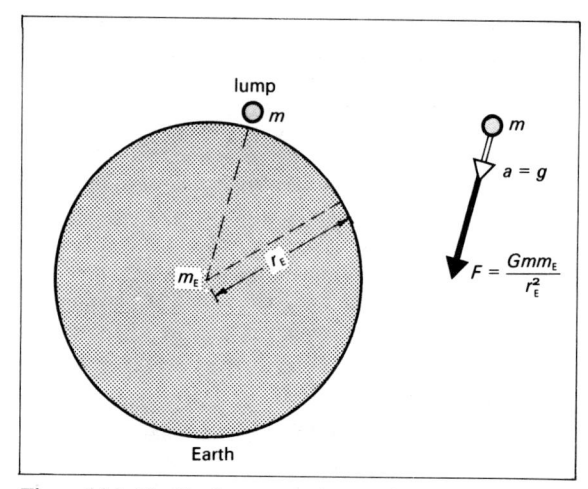

Figure 14-1 The Earth attracts a lump at its surface.

▶ **Example 14-1** What gravitational force does a billiard ball (of mass 0.10 kg) exert on another similar ball which is placed so that their centres are 0.10 m apart? (Treat the balls as particles—we shall see in Section 14-7 that this procedure is justified.)

Using Newton's law of gravitation, we have

$$F = \frac{(6.7 \times 10^{-11}\,\text{N}\,\text{m}^2\,\text{kg}^{-2})(0.10\,\text{kg})^2}{(0.10\,\text{m})^2}$$

$$= 6.7 \times 10^{-11}\,\text{N}.$$

This is roughly equal to the weight of a particle of smoke ash. In everyday life other forces (such as frictional forces) are nearly always much larger than gravitational forces (unless, of course, one of the bodies is of planetary size). ◀

Consider the gravitational pull of the Earth on a lump with a mass m (figure 14-1). We know that if the lump is released just above the Earth's surface it accelerates towards the centre of the Earth with an acceleration of g. Applying Newton's second law to the mass m we get

$$mg = G\frac{mm_E}{r_E^2}.$$

Dividing by m and rearranging

$$m_E = \frac{gr_E^2}{G} = \frac{(9.8\,\text{N}\,\text{kg}^{-1})(6.4 \times 10^6\,\text{m})^2}{6.7 \times 10^{-11}\,\text{N}\,\text{m}^2\,\text{kg}^{-2}}$$

$$= 6.0 \times 10^{24}\,\text{kg},$$

and we have found the mass of the Earth! If the free fall acceleration is known at a known distance from any other planet then its mass can similarly be found. If we examine this apparently simple calculation closely several difficulties arise. Does not Newton's law of gravitation apply only to particles?—the Earth is hardly that. Is it legitimate to divide by m? m in mg is the inertial mass: is m in Gmm_E/r_E^2 the inertial mass? In measuring g relative to the Earth's surface are we not using a non-inertial frame of reference? Such a list of possible difficulties is rather daunting. The difficulty with the reference frame has been discussed before on page 70 but the other two questions present more serious difficulties; we shall ignore them for the moment and assume that inertial masses can be used in the law of gravitation (see Section 14-9), and that a rigid body possessing spherical symmetry will gravitationally attract and be attracted by external particles as if all its mass were concentrated at its centre (see Section 14-7).

We might also note that in equation 14-1 the direction of $\boldsymbol{F}$ is parallel but in the opposite direction to the vector $\boldsymbol{r}$, if $\boldsymbol{F}$ is the pull of m_1 on m_2 and the origin of $\boldsymbol{r}$ is at the particle m_1. To express Newton's law of gravitation in vector form we thus have

$$\boldsymbol{F} = -G\frac{m_1 m_2}{r^2}\boldsymbol{n}$$

where $\boldsymbol{n}$ is the unit vector in the direction of $\boldsymbol{r}$.

▶ **Example 14-2** Assuming that the period T of orbit of a satellite round a body depends on the mass m of the body, the radius r of the orbit, and the universal gravitational constant G, use the method of dimensional analysis to find a possible form of the dependence of T on m, r, and G.

Let us write $T = km^x r^y G^z$.

Then $[T] = [m]^x [r]^y [G]^z$

or $T = M^x L^y (M^{-1} L^3 T^{-2})^z$.

Equating powers of the dimensions, we have

$$M: 0 = x - z$$
$$L: 0 = y + 3z$$

and $$T: 1 = -2z,$$

which give $z = -\frac{1}{2}, \quad y = \frac{3}{2}, \quad x = -\frac{1}{2},$

so that
$$T = k\sqrt{\left(\frac{r^3}{Gm}\right)}$$

or $GmT^2 = k^2 r^3$.

This method does not enable us to find the value of k: by other means we can show that $k = 2\pi$. ◂

14-3 Measuring G

It is worth noting here how Newton estimated G. He guessed that the average density of the Earth was between 5000 and 6000 kg m^{-3} and thus found a value for the mass of the Earth $m_E = \frac{4}{3}\pi r_E^3 \rho$, its radius being fairly well known at the time. He then equated mg with Gmm_E/r_E^2, as we did on page 226, and knowing m_E was able to deduce G. His guess for ρ was a good one (a recent value is 5522 kg m^{-3} —see table 14-1) and consequently so was his estimate of G. Incidentally we might also note that an experiment to measure G is sometimes referred to as an experiment to 'weigh' the Earth.

We can make only a rough measurement of G in the school laboratory, that is we can obtain only an order of magnitude for G, unless a great deal of time and care is taken. As we see from Example 14-1 the forces involved are minute. The following outline is taken from an experiment suggested in the Nuffield Advanced Physics course and the reader is referred to the course's students' laboratory book for greater detail. Two small metal spheres (of iron for example) are mounted about 100 mm apart on a springy light beam (springy to act as a shock absorber) and the beam is suspended by a *very* fine tungsten fibre about 75 mm long (see figure 14-2a). The dumbbell-like rod will not now remain still unless it is shielded from convection currents and mechanical vibrations. It is therefore hung in a case and the case closed. The top support for the tungsten fibre should not be rigid but of a spongy material—again to act as an absorber for mechanical vibration. The beam carries a small mirror which reflects a fixed incident beam of light on to a scale and thus registers any torsional movement of the beam. During the experiment electrostratic forces may be larger

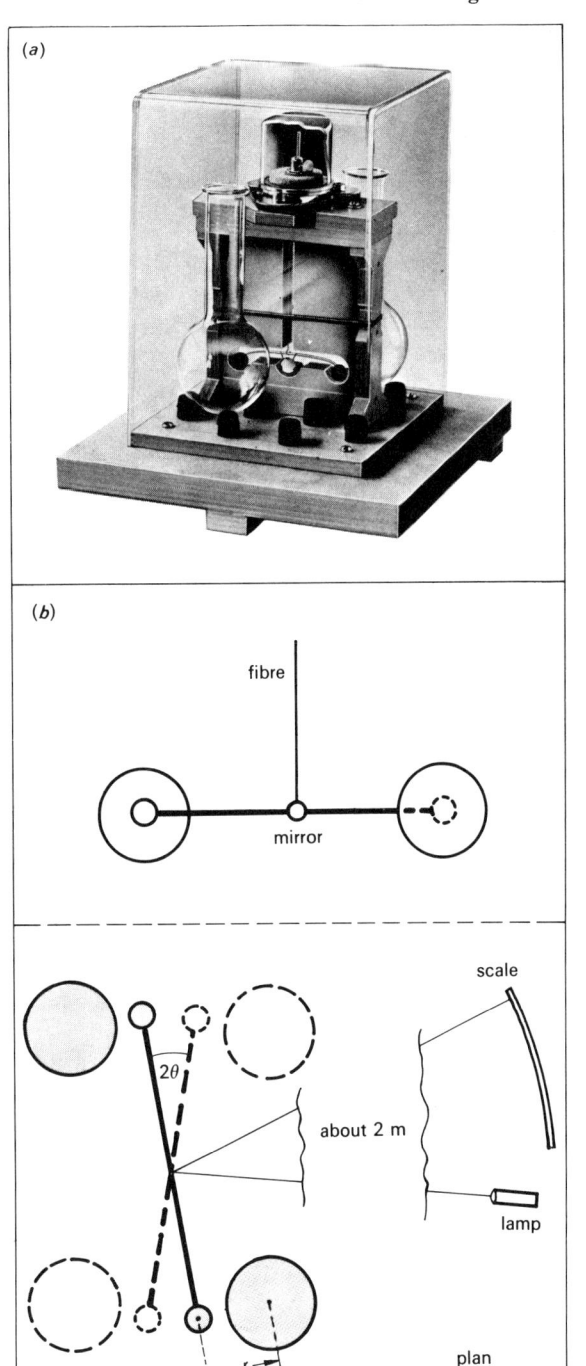

Figure 14-2 (*a*) A small torsion balance, based on Cavendish's original method, with which the gravitational constant G can be measured. The flasks are filled with mercury, and exert a torque on the small iron spheres. (*b*) illustrates the principle of the method.

228 14 Gravitation

than the forces being investigated and great care to avoid charging parts of the apparatus must be taken. It is also advisable to screen the apparatus electrostatically with aluminium foil.

If two large attracting metal spheres (such as round-bottomed flasks of mercury) are now placed as indicated in figure 14-2a then the beam should twist under the action of the gravitational torque. If the large spheres are then placed so as to rotate the beam in the opposite sense, the angle between the two positions of equilibrium, 2θ (see figure 14-2b), can be deduced from the movement of the light across the scale. The experimenter may have to wait for some time for the system to settle down in its new equilibrium position after the large spheres are moved. If the scale is a distance L from the mirror, and the light from the mirror moves a distance x, then

$$2(2\theta) \approx \frac{x}{L} \quad \text{if } \theta \text{ is small,}$$

therefore
$$\theta = \frac{x}{4L}.$$

To measure the torque it is necessary to know the torsional constant k of the suspending fibre, where

$$k = \frac{\text{applied torque}}{\text{angular displacement}}.$$

To find k the large attracting masses are removed and the beam is set into torsional oscillation (see Section 15-5); the period is then given by

$$T = 2\pi \sqrt{\frac{I}{k}},$$

where I is the moment of inertia of the oscillating system about the axis of rotation.

Thus
$$k = \frac{4\pi^2 I}{T^2} = \frac{\text{applied torque}}{\theta}.$$

As the applied torque $= G\frac{m_1 m_2}{r^2} d$ (see figure 14-2),

where d is the distance between the two suspended spheres,

we have
$$G\frac{m_1 m_2}{r^2} d = \frac{4\pi^2 I \theta}{T^2},$$

in which all the quantities are measurable except G, I being approximately $2m_1 (d/2)^2$.

To measure G more carefully no new principle is needed. We could make the attracting masses larger and make the torsion suspension more sensitive. If the *whole* apparatus is scaled up, however, we gain no advantage, as the moment of inertia of the beam increases and the fibre needs to be stronger and therefore less sensitive. Also the larger the apparatus, the more important the effects of temperature gradients between different parts of the apparatus. At the moment (1972) a large-scale experiment is underway in a subterranean 'laboratory' in north-east Italy; in a cave, the Grotta Gigante, so far below the surface as to have annual temperature variations of less than 1 K and to be free of man-made vibrations, an 80 m torsion pendulum is being set up which will be operated by remote control and be watched by closed-circuit television.

An analysis of measurements of G over the last hundred years shows convincingly that the measured value does *not* depend on the size, shape, temperature, or nature of the attracting materials. Further, it has been shown experimentally that one can *not* shield one body from the gravitational attraction of another by interposing, for instance, a lead screen. G seems truly to be a universal constant.

14-4 The Earth's gravitational field

The acceleration due to gravity, g, appears in the relation $W = mg$ for the weight of a body. Thus we can write

[5-4]
$$g = \frac{W}{m},$$

which expresses g as the gravitational pull per unit mass that the Earth exerts on a body. In this sense g is called the Earth's *gravitational field strength*. It is a vector quantity and has the unit $N\,kg^{-1}$, which is of course equivalent to $m\,s^{-2}$. For a spherically symmetrical Earth, $W = Gmm_E/r^2$, where m_E is the mass of the Earth and r the distance measured from its centre, so that

$$mg_r = G\frac{mm_E}{r^2},$$

$$g_r = G\frac{m_E}{r^2} = \text{constant for a given } r. \quad [14\text{-}2]$$

As $Gm_E = (6.67 \times 10^{-11}\,N\,m^2\,kg^{-2})(5.98 \times 10^{24}\,kg)$
$= 3.99 \times 10^{14}\,N\,m^2\,kg^{-1}$
$\approx 4 \times 10^{14}\,N\,m^2\,kg^{-1},$

then it is a simple matter to draw a graph of g_r against r for the Earth. Figure 14-3 shows such a graph where g_0 and r_E stand for the size of g_r at the Earth's surface and the radius of the Earth respectively. The problem of how g_r varies for $r < r_E$ is left to Example 14-8.

Let us consider the value of g at a height h above the

14-4 The Earth's gravitational field

Since $h \ll r_E$ we can write

$$g_h = g_0\left(1 - \frac{2h}{r_E} + \cdots\right) \quad \text{(see page 10),}$$

$$\approx g_0\left(1 - \frac{2h}{r_E}\right)$$

Thus at an altitude of 32 km,

$$\frac{2h}{r_E} = \frac{2 \times 32 \times 10^3 \text{ m}}{6.4 \times 10^6 \text{ m}} = \frac{1}{100},$$

and g_h is only $99g_0/100$, that is the gravitational field strength has fallen by one per cent.

If we consider the Earth's gravitational field on a larger scale it is useful to use the concept of gravitational lines of force. The idea is similar to that which the reader may have met in studying electromagnetism or electrostatics. We say that there is a gravitational field in any region of space in which a mass experiences a gravitational force and the size of the field is given by W/m, where m is a small mass. We represent the gravitational field by lines of force, the tangent to which at any point is the direction of W. An arrow is added to give the sense of the field. The gravitational field around the Earth would be radial but for the presence of the Moon, which, with a mass of about $m_E/80$, modifies the resultant field as shown in figure 14-4. On a yet larger scale the Earth itself produces a very tiny disturbance in the Sun's gravitational field.

On a smaller scale we find that there are variations with latitude in the Earth's gravitational field strength as

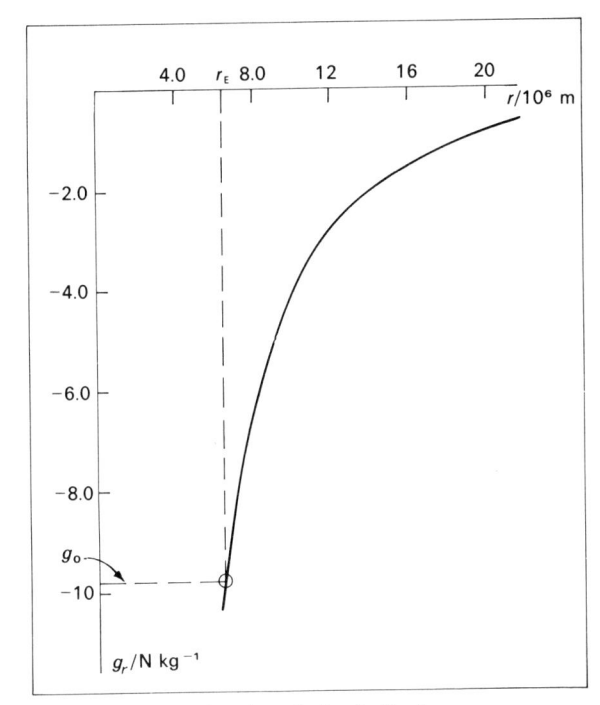

Figure 14-3 g_r as a function of r for the Earth.

Earth's surface; that is in the few kilometres in which man normally moves. If this point is a distance r from the Earth's centre we can write $r = r_E + h$ and get

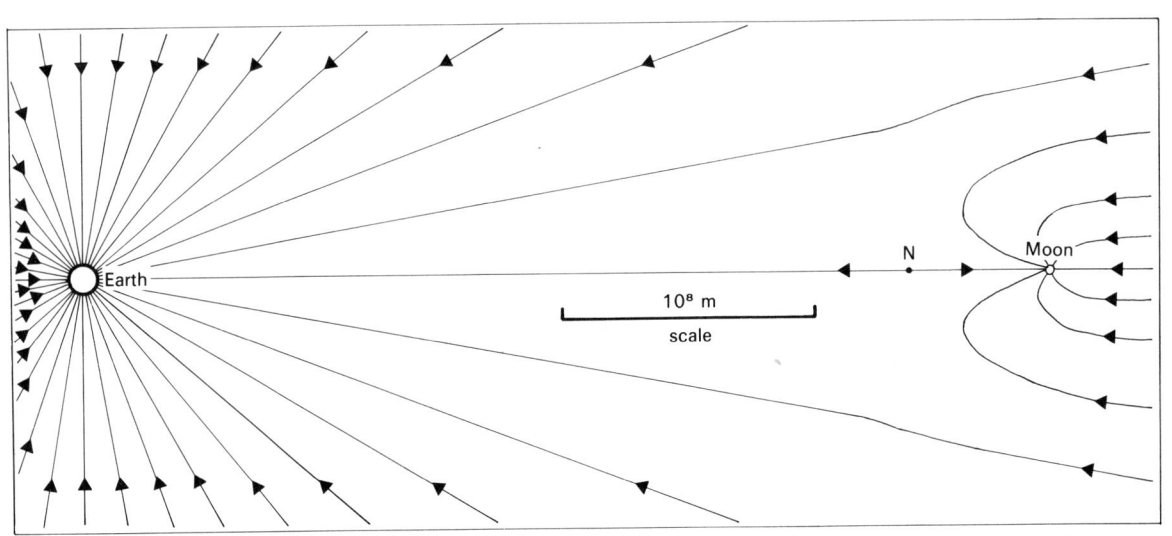

$$g_h = \frac{Gm_E}{(r_E + h)^2} = \frac{Gm_E}{r_E^2} \frac{1}{(1 + h/r_E)^2} = g_0\left(1 + \frac{h}{r_E}\right)^{-2}.$$

Figure 14-4 Lines of force for the Earth–Moon gravitational field. N (at which there is zero resultant gravitational field) is called a *neutral point*.

Latitude/°	g/N kg^{-1}
0	9.780
10	9.782
20	9.786
30	9.793
40	9.802
50	9.811
60	9.819
70	9.826
80	9.831
90	9.832

Table 14-2 The variation of g with latitude at sea-level. The value is given in N kg^{-1} but could equally well be given in m s^{-2}. The standard value is 9.805 65 N kg^{-1}.

the result of the Earth's lack of spherical symmetry. Its polar diameter is about 40 km less than its equatorial diameter, an eccentricity of about 1 in 300 (see figure 14-5). One result of this is that the Mississippi river which flows towards the Equator finishes further from the centre of the Earth than it started! Also, an observer on the Earth finds that at the Equator the value of g is 0.05 N kg^{-1} less than it is at the Poles; 0.03 N kg^{-1} of this is caused by the rotation of the Earth about its axis and was discussed in Section 5-7, but the remaining 0.02 N kg^{-1} is a result of the Earth's lack of spherical symmetry.

Apart from variations in g due to differences in altitude, there are also local variations in the Earth's gravitational field strength caused by mountains and by mineral or oil deposits: the Earth's mass is not distributed with perfect spherical symmetry. The geologist can use these variations in g to deduce what lies beneath the surface; *gravimeters* (which are simply very sensitive spring balances) are used to compare values of g in different places with an accuracy of better than 1 part in 10^8. Section 3-5 gives an account of an absolute measurement of g by free fall techniques, and table 14-2 lists its values at different latitudes. For reference purposes there is a standard gravitational field strength $g_s = 9.80565$ N kg^{-1} which is close to the measured value at sea-level and latitude 45°.

The orbits of artificial satellites are affected by variations in g, and from a study of the variations in their orbits has come new knowledge about the shape of the Earth and the presence of subterranean mineral deposits. The effect of local variations in the Moon's gravitational field on the early Apollo missions made it possible to identify the so-called *mascons*—local mass concentrations.

14-5 Satellites

In Section 5-7 we discussed free fall and weightlessness. Any body which is projected in such a way as to remain in a state of free fall for any length of time we shall call a *satellite* of the body in whose gravitational field it is moving. What can we deduce from Newton's mechanics about the motion of a satellite? Let us use the solar system as the basis of our discussion. If we can treat the Sun as being at rest, then the angular momentum of a planet about the Sun remains constant as there is no torque acting on the planet about its axis of rotation. Kinematically this means that the area swept out by the line joining the planet to the Sun in successive time intervals is constant—see Section 13-3. Thus Newton's laws of motion (in this case the principle of conservation of angular momentum) explain the motion stated by Kepler in his second law.

Suppose that the motion of a planet *is* circular with the Sun at the centre of its orbit; this is so nearly true of all the planets except Pluto (and possibly Mercury) as to be a reasonable assumption. A planet of mass m_P moving with (constant) speed $v = r\omega$ in a circle of radius r will be subject to a centripetal acceleration $r\omega^2$ produced by the gravitational pull of the Sun (mass m_S); this pull is $Gm_P m_S/r^2$. Applying Newton's second law to the planet

$$m_P r\omega^2 = G\frac{m_P m_S}{r^2},$$

or

$$r^3\omega^2 = Gm_S.$$

As Gm_S is the same for all the planets, then

$$r^3\omega^2 = \text{constant}, \qquad [14\text{-}3]$$

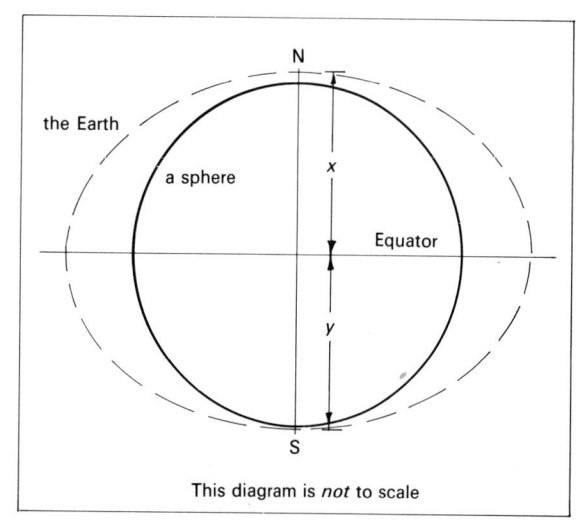

Figure 14-5 The shape of the Earth. The equatorial diameter is 42.77 km greater than the polar diameter. For the Northern bulge $x = y + 33$ m.

14-5 Satellites

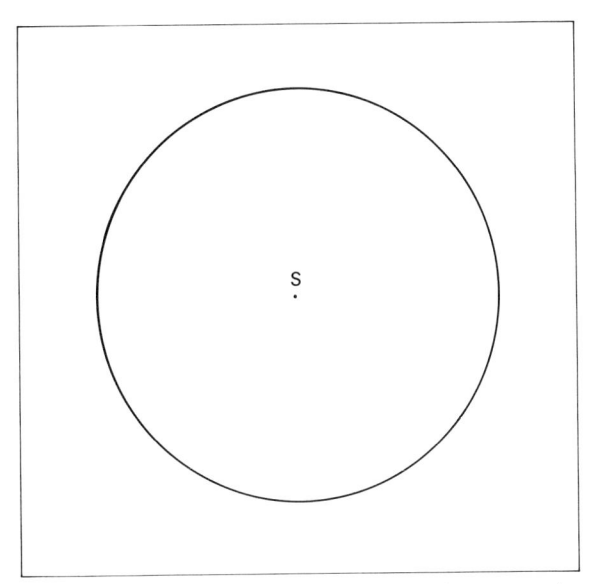

Figure 14-6 The Earth's orbit round the Sun drawn to scale. Can you see that it is *not* a circle with S at its centre?

and using $\omega = 2\pi/T$, where T is the period of the motion,

$$r^3 \frac{4\pi^2}{T^2} = \text{constant}$$

or

$$r^3 \propto T^2$$

for the planets of the solar system. This is Kepler's third law—another triumph for Newtonian mechanics. By measuring r^3/T^2, which is equal to $Gm_S/4\pi^2$, we can calculate the mass of the Sun, and similarly the mass of any object which possesses a satellite. If we take the Earth satellites listed in table 14-3 and plot a graph of $\log_{10}(r/m)$ against $\log_{10}(T/s)$ we should get a straight line with a slope of 2/3.

▶ **Example 14-3** What tangential speed on the Moon's equator would a rifle bullet need for it to make a complete orbit of the Moon? Take G to be 6.7×10^{-11} N m² kg⁻², the mass m_M of the Moon to be 7.3×10^{22} kg and its radius r to be 1.7×10^6 m.

Using Newton's law of gravitation, and his second law, we have

$$G\frac{mm_M}{r^2} = m\frac{v^2}{r}$$

where m is the mass of the bullet and v its speed.

Hence

$$v = \sqrt{\left(\frac{Gm_M}{r}\right)}$$

$$= \sqrt{\left(\frac{6.7 \times 10^{-11} \text{ N m}^2 \text{ kg}^{-2} \times 7.3 \times 10^{22} \text{ kg}}{1.7 \times 10^6 \text{ m}}\right)}$$

$$= 1.7 \times 10^3 \text{ m s}^{-1}. \qquad ◀$$

▶ **Example 14-4** Early Bird is one communications satellite which has been put into an orbit such that it appears stationary to an observer on the Earth. Find its speed, given that $G = 6.7 \times 10^{-11}$ N m² kg⁻² and that the mass m_E of the Earth is 6.0×10^{24} kg.

The force F of attraction is given by $F = Gmm_E/r^2$ where m is the mass of the satellite and r is the radius of its orbit. By Newton's second law we have $F = mv^2/r$ where v is the speed of the satellite: we also have $T = 2\pi r/v$ where T is the period of the orbit.

It is always best to perform the algebra before substituting values of the quantities, so eliminating F and m from the first two equations, we have

$$\frac{v^2}{r} = \frac{Gm_E}{r^2}$$

which gives

$$v^2 r = Gm_E.$$

Satellite	Date of launch	Period/s	Distance above Earth/km	Notes
Sputnik 1	4.10.57	5.80×10^3	220–950	first artificial satellite
Tiros 1	1.4.60	5.95×10^3	730	weather satellite
Vostok 1	12.4.61	5.35×10^3	180–320	man in Space (Yuri Gagarin)
Syncom 2	26.7.63	8.70×10^4	36 500	synchronous communications satellite
The Moon		2.40×10^6	380 000	how did it come to be there?

Table 14-3 Some Earth satellites. There are thousands of artificial satellites now orbiting the Earth.

232 14 Gravitation

Eliminating r from this and the third equation, we have

$$v^2 \left(\frac{vT}{2\pi}\right) = Gm_E$$

so that

$$v = \sqrt[3]{\left(\frac{2\pi Gm_E}{T}\right)}$$

$$= \sqrt[3]{\left(\frac{2\pi \times 6.7 \times 10^{-11}\,\text{N m}^2\,\text{kg}^{-2} \times 6.0 \times 10^{24}\,\text{kg}}{24 \times 3600\,\text{s}}\right)}$$

$$= 3.1 \times 10^3\,\text{m s}^{-1}.$$

The equation $v^2 r = Gm_E$ (which is a constant for all satellites of the Earth) implies that for a particular speed of the satellite in its orbit there is a particular radius of orbit and we could now determine this. ◀

14-6 Sun, Earth, and Moon

From table 14-1 we see that the relative masses of the Sun, Earth, and Moon are roughly 30 000 000 : 80 : 1, and the average Earth–Sun distance is 400 times the average Earth–Moon distance. From these numbers we can see the scale of the problems which involve the motions and interactions of these bodies.

▶ **Example 14-5** Newton would have known that the Moon was 60 times further from the centre of the Earth than we are, and that, in one second, the Moon deviated from a linear path by about 1.3 mm: that is, it fell, towards the Earth, about 1.3 mm in one second. Would he have thought that this fact supported his theory of gravitation?

If the law is inverse square, the force per unit mass at

so that in the first second of a body's fall, it should fall 1.3 mm × 3600, which is equal to 4.7 m, which compares well with the 4.9 m which a body does fall in the first second of its free fall at the surface of the Earth. The correspondence of these two values not only supports the form of the law, but its application to both terrestrial and planetary mechanics. ◀

The tides

The Sun is so massive that we are quite justified in thinking of the Earth revolving around its centre, but the same cannot be said of the Moon's motion around the Earth. The Moon revolves around the centre of mass of the Earth–Moon system and *so does the Earth*, each with a period of 27.3 days (see figure 14-7). Let us repeat this: each part of the Earth revolves in a circle of radius 4800 km with a period of about 27 days, a motion which is superimposed on its *daily* rotation about an axis through its centre of mass and its *annual* progression around the Sun. Now let us think of the forces involved; the gravitational pull of the Moon on the Earth produces the centripetal force for the Earth's monthly motion. A lump of mass m at the Earth's surface experiences a force $W = Gmm_E/r_E^2$ towards the Earth's centre and an

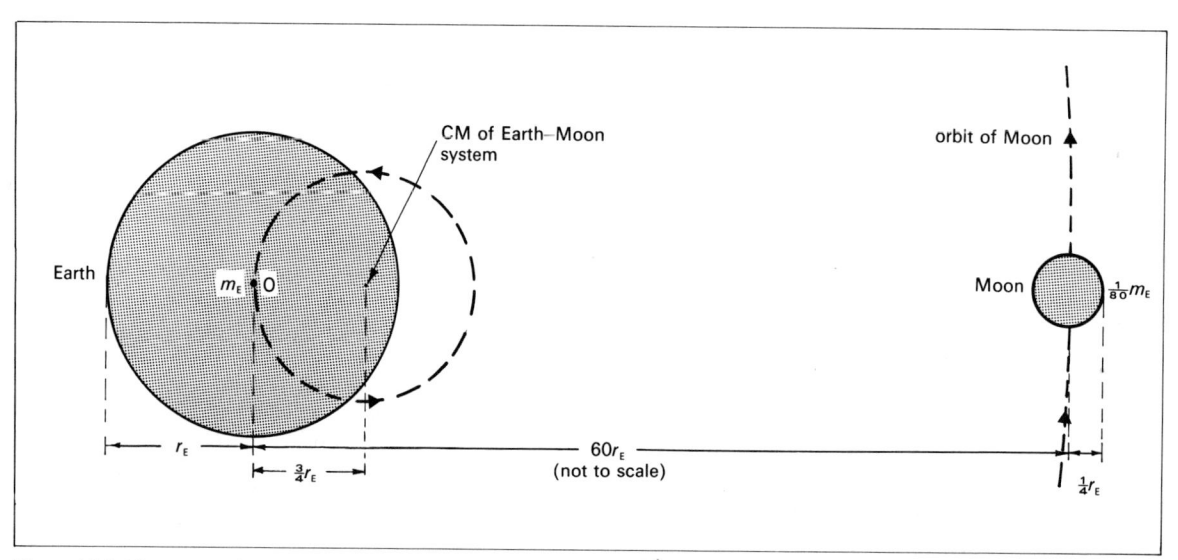

Figure 14-7 The centre of mass of the Earth–Moon system lies about 1600 km below the Earth's surface.

14-6 Sun, Earth, and Moon   233

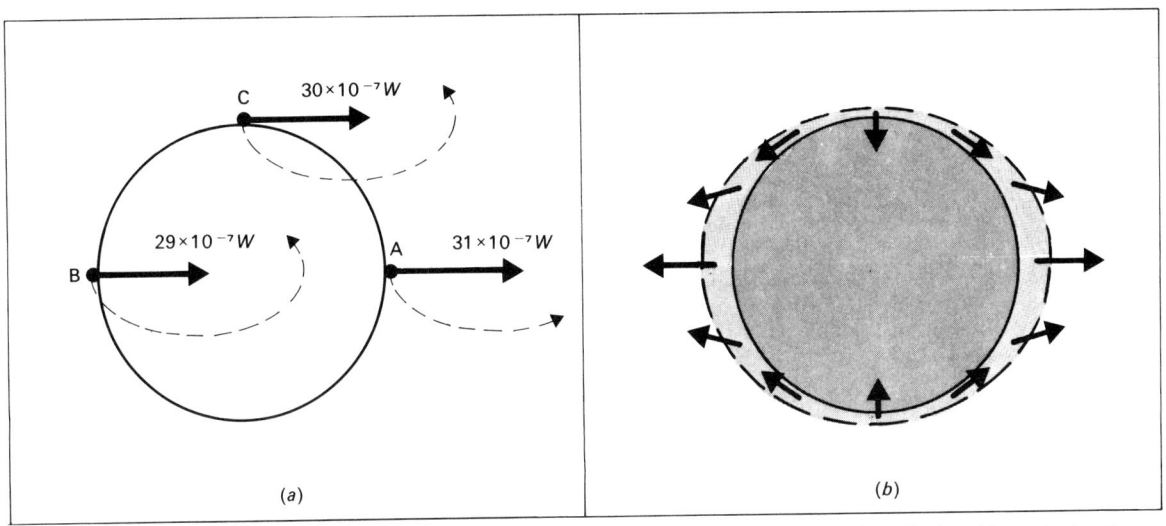

Figure 14-8 (a) A, B, and C all rotate with the same period in circles as shown. (b) shows the effective tide-producing forces.

average force

$$G\frac{mm_E/80}{(60r_E)^2} \approx 30 \times 10^{-7} W$$

towards the centre of the Moon (see figure 14-8). The size of the force exerted by the Moon, however, depends on whether the lump is on the side of the Earth facing the Moon, which would then be $59r_E$ away, or on the opposite side, when it would then be $61r_E$ away. The difference between $(59r_E)^2$ and $(61r_E)^2$ is between 6 and 7 per cent of $(60r_E)^2$, so the difference in these extreme 'Moon forces' is about $2 \times 10^{-7} W$. Thus, while $30 \times 10^{-7} W$ is the centripetal force needed to make a mass m rotate about the centre of mass of the Earth–Moon system, the Moon actually supplies forces varying from about $29 \times 10^{-7} W$ to $31 \times 10^{-7} W$. Referring to figure 14-8a, the effect on the non-rigid Earth is as follows: at A the extra force $10^{-7} W$ tends to pull the mass m away from the Earth's surface (and remember that W is the weight of the mass) and thus piles up the Earth's movable layer of water; at B an extra $10^{-7} W$ is needed to produce the monthly motion and so the mass m appears to be lighter, and again the water piles up. Similarly we can consider the difference in the pull of the Moon and the required centripetal force at all points on the Earth's surface. The (vector) difference between these two forces is represented in figure 14-8b, the net result being that the Moon produces *two tidal bulges* on the Earth, which we know are a few metres high. As the Earth rotates daily about *its* centre the tidal bulges or humps move across its surface, and as this rotation is in the same sense as that of the Moon in its orbit the time interval between tides is nearer 12.5 hours than the expected 12 hours. They do not occur along the line joining the centres of the Earth and Moon because of the inertia of the water, the frictional delaying forces, and the complicated modifying effect of the Earth's land masses.

An exactly similar argument holds for the pull of the Sun on the Earth and we would predict the existence of a further two tides. As the pull of the Sun on the Earth is much bigger than the pull of the Moon we might expect the Sun tides to be larger, but this is not the case, for it is the *difference* in Sun pulls experienced by bodies at midday and midnight which is relevant, that is the gravitational pull on bodies which are roughly $19\,999\,r_E$ and $20\,001\,r_E$ from the Sun. The Sun tides thus appear as minor modifications to Moon tides. When they are in phase we get large *spring* tides and, when they are out of phase, small *neap* tides. The so-called spring tides will, of course, occur twice a month!

The Earth's precession

★ In Section 13-7 we pointed out that the Earth acts like a huge gyroscope which is subject to an external torque about its centre of mass and perpendicular to its daily axis of rotation. In order to understand what follows the reader should be familiar with the behaviour of gyroscopes, at least descriptively—see Section 13-7. The torque is caused by the gravitational pull of the Sun on the non-spherical Earth. (The shape of the Earth was discussed in Section 14-4.)

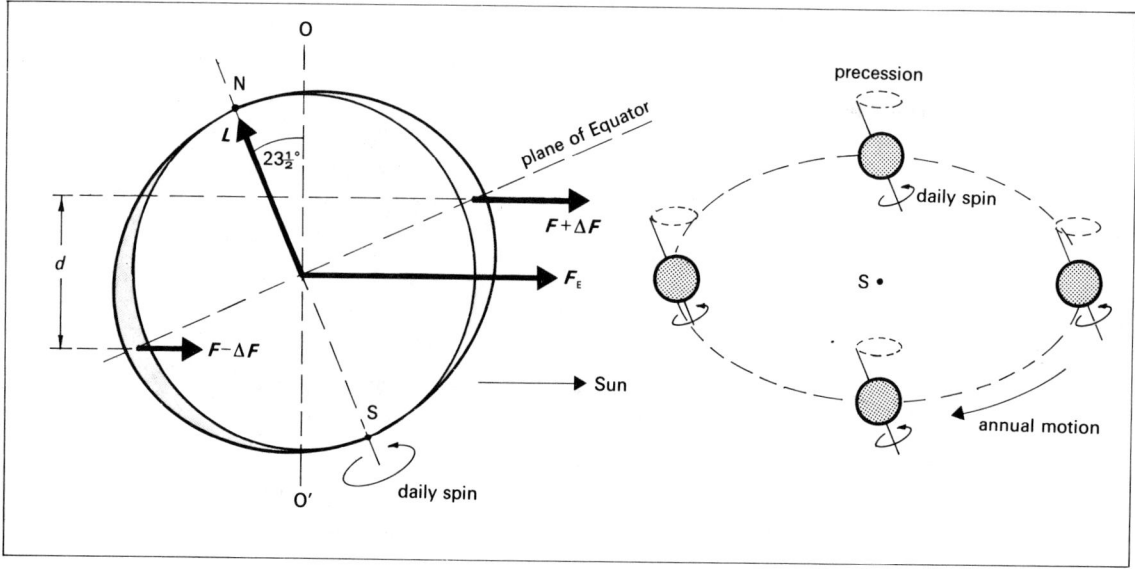

Figure 14-9 The Earth spins daily with its axis making an angle of $23\tfrac{1}{2}°$ to the ecliptic—the plane in which it revolves annually round the Sun.

Consider the Earth as a spherically symmetrical body to which is added an outer layer, thickest at the equator and vanishing at the poles. If the pull of the Sun on the central sphere is F_E and if we can represent the assymetrical pull of the Sun on the outer layer by forces $F+\Delta F$ and $F-\Delta F$ then the Earth is subject to a torque $T = d\Delta F$ (see figure 14-9). As the direction of T is out of the paper and perpendicular to L, the Earth's spin angular momentum, then the Earth's axis of rotation will precess as shown. The torque exerted on the Earth by the Moon is larger than T and the measured period of the precession, 26 000 years, is the result of the action of both bodies. As the axis precesses, that point in the sky which appears to be stationary when viewed from the Northern hemisphere varies. This point is close to a star which we call the Pole star, but 2000 years ago there was no prominent star to mark the place. ★

The Moon

The Moon now always turns the same face towards the Earth. The reader should consider why this is the inevitable fate of any planet or satellite which has non-rigid properties (such as a liquid core or oceans on its surface). For example the planet Mercury has already been reduced to a very slow rotation about its own axis by tides (or their equivalent) caused by the Sun.

Just as the Earth slowed down the spin of the Moon so now the Moon, by means of its tidal effect, is slowing down the spin of the Earth, that is a day is getting longer (by about 10^{-3} s per century). The energy could all become random internal energy but as the principle of conservation of angular momentum applies to the Earth–Moon system, when the Earth's spin angular momentum decreases the orbital angular momentum of the system must increase. In practice the Earth–Moon separation increases (see page 214). Some of the Earth's kinetic energy is thus becoming gravitational potential energy.

Man in Space

This is not the place for a detailed account of extra-terrestrial exploration.* We have considered the theory of the rocket and the need for multistage systems, weightlessness and free fall, orbiting Earth satellites, and the Earth–Moon gravitational field. In later stages of this chapter we shall say more about escape velocity and the shape of satellite orbits. Putting men on the Moon is really a technological achievement—a triumph of engineering skill and managerial organization—rather than a scientific one, for all the mechanics necessary for the project were performed by Newton or his successors years before there were any man-made satellites.

---

*See, for example, the book by Ryan cited in the bibliography to Chapter 8 or the many N.A.S.A. Education Publications especially numbers EP 71 and EP 95.

▶ **Example 14-6** What is the value of the gravitational acceleration g_M at the surface of the Moon? Take $G = 6.7 \times 10^{-11} \text{ N m}^2 \text{ kg}^{-2}$, the radius r_M of the Moon $= 1.7 \times 10^6$ m, and the average density ρ of its material $= 3.4 \times 10^3 \text{ kg m}^{-3}$.

At the Moon's surface the gravitational force on a mass m is given by

$$F = G\frac{mm_M}{r_M^2}$$

and using Newton's second law, we have

$$G\frac{mm_M}{r_M^2} = mg_M$$

where g_M is the acceleration of the mass m at the Moon's surface. Thus

$$\begin{aligned}g_M &= \frac{Gm_M}{r_M^2} \\ &= \frac{G(\tfrac{4}{3}\pi r_M^3 \rho)}{r_M^2} \\ &= \tfrac{4}{3}\pi G \rho r_M \\ &= \tfrac{4}{3}\pi (6.7 \times 10^{-11} \text{ N m}^2 \text{ kg}^{-2}) \\ &\quad \times (3.4 \times 10^3 \text{ kg m}^{-3})(1.7 \times 10^6 \text{ m}) \\ &= 1.6 \text{ m s}^{-2}.\end{aligned}$$

◀

▶ **Example 14-7** If a spacecraft travels directly from the Earth to the Moon, at what distance from the Earth is there no resultant gravitational force on it? Take the masses of the Earth and the Moon to be 6.0×10^{24} kg and 7.4×10^{22} kg respectively, and take the mean Earth–Moon distance to be 3.8×10^8 m.

Let the Earth–Moon distance be R, and let the distance of the gravitational neutral point from the Earth's centre be r. Then

$$G\frac{mm_E}{r^2} = G\frac{mm_M}{(R-r)^2}$$

which gives $(R-r)^2 = \dfrac{m_M}{m_E}r^2.$

Thus $R - r = \pm \left(\dfrac{m_M}{m_E}\right)^{1/2} r$

which gives $r = \dfrac{R}{1 + \sqrt{\dfrac{m_M}{m_E}}}$ (taking the positive sign)

$= 3.4 \times 10^8 \text{ m},$

(that is, the neutral point occurs when the spacecraft has travelled 0.90 of its total distance). What is the significance of the negative sign in the above equation? It cannot have any bearing on this problem, since it gives a value of r which is greater than the Earth–Moon distance. It arises because the initial equation would be obtained if the force of gravitation could be either attractive or repulsive: if the Earth repelled, and the Moon attracted, the neutral point would be on the far side of the Moon. ◀

14-7 Gauss's theorem

The results of this section are of great importance—some of them have already been used. Some readers may wish to omit the mathematics leading to them but they should nevertheless note the results expressed in the two sentences labelled equations 14-4 and 14-5.

★ How can we deduce the gravitational field strength at places in the vicinity of a number of particles or of a body? Knowing Newton's law of gravitation, we can place a small test mass Δm at the point where we require the field and evaluate the pull exerted on it by each particle m_1, m_2, etc. as

$$F_1 = +G\frac{m_1 \Delta m}{r_1^2}n_1, \quad F_2 = +G\frac{m_2 \Delta m}{r_2^2}n_2, \quad \text{etc.,}$$

where we take the origin at the test mass. Then from the definition of the gravitational field strength, we have $\mathbf{g}\Delta m = \Sigma \mathbf{F}$. The resulting problem hinges on evaluating $\Sigma \mathbf{F}$ which, as a problem in vector addition, will be very difficult for more than two or three particles even where the particles make up a body which possesses a high degree of symmetry.

Another approach to the problem is to reformulate Newton's law of gravitation, an inverse square law, as a statement known as *Gauss's theorem*. We define *the flux of a gravitational field through a small plane surface* as the product of the area of the surface and the resolved part of the gravitational field strength normal to it. Referring to figure 14-10 the gravitational flux through A is Φ, where

$$\Phi = g\cos\theta A = g_n A.$$

In vector terms $\quad \Phi = \mathbf{g} \cdot \mathbf{A}.$

Where the gravitational field strength is not constant over a plane surface or where a curved surface is involved, we can still evaluate the total gravitational flux by breaking the surface up into small areas ΔA_1, ΔA_2, etc., for, as Φ is a scalar quantity,

$$\begin{aligned}\Phi &= \sum \Delta \Phi = \sum g_n \Delta A \\ &= g_1 \cos\theta_1 \Delta A_1 + g_2 \cos\theta_2 \Delta A_2 + \cdots,\end{aligned}$$

g_n representing the resolved part of $\mathbf{g}$ for the area involved. Gauss's theorem states that

the total flux of the gravitational field outwards through any closed surface is equal to $4\pi G$ times the total mass enclosed by the surface.

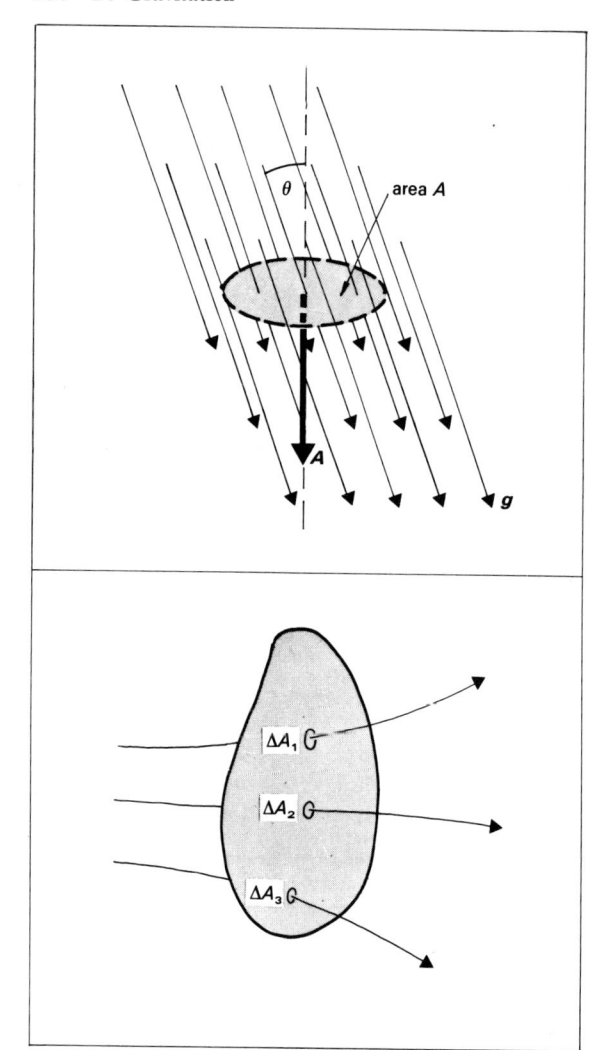

Figure 14-10 The flux of a gravitational field.

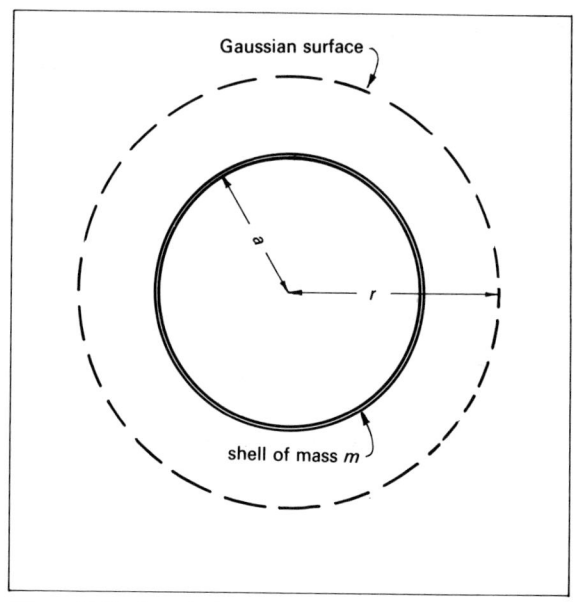

Figure 14-11 Gauss's theorem applies to a closed surface—we draw an imaginary surface before applying the theorem.

Let its strength be g_r a distance r from the centre of the sphere. When $r > a$, the gravitational flux through a spherical surface concentric with the shell

$$\Phi = \sum g_n \Delta A = g_r \sum \Delta A$$

for at every point the gravitational field strength is normal to the surface we have drawn. (Such a surface, constructed so that we may apply the theorem, is called a Gaussian surface.) Therefore, applying the theorem,

we have,
$$g_r \sum \Delta A = 4\pi G \sum \Delta m,$$
$$g_r (4\pi r^2) = 4\pi G m,$$

that is
$$g_r = G \frac{m}{r^2}.$$

The gravitational field outside a uniform spherical shell is the same as if all its mass were concentrated at its centre. It follows that a solid spherical body attracts as though all its mass were concentrated at its centre, provided it consists of layers each of which is of uniform density. The Earth is such a body: its density is not uniform but depends only on the distance from the centre. Thus, if we place a particle of mass m_1 in the gravitational field of a spherically symmetrical body of mass m_2 then the particle is pulled with a force $G m_1 m_2/r^2$, where r is the distance from the centre of the sphere to the particle. By Newton's third law, the sphere is pulled towards the particle with an equal force, that is $G m_1 m_2/r^2$, provided it is not distorted in any way.

A rigid spherically symmetrical body is attracted as though all its mass were concentrated at its centre. [14-4]

We have thus justified the use of Newton's law of gravitation

In symbols
$$\sum g_n \Delta A = 4\pi G \sum \Delta m,$$

or vectorially
$$\sum \mathbf{g} \cdot \Delta \mathbf{A} = -4\pi G \sum \Delta m,$$

the minus sign indicating that gravitational forces are always attractive. For a formal proof of the theorem which, with differing constants, can be applied to any inverse square law field, the reader is referred to texts on electricity and in particular to sections on the electric field.

To appreciate what the theorem means let us apply it to establishing the gravitational properties of a body which possesses spherical symmetry—the planets and stars of this chapter. Consider a uniform spherical shell of mass m and radius a. By symmetry its gravitational field must be radial.

(which is about particles) in Earth–Moon and similar situations providing we ignore the slight asymmetry and non-rigidity of the bodies. The Earth is certainly not a homogeneous sphere but has a density which varies as one moves away from its centre. For example, the outer crust or mantle has an average density which is less than half the average density of the whole Earth. Similarly other planets and stars are not homogeneous but they are approximately spherically symmetrical.

Let us return to figure 14-11. The gravitational flux Φ, through a concentric spherical surface for which $r < a$, is given by

$$\Phi = \sum g_n \Delta A = g_r \sum \Delta A$$

from symmetry considerations. Applying the theorem, we have

$$g_r \sum \Delta A = 4\pi G \sum \Delta m$$

$$g_r(4\pi r^2) = 4\pi G(0) \quad \text{(zero mass enclosed)}.$$

Therefore $\qquad g_r = 0.$

The gravitational field caused by a uniform spherical shell is zero inside the shell. [14-5]

This does not mean that a shell can be used to shield the space inside it from *other* gravitational fields but that its own field is zero. We might have guessed this result by trying to draw lines of force within a spherical shell.

Gauss's theorem can be applied to other distributions of mass but as our needs are nearly always for information about spheres we shall not proceed further. See Exercise 14-32. ★

▶ **Example 14-8** If the value of the gravitational acceleration g at the Earth's surface is 9.8 m s^{-2}, what is its value $5.8 \times 10^6 \text{ m}$ from its centre, assuming that the density of the material of the Earth is constant and that the Earth's radius is $6.4 \times 10^6 \text{ m}$? If in fact the value of g at this position is 10.0 m s^{-2}, what can be deduced about the material of the Earth?

At a point at a distance r from the centre of a spherical Earth of uniform density ρ, a mass m would be pulled by a force Gmm_r/r^2, where m_r is the mass of the Earth within the radius r. Suppose this gives it an acceleration g: using Newton's second law, we have

$$mg = \frac{Gm}{r^2}(\tfrac{4}{3}\pi r^3 \rho)$$

which gives $\qquad g = \tfrac{4}{3}\pi G \rho r,$

so that g varies directly as r, and at a distance of $5.8 \times 10^6 \text{ m}$ from the centre of a uniform Earth its value is

$$\frac{5.8}{6.4} \times 9.8 \text{ m s}^{-2} = 8.9 \text{ m s}^{-2}.$$

The actual value of g at this point is 10.0 m s^{-2}, so that the density of the core of the Earth must be greater than the density of the Earth's crust. ◀

14-8 Gravitational potential

The gravitational force is a conservative one, that is the work done by the gravitational pull on a particle as it moves from A to B is independent of the path taken between A and B. We can thus talk about the difference of a particle's gravitational potential energy between two points in a gravitational field (see Section 9-1), and (if we choose a suitable origin) of *the* gravitational potential energy of a particle.

We are mostly interested in the gravitational fields produced by planets. These fields are directed radially inward towards the centre of the planet and obey an inverse square law; at a distance r from *the centre* of the planet of mass m_P we have,

$$g_r = G\frac{m_P}{r^2} \qquad [14\text{-}6]$$

In particular for the Earth $Gm_E = 4.0 \times 10^{14} \text{ N m}^2 \text{ kg}^{-1}$, so that a graph of g_r against r is as shown on page 229 in figure 14-3. A further example giving quantitative information about the Earth's gravitational field and the forces it produces on a particular space probe is given in the graph of figure 7-6. We have therefore already developed many of the ideas which it is the purpose of this section to bring together and to use.

If we ignore the presence of other massive bodies, particularly the Moon (see figure 14-4), and the very small asymmetries produced near the Earth's surface by mountains, etc., the gravitational field of the Earth is as shown in figure 14-12 below. A particle of mass m placed at a

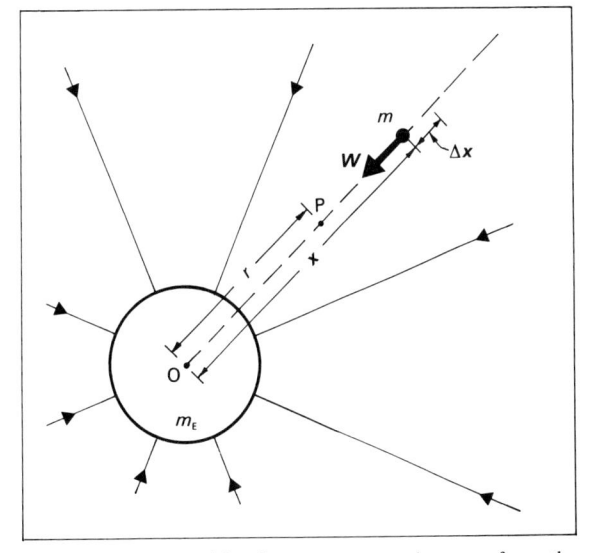

Figure 14-12 A particle of mass m moves Δx away from the centre of the Earth.

14 Gravitation

point P in the field

(a) experiences a gravitational force W in the direction of the field at P, and

(b) possesses a *gravitational potential energy* E.

It is important to realize that both (a) and (b) refer to a *particular body* at P: in fact, they depend on the mass of the body. A more generally useful approach would be to describe the field itself in terms which are independent of the mass of any special body. To do this we say that at a point P in a gravitational field

(c) the force per unit mass, g, at P is called the *gravitational field strength* at P, and

(d) the gravitational potential energy per unit mass, V, at P is called the *gravitational potential* at P.

Items (a) and (c) are already very familiar and of course

[5-4] $$g = \frac{W}{m}.$$

Items (b) and (d) are linked by the equation

$$V = \frac{E}{m}. \quad [14\text{-}7]$$

To calculate E and V we have to agree on a place of zero gravitational energy. For everyday purposes the surface of the Earth is convenient and we can calculate $\Delta E = mg\Delta h$ for small Δh above the ground—see Example 14-9. More generally we say that a body would have zero gravitational potential energy if it were infinitely distant from all other gravitationally attracting masses. As it then approaches, for example, the Earth its gravitational potential energy decreases and so we formally define E thus:

> the **gravitational potential energy** of a body at a point P is the work done by the gravitational field on the body as it moves from P to infinity.

For points in the Earth's gravitational field, referring to figure 14-12, the value of E at P, a distance r from the centre of the Earth is given by

$$E = \sum_{r}^{\infty} W \cdot \Delta x$$

$$= \sum_{r}^{\infty} (-mg_x) \Delta x$$

$$= \int_{r}^{\infty} -\frac{mGm_E}{x^2} dx$$

$$= \left[\frac{Gmm_E}{x} \right]_{r}^{\infty}.$$

So that at P $$E = -\frac{Gmm_E}{r}. \quad [14\text{-}8]$$

Note that E is negative, as we should expect having chosen our zero for E to be at infinity and remembering that gravitational interactions are always attractive. As $Gm_E \approx 4 \times 10^{14}\,\text{N m}^2\,\text{kg}^{-1}$ a graph of E against r for a space probe of mass, say, 5000 kg can be drawn. Such a graph is shown in figure 9-18.

The gravitational potential $V = E/m$ at the point P in the Earth's gravitational field is now seen to be

$$V = -\frac{Gm_E}{r}. \quad [14\text{-}9]$$

Both E and V are scalar quantities (the unit for V is the J kg^{-1}) so that we can write down the difference of gravitational potential energy ΔE between two points distant r_1 and r_2 from the centre of the Earth for a body of mass m:

$$\Delta E = Gmm_E \left(\frac{1}{r_1} - \frac{1}{r_2} \right). \quad [14\text{-}10]$$

The point further from the Earth is at the higher potential but it is not necessary to specify in what direction from the centre of the Earth the distances r_1 and r_2 are measured. Thus in figure 14-13 suppose an orbiting space satellite moves from the circular orbit marked 1 to that marked 2. The gravitational potential energy in orbit 1 is determined by the radius of the orbit (as is the kinetic energy

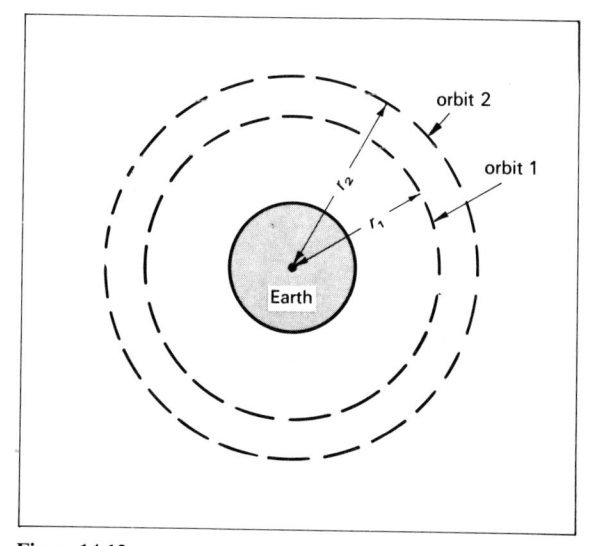

Figure 14-13

of the satellite, assuming there are no frictional forces acting on it) and so is the gravitational potential energy of the satellite in orbit 2. The transfer from orbit 1 to orbit 2 will thus involve a fixed change in potential energy regardless of where on its orbit the transfer takes place or even whether the transfer takes several orbits to achieve.

Following immediately from equation 14-10 we have the *gravitational potential difference* ΔV between two points in the Earth's field distant r_1 and r_2 from the centre of the Earth

$$\Delta V = Gm_E \left(\frac{1}{r_1} - \frac{1}{r_2} \right). \qquad [14\text{-}11]$$

The equations 14-8 to 14-11 hold for any other planet or star (because they all have a spherically symmetrical mass distribution) using the appropriate planetary mass in place of m_E. However, the definitions of E, V, ΔE, and ΔV are quite general and apply to *any* gravitational field, not only to fields which obey the inverse square law relationship $g_r = Gm/r^2$.

▶ **Example 14-9** Show that near the Earth's surface changes in gravitational potential energy can be calculated using $\Delta E = mg_0 \Delta h$ where g_0 is the gravitational field strength at the Earth's surface, that is about $10\,\text{N}\,\text{kg}^{-1}$.

[14-10] $\qquad \Delta E = Gmm_E \left(\frac{1}{r_1} - \frac{1}{r_2} \right).$

For a change ΔE near the Earth's surface let us write $r_1 = r_E$ and $r_2 = r_E + \Delta h$, where Δh is measured vertically upward.

Then $\qquad \Delta E = Gmm_E \left(\frac{1}{r_E} - \frac{1}{r_E + \Delta h} \right)$

$$= \frac{Gmm_E \Delta h}{r_E (r_E + \Delta h)}.$$

As $r_E \approx 6 \times 10^6\,\text{m}$, then for $\Delta h < 10^4\,\text{m}\,(10\,\text{km})$ we can safely write $r_E + \Delta h \approx r_E$, and hence

$$\Delta E = \frac{Gmm_E}{r_E^2} \Delta h.$$

But equation 14-2 tells us that $Gm_E/r_E^2 = g_0$, the gravitational field strength at the Earth's surface, and thus

$$\Delta E = mg_0 \Delta h.$$

Notice that the rate of change of E with height h, $\Delta E/\Delta h$, is equal to the gravitational force mg_0, which is consistent with the discussion in Section 9-7. ◀

Escape velocity

The gravitational potential energy E of a particle of mass m at the Earth's surface is given by $E = -Gmm_E/r_E$. If we project such a particle from the Earth's surface with kinetic energy $\frac{1}{2}mv_e^2$ in the Earth's gravitational field, then its subsequent speed v and distance r from the Earth's centre are given (if we ignore frictional forces) by

$$\tfrac{1}{2}mv^2 + \left(-\frac{Gmm_E}{r} \right) = \text{constant}$$

$$= \tfrac{1}{2}mv_e^2 + \left(-\frac{Gmm_E}{r_E} \right)$$

as the total energy of the particle must be conserved. As r increases, so v decreases and if the particle is still to be moving away from the Earth when $r = \infty$ (that is $\frac{1}{2}mv^2 > 0$ when $Gmm_E/r = 0$), we must have

$$\tfrac{1}{2}mv_e^2 + \left(-\frac{Gmm_E}{r_E} \right) > 0,$$

that is for all $m \neq 0$, $\quad v_e > \sqrt{\dfrac{2Gm_E}{r_E}}.$

Since $g_0 = \dfrac{Gm_E}{r_E^2},$ $\quad v_e > \sqrt{(2g_0 r_E)}$

$$> \sqrt{[2(9.8\,\text{m s}^{-2})(6.4 \times 10^6\,\text{m})]}$$

$$> 11\,\text{km s}^{-1}.$$

The least speed at which a particle can be projected at the Earth's surface in any direction above the horizontal so as never to return, $v_e = 11\,\text{km s}^{-1}$ (40 300 km per hour), is called the Earth's *escape velocity*. The expression used to calculate v_e is quite general and can be used to calculate the escape velocity from the surface of other planets or from the Moon, for which the escape velocity is about $2.4\,\text{km s}^{-1}$.

If we know the escape velocity from a planet's surface we can estimate whether it is possible for the planet's atmosphere to retain a given gas. The average speeds of hydrogen and oxygen molecules at the average temperature of the Earth's atmosphere would be about $1.9\,\text{km s}^{-1}$ and $0.5\,\text{km s}^{-1}$ respectively. Referring to figure 2-18 on page 26 we see that the random distribution of molecular speeds implies that it will be possible for both hydrogen and oxygen molecules in the upper atmosphere to escape, but that the rate of escape of the hydrogen molecules will be very much greater than that for oxygen. The rate of escape of gas molecules from the Moon is such that it has already lost its atmosphere completely.

Orbits

The path of a ball thrown in the air is usually said to be a parabola and can be shown to be one analytically under certain simplifying assumptions—see page 42. It is really part of an ellipse and would certainly be seen as one by an external inertial observer. To see what the paths of projected bodies are in general consider the total mechanical energy E_t of a satellite of mass m moving with speed v in the gravitational field of a planet of mass m_P when at a distance r from its centre. It is given by

$$E_t = \tfrac{1}{2}mv^2 + \left(-\frac{Gmm_P}{r}\right).$$

This expression justifiably ignores the kinetic energy of the planet as part of the mechanical energy of the system (see page 146). If E_t (which is constant) > 0, then the satellite escapes. In this case, its path is a hyperbola with the planet at one focus. Conversely, if $E_t < 0$, the satellite remains in the gravitational field of the planet and is said to be *bound*. In this case its path is an ellipse with the planet at one focus. Figure 14-14 illustrates this for a particle which is projected horizontally at a speed v_0 at a height h above the Earth's surface so that

$$E_t = \tfrac{1}{2}mv_0^2 + \left(-\frac{Gmm_E}{r_E + h}\right).$$

The boundary between elliptical and hyperbolic paths, $E_t = 0$, is shown as a dotted line and is a parabola with focus at O. This is a true parabola and should not be confused with the 'parabolic' path of a body thrown into the air as mentioned at the start of this paragraph. (The reader should refer to texts on analytical geometry for details of ellipses, parabolas, and hyperbolas; these curves are collectively called *conic sections*.) The total energy, E_t, does not uniquely determine a satellite orbit: in figure 14-14 $r_E + h$ and v_0 must be specified as well. In general we need to specify E_t and **L**, the angular momentum of the satellite. $L = m(r_E + h)v_0$ in figure 14-14. For a given E_t but varying L, a bound satellite could move in any one of a series of ellipses all having the same focus and major axis but different eccentricities. One of these ellipses will of course be a circle.

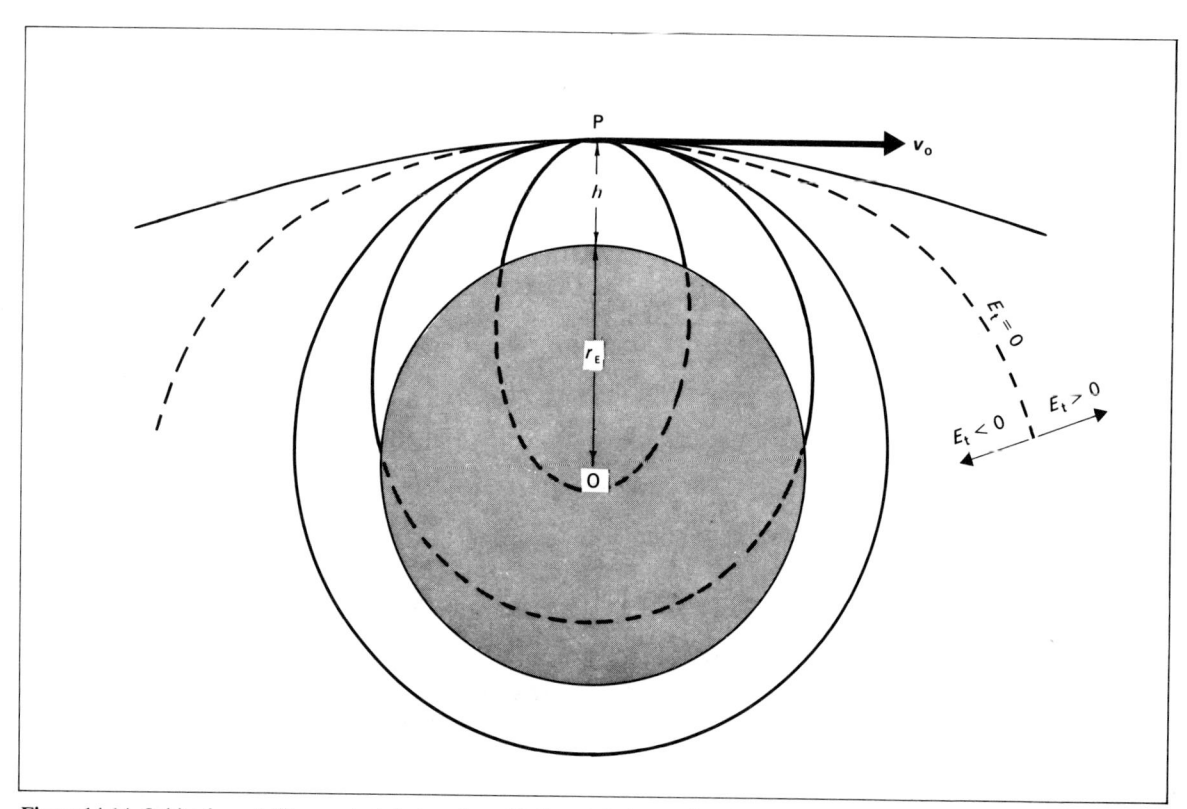

Figure 14-14 Orbits for satellites projected at v_0 from P. If $v_0 = 0$ the motion is linear towards O and if $v_0 = \infty$ the motion is linear to ∞.

14·9 Inertial and gravitational mass

Matter has two properties to which we have so far given the name mass: firstly, it is the measure of a body's inertia and, secondly, it is the measure of a body's gravitational charge. Let us call them the inertial mass, m_i, and the gravitational mass, m_g, respectively. m_i is defined by Newton's second law of motion

$$m_i \boldsymbol{a} = \boldsymbol{F},$$

while m_g is defined by Newton's law of gravitation

$$\boldsymbol{F} = -\left(G\frac{m_g M_g}{r^2}\right)\boldsymbol{n} = m_g \boldsymbol{g},$$

where $\boldsymbol{g}$ is the gravitational field strength. Suppose we drop a particle of inertial mass m_i and measure its acceleration $\boldsymbol{a}$ when it is pulled by a single force $m_g \boldsymbol{g}$. By Newton's second law

$$m_i \boldsymbol{a} = m_g \boldsymbol{g} \quad \text{or} \quad \frac{m_i}{m_g} = \frac{g}{a}.$$

If the experiment is repeated at the same place (same $\boldsymbol{g}$) with a particle of inertial mass m_i' and gravitational mass m_g' and we measure its acceleration to be $\boldsymbol{a}'$, then

$$\frac{m_i'}{m_g'} = \frac{g}{a'}.$$

But we know from such free fall experiments that $\boldsymbol{a} = \boldsymbol{a}'$, and so

$$\frac{m_i}{m_g} = \frac{m_i'}{m_g'} = \cdots = \text{constant}.$$

In fact a man can fall alongside a space capsule without being attached to it (and therefore having extra forces exerted on him) for long periods of time and so our experimental test of $\boldsymbol{a} = \boldsymbol{a}'$ is extremely sensitive (of the order of 1 part in 10^{12}).

It is clearly convenient to make $m_i/m_g = 1$, and this we can do (writing $m_i = m_g$) and then *measure* the universal constant of gravitation G. We could have written $G = 1$, but we should have then had a constant in Newton's second law which would have to be measured.

At this stage in mechanics we can convincingly say that a beam balance (see page 188) and an inertial balance (see page 65), although they compare gravitational masses and inertial masses respectively, are equally useful in comparing what we can now choose to call simply the 'mass' of two bodies.

General relativity

The equivalence of inertial and gravitational mass is now taken to be more than a fluke of nature. Let us refer to figure 6-25 on page 93 where a man sitting in a train observes a ball rolling away from him. Let us suppose that he cannot see out of the train. He may conclude that the train (that is his carriage and table) but not the ball is accelerating *or* he may conclude that the train is now going down an incline. In the first case he would be observing the inertial property of the matter constituting the ball and in the second case its gravitational property. As these are identical he has no way of distinguishing between his two possible solutions as to why the ball rolls away from him. This idea is known as *the principle of equivalence* and is formally stated as follows:

an observer has no means of distinguishing whether his laboratory is in a uniform gravitational field or in an accelerated frame of reference.

To illustrate the principle in a situation which offers the possibility of an experimental check of its validity consider the spaceship shown in figure 14-15a. Suppose

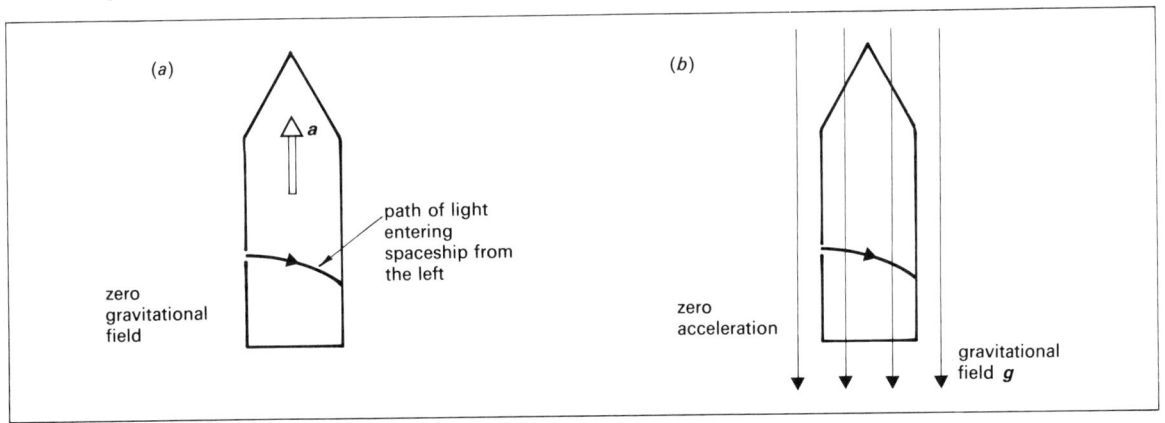

Figure 14-15 $\boldsymbol{a} = -\boldsymbol{g}$.

the ship is accelerating relative to an inertial frame of reference while moving in a region free from any gravitational field. To an observer inside the spaceship, light entering through a small hole in its side will be seen to follow a curved path, because the observer and the spaceship accelerate upwards. The observer in the spaceship cannot however know, by observing the curved path of the light, whether his spaceship is accelerating or is at rest in a downward gravitational field, because the principle of equivalence states that the real situation could be that shown in figure 14-15b, that is if the spaceship was at rest in a gravitational field the path of the light would again be curved.

These ideas suggest that we could test the principle of equivalence by observing light travelling from a distant star to an observer on the Earth. This light may pass through gravitational fields and in so doing have its direction of travel altered. We do observe an alteration in the apparent position of the star when light from it passes close to the Sun. To see the star at all in these circumstances it is necessary to perform the experiment during a total eclipse of the Sun by the Moon, but such measurements do confirm that the star appears to be displaced. The angular displacement is about 8.5×10^{-6} rad and is difficult to measure precisely. The displacement predicted by the theory of special relativity, where the inertial mass of the photons is used in applying Newton's laws of gravitation and motion, is only half the observed displacement. We therefore need the principle of equivalence to explain the observed displacement. This principle lies at the heart of Einstein's *theory of general relativity*.

Bibliography

Cook, A. H. (1970). 'A new determination of the constant of gravitation.' *Sources of physics teaching*, part 5. Taylor and Francis. Reprinted from *Contemporary Physics*.

Gamow, G. (1961). 'Gravity.' *Scientific American* offprint number 273.

Heiskanen, W. A. (1955) 'The Earth's gravity.' *Scientific American* offprint number 812.

King-Hele, D. (1967). 'The shape of the Earth.' *Scientific American* offprint number 873.

Titchmarsh, P. (1962). 'Travelling hopefully towards *G*.' *School Science Review*, number 152, page 58. A sobering account of the practical difficulties associated with this experiment.

Atkins, K. R. (1972). *Physics—once over—lightly.* John Wiley. Chapter 10 gives a delightful and non-mathematical review of the theory of general relativity.

Cook, A. H. (1969). *Gravity and the Earth.* Wykeham. Chapter 3 effectively links local variations in g with the geology of the Earth's crust.

French, A. P. (1971). *Newtonian mechanics.* Nelson. Chapter 8 deals with universal gravitation, and a discussion of tides appears in Chapter 12.

Holton, G. and Roller, D. H. D. (1958). *Foundations of modern physical science.* Addison-Wesley. The study of planetary systems in Part III stresses the historical and philosophic aspects of the subject.

Nuffield Advanced Physics (1971). Teachers' guide, Unit 3 *Field and potential.* Penguin. Part Two on gravitational field and potential contains much relevant quantitative information most of which also appears in the Students' book.

Nuffield Advanced Physics (1972). Students' laboratory book. Penguin. A school laboratory experiment for *G*.

Project Physics (1971). Reader, Unit 2 *Motion in the heavens.* Holt, Rinehart and Winston. Chapters 6, 12, 17, and 24 are relevant.

Project Physics (1971). Reader, Unit 5 *Models of the atom.* Chapter 9 is about general relativity.

Rogers, E. M. (1960). *Physics for the inquiring mind.* Oxford University Press. Part Two concerns astronomy and shows how it provides a clear example of the growth and use of theory in science. The approach is reflected in the Nuffield O-level Physics course.

Tricker, R. A. R. (1965). *Bores, breakers, waves and wakes.* Mills and Boon. See Chapters 1 and 3 for a non-mathematical discussion of tides.

Weidner, R. T. and Sells, R. L. (1965). *Elementary classical physics*, volume 1. Allyn and Bacon. Gravitation is covered in Chapter 16.

Wenham, E. J. (1969). *Planetary astronomy.* Longman. An excellently illustrated elementary account.

8 mm film loop. 'Measurement of *G*.' Ealing Scientific.

Exercises

Data (to be used unless otherwise directed):

$g = 9.8\,\text{m s}^{-2}$ at the surface of the Earth
$ = 9.8\,\text{N kg}^{-1}$ at the surface of the Earth.
$G = 6.7 \times 10^{-11}\,\text{N m}^2\,\text{kg}^{-2}$.

14-1 What would be the radius of two identical lead spheres if, when placed in contact, they are to exert a gravitational force of $1.0\,\text{N}$ on each other? (Density of lead $= 1.1 \times 10^4\,\text{kg m}^{-3}$.) ●

14-2 One early method of measuring G used apparatus which consisted essentially of a form of beam balance, from each end of which hung identical lead spheres of mass $23\,\text{kg}$. Vertically beneath each of these in turn was placed a mass of $160\,\text{kg}$, the centres of the spheres being $0.20\,\text{m}$ apart. The resulting deflection of the beam was observed. What mass would need to be added to either of the upper spheres to produce the same deflection? ●

14-3 The masses of the Sun and the Earth are $2.0 \times 10^{30}\,\text{kg}$ and $6.0 \times 10^{24}\,\text{kg}$ respectively. The mean Sun–Earth and Earth–Moon distances are $1.5 \times 10^{11}\,\text{m}$ and $3.8 \times 10^8\,\text{m}$ respectively. The Moon is attracted by both the Sun and the Earth: find the ratio of the gravitational pull exerted on the Moon by the Earth to that exerted on the Moon by the Sun. Are you surprised by the result? ●

14-4 When an electron revolves round a proton in the hydrogen atom, the particles exert gravitational and electric forces on each other. Calculate the ratio (electric force)/(gravitational force). (Consult Exercise 13-5 for details of the electric force and the mass of the electron; the mass of the proton $= 1.7 \times 10^{-27}\,\text{kg}$.) ●

14-5 to 14-10 In problems concerning satellites orbiting planets, it will be convenient to use the following notation:

- m_P mass of planet
- m mass of satellite
- r radius of orbit
- R radius of planet
- T period of orbit
- v speed of satellite
- ω angular velocity of radius to satellite
- g gravitational acceleration at distance r from planet
- g_0 gravitational acceleration at surface of planet
- ρ mean density of material of planet.

Show that

14-5 $\dfrac{g}{g_0} = \left(\dfrac{R}{r}\right)^2$

14-6 $v^2 = gr$

14-7 $gr^2 = Gm_P$

14-8 $g_0 = \tfrac{4}{3}\pi \rho G R$

14-9 $gT^2 = 4\pi^2 r$

14-10 $Gm_P\, T^2 = 4\pi^2 r^3$ (Kepler's third law).

(*Note:* these results, except possibly that to 14-5, should not be remembered, but in performing calculations it will be advantageous to derive these or similar results *before* substituting numerical values—see the Examples.)

14-11 A planet may be idealized as a sphere of radius R; the gravitational acceleration at its surface is g_0. At what distance from the centre is the gravitational acceleration
(a) $g_0/2$
(b) $g_0/4$
(c) $g_0/100$?
(Consider only points outside the planet.) ●

14-12 What is the value of g at the surface of the Sun? (Mass of Sun $= 2.0 \times 10^{30}\,\text{kg}$; radius of Sun $= 7.0 \times 10^8\,\text{m}$.) ●

14-13 Sketch a graph to illustrate the variation of the gravitational field strength g of a spherically symmetrical planet of uniform density with distance r from its centre, as r varies from zero to infinity. Let the planet have radius R.

If a particle were released from infinity, and attracted towards the planet, and can be imagined to be able to pass through the material of the planet to reach its centre
(a) where will it have its greatest acceleration?
(b) where will it have its greatest speed?
(c) will it ever have zero acceleration?

14-14 Find the period of a satellite which orbits just above the surface of a planet which is a perfect sphere of uniform density $5.0 \times 10^3\,\text{kg m}^{-3}$. ●

14-15 The radius of the Earth is $6.4 \times 10^6\,\text{m}$. Estimate the period of the orbit, and the speed, of the first man-made satellite, which orbited within a few hundred kilometres of the Earth's surface. ●

14-16 Find the radius of the orbit of a satellite of the Earth which orbits in an equatorial plane with a period of revolution of 24 hours. The mass of the Earth $= 6.0 \times 10^{24}\,\text{kg}$. Are there any uses to which such a satellite could be put? Is it necessary for the orbit to lie in an equatorial plane? ●

14-17 Before separation, the spacecraft of the Apollo 11 mission was orbiting the Moon at a speed of $1650\,\text{m s}^{-1}$. What was its mean distance from the surface of the Moon? (Mass of Moon $= 7.34 \times 10^{22}\,\text{kg}$; radius of Moon $= 1.74 \times 10^6\,\text{m}$.) ●

14-18 Newton knew that the mean Earth–Moon distance was $3.8 \times 10^8\,\text{m}$ and that the period of the Moon's revolution was $2.4 \times 10^6\,\text{s}$. He could therefore calculate the value of the gravitational acceleration (due to the Earth) at that distance from the Earth. He also knew the radius of the Earth ($6.4 \times 10^6\,\text{m}$) and the value of g at the surface of the Earth ($9.8\,\text{m s}^{-2}$). Would this data support the theory that the universal gravitational force varies inversely as the square of the distance between the attracting bodies?

14-19 The value of g at the equator is less than that at the poles because the equatorial radius is greater than the polar 'radius', by a distance of $22\,\text{km}$. Find the fractional change in g between the poles and the equator due to this equatorial bulge. Take the polar radius to be $6400\,\text{km}$. (*Hint:* write $gr^2 = $ constant and show that

$$\frac{\Delta g}{g} = -2\frac{\Delta r}{r}.\;)$$ ●

14-20 Show that the unit of acceleration, the m s^{-2}, is equivalent to the unit of gravitational field strength, the N kg^{-1}. What are the units of
(a) gravitational potential energy
(b) gravitational potential?

14 Gravitation

14-21 Find the escape velocity from the surfaces of the planets Mercury and Jupiter. The masses of the planets are 3.3×10^{23} kg and 1.9×10^{27} kg respectively, and their radii are 2.6×10^6 m and 7.2×10^7 m respectively. ●

14-22 Why is the escape velocity of a body from a planet independent of the direction in which the body is launched?

14-23 How much kinetic energy must be given to one kilogram of material at the Earth's surface to enable it to escape from the Earth's gravitational field? If this energy were converted into internal energy in the material, and the material did not melt, what would be its temperature rise? Take the specific heat capacity of the material to be 1.0×10^3 J kg^{-1} K^{-1}. ●

14-24 Ignoring air resistance, estimate the velocity with which a meteorite strikes the surface of the Earth. (Consult the paragraph in the text on escape velocity.) Is this a realistic calculation?

14-25 Consider a rocket-driven vehicle of mass 5.0×10^3 kg in a circular orbit about the Earth at distances from the Earth's centre of
(a) 8.0×10^6 m   (b) 9.0×10^6 m.
Find its gravitational potential energy and its kinetic energy in these orbits, and hence determine the chemical energy which must be used to increase its distance from the Earth's centre from 8.0×10^6 m to 9.0×10^6 m. Take Gm_E to be 4.0×10^{14} N m^2 kg^{-1}. ●

14-26 A satellite in an approximately circular orbit close to the Earth experiences forces of air resistance which cause the radius of its orbit to decrease. Is it possible for its speed to be greater in its new orbit? Explain.

14-27 Using $g = Gm_E/r^2$, draw a graph of g against r for the Earth, using the following values of r:
(a) 6.4×10^6 m (the radius of the Earth)
(b) 1.0×10^7 m
(c) 2.0×10^7 m
(d) 4.0×10^7 m
(e) 1.0×10^8 m,
and taking $Gm_E = 4.0 \times 10^{14}$ N m^2 kg^{-1}.
Use your graph to find the change in gravitational potential between $r = 1.0 \times 10^7$ m and $r = 2.0 \times 10^7$ m. (This is represented by the area under the graph between these values of r.) Hence find the change in kinetic energy of a spacecraft of mass 5600 kg travelling between these points on a journey from the Moon to the Earth. (The Moon is sufficiently distant for its effect to be ignored here.) ●

14-28 Find the gravitational potential V at distances $r/1.0 \times 10^7$ m $= 1, 2, 3, 4$ from the centre of the Earth. Take Gm_E to be 4.0×10^{14} N m^2 kg^{-1}. Plot a graph of V against r, and find the gradient dV/dr of the graph at the specified values of r. Also calculate the values of g (using equation 14-2) at these distances, and compare your answers. Do they suggest that

$$\frac{dV}{dr} = -g?$$

14-29 The masses of the Earth and the Moon are 6.0×10^{24} kg and 7.3×10^{22} kg respectively, and the mean Earth–Moon distance is 3.8×10^8 m. Find the total gravitational potential at the following distances from the Earth on a line joining the centres of the Earth and Moon:

(a) 1.0×10^8 m   (b) 3.0×10^8 m   (c) 3.4×10^8 m
(d) 3.6×10^8 m.
(At the point (c) the resultant force on a particle is zero.)
Sketch your results on a graph of gravitational potential V against r, the distance from the Earth. (The result should be of similar form to that shown in figure 14-16.) Superimpose on this diagram the curve which would be obtained in the absence of the Moon (you need not make any further calculations—a rough sketch will do), and comment on the curves with reference to the problems of sending spacecraft to the Moon.

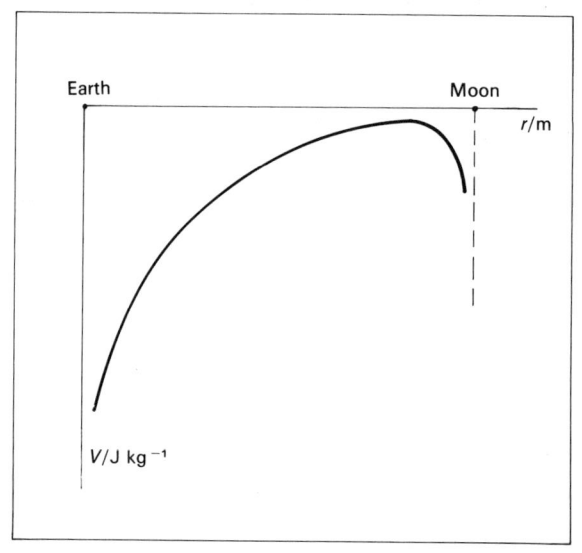

Figure 14-16

14-30 From your results of Exercise 14-29 deduce the minimum energy which must be given to a spacecraft to enable it to reach the Moon, if its mass when it is 3.4×10^8 m from the Earth is 2.8×10^4 kg. Why is it necessary to specify the mass at a particular distance?

14-31 When the command module of the Apollo 11 mission was returning to the Earth, the following data were recorded.

Ground elapsed time/hr	Distance from Moon/km	Speed/m s^{-1}
145	4.79×10^7	1318.8
146	5.26×10^7	1313.8

What is the average acceleration over this part of the flight? Account for the decrease in speed. ●

14-32 Some 'flat-Earth' scientists believe that the Earth consists of a sheet of material of uniform thickness h and uniform density ρ, extending infinitely in all directions. Use Gauss's theorem to show that the gravitational field strength g is given by $g = 2\pi\rho Gh$ in a direction normal to the Earth. (*Hint*: as a 'Gaussian' surface, imagine a cylinder, of cross-sectional area A, whose axis is perpendicular to the surface of the Earth, and whose end faces lie one on each side of the Earth.) Draw a diagram showing the gravitational lines of force around such a flat Earth.

What difference is there (apart from the size) between the gravitational fields of a spherical Earth and a flat Earth?

14-33 Refer to Exercise 14-32: what value of h would be required to produce a value of g of $10 \, \text{m s}^{-2}$, if the material had a density of $5.5 \times 10^3 \, \text{kg m}^{-3}$? ●

14-34 The gravitational field around the flat Earth of Exercise 14-32 is *uniform*, that is, it has the same size and the same direction at all points on one side of the sheet of material. Explain how it is possible for the field not to become weaker as one moves further from the Earth.

14-35 Suppose that the flat Earth of Exercise 14-32 consisted not of an infinite sheet but of a flat circular sheet of *very* large radius. What would then be the value of the 'vertical' component of g (in terms of ρ, G, h) at the edge of the sheet?

14-36 Geologists use 'gravity meters' (which can measure the value of g to 1 part in 10^8) to detect the presence of coal seams, oil fields, and so on by measuring the variation of the gravitational field strength near such deposits as a result of the difference in density between the deposit and the surrounding rocks. What would be the difference in the value of g caused by the presence of a coal seam 150 m thick, if the density of coal is $2500 \, \text{kg m}^{-3}$, and the density of the surrounding materials is $3000 \, \text{kg m}^{-3}$? (Make the approximation that the Earth is flat, and that the coal lies in a uniform horizontal layer which may be considered infinite in extent.) Why does the answer not depend on the distance of the coal seam below the surface of the Earth? ●

14-37 Why does the Moon always turn one face towards the Earth? If there were oceans on its surface, would they have tides?

14-38 What sort of universe would we live in if the value of G were one-hundredth of its actual value, all other physical constants remaining the same? How would our everyday life be affected? Try to give numerical estimates.

15 Mechanical oscillations

15-1 Repetitive motions	246	15-7 The energy of a simple harmonic oscillator	260
15-2 The kinematics of simple harmonic motion	246	15-8 Damped oscillations	263
15-3 Hooke's law	251	15-9 Resonance	266
15-4 The dynamics of simple harmonic motion	252	Bibliography	269
15-5 Pendulums	255	Exercises	270
15-6 Some oscillating systems	257		

15-1 Repetitive motions

In order to measure time we need to use a repetitive or periodic device or some repetitive natural phenomenon (see Section 1-5) which we call a *clock*. In order to investigate any phenomenon which is thought to have a repetitive or periodic property we need to use a clock. Until a standard clock has been chosen it is senseless to argue about whether, for example, a heart beats 'regularly', for, if you decide that your heartbeat shall be the standard clock for all measurements of time, then your pulse will *by definition* beat regularly, while you might think that the length of a day varies from, say, 108 000 heartbeats to 105 000 heartbeats. What criteria should we use in our choice of a standard clock? Apart from the properties discussed in Section 1-9 in choosing a subatomic time standard it is necessary that the motion should be *isochronous*, that is, its periodicity should not vary with the size of the oscillation. It is also convenient if it measures other 'regular' repetitive motions to be regular. Thus a bouncing ball does not have an isochronous motion for as the height to which it bounces becomes smaller, the times between successive impacts becomes smaller (as measured by a balance wheel in a wrist watch). Also, the time taken by the Earth to rotate once about its axis is not a regular repetitive motion as measured by the vibration of a quartz crystal.

Having chosen a standard clock (Section 1-5) and from it calibrated more useful and practical devices for measuring time in a laboratory, let us consider the number of mechanical systems which are periodic: a pendulum, a mass vibrating on the end of a spring, a violin string, a ruler clamped at one end, and so on. To study these and other mechanical systems we have two problems. What is the motion like? We must describe it kinematically. Why is the motion as it is? We must investigate the dynamics of the system. Figure 15-1 shows a demonstration which suggests that uniform circular motion, when viewed edge-on, looks exactly like the motion of a mass on the end of a light spring. This demonstration does not by itself prove anything, but it does suggest that some of the words and symbols we use in describing circular motion may appear in the kinematics of periodic motion.

15-2 The kinematics of simple harmonic motion

Consider the oscillation of a loaded air-track glider which is attached to two fixed posts by identical light springs as shown in figure 15-2a. If it is pulled to one side (for example, to the left) and released, the glider oscillates between two extreme positions. A multiflash photograph

15-2 The kinematics of simple harmonic motion 247

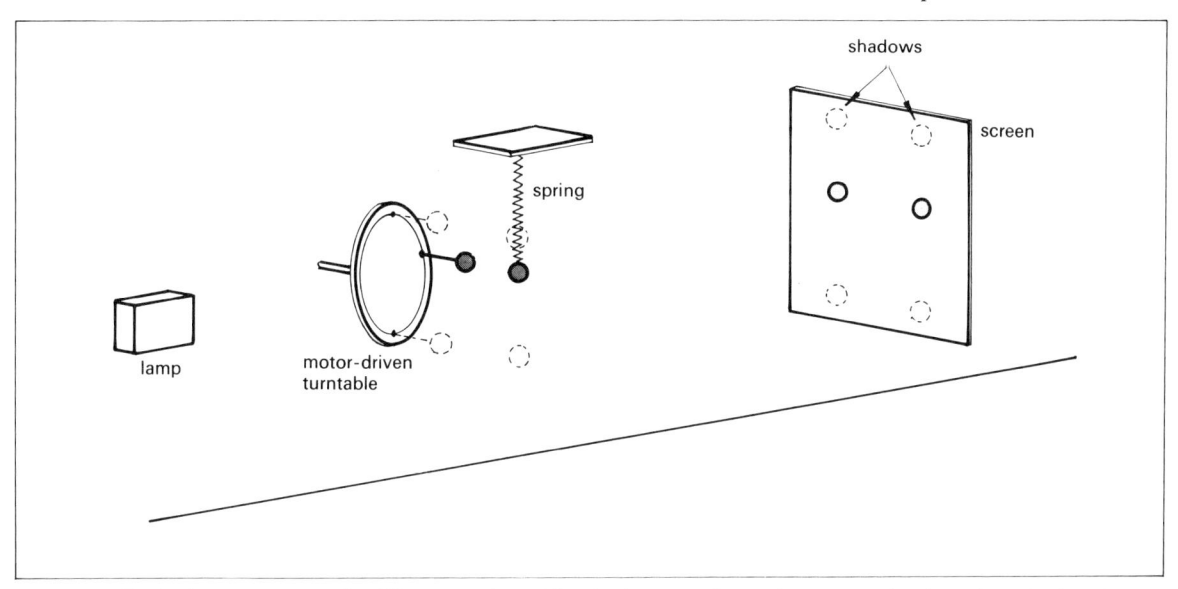

Figure 15-1 Projecting two apparently different motions. The shadows can be made to move in phase by suitably adjusting the motor speed. We notice that even when the amplitude of the mass on the spring dies down, its shadow still moves in phase with the motor-driven shadow.

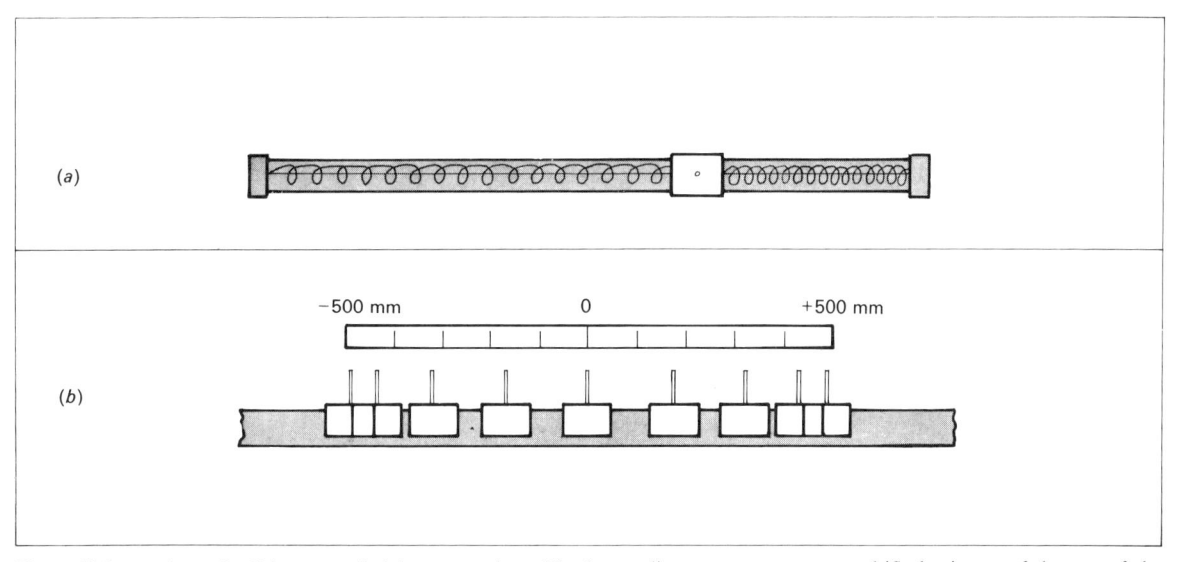

Figure 15-2 An air-track glider controlled by two springs. The lower diagram represents a multiflash picture of the top of the glider during half an oscillation.

exposed for the first half-oscillation, that is while the glider travels from its extreme left to its extreme right, will be like that represented in figure 15-2b. The experiment could be performed with a trolley, but the motion of the air-track glider is simpler, as it is virtually frictionless.

From the photograph we can draw a displacement–time graph for the glider, treating it as a particle. It is convenient to describe the displacement of the glider as zero when it is in its equilibrium position, and $t = 0$ can be taken as the moment of release. These conventions are

15 Mechanical oscillations

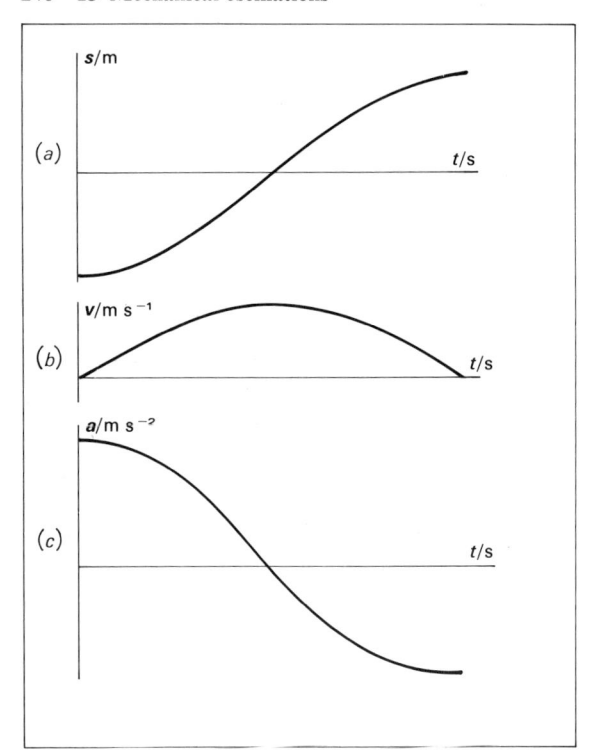

Figure 15-3 $s-t$, $v-t$, and $a-t$ graphs for the glider over half an oscillation. The graphs should be 'read' down as well as across, for example the acceleration is zero when the glider passes through the position of zero displacement.

adopted in figure 15-3. Figure 15-3a shows the displacement–time graph, and (see Section 3-4) we can *deduce* the velocity–time and acceleration–time graphs by measuring slopes,

for $$v = \frac{ds}{dt}, \quad \text{and} \quad a = \frac{dv}{dt}.$$

The most striking result of the motion curves for the glider is that the $a-t$ curve is, or seems to be, the inverse of the $s-t$ curve. To check this we could draw a graph of displacement against acceleration, and we find that we have a straight line passing through the origin (see figure 15-4).

Thus $$a \propto -s$$

or $$a = -(\text{constant})s,$$

the constant being a positive number: let us call it ω^2, which is sensible, since it must have s^{-2} as a unit, and we then have

$$a = -\omega^2 s. \qquad [15\text{-}1]$$

This equation defines *simple harmonic motion*, that is, if we can show that the acceleration of a particle is related to its displacement in this way then we can say it is moving with simple harmonic motion. For rigid bodies we shall have an *angular* displacement θ and an *angular* acceleration α: then

$$\alpha = -\omega^2 \theta \qquad [15\text{-}2]$$

describes a simple harmonic motion, perhaps of a pendulum or a balance wheel. (Note that ω is not an angular velocity in these equations, but a constant with units of s^{-1}.)

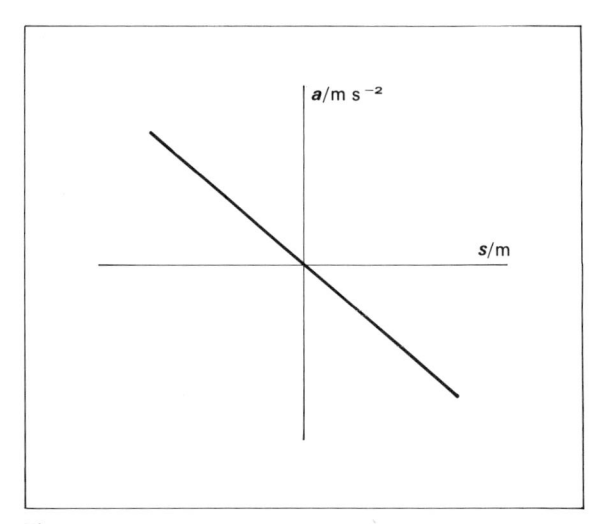

Figure 15-4 An $a-s$ graph plotted from figures 15-3a and (c).

By measuring the slope of the graph in figure 15-4 we can deduce the value of ω^2 and hence the value of ω. For the displacement–time graph of figure 15-3a we can measure the time T taken for the glider to complete one oscillation. T is called the *period* of the motion (the graph shown covers only half of one complete period).

We find that $$\omega = \frac{2\pi}{T},$$

and so $$T = \frac{2\pi}{\omega}, \qquad [15\text{-}3]$$

a deduction which can best be confirmed by repeating the whole experiment after altering the mass of the glider or the stiffness of the springs. Further, denoting the maximum values of s, v, and a by s_0, v_0, and a_0, we call s_0 the *amplitude* of the oscillation. For a true simple harmonic motion (where there is no damping) s_0 is constant.

All mechanical simple harmonic motions can be analysed in this way, and all graphs have the same form as those of figure 15-3. What equation describes the curve of figure 15-3a? It looks like a sine or cosine curve. Let us guess that it is a cosine curve and of the form

$$s = s_0 \cos \frac{2\pi}{T} t, \qquad [15\text{-}4]$$

for when $t = 0$,

$$\cos \frac{2\pi}{T} t = \cos 0 = 1, \quad \text{and} \quad s = s_0.$$

When $t = T/4$,

$$\cos \frac{2\pi}{T} t = \cos \frac{\pi}{2} = 0, \quad \text{and} \quad s = 0.$$

When $t = T/2$,

$$\cos \frac{2\pi}{T} t = \cos \pi = -1, \quad \text{and} \quad s = -s_0,$$

and so on. The guess seems a good one, since these results satisfy the curve of figure 15-3a. Guessing here is no different from guessing the solution of a differential equation such as

$$a = \frac{d^2 s}{dt^2} = -\omega^2 s.$$

If the glider in figure 15-2 had been at the centre point, moving to the right at v_0 when the clock started, the displacement–time graph drawn from the experiment would have been a sine curve instead of a cosine curve. The equation would then have been

$$s' = s_0 \sin \frac{2\pi}{T} t' = s_0 \cos \frac{2\pi}{T} \left(t + \frac{T}{4} \right),$$

that is $\quad s' = s_0 \cos \left(\dfrac{2\pi}{T} t + \dfrac{\pi}{2} \right).$

The only difference between this and equation 15-4 is the constant $\pi/2$, which is called their *phase difference*. In general,

$$s = s_0 \cos \frac{2\pi}{T} t \quad \text{and} \quad s' = s_0 \cos \left(\frac{2\pi}{T} t + \varepsilon \right)$$

are said to have a phase difference ε.

It is because sines and cosines come into the mathematical analysis that the periodic motion is said to be *harmonic*. It is *simple* in the sense that the displacement s depends on a sine and/or a cosine function of the same frequency, while more complex repetitive harmonic motions can be expressed only as the sum of a number of such functions of different frequencies. In this text we shall consider only simple harmonic motion in any detail: fortunately this does describe fairly accurately many oscillations found in nature.

If $s = s_0 \cos 2\pi t/T$, then we can deduce the corresponding equations for v and a from figure 15-3:

$$v = -v_0 \sin \frac{2\pi}{T} t \qquad [15\text{-}5]$$

and

$$a = -a_0 \cos \frac{2\pi}{T} t. \qquad [15\text{-}6]$$

In calculus terms, if

$$s = s_0 \cos \frac{2\pi}{T} t,$$

then

$$v = \lim_{\Delta t \to 0} \frac{\Delta s}{\Delta t} = \frac{ds}{dt}$$

$$\Rightarrow v = -s_0 \frac{2\pi}{T} \sin \frac{2\pi}{T} t, \qquad [15\text{-}7]$$

and

$$a = \lim_{\Delta t \to 0} \frac{\Delta v}{\Delta t} = \frac{dv}{dt}$$

$$\Rightarrow a = -s_0 \left(\frac{2\pi}{T} \right)^2 \cos \frac{2\pi}{T} t, \qquad [15\text{-}8]$$

which gives

$$a = -\left(\frac{2\pi}{T} \right)^2 s$$

or [15-1]

$$a = -\omega^2 s.$$

This confirms that a particle which moves with a displacement which varies with time as $s = s_0 \cos \omega t$ is executing simple harmonic motion of period $T = 2\pi/\omega$.

To find the velocity v for the particle at a given displacement s from the origin $s = 0$, we have

[15-7] $\qquad v = -\dfrac{2\pi}{T} s_0 \sin \dfrac{2\pi}{T} t$

$$= \pm \frac{2\pi}{T} s_0 \sqrt{\left(1 - \cos^2 \frac{2\pi}{T} t \right)}$$

$$= \pm \frac{2\pi}{T} \sqrt{\left(s_0^2 - s_0^2 \cos^2 \frac{2\pi}{T} t \right)}$$

$$= \pm \frac{2\pi}{T} \sqrt{(s_0^2 - s^2)}, \qquad [15\text{-}9]$$

the alternative, plus or minus, indicating that the velocity at a displacement s can have either of the two possible directions.

▶ **Example 15-1** A particle moves with simple harmonic motion of period 2.0 s and amplitude 80 mm. If its displacement is zero when $t = 0$, what is its change of displacement between
(a) $t = 0.40$ s and $t = 0.80$ s
(b) $t = 0.80$ s and $t = 1.20$ s?

(a) From equation 15-4

$$s = s_0 \cos \frac{2\pi}{T} t$$

so that the displacements s_1 and s_2 at the times $t = 0.40$ s and $t = 0.80$ s (respectively) are given by

$$s_1 = (80 \text{ mm}) \cos\left(\frac{2\pi}{2.0 \text{ s}} \times 0.40 \text{ s}\right)$$

$$= 80 \left(\cos \frac{2\pi}{5}\right) \text{mm} = 80 \cos 72° \text{ mm}$$

$$s_2 = (80 \text{ mm}) \cos\left(\frac{2\pi}{2.0 \text{ s}} \times 0.80 \text{ s}\right)$$

$$= 80 \left(\cos \frac{4\pi}{5}\right) \text{mm} = 80 \cos 144° \text{ mm}.$$

Therefore its change of displacement

$$\Delta s = s_2 - s_1 = 80[(-0.809) - (+0.309)] \text{ mm}$$

$$= (-64.7 \text{ mm}) - (+24.7 \text{ mm})$$

$$= -89.4 \text{ mm}.$$

(The negative sign means that the particle has moved to a point 89 mm further in the negative direction. There has been this change of displacement: it does not follow that the particle has travelled a distance of 89 mm, although on this occasion it has.)
(b) Similarly between $t = 0.80$ s and $t = 1.20$ s the change in displacement Δs is given by

$$\Delta s = 80\left(\cos \frac{6\pi}{5} - \cos \frac{4\pi}{5}\right) \text{mm}$$

$$= 80(\cos 216° - \cos 144°) \text{mm},$$

but as $\cos 216° = \cos 144°$ the change of displacement is zero. It is not that the particle has not moved: it merely happens to be in the same position (though moving in a different direction) when $t = 0.80$ s and when $t = 1.20$ s. ◀

▶ **Example 15-2** Refer to Example 15-1: find the acceleration of the particle at $t = 0.40$ s, $t = 0.80$ s, and $t = 1.20$ s.

From equation 15-8

$$a = -s_0 \left(\frac{2\pi}{T}\right)^2 \cos \frac{2\pi}{T} t$$

but since on this occasion we already know the values of the displacement at the given times it is simpler (and better physics) to use the fact that

$$a = -\left(\frac{2\pi}{T}\right)^2 s.$$

We know that the displacements at the times given are, respectively,

$$+24.7 \text{ mm}, \quad -64.7 \text{ mm}, \quad \text{and} \quad -64.7 \text{ mm}.$$

As $T = 2.0$ s, the value of $(2\pi/T)^2$ is $(2\pi/2.0 \text{ s})^2 = 9.85 \text{ s}^{-2}$, so that the three accelerations are

$$-243 \text{ mm s}^{-2}, \quad 637 \text{ mm s}^{-2}, \quad \text{and} \quad 637 \text{ mm s}^{-2},$$

the signs indicating that the acceleration of the particle is on each occasion opposite in direction to the displacement. The reader should notice that

(a) the acceleration *is* proportional to the displacement. It is *not* constant, and problems about simple harmonic motion *cannot* be solved using the equations for uniformly accelerated motion (for example, $v^2 = u^2 + 2as$).
(b) the value of the acceleration is precisely the same (in size *and* direction) at a particular displacement, whether the particle has a positive or a negative velocity.
(c) the smaller the value of T, the greater the acceleration at a particular displacement (and vice versa).
(d) the acceleration is zero when the displacement is zero, and has its maximum value when $s = \pm s_0$. The maximum acceleration of this particle occurs when $s = \pm 80$ mm:

when $\quad s = +80$ mm, $\quad a = -788 \text{ mm s}^{-2}$

and when $s = -80$ mm, $\quad a = +788 \text{ mm s}^{-2}$.

(e) the acceleration is zero when the velocity has its maximum size, and has its maximum size when the velocity is zero. ◀

▶ **Example 15-3** Refer to Example 15-1: find the velocity of the particle at $t = 0.40$ s, $t = 0.80$ s, and $t = 1.20$ s.

$$[15\text{-}7] \quad v = -s_0 \frac{2\pi}{T} \sin \frac{2\pi}{T} t.$$

When $t = 0.40$ s,

$$v = -(80 \text{ mm})\left(\frac{2\pi}{2.0 \text{ s}}\right) \sin\left(\frac{2\pi}{2.0 \text{ s}} \times 0.40 \text{ s}\right)$$

$$= -80\pi \left(\sin \frac{2\pi}{5}\right) \text{mm s}^{-1}$$

$$= -239 \text{ mm s}^{-1}.$$

When $t = 0.80$ s,

$$v = -80\pi \left(\sin \frac{4\pi}{5}\right) \text{mm s}^{-1}$$

$$= -148 \text{ mm s}^{-1}.$$

When $t = 1.20\,\text{s}$,

$$v = -80\pi \left(\sin \frac{6\pi}{5}\right) \text{mm s}^{-1}$$

$$= +148\,\text{mm s}^{-1}.$$

We see here that at a particular displacement (we saw in Example 15-1 that at both $t = 0.80\,\text{s}$ and $t = 1.20\,\text{s}$ the particle has the same displacement) the particle has a particular speed, independent of its direction of motion.

You should notice that the speed of the particle is a maximum when $\sin 2\pi t/T = 1$ (that is when $t = 0.50\,\text{s}$, $1.50\,\text{s}$ etc.) and then has the value $(80\,\text{mm})(2\pi/2.0\,\text{s}) = 251\,\text{mm s}^{-1}$. The velocity is zero when $\sin 2\pi t/T = 0$ (that is when $t = 0, 1.0\,\text{s}, 2.0\,\text{s}$, etc.). Thus the particle moves fastest when its displacement is zero, and stops (of course) when its displacement is a maximum. ◀

15-3 Hooke's law

Suppose that a solid body is subject to a pair of opposing forces or torques which stretch or twist it from an original equilibrium state to a final equilibrium state (see figure 15-5). In each case the body is deformed, the macroscopic change of shape or size depending on the microscopic properties of the specimen (its molecular structure). Here we are interested only in the relation between the deformation (as measured by x or θ in figure 15-5) and the deforming effect produced by a pair of forces F or a pair of torques T. Note that a body *cannot* be in equilibrium under the action of a *single* force or a *single* torque.

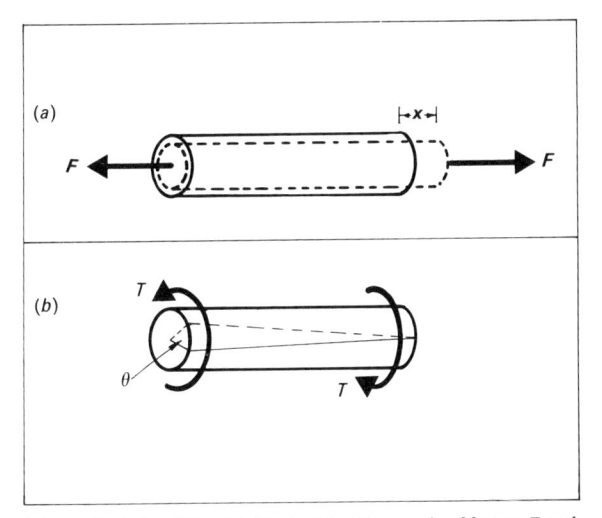

Figure 15-5 A solid rod is (a) stretched by a pair of forces F and (b) twisted by a pair of torques T (for small deformations $x \propto F$ and $\theta \propto T$ respectively). The rod is shown to be undisplaced at one end for convenience.

Figure 15-6 shows a simple apparatus for investigating the effect of stretching a wire with equal and opposite forces. The extension x of the wire is measured on the millimetre scale S, past which moves the vernier V which is fixed to the wire which is not under test. The stretching forces are altered by hanging different known masses from the lower end of the wire being tested. The mass at the end of the wire carrying the vernier is to ensure that the wire remains taut, and both wires are hung from the same beam so that any depression of the beam during the experiment will not affect the readings. A graph of x/m, plotted against F/N, is found to be a straight line *for small values of x*. Robert Hooke (1635–1703) was the first to record the linear relationship between F and x which is found to hold, for *small* values of x, for a wide variety of wires, of both metallic and amorphous materials, as well as for springs. We do not intend to discuss the relation between the structure of the materials and their *elasticity* in this text, nor shall we consider what happens for *large* values of x. The reader is referred to textbooks on the structure and strength of materials for the physics of this large and fascinating area of science.

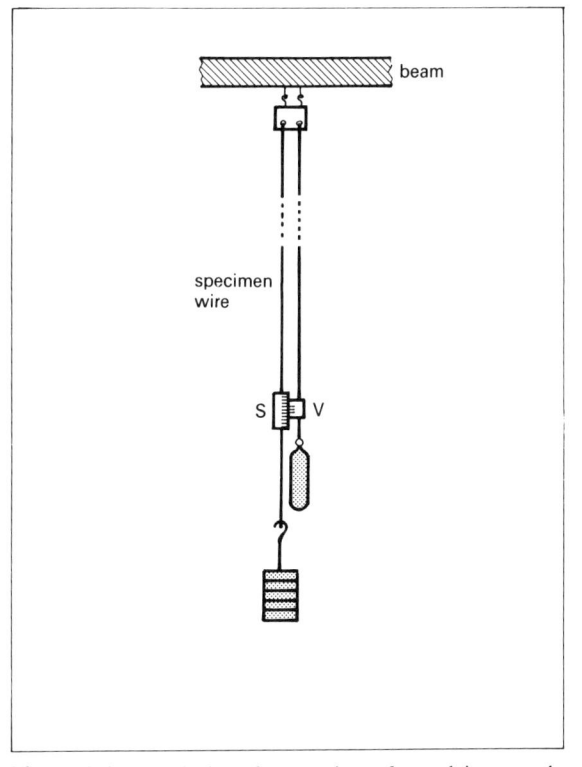

Figure 15-6 The principle of an experiment for applying extending forces to a wire and measuring its elongation.

15 Mechanical oscillations

Figure 15-7 shows a simple apparatus for investigating the effect of twisting a wire with equal and opposite torques. The difference in angular displacement θ of the wire between the points A and B is measured by fixing mirrors to it at these points, and reflecting beams of light to scales placed a few metres from them. In this way small values of θ can be measured. The torques are applied by fixing the top of the specimen, and attaching a heavy cylinder to its lower end. The cylinder is then twisted as shown. If the tension in each string is W, then the twisting torque is $T = Wd$: a solid transmits torque just as it transmits force. A graph of $\theta/°$ against $T/\text{N m}$ is found to be a straight line passing through the origin for small values of θ; the specimen can be twisted in a negative sense by re-setting the pulleys.

When a body is found to alter in size or shape in such a way that the size of the deformation is proportional to the deforming force or torque the body is said to obey *Hooke's law*. It normally holds only for small displacements.

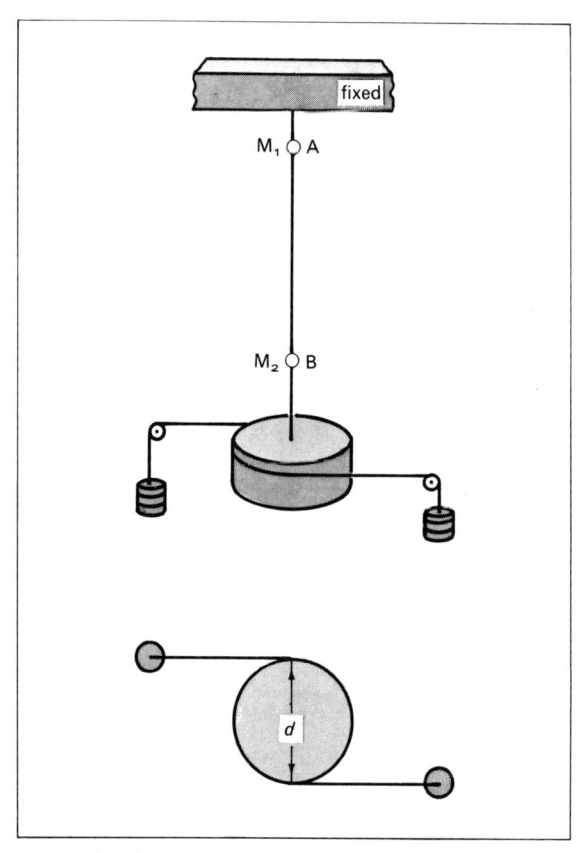

Figure 15-7 A static procedure for applying twisting torques to a wire and measuring its angular deformation.

By Newton's third law the force or torque exerted *by* a body is equal and opposite to the deforming force or torque. Thus for a body which obeys Hooke's law we can write

$$F = -kx \qquad [15\text{-}10]$$

and

$$T = -k'\theta, \qquad [15\text{-}11]$$

where F and T now represent respectively the force and torque exerted *by* the body, and k and k' are constants. k was called the 'spring constant' or 'stiffness' in Section 7-3, where the work done by a variable force was considered. Both the force and the torque are conservative for the displacements for which they obey Hooke's law, that is, no work is then done by internal forces.

15-4 The dynamics of simple harmonic motion

Let us consider the experiment described at the start of Section 15-2 from the dynamical point of view. When the glider is first released the resultant force of the springs on the glider accelerates it to the right (note that the displacement is negative and the acceleration is positive at first). As the trolley moves to the right the resultant force on it decreases, the springs obey Hooke's law, and so the acceleration, although still to the right, becomes smaller. At the centre of the motion, there is zero resultant force on the glider and so the acceleration is zero. Continuing this dynamical argument involving Newton's second law and Hooke's law we can see intuitively that the acceleration a is proportional to the displacement x, as was deduced experimentally on page 248. Further we can see that if the mass of the glider were doubled the acceleration at any given displacement would be halved, and that if the springs were made twice as 'strong', for example, if a second pair of identical springs were placed in parallel with the original springs, the acceleration at a given displacement would be doubled. Analytically we can represent the argument as follows.

Consider a particle of fixed mass m which is subject to a variable force F. By Newton's second law

$$ma = F,$$

where a is the acceleration of the particle. Suppose that there is only one force acting on the particle and that this force obeys Hooke's law for small displacements:

[15-10] $$F = -kx,$$

then the motion of the particle is described by the equation

$$ma = -kx$$

15-4 The dynamics of simple harmonic motion

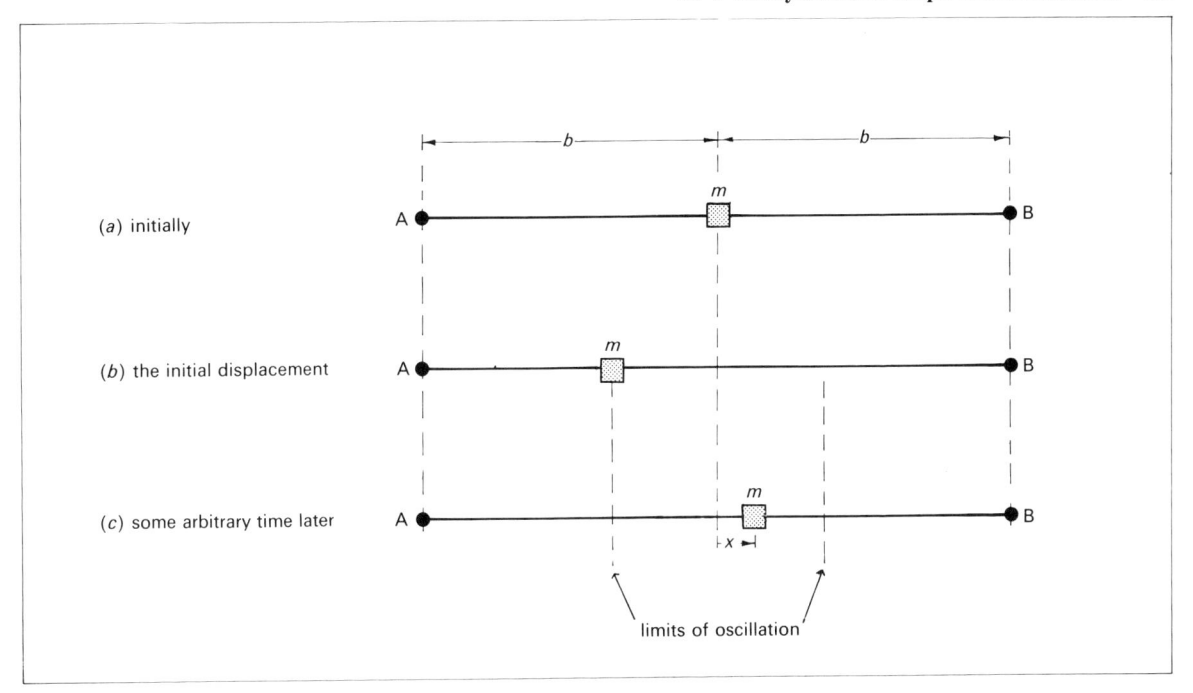

Figure 15-8

(a) initially

(b) the initial displacement

(c) some arbitrary time later

limits of oscillation

or
$$a = -\frac{k}{m}x,$$

which tallies with our intuitively derived results of the previous paragraph. By comparison with equation 15-1 which defines simple harmonic motion, we see that the particle is moving with simple harmonic motion of period T given by

[15-3]
$$T = \frac{2\pi}{\omega}$$
$$= 2\pi\sqrt{\frac{m}{k}}.$$

Although this tells us how the period depends on m and k, we do not know how fast the particle is moving as it passes a given point nor what is its maximum displacement, but the equation does tell us that the period T is *independent* of the initial displacement. Thus if $k = 10\,\text{N m}^{-1}$ and $m = 0.080\,\text{kg}$ we shall have an oscillation of period $T = 0.56\,\text{s}$, that is a frequency of oscillation f given by

$$f = \frac{1}{T} = 1.8\,\text{Hz},$$

whatever the amplitude of the motion.

▶ **Example 15-4** A particle of mass m is placed on a frictionless horizontal table and is attached, by two identical massless spiral springs of natural length l and stiffness k, to two fixed points A and B on the table. A and B are a distance $2b$ apart, where $2b > 2l$, so that the springs are stretched. The particle is then given a displacement along the line of the springs (but so that the spring which is now shorter is still stretched) and released. Prove that the motion which ensues is simple harmonic, and find its period.

In figure 15-8c let the displacement of the particle, at some arbitrary time, be x, and its acceleration a (its direction measured to be positive in the direction in which x is measured from the central origin) and let the pulls of the springs attached to A and B be T_1 and T_2 respectively. The lengths of the springs are now $b+x$ and $b-x$ respectively, and so their extensions are $b+x-l$ and $b-x-l$ respectively. Figure 15-9 is a free-body diagram for the particle.

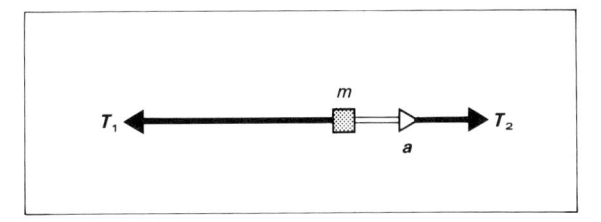

Figure 15-9

15 Mechanical oscillations

Using Newton's second law we have

$$ma = T_2 - T_1$$

where $T_1 = k(b+x-l)$ and $T_2 = k(b-x-l)$,

so that
$$ma = k[(b-x-l) - (b+x-l)]$$
$$= -2kx$$

and
$$a = -\frac{2k}{m}x.$$

k and m are constants for the system, so that we have shown that

$$a = -(\text{constant})x$$

which is the criterion of simple harmonic motion.

By comparison with the relations $a = -\omega^2 x$ and $T = 2\pi/\omega$, we can see that the period T of this motion is given by

$$T = 2\pi\sqrt{\left(\frac{m}{2k}\right)}.$$ ◀

▶ **Example 15-5** A particle of mass m is attached to one end of a massless spring of stiffness k, the other end of which is attached to a fixed point: the spring is allowed to hang vertically. The particle is then given a slight vertical displacement (but so that the spring always remains stretched). Show that the motion of the particle is simple harmonic and find its period.

Figure 15-10 shows (a) the spring before the particle is attached, (b) the spring after the particle is attached, and a free-body diagram for the particle then, and (c) the spring and particle at some subsequent (arbitrary) time, and a free-body diagram for the particle then.

In (b) we note that

$$T_0 = mg,$$

as the particle is in equilibrium and

$$T_0 = ke,$$

as the spring obeys Hooke's law, so that

$$ke = mg.$$

In (c) we have marked the displacement x from the *equilibrium position* of the particle; the free-body diagram shows the forces acting on the particle, and its acceleration marked in the same direction as x. Using Newton's second law we have

$$ma = mg - T$$

where
$$T = k(e+x)$$

so that
$$ma = mg - ke - kx.$$

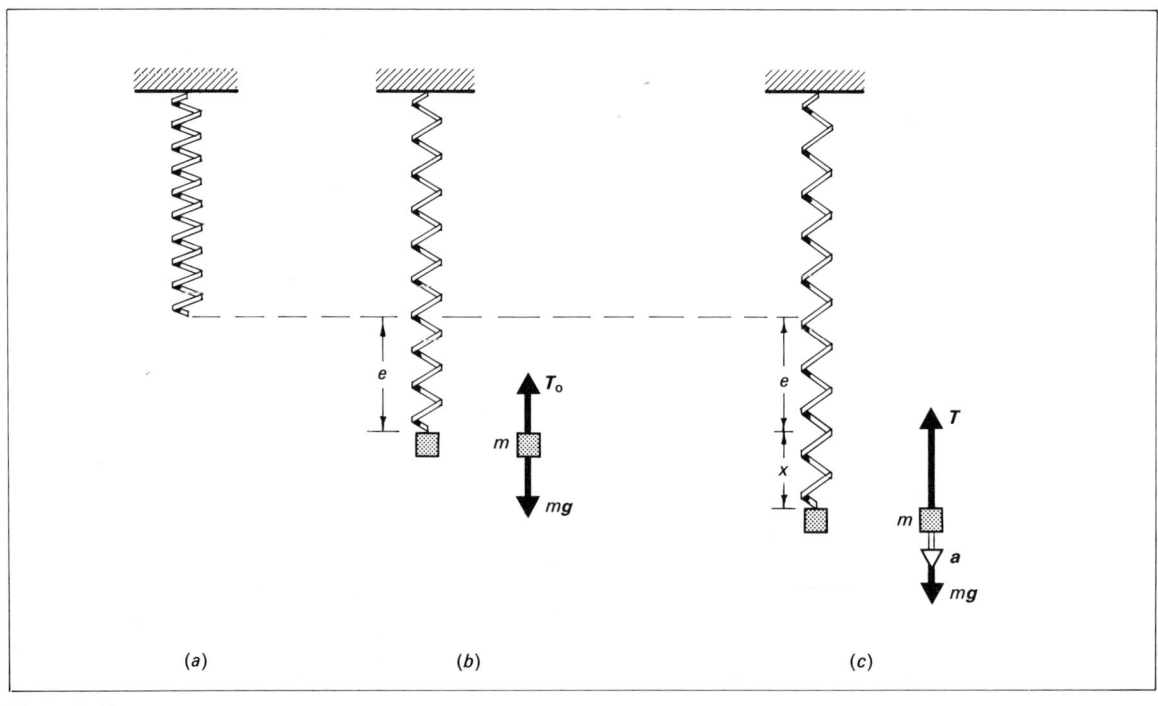

Figure 15-10

We know, however, that
$$mg = kc,$$
so that
$$a = -\frac{k}{m}x$$

and this equation satisfies the criterion for simple harmonic motion. The period T of the motion is given by
$$T = 2\pi\sqrt{\frac{m}{k}}.$$

(*Note:* if we had measured x from some point other than the equilibrium position of the particle, we should not have found that $a = -(\text{constant})x$.) ◀

15-5 Pendulums

Mechanical clocks are generally of two types. They consist of a rigid body which is either free to oscillate about a fixed horizontal axis in the Earth's gravitational field or free to oscillate about a fixed axis under an elastic restoring force. The first type is what the average person thinks of as a pendulum clock, but the physicist would say that the first type is a compound pendulum and the second type is a torsional pendulum. In this section we shall assume that time is measured by some standard instrument and we shall treat pendulums as oscillating systems rather than as clocks.

The compound pendulum

Consider a body rotating about a fixed axis. Suppose the body has a moment of inertia I about this axis, and that the body is subject to a variable resultant torque $\boldsymbol{T}$ about this axis. By Newton's second law

[12-4]
$$I\boldsymbol{\alpha} = \boldsymbol{T},$$

where $\boldsymbol{\alpha}$ is the angular acceleration of the body about the axis. Suppose there is only this one torque acting on the body and that this torque obeys Hooke's law for angular displacements: then

[15-11]
$$T = -k'\theta,$$

and the motion of the body is given by the equation
$$I\alpha = -k'\theta$$
or
$$\alpha = -\frac{k'}{I}\theta.$$

Comparing this with equation 15-2 which defines simple harmonic motion, we see that the body is moving with

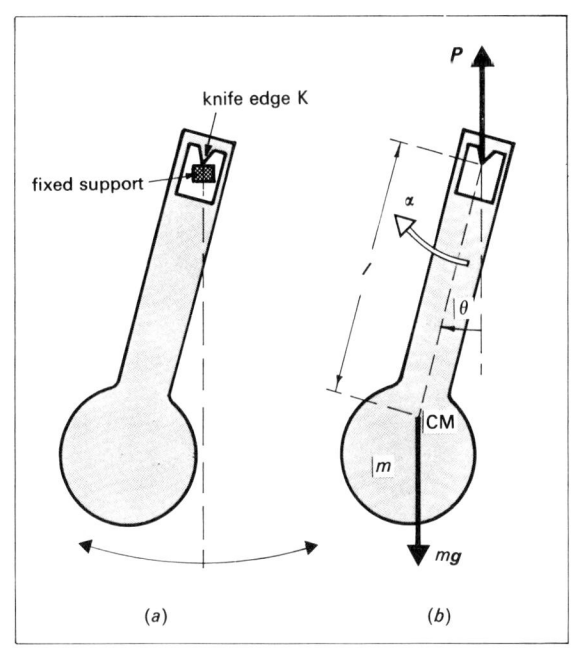

Figure 15-11 (*a*) A compound pendulum and (*b*) the forces acting on it.

simple harmonic motion of period T given by

[15-3]
$$T = \frac{2\pi}{\omega}$$
$$= 2\pi\sqrt{\frac{I}{k'}}.$$

The full motion can now be analysed if the angular amplitude of the oscillation is known.

Suppose the body shown in figure 15-11 has a moment of inertia I about a horizontal axis through the knife edge K. Applying Newton's second law to the body for rotation about this axis we have

$$I\boldsymbol{\alpha} = \sum \boldsymbol{T}$$
$$I\alpha = -mgl\sin\theta$$

where l is the distance from K to the centre of mass (CM) of the body. As we are taking the clockwise sense to be positive then the torque is $-mgl\sin\theta$. Rearranging,

$$\alpha = -\frac{mgl}{I}\sin\theta,$$

which does *not* represent a simple harmonic motion, as it is not of the form $\alpha = -\omega^2\theta$. It is repetitive, but it is not simple harmonic motion: we must not fall into the trap of assuming that all repetitive motions are necessarily simple harmonic motions. When θ_0 is very small, that is the maximum displacement or amplitude of the oscillation is small, we can write $\sin\theta \approx \theta$, where θ is measured in radians, and the relation between α and θ becomes approximately

$$\alpha = -\frac{mgl}{I}\theta.$$

So for small oscillations a compound pendulum performs a simple harmonic motion with a period T_c given by

$$T_c = 2\pi \div \sqrt{\frac{mgl}{I}}$$

or
$$T_c = 2\pi\sqrt{\frac{I}{mgl}}. \qquad [15\text{-}12]$$

The simplest practical realization of this pendulum is to hang a small lead sphere at the end of a long piece of thread. The moment of inertia of the system about the point at which the cotton is fixed is so nearly ml^2 (where m is the mass of the lead sphere and l is the length from the point of suspension to the centre of the sphere) that we can think of the system as a point mass m on the end of a massless suspension of length l. The system is then called a 'simple' pendulum and has a period T_s given by

$$T_s = 2\pi\sqrt{\frac{ml^2}{mgl}} = 2\pi\sqrt{\frac{l}{g}}.$$

Suppose such a simple pendulum is found to oscillate with a period of 2.00 s (as measured by an independently calibrated clock) in a laboratory where g is known to be 9.80 m s^{-2}, then the length of the pendulum is given by

$$l = \frac{T_s^2 g}{4\pi^2} = 0.993\,\text{m},$$

so that a simple pendulum which passes through its lowest point once each second is just less than one metre long. This calculation assumes that the amplitude of the pendulum is so small that the simple theory is applicable and

$$T_s = 2\pi\sqrt{\frac{l}{g}}.$$

The graph of figure 15-12 shows how the ratio T/T_s varies with amplitude θ up to $\theta = 90°$ (that is, whole swings from the horizontal position to the other horizontal position) and shows that the difference between T and T_s is less than one per cent for values of θ below about 20°.

★ The relation $T_s = 2\pi(l/g)^{1/2}$ involves another assumption. Looking back we see it is derived from

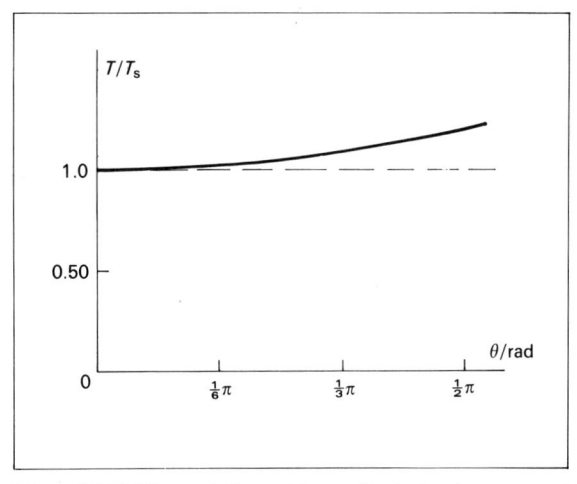

Figure 15-12 The variation with amplitude in the measured period T of a simple pendulum. T_s is the value at $\theta = 0$. The variation shown is not caused by air resistance but by the inherent non-isochronous nature of the oscillations for large θ.

$$T_s = 2\pi\sqrt{\frac{ml^2}{mgl}}.$$

If $l \neq 0$ we can say that

$$T_s = 2\pi\sqrt{\frac{ml}{mg}},$$

but can we cancel the masses m? Strictly speaking we have

$$T_s = 2\pi\sqrt{\frac{m_i l}{m_g g}}$$

where m_i and m_g represent, respectively, the inertial and gravitational masses of the pendulum bob. As, experimentally, we find that T is independent of the amount or nature of the material forming the bob of the pendulum, we deduce that the ratio m_i/m_g at a given place is fixed, and we define it to be unity (see also page 241). Newton himself considered this problem and measured T_s for a simple pendulum with a hollow bob into which he inserted a variety of materials. The reader should ask himself why Newton used this technique rather than simply substituting different bobs. ★

Compound pendulums can be used for laboratory determinations of **g**, the Earth's gravitational field strength, and indeed a quick experiment with a wristwatch and ruler would yield a value for g to within 10 per cent with a minimum of fuss. Historically the compound pendulum was developed to a point where g could be measured to a few parts in 10^6, and values of g at different locations could be compared even more reliably. Nowadays, however, the absolute measurement of g at a fixed station is achieved using free-fall methods (see page 40) while relative values over the Earth's surface can be deduced using gravimeters or from satellite orbits (see page 230). Details of pendulum experiments can be found in textbooks dealing with practical physics.

The torsion pendulum

Suppose the rigid disc shown in figure 15-13 has a moment of inertia I about a vertical axis through its centre of mass. If it is rigidly connected to a thin torsion wire which obeys Hooke's law for angular deformations, so that it can exert a torque T on the disc where $T = -k'\theta$, we have, applying Newton's second law to the disc, for rotational motion

$$I\alpha = -k'\theta$$

or

$$\alpha = -\frac{k'}{I}\theta.$$

This represents a simple harmonic motion and the disc therefore oscillates about the vertical axis with a period T_t given by

$$T_t = 2\pi \div \sqrt{\frac{k'}{I}}$$

$$T_t = 2\pi \sqrt{\frac{I}{k'}}. \qquad [15\text{-}13]$$

By making the torsion wire long enough we can achieve oscillations of very large amplitude (perhaps two or three whole revolutions) without damaging the material of the support or even taking it beyond the region in which it obeys Hooke's law. The torsion pendulum is used in a number of experiments to measure small torques (and therefore forces): for example, in the experiment in Section 14-3 to measure the value of G. The value of k' needs to be measured in any of these experiments and the procedure is to vary I to $I+I'$, where I' is known, deduce k' from measured values of the period in each case, and then use this value of k' to measure the unknown static torques (and hence perhaps forces) required. This may seem a tortuous process but the fact that it is used shows the reliability of the torsion pendulum as an example of a strictly simple harmonic oscillator.

15-6 Some oscillating systems

It is no exaggeration to say that any particle or body, when displaced from a position of stable equilibrium, undergoes oscillations of some sort. If the initial displacement is small enough we can go further and say that the oscillations will be simple harmonic. Apart from the pendulums of the last section and the examples in Section 15-4, consider the motion of a ball rolling on a concave surface, of a ruler clamped at one end to a bench, of the mercury in a U-tube manometer, of a violin string, or of one of the atoms in an oxygen molecule. All these systems have motion which is simple harmonic for small amplitudes, the reason being that the particles or bodies are acted on by pushes and pulls which tend to restore them to their equilibrium positions, and the size of the resultant restoring force is proportional (for small displacements) to the displacement of the particle or body from its equilibrium position. In analysing any of these systems we must first decide precisely what it is that moves and what forces act on it, as in the two examples which follow.

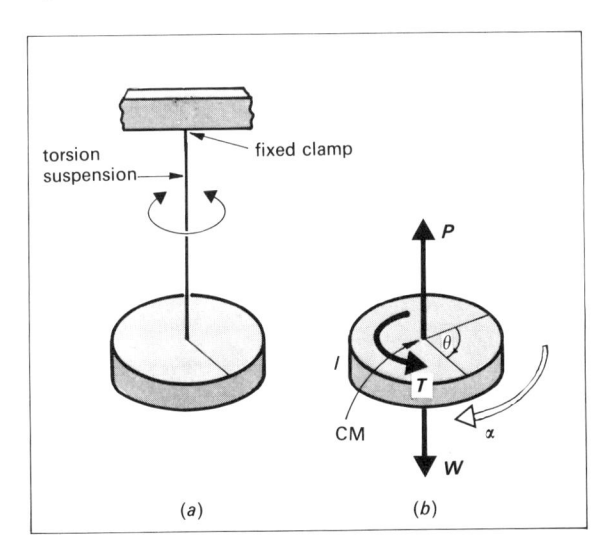

Figure 15-13 (*a*) A torsion pendulum and (*b*) the forces acting on it.

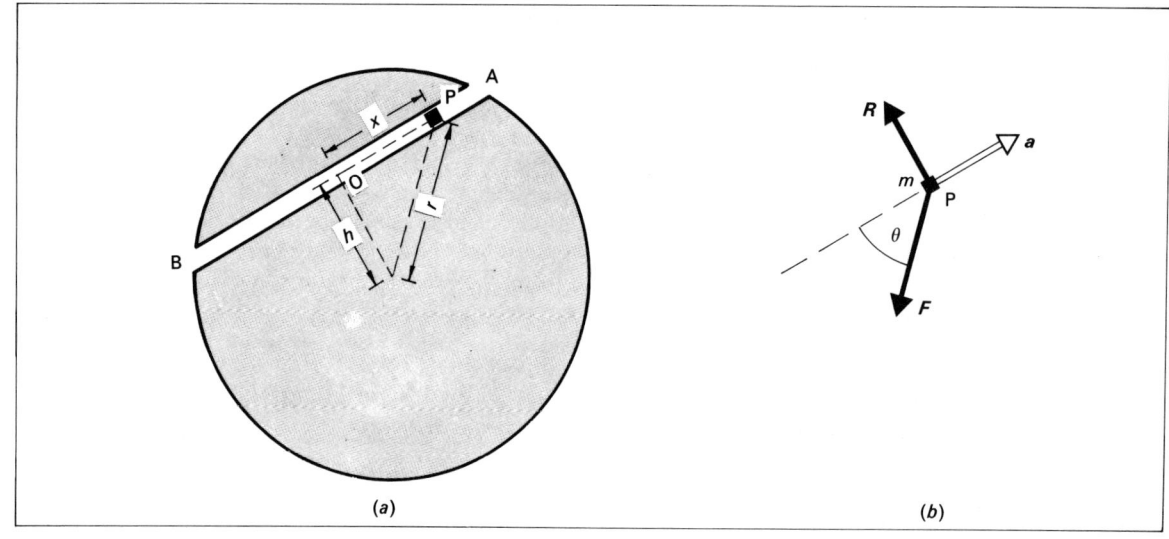

Figure 15-14 A parcel P moves through a tunnel. (b) is a free-body diagram for P.

▶ **Example 15-6** A parcel is placed at one end A of a straight tube connecting A to a second point B on the Earth's surface, as shown in figure 15-14. The tube may be supposed to be evacuated, the material of the Earth to be homogeneous, and the walls of the tube frictionless. (The problem is therefore hypothetical, but none the less interesting for that.) How long will it be before the parcel arrives at B?

Suppose the two points are so placed that the tube passes a distance h from the Earth's centre. Let us measure the displacement of the parcel from the centre O of the tube. When the parcel is at P, the pull F of the Earth on it is given by

$$F = G\frac{mm_E}{r^2},$$

where $m_E (= 4\pi r^3 \rho/3)$ is the mass of that part of the Earth (of density ρ) contained within a sphere whose centre is the centre of the Earth and whose radius is r. Applying Newton's second law,

$$ma = -F\cos\theta$$
$$= -G\frac{m}{r^2}(\tfrac{4}{3}\pi r^3 \rho)\frac{x}{r}$$
$$= -Gm\tfrac{4}{3}\pi\rho x,$$

so that
$$a = -(\tfrac{4}{3}\pi\rho G)x$$
$$= -(\text{constant})x$$

and the parcel moves with simple harmonic motion between the extreme positions A and B. By analogy with the general expression for the period $T = 2\pi/\omega$, the period T of the parcel's motion will be given by

$$T = 2\pi\sqrt{\frac{3}{4\pi\rho G}}$$

and so the time-interval between its being placed at A and its arrival at B will be

$$\frac{T}{2} = \sqrt{\frac{3\pi}{4\rho G}}.$$

The surprising thing about this result is that this time for the journey is independent of the positions of A and B on the Earth's surface. ◀

▶ **Example 15-7** A frictionless vertical cylinder of cross-sectional area A contains a gas which is trapped by a piston which fits the cylinder perfectly. The piston has a mass m, and the atmospheric pressure above the piston is p_0 and is assumed to be constant. The piston is slightly displaced and, when released, oscillates about its equilibrium position. Show that the oscillations are approximately simple harmonic.

From the free-body diagram in figure 15-15a we have

$$p'A = mg + p_0 A$$

where p' is the initial pressure of the gas in the cylinder when the piston is in equilibrium. When the piston has a displacement x, and the pressure of the gas is p, suppose the acceleration of the piston is a. By Newton's second

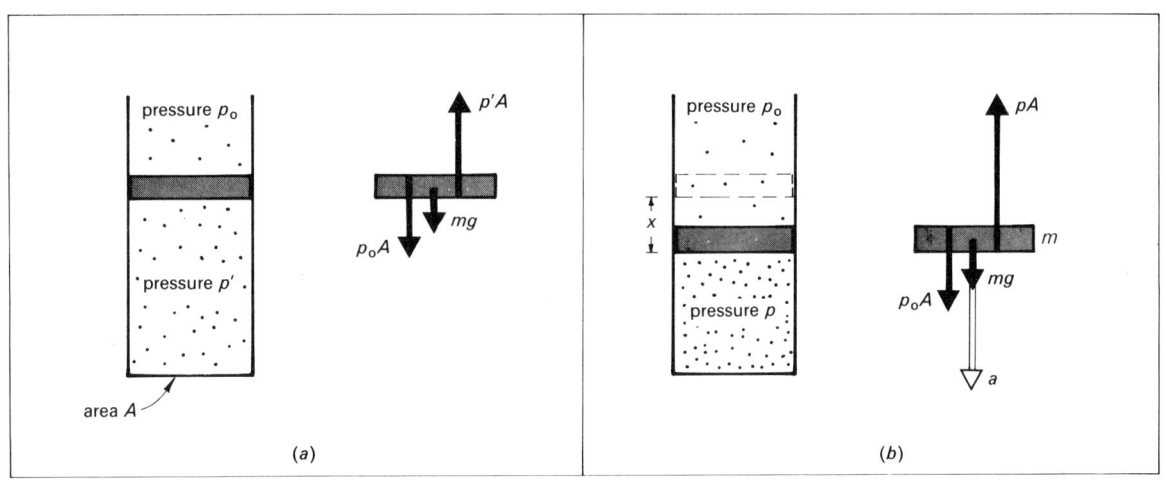

Figure 15-15 A freely moving piston (*a*) in equilibrium and (*b*) oscillating in a cylinder.

law we have (in figure 15-15*b*)

$$ma = mg + p_0 A - pA$$
$$= p'A - pA$$
$$= (p' - p)A$$
$$= A(\Delta p),$$

where Δp is the change of pressure when the piston has a displacement x. We now need to make some assumptions about the behaviour of the gas trapped in the cylinder. The simplest assumption is that the pressure is inversely proportional to its volume V, but here a better assumption is that

$$pV^\gamma = \text{constant},$$

(where γ is a constant for a particular gas). Differentiating we have

$$p\gamma V^{\gamma-1} + V^\gamma \frac{dp}{dV} = 0$$

and if Δp and ΔV are small, it is approximately true that

$$\Delta p = -\gamma \frac{p}{V} \Delta V$$
$$= -\gamma \frac{p}{V} Ax.$$

Substituting this expression for Δp in our earlier result we now have

$$ma = -A\gamma \frac{p}{V} Ax$$

so that (for small Δp and ΔV, and hence small amplitude oscillations) we have

$$a = -\frac{\gamma p A^2}{mV} x.$$

If the change of volume during the oscillation is small, we can assume that the values of p and V are both approximately constant, so that the motion *is* (approximately) simple harmonic. The number of assumptions we have made gives this problem an air of unreality, but does give a good idea of the number of complicating factors which there may be in an apparently simple problem. However, this does form the basis of one method of measuring the value of γ (the ratio of the principal specific heat capacities of the gas in the cylinder). ◀

★ **Two-body oscillations** Even the simplest of oscillating systems such as pendulums or loaded springs are more complex when examined closely. In each case the Earth should have been considered as part of the oscillating system: this is our recurring problem about frames of reference. Fortunately the Earth is so massive as not to alter significantly the numerical solutions, but we ought to consider further those cases where we can easily identify both parts of the oscillating system.

When two masses, m_1 and m_2, connected by a massless spring of stiffness k and resting on a frictionless horizontal surface (or in a state of free fall), are set oscillating, then the period as measured by an observer at the centre of mass of the system is not

$$2\pi \sqrt{\frac{m_1}{k}} \quad \text{nor} \quad 2\pi \sqrt{\frac{m_2}{k}}$$

nor

$$2\pi \sqrt{\frac{m_1 + m_2}{2k}}$$

but is

$$2\pi \sqrt{\frac{\mu}{k}}$$

where

$$\mu = \frac{m_1 m_2}{m_1 + m_2} = \frac{m_1}{1 + m_1/m_2}.$$

Note that $\mu \approx m_1$ if m_2 is very large compared with m_1. μ is called the *reduced mass* of the system and is of wide application in all situations where two bodies are subject only to forces of interaction.

For instance, an ammonia molecule NH_3 forms an oscillating system in which the single nitrogen atom vibrates with a frequency of 2.387×10^{10} Hz perpendicular to the plane containing the three hydrogen atoms (figure 15-16). The hydrogen atoms are not themselves fixed, so that this is really a two-body oscillation and we shall therefore not attempt any detailed analysis. The amplitude of the oscillation may vary, for example, with the temperature of the bulk ammonia, but the motion is perfectly isochronous, so much so that if it is chosen as a clock it can detect annual variations in the length of a day amounting to a few parts in 10^9 as well as a gradual decrease in the average length of a day over the years. The frequency of the oscillation of the nitrogen atom depends on the nature of the forces between it and the hydrogen atoms and also on the relative masses of hydrogen and nitrogen atoms. Thus an NH_3 molecule containing three deuterium atoms (a deuterium atom is a hydrogen atom with an additional neutron in the nucleus) would oscillate at a lower frequency than the ordinary ammonia molecule. ★

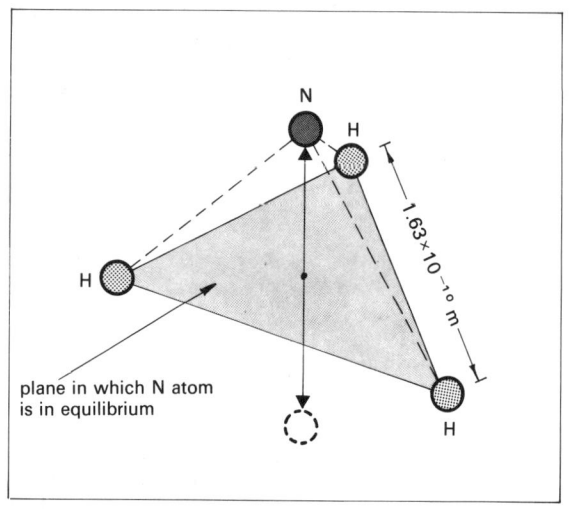

Figure 15-16 A representation of the natural vibrations of an ammonia molecule.

15-7 The energy of a simple harmonic oscillator

The kinetic energy of an oscillating body clearly varies: indeed at the two extremes of its motion the body is instantaneously at rest so that there it clearly has zero kinetic energy. Considering the bob of a simple pendulum we see that the gravitational potential energy of the bob also varies and that this is a maximum when the kinetic energy is zero, and vice versa. So a simple pendulum is a device which periodically transfers its stored mechanical energy from one of these types to the other, and, providing no dissipative damping forces act, continues to do so. Similarly, a mass oscillating on a frictionless horizontal surface transfers its stored mechanical energy from kinetic energy to elastic potential energy in the spring, and vice versa.

Here then is a good way of describing the physical properties of an oscillating body. What is the total energy of the oscillator? It is equal to the kinetic energy of the body as it passes through its equilibrium position and commonsense tells us that it is related in some way to the amplitude of its motion. To go further we need to express these statements more exactly. Let us consider a particle of mass m oscillating on a horizontal frictionless surface and attached to a spring which can be both stretched and compressed, and which has equal stiffness k for both extension and compression (figure 15-17a). We know that its kinetic energy T is given by

[7-3] $$T = \tfrac{1}{2}mv^2$$

when its speed is v, and its elastic potential energy E_e is given by

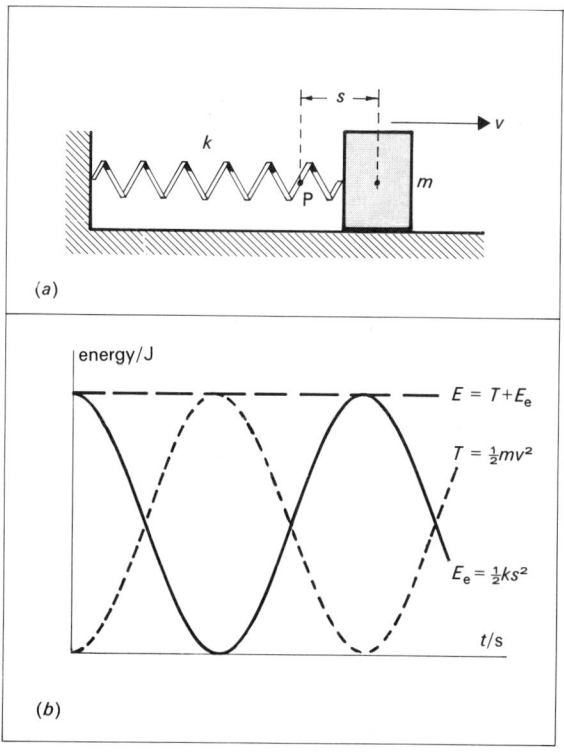

[9-2] $$E_e = \tfrac{1}{2}ks^2$$

Figure 15-17 (a) A mass vibrates about an equilibrium position P. (b) Energy changes with time for a simple harmonic oscillator.

when its displacement is s from its equilibrium position.

From the above discussion we get, for this oscillator with zero damping, a total mechanical energy E given by

$$E = T + E_e = \text{constant},$$

where
$$E = \tfrac{1}{2}ks_0^2$$

(or $E = \tfrac{1}{2}mv_0^2$, where v_0 is the maximum speed).

The total energy is therefore proportional to the *square*, s_0^2, of the amplitude, a result which is widely applicable in the study of physics.

For a simple harmonic oscillator,

[15-4] $s = s_0 \cos \omega t$ and

[15-5] $v = -v_0 \sin \omega t$,

so that $E_e = \tfrac{1}{2}ks^2 = \tfrac{1}{2}ks_0^2 \cos^2 \omega t$

and $T = \tfrac{1}{2}mv^2 = \tfrac{1}{2}mv_0^2 \sin^2 \omega t$.

Graphs of E_e/J and T/J against time, t/s, are shown in figure 15-17b. Each is always positive and their sum is constant.

Another way of representing energy relationships for an oscillator is shown in figure 15-18. For the case considered (simple harmonic motion) the graph is a parabola and for a motion of amplitude s_0 the relative sizes of T and E_e can be read off the graph. The graph of E_e/J against s/m will only be parabolic where the spring obeys Hooke's law. If, however, the graph of the potential energy of a particle against its displacement is *roughly* parabolic about a position of stable equilibrium (even if the curve does not follow the parabola for large displacements) the particle will oscillate with simple harmonic motion for small displacements. Such is the case for an atom in a solid, and the deviation of the curve from the parabolic shape for large displacements provides the explanation for the expansion of solids when their temperature is raised.

▶ **Example 15-8** Refer to Example 15-4: suppose $b = 0.50\,\text{m}$, $l = 0.20\,\text{m}$, $k = 5.0\,\text{N m}^{-1}$, and $m = 0.10\,\text{kg}$. Suppose also that the amplitude of the oscillation is $0.20\,\text{m}$. Find

(a) (i) the maximum kinetic energy of the system, and (ii) the potential energy of the system at this time
(b) the maximum potential energy of the system
(c) the total mechanical energy of the system at a time $0.10\,\text{s}$ after the particle has passed through its equilibrium position.

(a) (i) We have already shown that the period T of the oscillation is given by $T = 2\pi\sqrt{(m/2k)}$, so that here

$$T = 2\pi\sqrt{\frac{0.10\,\text{kg}}{2 \times 5.0\,\text{N m}^{-1}}} = 0.20\pi\,\text{s}.$$

The kinetic energy of the particle is greatest when it passes through the equilibrium position: then its velocity v is (as shown) given by (see equation 15-9)

$$v_0 = \pm s_0 \frac{2\pi}{T}$$

$$= \pm(0.20\,\text{m})\left(\frac{2\pi}{0.20\pi\,\text{s}}\right)$$

$$= \pm 2.0\,\text{m s}^{-1},$$

and the kinetic energy

$$T = \tfrac{1}{2}(0.10\,\text{kg})(2.0\,\text{m s}^{-1})^2$$

$$= 0.20\,\text{J}.$$

(ii) In the equilibrium position each spring has an extension of $0.30\,\text{m}$: using $E_e = \tfrac{1}{2}kx^2$, we have the potential energy E_e given by

$$E_e = 2 \times \tfrac{1}{2}(5.0\,\text{N m}^{-1})(0.30\,\text{m})^2$$

$$= 0.45\,\text{J}.$$

(b) The potential energy is a maximum when the particle has its maximum displacement: then one string has an extension of $0.10\,\text{m}$ and the other an extension of $0.50\,\text{m}$, so that the total potential energy E_e, given by $\tfrac{1}{2}kx_1^2 + \tfrac{1}{2}kx_2^2$, is

$$E_e = \tfrac{1}{2}(5.0\,\text{N m}^{-1})(0.10\,\text{m})^2 + \tfrac{1}{2}(5.0\,\text{N m}^{-1})(0.50\,\text{m})^2$$

$$= 0.65\,\text{J}$$

(that is the same as the total mechanical energy in the equilibrium position).

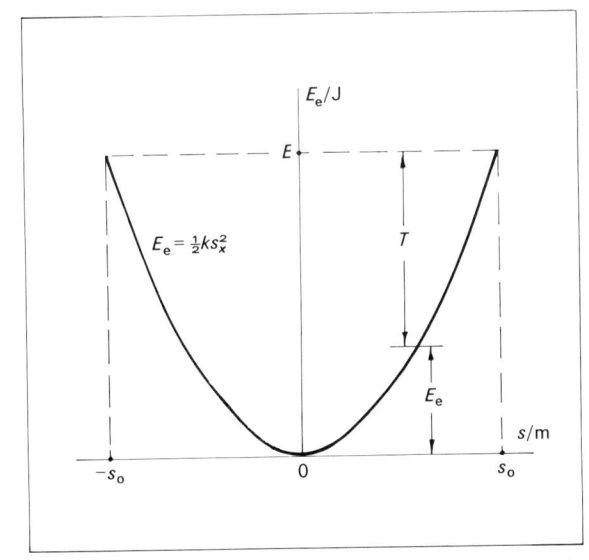

Figure 15-18 Energy and displacement for a simple harmonic oscillator. The equilibrium position is at 0.

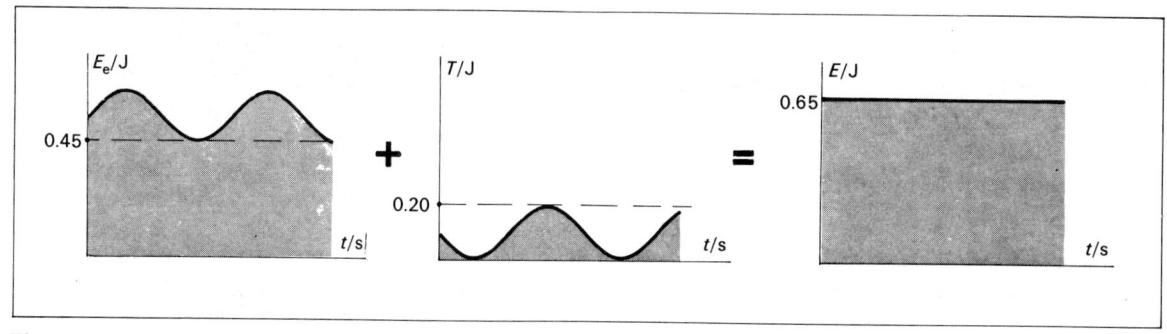

Figure 15-19

(c) At a time $t = 0.10\,\mathrm{s}$ after passing through the equilibrium position

$$s = s_0 \cos \frac{2\pi}{T} t$$

$$= (0.20\,\mathrm{m}) \cos\left(\frac{2\pi}{0.20\pi\,\mathrm{s}} \times 0.10\,\mathrm{s}\right)$$

$$= 0.108\,\mathrm{m}.$$

$$v = v_0 \sin \frac{2\pi}{T} t$$

$$= (2.0\,\mathrm{m\,s^{-1}}) \sin\left(\frac{2\pi}{0.20\pi\,\mathrm{s}} \times 0.10\,\mathrm{s}\right)$$

$$= 1.683\,\mathrm{m\,s^{-1}}.$$

The extensions of the strings are therefore $(0.30 + 0.108)\,\mathrm{m}$ and $(0.30 - 0.108)\,\mathrm{m}$ respectively, that is $0.408\,\mathrm{m}$ and $0.192\,\mathrm{m}$, and the potential energy E_e of the strings is given by

$$E_e = \tfrac{1}{2}[5.0\,\mathrm{N\,m^{-1}}][(0.408\,\mathrm{m})^2 + (0.192\,\mathrm{m})^2]$$

$$= 0.508\,\mathrm{J}.$$

At this point the kinetic energy T is given by

$$T = \tfrac{1}{2}(0.10\,\mathrm{kg})(1.683\,\mathrm{m\,s^{-1}})^2$$

$$= 0.142\,\mathrm{J}.$$

To three significant figures the total mechanical energy is again $0.650\,\mathrm{J}$, as we should have expected.

This example differs from that described in Section 15-7 in that the system has some energy even in the equilibrium position. Figure 15-19 shows the situation graphically. ◀

★ Where it is possible to write down the energy equation for an oscillator (or any mechanical system) in terms of a single variable quantity it is often possible to differentiate the energy equation with respect to time and thus obtain a relationship containing the acceleration of the oscillator. Consider a simple pendulum: a point mass m on the end of a massless string of length l fixed at O (figure 15-20).

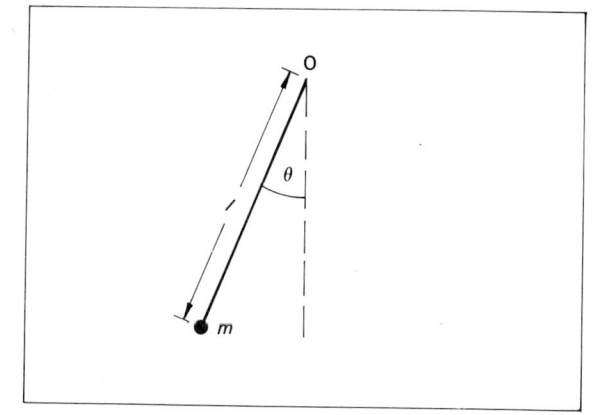

Figure 15-20

The speed v of the mass is given by $v = l(d\theta/dt)$ and if we measure the gravitational potential energy of the mass relative to O, then the energy equation

$$T + E_g = E$$

becomes

$$\tfrac{1}{2} m \left(l\frac{d\theta}{dt}\right)^2 + (-mgl\cos\theta) = E,$$

or

$$\tfrac{1}{2} m l^2 \left(\frac{d\theta}{dt}\right)^2 - mgl\cos\theta = E.$$

Differentiating this equation with respect to t (E is constant), gives

$$ml^2 \left(\frac{d\theta}{dt}\right)\frac{d^2\theta}{dt^2} + mgl\left(\frac{d\theta}{dt}\right)\sin\theta = 0,$$

so that either

$$ml\frac{d\theta}{dt} = 0,$$

which is possible, but a trivial solution, or

$$l\frac{d^2\theta}{dt^2} + g\sin\theta = 0.$$

Thus the angular acceleration α is given by

$$\alpha = -\frac{g}{l}\sin\theta$$

$$\approx -\frac{g}{l}\theta, \quad \text{for small } \theta.$$

This represents simple harmonic motion of period $T_s = 2\pi\sqrt{(l/g)}$, as derived in Section 15-4. ★

15-8 Damped oscillations

Real oscillatory motions die away. They are said to be *damped*. Dissipative forces do negative work on the oscillating system, always opposing the motion, and mechanical energy is converted into internal energy. To see how the amplitude changes with time during a damped oscillation we may clamp a long springy steel blade (of length about 0.5 m) so that it vibrates in a horizontal plane, and attach a small paintbrush to its free end (see figure 15-21). The

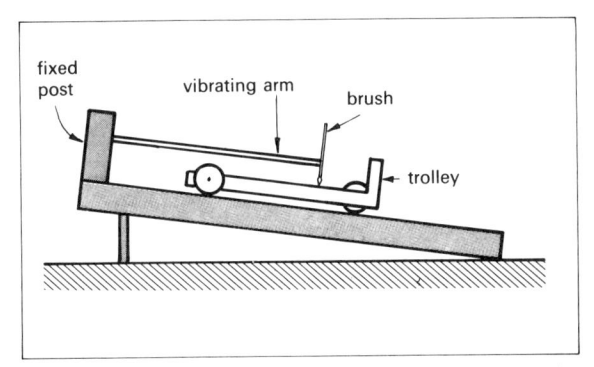

Figure 15-21 Obtaining a displacement–time curve for the motion of a vibrating brush.

blade is then mounted so that the brush can draw a trace on the horizontal surface of a long trolley which is able to run down a friction-compensated slope at a steady speed after being given an initial push (such a piece of apparatus is sometimes called a Fletcher's Trolley). A piece of paper pinned to the top of the trolley can now be used to obtain an ink trace which is a displacement–time graph for the motion of the brush. The result is rather beautiful (figure 15-22a). The oscillation is isochronous, or almost so, and the amplitude decreases in such a way that the ratio of successive maxima of displacement remains roughly constant. Mathematically this means that the dotted line in figure 15-22a follows an exponential decay curve. Not all damped oscillations are like this. Figure 15-22b shows the motion of a block of wood which is attached to a spring and vibrating on a *rough* horizontal surface. Here the period of the motion decreases

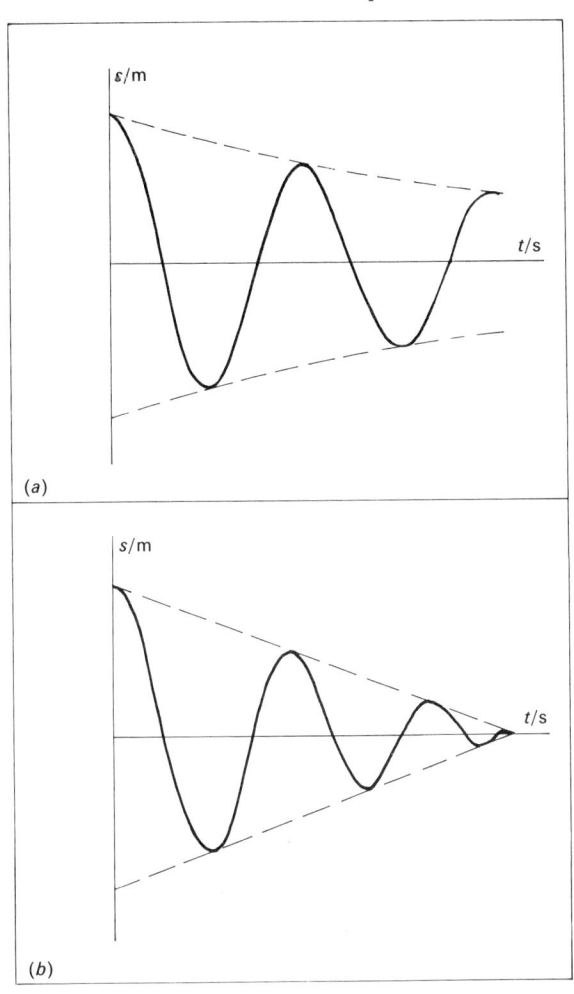

Figure 15-22

rapidly and the amplitude falls to zero in an approximately linear way.

We can never *in practice* remove all damping but the property of mechanical oscillations that is most important is that the period should be independent of the amplitude: it is therefore the first of these graphs which is the more interesting. What sort of vibrating systems produce exactly isochronous damped harmonic motions? It can be shown mathematically that when there is a small force whose size is proportional to the speed of the oscillator and which acts always in such a way as to slow it down, the motion is like that of figure 15-22a. In the vibrating-brush experiment the dissipative forces are internal forces in the blade and its support which do produce damping forces of this sort and thus a curve as in figure 15-22a. (The frictional forces exerted by the air in the experiment are very small, and are just as likely to be proportional to the square of the speed as to the speed itself, particularly for speeds of the order of a few metres per second.)

Figure 15-23 shows a system for which the damping can be studied in some detail. A torsion pendulum is made with a metal skirt attached to the underside of the disc. The pendulum is allowed to rotate with differing lengths of the skirt immersed in an oil bath. For slow torsional oscillations the viscous damping torque exerted by the oil on the skirt of the pendulum is exactly proportional to the angular velocity, and the isochronous nature of these damped oscillations can be verified. Even quite heavy damping, though lowering the frequency of the oscillations slightly, leaves the new greater period independent of their amplitude.

★ For a mathematical analysis the reader is referred to textbooks on differential equations. Applying Newton's second law to an oscillating particle of mass m acted upon by a force which obeys Hooke's law and a damping force which is proportional to the speed of the mass, we have

$$m\mathbf{a} = \sum \mathbf{F}$$
$$\Rightarrow ma = -kx - \lambda v$$

or

$$m\frac{d^2x}{dt^2} + \lambda\frac{dx}{dt} + kx = 0.$$

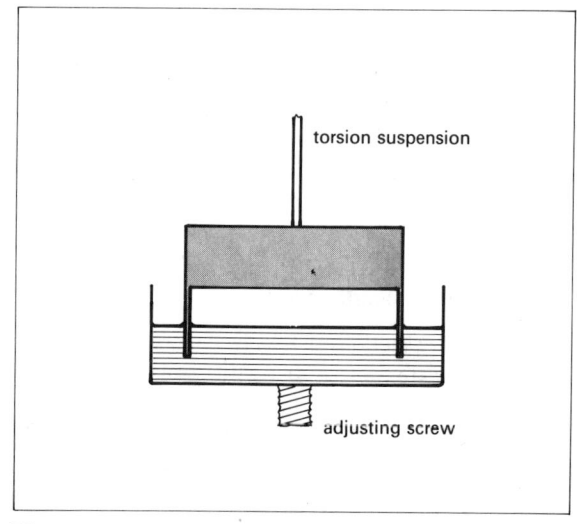

Figure 15-23 A cross-sectional diagram of a torsion pendulum arrangement with variable oil damping.

For a rotating oscillatory system the corresponding equation would be

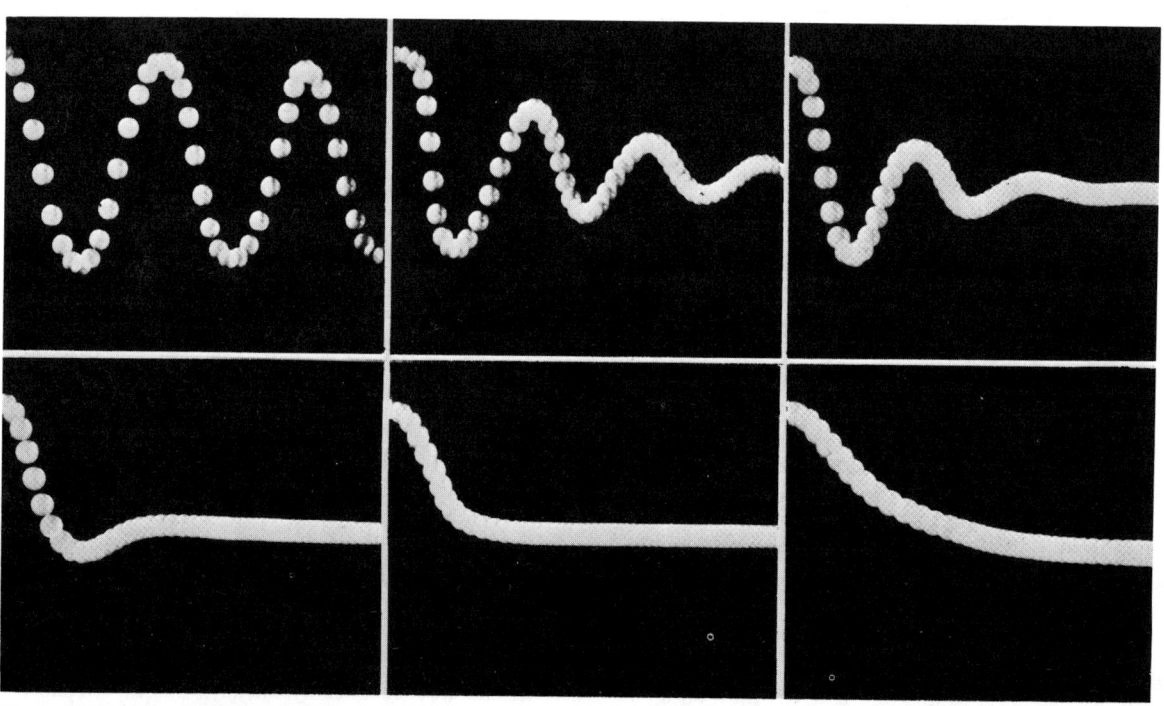

$$I\frac{d^2\theta}{dt^2} + \lambda'\frac{d\theta}{dt} + k'\theta = 0.$$

★

Figure 15-24 Damped harmonic motion.

Mechanical oscillations are often started in situations where it is desirable to damp the motion. Consider the springing of a car's suspension system: it would be disastrous if every bump set the car rocking and swaying for a matter of minutes, so special damping devices, called shock absorbers or dampers, are fitted. Similarly a galvanometer needle is set oscillating when a current begins to flow through the galvanometer, and it is clearly desirable that the needle should not oscillate about its final position for too long before coming to rest; in this case an electromagnetic damping technique is used.

Let us consider the car again. Suppose the wheel of a car hits a step of height h and continues to move at a height h above its original level. The spring at that corner of the car is thus suddenly compressed by an amount h and will then, in the absence of all damping, continue to oscillate about its new equilibrium with amplitude $s_0 = h$. Such springing would feel very soft and a passenger would feel very uncomfortable and perhaps sick. If there were a small amount of damping then the springing would still feel soft although noticeable vibration would die away after a few oscillations. Now consider a car with no springing at all (a difficult thing to realize in practice since the tyres, frame, axle, and seats all act as springs to some extent): on meeting the step a passenger in this car would be pushed violently by the seat as it moved up a distance h. There would not be any oscillation. Nor would very heavy damping be an acceptable solution, as the passenger would be left in the displaced position for some time, and if the car were to hit a series of bumps it would take so long to return to its original position that it would always be tilted and, worse, the spring would usually be considerably compressed and remain in that state for some time, effectively leaving that corner of the car without springing. The ideal is of course a compromise between too violent an oscillation and too long a recovery period. The five possibilities outlined above are shown in a displacement–time graph in figure 15-25; the graphs labelled a to e follow the order of the written discussion above. Where a mechanical system which can oscillate is damped so that it does not quite overshoot its original position when subjected to an impulsive blow it is said to be *critically* damped. In practice it is usually found preferable to have slightly less damping then this, since small oscillations about a new position of equilibrium are not noticeable.

Damping an oscillating system involves transferring the energy stored in the system and redistributing it. We can quantify the damping by defining a new term, the Q or quality factor of the oscillating system. It is defined by the equation

$$Q = 2\pi \frac{\text{energy stored in the system}}{\text{average energy lost per oscillation}}.$$

[15-14]

A high Q thus indicates a lightly damped system. Some typical values of Q for damped mechanical oscillators are:

seismograph for following the vibration of the Earth's surface	2
quartz crystal in water	8
loaded test-tube in water	10
air-damped mirror galvanometer	30
simple pendulum in air	400
piano string (middle C) in air	2000
quartz crystal in air	30 000

The oscillation shown in figure 15-22a has a Q of about 15. We shall use equation 15-14 in later sections as one means of describing a vibrating or oscillating system.

Where does the energy from the system go? Usually the mechanical energy is converted into internal energy of the system and its surroundings which thus become warmer. The mechanism for this energy transfer is of course frictional forces—either solid friction or more often fluid resistance and viscous forces. A system for varying the amount of viscous friction has been described in figure 15-23. Where very high damping is required, that is where the energy of the system needs to be rapidly dissipated as internal energy as in a railway truck buffer, fluid friction is usually employed using viscous liquids in situations where their flow is arranged to be very rapid by using narrow gaps. A number of high-Q solid materials are currently being developed which can be used to coat panels of steel or other mechanically stiff materials to produce a more rapid damping.

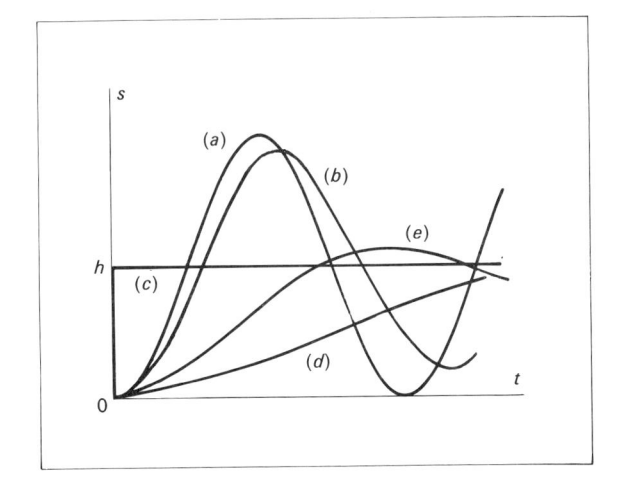

Figure 15-25

It is also possible to transfer mechanical energy from one oscillating system to another very rapidly under certain conditions. Such *coupled* oscillators form a subject the details of which are beyond the scope of this book. One of them, *Barton's pendulum*, will, however, be described in the next section, while the action of another, the *Wilberforce pendulum*, is outlined below. More generally the transfer of energy along ropes and springs or through solids (mechanical waves) are treated in Chapters 16 and 17.

Consider a long closely wound helical spring carrying a massive disc at its free lower end. This system can oscillate *either* linearly up and down *or* torsionally about a vertical axis (see figure 15-26). When the two periods of oscillation are *the same* then, after displacing the disc vertically, for example, the mechanical energy stored in the vibrating system is passed back and forth between the two possible modes of vibration. The coupling between the linear and angular modes occurs because when a coiled spring is stretched it tends to twist slightly. Thus the pendulum is sometimes undergoing purely linear oscillations and sometimes purely torsional oscillations. Seen from a distance the effect can be rather startling, as the torsional oscillations cannot be seen and so the effect is of a mass on the end of a spring undergoing fits of vibration and of rest.

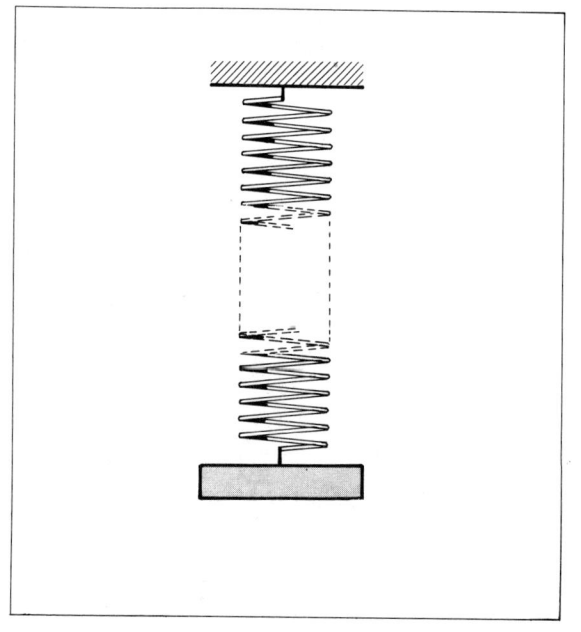

Figure 15-26 A Wilberforce pendulum.

15-9 Resonance

When a twin-tub washing machine spin-drier is started, the casing of the machine sometimes vibrates disturbingly at certain stages during the acceleration process. The effect can be so drastic that the machine fails to accelerate past one of these stages, and when this occurs the user knows that the remedy is to switch off, redistribute the clothes to be spun, and start again. The clue to what is happening lies in the solution to the problem. If the clothes are not symmetrically distributed in their tub then when they are rotating at a frequency f_t the tub is exerting a force on the casing of the spin-drier, which varies periodically in direction, the period T being given by $T = 1/f_t$. This causes the casing to vibrate at the frequency f_t but normally its motion is quite heavily damped, and the energy transfer from the rotating tub to the casing of the machine in each revolution is so small that the amplitude of the casing vibrations is negligible. Thus the motor accelerating the tub increases the kinetic energy of the tub and clothes, and the frequency of rotation increases. This argument can be repeated for any value of f_t. Suppose, however, that the casing of the spin-drier would itself naturally vibrate at a frequency f_0: that is, suppose that with the motor switched off you shook the machine and it then vibrated at a frequency f_0 (you would have to be quick to notice this vibration as the manufacturers try to damp these natural vibrations heavily). When the rotation of the tub now approaches a frequency f_0 there is an increasing transfer of mechanical energy from the tub to the casing of the machine in each revolution and the amplitude of the casing vibrations increases. When the tub is vibrating at a frequency *just below* f_0 the amplitude of these vibrations reaches a maximum, and when the tub rotates *at* f_0 the *transfer of energy* per revolution reaches a *maximum*. If this energy transfer is so large that all the work done by the motor on the tub per revolution is used to maintain the casing vibrations, then the motor fails to accelerate the tub past the frequency f_0. If the motor is now stopped and the clothes rearranged more symmetrically, then the periodic force of the tub on the casing will be reduced. This in turn reduces the energy transfer even at f_0, and the motor should now have enough power to accelerate the tub through the frequency f_0 even if it does so with some difficulty. As in practice the casing of a spin-drier may be able to vibrate naturally at other frequencies—f'_0 and f''_0, etc.—as well as at f_0, the above sequence of events may occur several times during a single period of acceleration to the required spin-drying speed.

The language used by a physicist in describing the situation would run as follows. An asymmetrically loaded spin-drier produces a *driving force* of frequency f_t on the casing of the machine. If the casing has a natural frequency of vibration f_0, then an *energy resonance* occurs when $f_t = f_0$ (an amplitude resonance occurs when f_t is just less than f_0). If the power capable of being transferred exceeds the power of the motor driving the tub of the drier there will be a limit $f < f_0$ to the frequency at which the drier can spin. To overcome this, the driving force must be reduced by loading the spin-drier symmetrically.

Resonance occurs in many physical situations. It involves forcing a system to oscillate: that is, instead of, for example, pulling a pendulum to one side and then allowing it to oscillate freely, we take hold of the pendulum near its top and push it to and fro periodically. Think of a child's swing: if we were to take hold of the ropes near the top, and then were to push to and fro horizontally with a frequency of 4 Hz, what would happen? We *would* make the swing oscillate at 4 Hz, but the child sitting on the swing would not enjoy it much because the amplitude of the swing's oscillations would be very small, perhaps a few centimetres. If we were to push with a frequency of 0.04 Hz the result would be equally disappointing. In both cases we would transfer little energy to the swing and the child. Anyone who has pushed a swing knows that one pushes in such a way as to build up the oscillations of the swing at its *natural* frequency. To demonstrate this in the laboratory the system known as the Barton's pendulum can be used. A pendulum with a massive bob is used to force the whole string ABC (see figure 15-27) to oscillate at a frequency which depends on the length OP. This massive pendulum is called the *driver pendulum*, and we want its motion to remain constant during the experiment; if necessary, it can be given occasional pushes. Let us say that the driver pendulum has a period T and a frequency f. Attached to ABC and thus forced to vibrate by the motion of AB, are several threads each carrying a paper cone (or a table-tennis ball). Each of these cones can swing as a pendulum, but the effective point of suspension of each is somewhere above AB (for example at o, for the cone at p). Viewed end-on, so that the motions of all the cones can be seen at the same time, the cones can be seen to oscillate, after some initial confusion, in such a way that

(a) they all have the same frequency f

(b) their amplitudes vary, the greatest being for the cone for which op is approximately equal to OP, and

(c) the cone with the greatest amplitude is oscillating approximately $T/4$ (one quarter of a period) behind (that is, later than) the driver pendulum.

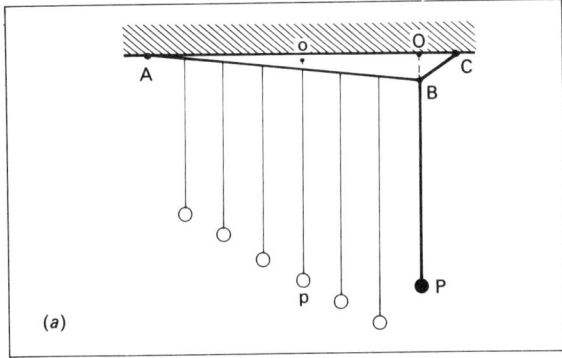

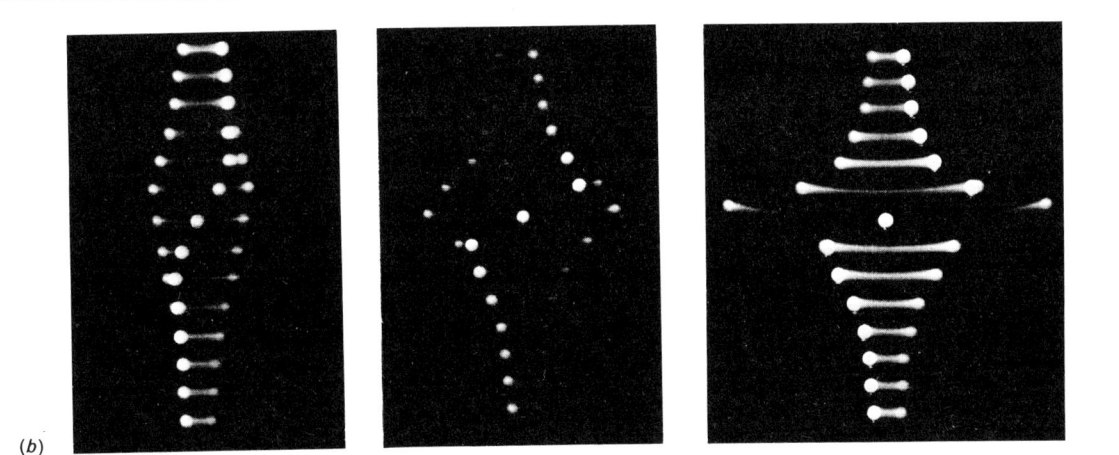

Figure 15-27 (a) Barton's pendulums. The massive bob P forces the whole system to oscillate. (b) Time-exposure photographs of Barton's pendulums. The pendulum bobs are light styrofoam spheres: when they are unloaded (as in the first photograph) they are heavily damped. In the second and third photographs they are increasingly heavily loaded, and the damping is less. We can see that the resonance becomes sharper as the damping decreases. An instantaneous flash photograph has been superimposed on the time exposure, and we can see the phase relationships between the driven pendulums.

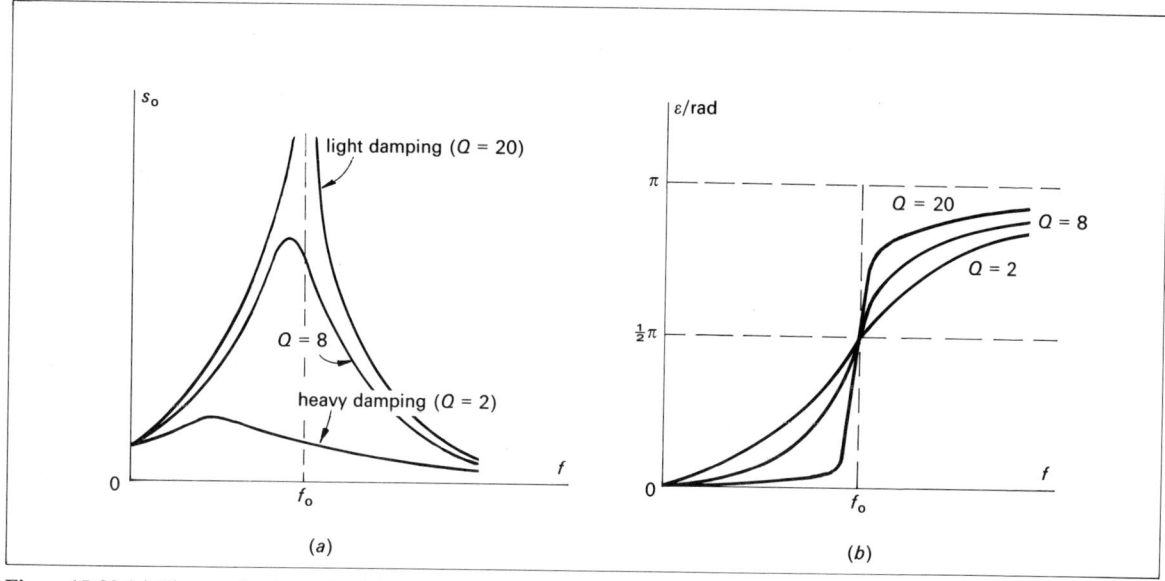

Figure 15-28 (a) The amplitude s_0 of a driven harmonic oscillator with a natural frequency f_0 when a simple harmonic driving force of frequency f is applied. As $f \to 0$, the amplitude tends to a value which depends on the maximum value of the driving force but is independent of the damping. (b) The phase difference ε (i.e. the *lag* of the driven oscillator) between a driven harmonic oscillator with a natural frequency f_0 and a driver of frequency f.

The conditions of the experiment can be varied, either by making the driven pendulums more massive and thus reducing the significance of the damping effect of the paper cones, as in figure 15-27b, or by altering the frequency of the driver pendulum by changing the length *OP*. If only one of the driven pendulums (for example one which has a natural frequency of f_0) is observed, and a whole series of experiments is performed for different frequencies f and different amounts of damping, then the curves shown in figure 15-28 can be produced. (For the definition of Q see equation 15-14 on page 265.)

The graphs in (a) show an *amplitude resonance* for $f \approx f_0$ when there is very little damping. When the damping is appreciable the amplitude resonance does not occur at f_0 but at a slightly lower frequency, $f = f_0 - \Delta f$. The situation where the amplitude of the driven pendulum is a maximum is easy to find when the system has only light damping, as can be seen from figure 15-27b. When the damping is high, so that for instance half the mechanical energy of the system is lost during a period ($Q \approx 12$) the resonance is not so 'sharp'. However it is still possible to pick out the resonant pendulum because it swings exactly $\pi/2$ rad *behind* the driver. The phase relationships between driver and driven pendulums are summarized in figure 15-28b, and illustrated in figure 15-27b. Those pendulums with a much higher natural frequency than the driver are almost in phase with the driver, while those pendulums with much smaller natural frequencies are almost half a period, π rad, behind. We must stress that although the discussion above is all given in terms of pendulums, the results, and in particular the graphs of figure 15-28, are quite general and refer to any (simple harmonic) oscillating system which is forced to vibrate by a sinusoidally varying driving force.

The maximum *energy* transfer from the driver to the driven pendulums occurs *at* $f = f_0$ whatever the damping. At $f = f_0$ the displacement of the driven pendulum is exactly $T/4$ behind the displacement of the driving system and thus the *velocity* of the driven pendulum is in phase with the driving *force*. The force then *always* does positive work on the driven pendulum. If f were not equal to f_0, the force and the velocity would sometimes have the same direction, but at other times would not, so that sometimes positive, sometimes negative, work would be done. The driver and driven pendulums therefore *must* have the same frequency for maximum energy transfer. This *energy resonance* is shown in figure 15-29.

Resonance (the study of resonant systems) must count as one of the most important physical concepts. Apart from mechanics, resonance has important applications in acoustical phenomena (see Chapter 18), in electrical circuits involving alternating currents, in the study of atoms and molecules, and in nuclear physics. In mechanics the often-quoted example of soldiers being ordered to break step when crossing a bridge is not a physicist's fantasy but a sensible precaution following, for example, the destruction of a suspension bridge at Angers in 1850, when a French infantry battalion lost 220 men. Mechanical resonance is often a nuisance: the rattling of loose parts in cars or in rotating machinery is usually a resonance phenomenon. Equally it can be put to use: a resonance condition can be sought when it is required to shake something.

Resonance can be a large-scale phenomenon (the Earth's atmosphere oscillates as a result of the Sun's daily heating, and the large amplitude of the oscillations suggests a resonant condition), or can occur on a small scale (the ions of a crystal such as sodium chloride oscillate, and for frequencies contained in infra-red radiation a resonant condition is produced). The reader should expect to find examples in all branches of physics. In the next three chapters numerous examples of mechanical resonance, and the study of the vibrating systems involved, occur.

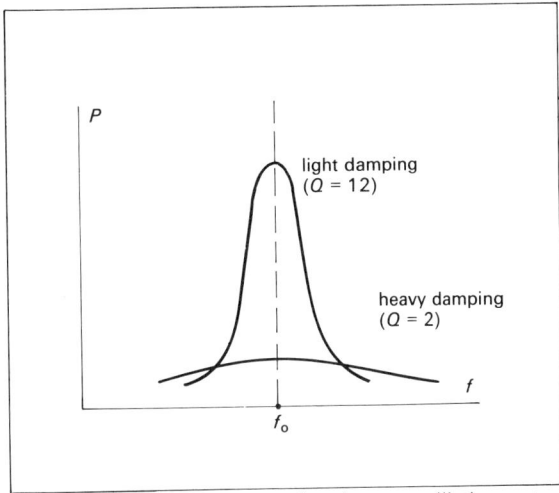

Figure 15-29 The power P transferred to an oscillating system with a natural frequency f_0. The width of the curve at half the maximum value of P determines how 'sharp' the resonance is. This width is approximately equal to f_0/Q, that is the lower the damping the sharper the resonance.

Bibliography

Essen, L. (1968). 'The measurement of time and frequency.' *Sources of physics teaching*, part 2. Taylor and Francis. This article is a reprint from *Contemporary Physics*.

Lyons, H. (1957). 'Atomic clocks.' *Scientific American* offprint number 225.

Bishop, R. E. D. (1965). *Vibration*. Cambridge University Press. A very fine non-mathematical account of vibrations and vibrating systems which stresses their relevance in engineering situations.

French, A. P. (1971). *Vibrations and waves*. Nelson. Chapters 3 and 4 on free and forced vibrations, though at first glance they seem fairly mathematical, contain some very worthwhile material.

Hopley, I. B. (1972). *Oscillations*. Methuen. This text links mechanical and electrical oscillations.

Jardine, J. (1967). *Physics is fun*. Book 4. Heinemann. Chapter 9 gives an elementary survey.

Nuffield Advanced Physics (1971). Teachers' guide, Unit 4 *Waves and oscillations*. Penguin. Mechanical oscillations are covered in Part Three which includes a technique for solving the equation for simple harmonic motion graphically.

Nuffield Advanced Physics (1971). Students' book, Unit 4 *Waves and oscillations*. Penguin. The article by D. E. Walshe and L. R. Wootton on the Severn bridge forms an excellent case study of an engineering project in which the study of oscillations forms an important part.

Resnick, R. and Halliday, D. (1966). *Physics*, part I. John Wiley. Mechanical oscillations are covered particularly clearly in Chapter 15.

Sears, F. W. and Zemansky, M. W. (1964). *College physics*. Addison–Wesley. Chapter 11 is about harmonic motion.

Weidner, R. T. and Sells, R. L. (1965). *Elementary classical physics*, volume 1. Allyn and Bacon. Chapter 17, entitled 'Elasticity and Simple Harmonic Motion', stresses the need for Hooke's law forces in simple vibrating systems.

Wenham, E. J., Dorling, G. W., Snell, J. A. N., and Taylor, B. (1972). *Physics, concepts and models*. Addison–Wesley. Chapters 19 and 20 on damped and forced oscillations are particularly valuable.

8 mm film loop. 'Coupled oscillators.' Ealing Scientific. A beautiful demonstration of energy being fed back and forth between two coupled pendulums.

8 mm film loop. 'Tacoma Narrows Bridge collapse.' Ealing Scientific.

16 mm film. 'Periodic motion.' Guild Sound and Vision. The film illustrates the relation between simple harmonic motion and uniform circular motion.

15 Mechanical oscillations

Exercises

Data (to be used unless otherwise directed):

$g = 10\,\mathrm{m\,s^{-2}} = 10\,\mathrm{N\,kg^{-1}}$.

15-1 A particle moves with simple harmonic motion of period 0.60 s and amplitude 10 mm.
  (a) What is its greatest speed, and where does this occur?
  (b) What is its greatest acceleration, and where does this occur? ●

15-2 If the particle of Exercise 15-1 has zero displacement at $t = 0$ and is moving so that its displacement is about to become positive, what is its displacement at
  (a) $t = 0.05\,\mathrm{s}$ (b) $t = 0.10\,\mathrm{s}$ (c) $t = 0.20\,\mathrm{s}$?
What is its velocity at
  (d) $t = 0.05\,\mathrm{s}$ (e) $t = 0.10\,\mathrm{s}$ (f) $t = 0.20\,\mathrm{s}$?
What is its acceleration at
  (g) $t = 0.05\,\mathrm{s}$ (h) $t = 0.10\,\mathrm{s}$ (i) $t = 0.20\,\mathrm{s}$? ●

15-3 Consider a 'simple pendulum', that is a massive particle suspended by a massless thread (of length l). Draw a free-body diagram for the particle in a displaced position, and use Newton's second law to prove that for a small displacement the angular acceleration of the thread is approximately proportional to, and directed in the opposite sense to, the angular displacement of the thread: in other words, prove that the pendulum moves with approximate angular simple harmonic motion. Also find the period of this simple harmonic motion, verifying that your result agrees with that obtained in Section 15-5.

15-4 A mass hangs in equilibrium from a light vertical spring, and when disturbed oscillates with simple harmonic motion. Would the period be increased or decreased if, separately,
  (a) the mass were doubled
  (b) a second identical spring were placed in parallel with the first
  (c) the spring were cut in two, and one half used to replace the original spring
  (d) the system were transferred from the Earth to the Moon? Explain your answers.

15-5 A mass of 4.0 kg is hung on the lower end of a vertical massless spring, and in the equilibrium position the extension is 0.10 m. A mass of 1.0 kg is hung on a second (different) spring and in equilibrium the extension is found to be 0.40 m. What is the ratio of the period of oscillation of the first and second springs when each, with its appropriate mass, is set into vertical oscillation? ●

15-6 A man leans on a car and finds that when he releases it the car vibrates vertically at a frequency of 2.0 Hz. If the mass of the car is 800 kg, what is the stiffness of the car's springs? If five people, each of mass 90 kg, now get into the car, what will be the new frequency of vertical vibration? ●

15-7 Suppose a point P is moving at constant speed v in a circle of radius s_0 and that its period is T. Suppose that when $t = 0$ the point is at one end B of a diameter AOB. Then at a time t, P is in a position such that

$$\mathrm{B}\hat{\mathrm{O}}\mathrm{P} = \frac{t}{T}\,2\pi \text{ radians} \quad \text{(see figure 15-30)}.$$

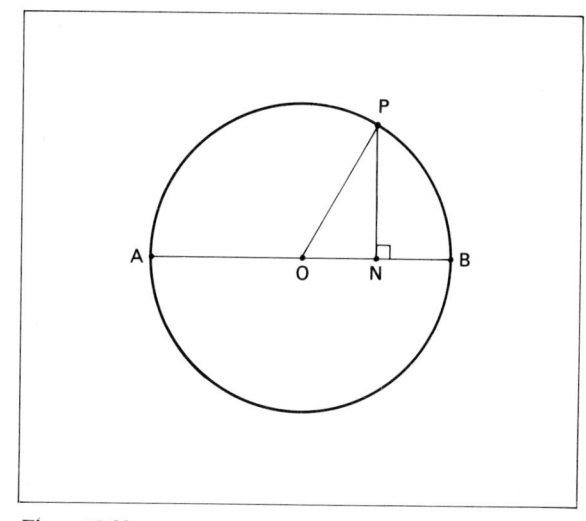

Figure 15-30

Consider a particle which moves with the projection N of P on the diameter AOB

Let $\quad ON = s:\quad$ then $s = s_0 \cos\left(\dfrac{2\pi}{T}\right)t$

and therefore N, and the particle, move with simple harmonic motion. We have thus established that a particle that moves with the projection, on a diameter, of a point moving in a circle at constant speed moves with simple harmonic motion. The instantaneous size and direction of the velocity and acceleration of the point P can be written down; by resolving suitably, find the velocity and acceleration of the particle, and verify that the results are consistent with the particle moving with simple harmonic motion.

15-8 In Exercise 15-7 we saw how we could relate the steady circular motion of a point to the simple harmonic motion of a particle moving along a diameter of the circle. It is sometimes helpful to relate a simple harmonic motion to the steady circular motion of a point, and any simple harmonic motion can be considered to have associated with it a point moving in a circle at a steady speed. For example, in figure 15-31 an *auxiliary circle* is superimposed on a diagram of a mass oscillating at the end of a vertical spring. This circle has no reality, but it is particularly useful if we want to find the time taken by the mass to move from one displacement to another. In figure 15-31 if we know the angles $P_2\hat{O}N_2$ and $P_1\hat{O}N_1$ (which we can calculate if we know ON_1, ON_2, and the amplitude of the simple harmonic motion), we can find the angle $P_2\hat{O}P_1$. This enables us to find the time taken for P to move from P_1 to P_2 which is equal to the time taken for the mass to move from N_1 to N_2.

If the amplitude of this particular simple harmonic motion is 30 mm, and the period $= 1.20\,\mathrm{s}$, what is the time taken for the mass to move between
  (a) $s = 0$ and $s = 15\,\mathrm{mm}$
  (b) $s = 15\,\mathrm{mm}$ and $s = 30\,\mathrm{mm}$
  (c) $s = 6.0\,\mathrm{mm}$ and $s = 21\,\mathrm{mm}$? ●

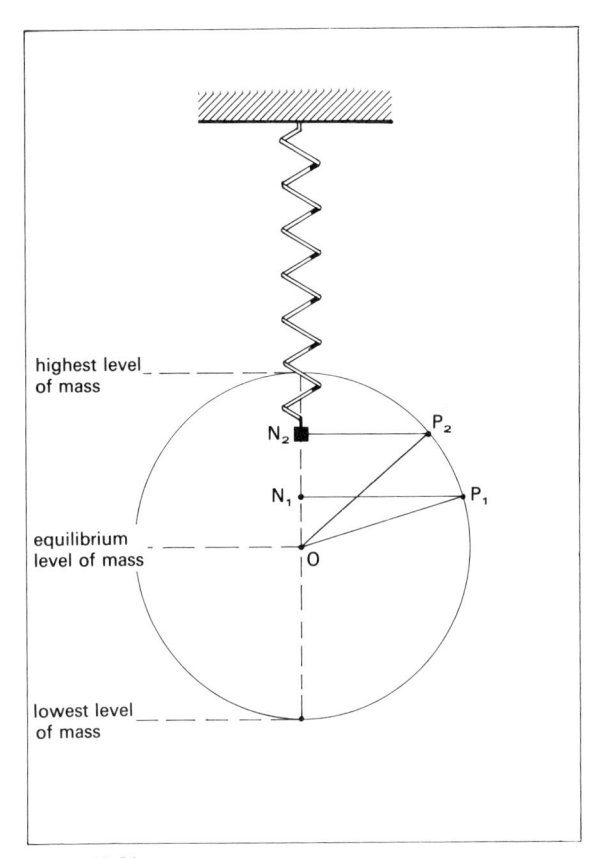

Figure 15-31

15-9 In a certain harbour the depth of water varies between 11 m and 5.0 m at high and low tides, and the time between high and low tides is 6.3 hours. If a ship needs 7.0 m of water to float, for what length of time may it float in the harbour? Assume that the rise and fall of the water is simple harmonic. If on a certain day high tide occurs at 0900 hours, when must the ship leave the harbour if it is not to become grounded? ●

15-10 An observer on Earth is in the plane in which Jupiter's satellites move. He observes that one of the satellites, Io, appears to move with simple harmonic motion of amplitude 4.2×10^8 m and period 1.5×10^5 s. What is the radius of the circle in which Io moves, and what is its speed? ●

15-11 An atom in a certain molecule vibrates with simple harmonic motion of amplitude 8.0×10^{-11} m and period 4.0×10^{-13} s. Find its maximum speed and its maximum acceleration. ●

15-12 Suppose that a tunnel could be drilled diametrically through a planet. If the planet were spherical and of uniform density, explain why a particle would move with simple harmonic motion if it were released from rest at one end of the tunnel. What would be the maximum acceleration of the particle?

Find the period of the simple harmonic motion of the particle in terms of the radius r of the planet and the gravitational acceleration g_0 at its surface. Find also the maximum speed in terms of these quantities.

How does the period of the simple harmonic motion compare with the period of a satellite in orbit very close to the surface of the planet? Comment on your answer.

15-13 A spring of stiffness 100 N m^{-1} is allowed to hang vertically, its upper end being attached to a fixed point. A mass of 6.0 kg is attached to the lower end, and allowed to reach its equilibrium position. What is the maximum displacement of the mass from this equilibrium position if it is to perform vertical simple harmonic oscillations? Assume Hooke's law is obeyed throughout. What would be the period of such a simple harmonic motion? Explain in a qualitative or semi-quantitative way (as you might to an intelligent layman) how it is possible for the period to be independent of the amplitude: 'commonsense' would suggest that the greater the amplitude, the greater the period. ●

15-14 Refer to Exercise 15-13. Suppose the mass is pulled down a distance of 0.40 m below the equilibrium position and released. (In this and in Exercises 15-15 and 15-16 we shall examine the same situation from different starting points.) From a knowledge of the period of the simple harmonic motion, find the initial acceleration of the mass, and its maximum speed. ●

15-15 Refer to Exercises 15-13 and 15-14. By considering the forces acting on the mass, find its initial acceleration and its maximum speed.

15-16 Refer to Exercises 15-13 and 15-14. Use the work–energy theorem to find the maximum speed of the mass.

15-17 Refer to Exercises 15-13 and 15-14. How long does it take for the mass to travel
(a) the first 0.20 m from rest
(b) the second 0.20 m? ●

15-18 Consider a cylinder of material of density ρ, cross-sectional area A, and height l, which floats upright with a length h immersed in a liquid of density σ (so that $\rho/\sigma = h/l$). Prove that when disturbed it moves with simple harmonic motion (in the absence of dissipative forces) and find its period. Assume that the level of the liquid is unaffected by the motion of the cylinder, and ignore the fact that some liquid inevitably also oscillates. What factors prevent it moving with exactly simple harmonic motion?

15-19 A mass m is attached to two equal massless elastic threads of stiffness k, and placed on a frictionless horizontal table. The other ends of the threads are attached to two points A and B on the table, a distance $2l$ apart, and the mass rests in equilibrium at the mid-point of AB, with both threads stretched. The mass is given a small displacement *perpendicular to* AB: if it can be assumed that the tension in each thread remains constant ($= T$) during the oscillation, prove that the mass moves with approximate simple harmonic motion, and find its period. ●

15-20 A flat strip of metal is placed in a horizontal position and clamped at one end; the other end is plucked so that it vibrates vertically in a simple harmonic motion of period 0.10 s. What restriction is there on the amplitude of the motion if a speck of dust, placed on the vibrating end of the strip, is to remain in contact throughout the motion? Explain at what point in the motion the speck is most likely to lose contact. ●

15 Mechanical oscillations

15-21 A U-tube has vertical arms of equal cross-sectional area A, and contains a length l (measured from one surface to the other round the bend in the tube) of non-viscous liquid of density ρ. Use the method of dimensions to find a possible form of the expression for the period of the simple harmonic motion which ensues when the liquid is disturbed.

15-22 A magnetic dipole (bar magnet) is pivoted so that it can rotate about a vertical axis through its centre; about this axis its moment of inertia is I, and its magnetic moment is m. Given that in a magnetic field of flux density B a magnet of moment m experiences a torque $mB\sin\theta$, where θ is the angle its axis makes with the field, prove that the bar magnet oscillates with approximately simple harmonic motion when given a *small* angular displacement from its equilibrium position, and find the period of the motion. ●

15-23 A horizontal platform vibrates horizontally with simple harmonic motion of amplitude 50 mm and period 0.50 s. What is the least value of the coefficient of static friction between the platform and objects placed on it at which the objects will not slide on the platform? ●

15-24 Refer to Example 15-5 and write down an expression for the energy of the mass–spring system when the mass has a displacement x from its equilibrium position, and a speed v. Equate this to a constant, and differentiate the resulting equation with respect to time to find a relationship between its acceleration and its displacement. (This technique provides us with an alternative method of proving that a particle has simple harmonic motion: it is a particular case of the general rule that differentiating an energy equation gives us an equation of motion, and integration of an equation of motion gives us an energy equation. See Section 15-7.) ●

15-25 A compound pendulum is any rigid pendulum which cannot be treated as a simple pendulum: for instance, a metre rule pivoted at a point near one end. Prove that such a pendulum will move with approximate angular simple harmonic motion (when the axis of rotation is horizontal) and find its period, if it has a mass m, and a moment of inertia I about its axis of rotation, and its centre of mass is a distance h from its axis of rotation. Derive your results
  (a) by differentiating the work–energy equation, and
  (b) by considering forces and using Newton's second law to form an equation of motion. ●

15-26 A thin uniform rod of length l and mass m is suspended by two vertical threads of length d, one attached at each end of the rod. Use the technique of Exercise 15-24 to prove that approximate angular simple harmonic motion occurs when the rod is disturbed so that it oscillates about a vertical axis through its centre, the rod remaining horizontal (though necessarily rising as it rotates) and find the period. The moment of inertia of a thin uniform rod of length l and mass m about an axis through its centre and perpendicular to its length is $ml^2/12$. ●

15-27 If a compound pendulum consists of a uniform rod of length l of negligible thickness, find the distance from its centre at which it should be pivoted in order that it may oscillate with (approximate) angular simple harmonic motion, about a horizontal axis, with as *small* a period as possible. A value for the moment of inertia of such a rod is given in Exercise 15-26. Sketch a rough graph of the variation of the period T of such a pendulum against the distance h of the axis of rotation from the centre of mass. ●

15-28 A spherical ball of radius $r/5$ rolls without slipping at the bottom of a hemispherical bowl of radius r. Show that, when the ball is given a small displacement from its lowest position, it oscillates with approximate simple harmonic motion, and find the period of this simple harmonic motion. The moment of inertia of a uniform sphere of radius r and mass m about a diameter is $2mr^2/5$. ●

15-29 A horizontal frictionless channel has a vertical cross section as shown in figure 15-32 and a mass is made to oscillate in it by being allowed to slide down one side from either of two positions A and B. An origin O is marked. Is this periodic motion simple harmonic? Draw a graph of the speed v of the mass against the time elapsed t for the two positions from which the mass may be released. Does the period of the oscillation depend on the height from which the mass is released? Does the period of a ball moving in a semicircular channel depend on the height from which the mass is released?

15-30 The answer to the last part of Exercise 15-29 was 'yes' that is, when the mass moves in a *circular* path, the motion is not *isochronous*. Try to discover from a mathematics textbook the curve on which the mass would need to move if its motion were to be isochronous. What is a *brachistochrone*?

15-31 The balance wheel of a watch moves with angular simple harmonic motion of period 0.50 s and amplitude 2.0 radians. Find its maximum angular velocity and its maximum angular acceleration. Find also the time taken for it to move through 1.0 radian from its central position. ●

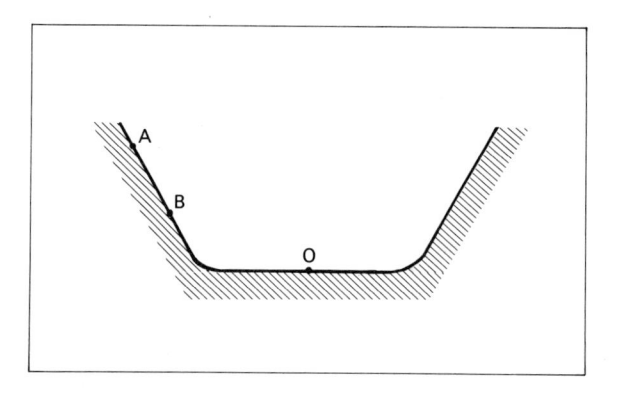

Figure 15-32

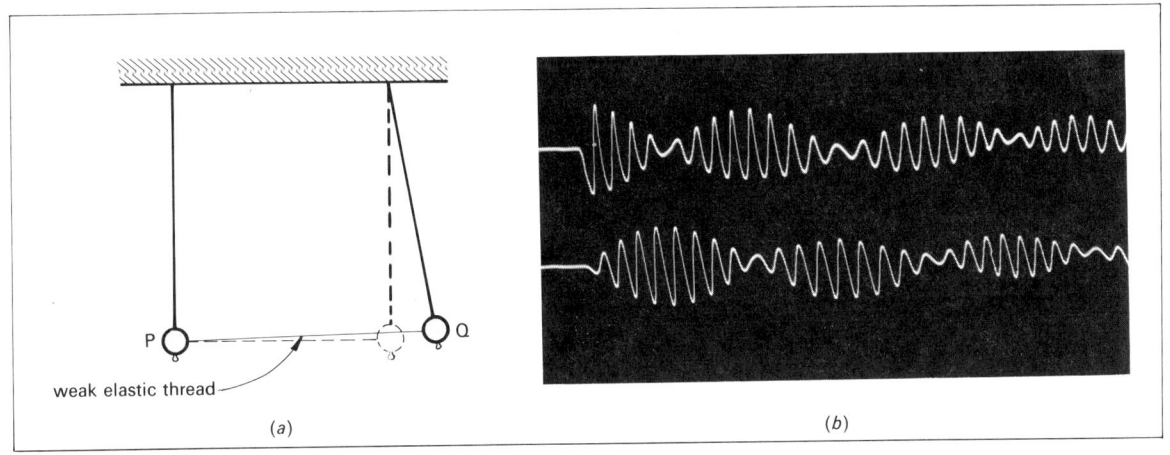

Figure 15-33 Coupled pendulums. Notice the damping which occurs as time progresses.

15-32 An empty child's swing has a certain period of oscillation. Is it altered when a child is placed on the swing? Explain.

15-33 When pendulum Q in figure 15-33a is pulled aside as shown (the movement being parallel to PQ) and released, the coupled pendulums exhibit a complex motion. Figure 15-33b is a photograph taken from below by a camera which is steadily moved along the floor when the pendulum bobs each consisted of a dry cell and a small torch bulb. Describe the behaviour of the pendulums as fully as possible. (*Hint:* the words 'energy transfer' and 'phase' should appear in your answer.)

15-34 Figure 15-34 shows two vibrating objects; one is a pendulum whose bob is of mass 1 kg. This is supported by a strip of metal XY which is fixed to a second strip AB, which rocks in a groove cut in the U-shaped wooden frame. The second vibrator is a steel strip which is clamped at its base to the wooden frame: a mass of about 0.1 kg can be slid vertically along this strip and clamped at different positions.

Explain qualitatively how the period of the pendulum depends on the depth of the bob below the point of support. Is its large mass a factor tending to increase or decrease its period? Also explain qualitatively how the period of the vibrating strip depends on the position of the clamped mass.

15-35 Refer to Exercise 15-34 and figure 15-34. Suppose that a horizontal elastic thread is used to join the upper part of XY to the lower part of the vertical vibrating strip, and that the pendulum is set into oscillation and its amplitude is maintained by occasional pushes. Discuss the variations in amplitude and phase of the oscillations of the end of the vibrating strip as the clamped mass is moved to successive positions along that strip. Discuss also what would be noticed by the person maintaining the constancy of the amplitude of the driver pendulum.

15-36 Use equation 15-14 to draw a graph of the total mechanical energy E of a freely oscillating system (for which $Q = 10$) against time t. Suppose that at $t = 0$, $E = 10$ J, and that the (constant) period T of the system is 1.0 s. Describe the shape of the graph.

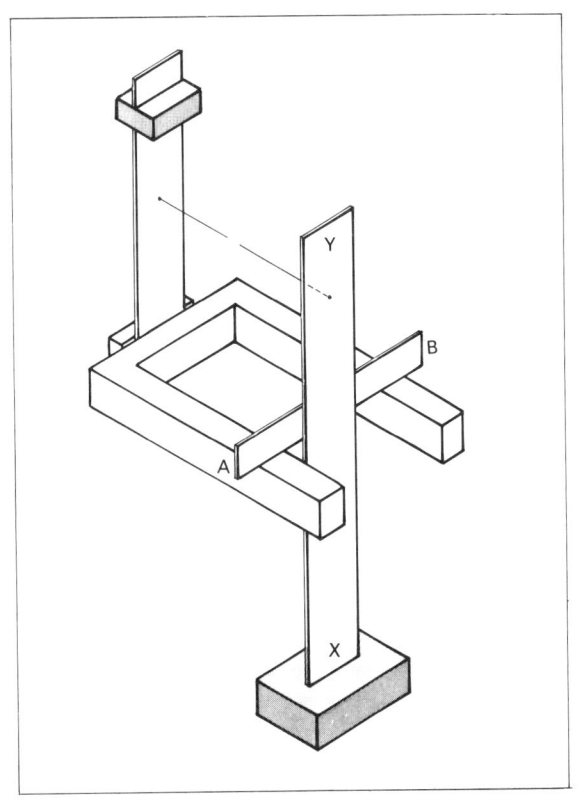

Figure 15-34

15-37 Sketch the general shape of the graph of the amplitude s_0 against time t for a freely oscillating system of constant Q. (*Hint:* see Exercise 15-36 and Section 15-7.)

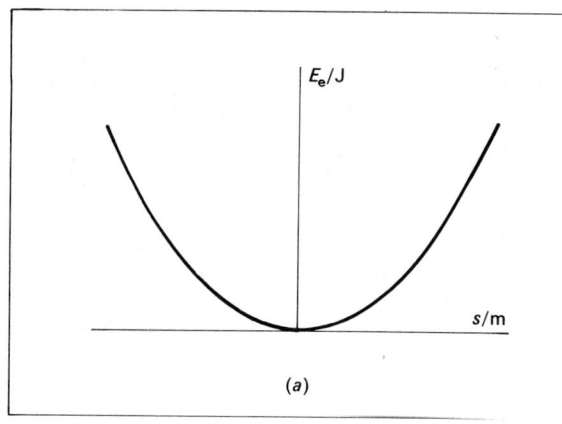

Figure 15-35

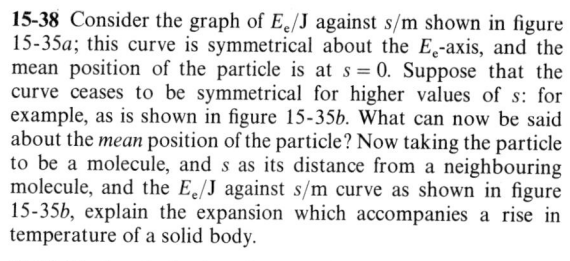

15-38 Consider the graph of E_e/J against s/m shown in figure 15-35a; this curve is symmetrical about the E_e-axis, and the mean position of the particle is at $s = 0$. Suppose that the curve ceases to be symmetrical for higher values of s: for example, as is shown in figure 15-35b. What can now be said about the *mean* position of the particle? Now taking the particle to be a molecule, and s as its distance from a neighbouring molecule, and the E_e/J against s/m curve as shown in figure 15-35b, explain the expansion which accompanies a rise in temperature of a solid body.

15-39 Find typical values for the dimensions and speeds of a motor-car engine, and assuming that the motion of a piston in the engine is simple harmonic, estimate the piston's maximum acceleration.

15-40 Find the length of a 'seconds-pendulum', that is a simple pendulum with a period of 2.000 s, at a place where $g = 9.800 \, \text{m s}^{-2}$.

15-41 Find the percentage change in the period of the pendulum of Exercise 15-40 when
(a) it is taken to the top of a tower of height 200 m, the radius of the Earth being 6.4×10^6 m
(b) there is a temperature rise of 10 K, and the linear expansivity of the material of the wire is $1.2 \times 10^{-5} \, \text{K}^{-1}$. (*Hint*: use calculus techniques to find the relationship between the change in period ΔT and the changes Δg and Δl in g and l respectively.)

15-42 Invent a device (which could be constructed in a school laboratory) which could be used to demonstrate that in simple harmonic motion the displacement of a body varies sinusoidally with time.

15-43 Suppose that a particle is moving in a straight line with simple harmonic motion of a certain amplitude and period. Suppose now that the particle simultaneously moves with simple harmonic motion of the same amplitude and period along a line at right angles to the first one, the centres of the simple harmonic motions coinciding. Describe the motion of the particle, considering the effect of possible differences of phase between the two simple harmonic motions.

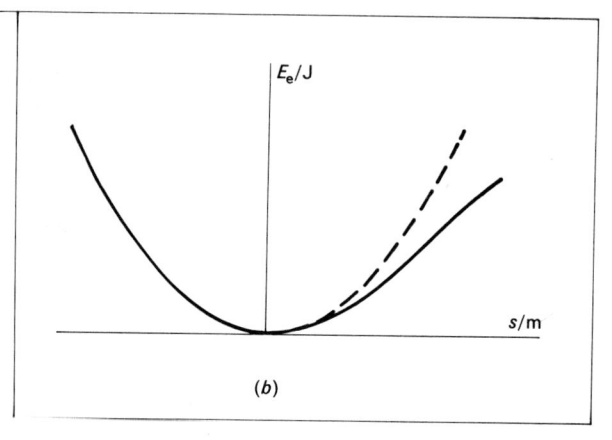

15-44 Suppose that one of the two simple harmonic motions of Exercise 15-43 has a period which is some multiple (such as 2, 3, etc.) of the other's. Describe what happens.

15-45 Some clocks have a pendulum and *also* a spring (which can be wound) or weights (which can be raised): watches have a balance wheel (the oscillations of which are controlled by hairsprings) and *also* a main-spring. What are the respective functions of
(a) the pendulum and the balance wheel, and
(b) the main-spring and the weights?

15-46 Consider the leg of an animal as a (compound) pendulum: how does the period of its natural swing depend on its length? Suppose that a giraffe has a leg which is similar in shape and mass-distribution to that of a horse, but that it is four times longer: find the ratio of the following quantities for the giraffe and the horse:
(a) the period of the leg's free swing
(b) the frequency of the leg's free swing
(c) the length of stride
(d) the speed of walking.

15-47 Discover the reason why the spectrum of light from the Sun is crossed by apparently dark lines (Fraunhofer lines) which correspond to particular frequencies of the radiation.

15-48 Why is electromagnetic radiation in the infra-red region more easily absorbed by solid matter than is light? (This is a complex question to answer fully.)

15-49 Write a brief account of resonance to explain it to a layman, including references to the following illustrative examples: a child on a swing, a man walking along a plank laid across a ditch, the reception of radio waves of a particular frequency.

15-50 The speed of a car may vary between $10 \, \text{m s}^{-1}$ and $25 \, \text{m s}^{-1}$: suppose lateral ridges occur on the road at regular intervals of 2 m. What range of resonant frequencies should the car manufacturer avoid? If he cannot avoid such a wide range, what other remedy is there? Do these remedies produce other problems?

16 Waves on a string

16-1 Mechanical waves	275	16-7 Superposition of sinusoidal waves	289
16-2 Travelling wave pulses	276	16-8 Stationary waves	291
16-3 Representing waves	279	16-9 Vibrating strings	293
16-4 The principle of superposition	280	Bibliography	296
16-5 The reflection of waves	283	Exercises	297
16-6 Periodic waves	286		

16-1 Mechanical waves

Waves—water waves, sound waves, radio waves—are very common and very important phenomena. Why are they important? Sound and light are the means by which animals, including man, learn most about their environments. These waves enable one person to communicate with another or with many others. Electromagnetic waves carry the energy from the Sun vital to man's presence on Earth. More fundamentally still, a physicist or a cosmologist could not describe his models for the existence of an atom or of the Universe without electromagnetic wave phenomena. Waves are clearly important.

In this text we have already learned a great deal about how *particles* can carry energy from A to B and how the mechanics of these particles can be built up from Newton's laws of motion. In this and succeeding chapters our aim is to consider the mechanics of wave motion. We shall deal with only those waves which travel in deformable media; for example, waves on the surface of water, waves on stretched strings and springs, waves in solid elastic materials, and sound waves in gases. All such waves are called *mechanical waves*. Other types of wave motion, principally electromagnetic waves such as radiated heat (including light) and radio waves, will not be considered. For a study of *electromagnetic waves* the reader is referred to texts on, for example, physical optics, or electricity and magnetism. It should be stressed however at the outset that most of the *properties* of waves considered in this text are quite general and *apply to all types of wave motions*.

A mechanical wave originates in the displacement of some part of an elastic medium from its equilibrium position, about which it then oscillates. As the particles forming the medium are coupled (that is they exert forces on one another, the size and direction of which tends to restore those displaced to their original positions), this disturbance is transmitted from one part of the medium to another. The moving disturbance constitutes our wave. (Clearly, mechanical waves cannot be transmitted through a vacuum.) If the medium is not perfectly elastic the mechanical (kinetic and potential) energy of the wave is gradually dissipated as internal energy. To give a definitive statement:

mechanical waves involve the transmission of mechanical energy through matter by means of a disturbance, the matter itself undergoing zero net displacement.

Waves in which the energy transfer takes place in two dimensions include the waves we see on the surface of water: in a swimming pool, a river, a lake, or in a

16 Waves on a string

laboratory ripple tank. Such waves serve to illustrate the above discussion. The waves are produced by setting a part of the water surface into oscillation and the disturbance can be *seen* moving away from the source. When the waves disturb an object floating on the water, for example a seagull or a float, we know that energy is transmitted to it because it starts to oscillate: it acquires kinetic energy. Further, its average position during the oscillation remains fixed and does not move away from its initial position (provided the amplitude of the wave disturbance is not too large). In this chapter, however, we are going to concentrate on a simple one-dimensional wave, that carried by a stretched string, thin spring, or rope.

16-2 Travelling wave pulses

Consider a uniform flexible spring which is stretched out on a well-polished table. If one end of the spring is given a brief flick to one side and back, a *wave pulse* travels along the spring (figure 16-1). The pulse is said to be *transverse*, as the displacement of a point on the spring as the pulse passes is perpendicular to the direction of motion of the energy carried by the pulse. The speed at which the pulse travels can be seen to be constant and the shape of the pulse remains unaltered except that its amplitude decreases slightly if the table is not frictionless.

If the spring is stretched to a greater extent, and another pulse produced, the pulse speed is now greater than before. In stretching the spring we have increased the tension, T, in it and lowered its mass per unit length m. Suppose pulses of differing shapes and sizes are sent down the spring for fixed values of T and m: we find little or no difference in the speed at which the pulses travel. In particular the speed, c_t, of a transverse travelling wave pulse does not seem to depend on y_0, the maximum sideways displacement of the spring. Such experiments are not easy to perform quantitatively as the speed of the pulse is high, of the order of several metres per second, and the tension awkward to measure because of the frictional force of the table on the spring. Suppose, however, we assume that c_t *does* depend on each of T, m, and y_0, and that these quantities are connected by the relation

$$c_t = kT^x m^y y_0^z,$$

where k is a dimensionless constant and x, y, and z are

Figure 16-1 A travelling wave pulse on a spring.

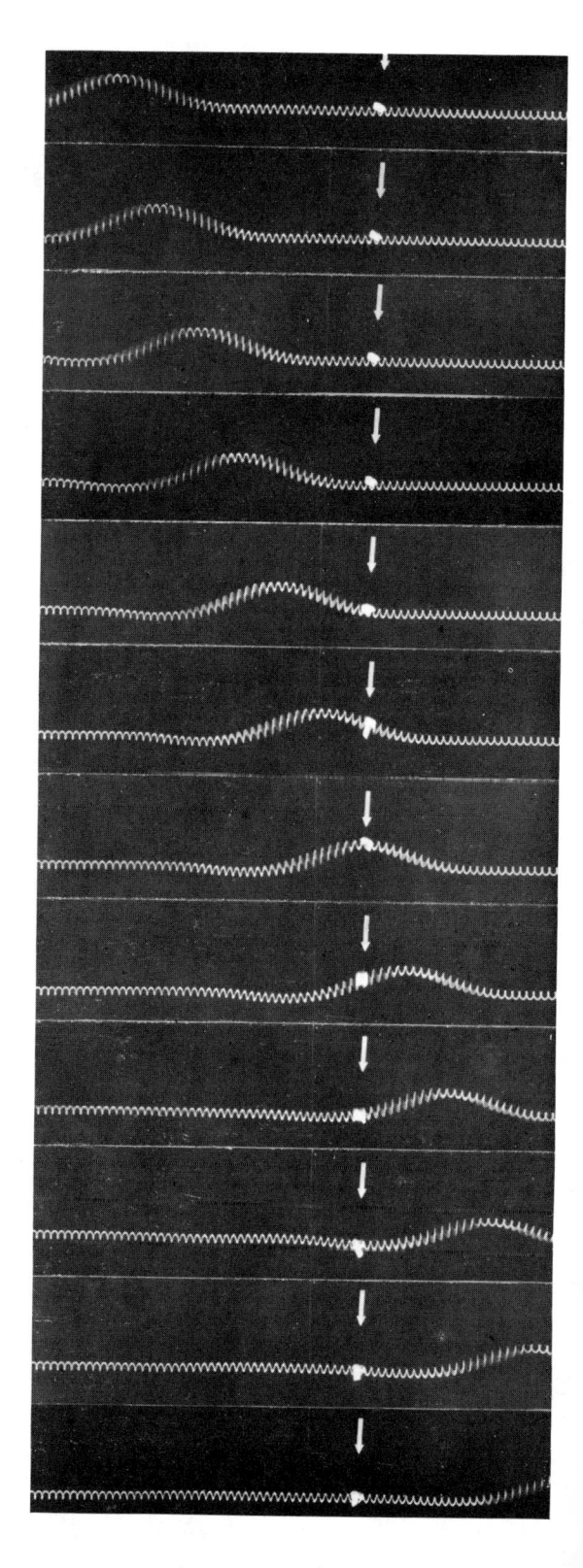

numbers. In dimensional terms this equation must be homogeneous (the units of the right-hand side must be m s^{-1}):

that is $\quad [c_t] = [T]^x[m]^y[y_0]^z$

or $\quad LT^{-1} = (MLT^{-2})^x(ML^{-1})^y(L)^z$,

whence $x = \frac{1}{2}$, $y = -\frac{1}{2}$, $z = 0$.

So that a *possible* relationship is

$$c_t = k\sqrt{\frac{T}{m}}$$

$$= k\sqrt{\frac{\text{tension in the spring}}{\text{mass per unit length of spring}}},$$

which agrees with the experimental conclusion that c_t does not depend on y_0. It is important to realize that the above relation has not been *proved*, but only shown to be a possible relation by considering the dimensions of the quantities involved.

Let us now think of the mechanism by which the pulse travels along the spring. How does one part of the spring affect the next part? If we sketch the position of the spring at two successive instants of time on top of one another we get the arrangement shown in figure 16-2. The lengths of the vertical arrows are proportional to the average velocity of points on the spring during the time interval considered. By the time the pulse is in the second position, the point A has been pulled down and stopped at A' while B has been pulled up to B' where it is still

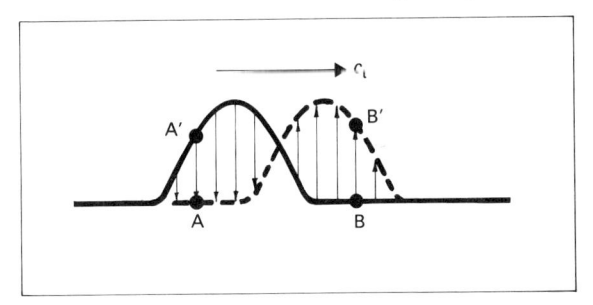

Figure 16-2

moving. We should be able to analyse the motions of A and B using Newton's laws of motion for the problem involves only force and inertia. It is the complicated shape of the wave pulse in figure 16-2 that prevents us tackling the problem. As, however, pulses of all shapes and sizes travel at the *same* speed let us consider the simplest possible pulse—a single *knee*. To create such a knee, one end of the stretched spring is moved horizontally and perpendicular to the spring at a uniform speed v. In practice we must soon stop the sideways movement but we can imagine the process continuing indefinitely provided the spring is infinitely long. The knee or kink in the spring now travels along the spring at a speed c_t (see figure 16-3). The part of the spring moving sideways must have a greater tension than the tension T in the stationary part of the spring, so if we consider a small part of the spring which includes the knee it will be

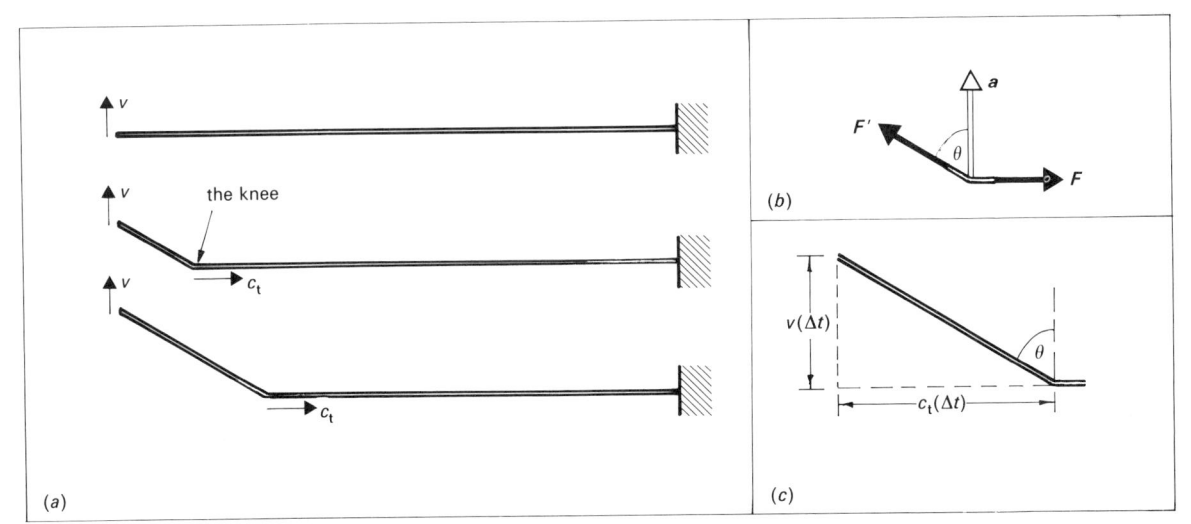

Figure 16-3 (*a*) A single knee (transverse wave pulse) travels along a horizontal stretched spring resting on a frictionless surface. (*b*) shows the horizontal force acting on a small part of the spring at the knee. After Δt the spring will be in the position shown in (*c*).

accelerated by a resultant force $F+F'$, where $F' > F$ and $F = T$ (see figure 16-3b). As we know it acquires a speed v which is perpendicular to the spring then this acceleration must be perpendicular to F and thus the accelerating force is simply $F' \cos \theta$.

By Newton's second law the rate of change of momentum of the spring must equal $F' \cos \theta$. If the knee moves at c_t and the mass per unit length of the spring is m, then in time Δt a mass $mc_t \Delta t$ of the spring is given a sideways velocity v. The rate of change of momentum is thus

$$\frac{\Delta p}{\Delta t} = \frac{mc_t \Delta t v}{\Delta t} = mc_t v,$$

and Newton's second law tells us that therefore

$$mc_t v = F' \cos \theta.$$

Referring to part (b) of figure 16-3 we have, as the spring does not accelerate in the direction parallel to F,

$$F' \sin \theta = F,$$

or

$$F' = \frac{F}{\sin \theta}.$$

The accelerating force $F' \cos \theta$ can be expressed as

$$F' \cos \theta = \frac{F}{\sin \theta}(\cos \theta) = \frac{F}{\tan \theta}.$$

Eliminating $F' \cos \theta$ between the two equations above in which it appears,

$$mc_t v = \frac{F}{\tan \theta},$$

while from part (c) of figure 16-3 we see that

$$\tan \theta = \frac{c_t \Delta t}{v \Delta t} = \frac{c_t}{v}$$

so that

$$mc_t v = \frac{Fv}{c_t}.$$

This implies that either

$$v = 0 \quad \text{(there is no wave pulse)}$$

or

$$mc_t = \frac{F}{c_t},$$

$$c_t^2 = \frac{F}{m},$$

so that

$$c_t = \sqrt{\frac{F}{m}}.$$

As $F = T$, the tension in the undisplaced part of the spring, then we can write

$$c_t = \sqrt{\frac{T}{m}}. \qquad [16\text{-}1]$$

This deduction of the speed of a mechanical wave pulse along a stretched spring confirms the result suggested by a consideration of dimensions and agrees with the experimental fact that the wave speed is independent of v. Thus we can (by altering v during the formation of the kink) make wave pulses of any shape and they will all travel with speed $c_t = (T/m)^{1/2}$.

▶ **Example 16-1** A man jerks one end of a length of garden hose which is slung between two posts, not touching the ground. Estimate the speed of the wave pulse which travels along the hose.

Let us estimate that the mass per unit length of the empty hose is 0.20 kg m^{-1} (a 20 m reel of plastic garden hose might weigh 40 N). Suppose that the tension in the hose is 50 N, and remains at this value approximately. Then using equation 16-1

$$c_t = \sqrt{\frac{T}{m}}$$

we have

$$c_t = \sqrt{\frac{50 \text{ N}}{20 \text{ kg m}^{-1}}}$$

$$= 1.6 \text{ m s}^{-1}.$$

If the hose had been full of water, both the mass per unit length *and* the tension (which depends directly on the weight of the hose) would have increased proportionately, so that the speed of the wave pulse would remain the same. ◀

An effective demonstration of the relationship, $c_t = (T/m)^{1/2}$, can be given by linking together a number of dynamics trolleys (such as those described on page 68) as shown diagrammatically in figure 16-4. In order to increase T, the number of springs used at each link can be increased and the speed of the wave pulse shown to increase, while by stacking trolleys the effect of increasing m can be demonstrated. These experiments are quantitative, although to show that c_t is equal to or at least proportional to $(T/m)^{1/2}$, m must be the mass of trolleys per unit length of *the springs* (not the mass of trolleys per unit length of *the system*); see connections of springs in figure 16-4. This model will be referred to several times in this chapter.

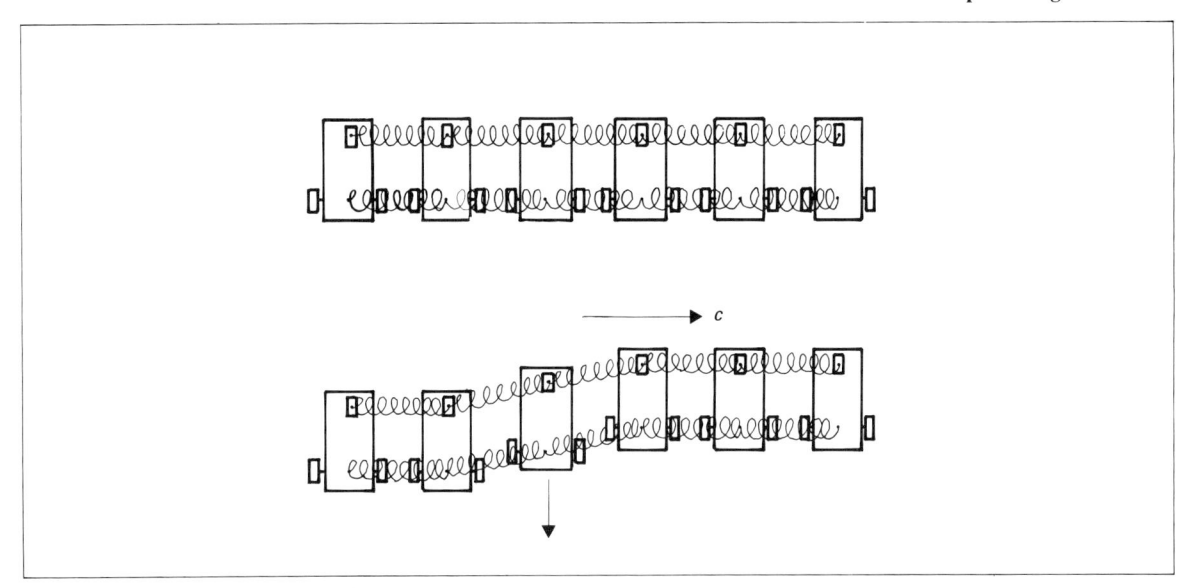

Figure 16-4 A trolley and spring model for transverse waves.

16-3 Representing waves

In representing the behaviour of travelling waves on ropes and springs (and other wave motions) we usually draw graphs. Two types of graph are commonly used, and these are illustrated in figure 16-5. In (b) a displacement–position graph shows what is happening to *every point* on the rope at *one* instant of time. A series of such graphs for instants $t = 0$, $t = 0.5\,\text{s}$, $t = 1.0\,\text{s}$, etc., would show the progression of the wave pulse. Such a series of

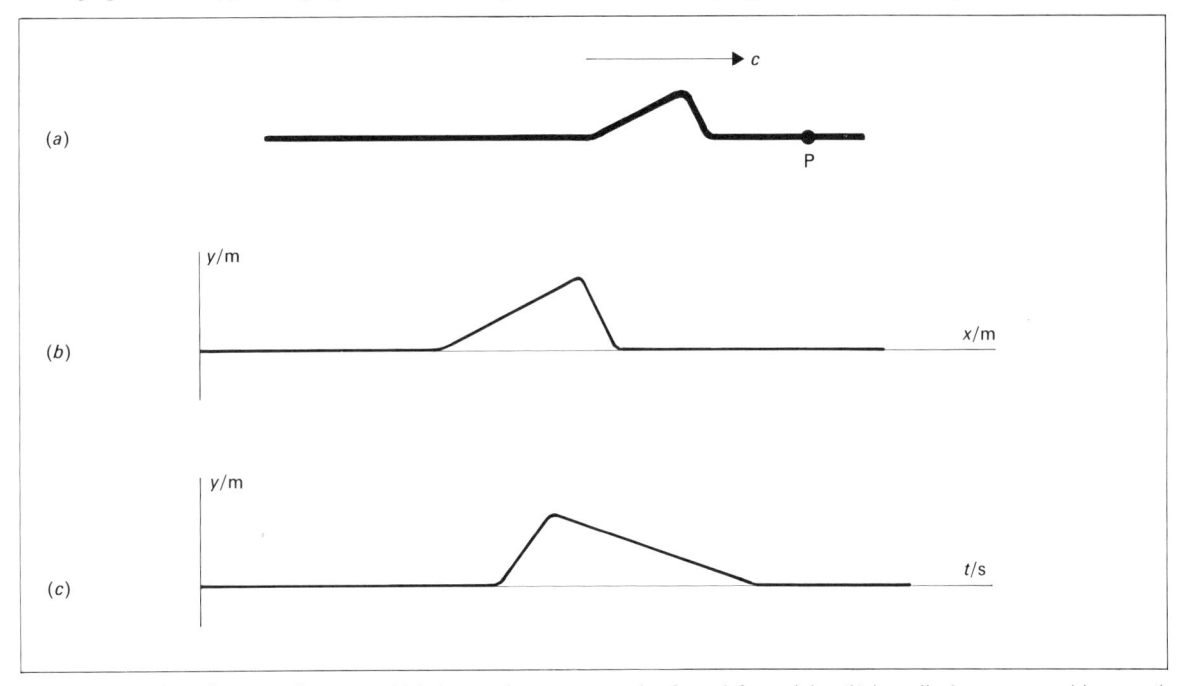

Figure 16-5 (a) is a diagram of a rope which is carrying a wave pulse from left to right. (b) is a displacement–position graph of all points on the rope at a certain instant in time, and (c) is a displacement–time graph for one point, for example P, on the rope.

graphs is tedious to draw but is sometimes the only way of producing a convincing written explanation of the behaviour of a wave or waves. In figure 16-5c a displacement–time graph shows what happens to *one point* on the rope as time passes. We could draw such a graph for every point on the rope and again it is sometimes helpful (though tedious) to choose several points and to draw displacement–time graphs for each. For brevity we shall sometimes refer to the graphs of figure 16-5b and (c) as y–x and y–t graphs respectively.

In displaying wave motions in the laboratory the reader may have met two techniques. Firstly a short-exposure photograph of a wave on a rope, which is equivalent to a y–x graph, and secondly an oscilloscope trace representing a sound wave received by a microphone, which is effectively a y–t graph. It is easy to be confused unless the difference between these two ways of representing wave motions graphically is fully appreciated.

The graphical representations of waves described so far are for *plane-polarized* waves, where the displacements of points on the string all lie in the same plane, for instance the x–y plane as shown in figure 16-6a. To produce such waves the source is disturbed in a plane perpendicular to the string. Figure 16-6b shows a much more complicated wave which can be produced by arranging for the source to move in several different directions. Such a disturbance produces a *non-polarized* wave pulse and the simple y–t and y–x graphs are inadequate to represent it. A special case of a non-polarized wave is when the source is moved in a circle. When produced on a string such a wave pulse moves along the string like a spiral. In this text we are chiefly interested in those transverse waves for which an explicit discussion of polarization is unimportant.

16-4 The principle of superposition

One of the most surprising things about waves is their ability to pass *through* one another. To illustrate this consider a long stretched string along which two wave pulses are travelling in opposite directions (figure 16-7). They appear to emerge unscathed after their meeting. There is no substitute for seeing this experiment performed in the laboratory. If it is tried with a row of linked trolleys such as that shown in figure 16-4 the speed of the wave pulses can be made slow enough to see what happens *as* the pulses cross. Alternatively, a long string or spring can be stretched out on the floor and pulses sent down it from each end—if necessary the process can be filmed. The waves emerge unaffected by the meeting; the energy of one wave pulse can be transmitted through other wave pulses. We can hear a person talking even

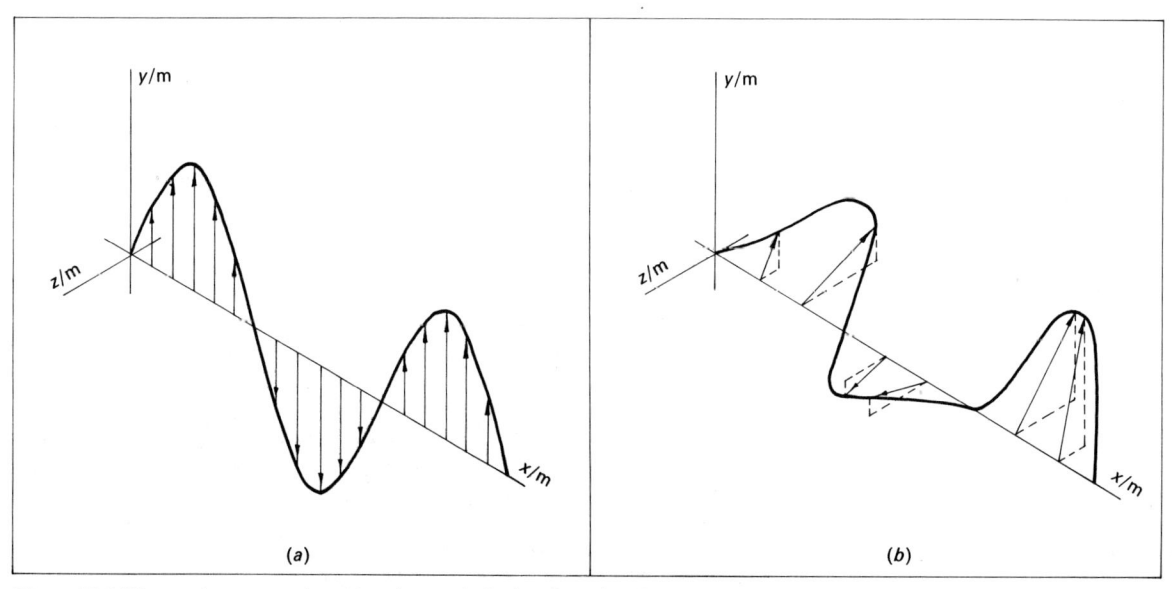

Figure 16-6 Wave pulses on a string: (a) a plane-polarized wave pulse; (b) a non-polarized wave pulse.

16-4 The principle of superposition

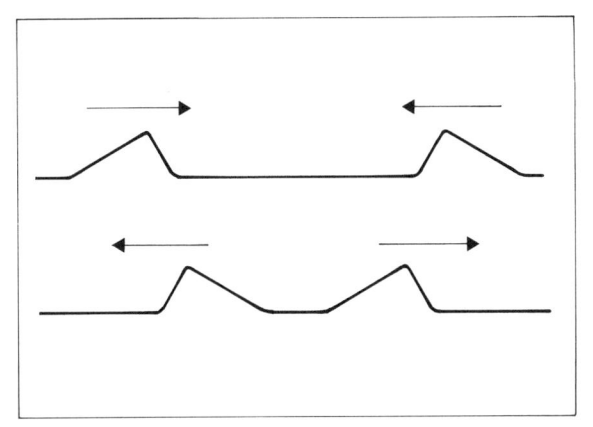

Figure 16-7 What happens during the time the pulses are interacting?

though other sound waves are crossing the line between our ear and the speaker. What would the world be like if we could not use waves, and if *all* communication were restricted to the transfer of material particles from place to place? They would inevitably bump into one another and chaos would ensue. Waves do not bump into one another unless, let us add, the displacement of the material carrying the wave pulse is so large as to permanently deform the material; then some of the mechanical energy of the waves becomes internal energy of the material, and the waves do *not* pass through each other unaffected.

But what can we say about the string at an instant during which more than one wave pulse is affecting the same part of it? The wave pulses are then said to *superpose* and the displacement of any point on the string is the vector sum of the displacements caused by each disturbance at that instant. This is called *the principle of superposition* and is the key to the understanding of many important wave phenomena. Providing the waves which are superposing are made up of displacements which lie in one plane—that is they are *polarized* in that plane— we can add the displacements algebraically. The more general cases of non-polarized waves or waves polarized in different planes necessitates the vector summation of displacements and will not be considered in this text.

Figure 16-8 illustrates the principle of superposition for waves on a string (*a*) and a spring (*b*). The photographs show the positions of the string or spring at successive instants of time and are thus really *y–x* graphs. When drawing graphs to illustrate the principle it is best to use idealized pulses of easily recognizable shape. In practice of course only more rounded pulses could be produced.

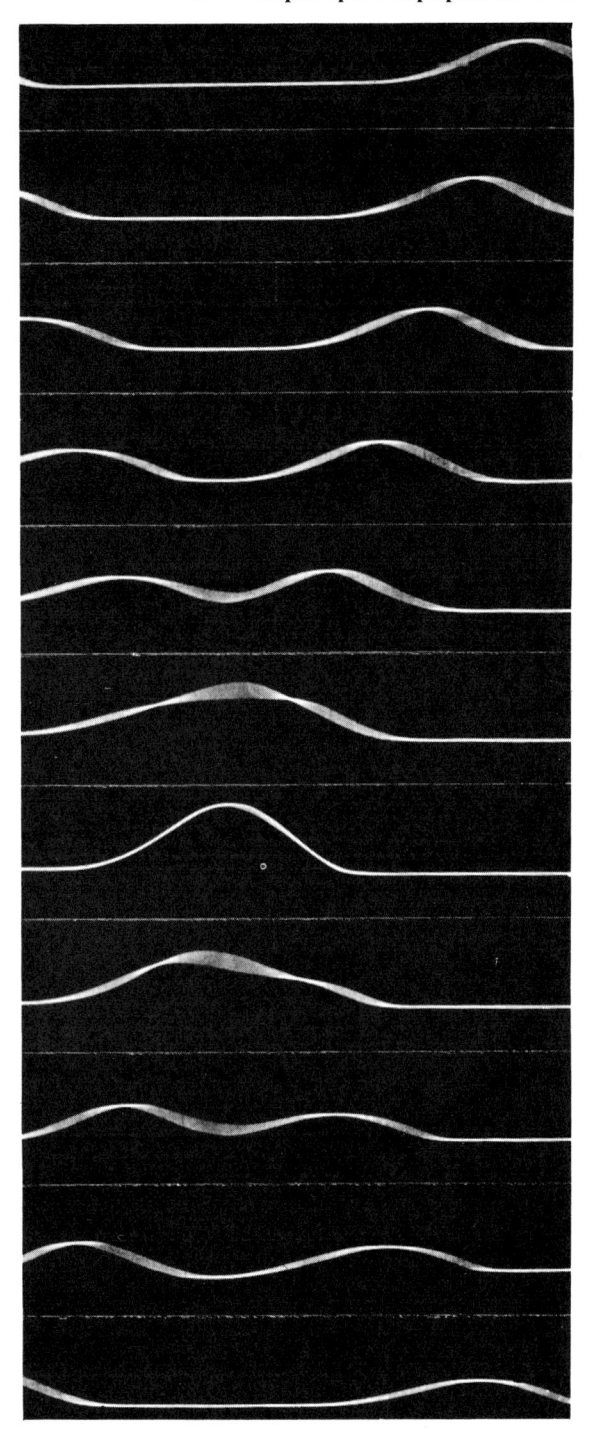

Figure 16-8a The principle of superposition for wave pulses on a string. Here, all displacements are positive.

16 Waves on a string

If we follow the displacement of a single point during the superposition of two waves, the y–t graph for the point can be drawn. Figure 16-9 shows two examples of this, the second being remarkable as the point chosen remains stationary throughout the process.

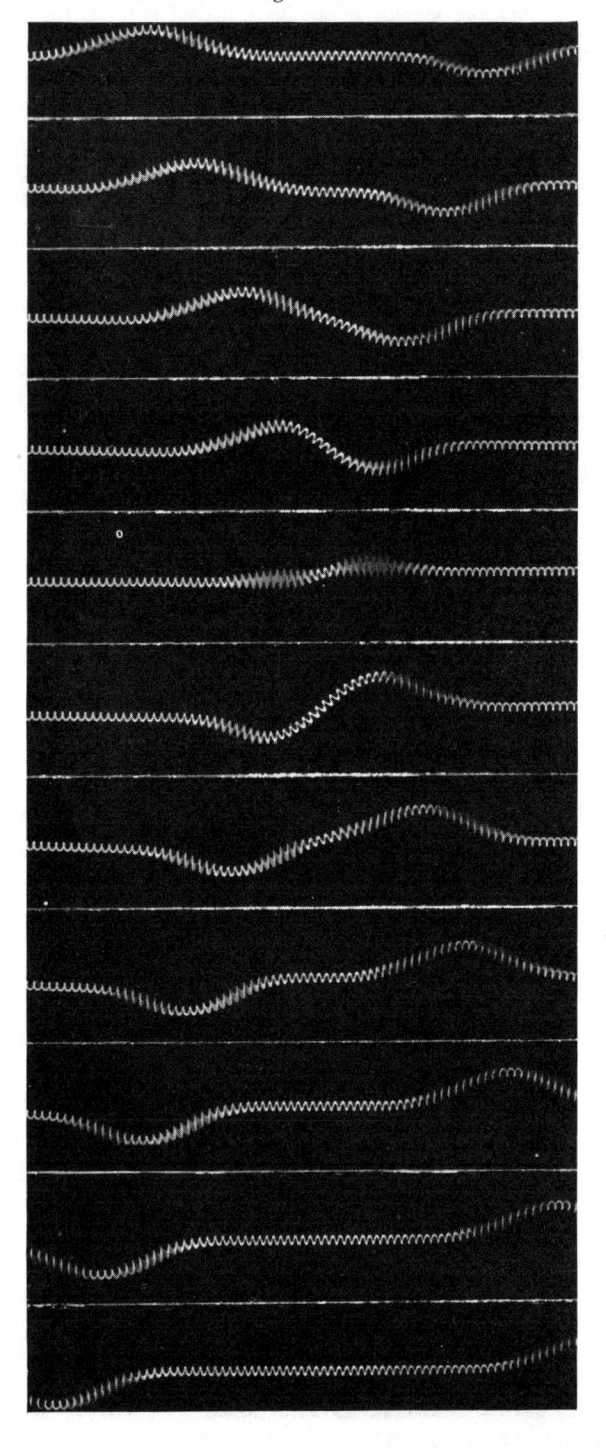

Figure 16-8b The principle of superposition for wave pulses on a spring. Both positive and negative displacements are occurring.

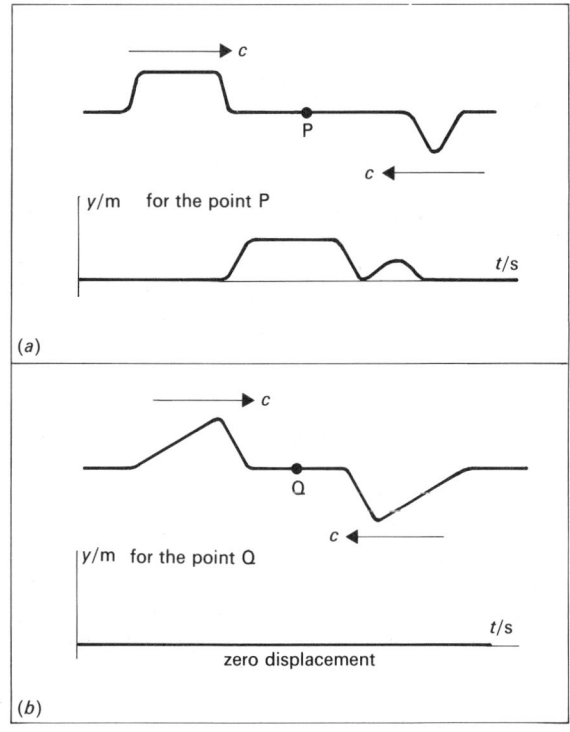

Figure 16-9 Analysing the displacement of a single point during the superposition of two wave pulses. Be quite sure you agree with the form of the graph in case (a)!

The principle of superposition of waves applies to all types of wave motion. For mechanical waves it follows from the principle of superposition (vector addition) of forces and the elastic properties of the medium carrying the waves. If the displacements are so large that Hooke's law is not obeyed, the principle becomes inapplicable. Superposition is sometimes referred to as *interference*. This is an unhappy choice of word to use in this context as the whole point is that the wave pulses continue unchanged after their 'collision'. We will continue to talk of waves superposing but will use the phrase *interference pattern* to describe some of the special effects which can result when continuous waves pass along the same string or through the same material.

16-5 The reflection of waves

As a wave pulse moves along a spring or string the leading part of the pulse in its displaced position pulls the next part of the spring sideways. We have shown how Newton's laws lead to the expression $c_t = (T/m)^{1/2}$ for the speed of the wave. What happens if the wave pulse reaches a fixed wall? Whereas at other points along the spring the leading part of the pulse pulls the next part of the spring up, here it finds itself pulling the wall so as to try to displace the wall sideways. The sideways pull of the spring on the wall must be equal to the sideways pull of the wall on the spring, by Newton's third law. Further it is in the opposite direction and so the sideways pull of the wall on the spring generates a reflected wave pulse which is identical in shape to the incident pulse (for the above arrangement holds at every instant during the process) but is upside down. It is also, of course, moving away from the wall at the same speed v as the incident pulse. Figure 16-10*a* shows the behaviour of the spring itself during this process. To equate this shape with the explanation of *how* the pulse is reflected consider the incident wave pulse continuing unaffected by the wall and a pulse generated at the wall as described. The spring assumes a position which is the result of the superposition of these two wave pulses. Figure 16-11 shows this in detail for one moment during the reflection of the pulse in figure 16-10*a*. If we wish to *predict* the shape of the spring close to the wall during the reflection then we take the incident wave pulse, fold it about the line of the wall, *invert* this folded pulse to produce the reflected pulse, and then superpose the incident and the reflected pulses in the region of the spring. The reader should try this for a moment other than that captured in figure 16-11.

If the end of the spring is quite free to move sideways instead of being attached to a wall the process of reflection can again be analysed using Newton's laws. In figure 16-10*b*, the spring is attached to a thin nylon thread. This time the arrival of the wave pulse pulls the last piece of the spring sideways and owing to the spring's inertia (Newton's first law) it overshoots. The pull of the spring on the last bit which has overshot now means that it in turn pulls on the spring, by Newton's third law. Further this pull is in the opposite direction and so a reflected wave pulse which is identical in shape to the incident wave pulse, and the same way up, is generated. As this reflected wave pulse moves away from the wall it produces the positions of the spring shown in figure 16-10*b* by superposing with the incident wave pulse. To predict the shape of the spring, then, we take the incident wave pulse and fold it about a line perpendicular to the end of the

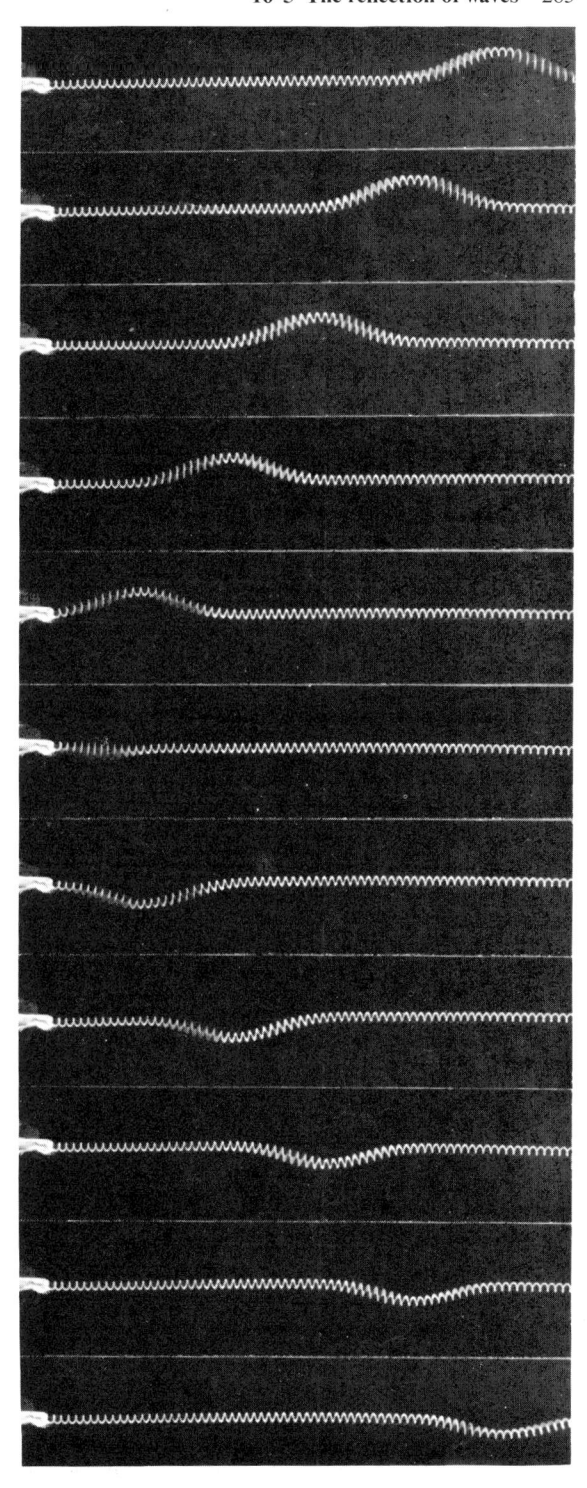

Figure 16-10a The reflection of a wave pulse at a fixed end.

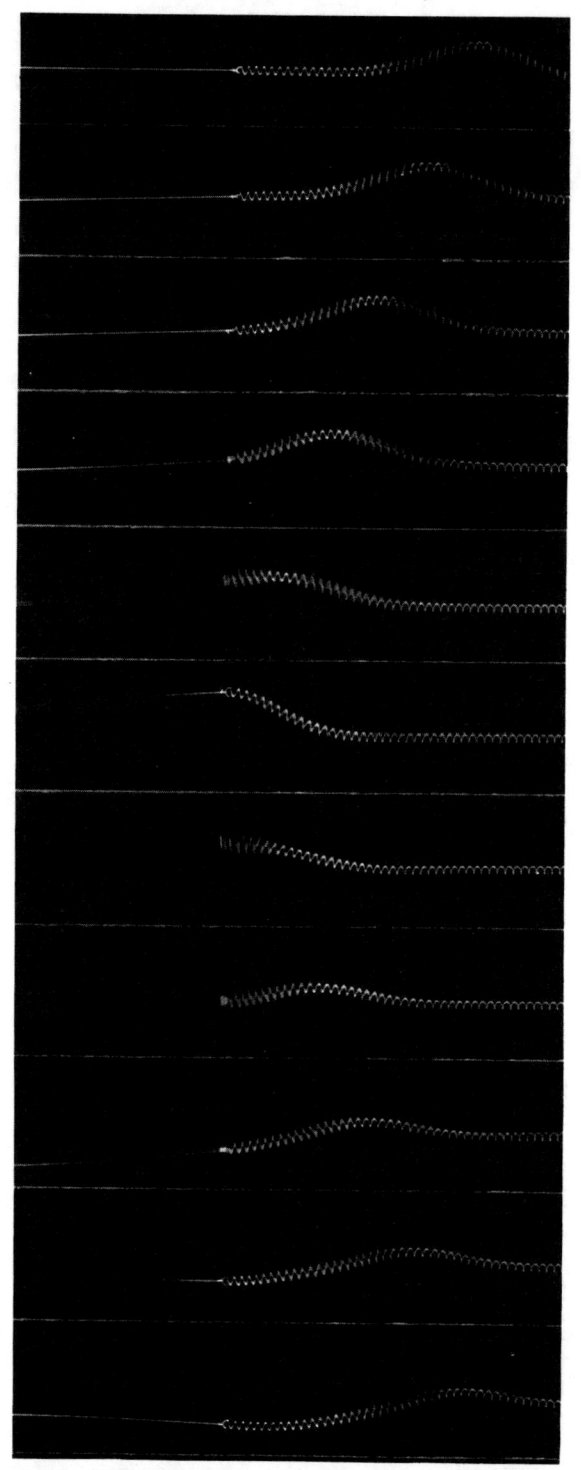

Figure 16-10b The reflection of a wave pulse at what approximates to a 'free' end.

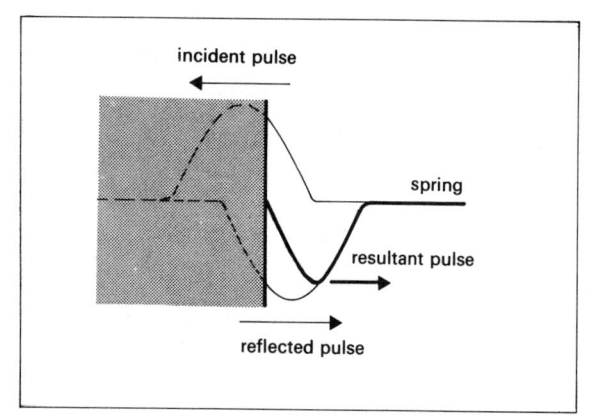

Figure 16-11 Reflection and the principle of superposition.

spring to produce the reflected pulse. We then superpose the incident and reflected wave pulses in the region of the spring. The reader is advised to try this—see Exercises 16-11 and 16-12.

In practice the spring can never be rigidly fixed or perfectly free at one end, although the fixed case is closely approached by attaching the spring to a massive object like the wall of a laboratory. Most situations are best described by thinking of the spring, of mass per unit length m_1 attached to another spring with a mass per unit length m_2. The speeds of a wave pulse are respectively

$$c_{t1} = \sqrt{\frac{T}{m_1}} \quad \text{and} \quad c_{t2} = \sqrt{\frac{T}{m_2}},$$

T being, of course, the same for each spring. Figure 16-12 shows the result of reflection at the boundary for two cases. The wave pulse which is transmitted is sometimes called the *refracted* wave pulse as its speed is different from the incident wave pulse. The energy of the incident wave pulse is shared between the reflected and refracted wave pulses—the ratio depending on the ratio c_{t1}/c_{t2}.

★ More strictly the fraction of energy reflected depends on the *mechanical impedance* Z of each spring. For a spring at tension T and of mass per unit length m,

$$Z = \frac{T}{c_t}$$
$$= \sqrt{(Tm)},$$

and the fraction of energy reflected can be shown to be

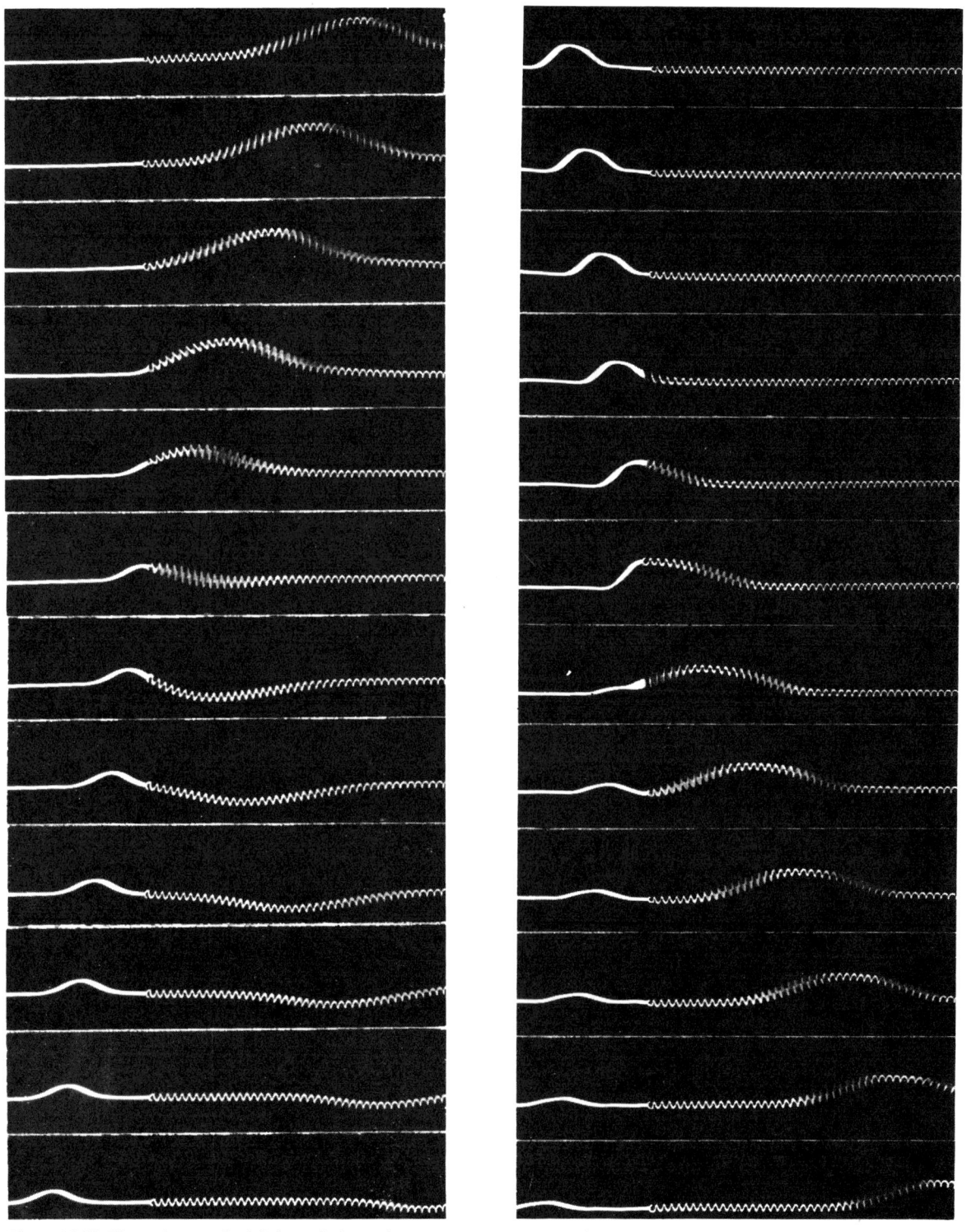

Figure 16-12 The spring on the left in each figure has a greater mass per unit length than that on the right, that is $m_1 > m_2$.

equal to

$$\frac{Z_1-Z_2}{Z_1+Z_2} = \frac{1-\sqrt{(m_2/m_1)}}{1+\sqrt{(m_2/m_1)}}$$

$$= \frac{1-(c_{t1}/c_{t2})}{1+(c_{t1}/c_{t2})}.$$

Thus the fraction of energy reflected can be predicted if we know either the ratio of the wave speeds or the ratio of the masses per unit length of the springs. ★

Throughout this section we have assumed that the mechanical energy of our wave pulses has not been dissipated in any way. In practice, of course, the energy of the wave pulse will gradually be converted to internal energy both in the spring itself and in the surrounding air. To realize the behaviour described above it is necessary to follow the behaviour of the pulses for short periods of time during which the dissipative forces have little noticeable effect.

16-6 Periodic waves

If one end of a very long string is made to vibrate in a plane perpendicular to the string in a repetitive periodic way then a series of transverse wave pulses, or a *wavetrain*, travels along the string. Let us suppose that the vibration is simple harmonic—the justification for dealing with this particularly simple case is given in the next section (see page 290). A displacement–distance graph for points on the string at an instant and a displacement–time graph for a single point on the string are given in figure 16-13.

For a source moving with simple harmonic motion the y–x graph is sinusoidal as is the y–t graph. This is difficult to show in the laboratory as experiments are confused both by reflections from the end of the string and by the dissipation of the energy of the wave as it travels along the string. If the amplitude of the source is y_0 then the maximum displacement of points on the string is also y_0, and this is called the *amplitude* of the wave. The frequency of the source, f, will also be the frequency of vibration of each point on the string, although adjacent points will not move in phase with one another. The distance between neighbouring points on the string which *are* moving in phase (that is, with the same displacement and velocity) is called the *wavelength* of the wave and is denoted by λ (see figure 16-14a). The *period* of the wave, $T (=1/f)$, is the period of oscillation of each point on the string (see figure 16-14b). Again we stress the need to distinguish carefully between y–x graphs and y–t graphs, that is between the shape of the wave or *waveform* and the motion of a point in the path of the wave.

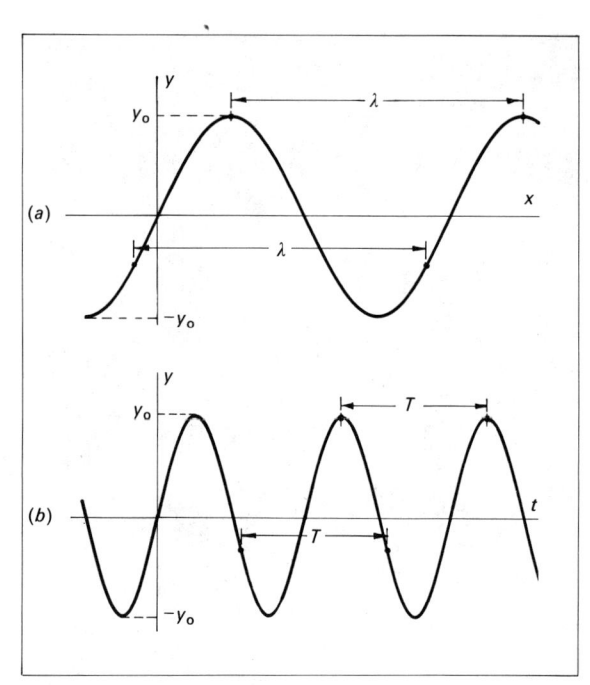

Figure 16-13 Graphs showing (a) the position of a string carrying a sinusoidal wave at time $t = 0$, and (b) the vibration of the point $x = 0$.

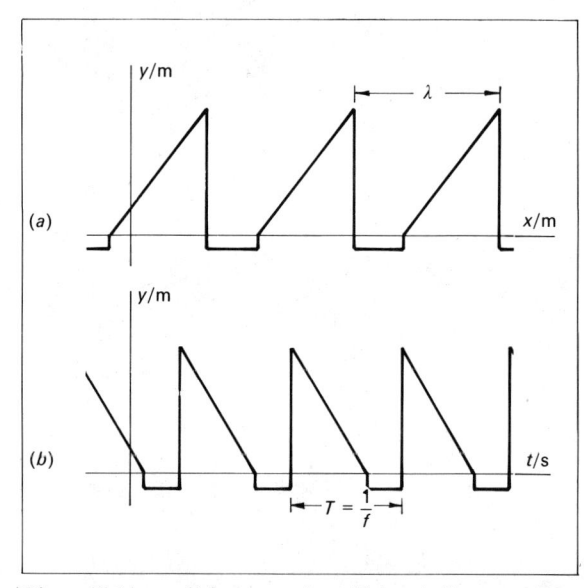

Figure 16-14 $c = f\lambda$ for a non-sinusoidal periodic wave.

If we draw a series of y–x graphs following figure 16-14a for times $t = \tfrac{1}{4}T$, $\tfrac{1}{2}T$, $\tfrac{3}{4}T$, T, etc., we find that the waveform advances a distance of one wavelength, λ, in a time interval T. The speed at which the waveform advances, c, is thus given by

$$c = \lambda/T,$$

or
$$c = f\lambda. \qquad [16\text{-}2]$$

That is, the velocity of propagation is equal to the product of the frequency and the wavelength. This relation holds for all types of waves, and for all periodic waves, not only sinusoidal ones. For example, figure 16-14 shows a periodic wave of wavelength λ and frequency $f = 1/T$. The wave is taken to move in the positive x-direction, thus producing the reversed shape of the graph in (b).

▶ **Example 16-2** Figure 16-15 shows two y–x graphs for a travelling wave moving with speed c through a point P. Draw the corresponding y–t graphs for the point P for the time that the wave passes through P, marking the scale on the time axis in terms of c and a.

(a) The wave first produces a positive displacement at P, and this lasts for a time a/c; this is succeeded by a negative displacement, again for a time a/c. These displacements are both repeated once, so that figure 16-16a can be drawn.
(b) A similar procedure gives figure 16-16b. ◀

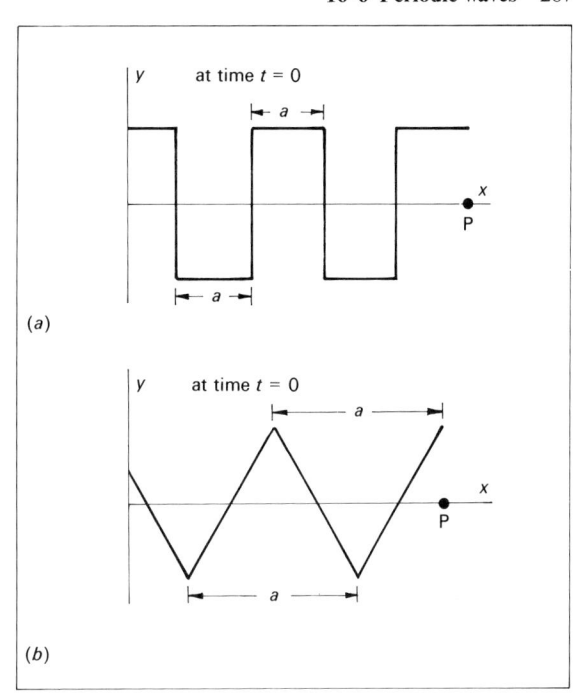

Figure 16-15

Phase and phase angle

When a wave travels along a string we say that the displacements at points on the string differ in *phase*. Take, for example, the row of trolleys as described in figure 16-4 to represent the string. As the trolleys have a large mass and the tension is small we can produce waves which move very slowly. By attaching, say, paper flags to any two trolleys A and B, and watching the flags as a wave pulse or a periodic wave travels along the trolleys, we are noting the *phase difference* between trolleys A and B. If the movements are identical in all respects then the trolleys A and B are said to be moving *in phase* with one another. For a periodic travelling wave (not necessarily a sinusoidal wave) the trolleys A and B will be in phase if they are separated by $\lambda, 2\lambda, 3\lambda, ..., n\lambda$ (where n is a whole number).

For sinusoidal waves let us refer to figure 16-13a on page 286. The y–x curve can be described by the equation

$$y = y_0 \sin \phi$$

for it is a sine curve, or by

$$y = y_0 \sin\left(\frac{2\pi}{\lambda}\right)x$$

for it repeats itself every time that ϕ increases by 2π

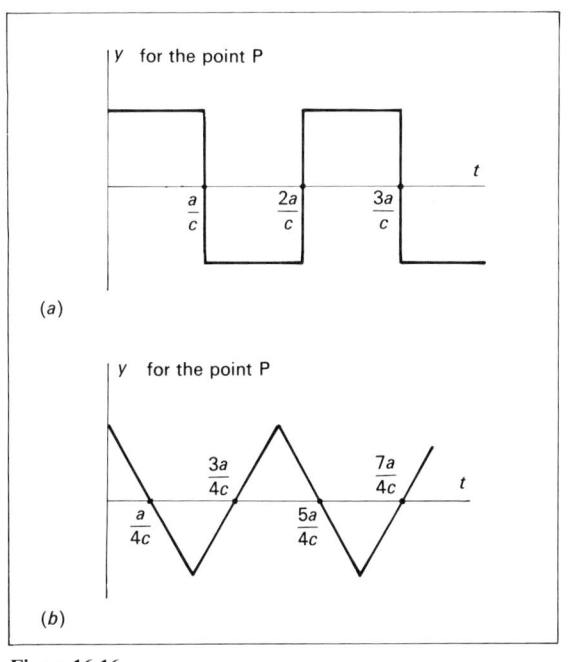

Figure 16-16

radians, that is every time that x increases by λ.
$\phi = (2\pi/\lambda)x$ is called the *phase angle* of the point at

16 Waves on a string

a distance x from the origin, and for two points in the path of this sinusoidal wave at distances x_1 and x_2 from the origin at which the displacements are

$$y_1 = y_0 \sin\left(\frac{2\pi}{\lambda}\right)x_1 \quad \text{and} \quad y_2 = y_0 \sin\left(\frac{2\pi}{\lambda}\right)x_2$$

the *phase difference* is given by

$$\phi_1 - \phi_2 = \frac{2\pi}{\lambda}(x_1 - x_2).$$

When $x_1 - x_2 = \lambda, 2\lambda, 3\lambda, \ldots, n\lambda$, the phase difference is an integral number of 2π radians, that is $x_1 - x_2 = n\lambda$ for points in phase at distances x_1, x_2. For sinusoidal waves we have a quantitative measure $\phi_1 - \phi_2$ for the phase difference between points which are not in phase. When the phase difference is π rad, 3π rad, $\ldots, (2n+1)\pi$ rad, where n is an integer, the points are said to be *out of phase*. This occurs when

$$(x_1 - x_2) = \frac{\lambda}{2}, \frac{3\lambda}{2}, \ldots, n\lambda + \frac{\lambda}{2},$$

that is

$$x_1 - x_2 = n\lambda + \frac{\lambda}{2}$$

for points out of phase at distances x_1, x_2.

The wave equation

Referring to figure 16-13b we see that the y–t graph for a point in the path of a sinusoidal wave has the equation

$$y = y_0 \sin \theta$$

for it is a sine curve; that is

$$y = y_0 \sin\left(\frac{2\pi}{T}\right)t$$

for it repeats itself every $\theta = 2\pi$ rad, that is every $t = T$. Equally we could, as $T = 1/f$, write

$$y = y_0 \sin(2\pi f t).$$

In general the displacement of points in the path of a sinusoidal travelling wave depends on *both* x and t. When t is constant (that is, at an instant) we should have the y–x graph

$$y_x = y_0 \sin\left(\frac{2\pi}{\lambda}\right)x, \qquad [16\text{-}3]$$

and when x is constant (that is, at a point) the y–t graph

$$y_t = y_0 \sin\left(\frac{2\pi}{T}\right)t. \qquad [16\text{-}4]$$

If the displacement at a chosen origin of x is written as equation 16-4, then at a distance x to the right of this origin (that is $x > 0$, if we adopt the usual sign convention that x is positive to the right), the displacement will show a phase *lag* $\delta (\delta > 0)$ where

$$y_{x,t} = y_0 \sin\left[\left(\frac{2\pi}{T}\right)t - \delta\right]$$

(notice the minus sign).

If the wave speed is constant for the wave travelling from the origin to the point x, then

$$\delta \propto x$$

or

$$\delta = kx,$$

where k is known as the *wave number*. Therefore

$$y_{x,t} = y_0 \sin\left[\left(\frac{2\pi}{T}\right)t - kx\right].$$

Two adjacent points on the wave which are in phase are separated by a distance λ; thus if x changes by λ, δ must change by 2π rad. Thus

$$k\lambda = 2\pi$$

$$k = \frac{2\pi}{\lambda},$$

and we get

$$y_{x,t} = y_0 \sin\left(\frac{2\pi t}{T} - \frac{2\pi x}{\lambda}\right)$$

or

$$y_{x,t} = y_0 \sin 2\pi\left(\frac{t}{T} - \frac{x}{\lambda}\right). \qquad [16\text{-}5]$$

This is the *wave equation* for a wave travelling in one dimension. It enables us to calculate the displacement $y_{x,t}$ for chosen values of x and t, that is to predict the displacement at a particular point in the path of the wave at a particular time. For the same wave travelling in the opposite direction, that is in the negative x-direction, the equation would be

$$y = y_0 \sin 2\pi\left(\frac{t}{T} + \frac{x}{\lambda}\right).$$

There are many ways of writing these equations by combining them with

$$c = \frac{\lambda}{T} \quad \text{or writing} \quad T = \frac{1}{f}.$$

It is more important to understand the separate equations 16-3 and 16-4 than to remember equation 16-5.

Sine or cosine?

Figure 16-17a shows a graph without an origin for θ. The graph is a sinusoidal one and has the characteristic 'wavy' shape of the graphs studied in this section. Before we can use the graph we need to describe it mathematically and to do that we choose an origin for the phase angle θ. Parts (b) and (c) show two of the many positions we might choose. In (b) the origin, O_s, is placed in such a position that the graph will be of the form $y = y_0 \sin \theta$, while in (c) the origin, O_c, is such as to produce the equation $y = y_0 \cos \theta$. We have not changed the graph itself but only the particular function needed to describe it. This shows that in studying waves it does not matter whether we use sine or cosine functions—we have chosen to use sine.

$$\phi = \left(\frac{2\pi}{\lambda}\right) SP \quad \text{and} \quad \phi' = \left(\frac{2\pi}{\lambda}\right) S'P.$$

The phase difference between the waves at P is thus given by

$$\phi - \phi' = \frac{2\pi}{\lambda}(SP - S'P).$$

The two waves are in phase at P if $SP - S'P = n\lambda$ and out of phase if $SP - S'P = n\lambda + \lambda/2$. Note that $SP - S'P$ represents the difference in distances from *one point* P to separate origins (the sources), while the phase difference between *two points* on the *same* wave was written in terms of $x_1 - x_2$, the distance between the points in the previous section.

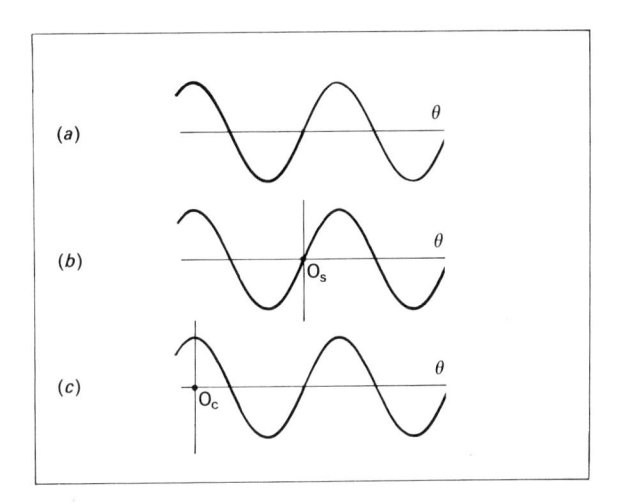

Figure 16-17

16-7 Superposition of sinusoidal waves

When two (or more) sinusoidal waves are superposed we follow the methods of Section 16-4 to find either the resultant waveform at a certain instant or the resulting displacement of a certain point in the path of the waves as time passes. No new principle is involved. The two waves may differ in frequency, in amplitude, or in phase. When we talk of the phase difference *between two travelling waves* we mean the phase difference between the displacements the two waves are producing at a given moment in time at a given point in their paths. The concept is usually of little value unless this phase difference is the same at all times. If two sources S and S' are themselves in phase, the phase angles of the two waves at the point P are

Coherence

If the two sources S and S' themselves have a phase difference ε which remains constant in time and they also have the same frequency, they are said to be *coherent* sources. ε need not be zero and the two sources can 'stop and start' in a random way providing that S' follows exactly what S does, that is ε remains constant. Sources for which the above conditions do not hold are said to be *incoherent*. In calculating the phase difference between two waves from coherent sources at a point P we must take ε into account and write

$$\text{phase difference} = \phi - \phi' \pm \varepsilon,$$

that is, if S leads S' by ε the phase difference

$$= \frac{2\pi}{\lambda}(SP - S'P) + \varepsilon.$$

290 16 Waves on a string

▶ **Example 16-3** What is the result of superposing two travelling waves of the same frequency but different amplitude at a place where the waves arrive out of phase by $\pi/6$ rad?

A graphical solution will convey most meaning. In figure 16-18 are drawn (solid lines) two travelling waves which are $\pi/6$ rad out of phase. They are displacement–time graphs because they represent what happens at a particular point at different times. The dots on the graphs indicate the points where it is easiest to calculate the sum of the displacements caused by the two waves, and the dotted line represents the sum of the waves, and is drawn by joining the points. We see that at this point the total displacement is periodic, with a frequency equal to that of either travelling wave, and an amplitude which is just less than the sum of the amplitudes of the individual waves. ◀

Let us consider what happens when the two travelling waves have

(a) the same frequency (and wavelength)
(b) slightly different frequencies (and wavelengths)
(c) widely different frequencies (and wavelengths).

Case (a) is very important, as we shall see when we come to discuss *stationary waves* in Section 16-8 and *sound waves* in Chapter 18. Case (b) is known as the *beat phenomenon*, which we shall discuss in Section 18-5, and case (c) is illustrated in figure 16-19, where the graph of the superposition is drawn for only one instant.

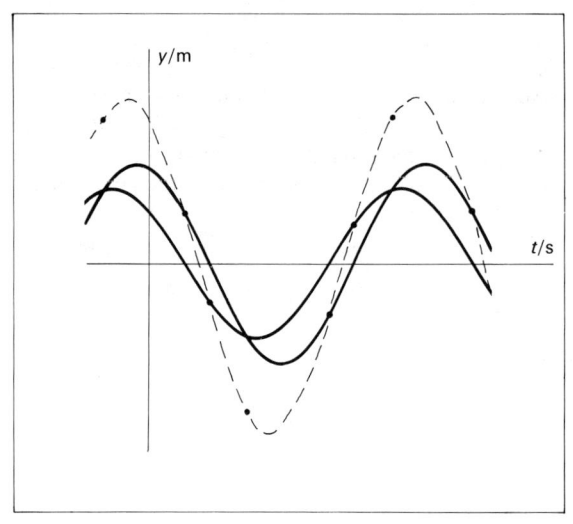

Figure 16-18

Fourier series

Any *periodic* wave motion is equivalent to the superposed sum of a number of sinusoidal wave motions of suitably chosen amplitudes, frequencies, and phase. This very sweeping generalization, due to Fourier, is the reason why it is necessary to study only sinusoidal waves in any detail.

The proof of this result is well beyond the scope of this text but, by working through Exercise 16-16, you can begin to see how apparently complex waves can be built up by superposing a series of sinusoidal waves.

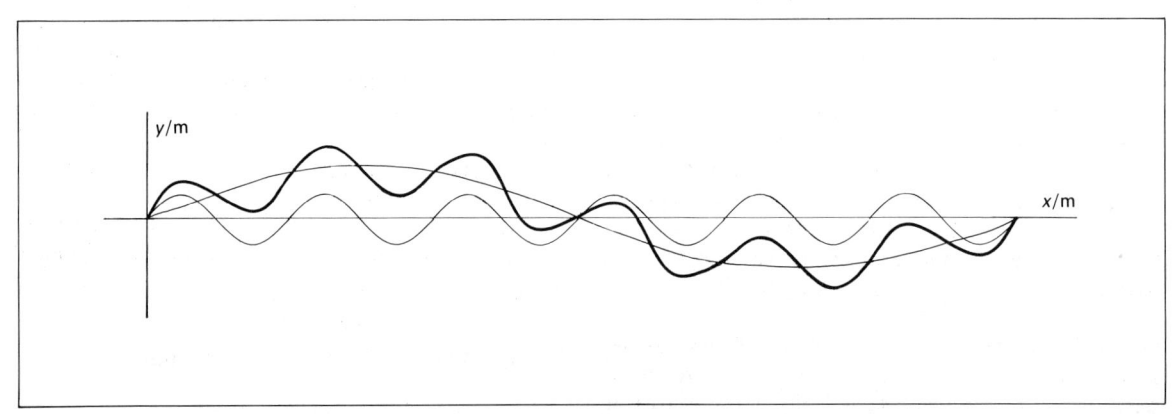

Figure 16-19 This shows the superposition of two waves of very different frequencies.

16-8 Stationary waves

One of the most elegant demonstrations in physics is to view a vibrating thread such as that described in figure 16-20. The frequency f of the source S should be slowly varied and the amplitude of the thread's transverse motion watched. For certain values of f this amplitude is large and if at these frequencies the frequency of the stroboscope is adjusted to match that of the source a 'frozen' pattern is seen. If the frequency of the stroboscope is now varied to $f \pm \Delta f$, sinuous movements of the thread are seen. As a physics demonstration it is not immediately clear whether it illustrates a wave phenomenon or a resonance phenomenon (see Section 15-9). Let us first try to analyse it in terms of the wave(s) on the thread and then consider the thread PQ as a driven oscillator.

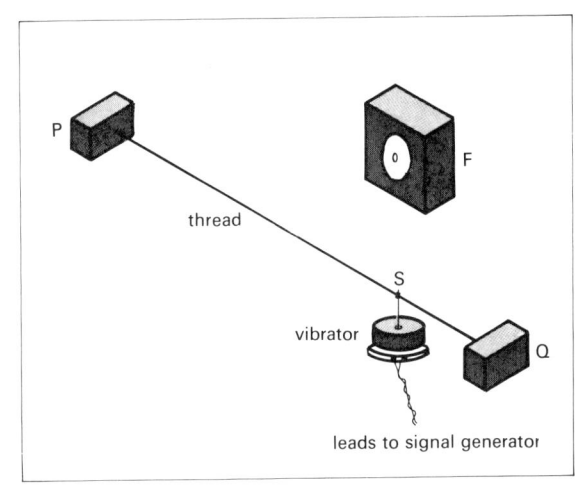

Figure 16-20 A xenon flashing stroboscope F being used to illuminate a thread stretched between P and Q along which travel sinusoidal transverse waves from a vibrating source S.

Transverse waves move from the source S to the fixed ends P and Q of the thread, where they are reflected as described in Section 16-5. The incident and reflected waves superpose and form an interference pattern. Let us consider the superposition of two waves of equal speed, frequency, and amplitude which are travelling along the same thread in opposite directions, and ignore for the moment the restrictions imposed by the relative positions of P, Q, and S. Figure 16-21 shows a series of y–x graphs for a point on the thread at successive moments of time separated by $T/8$, that is an eighth of the period of the wave.

From figure 16-21 it is immediately apparent that there are some points on the thread which have zero displacement *at all times*, for which a y–t graph would look like figure 16-22a. Such points are called nodal points or *nodes*, N, and are separated by a distance $\lambda/2$, where λ is the common wavelength of the waves. If the stroboscope is not used in the demonstration of figure 16-20 the positions of the nodes are still obvious. As there is no vibration of the thread *at* the nodes a paper rider may be placed on, and will remain on, the thread at such points. Equally from figure 16-21 there are some points on the thread which suffer maximum displacements, for which a y–t graph would look like figure 16-22b. These points are called antinodal points, or *antinodes*, A. They, too, are separated by a distance $\lambda/2$.

One further point to notice is that between adjacent nodes, N_1 and N_2, *all points* on the thread move in phase. Labelling successive nodes N_1, N_2, N_3, etc., then when the thread between N_1 and N_2, between N_3 and N_4, etc., is all moving (say) up, the thread between N_2 and N_3, between N_4 and N_5, etc., is all moving down. This lack of phase difference between successive points tells us that the result of the superposition is not itself a travelling wave; it is called a *stationary* (or standing) *wave*. Energy cannot *pass along* it, but is *stored in* it. These points can be demonstrated more simply than in figure 16-20 by holding a slinky or (better still) a set of trolleys, such as that shown in figure 16-4, fixed at both ends, and forcing it to oscillate in a transverse way by displacing it periodically close to one end. A number of spring-linked air pucks can also be set to oscillate in this manner.

To establish these results analytically let us take equation 16-5 representing a travelling wave. For waves of equal amplitude moving to the right it is

$$y_1 = y_0 \sin 2\pi \left(\frac{t}{T} - \frac{x}{\lambda} \right)$$

and to the left it is

$$y_2 = y_0 \sin 2\pi \left(\frac{t}{T} + \frac{x}{\lambda} \right).$$

Their resultant, by the principle of superposition, is

$$y = y_1 + y_2 = y_0 \left[\sin 2\pi \left(\frac{t}{T} - \frac{x}{\lambda} \right) + \sin 2\pi \left(\frac{t}{T} + \frac{x}{\lambda} \right) \right]$$

$$y = 2y_0 \left[\cos \frac{2\pi x}{\lambda} \right] \left[\sin \frac{2\pi t}{T} \right],$$

using the trigonometric relation

$$\sin A + \sin B = 2 \sin \tfrac{1}{2}(A+B) \cos \tfrac{1}{2}(A-B).$$

This is the equation of a stationary wave. At $x = \lambda/4, 3\lambda/4, 5\lambda/4$, etc., $\cos(2\pi x/\lambda)$ will be zero at all times.

16 Waves on a string

(i) $t = 0$

(ii) $t = \dfrac{T}{8}$

(iii) $t = \dfrac{2T}{8}$

(iv) $t = \dfrac{3T}{8}$

(v) $t = \dfrac{4T}{8}$

etc.

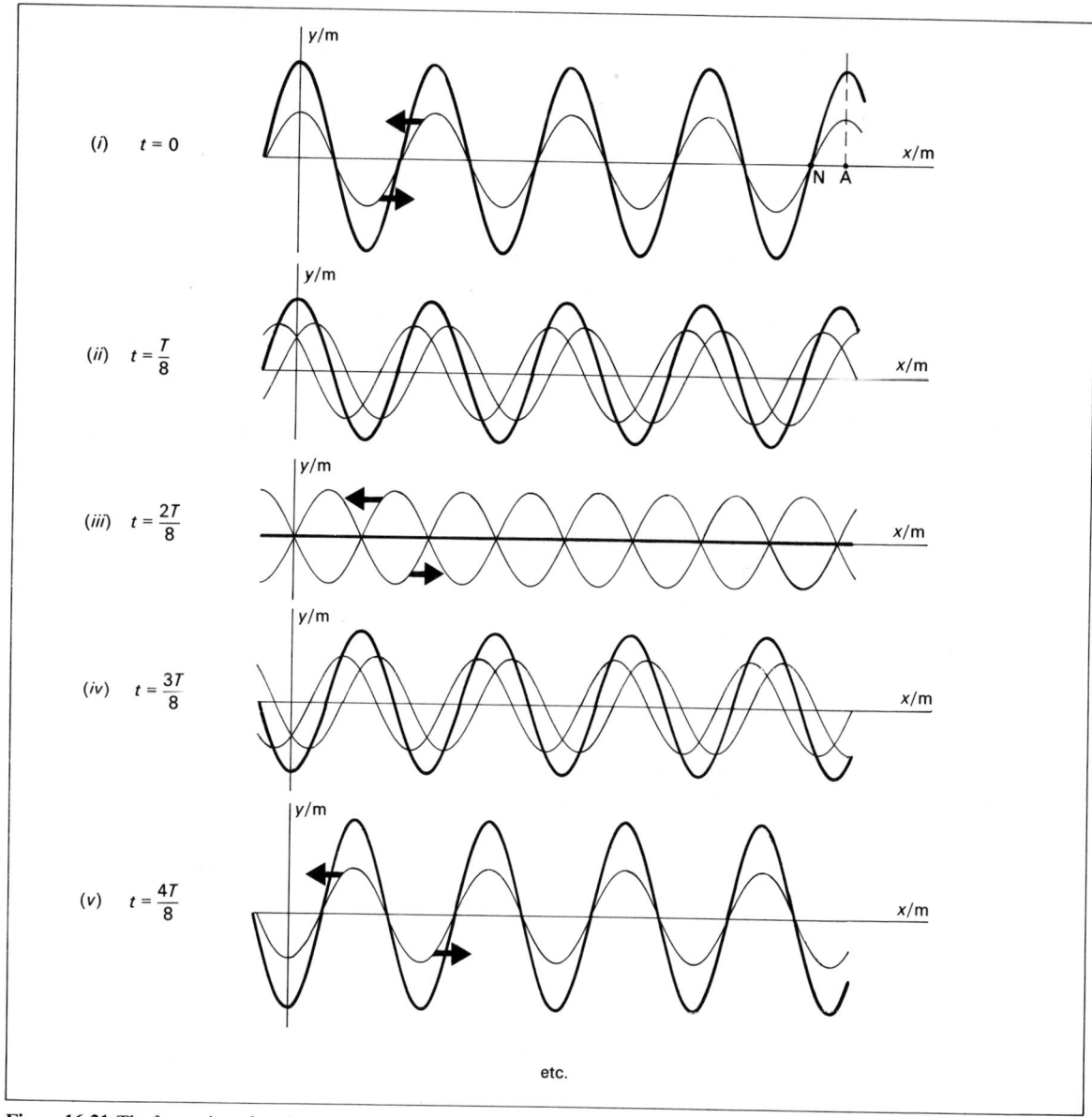

Figure 16-21 The formation of stationary or standing waves. y–t graphs for points such as (a) N, and (b) A, are shown in figure 16-22.

These are the nodes and are separated by $\lambda/2$. Similarly the antinodes are at $x = 0, \lambda/2, \lambda$, etc. Writing

$$y = \left[2y_0 \sin \dfrac{2\pi t}{T}\right]\left[\cos \dfrac{2\pi x}{\lambda}\right]$$

we see that a standing wave has a cosine profile which varies with time.

So far we have ignored the fact that it is not possible in practice to have a straight thread of infinite length—that is we have ignored the constraints imposed by the fixed ends P and Q in the original demonstration. If the frequency of the signal generator driving the vibrator in that experiment is set at random the characteristic stationary wave pattern, such as that of figure 16-23, does not appear. The reason is immediately clear if we consider

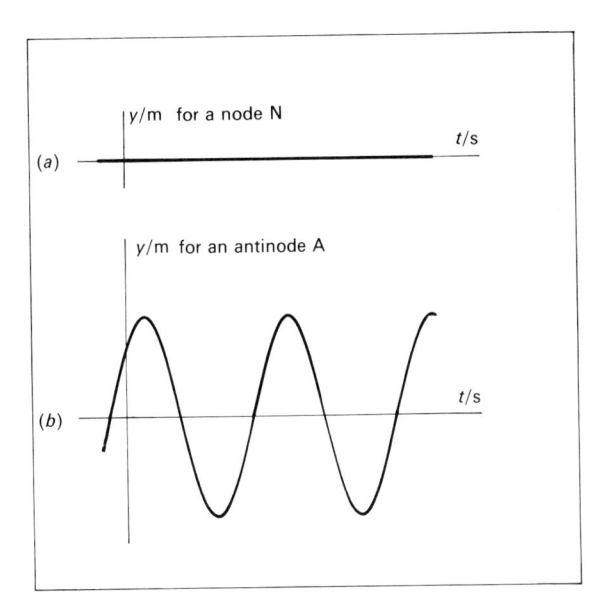

Figure 16-22 The frequency of the disturbance of A is f, the same as that of the waves.

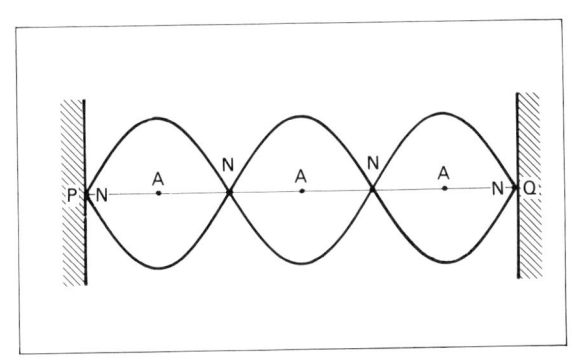

Figure 16-23 The envelope of a stationary wave pattern on a thread. If the frequency of the waves is greater than about 20 Hz; the envelope is seen by the eye as a solid form.

the ends P and Q of the thread: if they are fixed then P and Q must be nodal points in the pattern. Therefore the distance

$$PQ = l = n\left(\frac{\lambda}{2}\right)$$

where n is an integer, for nodes are separated by $\lambda/2$. For a thread on which waves travel at a speed c

[16-2] $$c = f\lambda$$

and so $$l = n\left(\frac{c}{2f}\right),$$

or $$f = n\left(\frac{c}{2l}\right) \qquad [16\text{-}6]$$

if a stationary wave pattern is to appear, that is f must be a whole number multiple of $c/2l$, and this limits the frequencies at which a stationary wave pattern will appear. For values of $f \neq n(c/2l)$ the result of the superposition will be constantly and chaotically changing.

In practice the situation is not quite as clear-cut as this analysis suggests; in a perfect world there would be *zero* displacement at the nodes, and the thread would need to be driven at the precise frequency f. However, when we perform the experiment we find that

(*a*) there is *not* zero displacement at the nodes, and
(*b*) f can differ significantly from the integral multiples of $c/2l$.

The reason in both cases is that

(*a*) the reflected waves do not have as large an amplitude as the incident waves and, because they cannot then annul each other, we get non-zero displacements at the nodes,
(*b*) there is damping because energy is transferred from the thread to the surroundings, and we have already seen that the damping of an oscillating system decreases the 'sharpness' of the resonance peaks. See figure 15-28a.

Thus with a real thread stretched between real supports we do not have to make very precise adjustments of length, tension, etc., to get a recognizable stationary wave pattern, but we must be content with some displacement at the nodes.

16-9 Vibrating strings

A transverse stationary wave pattern on a stretched string of length l is only possible at or near certain frequencies of vibration of the source of the waves. Put another way, a stretched string of length l has a number of possible transverse modes of vibration corresponding to certain frequencies of the driving mechanism. From the last section

$$f = n\left(\frac{c}{2l}\right), \text{ and}$$

[16-1] $$c_t = \sqrt{\frac{T}{m}},$$

so that $$f = \frac{n}{2l}\sqrt{\frac{T}{m}} \qquad [16\text{-}7]$$

is the relation between the possible frequencies and the

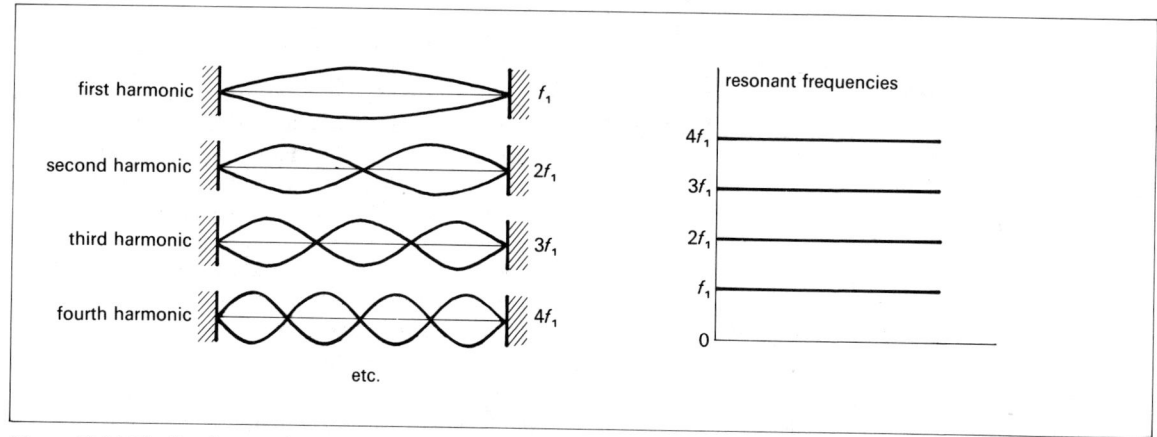

Figure 16-24 The first four modes of vibration of a stretched string fixed at both ends.

mechanical properties of the vibrating system (the string).

Writing, for $n = 1$,

$$f_1 = \frac{1}{2l}\sqrt{\frac{T}{m}},$$

we get possible modes of vibration at $f_2 = 2f_1$, $f_3 = 3f_1$, $f_4 = 4f_1$, etc. These are illustrated in figure 16-24. They can be demonstrated with the apparatus of figure 16-20, though care must be taken that S is not at a position which would be a node—it is safest to have S fairly close to one end of the string and to move it about until the greatest amplitude of vibration is produced on the string. This adjustment should be repeated when investigating each higher *harmonic*. The natural modes of vibration are clearly seen here to be the *resonant* frequencies at which the source S transfers energy to the system most effectively, and a large amplitude oscillation is then built up. There are many resonant frequencies and they correspond to the frequencies for which the string can support a stationary wave. At the lowest resonant frequency f_1 the system is sometimes said to be vibrating in its *fundamental* mode. f_1 is called the fundamental frequency and the higher frequencies are called *overtones*.

▶ **Example 16-4** A demonstrator wishes to show the production of stationary waves using a slinky spring. If its mass is 0.45 kg and its stiffness is 0.20 N m^{-1}, find the three lowest frequencies with which he must vibrate it if both ends are fixed and it is stretched to a length of 3.0 m. (The original length of the spring is negligible.) Would the frequencies be different if the slinky were stretched more?

For the fundamental mode of vibration there is a node at each end of the slinky, where it is fixed, and an antinode at its centre. Thus the length of the slinky is equal to one half-wavelength for the fundamental mode of vibration.

$$\tfrac{1}{2}\lambda = 3.0 \text{ m},$$

therefore

$$\lambda = 6.0 \text{ m}.$$

The speed c_t of the wave pulses is given by

$$[16\text{-}1] \qquad c_t = \sqrt{\frac{T}{m}}$$

$$= \sqrt{\frac{(0.20 \text{ N m}^{-1})(3.0 \text{ m})}{0.45 \text{ kg}/3.0 \text{ m}}}$$

$$= \sqrt{(4.0 \text{ m}^2 \text{ s}^{-2})}$$

$$= 2.0 \text{ m s}^{-1}.$$

The frequency f is given by

$$f = \frac{c_t}{\lambda}$$

$$= \frac{2.0 \text{ m s}^{-1}}{6.0 \text{ m}}$$

$$= 0.33 \text{ Hz},$$

that is the demonstrator must move his hand to and fro so as to perform one complete cycle every 3.0 s. This is the lowest frequency (associated with the largest wavelength). For the next two modes of vibration $\lambda = 3.0$ m and $3\lambda/2 = 3.0$ m respectively, so that $f = 0.67$ Hz and 1.00 Hz respectively. In general, for the fundamental mode of vibration, with a spring of length l, stiffness k, and mass m,

$$f = \frac{c_t}{2l}$$

$$= \frac{1}{2l}\sqrt{\frac{kl}{m/l}}$$

$$= \frac{1}{2}\sqrt{\frac{k}{m}},$$

so that the fundamental frequency is independent of the tension in the spring and its length. But note that this result is true only for this particular case, where the tension was proportional to the length and not the extension, because we took the initial length of the slinky to be negligible. ◀

One piece of apparatus designed to investigate the fundamental mode of vibration quantitatively is the *sonometer* (see figure 16-25). A wire is stretched to a measured tension T by adjusting the screw beyond P. A variable length of wire $l = PQ$ is used by adjusting the position of the bridge Q. The variation of f_1 with T or with l can now be studied and detailed descriptions of such experiments can be found in books on practical physics. The sonometer is a crude musical instrument; let us discuss briefly the relation between the physics of this section and the music of violins and pianos.

Where the scientist says the frequency of a vibrating string increases a musician says that the sound (transmitted by the air and detected by his ear) produced by the string rises in *pitch*. A doubling of frequency corresponds to a rise in pitch of one *octave*, so that, starting at any note, the musical progression doh:doh':doh" represents notes of frequencies $f_1:2f_1:4f_1$. We shall see later that the human ear can detect vibrations in the air between roughly 20 Hz and 20000 Hz, so that as $20000\,\text{Hz} \approx 20 \times 2^{10}\,\text{Hz}$ the ear covers a range of about 10 octaves (the reader might like to check that a piano covers a smaller number of octaves). The interval doh' to soh' corresponds to the frequency change $2f_1$ to $3f_1$ and it would be possible to build up a musical scale starting from a given fundamental f_1, in which all the notes were defined mathematically as simple fractions, $\frac{5}{4}$, $\frac{6}{5}$, etc., of f_1. Two problems arise in musical practice:

(*a*) It does not happen to be possible for instruments, such as pianos as we know them, which use strings of fixed lengths, to play in all musical *keys*—in effect we should need a separate piano for each of several scales starting at points f_1, f'_1, etc.

(*b*) If problem (*a*) is removed by such harmonic compromises as our present *equal-temperament* system (Bach's well-tempered clavier), there is still the problem that not all countries will adopt the same starting point, the same frequency for the note called *concert A*. This second problem is now (but only since 1939) resolved and concert A is defined to be 440 Hz. This leads to middle C in the equal-temperament scale used by musicians having a frequency of 261 Hz while the scientists' middle C is still usually quoted as 256 Hz. For a discussion of musical pitch, harmony, and temperament at a level which can be understood by the non-musician the interested reader is referred to *Sound* by F. G. Mee. (*Note:* the musical scales referred to here and elsewhere do not take into account non-European music, nor the bagpipes.)

Stringed instruments

When a piano string is struck or a violin string is bowed there is no oscillator of fixed frequency forcing the string to vibrate. On the strings of the piano a wave disturbance is set up and an infinite number of waves of different wavelength travel on the string; this is possible as waves do not interact but simply add according to the principle of superposition to give a single resulting position for the string at any instant. Very quickly those wavelengths which do not correspond to allowed stationary wave patterns dissipate their energy and the string then vibrates in its fundamental mode with frequency f_1 *and* with all its overtones nf_1. Not all the overtones, however, have equal amplitude, and it is the relative importance of those noticeably present which gives the piano its particular sound or *quality*; figure 16-26a shows the overtones we might expect from a particular piano string. Which overtones predominate depends on the design of the instrument as a whole and on the materials used in its construction.

For the violin the process of bowing causes the resined bow to grip the string and then release it. As it oscillates the friction between the bow and the string is not enough (see page 84) for the bow again to grip it until its speed falls below a certain value; the process is then repeated so that a repetitive plucking is achieved and thus

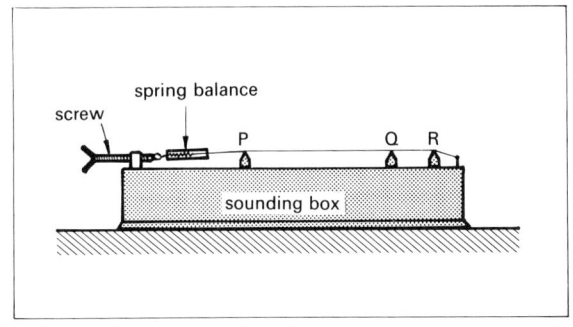

Figure 16-25 A sonometer or monochord.

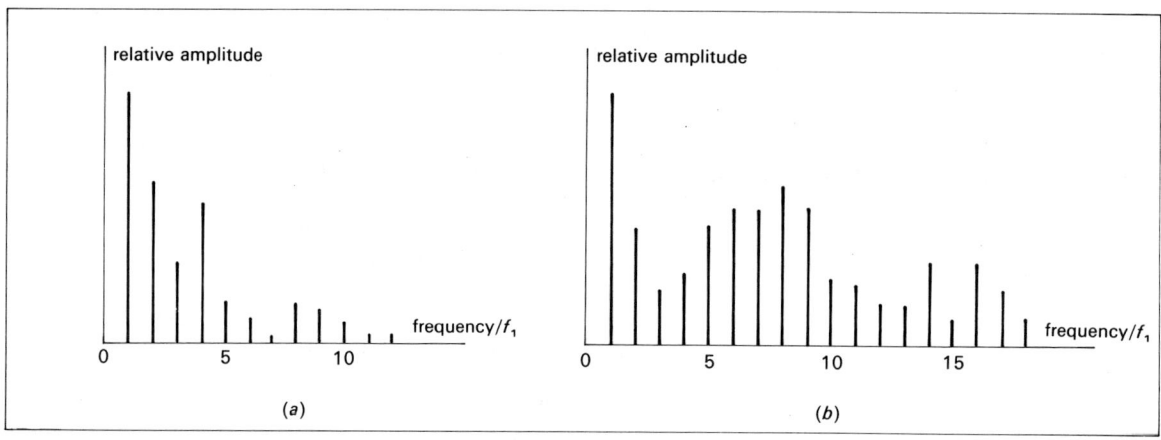

Figure 16-26 Typical frequency spectra for (a) a piano and (b) a violin. Notice (i) the weak seventh harmonic for the piano—it is struck about one-seventh of the way along the string, (ii) the strength of the high harmonics in the violin.

a continuous note. Figure 16-26b shows the overtones we might expect from a particular violin string. The quality of the note depends on the wood of the violin box and many other factors; even the way in which the varnish was dried during manufacture is said to affect the issue.

For both the piano with a fixed range of notes and a violin with its continuous range of possible notes the initial design of strings with a given fundamental frequency, the tuning of the instrument, and (with the violin) the fingering, depend on

$$f_1 = \frac{1}{2l}\sqrt{\frac{T}{m}}.$$

The reader is referred to Exercises 16-25 to 16-27 which bring out the details. A violinist has the further possibility of producing, for example, the harmonic $f_4 = 4f_1$ by lightly touching the vibrating string $\frac{1}{4}$ of the way along so as to damp the notes of frequency f_1, f_2, and f_3. He reaches his highest notes by using this technique.

Bibliography

Hutchins, C. M. (1962). 'The physics of violins.' *Scientific American* offprint number 289.

PSSC (1971). *Physics*, 3rd edition. Heath. Chapter 5—an introduction to waves—is particularly good.

Resnick, R. and Halliday, D. (1966). *Physics*, part I. John Wiley. Chapter 19 develops basic wave behaviour from mechanical principles.

Rogers, E. M. (1960). *Physics for the inquiring mind*. Oxford University Press. Though mechanical waves are not widely dealt with in this text a nice proof of the speed of transverse waves on a string is given on page 189.

Sears, F. W. and Zemansky, M. W. (1960). *College physics*. Addison–Wesley. Chapters 21 and 22 contain much of relevance to this and to the next chapter.

Weidner, R. T. and Sells, R. L. (1965). *Elementary classical physics*, volume 2. Allyn and Bacon. Chapter 39 is called waves on a string and Chapter 40 covers other elastic waves.

Wood, A. (1944). *The physics of music*. Methuen. Stringed instruments are covered in Chapter 7.

8 mm film loop. 'Transverse waves.' Gateway. An elementary film showing wave pulses travelling along coupled trolleys.

8 mm film loop. 'Superposition.' Ealing Scientific.

8 mm film loop. 'Standing waves on a string.' Ealing Scientific.

Exercises

16-1 Figure 16-27 shows y–x graphs for two travelling waves about to pass through a point P. Draw the corresponding y–t graphs for the point P. Taking the speed of the waves as $2.0\,\text{m s}^{-1}$, use the scale on the x-axis to mark a scale on the t-axis.

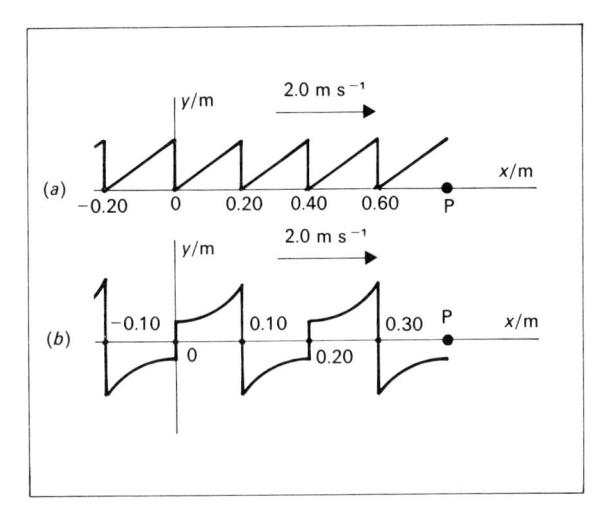

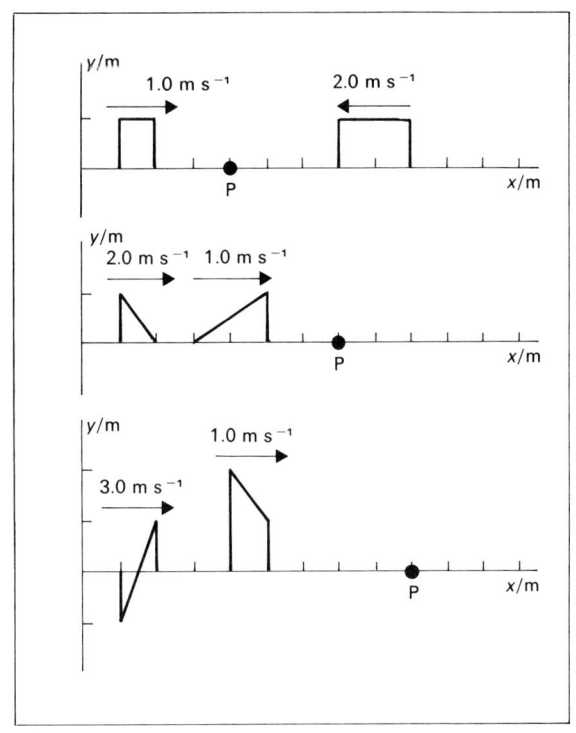

Figure 16-27

Figure 16-28 The markings on the x-axis are 1.0 m apart.

16-2 Figure 16-28 shows wave pulses moving along a stretched string at time $t = 0$. Use the principle of superposition to draw y–x graphs for each string at time $t = 2.0\,\text{s}$.

16-3 Refer to figure 16-28. Draw y–t graphs for the point P for a range of times $t = 0$ to $t = 6.0\,\text{s}$.

16-4 'Interference is an unfortunate term to choose when describing the interaction of waves.' Explain.

16-5 Figure 16-29 shows a y–x graph at time $t = 0$ for a pulse moving with speed $10\,\text{m s}^{-1}$ on a stretched string and about to be (perfectly) reflected. If the length of the pulse is 0.10 m, draw the y–x graphs for times $t/10^{-3}\,\text{s} = 5, 10, 15, 20, 25$.

16-6 Refer to figure 16-29. Draw the y–t graphs for the range of times $t/10^{-3}\,\text{s} = 0$ to 25
(a) for the point P   (b) for the point Q.

16-7 Repeat Exercises 16-5 and 16-6 for the situation where the end Q of the string is free to move transversely.

16-8 Write down the wave equation for a wave travelling in the positive direction of the x-axis, taking its amplitude as 0.10 m, its wavelength 0.50 m, and its frequency 3.0 Hz. Also write down the wave equation for a similar wave travelling in the opposite direction.

16-9 Sum the wave equations of Exercise 16-8 (using the trigonometrical relation $\sin A + \sin B = 2\sin\frac{1}{2}(A+B)\cos\frac{1}{2}(A-B)$) and interpret the result.

16-10 What is the phase difference for the oscillation of two points a distance 50 mm apart on a string along which a wave of frequency 100 Hz is travelling at a speed of $20\,\text{m s}^{-1}$? ●

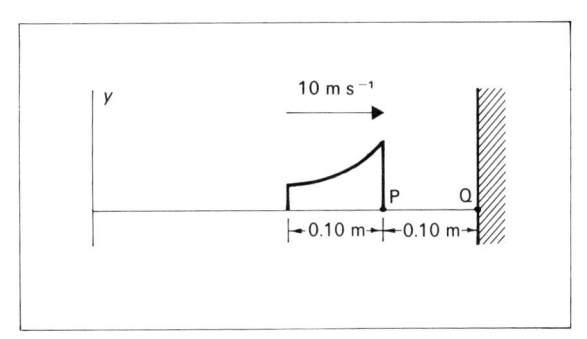

Figure 16-29

16-11 Sketch a few cycles of a travelling sinusoidal wave which is about to be reflected from a fixed boundary, and draw also a few cycles of the wave which has already been reflected and which is moving in the reverse direction. Use the principle of superposition to find the resultant wave. Repeat for two or three different positions of the incident wave, and show that the displacement produced by the resultant wave is always zero at all points (nodes) which are a whole number of half wavelengths from the boundary, and that the points at which the maximum displacement occurs (antinodes) are $\lambda/4$, $3\lambda/4$, $5\lambda/4$, etc., from the boundary.

16 Waves on a string

16-12 Repeat Exercise 16-11 for a wave being reflected from a free end, and show that now the nodes occur at distances $\lambda/4$, $3\lambda/4$, $5\lambda/4$, etc., from the free end, and that the antinodes occur at distances $\lambda/2$, $3\lambda/2$, $5\lambda/2$, etc., from that end.

16-13 A stretched string ABC consists of two sections AB and BC whose masses per unit length are in the ratio 1:4. The string can be given a periodic transverse vibration by a suitably placed vibrator. Describe the appearance of the string when the simplest stationary wave is formed on the string.

16-14 A heavy chain hangs vertically with its upper end fixed to the ceiling. It is given a transverse disturbance near its upper end: discuss the variation in speed of the pulse as it moves along the chain. If the upper end is made to oscillate sinusoidally from side to side, what sort of stationary wave patterns are possible on the chain? Draw sketches to illustrate your answer.

16-15 Draw the y–x graphs (marking the x-axis carefully) which represent the superposition of the following travelling sinusoidal waves which have the same speed of $9\,\mathrm{m\,s^{-1}}$ and the same amplitude:
(a) waves of frequency 9 Hz and 10 Hz
(b) waves of frequency 2 Hz and 10 Hz.

16-16 Draw to scale one half-cycle of a sinusoidal wave: let its amplitude be 100 mm and its wavelength 200 mm, so that your diagram occupies a square of side 100 mm. Suppose that this represents part of the travelling wave $y = a\sin 2\pi x/\lambda$ (where $a = 100$ mm, $\lambda = 200$ mm). Draw on the same diagram the graph of the travelling wave $y = a/3 \sin 3(2\pi x/\lambda)$, and draw the graph obtained by superposition. Now draw and add to the already superposed waves the wave $y = a/5 \sin 5(2\pi x/\lambda)$, and then the wave $y = a/7 \sin 7(2\pi x/\lambda)$. You should see that the resultant wave is beginning to assume a rectangular form, the amplitude of which can be shown to be 25π mm. The series of sine terms is called a *Fourier series*—see Section 16-7.

16-17 A sonometer has a steel wire which produces a fundamental note of frequency 200 Hz. What does the frequency become if each of the following changes is made in turn:
(a) the tension is doubled?
(b) the wire is replaced by another steel wire of half the diameter?
(c) the length is halved? ●

16-18 Suppose a stretched string has a stationary wave established on it. Discuss the forms in which mechanical energy is stored in it, and identify the parts of the string which have maximum and minimum amounts of the different forms of mechanical energy. Why does the string need to be continuously vibrated by an external periodic force?

16-19 Consider three stretched strings each with a fundamental frequency of vibration for transverse waves of f_0; one has two fixed ends, the second has one fixed end and one free end, and the third has both ends free. (The 'free' ends are free to move perpendicular to the initial position of the string.) When a stationary wave is set up in each, what frequencies (in terms of f_0, the fundamental frequency of each string) are possible in each system? ●

16-20 A steel wire of length 0.60 m and mass per unit length $0.010\,\mathrm{kg\,m^{-1}}$ is stretched horizontally so that its centre is between the poles of a permanent magnet. If the wire carries an alternating current of frequency 50 Hz, find the tension in the wire if it is to vibrate in its fundamental mode. ●

16-21 Find the speed of the waves which travel along a violin string which has a mass per unit length of $3.75 \times 10^{-4}\,\mathrm{kg\,m^{-1}}$ and a tension of 15 N. If its length is 0.33 m, what is the frequency of its fundamental note? ●

16-22 A steel wire of length 0.80 m is stretched between two fixed points, and its fundamental frequency is found to be 150 Hz. Find the speed of the waves in the wire. If the breaking stress of steel is $1.6 \times 10^9\,\mathrm{N\,m^{-2}}$, what is the highest fundamental frequency which can be produced in this wire by increasing the tension? Density of steel $= 8.0 \times 10^3\,\mathrm{kg\,m^{-3}}$. ●

16-23 A manufacturer wishes to make a violin which can be used by children. It is to play the same range of notes as a full-size violin. If the linear dimensions of the child's violin are to be half those of the full-size violin, how would you advise the manufacturer to string the child's violin?

16-24 Examine a guitar and a violin and explain why for a particular tension in a string the violin can play an infinitely variable range of notes whereas the guitar can play only a few distinct notes.

16-25 The twelve notes of the *equal-temperament* scale are labelled C, C♯, D, D♯, E, F, F♯, G, G♯, A, A♯, B, C′, and the frequency corresponding to each is $2^{1/12}$ times that of the previous note. If a piano contains strings of different lengths but the same tension and mass per unit length, how much longer than the C string is
(a) the E string   (b) the F string? ●

16-26 The notes of the *just intonation* scale C, D, E, F, G, A, B, C′ have frequencies defined by the relations C:C′ = 1:2, F:A:C′ = C:E:G = G:B:D′ = 4:5:6. If the frequency of C is f, find the frequencies of the other notes. How similar is G on this scale to G of the equal temperament scale (see Exercise 16-25)? If these notes are to be produced by the strings of a piano, all of which have the same tension and mass per unit length, find the lengths of the strings if l is the length of the string which produces note C. ●

16-27 Refer to Exercise 16-26. Show that the third harmonic of F is the same as the fourth harmonic of C. Find another similar relationship between harmonics. How would these facts be useful to piano tuners?

16-28 A circus ringmaster often has a whip which he 'cracks' during the circus horses' routine. This crack is produced by the end of the whip moving fast enough to break the sound barrier, that is, it is moving at more than $330\,\mathrm{m\,s^{-1}}$. Discuss how this very high speed arises.

17 Mechanical waves

17-1	Longitudinal waves	299	17-7 Other mechanical waves	312
17-2	Stationary longitudinal waves	302	17-8 Vibrating bodies	314
17-3	Waves in solids	304	17-9 Summary of wave-speed formulae	318
17-4	Energy and mechanical waves	306	Bibliography	319
17-5	Wavefronts	307	Exercises	320
17-6	Water waves	308		

17-1 Longitudinal waves

The division between this chapter and the last is for convenience rather than because there is any particular difference between waves on strings and other mechanical waves. A wave for which the displacement of a particle of the medium carrying the wave is parallel to the direction of energy propagation is called a *longitudinal* wave. Let us take as our prototype longitudinal wave the compressions which we can produce on a long open-coiled spring such as a slinky. The situation can be investigated experimentally using a suspended slinky as shown in figure 17-1, where the dissipation of the energy of the wave pulse by friction effects is greatly reduced. We need to reconsider all the material in Sections 16-2 to 16-8 from the point of view of longitudinal waves but as so much of Chapter 16 is of general relevance to *all* wave phenomena the task is relatively light.

Firstly, however, how fast do longitudinal wave pulses travel along a slinky? If the slinky is first stretched and then one end moved sharply a short distance parallel to the spring a longitudinal wave pulse travels along the spring. If the movement is such as to squash the spring the pulse is one of *compression* while if the movement is such as to stretch the spring the pulse is one of *rarefaction*. In figure 17-1 the end of the spring was moved to the right and then back to where it started—see also figure 17-4. Fortunately *all* such pulses of whatever shape are found to travel at the same speed along a particular spring (that is one with a particular tension and a particular mass per unit length), so that as in Section 16-2 we are justified in analysing only one simple shape of pulse in any detail. We start with a slinky stretched to a length PQ (see figure 17-2). We then move the end P *steadily* towards Q at speed v: this is the longitudinal equivalent of the 'knee' used in Section 16-2 (ensuring that the spring is meanwhile still in tension). Consider the situation after a time Δt. A part of the spring whose original length was $c_1 \Delta t$ and tension T is compressed to a length $c_1 \Delta t - v \Delta t$ and tension T'. Provided $c_1 > v$, the front of the wave pulse R will move along the spring ahead of P'. As the spring is stretched more in the section QR than in the section P'R then $T > T'$, and a small part of the spring around R will be subject to a resultant force

$$F + F',$$

where $\qquad F = T$

and $\qquad F' = T',$

that is a resultant force of size $T - T'$ to the right.

If the spring has an initial mass per unit length m then

17 Mechanical waves

Figure 17-1 A longitudinal wave pulse travelling along a spring.

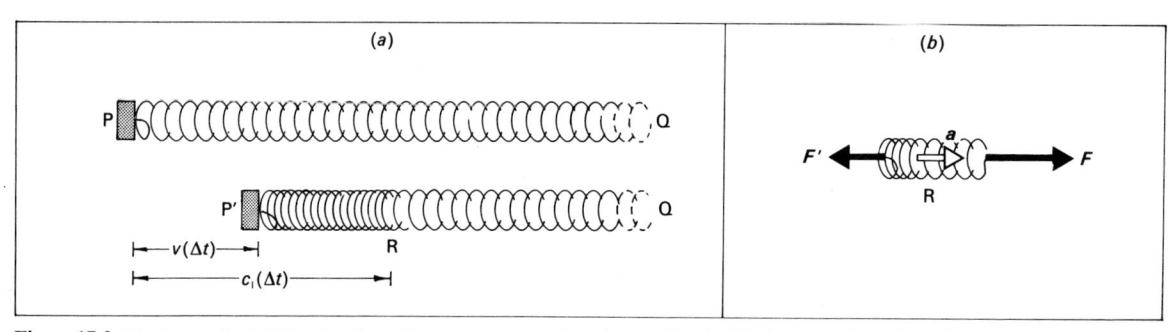

Figure 17-2 (a) A stretched slinky is allowed to contract so that the tension in PR becomes less than the tension T in RQ, the initial tension in the whole spring. (b) A small part of the slinky around R, the position of the wave pulse.

in time Δt a mass $mc_1 \Delta t$ has been given a velocity v to the right by a resultant force $F - F'$. By Newton's second law the rate of change of momentum is

$$\frac{mc_1 \Delta t v}{\Delta t} = F - F',$$

$$mc_1 v = F - F',$$

or $\qquad mc_1 v = T - T'.$

If the stiffness of the spring is k then a change in tension from T to T' would produce a change in the length of a spring which depended on how long the spring was. For a spring of length l, the change in length Δl would be given by

$$T - T' = k\Delta l.$$

In this case $\qquad \dfrac{\Delta l}{l} = \dfrac{v}{c_1},$

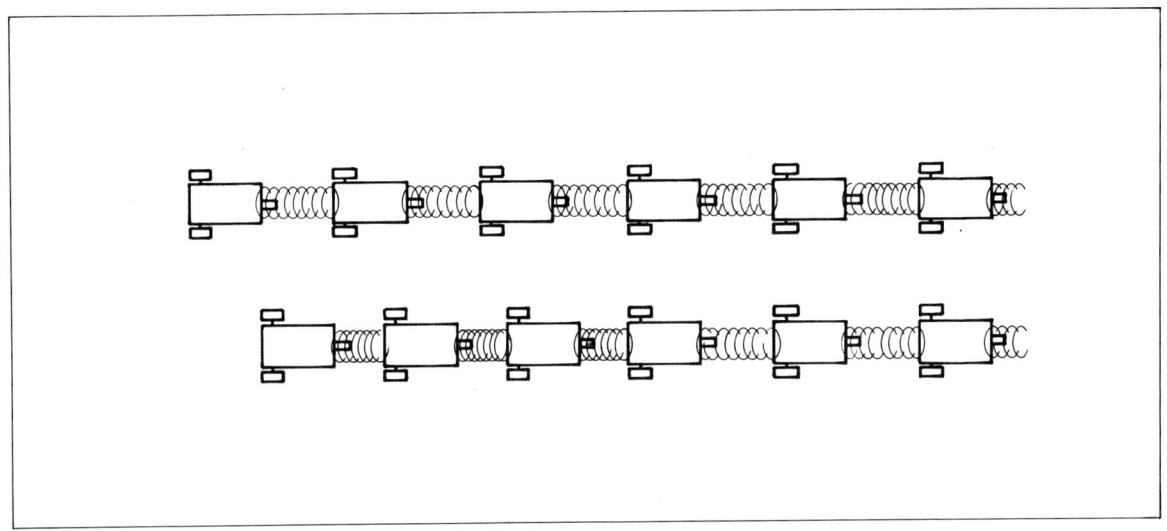

Figure 17-3 A trolley and spring model for longitudinal waves.

so that $$T - T' = k\frac{vl}{c_1}.$$

Eliminating $T - T'$ from the two equations above,

$$mc_1 v = \frac{kvl}{c_1}$$

so that either $v = 0$ (no wave pulse)

or $$c_1^2 = \frac{kl}{m},$$

that is $$c_1 = \sqrt{\frac{kl}{m}}. \qquad [17\text{-}1]$$

Note that, as expected, the speed of the pulse c_1 does *not* depend on v, the speed at which P is moved to produce the pulse, and further that if k is the same for compressing forces as for extending forces the pulse speed has the same value whether the spring is stretched or compressed initially or during the motion.

Checking the dimensions of the relation we get for the right-hand side

$$[(k)^{1/2}(l)^{1/2}(m)^{-1/2}] = (MT^{-2})^{1/2}(L)^{1/2}(ML^{-1})^{-1/2}$$
$$= LT^{-1}$$

and for the left-hand side $[c_1] = LT^{-1}$.

An effective demonstration of a *slow* longitudinal wave can be managed by linking a number of trolleys together as shown in figure 17-3. The wave can be slowed down further by adding extra mass to each trolley, for instance by stacking a second trolley on top of each. The reader is referred to Exercise 17-4 for a question which helps to relate the formula $c_1 = (kl/m)^{1/2}$ derived for a continuous slinky to the lumped-mass spring model.

Representing longitudinal waves

In representing longitudinal waves, sketches of what is really happening on a slinky, such as figure 17-4b, are not at all easy to draw. It becomes easier if we use y- and x-axes and let the y-axis represent the *longitudinal* displacement of the particles of the medium. Figure 17-4c shows two typical displacements AA' and BB', and the rest of the graph is sketched in. The graph now *looks* like that of a transverse wave pulse which is both a danger and a help; a danger in that we may think that the displacements *are* transverse, but a help in that we can use all our graphical techniques (such as when handling superposition) for longitudinal waves. As for transverse waves, both y–x graphs at an instant and y–t graphs for a point can be drawn.

As the displacement of all particles in the path of a longitudinal wave is parallel to the direction of energy propagation there can be no equivalent to the concept of polarizing the waves in a plane. Transverse waves can be plane-polarized; for longitudinal waves this has no meaning.

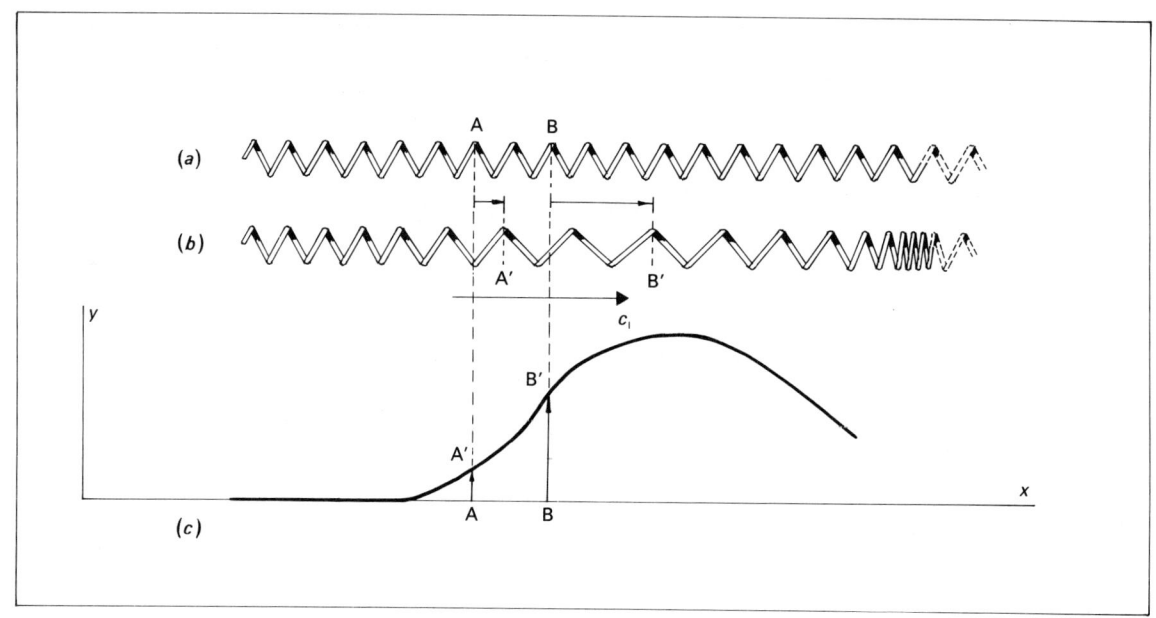

Figure 17-4 (c) is a y–x graph for the displaced spring carrying the longitudinal wave pulse shown in (b). Displacements to the right from the equilibrium positions are conventionally measured as positive.

17-2 Stationary longitudinal waves

Longitudinal mechanical waves obey the principle of superposition, that is when two waves meet the displacement of a particle on the wave is the vector sum of the displacements caused by each disturbance. This can be demonstrated with the slinky shown in figure 17-1 or using a long line of longitudinally linked trolleys as described in figure 17-3. It is essential to *see* a demonstration of two pulses going 'through' one another. In describing the effect we draw displacement–distance graphs for the wave at several moments during the superposition and such graphs will look like figure 16-8, though we must remember that whereas for transverse waves the graphs show what we should see, this is not the case with graphs describing longitudinal wave phenomena. The graphs for longitudinal waves are no less correct but perhaps a little more difficult to appreciate.

A source can be made to produce a sinusoidal longitudinal wave by oscillating with simple harmonic motion along the line of the spring or medium which is to carry the wave. All the graphs and mathematics of Section 16-6 are relevant. Thus we talk of the wavelength λ, period T, frequency f, and amplitude y_0 of longitudinal waves, and for sinusoidal waves the wave equation

[16-5] $$y = y_0 \sin 2\pi \left(\frac{t}{T} - \frac{x}{\lambda} \right)$$

holds as does the associated concept of phase angle. Points on a travelling wave separated by a distance of $\lambda, 2\lambda, 3\lambda, \ldots$, etc. are said to be moving in phase.

To show travelling sinusoidal waves in the laboratory is difficult because of reflections but we can make use of these same reflections to demonstrate longitudinal stationary waves (see figure 17-5). The source S should be set at a frequency for which the spring exhibits a definite pattern of blurred regions and still regions. The nodes and antinodes are obvious in figure 17-5b, the fixed end

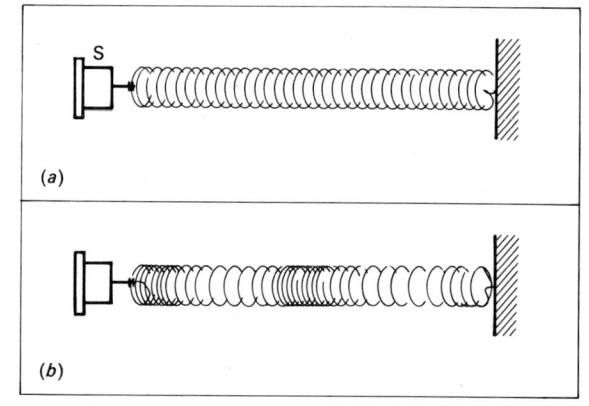

Figure 17-5 Demonstrating stationary longitudinal waves on a spring. The spring is shown in its undisturbed state, and as it is seen when the stationary wave has been formed.

17-2 Stationary longitudinal waves

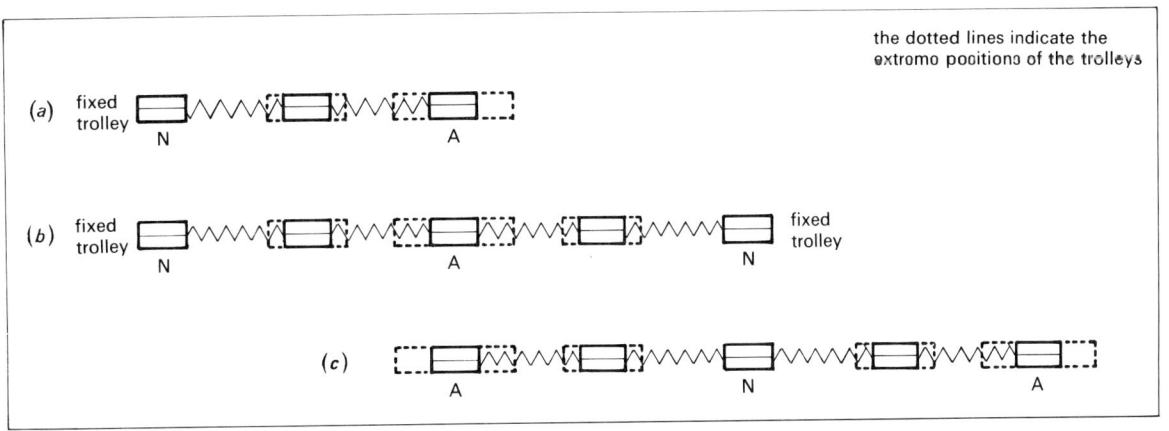

Figure 17-6 Diagrammatic representation of stationary wave patterns on a spring-linked trolley system. All the trolleys are free to oscillate except the three indicated as being fixed.

of the spring being a node and the end attached to the source being neither a node nor an antinode. The nodes are separated by $\lambda/2$, as are the antinodes, and the mathematics of the superposition producing this interference pattern is just like that on page 291. The number of nodes occurring depends, of course, on the frequency chosen for the experiment. λ is very easily measured in this experiment and reading f from the signal generator driving S we can deduce $c_1 = f\lambda$ and check that

$$c_1 = \sqrt{\frac{kl}{m}}$$

for the spring under test. This is probably the best laboratory test for this relation.

Stationary longitudinal waves can also be demonstrated using a number of trolleys linked end-to-end or a number of spring-linked gliders on an air track. The hand can be used to set the system into vibration. Unlike a stretched string there is no need in this case for the springs linking the trolleys to be under any initial extension or compression so that the ends of the line may be either fixed or free (the next paragraph explains how longitudinal waves reflect). Figure 17-6 shows in diagrammatic form three possible stationary wave interference patterns using a fixed frequency and varying the number of trolleys (or gliders). The reader will find the experimental investigation of the possible modes of vibration of such systems, particularly case (c), fascinating. See also Section 17-7.

All types of wave motion can be used to produce stationary waves and we must stress that all the basic wave concepts developed in the last chapter are of general relevance not only to the mechanical waves of this text but also to electromagnetic waves.

Reflection

When a longitudinal wave on a spring is reflected the exact nature of the reflection depends on whether the end of the spring is fixed or free. In Section 16-5 we applied Newton's laws—concepts of force and inertia—to the reflection of a transverse wave pulse on a string. Similar arguments (see Exercise 17-3) lead to the conclusions, verified in practice, that for longitudinal waves:

(a) at a free boundary a compression pulse is reflected as a rarefaction pulse (that is there is a phase change of π rad on reflection) and vice versa.

(b) at a fixed boundary a compression pulse is reflected as a compression pulse and a rarefaction pulse is reflected as a rarefaction pulse.

These effects can be demonstrated on the slinky shown in figure 17-1 but a slower wave pulse makes the results easier to see. The train of trolleys shown in figure 17-7

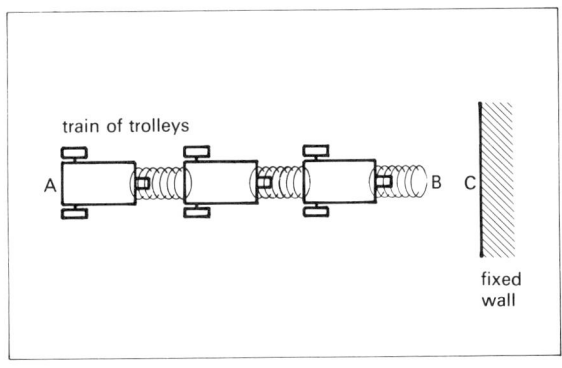

Figure 17-7 A train buffer, B, strikes a fixed contact at C.

is rolled at a steady speed towards a fixed barrier. It is quite difficult to achieve this but a little practice soon produces the desired result if each of the trolleys is set in motion at the same time. When the spring at B hits the wall at C it is compressed and a compression pulse starts at B and travels to the end A of the train where it is reflected as a rarefaction pulse which travels back to B. On arriving at A this rarefaction pulse 'pulls' the buffer B away from the wall and the train sets off to the left. The mechanical wave idea shown by this experiment is widely relevant to 'bouncing'. If the time of contact of C at B is recorded, for example by arranging for an electric circuit to be made when C hits B and broken when C leaves B, the experiment yields a measurement of the speed of the longitudinal wave along the line of trolleys. This experiment shows that the time of contact of two colliding objects is equal to the time for a wave pulse to travel across one of them and back. (Such an idea is used in the experiment described in the next section.)

17-3 Waves in solids

A solid rod is structurally analogous to a slinky and if struck at one end a wave pulse will travel along a rod just as it does along the slinky described in Section 17-1. The formula $c_1 = \sqrt{(kl/m)}$ for the wave speed applies. We write $F = kx$ for a spring; the corresponding expression for a solid rod or wire of length l and cross-sectional area A is

$$\frac{F}{A} = E\left(\frac{x}{l}\right) \qquad [17\text{-}2]$$

where E is the *Young modulus* and is a property of the material of which the rod is made.
Rearranging we get

$$F = \left(\frac{AE}{l}\right)x$$

and so the stiffness k of a rod of length l and cross section A is given by $k = AE/l$. For a rod of cross section A and density ρ (ρ again being a property of the material and not of a particular rod or wire) clearly the mass per unit length $m = A\rho$. Substituting in the formula for c_1 we get

[17-1] $\qquad c_1 = \sqrt{\dfrac{kl}{m}} = \sqrt{\left(\dfrac{AE}{l}\dfrac{l}{A\rho}\right)}$

$$c_1 = \sqrt{\frac{E}{\rho}}. \qquad [17\text{-}3]$$

Thus for a copper rod, where $E = 1.3 \times 10^{11}\,\text{N m}^{-2}$ and $\rho = 8.9 \times 10^3\,\text{kg m}^{-3}$,

$$c_1 = \sqrt{\frac{1.3 \times 10^{11}\,\text{N m}^{-2}}{8.9 \times 10^3\,\text{kg m}^{-3}}}$$

$$= 3800\,\text{m s}^{-1}.$$

This value will, of course, depend on the temperature of the copper rod for both E and ρ are functions of the temperature. It should be emphasized that the relation $c_1 = \sqrt{(E/\rho)}$ is of the form

$$\text{wave speed} = \sqrt{\frac{\text{elastic property}}{\text{inertial property}}} \qquad [17\text{-}4]$$

of the material, just as was equation 16-1 for transverse waves on a string. Any relation for the speed of a mechanical wave in an elastic medium will be of this form.

Can we test this result experimentally? Figure 17-8 shows a possible arrangement. A signal generator is set to give about 5 V output at 25 kHz and connected to one end of the rod under test. The rest of the circuit is arranged as shown with the c.r.o. stability control set so that a trace appears when the hammer is placed in contact with the rod but disappears when the contact is broken. The experiment is now a simple one; the hammer is used to strike the rod and the number of oscillations on the c.r.o. is counted and the calibration of the signal generator used to find the period of contact Δt. Alternatively, the calibrated timebase itself can be used to measure the period of contact. If the length of the rod is l then $c_1 = 2l/\Delta t$, for the hammer remains in contact with the rod while the compression pulse travels down the rod and the reflected rarefaction pulse (see page 303) travels back to push the hammer away. The experiment once set up is easy to repeat for different materials. Typically if $l \approx 1$ m, then $\Delta t \approx 0.6$ ms, so that using a signal generator set at 25 kHz about 15 oscillations appear on the screen. The hammer should be heavy and loosely held in the hand so as to damp the wave which travels across the hammer head and back.

★ When a longitudinal wave is sent through a solid body such as a wall which extends a large distance in directions perpendicular to the wave propagation, the wave speed is different from $c_1 = \sqrt{(E/\rho)}$ because for a rod the solid is able to alter its cross section while for a wave in the bulk material any volume change which occurs when the wave passes must be only the result of longitudinal strain. We can define a longitudinal modulus M for which

$$c_1 = \sqrt{\frac{M}{\rho}}; \qquad [17\text{-}5]$$

17-3 Waves in solids

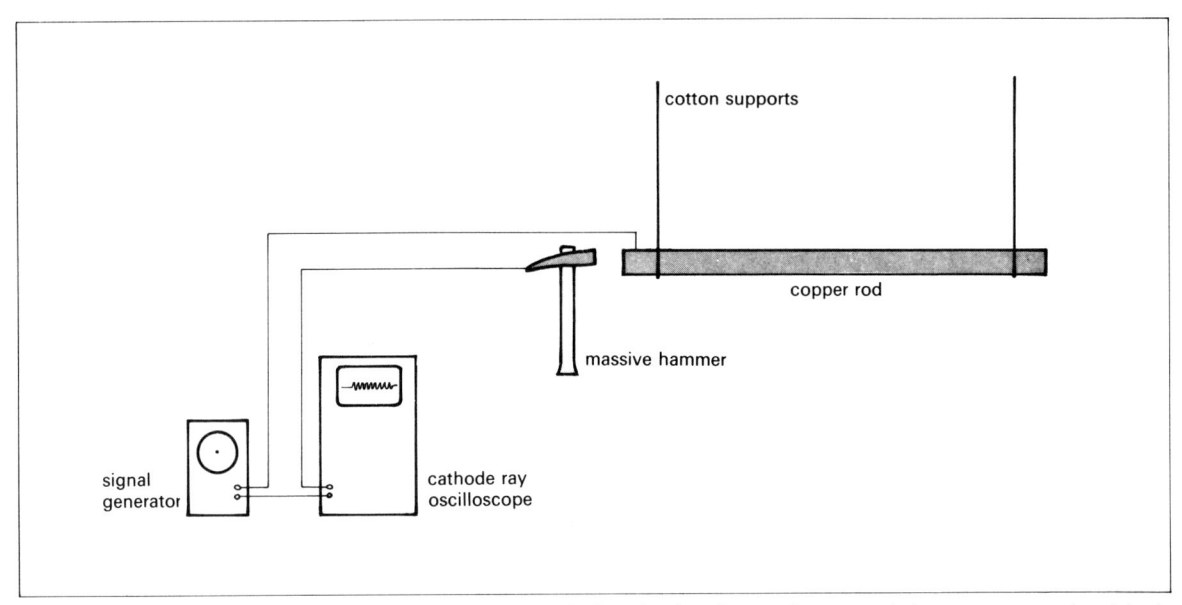

Figure 17-8 Measuring the speed of a longitudinal wave by finding the time for a pulse to travel down a copper rod and back.

M is typically greater than E by perhaps 25 per cent so that we must expect the experimental values of c_1 to be greater by more than 10 per cent than those deduced from equation 17-3. This area of study requires a much more detailed knowledge of elastic moduli than we have provided in this text. ★

It is possible to produce longitudinal waves on a rod by stroking the rod with a resined cloth as well as by striking it at one end. This is because the cross section of the rod is altered slightly during the grip–slip–grip stroking and just as striking the rod produces longitudinal waves plus a variation in cross section, so varying the cross section produces longitudinal waves.

▶ **Example 17-1** Suppose we could look at a solid copper rod at a sub-microscopic level and see a longitudinal wave pulse passing along it. In an ordered crystal we should see a series of masses, the molecules of the crystal, linked together by springs, the intermolecular electromagnetic forces. The speed of a wave pulse along a copper rod at 20 °C is $3.75 \times 10^3 \text{ m s}^{-1}$: estimate the intermolecular spring constant k_1 using the relation $c_1 = l_1 \sqrt{(k_1/m_1)}$ derived in Exercise 17-4.

Consider a single row of copper atoms. They are spaced at intervals of about 2.5×10^{-10} m, and as the relative molecular mass of copper is 63.6, the mass of one copper atom is

$$\frac{63.6 \text{ g mol}^{-1}}{6.02 \times 10^{23} \text{ mol}^{-1}} = 1.06 \times 10^{-22} \text{ g}$$

$= 1.06 \times 10^{-25}$ kg.

So if $c_1 = l_1 \sqrt{\left(\dfrac{k_1}{m_1}\right)}$

$$k_1 = \frac{c_1^2 m_1}{l_1^2}$$

$$= \frac{(3.75 \times 10^3 \text{ m s}^{-1})^2 (1.06 \times 10^{-25} \text{ kg})}{(2.5 \times 10^{-10} \text{ m})^2}$$

$= 24 \text{ N m}^{-1}$.

(In this example we have considered a single row of atoms, and it might be thought that the analysis would not apply to an actual three-dimensional crystal. In fact the crystal behaves just as an aligned group of single rows of atoms.) ◀

To set up a stationary longitudinal wave in a solid rod the arrangement of figure 17-8 (without the signal generator and c.r.o.) can be used. A few blows with the hammer will soon set the rod ringing as the wave pulses reflect successively at both ends. Alternatively, the rod can be clamped at its centre and one side stroked longitudinally with a resined cloth. In either case it is clear that the free ends of the rod must be antinodes and for the simplest longitudinal mode of vibration the length of the rod will be $\lambda/2$—see figure 17-6c. Thus for a rod 1 m long, $\lambda = 2$ m and if the rod is copper, $c_1 = 3800 \text{ m s}^{-1}$. The frequency associated with this stationary wave pattern is given by

$$f = \frac{c_1}{\lambda} = \frac{3800 \text{ m s}^{-1}}{2 \text{ m}} = 1900 \text{ Hz}.$$

The ends of the rod will be oscillating in and out at this frequency and will produce a sound wave in the air of the same frequency.

★ When *one* atom of a solid oscillates, typically with a frequency of about 10^{-13} Hz, it sends elastic waves of wavelengths 10^{-10} m to 10^{-11} m through the solid. In this sense the *internal* (vibrational) *energy* of the solid can be thought of as the energy of the elastic waves travelling within the solid. The mechanical energy of the atom is quantized and therefore the wave energy is also quantized and we talk of *phonons* carrying the energy within the solid. The analogy is with photons of electromagnetic energy. The thermal properties of solid (particularly crystalline) materials have been explored, in recent years, using the phonon concept and, for example, the size of the thermal conductivity of a material adequately explained. (See Section 18-7 for a spectrum of longitudinal mechanical waves.) ★

17-4 Energy and mechanical waves

In a periodic travelling (or progressive) wave motion the energy contained within a section of length λ leaves the section in a period of time T. The energy of the wave is partly the kinetic energy of the oscillating material and partly the elastic potential energy of the material. If we consider the material to be made up of a row of particles each of mass m_0 executing simple harmonic motion of period T and amplitude y_0, then the total mechanical energy per particle E is equal to its *maximum* kinetic energy. If it passes through its equilibrium position with a speed v_0 then the maximum kinetic energy is

$$E = \tfrac{1}{2} m_0 v_0^2.$$

But $$v_0 = \pm y_0 \frac{2\pi}{T}$$ from equation 15-9,

and so $$E = \tfrac{1}{2} m_0 \left(\frac{2\pi y_0}{T}\right)^2.$$

If the mass per unit length of the material is m then a length λ contains n particles where

$$n = \lambda \left(\frac{m}{m_0}\right)$$

and thus the total energy of a length λ is

$$E_\lambda = nE = \left(\frac{\lambda m}{m_0}\right) \frac{m_0}{2} \left(\frac{2\pi y_0}{T}\right)^2$$

$$= \tfrac{1}{2} \lambda m \left(\frac{4\pi^2}{T^2}\right) y_0^2.$$

As this energy is transferred to the next segment of length λ in a time T the average *power* transmitted is

$$P_{av} = \frac{E_\lambda}{T} = \tfrac{1}{2} \lambda m \left(\frac{4\pi^2}{T^3}\right) y_0^2.$$

But $f = 1/T$ and $c = f\lambda$ where f is the frequency of the wave motion and c its speed, so, more simply,

$$P_{av} = \tfrac{1}{2} m (4\pi^2 f^2 c) y_0^2$$

$$P_{av} = 2\pi^2 mcf^2 y_0^2. \qquad [17\text{-}6]$$

Thus the rate of energy transmission is, as expected, proportional to c, the wave speed, and is also proportional to the *square* of both the frequency and the amplitude of the wave motion. A high frequency (low wavelength) wave can transfer much more power than a low frequency wave of comparable amplitude.

The relation derived above for the average rate of energy transfer holds for both transverse and longitudinal sinusoidal wave motions. It is in a form which applies to waves along ropes and springs. For a longitudinal wave in a solid rod of density ρ and cross-sectional area A, the mass per unit length m is given by $m = \rho A$ and so (any variation of A being assumed negligible)

$$P_{av} = 2\pi^2 \rho A c f^2 y_0^2.$$

The power transferred per unit area (measured perpendicular to the energy flow) is called the *intensity* I of the wave. The average intensity of a longitudinal wave in a rod is thus

$$I = \frac{P_{av}}{A} = 2\pi^2 \rho c f^2 y_0^2. \qquad [17\text{-}7]$$

In particular, when ρ, c, and y_0 are constant,

$$I \propto f^2$$

and, when ρ, c, and f are constant,

$$I \propto y_0^2.$$

Energy is *not* propagated in a *perfect* stationary wave system. The system simply vibrates and in so doing there is an interchange of energy between kinetic energy and elastic potential energy. Consider the extreme cases shown in figure 16-21. In part (*iii*) the string is in an undisplaced position while in parts (*i*) and (*v*) the string is instantaneously at rest. In many practical examples a stationary wave system is not perfect in this sense and does feed energy to some surrounding object, for example the sound box of a violin.

17-5 Wavefronts

When a wave travels along a spring, a string, or a rod the direction of energy propagation is in one dimension, namely along the spring, string, or rod. (For the spring and the string the one-dimensional nature of the wave is inevitable but for the rod this is not so. For the energy to travel in one dimension the source at the end of the rod must extend over the surface of the end of the rod—it must not, for example, be a point source.) Figure 17-9 shows a one-dimensional wave. A set of points in the path of the wave all of which have the same phase define a surface called a *wavefront*. In the case of one-dimensional waves the wavefronts will be planes at right angles to the direction of energy propagation. When the source oscillates periodically the distance between wavefronts which differ in phase angle by 2π rad is, of course, the wavelength. A *ray* is a line drawn from the source which is perpendicular to the wavefronts; such a line shows the path along which the energy travels. In figure 17-9 the rays are a set of parallel straight lines.

But wave energy is often propagated in two dimensions (for instance on a water surface) or three dimensions (for instance in air). Figure 17-10 illustrates the relations between the source, the direction of energy propagation (the rays), and the wavefronts for two- and three-dimensional waves. In each case the wave speed is the same in all directions thus producing the high degree of symmetry shown in the diagrams. A medium which carries the wave energy at the same speed in all directions is said to be *isotropic*. Where a non-isotropic medium carries a wave, a complex wavefront will usually result. The wavefront is, however, still identifiable as *the locus of points which have the same phase*. At places at a great distance from a source any wavefront will, over a small area, appear to be plane. Thus a water wave caused by a boy jumping off a boat into a lake will, on arriving at the beach, look like a plane wavefront.

As a wavefront travels away from the source of the waves the intensity of the wave energy will decrease. One

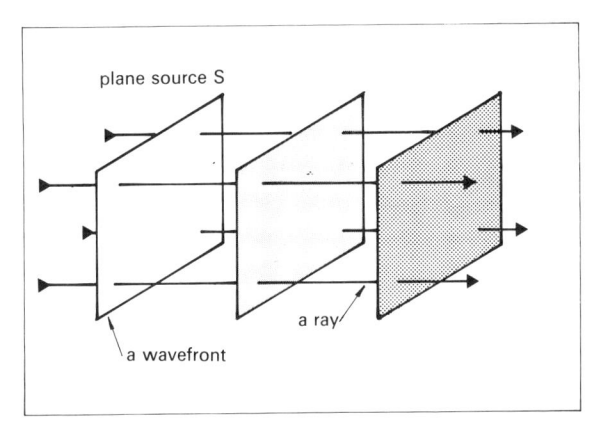

Figure 17-9 A plane wavefront. The rays are perpendicular to the wavefronts.

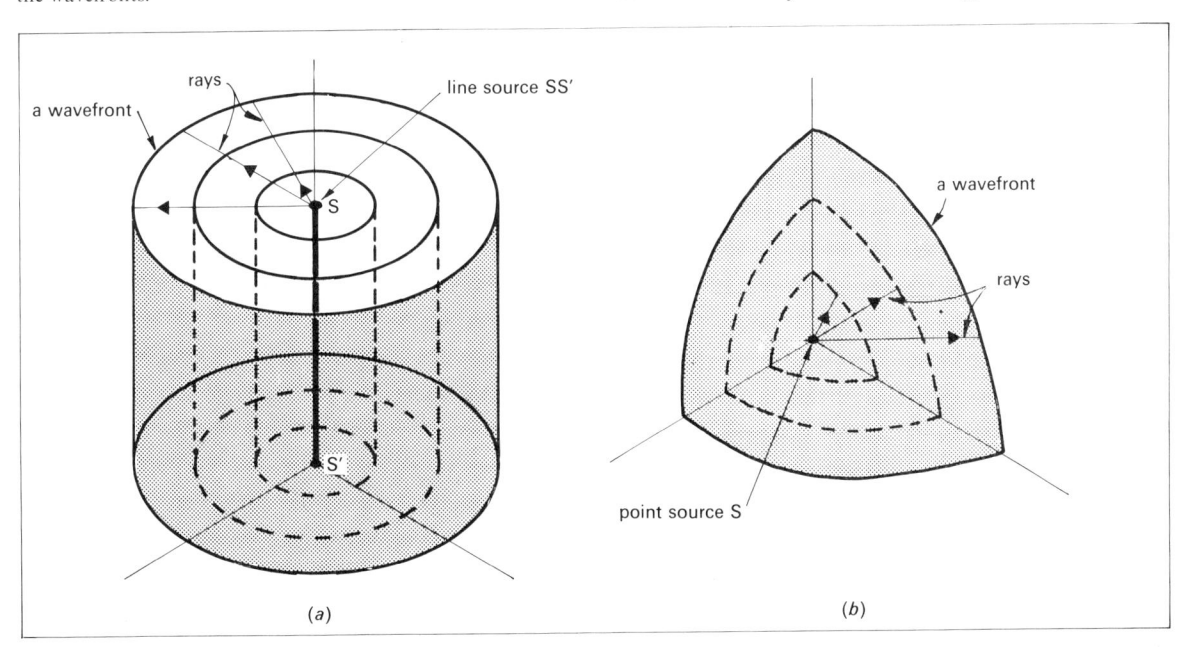

Figure 17-10 (*a*) Cylindrical and (*b*) spherical wavefronts.

cause of this is the dissipation of the wave energy as internal energy of the carrying medium; if the wavefront spreads out, that will also reduce the intensity. The dissipation of the wave energy is impossible to evaluate in the general case: we shall often assume it to be negligible although in particular cases we may choose to estimate the effect. The intensity or energy flux of a wave is defined as

$$I = \frac{P_{av}}{A} \qquad [17\text{-}8]$$

$$= \frac{\text{energy passing through an area } A \text{ in a time } t}{(\text{the area } A) \times (\text{the time } t)}.$$

Consider first a plane wavefront initially of area A (we shall assume there is no dissipation of energy). At some later time (see figure 17-9) all the energy associated with the wavefront still covers an area A (the rays are parallel) and so the intensity of the wave is unaltered. For cylindrical and spherical wavefronts the rays spread out and the intensity diminishes with the distance r from the source. For a cylindrical wavefront the areas of a length of cylinder l at radial distances r_1 and r_2 from the source are $2\pi r_1 l$ and $2\pi r_2 l$ respectively. As the total energy flux through these areas is constant then clearly

$$I_1 \times 2\pi r_1 l = I_2 \times 2\pi r_2 l$$

that is

$$I \propto \frac{1}{r}.$$

A similar geometric argument for spherical wavefronts leads to the equation

$$I_1 \times 4\pi r_1^2 = I_2 \times 4\pi r_2^2$$

that is

$$I \propto \frac{1}{r^2}.$$

Summarizing, and remembering that the intensity of a wave motion is proportional to the square of the wave amplitude y_0 we have:

	Amplitude y_0	Intensity I
Plane wavefront	y_0 independent of r	I independent of r
Cylindrical wavefront	$y_0 \propto \frac{1}{\sqrt{r}}$	$I \propto \frac{1}{r}$
Spherical wavefront	$y_0 \propto \frac{1}{r}$	$I \propto \frac{1}{r^2}$

Table 17-1

▶ **Example 17-2** A loudspeaker in a dance hall emits energy at a rate of 5.0 W. Assuming that it behaves as a point source, and that 80 per cent of the energy is transmitted uniformly in a cone whose solid angle is 0.25π steradian, and the remaining 20 per cent is transmitted uniformly in the remaining 3.75π steradians, find the intensity at points (a) 1 m directly in front of the loudspeaker (b) 4 m directly in front of the loudspeaker and (c) 1 m directly behind the loudspeaker.

The power transmitted into the cone in front of the loudspeaker is 4.0 W. At a point 1 m in front of the loudspeaker, the surface area of the sphere (whose centre is the loudspeaker) is

$$\frac{0.25\pi \text{ sr}}{4\pi \text{ sr}} \times 4\pi(1 \text{ m})^2 = 0.25\pi \text{ m}^2,$$

so that the intensity

$$I\left(= \frac{P_{av}}{A}\right) = \frac{4.0 \text{ W}}{0.25\pi \text{ m}^2} = 5.1 \text{ W m}^{-2}.$$

At a distance of 4 m in front of the loudspeaker, the intensity, varying inversely as the square of the distance, is $\frac{1}{16}$ of its value at 1 m, so $I = 0.32$ W m^{-2}.

At points behind the loudspeaker, the power has $\frac{1}{4}$ of its value in front and is distributed over 15 times the area (because the solid angle ratio is 3.75 sr: 0.25 sr = 15:1), so that the intensity $= \frac{1}{15} \times \frac{1}{4} \times 5.1$ W m^{-2} = 0.085 W m^{-2}. ◀

17-6 Water waves

Waves on the surface of water form one of the most fascinating of natural phenomena. Although apparently always changing, their behaviour does follow a pattern, and there are some general physical laws to help us understand them, but let us not lose sight of their beauty. In this text we shall be able to give only a brief glimpse into the characteristic properties of various types of water waves and the interested reader is referred to a glorious book by Tricker for a fuller treatment (see the bibliography).

Let us list a few naturally observed wave phenomena: ripples in a tea cup; breakers at the seaside; a river bore; a big sea swell; waves from a stone thrown into a lake; the wake of a rowing boat. The list is almost without end. Let us consider one of these in detail: why does a wave break at a beach? We begin by examining whether water waves are transverse or longitudinal mechanical waves. Figure 17-11 shows that the particle displacement is neither. In the water surface the particles move in a circle of radius y_0, where y_0 is the amplitude of the surface wave. Below the surface the circles rapidly get smaller—at a depth equal to half a wavelength the radius of the particles' movement has

17-6 Water waves

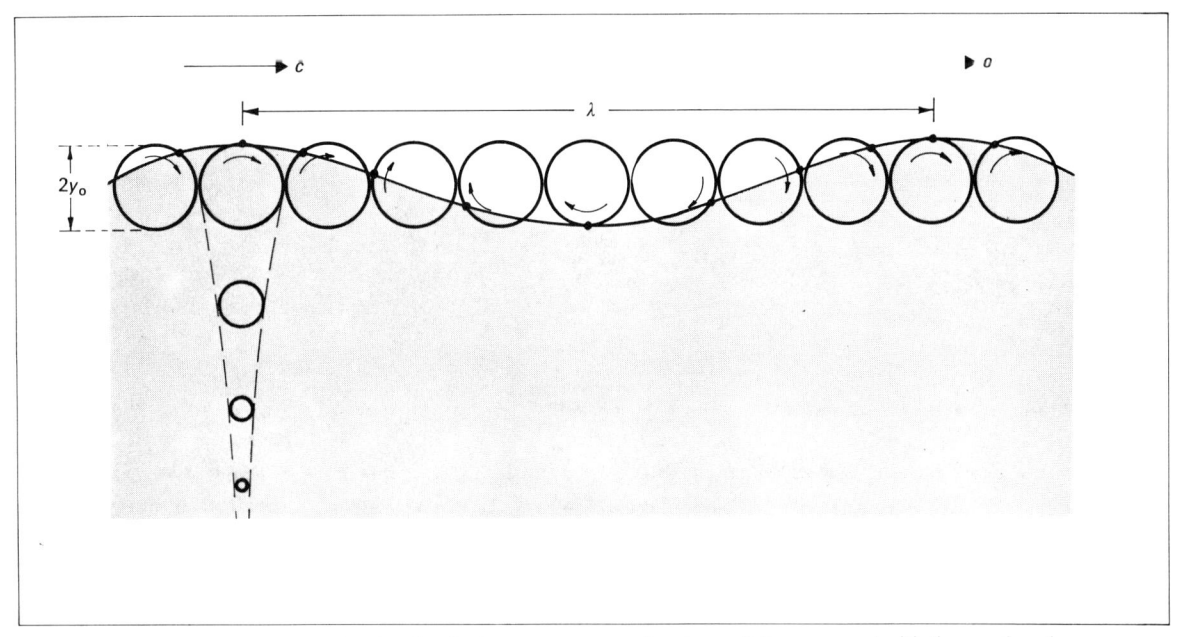

Figure 17-11 A wave in deep water showing the displacement pattern of water particles compared with the wavelength.

diminished to less than $y_0/20$. If the water is not deep and the bottom influences the water particles' displacement then the circles are flattened into ellipses. Further, for large amplitudes y_0, the shape of the wave is no longer symmetrical but the crests seem to be pointed and the troughs smoothly curved as one notices with waves moving along a sea wall.

We can now see that a wave would want to break at its crest if a water particle in the water surface has a horizontal speed at the top of its circle which is greater than the wave speed c. That each one of a train of waves should reach this condition must depend on the speed of the particle in its circular motion increasing and/or the speed of the wave c decreasing as the wave arrives at the beach. Suppose the wave frequency is f; this cannot change as the wave reaches a beach. The speed of the water particles in the surface is thus

$$v = \frac{\text{circumference of circle}}{\text{period}} = \frac{2\pi y_0}{1/f} = 2\pi f y_0.$$

Now it is a matter of common (seaside) experience that a wave slows down as it runs up a sandy beach. The wavelength λ of a wave drops to a fraction of a metre at the sea edge, is a metre or two where the paddler stands, and may be several metres where the swimmers play. The wave speed c thus decreases with decreasing water depth. The intensity of the plane wavefronts does not however drop until noticeable internal energy dissipation occurs in the breaking wave. This means that with reduced wave speed comes increased wave amplitude y_0 (a slower wave has to be taller) in order to maintain the same energy flux. We thus have

(a) c becomes smaller, and
(b) y_0, and thus v, becomes larger

as the water wave reaches the beach. Both (a) and (b) lead to a condition where $v > c$ and the top of the wave tips over, that is the wave breaks. A detailed study reveals that a wave breaks when y_0 is about two-thirds of the average depth of the water. This condition is indicated in figure 17-12.

The waves we have discussed above in considering just one of the many water wave phenomena are waves for which the wavelength $\lambda \gg h$, the depth of water in which the waves are travelling. If we further restrict the amplitude of the wave so that $h \gg y_0$, that is the depth is much the same at crest and trough, then it can be shown that the wave speed c is given by

$$c = \sqrt{(gh)}. \qquad [17\text{-}9]$$

The wave speed does not depend on the wavelength. A knowledge of this relation can tell us about the speed of tidal bores such as that on the River Severn (which is most easily observable between Newnham and

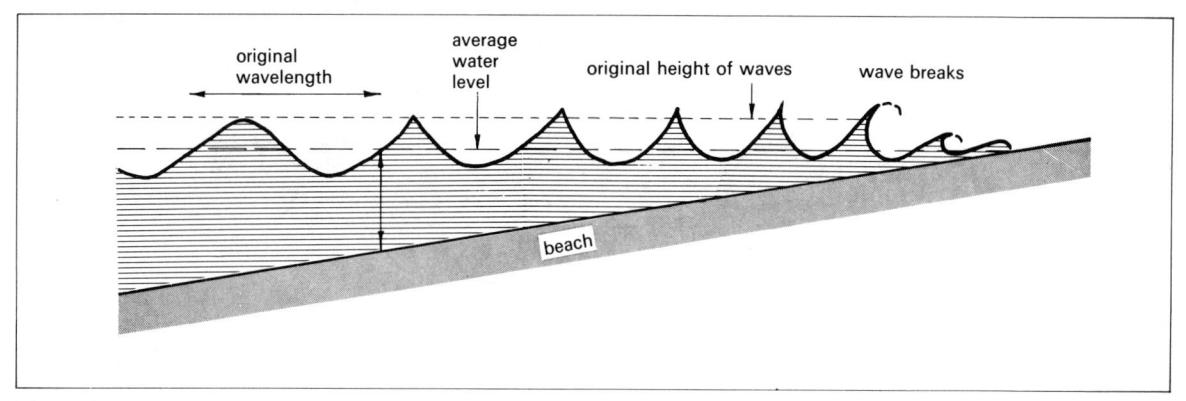

Figure 17-12 A schematic diagram of a wave reaching a beach.

Gloucester) and about the shape of wakes left by boats travelling in shallow water (see Section 19-7). The refraction of waves (see Section 19-3) which are incident obliquely on a shelving beach also depends on $c \propto \sqrt{h}$. See Exercise 17-20.

Apart from the long-wavelength waves in shallow water already discussed it is possible to isolate two main types of wave which travel on the surface of water (see figure 17-13). Firstly there are the *ripples* or capillary waves experienced in a laboratory ripple tank and secondly there are *gravity waves* or ocean waves found in open water. There are also the earthquake-caused water waves or *tsunamis* (which we shall not mention further but see the bibliography). Water waves which have speeds intermediate between those of ripples and gravity waves do of course exist but their properties are complex.

Gravity waves

The feature which distinguishes gravity waves from ripples is the type of controlling restoring mechanism. A gravity wave crest experiences a force; that is, its weight, accelerating it back to the average water level. Suppose the speed of gravity waves, c_g, depends only on the Earth's gravitational field strength g, the wavelength λ of the wave, and the density ρ of the liquid involved.

If
$$c_g = k g^x \lambda^y \rho^z$$

where k is a dimensionless constant, then the dimensions of the right-hand side are

$$(LT^{-2})^x (L)^y (ML^{-3})^z$$

and as this must be equal to LT^{-1} for the equation to be dimensionally homogeneous we get $x = \tfrac{1}{2}$, $y = \tfrac{1}{2}$, $z = 0$

and thus
$$c_g = k\sqrt{(g\lambda)}.$$

That $c_g \propto \sqrt{\lambda}$ can be tested by noting the period T of ocean waves and the distance λ between their crests ($c_g = \lambda/T$). A detailed theoretical analysis gives $k = \sqrt{(1/2\pi)}$ and thus

$$c_g = \sqrt{\frac{g\lambda}{2\pi}}. \qquad [17\text{-}10]$$

See Exercise 17-13 for some help in deriving this equation.

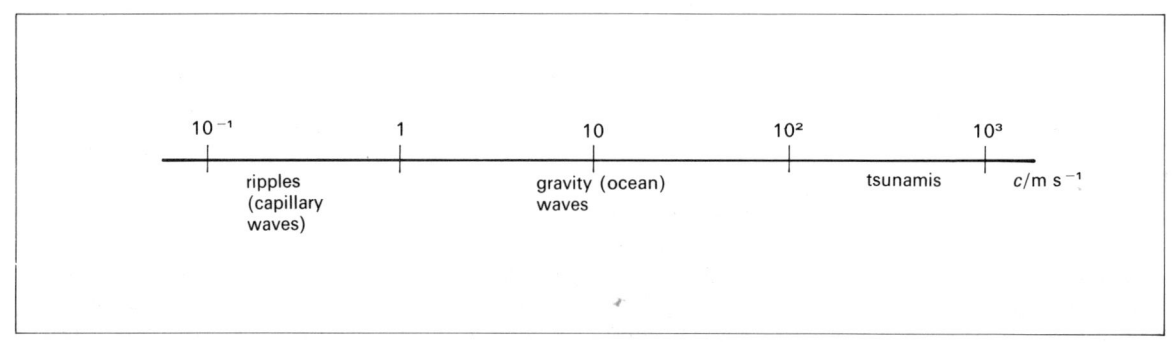

Figure 17-13 The speed of surface waves in deep water (more than one wavelength deep).

17-6 Water waves

The dependence of c_g on λ explains why when watching the water waves arriving at the edge of a river or an estuary from a distant source such as a boat the long wavelength waves arrive first and the short wavelength ones much later even though they all started from the same place at the same time.

At sea, waves are believed to be caused by the wind transferring energy to the sea. Both the wave speed and the wave amplitude can be empirically related to the (steady) wind speed. The largest reported wave seems to be one of period 14.8 seconds (wavelength 350 m, speed 24 m s^{-1}) with crest-to-trough height of 35 m. Such a wave was created by a gale of (Beaufort scale) storm force 11!

We must not lose sight of the usual wave properties possessed by gravity waves. They obey the principle of superposition and exhibit the phenomena such as refraction and diffraction described in Chapter 19. Stationary wave patterns can be produced.

Figure 17-14 A stone has been dropped into a pond. The ripples of greatest wavelength have travelled furthest.

Ripples

Ripples or capillary waves rely on the surface tension of the liquid surface to provide their elastic property* and for small wavelengths, say, less than 10 mm, they can be treated separately from gravity waves. The laboratory ripple tank provides an excellent apparatus for studying these waves and thus for studying conveniently the general behaviour of waves in two dimensions. The ripple tank will be widely used in Chapter 19 and is described in Section 19-1; in this section we shall consider the properties of ripples as surface tension water waves.

The first thing we note is that ripples of different wavelengths travel at different speeds. Figure 17-14 illustrates this phenomenon which can be seen on the surface of a ripple tank or by viewing the shadows of the surface projected on to a screen. This phenomenon will be discussed further in Section 19-6. Secondly, if waves of the same frequency can be produced on the surface of different liquids, for example on water, on ethanol, and on mercury, it is clear that the waves travel at different speeds. Both the elastic property (surface tension γ) and the inertial property (density ρ) vary from liquid to liquid. It is left as an exercise for the reader to show, using the method of dimensions, that the speed of a ripple c_r can be expressed as

$$c_r = k\sqrt{\frac{\gamma}{\lambda\rho}}.$$

That $c_r \propto 1/\sqrt{\lambda}$ can be readily tested for water in a ripple tank. A full theoretical analysis shows that

$$c_r = \sqrt{\frac{2\pi\gamma}{\rho\lambda}} \qquad [17\text{-}11]$$

providing the liquid is deep compared with λ.

Two-dimensional stationary wave patterns are often produced in cups of tea and are of a similar form to those described for rubber membranes in Section 17-8. Perhaps one of the most beautiful phenomena in physics occurs when a ripple is initiated in a liquid surface by a drop of the liquid striking the surface.

★ The most general relation for the speed of a surface wave on a liquid is

$$c = \sqrt{\left[\left(\frac{g\lambda}{2\pi} + \frac{2\pi\gamma}{\rho\lambda}\right)\tanh\frac{2\pi h}{\lambda}\right]} \qquad [17\text{-}12]$$

and it is the appearance of g and γ in the first two terms of this equation which gives us the terms gravity waves and capillary waves (ripples). The function $\tanh(2\pi h/\lambda)$ has the following properties.

As $\dfrac{h}{\lambda} \to 0$ (shallow water), $\tanh\dfrac{2\pi h}{\lambda} \to \dfrac{2\pi h}{\lambda}$

As $\dfrac{h}{\lambda} \to \infty$ (deep water), $\tanh\dfrac{2\pi h}{\lambda} \to 1$.

---

*For an account of the molecular mechanism of surface tension see Berry, M. V. (1971), *Physics Education*, **6**, page 79, and for a summary of surface tension effects see a text on the mechanical properties of matter.

(a) For shallow water gravity waves we get

$$c \approx \sqrt{\left[\left(\frac{g\lambda}{2\pi}\right)\left(\frac{2\pi h}{\lambda}\right)\right]} = \sqrt{(gh)}$$

which was equation 17-9.

(b) For ripples in very shallow water we get

$$c \approx \frac{2\pi}{\lambda}\sqrt{\frac{\gamma h}{\rho}}$$

and so $c \propto \sqrt{h}$ for waves of a given λ. This is used in Section 19-3 to illustrate how the refraction of waves can be demonstrated in a ripple tank.

(c) By deep water we only mean $h > \lambda$ for when $h = \lambda/2$, $\tanh 2\pi h/\lambda$ is already greater than 0.99. ★

17-7 Other mechanical waves

A list of mechanical waves would include waves on strings and springs, longitudinal waves in solids, waves on the surface of water, sound waves in air, earthquake or seismic waves, torsional waves, waves on membranes, and so on. The first few have been discussed already and sound waves in air have Chapter 18 to themselves. For the others we can only glance quickly at some features and offer the reader some references.

Seismic waves

The Earth's crust is not static. Occasionally the stresses which are built up cause a fracture or sudden deformation in the crust and the energy thus released ($\approx 10^{18}$ J in the largest earthquakes of which there are up to ten or so each year) is transmitted away from its source by elastic waves, mainly as a wave pulse or short series of pulses. The waves can be either longitudinal or transverse and as the longitudinal waves travel with a greater speed they arrive first at a recording station and are called the primary (P) waves. The transverse waves are called secondary (S) waves. The transverse S waves can be polarized when reflected from layers of varying composition and the vertical and horizontal components are referred to as the SV and SH waves respectively.

Both the P and S wave pulses produce three-dimensional wavefronts travelling away from (effectively) a point source called the *focus* of the earthquake (the point on the Earth's surface immediately above the focus is called the *epicentre*). Their intensity, I, obeys an inverse square law and since $I \propto y_0^2$, the amplitude of the wave, y_0, is proportional to $1/r$, r being the distance from the focus to the recording station. Detecting devices called *seismographs* register the amplitude of vibration of the Earth's crust and typically detect amplitudes down to 10^{-8} m, any smaller movements usually being swamped by motions caused by local traffic or the pounding of waves on a nearby shore—in fact all background 'noise' must be small for earthquake waves of amplitude 10^{-8} m to be readily observed. Figure 17-15 gives a typical displacement–time graph. The P and S wave pulses arrive as shown and are followed by waves of a relatively long period of several seconds. These travel *in* the surface layers of the Earth (rather than directly from place to place) and are thus spreading their energy in only two dimensions, they therefore remain of relatively large amplitude ($y_0 \propto 1/\sqrt{r}$) compared to the P and S waves.

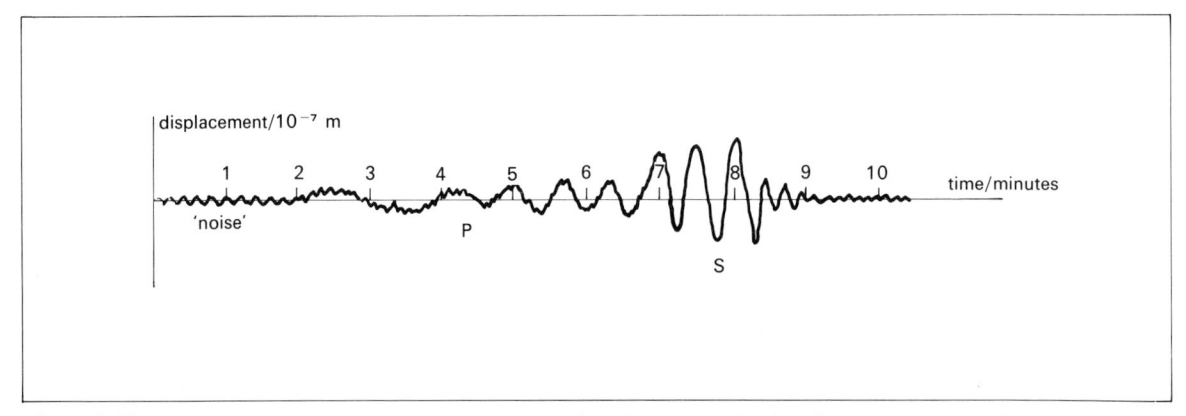

Figure 17-15 A (diagrammatic) typical seismic record of an earthquake. Some 'noise' is indicated before the arrival of the P waves.

As indicated by figure 17-15 the P and S waves travel at different speeds. A detailed knowledge of the times of arrival of the P and S waves and of their reflected, refracted, and diffracted products can both locate the focus of the earthquake and provide much information about the Earth's composition—the density and elastic properties of the material of which the Earth is made at various places and different depths. Thus the depth at which the Earth's fluid core begins is known. Further, by deliberately producing underground explosions the geophysical prospector may locate large-scale features such as salt domes which may have deposits of oil on their flanks.

▶ **Example 17-3** A recording station observes that there is a three minute interval between the reception of the primary and secondary waves from an earthquake. Assuming that the speeds of these waves near the surface of the Earth are roughly $8 \times 10^3 \, \text{m s}^{-1}$ and $5 \times 10^3 \, \text{m s}^{-1}$, find the distance of the earthquake from the recording station.

Let t be the time taken by the primary wave to travel from the earthquake to the recording station: then

$$(8 \times 10^3 \, \text{m s}^{-1})t = (5 \times 10^3 \, \text{m s}^{-1})(t + 180 \, \text{s})$$

which gives $t = 300 \, \text{s}$,

and hence the distance of the earthquake from the recording station is given by

$$s = (8 \times 10^3 \, \text{m s}^{-1})(300 \, \text{s})$$
$$= 2.4 \times 10^6 \, \text{m}$$
$$= 2400 \, \text{km}.$$

This solution assumes the P and S waves have travelled along the same path. This is not true owing to refraction (see page 344) and so the result can only be taken as very approximate. ◀

Torsional waves

The transverse earthquake waves, S waves, rely for their propagation on the resistance of the material of the Earth's crust to shearing. The speed c of such a wave depends upon the shear (or rigidity) modulus G and on the density ρ of the material carrying the wave disturbance and it can be shown that

$$c = \sqrt{\frac{G}{\rho}}. \qquad [17\text{-}13]$$

This sort of wave would best be called a *shear* wave; figure 17-16a shows a shear wave on a rod.

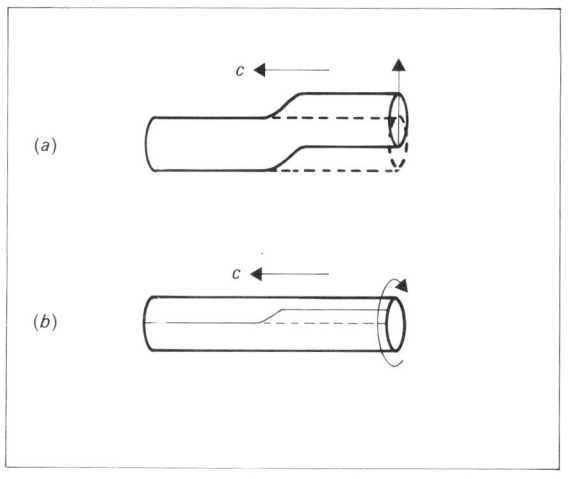

Figure 17-16 (a) A shear and (b) a torsional wave pulse on a rod.

Another way in which a rod can be deformed is to twist it. In this case the motion of the parts of the rod is perpendicular to its length and if a wave pulse is produced travelling along the rod it is called a *torsional* wave—see figure 17-16b. Again the speed of the wave is given by equation 17-13, showing the mathematically similar nature of apparently different dynamical motions. The reader should also note that again the right-hand side of the equation contains an elastic property G divided by an inertial property. In all the above we are assuming that the rod is not deformed beyond displacements for which it obeys Hooke's law. As E (the Young modulus) is greater than G by a factor of about 2.5 for metals, then longitudinal waves travel faster than both shear and torsional waves by a factor of about 1.6.

It is possible to produce torsional waves travelling at very slow speeds by taking a thin rod or thick wire and artificially increasing its moment of inertia about the axis of the wire by fixing rods at right angles to the wire. The arrangement is indicated in figure 17-17, the effect of the transversely mounted rods being to increase the value of ρ in $c = \sqrt{(G/\rho)}$. Using this device, waves with $f \approx 0.5 \, \text{Hz}$ travelling at about $0.25 \, \text{m s}^{-1}$ can be produced. The beautiful 'slow motion' effect is ideal for many demonstrations of the properties of mechanical waves but a long version of the system is not easily set up in the laboratory. A simple arrangement is to use a vertical length of flexible steel tape and to attach wooden cross pieces about 0.3 m long at intervals of 0.1 m. Torsional waves have been put to best effect in a film by J. N. Shive of Bell Telephone Laboratories—see the bibliography.

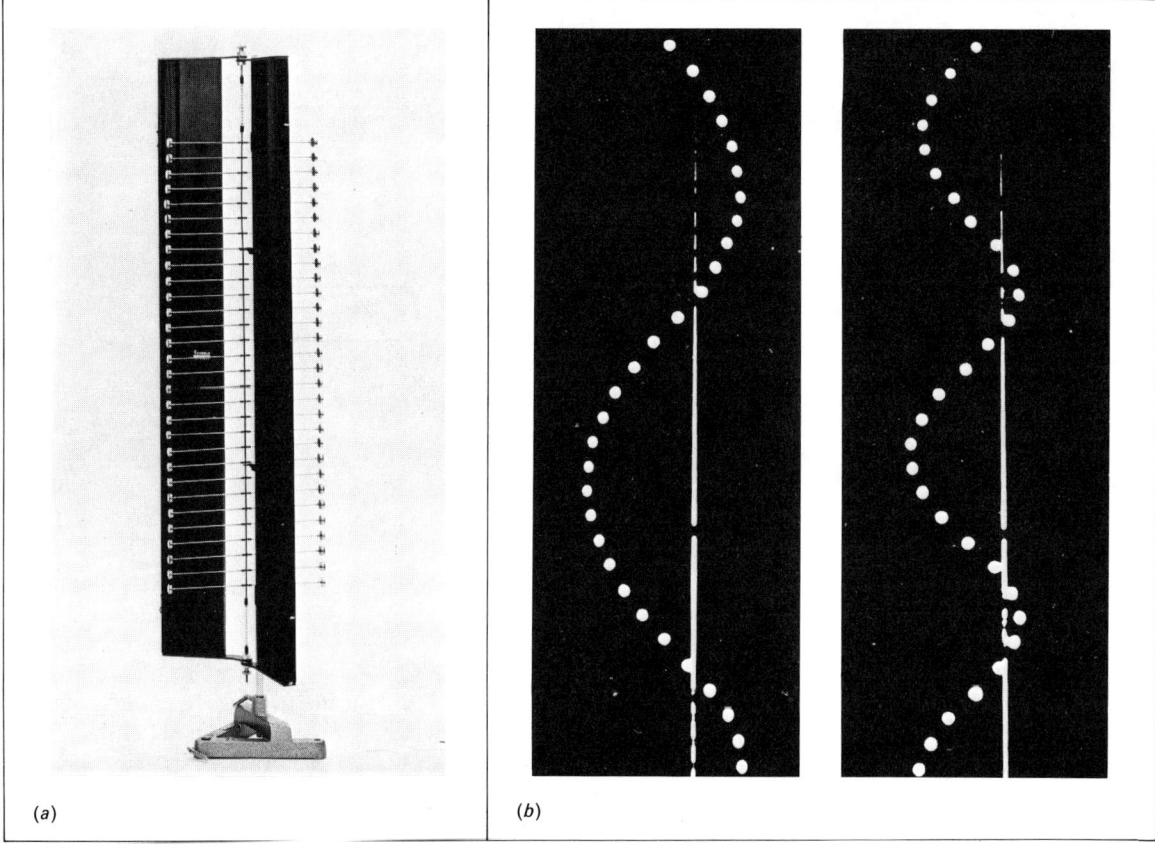

Figure 17-17 (*a*) A torsion-bar wave machine. (*b*) Instantaneous flash photographs of the bobs at the ends of the bars for two different wave speeds.

Drumskin waves

A stretched elastic membrane such as a stretched rubber sheet or a soap film will carry waves in two dimensions over its surface. In many ways the propagation of the waves is like that of water ripples. The more interesting results of these waves lie in the stationary wave patterns which can be produced on membranes limited in extent and of various shapes—this is taken up in the next section.

17-8 Vibrating bodies

When a periodic mechanical wave is produced in or on a body of limited extent the superposition of the wave and its reflection(s) can give rise to a stationary wave system. Equally we might say the body is vibrating in a resonant mode. The two descriptions are physically identical. We have already considered some resonant systems in Section 15-9 and have dealt with vibrating strings in Section 16-9; here we shall look at some more stationary wave or resonant vibrating systems—particularly those resulting from the elastic waves met in this chapter. We shall do no more than mention two extreme cases. Firstly let us consider a freely falling drop of water. The drop, having broken from a jet, will oscillate. This can be viewed in the laboratory without high-speed photography by first pulsing a fine water jet and then illuminating the resulting 'string' of water drops stroboscopically. The pulsation of a drop is controlled by the same factors as those which control the speed of ripples travelling along the surface of water (see Exercise 17-23). Secondly consider a huge freely falling body—the Moon. At the time of writing the Moon is known to 'ring' when a massive object, perhaps a discarded space vehicle, crashes into it. In this case the seismic wave(s) set up by the impact of the object travel repeatedly across (or round) the Moon, in effect setting the Moon itself into oscillation.

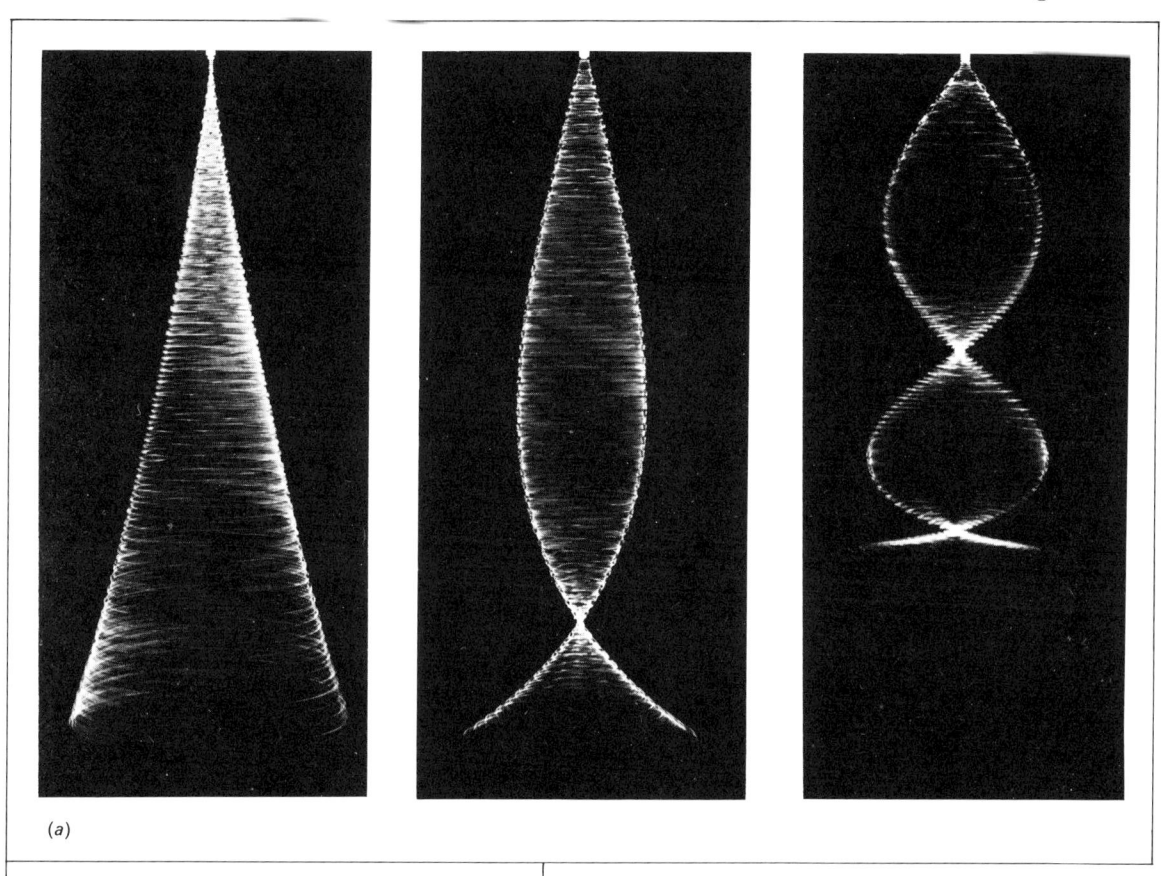

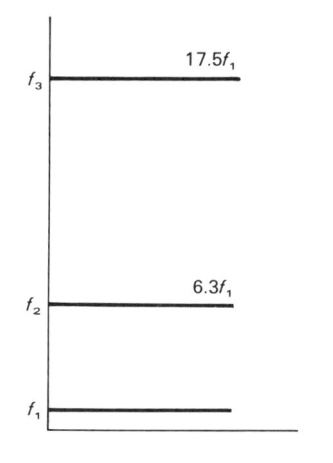

Vibrating rods

A more mundane example but one of great practical significance is the stationary wave pattern set up by shear waves on chains, rods, and blades fixed at one end. Figure 17-18 shows the first three possible modes of vibration. A shear wave may be set travelling along the rod by sudden displacements of the fixed end such as might occur when the rod is fixed to a piece of vibrating or rotating machinery, or by the free end undergoing a sideways push from an external force. If the source of the wave is periodic then at frequencies f_1, f_2, etc. a violent resonant

Figure 17-18 (a) A vibrating chain supported at one end. (b) shows how the characteristic frequencies of the first three modes are related—the overtones are not harmonics.

17 Mechanical waves

condition will result. This is a cause of considerable difficulty in the design of turbine and compressor blades for jet engines where the periodic impulses are related to the speed of rotation of the shaft. The resonant frequencies will differ from blade to blade and will not necessarily be those shown in figure 17-18b. Similarly steel chimney stacks can be set oscillating by steady winds, the eddies from the wind passing the chimney acting as periodic external forces. To prevent large-amplitude, and sometimes destructive, oscillations building up a designer tries to decrease the Q of the vibrating blade, that is to increase the energy per cycle which is dissipated as internal energy in the structure and its surroundings. Thus the optimum material for a compressor blade will have (among many other properties) high vibration damping (a sort of internal sogginess), a property possessed by resin-bonded carbon fibre material. With a steel chimney the designer will try to remove the cause of the vibration by discouraging the formation of eddies. One way of doing this is to fit *strakes* to the chimney; these consist of helical fins (like a helter-skelter at a fair) wound around the top of the chimney.

A set of metal blades of different lengths and/or mass per unit length all fixed to the same base and arranged so that their fundamental frequencies of vibration form a continuous series of whole numbers is called a *vibrating reed tachometer*. If the base is forced to oscillate with a small amplitude the frequency of the oscillation can be measured by noting which blade is set into a resonant vibration. More important than this is the property of the instrument that if a complex periodic vibration is fed to the base then the tachometer unscrambles the vibration and blades corresponding to the component sinusoidal vibrations are set into motion. The device can further be used to indicate the relative amplitudes of the components. It is truly a vibration spectrometer. (See also page 290 for a note on Fourier analysis.)

trolley system which is free at both ends. Thus for a deep tank, 2 m long, the fundamental mode will have a wavelength of 4 m and will thus be produced by waves of speed

$$c \left(= \sqrt{\frac{g\lambda}{2\pi}} \right) = \sqrt{\frac{10 \, \text{m s}^{-2} \times 4 \, \text{m}}{2\pi}} \quad [17\text{-}10]$$

$$= 2.5 \, \text{m s}^{-1}.$$

The period of these waves, T, and thus the period of oscillation of the water, is given by

$$T = \frac{\lambda}{c}$$

$$= \frac{4 \, \text{m}}{2.5 \, \text{m s}^{-1}}$$

$$= 1.6 \, \text{s},$$

and to produce the sloshing the tank should be pushed and pulled at this time interval. The reader should try similar calculations for any available tank or pan remembering that

$$c = \sqrt{(gh)} \quad [17\text{-}9]$$

if the depth of the water is less than half a wavelength. The higher-frequency sloshes will be readily noticed (and they are harmonic, that is of frequencies which are integral multiples of the fundamental frequency) but tend to be quickly damped and die away.

Very large-scale sloshes can take place in lakes. The fundamental mode is called a *seiche* (pronouced saysh). A wind or, for large lakes, a local difference of atmospheric pressure, initiates the motion and the fundamental mode, which will have a period of about a minute for a small lake, gives the impression of a tide. The seiche on Lake Geneva (60 km long and about 150 m deep) is particularly impressive, having a period of just more than one hour.

Sloshes

We all know the verb to *slosh*—bath water can be made to do it and the near impossibility of preventing water held in a shallow tray from sloshing over the edge will be well known to anyone who has, for instance, tried to carry a full ripple tank from a laboratory bench to a sink. A slosh is a noun we shall use to describe a resonant mode of vibration of a vessel of liquid. If the water in a large rectangular tank is made to slosh by producing waves parallel to one side, the stationary modes are very similar to those which can be demonstrated by a spring–

Chladni vibrations

The stationary wave patterns produced with two-dimensional transverse waves on plates and membranes were first investigated by E. F. F. Chladni in 1878. The vibration of circular discs and membranes is widely relevant in the design of circularly symmetrical parts in rotating machinery. Figure 17-19 shows a classic experimental investigation, the sand settling along the nodes—the places of zero displacement in the stationary wave pattern. To investigate the patterns on circular plates we can use a circular stretched rubber membrane.

17-8 Vibrating bodies

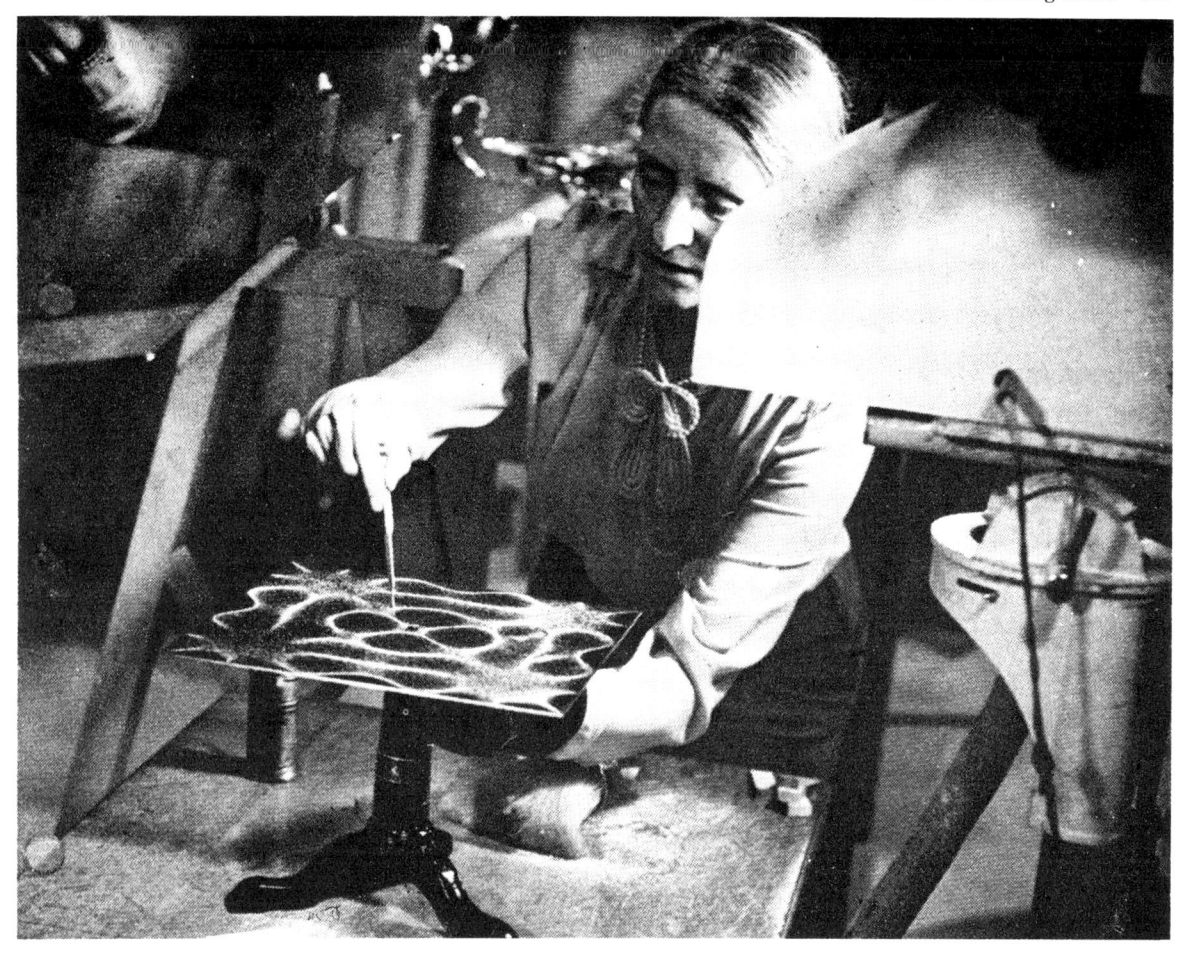

Figure 17-19 Miss Mary Waller producing Chladni figures using dry sand on an iron plate. She is touching the underside of the plate with a piece of solid carbon dioxide. The demonstration formed part of a television broadcast on 11 November 1937.

Figure 17-20 shows such a membrane clamped all round its periphery and vibrating in four of its simpler modes. The driving force can conveniently be a large loudspeaker placed under the sheet and connected to a signal generator. If the sheet is illuminated stroboscopically the pulsating sheet can be closely examined. The difference between this sheet and a plate vibrating in a circular mode is that the clamping of the plate is different from that of the sheet. This alters the relation between the resonant frequencies but does not prevent the principles being demonstrated. Incidentally, the rubber sheet can be replaced with a stable soap film and the circular frame oscillated manually. There are no simple relationships between the resonant frequencies found in Chladni vibrations.

Tuning forks

All vibrating bodies communicate their vibration to the air around them and the next chapter deals with this phenomenon of *sound*. One common sound source is the *tuning fork* and we end this chapter by considering its fundamental vibrating mode. A tuning fork is essentially a rod which is free to oscillate without constraint in a

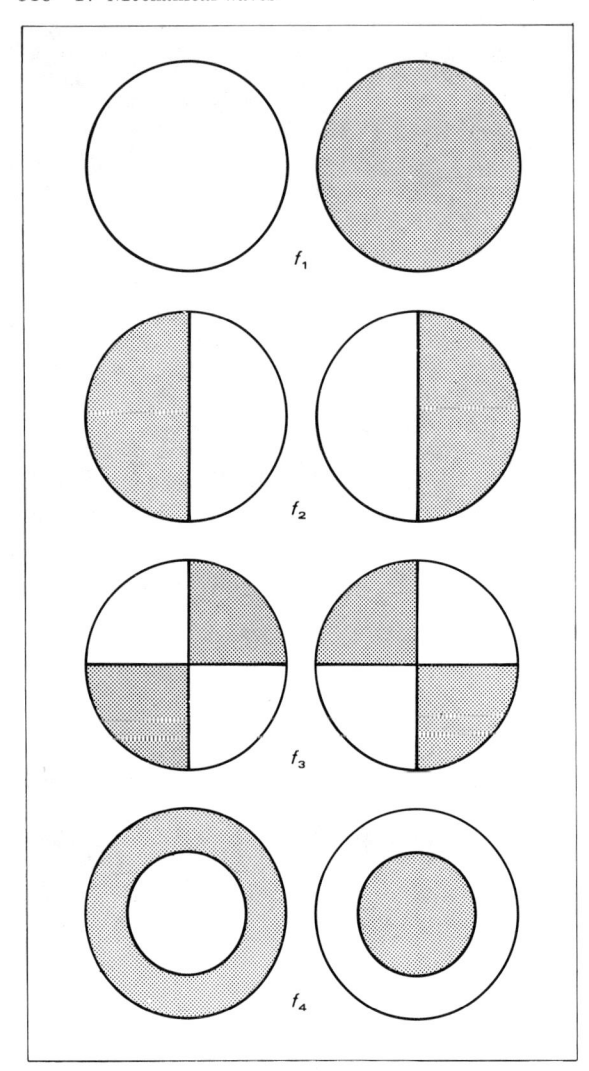

Figure 17-20 Nodal patterns for the first four transverse vibrational modes of a circular membrane clamped at its edge. The shaded areas represent zones which are in phase; the unshaded areas are in antiphase.

transverse mode—see figure 17-21a. As the ends of the rod are bent round into the familiar tuning fork shape the fundamental mode becomes like (c) and this is the only mode in which the fork can vibrate when it is struck near one end—there is a complete absence of overtones. The base of the tuning fork clearly oscillates up and down when its prongs vibrate from side to side.

17-9 Summary of wave-speed formulae

The following list contains equations from Chapters 16, 17, and 18. The equation numbers at the left of the page refer the reader to their location. The list is not exhaustive.

Transverse waves on a string or spring:

[16-1] $$c_t = \sqrt{\frac{T}{m}}.$$

Longitudinal waves on a spring:

[17-1] $$c_l = \sqrt{\frac{kl}{m}}.$$

Longitudinal waves in solid rods:

[17-3] $$c_l = \sqrt{\frac{E}{\rho}}.$$

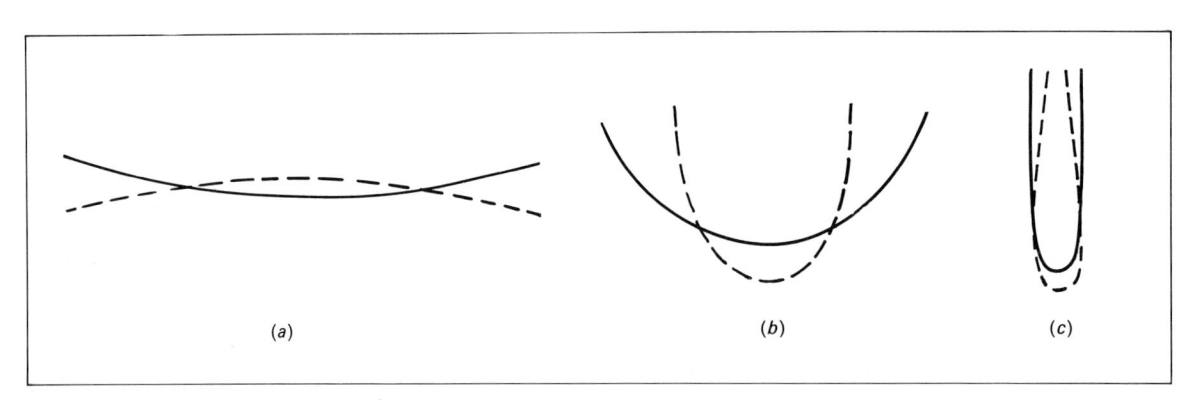

Figure 17-21 A tuning fork as a bent rod.

Longitudinal waves in bulk solid (earthquake P waves):

[17-5] $\quad c_l = \sqrt{\dfrac{M}{\rho}} \quad (M > E)$.

Surface waves on a liquid:

[17-12] $\quad c = \sqrt{\left[\left(\dfrac{g\lambda}{2\pi} + \dfrac{2\pi\gamma}{\rho\lambda}\right)\tanh\dfrac{2\pi h}{\lambda}\right]}$.

Shallow water gravity waves:

[17-9] $\quad c = \sqrt{(gh)}$.

Deep water gravity waves:

[17-10] $\quad c_g = \sqrt{\dfrac{g\lambda}{2\pi}}$.

Ripples (in water deep compared to λ):

[17-11] $\quad c_r = \sqrt{\dfrac{2\pi\gamma}{\rho\lambda}}$.

Torsional waves on rods (earthquake S waves):

[17-13] $\quad c = \sqrt{\dfrac{G}{\rho}} \quad (E > G)$.

Longitudinal waves in a fluid:

[18-4] $\quad c = \sqrt{\dfrac{K_{ad}}{\rho}}$.

Sound waves in a gas:

[18-7] [18-8] $\quad c = \sqrt{\dfrac{\gamma p}{\rho}} = \sqrt{\dfrac{\gamma RT}{M}}$.

(Note that γ here does *not* represent surface tension—see page 326.)

In general

[17-4] $\quad c = \sqrt{\dfrac{\text{elastic property}}{\text{inertial property}}}$.

Bibliography

Bascom, W. (1959). 'Ocean waves.' *Scientific American* offprint number 828.

Bernstein, J. (1954). 'Tsunamis.' *Scientific American* offprint number 829.

Bullen, K. E. (1955). 'The interior of the Earth.' *Scientific American* offprint number 804.

Frischmann, W. W. (1973). 'Tall buildings.' Nuffield Advanced Physics, *Physics and the engineer*. Penguin. This article is reprinted from *Science Journal*.

Long, R. E. (1970). 'Seismic waves and the Earth's interior.' *Physics Education*, **5**, page 162.

Oliver, J. (1959). 'Long earthquake waves.' *Scientific American* offprint number 827.

Sproull, R. L. (1962). 'The conduction of heat in solids.' *Scientific American* offprint number 288. This article includes a discussion of phonons.

Barber, N. F. (1969). *Water waves*. Wykeham. A comprehensive study containing both descriptive and mathematical treatments.

Bishop, R. E. D. (1965). *Vibration*. Cambridge University Press. Many and varied vibrating systems are described in this text.

Nuffield Advanced Physics (1971). Teachers' guide, Unit 4 *Waves and oscillations*. Penguin. Part Two deals with mechanical waves, especially longitudinal waves in solids.

Tricker, R. A. R. (1965). *Bores, breakers, waves and wakes*. Mills and Boon. A glorious study of waves on water. The treatment is comprehensive and the text contains many original colour photographs.

Waller, M. D. (1961). *Chladni figures*. Bell.

Wenham, E. J., Dorling, G. W., Snell, J. A. N., and Taylor, B. (1972). *Physics, concepts and models*. Addison–Wesley. Chapter 21 approaches mechanical waves by considering the transmission of energy by a series of coupled oscillators.

Wood, A. (1944). *The physics of music*. Methuen. Chapters 8 and 9 deal with non-stringed musical instruments.

8 mm film loop. 'Drops and splashes.' Ealing Scientific. The perfect use for high speed photography.

8 mm film loop. 'Vibration of a drum.' Ealing Scientific.

8 mm film loop. 'Wind-induced oscillations.' Penguin. This loop explains how structures such as bridges can be set to vibrate by steady winds.

16 mm film. 'Simple waves.' Guild Sound and Vision. The film uses a torsion-bar wave-machine to illustrate wave properties.

17 Mechanical waves

Exercises

Data (to be used unless otherwise directed):
$$g = 10\,\text{m s}^{-2} = 10\,\text{N kg}^{-1}.$$

17-1 Figure 17-22 shows two methods of representing the displacements of particles through which a *longitudinal* wave is passing. A, B, C, etc. are the undisturbed positions of particles $\lambda/8$ apart, and A', B', C', etc. are the disturbed positions. In (b) the length AA' is drawn half the size of AA' in (a). Copy diagrams (a) and (b) and complete (b), but omitting the original positions A, B, C, etc. of the particles.

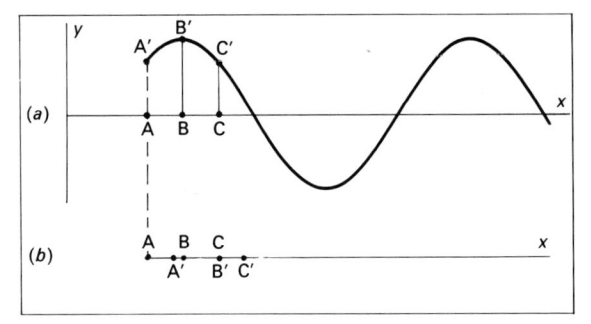

Figure 17-22

17-2 A slinky is stretched to a length of 3.0 m, has a stiffness of $0.20\,\text{N m}^{-1}$, and a mass of 0.45 kg. Assuming its original length is negligible, find the speed of longitudinal waves in the slinky. What are the first three frequencies of vibration which will set up a longitudinal stationary wave in the slinky if
(a) both ends are fixed
(b) one end is fixed but the other end is free
(c) both ends are free? ●

17-3 Consider a lumped-mass spring system (for example railway trucks with spring buffers between them). Use Newton's laws of motion to produce a qualitative description of what happens when a compression pulse travels to one end which is
(a) free   (b) fixed.
Compare your results with the results obtained when a *transverse* pulse is reflected from free and fixed ends of a string.

17-4 Consider a lumped-mass spring system such as the series of trolleys in figure 17-3. Show that the formula $c_1 = \sqrt{(kl/m)}$ (for longitudinal waves along a *non*-lumped system) becomes $c_1 = l_1\sqrt{(k_1/m_1)}$ (where k_1 is the natural length of *one* of the small springs, l_1 is the distance between trolley centres, and m_1 is the mass of one trolley) for a lumped-mass spring system. (*Hint:* if there are n springs and n masses in a length l, $k = k_1/n$ and $l = nl_1$.)

17-5 Refer to Example 17-1. If you are given the additional information that the Young modulus for copper is $1.3 \times 10^{11}\,\text{N m}^{-2}$ and that the atomic spacing in copper $2.6 \times 10^{-10}\,\text{m}$, make another estimate of the value of k_1. (Use the fact that k_1 is related to E by $k_1 = EA/l_1$ and that it would be reasonable to assume that A is roughly equal to l_1^2.) Are you surprised that your two values of k_1 are different? ●

17-6 Repeat the methods of Example 17-1 and Exercise 17-5 for a row of aluminium atoms, using the following data:
  speed of longitudinal waves in aluminium at 293 K = $5.1 \times 10^3\,\text{m s}^{-1}$
  atomic spacing in aluminium = $2.9 \times 10^{-10}\,\text{m}$
  relative molecular mass of aluminium = 27
  Young modulus for aluminium = $7 \times 10^{10}\,\text{N m}^{-2}$. ●

17-7 One way of establishing stationary waves in a gas in a tube is to connect a piston in the tube to a rod as shown in figure 17-23. The rod is clamped at its mid-point, and stroked with a resined cloth, thus creating a longitudinal wave in the rod.
In a particular experiment it is found that the frequency of the fundamental mode of vibration is 1070 Hz. If a brass rod of length 1.50 m is used, what is the speed of longitudinal waves in brass? What value does this give for the Young modulus of brass, if the density of brass is $8.5 \times 10^3\,\text{kg m}^{-3}$? ●

17-8 A sonar beam is used to find the depth of objects below the surface of the sea: a longitudinal wave pulse is reflected from the object and the depth found from a measurement of the time interval and a knowledge of the speed of sound in water. If on a particular occasion the time interval is 0.17 s and the speed of sound in water is $1450\,\text{m s}^{-1}$, how deep is the object reflecting the pulse? Assuming that the density of sea water is $1.02 \times 10^3\,\text{kg m}^{-3}$, find the appropriate modulus of elasticity for sea water. ●

17-9 A wave transmits a power of 5.0 W. Find the power which it can transmit if
(a) its amplitude is doubled, its frequency remaining the same, or
(b) its frequency is doubled, its amplitude remaining the same. ●

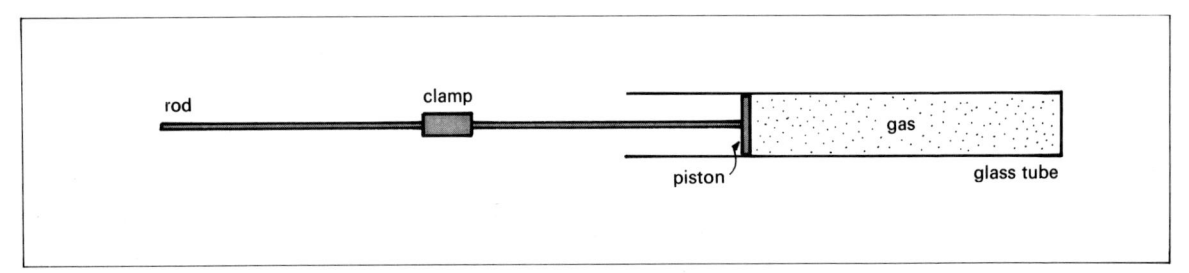

Figure 17-23

17-10 Given that the approximate speed of the secondary seismic waves (which are transverse and therefore rely on the resistance of the material of the Earth's crust to shearing) is 5×10^3 m s^{-1}, and that a rough value for the density of the material of the Earth's crust is 3.5×10^3 kg m^{-3}, estimate the shear modulus of the material of the Earth's crust. ●

17-11 Check the dimensional consistency of the equation $c = \sqrt{[(g\lambda/2\pi + 2\pi\gamma/\lambda\rho)\tanh 2\pi h/\lambda)]}$.

17-12 A man on the side of a stationary ship in deep water sees five complete waves at any one time along the side of the ship. It takes 4.0 s for one wave to pass him: find the wavelength of the waves and hence the length of the ship. ●

17-13 Refer to figure 17-11, where the wave speed is c. Let the circumferential speed of the particles moving in the circles be u: then the crest particles appear to an observer moving with the wave to have a speed of $c-u$, and the trough particles appear to have a speed of $c+u$. Find the kinetic energies of typical crest and trough particles (of mass m) and, by equating the loss of kinetic energy of a trough particle to its gain of potential energy when it becomes a crest particle, derive the expression $c = \sqrt{(g\lambda/2\pi)}$. (Remember that $u = 2\pi r/T$, where r is the radius of the circles in which the particles move, and T is the period, and that $T = 1/f = \lambda/c$.)

17-14 Use the methods of the differential calculus to show that the minimum speed of waves in a *deep* liquid (density ρ, surface tension γ) occurs when $\lambda^2 = 4\pi^2\gamma/g\rho$, and that the minimum speed c_{min} is given by $c_{min} = (4g\gamma/\rho)^{1/4}$. Estimate the value of λ for which the minimum value occurs in water ($\rho = 10^3$ kg m^{-3} and $\gamma = 7 \times 10^{-2}$ N m^{-1}), and estimate c_{min} for water. ●

17-15 Check the dimensional consistency of the two expressions derived in Exercise 17-14.

17-16 Take the equation $c = \sqrt{(g\lambda/2\pi + 2\pi\gamma/\lambda\rho)}$ for deep liquid waves and find the values of c for water ($\rho = 10^3$ kg m^{-3}, $\gamma = 7 \times 10^{-2}$ N m^{-1}) for $\lambda = 10^n$ m where $n = 1, 0, -1, -2, -3$. Sketch a graph of c against λ, and verify your numerical answers to Exercise 17-14.

17-17 Waves break on a seashore at a frequency of 0.35 Hz. Assuming that the original waves in the ocean had the same frequency, find their wavelength and hence their speed in deep water. ●

17-18 Write an essay on tsunamis.

17-19 Find the speed of a tsunami if it is generated by an earthquake on the sea bed when the water is 4×10^4 m deep. ●

17-20 Figure 17-24 is a map of the area around the River Severn where the bore occurs. Given that on a certain day the depths of the river at Framilode and Stone Bench were 1.6 m and 3.6 m respectively, estimate the time taken for the bore to travel from Upper Framilode to Stone Bench, assuming that the height of the bore is small compared with the depth of the river. Is it possible for a motorist to see the same bore at both places?

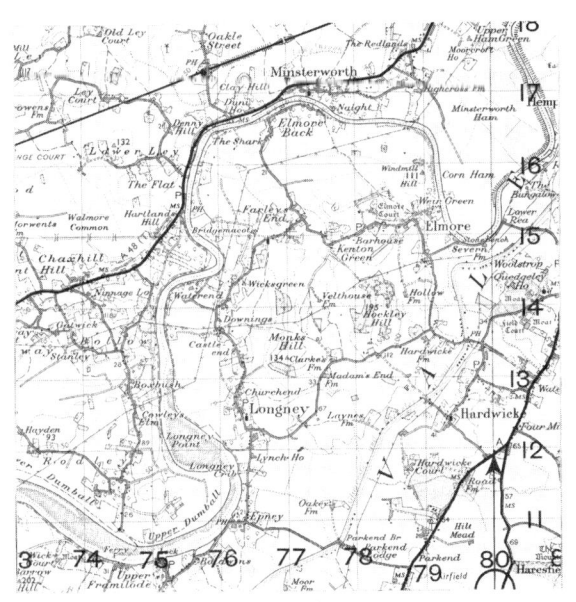

Figure 17-24 A map of the area around the River Severn between Upper Framilode and Stone Bench. The grid lines are 1.0 km apart. *Crown Copyright Reserved.*

17-21 Estimate the gravitational potential energy lost by a wave arriving on a beach, if the height of the wave is 0.50 m, and it is 50 m long. For a typical frequency of arrival, estimate the rate of arrival of energy on a 50 metre length of beach.

17-22 How is surfing possible?

17-23 Make reasonable assumptions as to the quantities on which the period of vibration of a *freely falling* liquid drop depends, and use the method of dimensions to find the form of a possible relationship between the period and these quantities.

17-24 The speed c of waves on a drumskin is given by $c = \sqrt{(T/\sigma)}$, where σ is the surface density (or mass per unit area) of the material of the drumskin. Find the dimensions of T, and hence guess the meaning of this symbol.

17-25 Discover what happens when a body moves through a fluid at a speed higher than that of the speed of waves in the fluid. (The same phenomenon occurs in several different situations.)

17-26 Consider a length of steel wire, bent into a circle and held so that it is horizontal. If it is given a periodic disturbance at some suitable point on its circumference, what modes of stationary wave are possible? The three-dimensional equivalent of this would be a hollow ball with an elastic cover (for example a tennis ball). Suggest one possible stationary wave mode for this type of object.

18 Sound waves

18-1	Waves in a fluid	322	18-6 Vibrating air columns	333
18-2	The speed of sound waves in air	323	18-7 The acoustic spectrum	336
18-3	Sound intensity	326	18-8 Architectural acoustics	337
18-4	The sense of hearing	329	Bibliography	338
18-5	Beats	332	Exercises	339

18-1 Waves in a fluid

What types of wave are possible in the body of a fluid? There *can* be longitudinal waves which require only that the substance should have an elastic property (which implies that it should be springy and compressible). There cannot, however, be transverse waves, since these require that the substance should have a structure in which each molecule is linked to a particular set of neighbouring molecules. The elastic property which enables a fluid to transmit energy in the form of waves must therefore be its bulk modulus K which is defined by the equation

$$\Delta p = -K \frac{\Delta V}{V}. \qquad [18\text{-}1]$$

K thus tells us by what fraction the volume decreases $(-\Delta V/V)$ when the pressure in the fluid increases by Δp. The inertial property possessed by a fluid can be represented as with a solid by its density ρ.

This all tells us that fluids will transmit longitudinal but not transverse mechanical waves. Longitudinal mechanical waves which can be detected by the human ear are called sound waves. It is readily observable that they travel fast but at a finite speed; we note this from echo phenomena and from the interval between receiving the flash and the bang from the starter's gun at an athletics meeting. More remarkably, sound waves of all wavelengths travel at the *same* speed, for if we listen to music coming from a distant source, such as a marching band, we hear the high- and low-frequency notes simultaneously.

To enable us to calculate the speed of a sound wave, let us consider a pipe of uniform cross-sectional area A containing a fluid of uniform density ρ and bulk modulus K at a pressure p (figure 18-1). Suppose a close-fitting piston is pushed steadily in at a speed v and that the wave pulse so formed moves along the tube at a speed c. If the force needed to do this is F and the pressure of the compressed fluid to the right of the piston is $p + \Delta p$ then

$$\Delta p = \frac{F}{A}.$$

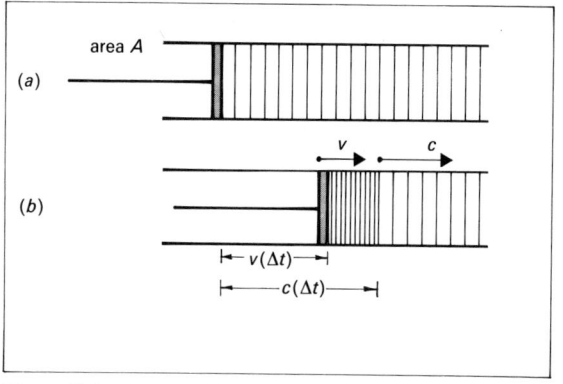

Figure 18-1

Referring to figure 18-1b, we see that for the fluid, initially of volume $A(c\Delta t)$, the decrease in volume in time Δt is $A(v\Delta t)$, that is the fractional change in volume

$$\frac{\Delta V}{V} = -\frac{Av\Delta t}{Ac\Delta t}$$

$$= -\frac{v}{c}$$

and so
$$K = \frac{\Delta p}{-\Delta V/V}$$

$$= \frac{Fc}{Av}. \qquad [18\text{-}2]$$

The gain of momentum of the fluid in time $\Delta t = (c\Delta t A\rho)v$, and so the rate of change of momentum, which by Newton's second law is equal to the accelerating force, is

$$cA\rho v = F. \qquad [18\text{-}3]$$

Eliminating F, A, and v from equations 18-2 and 18-3:

$$\frac{K}{c} = c\rho,$$

and so
$$c^2 = \frac{K}{\rho}$$

or
$$c = \sqrt{\frac{K}{\rho}}. \qquad [18\text{-}4]$$

This expression does not contain v and so if the motion of the piston can be adjusted to produce wave pulses of all shapes, all will travel at this speed c. There is a limiting condition, namely that $v \ll c$, for if this is not so the volume strain $\Delta V/V$ is not small and the bulk modulus K will not be a constant. As c is large (see table 18-1) there is no heat transfer during the passage of the wave and so K represents the adiabatic bulk modulus.

The above proof is for sound waves travelling in one dimension. The result holds, however, in the general (and usual) case of three-dimensional wavefronts. Table 18-1 gives some typical values for the speed of sound in fluids at 273 K.

The mechanism of longitudinal wave propagation in a liquid is different from the mechanism in a gas. In a liquid the molecules, though in a state of random motion, are close to their neighbours. Thus when a compression wave acts on a layer of liquid molecules, such as would be produced by a piston pushed into a tube, the liquid behaves effectively as a solid would, and the immediate interactions between the molecules transmit the wave energy. The same is not true of a gas, for gas molecules have a mean free path $l \approx 10^{-7}$ m, that is a gas molecule travels, on

Fluid	Speed/m s^{-1}
carbon dioxide	260
air	330
helium	970
distilled water	1 400
sea water	1 450

Table 18-1 The speed of sound waves at 273 K. The pressure is not relevant.

average, a distance l between collisions. (The diameter of a molecule $\approx 10^{-10}$ m.) This means that the gas molecule spends most of the time in free motion between collisions at an average speed v_{av} of about 5×10^2 m s^{-1} for typical gases at s.t.p. It is of course only *during* a collision (of which it makes about 10^{10} s^{-1}) that the molecule interacts with other molecules. When a gas is compressed the molecules are crowded together and in this higher-density, higher-pressure, situation a number of molecules will move to places of lower density and pressure. They will presumably do this at speeds of about 500 m s^{-1}. The process will continue and so a pulse of higher density and higher pressure will travel through the gas at a wave speed c which we should expect to be the same as v_{av}. In fact $c \approx 0.6 v_{av}$ which is in satisfying close agreement with what we expected. There appears to be a net transfer of molecules away from the source in the above discussion. This is what happens when there is a single compressional wave pulse (see figure 18-1), but for a periodic wave there is no such net movement. The oscillatory motion of, for example a piston, enables molecules to return to areas of rarefaction.

A sound wave in a gas can thus be thought of as a series of periodic variations in the density and pressure of the gas superimposed on the random motion of the gas molecules.

That the above argument cannot hold when the source moves with a speed greater than v_{av} is obvious. There will be a piling up of the molecules around the moving source and a *shock wave* (see Section 19-8) will be formed. The term shock wave is unfortunate as it is not a wave at all.

18-2 The speed of sound waves in air

Table 18-1 gives the speed of sound in air at 273 K as 330 m s^{-1}. To determine this value many methods are available. Some are direct length-divided-by-time determinations and some involve an indirect frequency-times-wavelength approach. Further, the speed of sound in the open air is greater than the speed of sound in a pipe. A historical study of measurements of the speed of sound in air could well be used to illustrate the improvement in experimental technique and the improvement in the accuracy and sensitivity of apparatus over the last 250 years. Faced with so many possibilities we shall describe only one direct and one indirect method, each in free air. Some other methods are suggested by Exercises 18-3 and 18-20, while other indirect methods will arise from the material considered in Sections 18-5 and 19-5.

Firstly a simple direct method involving no complex apparatus but capable of giving c to about 10 per cent, that is to $\pm 30 \text{ m s}^{-1}$. On an open field one experimenter at a point P produces a regular series of sharp claps, for example by striking two wooden blocks together in time with a metronome. A second experimenter at P measures the interval between claps with a stopclock or stopwatch (it is best not to trust any metronome calibrations without a check). A third experimenter, the observer, walks away from P across the field. As he does so he will notice that he sees the blocks being clapped before he hears the sound of the clap. Eventually he reaches a point where he sees one clap and hears the previous clap *simultaneously*. If he is now a distance l from P then the time Δt taken for the sound to travel from P to him must be equal to the metronome interval measured at P.

Thus $$c = \frac{l}{\Delta t}.$$

If $\Delta t \approx 0.5 \text{ s}$ then l will be $\approx 160 \text{ m}$. The method is not very precise but it is simple. If a metronome is not available then a simple pendulum can be used as a regulator.

Secondly we describe an indirect method which aims to measure λ for a periodic sound wave. Figure 18-2 shows the arrangement of the apparatus. A signal generator has its low-impedance output connected to a loudspeaker and its high-impedance output to the X-plates of a c.r.o. which has its timebase switched off. A microphone placed two or three metres away from the speaker picks up the sound and, after any necessary amplification, is connected to the Y-plates of the oscilloscope. The two signals at the X- and Y-inputs of the c.r.o. are bound to be *coherent*, that is they will have a constant phase relation at different times for a given distance between the speaker and the microphone. This means that the oscilloscope trace will

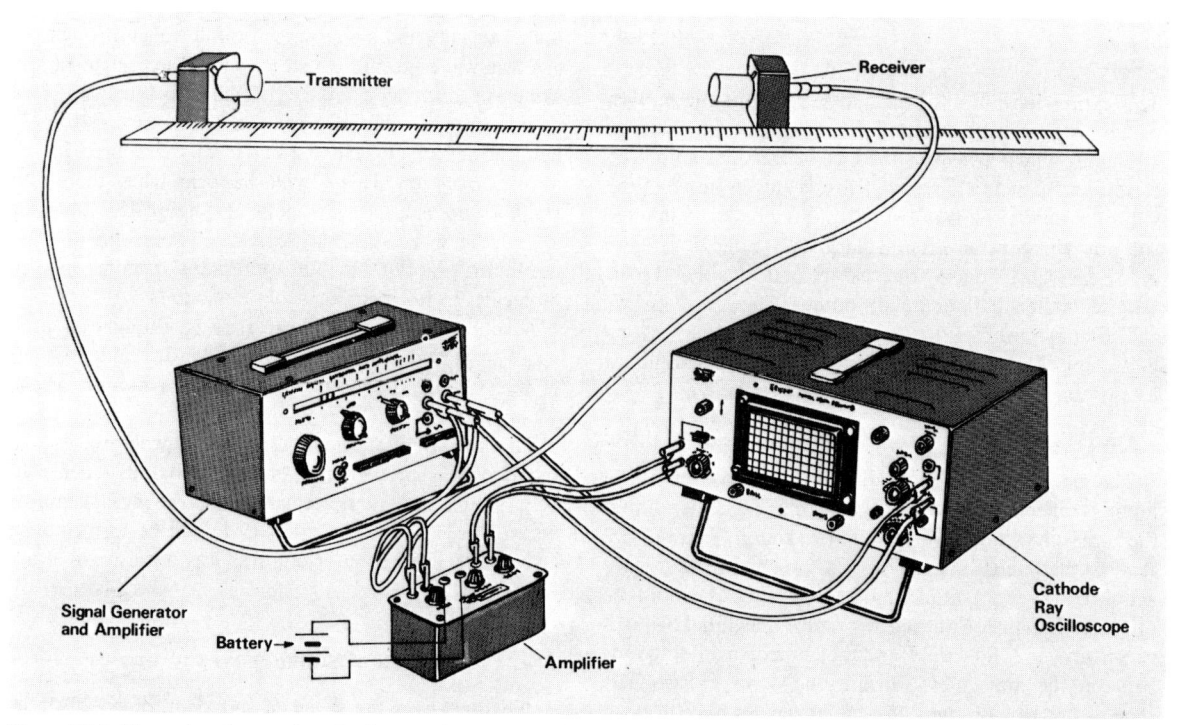

Figure 18-2 Measuring the wavelength of a sound wave. The distance between the speaker and the microphone can be varied.

18-2 The speed of sound waves in air

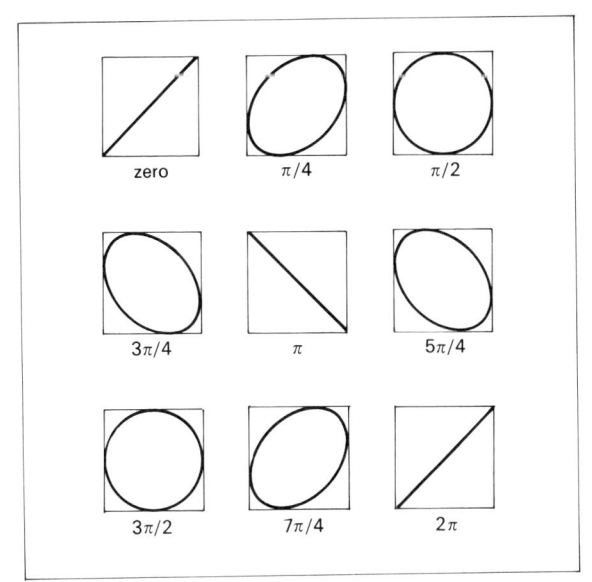

Figure 18-3 A Lissajous figure sequence for two simple harmonic motions of equal frequency and of the phase difference given.

remain stationary in or near one of the forms shown in figure 18-3 if the signal generator is providing a simple harmonic wave form. Such a trace is called a *Lissajous figure*. If the loudspeaker is now moved directly away from the microphone the phase difference between the signals will alter, but if the loudspeaker is moved a distance λ the pattern on the c.r.o. screen will go through all the positions shown in figure 18-3 and return to its initial position: this corresponds to a total phase change of 2π rad. To measure λ we therefore move the loudspeaker directly away from the microphone until the c.r.o. trace pulses through n complete cycles of 2π rad. If this distance is x,

$$x = n\lambda.$$

If x is of the order of 1 m then λ is being measured to about a half of one per cent, because moving the speaker by ± 1 mm is enough to create or destroy a straight-line trace: the measurement is precise. To find the speed of sound, c, we now use $c = f\lambda$, where f is the frequency of the signal generator.

The probable error in c depends largely on how reliable are the signal generator's calibrations. We can do one of the following (in order of increasing difficulty and reliability):

(*i*) assume that they are correct
(*ii*) compare the reading at 50 Hz with the frequency of the mains supply
(*iii*) compare the calibrations with those of another signal generator (they are unlikely to be wrong in exactly the same way)
(*iv*) compare the reading at f_s with a standard tuning fork.

For methods (*ii*), (*iii*), and (*iv*) the comparison is best made by producing the Lissajous figures of figure 18-3, while for (*ii*) and (*iv*) more complex Lissajous figures* enable the calibrations to be tested at values $50n$ Hz or nf_s respectively. Overall the value found for c should be better than 1 per cent at any given frequency.

If, moreover, a graph of f against $1/\lambda$ is plotted for a wide range of frequencies (and this is quickly done with this apparatus) then a straight line results. This shows that sound waves, in the range of audio-frequencies, do *not* disperse, that is sound waves of all frequencies travel at the same speed. By measuring the slope of this straight line, c can be found to ± 1 m s^{-1} in free air in the laboratory.

Qualitative investigations of the effects of temperature and of the presence of gases other than air can be made simply by warming the air between the speaker and microphone or by blowing some other gas into the space without moving either. The direction of drift of the c.r.o. trace can be interpreted as an increase or a decrease in λ and thus of c.

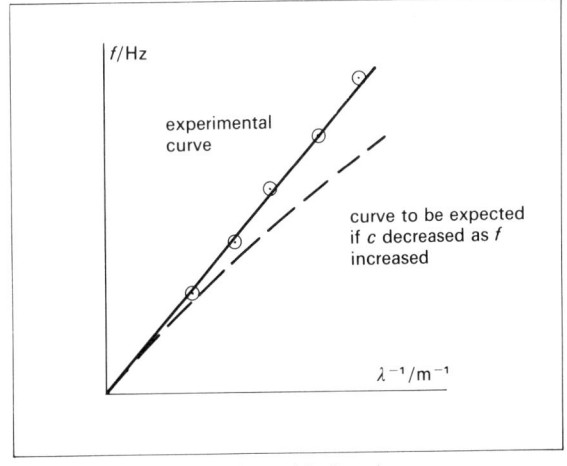

Figure 18-4 The speed of sound in free air.

---

*See for example Bennet, G. A. G. (1968). *Electricity and modern physics: m.k.s. version*. Arnold.

18 Sound waves

▶ **Example 18-1** An experiment similar to that shown in figure 18-2 is performed. On the first occasion the microphone has to be moved 3.00 m nearer the speaker to reproduce the same straight-line trace on the c.r.o. as before. The air between the speaker and the microphone is then enclosed in a pipe and it is found that the trace on the c.r.o. is no longer a straight line: the microphone must be moved 50 mm nearer the speaker to reproduce the straight-line trace. If the frequency of the signal generator is 110 Hz, what are the speeds of sound in air (at that temperature) when the air is (a) free (b) enclosed in this particular pipe?

The fact that the speaker must be moved a distance of 3.00 m to produce the same trace indicates that the wavelength $\lambda = 3.00$ m. Since the frequency $f = 110$ Hz, the speed of sound in air in these conditions

$$= (110 \text{ Hz})(3.00 \text{ m}) = 330 \text{ m s}^{-1}.$$

On the second occasion the wavelength is reduced by 50 mm, so that the speed of sound in the pipe is

$$(110 \text{ Hz})(2.95 \text{ m}) = 325 \text{ m s}^{-1},$$

less than the speed in free air. ◀

We can show theoretically how c should vary for various gases and for various conditions of temperature and pressure. We shall need

[18-4] $$c = \sqrt{\frac{K}{\rho}},$$

[18-1] $$K = \frac{\Delta p}{-\Delta V/V} = -V \frac{dp}{dV}$$

and, for an ideal gas

$$pV = \frac{m}{M} RT, \quad [18\text{-}5]$$

where m is the mass of the gas, V its volume, M the molar mass, R the gas constant, and T the kelvin temperature.

When sound waves produce pressure variations in a gas the process is adiabatic; the temperature T is not constant but

$$pV^\gamma = \text{constant} \quad [18\text{-}6]$$

γ being a dimensionless constant for a given gas. Differentiating with respect to V we get

$$V^\gamma \frac{dp}{dV} + \gamma V^{\gamma-1} p = 0$$

or

$$-V \frac{dp}{dV} = \gamma p,$$

that is

$$K_{\text{ad}} = \gamma p.$$

Thus

$$c = \sqrt{\frac{\gamma p}{\rho}} \quad [18\text{-}7]$$

but

$$\frac{p}{\rho} = \frac{pV}{m} = \frac{RT}{M}$$

from equation 18-5, and so

$$c = \sqrt{\frac{\gamma RT}{M}}. \quad [18\text{-}8]$$

This equation tells us that c

(i) does *not* depend on the pressure of the gas ($c = \sqrt{(\gamma p/\rho)}$ would suggest that it does but of course if p changes, so does ρ in proportion)

(ii) depends on the kelvin temperature in that $c \propto \sqrt{T}$, and

(iii) depends on the nature of the gas in that $c \propto \sqrt{(\gamma/M)}$.

These quantitative conclusions can be used to explain various observed phenomena; see Exercises 18-5 and 18-6.

Table 18-1 on page 323 gives the speed of sound in distilled water and sea water. The latter quantity was important when sonar was used for depth sounding at sea. The speed of sound in water increases by about 3 m s^{-1} for a 1 K rise in the water temperature and is also found to increase slightly with depth. Both increases can be attributed to the fact that the value of K for water changes more rapidly than its density ρ. The speed of sound in liquids drops considerably if the liquid is in a trough or tube, relatively much more than for gases.

18-3 Sound intensity

The intensity I of a wave is defined by the equation

$$I = \frac{P_{\text{av}}}{A} = \frac{E}{At} \quad [18\text{-}9]$$

where E is the energy crossing an area A perpendicular to the direction of wave propagation in time t. In Section 17-4 this was shown to be related to the properties of a mechanical wave by the equation

[17-7] $$I = 2\pi^2 c\rho f^2 y_0^2, \quad [18\text{-}10]$$

the symbols having their usual meanings. It is not easy to find the value of I by measuring each of the quantities on the right of this equation because we know nothing of y_0. We can set up a stationary wave in a pipe (see Section 18-6) and observe through a microscope the oscillations of smoke or dust particles in the air at one of the antinodes.

The order of magnitude of the amplitude of these oscillations is 0.01 mm at 300 Hz for a very loud sound (a sound at the threshold of feeling) and this amplitude is found to be independent of the size of the particles involved. In this case the displacement amplitude of a progressive sound wave is not being measured directly but it is quite reasonable to say that for a *very* loud sound $y_0 \approx 10^{-5}$ m. Substituting this value and the values of the other quantities into equation 17-7 we get

$$I = 2\pi^2 \times 330 \, \text{m s}^{-1} \times 1.3 \, \text{kg m}^{-3}$$
$$\times (300 \, \text{s}^{-1})^2 \times (10^{-5} \, \text{m})^2$$
$$= 0.08 \, \text{kg s}^{-3} = 0.08 \, \text{W m}^{-2}$$

that is $\quad I \approx 10^{-1} \, \text{W m}^{-2}$

which is close to the *loudest* sound which the ear can tolerate at this frequency. The intensity of the *smallest* sound which the ear can detect is $\approx 10^{-13} \, \text{W m}^{-2}$ at a frequency of about 3500 Hz, and this corresponds to a displacement amplitude $y_0 < 10^{-11}$ m (less than the diameter of a typical atom). See page 330 for further discussion of the range of audibility for normal ears.

The ear in responding to such small displacements acts not as a detector of the displacements themselves but as a detector of the pressure variations which accompany them. On page 323 the local variation of density and pressure as the number of molecules per unit volume varies was seen to be a necessary part of the propagation of a sound wave in a gas. Suppose the fluid is initially at a pressure p, and let us consider a layer of thickness Δx and cross section A. Suppose it is compressed by a length Δy, and that the new pressure is $p + \Delta p$. If K is the (adiabatic) bulk modulus then, then referring to figure 18-5b,

[18-1] $\quad \Delta p = -K \dfrac{\Delta V}{V} = -K \dfrac{(-A\Delta y)}{A \Delta x}$,

that is $\quad \Delta p = K \dfrac{\Delta y}{\Delta x}$

or in calculus notation

$$\Delta p = K \dfrac{dy}{dx}.$$

As for a progressive wave the displacement

[16-5] $\quad y = y_0 \sin 2\pi \left(\dfrac{x}{\lambda} - \dfrac{t}{T} \right)$,

then differentiating with respect to x gives

$$\dfrac{dy}{dx} = \dfrac{2\pi}{\lambda} y_0 \cos 2\pi \left(\dfrac{x}{\lambda} - \dfrac{t}{T} \right)$$

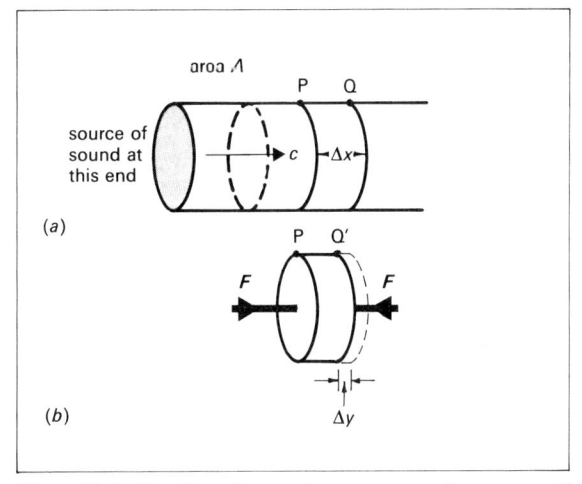

Figure 18-5 The effect of a sound wave compression on a small column of fluid PQ.

whence $\quad \Delta p = K \left(\dfrac{2\pi y_0}{\lambda} \right) \cos 2\pi \left(\dfrac{x}{\lambda} - \dfrac{t}{T} \right).$

Substituting for K from $c^2 = K/\rho$ where ρ is the mean density, we get

$$\Delta p = \left(\dfrac{2\pi y_0}{\lambda} \right) \rho c^2 \cos 2\pi \left(\dfrac{x}{\lambda} - \dfrac{t}{T} \right)$$
$$= \Delta p_0 \cos 2\pi \left(\dfrac{x}{\lambda} - \dfrac{t}{T} \right), \qquad [18\text{-}11]$$

where we write

$$\Delta p_0 = \left(\dfrac{2\pi y_0}{\lambda} \right) \rho c^2. \qquad [18\text{-}12]$$

Δp_0 is called the *pressure amplitude*, or the acoustic pressure amplitude. Thus a sound wave can be considered as a wave of displacement

$$y = y_0 \sin 2\pi \left(\dfrac{x}{\lambda} - \dfrac{t}{T} \right)$$

or as a pressure wave,

$$\Delta p = \Delta p_0 \cos 2\pi \left(\dfrac{x}{\lambda} - \dfrac{t}{T} \right).$$

Notice that the pressure wave is $\pi/2$ rad out of phase with the wave of displacement. Thus at places where the displacement is a maximum the excess or acoustic pressure is zero (that is the pressure is atmospheric) and where the excess pressure is a maximum the displacement is zero,

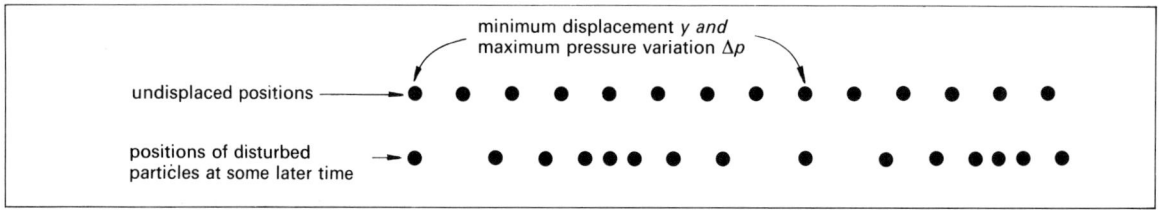

Figure 18-6 Positions of maximum Δp correspond to positions of minimum y during the passage of a longitudinal wave.

and so on (see figure 18-6). This result is of considerable importance as the detectable property of sound waves in air is usually Δp rather than y. These results are shown graphically in figures 18-7a and 18-7b. A graph of the excess density $\Delta \rho$ against x or t would have the same phase as the graph of Δp, that is

$$\Delta \rho = \Delta \rho_0 \cos 2\pi \left(\frac{x}{\lambda} - \frac{t}{T} \right) \qquad [18\text{-}13]$$

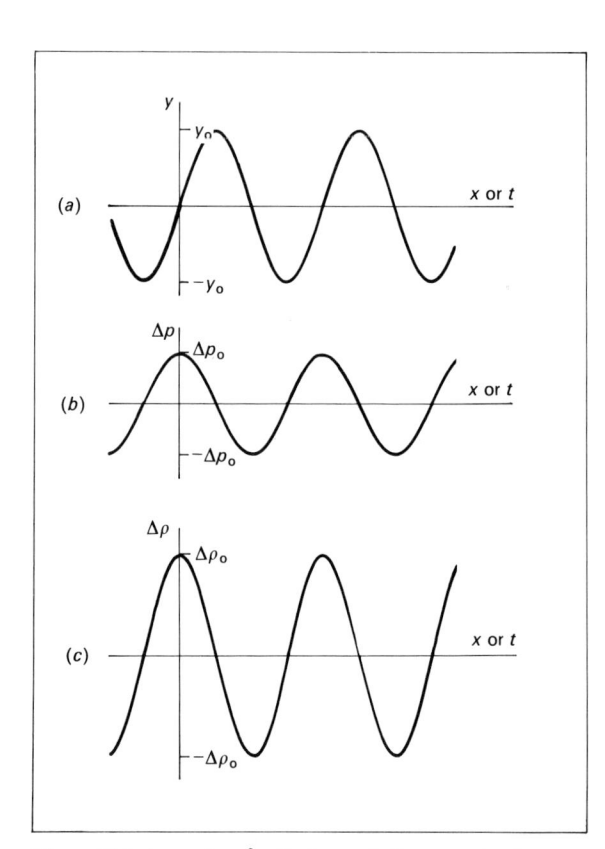

as shown in figure 18-7c.

Figure 18-7 $\Delta p_0 = 2\pi \rho c^2 y_0 / \lambda$ where ρ is the mean density.

Returning to the intensity of the wave and substituting for y_0 in terms of Δp_0, we have

$$[18\text{-}10] \quad I = 2\pi^2 c \rho f^2 y_0^2 = 2\pi c \rho f^2 \left(\frac{\lambda \Delta p_0}{2\pi \rho c^2} \right)^2$$

or as $c = f\lambda$

$$I = \frac{(\Delta p_0)^2}{2c\rho}. \qquad [18\text{-}14]$$

Note that in this expression I is *independent* of the frequency of the wave and depends only on Δp_0, whereas in equation 18-10 I depends on both f and y_0. For a very loud sound $I \approx 10^{-1}$ W m^{-2} and so in air

$$(\Delta p_0)^2 = 10^{-1} \text{ W m}^{-2} \times 2 \times 340 \text{ m s}^{-1} \times 1.3 \text{ kg m}^{-3}$$

and $\qquad \Delta p_0 \approx 10 \text{ N m}^{-2}$,

which is still only a tiny fraction of atmospheric pressure, $p_A = 10^5$ N m^{-2}. Figure 18-8 on page 329 gives more information about the ear.

The pressure variations produced by sound waves in air are (although small) readily detectable using different types of microphone which convert variations of pressure over the surface of a membrane or diaphragm into variations of electric potential difference. The sensitive surface of the microphone is forced to execute periodic oscillations by the incident wave, the amplitude of the forced oscillation being independent of the orientation of the surface with respect to the wave, for air pressure is a scalar quantity. The oscillating microphone surface may

(a) alter the resistance of a body of carbon granules as in a carbon microphone, or

(b) alter the capacitance of a parallel-plate capacitor as in an electrostatic microphone, or

(c) produce an induced e.m.f. by causing a relative motion between a coil and a magnetic field as in a moving-coil microphone.

In each case the oscillating electric potential difference produced may have to be amplified before being fed to a loudspeaker or a c.r.o. The trace on a c.r.o. is, if there is no distortion from the microphone or the amplifying system, a graph of excess pressure (acoustic pressure) against time for the sound wave incident on the microphone.

Source	Maximum total power/W
Orchestra (75 performers)	70
Clarinet	5×10^{-2}
Average speech	3×10^{-5}

Table 18-2 The energy radiated as sound is a tiny fraction of the listed energy used to produce the sound. The human voice is one of the most efficient transformers, yet 99 per cent of its energy becomes internal energy and only 1 per cent radiated sound.

18-4 The sense of hearing

The ear–brain system is a most remarkable device in that we can listen to an orchestral concert coming from the single loudspeaker of a radio and yet hear all the individual instruments of that orchestra. Contrast the eye–brain system which uses light waves. A single ear does not, however, distinguish the direction from which a sound comes, as an eye does. To judge the direction of a sound source we need to have the use of both ears.

(a) At high frequencies we use the fact that the sound from a source will have different intensities at the two ears unless the source lies directly in front or behind the head. This method works at high frequencies as there is then only a little diffraction round the head—see Section 19-4.

(b) At low frequencies we use the fact that a wave will arrive at one ear before the other unless it lies directly in front or behind. The time difference may be as great as 600 μs for a source at one side of the head, and the brain can detect differences as small as 30 μs.

Returning to the first point the eye–brain system acts as a sort of acoustic spectrometer in a manner similar to the behaviour of the tachometer mentioned on page 316.

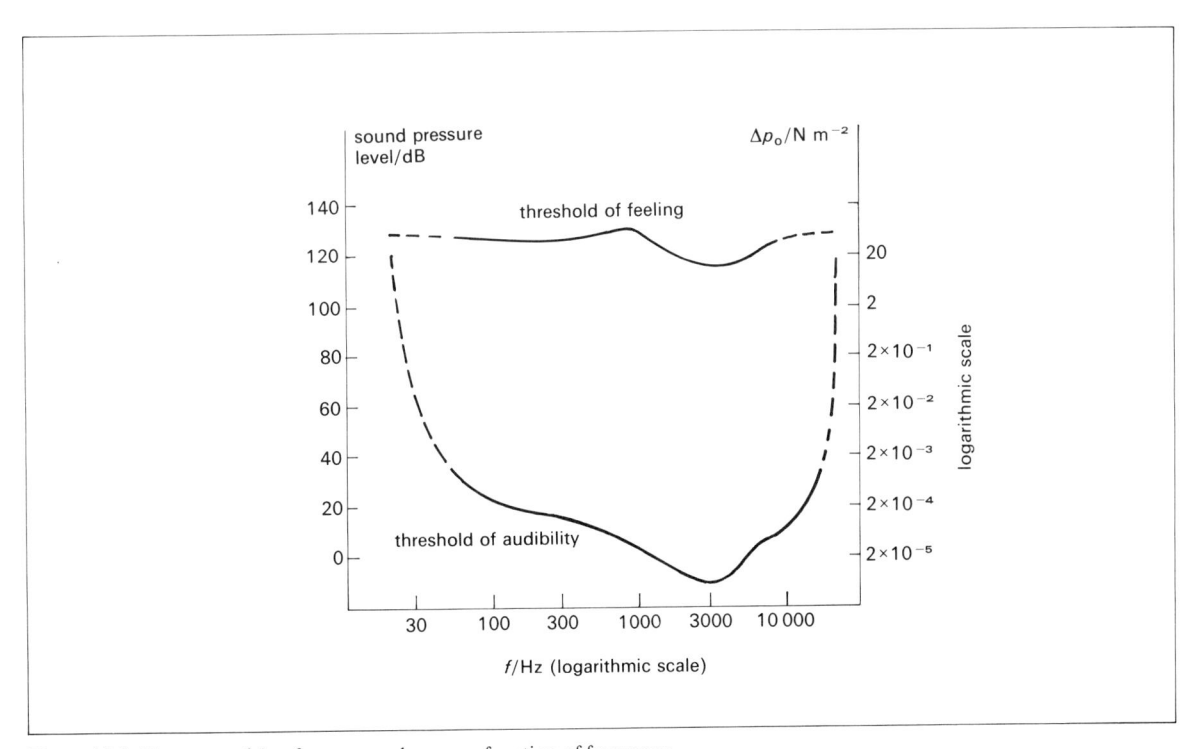

Figure 18-8 The range of Δp_0 for a normal ear as a function of frequency.

Further, if for example only two periodic sounds of frequencies f and $2f$ are present the ear–brain not only detects these frequencies but fortunately registers the notes without reference to the phase relation between them. This produces an enormous simplification in the sound vocabulary we need to learn. The reader can consider this concept by working through Exercise 18-15.

The ear–brain system is also a microphone-display system. The ear responds to pressure waves over a range of frequency from about 20 Hz to about 20 000 Hz (the maximum falling with age) and is most sensitive in the range 2 kHz to 5 kHz. The overall frequency range represents almost 10 octaves since $20\,000\,\text{Hz} \approx 2^{10} \times 20\,\text{Hz}$ (20 Hz to 40 Hz represents an octave, 40 Hz to 80 Hz the next octave, and so on). The ear responds to pressure waves over (see figure 18-8) a range of excess-pressure amplitudes from a maximum of $50\,\text{N m}^{-2}$, over a wide range of low frequencies, down to about $10^{-5}\,\text{N m}^{-2}$ at 3000 Hz. The greatest value of the ratio $(\max I)/(\min I)$ at one frequency $\approx 10^{12}$, and the corresponding ratio for sound-pressure amplitudes is $\approx 10^6$. A simple way of measuring this range of I at any frequency is, treating a loudspeaker as a point source, to use the inverse square law. The observer stands (say) 2 m from a speaker arranged to give him a painful sound sensation. He then moves back to just over 6 m $[(6\text{m}/2\text{m})^2 \approx 10]$, judges the sound intensity there, and then as he moves back to 2 m reduces the volume control on the speaker to maintain that intensity. Repeating the process reduces the intensity by a factor of 10 each time and this is continued until he cannot detect the sound at all. In figure 18-8 the upper line shows the *threshold of feeling*, and the lower line shows the *threshold of audibility*.

▶ **Example 18-2** Use the graph of figure 18-8 to find the greatest tolerable sound intensity and the frequency at which it occurs. Hence find the corresponding displacement amplitude. Assume that air has a density of 1.3 kg m^{-3} and that the speed of sound in air is 340 m s^{-1}.

We can estimate from the graph (remembering that the scales are logarithmic) that the greatest tolerable excess pressure is about $40\,\text{N m}^{-2}$ and that this occurs at a frequency of about 750 Hz. Equation 18-14 gives

$$I = \frac{(\Delta p_0)^2}{2c\rho}$$

$$= \frac{(40\,\text{N m}^{-2})^2}{2 \times 340\,\text{m s}^{-1} \times 1.3\,\text{kg m}^{-3}}$$

$$= 1.8\,\text{W m}^{-2}.$$

To find the displacement amplitude we eliminate I between equations 18-10 and 18-14, whence

$$y_0 = \frac{\Delta p_0}{2\pi f \rho c} \qquad [18\text{-}15]$$

$$= \frac{40\,\text{N m}^{-2}}{2\pi \times 750\,\text{Hz} \times 1.3\,\text{kg m}^{-3} \times 340\,\text{m s}^{-1}}$$

$$= 1.9 \times 10^{-5}\,\text{m}. \qquad \blacktriangleleft$$

Loudness

When we come to consider the relation between loudness (a subjective measure) and intensity (a defined quantity) we must take account of the fact that although a large orchestra is clearly louder than a single clarinet it is not (see table 18-2) 1400 times louder. In order to establish a scale of loudness we need some standard or reference level and a method of defining how much louder a sound is than the chosen standard.

The ear is part of the nervous system and it is found that there is a particular relationship between the intensity of a stimulus to any part of the nervous system and resulting physiological sensation. Consider the following experiment. One person places a hand on a table and rests a book of weight W on his hand. Then a second person gently places extra masses on the book and the first person (without looking) notes the least extra weight ΔW which can be reliably detected as a pressure sensation—the least weight for which he can say 'this is heavier'. Now the experiment is repeated with a heavier book. A series of such very simple experiments suggest that the least detectable extra weight is proportional to the initial weight of the book. If we quantify the least perceptible increase in feeling as ΔF then

$$\Delta F \propto \frac{\Delta W}{W}$$

or

$$\Delta F = k\frac{\Delta W}{W}$$

where k is a constant. This is mathematically equivalent to the statement

$$F = k\ln\left(\frac{W}{W_0}\right)$$

where W_0 is an (arbitrarily) agreed standard weight,

or

$$F = k'\log_{10}\left(\frac{W}{W_0}\right), \qquad [18\text{-}16]$$

and is called the *Weber–Fechner law*. For sound the stimulus is that provided by a sound wave, so our ear measures sound intensity on a logarithmic scale.

For two sounds of intensities I_1 and I_2 of the same frequency we can therefore say that a useful measure of the second is that it has a subjective intensity which is $\log_{10}(I_2/I_1)$ above that of the first. As measurement of intensity is seldom as convenient as measurement of excess pressure amplitude it is common to express

$$\log_{10}\frac{I_2}{I_1} = \log_{10}\frac{(\Delta p_2)^2}{(\Delta p_1)^2} = 2\log_{10}\frac{\Delta p_2}{\Delta p_1}.$$

For example if $\Delta p_2 = 10^{-1}\,\mathrm{N\,m^{-2}}$ and $\Delta p_1 = 10^{-3}\,\mathrm{N\,m^{-2}}$ we have

$$\log_{10}\frac{\Delta p_2}{\Delta p_1} = \log_{10}\frac{10^{-1}\,\mathrm{N\,m^{-2}}}{10^{-3}\,\mathrm{N\,m^{-2}}} = 2,$$

so that $\log_{10}(I_2/I_1) = 4$.

We say the subjective intensity of the second sound is 4 bels above the first; we have here strictly only a ratio but for convenience we supply a unit (the *bel*). As there is a maximum of 12 bels between the limits of the ear's range it is usual to quote the above result not as 4 bels but as 40 decibels (dB), thus giving a wider range of integral values. Further we define the *sound-pressure level* (SPL) of a sound as

$$SPL = 20\log_{10}\left(\frac{\Delta p_0}{2\times 10^{-5}\,\mathrm{N\,m^{-2}}}\right)\mathrm{dB} \quad [18\text{-}17]$$

where Δp_0 is the excess pressure amplitude of the sound and $2\times 10^{-5}\,\mathrm{N\,m^{-2}}$ is an agreed reference level.* For sound waves which are not simple harmonic waves $\Delta p_2/\Delta p_1$ should be replaced by the ratio of the root mean square values of the excess pressure Δp, taken over small time intervals, and Δp_0 replaced by $\sqrt{2}\times \Delta p_{\mathrm{r.m.s.}}$.

Unfortunately the procedure outlined above does not provide an entirely satisfactory scale of *loudness*. One accepted technique is to measure the ratio

$$SL = 10\log_{10}\left(\frac{\text{intensity of sound}}{\begin{array}{c}\text{intensity of sound of same pitch and}\\ \text{type at the threshold of hearing}\end{array}}\right)\mathrm{dB}$$

[18-18]

which is called the *sensation level* and is again in decibels (dB). This provides a system which tallies well with the physiological concept of loudness for sounds of a given frequency.

---

*Kaye and Laby (1966). *Tables of physical and chemical constants*. 13th edition. Longman.

Noise

When trying to give a single number to represent a noise level it is immediately apparent that a straight measure of I or $\Delta p_{\mathrm{r.m.s.}}$ relative to an agreed base is inadequate. The noise will contain a wide range of frequencies and some frequencies will be judged to be 'noisier' than others for a given value of $\Delta p_{\mathrm{r.m.s.}}$. And may not noise to one person be music to another? We are thus faced with the problem of putting a number to a *subjectively* judged quantity. In general, however, it is agreed that the degree of noise depends on such factors as its intensity, frequency, and duration. The whine of a jet engine or the squeak of a piece of chalk are both sounds in which high frequencies predominate and these noises are especially unpleasant. A new scale for measuring sound intensities is thus defined where *noise* levels are being investigated; this is the *A* scale with units of dB(A) and involves a weighting on the measuring instrument which accentuates the higher frequencies. In other respects it can be treated like the decibel defined above, that is doubling the noise (by moving closer to its source, for instance) will produce an increase of 10 dB(A), and the weighting is such that a *normal ear* will now subjectively judge the noise to be twice as loud. On this A scale a normal ear can just detect changes of $\pm 2\,\mathrm{dB(A)}$.

Change in noise level	$\pm 2\,\mathrm{dB(A)}$	a barely perceptible change
	$-5\,\mathrm{dB(A)}$	normal hearing loss, age 45–55
	$+10\,\mathrm{dB(A)}$	a doubling of the noise level
	$-20\,\mathrm{dB(A)}$	serious hearing loss
Noise level	$30\,\mathrm{dB(A)}$	a whisper
	$60\,\mathrm{dB(A)}$	normal conversation
	$80\,\mathrm{dB(A)}$	a busy street
	$95\,\mathrm{dB(A)}$	a dangerously noisy factory

Table 18-3 Some noise levels and changes in noise levels (representative values).

The noise that a car is permitted to make in Great Britain is defined by law (1973) to be not more than 80 dB(A), the noise level being measured 10 m from the road across open ground. The car may be noisiest when going up a steep hill and it is common to test for engine noise under these circumstances. For aircraft, in particular those with jet engines, yet another way of measuring noise

18-5 Beats

Suppose we connect two signal generators to two loudspeakers and try to produce sounds of equal frequencies (and roughly equal intensities) by adjusting the controls of the signal generators. It is very unlikely that the frequencies f_1 and f_2 will be exactly the same; for example a difference of 0.1 per cent at a frequency of about 2000 Hz would give $f_1 \sim f_2 = 2$ Hz. What would we hear with, for example, this frequency difference? We would hear a pulsating sound, one which rises and falls in loudness twice every second. If the intensities of the sounds from the speakers were equal the *beats* would be very pronounced, reducing to complete silence at each minimum. It now proves a simple matter to adjust the two signal generators to be at exactly the same frequency; all we have to do is to adjust, say, f_1 until the period of the beats is so large that they cannot readily be heard. $f_2 - f_1$ will then be perhaps less than 0.1 Hz and so f_1 and f_2 are within

$$\frac{0.1 \text{ Hz}}{2000 \text{ Hz}} \times 100\% = 0.005\%$$

at 2000 Hz—the adjustment is *extremely* precise.

In order to 'see' what is happening the ear-brain system could be replaced by a microphone and c.r.o., with, if necessary, any extra amplification. The microphone is connected to the Y-plates of the c.r.o. and its timebase set to display 30 or so periods of the separate waves. The c.r.o. trace is now a pressure–time graph for the point in the path of the waves at which the microphone is placed. Figure 18-9 shows a $\Delta p - t$ graph when $f_1 = 600$ Hz and $f_2 = 700$ Hz.

This is an example of the principle of superposition of two waves (see Section 16-7). In principle it could be produced on a *very* long string or spring with waves of slightly differing frequencies being produced at the ends, but in practice such an example is confused by reflections and the consequent stationary wave patterns. It is most

---

*See Committee on the problem of noise (1963). *Noise: final report.* HMSO.

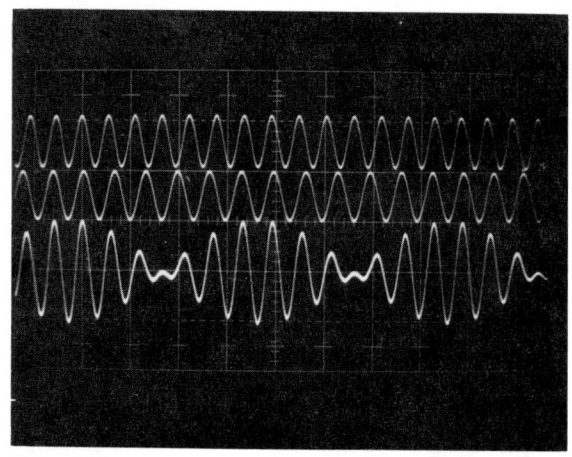

Figure 18-9 The beat phenomenon. The lower trace shows the superposition of two sinusoidal waves of frequency 600 Hz and 700 Hz which are shown in the upper two traces.

easily demonstrated using sound waves but beats are also observed when elastic waves in rods, plates, and shafts are produced by two sources of different frequencies.

If will be shown (page 333) that the frequency f_{amp} of the amplitude variation is related to the frequencies of the two waves by the relation

$$f_{amp} = \frac{|f_1 - f_2|}{2}.$$

The number of times the amplitude of this resultant wave reaches a maximum value per unit time is called the *beat frequency*. It is the frequency with which successive intensity maxima are heard and is *twice* as great as f_{amp}. The reader should be able to deduce this by considering the envelope of the lowest trace in figure 18-9. So we have

$$\text{beat frequency} = |f_1 - f_2|. \quad [18\text{-}19]$$

Piano tuners use beats both to tune two notes to be of exactly the same frequency (or the first harmonic of one note to have exactly the same frequency as the fundamental of a second note which they want to be one octave higher). They also count beats (the fastest rate of beating the ear can detect is about seven per second) in order that there may be the proper frequency differences between various notes on an equal-temperament scale. It is often possible to produce beats in the laboratory with tuning forks of nominally equal frequencies. Beats between the forks can be eliminated by loading one of them with small pieces of plasticine.

Analytically, beats occur when two waves superpose *at a point*. Taking waves of equal amplitude for convenience and using pressure waves rather than waves of displacement we have

$$\Delta p_1 = \Delta p_0 \sin \frac{2\pi}{T_1} t = \Delta p_0 \sin 2\pi f_1 t,$$

and $\quad \Delta p_2 = \Delta p_0 \sin \frac{2\pi}{T_2} t = \Delta p_0 \sin 2\pi f_2 t.$

Therefore, by the principle of superposition,

$$\Delta p = \Delta p_1 + \Delta p_2 = \Delta p_0 (\sin 2\pi f_1 t + \sin 2\pi f_2 t)$$

$$= 2\Delta p_0 \left[\cos 2\pi \left(\frac{f_1 - f_2}{2} \right) t \right] \left[\sin 2\pi \left(\frac{f_1 + f_2}{2} \right) t \right]$$

$$= \Delta P_0 \sin 2\pi \left(\frac{f_1 + f_2}{2} \right) t,$$

where

$$\Delta P_0 = 2\Delta p_0 \cos 2\pi \left(\frac{f_1 - f_2}{2} \right) t$$

is the 'amplitude' of a sinusoidal wave of frequency $(f_1 + f_2)/2$: the 'amplitude' itself varies, and has a frequency $(f_1 - f_2)/2$.

The phenomenon of beats also occurs when two mechanical oscillating system (which have similar but not identical frequencies) are loosely connected so that they can gradually transfer energy from one to the other. Such *coupled oscillators* are mentioned in Section 15-8 and Exercise 15-33. Suppose two identical pendulums P and Q of roughly equal mass are set up as shown in figure 18-10 and P is set oscillating in a plane perpendicular to the paper. Pendulum Q, initially undisturbed, gradually begins to swing and its amplitude increases while that of P decreases. The transfer of energy from P to Q does not, however, stop when their amplitudes are equal but Q's amplitude continues to rise and P's to fall until P is almost at rest. The process then happens in reverse. Figure 15-33b shows the result of a similar experiment in which the pendulums swing in the same plane and each carries a small lamp. As the motion continues the camera is moved below the pendulums so recording an extended trace which is actually a displacement–time graph.

The effect is as if each pendulum were exhibiting the result of beats between two simple harmonic motions of different frequencies. The energy is fed from P to Q and back at the beat frequency which depends upon many variables such as the mass of each pendulum, the nature of the coupling, and the natural frequency of the pendulums.

18-6 Vibrating air columns

Sections 16-8 and 17-2 deal with the phenomenon of stationary waves. A vibrating air column is a stationary wave system involving sound waves in a tube. As sound is a longitudinal wave the spring–trolley system shown in figure 17-3 illustrates the form of some possible modes of vibration. The apparatus of figure 18-11 below can

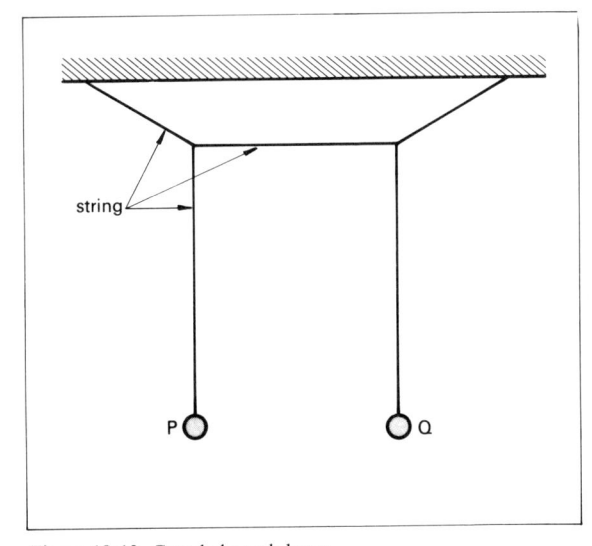

Figure 18-10 Coupled pendulums.

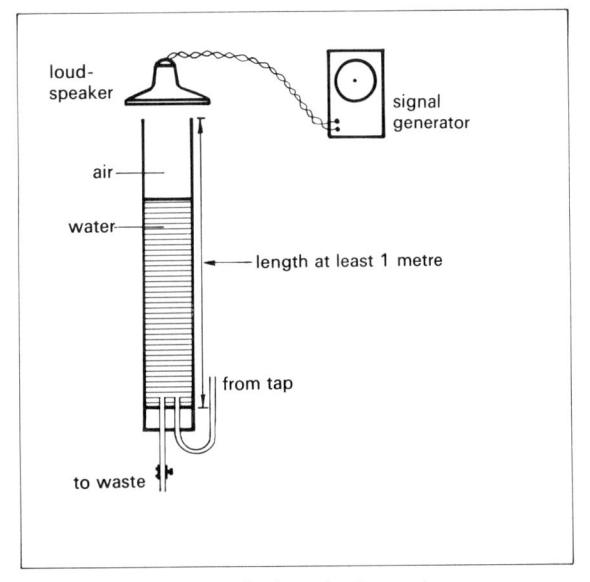

Figure 18-11 Apparatus for investigating stationary wave conditions for a column of air.

very readily be used to investigate such modes of vibration for sound waves in a tube. By adjusting the rate of delivery of water to the (vertical) tube, which should be at least a metre long, the level of the water can be made to rise or fall, quickly or slowly, or simply to remain at one level. The low-impedance output of the signal generator should be connected to a small loudspeaker fixed a few millimetres above the top of the tube. The frequency, f, of the signal generator is set at a particular value (or a tuning fork is used), and the water is made to rise rapidly to near the top of the tube. At least one sharp increase in loudness of the sound will be heard, for $f > 100\,\text{Hz}$. This occurs when a stationary wave pattern is set up between the wave travelling down the tube and its reflection from the water surface. If the tube is long, or the frequency high, more than one position where the sound rises to a maximum will be noted. The same intensity peaks will occur as the water level is lowered.

An alternative experiment is to keep the water level constant and vary the frequency of the signal generator. Again there will be a sharp increase in the loudness of the sound heard at certain frequencies. In this case the experiment is perhaps best described as an investigation of the resonant frequencies of a vibrating system (the column of air). In both experiments the variation of water level or frequency should be quite fast as it is then easier to detect the condition of stationary wave formation. Having noted roughly where the 'interesting' regions are, the experiments can be repeated more slowly paying particular attention to these regions. Figure 18-12 shows the behaviour of the air in the tube with the air vibrating in its fundamental mode. As we can consider either the particle displacement or the variation of excess pressure at points in the tube both are given for this case. The water level, level B in figure 18-12, is a place of *zero particle displacement* and of maximum variation in excess pressure; the top of the tube, level A, is approximately a place of *maximum variation in particle displacement* and of zero excess pressure. The reasons for these boundary conditions at B are obvious: the air particles cannot be displaced longitudinally into the water surface (so there is a displacement node), and as Δp is $\pi/2$ rad out of phase with y, an excess pressure antinode must occur at a particle displacement node. Similarly at A we can argue that as the pressure in the stationary wave system must be atmospheric, that is an excess pressure node, then A is a particle displacement antinode.

For sound waves in air at 273 K, $c(=f\lambda) = 330\,\text{m s}^{-1}$, and so at a frequency of 1000 Hz the wavelength is about 0.3 m. For tubes whose lengths are rather more than one metre there will thus for frequencies above 1000 Hz be a fundamental mode and several overtones. The particle displacement nodes in a tube in which the air is vibrating at the frequency of one of its overtones can be located directly by placing the tube in a horizontal position, closing one end, and placing a small loudspeaker at the other end. Some fine powder, such as lycopodium powder, is sprinkled along the tube and the loudspeaker is excited. This demonstration is a traditional experiment first performed by Kundt (1830–1894). At air particle displacement nodes the powder also experiences no displacement when a stationary wave condition is produced but between these nodes the dust is agitated. The precise patterns formed by the dust are complex but the violence of their motion can be used to tune the tube to a stationary mode and the distance between the nodes is easily measured.

As successive nodes are separated by half a wavelength, the wavelength of the sound waves in the tube can be measured. If the frequency f is also known, then the speed of sound in the tube can be deduced. It is possible to alter the nature of the gas in the tube and also to control its temperature, so that this experiment affords a method of testing equation 18-8, $c = \sqrt{(\gamma RT/M)}$, or of measuring γ.

The length of the arrow, and the size of Δp, indicate the amplitude of the particle displacement and the excess pressure variation respectively

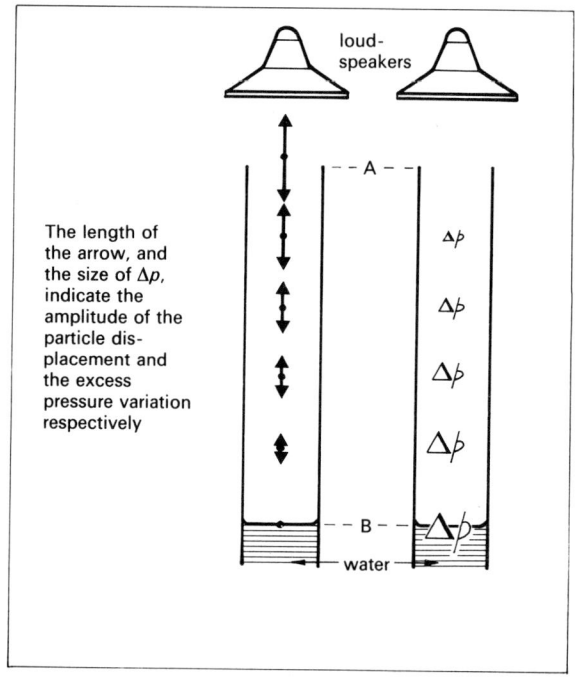

Figure 18-12 Two ways of illustrating the existence of a stationary sound wave in a tube.

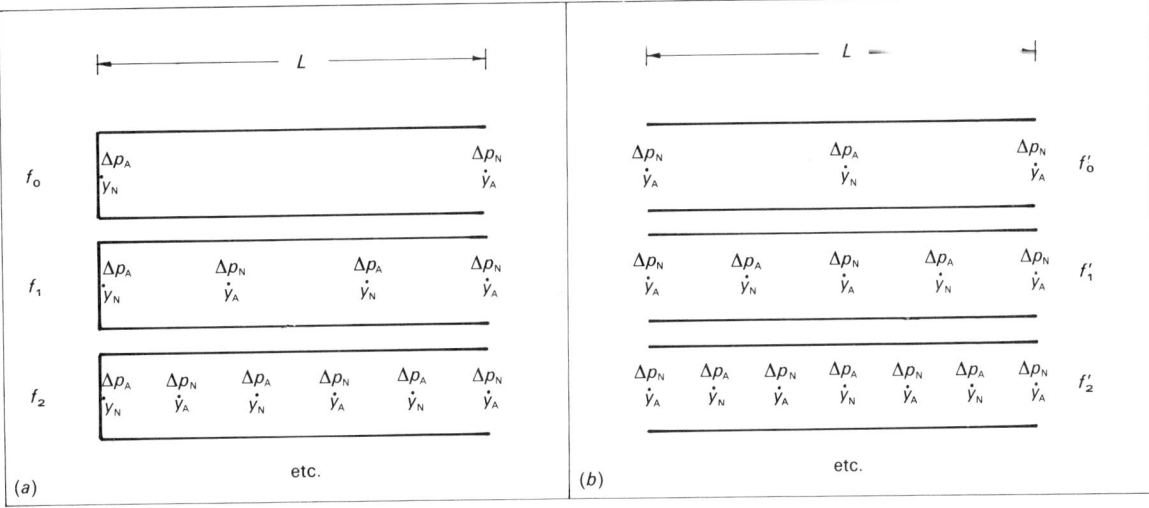

Figure 18-13 Overtones for tubes of length L (a) closed and (b) open.

Figure 18-13 illustrates the possible modes for (a) a tube closed at one end and (b) a tube open at both ends. Particle-displacement antinodes y_A and excess pressure antinodes Δp_A are indicated. Nodes of each are similarly shown by y_N and Δp_N. For the closed tube (closed at one end, that is) the wavelength λ_0 of the fundamental mode is given by $\lambda_0 = 4L$ and so $f_0 (= c/\lambda_0) = c/4L$. A study of figure 18-13a shows that the overtones have frequencies $f = (2n+1)f_0$, where $n = 1, 2, 3$, etc. For the open tube (open at both ends, that is) the fundamental frequency f'_0 is given by $\lambda'_0 = 2L$ and so $f'_0 (= c/\lambda'_0) = c/2L$ and the overtones (figure 18-13b) are given by $f' = (n+1)f'_0$, where $n = 1, 2, 3$, etc. Closed tubes produce only the *odd* harmonics but all the harmonics are present in an open tube.

The open end of a tube vibrating in a resonant mode is not quite a displacement antinode. The plane wavefronts in the tube give rise to approximately spherical wavefronts in the free air. This results in the displacement antinode being a short distance *beyond* the end of the tube: about $0.6\,r$ for cylindrical tubes of radius r. For tubes of elliptic or other cross sections or for tubes with flared ends there is no simple relation between this *end correction* and the tube's dimensions.

▶ **Example 18-3** A glass tube is mounted vertically as in figure 18-11. A tuning fork which is reliably marked 384 Hz is held above the tube, and when the water level is lowered from the top, an increase in loudness is heard when the water level is 203 mm below the top and again when the level is 635 mm below the top. Find the speed of sound in the (damp) air in the tube.

We expect the first increase in loudness to occur when the air column vibrates in its fundamental mode, that is when there is a node at the closed end and an antinode at the open end or, more accurately, just outside the open end. The second increase in loudness corresponds to the third harmonic. Thus if λ is the wavelength of the sound waves produced by the tuning fork and x is the correction for the end-effect,

and
$$\tfrac{1}{4}\lambda = 203 \text{ mm} + x$$
$$\tfrac{3}{4}\lambda = 635 \text{ mm} + x,$$

so that
$$\tfrac{1}{2}\lambda = 432 \text{ mm}$$
and
$$\lambda = 864 \text{ mm}.$$

Thus
$$c = (384 \text{ Hz})(0.864 \text{ m})$$
$$= 332 \text{ m s}^{-1}.$$

Notes: (a) $\tfrac{1}{4}\lambda = 216$ mm, so that $x = 13$ mm. If x is roughly $0.6\,r$ (where r is the radius of the tube), r is roughly 20 mm.

(b) This calculation indicates that the simplest experimental technique is to measure the distance between the water levels for the first and second increases in loudness. This gives $\tfrac{1}{2}\lambda$, and we can ignore the end-effect of the tube. ◀

Wind instruments

As with stringed musical instruments (see Section 16-9) the quality of a wind instrument depends on the number and relative amplitude of the harmonics which are present. Some wind instruments, such as the clarinet, act as closed pipes and thus have the even harmonics absent—this (plus the predominance of the fundamental in the frequency spectrum) produces the so-called fruity tone of the clarinet. Which particular overtones predominate in a wind instrument depends both on the way in which it is blown, its construction, and the materials of which it is made. In some wind instruments, for example the oboe, the amplitude of the fundamental may be very small (carrying less than 1 per cent of the sound energy). The reason why we still 'hear' the fundamental frequency f_0 is because the *difference tones*—the beat frequency between *adjacent* harmonics—all have a frequency f_0. When a wind instrument is 'overblown' the fundamental is absent. In the case of closed-tube instruments this means that the new 'fundamental' note is of frequency three times the fundamental, but in an open tube the new 'fundamental' frequency is only twice the fundamental frequency.

To excite the air in a wind instrument we can use

(*a*) edge tones as in a flute or an organ. In this system air is blown at a thin wedge (so that the wedge divides the air stream) and the eddies so formed initiate the vibration of the air in the tube,

(*b*) reeds as in a clarinet or saxophone,

(*c*) the lips as in brass instruments. The vibration of the lips is controlled by the tension in them and the reader should try to experience the 'tickling' feeling when trying to blow a trumpet.

Most wind instruments have a fixed range of possible notes controlled by opening holes to alter the length of the resonating air column. The trombone is an exception: its length can be continuously varied.

18-7 The acoustic spectrum

We have used the word sound to represent longitudinal mechanical waves of frequencies to which the human ear is sensitive. If we treat all longitudinal mechanical waves together we can produce the spectrum shown in figure 18-14.

Infrasonics

Infrasonic or subsonic waves in air are generated by any vibrating object, even the ground itself, but we feel such waves not with the ear but only by tactile sensations (touch), giddiness, or body resonances such as may be experienced by the stomach when we become 'travel sick' (the stomach has a natural frequency of vibration of about 3 Hz). The effects of these vibrations on human beings is important in the design of any machinery with which human beings may come into contact: for example hand-held machine tools, cars, aeroplanes, and manned space probes. Earthquake waves have been briefly considered earlier in Section 17-7.

Ultrasonics

Surfaces which vibrate with frequencies greater than about 20 kHz produce waves in air which are said to be ultrasonic. Their wavelength in air will be less than 15 mm or so. Two types of ultrasonic *transducers* (sources of ultrasonic waves) are common. Up to about 10^5 Hz the transducer is a ferromagnetic rod (usually nickel) which can be magnetized and demagnetized in an alternating magnetic field. The field can be produced by passing an alternating current through a solenoid wrapped round the rod. In following this magnetic cycle the dimensions of the rod change (the effect is called *magnetostriction*). If one of the resonant frequencies of the rod for longitudinal stationary waves is arranged to equal the frequency of the alternating field a large amplitude ($\approx 10^{-2}$ mm) displacement of the ends of the rod can be produced. Above 10^5 Hz and up to more than 10^{10} Hz a quartz crystal is used as the transducer. If a small slab of quartz is subject to an alternating *electric* field it too changes its dimensions: this is the *piezo-electric* effect. The electric field can be produced by silvering the faces of the slab and applying an alternating potential difference across it. Again a resonant condition is sought to produce large-amplitude oscillations.

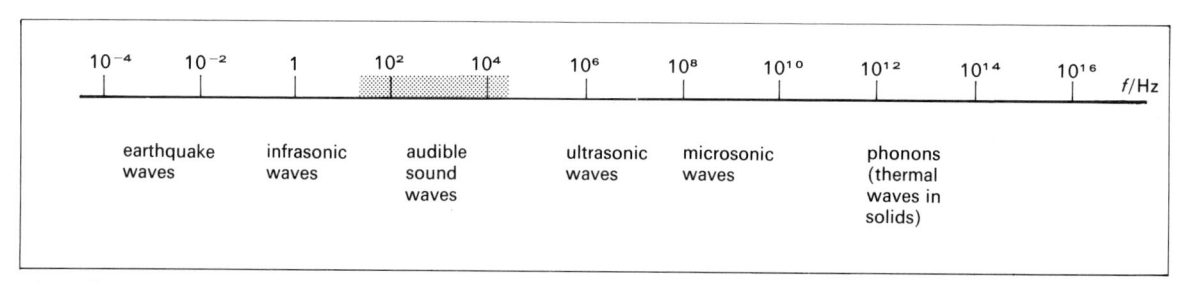

Figure 18-14 The acoustic spectrum from very long earthquake waves ($f \approx 10^{-3}$ Hz) to waves in crystals produced by atomic vibrations ($f \approx 10^{13}$ Hz).

As the intensity of a wave is proportional to the product of the squares of the amplitude and the frequency of the particle displacement it is generally possible to generate ultrasonic waves of much higher intensity than sound waves. Further as they have small wavelengths it is possible to produce parallel beams of ultrasonic waves and to focus them, for they do not diffract (see Section 19-4) as readily as sound waves. These two possibilities lead to many uses for ultrasonic waves, only some of which will be mentioned here.

(a) Bats use echo techniques with ultrasonic waves to locate obstacles and small objects such as insects. The principle is to produce a short pulse of waves and to measure the time interval before a reflected pulse returns. Sonar, a system for measuring the depth of water below a boat, uses the echo technique at about 40 kHz, displaying the outgoing and returning pulse on an oscilloscope. Similarly ultrasonic echoes can be used to measure the thickness of materials and to detect flaws in metal objects such as railway lines.

(b) In both solids and liquids ultrasonic waves can be used to produce destructive effects. Thus a focused beam of high intensity waves can be used to 'drill' square holes in glass or steel if a suitable abrasive powder is fed into the shaped beam. In liquids a strong beam produces cavitation—the formation of bubbles—and this can be used to scrub off material clinging to any surface immersed in the liquid. Cavitation is also used in low-temperature sterilizing processes as bacteria are killed by the action.

Ultrasonic waves in air, like sound waves, do not disperse, except to a small extent at very high frequencies, that is they travel at a fixed speed independent of their wavelength. However, as the wavelength decreases the *attenuation* of the wave increases, that is the dissipation of the sound energy as internal energy of the gas molecules increases, and above 10^8 Hz a mechanical longitudinal wave in air ceases to be a practical possibility of any significance. Longitudinal waves of higher frequencies in liquids and solids are called *microsonic* waves.

For a brief discussion of thermal waves in solids (phonons) see Section 17-3.

18-8 Architectural acoustics

When a steady sound is produced in a closed room energy is fed into the ordered oscillations of the air molecules. If the walls of the room reflected the sound perfectly and there was no loss of energy to internal energy in the air (the random motion of the molecules) then the intensity of the sound detected by a microphone placed in the room would become greater and greater. This does not happen. The two factors idealized above both, in practice, dissipate the sound energy so that an equilibrium condition is rapidly reached when the intensity at the microphone remains constant. If the source is now switched off there is a measurable time during which the intensity at the microphone remains detectable. The room is said to *reverberate*, and the most important acoustic property of a room or a concert hall is the time of reverberation.

We define the *reverberation time*, T_r, to be the time taken for the intensity of a sound of a given frequency to fall from a sensation level of 60 dB to the threshold of hearing for that sound, that is an intensity drop by a factor of 10^6. The intensity decreases exponentially. W. C. Sabine investigated the dependence of T_r on the volume V of the room and the area A of its walls; he found

$$T_r \propto \frac{V}{A}$$

where $\quad A = \alpha_1 A_1 + \alpha_2 A_2 + \alpha_3 A_3 + \cdots,$

α_a being the absorption coefficient of the material forming an area of the walls. For a room with perfectly absorbing walls A is simply the total area of those walls; it is sometimes referred to as the *equivalent open-window area*, as an open window clearly allows all the sound incident on it to pass through.

Further, $\quad T_r = \dfrac{kV}{A} \quad$ [18-20]

where k is a constant whose value is found to be $0.17\,\text{s}\,\text{m}^{-1}$. A typical value of T_r for a large bare room or a small hall is 3 s or 4 s, while for the same room or hall full of (about 50) people the reverberation time is only half that value. It is possible to calculate the effect of an audience by assuming that each person is equivalent to about $0.5\,\text{m}^2$ of totally absorbing area.

Material	α_a at 250 Hz	α_a at 1000 Hz
Brickwork	0.02	0.04
Flat wood	0.01	0.05
Carpet on underlay	0.05	0.40
Heavy curtains	0.35	0.72
Perforated tiles (or other acoustic absorber)	0.35	0.75

Table 18-4 Some approximate values for α_a. The values at other frequencies cannot be accurately deduced by extrapolation.

▶ **Example 18-4** An assembly hall is 20 m wide, 50 m long, and 10 m high. The walls are bare brickwork (except for one end, which has curtaining), the floor is wooden, and the ceiling is plastered. Taking data from the text or from table 18-4, find the reverberation time T_r for a note of 250 Hz when the hall is empty and when it contains 600 people.

We use equation 18-20,

$$T_r = \frac{(0.17 \text{ s m}^{-1})V}{A},$$

where $V = (20 \text{ m})(50 \text{ m})(10 \text{ m}) = 10^4 \text{ m}^3$.

There are 200 m² of curtaining, 1000 m² of wood, and 200 m² + 1000 m² + 2(500 m²) = 2200 m² of reflective material such as brick or plaster. The absorption coefficients for a note of 250 Hz are 0.35, 0.01, and 0.020 respectively, so that the equivalent open-window area A is given by

$$A = (200 \text{ m}^2)(0.35) + (1000 \text{ m}^2)(0.010) + (2200 \text{ m}^2)(0.020)$$

$$= 124 \text{ m}^2.$$

Therefore

$$T_r = \frac{(0.17 \text{ s m}^{-1})(10^4 \text{ m}^3)}{124 \text{ m}^2}$$

$$= 14 \text{ s}$$

when the hall is empty. When the hall contains 600 people, they add an effective 600(0.5 m²) of totally absorbing area, so that now

$$T_r = \frac{(0.17 \text{ s m}^{-1})(10^4 \text{ m}^3)}{424 \text{ m}^2}$$

$$= 4.0 \text{ s}.$$

This is high for a hall of this size if it is used for an orchestral concert, though for notes of higher frequencies T_r would be less. ◀

If T_r is made very small, then although speech, for example, will be easily intelligible, it may be almost inaudible, for we normally rely on reflections to increase the intensity at our ears. It is thus necessary not to put surfaces which absorb (and thus lower the value of T_r) at places where they will prevent the sound from reaching an audience by reflection. In some concert halls large angled reflecting surfaces are placed above the performers and absorbing surfaces placed behind the audience. To study the way in which sound travels from a point source to all corners of a hall it is possible to build two-dimensional models of the hall and use ripple tank experiments or Schlieren photography to investigate the multiple reflections when waves are produced in the model.

Bibliography

Békésy, G. von. (1957). 'The ear.' *Scientific American* offprint number 44.

Beranek, L. L. (1966). 'Noise.' *Scientific American* offprint number 306.

Blitz, J. (1967). 'Ultrasonics.' *Physics Education*, **2**, page 268.

Dobbs, E. R. (1971). 'The place of acoustics in education.' *Physics Education*, **6**, page 153.

Leventhall, H. G. (1967). 'The acoustics of rooms.' *Physics Education*, **2**, page 101.

Smith, M. J. T. (1971). 'A look into the aero engine noise problem.' *Physics Education*, **6**, page 193.

Blitz, J. (1971). *Ultrasonics: methods and applications*. Butterworth. A not too mathematical account with up-to-date details of the uses of ultrasonic waves.

Griffin, D. R. (1960). *Echoes of bats and men*. Heinemann. A book from the Science Study Series.

Jardine, J. (1965). *Physics is fun*, Book 2. Heinemann. Chapter 5 is a well-illustrated elementary account.

Mee, F. J. (1967). *Sound*. Heinemann. Much of this book is relevant; in particular see Chapter 4 on the velocity of sound and Chapter 10 on the acoustics of buildings.

Project Physics (1970). Reader, Unit 3 *The triumph of mechanics*. Holt, Rinehart and Winston. See Chapters 15 and 16.

Sears, F. W. and Zemansky, M. W. (1964). *College physics*. Addison-Wesley. Chapter 23 is on acoustical phenomena.

Taylor, C. A. (1965). *The physics of musical sounds*. English Universities Press. A book rich in relevant material presented in such a way that the more mathematical parts can be avoided. The book is accompanied by a gramophone record.

8 mm film loop. 'Wave motion interference—change of frequency.' Gateway. This loop shows beats as a moving interference pattern.

Exercises

Data (use the following values unless otherwise directed):
$g = 10 \text{ m s}^{-2} = 10 \text{ N kg}^{-1}$.
Density of air = 1.3 kg m^{-3}.
Speed of sound in air = 340 m s^{-1} (which is its value at 290 K).
Values of γ: helium, 1.7; water vapour, 1.3 (mean value); air, 1.4 (mean value).
Relative molecular mass: helium, 4; water, 18; air, 29 (mean value).

18-1 Check the dimensional consistency of the equation $c = \sqrt{(K/\rho)}$, where c is the speed of sound in a gas, K the adiabatic bulk modulus of the gas, and ρ its density.

18-2 A group of people measuring the speed of sound in air, using the technique described on page 324, find that the observer is 100 m from the clapper when he first sees and hears claps simultaneously. The rate of clapping is 3 Hz. What value do they record for the speed of sound in air?

18-3 A man who wishes to measure the speed of sound in air stands some distance (which he will measure) from an isolated wall: he has two blocks of wood which he will clap together at regular intervals, timing each clap to coincide with the echo he hears of the previous clap. A friend will time his rate of clapping. Advise him as to the distance he should stand from the wall in order that the rate of clapping may be slow enough to be physically possible, showing how you arrived at your estimate of the distance.

18-4 Given that the speed of sound in air is 330 m s^{-1} at 273 K, find
(a) the speed of sound in air at 373 K
(b) the speed of sound in helium at 273 K.

18-5 Discuss qualitatively the effect on the speed of sound in air if the air becomes moist.

18-6 A man breathes in a lungful of helium gas and tries to sing a note which he intends to be C(256 Hz). Assuming that the wavelength of the sound waves is unchanged, find the frequency of the waves in the helium.

18-7 Given that the speed of sound in air at a pressure of 1 atmosphere and a temperature of 273 K is 330 m s^{-1}, find the speed of sound in air
(a) at a pressure of 4 atmospheres and a temperature of 273 K
(b) at a pressure of 2 atmospheres and a temperature of 1092 K.
Comment on your answers.

18-8 A source of sound of frequency 2000 Hz is placed in air at a certain distance from a rigid reflecting plate. A small microphone is moved along the line from the source which is perpendicular to the plate, and maxima of intensity are registered on a cathode ray oscilloscope, which is connected to the microphone, at intervals of 80 mm. Explain this, and find a value for the speed of sound in air.
If the microphone is placed against the plate, will the cathode ray oscilloscope record a maximum or a minimum of intensity?

18-9 For sound waves in air draw a graph of the intensity I against the excess-pressure amplitude Δp_0. Plot I and Δp_0 along the y- and x-axes respectively, for values of $\Delta p_0 / \text{N m}^{-2} = 2 \times 10^n$ where $n = -5, -3, -1, 1$.

18-10 A loudspeaker is emitting energy at a rate of 10 W. Treating it as a point source, find the intensity at a distance of 2 m from it, and hence the excess pressure amplitude at that point. If the area of a human ear-drum is about 10^{-4} m^2, find the amplitude of the excess force exerted on the ear-drum.

18-11 Use the graph of figure 18-8 to determine the smallest detectable sound intensity, and the frequency at which this occurs, and hence calculate
(a) using equation 18-14, the corresponding excess pressure amplitude
(b) using equation 18-10, the corresponding displacement amplitude.
Does your answer to (a) agree with an estimate made from the graph?

18-12 Use the graph of figure 18-8 to find the range of audibility (in dB) at the following frequencies:
(a) 100 Hz   (b) 600 Hz   (c) 1000 Hz.

18-13 Use the graph of figure 18-8 to determine the sensation level (*SL*) at the threshold of feeling for sound of frequency
(a) 100 Hz   (b) 400 Hz   (c) 1000 Hz.

18-14 To comply with legal requirements, motor manufacturers in Great Britain must design their cars so that the maximum loudness is 80 dB(A). A road test of a particular car reveals that the maximum loudness is 83 dB(A). The manufacturer claims that this is a negligible amount above the legal limit: 'less than 1 part in 25'. A consumer association claims that, on the contrary, an increase from 80 dB(A) to 83 dB(A) means a *doubling of intensity*. Who is right?

18-15 Sketch the sine waves $y = y_0 \sin(2\pi/T)t$ when y_0 is 20 mm and T is (a) 2.0 s, and (b) 2.5 s, for values of t/s from 0 to 10. Use the same axes for both graphs. Find by superposition the result of adding the two waves.
Now draw the graph (a) again, but instead of repeating (b) draw the graph of $y = y_0 \sin[(2\pi t/T) + (\pi/2)]$ for $y_0 = 20$ mm and $T = 2.5$ s and values of t/s from 0 to 10. This of course has the same shape as the original graph (b), but is moved along by one quarter-cycle. Now superpose these two waves. The results of the two superpositions do not *look* the same, yet when these are sound waves we hear the same result in either case. The first statement of this result is due to G. S. Ohm (1787–1854).

18-16 Draw (accurately to scale) a y–t graph of a periodic wave of period 0.50 s (that is, frequency 2.0 Hz) and amplitude about 20 mm. Arrange to have at least 10 complete waves in your diagram. The waves need not be sinusoidal; a sawtooth, or zig-zag, wave will do. On the same diagram draw a second wave of the same amplitude, but of period 0.40 s (and frequency 2.5 Hz). Use the principle of superposition to add the waves, and find from your diagram
(a) the period of the resultant wave, and hence its frequency; compare this frequency with the frequency of the original waves
(b) the beat frequency.

18-17 An amateur violinist is using a tuning fork of frequency 440 Hz to tune a string on his violin to produce a note of frequency 440 Hz. At his first attempt he hears beats of frequency 3 Hz. What are the possible frequencies of his violin string?

If he now tightens his string, and the beat frequency increases to 5 Hz, what is now the frequency of his violin string?

18-18 Draw a frequency spectrum (similar to that in figure 16-26) for the harmonics of
(a) an open tube   (b) a closed tube.

18-19 The speed of sound in carbon dioxide at 273 K is 260 m s^{-1}. What would need to be the length of a resonance tube (as shown in figure 18-11) if an observer is to hear seven increases in loudness when he uses a tuning fork of frequency 320 Hz and lowers the water level from the top?

18-20 In a Kundt tube experiment to measure the speed of sound in carbon dioxide at 290 K, one end of the tube was closed and the other fitted with a loudspeaker connected to a signal generator of variable frequency. Resonance was observed at a frequency of 650 Hz, and then the piles of lycopodium powder (at the nodes) were 0.21 m apart. Use this data to find the speed of the sound.

18-21 Describe and explain the variation in sound heard when a large can is steadily filled with water.

18-22 If a source of sound is placed at one end of a tube which is open at the other end, much of the sound will be reflected at the open end. How are instruments designed so as to allow the sound to escape into the surrounding air?

18-23 Figure 18-15 shows the sound from a loudspeaker being passed through a system of tubing (Quincke's tube) to reach a listener through headphones. The slide S can be moved so that the sound passing through it takes a shorter or longer path than it previously did. When S is moved, the intensity of sound heard by the listener varies from a minimum to a maximum to a minimum again, and so on. Explain this.

If the frequency of the sound is 500 Hz, and the speed of sound in the tube at that temperature is 320 m s^{-1}, and the listener first hears a minimum of intensity, what is the least distance S must be moved for him to again hear a minimum of intensity?

18-24 A quartz transducer capable of transmitting ultrasonic waves of frequency 2.0×10^7 Hz (the upper limit for quartz) is to be designed. Find the width of the crystal (between its silvered faces) in order that it may resonate in its fundamental mode. Take the density and bulk modulus of quartz to be 2600 kg m^{-3} and 7.9×10^{10} N m^{-2} respectively.

18-25 Write an essay on the use of ultrasonic waves by bats for locating objects.

18-26 Petrol pumps can be made to cut off the supply of petrol automatically when the tank is full. The mechanism uses ultrasonic waves. Suggest how it might work and estimate the numerical values of the quantities involved.

18-27 Estimate the reverberation time for the room in which you are working.

18-28 Suggest an experimental arrangement with which you could measure the absorption coefficient α_a of polystyrene ceiling tiles. What would be the main experimental difficulties?

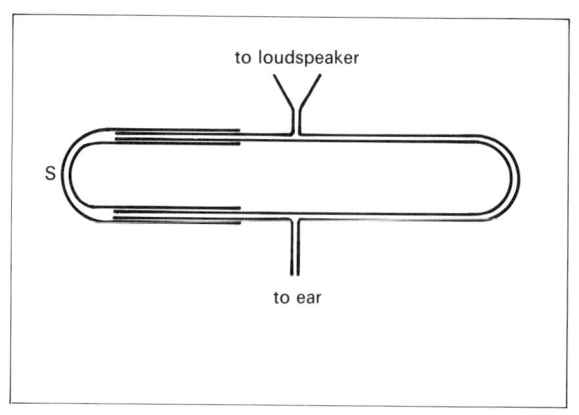

Figure 18-15 Quincke's tube.

19 Wave phenomena

19-1 Seeing waves	341	19-6 Dispersion	353
19-2 Huygens's construction	343	19-7 Doppler effect	353
19-3 Reflection and refraction	344	19-8 Shock waves	357
19-4 Diffraction	347	Bibliography	359
19-5 Two-source interference patterns	350	Exercises	359

19-1 Seeing waves

Most readers will be familiar with the *ripple tank* as a useful piece of laboratory equipment for the study of wavefronts which can travel in two dimensions. It is because the phenomena exhibited by the ripples on the water surface can be so easily made visible that the system is so useful. We shall not attempt a full description of all possible ripple tank experiments but many of the phenomena mentioned in this chapter can be demonstrated with this device. Ripple tanks are not, however, as straightforward as they seem. The choice of depths and the structure of the sides of the tanks are important details, and the optics which produce the projected 'shadows' of the water waves are complicated. Further the difference between the wave speed and the group speed (see Section 19-6) in a wave pulse is confusing.

The speed of periodic wave ripples is given in figure 19-1 for differing frequencies and depths of water. A normal ripple tank will be filled to a depth of about 5 mm. If the depth of water is less than 2 mm the energy of the wave is rapidly dissipated (this phenomenon is called *attenuation*); for depths greater than about 7 mm the opposite is true and so the experiment may be confused by reflections from the sides of the tank. An intermediate depth, say 4 mm to 5 mm, is a good compromise (unless the refraction of the waves is to be studied when the dependence of their speed on the depth of the water is the relevant wave property). Reflections from the sides of the tank can be reduced by using angled gauze or porous foam *beaches* though neither is wholly satisfactory. A better design of beach is one which in the vertical cross section is of parabolic shape; in this case the energy of the wave is absorbed rather than reflected.

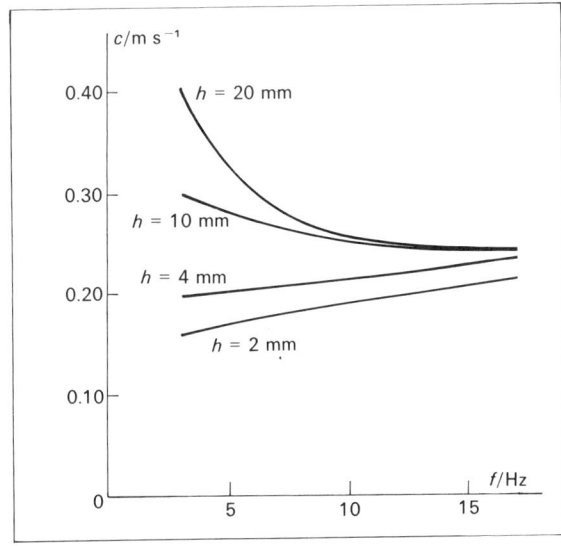

Figure 19-1 The variation with frequency f of the speed c of ripples on water. h represents the depth of the water. The usual range of f is from 3 Hz up to about 20 Hz.

342 19 Wave phenomena

The optical principle of a ripple tank is illustrated in figure 19-2. The diagram is idealized because it suggests a sharp focusing effect produced by the curved water surface on the screen. However, altering the distance b (or a) still enables a recognizable pattern to be seen on the screen. We must beware of too literal an interpretation of the screen pattern: the simple projection ratio $a/(a+b)$ does not always tell us what is happening at the water surface. If we remember these practical difficulties we can nevertheless make considerable use of the ripple tank for qualitative demonstration experiments.

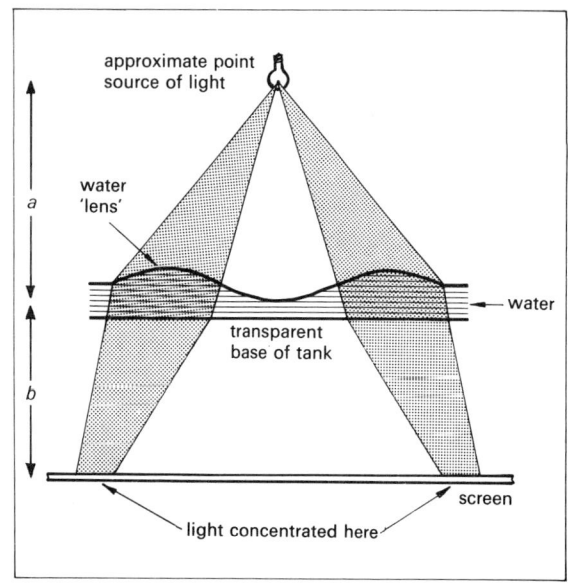

Figure 19-2 The optical principle of the ripple tank. The diagram shows light being converged by the crests and diverged by the troughs: so bright and dull areas on the screen correspond to the waves in the tank.

Ultrasonic waves

For mechanical wavefronts which travel in three dimensions we must use sound waves. For worthwhile experiments ultrasonic frequencies are essential and 40 kHz equipment is available in a simple form. At the corresponding wavelength (less than 10 mm) the apparatus can be used in a laboratory without too much danger of reflections confusing the issue. The horns provide a useful directional property and the signal received from a microphone is displayed on a galvanometer or a c.r.o.* The wavelength

---

*One set of ultrasonic apparatus by Unilab gives a 1 mA reading on a galvanometer when the distance TR is about 30 metres. A classic series of experiments using waves of ≈ 15 mm is described by Pohl (see the bibliography).

of ripples in a ripple tank can conveniently be made of the same order as that of these ultrasonic waves, thus enabling the same phenomenon to be illustrated with different mechanical wave systems. For sound waves of audible frequencies, signal generators and loudspeakers can, of course, be used.

Figure 19-3 Ultrasonic transmitter and receiver. The receiver is connected to a galvanometer.

Schlieren photography

Sound waves are not directly visible: we cannot follow the progress of a wavefront as in a ripple tank. Instead we investigate the variation of pressure amplitude at points in the path of the wave. It is possible to photograph the position of the wavefront of a wave pulse if the density changes in the air are great enough to bend a beam of light passing through it. The wave pulse is usually produced by a spark between two electrodes; this produces a sharp and violent bang. The wavefront from the spark is illuminated and the shutter of a camera synchronized so as to record its position at a given moment on a photographic plate. The technique is called the Schlieren–Töpler or simply the *Schlieren method* (see figure 19-4). At D is placed a continuous source of light and the experimenter looks into the mirror from the camera position. He sees a bright field of view if the mirror is properly adjusted to give the light paths shown. The *Schlieren stop*, S, a finely ground edge like a razor blade, is then moved slowly across the field of view until it is as dark as possible. This requires great care and a good-quality mirror free from spherical aberration. If now any disturbance occurs in the experimental area which alters the light paths, some of the rays which are bent will pass the Schlieren stop and reach the film. Thus, for instance, if a lighted match is used to warm the air in the experimental area an observer will 'see' the air rising. In

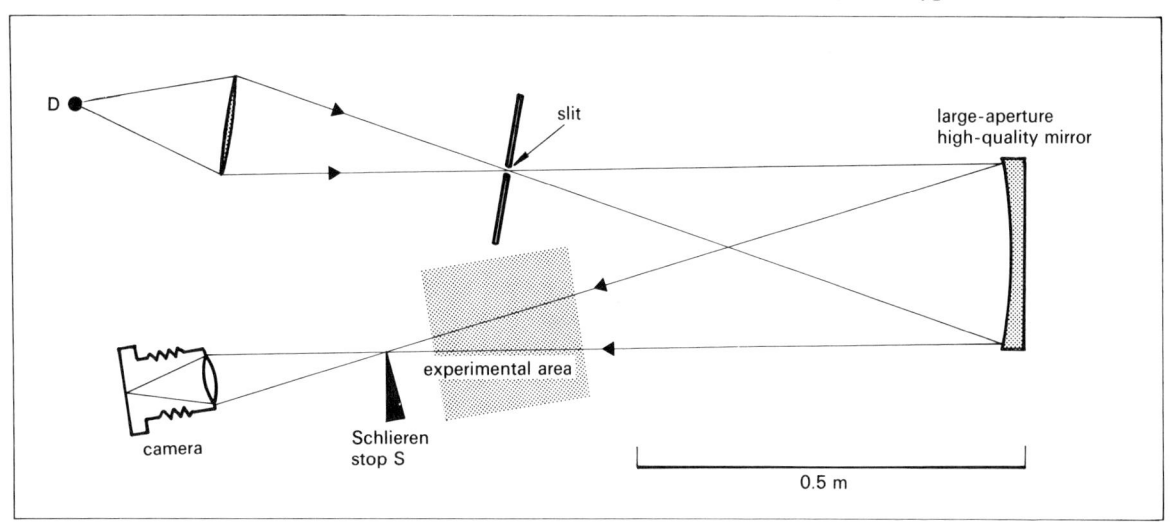

Figure 19-4 The principle of Schlieren photography.

this way the acoustic properties of halls can be studied (using models) as can many of the non-periodic wave properties outlined in this chapter.

19-2 Huygens's construction

If we know where a wavefront is at time t, how can we predict where it will be at a time $t + \Delta t$? So far we have answered this question by applying Newton's laws of motion and the principle of superposition to the material carrying the wave. Huygens suggested (in 1690) an intuitive geometrical way of locating the new wavefront. His method can best be thought of in two steps.

(a) Suppose that each point on an advancing wavefront acts as a source of secondary *wavelets*. In three dimensions these will be spherical wavelets, and in two dimensions circles (see figure 19-5), providing the medium carrying the waves is isotropic. In a time Δt the secondary wavelets will have moved a distance $c\Delta t$ from their sources on the old wavefront.

(b) After the time interval Δt, the new wavefront can be located by finding the *envelope* of the secondary wavelets *in the forward direction*. Thus a diverging spherical wavefront moves outwards as a spherical wavefront, and so forth.

The lines joining corresponding points on two wavefronts are called *rays* and are perpendicular to the wavefronts.

The usefulness of this idea lies in its application. Apart from the example given in the next section, consider a plane wavefront of infinite extent which reaches a barrier with a hole in it. Only that part of the wavefront incident on the hole will get through but Huygens's construction immediately predicts that the wave will spread out in the region beyond the hole. This phenomenon, *diffraction*, is considered further in Section 19-4.

Such a successful geometrical construction must have a sound physical basis. Kirchhoff showed (but not until nearly 200 years later) that Huygens's construction was not a fluke. He suggested that:

(a) Each point on an existing wavefront acts as a source of secondary waves the amplitude of which varies with the

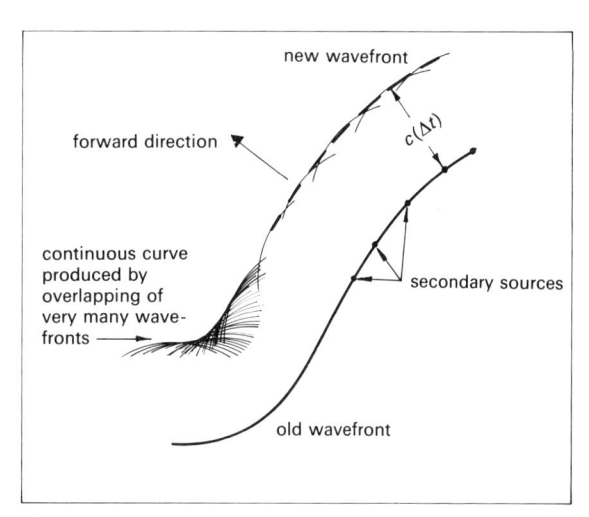

Figure 19-5 Huygens's construction.

angle θ between the (forward) normal to the wavefront according to an *obliquity* factor $(1+\cos\theta)$. This factor (which is zero for $\theta = \pi$ rad, the backward direction) must be multiplied by any other factor on which the amplitude depends, for example a suitable function of distance.

(b) The secondary wave sources are all of phase $\pi/2$ rad ahead of the wavefront on which they lie.

(c) The resultant wave amplitude at any point is the (vector) sum of all the secondary wavelets arriving there at any instant in time, that is the principle of superposition applies to the secondary wavefronts.

The mathematics involved in applying this method is too complex for this text and we shall usually be content to use Huygens's construction.

19-3 Reflection and refraction

Huygens's construction leads to the well-known law of reflection; its use to prove this is left as an exercise for the reader (see Exercise 19-4, or the proof can be found in many texts on optics). As well as locating the new wavefront as the envelope of secondary wavelets the proof involves using the idea that the time separation between corresponding points of two wavefronts (points, that is, on the same ray) is the same for all such pairs of points. This is sometimes known as *Malus's law*. Its use together with Huygens's construction is illustrated below for refraction.

The *reflection* of mechanical waves in one dimension has been considered at various points in the text (the reader should refer to the index), particularly when a stationary wave pattern results. In two and three dimensions we have mentioned the reflection of sound waves as they affect, for instance, the acoustics of rooms. We have considered stationary waves on water surfaces and elastic membranes. An interesting example of the reflection of sound waves exists in the Whispering Gallery in the dome of St Paul's Cathedral. The successive reflections or echoes keep the intensity of the sound near the circular wall of the gallery very high.

Refraction occurs when the speed of a wave changes, and the refractive index (n) of one material relative to another is defined as the ratio of the wave speeds. If c_1 and c_2 are the wave speeds in the first and second media, and $_1n_2$ is the refractive index of the second medium relative to the first,

$$_1n_2 = c_1/c_2. \qquad [19\text{-}1]$$

The interesting consequence of such a change of speed is the bending of the direction of propagation of the wave energy where a wavefront strikes the boundary between two media obliquely. In figure 19-6 consider the part AB of a wavefront PQ which refracts in time Δt to a new wavefront A'B'. Parts of secondary wavelets from A and B are shown.

Clearly $\qquad BB' = c_1 \Delta t \qquad$ and $\qquad AA' = c_2 \Delta t,$

so that $\qquad _1n_2 \left(= \dfrac{c_1}{c_2} \right) = \dfrac{BB'}{AA'}.$

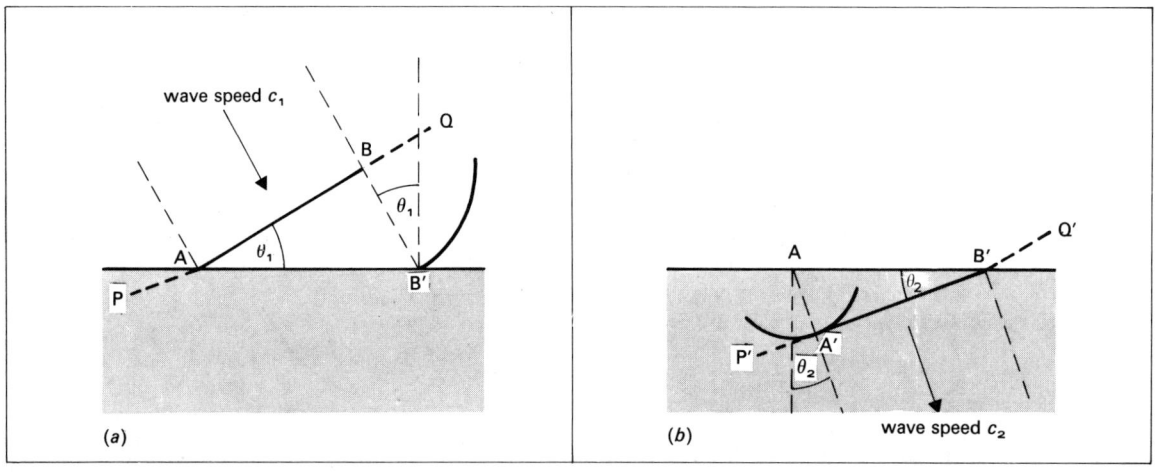

But $\qquad \sin\theta_1 = \dfrac{BB'}{AB'} \qquad$ and $\qquad \sin\theta_2 = \dfrac{AA'}{AB'}$

so that $\qquad \dfrac{BB'}{AA'} = \dfrac{\sin\theta_1}{\sin\theta_2}$

Figure 19-6 A wavefront PQ moves to P'Q' in a time Δt. There will also be a (partially) reflected wavefront which is not shown.

19-3 Reflection and refraction

and
$$_1n_2 = \frac{\sin\theta_1}{\sin\theta_2}, \quad [19\text{-}2]$$

a result familiar in optics as *Snell's law of refraction*. As c_1/c_2 is constant for two given isotropic media then so is $\sin\theta_1/\sin\theta_2$.

Suppose that in figure 19-6b c_2 had been greater than c_1 in such a way that in drawing the secondary wave from A we had produced a slightly different diagram with

$$AA' > AB'.$$

This would have occurred if

$$c_2 \Delta t > \frac{BB'}{\sin\theta_1}$$
$$> \frac{c_1 \Delta t}{\sin\theta_1},$$

that is
$$c_2 > \frac{c_1}{\sin\theta_1}.$$

With $AA' > AB'$ we cannot construct the new wavefront from B' tangential to the secondary wave from A, that is there is now *no envelope* to the secondary waves. Either Huygens's construction does not apply or there is no refracted wavefront: the latter is the case. The wave is totally reflected at the barrier and the phenomenon is called *total internal reflection*. It occurs when $c_1 < c_2 \sin\theta_1$. This expresses the idea that total internal reflection can *not* occur for a wave moving from a medium in which it moves quickly towards one in which it moves more slowly, and that in cases where it can occur it does so only for values of $\theta_1 > \sin^{-1}(c_1/c_2)$.

▶ **Example 19-1** Figure 19-7a shows the paths of some seismic waves through the Earth, and figure 19-7b shows how the speed of P and S waves varies with distance from the Earth's surface. (a) Taking measurements from figure 19-7a and readings from figure 19-7b, verify that the refraction of ray ABC obeys Snell's law of refraction. (b) What is the critical angle for the interface between the mantle and the liquid core? Is its measured value

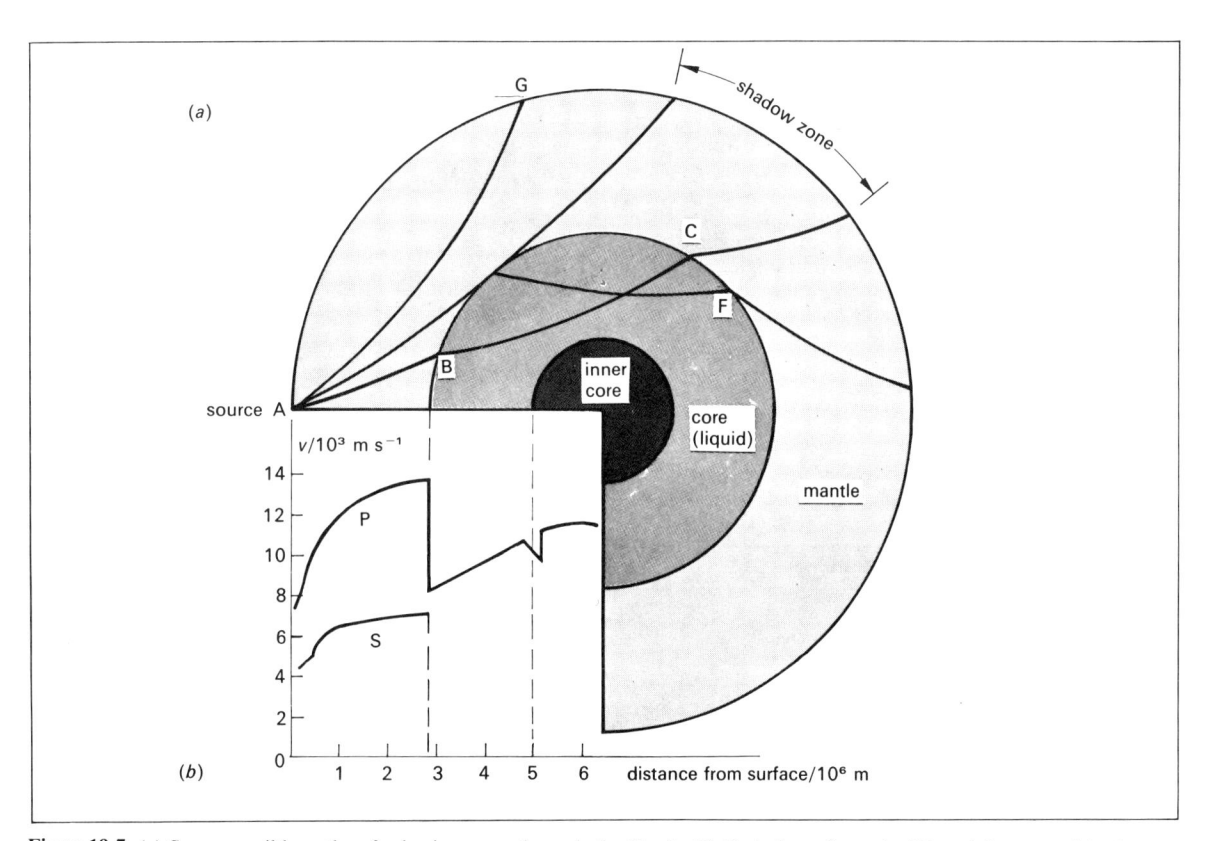

Figure 19-7 (a) Some possible paths of seismic waves through the Earth. (b) Variation of speed of P and S waves with distance from the Earth's surface.

what you would expect? (c) Account for the curving of the rays which leave A. Is a ray such as AG symmetrical?

(a) The angles between the tangents at B to the curves AB and BC make angles of 44° and 25° with the Earth's radius through B. The ratio of these sines = $\sin 44°/\sin 25°$ = $0.695/0.423 = 1.64$, and the ratio of the speeds = $13\,700\,\text{m s}^{-1}/8200\,\text{m s}^{-1} = 1.67$. This is a good agreement, considering the lack of precision in measuring the angles on the figure.

(b) Ray ADE grazes the surface of the core, and coincides with ray ADF along AD. Therefore the angle between the normal at D and the tangent to DF at D is the critical angle. (Strictly, there are two *almost* coincident rays which pass along AD, but we cannot distinguish these on this diagram.) This angle is 37°, and its sine is 0.602: the reciprocal of this is 1.67. This is the same (to three significant figures) as our value for the ratio of the speeds in the two media.

(c) The velocity of the wave increases with depth (because both the density and the elasticity of the mantle increase with depth, though not proportionally). If a ray meets obliquely a *dis*continuous change of medium, its direction will change *dis*continuously; here, where the medium changes continuously, there will be a continuous change of direction. Considerations of symmetry are enough to tell us that the curve will be symmetrical about the radius through the point on the ray where it is moving tangentially to the Earth's surface.

Note:
(i) the graph for the speeds of the S waves stops where the core begins, because shear waves cannot be transmitted through a liquid.
(ii) the liquid core behaves like a lens. Waves are concentrated into the region whose angles are greater than 142° (up to an angle of 180° + 38°), and are missing from the region between 103° and 142°, although some are diffracted into this region.

Water waves

The graph of figure 19-1 shows how the speed of ripples in a ripple tank varies with depth. A quantitative demonstration of total internal reflection is thus possible. Firstly the ratio of the speeds of ripples of frequency f (say about 8 Hz) in deep and shallow water is measured. By a suitable choice of h_1 and h_2 (see figure 19-8) a ratio c_1/c_2 of about 0.5 can be achieved. To measure c_1/c_2 we do not need to measure either c_1 or c_2 directly but use

$$c_1 = f\lambda_1$$

and

$$c_2 = f\lambda_2,$$

and measure $\lambda_1/\lambda_2 (= c_1/c_2)$ by observing the projection of the water surface under stroboscopic illumination. With the waves now incident from the shallow water obliquely on the refracting boundary the angle θ_1 (see figure 19-8) is gradually increased until total internal reflection occurs. Then θ_1 is equal to the critical angle, and we can verify that this is equal to $\sin^{-1}(\lambda_1/\lambda_2)$. The experiment, though not very precise, is particularly interesting, for the total internal reflection seems to occur not at any real barrier but in the surface above the step in the water level.

Gravity water waves (see page 310) also exhibit refraction. When a sea wave meets a shelving beach at an angle (that is with a wavefront not parallel to the shore) the wave bends as indicated in figure 19-9a.

Earthquake waves

The Earth's crust is not homogeneous and the speed of

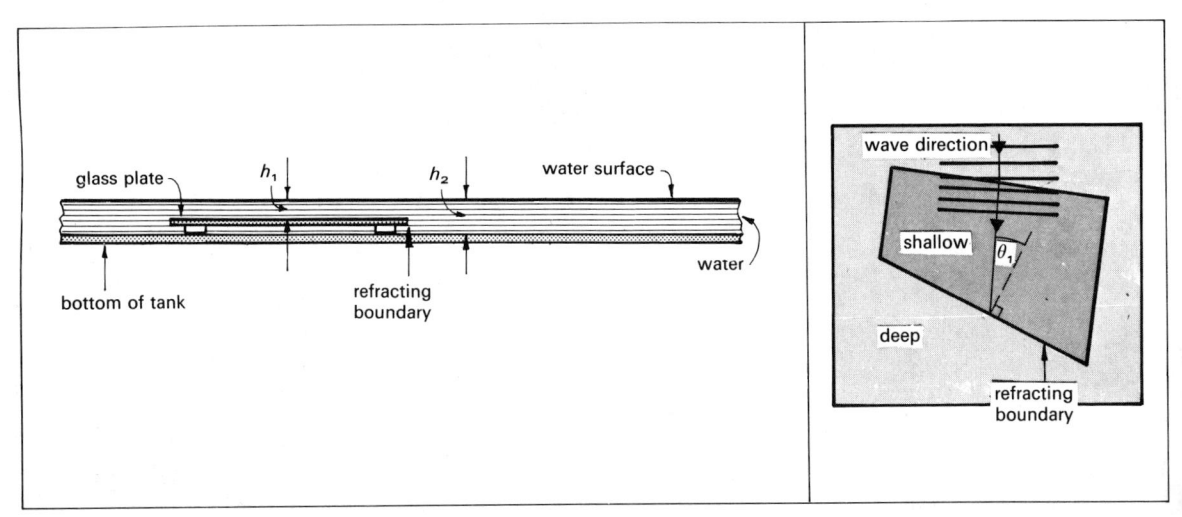

Figure 19-8 Arrangement for refraction in a ripple tank.

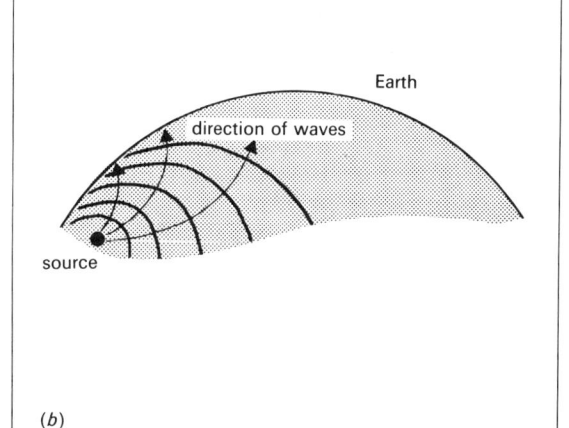

elastic waves, both P and S, varies with depth. The resulting refraction is indicated for one sort of wave in figure 19-9b and considerably complicates the problems of locating the focus of an earthquake from seismographic records (see also examples 17-3 and 19-1). The P waves travel at about $8000\,\mathrm{m\,s^{-1}}$ near the Earth's surface. When these longitudinal waves strike the surface of the Earth they could be refracted into the atmosphere where they would travel at about $330\,\mathrm{m\,s^{-1}}$. Such a large change of speed means that only a small percentage of the wave energy would be refracted; most is reflected.

Sound waves

Exercises 19-13, 19-14, and 19-15 deal with some of the phenomena which occur when sound waves are refracted in moving air and in air in which there is a temperature gradient. The reader is advised to attempt these exercises. The speed of the waves in a gas depends on the properties of the gas: at a boundary between gases there will therefore be refraction if the direction of the waves is not normal to the boundary. It is hard to find the relative refractive index of two gases by measuring the angles of incidence and refraction of a beam of sound waves. However, silk (which is not opaque to the sound waves) can be used to enclose the gas, and the deviation of a beam of ultrasonic waves incident normally in air on one face of a prism of CO_2 can be measured. Using rubber, only a very small fraction of the sound energy will be transmitted from one gas to the other.

As sound waves travel faster in a solid material (such as iron) than in air, sound travelling in air and meeting an iron plate can be totally internally reflected if the angle of incidence is above the critical angle. This idea is employed in the design of speaking tubes (a *sound pipe*) such as those used on ships.

19-4 Diffraction

It is a matter of common experience that sound waves bend round corners and spread out beyond doors and windows. Whenever a wavefront is limited or partly stopped in some way we get diffraction. Huygens's construction, which indicates that every point on the wavefront acts as a source of secondary wavelets, together with the principle of superposition, enables us to predict the result of diffraction in simple cases.

Figure 19-9 Refraction: (a) gravity waves 'beaching'; (b) earthquake P waves.

19 Wave phenomena

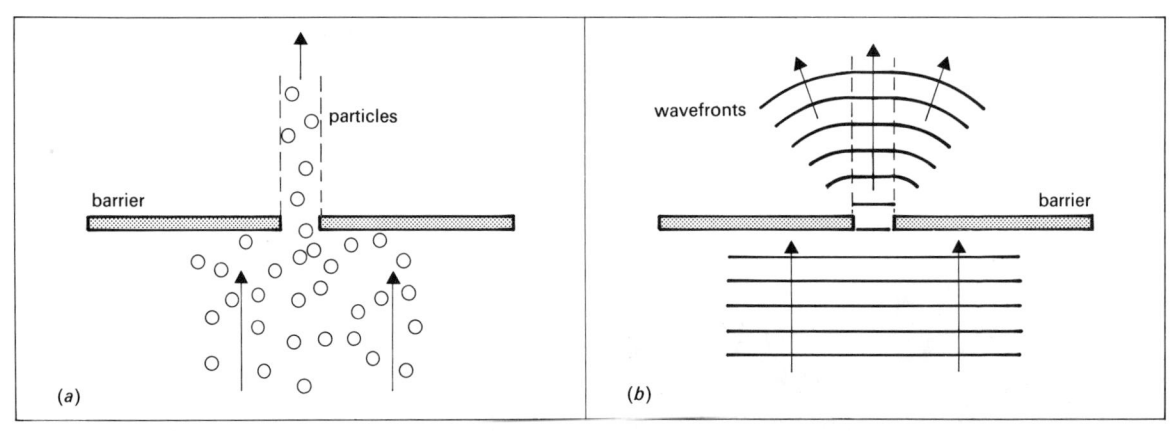

Figure 19-10 The contrast between particle and wave behaviour.

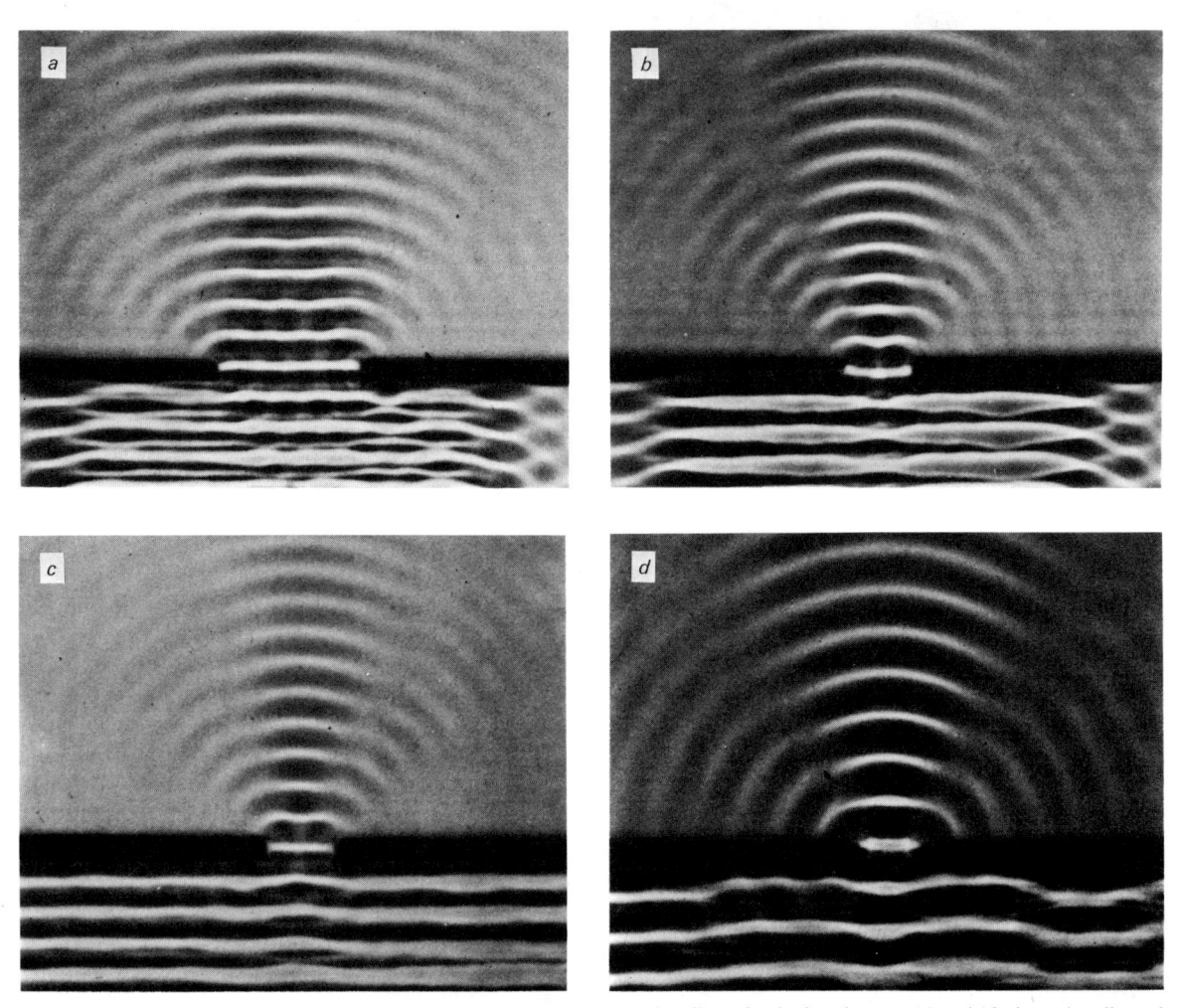

Figure 19-11 The diffraction of straight waves at a gap. (*a*) and (*b*) show the effect of reducing the gap; (*c*) and (*d*) show the effect of increasing the wavelength.

19-4 Diffraction

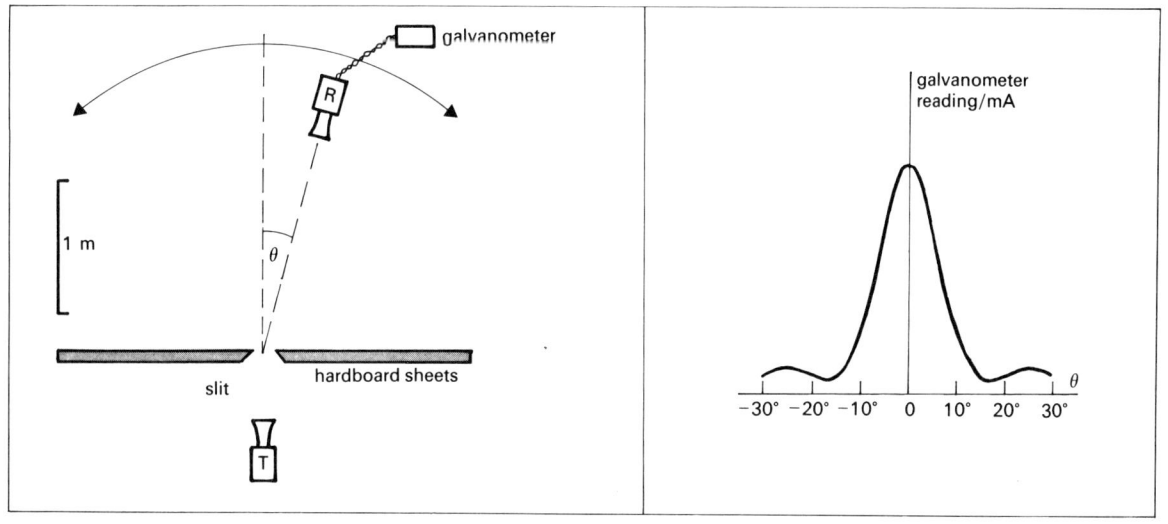

Figure 19-12 A diffraction experiment for ultrasonic waves of $\lambda \approx 8$ mm. The graph shows the relative intensity at the receiver against θ as R is moved on an arc centred at the slit.

Consider figure 19-10b: is it possible that a thin strip of wavefront equal in width to the gap could continue beyond the barrier in the ripple tank? What would happen to the 'edges' of the strip? They would have to be vertical. This sort of thinking leads us to see the inevitability of diffraction in this case. The energy of the water wave *must* spread out round the barrier and similar thinking predicts diffraction for any mechanical waves. What is more, the higher the frequency of oscillation of particles in the water surface the less time they have to 'fall sideways' away from the straight-through position and so we might expect a smaller proportion of the wave energy diffracted for high f (and low λ) than for low f. This last prediction can readily be shown to be true for water waves in a ripple tank. A set of plane waves is generated using an eccentric motor mounted on a loosely supported rod. The frequency can be altered by controlling the speed of rotation of the motor while the width of the gap, d, is easily adjusted. The way in which the wave energy is spread beyond the gap can be shown to depend on the ratio λ/d.

The ripple tank, however, does not give us a sufficiently detailed picture. The arrangement shown in figure 19-12 can be used to investigate how the intensity of an ultrasonic wave varies over a distance of many hundreds of wavelengths to either side of a slit of width $d \approx 3\lambda$. There is not a sharp acoustic shadow but a continuous variation of intensity as the receiver is moved across in front of the gap. The important experimental result is that the intensity reaches a minimum (at about 20° in the graph) *and then rises again.* Further maxima and minima are suggested but even this experiment is not really sensitive enough to show them convincingly.

To show why the minima arise, consider the plane wavefront incident at the slit of figure 19-13. Suppose we imagine ten secondary (Huygens) sources p, q, r, s, t and j, k, l, m, n as shown (and ignore any variation of amplitude with θ). The waves from the sources p and j will each send energy in a direction making an angle θ with the original direction, but these waves will have a phase difference ϕ, the value of ϕ depending on how much further the wave from source p travels than the wave from

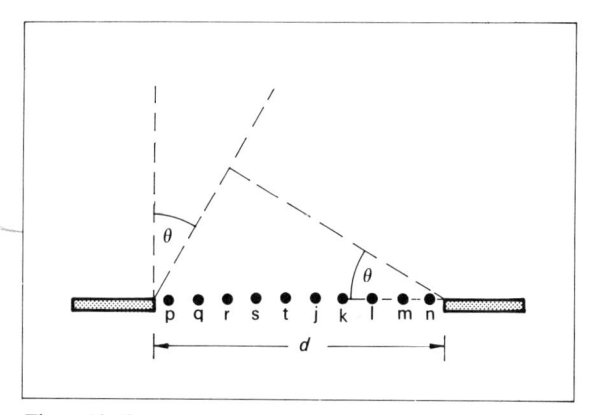

Figure 19-13 Huygens's principle and diffraction.

source j. From the geometry shown in the diagram, this distance is x where

$$x = \frac{d}{2}\sin\theta$$

and so

$$\phi = \frac{2\pi}{\lambda}\left(\frac{d}{2}\sin\theta\right).$$

If $\phi = 2\pi$ rad, 4π rad, etc., the two waves will be in phase, but if $\phi = \pi$ rad, 3π rad, etc., they will be out of phase. The first interesting case occurs when $\phi = \pi$ rad: the corresponding value (θ_1) of θ is given by

$$\pi = \frac{2\pi}{\lambda}\left(\frac{d}{2}\sin\theta_1\right)$$

or

$$\sin\theta_1 = \frac{\lambda}{d} \qquad [19\text{-}3]$$

and then the waves from the sources p and j are *out of phase*. If these two waves were to superpose they would produce zero displacement. At large distances (compared to d) from the slit in figure 19-13, the waves at θ_1 from p and j are gathered by R. This argument for sources p and j applies exactly to each of the pairs of sources qk, rl, sm, tn or to any secondary source on the left-hand half of the wavefront at the slit and the corresponding source on the right-hand half of the wavefront. Thus in a direction θ_1 given by $\sin\theta_1 = \lambda/d$, there will be a minimum amplitude at a great distance from the slit. The intensity will then also be a minimum, so that for $d = 3\lambda$,

$$\theta_{min} = \sin^{-1}\left(\frac{\lambda}{3\lambda}\right) \approx 20°$$

as shown on the graph in figure 19-12. The intensity is not zero as the receiver gathers waves from a finite area and so waves leaving p or j at $\theta_1 \pm \Delta\theta_1$. Lowering λ and d compared to the distance from slit to receiver produces a better experiment and this detailed work on diffraction is usually dealt with in texts on physical optics, where the (electromagnetic) waves have wavelengths of the order of 10^{-7} m. In the case of ripples on the surface of water we have only a relatively small distance beyond the slit available for observation, for example for a ripple tank 0.7 m long, there is not more than about 0.5 m beyond a gap and for $\lambda \approx 0.02$ m this is only 25 wavelengths. The simple theory does not hold in this case and it is difficult to draw any *detailed* conclusions from ripple tank diffraction experiments.

Most of the mechanical waves we have met in this text have wavelengths which are large compared with the dimensions of any objects or gaps they might meet so that they readily exhibit diffraction effects. The basic concept that 'waves bend round corners' is of great importance: diffraction is fundamental to a knowledge of the behaviour of waves.

Scattering

In the diffraction of waves round an object (see Exercises 19-16 to 19-19) it is quite possible that some wave energy may be given to the object so that it in turn becomes a source of waves: a real source and not a Huygens secondary source. When this happens the object is said to *scatter* the wave. When a sound wave strikes a suspended elastic sphere the sphere is set into oscillation, and now acts as a sound source with a frequency which is related (but not in any simple way) to that of the incident sound wave. The scattering of phonons (thermal waves in solids) controls the ability of solid material to conduct heat.

19-5 Two-source interference patterns

When two (or more) waves reach the same point we apply the principle of superposition to establish the resultant displacement at that point. Figure 19-14 shows a two-source experiment (an *interference* experiment) where the two sources are of the same frequency. They can further be adjusted to have roughly equal amplitudes by placing a variable resistor in series with one of the loudspeakers. As shown the sources, S_1 and S_2, are in phase but by reversing the connections to one of the

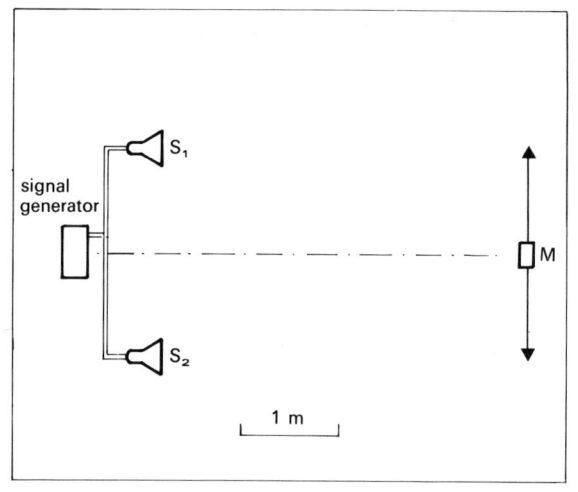

Figure 19-14 A three-dimensional superposition experiment with sound waves.

loudspeakers they can be arranged to be π rad out of phase (that is, in antiphase). In each case the sources have a phase relationship which does not vary with time: they are said to be *coherent*. The result of the superposition can be demonstrated with a microphone and c.r.o., or simply by listening. One difficulty is that reflected waves confuse the results; in a bare room a group of people can help to reduce reflections but they must be careful not to add to the background noise. A frequency of a few kilohertz ($\lambda \approx 0.1$ m) enables the experiment to be performed in a small space but lower frequencies should be used if the ear–brain is to be used as the detecting system.

As the microphone M is moved about, a pattern of maxima and minima of sound intensity is found. At places of maximum intensity clearly the phase difference between the excess pressures produced by the two waves is 0 or 2π rad (or, more generally, $2\pi n$ rad, where n is an integer). The path difference $S_1 M - S_2 M$ corresponds to a phase difference

$$\frac{2\pi}{\lambda}(S_1 M - S_2 M)\,\text{rad}$$

and so $\quad \dfrac{2\pi}{\lambda}(S_1 M - S_2 M) = 2\pi n$

that is $\quad S_1 M - S_2 M = n\lambda \qquad$ [19-4]

(for maximum I).

Similarly, $\quad S_1 M - S_2 M = (2n+1)\dfrac{\lambda}{2} \qquad$ [19-5]

(for minimum I).

A tape measure can be used to find the distances $S_1 M$ and $S_2 M$ at a minimum (which is more sensitively located than a maximum). If $S_1 M'$ and $S_2 M'$ are now measured to the *next* minimum, λ can be found as it is the *change* in the path difference. If λ is known the above equations can be tested. Figure 19-15 shows the *nodal lines* (lines of minimum intensity) and *antinodal lines* (lines of maximum intensity) in any plane containing the speakers for the particular case where they are in phase.

This experiment is perhaps the most convincing demonstration of the principle of superposition. If, with M on a nodal line, S_1 is disconnected, the oscilloscope records the arrival of sound energy; when S_1 is reconnected the trace reduces to a minimum. With M on an antinodal line the trace halves on disconnecting S_1. As the sound intensity $I = (\Delta p_0)^2/2\rho c$ (see page 328) and the c.r.o. trace height h_0 is proportional to Δp_0 (the excess pressure amplitude at M) we see that at a minimum (assumed zero for simplicity) $h_0 (\propto \Delta p_0)$ is zero, therefore

$$I = 0,$$

while at a maximum $h_0 (\propto \Delta p_0)$ is twice the height produced by S_1 or S_2 alone, therefore

$$I = 2^2 I_1$$
$$= 4 I_1 (\text{or } 4 I_2).$$

In this way the sound energy is *redistributed* when both S_1 and S_2 are emitting sound waves; energy is not lost. The energy flow away from S_1 and S_2 takes place along the antinodal lines. Adjacent antinodal lines are π rad out of phase.

Two-dimensional interference patterns for two sources on the surface of a ripple tank are readily demonstrated. Although the space is limited the hyperbolic shape of the nodal lines is very marked and the dependence of the form of the hyperbolae for differing λ and various separations $S_1 S_2$ can be investigated. These experiments can be

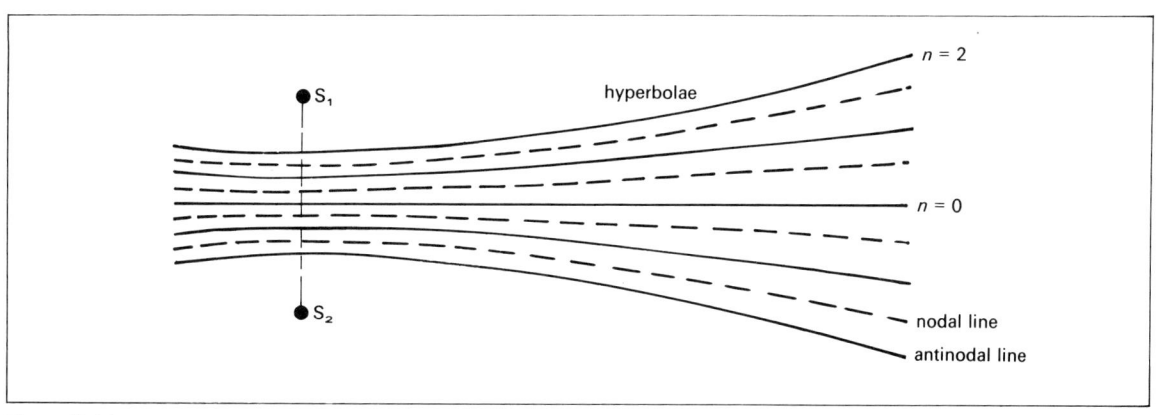

Figure 19-15 The sound intensity interference pattern for two in-phase sources.

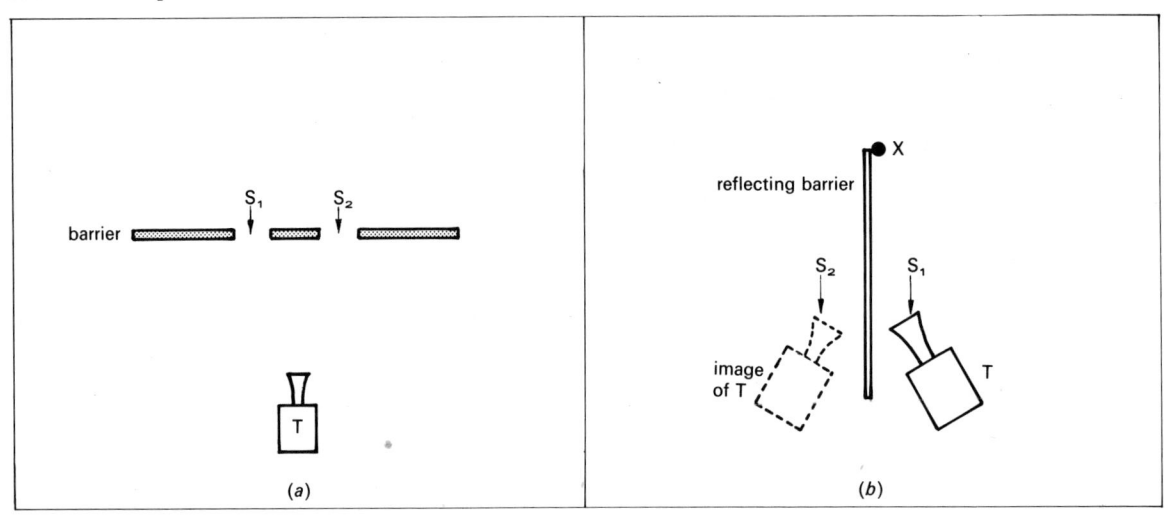

Figure 19-16 Two sources from one. In (b) there will be a minimum at X (because of the π radians phase change which occurs on reflection), that is the line of symmetry is a nodal line.

repeated with 40 kHz ultrasonic waves. Figure 19-16 indicates two ways of producing two coherent sources from a single ultrasonic transmitter using (a) diffraction and (b) reflection. For two sound waves of equal amplitude and frequency arriving at the same point with a phase difference ϕ we have

$$\Delta p_1 = \Delta p_0 \sin \frac{2\pi}{T} t$$

and

$$\Delta p_2 = \Delta p_0 \sin \left(\frac{2\pi}{T} t - \phi \right).$$

By the principle of superposition

$$\Delta p = \Delta p_1 + \Delta p_2 = \Delta p_0 \left[\sin \frac{2\pi}{T} t + \sin \left(\frac{2\pi}{T} t - \phi \right) \right]$$

$$= 2\Delta p_0 \cos \frac{\phi}{2} \sin \left(\frac{2\pi}{T} t - \frac{\phi}{2} \right). \qquad [19\text{-}6]$$

The pressure amplitude of this new wave is given by

$$\Delta P = 2\Delta p_0 \cos \frac{\phi}{2}$$

and the intensity of the wave by

$$I = \frac{(\Delta P)^2}{2\rho c}$$

$$= \frac{(2\Delta p_0 \cos \phi/2)^2}{2\rho c}$$

$$= 4 \cos^2 \frac{\phi}{2} \frac{(\Delta p_0)^2}{2\rho c}$$

$$= \left(4 \cos^2 \frac{\phi}{2} \right) I_0,$$

where I_0 is the intensity produced by either wave separately. (A similar proof holds for particle displacements y_1 and y_2; if these displacements are transverse, they must be polarized in the same plane.)

Figure 19-17 shows clearly that the average intensity as ϕ varies is $2I_0 = I_0 + I_0$ the sum of the intensities from S_1 and S_2. The second factor of equation 19-6,

$$\sin \left[\left(\frac{2\pi}{T} \right) t - \frac{\phi}{2} \right],$$

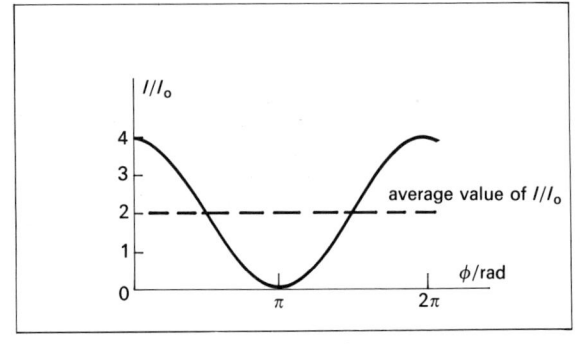

Figure 19-17 Graph of $I = I_0 (4 \cos^2 \phi/2)$ illustrating the redistribution of energy in a two-source interference pattern.

shows that adjacent antinodal lines, which occur for $\phi = 0$, $\phi = 2\pi$ rad, $\phi = 4\pi$ rad, etc., differ by π rad, that is they are in antiphase.

19-6 Dispersion

When the speed of a wave depends on its wavelength the wave is said to be travelling in a *dispersive medium*. By the speed of a wave in this context we mean the speed c at which the shape of an infinitely long sinusoidal wave advances: $c = f\lambda$. This is strictly called the *phase speed* of the wave. Thus we say that dispersion occurs when the phase speed c depends on the wavelength λ.

We have already noted the following results:

(a) sound waves in free air—no dispersion
(b) ripples on water—dispersion
(c) gravity waves in deep water—dispersion
(d) gravity waves in shallow water—no dispersion
(e) waves on strings and springs—no dispersion.

In each case the equation relating the speed c to the inertial and elastic properties of the medium either contains λ as in (b) and (c) or does not contain λ as in (a), (d), and (e). For some other waves:

(f) P and S earthquake waves—no dispersion
(g) long earthquake waves—dispersion
(h) sound waves in tubes—dispersion

and so on.

Where a wave is not dispersed the speed of the wave as measured by the speed at which a signal is transmitted from A to B is equal to the phase speed c. The wave also has the same shape during its journey, a result which has important implications for the transmission of sound waves. For waves which are dispersed the situation is quite different. Consider a wave pulse such as might be formed by throwing a stone into a deep pond. According to the Fourier theorem (see Exercise 16-16) a wave pulse may be considered to be the result of superposing a series of simple harmonic waves. Thus the initial wave pulse of figure 19-18 may contain waves of long wavelength and of short wavelength and if the waves are gravity water waves, for which $c = \sqrt{(g\lambda/2\pi)}$, then the waves of long wavelength will travel faster than those of short wavelength. An extreme example of this dispersion effect is given by ocean waves from distant storms; for example, long waves arriving on the coast of Cornwall from a storm near the Falkland Islands have been found to arrive four days before the shortest waves from the same storm.

As a result of dispersion a group of gravity water waves a long way from their source behaves in an odd way

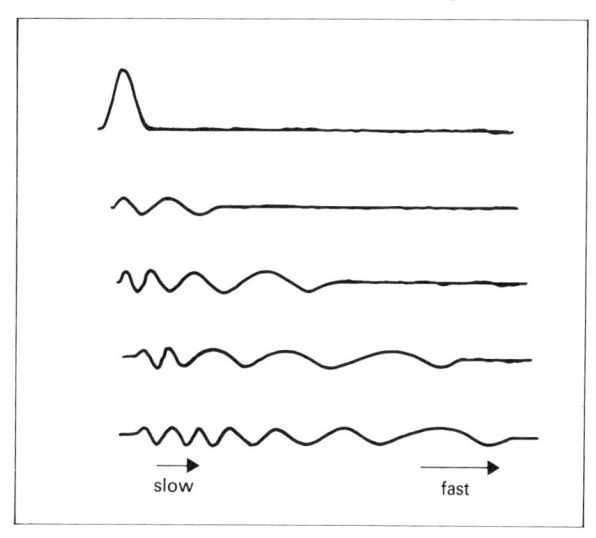

Figure 19-18 A diagrammatic illustration of the effect of dispersion on the propagation of a wave pulse.

(such a group will contain waves with only a small spread of wavelength). The leading wave of the group seems to disappear and a new wave to appear at the back. As a result the speed of the wave group—the speed at which the energy associated with the waves moves forward—is less than the phase speed c_λ, while the energy of the wave group remains constant. This new speed is called the group speed, v, and is the speed at which an observer would measure the group of waves to move past him. Since for gravity waves c increases as λ increases, then $v < c$.

Figure 17-14 shows dispersion on the surface of a pond. For ripples the phase speed decreases as the wavelength increases [$c = \sqrt{(2\pi\gamma/\rho\lambda)}$], so that an observer watching a group of ripples would see waves disappearing at the back of the group and reappearing at the front; the group speed is greater than the phase speed. In general if $c_{\lambda+\Delta\lambda} >$ or $< c_\lambda$ then $v <$ or $> c$. This phenomenon of dispersion and group velocity is of no importance for sound waves in air but is important for light waves travelling in glass.

19-7 Doppler effect

Moving source

The pitch of a train whistle heard by an observer standing on a station platform seems to fall at the moment the whistle rushes past him. The frequency of the sound waves reaching him depends on the relative motion between himself and the train. The frequency of the whistle on the train, of course, remains fixed.

To analyse what is happening let us consider a source S of sound waves of frequency f_S. Suppose these waves travel at a speed c and are of wavelength $\lambda_S : c = f_S \lambda_S$. Two different simple situations are possible: firstly, where an observer O is at rest in the air and the source moves directly towards him at a speed v_S; and, secondly, where the source is at rest in the air but the observer moves towards it at a speed v_O.

Figure 19-19 clearly shows that the observer will hear a high frequency note, for the waves are 'compressed' in the direction SO while their speed is unchanged. During each period of vibration of the source, a time $1/f_S$, S moves forward a distance v_S/f_S and so the wavelength is shortened by this amount in the forward direction. If the wavelength observed at O is λ_O then

$$\lambda_O = \lambda_S - \frac{v_S}{f_S}.$$

If the observed frequency is f_O (and $\lambda_O = c/f_O$ and $\lambda_S = c/f_S$), then

$$\frac{c}{f_O} = \frac{c}{f_S} - \frac{v_S}{f_S};$$

therefore
$$f_O = f_S \left(\frac{c}{c - v_S} \right)$$
$$= f_S \left(\frac{1}{1 - v_S/c} \right). \quad [19\text{-}7]$$

Similar reasoning leads to

$$f_O = f_S \left(\frac{1}{1 + v_S/c} \right)$$

when the source is receding from the observer at a speed v_S.

▶ **Example 19-2** An observer stands by the side of a railway track while a train approaches him at a steady speed of $34 \, \text{m s}^{-1}$. It continuously sounds its whistle, which has a frequency of 500 Hz. What are the frequencies heard by the observer as the train approaches and recedes? Take the speed of sound in air to be $340 \, \text{m s}^{-1}$.

The wavelength of the whistle would be $(340 \, \text{m s}^{-1}/500 \, \text{m s}^{-1}) = 0.68 \, \text{m}$ if it were stationary. But in each $1/500 \, \text{s}$, the whistle moves a distance of $(34 \, \text{m s}^{-1})(1/500 \, \text{s}) = 0.068 \, \text{m}$, so that the wave's length is only $0.68 \, \text{m} - 0.068 \, \text{m} = 0.612 \, \text{m}$. The speed of the sound is still $340 \, \text{m s}^{-1}$, so the observed frequency is $(340 \, \text{m s}^{-1}/0.612 \, \text{m}) = 556 \, \text{Hz}$.

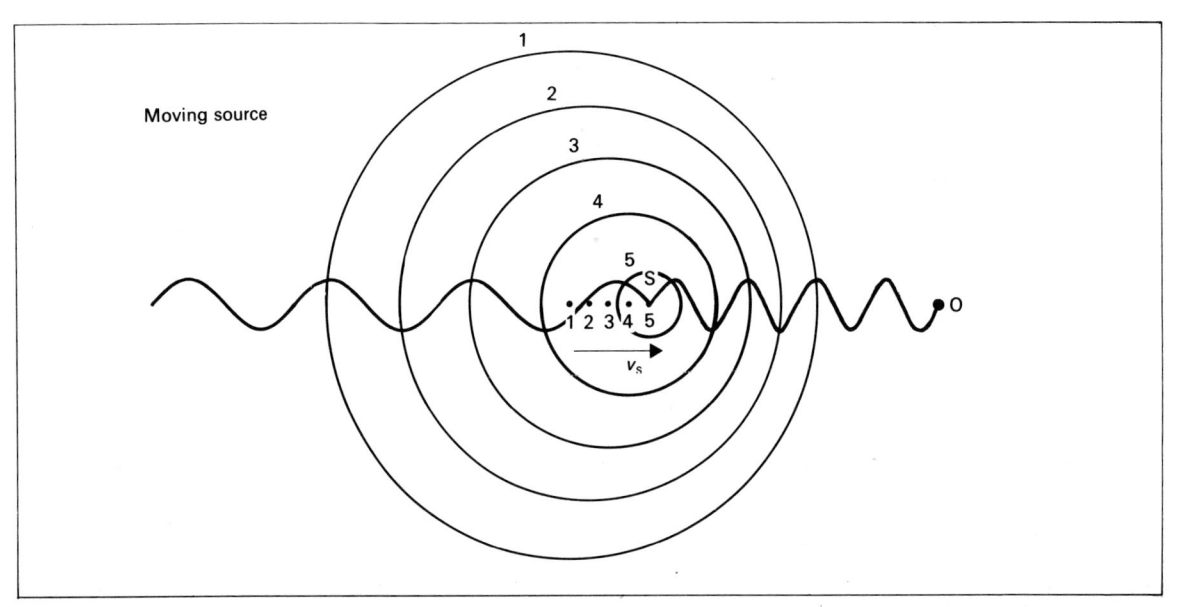

Figure 19-19 A moving source. The wavefronts for five successive positions of the source are shown and numbered. A stationary observer is at O.

19-7 Doppler effect

When the whistle is moving away, the wavelength is lengthened by the same amount, so that the length of the wave becomes $0.68\,\text{m} + 0.068\,\text{m} = 0.748\,\text{m}$, and the observed frequency is $(340\,\text{m s}^{-1}/0.748\,\text{m}) = 455\,\text{Hz}$. Thus there is a change in frequency of 101 Hz when the whistle passes the observer. The change is sudden but it is not instantaneous as the observer is not on the line of movement of the whistle. ◀

Moving observer

From figure 19-20 we see that in a time interval Δt the observer moves $v_O \Delta t$ and so 'gathers' $v_O \Delta t / \lambda_S$ extra waves. He would anyway receive $f_S \Delta t$ waves in this time and so if the observed frequency is f_O, then

$$f_O \Delta t = f_S \Delta t + \frac{v_O \Delta t}{\lambda_S}.$$

But $c = \lambda_S f_S$,

therefore $\quad f_O = f_S + \dfrac{v_O f_S}{c}$

or $\quad f_O = f_S \left(1 + \dfrac{v_O}{c}\right).$ [19-8]

Similar reasoning leads to

$$f_O = f_S \left(1 - \frac{v_O}{c}\right)$$

when the observer is moving away from the source.

Where the motion of the source is not along the line OS there is still a frequency change though now f_O varies continuously. If the component of the velocity v_S along SO is $v_S \cos\theta$, where θ is the angle between v_S and SO, then

$$f_O = \frac{f_S}{1 - v_S \cos\theta / c} \quad [19\text{-}9]$$

and so on. (See Exercises 19-28 and 19-29.) The fact that $f_O \neq f_S$ if v_S or $v_O \neq 0$ is called the *Doppler effect* and the above discussion holds for all mechanical waves. The cases for which v_O increases to become of the order of c are most easily visualized for water waves. Consider a source producing ripples which travel on a water surface at $0.25\,\text{m s}^{-1}$. If we fix our attention on a point just above the surface which is moving *away* from the source at $0.25\,\text{m s}^{-1}$, the water surface beneath it will always be the same shape: $f_O = 0$. On the other hand, if we fix our attention on a point which moves towards the source at $0.25\,\text{m s}^{-1}$ the water surface beneath it pulses up and down with a frequency $f_O = 2f_S$. The case for which v_S increases beyond c is discussed in the next section.

If a stationary source S sends waves to a reflecting barrier R a stationary wave pattern is produced in the region between S and R. If R is now moved towards S at a speed v an observer who receives both the sound direct from S and the reflected sound from R will hear a beat phenomenon. If the $f_S = 1000\,\text{Hz}$ and we take $v_R/c = 1/1000$ (that is $v_R \approx 0.3\,\text{m s}^{-1}$) then the frequency of the wave as received at the reflector is $1000\,\text{Hz} \times (1 + 1/1000) = 1001\,\text{Hz}$. R is now acting as a second source (of frequency 1001 Hz) approaching S at $0.3\,\text{m s}^{-1}$. The frequency of the waves from R as measured by an observer at rest relative to S is $1001\,\text{Hz} \times [1/(1 - 1/1000)] \approx 1002\,\text{Hz}$, and so the waves from S and R beat at a frequency $(1002 - 1000)\,\text{Hz} = 2\,\text{Hz}$. This experiment is quite easily performed in the laboratory and the idea is the basis of using sound echoes to measure the speed of, for example, a submarine.

The relativistic Doppler effect

Light is an electromagnetic wave motion. The energy travels in wave packets called *photons* which are characterized by a certain frequency corresponding to the colour of the light. Photons obey the principle of the constancy of the limiting speed of particles (Section 10-6), that is the speed of light *in vacuo* is the same, $3.0 \times 10^8\,\text{m s}^{-1}$, for all observers in inertial frames of reference.

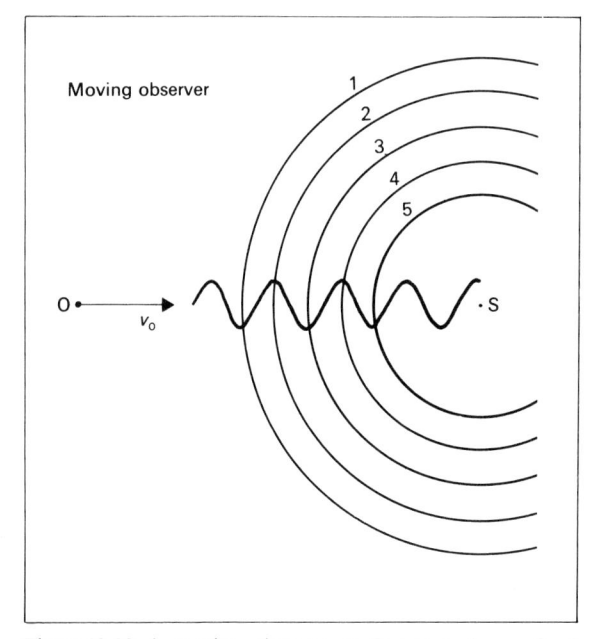

Figure 19-20 A moving observer at O approaches a fixed source.

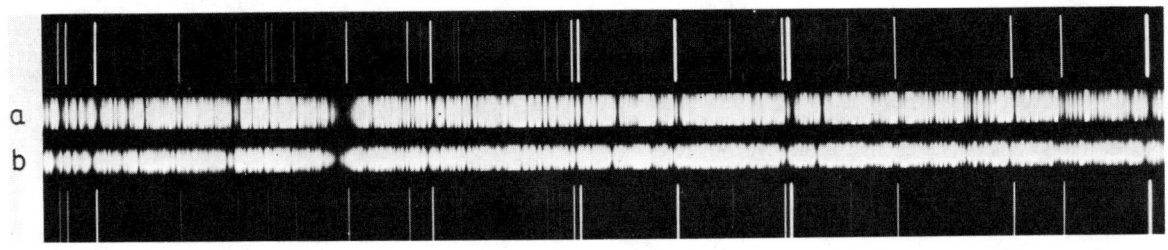

Figure 19-21 Spectra ($\lambda = 4.200 \times 10^{-7}$ m to $\lambda = 4.300 \times 10^{-7}$ m) of the constant-velocity star Arcturus. The photographs were taken from the Earth at an interval of six months. On the first occasion (a) the velocity of the star was $+18\,\text{km s}^{-1}$ relative to the Earth, and on the second occasion (b) it was $-32\,\text{km s}^{-1}$, the difference being due to the speed of the Earth in its orbit round the Sun. The effect on the spectra can be seen by comparing the positions of the spectral lines with those in the reference spectra above and below.

In developing the Doppler relationships for sound, the speed of these mechanical waves was measured relative to the air in which they travelled. No equivalent medium exists for electromagnetic waves, and so for light we *cannot* adopt equations 19-7 to 19-9 but must start again.

In Section 10-6 we considered the way in which our classical view of time must be altered because of the principle of the constancy of the limiting speed of particles. In the argument leading to the time dilation formula we showed that the ratio

$$\frac{\Delta t_b}{\Delta t_a} = k$$

$$= \sqrt{\frac{1 + v/c}{1 - v/c}},$$

where Δt_a is the (correct) time interval between an observer A sending signals (at $3.0 \times 10^8\,\text{m s}^{-1}$) and Δt_b is the (correct) time interval at which a second observer B receives them, when A and B are moving apart at a speed v. The quantity k is called the *relativistic Doppler factor*: its value depends only on the relative speeds of A and B.

As $T = 1/f$ then (A emitting and B receiving),

$$\frac{\Delta t_b}{\Delta t_a} = \frac{f_{\text{emitted}}}{f_{\text{received}}}.$$

or in the notation of this section (S emitting and O observing)

$$\frac{f_s}{f_o} = \sqrt{\frac{1 + v/c}{1 - v/c}},$$

that is

$$f_o = f_s \sqrt{\frac{1 - v/c}{1 + v/c}}. \qquad [19\text{-}10]$$

This implies that if a source, such as a distant star, is emitting photons of frequency f_s, these photons will be observed on Earth to have a frequency which is *lower* than f_s if the star is receding from the Earth.* Characteristic lines in a spectrum will therefore be displaced towards the red end of the spectrum. This is the *Doppler red shift* on which so much of our knowledge of the Universe depends. For source and observer approaching at a relative speed v, we simply replace v by $-v$ in the above relations.

The relativistic Doppler effect is used to measure the speed of vehicles such as cars and satellites. For $v \ll c$ the quantity

$$1 - \frac{f_o}{f_s} = \frac{f_s - f_o}{f_s} = \frac{\Delta f}{f_s}.$$

But

$$\frac{f_s - f_o}{f_s} = \frac{f_s - f_s \sqrt{[(1 - v/c)/(1 + v/c)]}}{f_s}$$

$$= 1 - \left(1 - \frac{v}{c}\right)^{1/2} \left(1 + \frac{v}{c}\right)^{-1/2}.$$

Expanding, using the binomial theorem,

$$\frac{f_s - f_o}{f_s} = 1 - \left(1 - \frac{v}{2c} + \cdots\right)\left(1 - \frac{v}{2c} - \cdots\right)$$

$$= 1 - \left(1 - \frac{v}{c} + \cdots\right)$$

$$\approx \frac{v}{c} \text{ ignoring terms in } \frac{v^2}{c^2} \text{ or above.}$$

Thus $\quad \dfrac{\Delta f}{f_s} \approx \dfrac{v}{c} \qquad [19\text{-}11]$

---

*The star must have no transverse velocity for these statements to hold exactly—for a brief comment on the transverse relativistic Doppler effect see *The teaching of physics* by J. W. Warren.

and so for $f_s = 10^{10}$ Hz, $c = 3.0 \times 10^8$ m s^{-1}, and $v = 15$ m s^{-1} we get $\Delta f = 500$ Hz. This *beat frequency*, Δf, can readily be converted into a dial reading for easy use in a police speed-trap. Further suggested uses, both practical and theoretical, for the k factor are suggested in the exercises at the end of this chapter.

19-8 Shock waves

When $v_s > c$ for mechanical waves a situation like that shown in figure 19-22 arises. The source might be a vibrating prong moving across the surface of a ripple tank or a bullet in air or (more easily observed) a boat on a lake.

Consider the example of the bullet in air where the waves are sound waves for which $c = 330$ m s^{-1}. To produce a shock wave the source must travel at more than 330 m s^{-1}, which is why it is convenient to consider a bullet, though of course supersonic aeroplanes can by definition travel at speeds greater than 330 m s^{-1}. Shock waves of high amplitude travel faster than the speed of ordinary sound waves but we shall ignore this here. The nose of the bullet will initiate a disturbance in the air and the wavefronts will, according to Huygens's construction, produce an envelope which will be the resulting wavefront. This shock wave envelope shows up clearly enough in figure 19-22a; in (b) we see the geometry and clearly

$$\operatorname{cosec} \theta = \frac{v_s \Delta t}{c \Delta t} = \frac{v_s}{c}. \qquad [19\text{-}12]$$

This ratio is called the *Mach number* (Ma); Ma 2, for example, means that the source is moving at twice the speed of sound. The Anglo–French Concorde cruises at just over Ma 2; this does not however mean that it flies at 2×330 m s^{-1} for it flies high up in the Earth's atmosphere where the speed of sound is only about 280 m s^{-1}. A great deal of energy is associated with a shock wave giving rise to the sonic bang associated with supersonic aircraft.

Shock waves produced by bullets and other small objects can be photographed using the Schlieren technique. Both the nose and the tail of a bullet produce conical shock waves. By measuring θ (see figure 19-22b) from such a photograph the speed of the bullet can be measured and this technique is a standard one in ballistics laboratories. As noted on page 298 the crack of a whip occurs when the tip of the whip reaches a speed of more than Ma 1, so producing a shock wave. Figure 19-23 shows the way in which the shock wave cones from a supersonic aeroplane meet the ground.

The shock waves produced by boats are part of a more complex wave phenomenon called a *wake*. Most of the energy of a ship or boat goes into producing the wake and a detailed understanding of its formation enables us

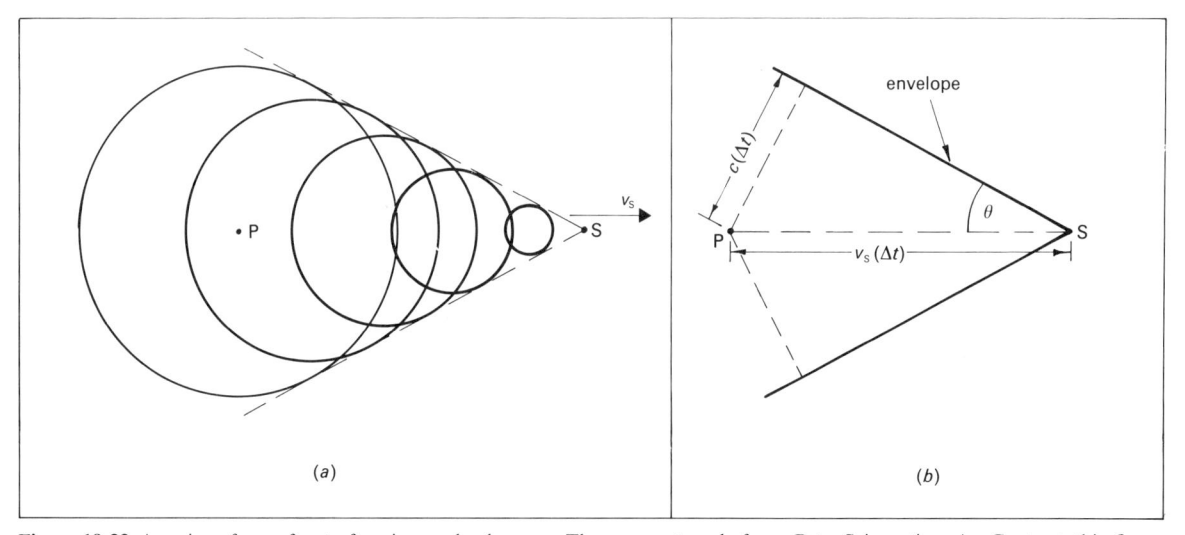

Figure 19-22 A series of wavefronts forming a shock wave. The source travels from P to S in a time Δt. Contrast this figure with figure 19-19.

358   19 Wave phenomena

Figure 19-23 Shock waves formed by an aircraft flying at about Ma 2. Both the leading and trailing parts of the aircraft form shock waves.

to design vessels more efficiently. However, water waves disperse (that is their speed depends on their wavelength) and this makes the analysis of wakes very much more difficult than for non-dispersive sound waves. One argument* is that the shock waves of this paragraph occur only in shallow water where $c = \sqrt{(gh)}$, h being the depth. In water that is deep compared to the wavelength of the waves being generated the wake is always of the form indicated in figure 19-24 and this can be observed both for swans on a lake and for tankers at sea.

*See *Bores, Breakers, Waves and Wakes* by R. A. R. Tricker.

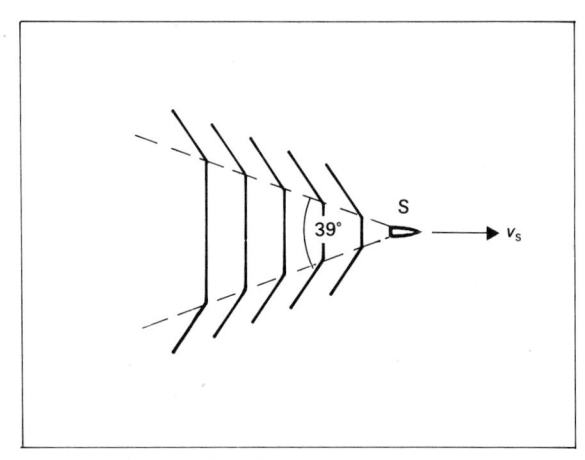

Figure 19-24 The wake of a ship or a swan. The 39° angle between the arms of the wake is independent of v_s.

Bibliography

Mendoza, M. (1968). 'Waves.' *Sources of physics teaching*, part 2. Taylor and Francis. This article is reprinted from *Contemporary Physics*.

Sandage, A. R. (1956). 'The red shift.' *Scientific American* offprint number 240.

Arons, A. B. (1965). *Development of concepts of physics*. Addison–Wesley. Chapter 22 covers waves.

Chaundy, D. C. F. (1972). *Waves*. Longman. An excellent well-illustrated elementary text.

French, A. P. (1971). *Vibrations and waves*. Nelson. The last chapter covers the relevant subject matter.

Llowarch, W. (1961). *Ripple tank studies of wave motion*. Oxford University Press. A superb book containing numerous original photographs and detailed non-mathematical discussion of all the material mentioned in this chapter.

Nuffield O-level Physics (1967). *Guide to experiments III*. Longman/Penguin. Numerous ripple tank experiments are described.

Pohl, R. W. (1932). *Physical principles of mechanics and acoustics*. Blackie (out of print). A textbook rooted in experiment. The last chapter is relevant here and includes among much of interest the details of quantitative experiments using ultrasonic waves.

Project Physics (1970). Text and handbook, Unit 3 *The triumph of mechanics*. Holt, Rinehart and Winston. Chapter 12 is on waves. See also the handbook section.

PSSC (1971). *Physics*, 3rd edition. Raytheon. Chapters 6 and 7 of this text or of *College Physics*.

Tricker, R. A. R. (1964). *Bores, breakers, waves and wakes*. Mills and Boon. The behaviour of water waves in their natural surroundings.

8 mm film loop. 'Diffraction at an aperture.' Gateway. The film shows how the diffraction of water waves in a ripple tank depends upon the width of the aperture.

8 mm film loop. 'Formation of shock waves.' Ealing Scientific.

8 mm film loop. 'Refraction of waves.' Ealing Scientific. A convincing film showing a ripple tank with two sections of different depths. The film includes a demonstration of total internal reflection.

16 mm film. 'Sound waves.' Guild Sound and Vision. The film uses sound waves at 5000 Hz to illustrate wave properties.

Exercises

Data (to be used unless otherwise directed):

$g = 10 \text{ m s}^{-2} = 10 \text{ N kg}^{-1}$.
Speed of sound in air at 290 K $= 3.4 \times 10^2 \text{ m s}^{-1}$.
Speed of electromagnetic radiation *in vacuo* $= 3.0 \times 10^8 \text{ m s}^{-1}$.

19-1 A stroboscope disc is placed between a lamp and a ripple tank surface: the disc has 5 slits and is rotated steadily at 2 revolutions per second. If the ripple tank pattern appears stationary, what are the possible frequencies of the wave on the water surface? ●

19-2 Figure 19-25 shows the pattern observed under stroboscopic illumination on a ripple tank when a straight vibrator V is used with a fixed barrier B. When the stroboscope is removed, the top half of the diagram is still visible. Explain this. If the distance between V and B is 150 mm, what is the wavelength of the waves? What would be seen if the stroboscope were used at twice the original frequency? ●

19-3 A ripple tank is to be used to demonstrate the fact that when waves move from deep water to shallow water their wavelength changes. Use the expressions $c = 2\pi/\lambda \sqrt{(\gamma h/\rho)}$ and $c = f\lambda$ (where f and λ are the frequency and wavelength of the waves, γ is the surface tension of the water, h its depth, and ρ its density) to find the wavelength of ripples when the frequency of the vibrator is 10 Hz and the depth of the water is (*a*) 8.0 mm (*b*) 2.0 mm. (Take $\gamma = 7.0 \times 10^{-2} \text{ N m}^{-1}$, $\rho = 1.0 \times 10^3 \text{ kg m}^{-3}$.) ●

19-4 Use Huygens's construction to prove that when a plane wave is incident obliquely on a plane reflecting surface, the angle of incidence is equal to the angle of reflection. (Start by copying figure 19-6*a*.)

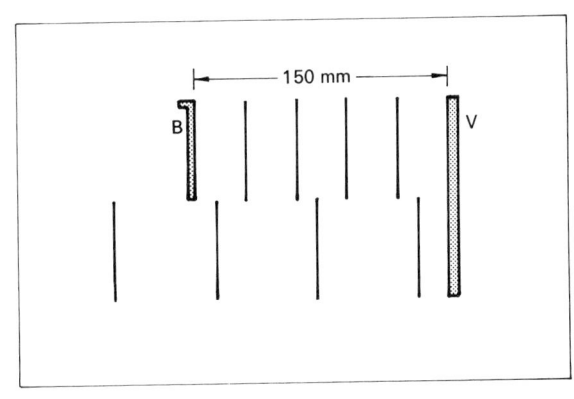

Figure 19-25

19 Wave phenomena

19-5 Railings along the edge of a pavement are spaced at regular intervals of 200 mm for a considerable distance. A man walking along the pavement who occasionally strikes the pavement with his walking stick hears a faint musical note when he does so, by reflection of sound from the railings. What is its approximate frequency? Explain. ●

19-6 If longitudinal seismic waves (with a speed of 8.0×10^3 m s^{-1}) have an angle of incidence of $70°$ when they strike the Earth's surface, what is the angle of refraction? Could they ever be totally internally reflected at the Earth's surface? ●

19-7 The bulk modulus and density of iron are, respectively, 1.1×10^{11} N m^{-2} and 7.6×10^3 kg m^{-3}. Find the critical angle for sound waves travelling from air towards iron. Does this value suggest that it would be relatively hard to construct a 'sound pipe' for use as a speaking tube? ●

19-8 Explain the refraction of water waves illustrated in figure 19-9a.

19-9 A thin plane membrane is used to separate some gas at 288 K from the same gas at 392 K. A plane sound wave travels in the cooler gas and is incident on the membrane at an angle of $20°$. Find the angle of refraction. In which gas would the wave need to travel if total internal reflection were to be possible? What is the critical angle? ●

19-10 Refer to the last paragraph of Section 19-3. What is a *light* pipe? In what way is the principle of its operation similar to that of a sound pipe?

19-11 Figure 19-26 shows plane sound waves being deviated by an equiangular prism, filled with hydrogen, in air. Find the angle of incidence θ in order that the waves may pass through the prism symmetrically. The speed of sound in hydrogen is 3.9 times greater than it is in air at the same temperature. (*Hint:* the time taken for the point A on the wavefront to move to A' through the hydrogen is equal to the time taken for point B on the wavefront to move to B' through air.) ●

19-12 It is proposed to construct a carbon dioxide lens to bring plane sound waves to a point, as shown in figure 19-27. Given that AB is to be 0.50 m, and OF (the focal length) is to be 1.50 m, find the thickness OX of the lens, given that the speed of sound in air is 1.3 times greater than the speed of sound in carbon dioxide at the same temperature. What assumptions does your solution involve? Are they reasonable assumptions in this situation? ●

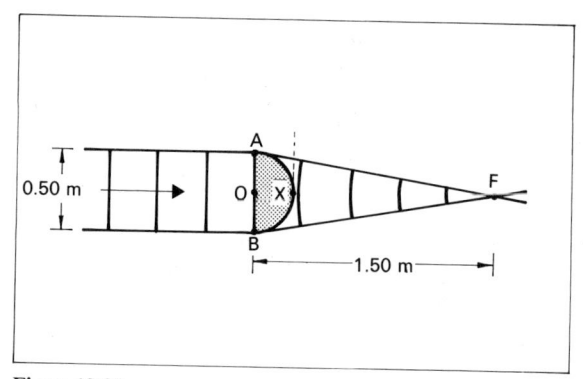

Figure 19-27

19-13 Figure 19-28 shows the wavefronts from a source of sounds when the waves are in a medium which is such that they have a higher speed at greater distances from the surface. Copy the diagram and draw on it the directions in which the sound travels (the 'rays' of sound). This situation occurs in practice in the evening of a hot day when the ground (and the air near it) cools first. Explain why it is sometimes easier to hear sounds at a distance on such an evening.

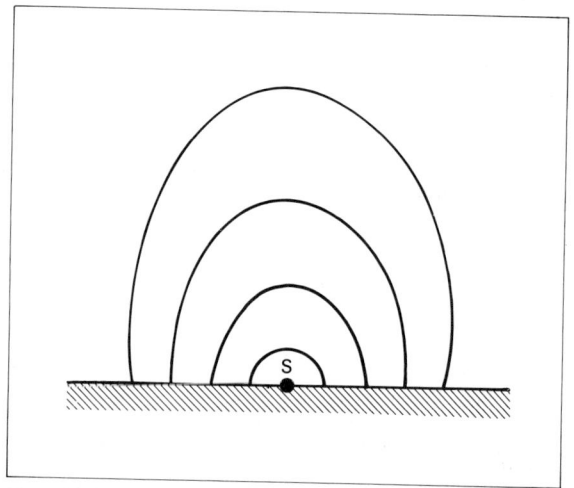

Figure 19-28

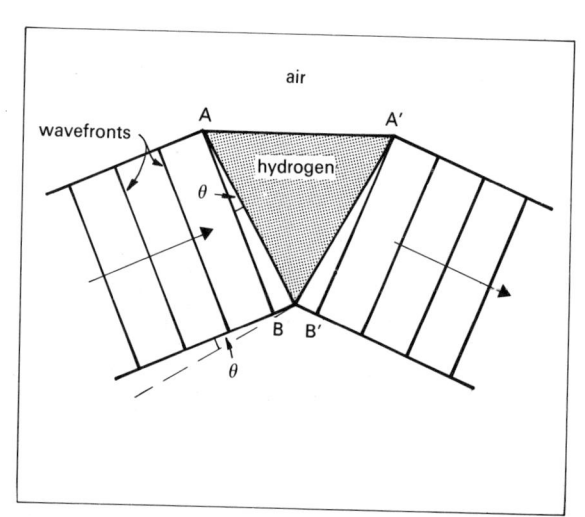

Figure 19-26

19-14 Draw a diagram similar to figure 19-28 to explain why it is easier to hear a sound when one is downwind of it. (The speed of a wind increases with height above the Earth's surface, for a short distance.)

19-15 The temperature of the atmosphere decreases to a height of about 11 km and then increases again. Use this fact to explain why there is sometimes a 'silent zone' a few kilometres from an explosion, but the explosion can again be heard at greater distances.

19-16 Draw diagrams to illustrate what happens when plane waves of wavelength λ strike head-on an obstacle of width d when
(a) the ratio λ/d is small, and
(b) the ratio λ/d is large.

19-17 Use the information conveyed by figure 19-12 to draw a polar diagram showing how the intensity varies with direction. Figure 19-29 shows the beginning of the polar diagram: the amplitudes at $\theta = 0°, 10°, 20°$ are shown. The diagram should be completed, and the points joined with a line.

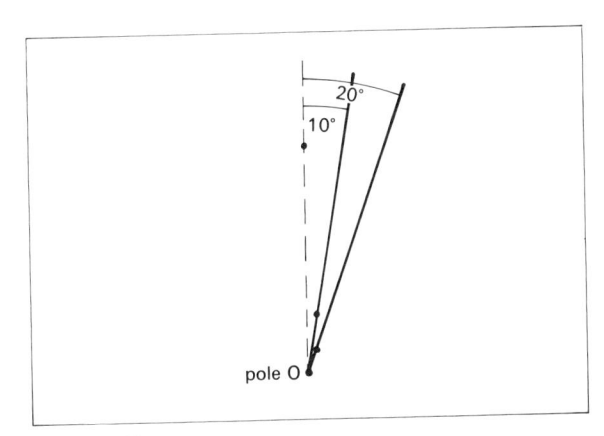

Figure 19-29

19-18 Water waves of wavelength 25 mm arrive at a gap of width 100 mm in a barrier: the waves are parallel to the barrier. Find the first three angles on either side of the centre line of the gap at which there will be a minimum of amplitude.
What happens if the width of the gap is reduced to
(a) 50 mm   (b) 25 mm   (c) less than 25 mm?

19-19 A man lies on the ground near the edge of a cliff, and a seagull perches on a ledge a few metres below the top of the cliff. It makes two kinds of noise: high-pitched cries, and a low-pitched noise from the beating of its wings. Assuming that the two noises have similar intensities, which is the man more likely to hear, and why?

19-20 Draw two points, S_1 and S_2, 20 mm apart. With centres S_1 and S_2 draw semicircular arcs (on one side of the line $S_1 S_2$) of radii 10 mm to 100 mm, at 10 mm intervals. Locate the points A_1, A_2, etc. which are the intersections of those points equidistant from S_1 and S_2. Also locate those points B_1, B_2, etc. which are 10 mm further from S_1, and the points C_1, C_2, etc. which are 20 mm further from S_1 than they are from S_1. Join the points A_1, A_2, etc. (with a straight line) and use smooth curves to join the points B_1, B_2, etc. and the points C_1, C_2, etc. What is the significance of the diagram you now have?

19-21 Refer to Exercise 19-20. Use the mid-point of $S_1 S_2$ as an origin and impose rectangular axes on the diagram so that the coordinates of S_1 and S_2 (in cm) are (0, 1) and (0, −1) respectively. Consider any point B which is 1 cm further from S_2 than it is from S_1, and assign the coordinates (x, y) to it. Show that x and y are related by the equation $y^2 - x^2/3 = 1/4$. (This equation has the form of a hyperbola: any other point such that its distances from S_1 and S_2 have a constant difference also lies on a hyperbola, so that the nodal and antinodal lines of such a two-source interference pattern are hyperbolic.)

19-22 Refer to figure 19-15. Sketch the positions of the nodal and antinodal lines when S_1 and S_2 are in antiphase.

19-23 Use your experience of Exercise 19-20 to discover what happens to the interference pattern of figure 19-15 when
(a) the distance $S_1 S_2$ is increased, the wavelength remaining the same, or
(b) the wavelength is increased, the distance $S_1 S_2$ remaining the same, or
(c) the distance $S_1 S_2$ is decreased, *and* the wavelength is decreased, both by the same factor.

19-24 Two identical in-phase sources of sound S_1 and S_2 are placed a certain distance apart. At a point on the perpendicular bisector of $S_1 S_2$, and some distance from them, a microphone detects a maximum of intensity of sound: and it is then moved some distance parallel to $S_1 S_2$ until a maximum is again detected. The distances of this point from S_1 and S_2 are found to be 10.0 m and 8.0 m. What is the wavelength of the sound? ●

19-25 It can be shown that $v = c - \lambda(dc/d\lambda)$, where v and c are the group velocity and phase velocity of a wave motion respectively, and λ is the wavelength. Prove that for water waves
(a) of short wavelength (ripples), $v = 3c/2$, and
(b) of long wavelength (gravity waves), $v = c/2$.
What are the implications of these results?

19-26 Find from first principles the frequencies heard by a stationary observer when a horn of frequency 400 Hz attached to a sports car moving down the straight of a race track at a speed of 50 m s^{-1} passes close to him. ●

19-27 Repeat Exercise 19-26 but now with a wind of speed 15 m s^{-1} blowing in the direction in which the car is moving. ●

19-28 An observer's perpendicular distance from a point A on a railway track is 100 m. An express train moves along the track at a steady speed of 50 m s^{-1}, continuously sounding a whistle of frequency 600 Hz. Draw a graph to show the frequency f heard by the observer against x, the distance of the train from A, for values of x = 200 m, 100 m, 50 m, 20 m, 0.
Use your graph to find the distance of the train from A when the frequency heard is 625 Hz.
Complete your graph by sketching its form for negative values of x. ●

19-29 Refer to Exercise 19-28. Sketch the form of this graph again, and then on the same diagram draw a few of the curves which would be obtained for smaller distances of the observer from the track, including the case when the observer is actually on the line of motion of the train.

19 Wave phenomena

19-30 A policeman sounds a whistle of frequency 400 Hz. Find from first principles the frequencies of the whistle as heard by the occupants of a car moving in a straight line past (and close to) the policeman at a speed of $50\,\mathrm{m\,s^{-1}}$. Compare your answers with those to Exercise 19-26; they should be different. A knowledge of the relative speeds of source and observer is not enough: their own speeds relative to the Earth must be known.

19-31 Derive an expression for the apparent frequency f_O of a source of frequency f when the source and observer are both moving towards each other with speeds relative to the Earth of v_S and v_O respectively. Let the speed of sound be c. Hence find the frequency heard by an observer on train A when a whistle of frequency 600 Hz is blown on train B, both trains having the same speed of $40\,\mathrm{m\,s^{-1}}$,
  (a) if the trains are approaching each other, and
  (b) if the trains are moving away from each other.

19-32 A car, continuously sounding its horn of frequency 500 Hz, is moving away from an observer at a steady speed of $5\,\mathrm{m\,s^{-1}}$ and towards a plane wall which reflects the sound. What is the frequency of the beats which the observer hears? (*Hint:* consider the reflected waves as coming from a moving virtual image of the source on the far side of the wall.)

19-33 A source of sound of frequency 2000 Hz is placed near a plane reflector which is moving towards the source at constant speed. If beats of frequency 20 Hz are heard by a stationary observer, what is the speed of the reflector? (*Hint:* the image of the source does *not* move at the same speed as the reflector.)

19-34 A police speed-trap uses radar waves of length 100 mm: what are the changes of frequency observed when a car approaches it having a speed of
  (a) $13.4\,\mathrm{m\,s^{-1}}$ (30 mile hr^{-1}) and
  (b) $17.9\,\mathrm{m\,s^{-1}}$ (40 mile hr^{-1})?

19-35 Light of wavelength 6.56×10^{-7} m comes from a hydrogen atom in a distant star. With what speed must the star be moving (directly away from the Earth) if there is to be an increase of 1 per cent in its observed wavelength?

19-36 The Sun has a period of rotation about its own axis of 2.3×10^6 s, and a mean diameter of 1.4×10^9 m. Assuming that the Earth lies in the equatorial plane of the Sun, find the Doppler change in wavelength for light of wavelength 5.0×10^{-7} m which comes from one edge of the Sun. (*Hint:* first decide if the ratio v/c is small enough for approximations to be made.)

19-37 We have shown in Section 19-7 that the Doppler factor for recession is $k = \sqrt{[(1+v/c)/(1-v/c)]}$: refer to page 356. Suppose there is a third observer C who is at rest relative to A and situated on the line AB produced, and suppose that he receives signals from B as A receives them, that is B sends them on at intervals $\Delta t_b = k\Delta t_a$. Use the fact that $\Delta t_c = \Delta t_a$ to show that the Doppler factor for signals received by C from B is $1/k$, that is that the Doppler factor for approach is $\sqrt{[(1-v/c)/(1+v/c)]}$.

19-38 Suppose now that the observers A, B, and C of Exercise 19-37 are again situated in a straight line, with B moving away from A at relative speed u, and C moving away from B with relative speed v. Show that the speed v' of C relative to A is given by $v' = (u+v)/(1+uv/c^2)$. (*Hint:* if the Doppler factors for signals received by B from A, and by C from B, are k_1 and k_2, the factor for signals received direct by C from A is $k_1 k_2$.)

19-39 Consider the result of Exercise 19-38: is it possible for two observers to have a relative velocity which is greater than c?

19-40 A supersonic aircraft is flying at a constant height of 1.6×10^4 m in a straight line at a speed of $600\,\mathrm{m\,s^{-1}}$, passing directly over a point X. Suppose that the speed of sound at that height is $280\,\mathrm{m\,s^{-1}}$. What is the horizontal distance of the aircraft from X when a shock 'wave' is received at X?

Appendix

Conversion factors for non-SI units of energy, and related quantities, to joules (to three significant figures)

Each of these quantities is *defined* in terms of the joule, the SI unit, except for the last four, whose values depend on experimental measurement.

1 erg	$= 1.00 \times 10^{-7}$ J
1 calorie (cal)$_1$	$= 4.19$ J
1 Calorie (kcal $\equiv 10^3$ cal)	$= 4.19 \times 10^3$ J
1 British thermal unit (Btu)$_2$	$= 1.06 \times 10^3$ J
1 therm ($\equiv 10^5$ Btu)	$= 1.06 \times 10^8$ J
1 Q ($\equiv 10^{18}$ Btu)	$= 1.06 \times 10^{21}$ J
1 foot pound force (ft lbf)	$= 1.36$ J
1 foot poundal (ft pdl)	$= 4.21 \times 10^{-2}$ J
1 watt second (W s)	$= 1.00$ J
1 kilowatt hour (kW h)$_3$	$= 3.60 \times 10^6$ J
1 horse power hour (h.p. h)	$= 2.69 \times 10^6$ J
1 electronvolt (eV)	$= 1.60 \times 10^{-19}$ J
1 MeV ($\equiv 10^6$ eV)	$= 1.60 \times 10^{-13}$ J
1 kilogram (kg)$_4$	$= 8.99 \times 10^{16}$ J
1 unified atomic mass unit (u)$_4$	$= 1.49 \times 10^{-10}$ J

$_1$ the 15 °C calorie
$_2$ the international steam table Btu
$_3$ sometimes called a 'unit'
$_4$ mass–energy equivalence, $\Delta E = c^2 \Delta m$

Answers

Chapter 1
1-11 (a) 3.0×10^{-8} s;
(b) 2.8×10^8 m s^{-1}
1-18 (a) DL^3; (b) DL^{4}T^{-2}
1-19 (a) den m^3; (b) den m^4 s^{-2}
1-24 (1.20 ± 0.07) kg m^{-3}
1-25 9.8 m s^{-2}; $\pm 20\%$
1-26 120 mm; 1.0 mm
1-27 4.8%; 1.0%
1-30 36 mm^3
1-31 $\approx 9\%$
1-32 4%
1-33 1.5%
1-35 2.0 rad; 114°
1-36 0.70 m

Chapter 2
2-1 (a) 50 m, N 37° E;
(b) 75 m, S 53° W;
(c) 30.4 m, N $80\frac{1}{2}$° E;
no
2-2 80 m SW; no
2-3 250 m, N 53° E
2-4 (a) 20 m east; (b) 20 m west;
(c) 20 m west; (d) 80 m west
2-5 (a) 11.9 km, N $4\frac{1}{2}$° W;
(b) 4.6 m, N 60° W
2-6 (a) 2.0 m, N $83\frac{1}{2}$° E;
(b) 2.1 km, S 13° W
2-7 49 m, N 16° E; no
2-8 49 m, N 16° E
2-10 10 m s^{-1}, N 37° E;
3.0 m s^{-1}, S 53° W;
15.2 m s^{-1}, N $80\frac{1}{2}$° E; zero
2-11 (a) 8.0 m s^{-1};
(b) 4.0 m s^{-1} upwards
2-13 (a) 33.5 m s^{-1}, $26\frac{1}{2}$° with the horizontal; (b) 30.4 m s^{-1}, $9\frac{1}{2}$° with the horizontal; (c) 31.6 m s^{-1}, $18\frac{1}{2}$° with the horizontal
2-14 39 m s^{-1} northwards, at an angle of 40° above the horizontal
2-15 (a) 50 m s^{-1}; (b) 50 m s^{-1};
(c) 45 m s^{-1} SE; (d) 32 m s^{-1} south;
(e) zero
2-18 (a) 70 m; (b) 100 m
2-19 (a) 2.0 m; (b) -10 m
2-20 400 m s^{-1}
2-25 5080 s; 5000 s
2-26 1.25 m s^{-1}, N 37° W; 1200 s; 1200 m
2-27 North; 1800 m
2-28 At least 1.0 m s^{-1}; 900 s
2-29 36 m s^{-1}, S 34° W;
36 m s^{-1}, N 34° E; 36 m s^{-1}, S 34° E;
36 m s^{-1}, N 34° W
2-30 7.8 m s^{-1}, S $79\frac{1}{2}$° W;
7.8 m s^{-1}, N $79\frac{1}{2}$° E; 870 m; 960 s

Chapter 3
3-1 (a) 3.5 m s^{-2} SE;
(b) 11 m s^{-2} S 63° E;
(c) 5.0 m s^{-2} south
3-2 (a) 180 m s^{-2} SW;
(b) 180 m s^{-2} NW;
(c) 130 m s^{-2} west; (d) zero
3-7 4.0 m s^{-2} south
3-8 10 m s^{-2} vertically downwards
3-9 (a) 40 m s^{-1} north;
(b) 70 m s^{-1} north
3-13 200 m
3-14 140 m
3-15 40 s; 800 m
3-16 45 s; 900 m
3-17 0.88 m s^{-2}; 44 m s^{-1}
3-18 (a) 30 m s^{-1}; (b) 20 s; (c) 500 m
3-19 200 m
3-23 1.25 m s^{-2}; 16 s
3-24 3.0 s; 45 m
3-25 5.0 s
3-26 (a) 2.0 s; (b) 8.0 s
3-27 -0.50 m s^{-2}; 2400 m
3-35 2.0×10^{-8} s;
5.4×10^6 m s^{-1}, N 22° W;
2.0×10^{-15} m
3-43 8000 m

Chapter 4
4-1 100π rad s^{-1}
4-2 0.40π rad s^{-1}; 4.0π m s^{-1}
4-4 (a) 0.225 m s^{-2}; (b) 40 m s^{-2}
4-6 -52 rad s^{-2}; 67 revolutions
4-7 150 rad s^{-1}
4-8 4.0 s; 400 rad
4-9 $400g$
4-11 8000 m s^{-1}; 4750 s; 5040 s
4-12 3.0×10^4 m s^{-1};
6.0×10^{-3} m s^{-2}
4-13 1.0×10^3 m s^{-1};
2.7×10^{-3} m s^{-2}
4-14 (a) 4.7×10^2 m s^{-1};
3.4×10^{-2} m s^{-2};
(b) 3.3×10^2 m s^{-1};
1.7×10^{-2} m s^{-2}
4-15 (a) 2.2×10^6 m s^{-1};
(b) 9.3×10^{22} m s^{-2}

Chapter 5
5-7 (a) 1.0 m s^{-2}; 1.0 N kg^{-1};
(b) 10 m s^{-2}; 10 N kg^{-1};
(c) 200 m s^{-2}; 200 N kg^{-1}
5-8 (a) 20 m s^{-2}; (b) 5.0 m s^{-2}
5-9 (a) 9.2 m s^{-2}; (b) 2.6×10^6 m

Chapter 6
6-7 2.0 m s^{-2}; 48 N
6-8 1.9×10^4 N
6-10 19 N; 1.1 m s^{-2}
6-11 2.5×10^{-1} m s^{-2};
4.5×10^4 N; 2.3×10^4 N
6-14 9.4×10^{-3} m s^{-2}
6-16 15 m s^{-2}; 6.0 m s^{-2}
6-18 2.3 m; 2.3 m
6-19 No; 30°; 5.5 m s^{-1}
6-20 $g \sin \alpha$; $g \tan \alpha$
6-21 $x = 1$, $y = 0$, $z = 1$
6-23 1.65×10^3 m
6-24 45°
6-27 3.2 rad s^{-1};
(a) 4000 N inwards;
(b) 4000 N outwards
6-28 8.5×10^{-5} m
6-31 1.5×10^{19} N
6-34 0.22
6-35 3.2 m s^{-1}
6-37 (a) 1.1 N; (b) 0.98 N
6-39 685 N
6-41 2.0×10^5 N

Chapter 7
7-5 (a) $+0.12$ J; (b) -0.12 J; zero
7-7 (a) 3.0×10^4 J;
(b) 2.8×10^4 J; (c) -2.5×10^4 J
7-8 $mgl(1 - \cos \theta)$
7-9 (a) 3.2×10^2 J; (b) zero;
(c) -1.1×10^2 J
7-10 (a) -4.0×10^{-2} J;
(b) -1.2×10^{-1} J;
(c) -2.0×10^{-1} J
7-11 (a) 2.5 J; (b) -1.0 J;
1.25 m; no
7-12 4.5 J
7-13 (a) 5.2×10^4 J;
(b) -4.0×10^3 J; (c) zero
7-14 -1.3×10^{10} J
7-15 40 N; 50 N
7-18 3.5 kW
7-19 (a) 10 m s^{-1} east; (b) 10 m s^{-1} east
7-20 0.89 m s^{-1}
7-24 7.0 m s^{-1}

7-25 (a) 5.0 J; (b) -3.75 J; $1.62\,\text{m s}^{-1}$
7-27 $35\,\text{m s}^{-1}$
7-28 (a) $2.2\,\text{m s}^{-1}$; (b) $3.9\,\text{m s}^{-1}$; (c) $2.2\,\text{m s}^{-1}$; (d) zero
7-30 1.4 m
7-33 (a) $10\,\text{m s}^{-1}$; (b) $8.9\,\text{m s}^{-1}$; (c) $8.9\,\text{m s}^{-1}$; (d) $10\,\text{m s}^{-1}$
7-34 (a) $1.8\,\text{m s}^{-1}$; (b) $2.6\,\text{m s}^{-1}$
7-35 $2.3\,\text{m s}^{-1}$
7-37 $2.5r$
7-38 4.5×10^4 N
7-39 100 W; 1.0×10^4 N
7-40 1.3 m; 3.6 J
7-41 -1.1×10^2 J
7-42 2.6×10^3 N; 1.7×10^4 W
7-43 21°
7-44 5×10^5 J

Chapter 8
8-5 10 N s; $2.2 \times 10^2\,\text{m s}^{-1}$
8-6 20 s; 60 s
8-8 1.0×10^5 N
8-9 3.6×10^3 N
8-10 5.0×10^3 N
8-13 (a) 1.7×10^4 N s; $17\,\text{m s}^{-1}$; (b) 3.2×10^4 N s; $32\,\text{m s}^{-1}$
8-14 (a) 63 N s, N 3° W; (b) 17 N s, S 9° E; (c) 75 N s, S 14° W
8-15 5.1×10^4 N s SE
8-16 1.2 N s in a direction making 57° with the velocity of $1.8\,\text{m s}^{-1}$; same size in opposite direction
8-18 $3.5\,\text{m s}^{-1}$ to the right; 3.4 N s to the left (first ball); 3.4 N s to the right (second ball)
8-19 -1.7 J
8-22 $1.6\,\text{m s}^{-1}$
8-23 $0.40\,\text{m s}^{-1}$ in its original direction
8-24 $2.5\,\text{m s}^{-1}$; $\tfrac{1}{4}$
8-25 3.0
8-27 $50\,\text{m s}^{-1}$ in the opposite direction
8-28 $+2.25 \times 10^7$ J
8-29 $3.0\,\text{m s}^{-1}$; -36 J
8-33 0.50 kg
8-34 $440\,\text{m s}^{-1}$ straight on, but $28\tfrac{1}{2}°$ below the horizontal
8-35 $1.25 \times 10^{-1}\,\text{m s}^{-2}$
8-37 1.6×10^3 N; yes
8-38 $10\,\text{m}^2$
8-39 $14\,\text{m s}^{-1}$
8-40 Straight line joining the point ($t = 0$, $F = 0.10$ N) to the point ($t = 20$ s, $F = 2.1$ N)
8-41 $1.6 \times 10^3\,\text{m s}^{-1}$
8-43 3.2 N
8-44 $50\,\text{kg s}^{-1}$
8-45 1.8
8-46 $6.9 \times 10^3\,\text{m s}^{-1}$
8-47 $10\,\text{m s}^{-2}$
8-48 17; 0.94; 5.9%; 0.61; 1.3×10^6 kg; 2×10^7 N

Chapter 9
9-1 (a) 2.0×10^3 J; (b) 1.0×10^{-2} J
9-2 (a) 4.0×10^{-1} J; (b) 1.6 J
9-3 1.0 m; $2.2\,\text{m s}^{-1}$
9-4 $6.3\,\text{m s}^{-1}$
9-5 $28\,\text{m s}^{-1}$
9-6 $10\,\text{m s}^{-1}$
9-7 $1.0\,\text{m s}^{-1}$
9-8 $15\,\text{m s}^{-1}$
9-9 1.4×10^5 J
9-10 (a) 1.0 m from A; (b) yes; (c) $1.0\,\text{m s}^{-1}$
9-12 Zero; $0.50\,\text{m s}^{-1}$
9-14 $h_2 = e^2 h_1$
9-15 $0.10\,\text{m s}^{-1}$ to the left; $0.80\,\text{m s}^{-1}$ to the right
9-16 $2m_A/(m_A - m_B)$
9-17 $2m_A/(m_A + m_B)$; $4m_A m_B/(m_A + m_B)^2$; 0.18; 1.0; 0.18
9-21 $u \sin \theta$, $u \cos \theta$; along line of centres, perpendicular to the line of centres
9-23 $7.0\,\text{m s}^{-1}$
9-24 54 J; 6.0 J; 48 J
9-26 $122.5\,\text{J} \leqslant T \leqslant 137.5\,\text{J}$
9-27 7.8×10^2 K
9-28 4.3 K; 0.74 K
9-29 1.4 K
9-30 $mg/k + l$
9-31 $\theta = 0$, $\theta = 2 \arccos[kl/(2kl - mg)]$
9-33 $x_1 = \sqrt[6]{\left(\dfrac{26B}{7A}\right)}$; 0.12

Chapter 10
10-2 (a) 4.6×10^{-24} kg; 4.1×10^{-12} J; (b) 1.2×10^{-20} kg; 1.1×10^{-11} J; (c) 5.5×10^{-30} kg; 5.0×10^{-11} J
10-4 8.9×10^{-33} kg
10-5 1.0×10^4 V
10-6 (a) 8.2×10^{-14} J; (b) 1.5×10^{-10} J; $0.87c$
10-7 (a) 3.5×10^{-10} J; (b) 1.1×10^{-9} J
10-8 (a) 6.3×10^{-16} J; (b) 2.4×10^{-11} J; (c) 2.2×10^{-12} kg
10-9 2.4×10^{-35} kg
10-10 $4.7 \times 10^{-6}\,\text{N m}^{-2}$
10-11 8.6×10^{-13} J
10-12 1.5×10^{-18} N s
10-13 $500\,\text{m s}^{-1}$; 2.5×10^{-20} J; 3.3×10^{-31} kg
10-14 1.6×10^{-13} J; 1.2×10^{-20} Hz
10-16 0.9957
10-17 1.6×10^{-13} J
10-18 4×10^6 J
10-19 2×10^{-14} J

Chapter 11
11-1 (a) -16 N m, zero, -16 N m; (b) $+5.0$ N m, zero, -2.0 N m; (c) zero, -16 N m, -32 N m
11-2 None
11-3 100 N, 60 N
11-4 200 N
11-5 (a) $+0.40$ N m; (b) $+0.40$ N m; (c) $+0.40$ N m
11-6 (a) 1.0 N upwards; (b) $+0.30$ N m
11-7 No; a torque of -10 N m
11-8 (a) 200 N upwards; (b) $+300$ N m
11-9 324 N; 2.2 m from the apex of the triangle
11-10 610 N; 1.9 from the base of the figure
11-12 9.0 N, 6.0 N
11-13 100 N, 200 N, 400 N; at A, at 45° to the horizontal, upwards; 71 N
11-15 (a) 37 N horizontally; 106 N at 70° with the horizontal
11-16 50 N; 100 N
11-17 (a) 67 N; (b) 134 N at $63\tfrac{1}{2}°$ with the horizontal
11-18 110 N; 170 N; no
11-19 (a) 193 N; (b) 124 N at 66° above the horizontal; no
11-20 56 N; 0.37
11-21 The other leg; 0.72 m
11-22 $W \cos \theta / [2 \cos(45° - \tfrac{1}{2}\theta)]$
11-23 6.0 N; 10 N
11-25 8600 N, 80 N; $+1640$ N m
11-26 45 N
11-29 $\sqrt{(m_1 m_2)}$

Chapter 12
12-2 (a) 0.21 m; (b) 0.46 m; (c) 0.20 m
12-3 $1.5 \times 10^{-3}\,\text{kg m}^2$ in each case
12-4 $0.50\,\text{kg m}^2$; $0.50\,\text{kg m}^2$
12-5 $1.0 \times 10^{-3}\,\text{kg m}^2$
12-6 6.7 J
12-7 190 J
12-8 9.3 J
12-9 17 rad s^{-1}
12-10 7.7 rad s^{-1}
12-11 20 rad s^{-1}
12-13 10 rad s^{-1}; 10 J; 9.0 J; 19 J
12-14 6.0×10^2 J
12-15 4.2×10^4 J; 4.5×10^{-2}
12-17 $5.2\,\text{m s}^{-1}$; $6.3\,\text{m s}^{-1}$
12-20 0.19 J
12-21 2.7 rad s^{-1}; no
12-22 (a) 40 rad s^{-2}; (b) 29 rad s^{-2}
12-23 $1.05\,\text{m s}^{-2}$; 33 N; 45 N
12-24 1000 N m
12-25 8.0 rad s^{-2}; 72 rad s^{-2}
12-26 3.9 rad s^{-1}; 26 rad s^{-2}
12-27 1400 N m
12-28 3.5 revolutions; -45 rad s^{-2}
12-29 $0.60g$, $0.75g$, $0.80g$, $1.25g$, $1.33g$, $1.67g$

12-31 $P = 6000\,\text{N}$, $Q = 4000\,\text{N}$; $P = Q = 5000\,\text{N}$
12-32 0.20; 11°
12-34 $5g/7\sin\alpha$; $2mg/7\sin\alpha$ up the slope
12-35 $2g/3$; $2g/3a$; $mg/3$
12-36 2.0 N; $-8.0\,\text{m}\,\text{s}^{-2}$; $625\,\text{rad}\,\text{s}^{-2}$; $1.4\,\text{m}\,\text{s}^{-1}$; 0.12 m
12-37 $400\,\text{rad}\,\text{s}^{-1}$

Chapter 13
13-2 $4.0\,\text{kg}\,\text{m}^2\,\text{s}^{-1}$ west
13-3 $2.7 \times 10^{40}\,\text{kg}\,\text{m}^2\,\text{s}^{-1}$
13-4 $4.0 \times 10^{10}\,\text{kg}\,\text{m}^2\,\text{s}^{-1}$
13-5 $2.6 \times 10^{-25}\,\text{kg}\,\text{m}^2\,\text{s}^{-1}$
13-6 33
13-7 $3.3\,\text{rad}\,\text{s}^{-1}$; yes
13-8 $4.1\,\text{rad}\,\text{s}^{-1}$
13-9 $1.0\,\text{rad}\,\text{s}^{-1}$
13-11 $7.2\,\text{rad}\,\text{s}^{-2}$; 1800 N m
13-19 The normal reaction at the front and rear wheels is increased and decreased, respectively, by 128 N
13-23 OA should be made to rotate in a horizontal plane about O with an angular velocity of $1.0\,\text{rad}\,\text{s}^{-1}$, clockwise, as seen from above

Chapter 14
14-1 $2.3 \times 10^{-1}\,\text{m}$
14-2 $6.3 \times 10^{-7}\,\text{kg}$
14-3 0.47
14-4 3.8×10^{39}
14-11 (a) $\sqrt{2}R$; (b) $2R$; (c) $10R$
14-12 $2.7 \times 10^2\,\text{N}\,\text{kg}^{-1}$
14-14 $5.3 \times 10^3\,\text{s}$
14-15 $5 \times 10^3\,\text{s}$; $8 \times 10^3\,\text{m}\,\text{s}^{-1}$
14-16 $4.2 \times 10^7\,\text{m}$
14-17 $6 \times 10^4\,\text{m}$
14-19 6.9×10^{-3}
14-21 $4.1 \times 10^3\,\text{m}\,\text{s}^{-1}$; $5.9 \times 10^4\,\text{m}\,\text{s}^{-1}$
14-23 $6.3 \times 10^7\,\text{J}$; $6.3 \times 10^4\,\text{K}$
14-25 $1.5 \times 10^{10}\,\text{J}$
14-27 $2.0 \times 10^7\,\text{J}\,\text{kg}^{-1}$; $1.1 \times 10^{11}\,\text{J}$
14-31 $1.4 \times 10^{-3}\,\text{m}\,\text{s}^{-2}$
14-33 $4.3 \times 10^6\,\text{m}$
14-36 $3.1 \times 10^{-5}\,\text{m}\,\text{s}^{-2}$

Chapter 15
15-1 (a) $1.0 \times 10^{-1}\,\text{m}\,\text{s}^{-1}$; (b) $1.1\,\text{m}\,\text{s}^{-2}$
15-2 (a) $+5.0\,\text{mm}$; (b) $+8.7\,\text{mm}$; (c) $+8.7\,\text{mm}$; (d) $+91\,\text{mm}\,\text{s}^{-1}$; (e) $+52\,\text{mm}\,\text{s}^{-1}$; (f) $-52\,\text{mm}\,\text{s}^{-1}$; (g) $-5.5\,\text{mm}\,\text{s}^{-2}$; (h) $-9.5\,\text{mm}\,\text{s}^{-2}$; (i) $-9.5\,\text{mm}\,\text{s}^{-2}$
15-5 0.50
15-6 $3.2 \times 10^4\,\text{N}\,\text{m}^{-1}$; 1.6 Hz
15-8 (a) 0.10 s; (b) 0.20 s; (c) 0.11 s
15-9 7.7 hours; 16 40 hours
15-10 $4.2 \times 10^8\,\text{m}$; $1.8 \times 10^4\,\text{m}\,\text{s}^{-1}$
15-11 $1.3 \times 10^3\,\text{m}\,\text{s}^{-1}$; $2.0 \times 10^{16}\,\text{m}\,\text{s}^{-2}$
15-13 0.60 m; 1.5 s
15-14 $6.7\,\text{m}\,\text{s}^{-2}$; $1.6\,\text{m}\,\text{s}^{-1}$
15-17 (a) 0.13 s; (b) 0.26 s
15-18 $2\pi\sqrt{(h/g)}$
15-19 $\pi\sqrt{(2ml/T)}$
15-20 amplitude $< 2.5\,\text{mm}$
15-22 $2\pi\sqrt{(I/mB)}$
15-23 0.79
15-24 $E = \tfrac{1}{2}mv^2 + \tfrac{1}{2}k(e+x)^2 - mg(e+x)$
15-25 $2\pi\sqrt{(I/mgh)}$
15-26 $\pi\sqrt{(2l/3g)}$
15-27 $l/\sqrt{6}$
15-28 $2\pi\sqrt{(2r/5g)}$
15-31 $25\,\text{rad}\,\text{s}^{-1}$; $3.1 \times 10^2\,\text{rad}\,\text{s}^{-2}$; $4.2 \times 10^{-2}\,\text{s}$
15-40 0.993 m
15-41 $3.1 \times 10^{-3}\%$; $6.0 \times 10^{-3}\%$

Chapter 16
16-10 $\pi/2$ rad
16-17 (a) $2.8 \times 10^2\,\text{Hz}$; (b) $4.0 \times 10^2\,\text{Hz}$; (c) $4.0 \times 10^2\,\text{Hz}$
16-19 nf_0; $(2n-1)f_0$; nf_0; where $n = 1, 2, 3, \ldots$
16-20 36 N
16-21 $200\,\text{m}\,\text{s}^{-1}$; 303 Hz
16-22 $240\,\text{m}\,\text{s}^{-1}$; $3.1 \times 10^2\,\text{Hz}$
16-25 (a) 1.26; (b) 1.33
16-26 f, $9f/8$, $5f/4$, $4f/3$, $3f/2$, $5f/3$, $15f/8$, $2f$; $1.500f$, $1.495f$; l, $8l/9$, $4l/5$, $3l/4$, $2l/3$, $3l/5$, $8l/15$, $1l/2$

Chapter 17
17-2 (a) 0.33 Hz, 0.67 Hz, 1.0 Hz; (b) 0.17 Hz, 0.50 Hz, 0.83 Hz; (c) 0.33 Hz, 0.67 Hz, 1.0 Hz
17-5 $34\,\text{N}\,\text{m}^{-1}$
17-6 $14\,\text{N}\,\text{m}^{-1}$; $20\,\text{N}\,\text{m}^{-1}$
17-7 $3.2 \times 10^3\,\text{m}\,\text{s}^{-2}$; $8.8 \times 10^{10}\,\text{N}\,\text{m}^{-2}$
17-8 120 m; $K = 2.1 \times 10^9\,\text{N}\,\text{m}^{-2}$
17-9 (a) 20 W; (b) 20 W
17-10 $8.8 \times 10^{10}\,\text{N}\,\text{m}^{-2}$
17-12 25 m; 125 m
17-14 $1.7 \times 10^{-2}\,\text{m}$; $0.23\,\text{m}\,\text{s}^{-1}$
17-17 13 m; $4.6\,\text{m}\,\text{s}^{-1}$
17-19 $630\,\text{m}\,\text{s}^{-1}$

Chapter 18
18-2 $300\,\text{m}\,\text{s}^{-1}$
18-4 (a) $390\,\text{m}\,\text{s}^{-1}$; (b) $980\,\text{m}\,\text{s}^{-1}$
18-6 760 Hz
18-7 (a) $330\,\text{m}\,\text{s}^{-1}$; (b) $660\,\text{m}\,\text{s}^{-1}$
18-8 $320\,\text{m}\,\text{s}^{-1}$
18-10 $0.20\,\text{W}\,\text{m}^{-2}$; $4.2\,\text{N}\,\text{m}^{-2}$; $4.2 \times 10^{-4}\,\text{N}$
18-17 437 Hz; 443 Hz; 445 Hz
18-19 More than 2.6 m
18-20 $270\,\text{m}\,\text{s}^{-1}$
18-23 0.32 m
18-24 $1.4 \times 10^{-4}\,\text{m}$

Chapter 19
19-1 Multiples of 10 Hz
19-2 60 mm
19-3 (a) $2.2 \times 10^{-2}\,\text{m}$; (b) $1.5 \times 10^{-2}\,\text{m}$
19-5 850 Hz
19-6 2.3°
19-7 5.1°
19-9 $23\tfrac{1}{2}°$; 59°
19-11 7.4°
19-12 0.27 m
19-18 (a) $14\tfrac{1}{2}°$; (b) 30°; (c) $48\tfrac{1}{2}°$
19-24 2.0 m
19-26 470 Hz; 349 Hz
19-27 466 Hz; 347 Hz
19-28 28 m
19-30 459 Hz; 361 Hz
19-31 (a) 760 Hz; (b) 470 Hz
19-32 15 Hz
19-33 $1.7\,\text{m}\,\text{s}^{-1}$
19-34 (a) 268 Hz; (b) 358 Hz
19-35 $3.0 \times 10^6\,\text{m}\,\text{s}^{-1}$
19-36 $6.4 \times 10^{-12}\,\text{m}$, i.e. a fractional change of 1.28×10^{-5}
19-40 $3.0 \times 10^4\,\text{m}$

Index

Key: 74*e* refers to an exercise.

A

absorption coefficient 337
accelerating reference frame 92
acceleration 32
    angular 52, 55, 198
    average 32
    centripetal 56
    circular motion 56
    constant 33, 35, 42
    due to gravity 70
    in s.h.m. 248
    instantaneous 32
    measurement of 39
    radial 56, 59
    tangential 59
    –time graphs 38
    unit of 32
accelerometer 39
accuracy 2
acoustic pressure 327
acoustic spectrometer 329
acoustic spectrum 336
acoustics of buildings 337
action and reaction 72
air columns, vibrating 333
air track 25, 106, 120, 246
algebra, vector 16
amplitude,
    of a wave 286
    of s.h.m. 248
    pressure 327
    resonance 268
angle,
    definition of 11
    small 10
    trigonometric relationships 10
angular acceleration 52, 55, 198
    average 52
    constant 56
    instantaneous 52
angular displacement 52
angular kinetic energy 194
angular momentum 207
    conservation of 211
    orbital 208
    rate of change of 208
    spin 208
    vector nature of 218
angular velocity,
    average 52

    instantaneous 52
    measurement of 53
antinodal lines 351
antinode 291
Apollo missions 230, 234, 244*e*
architectural acoustics 339
area as a vector 82
atomic clock 2
attenuation of waves 337, 341
audible range of frequency 330
auxiliary circle 270*e*
axial vector 179, 208

B

balance,
    beam 188
    inertial 65
Barton's pendulum 267
beam balance 188
beats 332
    in radar speed trap 357, 362*e*
    sound 332
bel 331
Bertozzi experiment 155
binomial expansion 10
bodies,
    and particles 177
    non-rigid 215
    vibrating 314
bores 321*e*
bound orbit 240
bubble chamber 144, 170

C

cat, falling 215, 217, 218
central forces 89, 209
centre of gravity 181
    values of 182
centre of mass 130
    kinetic energy 143, 146
centrifugal force 89
centripetal acceleration 56
centripetal force 89
CERN 170
change of phase 283
Chladni vibrations 316
circular motion 52
    with constant speed 56
    with varying speed 58

circular orbits 230
clocks 4, 246, 255
    moving 169, 170
cloud chamber 144
coefficient of friction,
    kinetic 83
    static 84
coefficient of restitution 141
coherence 289, 351
coherent sources 289, 351
collisions 141
    elastic 141
    explosive 123, 125
    nuclear 143
    plastic 141
    two-dimensional 124, 143
comet's tail 163
compound pendulum 255
compression pulse 299
Compton effect 166
concert 'A' 195
conservation laws,
    angular momentum 211
    linear momentum 117
    mass 66
    mass–energy 161
    mechanical energy 138
    total energy 139
conservative force 138
constancy of limiting speed 166
contact force, normal 80
coplanar forces 182
Coriolis forces 93
cosmic rays 157
couple 186
coupled oscillators 259, 266, 273*e*, 333
critical damping 265
cross product of vectors 22

D

damped oscillations 263
damping,
    critical 265
    effect on forced vibration 268
decibel 331
derived quantity 5
difference tones 336

368 Index

diffraction,
   and Huygens's construction 347
   by a slit 349
dimensional analysis 95e, 272e, 276
dimensions, uses of 5
dispersion 353
   of sound 353
   of water waves 353
displacement 15
   adding 16
   angular 52
   –position graphs 279
   –time graphs 36, 279
distance 15
   –time graphs 38
Doppler effect,
   electromagnetic waves 355
   mechanical waves 353
dot product of vectors 21
drumskin waves 314
dry friction 82

E

ear,
   normal 331
   sensitivity of 329
Earth,
   gravitational field of 228
   mass of 226
   –Moon system 229, 232, 244e
   rotation of 70, 230
   shape of 230
earthquake waves 312, 346
efficiency of a machine 104
elastic collision 141
end-correction in air columns 335
energy,
   and s.h.m. 260
   chemical 139
   conservation principle 138
   conversions 139
   elastic potential 137
   equation 262, 272e
   flow diagrams 107, 141
   from Sun 139
   gravitational potential 136
   inertia of 157
   internal 139, 145
   kinetic 106
   mass– 157
   nuclear 139
   orders of magnitude of 140
   photon 165
   resources 139
   rest 161
   wave 275
equal-temperament system 295, 298e
equation of a straight line 8
equations, dimensions in 5
equilibrium,
   conditions for 178, 182
   stable and unstable 149

equivalence of mass and energy 161, 163
equivalence, principle of 241
errors,
   possible and probable 7
   random and systematic 2
escape velocity 239
expansion of solids 274e

F

field, gravitational 228
field strength, gravitational 228, 238
first law of thermodynamics 148
fission 163
flat Earth 244e
fluid friction 86
fluids, sound waves in 322
focus of earthquake 312
force,
   action–reaction 72
   central 89, 209
   centrifugal 89
   centripetal 89
   conservative 138
   coplanar 182
   Coriolis 93
   definition of 126, 160
   dissipative 138
   fictitious 93
   frictional (dry) 82
   gravitational 225
   gravitational unit of 71
   idea of 61
   impulse of 115
   impulsive 115
   intermolecular 81
   internal 110
   moment of 178
   normal contact 80
   representing 73
   types of 61
   unit of 67
   vector nature of 76
   viscous 86
forced oscillations 267
fossil fuels 139
Foucault pendulum 93
Fourier series 290, 298e
frame of reference 46, 92, 109, 119, 131, 154
free fall 70, 91
free vector 17
free-body diagram 64, 75e
frequency,
   audible range 330
   beat 357
   fundamental 294
   natural 267
   of a wave motion 286
   resonant 266, 294, 315, 334
   rotational 53
   spectrum 296

friction,
   coefficients of 83, 84
   dry 82
   fluid 86
   kinetic 83
   laws of 83
   rolling 85
   static 84
   tidal 214
Frisch and Smith's experiment 171
fundamental frequency 294
fundamental mode of vibration 294
fundamental quantity 5
fusion, nuclear 163

G

g, measurement of 40, 256
G, measurement of 227
   value of 226
Gauss's theorem 233
general relativity 241
graphs,
   intercept 8
   slope 8
gravimeters 230
gravitation, Newton's law of 101, 225
gravitational constant G,
   measurement of 227
   value of 226
gravitational effect of spherical shell 236
gravitational field,
   flux of 233
   of Earth 228
gravitational field strength 228, 238
gravitational interaction 80
gravitational mass 241, 256
gravitational potential 237
   difference 239
   energy 136, 238
gravity, acceleration caused by,
   effect of Earth's rotation on 70, 230
   inside the Earth 237
   measurement of 40, 256
   standard 71
   variation with altitude 229
   variation with latitude 229
gravity, centre of 181
gravity waves 310
group speed 353
gyration, radius of 197
gyroscope 218
   Earth as a 221, 233

H

half-life 4
harmonic motion,
   damped 263
   simple 246
harmonics 294, 315, 335
hearing, sense of 329
hertz, the 53

Hooke's law 251, 257
   as cause of s.h.m. 252
hot potato, increased mass of 163
human ear, audible range of 330
Huygens's construction 343
   diffraction 347
   reflection 344
   refraction 344
   shock wave 357
   total internal reflection 345
hyperbolic fringe locus 351

I

impact, Newton's law of 141
impedance 284
impulse,
   of force 115
   of torque 208
   unit of 115
impulse–momentum equation 117
inelastic collision 141
inertia,
   of energy 161
   moment of 195
inertial balance 65
inertial mass 65, 241, 256
inertial reference frame 48, 93, 119, 131, 154
infrasonics 336
intensity of a wave 306
   and amplitude 306, 308
interactions 117
   gravitational 80
   sub-atomic 125
   two-dimensional 124
interfacial pressure 82
interference,
   of wave pulses 282
   two-source 350
   redistribution of energy in 351
intermolecular forces 81
internal,
   energy 139, 145
   force 110
   work 110
internal reflection, total 345
International System of Units (SI) 6
inverse square law,
   gravitation 225
   wave motion 308
isochronous motion 246

J

jet engine 128
joule, the 98
just-intonation scale 298e

K

Kepler's laws 224
   second law 210, 230
   third law 231

kilogram, the 5
kilogram force 71
kilowatt hour 103
kinematics 46
   simple harmonic motion 246
kinetic energy 106
   angular 194
   centre of mass 143, 146
   relativistic 158, 161
kinetic friction 83
Kundt's dust tube 334, 340e

L

length,
   measurement of 3
   orders of magnitude of 4
   standard of 2
light pipe 360e
limiting speed 157, 166, 167
linear motion 35
   graphs 35
Lissajous figures 325
longitudinal wave 299
   graphical representation 301
   reflection of 303
   speed of 299
   stationary 302
Lorentz contraction 172
loudness 330
lumped-mass spring system 278, 303, 320e

M

Mach number 357
machine,
   perpetual motion 104
   principle of 103
magnetostriction 336
Malus's law 344
mass,
   centre of 130
   conservation of 66
   contrasted with weight 91
   –energy 157
   –energy, conservation of 161
   gravitational 241
   gravitational and inertial 241, 256
   increase equation 159
   inertial 65, 241
   measurement of 66, 122
   of photon 165
   reduced 260
   relativistic 160
   rest 126, 159
   standard of 5
measurement,
   accurate 2
   precise 2
mechanical advantage 104
mechanical impedance 284
mechanical waves 275

mechanics,
   relativistic 154
method of dimensions 5, 272e 276
metre, the 2
micrometer 3
model 1
   spring and trolley 278, 303
modes of vibration,
   air columns 334
   stretched strings 294
molecules, forces between 81
moment as a vector 179
moment of a couple 186
moment of a force 178
moment of inertia 195
   measurement of 214
   values of 197
moments, principle of 182
momentum,
   angular 207
   conservation of angular 211
   conservation of linear 117
   force and rate of change of 126
   linear 116
   of particle 116
   of photon 165
   relativistic 160
monkey and hunter 44
Moon–Earth system 229, 232
motions, repetitive 246
moving clocks 169, 170
multiflash photographs 27, 54
musical note 295
musical scales 295, 298e

N

natural frequency 267
newton, the 67
Newton's law of gravitation 101, 225
Newton's law of impact 141
Newton's laws of motion,
   first law 61, 65
   second law 67, 87, 178
   third law 72
nodal lines 351
node 291
nodes,
   distance between adjacent 291
   in air columns 334
   on strings 291
noise 331
   perceived level of 332
non-rigid bodies 215
normal contact force 80
normal ear 331
note, musical 295
nuclear fission 163
nuclear fusion 163
nuclear reaction 162
nutation 219

Index

O

octave 295
open-window area, equivalent 337
orbits 240
orders of magnitude 4, 5
oscillating systems 257
oscillations,
    damped 263
    forced 267
    simple harmonic 246
    two-body 259, 266, 273e
overhauling of machine 104
overtones 294, 315, 335

P

pair annihilation 166
pair production 166
parabolic motion 42, 44
parallax 3
parallel axis theorem 198, 205e
pascal, the 82
pendulum 255
    Barton's 267
    compound 255
    Foucault 93
    simple 256
    torsion 257
    Wilberforce 266
perceived noise level 332
percentage error 7, 13e
period 248
periodic motion 246
periodic waves 286
perpetual motion 104
phase,
    angle 287
    change on reflection 283
    difference 249, 287, 289
    speed 353
phonon 306
photoelectric effect 164
photoelectric switching 25, 55
photographic techniques 27, 54
photon 164, 355
    –electron interactions 166
    energy 165
    momentum 165
piezo-electric effect 336
pitch of a note 295
Planck constant, the 165
planetary motion, Kepler's laws of 224
polar vector 22
polarized waves 280
potential,
    and field strength 238
    gravitational 237
potential energy,
    elastic 137
    graphs 148
    gravitational 136
power 103
    of a wave 306
    unit of 103
precession 219
precision 2
prefixes 6
pressure,
    acoustic 327
    amplitude 327
    effect on the speed of sound 326
    interfacial 82
    radiation 163
    unit of 82
principle of equivalence 241
principle of moments 182
principle of special relativity 47, 154
principle of superposition 280, 289, 302, 351
projectile motion 42, 44
proportionality 8
pseudovector 22, 179, 208
pulses,
    compression and rarefaction 299
    wave 276

Q

Q of oscillating system 265
Q unit of energy 139
quality factor 265
quality of a note 295
Quincke's tube 340e

R

radian, the 10
radiation pressure 163
radioactive clock 4
radius of gyration 197
random error 2
rarefaction pulse 299
ray 307
recoil 121
red shift 356
reduced mass 260
reference frame 46
    accelerating 92
    inertial 48, 93, 119, 131, 154
reflection of waves,
    as cause of stationary waves 291, 302
    Huygens's construction for 344
    on strings 283
    phase change on 283
    total internal 345
refraction of waves 284
    continuous 346, 360e
    Huygens's construction for 344
    Snell's law 345
relationships 8
relative velocity 28, 362e
relativistic Doppler effect 355
relativity, general 241
repetitive motions 246
representing waves 279, 301
resolving vectors 19
resonance 266
    amplitude 268
    energy 268
    of air columns 334
    of strings 294
    phase relationships in 267
    sharpness of 269
resonant frequencies 266, 294, 315, 334
rest mass 159
restitution, coefficient of 141
resultant of vector combination 16
reverberation time 337
rigid body 177
ripple tank 341
ripples 311
rockets 128
rods, vibrating 315
rolling friction 85
rotation of Earth (and g) 70, 230
rotational dynamics 193

S

satellites 230
    data for 231
Saturn V rocket 131, 135e
scalar product 21
scalar quantity 15
scaler 25
scattering 349
Schlieren photography 342, 357
screw gauge 3
second, the 2
seiche 316
seismic waves 312, 346
seismograph 312
sensation level 331
sensitivity 2, 59
    of ear 239
shear wave 313
shock wave 323
SI units 6
simple harmonic motion,
    and Hooke's law 252
    angular 248
    approximate 256
    combination of 274e
    damped 263
    definition of 248
    dynamics of 252
    energy in 260
    kinematics of 246
simple pendulum 256
single slit diffraction 349
sinusoidal waves,
    equation for 288
    superposition of 289
sliding and toppling 200
slope of a graph 8
sloshes 316
Snell's law 345
solar system, data for 225

solid,
  pressure exerted by 82
  speed of sound in 304
sonometer 295
sound,
  adiabatic nature of 323, 326
  Doppler effect in 353
  intensity of 326
  loudness of 330
  mechanism of 323
  no dispersion of 322
  pipe 347
  -pressure level 330
  spectrum 336
  speed in fluids 322
space contraction 172
special relativity, principle of 47, 154
spectrum,
  acoustic 329, 336
  frequency 296
  velocity 25
speed,
  and velocity 22
  average 22
  group 353
  instantaneous 23
  limiting 157, 166, 167
  measurement of 25, 120
  phase 353
  -time graphs 38
  unit of 22
speed of,
  longitudinal wave 299
  sound waves 323
  transverse wave 277
  waves, formulae 318
spherical wave front 307
spring,
  and Hooke's law 252
  constant 102, 252
  energy stored by 102, 137
  stiffness of 102, 252
  waves on 276, 299
stability of equilibrium 149
standard gravity 71
standards of measurement 2, 7
standing waves (*see* stationary waves)
static friction 84
stationary waves,
  in sound 333
  on strings 291
stiffness of spring 102, 252
stringed instruments 295
strings, vibrating 293
stroboscope 27, 54
subtraction of vectors 18
Sun,
  source of energy 139
  tides caused by 233
superposition, principle of 280, 289, 302, 351
supersonic boom 357
systematic error 2

T
tachometer, vibrating reed 316
tension 78
theorem of parallel axes 198, 205
thermodynamics,
  first law 148
  second law 140
threshold of audibility 330
threshold of feeling 330
ticker-timer 26, 54
tides, theory of 232
time, standard of 2
time dilation 169
time interval,
  measurement of 4
  orders of magnitude of 5
time period 248
toppling 200
torque 187, 198
  definition of 208
  impulse of 208
  vector nature of 179
  work done by 201
torquemeter 202
torsion pendulum 257
torsional wave 313
torsion-bar wave machine 314
total internal reflection,
  sound waves 347
  water waves 346
transducers 336
transverse waves,
  reflection of 283
  representing 279
  speed of 277
triangle of forces 191*e*
tsunamis 310
tuning fork 317
turntable 54
two-source interference patterns 350

U
ultimate speed 157
ultrasonic waves 336, 342
ultrasonics 336
uniform circular motion 56
unit vector 31*e*
units 6
  derived 5
  fundamental 5
  SI 6
universal gravitation, law of 226
unstable equilibrium 149

V
vector product 21, 22
vector quantity 15
vectors,
  addition of 16
  axial 22, 179, 208
  force as a 76
  moment as a 179
  multiplication of 21, 22
  polar 22
  resolving 19
  subtraction of 18
velocity (*see also* speed) 22
  and speed 22
  angular 52
  average 22
  escape 239
  instantaneous 23
  ratio 104
  relative 28
  selector 25
  spectrum 25
  -time graphs 36
vibrations,
  Chladni 316
  damped 263
  forced 266
  of air columns 333
  of rods 315
  of strings 293
viscous force 86

W
wakes 357
water waves 308, 346
  breaking of 308
  dispersion of 353
  speed of 309
watt, the 103
wave equation 286
wave number 288
wave pulse 276
waveform 286
wavefront 307
wavelength 286
wavelets 343
waves,
  drumskin 314
  earthquake 312, 346
  frequency of 286
  gravity 310
  in a fluid 322
  in solids 304
  intensity of 306
  interference of 282, 350
  longitudinal 299
  mechanical 275
  models 278, 303
  periodic 286
  polarized 280
  power of 306
  properties of 275
  reflection of 283
  seismic 312, 346
  shear 313
  shock 323, 357
  sinusoidal 288
  sound 322, 347
  speed of 277, 299
  stationary (standing) 291, 302

Waves—*continued*
  torsional 313
  transverse 276
  water 308, 346
wavetrain 286
Weber–Fechner Law 330
weight 70, 91
  and rotating Earth 70
weightlessness 70, 91
wheels, rolling, driven and braked 85
Wilberforce pendulum 266
wind instruments 335
work done, by
  constant force 98
  force 97
  internal force 98, 110
  resultant force 100
  torque 201
  variable force 100
work done in stretching a spring 137
work–energy theorem 107
work, unit of 98

X

X-ray production 166

Y

Young modulus, the 304

Z

zero of potential 238